# Members of Congress

# Members of Congress
## A Bibliography

**Robert U. Goehlert**
*Indiana University*

**Fenton S. Martin**
*Indiana University*

**John R. Sayre**
*Phillips University*

Congressional Quarterly
Washington, D.C.

## Congressional Quarterly

Congressional Quarterly Inc., an editorial research service and publishing company, serves clients in the fields of news, education, business, and government. It combines the specific coverage of Congress, government, and politics contained in the *Congressional Quarterly Weekly Report* with the more general subject range of an affiliated service, the *CQ Researcher.*

Congressional Quarterly also publishes a variety of books, including college political science textbooks and public affairs paperbacks on developing issues and events under the CQ Press imprint. CQ Books researches, writes, and publishes information directories and reference books on the federal government, national elections, and politics, including the *Guide to the Presidency,* the *Guide to Congress,* the *Guide to the U.S. Supreme Court,* the *Guide to U.S. Elections,* and *Politics in America. CQ's Encyclopedia of American Government* is a three-volume reference work providing essential information about the U.S. government. The *CQ Almanac,* a compendium of legislation for one session of Congress, is published each year. *Congress and the Nation,* a record of government for a presidential term, is published every four years.

CQ publishes the *Congressional Monitor,* a daily report on current and future activities of congressional committees, and several newsletters. The CQ FaxReport is a daily update available every afternoon when Congress is in session. An electronic on-line information system, Washington Alert, provides immediate access to CQ's databases of legislative action, votes, schedules, profiles, and analyses.

Printed in the United States of America.

ISBN 0-87187-865-8

Library of Congress Cataloging-in-Publication Data
*(in process)*

# Contents

# Introduction

*Members of Congress: A Bibliography* is an extensive listing of biographical references of individuals who have served in the U.S. Congress from 1774 through 1995. Although we searched for scholarly works published through 1995 about each individual who has served in Congress not all members are represented in this volume. There was a wealth of publications found for some members, while for others there were none.

The citations to biographical materials about the members cover their public and private lives, both in and out of Congress. We included autobiographical materials whenever we came across them, but we did not make an exhaustive attempt to identify all autobiographies. We included other writings by members whenever the works had anything to do with their public careers, but we did not include items that were on other topics, such as works of fiction, policy statements, or nonbiographical material. We listed items about members' lives prior and subsequent to their careers in Congress, so the bibliography is not limited to citations covering an individual's career in Congress. If an individual also served in other government positions, at any level, we have included those materials.

The bibliography includes citations to books, articles, dissertations, and essays within edited volumes. Although we have included numerous citations to chapters in books or edited volumes, we did not systematically search for them. We included what we came across as we searched for scholarly books and articles.

For some members of Congress, particularly those who were either presidents or Supreme Court justices, we have listed only a select number of citations. For example, the volume of literature on Lincoln is enormous, so we decided to include only those citations that are representative of all aspects of Lincoln's life. For additional citations to those members of Congress who were presidents or Supreme Court justices, consult two of our earlier bibliographies that contain citations to biographical materials: *The American Presidents: A Bibliography* (Congressional Quarterly, 1987) and *The U.S. Supreme Court: A Bibliography* (Congressional Quarterly, 1990).

This volume does not include government documents, newspaper articles, eulogies, obituaries, or articles from popular magazines. There is an abundance of information about members of Congress in popular magazines. One can use the *Reader's Guide to Periodical Literature, Magazine Index,* and *Public Affairs Information Service Bulletin,* and other general magazine indexes to find those articles. We did not include any references to the *National Journal* or *Congressional Quarterly Weekly Report,* although they contain a large amount of information about individuals who have served in Congress. *Public Affairs Information Service Bulletin* indexes the *National Journal* and *Congressional Quarterly Weekly Report,* which are also indexed by their publishers.

For dissertations, we made an exhaustive search of *Dissertation Abstracts OnDisc, Comprehensive Dissertation Index,* and *Disser-*

*tation Abstracts.* For books, we checked *Books in Print, Cumulative Book Index, American Book Publishing Record, Public Affairs Information Service Bulletin, National Union Catalog, Biographical Books 1876–1949,* and *Biographical Books 1950–1980,* as well as holdings of the Indiana University Libraries. We also searched various online databases, primarily RLIN and OCLC for books.

In compiling this bibliography, we checked a variety of print, CD-ROM, and online indexes. In particular, we searched the following twenty-five indexes:

*ABC POL SCI*

*America: History and Life*

*Annual Legal Bibliography*

*Arts and Humanities Citation Index*

*British Humanities Index*

*Combined Retrospective Index to Journals in History*

*Combined Retrospective Index to Journals in Political Science*

*Current Index to Journals in Education*

*Current Law Index*

*Education Index*

*Humanities Index*

*Index to Legal Periodicals*

*Index to Periodical Articles Related to Law*

*International Bibliography of the Social Sciences: Political Science*

*International Political Science Abstracts*

*Legal Resource Index*

*Psychological Abstracts*

*Public Affairs Information Service Bulletin*

*Religion Index One*

*Social Sciences Citation Index*

*Social Sciences Index*

*Sociological Abstracts*

*United States Political Science Documents*

*Women's Studies Abstracts*

*Writings on American History*

Each entry includes the name of the member of Congress, the dates of birth and death, the political party (if the member belonged to one), the state from which the member was elected, and the years of service in either the Senate or House of Representatives. (Please note that the party affiliation listed is the party the member belonged to at the end of his or her political career, or currently, if the person is still a member of Congress. Some members changed political parties over the course of their careers.) At the end of this introduction is a table of the abbreviations for political parties.

The best source for additional biographical information is the Bicentennial edition of the *Biographical Directory of the United States Congress, 1774–1989.* For biographical information about current members of Congress, consult the *Almanac of American Politics* or *Politics in America.* These reference tools are published every two years. Biographical information about members of earlier Congresses appears in the *Dictionary of American Biography.* The best way to determine whether there is any biographical information about a member of Congress in other biographical tools is to use the *Biography and Genealogy Master Index 1995* or the *Biography and Genealogy Master Index CD-ROM 1995 Cumulation.* These tools locate citations to biographical articles appearing in biographical dictionaries and *Who's Who.*

# Party Abbreviations

| | | | |
|---|---|---|---|
| AD | Anti-Democrat | Jeff.R | Jeffersonian Republican |
| Ad.D | Adams Democrat | L | Liberal |
| AF | Anti-Federalist | Lab. | Laborite |
| AJ | Anti-Jacksonian | L&O | Law & Order |
| AL | American Laborite | LR | Liberal Republican |
| ALD | Anti-Lecompton Democrat | N | Nullifier |
| ALot. | Anti-Lottery Democrat | Nat. | Nationalist |
| AM | Anti-Monopolist | New Prog. | New Progressive |
| AMas. | Anti-Mason | Nonpart. | Nonpartisan |
| AP | American Party | NR | National Republican |
| C | Conservative | O | Opposition Party |
| Coal. | Coalitionist | P | Populist |
| Confed. D | Confederate Democrat | PD | Popular Democrat |
| Const U | Constitutional Unionist | PR | Progressive Republican |
| CR | Conservative Republican | Prog. | Progressive |
| D | Democrat | Prohib. | Prohibitionist |
| DFL | Democrat Farmer Labor | R | Republican |
| DR | Democratic Republican | Read | Readjuster |
| F | Federalist | Sil.R | Silver Republican |
| FL | Farmer Laborite | Soc. | Socialist |
| FS | Free-Soiler | SR | State Rights Party |
| FSD | Free Soil Democrat | SRD | States Rights Democrat |
| FSil. | Free-Silver | SRFT | State Rights Free-Trader |
| G | Greenbacker | U | Unionist |
| I | Independent | UD | Union Democrat |
| ID | Independent Democrat | UL | Union Laborite |
| IP | Independent Populist | UR | Union Republican |
| IR | Independent Republican | UU | Unconditional Unionist |
| IRad. | Independent Radical | UW | Union Whig |
| IW | Independent Whig | W | Whig |
| J | Jacksonian | | |

# Members of Congress

**ABEL, HAZEL HEMPELL** (1888–1966)
R-NE, Senate 1954.

1. Parshalle, Eve. "Abel, Hazel." In her *The Kashmir Bridge-Women*, 101–104. Los Angeles: Oxford Press, 1965.

**ABERCROMBIE, JOHN WILLIAM** (1866–1940) D-AL, House 1913–1917.

2. Richardson, Jesse M. *The Contributions of John William Abercrombie to Public Education*. Nashville, TN: Bureau of Publications, George Peabody College for Teachers, 1949.

**ABOUREZK, JAMES GEORGE** (1931– ) D-SD, House 1971–1973, Senate 1973–1979.

3. Abourezk, James. *Advise and Consent: Memoirs of South Dakota and the U.S. Senate*. Chicago: Lawrence Hill Books, 1989.

**ABZUG, BELLA SAVITZKY** (1920– ) D-NY, House 1971–1977.

4. Abzug, Bella. *Bella! Ms. Abzug Goes to Washington*. Edited by Mel Ziegler. New York: Saturday Review Press, 1972.

5. Faber, Doris. *Bella Abzug*. New York: Lothrop, 1976.

**ADAIR, JOHN** (1757–1840) J-KY, House 1831–1833, Senate 1805–1806.

6. Gillig, John S. "In the Pursuit of Truth and Honor: The Controversy between Andrew Jackson and John Adair in 1817." *Filson Club History Quarterly* 58 (April 1984): 177–201.

7. Leger, William G. "The Public Life of John Adair." Ph.D. dissertation, University of Kentucky, 1953.

**ADAMS, CHARLES FRANCIS** (1807–1886) R-MA, House 1859–1861.

8. Adams, Brooks. *Charles Francis Adams: An American Statesman*. Boston: N.p., 1912.

9. Adams, Charles F. *Diary of Charles Francis Adams*. 6 vols. Edited by William T. Doherty, Marc Friedlaender, and Lyman H. Butterfield. Cambridge, MA: Harvard University Press, 1975.

10. Adams, James T. *The Adams Family*. Boston: Little, Brown, 1930.

11. Burt, Nathaniel. "Charles Francis Adams." In his *First Families: The Making of an American Aristocracy*, 230–240. Boston: Little, Brown, 1970.

12. Collins, Patrick A. *Charles Francis Adams as Minister to England, and an Anti-Know-Nothing*. Boston: Post Publishing Company, 1876.

13. Duberman, Martin B. "Charles Francis Adams, Antimasonry, and the Presidential Election of 1836." *Mid-America* 43 (April 1961): 114–126.

14. ———. *Charles Francis Adams, 1807–1886*. Boston: Houghton Mifflin, 1961.

15. Ferris, Norman B. "American Diplomatist Confronts Victorian Society." *History Today* 15 (August 1965): 550–558.

16. Friedlaender, Marc. "Charles Francis Adams, Numismatist, Brought to the Bar: Groux vs. Adams." *Massachusetts Historical Society Proceedings* 86 (1974): 3–27.

17. Harbert, Earl N. "Charles Francis Adams (1807–1886): A Forgotten Family Man of Letters." *Journal of American Studies* 6 (December 1972): 249–265.

**18.** Nagel, Paul C. "Reconstruction, Adams Style." *Journal of Southern History* 52 (February 1986): 3–18.

**19.** Perling, Joseph J. "Sons of John Quincy Adams." In his *Presidents' Sons: The Prestige of Name in a Democracy,* 30–49. New York: Odyssey Press, 1947.

**20.** Russell, Francis. "Charles Francis Adams: Voice of Honor." In his *Adams: An American Dynasty,* 235–281. New York: American Heritage, 1976.

**21.** Shepherd, Jack. "The Union Is Not Destroyed." In his *The Adams Chronicles: Four Generations of Greatness,* 343–373. Boston: Little, Brown, 1975.

**22.** Stark, Bruce P. "The Development of a Historical Stance: The Civil War Correspondence of Henry and Charles Francis Adams, Jr." *Clio* 4 (June 1975): 383–397.

**ADAMS, JOHN** (1735–1826) F-MA,
Continental Congress 1774–1778.

**23.** Adams, John. *Diary and Autobiography.* 4 vols. Edited by Lyman H. Butterfield. Cambridge, MA: Harvard University Press, 1961.

**24.** ———. *Familiar Letters of John Adams and His Wife Abigail Adams, During the Revolution.* Edited by Charles F. Adams. Boston: Houghton Mifflin, 1875.

**25.** ———. *John Adams Papers.* Edited by Frank Donovan. New York: Dodd, Mead, 1965.

**26.** ———. *Legal Papers of John Adams.* 3 vols. Edited by L. Kinvin Wroth and Hiller B. Zobel. Cambridge, MA: Harvard University Press, 1965.

**27.** ———. *The Works of John Adams, Second President of the United States.* 10 vols. Boston: Little, Brown, 1850–1856.

**28.** Adams, John, Abigail Adams, and Thomas Jefferson. *The Adams-Jefferson Letters: The Complete Correspondence between Thomas Jefferson and Abigail and John Adams.* 2 vols. Edited by Lester J. Cappon. Chapel Hill: University of North Carolina Press, 1959.

**29.** Adams, John, and Benjamin Rush. *The Spur of Fame: Dialogues of John Adams and Benjamin Rush, 1805–1813.* Edited by John A. Schutz and Douglas Adair. San Marino, CA: Huntington Library, 1966.

**30.** Bailyn, Bernard. "Butterfield's Adams." *William and Mary Quarterly* 19 (April 1962): 238–256.

**31.** Bowen, Catherine D. *John Adams and the American Revolution.* Boston: Little, Brown, 1950.

**32.** Brown, Ralph A. *The Presidency of John Adams.* Lawrence: University Press of Kansas, 1975.

**33.** Chamberlain, Mellen. *John Adams, the Statesman of the American Revolution: With Other Essays and Addresses, Historical and Literary.* Boston: Houghton Mifflin, 1898.

**34.** Chinard, Gilbert. *Honest John Adams.* Boston: Little, Brown, 1933.

**35.** Ellis, Joseph J. *Passionate Sage: The Character and Legacy of John Adams.* New York: Norton, 1993.

**36.** Ferling, John E. *John Adams: A Life.* Knoxville: University of Tennessee Press, 1992.

**37.** Ferling, John E. "An Office of Unprofitable Dignity." *American History Illustrated* 24 (March 1989): 12–23, 52.

**38.** Guerrero, Linda. "John Adams' Vice Presidency, 1789–1797." Ph.D. dissertation, University of California, Santa Barbara, 1978.

**39.** Handler, Edward. *America and Europe in the Political Thought of John Adams.* Cambridge, MA: Harvard University Press, 1964.

**40.** Haraszti, Zoltan. *John Adams and the Prophets of Progress.* Cambridge, MA: Harvard University Press, 1952.

**41.** Howe, John R. *The Changing Political Thought of John Adams.* Princeton, NJ: Princeton University Press, 1966.

**42.** Kunstler, William M. "John Adams." In his *The Case for Courage*, 46–81. New York: William Morrow, 1962.

**43.** Kurtz, Stephen G. "Political Science of John Adams." *William and Mary Quarterly* 25 (October 1968): 605–613.

**44.** Miroff, Bruce. "John Adams: Merit, Fame, and Political Leadership." In his *Icons of Democracy: American Leaders as Heroes, Aristocrats, Dissenters, and Democrats.* New York: Basic Books, 1993.

**45.** Morse, John T. *John Adams.* Boston: Houghton Mifflin, 1884.

**46.** Myers, J. Jay. "John Adams: Atlas of Independence." In his *The Revolutionists*, 26–46. New York: Washington Square Press, 1971.

**47.** Padover, Saul K. "The American as Aristocrat: John Adams." In his *The Genius of America: Men Whose Ideas Shaped Our Civilization*, 43–54. New York: McGraw-Hill, 1960.

**48.** Ryerson, Richard A. "John Adams' First Diplomatic Mission: Philadelphia 1774." *Massachusetts Historical Society Proceedings* 95 (1983): 17–28.

**49.** Shepherd, Jack. *The Adams Chronicles: Four Generations of Greatness.* Boston: Little, Brown, 1975.

**50.** Smith, Page. *John Adams.* 2 vols. Garden City, NY: Doubleday, 1962.

**51.** Umbreit, Kenneth B. "John Adams." In his *Founding Fathers: Men Who Shaped Our Tradition*, 104–161. Port Washington, NY: Kennikat, 1969.

**52.** Wildman, Edwin. "John Adams: Who Devoted His Life to His Country." In his *The Founders of America in the Days of the Revolution*, 194–214. Freeport, NY: Books for Libraries, 1968.

**53.** Young, Donald. "John Adams-Thomas Jefferson-Aaron Burr." In his *American Roulette: The History and Dilemma*

of the Vice Presidency, 5–23. New York: Holt, Rinehart and Winston, 1965.

**ADAMS, JOHN QUINCY** (1767–1848)
**F-MA, Senate 1803–1808, House 1831–1848.**

**54.** Adams, Charles F., ed. "John Quincy Adams and Speaker Andrew Stevenson, of Virginia: An Episode of the Twenty-Second Congress (1832)." *Massachusetts Historical Society Proceedings* 39 (1906): 504–553.

**55.** Adams, John Q. *The Diary of John Quincy Adams, 1794–1845: American Diplomacy, and Political, Social, and Intellectual Life, from Washington to Polk.* Edited by Allan Nevins. New York: Ungar, 1969.

**56.** ———. *Memoirs of John Quincy Adams, Comprising Portions of His Diary from 1795 to 1848.* Edited by Charles F. Adams. 12 vols. Freeport, NY: Books for Libraries, 1969.

**57.** ———. *Writings of John Quincy Adams.* 7 vols. Edited by Worthington C. Ford. New York: Greenwood, 1968.

**58.** Banninga, Jerald L. "John Quincy Adams: A Critic in the Golden Age of American Oratory." Ph.D. dissertation, Indiana University, 1963.

**59.** ———. "John Quincy Adams' Address of July 4, 1821." *Quarterly Journal of Speech* 53 (February 1967): 44–49.

**60.** ———. "John Quincy Adams on the Right of a Slave to Petition Congress." *Southern Speech Communication Journal* 38 (Winter 1972): 151–163.

**61.** Baron, Stephen M. "John Quincy Adams and the American Party System." Ph.D. dissertation, Northern Illinois University, 1978.

**62.** Bates, Jack W. "John Quincy Adams and the Antislavery Movement." Ph.D. dissertation, University of Southern California, 1953.

**63.** Bemis, Samuel F. *John Quincy Adams and the Foundations of American Foreign Policy.* New York: Knopf, 1949.

**64.** ———. "John Quincy Adams and George Washington." *Massachusetts Historical Society Proceedings* 67 (1941–1944): 365–384.

**65.** ———. "John Quincy Adams and Russia." *Virginia Quarterly Review* 21 (October 1945): 553–568.

**66.** ———. *John Quincy Adams and the Union.* New York: Knopf, 1956.

**67.** Bergquist, Harold E., Jr. "John Quincy Adams and the Promulgation of the Monroe Doctrine, October-December, 1823." *Essex Institute of Historical Collections* 3 (January 1975): 37–52.

**68.** Bobbe, Dorothie. *Mr. and Mrs. John Quincy Adams: An Adventure in Patriotism.* New York: Minton Balch, 1930.

**69.** Branton, Harriet K. "Another Album Leaf by John Quincy Adams." *Western Pennsylvania Historical Magazine* 60 (October 1977): 415–418.

**70.** Callanan, Harold J. "The Political Economy of John Quincy Adams." Ph.D. dissertation, Boston University, 1975.

**71.** Clark, Bennett C. *John Quincy Adams, "Old Man Eloquent."* Boston: Little, Brown, 1932.

**72.** Collins, Herbert R., and David B. Weaver. "Wills of the U.S. Presidents: John Quincy Adams." *Trusts and Estates* 115 (January 1976): 18–34.

**73.** Crapol, Edward P. "John Quincy Adams and the Monroe Doctrine: Some New Evidence." *Pacific Historical Review* 48 (August 1979): 413–419.

**74.** Downey, William G., Jr. "John Quincy Adams' Monroe Doctrine." *Thought* 14 (December 1939): 620–632.

**75.** East, Robert A. *John Quincy Adams: The Critical Years: 1785–1794.* New York: Bookman Associates, 1962.

**76.** Farnum, George R. "Historical New England Shrines of the Law: Otis, Adams, and Hancock." *American Bar Association Journal* 22 (June 1936): 383–388.

**77.** ———. "Historical New England Shrines of the Law: Quincy and the Adamses." *American Bar Association Journal* 22 (May 1936): 309–312.

**78.** Ford, Worthington C. "John Quincy Adams and the Monroe Doctrine." *American Historical Review* 7 (July 1902): 676–696.

**79.** ———. "The Recall of John Quincy Adams in 1808." *Massachusetts Historical Society Proceedings* 45 (1912): 354–373.

**80.** Glick, Wendell. "The Best Possible World of John Quincy Adams." *New England Quarterly* 37 (March 1964): 3–17.

**81.** Goodfellow, Donald M. "Your Old Friend, J. Q. Adams." *New England Quarterly* 21 (June 1948): 217–231.

**82.** Hargreaves, Mary W. *The Presidency of John Quincy Adams.* Lawrence: University Press of Kansas, 1985.

**83.** Harrison, Lowell H. "Old Man Eloquent Takes the Floor." *American History Illustrated* 13 (February 1979): 22–29.

**84.** Hecht, Marie B. *John Quincy Adams: A Personal History of an Independent Man.* New York: Macmillan, 1972.

**85.** Illick, Joseph E. "John Quincy Adams: The Maternal Influence." *Journal of Psychohistory* 4 (Fall 1976): 185–195.

**86.** Jenkins, Starr. "American Statesmen as Men of Letters: Franklin, Adams, Jefferson, John Quincy Adams, Lincoln, Theodore Roosevelt, and Wilson Considered as Writers." Ph.D. dissertation, University of New Mexico, 1972.

**87.** Johannesen, Richard L. "John Quincy Adams' Speaking on Territorial Expansion, 1836–1848." Ph.D. dissertation, University of Kansas, 1964.

**88.** Johnson, Willis F. "John Quincy Adams and Secession, 1842." *Magazine of History* 25 (September 1917): 96–99.

**89.** Jones, Maldwyn A. "John Quincy Adams." *History Today* 30 (November 1980): 5–8.

**90.** Kaye, Jacqueline. "John Quincy Adams and the Conquest of Ireland." *Eire-Ireland* 16 (1981): 34–54.

**91.** Kennedy, John F. "'The Magistrate Is the Servant Not . . . of the People But of his God': John Quincy Adams." In his *Profiles in Courage*, 31–54. New York: Harper and Row, 1956.

**92.** Ketcham, Ralph L., ed. "Jefferson and Madison and the Doctrine of Interposition and Nullification: A Letter of John Quincy Adams." *Virginia Magazine of History and Biography* 66 (April 1958): 178–182.

**93.** Kline, Sherman J. "John Quincy Adams—The Old Man Eloquent." *Americana* 21 (October 1927): 479–497.

**94.** Klingelhofer, Herbert E. "John Quincy Adams, Literary Editor." *Manuscripts* 35 (Fall 1983): 265–272.

**95.** Knapp, Frank A., Jr. "John Quincy Adams: Defensor de Mexico?" *Historia Mexicana* 7 (September 1957): 116–123.

**96.** Lewis, Mary E. "An Annotated Reference to John Quincy Adams' Letters on Rhetoric and Oratory Based on the Requirements of the Boyeston Chair Committee." Master's thesis, California State University, 1972.

**97.** Lipsky, George A. *John Quincy Adams, His Theory and Ideas.* New York: Crowell, 1950.

**98.** MacLean, William J. "John Quincy Adams and Reform." Ph.D. dissertation, University of North Carolina, 1971.

**99.** ———. "Othello Scorned: The Racial Thought of John Quincy Adams." *Journal of the Early Republic* 4 (Summer 1984): 143–160.

**100.** Macoll, John D. "Congressman John Quincy Adams, 1831–1833." Ph.D. dissertation, Indiana University, 1973.

**101.** ———. "Representative John Quincy Adams's Compromise Tariff of 1832." *Capitol Studies* 1 (Fall 1972): 41–58.

**102.** Martin, Dan M. "John Quincy Adams and the Whig Ideology." Ph.D. dissertation, Princeton University, 1968.

**103.** Mayo, Lawrence S. "Jeremy Belknap and J. Q. Adams, 1787." *Massachusetts Historical Society Proceedings* 59 (February 1926): 203–209.

**104.** McLaughlin, Andrew C., ed. "Letters of John Quincy Adams to Alexander Hamilton Everett, 1811–1837." *American Historical Review* 11 (October 1905): 88–116.

**105.** Morgan, H. Wayne. "John Quincy Adams as Minister to Russia, 1809–1814." *Western Humanities Review* 10 (Autumn 1956): 375–382.

**106.** Morgan, William G. "John Quincy Adams versus Andrew Jackson: Their Biographers and the Corrupt Bargain Charge." *Tennessee Historical Quarterly* 26 (Spring 1967): 43–58.

**107.** Morris, Walter J. "John Quincy Adams: Germanophile." Ph.D. dissertation, Pennsylvania State University, 1963.

**108.** ———. "John Quincy Adams's German Library with a Catalog of His German Books." *American Philosophical Society Proceedings* 118 (September 1974): 321–333.

**109.** Morrison, Katherine L. "A Reexamination of Brooks and Henry on John Quincy Adams." *New England Quarterly* 54 (June 1981): 163–179.

**110.** Morse, John T. *John Quincy Adams.* Boston: Houghton Mifflin, 1882.

**111.** Musto, David F. "The Youth of John Quincy Adams." *American Philosophical Society Proceedings* 113 (August 1969): 269–282.

**112.** Nagel, Paul C. *Descent from Glory: Four Generations of the John Adams Family.* Oxford: Oxford University Press, 1983.

**113.** Noonan, John T., Jr. *The Antelope: The Ordeal of the Recaptured Africans in the Administrations of James Monroe and John Quincy Adams.* Berkeley: University of California Press, 1977.

**114.** Owens, Patrick J. "John Quincy Adams and American Utilitarianism." Ph.D. dissertation, University of Notre Dame, 1976.

**115.** Parsons, Lynn H. "Censoring Old Man Eloquent: Foreign Policy and Disunion, 1842." *Capitol Studies* 3 (Fall 1975): 89–106.

**116.** ———. "A Perpetual Harrow upon My Feeling: John Quincy Adams and the American Indian." *New England Quarterly* 46 (September 1973): 339–379.

**117.** ———. "The Splendid Pageant: Observations on the Death of John Quincy Adams." *New England Quarterly* 53 (December 1980): 464–482.

**118.** Quincy, Josiah. *Memoir of the Life of John Quincy Adams.* Boston: Phillips, Sampson, 1858.

**119.** Rahskopf, Horace G. "John Quincy Adams' Theory and Practice of Public Speaking." *Archives of Speech* 1 (September 1936): 7–98.

**120.** Reingold, Nathan. "The Scientific Mixed with the Political: John Quincy, Brooks, and Henry Adams." Ph.D. dissertation, University of Pennsylvania, 1951.

**121.** Richards, Leonard L. *The Life and Times of Congressman John Quincy Adams.* New York: Oxford University Press, 1986.

**122.** Rodesch, Jerold C. "America and the Middle Ages: A Study in the Thought of John and John Quincy Adams." Ph.D. dissertation, Rutgers University, 1971.

**123.** Russell, Francis. "John Quincy Adams." In his *Adams: An American Dynasty,* 140–233. New York: American Heritage, 1976.

**124.** Seward, William H. *Life and Public Services of John Quincy Adams, Sixth President of the United States.* Auburn, NY: Derby, Miller, 1849.

**125.** Shepherd, Jack. *The Adams Chronicles: Four Generations of Greatness.* Boston: Little, Brown, 1975.

**126.** ———. *Cannibals of the Heart: A Personal Biography of Louisa Catherine and John Quincy Adams.* New York: McGraw-Hill, 1981.

**127.** Smoot, Joseph G. "A Presbyterian Minister Calls on President John Quincy Adams." *New England Quarterly* 34 (September 1961): 379–382.

**128.** Stenberg, Richard R. "J. Q. Adams: Imperialist and Apostate." *Southwestern Social Science Quarterly* 16 (March 1936): 37–49.

**129.** Stirk, Samuel D. "John Quincy Adams's Letters on Silesia." *New England Quarterly* 9 (September 1936): 485–499.

**130.** Weeks, William E. *John Quincy Adams and American Global Empire.* Lexington: University Press of Kentucky, 1992.

**131.** Wiltse, Charles M. "John Quincy Adams and the Party System: A Review Article." *Journal of Politics* 4 (August 1942): 407–414.

## ADAMS, SAMUEL (1722–1803) MA, Continental Congress 1774–1782.

**132.** Adams, Samuel. *The Writings of Samuel Adams.* 4 vols. Edited by Harry A. Cushing. New York: Putnam's, 1904–1908.

**133.** Archer, Jules. "The Sly Fox . . . Sam Adams." In his *They Made a Revolution: 1776,* 9–26. New York: St. Martin's Press, 1973.

**134.** Beach, Stewart. *Samuel Adams: The Fateful Years, 1764–1776.* New York: Dodd, 1965.

**135.** Canfield, Cass. *Samuel Adams' Revolution, 1765–1776, with the Assistance of George Washington, Thomas Jefferson, Benjamin Franklin, John Adams, George III and the People of Boston.* New York: Harper, 1976.

**136.** Chidsey, Donald B. *World of Samuel Adams.* Nashville: Nelson, 1974.

**137.** Galvin, John R. *Three Men of Boston.* New York: Crowell, 1976.

**138.** Gerson, Noel B. *Grand Incendiary: A Biography of Samuel Adams.* New York: Dial, 1973.

**139.** Guedalla, Philip. "Mr. Samuel Adams." In his *Fathers of the Revolution,* 235–249. New York: Putnam's, 1926.

**140.** Harlow, Ralph V. *Samuel Adams, Promoter of the American Revolution: A Study in Psychology and Politics.* New York: Octagon Books, 1975.

**141.** Hosmer, James. *Samuel Adams.* Boston: Houghton Mifflin, 1885.

**142.** ———. *Samuel Adams, The Man of the Town-Meeting.* Baltimore, MD: Johns Hopkins University Press, 1884.

**143.** Hubbard, Elbert. "Samuel Adams." In his *Little Journeys to the Homes of the Great,* vol. 3, 77–95. Chicago: W. H. Wise, 1916.

**144.** Lodge, Henry C. "Samuel Adams." In his *A Frontier Town and Other Essays,* 128–161. New York: Charles Scribner's Sons, 1906.

**145.** Magoon, Elias L. "Samuel Adams." In his *Orators of the American Revolution,* 95–120. New York: Charles Scribner, 1853.

**146.** Maier, Pauline. "Coming to Terms with Samuel Adams." *American Historical Review* 81 (February 1976): 12–37.

**147.** ———. "A New Englander as Revolut-ionary: Samuel Adams." In her *The Old Revolutionaries,* 3–50. New York: Knopf, 1980.

**148.** Marson, Philip. "Voices of Freedom: James Otis and Samuel Adams." In his *Yankee Voices,* 89–134. Cambridge, MA: Schenkman, 1967.

**149.** Miller, John C. *Sam Adams: Pioneer in Propaganda.* Boston: Little, Brown, 1936.

**150.** Myers, J. Jay. "Sam Adams: The Greatest Saboteur." In his *The Revolutionists,* 1–13. New York: Washington Square Press, 1971.

**151.** Nicholas, Edward. "The Puritans." In his *Hours and the Ages,* 61–94. New York: W. Sloane Associates, 1949.

**152.** O'Toole, James M. "The Historical Interpretations of Samuel Adams." *New England Quarterly* 49 (March 1976): 82–96.

**153.** Parrington, Vernon L. "Sam Adams: The Mind of the American Democrat." In his *Main Currents in American Thought,* vol. 1, 233–247. New York: Harcourt, Brace, 1927.

**154.** Rich, Andrea. *Rhetoric of Revolution: Samuel Adams, Emma Goldman, Malcolm X.* Durham, NC: Moore, 1970.

**155.** Sanderson, John. "Samuel Adams." In *Sanderson's Biography of the Signers of the Declaration of Independence,* edited by Robert T. Conrad, 67–80. Philadelphia: Thomas, Cowperthwait, 1848.

**156.** Seccombe, Matthew. "From Revolution to Republic: The Later Political Career of Samuel Adams, 1774–1803." Ph.D. dissertation, Yale University, 1978.

**157.** Sparks, Edwin E. "Sam Adams, the Man of the Town Meeting." In his *The Men Who Made the Nation,* 47–78. New York: Macmillan, 1901.

**158.** Stanley, Owen R. "Samuel Adams: A Case Study in the Strategies of Revolution." Ph.D. dissertation, Washington State University, 1975.

**159.** Thacher, Thomas. *A Tribute of Respect to the Memory of Samuel Adams.* Dedham, MA: Mann, 1804.

**160.** Umbreit, Kenneth B. "Samuel Adams." In his *Founding Fathers: Men Who*

*Shaped Our Tradition*, 175–199. Port Washington, NY: Kennikat, 1969.

**161.** Wells, William V. *Life and Public Services of Samuel Adams*. 2d ed. 3 vols. Freeport, NY: Books for Libraries, 1969.

**162.** Wildman, Edwin. "Samuel Adams: Who Organized the Revolutionary Idea." In his *Founders of America*, 27–45. Freeport, NY: Books for Libraries, 1968.

**163.** Wright, Esmond. "The Man from Harvard College." In his *Time for Courage*, 30–40. New York: Putnam's, 1971.

**ADAMS, SHERMAN (1899–1986) R-NH, House 1945–1947.**

**164.** Adams, Rachel. *On the Other Hand*. New York: Harper and Row, 1963.

**165.** Adams, Sherman. *Firsthand Report: The Story of the Eisenhower Administration*. New York: Harper, 1961.

**166.** Anderson, Patrick. "The Incorruptible Man: Adams." In his *Presidents' Men*, 149–166. Garden City, NY: Doubleday, 1968.

**167.** Koenig, Louis W. *The Invisible Presidency*, 338–404. New York: Rinehart, 1960.

**168.** Mooney, Booth. "Ike's Decline and Adam's Fall." In his *Politicians: 1945–1960*, 164–165, 288–297. New York: Lippincott, 1970.

**ADDABBO, JOSEPH PATRICK (1925–1986) D-NY, House 1961–1986.**

**169.** Kuttner, Robert L. "Congressman Joe vs. the Pentagon." *New York* 12 (February 12, 1979): 61–66.

**AIKEN, DAVID WYATT (1828–1887) D-SC, House 1877–1887.**

**170.** Hand, Samuel B. *Friends, Neighbors, and Political Allies*. Burlington: University of Vermont, 1986.

**171.** Pritchard, Claudius H. *Colonel D. Wyatt Aiken, 1828–1877, South Carolina's*

*Militant Agrarian*. Hampden-Sydney, VA: Privately printed, 1970.

**AIKEN, GEORGE DAVID (1892–1984) R-VT, Senate 1941–1975.**

**172.** Aiken, George D. *Aiken: Senate Diary, January 1972–January 1975*. Brattleboro, VT: Stephen Greene Press, 1976.

**173.** ———. *Speaking from Vermont*. New York: Stokes, 1938.

**174.** Gallagher, Connell. "The Senator George D. Aiken Papers: Sources for the Study of Canadian-American Relations." *Archivaria* (Canada) 21 (Winter 1985/1986): 176–179.

**175.** Stoler, Mark. "Aiken, Mansfield and the Tonkin Gulf Crisis: Notes from the Congressional Leadership Meeting at the White House, August 4, 1964." *Vermont History* 50 (Spring 1982): 80–94.

**ALBERT, CARL BERT (1908–   ) D-OK, House 1947–1977.**

**176.** Albert, Carl, and Danney Goble. *Little Giant: The Life and Times of Speaker Carl Albert*. Norman: University of Oklahoma Press, 1990.

**177.** Grant, Philip A., Jr. "A Tradition of Political Power: Congressional Committee Chairmen from Oklahoma, 1945–1972." *Chronicles of Oklahoma* 60 (Winter 1982/1983): 438–447.

**ALCORN, JAMES LUSK (1816–1894) R-MS, Senate 1871–1877.**

**178.** Pereyra, Lillian A. *James Lusk Alcorn: A Persistent Whig*. Baton Rouge: Louisiana State University Press, 1966.

**179.** Tubb, Jackson M. "Senatorial Career of James Lusk Alcorn." Ph.D. dissertation, University of Mississippi, 1927.

**ALDRICH, NELSON WILMARTH**
**(1841–1915) R-RI, House 1879–1881,**
**Senate 1881–1911.**

**180.** Demetropoulos, Nicholas A. "Nelson Wilmarth Aldrich: An Appraisal." Master's thesis, Brown University, 1962.

**181.** Rosmond, James A. "Nelson Aldrich, Theodore Roosevelt, and the Tariff, A Study to 1905." Ph.D. dissertation, University of North Carolina, 1974.

**182.** Stephenson, Nathaniel W. *Nelson W. Aldrich: A Leader in American Politics.* New York: Scribner's, 1930.

**183.** Sternstein, Jerome L. "Corruption in the Gilded Age Senate: Nelson W. Aldrich and the Sugar Trust." *Capitol Studies* 6 (Spring 1978): 13–37.

**184.** ———. "King Leopold II, Senator Nelson W. Aldrich, and the Strange Beginning of American Economic Penetration of the Congo." *African Historical Studies* 2 (1969): 189–204.

**185.** ———. "Nelson W. Aldrich: The Making of the General Manager of the United States, 1841–1886." Ph.D. dissertation, Brown University, 1968.

**ALEXANDER, JOSHUA WILLIS**
**(1852–1936) D-MO, House 1907–1919.**

**186.** Sponaugle, Gail A. "The Congressional Career of Joshua W. Alexander." Master's thesis, Northeast Missouri State University, 1979.

**ALGER, BRUCE REYNOLDS (1918– )**
**R-TX, House 1955–1965.**

**187.** Cain, Edward R. "Honorable Bruce Alger." In his *They'd Rather Be Right,* 269–271. New York: Macmillan, 1963.

**ALGER, RUSSELL ALEXANDER**
**(1836–1907) R-MI, Senate 1902–1907.**

**188.** Bell, Rodney E. "A Life of Russell Alexander Alger, 1836–1907." Ph.D. dissertation, University of Michigan, 1975.

**ALLEN, HENRY JUSTIN (1868–1950)**
**R-KS, Senate 1929–1930.**

**189.** Allen, John B. *Allen's Political Essays.* Walla Walla, WA: Allen-Chancey Agency, 1909.

**190.** Clugston, William G. "A Mid-American D'Artagnan." In his *Rascals in Democracy,* 114–140. New York: R. R. Smith, 1940.

**ALLEN, JOHN MILLS (1846–1917) D-MS,**
**House 1885–1901.**

**191.** Armstrong, Walter P. "Private John Allen: A Lawyer Who Had the Saving Grace." *American Bar Association Journal* 33 (October 1947): 990–994.

**192.** Faries, Clyde J. "Private Allen's Strategy of Reconciliation." *Quarterly Journal of Speech* 52 (December 1966): 358–363.

**193.** ———. "Redneck Rhetoric and the Last of the Redeemers: The 1899 McLaurin-Allen Campaign." *Journal of Missouri History* 33 (November 1971): 283–298.

**194.** ———. "The Rhetoric of Private John Allen." Ph.D. dissertation, University of Missouri, 1965.

**195.** Gentry, Claude. *Private John Allen: Gentleman, Statesman, Sage, Prophet.* Baldwyn, MS: The author, 1951.

**ALLEN, NATHANIEL (1780–1832) NY,**
**House 1819–1821.**

**196.** Baldwin, Aubrey H. "Commissioner Nathaniel Allen, Citizen of Two Worlds." *Pennsylvania Genealogical Magazine* 32 (1982): 189–218.

**ALLEN, WILLIAM (1803–1879) D-OH,**
**House 1833–1835, Senate 1837–1849.**

**197.** McGrane, Reginald C. "William Allen, 1874–1876." In *Governors of Ohio,* 101–104. Columbus: Ohio Historical Society, 1954.

**198.** ———. *William Allen: A Study in Western Democracy.* Columbus: Ohio State Archaeological and Historical Society, 1925.

## ALLISON, WILLIAM BOYD (1829–1908) R-IA, House 1863–1871, Senate 1873–1908.

199. Cooper, Vernon. "The Public Career of William Boyd Allison." Ph.D. dissertation, State University of Iowa, 1927.

200. Sage, Leland. *William Boyd Allison: A Study in Practical Politics.* Iowa City: State Historical Society of Iowa, 1956.

## AMES, ADELBERT (1835–1933) R-MS, Senate 1870–1874.

201. Ames, Blanche. *Adelbert Ames, 1835–1933, General, Senator, Governor: The Story of His Life and Times and His Integrity as a Soldier and Statesman in the Service of the United States of America, throughout the Civil War and in Mississippi in the Years of Reconstruction.* North Easton, MA: The author, 1964.

202. Benson, Harry K. "The Public Career of Adelbert Ames, 1861–1876." Ph.D. dissertation, University of Virginia, 1975.

203. Current, Richard N. "The Carpetbagger as Man of Conscience: Adelbert Ames." In his *Three Carpetbag Governors,* 67–98. Baton Rouge: Louisiana State University Press, 1967.

204. Lord, Stuart B. "Adelbert Ames: Soldier and Politician: A Reevaluation." *Maine Historical Society Quarterly* 13 (Fall 1973): 81–97.

## AMES, FISHER (1758–1808) F-MA, House 1789–1797.

205. Adams, John Q. *American Principles: A Review of Works of Fisher Ames.* Boston, MA: Everett and Monroe, 1809.

206. Allen, William B., ed. *Works of Fisher Ames.* Indianapolis: Liberty Classics, 1983.

207. Bernhard, Winfred E. *Fisher Ames: Federalist and Statesman, 1758–1808.* Chapel Hill: University of North Carolina Press, 1965.

208. Douglass, Elisha P. "Fisher Ames, Spokesman for New England Federalism." *American Philosophical Society Proceedings* 103 (October 1959): 693–715.

209. Hauth, Luster E. "A Critical Study of Fisher Ames's Management of Ideas in His Congressional Speeches on Alexander Hamilton's Economic System." Ph.D. dissertation, University of Iowa, 1962.

210. Magoon, Elias L. "Fisher Ames: Orator of Genius and Elaborate Beauty." In his *Orators of the American Revolution,* 311–342. New York: Charles Scribner, 1853.

211. Morison, Samuel E. "The India Ventures of Fisher Ames, 1794–1804." *Proceedings of the American Antiquarian Society* (Worcester, MA) 37 (April 1927): 14–23.

212. ———. "Squire Ames and Dr. Ames." In his *By Land and Sea,* 200–218. New York: Knopf, 1953.

213. Parrington, Vernon L. "Fisher Ames: The Oracle of the Tie-Wig School." In his *Main Currents in American Thought,* vol. 2, 279–288. New York: Harcourt, Brace, 1927.

## AMES, OAKES (1804–1873) R-MA, House 1863–1873.

214. Ames, Oakes. *A Memoir.* Cambridge, MA: Riverside Press, 1883.

215. Crawford, Jay B. *The Credit Mobilier of America.* New York: Greenwood, 1969.

## AMLIE, THOMAS RYUM (1897–1973) PROG-WI, House 1931–1933, 1935–1939.

216. Amlie, Thomas R. *Let's Look at the Record.* Madison, WI: Capital City Press, 1950.

217. Long, Robert E. "Thomas Amlie: A Political Biography." Ph.D. dissertation, University of Wisconsin, 1970.

218. Lovin, Hugh T. "Thomas R. Amlie's Crusade and the Dissonant Farmers: A New Deal Wind Fall." *North Dakota Quarterly* 49 (Winter 1981): 91–105.

**219.** Rosenof, Theodore. "The Political Education of an American Radical: Thomas R. Amlie in the 1930's." *Wisconsin Magazine of History* 58 (Autumn 1974): 1930.

**220.** Weiss, Stuart L. "Thomas Amlie and the New Deal." *Mid-America* 59 (January 1977): 19–38.

**ANDERSON, CLINTON PRESBA**
**(1895–1975) D-NM, House 1941–1945,**
**Senate 1949–1973.**

**221.** Anderson, Clinton P. *Outsider in the Senate: Senator Clinton Anderson's Memoirs.* New York: World, 1970.

**222.** Baker, Richard A. "The Conservation Congress of Anderson and Aspinall, 1963–64." *Journal of Forest History* 29 (July 1985): 104–119.

**223.** ———. *Conservation Politics: The Senate Career of Clinton P. Anderson.* Albuquerque: University of New Mexico Press, 1985.

**224.** Forsythe, James L. "Clinton P. Anderson, Politician and Businessman as Truman's Secretary of Agriculture." Master's thesis, University of New Mexico, 1970.

**225.** Fox, Richard L. "New Mexico Senators: A History of Power." *New Mexico Magazine* 63 (November 1985): 82–90.

**ANDERSON, JOHN ALEXANDER**
**(1834–1892) R-KS, House 1879–1891.**

**226.** Martin, George W. "John Anderson: A Character Sketch." *Kansas State Historical Society Collections* 8 (1904): 315–323.

**ANDERSON, JOHN BAYARD (1922–    )**
**R-IL, House 1961–1981.**

**227.** Anderson, John B. *Congress and Conscience.* Philadelphia: Lippincott, 1970.

**228.** ———. *A Congressman's Choice: Between Two Worlds.* Grand Rapids, MI: Zondervan Publishing House, 1972.

**229.** Bisnow, Mack. *Diary of a Dark Horse: The 1980 Anderson Presidential Campaign.* Carbondale: Southern Illinois University Press, 1983.

**230.** Brown, Clifford W., Jr., and Robert J. Walker. *A Campaign of Ideas: The 1980 Anderson/Lucey Platform.* Westport, CT: Greenwood, 1984.

**231.** Kotche, James R. *John B. Anderson, Congressman and Presidential Candidate.* Rockford, IL: J. Kotche, 1981.

**ANDERSON, LUCIAN (1824–1898)**
**UU-KY, House 1863–1865.**

**232.** Hood, James L. "For the Union: Kentucky's Unconditional Unionist Congressman and the Development of the Republican Party in Kentucky, 1863–1865." *Register of the Kentucky Historical Society* 76 (July 1978): 197–215.

**ANDERSON, RICHARD CLOUGH JR.**
**(1788–1826) R-KY, House 1817–1821.**

**233.** Anderson, Richard C., Jr. *Diary and Journal, 1814–1826.* Edited by Alfred P. Tischendorf and E. Taylor Parks. Durham, NC: Duke University Press, 1964.

**234.** Park, E. Taylor, and Alfred A. Tischendorf. "Cartagena to Bogota, 1825–1826: Richard Clough Anderson, Jr." *Hispanic American Historical Review* 42 (May 1962): 217–230.

**235.** Rubenstein, Asa L. "Richard Clough Anderson, Nathaniel Massie, and the Impact of Government on Western Land Speculation and Settlement, 1774–1830." Ph.D. dissertation, University of Illinois, 1986.

**ANDREWS, MARK (1926–    ) R-ND,**
**House 1963–1981, Senate 1981–1987.**

**236.** Fenno, Richard F. *When Incumbency Fails: The Senate Career of Mark Andrews.* Washington, DC: CQ Press, 1992.

**ANDREWS, SAMUEL GEORGE**
**(1796–1863) R-NY, House 1857–1859.**

**237.** Andrews, James S. *Samuel George Andrews and Family.* N.p., 1920.

**238.** McKelvey, Blake. *Rochester Mayors before the Civil War,* 7–8, 18. Rochester, NY: Rochester Public Library, 1964.

**ANDRUS, JOHN EMORY (1841–1934)**
**R-NY, House 1905–1913.**

**239.** Morrill, George P. *Multimillionaire Straphanger: A Life of John Emory Andrus.* Middletown, CT: Wesleyan University Press, 1971.

**APPLETON, NATHAN (1779–1861)**
**W-MA, House 1831–1833, 1842.**

**240.** Gregory, Francis W. *Nathan Appleton, Merchant and Entrepreneur, 1779–1861.* Charlottesville: University Press of Virginia, 1975.

**241.** ———. "Nathan Appleton, Yankee Merchant 1779–1861." Ph.D. dissertation, Radcliffe College, 1949.

**242.** Sheppard, John H. *Sketch of Hon. Nathan Appleton, LL.D.* Boston: New England Historic Genealogical Society, 1862.

**243.** Tharp, Louise H. *The Appletons of Beacon Hill.* Boston: Little, Brown, 1973.

**244.** Winthrop, Robert C. *Memoir of the Hon. Nathan Appleton, LL.D.* Westport, CT: Greenwood, 1969.

**ARCHER, JOHN (1741–1810) R-MD,**
**House 1801–1807.**

**245.** McLachlan, James. "John Archer." In his *Princetonians, 1748–1768,* 300–302. Princeton, NJ: Princeton University Press, 1976.

**ARMSTRONG, JOHN JR. (1758–1843)**
**NY, Senate 1800–1802, 1803–1804.**

**246.** Skeen, C. Edward. *John Armstrong, Jr., 1758–1843: A Biography.* Syracuse, NY: Syracuse University Press, 1981.

**247.** ———. "Monroe and Armstrong: A Study in Political Rivalry." *New York Historical Society Quarterly* 57 (April 1973): 121–147.

**248.** Van Rensselaer, Solomon. *A Narrative of the Affair of Queenstown: In the War of 1812.* New York: Leavitt, Lord, 1836.

**ARNOLD, ISAAC NEWTON (1815–1884)**
**R-IL, House 1861–1865.**

**249.** Thomas, Benjamin P. "Romanticism Is the Vogue." In his *Portrait for Posterity: Lincoln and His Biographers,* 91–94. New Brunswick, NJ: Rutgers University Press, 1947.

**ARNOLD, THOMAS DICKENS**
**(1798–1870) W-TN, House 1831–1833,**
**1841–1843.**

**250.** Temple, Oliver P. "Thomas D. Arnold." In his *Notable Men of Tennessee, from 1833 to 1875,* 56–65. New York: Cosmopolitan Press, 1912.

**ASHLEY, JAMES MITCHELL (1824–1896)**
**R-OH, House 1859–1869.**

**251.** Ashley, Charles S. "Governor Ashley's Biography and Messages." *Montana Historical Society Contributions* 6 (1907): 143–223.

**252.** Horowitz, Robert F. *Great Impeacher: A Political Biography of James M. Ashley.* New York: Brooklyn College Press, 1979.

**253.** Jackson, W. Sherman. "Representative James M. Ashley and the Midwestern Origins of Amendment Thirteen." *Lincoln Herald* 80 (Summer 1978): 83–95.

**254.** Kahn, Maxine B. "Congressman Ashley in the Post-Civil War Years." *Northwest Ohio Quarterly* 36 (Summer 1964): 116–33, 194–210.

**ASHLEY, WILLIAM HENRY (1778–1838)**
**J-MO, House 1831–1837.**

**255.** Bechdolt, Frederick R. "Ashley and His Young Men." In his *Giants of the Old West,* 25–45. New York: Century, 1930.

**256.** Clokey, Richard M. "The Life of William H. Ashley." Ph.D. dissertation, University of Wisconsin, 1969.

**257.** ———. *William H. Ashley: Enterprise and Politics in the Trans-Mississippi West.* Norman: University of Oklahoma Press, 1980.

**258.** Frost, Donald M. *Notes on General Ashley, the Overland Trail and South Pass.* Barre, MA: Barre Gazette, 1960.

**259.** Glavert, Ralph E. "The Life and Activities of William Henry Ashley and His Associates, 1822–1826." Master's thesis, Washington University, 1950.

**260.** Monaghan, James. "Ashley's Men." In his *Overland Trail,* 118–138. Indianapolis: Bobbs, 1947.

**261.** Morgan, Dale L. "The Diary of William H. Ashley." *Missouri Historical Society Bulletin* 11 (1954/1955): 9–40, 158–186, 279–302.

**262.** ———. "New Light on Ashley and Jedediah Smith." *Pacific Historian* 12 (May 1968): 14–23.

**263.** ———. *The West of William H. Ashley: The International Struggle for the Fur Trade of the Missouri, the Rocky Mountains, and the Columbia, with Explorations beyond the Continental Divide, Recorded in the Diaries and Letters of William H. Ashley and His Contemporaries, 1822–1838.* Denver: Old West, 1964.

**264.** Moss, James E. "William Henry Ashley: A Jackson Man with Feet of Clay: Missouri's Special Election of 1831." *Missouri Historical Review* 61 (October 1966): 1–20.

**265.** Rawling, Gerald. "William Ashley: The Arikara Campaign." In his *Pathfinders,* 123–139. New York: Macmillan, 1964.

**ASHURST, HENRY FOUNTAIN**
**(1874–1962) D-AZ, Senate 1912–1941.**

**266.** Ashurst, Henry F. *A Many-Colored Toga: Diary of Henry Fountain Ashurst.* Edited by George F. Sparks. Tucson: University of Arizona Press, 1962.

**267.** Taylor, Christian A. *Ashurst of Arizona.* New York: N.p., 1916.

**ASPIN, LESLIE (1938–1995) D-WI, House 1971–1993.**

**268.** Hart, Benjamin. "Tip's Iceberg: The Emerging Democratic Leadership in the House." *Policy Review* 35 (Winter 1986): 66–70.

**ASPINALL, WAYNE NORVIEL**
**(1896–1983) D-CO, House 1949–1973.**

**269.** Baker, Richard A. "The Conservation Congress of Anderson and Aspinall, 1963–64." *Journal of Forest History* 29 (July 1985): 104–119.

**270.** Edmonds, Carol. *Wayne Aspinall, Mr. Chairman.* Lakewood, CA: Crown Point, 1980.

**271.** Gates, Paul W. "Pressure Groups and Recent American Land Policies." *Agricultural History* 55 (April 1981): 103–127.

**272.** McCarthy, Michael. "He Fought for His West: Colorado Congressman Wayne Aspinall." *Colorado Heritage* (1988): 33–44.

**ATCHISON, DAVID RICE (1807–1886) W-MO, Senate 1843–1855.**

**273.** Atchison, Theodore. "David R. Atchison, A Study in American Politics." *Missouri Historical Review* 24 (July 1930): 502–515.

**274.** Parrish, William E. *David Rice Atchison of Missouri, Border Politician.* Columbia: University of Missouri Press, 1961.

**AUSTIN, WARREN ROBINSON**
**(1877–1962) R-VT, Senate 1931–1946.**

**275.** Finger, Seymour M. "The Early Years: Stettinius and Austin." In his *Your Man at the UN: People, Politics, and Bureaucracy in Making Foreign Policy,* 41–71. New York: New York University Press, 1980.

**276.** Fisher, Dorothy C. "Warren Austin." In her *Vermont Tradition,* 357–366. Boston: Little, Brown, 1953.

**277.** Mazuzan, George T. "Warren R. Austin: A Republican Internationalist and United States Foreign Policy." Ph.D. dissertation, Kent State University, 1970.

**278.** ———. *Warren R. Austin at the UN, 1946–1953.* Kent, OH: Kent State University Press, 1977.

**279.** Porter, David L. "Senator Warren R. Austin and the Neutrality Act of 1939." *Vermont History* 42 (Summer 1974): 228–238.

🕊

## BACON, AUGUSTUS OCTAVIUS
(1839–1914) D-GA, Senate 1895–1914.

**280.** Steelman, Lala C. "The Public Career of Augustus Octavius Bacon." Ph.D. dissertation, University of North Carolina, 1950.

**281.** ———. "Senator Augustus O. Bacon, Champion of Philippine Independence." *East Carolina College Publications in History* 2 (1965): 91–113.

**282.** Ward, Judson C. "Augustus Octavius Bacon and Joseph E. Brown: An Exchange of Letters." *Atlanta Historical Journal* 26 (Winter 1982–1983): 64–67.

## BACON, EZEKIEL (1776–1870) R-MA, House 1807–1813.

**283.** Barlow, William, and David O. Powell. "Congressman Ezekiel Bacon of Massachusetts and the Coming of the War of 1812." *Historical Journal of Western Massachusetts* 6 (Spring 1978): 28–41.

## BADGER, GEORGE EDMUND
(1795–1866) W-NC, Senate 1846–1855.

**284.** London, Lawrence F. "George Edmund Badger in the United States Senate, 1846–1849." *North Carolina Historial Review* 15 (January 1938): 1–22.

**285.** ———. "The Public Career of George E. Badger." Ph.D. dissertation, University of North Carolina, 1936.

## BADILLO, HERMAN (1929–    ) D-NY, House 1971–1977.

**286.** Neidle, Cecyle S. "Herman Badillo 1929–    : Congressman from New York." In her *Great Immigrants,* 245–274. Boston: Twayne, 1973.

## BAER, JOHN MILLER (1886–1970) R-ND, House 1917–1921.

**287.** Reid, Bill G. "John Miller Baer: Nonpartisan League Cartoonist and Congressman." *North Dakota History* 44 (Winter 1977): 4–13.

## BAGBY, ARTHUR PENDLETON
(1794–1858) D-AL, Senate 1841–1848.

**288.** Martin, John M. "The Senatorial Career of Arthur Pendleton Bagby." *Alabama History Quarterly* 42 (Fall/Winter 1980): 125–156.

## BAILEY, JAMES EDMUND (1822–1885) D-TN, Senate 1877–1881.

**289.** McCord, Franklin. "J. E. Bailey: A Gentleman of Clarksville." *Tennessee Historical Quarterly* 23 (September 1964): 246–268.

## BAILEY, JOSEPH WELDON (1862–1929) D-TX, House 1891–1901, Senate 1901–1913.

**290.** Acheson, Sam H. *Joe Bailey: The Last Democrat.* New York: Macmillan, 1932.

**291.** Cocke, William A. *The Bailey Controversy in Texas with Lessons from the Political Life Story of a Fallen Idol.* San Antonio, TX: Cocke, 1908.

**292.** Crawford, William L. *Crawford on Baileyism: The Greatest Expose of Political Degeneracy Since the Credit Mobilier Scandal: The Whole Story of the Unholy Alliance between Senator Bailey and Standard Oil.* Dallas, TX: Eclectic News Bureau, 1897.

**293.** Holcomb, Bob C. "Senator Joe Bailey: Two Decades of Controversy." Ph.D. dissertation, Texas Tech University, 1968.

**294.** Parks, Ruth. "Joseph W. Bailey as Defender of State Rights." Master's thesis, University of Texas, 1940.

**295.** Presley, James. "The Scandal of the Senator and Standard Oil." In his *Saga of Wealth*, 73–88. New York: Putnam's, 1978.

**296.** Senter, E. G., comp. *The Bailey Case Boiled Down: A Synopsis of the Material Evidence*. Dallas, TX: Flag Publishing Company, 1908.

**297.** Welch, June R. "Joe Bailey Could Have Had Any Office." In her *The Texas Senator*, 106–113. Dallas: G.L.A. Press, 1978.

**BAILEY, JOSIAH WILLIAM (1873–1946)**
**D-NC, Senate 1931–1946.**

**298.** Marcello, Ronald G. "Senator Josiah Bailey, Harry Hopkins, and the WPA: A Prelude to the Conservative Coalition." *Southern Studies* 22 (Winter 1983): 321–339.

**299.** Moore, John R. "Senator Josiah W. Bailey and the Conservative Manifesto of 1937." *Journal of Southern History* 31 (February 1965): 21–39.

**300.** ———. *Senator Josiah William Bailey of North Carolina: A Political Biography*. Durham, NC: Duke University Press, 1968.

**BAKER, EDWARD DICKINSON**
**(1811–1861) R-OR, House 1845–1847**
**(Whig-IL), 1849–1851 (Whig-IL), Senate**
**1860–1861 (R-OR).**

**301.** Baltz, John D. *Hon. Edward D. Baker, U.S. Senator from Oregon*. Lancaster, PA: Inquirer Printing Co., 1888.

**302.** Blair, Harry C., and Rebecca Tarshis. *Life of Colonel Edward D. Baker, Lincoln's Constant Ally, Together with Four of His Great Orations*. Portland: Oregon Historical Society, 1960.

**303.** Braden, Gayle A. "The Public Career of Edward Dickinson Baker." Ph.D. dissertation, Vanderbilt University, 1960.

**304.** Burns, Jeremiah. *The Patriot's Offering; or, the Life, Services, and Military Career of the Noble Trio, Ellsworth, Lyon and Baker*. New York: Baker and Godwin, 1862.

**305.** Conmy, Peter T. *Edward Dickinson Baker, a California Pioneer, a National Hero*. San Francisco: California History Board of the Native Sons of the Golden West, 1939.

**306.** Hunt, Rockwell D. "Edward Dickinson Baker." In his *California's Stately Hall of Fame*, 321–325. Stockton, CA: College of the Pacific, 1950.

**307.** Kennedy, Elijah R. *The Contest for California in 1861: How Colonel E. D. Baker Saved the Pacific States to the Union*. Boston: Houghton Mifflin, 1912.

**308.** Matheny, James H. "A Modern Knight Errant: Edward Dickinson Baker." *Illinois State Historical Society Journal* 9 (April 1916): 23–42.

**309.** Shutes, Milton H. "Colonel E. D. Baker." *California Historical Society Quarterly* 17 (December 1938): 303–324.

**310.** Stanley, Edward. "Edward Dickinson Baker." In *Representative and Leading Men of the Pacific*, edited by Oscar T. Shuck, 63–83. San Francisco: Bacon, 1870.

**311.** Sumner, Charles. *Bingham and Baker*. Washington, DC: Scammell, 1861.

**312.** Vandenhoff, Anne. *Edward Dickinson Baker, Western Gentleman, Frontier Lawyer, American Statesman*. Auburn, CA: Pony Express Printers, 1979.

**313.** Wallace, Joseph. *Sketch of the Life and Public Services of Edward D. Baker: United States Senator from Oregon, and Formerly Representative in Congress from Illinois Who Died in Battle near Leesburg, VA, October 21, 1861*. Springfield, IL: N.p., 1870.

**BAKER, HOWARD HENRY JR.** (1925–  )
R-TN, Senate 1967–1985.

**314.** Annis, James L. "Howard H. Baker, Jr.: A Public Biography." Ph.D. dissertation, Ball State University, 1985.

**315.** Myers, Stacy C. "Howard Baker: A Rhetoric of Leadership." Ph.D. dissertation, Southern Illinois University, 1972.

**BALDWIN, ABRAHAM** (1754–1807) F-GA, **House 1789–1799, Senate 1799–1807, Continental Congress 1785, 1787–1788.**

**316.** Coulter, E. Merton. *Abraham Baldwin: Patriot, Educator, and Founding Father.* Arlington, VA: Vandamere Press, 1987.

**317.** Furlong, Patrick J. "Abraham Baldwin: A Georgia Yankee as Old-Congress Man." *Georgia Historical Quarterly* 56 (Spring 1972): 51–71.

**BALDWIN, JOSEPH CLARK** (1897–1957) **R-NY, House 1941–1947.**

**318.** Baldwin, Joseph C. *Flowers for the Judge.* New York: Coward-McCann, 1950.

**BALDWIN, RAYMOND EARL** (1893–1986) R-CT, Senate 1946–1949.

**319.** Johnson, Curtis S. *Raymond E. Baldwin: Connecticut Statesman.* Chester, CT: Pequot Press, 1972.

**BALDWIN, SIMEON** (1761–1851) F-CT, **House 1803–1805.**

**320.** Baldwin, Simeon E. *Life and Letters of Simeon Baldwin.* New Haven, CT: Tuttle, Morehouse and Taylor, 1919.

**BALL, JOSEPH HURST** (1905–1993) **R-MN, Senate 1940–1942, 1943–1949.**

**321.** Finney, Nat S. "Joseph H. Ball." In *Public Men In and Out of Office,* edited by John T. Salter, 297–310. Chapel Hill: University of North Carolina Press, 1946.

**322.** Stuhler, Barbara. "Senator Joseph H. Ball: Pioneering Internationalist." In her *Ten Men in Minnesota and American Foreign Policy,* 1898–1968, 123–144. St. Paul: Minnesota Historical Society, 1973.

**BANKHEAD, JOHN HOLLIS II** (1872–1946) D-AL, Senate 1931–1946.

**323.** Johnson, Evans C. "John H. Bankhead 2d: Advocate of Cotton." *Alabama Review* 41 (January 1988): 30–58.

**324.** Key, Jack B. "John H. Bankhead, Jr. of Alabama: The Conservative as Reformer." Ph.D. dissertation, Johns Hopkins University, 1966.

**BANKHEAD, WILLIAM BROCKMAN** (1874–1940) D-AL, House 1917–1940.

**325.** Heacock, Walter J. "William B. Bankhead and the New Deal." *Journal of Southern History* 21 (August 1955): 347–359.

**326.** ———. "William Brockman Bankhead: A Biography." Ph.D. dissertation, University of Wisconsin, 1953.

**BANKS, NATHANIEL PRENTICE** (1816–1894) R-MA, House 1853–1857, 1865–1873, 1875–1879, 1889–1891.

**327.** Bartlett, David V. "N. P. Banks." In his *Presidential Candidates: Containing Sketches, Biographical, Personal and Political, of Prominent Candidates for the Presidency in 1860,* 198–204. New York: A.B. Burdick, 1859.

**328.** Flinn, Frank M. *Campaigning with Banks in Louisiana, '63 and '64, and with Sheridan in the Shenandoah Valley in '64 and '65.* Lynn, MA: Thomas P. Nichols, 1887.

**329.** Harrington, Fred H. *Fighting Politician: Major General N. P. Banks.* Philadelphia: University of Pennsylvania Press, 1948.

**330.** Landers, Howard L. "Wet Sands and Cotton: Banks's Red River Campaign." *Louisiana Historical Quarterly* 19 (January 1936): 150–195.

**331.** Malin, James C. "Speaker Banks Courts the Free Soilers: The Fremont-Robinson Letter of 1856." *New England Quarterly* 12 (March 1939): 103–112.

**332.** Smith, George W. "The Banks Expedition of 1862." *Louisiana Historical Quarterly* 26 (April 1943): 341–360.

**333.** Williams, Richard H. "General Banks's Red River Campaign." *Louisiana Historical Quarterly* 32 (January 1939): 103–144.

**334.** Williams, T. Harry. "General Banks and the Radical Republicans in the Civil War." *New England Quarterly* 12 (June 1939): 268–280.

**BARBOUR, JAMES (1775–1842)**
**AD/SR-VA, Senate 1815–1825.**

**335.** Lowery, Charles D. *James Barbour: A Jeffersonian Republican.* University: University of Alabama Press, 1984.

**BARBOUR, JOHN STRODE JR.**
**(1820–1892) D-VA, House 1881–1887, Senate 1889–1892.**

**336.** Quinn, James T. "John S. Barbour, Jr. and the Restoration of the Virginia Democracy, 1883–1892." Master's thesis, University of Virginia, 1966.

**BARBOUR, PHILIP PENDLETON**
**(1783–1841) J-VA, House 1814–1825, 1827–1830.**

**337.** Cynn, Paul P. "Philip Pendleton Barbour." *John P. Branch Historical Papers of Randolph-Macon College* 4 (1913): 67–77.

**338.** Gatell, Frank O. "Philip Pendleton Barbour." In *The Justices of the United States Supreme Court, 1789–1969.* Vol. 5, compiled by Leon Friedman, 717–727. New York: R. R. Bowker, 1969.

**BARD, THOMAS ROBERT (1841–1915)**
**R-CA, Senate 1900–1905.**

**339.** Hutchinson, William H. *Oil, Land and Politics, The California Career of Thomas Robert Bard.* 2 vols. Norman: University of Oklahoma Press, 1965.

**340.** Westergaard, Waldemar. "Thomas R. Bard and Ventura County's Sheep Industry, 1870–1884." *Historical Society of Southern California* 11 (1920): 5–11.

**BARDEN, GRAHAM ARTHUR**
**(1896–1967) D-NC, House 1935–1961.**

**341.** Puryear, Elmer L. *Graham A. Barden, Conservative Carolina Congressman.* Buie's Creek, NC: Campbell University Press, 1979.

**342.** Reeves, Andree E. "The Committee during the Barden Years." In his *Congressional Committee Chairmen: Three Who Made an Evolution,* 20–75. Lexington: University Press of Kentucky, 1993.

**BARKLEY, ALBEN WILLIAM**
**(1877–1956) D-KY, House 1913–1927, Senate 1927–1949, 1955–1956.**

**343.** Barkley, Alben W. *That Reminds Me.* Garden City, NY: Doubleday, 1954.

**344.** Barkley, Jane H. *I Married the Veep.* New York: Vanguard, 1958.

**345.** Barzman, Sol. "Alben W. Barkley." In his *Madmen and Geniuses: The Vice-Presidents of the United States,* 245–252. Chicago: Follett, 1974.

**346.** Claussen, E. Neal. "Alben Barkley's Rhetorical Victory in 1978." *Southern Speech Communication Journal* 45 (Fall 1979): 79–92.

**347.** Clevenger, Theodore. "Alben W. Barkley's Use of Humor in Public Speaking." *Western Speech* 20 (Winter 1956): 15–22.

**348.** Davis, Polly A. *Alben W. Barkley, Senate Majority Leader and Vice President.* New York: Garland, 1979.

**349.** ———. "Alben W. Barkley: Vice President." *Register of the Kentucky Historical Society* 76 (April 1978): 112–132.

**350.** ———. "Alben W. Barkley's Public Career in 1944." *Filson Club History Quarterly* 51 (April 1977): 143–157.

**351.** ———. "Court Reform and Alben W. Barkley's Election as Majority Leader." *Southern Quarterly* 15 (October 1976): 15–31.

**352.** Grant, Philip A. "Editorial Reaction to the Harrison-Barkley Senate Leadership Contest, 1937." *Journal of Mississippi History* 36 (May 1974): 127–141.

**353.** Grinde, Gerald S. "The Early Political Career of Alben W. Barkley, 1877–1937." Ph.D. dissertation, University of Illinois, 1976.

**354.** ———. "The Emergence of the Gentle Partisan: Alben W. Barkley and Kentucky Politics, 1919." *Register of the Kentucky Historical Society* 78 (Summer 1980): 243–258.

**355.** ———. "Politics and Scandal in the Progressive Era: Alben W. Barkley and the McCracken County Campaign of 1909." *Filson Club History Quarterly* 50 (April 1976): 36–51.

**356.** Hatcher, John H. "Alben Barkley, Politics in Relief and the Hatch Act." *Filson Club History Quarterly* 40 (July 1966): 249–264.

**357.** Hixson, Walter L. "The 1938 Kentucky Senate Election: Alben W. Barkley, 'Happy' Chandler, and the New Deal." Register of the Kentucky Historical Society 80 (Summer 1982): 309–329.

**358.** Kornitzer, Bela. "Vice President Barkley and His Father: John W. Barkley - Alben W. Barkley." In his *American Fathers and Sons,* 85–107. Lawrence, MA: Hermitage, 1952.

**359.** Libbey, James K. *Dear Alben: Mr. Barkley of Kentucky.* Lexington: University Press of Kentucky, 1979.

**360.** Reichert, William O. "The Political and Social Thought of Alben W. Barkley." Master's thesis, University of Kentucky, 1950.

**361.** Ritchie, Donald A. "Alben W. Barkley: The President's Man." In *First Among Equals: Outstanding Senate Leaders of the Twentieth Century,* edited by Richard A. Baker and Roger H. Davidson, 127–162. Washington, DC: Congressional Quarterly, 1991.

**362.** Robinson, George W. "The Making of a Kentucky Senator: Alben W. Barkley and the Gubernatorial Primary of 1923." *Filson Club Historical Quarterly* 40 (April 1966): 123–135.

**363.** Shannon, Jasper B. "Alben W. Barkley: Reservoir of Energy." In *Public Men In and Out of Office,* edited by John T. Salter, 240–256. Chapel Hill: University of North Carolina Press, 1946.

**364.** Wallace, H. Lew. "Alben Barkley and the Democratic Convention of 1948." *Filson Club Historical Quarterly* 55 (July 1981): 231–252.

**BARKSDALE, ETHELBERT** (1824–1893)
**D-MS, House 1883–1887.**

**365.** Peterson, Owen M. "Ethelbert Barksdale in the Democratic National Convention of 1860." *Journal of Mississippi History* 14 (October 1952): 257–278.

**BARKSDALE, WILLIAM** (1821–1863)
**D-MS, House 1853–1861.**

**366.** McKee, James W. "William Barksdale and the Congressional Election of 1853." *Journal of Mississippi History* 34 (May 1972): 129–158.

**367.** Tyson, Raymond W. "William Barksdale and the Brooks-Sumner Assault." *Journal of Mississippi History* 26 (May 1964): 135–140.

**BARNARD, DANIEL DEWEY (1797–1861) W-NY, House 1827–1829, 1839–1845.**

368. Penny, Sherry H. "Dissension in the Whig Ranks: Daniel Dewey Barnard Versus Thurlow Weed." *New York Historical Society Quarterly* 59 (January 1975): 71–92.

369. ———. *Patrician in Politics: Daniel Dewey Barnard of New York.* Port Washington, NY: Kennikat, 1974.

**BARNWELL, ROBERT WOODWARD (1801–1882) SC, House 1829–1833, Senate 1850.**

370. Barnwell, John, ed. "Hamlet to Hotspur: Letters of Robert Woodward Barnwell to Robert Barnwell Rhett." *Carolina Historical Magazine* 77 (October 1976): 236–237, 247.

371. ———. "In the Hands of Compromisers: Letters of Robert W. Barnwell to James H. Hammond." *Civil War History* 229 (June 1983): 154–168.

**BARRINGER, DANIEL MOREAU (1806–1873) W-NC, House 1843–1849.**

372. Barringer, Daniel M. *Heroic Efforts at Meteor Crater, Arizona: Selected Correspondence between Daniel Moreau Barringer and Elihu Thomson.* Edited by Harold J. Abrahams. Rutherford, NJ: Fairleigh Dickinson University Press, 1981.

**BARROW, GEORGE WASHINGTON (1807–1866) W-TN, House 1847–1849.**

373. McGlone, John. "What Became of General Barrow? The Forgotten Story of George Washington Barrow." *Tennessee Historical Quarterly* 48 (Spring 1989): 37–45.

**BARTHOLDT, RICHARD (1855–1932) R-MO, House 1893–1915.**

374. Adams, Willi P. "Ethnic Politicians and American Nationalism During the First World War: Four German-Born Members of the U.S. House of Representatives." *American Studies International* 29 (April 1991): 20–34.

**BARTLETT, EDWARD LEWIS "BOB" (1904–1968) D-AK, House 1945–1959, Senate 1959–1968.**

375. Naske, Claus M. *Edward Lewis Bob Bartlett of Alaska: A Life in Politics.* Fairbanks: University of Alaska Press, 1979.

**BARTLETT, JOSIAH (1729–1795) NH, Continental Congress 1775, 1776, 1778.**

376. Bartlett, Josiah, ed. *The Papers of Josiah Bartlett.* Hanover, NH: University Press of New England, 1979.

377. Maier, Pauline. "From the Letters of Josiah and Mary Bartlett." In her *The Old Revolutionaries,* 139–163. New York: Knopf, 1980.

378. Mevers, Frank C. "Josiah Bartlett." In *Physician Signers of the Declaration of Independence,* edited by George E. Gifford, 99–121. New York: Science History Publications, 1976.

379. Page, Elwin L. "Josiah Bartlett and the Federation." *Historical New Hampshire* 2 (October 1947): 1–6.

380. Sanderson, John. "Josiah Bartlett." In *Sanderson's Biography of the Signers of the Declaration of Independence,* edited by Robert T. Conrad, 168–177. Philadelphia: Thomas, Cowperthwait, 1848.

**BARTLEY, MORDECAI (1783–1870) OH, House 1823–1831.**

381. Smith, S. Winifred. "Mordecai Bartley, 1844–1846." In *Governors of Ohio,* 53–56. Columbus: Ohio Historical Society, 1954.

**BARTON, BRUCE (1886–1967) R-NY, House 1937–1941.**

382. Nuechterlein, James A. "Bruce Barton and the Business Ethos of 1920's." *South Atlantic Quarterly* 76 (Summer 1977): 293–308.

**BARTON, DAVID** (1783–1837) MO, Senate 1821–1831.

383. McCandless, Perry G. "Benton v. Barton: The Formation of the Second-Party System in Missouri." *Missouri Historical Review* 79 (July 1985): 425–438.

384. Shoemaker, Floyd C. "David Barton, John Rice Jones, and Edward Bates: Three Missouri State and Statehood Founders." *Missouri Historical Review* 65 (July 1971): 527–543.

385. Van Ravenswaay, Charles. "The Tragedy of David Barton." *Missouri Historical Society Bulletin* 7 (October 1950): 35–56.

**BASSETT, RICHARD** (1745–1815) DE, Senate 1789–1793.

386. Pattison, Robert E. *The Life and Character of Richard Bassett.* Wilmington: Historical Society of Delaware, 1900.

**BATE, WILLIAM BRIMAGE** (1826–1905) D-TN, Senate 1887–1905.

387. Chesney, William N. "The Public Career of William B. Bate." Master's thesis, University of Tennessee, 1951.

388. Marshall, Park. *A Life of William B. Bate, Citizen, Soldier and Statesman.* Nashville, TN: Cumberland Press, 1908.

**BATES, EDWARD** (1793–1869) MO, House 1827–1829.

389. Bartlett, David V. "Edward Bates." In his *Presidential Candidates: Containing Sketches, Biographical, Personal and Political, of Prominent Candidates for the Presidency in 1860,* 118–126. New York: A. B. Burdick, 1859.

390. Beale, Howard K., ed. *The Diary of Edward Bates, 1859–1866.* Washington, DC: Government Printing Office, 1933.

391. Cain, Marvin R. "Edward Bates: The Rise of a Western Politician, 1814–1850." Master's thesis, University of Missouri, 1957.

392. ———. *Lincoln's Attorney General: Edward Bates of Missouri.* Columbia: University of Missouri Press, 1965.

393. Luthin, Reinhard H. "Organizing the Republican Party in the 'Border-Slave' Regions: Edward Bates's Presidential Candidacy in 1860." *Missouri Historical Review* 38 (January 1944): 138–161.

394. Macartney, Clarence E. "Edward Bates: Lincoln and His First Choice." In his *Lincoln and His Cabinet,* 59–82. New York: Charles Scribner's Sons, 1931.

**BAYARD, JAMES ASHETON SR.** (1767–1815) F-DE, House 1797–1803, Senate 1804–1813.

395. Borden, Morton. *The Federalism of James A. Bayard.* New York: Columbia University Press, 1955.

396. Conrad, Henry C., ed. *Letters of James Asheton Bayard, 1802–1814.* Wilmington: Historical Society of Delaware, 1901.

397. Donnan, Elizabeth, ed. *Papers of James A. Bayard, 1796–1815.* New York: Da Capo, 1971.

**BAYARD, JOHN BUBENHEIM** (1738–1807) PA, Continental Congress 1785–1787.

398. Wilson, James E. *A Maryland Manor: A Paper Read Before the Maryland Historical Society.* Baltimore, MD: J. Murphy, 1890.

**BAYARD, THOMAS FRANCIS SR.** (1828–1898) D-DE, Senate 1869–1885.

399. Bayard, Richard H. *Bayard Papers.* Washington, DC: American Historical Association, 1913.

400. Shippee, Lester B. "Thomas Francis Bayard. . . ." In *The American Secretaries of State and Their Diplomacy,* vol. 8, edited by Samuel F. Bemis, 45–106. New York: Knopf, 1928.

401. Tansill, Charles C. *The Congressional Career of Thomas F. Bayard, 1869–1885.*

Washington, DC: Georgetown University Press, 1946.

402. ———. *The Foreign Policy of Thomas F. Bayard, 1885–1897.* New York: Fordham University Press, 1940.

403. Willson, Beckles. "Lincoln, Bayard and Hay." In his *America's Ambassadors to England (1785–1928),* 402–411. London: J. Murray, 1928.

**BAYH, BIRCH EVAN** (1928–  ) **D-IN, Senate 1963–1981.**

404. Bayh, Marvella. *Marvella, A Personal Journey.* New York: Harcourt Brace Jovanovich, 1979.

405. Lubalin, Eve. "Presidential Ambition and Senatorial Behavior: The Impact of Ambition on the Behavior of Incumbent Politicians." Ph.D. dissertation, Johns Hopkins University, 1981.

**BAYLY, THOMAS HENRY** (1810–1856) **D-VA, House 1844–1856.**

406. Wheeler, Henry G. "Bayle, Thomas Henry." In his *History of Congress,* vol. 1, 493–509. New York: Harper, 1848.

**BEATTY, JOHN** (1749–1826) **NJ, Continental Congress 1784–1785, House 1793–1795.**

407. Rogers, Fred B. "General John Beatty (1749–1826): Patriot and Physician." In his *Help-Bringers: Versatile Physicians of New Jersey,* 45–53. New York: Vantage, 1960.

**BECK, JAMES MONTGOMERY** (1861–1936) **R-PA, House 1927–1934.**

408. Keller, Morton. *In Defense of Yesterday: James M. Beck and the Politics of Conservatism, 1861–1936.* New York: Coward-McCann, 1958.

409. ———. "Journey to Disillusion: James M. Beck and the Course of Modern American Conservatism, 1861–1936." Ph.D. dissertation, Harvard University, 1956.

**BECKHAM, JOHN CREPPS WICKLIFFE** (1869–1940) **D-KY, Senate 1915–1921.**

410. Finch, Glenn. "The Election of United States Senators in Kentucky: The Beckham Period." *Filson Club History Quarterly* 44 (January 1970): 38–50.

**BECKWORTH, LINDLEY GARRISON "GARY" SR.** (1913–1984) **D-TX, House 1939–1953, 1957–1967.**

411. Kemper, Billie B. "Lindley Beckworth: Grassroots Congressman." Master's thesis, Stephen F. Austin State University, 1980.

**BEDFORD, GUNNING JR.** (1747–1812) **DE, Continental Congress 1783–1785.**

412. Conrad, Henry C. *Gunning Bedford, Junior.* Wilmington: Historical Society of Delaware, 1900.

**BEDINGER, HENRY** (1812–1858) **D-VA, House 1845–1849.**

413. Levin, Alexandra L. "Henry Bedinger of Virginia: First United States Minister to Denmark." *Virginia Cavalcade* 29 (Spring 1980): 184–191.

**BELL, JOHN** (1797–1869) **W-TN, House 1827–1841, Senate 1847–1859.**

414. Bartlett, David V. "John Bell." In his *Presidential Candidates: Containing Sketches, Biographical, Personal and Political, of Prominent Candidates for the Presidency in 1860,* 150–160. New York: A.B. Burdick, 1859.

415. Caldwell, Joshua W. "John Bell of Tennessee: A Chapter of Political History." *American Historical Review* 4 (July 1898/1899): 652–664.

416. ———. *Sketches of the Bench and Bar of Tennessee.* Knoxville, TN: Ogden Brothers, 1898.

**417.** Foote, Henry S. *The Bench and Bar of the South and South West.* St. Louis, MO: Soule, Thomas, and Wentworth, 1876.

**418.** Goodpasture, Albert V. "John Bell's Political Revolt and His Vauxhall Garden Speech." *Tennessee Historical Magazine* 2 (December 1916): 254–263.

**419.** Grim, Mark S. "The Political Career of John Bell." Master's thesis, University of Tennessee, 1930.

**420.** Grimsley, Thornton. "Letters of Colonel Thornton Grimsley to Secretary of War John Bell (1841)." Edited by T. C. Elliot. *Quarterly of the Oregon Historical Society* 24 (December 1923): 434–442.

**421.** McKellar, Kenneth D. *Tennessee Senators as Seen by One of Their Successors.* Kingsport, TN: Southern Publishers, 1942.

**422.** Ordway, Sallie F. "John Bell." *Gulf States Historical Magazine* 2 (July 1903): 35–44.

**423.** Parks, Joseph H. "John Bell and Secession." *East Tennessee Historical Society Publications* 16 (1944): 30–47.

**424.** ———. *John Bell of Tennessee.* Baton Rouge: Louisiana State University Press, 1950.

**425.** Parks, Norman L. "The Career of John Bell as Congressman from Tennessee, 1827–1841." *Tennessee Historical Quarterly* 1 (September 1942): 229–249.

**426.** ———. "The Career of John Bell of Tennessee in the United States House of Representatives." Ph.D. dissertation, Vanderbilt University, 1942.

**427.** Scott, Jesse W. "John Bell: A Tennessee Statesman in National Politics from 1840 to 1860." Master's thesis, Tennessee State A & I University, 1950.

## BELLMON, HENRY LOUIS (1921–    ) R-OK, Senate 1969–1981.

**428.** Bellmon, Henry. *The Life and Times of Henry Bellmon.* Tulsa, OK: Council Oak Books, 1992.

## BELMONT, PERRY (1851–1947) D-NY, House 1881–1888.

**429.** Belmont, Perry. *American Democrat: The Recollections of Perry Belmont.* 2d ed. New York: Columbia University Press, 1941.

## BENJAMIN, JUDAH PHILIP (1811–1884) D-LA, Senate 1853–1861.

**430.** Abrahams, Robert D. *Mr. Benjamin's Sword.* Philadelphia: Jewish Publishing Society of America, 1948.

**431.** Butler, Pierce. "Judah P. Benjamin." In *Library of Southern Literature,* edited by Edwin A. Alderman and Joel C. Harris, vol. 1, 303–307. New Orleans: Martin and Hoyt, 1909.

**432.** ———. *Judah P. Benjamin.* Philadelphia: Jacobs, 1907.

**433.** Delmar, Vina. *Beloved.* New York: Dell, 1958.

**434.** Evans, Eli N. *Judah P. Benjamin: The Jewish Confederate.* New York: Free Press, 1988.

**435.** Kahn, Edgar M. *Judah Philip Benjamin in California.* San Francisco: E.M. Kahn, 1968.

**436.** Madison, Charles A. "Judah Philip Benjamin: 'The Brains of the Confederacy.'" In his *Eminent American Jews: 1776 to the Present,* 42–56. New York: Frederick Ungar Publishing Co., 1970.

**437.** Meade, Robert D. *Judah P. Benjamin: Confederate Statesman.* New York: Oxford University Press, 1943.

**438.** Neiman, Simon I. *Judah Benjamin.* Indianapolis: Bobbs-Merrill, 1963.

**439.** Osterweis, Rollin G. *Judah P. Benjamin, Statesman of the Lost Cause.* New York: Putnam's, 1935.

**440.** Winston, James H. *Judah P. Benjamin: Distinguished at the Bars of Two Nations: An Address Delivered before the Law Club of Chicago on March 22, 1929.* Chicago: Privately published, 1930.

**BENNET, HIRAM PITT (1826–1914) CR-CO, House 1861–1865.**

**441.** Bennet, Hiram P. *Hiram Pitt Bennet: Pioneer, Frontier Lawyer, Politician.* Edited by Liston E. Leyendecker. Denver: Colorado Historical Society, 1988.

**442.** Silverman, Jason H. "Making Brick Out of Straw: Delegate Hiram P. Bennet." *Colorado Magazine* 53 (Fall 1976): 310–327.

**BENNETT, WALLACE FOSTER (1898–1993) R-UT, Senate 1951–1974.**

**443.** Abramson, Marcia. *Wallace F. Bennett, Republican Senator from Utah.* Washington, DC: Grossman, 1972.

**444.** Bennett, Frances M. *Glimpses of a Mormon Family.* Salt Lake City, UT: Deseret Book Co., 1968.

**445.** Bennett, Wallace G. *Faith and Freedom: The Pillars of American Democracy.* New York: Scribner's, 1950.

**446.** ———. *Why I Am a Mormon.* New York: T. Nelson, 1958.

**BENSON, ELMER AUSTIN (1895–1985) FL-MN, Senate 1935–1936.**

**447.** Benson, Elmer A. "Politics in My Lifetime." *Minnesota History* 47 (Winter 1980): 154–160.

**448.** Shields, James M. *Mr. Progressive: A Biography of Elmer Austin Benson.* Minneapolis, MN: Denison, 1971.

**BENTON, THOMAS HART (1782–1858) D-MO, Senate 1821–1851, House 1853–1855.**

**449.** Bates, Edward. *Edward Bates against Thomas H. Benton.* St. Louis, MO: Charless and Paschall, 1828.

**450.** Benton, Thomas H. *Thirty Years View: Or a History of the Workings of the American Government for Thirty Years, 1820–1850.* 2 vols. New York: Appleton, 1854–1856.

**451.** Brewer, John E. "Thomas Hart Benton and American Nationalism." Ph.D. dissertation, Florida State University, 1970.

**452.** Brooks, Noah. "Thomas H. Benton." In his *Statesmen*, 91–118. New York: Scribner's, 1894.

**453.** Castel, Albert E. "Thomas Hart Benton: A Profile." *American History Illustrated* 2 (July 1967): 12–19.

**454.** Chambers, William N. "The Education of a Democrat: Formative Years of Thomas Hart Benton and the Development of His Political Ideas, 1782–1826." Ph.D. dissertation, Washington University, 1949.

**455.** ———. *Old Bullion Benton, Senator from the New West: Thomas Hart Benton, 1782–1858.* New York: Russell and Russell, 1956.

**456.** Clark, Champ. "Thomas Hart Benton." In *Library of Southern Literature*, edited by Edwin A. Alderman and Joel C. Harris, vol. 1, 345–350. New Orleans, LA: Martin and Hoyt, 1909.

**457.** Fremont, Jessie. "Biographical Sketch of Senator Benton in Connection with Western Expansion." In *Memoirs of My Life*, by John C. Fremont, 1–17. Chicago: Belford, Clark, 1887.

**458.** Hansen, William A. "Thomas Hart Benton and the Oregon Question." *Missouri Historical Review* 63 (July 1969): 489–497.

**459.** Jones, William C. *Colonel Benton and His Contemporaries.* Washington, DC: Polkinhorn, Printer, 1858.

**460.** Kennedy, John F. "'I Despise the Bubble Popularity . . . .': Thomas Hart Benton." In his *Profiles in Courage,* 81–99. New York: Harper and Row, 1956.

**461.** Magoon, Elias L. "Thomas H. Benton." In his *Living Orators in America,* 302–407. New York: Baker and Scribner, 1849.

**462.** McCandless, Perry G. "Benton V. Barton: The Formation of the Second-Party System in Missouri." *Missouri Historical Review* 79 (July 1985): 425–438.

**463.** ———. "The Political Philosophy and Political Personality of Thomas H. Benton." *Missouri Historical Review* 50 (January 1956): 145–158.

**464.** ———. "The Rise of Thomas Hart Benton in Missouri Politics." *Missouri Historical Review* 50 (October 1955): 16–29.

**465.** ———. "Thomas Hart Benton: His Source of Political Strength in Missouri from 1815–1838." Ph.D. dissertation, University of Missouri, 1953.

**466.** McClure, Clarence H. "Early Opposition to Thomas Hart Benton." *Missouri Historical Review* 10 (April 1916): 151–196.

**467.** ———. "Opposition in Missouri to Thomas Hart Benton." Ph.D. dissertation, George Peabody College for Teachers, 1926.

**468.** Meigs, William M. *The Life of Thomas Hart Benton.* Philadelphia: Lippincott, 1904.

**469.** Mills, Douglas E. "The Currency and Fiscal Ideas of Thomas Hart Benton." Master's thesis, University of California, Berkeley, 1950.

**470.** Parrish, William E. *Thomas Hart Benton.* Parkville: Missouri Council for Social Studies, Park College, 1959.

**471.** Ray, Perley O. "The Retirement of Thomas H. Benton from the Senate and Its Significance." *Missouri Historical Review* 2 (January 1908): 97–111.

**472.** Rogers, Joseph M. *Thomas H. Benton.* Philadelphia: G. W. Jacobs, 1905.

**473.** Roosevelt, Theodore. *The Life of Thomas Hart Benton.* Boston: Houghton Mifflin, 1887.

**474.** Shalhope, Robert E. "Thomas Hart Benton and Missouri State Politics: A Re-Examination." *Missouri Historical Society Bulletin* 25 (1969): 171–191.

**475.** Smith, Elbert B. *Magnificent Missourian: The Life of Thomas Hart Benton.* Philadelphia: Lippincott, 1957.

**476.** ———. "Thomas Hart Benton: The First Civil War Revisionist." *Midwest Quarterly* 6 (Autumn 1964): 45–56.

**477.** ———. "Thomas Hart Benton: Southern Realist." *American Historical Review* 58 (July 1953): 795–807.

**478.** Wheat, Francis M. "Senator Benton Lays His Plans." *California Historical Society Quarterly* (San Francisco) 13 (June 1934): 150–154.

**BENTON, WILLIAM (1900–1973) D-CT, Senate 1949–1953.**

**479.** Gunther, Max. "William Benton: One-Hundred-Fifty Million Dollars." In his *The Very, Very Rich and How They Got That Way,* 20–30. Chicago: Playboy Press Book, 1972.

**480.** Hyman, Sidney. *The Lives of William Benton.* Chicago: University of Chicago Press, 1969.

**BENTSEN, LLOYD MILLARD JR. (1921– ) D-TX, House 1948–1955, Senate 1971–1993.**

**481.** Banks, Jimmy. "Anatomy of a Campaign." In his *Money, Marbles, and Chalk: The Wondrous World of Texas Politics,* 199–212. Austin: Texas Publishing Company, 1971.

**482.** Lubalin, Eve. "Presidential Ambition and Senatorial Behavior: The Impact of Ambition on the Behavior of Incumbent Politicians." Ph.D. dissertation, Johns Hopkins University, 1981.

**483.** Welch, June R. "Lloyd Bentsen Was the Valley's First Senator." In her *The Texas Senator,* 72–75. Dallas: G.L.A. Press, 1978.

**BERGER, VICTOR LUITPOLD**
**(1860–1929) SOC-WI, House 1911–1913,**
**1923–1929.**

**484.** Bedford, Henry F. "A Case Study in Hysteria: Victor L. Berger, 1917–1921." Master's thesis, University of Wisconsin, 1953.

**485.** Chafee, Zechariah. "Exclusion of Victor L. Berger from the House of Representatives." In his *Freedom of Speech,* 315–332. New York: Harcourt, Brace and Howe, 1920.

**486.** De Leon, Daniel. *A Socialist in Congress: His Conduct and Responsibilities: 'Parliamentary Idiocy' vs. Marxian Socialism.* New York: New York Labor News Co.: 1963.

**487.** Miller, Sally M. *Victor Berger and the Promise of Constructive Socialism, 1910–1920.* Westport, CT: Greenwood, 1973.

**488.** Muzik, Edward J. "Victor L. Berger: Congress and the Red Scare." *Wisconsin Magazine of History* 47 (Summer 1964): 309–318.

**489.** Olson, Frederick I. "Victor Berger's Friends at Court." *Milwaukee History* 13, no. 1 (1990): 11–17.

**BERNHISEL, JOHN MILTON**
**(1799–1881) W-UT, House 1851–1859,**
**1861–1863.**

**490.** Barnett, Gwynn W. "Dr. John M. Bernhisel: Mormon Elder in Congress." *Utah Historical Quarterly* 36 (Spring 1968): 143–167.

**491.** ———. "John M. Bernhisel: Mormon Elder in Congress." Ph.D. dissertation, Brigham Young University, 1968.

**492.** Cartwright, James F., and James B. Allen. "John M. Bernhisel Letter to Brigham Young." *Brigham Young University Studies* 22 (Summer 1982): 357–362.

**BERRIEN, JOHN MACPHERSON**
**(1781–1856) W-GA, Senate 1825–1829,**
**1841–1845, 1845–1852.**

**493.** Govan, Thomas P. "John M. Berrien and the Administration of Andrew Jackson." *Journal of Southern History* 5 (November 1939): 447–467.

**494.** McCrary, Royce C. "John Macpherson Berrien of Georgia (1781–1856): A Political Biography." Ph.D. dissertation, University of Georgia, 1971.

**495.** ———. "John Macpherson Berrien and the Know-Nothing Movement in Georgia." *Georgia Historical Quarterly* 61 (Spring 1977): 35–42.

**496.** Smith, C. Jay. "John Macpherson Berrien." In *Georgians in Profile: Historical Essays in Honor of Ellis Merton Coulter,* edited by Horace Montgomery, 168–191. Athens: University of Georgia Press, 1958.

**BERRY, ELLIS YARNAL (1902–   )**
**R-SD, House 1951–1971.**

**497.** Schulte, Steven C. "Removing the Yoke of Government: E. Y. Berry and the Origins of Indian Termination Policy." *South Dakota History* 14 (Spring 1984): 48–67.

**BERRY, JAMES HENDERSON**
**(1841–1913) D-AR, Senate 1885–1907.**

**498.** Berry, James. *An Autobiography of James Berry.* Bentonville, AR: Democrat Press, 1913.

## BEVERIDGE, ALBERT JEREMIAH
**(1862–1927) R-IN, Senate 1899–1911.**

**499.** Alderson, William T., and Kenneth K. Baily. "Correspondence between Albert J. Beveridge and Jacob M. Dickinson on the Writing of Beveridge's Life of Lincoln." *Journal of Southern History* 20 (May 1954): 210–237.

**500.** Barbee, David R. *An Excursion in Southern History, Briefly Set Forth in the Correspondence between Senator A. J. Beveridge and David Rankin Barbee.* Richmond, VA: Williams, 1928.

**501.** Beveridge, Albert J. *The Meaning of the Times and Other Speeches.* Indianapolis: Bobbs-Merrill, 1908.

**502.** Bowers, Claude G. *Beveridge and the Progressive Era.* New York: Library Guild, 1932.

**503.** Braeman, John. *Albert J. Beveridge: American Nationalist.* Chicago: University of Chicago Press, 1971.

**504.** ———. "Albert J. Beveridge and the First National Child Labor Bill." *Indiana Magazine of History* 60 (March 1964): 1–36.

**505.** Carlson, A. Cheree. "Albert J. Beveridge as Imperialist and Progressive: The Means Justify the End." *Western Journal of Speech Communication* 52 (Winter 1988): 46–62.

**506.** De La Cruz, Jesse. "Rejection Because of Race: Albert J. Beveridge and Nuevo Mexico's Struggle for Statehood, 1902–1909." *Aztlan* 7 (Spring 1976): 79–97.

**507.** Donnan, Elizabeth, and Leo F. Stock, eds. "Senator Beveridge, J. Franklin Jameson, and Abraham Lincoln." *Mississippi Valley Historical Review* 35 (March 1949): 639–673.

**508.** ———. "Senator Beveridge, J. Franklin Jameson, and John Marshall." *Mississippi Valley Historical Review* 34 (December 1948): 453–492.

**509.** Gulley, Halbert E. "Speaking of Albert J. Beveridge." In *American Public Address,* edited by Loren Reid, 171–188. Columbia: University of Missouri Press, 1961.

**510.** Hileman, Byron P. "Albert J. Beveridge and the Labor Movement: The Evolution of a Progressive, 1899–1912." Master's thesis, University of Florida, 1967.

**511.** Levine, Daniel. "The Social Philosophy of Albert J. Beveridge." *Indiana Magazine of History* 58 (June 1962): 101–116.

**512.** Mangelsdorf, Karen U. "The Beveridge Visit to Arizona in 1902." *Journal of Arizona History* 28 (1987): 243–260.

**513.** Palermo, Patrick F. "Albert Beveridge and the Republican Rhetorical Tradition: The Making of a Senator." *Hayes Historical Journal* 5 (Spring 1985): 29–43.

**514.** Parker, James R. "Beveridge and the Election of 1912: Progressive Idealist or Political Realist." *Indiana Magazine of History* 63 (June 1967): 103–114.

**515.** Remy, Charles F. "The Election of Beveridge to the Senate." *Indiana Magazine of History* 36 (June 1940): 123–135.

**516.** Thomas, Benjamin P. "The Rout of the Romanticists." In his *Portrait for Posterity: Lincoln and His Biographers,* 243–266. New Brunswick, NJ: Rutgers University Press, 1947.

**517.** Thompson, J. A. "An Imperialist and the First World War: The Case of Albert J. Beveridge." *Journal of American Studies* 5 (August 1971): 133–150.

## BIBB, GEORGE MORTIMER
**(1776–1859) J-KY, Senate 1811–1814, 1829–1835.**

**518.** Goff, John S. "The Last Leaf: George Mortimer Bibb." *Register of the Kentucky Historical Society* 59 (October 1961): 331–342.

**BIBB, WILLIAM WYATT** (1781–1820)
R-GA, House 1807–1813, Senate 1813–1816.

**519.** Mellichamp, Josephine. "William Bibb." In her *Senators from Georgia,* 72–74. Huntsville, AL: Strode Publishers, 1976.

**BIBLE, ALAN HARVEY** (1909–1988)
D-NV, Senate 1954–1974.

**520.** Elliott, Gary E. "A Legacy of Support: Senator Alan Bible and the Nevada Mining Industry." *Nevada Historical Society Quarterly* 31 (Fall 1988): 183–197.

**521.** ———. "Senator Alan Bible and the Southern Nevada Water Project, 1954–1971." *Nevada Historical Society Quarterly* 32 (Fall 1989): 181–197.

**522.** ———. *Senator Bible and the Politics of the West.* Reno: University of Nevada Press, 1994.

**BIDDLE, RICHARD** (1796–1847) AMS-PA,
House 1837–1840.

**523.** Tyler, Patrick F. *Historical View of the Progress of Discovery on the More Northern Coasts of America, from the Earliest Period to the Present.* New York: Harper, 1860.

**BIDWELL, JOHN** (1819–1900) R-CA,
House 1865–1867.

**524.** Benjamin, Marcus. *John Bidwell, Pioneer.* Louisville, KY: Lost Cause Press, 1907.

**525.** Bidwell, Annie E. "The Character of John Bidwell: Two Letters Written by His Widow, Mrs. Annie E. K. Bidwell." *Historical Society of California Publications* (Los Angeles) 11 (1919): 53–55.

**526.** Cleland, Robert G. "The First of the Overland Pioneers." In his *Pathfinders,* 288–307. Los Angeles: Powell Publishing Company, 1929.

**527.** Cody, Cora E. "John Bidwell: His Early Career in California." Master's thesis, University of California, Berkeley, 1927.

**528.** Dillon, Richard. "John Bidwell." In his *Humbugs and Heroes,* 43–49. Garden City, NY: Doubleday, 1970.

**529.** Hunt, Rockwell D. *John Bidwell, Prince of California Pioneers.* Caldwell, ID: Caxton Printers, 1942.

**530.** Royce, Charles C. *John Bidwell; Pioneer Statesman, Philanthropist: A Biographical Sketch.* Chico, CA: N.p., 1906.

**BIGELOW, ABIJAH** (1775–1860) F-MA,
House 1810–1815.

**531.** Scotti, N. David. "Abijah Bigelow." *American Antiquarian Society Proceedings* 79 (1969): 245–252.

**BIGGS, ASA** (1811–1878) D-NC, House
1845–1847, Senate 1855–1858.

**532.** Biggs, Asa. *Autobiography, Including a Journal of a Trip from North Carolina to New York in 1832.* Edited by Robert D. Connor. Raleigh, NC: State Printers, 1915.

**BILBO, THEODORE GILMORE**
(1877–1947) D-MS, Senate 1935–1947.

**533.** Bailey, Robert J. "Theodore G. Bilbo and the Fair Employment Practices Controversy: A Southern Senator's Reaction to a Changing World." *Journal of Mississippi History* 42 (February 1980): 27–42.

**534.** ———. "Theodore G. Bilbo and the Senatorial Election of 1934." *Southern Quarterly* 10 (October 1971): 91–105.

**535.** Balsamo, Larry T. "Theodore G. Bilbo and Mississippi Politics, 1877–1932." Ph.D. dissertation, University of Missouri, 1967.

**536.** Boulard, Garry. "The Man versus the Quisling: Theodore Bilbo, Hodding Carter, and the 1946 Democratic Primary." *Journal of Mississippi History* 51 (August 1989): 201–217.

**537.** Ethridge, Richard C. "The Fall of the Man: The United States Senate's Probe of Theodore G. Bilbo in December 1946, and Its Aftermath." *Journal of Mississippi History* 38 (August 1976): 241–262.

**538.** Giroux, Vincent A. "The Rise of Theodore G. Bilbo (1908–1932)." *Journal of Mississippi History* 43 (August 1981): 180–209.

**539.** ———. "Theodore G. Bilbo: Progressive to Public Racist." Ph.D. dissertation, Indiana University, 1984.

**540.** Grant, Philip A., Jr. "The Mississippi Congressional Delegation and the Formation of the Conservative Coalition." *Journal of Mississippi History* 50 (February 1988): 21–28.

**541.** Green, A. Wigfall. *The Man Bilbo.* Baton Rouge: Louisiana State University Press, 1963.

**542.** Hobbs, Gambrell A. *Bilbo, Brewer, and Bribery in Mississippi Politics.* 2d ed. Memphis, TN: Dixon-Paul Printing Co., 1918.

**543.** Luthin, Reinhard H. "Theodore G. Bilbo: 'The Man' of Mississippi." In his *American Demagogues,* 44–76. Boston: Beacon Press, 1954.

**544.** Morgan, Chester M. *Redneck Liberal: Theodore G. Bilbo and the New Deal.* Baton Rouge: Louisiana State University Press, 1985.

**545.** ———. "Senator Theodore G. Bilbo, the New Deal, and Mississippi Politics (1934–1940)." *Journal of Mississippi History* 47 (August 1985): 147–164.

**546.** Saucier, Bobby W. "The Public Career of Theodore G. Bilbo." Ph.D. dissertation, Tulane University, 1971.

**547.** Skates, John R. "Journalist vs. Politician: Fred Sullens and Theodore B. Bilbo." *Southern Quarterly* 8 (April 1970): 273–292.

**548.** Smith, Charles P. "Theodore G. Bilbo's Senatorial Career: The Final Years 1941–1947." Ph.D. dissertation, University of Southern Mississippi, 1983.

**549.** Zorn, Roman J. "Theodore G. Bilbo." In *Public Men In and Out of Office,*

edited by John T. Salter, 277–296. Chapel Hill: University of North Carolina Press, 1946.

### BINGHAM, HIRAM (1875–1956) R-CT, Senate 1924–1933.

**550.** Bingham, Woodbridge. *Hiram Bingham: A Personal History.* Boulder: Bin Lan Zhen Publishers, 1989.

**551.** Cohen, Daniel. *Hiram Bingham and the Dream of Gold.* New York: M. Evans, 1984.

**552.** Miller, Frank L. "Fathers and Sons: The Binghams and American Reform, 1790–1970." Ph.D. dissertation, Johns Hopkins University, 1970.

**553.** Von Hagen, Victor W. "Hiram Bingham and the Lost Cities." *Archaeology* 2 (March 1949): 42–46.

### BINGHAM, JOHN ARMOR (1815–1900) R-OH, House 1855–1863, 1865–1873.

**554.** Beauregard, Erving E. *Bingham of the Hills: Politician and Diplomat Extraordinary.* New York: P. Lang, 1989.

**555.** ———. "The Chief Prosecutor of President Andrew Johnson." *Midwest Quarterly* 31 (Spring 1990): 408–422.

**556.** ———. "John A. Bingham and the Fourteenth Amendment." *Historian* 50 (November 1987): 67–76.

**557.** ———. "John A. Bingham: Scourge of the Slavocracy, Freemasonry and Papacy." *Maryland Historian* 21 (Fall/Winter 1990): 12–25.

**558.** ———. "Secretary Stanton and Congressman Bingham." *Lincoln Herald* 91 (Winter 1989): 141–150.

**559.** Riggs, C. Russell. "The Ante-Bellum Career of John A. Bingham: A Case Study in the Coming of the Civil War." Ph.D. dissertation, New York University, 1959.

**560.** Shotwell, Walter G. "Bingham." In his *Driftwood,* 175–233. New York: Longmans, Green, 1927.

**BINGHAM, KINSLEY SCOTT**
**(1808–1861) R-MI, House 1847–1851,**
**Senate 1859–1861.**

**561.** Sumner, Charles. *Bingham and Baker.*
Washington, DC: Scammell, 1861.

**562.** ———. "The Late Senator Bingham." In his *Works,* vol. 6, 124–129.
Boston: Lee and Shepard, 1880.

**BINGHAM, WILLIAM** (1752–1804) **F-PA,**
**Senate 1795–1801, Continental Congress**
**1786–1788.**

**563.** Alberts, Robert C. *Golden Voyage: The
Life and Times of William Bingham,
1752–1804.* Boston: Houghton Mifflin,
1969.

**564.** Roberson Center for the Arts and
Sciences. *William Bingham: America, a Good
Investment.* Binghamton, NY: The Center,
1975.

**565.** Sawtelle, William O. *William Bingham of Philadelphia and His Maine Lands,
an Address Delivered before the Genealogical
Society of Pennsylvania at the Annual Meeting, March 1, 1926.* Lancaster, PA: Wickersham Press, 1926.

**BINNEY, HORACE** (1780–1875) **AJ-PA,**
**House 1833–1835.**

**566.** Binney, Charles C. *Life of Horace Binney, with Selections from His Letters.* Philadelphia: Lippincott, 1903.

**567.** Montgomery, John T. *The Writ of
Habeas Corpus, and Mr. Binney.* 2d ed.
Philadelphia: John Campbell, 1862.

**BISBEE, HORATIO JR.** (1839–1916) **R-FL,**
**House 1877–1879, 1881, 1882–1885.**

**568.** Klingman, Peter D. "Inside the Ring:
Bisbee-Lee Correspondence, February–
April 1880." *Florida Historical Quarterly* 57
(October 1978): 187–204.

**BLACK, FRANK SWETT** (1853–1913)
**R-NY, House 1895–1897.**

**569.** Griffith, William M. "Administration
of Frank S. Black." In *Official New York,
From Cleveland to Hughes,* edited by Charles
E. Fitch, vol. 1, 149–164. New York: Hurd,
1911.

**BLACK, HUGO LAFAYETTE** (1886–1971)
**D-AL, Senate 1927–1937.**

**570.** Anastaplo, George. "Mr. Justice
Black, His Generous Common Sense, and
the Bar Admission Cases." *Southwestern
University Law Review* 9, no. 4 (1977):
977–1048.

**571.** Armstrong, Walter P. "Mr. Justice
Black." *Tennessee Law Review* 20 (April
1949): 638–643.

**572.** Ash, Michel. "The Growth of Justice
Black's Philosophy on Freedom of
Speech, 1962–1966." *Wisconsin Law Review*
(Fall 1967): 860–862.

**573.** Atkins, Burton M., and Terry
Sloope. "The 'New' Hugo Black and the
Warren Court." *Polity* 18 (Summer 1986)
621–637.

**574.** Ball, Howard. "Hugo L. Black: A
Twentieth Century Jeffersonian." *Southwestern University Law Review* 9, no. 4
(1977): 1049–1068.

**575.** ———. "Justice Hugo L. Black: A
Magnificent Product of the South." *Alabama Law Review* 36 (Spring 1985): 791–834.

**576.** ———. *The Vision and the Dream of
Justice Hugo L. Black: An Examination of a
Judicial Philosophy.* Tuscaloosa: University
of Alabama Press, 1975.

**577.** Ball, Howard, and Phillip J. Cooper.
*Of Power and Right: Hugo Black, William O.
Douglas and America's Constitutional Revolution.* Oxford: Oxford University Press,
1992.

**578.** Barnett, Vincent M., Jr. "Mr. Justice
Black and the Supreme Court." *University
of Chicago Law Review* 8 (December 1940):
20–41.

**579.** Berman, Daniel M. "Freedom and Mr. Justice Black: The Record after Twenty Years." *Missouri Law Review* 25 (1960): 155–174.

**580.** ———. "Hugo Black, Southerner." *American University Law Review* 10 (January 1961): 35–42.

**581.** ———. "Hugo L. Black: The Early Years." *Catholic University of America Law Review* 8 (May 1959): 103–116.

**582.** ———. "Hugo L. Black at Seventy-Five." *American University Law Review* 10 (January 1961): 43–52.

**583.** ———. "The Political Philosophy of Hugo L. Black." Ph.D. dissertation, Rutgers University, 1957.

**584.** ———. "The Racial Issue and Mr. Justice Black." *American University Law Review* 16 (June 1967): 386–402.

**585.** Beth, Loren P. "Mr. Justice Black and the First Amendment: Comments on the Dilemma of Constitutional Interpretation." *Journal of Politics* 41 (November 1979): 1105–1124.

**586.** Black, Elizabeth. "Hugo Black: The Magnificent Rebel." *Southwestern University Law Review* 9, no. 4 (1977): 889–898.

**587.** ———. "Hugo Black: A Memorial Portrait." *Supreme Court Historical Society Yearbook* (1982): 72–94.

**588.** Black, Hugo L. *Mr. Justice and Mrs. Black: The Memoirs of Hugo L. Black and Elizabeth Black.* New York: Random House, 1986.

**589.** Black, Hugo L., Jr. *My Father, a Remembrance.* New York: Random House, 1975.

**590.** Bloch, Charles J. "Mr. Justice Hugo L. Black." *Georgia Bar Journal* 25 (August 1962/1963): 56–59.

**591.** Burke, Andrew F. "Discussion of Senator Black's Legal Position under the Constitution of the United States." *Massa chusetts Law Quarterly* 22 (July/September 1937): 1–5.

**592.** Cahn, Edmond N. "Justice Black and the First Amendment 'Absolutes.'" *New York University Law Review* 37 (1962): 549–563.

**593.** Campbell, Jeter L. "Justices Douglas and Black and the Democratic Ethos: Rhetorical Criticism of Concurring and Dissenting Opinions on Obscenity, 1954–1975." Ph.D. dissertation, University of Minnesota, 1979.

**594.** Cole, Kenneth C. "Mr. Justice Black and 'Senatorial Courtesy.'" *American Political Science Review* 31 (December 1937): 1113–1115.

**595.** Cooper, Jerome A. "Mr. Justice Hugo Lafayette Black of Alabama." *Alabama Law Review* 24 (Fall 1972): 1–9.

**596.** ———. "Mr. Justice Hugo Lafayette Black of Alabama." *Alabama Lawyer* 33 (January 1972): 17–22.

**597.** ———. *"Sincerely Your Friend:" Letters from Mr. Justice Hugo L. Black to Jerome A. Cooper.* Tuscaloosa: University of Alabama Press, 1973.

**598.** Davis, Hazel B. *Uncle Hugo: An Intimate Portrait of Mr. Justice Black.* Amarillo, TX: N.p., 1965.

**599.** Decker, Raymond G. "Justice Hugo L. Black: The Balancer of Absolutes." *California Law Review* 59 (November 1971): 1335–1355.

**600.** Dennis, Everette E., Donald M. Gillmor, and David L. Grey, eds. *Justice Hugo Black and the First Amendment.* Ames: Iowa State University Press, 1978.

**601.** Dilliard, Irving. "Hugo Black and the Importance of Freedom." *American University Law Review* 10 (January 1961): 7–26.

**602.** ———. "Mr. Justice Black and *In Re Anastaplo.*" *Southwestern University Law Review* 9, no. 4 (1977): 953–976.

**603.** ———, ed. *One Man's Stand for Freedom: Mr. Justice Black and the Bill of Rights.* New York: Knopf, 1963.

**604.** Dommici, Peter J. "Protector of the Minorities: Mr. Justice Hugo L. Black." *University of Missouri at Kansas City Law Review* 32 (Summer 1964): 266–291.

**605.** Dorsen, Norman. "Mr. Justice Black and Mr. Justice Harlan." *New York University Law Review* 46 (October 1971): 649–652.

**606.** Douglas, William O. "Mr. Justice Black." *Yale Law Journal* 65 (February 1956): 449–450.

**607.** Dunne, Gerald T. *Hugo Lafayette Black and the Judicial Revolution.* New York: Simon and Schuster, 1976.

**608.** ———. "Justice Hugo Black and Robert Jackson: The Great Feud." *St. Louis University Law Journal* 19 (Summer 1975): 465–487.

**609.** Durr, Clifford J. "Hugo Black, Southerner, the Southern Background." *American University Law Review* 10 (January 1961): 27–42.

**610.** ———. "Hugo L. Black: A Personal Appraisal." *Georgia Law Review* 6 (Fall 1971): 1–13.

**611.** Frank, John P. "Hugo L. Black: He Has Joined the Giants." *American Bar Association Journal* 58 (January 1972): 21–25.

**612.** ———. "Justice Black and the New Deal." *Arizona Law Review* 9 (Summer 1967): 26–58.

**613.** ———. "Mr. Justice Black: A Biographical Appreciation." *Yale Law Journal* 65 (February 1956): 454–463.

**614.** ———. *Mr. Justice Black: The Man and His Opinion.* New York: Knopf, 1949.

**615.** Freund, Paul A. "Mr. Justice Black and the Judicial Function." *UCLA Law Review* 14 (January 1967): 467–474.

**616.** Freyer, Tony A. "Hugo L. Black: Alabamian and American, 1886–1937." *Alabama Law Review* 36 (Spring 1985): 789–926.

**617.** ———. *Hugo L. Black and the Dilemma of American Liberalism.* Glenview, IL: Scott Foresman, 1990.

**618.** ———. *Justice Hugo Black and Modern America.* Tuscaloosa: University of Alabama Press, 1990.

**619.** Gambill, Joel T. "Hugo Black: The First Amendment and the Mass Media." Ph.D. dissertation, Southern Illinois University, 1973.

**620.** Gordon, Murray A. "Justice Hugo Black: First Amendment Fundamentalist." *Lawyers Guild Review* 20 (Spring 1960): 1–5.

**621.** Grant, Philip. "The Constitutional Thought of Hugo Lafayette Black." Ph.D. dissertation, University of California, Santa Barbara, 1974.

**622.** Green, Leon. "Jury Trial and Mr. Justice Black." *Yale Law Journal* 65 (February 1956): 482–494.

**623.** Green, Richard F. "Mr. Justice Black Versus the Supreme Court." *University of Newark Law Review* 4 (Winter 1939): 113–138.

**624.** Gregory, William A., and Rennard Strickland. "Hugo Black's Congressional Investigation of Lobbying and the Public Utilities Holding Company Act: A Historical View of the Power Trust, New Deal Politics, and Regulatory Propaganda." *Oklahoma Law Review* 29 (Summer 1976): 543–576.

**625.** Grinnell, Frank W. "Can Senator Black Become a Member of the Supreme Court under the Constitution?" *Massachusetts Law Quarterly* 22 (July/September 1937): 20–23.

**626.** Hackney, Sheldon. "The Clay County Origins of Mr. Justice Black: The Populist as Insider." *Alabama Law Review* 36 (Spring 1985): 835–844.

**627.** Haigh, Roger W. "Defining Due Process of Law: The Case of Mr. Justice Hugo Black." *South Dakota Law Review* 17 (Winter 1972): 1–40.

**628.** ———. "The Judicial Opinions of Mr. Justice Hugo L. Black." *Southwestern University Law Review* 9, no. 4 (1977): 1069–1126.

**629.** ———. "Mr. Justice Black and the Written Constitution." *Albany Law Review* 24 (Fall 1972): 15–44.

**630.** ———. "Mr. Justice Hugo L. Black, Due Process of Law and the Judicial Role." Ph.D. dissertation, Fordham University, 1971.

**631.** Hamilton, Virginia V. *Hugo Black: The Alabama Years.* Baton Rouge: Louisiana State University Press, 1972.

**632.** ———, ed. *Hugo Black and the Bill of Rights: Proceedings of the First Hugo Black Symposium in American History on "The Bill of Rights and American Democracy."* Tuscaloosa: University of Alabama Press, 1978.

**633.** ———. "Hugo Black: The Road to the Court." *Southwestern University Law Review* 9, no. 4 (1977): 859–888.

**634.** ———. "Listen Hill, Hugo Black, and the Albatross of Race." *Alabama Law Review* 36 (Spring 1985): 845–860.

**635.** ———. "The Senate Career of Hugo L. Black." Ph.D. dissertation, University of Alabama, 1968.

**636.** Hudon, Edward G. "John Libburne, the Levellers, and Mr. Justice Black." *American Bar Association Journal* 60 (June 1974): 686–689.

**637.** Johnson, Nicholas. "Senator Black and the American Merchant Marine." *UCLA Law Review* 14 (January 1967): 399–427.

**638.** Kalven, Harry, Jr. "Upon Rereading Mr. Justice Black on the First Amendment." *UCLA Law Review* 14 (January 1967): 428–445.

**639.** Kalven, Harry, Jr., and Roscoe T. Steffen. "The Bar Admission Cases: An Unfinished Debate between Justice Frankfurter and Justice Black." *Law in Transition* 21 (Fall 1961): 155–196.

**640.** Kirkpatrick, W. Wallace. "Justice Black and Antitrust." *UCLA Law Review* 14 (January 1967): 475–500.

**641.** Klein, Michael. "Hugo L. Black: A Judicial View of American Constitutional Democracy." *University of Miami Law Review* 22 (Spring 1968): 753–799.

**642.** Krislov, Samuel. "Mr. Justice Black Reopens the Free Speech Debate." *UCLA Law Review* 11 (January 1964): 189–211.

**643.** Lee, David D. "Senator Black's Investigation of the Airmail, 1933–1943." *Historian* 53 (Spring 1991): 423–442.

**644.** Lerner, Max. "Mr. Justice Black." In *Ideas Are Weapons: The History and Uses of Ideas,* edited by Max Lerner, 254–266. New York: Viking, 1939.

**645.** Leuchtenburg, William E. "A Klansman Joins the Court: The Appointment of Hugo L. Black." *University of Chicago Law Review* 41 (Fall 1973): 1–31.

**646.** Madison, Charles A. "Hugo L. Black: Defender of the Bill of Rights." In his *Critics & Crusaders: A Century of American Protest,* 601–640. 2d. ed. New York: Frederick Ungar Publishing Co., 1959.

**647.** ———. "Hugo L. Black: New Deal Justice." In his *Leaders and Liberals in 20th Century America,* 315–363. New York: Frederick Ungar Publishing Co., 1961.

**648.** ———. "Justice Black: Defender of the Bill of Rights." *Chicago Jewish Forum* 12 (Spring 1954): 175–181.

**649.** Magee, James J. *Mr. Justice Black, Absolutist on the Court.* Charlottesville: University Press of Virginia, 1980.

**650.** ———. "Mr. Justice Black and the First Amendment: The Development and Dilemmas of an Absolutist." Ph.D. dissertation, University of Virginia, 1976.

**651.** Mason, Gene L. "Hugo Black and the United States Senate." Master's thesis, University of Kansas, 1964.

**652.** Mauney, Connie. "Mr. Justice Black and the First Amendment Freedoms: A Study in Constitutional Interpretation." Ph.D. dissertation, University of Tennessee, 1975.

**653.** McBride, Patrick. "Justice Black's Jurisprudence: A Study of His Interpretations of the Bill of Rights and the Due Process Clause of Amendment XIV." Ph.D. dissertation, University of California, Los Angeles, 1969.

**654.** ———. "Mr. Justice Black and His Qualified Absolutes." *Loyola University of Los Angeles Law Review* 2 (April 1969): 37–70.

**655.** McGovney, Dudley O. "Is Hugo L. Black a Supreme Court Justice de Jure?" *California Law Review* 26 (November 1937): 1–32.

**656.** Meador, Daniel J. "Justice Black and His Law Clerks." *Alabama Law Review* 15 (Fall 1962): 57–63.

**657.** ———. *Mr. Justice Black and His Books.* Charlottesville: University Press of Virginia, 1974.

**658.** Meek, Roy L. "Justices Douglas and Black: Political Liberalism and Judicial Activism." Ph.D. dissertation, University of Oregon, 1964.

**659.** Meiklejohn, Donald. "Public Speech in the Burger Court: The Influence of Mr. Justice Black." *University of Toledo Law Review* 8 (Winter 1977): 301–341.

**660.** Mendelson, Wallace. "Hugo Black and Judicial Discretion." *Political Science Quarterly* 85 (March 1970): 17–39.

**661.** ———. *Justices Black and Frankfurter: Conflict in the Court.* 2d ed. Chicago: University of Chicago Press, 1966.

**662.** ———. Justices Black and Frankfurter: Supreme Court Majority and Minority Trends." *Journal of Politics* 12 (February 1950): 66–92.

**663.** ———. "Mr. Justice Black and the Rule of Law." *Midwest Journal of Political Science* 4 (April 1960): 250–266.

**664.** ———. "Mr. Justice Black's Fourteenth Amendment." *Minnesota Law Review* 53 (March 1969): 711–727.

**665.** Murphy, Paul L. "The Early Social and Political Philosophy of Hugo Black: Liquor as a Test Case." *Alabama Law Review* 36 (Spring 1985): 861–880.

**666.** Mykkeltvedt, Ronald Y. "Justice Black and the Intentions of the Framers of the Fourteenth Amendment's First Section." *Mercer Law Review* 20 (Spring 1969): 423–442.

**667.** Nelson, Paul E. "The Rhetoric of Judicial Dissent in Selected First Amendment Opinions by Justice Hugo Lafayette Black." Master's thesis, University of Minnesota, 1966.

**668.** Newman, Roger K. *Hugo Black: A Biography.* New York: Pantheon Books, 1994.

**669.** Olivarius, Ann. "Absolutely Black: A Judicial Philosophy." *Beverly Hills Bar Association Journal* 11 (November/December 1977): 11–24.

**670.** Paul, Randolph E. "Mr. Justice Black and Federal Taxation." *Yale Law Journal* 65 (February 1956): 495–528.

**671.** Perry, Barbara A. "Justice Hugo Black and the 'Wall of Separation between Church and State.'" *Journal of Church and State* 31 (Winter 1989): 55–72.

**672.** Pruden, Durward. "The Opposition of the Press to the Ascension of Hugo

Black to the Supreme Court of the United States." Ph.D. dissertation, New York University, 1945.

**673.** Ray, Ben F. "Justice Black Adorns the Bench." *Alabama Lawyer* 10 (October 1949): 455–457.

**674.** Reich, Charles A. "Mr. Justice Black and the Living Constitution." *Harvard Law Review* 76 (February 1963): 673–754.

**675.** ———. "Mr. Justice Black as One Who Saw the Future." *Southwestern University Law Review* 9, no. 4 (1977): 845–858.

**676.** Resnik, Solomon. "Black and Douglas: Variations in Dissent." *Western Political Quarterly* 16 (June 1963): 305–322.

**677.** Rice, Charles E. "Justice Black, the Demonstrators, and a Constitutional Rule of Law." *UCLA Law Review* 14 (January 1967): 454–466.

**678.** Rodell, Fred. "A Sprig of Laurel for Hugo Black at 75." *American University Law Review* 10 (January 1961): 1–6.

**679.** Rostow, Eugene V. "Mr. Justice Black: Some Introductory Observations." *Yale Law Journal* 65 (February 1956): 450–453.

**680.** Rutledge, Ivan C. "Justice Black and Labor Law." *UCLA Law Review* 14 (January 1967): 501–523.

**681.** Schwartz, Thomas A. *Measuring Absolutists: Justices Hugo L. Black and William O. Douglas and Their Differences of Opinion on Freedom of the Press.* N.p., 1979.

**682.** Shannon, David A. "Hugo Lafayette Black as United States Senator." *Alabama Law Review* 36 (Spring 1985): 881–898.

**683.** Silverstein, Mark. *Constitutional Faiths: Felix Frankfurter, Hugo Black, and the Process of Judicial Decision-Making.* Ithaca, NY: Cornell University Press, 1984.

**684.** Simon, James F. *The Antagonists: Hugo Black, Felix Frankfurter and Civil Liberties in Modern America.* New York: Simon and Schuster, 1989.

**685.** Slayman, Charles H., Jr. "Speeches and Articles by Mr. Justice Hugo L. Black." *American University Law Review* 10 (January 1961): 116–119.

**686.** Snowiss, Sylvia. "Justice Black and the First Amendment." Ph.D. dissertation, University of Chicago, 1968.

**687.** ———. "The Legacy of Justice Black." *Supreme Court Review* 1973 (1973): 187–252.

**688.** Soles, James R. "Mr. Justice Black and the Defendant's Constitutional Rights." Ph.D. dissertation, University of Virginia, 1968.

**689.** Strickland, Stephen P. "Mr. Justice Black: A Reappraisal." *Federal Bar Journal* 25 (Fall 1965): 365–382.

**690.** ———, ed. *Hugo Black and the Supreme Court: A Symposium.* Indianapolis, IN: Bobbs-Merrill, 1967.

**691.** Suitts, Steve. "Hugo Black's Constitution." *Alabama Heritage* 9 (Summer 1988): 42–55.

**692.** Sutherland, Arthur E. "Justice Black on Counsel and Nonvoluntary Confessions." *UCLA Law Review* 14 (1967): 536–552.

**693.** Targan, Donald G. "Justice Black, Inherent Coercion: An Analytical Study of the Standard for Determining the Voluntariness of a Confession." *American University Law Review* 10 (January 1961): 53–61.

**694.** Thornton, J. Mills. "Hugo Black and the Golden Age." *Alabama Law Review* 36 (Spring 1985): 899–914.

**695.** Tillet, Paul. "Mr. Justice Black, Chief Justice Marshall and the Commerce Clause." *Nebraska Law Review* 43 (December 1963): 1–26.

**696.** Ulmer, S. Sidney. "The Longitudinal Behavior of Hugo Lafayette Black: Parabolic Support for Civil Liberties, 1937–1971." *Florida State University Law Review* 1 (Winter 1973): 131–153.

**697.** Van Alstyne, William W. "Mr. Justice Black, Constitutional Review, and the Talisman of State Action." *Duke Law Journal* 1965 (Spring 1965): 219–247.

**698.** Williams, Charlotte. "Hugo L. Black: A Study in the Judicial Process." Ph.D. dissertation, Johns Hopkins University, 1949.

**699.** Winters, John W. "Opinion Variation as a Measure of Attitude Change in the Supreme Court: A Study of the Opinions of Justice Hugo L. Black from 1957 to 1968." Ph.D. dissertation, University of Kentucky, 1974.

**700.** Wright, Charles A. "Hugo L. Black: A Great Man and a Great American." *Texas Law Review* 50 (December 1971): 1–5.

**701.** Wright, J. Skelly. "Justice at the Dock: The Maritime Worker and Justice Black." *UCLA Law Review* 14 (1967): 521–535.

**702.** Wyatt-Brown, Bertram. "Ethical Background of Hugo Black's Career: Thoughts Prompted by the Articles of Sheldon Hackney and Paul L. Murphy." *Alabama Law Review* 36 (Spring 1985): 915–926.

**703.** Yarbrough, Tinsley E. "Justice Black and Equal Protection." *Southwestern University Law Review* 9, no.4 (1977): 899–936.

**704.** ———. "Justice Black, the First Amendment, and the Burger Court." *Mississippi Law Journal* 46 (Spring 1975): 203–246.

**705.** ———. "Justice Black, the Fourteenth Amendment and Incorporation." *University of Miami Law Review* 30 (Winter 1976): 231–276.

**706.** ———. "Justices Black and Douglas: The Judicial Function and the Scope of Constitutional Liberties." *Duke Law Journal* 1913 (January 1973): 441–486.

**707.** ———. *Mr. Justice Black and His Critics.* Durham, NC: Duke University Press, 1988.

**708.** ———. "Mr. Justice Black and Legal Positivism." *Virginia Law Review* 57 (April 1971): 375–407.

**BLACKBURN, JOSEPH CLAY STILES** (1838–1918) D-KY, House 1875–1885, Senate 1885–1897, 1901–1907.

**709.** Schlup, Leonard. "Joseph Blackburn of Kentucky and the Panama Question." *Filson Club Quarterly* 51 (October 1977): 350–362.

**BLAINE, JAMES GILLESPIE** (1830–1893) R-ME, House 1863–1876, Senate 1876–1881.

**710.** Balch, William R. *An American Career and Its Triumph: The Life and Public Services of James G. Blaine, with the Story of John A. Logan's Career.* Fond du Lac, WI: G. L. Benjamin, 1884.

**711.** Balestier, Charles W. *James G. Blaine, a Sketch of His Life: With a Brief Record of the Life of John A. Logan.* New York: J. W. Lovell, 1884.

**712.** Beale, Harriet S. "James G. Blaine." In *Just Maine Folks,* 26–38. Lewiston, ME: Journal Printshop, 1924.

**713.** Blaine, James G. *Political Discussions, Legislative, Diplomatic and Popular, 1856–1886.* Norwich, CT: Henry Bill, 1887.

**714.** ———. *Twenty Years of Congress: From Lincoln to Garfield.* 2 vols. Norwich, CT: Henry Bill, 1884–1886.

**715.** Bliss, George. *The Charges against Mr. Blaine Examined by a Republican.* New York: N.p., 1884.

**716.** Boyd, James P. *Life and Public Services of Hon. James G. Blaine, the Illustrious American Orator, Diplomat, and Statesman.* Philadelphia: Publisher's Union, 1893.

**717.** Bradford, Gamaliel. "James Gillespie Blaine." In his *American Portraits*, 113–141. Boston: Houghton Mifflin, 1922.

**718.** Brooks, Noah. "James G. Blaine." In his *Statesmen*, 281–312. New York: Scribner's, 1894.

**719.** Cook, Vincent S. *The Life and Public Services of Our Greatest Living Statesman, Hon. James G. Blaine, 'the plumed knight': To Which Is Added the Life of Gen'l John A. Logan.* Rochester, NY: H.B. Graves, 1884.

**720.** Conwell, Russell H. *The Life and Public Services of James G. Blaine.* Hartford, CT: S. S. Scranton, 1884.

**721.** Coulter, E. Merton. "Amnesty for All Except Jefferson Davis: The Hill-Blaine Debate of 1876." *Georgia Historical Quarterly* 56 (Winter 1872): 453–494.

**722.** Craig, Hugh. *The Biography and Public Services of Hon. James G. Blaine.* Authorized ed., New York: H. S. Goodspeed, 1884.

**723.** Crawford, Theron C. *James G. Blaine: A Study of His Life and Career.* Philadelphia: Edgewood Publishing, 1893.

**724.** Dodge, Mary A. *Biography of James G. Blaine.* Norwich, CT: Henry Bill, 1895.

**725.** Ford, Trowbridge H. "The Political Crusade against Blaine in 1884." *Mid-America* 57 (January 1975): 38–55.

**726.** Fry, James B. *The Conkling and Blaine-Fry Controversy, in 1866: The Outbreak of the Life-Long Feud between the Two Great Statesmen, Roscoe Conkling and James G. Blaine.* New York: Press of Sherwood, 1893.

**727.** Fuller, Hubert B. "James G. Blaine." In his *The Speakers of the House*, 169–192. Boston: Little, Brown, 1909.

**728.** Gay, James T. "Harrison, Blaine, and Cronyism . . . Some Facets of the Bering Sea Controversy of the Late Nineteenth Century." *Alaska Journal* 3 (Winter 1973): 12–19.

**729.** Green, Steven K. "The Blaine Amendment Reconsidered." *American Journal of Legal History* 36 (January 1992): 38–69.

**730.** Ham, Edward B. "Amnesty and Blaine of Maine." *New England Quarterly* 28 (June 1955): 255–258.

**731.** Hamilton, Gail. *Biography of James G. Blaine.* Norwich, CT: Henry Bill, 1895.

**732.** Harrison, Robert. "Blaine and the Camerons: A Study in the Limits of Machine Power." *Pennsylvania History* 49 (July 1982): 157–175.

**733.** Haughton, Walter R. *Early Life and Public Career of Hon. James G. Blaine, Patriot, Statesman, and Historian.* Chicago, IL: A. G. Nettleton, 1884.

**734.** Hoyer, Eva. "James Gillespie Blaine: The Father of the Pan American Union, 1830–1898." In her *Sixteen Exceptional Americans*, 129–150. New York: Vantage, 1959.

**735.** Hoyt, Edwin P. "James G. Blaine." In his *Lost Statesmen*, 129–146. Chicago: Reilly and Lee, 1961.

**736.** Johnson, Willis F. *An American Statesman: The Works and Words of James G. Blaine.* Philadelphia: A. R. Keller, 1892.

**737.** Kitson, James T. "The Congressional Career of James G. Blaine, 1862–1876." Ph.D. dissertation, Case Western Reserve University, 1971.

**738.** Klinkhamer, Marie C. "The Blaine Amendment of 1875: Private Motives for Political Action." *Catholic Historical Review* 42 (April 1956): 15–49.

**739.** Knox, Thomas W. *The Lives of James G. Blaine and John A. Logan: Republican Presidential Candidates of 1884*, 52–241. Hartford, CT: Hartford Publishing Company, 1884.

**740.** Landis, John H. *The Life of James Gillespie Blaine.* Lancaster, PA: New Era Printing House, 1884.

**741.** Langley, Lester D. "James Gillespie Blaine: The Ideologue as Diplomatist." In *Makers of American Diplomacy,* edited by Frank J. Merli and T. A. Wilson, 253–278. New York: Scribner's, 1974.

**742.** Lockey, James B. "James Gillespie Blaine." In his *The American Secretaries of State and Their Diplomacy,* edited by Samuel F. Bemis, vol. 7, 260–297; vol. 8, 107–184. New York: Knopf, 1928.

**743.** Long, John D. "James G. Blaine." *Education* 8 (April 1893): 455–461.

**744.** Macartney, Clarence E. "James G. Blaine." In *Men Who Missed It,* 87–95. Philadelphia: Dorrance, 1940.

**745.** Mann, Edward C. *Hon. James G. Blaine's Place in American History.* Albany, NY: Matthew Bender, 1893.

**746.** Mead, Edwin D. *The Case of Mr. Blaine.* Philadelphia: Avil and Co., 1884.

**747.** Meyer, Alfred W. "The Blaine Amendment and the Bill of Rights." *Harvard Law Review* 64 (April 1951): 939–945.

**748.** Mills, Roger Q. "The Gladstone-Blaine Controversy." *North American Review* 150 (February 1890): 145–176.

**749.** Morris, Charles. "James G. Blaine, the Plumed Knight of Republicanism." In his *Heroes of Progress in America,* 278–286. Philadelphia: Lippincott, 1906.

**750.** Muzzey, David. *James G. Blaine: A Political Idol of Other Days.* New York: Dodd, Mead, 1934.

**751.** Peel, Roy V. "James Gillespie Blaine: A Study in Political Leadership." Ph.D. dissertation, University of Chicago, 1927.

**752.** Pierce, James W. *Life of the Hon. James G. Blaine.* Baltimore: M. R. N. Woodward, 1893.

**753.** Ramsdell, Henry J. *Life and Public Service of Hon. James G. Blaine.* Deposit, NY: Phillips and Burrows, 1884.

**754.** Ridpath, John C. *Life and Work of James G. Blaine.* Philadelphia: Historical Publishing, 1893.

**755.** Roberts, Henry G. "James G. Blaine." In *A History and Criticism of American Public Address,* edited by William N. Brigance, 878–890. New York: McGraw-Hill, 1943.

**756.** Romero, M. "Mr. Blaine and the Boundary Question between Mexico and Guatemala." *Bulletin of the American Geographic Society* 29, no. 3 (1897): 281–330.

**757.** Russell, Charles E. *Blaine of Maine: His Life and Times.* New York: Cosmopolitan Book, 1931.

**758.** Seitz, Don C. "James G. Blaine." In his *The 'Also Rans': Great Men Who Missed Making the Presidential Goal,* 282–297. New York: Thomas Y. Crowell, 1928.

**759.** Sherman, Thomas H. *Twenty Years with James G. Blaine: Reminiscences by His Private Secretary.* New York: Grafton Press, 1928.

**760.** Smith, Theodore C. "The Garfield-Blaine Tradition." *Massachusetts Historical Society Proceedings* 57 (March 1924): 291–307.

**761.** Spetter, Allan B. "Harrison and Blaine: Foreign Policy, 1889–1893." *Indiana Magazine of History* 65 (September 1969): 215–228.

**762.** ———. "Harrison and Blaine: Foreign Policy, 1889–1893." Ph.D. dissertation, Rutgers University, 1967.

**763.** ———. "Harrison and Blaine: No Reciprocity for Canada." *Canadian Review of American Studies* 12 (Fall 1981): 143–156.

**764.** Stanwood, Edward. *James Gillespie Blaine.* New York: AMS Press, 1972.

**765.** Stoddard, Henry L. "Blaine! Blaine!—James G. Blaine." In his *As I Knew Them,* 93–101. New York: Harper Brothers, 1927.

**766.** Strobel, Edward H. *Mr. Blaine and His Foreign Policy: An Examination of His Most Important Dispatches While Secretary of State.* Boston: H. W. Hall, 1884.

**767.** Tyler, Alice F. "The Foreign Policy of James G. Blaine." Ph.D. dissertation, University of Minnesota, 1927.

**768.** Volwiler, Albert Y. "Harrison, Blaine, and American Foreign Policy, 1889–1893." *Proceedings of the American Philosophical Society* 79 (November 1938): 637–648.

**769.** Wilgus, A. Curtis. "James G. Blaine and the Pan American Movement." *Hispanic American Historical Review* 5 (November 1922): 622–708.

**770.** Winchester, Richard C. "James G. Blaine and the Ideology of American Expansionism." Ph.D. dissertation, University of Rochester, 1966.

**771.** Windle, Jonathan C. "James G. Blaine: His American Policy and Its Effect upon the McKinley Tariff Act of 1890." Master's thesis, Florida Atlantic University, 1976.

**BLAINE, JOHN JAMES (1875–1934) R-WI, Senate 1927–1933.**

**772.** O'Brien, Patrick G. "Senator John J. Blaine: An Independent Progressive During Normalcy." *Wisconsin Magazine of History* 60 (Autumn 1976): 25–41.

**BLAIR, AUSTIN (1818–1894) R-MI, House 1867–1873.**

**773.** Crofts, Daniel W. "The Blair Bill and the Elections Bill: The Congressional Aftermath to Reconstruction." Ph.D. dissertation, Yale University, 1968.

**774.** Harris, Robert C. "Austin Blair of Michigan: A Political Biography." Ph.D. dissertation, Michigan State University, 1969.

**BLAIR, FRANCIS PRESTON, JR.** (1821–1875) D-MO, House 1857–1859, 1860, 1861–1862, 1863–1864, Senate 1871–1873.

**775.** Craly, David G. *Seymour and Blair, Their Lives and Services with an Appendix Containing a History of Reconstruction.* New York: Richardson, 1868.

**776.** Kirkland, Edward C. "The Politician's Dream of Peace." In his *The Peacemakers of 1864,* 141–205. New York: Macmillan, 1927.

**777.** McCabe, James D. *The Life and Public Services of Horatio Seymour: Together with a Complete and Authentic Life of Francis P. Blair, Jr.* Cincinnati, OH: Jones Brothers, 1868.

**778.** Phillips, Christopher. "The Radical Crusade: Blair, Lyon, and the Advent of the Civil War in Missouri." *Gateway Heritage* 10 (Spring 1990): 22–43.

**779.** Smith, Elbert B. *Francis Preston Blair.* New York: Free Press, 1980.

**780.** Smith, William E. *The Francis Preston Blair Family in Politics.* 2 vols. New York: Macmillan, 1933.

**781.** Wurthman, Leonard B. "Frank Blair: Lincoln's Congressional Spokesman." *Missouri Historical Review* 64 (April 1970): 263–288.

**BLAIR, JOHN (1790–1863) J-TN, House 1823–1835.**

**782.** Bloomer, Faye T. "The Legislative Career of John Blair." Master's thesis, East Tennessee State University, 1956.

**BLAKLEY, WILLIAM ARVIS (1898–1976) D-TX, Senate 1957, 1961.**

**783.** Welch, June R. "Bill Blakley Looked Like a Texas Senator." In her *The Texas Senator,* 64–65. Dallas, TX: G. L. A. Press, 1978.

**784.** ———. "Bill Blakley Served in Both Senatorial Lines." In her *The Texas Senator,* 144–147. Dallas, TX: G. L. A. Press, 1978.

**BLANCHARD, NEWTON CRAIN**
(1849–1922) D-LA, House 1881–1894,
Senate 1894–1897.

**785.** Reeves, Miriam G. "Newton Crain Blanchard (1904–1908)." In her *Governors of Louisiana,* 89–91. Gretna, LA: Pelican Publishing, 1972.

**BLAND, RICHARD** (1710–1776) VA,
Continental Congress 1774–1775.

**786.** Detweiler, Robert C. "Richard Bland: Conservator of Self-Government in Eighteenth-Century Virginia." Ph.D. dissertation, University of Washington, 1968.

**787.** Rossiter, Clinton L. "Richard Bland: The Whig in America." *William and Mary Quarterly* 19 (January 1953): 33–79.

**BLAND, RICHARD PARKS** (1835–1899)
D-MO, House 1873–1895, 1897–1899.

**788.** Byars, William V. *"An American Commoner": The Life and Times of Richard Parks Bland.* Columbia, MO: E. W. Stephens, 1900.

**789.** Haswell, Harold A. "The Public Life of Congressman Richard Parks Bland." Ph.D. dissertation, University of Missouri, 1951.

**790.** Hollister, Wilfred R., and Harry Norman. "Richard P. Bland." In their *Five Famous Missourians,* 87–172. Kansas City, MO: Hudson-Kimberly Publishing Co., 1900.

**BLEASE, COLEMAN LIVINGSTON**
(1868–1942) D-SC, Senate 1925–1931.

**791.** Burnside, Ronald D. "The Governorship of Coleman Livingston Blease of South Carolina, 1911–1915." Ph.D. dissertation, Indiana University, 1963.

**792.** Hollis, Daniel W. "Cole Blease: The Years between the Governorship and the Senate, 1915–1924." *South Carolina Historical Magazine* 80 (January 1979): 1–17.

**793.** ———. "Cole L. Blease and the Senatorial Campaign of 1924." *Proceedings of the South Carolina Historical Association* 48 (1978): 53–68.

**BLOOM, SOL** (1870–1949) D-NY, House 1923–1949.

**794.** Bloom, Sol. *The Autobiography of Sol Bloom.* New York: Putnam's, 1948.

**795.** ———. "Boyhood in San Francisco." In *Autobiographies of American Jews,* compiled by Harold U. Ribalow, 16–25. Philadelphia: Jewish Publishing, 1965.

**796.** Bone, Hugh A. "Sol Bloom." In *Public Men In and Out of Office,* edited by John T. Salter, 225–239. Chapel Hill: University of North Carolina Press, 1946.

**797.** Dickson, Samuel. "Sol Bloom." In his *Tales of San Francisco,* 683–693. Stanford, CA: Stanford University Press, 1957.

**BLOOMFIELD, JOSEPH** (1753–1823)
R-NJ, House 1817–1821.

**798.** Bloomfield, Joseph. *Citizen Soldier: The Revolutionary War Journal of Joseph Bloomfield.* Edited by Mark E. Lender and James K. Martin. Newark: New Jersey Historical Society, 1982.

**799.** Elmer, Lucius Q. "Governors I Have Known: Joseph Bloomfield." In *The Constitution and Government of the Province and State of New Jersey,* 114–137. Newark, NJ: M. R. Dennis, 1872.

**800.** Schluter, William E. "An Analysis of Joseph Bloomfield's Emergence as a Jeffersonian Republican." Master's thesis, Temple University, 1982.

**BLOUNT, WILLIAM** (1749–1800) TN,
Senate 1796–1797, Continental Congress
1782–1783, 1786–1787.

**801.** Heiskell, Samuel G. *Andrew Jackson and Early Tennessee History,* 79–101. Nashville, TN: Ambrose Printing Company, 1920.

**802.** Keith, Arthur B. "William Blount in North Carolina Politics, 1781–1789." In *Studies in Southern History*, edited by Joseph C. Sitterson, 47–61. Chapel Hill: University of North Carolina Press, 1957.

**803.** Masterson, William H. *William Blount.* Baton Rouge: Louisiana State University Press, 1954.

**804.** Melton, Buckner F., Jr. "The First Impeachment: The Constitution's Framers and the Case of Senator William Blount." Ph.D. dissertation, Duke University, 1990.

**805.** Wright, Marcus J. *Some Account of the Life and Services of William Blount.* Washington, DC: Gray, 1884.

**BOGGS, CORINNE CLAIBORNE "LINDY" (1916–    ) D-LA, House 1973–1991.**

**806.** Boggs, Lindy. *Washington through a Purple Veil: Memoirs of a Southern Lady.* New York: Harcourt Brace, 1994.

**BOGGS, THOMAS HALE SR. (1914–1972) D-LA, House 1941–1943, 1947–1973.**

**807.** Balias, Scott E. "The Courage of His Convictions: Hale Boggs and Civil Rights." Master's thesis, Tulane University, 1993.

**808.** Eggler, Bruce. *Life and Career of Hale Boggs.* New Orleans, LA: States-Item, 1973.

**809.** Engstrom, Richard L. "The Hale Boggs Gerrymander: Congressional Redistricting, 1969." *Louisiana History* 21 (Winter 1980): 59–66.

**810.** Gibson, Dirk C. "Hale Boggs on J. Edgar Hoover: Rhetorical Choice and Political Denunciation." *Southern Speech Communication Journal* 47 (Fall 1981): 54–66.

**811.** Shryer, Molly. *Hale Boggs: Democratic Representative from Louisiana.* Washington, DC: Grossman, 1972.

**BOILEAU, GERALD JOHN (1900–1981) PROG-WI, House 1931–1939.**

**812.** Lorence, James J. "Gerald J. Boileau and the Politics of Sectionalism: Dairy Interests and the New Deal, 1933–1938." *Wisconsin Magazine of History* 71 (Summer 1988): 276–295.

**813.** ———. *Gerald J. Boileau and the Progressive-Farmer-Labor Alliance: Politics of the New Deal.* Columbia: University of Missouri Press, 1993.

**BOLLING, RICHARD WALKER (1916–1991) D-MO, House 1949–1983.**

**814.** Bolling, Richard. *House Out of Order.* New York: Dutton, 1965.

**815.** ———. *Power in the House: A History of the Leadership of the House of Representatives.* New York: Putnam's, 1974.

**816.** Gergen, David, and Theodore C. Sorenson. "Governing America: A Conversation with Richard Bolling." *Public Opinion* 7 (February/March 1984): 2–8.

**BOLTON, FRANCES PAYNE (1885–1977) R-OH, House 1940–1969.**

**817.** Lamson, Peggy. "Lady of the House: Frances P. Bolton." In her *Few Are Chosen: American Women in Political Life Today,* 33–60. Boston: Houghton Mifflin, 1968.

**818.** Loth, David G. *A Long Way Forward: The Biography of Congresswoman Frances P. Bolton.* New York: Longmans, 1957.

**BOND, SHADRACK (1773–1832) IL, House 1812–1813.**

**819.** Bloom, Jo T. "Peaceful Politics: The Delegates from Illinois Territory, 1809–1818." *Old Northwest* 6 (Fall 1980): 203–215.

**BOOTH, NEWTON (1825–1892) AM-CA, Senate 1875–1881.**

**820.** Booth, Newton. *Newton Booth of California, His Speeches and Addresses.* New York: Putnam's, 1894.

**821.** Melendy, Howard B., and Benjamin F. Gilbert. "Newton Booth." In their *Governors of California: Peter H. Burnett to Edmund G. Brown,* 156–165. Georgetown, CA: Talisman Press, 1965.

**BORAH, WILLIAM EDGAR** (1865–1940)
**R-ID, Senate 1907–1940.**

**822.** Ashby, Darrel L. "William E. Borah and the Politics of Constitutionalism." *Pacific Northwest Quarterly* 58 (July 1967): 119–129.

**823.** Ashby, Leroy. *The Spearless Leader: Senator Borah and the Progressive Movement in the 1920's.* Urbana: University of Illinois Press, 1972.

**824.** Berger, Henry W. "Laissez Faire for Latin America: Borah Defines the Monroe Doctrine." *Idaho Yesterdays* 9 (Summer 1965): 10–17.

**825.** Berman, Averill J. "Senator William Edgar Borah: A Study in Historical Agreements and Contradictions." Ph.D. dissertation, University of Southern California, 1955.

**826.** Braden, Waldo W. "Bases of William E. Borah's Speech Preparation." *Quarterly Journal of Speech* 33 (February 1947): 28–30.

**827.** ———. "Political Speaking of William E. Borah." In *American Public Address,* edited by Loren Reid, 189–208. Columbia: University of Missouri Press, 1961.

**828.** Brune, Lester H. "Borah and the Airplanes." *Idaho Yesterdays* 12 (Spring 1968): 22–24.

**829.** Church, Frank F. "Borah the Statesman." *Idaho Yesterdays* 9 (Summer 1965): 2–9.

**830.** Cooper, John M., Claudius O. Johnson, and Merle W. Wells. "William E. Borah, Political Thespian." *Pacific Northwest Quarterly* 56 (October 1965): 145–158.

**831.** Debenedetti, Charles. "Borah and the Kellogg-Briand Pact." *Pacific Northwest Quarterly* 63 (January 1972): 22–29.

**832.** Gilbert, Clinton W. "William E. Borah." In his *The Mirrors of Washington,* 245–256. New York: Putnam's, 1921.

**833.** Godfrey, Donald G., and Val E. Limburg. "The Rogue Elephant of Radio Legislation: Senator William E. Borah." *Journalism Quarterly* 67 (Spring 1990): 214–224.

**834.** Griffith, Will. "Senator-at-Large: William E. Borah." In *Idols of Egypt,* edited by Will Griffith, 61–76. Carbondale, IL: Egypt Book House, 1947.

**835.** Grover, David H. "Borah and the Haywood Trial." *Pacific Historical Review* 32 (February 1963): 65–77.

**836.** ———. *Debaters and Dynamiters: The Story of the Haywood Trial.* Corvallis: Oregon State University Press, 1964.

**837.** Hewes, James E. "William E. Borah and the Image of Isolation." Ph.D. dissertation, Yale University, 1955.

**838.** Hill, Sidney R. "The Rhetorical Theory of William Edgar Borah as Seen through His Senate Speeches on the League of Nations." Master's thesis, University of Florida, 1971.

**839.** Johnson, Claudius O. *Borah of Idaho.* New York: Longmans, Green, 1936.

**840.** ———. "When William E. Borah Was Defeated for the United States Senate, in 1903." *Pacific Historical Review* 12 (June 1943): 125–138.

**841.** ———. "William E. Borah: The People's Choice." *Pacific Northwest Quarterly* 44 (January 1953): 15–22.

**842.** Kneeshaw, Stephen J. "Borah and the Outlawry of War: Another Look." *Idaho Yesterdays* 27 (Spring 1983): 2–10.

**843.** Lippmann, Walter. "Borah." In his *Men of Destiny,* 140–161. New York: Macmillan, 1927.

**844.** Maddox, Robert J. "Borah and the Battleships." *Idaho Yesterdays* 9 (Summer 1965): 20–27.

**845.** ———. *William E. Borah and American Foreign Policy.* Baton Rouge: Louisiana State University Press, 1970.

**846.** ———. "William E. Borah and the Crusade to Outlaw War." *Historian* 29 (February 1967): 200–220.

**847.** McKenna, Marian C. *Borah.* Ann Arbor: University of Michigan Press, 1961.

**848.** Owens, John W. "Why They Love Borah." *In Faces of Five Decades,* edited by Robert B. Luce, 103–105. New York: Simon and Schuster, 1964.

**849.** Pinckney, Orde S. "Lion Triumphant." *Idaho Yesterdays* 3 (Summer 1959): 12–24.

**850.** ———. "William E. Borah: Critic of American Foreign Policy." *Studies on the Left* 1, no. 3 (1960): 48–61.

**851.** ———. "William E. Borah and the Republican Party, 1932–1940." Ph.D. dissertation, University of California, 1958.

**852.** Villard, Oswald G. "William E. Borah: The Idaho Lion." In his *Prophets True and False,* 51–63. New York: Knopf, 1928.

**853.** Vinson, John C. *William E. Borah and the Outlawry of War.* Athens: University of Georgia Press, 1957.

**854.** Weinberger, James M. "The British on Borah: Foreign Office and Embassy Attitudes toward Idaho's Senior Senator, 1935–1940." *Idaho Yesterdays* 25 (Fall 1981): 2–14.

**855.** Whitehead, Albert. "The Oratory of William Edgar Borah." *Quarterly Journal of Speech* 32 (October 1946): 292–297.

**856.** Williams, William A. "A Note on the Isolationism of Senator William E. Borah." *Pacific Historical Review* 22 (November 1953): 391–392.

**BOREMAN, ARTHUR INGHRAM** (1823–1896) R-WV, Senate 1869–1875.

**857.** Woodward, Isaiah A. "Arthur Inghram Boreman: A Biography." Ph.D. dissertation, University of Virginia, 1970.

**858.** ———. "Arthur Inghram Boreman: A Biography." *West Virginia History* 31 (July 1970): 206–269; 32 (October 1970): 10–48.

**BOSONE, REVA ZILPHA BECK** (1895–1983) D-UT, House 1949–1953.

**859.** Clopton, Beverly B. *Her Honor, The Judge: The Story of Reva Beck Bosone.* Ames: Iowa State University Press, 1980.

**BOTTS, JOHN MINOR** (1802–1869) W-VA, House 1839–1843, 1847–1849.

**860.** Bartlett, David V. "John Minor Botts." In his *Presidential Candidates: Containing Sketches, Biographical, Personal and Political, of Prominent Candidates for the Presidency in 1860,* 316–321. New York: A. B. Burdick, 1859.

**BOTTUM, JOSEPH H.** (1903–1984) R-SD, Senate 1962–1963.

**861.** Clem, Alan L. *The Nomination of Joe Bottum.* Vermillion, SD: Governmental Research Bureau, 1963.

**BOUDINOT, ELIAS** (1740–1821) NJ, House 1789–1795, Continental Congress 1778, 1781–1783.

**862.** Boudinot, Elias. *The Life, Public Services, Addresses, and Letters of Elias Boudinot.* 2 vols. New York: Da Capo Press, 1971.

**863.** Boyd, George A. *Elias Boudinot: Patriot and Statesman, 1740–1821.* Princeton, NJ: Princeton University Press, 1952.

**864.** Clark, Barbara L. *E. B.: The Story of Elias Boudinot IV, His Family, His Friends,* *and His Country.* Ardmore, PA: Dorrance, 1977.

**865.** Whisenhunt, Donald W. *Elias Boudinot.* Trenton: New Jersey Historical Commission, 1975.

**BOURNE, JONATHAN JR.** (1855–1940) R-OR, Senate 1907–1913.

**866.** Pike, Albert. "Jonathan Bourne, Jr., Progressive." Ph.D. dissertation, University of Oregon, 1957.

**BOUTWELL, GEORGE SEWEL** (1818–1905) R-MA, House 1863–1869, Senate 1873–1877.

**867.** Beisner, Robert L. "The Old Stalwart." In his *Twelve Against Empire,* 193–197. New York: McGraw-Hill, 1968.

**868.** Boutwell, George S. *Reminiscences of Sixty Years in Public Affairs.* New York: McLure, Philips, 1902.

**869.** Brown, Thomas H. "George Sewel Boutwell: Public Servant (1818–1905)." Ph.D. dissertation, New York University, 1979.

**870.** Domer, Thomas. "Role of George S. Boutwell in the Impeachment and Trial of Andrew Johnson." *New England Quarterly* 49 (December 1976): 596–617.

**BOWLES, CHESTER BLISS** (1901–1986) D-CT, House 1959–1961.

**871.** Bowles, Chester. *Promises to Keep: My Years in Public Life, 1941–1969.* New York: Harper and Row, 1971.

**872.** Schaffer, Howard B. *Chester Bowles: New Dealer in the Cold War.* Cambridge, MA: Havard University Press, 1993.

**BOWLIN, JAMES BUTLER** (1804–1874) D-MO, House 1843–1851.

**873.** Wheeler, Henry G. "Bowlin, James Butler." In his *History of Congress,* vol. 1, 446–456. New York: Harper, 1848.

**BOYD, LINN** (1800–1859) D-KY, House 1835–1837, 1839–1855.

**874.** Clift, Garrett G. "Linn Boyd." In his *Governors of Kentucky, 1792–1942,* 194–198. Cynthiana, KY: Hobson Press, 1942.

**875.** Hamilton, Holman. "Kentucky's Linn Boyd and the Dramatic Days of 1850." *Register of the Kentucky Historical Society* 55 (July 1957): 185–195.

**876.** Thompson, George W. *Biographical Sketch of Hon. Linn Boyd, of Kentucky, the Present Speaker of the House of Representatives of the United States.* Washington, DC: Congressional Globe Office, 1855.

**BOYKIN, FRANK WILLIAM** (1885–1969) D-AL, House 1935–1963.

**877.** Boykin, Edward. *Everything's Made from Love in This Man's World: Vignettes from the Life of Frank W. Boykin.* Mobile, AL: Privately printed, 1973.

**BRABSON, REESE BOWEN** (1817–1863) O-TN, House 1859–1861.

**878.** Temple, Oliver P. "Reese B. Brabson." In his *Notable Men of Tennessee from 1833 to 1875: Their Times and Their Contemporaries,* 75–76. New York: Cosmopolitan Press, 1912.

**BRACKENRIDGE, HENRY MARIE** (1786–1871) W-PA, House 1840–1841.

**879.** Brackenridge, Henry M. *Recollections of Persons and Places in the West.* Philadelphia: J. Kay, 1834.

**880.** Keller, William F. *The Nation's Advocate: Henry Marie Brackenridge and Young America.* Pittsburgh, PA: University of Pittsburgh Press, 1956.

**BRADEMAS, JOHN** (1927–  ) D-IN, House 1959–1981.

**881.** Brademas, John. *Washington, D.C. to Washington Square.* New York: Weidenfield and Nicolson, 1986.

**BRADLEY, WILLIAM O'CONNELL**
(1847–1914) R-KY, Senate 1909–1914.

882. Barker, Adelaide A. "William O'Connell Bradley." Master's thesis, University of Kentucky, 1927.

**BRADLEY, WILLIAM WARREN "BILL"**
(1943–    ) D-NJ, Senate 1979–   .

883. Bradley, William W. *Life on the Run.* New York: Quadrangle, 1976.

884. Jaspersohn, William. *Senator: A Profile of Bill Bradley in the U.S. Senate.* San Diego, CA: Harcourt Brace Jovanovich, 1992.

885. McPhee, John A. *Sense of Where You Are: A Profile of William Warren Bradley.* 2d ed. New York: Farrar, Strauss, 1978.

**BRAGG, JOHN** (1806–1878) D-AL, House 1851–1853.

886. McGregor, Robert C. "Between the Two Wars: Alabama in the House of Representatives 1849–1861." *Alabama Historical Quarterly* 42 (Fall/Winter 1980): 167–200.

**BRAGG, THOMAS** (1810–1872) D-NC, Senate 1859–1861.

887. Cowper, Pulaski. "Thomas Bragg." In *Lives of Distinguished North Carolinians,* edited by William Peele. Raleigh: North Carolina Publishing Society, 1898.

**BRANDEGEE, FRANK BOSWORTH**
(1864–1924) R-CT, House 1902–1905, Senate 1905–1924.

888. Janick, Herbert. "Senator Frank B. Brandegee and the Election of 1920." *Historian* 35 (May 1973): 434–451.

**BRATTON, SAM GILBERT** (1888–1963) D-NM, Senate 1925–1933.

889. Fox, Richard L. "New Mexico Senators: A History of Power." *New Mexico Magazine* 63 (November 1985): 82–90.

**BRAWLEY, WILLIAM HUGGINS**
(1841–1916) D-SC, House 1891–1894.

890. Brawley, William H. *Journal of William H. Brawley,* 1864–1865. Edited by Francis P. Brawley. Charlottesville, VA: Privately published, 1970.

**BRAXTON, CARTER** (1736–1797) VA, Continental Congress 1775–1776, 1777–1783, 1785.

891. Dill, Alonzo T. *Carter Braxton: Last Virginia Signer.* Richmond: Virginia Independence Bicentennial Commission, 1976.

892. ———. *Carter Braxton, Virginia Signer: A Conservative in Revolt.* Lanham, MD: University Press of America, 1983.

893. Sanderson, John. "Carter Braxton." In *Sanderson's Biography of the Signers of the Declaration of Independence,* edited by Robert T. Conrad, 748–757. Philadelphia: Thomas, Cowperthwait, 1848.

894. Stevens, L. Tomlin. "Carter Braxton, Signer of the Declaration of Independence." Ph.D. dissertation, Ohio State University, 1969.

**BRECK, SAMUEL** (1771–1862) PA, House 1823–1825.

895. Wainwright, Nicholas B. "The Diary of Samuel Breck, 1814–1838." *Pennsylvania Magazine of History and Biography* 102 (October 1978): 469–508; 103 (January 1979): 85–113; 103 (April 1979): 222–251; 103 (July 1979): 356–382.

896. Winslow, Stephen N. "Samuel Breck." In his *Biographies of Successful Philadelphia Merchants,* 61–69. Philadelphia: J. K. Simon, 1864.

**BRECKINRIDGE, JOHN** (1760–1806) R-KY, Senate 1801–1805.

897. Durrett, Reuben T. "John Breckinridge." In *Library of Southern Literature,* edited by Edwin A. Alderman and Joel C.

Harris, vol. 4, 1462–1476. New Orleans: Martin and Hoyt, 1909.

**898.** Harrison, Lowell H. *John Breckinridge: Jeffersonian Republican.* Louisville, KY: Filson Club, 1969.

**899.** ———. "John Breckinridge: Western Statesman." *Journal of Southern History* 18 (May 1952): 137–151.

**BRECKINRIDGE, JOHN CABELL (1821–1875) D-KY, House 1851–1855, Senate 1861.**

**900.** Bartlett, David V. "John C. Breckinridge." In his *Presidential Candidates: Containing Sketches, Biographical, Personal and Political, of Prominent Candidates for the Presidency in 1860,* 336–345. New York: A. B. Burdick, 1859.

**901.** Barzman, Sol. "John Cabell Breckinridge." In his *Madmen and Geniuses: The Vice-Presidents of the United States,* 97–102. Chicago: Follett, 1974.

**902.** Burger, Nash K., and John K. Bettersworth. "Militant Moderate: John C. Breckinridge." In their *South of Appomattox,* 80–111. New York: Harcourt, 1959.

**903.** Davis, William C. *Breckinridge: Statesman, Soldier, Symbol.* Baton Rouge: Louisiana State University Press, 1974.

**904.** ———. "John C. Breckinridge." *Register of the Kentucky Historical Society* 85 (Summer 1987): 197–212.

**905.** Heck, Frank H. "John C. Breckinridge in the Crisis of 1860–1861." *Journal of Southern History* 21 (August 1955): 316–346.

**906.** ———. *Proud Kentuckian: John C. Breckinridge, 1821–1875.* Lexington: University Press of Kentucky, 1976.

**907.** Stillwell, Lucille. *John Cabell Breckinridge.* Caldwell, ID: Caxton Printers, 1936.

**908.** Young, Bennett H. "John Cabell Breckinridge." In *Library of Southern Literature,* edited by Edwin A. Alderman and Joel C. Harris, vol. 2, 491–494. New Orleans, LA: Martin and Hoyt, 1909.

**BRECKINRIDGE, WILLIAM CAMPBELL PRESTON (1837–1904) D-KY, House 1885–1895.**

**909.** Fuller, Paul E. "An Early Venture of Kentucky Women in Politics: The Breckinridge Congressional Campaign of 1894." *Filson Club History Quarterly* 63 (April 1989): 224–242.

**910.** Klotter, James C. *The Breckinridges of Kentucky,* 1760–1981. Lexington: University Press of Kentucky, 1986.

**911.** ———. "Sex, Scandal, and Suffrage in the Gilded Age." *Historian* 42 (February 1980): 225–243.

**BREESE, SIDNEY (1800–1878) D-IL, Senate 1843–1849.**

**912.** McNulty, John W. "Sidney Breese: His Early Career in Law and Politics in Illinois." *Journal of the Illinois State Historical Society* 61 (Summer 1968): 164–181.

**BRENTON, SAMUEL (1810–1857) R-IN, House 1851–1853, 1855–1857.**

**913.** Mather, George R. "Clergyman and Congress." *Old Fort News* 52, no. 1 (1989): 2–9.

**BRICE, CALVIN STEWART (1845–1898) D-OH, Senate 1891–1897.**

**914.** Havighurst, Walter. "The World of Calvin Brice." In his *Men of Old Miami, 1809–1873,* 209–224. New York: Putnam's, 1974.

**BRICKER, JOHN WILLIAM (1893–1986) R-OH, Senate 1947–1959.**

**915.** Davies, Richard S. *Defender of the Old Guard: John Bricker and American Politics.* Columbus: Ohio State University Press, 1993.

**916.** Grant, Philip A., Jr. "The Bricker Amendment Controversy." *Presidential Studies Quarterly* 15 (Summer 1985): 572–582.

**917.** Pauly, Karl B. *Bricker of Ohio, the Man and His Record.* New York: Putnam's, 1944.

**918.** ———. "John W. Bricker, 1939–1945." In *Governors of Ohio,* 184–188. Columbus: Ohio Historical Society, 1954.

**919.** Schueneman, Bruce R. "John Bricker, Conservative." Master's thesis, Texas A&I University, 1983.

**920.** Seasongood, Murray. "John W. Bricker." In *Public Men In and Out of Office,* edited by John T. Salter, 395–414. Chapel Hill: University of North Carolina Press, 1946.

**921.** Tananbaum, Duane A. "The Bricker Amendment Controversy: Its Origins and Eisenhower's Role." *Diplomatic History* 9 (Winter 1985): 73–93.

**922.** ———. *The Bricker Amendment Controversy: A Test of Eisenhower's Political Leadership.* Ithaca, NY: Cornell University Press, 1988.

**923.** Zahniser, Marvin R., ed. "John W. Bricker Reflects upon the Fight for the Bricker Amendment." *Ohio History* 87 (Summer 1978): 322–333.

**BRIDGES, HENRY STYLES** (1898–1961) R-NH, Senate 1937–1961.

**924.** Cater, Douglass. "Senator Styles Bridges and His Farflung Constituents." *Reporter* 11 (July 20, 1954): 8–21.

**BRIGHT, JESSE DAVID** (1812–1875) D-IN, Senate 1845–1862.

**925.** Murphy, Charles B. *The Political Career of Jesse D. Bright.* Indianapolis: Indiana Historical Society, 1931.

**926.** Sumner, Charles. *The Expulsion of a Senator.* Washington, DC: Office of the Congressional Globe, 1862.

**927.** Van Der Weele, Wayne J. "Jesse David Bright: Master Politician from the Old Northwest." Ph.D. dissertation, Indiana University, 1958.

**BRISTOW, FRANCIS MARION** (1804–1864) O-KY, House 1854–1855, 1859–1861.

**928.** Webb, Ross A. "Francis Marion Bristow, A Study in Unionism." *Filson Club History Quarterly* 37 (April 1963): 142–158.

**BRISTOW, JOSEPH LITTLE** (1861–1944) R-KS, Senate 1909–1915.

**929.** Easterling, Larry J. "Sen. Joseph L. Bristow and the Seventeenth Amendment." *Kansas Historical Quarterly* 41 (Winter 1975): 488–511.

**930.** Sageser, Adelbert B. *Joseph L. Bristow: Kansas Progressive.* Lawrence: University Press of Kansas, 1968.

**BRITTEN, FREDERICK ALBERT** (1871–1946) R-IL, House 1913–1935.

**931.** VanderMeer, Philip R. "Congressional Decision-Making and World War I: A Case Study of Illinois." *Congressional Studies* 8, no. 2 (1981): 59–79.

**BRODERICK, DAVID COLBRETH** (1820–1859) D-CA, Senate 1857–1859.

**932.** Conmy, Peter T. *David C. Broderick and the Re-location of the Broderick Monument, Why a Monument to Broderick?* San Francisco: History Board, Native Sons of the Golden West, 1942.

**933.** Fredman, Lionel E. "Broderick: A Reassessment." *Pacific Historical Review* 30 (February 1981): 39–46.

**934.** Hall, Carroll D. *The Terry-Broderick Duel.* San Francisco: Colt Press, 1939.

**935.** Lynch, Jeremiah. *The Life of David C. Broderick, A Senator of the Fifties.* New York: Baker and Taylor, 1911.

**936.** O'Meara, James. *Broderick and Gwin.* San Francisco: Bacon and Company, Printers, 1881.

**937.** Williams, David A. *David C. Broderick, a Political Portrait.* San Marino, CA: Huntington Library, 1969.

**BROMBERG, FREDERICK GEORGE**
(1837–1930) LR-AL, House 1873–1875.

**938.** Sizemore, Margaret D. "Frederick G. Bromberg of Mobile: An Illustrious Character, 1837–1928." *Alabama Review* 29 (April 1976): 104–112.

**BROOKE, EDWARD WILLIAM III**
(1919–   ) R-MA, Senate 1967–1979.

**939.** Becker, John F., and Eugene E. Heaton, Jr. "The Election of Senator Edward W. Brooke." *Public Opinion Quarterly* 31 (Fall 1967): 346–358.

**940.** Christopher, Maurine. "Edward W. Brooke/Massachusetts." In her *Black Americans in Congress,* 228–236. Rev. ed. New York: Thomas Y. Crowell, 1976.

**941.** Cutler, John H. *Ed Brooke: Biography of a Senator.* Indianapolis: Bobbs-Merrill, 1972.

**942.** Flynn, James J. *Negroes of Achievement in Modern America,* 138–143. New York: Dodd, Mead, 1970.

**943.** Hartshorn, Elinor C. "The Quiet Campaigner: Edward W. Brooke in Massachusetts." Ph.D. dissertation, University of Massachusetts, 1973.

**944.** Metcalf, George R. "Edward W. Brooke." In his *Black Profiles,* 279–305. New York: McGraw-Hill, 1968.

**945.** Toppin, Edgar A. "Brooke, Edward W." In his *Biographical History of Blacks in America since 1528,* 257–258. New York: McKay, 1971.

**BROOKHART, SMITH WILDMAN**
(1869–1944) R-IA, Senate 1922–1926,
1927–1933.

**946.** Briley, Ronald F. "Smith W. Brookhart and the Limits of Senatorial Dissent." *Annals of Iowa* 48 (Summer/Fall 1985): 56–79.

**947.** Cook, Louis H. "Brookhart, Insurgent." *North American Review* 231 (February 1931): 178–184.

**948.** Dennis, Alfred P. "The European Education of Senator Brookhart." In his *Gods and Little Fishes.* Indianapolis: Bobbs-Merrill, 1931.

**949.** Luthin, Reinhard H. "Smith Wildman Brookhart of Iowa: Insurgent Agrarian Politician." *Agricultural History* 25 (October 1951): 187–197.

**950.** McDaniel, George W. "Prohibition Debate in Washington County, 1890–1894: Smith Wildman Brookhart's Introduction to Politics." *Annals of Iowa* 45 (Winter 1981): 519–536.

**951.** ———. "The Republican Party in Iowa and the Defeat of Smith Wildman Brookhart, 1924–1926." *Annals of Iowa* 48 (Winter/Spring 1987): 413–434.

**952.** ———. "Smith Wildman Brookhart." *Palimpsest* 63 (November/December 1982): 174–183.

**953.** ———. "Smith Wildman Brookhart: Agrarian Radical in New Era America." Ph.D. dissertation, University of Iowa, 1985.

**954.** Neprash, Jerry A. *The Brookhart Campaigns in Iowa, 1920–1926: A Study in Motivation in Political Attitudes.* New York: Columbia University Press, 1932.

**955.** Porter, David L. "Iowa Congressional Delegation and the Great Economic Issues, 1929–1933." *Annals of Iowa* 46 (Summer 1982): 337–354.

**BROOKS, PRESTON SMITH**
(1819–1857) D-SC, House 1853–1856,
1856–1857.

**956.** Gienapp, William E. "Crime against Sumner: The Caning of Charles Sumner and the Rise of the Republican Party." *Civil War History* 25 (September 1979): 218–245.

**957.** Mathis, Robert N. "Preston Smith Brooks: The Man and His Image." *South Carolina Historical Magazine* 79 (October 1978): 296–310.

**BROWN, ALBERT GALLATIN** (1813–1880) D-MS, House 1839–1841, 1847–1853, Senate 1854–1861.

**958.** Cluskey, Michael W. "Biographical Sketch." *Speeches, Messages and Other Writings, by Albert G. Brown,* 5–17. Philadelphia: J. B. Smith, 1859.

**959.** McCutchen, Samuel P. "The Political Career of Albert Gallatin Brown." Ph.D. dissertation, University of Chicago, 1930.

**960.** Ranck, James B. *Albert Gallatin Brown: Radical Southern Nationalist.* New York: Appleton, 1937.

**BROWN, ARTHUR** (1843–1906) R-UT, Senate 1896–1897.

**961.** Thatcher, Linda. "The 'Gentile Polygamist': Arthur Brown, Ex-Senator from Utah." *Utah Historical Quarterly* 52 (Summer 1984): 231–245.

**BROWN, BEDFORD** (1795–1870) D-NC, Senate 1829–1840.

**962.** Jones, Houston G. "Bedford Brown: State Rights Unionist." *North Carolina Historical Review* 32 (July 1955): 321–345; 32 (October 1955): 483–511.

**BROWN, BENJAMIN GRATZ** (1826–1885) UU-MO, Senate 1863–1867.

**963.** Peterson, Norma L. *Freedom and Franchise: The Political Career of B. Gratz Brown.* Columbia: University of Missouri Press, 1968.

**BROWN, ETHAN ALLEN** (1776–1852) OH, Senate 1822–1825.

**964.** Still, John S. "Ethan A. Brown, 1818–1822." In *Governors of Ohio,* 20–23. Columbus: Ohio Historical Society, 1954.

**BROWN, JAMES** (1776–1835) LA, Senate 1813–1817, 1819–1823.

**965.** Padgett, James A., ed. "Letters of James Brown to Henry Clay, 1804–1835." *Louisiana Historical Quarterly* 24 (October 1941): 921–1177.

**BROWN, JOHN** (1757–1837) VA/KY, House 1789–1792, Senate 1792–1805, Continental Congress 1787–1788.

**966.** Sprague, Stuart S. "Senator John Brown of Kentucky, 1757–1837: A Political Biography." Ph.D. dissertation, New York University, 1972.

**967.** Warren, Elizabeth. "John Brown and His Influence on Kentucky Politics: 1784–1805." Ph.D. dissertation, Northwestern University, 1937.

**BROWN, JOSEPH EMERSON** (1821–1894) D-GA, Senate 1880–1891.

**968.** Bragg, William H. *Joe Brown's Army: The Georgia State Line, 1862–1865.* Macon, GA: Mercer University Press, 1987.

**969.** Bryant, James C. "Governor Joseph Emerson Brown: Reconstructed Layman." *Georgia Baptist History* 12 (1990): 57–69.

**970.** Fielder, Herbert. *A Sketch of the Life and Times and Speeches of Joseph E. Brown.* Springfield, MA: Springfield Printing Company, 1883.

**971.** Hay, Thomas R. *Joseph Emerson Brown: Governor of Georgia, 1857–1865* Savannah: Georgia Historical Society, 1929.

**972.** Hill, Louise B. *Joseph E. Brown and the Confederacy.* Chapel Hill: University of North Carolina Press, 1939.

**973.** Lanier, Doris. "Joe Brown and Pumpkin Pie: Bill Nye's Sketch." *Atlanta Historical Journal* 30 (Summer 1986): 83–86.

**974.** Parks, Joseph H. *Joseph E. Brown of Georgia.* Baton Rouge: Louisiana State University Press, 1976.

**975.** Roberts, Derrell C. *Joseph E. Brown and the Politics of Reconstruction.* University: University of Alabama Press, 1973.

**976.** Speer, Emory. *Joseph E. Brown, of Georgia.* Atlanta, GA: Foote and Davies, 1905.

**977.** Ward, Judson C. "Augustus Octavius Bacon and Joseph E. Brown: An Exchange of Letters." *Atlanta Historical Journal* 26 (Winter 1982–1983): 64–67.

**BROWN, PRENTISS MARCH**
**(1889–1973) D-MI, House 1933–1936, Senate 1936–1943.**

**978.** Cisler, Walker L. *Michigan's Giant Stride: The Story of the Mackinac Bridge.* New York: Newcomen Society in North America, 1967.

**BROWNE, EDWARD EVERTS**
**(1868–1945) R-WI, House 1913–1931.**

**979.** Sellery, George C. "Edward E. Browne, 1868–1945." *Wisconsin Magazine of History* 30 (December 1946): 186.

**BROWNE, THOMAS McLELLAND**
**(1829–1891) R-IN, House 1877–1891.**

**980.** Barnes, William H. "Thomas M. Browne." In his *Lives of Gen. Ulysses S. Grant and Hon. Henry Wilson, Together with Sketches of Republican Candidates for Congress in Indiana,* 31–36. New York: W. H. Barnes, 1872.

**BROWNING, GORDON WEAVER**
**(1889–1976) D-TN, House 1923–1935.**

**981.** Adams, J. W. "Governor Gordon Browning, Campaigner Extraordinary: The 1936 Election for Governor." *West Tennessee Historical Society Papers* 30 (October 1976): 5–23.

**982.** Majors, William R. *The End of Arcadia: Gordon Browning and Tennessee Politics.* Memphis, TN: Memphis State University Press, 1982.

**BROWNING, ORVILLE HICKMAN**
**(1806–1881) R-IL, Senate 1861–1863.**

**983.** Baxter, Maurice G. *Orville H. Browning, Lincoln's Friend and Critic.* Bloomington: Indiana University, 1957.

**984.** Browning, Orville H. *The Diary of Orville Hickman Browning. 1850–81.* 2 vols. Edited by Theodore C. Pease and James G. Randall, Springfield: Trustees of the Illinois State Historical Society, 1925–1931.

**BROWNLOW, WALTER PRESTON**
**(1851–1910) R-TN, House 1897–1910.**

**985.** Beeson, Helen S. "Walter P. Brownlow, Republican." Master's thesis, East Tennessee State University, 1967.

**BROWNLOW, WILLIAM GANNAWAY**
**(1805–1877) R-TN, Senate 1869–1875.**

**986.** Alexander, Thomas B. "Strange Bedfellows: The Interlocking Careers of T. A. R. Nelson, Andrew Johnson and W. G. (Parson) Brownlow." *East Tennessee Historical Society's Publications* 51 (1979): 54–77.

**987.** Brownlow, William G. *Brownlow, the Patriot and Martyr: Showing His Faith, and Works, As Reported by Himself.* Philadelphia: R. Weir, 1862.

**988.** Conkin, Royal F. "The Public Speaking Career of William Gannaway Brownlow." Ph.D. dissertation, Ohio University, 1967.

**989.** Coulter, E. Merton. *William G. Brownlow: Fighting Parson of the Southern Highlands.* Chapel Hill: University of North Carolina Press, 1937.

**990.** Heiskell, Samuel G. *Andrew Jackson and Early Tennessee History,* vol. 3, 203–272. Nashville, TN: Ambrose Printing Company, 1921.

**991.** Humphrey, Steven. *That D....d Brownlow.* Boone, NC: Appalachian Consortium Press, 1987.

**992.** Kelly, James C. "William Gannaway Brownlow, Part I." *Tennessee Historical Quarterly* 43 (Spring 1984): 25–43.

**993.** ———. "William Gannaway Brownlow, Part II." *Tennessee Historical Quarterly* 43 (Summer 1984): 155–172.

**994.** Patton, James W. "The Senatorial Career of William G. Brownlow." *Tennessee Historical Magazine* 1 (April 1931): 153–164.

**995.** ———. *Unionism and Reconstruction in Tennessee, 1860–1869.* Chapel Hill: University of North Carolina Press, 1934.

**996.** Temple, Oliver P. "William Gannaway Brownlow." In *Notable Men of Tennessee from 1833 to 1875: Their Times and Their Contemporaries,* compiled by Mary B. Temple, 271–356. New York: Cosmopolitan Press, 1912.

## BRUCE, BLANCHE KELSO (1841–1898)
### R-MS, Senate 1875–1881.

**997.** Christopher, Maurine. "Blanche K. Bruce/Mississippi." In her *Black Americans in Congress,* 15–24. Rev. ed. New York: Thomas Y. Crowell, 1976.

**998.** Gatewood, Willard B. *Aristocrats of Color: The Black Elite, 1880–1920.* Bloomington: Indiana University Press, 1990.

**999.** Mann, Kenneth E. "Blanche Kelso Bruce: United States Senator without a Constituency." *Journal of Mississippi History* 38 (May 1976): 183–198.

**1000.** St. Clair, Sadie D. "The National Career of Blanche Kelso Bruce." Ph.D. dissertation, New York University, 1947.

**1001.** Shapiro, Samuel. "A Black Senator from Mississippi: Blanche K. Bruce." *Review of Politics* 44 (January 1982): 83–109.

**1002.** Simmons, William J. "Senator Blanche K. Bruce." In his *Men of Mark,* 483–487. Lincoln, NE: Johnson, 1970.

**1003.** Smith, Frank E., and Audrey Warren. "Blanche Kelso Bruce." In their *Mississippians All,* 45–58. Gretna, LA: Pelican, 1968.

**1004.** Sterling, Philip. *Four Took Freedom: The Lives of Harriet Tubman, Frederick Douglass, Robert Smalls, and Blanche K. Bruce.* Garden City, NY: Doubleday, 1967.

**1005.** Toppin, Edgar A. "Bruce, Blanche K." In his *Biographical History of Blacks in America since 1528,* 259–260. New York: McKay, 1971.

**1006.** Urofsky, Melvin I. "Blanche K. Bruce: United States Senator, 1875–1881." *Journal of Mississippi History* 29 (May 1967): 118–141.

## BRUCE, WILLIAM CABELL (1860–1946)
### D-MD, Senate 1923–1929.

**1007.** Bruce, William C. *Recollections.* Baltimore: King Brothers, 1936.

## BRYAN, WILLIAM JENNINGS
### (1860–1925) D-NE, House 1891–1895.

**1008.** Alcorn, Gay D. "William Jennings Bryan's Visits to Saratoga and the Encampment Valley." *Annals of Wyoming* 56 (Spring 1984): 35–38.

**1009.** Allen, Leslie H., ed. *Bryan and Darrow at Dayton: The Record and Documents of the Bible-Evolution Trial.* New York: Russell and Russell, 1967.

**1010.** Anderson, David D. *William Jennings Bryan.* Boston: Twayne, 1981.

**1011.** Barcus, James S. *The Boomerang: Or, Bryan's Speech with the Wind Knocked Out.* New York: J. S. Barcus, 1896.

**1012.** Barnes, James A. "Myths of the Bryan Campaign." *Mississippi Valley Historical Review* 34 (December 1947): 367–404.

**1013.** Beals, Carleton. "Silver Knight on a Cross of Gold." In his *Great Revolt and Its Leaders,* 299–322. New York: Abelard-Schuman, 1968.

**1014.** Bryan, William J., and Mary B. Bryan. *Memoirs of William Jennings Bryan.* 2 vols. Philadelphia: John Winston, 1925.

**1015.** Challener, Richard D. "William Jennings Bryan." In *Uncertain Tradition: American Secretaries of State in the Twentieth Century,* edited by Norman A. Graebner, 79–100. New York: McGraw-Hill, 1961.

**1016.** Cherny, Robert W. ed. "Dan Bride's Memoirs of William Jennings Bryan." *Nebraska History* 66 (Fall 1985): 257–271.

**1017.** ———. *A Righteous Cause: The Life of William Jennings Bryan.* Boston: Little, Brown, 1985.

**1018.** Clark, Champ. "Baltimore." In his *My Quarter Century of American Politics,* vol. 2, 392–443. New York: Harper and Brothers, 1920.

**1019.** Clements, Kendrick A. "'A Kindness to Carranza': William Jennings Bryan, International Harvester and Intervention in Yucatan." *Nebraska History* 57 (Winter 1976): 479–490.

**1020.** ———. *William Jennings Bryan, Missionary Isolationist.* Knoxville: University of Tennessee Press, 1982.

**1021.** Coletta, Paolo E. "Bryan, Anti-imperialism and Missionary Diplomacy." *Nebraska History* 44 (September 1963): 167–188.

**1022.** ———. "Bryan at Baltimore, 1912: Wilson's Warwick?" *Nebraska History* 57 (Summer 1976): 201–225.

**1023.** ———. "Bryan, McKinley, and the Treaty of Paris." *Pacific Historical Review* 26 (May 1957): 131–146.

**1024.** ———. "The Most Thankless Task: Bryan and the California Alien Land Legislation." *Pacific Historical Review* 36 (May 1967): 163–188.

**1025.** ———. "The Patronage Battle between Bryan and Hitchcock." *Nebraska History* 49 (Summer 1968): 121–137.

**1026.** ———. "Secretary of State William Jennings Bryan and Deserving Democrats." *Mid-America* 48 (April 1966): 75–98.

**1027.** ———. "Will the Real Progressive Stand Up? William Jennings Bryan and Theodore Roosevelt to 1909." *Nebraska History* 65 (Spring 1984): 15–57.

**1028.** ———. *William Jennings Bryan.* 2 vols. Lincoln: University of Nebraska Press, 1964–1969.

**1029.** ———. "William Jennings Bryan and Currency and Banking Reform." *Nebraska History* 45 (March 1964): 31–58.

**1030.** ———. "William Jennings Bryan and the United States-Columbia Impasse, 1903–1921." *Hispanic-America Historical Review* 47 (November 1967): 486–501.

**1031.** ———. "William Jennings Bryan's Plans for World Peace." *Nebraska History* 58 (Summer 1977): 193–217.

**1032.** Curti, Merle E. *Bryan and World Peace.* New York: Octagon Books, 1969.

**1033.** Daly, James J. "William Jennings Bryan and the Red River Valley Press, 1890–1896." *North Dakota History* 42 (Winter 1975): 26–37.

**1034.** Daniels, Roger. "William Jennings Bryan and the Japanese." *Southern California Quarterly* 48 (Fall 1966): 227–240.

**1035.** Davis, Hayne, ed. *Bryan among the Peace-Makers: Special Edition Issued in Connection with the Ovation to Mr. Bryan by Thousands of His Countrymen, Aug. 30, 1906.* New York: Progressive Publishing, 1906.

**1036.** Fite, Gilbert C. "William Jennings Bryan and the Campaign of 1896: Some Views and Problems." *Nebraska History* 47 (September 1966): 247–264.

**1037.** Fitzpatrick, James K. "William Jennings Bryan: The Great Commoner." In his *Builders of the American Dream,* 131–157. New Rochelle, NY: Arlington House, 1977.

**1038.** Gale, Albert L., and George W. Kline. *Bryan the Man: The Great Commoner at Close Range.* St. Louis, MO: Thompson, 1908.

**1039.** Ginger, Raymond. *Six Days or Forever? Tennessee v. John Thomas Scopes.* Boston: Beacon, 1958.

**1040.** Glad, Paul W. *McKinley, Bryan, and the People.* New York: Lippincott, 1964.

**1041.** ———. *Trumpet Soundeth: William Jennings Bryan and His Democracy, 1896–1912.* Lincoln: University of Nebraska Press, 1960.

**1042.** ———, ed. *William Jennings Bryan: A Profile.* New York: Hill and Wang, 1968.

**1043.** Grant, Philip A. "William Jennings Bryan and the Presidential Election of 1916." *Nebraska History* 63 (Winter 1982): 531–541.

**1044.** Griffith, Will. "Great Commoner—William Jennings Bryan." In *Idols of Egypt,* edited by Griffith Will, 13–30. Carbondale, IL: Egypt Book House, 1947.

**1045.** Hanson, John W., Jr. "Life and Services of Hon. William J. Bryan." In his *The Parties and the Men,* 499–515. Chicago: W. B. Conkey Company, 1896.

**1046.** Haynes, Frederick E. "The Pioneer Progressives: Bryan and La Follette." In his *Third Party Movements Since the Civil War,* 379–390. Iowa City: State Historical Society of Iowa, 1916.

**1047.** Herrick, Genevieve F., and John O. Herrick. *The Life of William Jennings Bryan.* Chicago: Buxton, 1925.

**1048.** Hibben, Paxton. *The Peerless Leader: William Jennings Bryan.* New York: Farrar and Rinehart, 1929.

**1049.** Himmelberg, Robert R., and Raymond J. Cunningham, eds. "William Jennings Bryan, Orlando Jay Smith, and the Founding of the Commoner: Some New Bryan Letters." *Nebraska History* 48 (Spring 1967): 69–79.

**1050.** Hofstadter, Richard. "William Jennings Bryan: The Democrat as Revivalist." In his *American Political Tradition and the Men Who Made It,* 183–202. New York: Knopf, 1948.

**1051.** Hollingsworth, Joseph R. "William Jennings Bryan." In his *The Whirligig of Politics: The Democracy of Cleveland and Bryan.* Chicago: University of Chicago Press, 1963.

**1052.** Hoyt, Edwin P. "William Jennings Bryan." In his *Lost Statesmen,* 147–168. Chicago: Reilly and Lee, 1961.

**1053.** Johnson, John R. "William Jennings Bryan (Crusader) 1860–1925." In his *Representative Nebraskans,* 29–33. Lincoln, NE: Johnsen, 1954.

**1054.** Kaplan, Edward S. "The Latin American Policy of William Jennings Bryan, 1913–1915." Ph.D. dissertation, New York University, 1970.

**1055.** ———. "William Jennings Bryan and the Panama Canal Tools Controversy." *Mid-America* 56 (April 1974): 100–108.

**1056.** Kent, Frank R. "Beginnings of the Bryan Era." In his *The Democratic Party: A History,* 338–375. New York: Century, 1928.

**1057.** Koenig, Louis W. *Bryan: A Political Biography of William Jennings Bryan.* New York: Putnam's, 1971.

**1058.** Levine, Lawrence W. *Defender of the Faith: William Jennings Bryan: The Last Decade, 1915–1925.* New York: Oxford University Press, 1965.

**1059.** Lindeen, Shirley A. "The Political Philosophies of William Jennings Bryan and George W. Norris." Ph.D. dissertation, University of Nebraska, 1971.

**1060.** Lindeen, Shirley A., and James W. Lindeen. "Bryan, Norris and the Doctrine of Party Responsibility." *American Studies* 11 (Spring 1970): 45–53.

**1061.** Lippmann, Walter. "Bryan and the Dogma of Majority Rule." In his *Men of Destiny*, 45–60. New York: Macmillan, 1927.

**1062.** Long, John C. *Bryan, the Great Commoner.* New York: Appleton, 1928.

**1063.** Merriam, Charles E. *Four American Party Leaders: Henry Ward Beecher Foundation Lectures, Delivered at Amherst College by Charles Edward Merriam.* New York: Macmillan, 1926.

**1064.** Metcalf, Richard L. *The Life and Patriotic Services of Hon. William J. Bryan, Also the Life of Hon. Arthur Sewall.* Omaha, NE: Edgewood, 1896.

**1065.** Miller, Karl P. "William Jennings Bryan." In his *How in the World Do Americans: A Biographical Inquiry*, 203–214. New York: Pageant, 1957.

**1066.** Nagle, Roger. "An Historical Evaluation of William Jennings Bryan: His Public Career and Political Ideals, 1891–1915." Ph.D. dissertation, St. John's University, 1955.

**1067.** Newbranch, Harvey E. *William Jennings Bryan: A Concise but Complete History of His Life and Services.* Lincoln, NE: University Publishing Co., 1900.

**1068.** Ogle, Arthur B. "Above the World: William Jennings Bryan's View of the American Nation in International Affairs." *Nebraska History* 61 (Summer 1980): 152–171.

**1069.** Potter, Rex M. *William Jennings Bryan: The Great Commoner.* Fort Wayne, IN: Allen County-Fort Wayne Historical Society, 1961.

**1070.** Prescott, Lawrence F. "Hon. William J. Bryan." In his *Living Issues of the Campaign of 1900*, 1–17. New York: Mighill, 1900.

**1071.** Rosser, Charles M. *The Crusading Commoner, a Close-Up of William Jennings Bryan and His Times.* Dallas, TX: Mathis, Van Nort, and Company, 1937.

**1072.** Russell, C. Allyn. "William Jennings Bryan: Statesman Fundamentalist." *Journal of Presbyterian History* 53 (Summer 1975): 93–119.

**1073.** Seitz, Don C. "William Jennings Bryan." In his *The 'Also Rans': Great Men Who Missed Making the Presidential Goal*, 320–338. New York: Thomas Y. Crowell, Co., 1928.

**1074.** Smith, Willard H. "The Pacifist Thought of William Jennings Bryan." *Mennonite Quarterly Review* 45 (January 1971): 33–81.

**1075.** ———. "The Pacifist Thought of William Jennings Bryan." *Mennonite Quarterly Review* 45 (April 1971): 152–181.

**1076.** ———. "William Jennings Bryan and Racism." *Journal of Negro History* 54 (April 1969): 127–149.

**1077.** ———. "William Jennings Bryan and the Social Gospel." *Journal of American History* 53 (June 1966): 41–60.

**1078.** Springen, Donald K. *William Jennings Bryan: Orator of Small Town America.* Westport, CT: Greenwood, 1991.

**1079.** Stevenson, Marietta. "William Jennings Bryan as a Political Leader." Ph.D. dissertation, University of Chicago, 1926.

**1080.** Stoddard, Henry L. "Bryan: A Career of Protest." In his *As I Knew Them*, 273–290. New York: Harper Brothers, 1927.

**1081.** Supple, Robert V. "The Political Rise of William Jennings Bryan from 1888 to the Nomination for the Presidency of the Democratic Party in 1896." Ph.D. dissertation, New York University, 1951.

**1082.** Sutton, Walter A. "Bryan, La Follette, Norris: Three Mid-Western Politicians." *Journal of the West* 8 (October 1969): 613–630.

**1083.** Thompson, Charles W. "Bryan." In his *Presidents I've Known and Two Near Presidents*, 41–110. Indianapolis: Bobbs-Merrill, 1929.

**1084.** Villard, Oswald G. "William J. Bryan: Cabinet Officer." In his *Prophets True and False*, 202–214. New York: Knopf, 1928.

**1085.** Vivian, James F. "Wilson, Bryan, and the American Delegation to the Abortive Fifth Pan American Conference, 1914." *Nebraska History* 59 (Spring 1978): 56–69.

**1086.** Wecter, Dixon. "Commoner and Rough Rider." In his *Hero in America*, 364–391. New York: Scribner's, 1972.

**1087.** Weisbord, Marvin R. "Silver Tongue on the Stump: William Jennings Bryan." In his *Campaigning for President: A New Look at the White House*, 41–54. Washington, DC: Public Affairs Press, 1964.

**1088.** Wener, Morris R. *Bryan.* New York: Harcourt, Brace, 1929.

**1089.** Whicher, George F., ed. *William Jennings Bryan and the Campaign of 1896.* Boston: Heath, 1953.

**1090.** White, William A. "Bryan." In his *Masks in a Pageant*, 233–279. New York: Macmillan, 1928.

**1091.** "William Jennings Bryan." In *The American Secretaries of State and Their Diplomacy*, edited by Samuel F. Bemis, vol. 10, 1–44. New York: Knopf, 1929.

**1092.** Williams, Wayne C. *William Jennings Bryan: A Study in Political Vindication.* New York: Fleming H. Revell, 1923.

**1093.** Wilson, Charles M. *Commoner William Jennings Bryan.* Garden City, NY: Doubleday, 1970.

**1094.** Wood, M. "William Jennings Bryan: Crusader for the Common Man." In *American Public Address*, edited by Loren Reid, 151–169. Columbia: University of Missouri Press, 1961.

**1095.** Woodcock, George. "William Jennings Bryan: The Great Commoner." *History Today* 7 (July 1957): 443–449.

**1096.** Worthen, Edward H. "The Mexican Journeys of William Jennings Bryan, a Good Neighbor." *Nebraska History* 59 (Winter 1978): 485–500.

## BUCHANAN, JAMES (1791–1868) D-PA, House 1821–1831, Senate 1834–1845.

**1097.** Auchampaugh, Philip G. "James Buchanan, the Bachelor of the White House: An Inquiry on the Subject of Feminine Influence in the Life of Our Fifteenth President." *Tyler's Quarterly Historical and Genealogical Magazine* 20 (January 1939): 154–166, 218–234.

**1098.** ———. *James Buchanan and His Cabinet on the Eve of the Secession.* Lancaster, PA: Privately printed, 1926.

**1099.** ———. "James Buchanan, the Squire from Lancaster." *Pennsylvania Magazine of History and Biography* 56 (1932): 15–32.

**1100.** ———. "James Buchanan, the Squire of Lancaster." *Pennsylvania Magazine of History and Biography* 55 (1931): 289–300.

**1101.** Baylen, Joseph O. "James Buchanan's Calm of Despotism." *Pennsylvania Magazine of History and Biography* 77 (July 1953): 294–310.

**1102.** Binder, Frederick M. *James Buchanan and the American Empire.* Selinsgrove, PA: Susquehanna University Press, 1994.

**1103.** Buchanan, James. *Mr. Buchanan's Administration on the Eve of the Rebellion.* New York: Appleton, 1866.

**1104.** ———. *Works.* 12 vols. Edited by John B. Moore. Philadelphia: Lippincott, 1908–1911.

**1105.** Claussen, E. Neal. "Hendrick B. Wright and the Nocturnal Committee." *Pennsylvania Magazine of History and Biography* 89 (April 1965): 199–206.

**1106.** Curtis, George T. *Life of James Buchanan, Fifteenth President of the United States.* 2 vols. New York: Harper, 1883.

**1107.** Hensel, William U. *The Attitude of James Buchanan, a Citizen of Lancaster County, toward the Institution of Slavery in the United States.* Lancaster, PA: New Era Printing Company, 1911.

**1108.** ———. "James Buchanan as a Lawyer." *University of Pennsylvania Law Review* 60 (May 1912): 546–573.

**1109.** ———. "A Pennsylvania Presbyterian President: An Inquiry into the Religious Sentiments of James Buchanan, Fifteenth President of the United States." *Presbyterian Historical Society Journal* 4 (March 1908): 203–216.

**1110.** ———. *The Religious Convictions and Character of James Buchanan, Fifteenth President of the United States—A Citizen of Lancaster County—A Member of the Presbyterian Church.* Lancaster, PA: Intelligencer Print, 1912.

**1111.** Hillman, Frank P. "The Diplomacy Career of James Buchanan." Ph.D. dissertation, George Washington University, 1953.

**1112.** Hoyt, Edwin P. *James Buchanan.* Chicago: Reilly and Lee, 1966.

**1113.** Hutton, Amy. "Buchanan Family Reminiscences." *Maryland Historical Magazine* 35 (September 1940): 262–269.

**1114.** Klein, Philip S. "Bachelor Father: James Buchanan as a Family Man." *Western Pennsylvania Historical Magazine* 50 (July 1967): 199–214.

**1115.** ———. "James Buchanan and Ann Coleman." *Pennsylvania History* 21 (January 1954): 1–20.

**1116.** ———. *President James Buchanan: A Biography.* University Park: Pennsylvania State University Press, 1962.

**1117.** ———. *The Story of Wheatland.* Lancaster, PA: Junior League of Lancaster, 1936.

**1118.** McFarlane, Ian D. *Buchanan.* London: Duckworth, 1981.

**1119.** McMurtry, R. Gerald. "James Buchanan in Kentucky, 1813." *Filson Club History Quarterly* 8 (April 1934): 73–87.

**1120.** Meerse, David E. "Origins of the Buchanan-Douglas Feud Reconsidered." *Illinois State Historical Society Journal* 67 (April 1974): 154–174.

**1121.** Miller, C. L. "The Importance of the Adoption of Buchanan's Minority Report on the Repeal of the Twenty-Fifth Section of the Judiciary Act of 1789." *University of Pennsylvania Law Review* 60 (May 1912): 574–581.

**1122.** Pendleton, Lawson A. "James Buchanan's Attitude toward Slavery." Ph.D. dissertation, University of North Carolina, 1964.

**1123.** Ranck, James B. "The Attitude of James Buchanan toward Slavery." *Pennsylvania Magazine of History* 51 (April 1927): 126–142.

**1124.** Smith, Elbert B. *The Presidency of James Buchanan.* Lawrence: University Press of Kansas, 1975.

**1125.** Sternberg, Richard R. "Jackson, Buchanan, and the Corrupt Bargain Calumny." *Pennsylvania Magazine of History and Biography* 58 (1934): 61–85.

**1126.** Worner, William F. "James Buchanan." *Lancaster County Historical Society Papers* 36 (1932): 59–83.

**1127.** ———. "James Buchanan." *Lancaster County Historical Society Papers* 38 (1934): 103–144.

**BUCK, ALFRED ELIAB** (1832–1902) R-AL, House 1869–1871.

**1128.** Bhurtel, Shyam K. "Alfred Eliab Buck: Carpetbaggers in Alabama and Georgia." Ph.D. dissertation, Auburn University, 1981.

**BUCKALEW, CHARLES ROLLIN**
(1821–1899) D-PA, Senate 1863–1869, House 1887–1891.

1129. Hummel, William W. "Charles R. Buckalew: Democratic Statesman in a Republican Era." Ph.D. dissertation, University of Pittsburgh, 1963.

**BUCKINGHAM, WILLIAM ALFRED**
(1804–1875) R-CT, Senate 1869–1875.

1130. Buckingham, Samuel. *The Life of William A. Buckingham.* Springfield, MA: W. F. Adams. 1894.

1131. Stowe, Harriet B. "William Alfred Buckingham." In *Men of Our Time,* 463–479. Hartford, CT: Hartford Publishing Company, 1868.

**BUCKLEY, JAMES LANE** (1923– ) C-NY, Senate 1971–1977.

1132. Buckley, James L. *If Men Were Angels: A View from the Senate.* New York: Putnam's, 1975.

1133. Markmann, Charles L. *The Buckleys: A Family Examined.* New York: Morrow, 1973.

1134. Paone, Arthur J. *Conflict of Interest: James L. Buckley in the U.S. Senate.* Brooklyn, NY: Paone, 1976.

**BULKLEY, ROBERT JOHNS** (1880–1965) D-OH, House 1911–1915, Senate 1930–1939.

1135. Jenkins, William D. "Robert Bulkley: Progressive Profile." *Ohio History* 88 (Winter 1979): 57–72.

1136. ———. "Robert Bulkley, Progressive Profile." Ph.D. dissertation, Case Western Reserve University, 1969.

1137. Stegh, Leslie J. "A Paradox of Prohibition: Election of Robert J. Bulkley as Senator from Ohio, 1930." *Ohio History* 83 (Summer 1974): 170–182.

1138. ———. "Wet and Dry Battles in the Cradle State of Prohibition: Robert J. Bulkley and the Repeal of Prohibition in Ohio." Ph.D. dissertation, Kent State University, 1975.

**BULLARD, HENRY ADAMS** (1788–1851) W-LA, House 1831–1834, 1850–1851.

1139. Bonquois, Dora J. "The Career of Henry Adams Bullard, Louisiana Jurist, Legislator and Educator." *Louisiana Historical Quarterly* 23 (October 1940): 999–1106.

**BUMPERS, DALE LEON** (1925– ) D-AR, Senate 1975– .

1140. Smith, Harold T. "J. William Fulbright and the Arkansas 1974 Senatorial Election." *Arkansas Historical Quarterly* 44 (Summer 1985): 103–117.

**BURDICK, QUENTIN NORTHROP**
(1908–1992) D-ND, House 1959–1960, Senate 1960–1992.

1141. Burdick, Quentin. "Impressions of Congress." *North Dakota Quarterly* 27 (Spring 1959): 29–32.

**BURKE, AEDANUS** (1743–1802) SC, House 1789–1791.

1142. Meleney, John C. *The Public Life of Aedanus Burke: Revolutionary Republican in Post-revolutionary South Carolina.* Columbia: University of South Carolina Press, 1989.

**BURKE, CHARLES HENRY** (1861–1944) R-SD, House 1899–1907, 1909–1915.

1143. Flynn, Sean J. "Western Assimilationist: Charles H. Burke and the Burke Act." *Midwest Review* 11 (1989): 1–15.

**BURKE, THOMAS** (1747–1783) NC, Continental Congress 1776–1781.

1144. Sanders, Jennings B. "Thomas Burke in the Continental Congress." *North Carolina Historical Review* 9 (January 1932): 22–37.

1145. Watterson, John S. "Thomas Burke, Paradoxical Patriot." *Historian* 41 (August 1979): 664–681.

**1146.** ———. *Thomas Burke, Restless Revolutionary.* Washington, DC: University Press of America, 1980.

**BURKE, YVONNE BRATHWAITE**
(1932–   ) D-CA, House 1973–1979.

**1147.** Christopher, Maurine. "Yvonne Brathwaite Burke/California." In her *Black Americans in Congress,* 278. Rev. ed. New York: Thomas Y. Crowell, 1976.

**1148.** Gray, Pamela L. "Yvonne Braithwaite Burke: The Congressional Career of California's First Black Congresswoman, 1972–1978." Ph.D. dissertation, University of Southern California, 1987.

**BURLESON, ALBERT SIDNEY**
(1863–1937) D-TX, House 1899–1913.

**1149.** Anderson, Adrian N. "Albert Sidney Burleson: A Southern Politician in the Progressive Era." Ph.D. dissertation, Texas Tech University, 1967.

**1150.** ———. "President Wilson's Politician: Albert Sidney Burleson of Texas." *Southwestern Historical Quarterly* 77 (January 1974): 339–354.

**1151.** Spero, Sterling D. "The Burleson Economy Program." In his *The Labor Movement in a Government Industry,* 186–228. New York: George H. Doran, 1924.

**BURLINGAME, ANSON** (1820–1870)
R-MA, House 1855–1861.

**1152.** Anderson, David L. "Anson Burlingame: American Architect of the Cooperative Policy in China, 1861–1871." *Diplomatic History* 1 (Summer 1977): 239–256.

**1153.** ———. "Anson Burlingame: Reformer and Diplomat." *Civil War History* 25 (December 1979): 293–308.

**1154.** Kim, Samuel S. "Anson Burlingame: A Study in Personal Diplomacy." Ph.D. dissertation, Columbia University, 1966.

**1155.** Koo, Telly H. "The Life of Anson Burlingame." Ph.D. dissertation, Harvard University, 1922.

**1156.** Ring, Martin R. "Anson Burlingame, S. Wells Williams and China, 1861–1870: A Great Era in Chinese-American Relations." Ph.D. dissertation, Tulane University, 1972.

**1157.** Williams, Frederick W. *Anson Burlingame and the First Chinese Mission to Foreign Powers.* New York: Russell and Russell, 1972.

**BURNET, JACOB** (1770–1853) F-NJ, Senate 1828–1831.

**1158.** Fisher, Samuel W. *History, The Unfolding of God's Providence: A Discourse Occasioned by the Death of Hon. Jacob Burnet.* Cincinnati, OH: Ben Franklin Printing House, 1853.

**BURNETT, HENRY CORNELIUS**
(1825–1866) D-KY, House 1855–1861.

**1159.** Craig, Berry F. "Henry Cornelius Burnett: Champion of Southern Rights." *Register of the Kentucky Historical Society* 77 (Autumn 1979): 266–274.

**BURNETT, JOHN LAWSON** (1854–1919)
D-AL, House 1899–1919.

**1160.** Johnson, Timothy D. "Anti-war Sentiment and Representative John Lawson Burnett of Alabama." *Alabama Review* 39 (July 1986): 187–195.

**BURNS, JOHN ANTHONY** (1909–1975)
D-HI, House 1957–1959.

**1161.** Amalu, Sammy. *Jack Burns: A Portrait in Transition.* Honolulu: Mamalahoa Foundation, 1974.

**1162.** Coffman, Tom. *Catch a Wave: A Case Study of Hawaii's New Politics.* 2d ed. Honolulu: University Press of Hawaii, 1973.

## BURNSIDE, AMBROSE EVERETT
(1824–1881) R-RI, Senate 1875–1881.

**1163.** Hassler, Warren W., Jr. "Ambrose E. Burnside." In his *Commanders of the Army of the Potomac,* 97–125. Baton Rouge: Louisiana State University Press, 1962.

**1164.** Macartney, Clarence E. "Grant and Burnside." In his *Grant and His Generals,* 245–266. New York: McBride, 1953.

**1165.** ———. "Lincoln and Burnside." In his *Lincoln and His Generals,* 117–134. Philadelphia: Dorrance, 1925.

**1166.** Marvel, William. *Burnside.* Chapel Hill: University of North Carolina Press, 1991.

**1167.** Morton, Julia J. "Trusting to Luck: Ambrose E. Burnside and the American Civil War." Ph.D. dissertation, Kent State University, 1992.

**1168.** Poore, Benjamin P. *Life and Public Service of Ambrose Burnside.* Providence, RI: J. A. and R. A. Reid, 1882.

**1169.** Thomas, Donna. "Ambrose E. Burnside and Army Reform, 1850–1881." *Rhode Island History* 37 (February 1978): 3–13.

## BURR, AARON (1756–1836) D-NY, Senate 1791–1797.

**1170.** Abernethy, Thomas P. *The Burr Conspiracy.* New York: Oxford University Press, 1954.

**1171.** Alexander, Holmes M. *Aaron Burr, the Proud Pretender.* New York: Harper, 1937.

**1172.** Barzman, Sol. "Aaron Burr." In his *Madmen and Geniuses: The Vice-Presidents of the United States,* 27–34. Chicago: Follett, 1974.

**1173.** Beirne, Francis F. *Shout Treason: The Trial of Aaron Burr.* New York: Hastings House, 1959.

**1174.** Bowers, Claude G. "The Trial of Treason." In his *Jefferson in Power,* 366–426. Boston: Houghton Mifflin, 1936.

**1175.** Bradford, Gamaliel. "Aaron Burr." In his *Damaged Souls,* 85–120. Boston: Houghton Mifflin, 1923.

**1176.** Brown, William H. *The Glory Seekers: The Romance of Would-Be Founders of Empire in the Early Days of the Great Southwest.* Chicago: McClure, 1906.

**1177.** Burr, Aaron. *Memoirs, with Miscellaneous Selections from Correspondence.* 2 vols. Edited by Matthew L. Davis. New York: Harper, 1836–1837.

**1178.** Burr, Samuel E. *The Burr-Hamilton Duel and Related Matters.* San Antonio, TX: Naylor, 1971.

**1179.** Chidsey, Donald B. *The Great Conspiracy: Aaron Burr and His Strange Doings in the West.* New York: Crown, 1967.

**1180.** Clark, Champ. "Aaron Burr." In *Modern Eloquence,* edited by Thomas B. Reed, vol. 7, 230–246. Philadelphia: J. D. Morris, 1900.

**1181.** Clemens, Jeremiah. *The Rivals: A Tale of the Times of Aaron Burr and Alexander Hamilton.* Philadelphia: Lippincott, 1860.

**1182.** Corwin, Edward S. "The Trial of Aaron Burr." In his *John Marshall and the Constitution,* 86–120. New Haven, CT: Yale University Press, 1919.

**1183.** Daniels, Jonathan. *Ordeals of Ambition: Jefferson, Hamilton, Burr.* Garden City, NY: Doubleday, 1970.

**1184.** Galloway, Charles B. "Aaron Burr in Mississippi." *Mississippi Historical Society Publications* 10 (1909): 237–245.

**1185.** Geissler, Suzanne. *Jonathan Edwards to Aaron Burr, Jr.: From the Great Awakening to Democratic Politics.* New York: Mellen Press, 1981.

**1186.** Henshaw, L. "The Aaron Burr Conspiracy in the Ohio Valley." *Ohio Valley Historical Association Annual Report* 7 (1913): 40–52.

**1187.** Hoyt, Edwin P. "Aaron Burr." In his *Lost Statesmen*, 23–44. Chicago: Reilly and Lee, 1961.

**1188.** Jenkinson, Isaac. *Aaron Burr, His Personal and Political Relations with Thomas Jefferson and Alexander Hamilton*. Richmond, IN: Cullaton, 1902.

**1189.** Judd, Jacob. "The Papers of Aaron Burr." *New York History* 65 (October 1985): 377–383.

**1190.** Kerkhoff, Johnston D. *Aaron Burr: A Romantic Biography*. New York: Greenberg, 1831.

**1191.** Knapp, Samuel L. *The Life of Aaron Burr*. New York: Wiley and Long, 1835.

**1192.** Kunstler, Laurence S. *The Unpredictable Mr. Aaron Burr*. New York: Vantage, 1974.

**1193.** Lewis, Alfred H. *An American Patrician: Or, the Story of Aaron Burr*. New York: Appleton, 1908.

**1194.** Lomask, Milton. *Aaron Burr: The Conspiracy and Years of Exile, 1805–1836*. New York: Farrar, Straus and Giroux, 1982.

**1195.** ———. *Aaron Burr: The Years from Princeton to Vice-President, 1756–1805*. New York: Farrar, Straus and Giroux, 1979.

**1196.** McCaleb, Walter F. *The Aaron Burr Conspiracy*. New York: Wilson-Erickson, 1936.

**1197.** ———. "The Aaron Burr Conspiracy and New Orleans." *American Historical Association Annual Report* 1903 (1903): 131–143.

**1198.** Merwin, Henry C. *Aaron Burr*. Boston: Small Maynard, 1899.

**1199.** Orth, Samuel P. "Aaron Burr, Father of the Political Machine." In his *Five American Politicians: A Study in the Evolution of American Politics*, 11–68. Cleveland, OH: Burrows Brothers, 1906.

**1200.** Parmet, Herbert S., and Marie B. Hecht. *Aaron Burr: Portrait of an Ambitious Man*. New York: Macmillan, 1967.

**1201.** Parton, James. *The Life and Times of Aaron Burr*. Boston: Houghton Mifflin, 1884.

**1202.** ———. *The Life and Times of Aaron Burr, Lieutenant-Colonel in the Army of the Revolution, United States Senator, Vice-President of the United States, etc.* New York: Mason Brothers, 1858.

**1203.** Peterson, Charles J. "Aaron Burr." In his *The Military Heroes of the Revolution*, 477–487. Philadelphia: J. B. Smith, 1856.

**1204.** Pidgin, Charles F. *Blennerhassett: Or the Decrees of Fate*. Boston: C. M. Clark, 1902.

**1205.** Reed, V. B., and James D. Williams, eds. *The Case of Aaron Burr*. Boston: Houghton Mifflin, 1960.

**1206.** Risher, James F. *Interview with Honor: The Burr-Hamilton Duel*. Philadelphia: Dorrance, 1975.

**1207.** Safford, William H. *The Blennerhassett Papers. . . Developing the Purposes and Aims of those Engaged in the Attempted Wilkinson and Burr Revolution*. Cincinnati, OH: Moore, Wilstach, Keys, 1861.

**1208.** Schachner, Nathan. *Aaron Burr: A Biography*. New York: Frederick A. Stokes, 1937.

**1209.** Seitz, Don C. "Aaron Burr." In his *The 'Also Rans': Great Men Who Missed Making the Presidential Goal*, 1–37. New York: Thomas Y. Crowell, 1928.

**1210.** Sheehan, Helena M. "Aaron Burr Conspiracy." Master's thesis, New York State College for Teachers, 1940.

**1211.** Slaughter, Thomas P. "Conspiratorial Politics: The Public Life of Aaron Burr." *New Jersey History* 103 (Spring/Summer 1985): 68–81.

**1212.** Spring, Samuel. *The Sixth Commandment Friendly to Virtue, Honor and Politeness*. Newburyport, MA: Allen, 1804.

**1213.** Swiggett, Howard G. "A Nondescript of Humanity: Aaron Burr." In his *The Forgotten Leaders of the Revolution*, 215–240. New York: Doubleday, 1955.

**1214.** Syrett, Harold C. ed. *Interview in Weehawken: The Burr-Hamilton Duel, as Told in the Original Documents*. Middletown, CT: Wesleyan University Press, 1960.

**1215.** Thomas, Gordon L. "Aaron Burr's Farewell Address." *Quarterly Journal of Speech* 39 (October 1953): 273–282.

**1216.** Todd, Charles B. *The True Aaron Burr: A Biographical Sketch*. New York: Barnes, 1902.

**1217.** Tompkins, Hamilton B. *Burr Bibliography*. Brooklyn, NY: Historical Printing Club, 1892.

**1218.** Vail, Philip. *The Great American Rascal: The Turbulent Life of Aaron Burr*. New York: Hawthorn Books, 1973.

**1219.** Wandell, Samuel H. *Aaron Burr: A Biography Written in Large Part from Original and Hitherto Unused Material*. New York: Putnam's, 1925.

**1220.** Wirt, William. *The Two Principle Arguments of William Wirt, Esquire, on the Trial of Aaron Burr, for High Treason*. Richmond, VA: S. Pleasants, 1808.

**1221.** Young, Donald. "John Adams-Thomas Jefferson-Aaron Burr." In his *American Roulette: The History and Dilemma of the Vice Presidency*, 5–23. New York: Holt, Rinehart and Winston, 1965.

## BURROWS, JULIUS CAESAR
**(1837–1915) R-MI, House 1873–1875, 1879–1883, 1885–1895, Senate 1895–1911.**

**1222.** Holsinger, M. Paul. "J. C. Burrows and the Fight against Mormonism: 1903–1907." *Michigan History* 52 (Fall 1968): 181–195.

**1223.** Orcutt, William D. *Burrows of Michigan and the Republican Party: A Biography and a History*. New York: Longmans, Green, 1917.

## BURSUM, HOLM OLAF (1867–1953)
**R-NM, Senate 1921–1925.**

**1224.** Fernlund, Kevin J. "Senator Holm O. Bursum and the Mexican Ring, 1921–1924." *New Mexico Historical Review* 66 (October 1991): 433–453.

**1225.** Moorman, Donald R. "A Political Biography of Holm O. Bursum: 1899–1924." Ph.D. dissertation, University of New Mexico, 1962.

## BURTON, HAROLD HITZ (1888–1964)
**R-OH, Senate 1941–1945.**

**1226.** Atkinson, David N. "American Constitutionalism under Stress: Mr. Justice Burton's Response to National Security Issues." *Houston Law Review* 9 (November 1971): 271–288.

**1227.** ———. "Justice Harold H. Burton and the Work of the Supreme Court." *Cleveland State Law Review* 27 (1978): 69–83.

**1228.** Berry, Mary F. *Stability, Security, and Continuity: Mr. Justice Burton and Decision-Making in the Supreme Court, 1945–1958*. Westport, CT: Greenwood, 1978.

**1229.** Forrester, Ray. "Mr. Justice Burton and the Supreme Court." *Tulane Law Review* 20 (October 1945): 1–21.

**1230.** Hudson, Edward G. *The Occasional Papers of Mr. Justice Burton*. Brunswick, ME: Bowdoin College, 1969.

**1231.** Marquardt, Ronald G. "The Judicial Justice: Mr. Justice Burton and the Supreme Court." Ph.D. dissertation, University of Missouri, 1973.

**1232.** McHargue, Daniel S. "One of Nine: Mr. Justice Burton's Appointment to the Supreme Court." *Western Reserve Law Review* 4 (Winter 1953): 128–131.

**1233.** Wilkin, Robert, and John Hadden. "Harold Hitz Burton, 1888–1964." *American Bar Association Journal* 50 (December 1964): 1148–1149.

**BURTON, PHILLIP** (1926–1983) D-CA, House 1964–1983.

**1234.** Leamer, Laurence. "Bongo." In his *Playing for Keeps in Washington*, 349–403. New York: Dial, 1977.

**BURTON, THEODORE ELIJAH** (1851–1929) R-OH, House 1889–1891, 1895–1909, 1921–1928, Senate 1909–1915, 1928–1929.

**1235.** Crissey, Forrest. *Theodore E. Burton, American Statesman.* Cleveland, OH: World, 1956.

**1236.** Schoenrich, Otto. *Former Senator Burton's Trip to South America, 1915.* Washington, DC: Carnegie Endowment for International Peace, 1915.

**1237.** Stay, Clarence R. "Theodore E. Burton on Navigation and Conservation: His Role as Chairman of the Committee on Rivers and Harbors, 1898–1909." Ph.D. dissertation, Case Western Reserve University, 1975.

**BUSH, GEORGE HERBERT WALKER** (1924– ) R-TX, House 1967–1971.

**1238.** Banks, Jimmy. "Big League." In his *Money, Marbles and Chalk: The Wondrous World of Texas Politics*, 187–198. Austin: Texas Publishing Company, 1971.

**1239.** Bush, George. *Looking Forward.* New York: Bantam Books, 1987.

**1240.** Duffy, Michael, and Dan Goodgame. *Marching in Place: The Status Quo Presidency of George Bush.* New York: Simon and Schuster, 1992.

**1241.** Finger, Seymour M. "George Bush." In his *Your Man at the UN: People, Politics and Bureaucracy in Making Foreign Policy*, 216–226. New York: New York University Press, 1980.

**1242.** Green, Fitzhugh. *George Bush: An Intimate Portrait.* New York: Hippocrene Books, 1989.

**1243.** Hedra, Tony. *Born to Run Things: An Utterly Unauthorized Biography of George Bush.* New York: Villard, 1992.

**1244.** King, Nicholas. *George Bush, a Biography.* New York: Dodd, Mead, 1980.

**1245.** Perry, Mark. *Eclipse: George Bush and the Decline of the CIA.* New York: Morrow, 1992.

**1246.** Ridley, Matt. *Warts and All: The Men Who Would Be Bush.* New York: Viking, 1989.

**BUTLER, BENJAMIN FRANKLIN** (1818–1893) R-MA, House 1867–1875, 1877–1879.

**1247.** Bland, Thomas A. *Life of Benjamin F. Butler.* Boston: Lee and Shepard, 1879.

**1248.** Bradford, Gamaliel. "Benjamin Franklin Butler." In his *Damaged Souls*, 221–258. Boston: Houghton Mifflin, 1923.

**1249.** Butler, Benjamin F. *Autobiography and Personal Reminiscences.* Boston: A. M. Thayer, 1892.

**1250.** ———. *Private and Official Correspondence During the Period of the Civil War.* 5 vols. Edited by Jessie A. Marshall. Norwood, MA: Plimpton Press, 1917.

**1251.** Conwell, Russell H. *Hon. Benjamin F. Butler.* Boston: Aurora Club, 1874.

**1252.** Driscoll, William D. "Benjamin F. Butler: Lawyer and Regency Politician." Ph.D. dissertation, Fordham University, 1965.

**1253.** France, A. F. "Admiral Farragut and General Butler." *U.S. Naval Institute Proceedings* 83 (February 1957): 214–215.

**1254.** Gordon, L. Thomas. "Benjamin F. Butler, Prosecutor." *Quarterly Journal of Speech* 45 (October 1959): 288–298.

**1255.** Griffin, Solomon B. *People and Politics Observed by a Massachusetts Editor.* Boston: Little, Brown, 1923.

**1256.** Holzman, Robert S. "Ben Butler in the Civil War." *New England Quarterly* 30 (September 1957): 330–345.

**1257.** ———. "Benjamin F. Butler: His Public Career." Ph.D. dissertation, New York University, 1953.

**1258.** ———. *Stormy Ben Butler.* New York: Macmillan, 1954.

**1259.** James, Edward T. "Ben Butler Runs for President: Labor, Greenbackers, and Anti-monopolists in the Election of 1884." *Essex Institute Historical Collections* 113 (April 1977): 65–88.

**1260.** Johnson, Howard P. "New Orleans under General Butler." *Louisiana Historical Quarterly* 24 (April 1941): 434–536.

**1261.** Macartney, Clarence E. "Grant and Butler." In his *Grant and His Generals,* 166–188. New York: McBride, 1953.

**1262.** ———. "Lincoln and Butler." In his *Lincoln and His Generals,* 46–67. Philadelphia: Dorrance, 1925.

**1263.** Mackenzie, William L. *The Lives and Opinions of Benjamin Franklin Butler and Jesse Hoyt.* Boston: Cook and Company, 1845.

**1264.** Mallam, William D. "Benjamin Franklin Butler, Machine Politician and Congressman." Ph.D. thesis, University of Minnesota, 1941.

**1265.** ———. "Butlerism in Massachusetts." *New England Quarterly* 33 (June 1960): 186–206.

**1266.** ———. "Fight for the Old Granite Block." *New England Quarterly* 36 (March 1963): 42–62.

**1267.** ———. "Grant-Butler Relationship." *Mississippi Valley Historical Review* 41 (September 1954): 259–276.

**1268.** Merrill, Louis T. "General Benjamin F. Butler as a Radical Leader During the Administration of President Andrew Johnson." Ph.D. dissertation, University of Chicago, 1937.

**1269.** Nash, Howard P. *Stormy Petrel: The Life and Times of Gen. Benjamin F. Butler, 1818–1893.* Rutherford, NJ: Fairleigh Dickinson University Press, 1969.

**1270.** Nolan, Dick. *Benjamin Franklin Butler: The Damnedest Yankee.* Novato, CA: Presidio, 1991.

**1271.** Parton, James. *General Butler in New Orleans: History of the Administration of the Department of the Gulf in the Year 1862; with an Account of the Capture of New Orleans, and a Sketch of the Previous Career of the General, Civil and Military.* 14th ed. New York: Mason Brothers, 1864.

**1272.** Pomeroy, Marcus M. *The Life and Public Services of Benjamin F. Butler, Major-General in the Army and Leader of the Republican Party.* New York: N.p., 1868.

**1273.** Seitz, Don C. "Benjamin F. Butler." In his *The 'Also Rans': Great Men Who Missed Making the Presidential Goal,* 298–319. New York: Thomas Y. Crowell, 1928.

**1274.** Thomas, Gordon L. "Benjamin F. Butler, Prosecutor." *Quarterly Journal of Speech* 45 (October 1959): 288–298.

**1275.** Thompson, Margaret S. "Ben Butler Versus the Brahmins: Patronage and Politics in Early Gilded Age Massachusetts." *New England Quarterly* 55 (June 1982): 163–186.

**1276.** Trefousse, Hans L. *Ben Butler: The South Called Him Beast!* Boston: Twayne, 1957.

**1277.** Weiss, Nathan. "General Benjamin Franklin Butler and the Negro: The Evolution of the Racial Views of a Practical Politician." *Negro History Bulletin* 29 (October 1965): 3–4.

**1278.** Werlich, Robert. *Beast Butler: The Incredible Career of Benjamin Franklin Butler.* Washington, DC: Quaker Press, 1962.

**1279.** West, Richard S. "Admiral Farragut and General Butler." *U.S. Naval Institute Proceedings* 82 (June 1956): 635–643.

**1280.** ———. *Lincoln's Scapegoat General: A Life of Benjamin F. Butler, 1818–1893.* Boston: Houghton Mifflin, 1965.

**BUTLER, HUGH ALFRED (1878–1954)**
**R-NE, Senate 1941–1954.**

**1281.** Paul, Justus F. "The Making of a Senator: The Early Life of Hugh Butler." *Nebraska History* 49 (Autumn 1968): 247–267.

**1282.** ———. "The Political Career of Senator Hugh Butler, 1940–1954." Ph.D. dissertation, University of Nebraska, 1966.

**1283.** ———. "The Power of Seniority: Senator Hugh Butler and Statehood for Hawaii." *Hawaiian Journal of History* 9 (1975): 140–147.

**1284.** ———. *Senator Hugh Butler and Nebraska Republicanism.* Lincoln: Nebraska State Historical Society, 1976.

**BUTLER, MARION (1863–1938) P-NC,**
**Senate 1895–1901.**

**1285.** Durden, Robert F. *Reconstruction Bonds and Twentieth-Century Politics: South Dakota v. North Carolina, 1904.* Durham, NC: Duke University Press, 1962.

**1286.** Hunt, James L. "The Making of a Populist: Marion Butler, 1863–1895." *North Carolina Historical Review* 62 (January 1985): 53–77; 62 (April 1985): 179–202; 62 (July 1985): 317–343.

**1287.** ———. "Marion Butler and the Populist Ideal, 1863–1938 (North Carolina)." Ph.D. dissertation, University of Wisconsin, 1990.

**BUTLER, PIERCE (1744–1822) D-SC,**
**Senate 1789–1796, 1802–1804, Continental**
**Congress 1787.**

**1288.** Bell, Malcolm. *Major Butler's Legacy: Five Generations of a Slaveholding Family.* Athens: University of Georgia Press, 1987.

**1289.** Coglan, Francis. "Pierce Butler, 1744–1822, First Senator from South Carolina." *South Carolina Historical Magazine* 78 (April 1977): 104–119.

**1290.** Richards, Miles S. "Pierce Mason Butler: The South Carolina Years, 1830–1841." *South Carolina Historical Magazine* 87 (January 1986): 14–29.

**1291.** Sikes, Lewright B. *The Public Life of Pierce Butler, South Carolina Statesman.* Washington, DC: University Press of America, 1979.

**BUTLER, WILLIAM ORLANDO**
**(1791–1880) D-KY, House 1839–1843.**

**1292.** Blair, Francis, Jr. "Sketch of the Public Services of Major-General W. O. Butler." In *Life of General Lewis Cass,* by George H. Hickman, 161–197. Baltimore: N. Hickman, 1848.

**1293.** Roberts, Gerald F. "William O. Butler: Kentucky Cavalier." Master's thesis, University of Kentucky, 1962.

**BYRD, HARRY FLOOD (1887–1966)**
**D-VA, Senate 1933–1965.**

**1294.** Fry, Joseph A., and Brent Tarter. "The Redemption of the Fighting Ninth: The 1922 Congressional Election in the Ninth District of Virginia and the Origins of the Byrd Organization." *South Atlantic Quarterly* 77 (Summer 1978): 352–370.

**1295.** Hatch, Alden. *The Byrds of Virginia.* New York: Holt, Rinehart and Winston, 1969.

**1296.** Hawkes, Robert T., Jr. "The Career of Harry Flood Byrd, Sr., to 1933." Ph.D. dissertation, University of Virginia, 1975.

**1297.** Heinemann, Ronald L. *Depression and New Deal in Virginia: The Enduring Dominion.* Charlottesville: University Press of Virginia, 1983.

**1298.** Henriques, Peter R. "The Byrd Organization Crushes a Liberal Challenge, 1950–1953." *Virginia Magazine of History and Biography* 87 (January 1979): 3–29.

**1299.** Koeniger, A. Cash. "The New Deal and the States: Roosevelt Versus the Byrd Organization in Virginia." *Journal of American History* 68 (March 1982): 876–896.

**1300.** Sweeney, James R. "Byrd and Anti-Byrd: The Struggle for Political Supremacy in Virginia, 1945–1954." Ph.D. dissertation, University of Notre Dame, 1973.

**1301.** ———. "Harry Byrd: Vanished Policies and Enduring Principles." *Virginia Quarterly Review* 52 (Autumn 1976): 596–612.

**1302.** ———. "Revolt in Virginia: Harry Byrd and the 1952 Presidential Election." *Virginia Magazine of History and Biography* 86 (April 1978): 180–195.

**1303.** Wilkinson, J. Harvie. *Harry Byrd and the Changing Face of Virginia Politics, 1945–1966.* Charlottesville: University Press of Virginia, 1968.

**BYRD, ROBERT CARLYLE (1917–    )**
**D-WV, House 1953–1959, Senate 1959–    .**

**1304.** Leamer, Laurence. "The Lion and the Waterhole." In his *Playing for Keeps in Washington,* 75–138. New York: Dial, 1977.

**1305.** Viorst, Milton. "Robert C. Byrd: Hillbilly in the Service of the Lord." In his *Hustlers and Heroes: An American Political Panorama,* 77–96. New York: Simon and Schuster, 1971.

**BYRNES, JAMES FRANCIS (1879–1972)**
**D-SC, House 1911–1925, Senate 1931–1941.**

**1306.** Brown, Walter J. *James F. Byrnes of South Carolina: A Remembrance.* Macon, GA: Mercer University Press, 1991.

**1307.** Burns, Richard D. "James F. Byrnes." In *Uncertain Tradition: American Secretaries of State in the Twentieth Century,* edited by Norman A. Graebner, 223–244. New York: McGraw, 1961.

**1308.** ———. *James F. Byrnes.* New York: McGraw, 1961.

**1309.** Byrnes, James F. *All in One Lifetime.* New York: Harper and Row, 1958.

**1310.** Byrnes, Winfred B., Jr. "New South Statesmen: The Political Career of James Francis Byrnes, 1911–1941." Ph.D. dissertation, Duke University, 1976.

**1311.** Clements, Kendrick A., ed. *James F. Byrnes and the Origins of the Cold War.* Durham, NC: Carolina Academic Press, 1982.

**1312.** Conover, Denise O. "James F. Byrnes and the Four-Power Disarmament Treaty." *Mid-America* 70 (January 1988): 19–34.

**1313.** ———. "James F. Byrnes, Germany, and the Cold War, 1946." Ph.D. dissertation, Washington State University, 1978.

**1314.** Curry, George. "James F. Byrnes." In *American Secretaries of State and Their Diplomacy,* edited by Robert H. Ferrell, vol. 14, 85–317, 340–396, 405–413. New York: Cooper Square, 1965.

**1315.** Figg, Robert M., Jr. "James F. Byrnes and the Supreme Court 1941–1942." *South Carolina Law Review* 25 (1973): 543–548.

**1316.** Gardner, Lloyd C. "James F. Byrnes: Collective Security through Public Diplomacy." In his *Architects of Illusion: Men and Ideas in American Foreign Policy, 1941–1949,* 84–112. Chicago: Quadrangle Books, 1970.

**1317.** Hogan, Frank J. "Associate Justice James F. Byrnes." *American Bar Association Journal* 27 (August 1941): 475–478.

**1318.** Messer, Robert L. *The End of an Alliance: James F. Byrnes, Roosevelt, Truman, and the Origins of the Cold War.* Chapel Hill: University of North Carolina Press, 1982.

**1319.** Moore, Winfred B., Jr. "James F. Byrnes: The Road to Politics, 1882–1910." *South Carolina Historical Magazine* 84 (April 1983): 72–88.

**1320.** ———. "New South Statesman: The Political Career of James Francis Byrnes, 1911–1941." Ph.D. dissertation, Duke University, 1976.

**1321.** Partin, John W. " 'Assistant President' for the Home Front: James F. Byrnes and World War II." Ph.D. dissertation, University of Florida, 1977.

**1322.** ———. "Roosevelt, Byrnes, and the 1944 Vice-Presidential Nomination." *Historian* 42 (November 1979): 85–100.

**1323.** Pettit, William. "Justice Byrnes and the United States Supreme Court." *South Carolina Law Quarterly* 6 (June 1954): 423–428.

**1324.** Placone, Ronald J. "Harry Truman, James Byrnes, and the Open Door: A Content Analysis of the Foreign Policy Speaking of the Truman Administration, 1945–1946." Master's thesis, Indiana University, 1978.

**1325.** Robertson, David. *Sly and Able: A Political Biography of James F. Byrnes.* New York: Norton, 1994.

**1326.** Ward, Patricia D. *The Threat of Peace: James F. Byrnes and the Council of Foreign Ministers, 1945–1946.* Kent, OH: Kent State University Press, 1979.

**BYRNS, JOSEPH WELLINGTON** (1869–1936) D-TN, House 1909–1936.

**1327.** Galloway, Jewell M. "The Public Life of Joseph W. Byrns." Master's thesis, University of Tennessee, 1962.

**1328.** ———. "Speaker Joseph W. Byrns: Party Leader in the New Deal." *Tennessee Historical Quarterly* 25 (Spring 1966): 63–76.

ॐ

**CABELL, EDWARD CARRINGTON** (1816–1896) W-FL, House 1845–1846, 1847–1853.

**1329.** Wheeler, Henry G. "Cabell, Edward Carrington." In his *History of Congress,* vol. 1, 431–445. New York: Harper and Brothers, 1848.

**CABOT, GEORGE** (1752–1823) MA, Senate 1791–1796.

**1330.** Lodge, Henry C. *Life and Letters of George Cabot.* New York: Da Capo Press, 1974.

**CAIN, RICHARD HARVEY** (1825–1887) R-SC, House 1873–1875, 1877–1879.

**1331.** Christopher, Maurine. "Richard H. Cain/South Carolina." In her *Black Americans in Congress,* 87–96. Rev. ed. New York: Thomas Y. Crowell, 1976.

**1332.** Lewis, Ronald L. "Cultural Pluralism and Black Reconstruction: The Public Career of Richard H. Cain." *Crisis* 85 (February 1978): 57–60.

**1333.** Mann, Kenneth E. "Richard Harvey Cain, Congressman, Minister and Champion for Civil Rights." *Negro History Bulletin* 35 (March 1972): 64–66.

**1334.** Simmons, William J. "Rt. Rev. Richard Harvey Cain, D.D." In his *Men of Mark,* 613–616. Lincoln, NE: Johnson Publishing Company, 1970.

**1335.** Thornbrough, Emma L. "Cain, Richard Harvey." In her *Black Reconstructionists,* 173–174. Englewood Cliffs, NJ: Prentice-Hall, 1972.

## CALHOUN, JOHN CALDWELL
(1782–1850) R-SC, House 1811–1817, Senate 1832–1843, 1845–1850.

**1336.** Alexander, Holmes M. "John Caldwell Calhoun." In his *The Famous Five*, 87–121. New York: Bookmailer, 1958.

**1337.** Ames, Herman V. *John C. Calhoun and the Secession Movement of 1850.* Worcester, MA: American Antiquarian Society, 1918.

**1338.** Atwell, Priscilla A. "Freedom and Diversity: Continuity in the Political Tradition of Thomas Jefferson and John C. Calhoun." Ph.D. dissertation, University of California, 1967.

**1339.** Bancroft, Frederic. *Calhoun and the South Carolina Nullification Movement.* Baltimore: Johns Hopkins University Press, 1928.

**1340.** Barsness, Richard W. "John C. Calhoun and the Military Establishment, 1817–1825." *Wisconsin Magazine of History* 50 (Autumn 1966): 43–53.

**1341.** Bartlett, Irving H. *Calhoun: A Biography.* New York: W. W. Norton, 1993.

**1342.** Barzman, Sol. "John C. Calhoun." In his *Madmen and Geniuses: The Vice-Presidents of the United States,* 53–60. Chicago: Follett, 1974.

**1343.** Baskin, Darryl B. "The Pluralist Vision of John C. Calhoun." *Polity* 2 (Fall 1969): 49–64.

**1344.** Bergeron, Paul H., ed. "A Tennessean Blasts Calhoun and Nullification." *Tennessee Historical Quarterly* 26 (Winter 1967): 383–386.

**1345.** Boller, Paul F. "Calhoun on Liberty." *South Atlantic Quarterly* 66 (Summer 1967): 395–408.

**1346.** Boucher, Chauncey S., and Robert P. Brooks, eds. *Correspondence Addressed to John C. Calhoun, 1837–1849.* Washington, DC: Government Printing Office, 1929.

**1347.** Bradford, Gamaliel. "John Caldwell Calhoun." In his *As God Made Them: Portraits of Some Nineteenth-Century Americans,* 87–128. Boston: Houghton Mifflin, 1929.

**1348.** Bradley, Bert E. "Refutative Techniques of John C. Calhoun." *Southern Speech Communication Journal* 37 (Summer 1972): 413–423.

**1349.** Brooks, Noah. "John C. Calhoun." In his *Statesmen*, 69–90. New York: Scribner's, 1894.

**1350.** Calhoun, John C. *Basic Documents.* Edited by John M. Anderson. State College, PA: Bald Eagle Press, 1952.

**1351.** ———. *Papers.* 8 vols. Edited by Robert L. Meriwether and W. Edwin Hemphill. Columbia: University of South Carolina Press, 1959–1975.

**1352.** ———. *Works.* 6 vols. Edited by Richard K. Cralle. New York: Appleton, 1851–1856.

**1353.** Capers, Gerald M. *John C. Calhoun Opportunist: A Reappraisal.* Gainesville: University of Florida Press, 1960.

**1354.** ———. "A Reconsideration of John C. Calhoun's Transition from Nationalism to Nullification." *Journal of Southern History* 14 (February 1948): 34–48.

**1355.** Celsi, Teresa N. *John C. Calhoun and the Roots of War.* Morristown, NJ: Silver Burdett Press, 1991.

**1356.** Coit, Margaret L., ed. *John C. Calhoun.* Englewood Cliffs, NJ: Prentice-Hall, 1991.

**1357.** ———. *John C. Calhoun, American Portrait.* Boston: Houghton Mifflin, 1950.

**1358.** Current, Richard N., ed. *John C. Calhoun.* New York: Washington Square Press, 1963.

**1359.** Dodd, William E. "John C. Calhoun." In his *Statesmen of the Old South: Or, from Radicalism to Conservative Revolt,* 91–170. New York: Macmillan, 1911.

**1360.** Donoghue, Francis J. "The Economic and Social Philosophies of John C. Calhoun." Ph.D. dissertation, Columbia University, 1969.

**1361.** Drucker, Peter F. "A Key to American Politics: Calhoun Pluralism." *Review of Politics* 10 (October 1948): 412–426.

**1362.** Elliott, Edward. "John C. Calhoun: Retardation through Sectional Influence." In his *Biographical Story of the Constitution,* 189–208. New York: Putnam's, 1910.

**1363.** Ewing, Gretchen G. "Duff Green, John C. Calhoun, and the Election of 1828." *South Carolina Historical Magazine* 79 (April 1978): 126–137.

**1364.** Ford, Lacy K. "Recovering the Republic: Calhoun, South Carolina, and the Concurrent Majority." *South Carolina Historical Magazine* 89 (July 1988): 146–159.

**1365.** Freehling, William W. "Spoilsmen and Interests in the Thought of John C. Calhoun." *Journal of American History* 52 (June 1965): 25–42.

**1366.** Hay, Thomas R. "John C. Calhoun and the Presidential Campaign of 1824." *North Carolina Historical Review* 12 (January 1935): 20–44.

**1367.** ———, ed. "John C. Calhoun and the Presidential Campaign of 1824: Some Unpublished Letters." *American Historical Review* 40 (October 1934): 82–96; (January 1935): 287–300.

**1368.** Hollis, Christopher. "John Caldwell Calhoun." In his *The American Heresy,* 82–145. New York: Minton, Balch, 1930.

**1369.** Hunt, Gaillard I. *John C. Calhoun.* Philadelphia: G. W. Jacobs, 1908.

**1370.** Jameson, J. Franklin, ed. *Correspondence of John C. Calhoun.* Washington, DC: American Historical Association, 1900.

**1371.** Jenkins, John S. *The Life of John Caldwell Calhoun.* Auburn: Alden and Beardsley, 1857.

**1372.** Kateb, George. "The Majority Principle: Calhoun and His Antecedents." *Political Science Quarterly* 84 (December 1969): 583–605.

**1373.** Lander, Ernest M. *The Calhoun Family and Thomas Green Clemson: The Decline of a Southern Patriarchy.* Columbia: University of South Carolina Press, 1983.

**1374.** ———. *Reluctant Imperials: Calhoun, the South Carolinians and the Mexican War.* Baton Rouge: Louisiana State University Press, 1980.

**1375.** Lerner, Ralph. "Calhoun's New Science of Politics." *American Political Science Review* 57 (December 1963): 918–932.

**1376.** Lodge, Henry C. "John C. Calhoun." In his *The Democracy of the Constitution, and Other Addresses and Essays,* 160–185. New York: Scribner's, 1915.

**1377.** Lytle, Andrew N. "John C. Calhoun." *Southern Review* 3 (Winter 1938): 510–530.

**1378.** Magoon, Elias L. "John C. Calhoun." In his *Living Orators in America,* 182–270. New York: Baker and Scribner, 1849.

**1379.** Marmor, Theodore R. "Anti-industrialism and the Old South: The Agrarian Perspective of John C. Calhoun." *Comparative Studies in Society and History* 9 (July 1967): 377–406.

**1380.** ———. *The Career of John C. Calhoun: Politician, Social Critic, Political Philosopher.* New York: Garland Publishers, 1988.

**1381.** Meigs, William M. *The Life of John Caldwell Calhoun.* 2 vols. New York: Neale, 1917.

**1382.** Moore, Frederick W., ed. *Calhoun as Seen by His Political Friends: Letters of Duff Green, Dixon H. Lewis, Richard K. Cralle, during the Period from 1831–1848,* Vol. 7, 159–169, 269–291, 353–361, 419–426. Washington, DC: Southern Historical Association, 1903.

**1383.** Niven, John. *John C. Calhoun and the Price of Union: A Biography.* Baton Rouge: Louisiana State University, 1988.

**1384.** Ogburn, Charlton. "The Constitutional Principles of John C. Calhoun." *Journal of Public Law* 2 (Fall 1953): 303–313.

**1385.** Padover, Saul K. "The American as States' Righter: John C. Calhoun." In his *The Genius of America: Men Whose Ideas Shaped Our Civilization,* 138–155. New York: McGraw-Hill, 1960.

**1386.** Parrington, Vernon L. "John C. Calhoun." In his *Main Currents in American Thought,* vol. 2, 69–82. New York: Harcourt, Brace, 1927.

**1387.** Parton, James. "John C. Calhoun." In his *Famous Americans of Recent Times,* 113–171. Boston: Houghton Mifflin, 1895.

**1388.** Peterson, Merrill D. *The Great Triumvirate: Webster, Clay and Calhoun.* New York: Oxford University Press, 1987.

**1389.** Phillips, Ulrich B. "John Caldwell Calhoun." In *American Plutarch,* edited by Edward T. James, 209–225. New York: Scribner's, 1965.

**1390.** Pickney, Gustavus M. *Life of John C. Calhoun.* Charleston, SC: Walker, Evans and Cogswell, 1903.

**1391.** Pritchett, John P. *Calhoun, His Defense of the South.* Poughkeepsie: Printing House of Harmon, 1937.

**1392.** Seitz, Don C. "John C. Calhoun." In his *The "Also Rans": Great Men Who Missed Making the Presidential Goal,* 53–76. New York: Crowell, 1928.

**1393.** Silbey, Joel H. "John C. Calhoun and the Limits of Southern Congressional Unity, 1841–1850." *Historian* 30 (November 1967): 58–71.

**1394.** Sioussat, St. George L. "John Caldwell Calhoun." In *The American Secretaries of State and Their Diplomacy,* edited by Samuel F. Bemis, vol. 5, 125–233. New York: Knopf, 1928.

**1395.** Skeen, C. Edward. "Calhoun, Crawford, and the Politics of Retrenchment." *South Carolina Historical Magazine* 73 (July 1972): 141–155.

**1396.** Spain, August O. *The Political Theory of John C. Calhoun.* New York: Bookman Associates, 1951.

**1397.** Spiller, Roger J. "John C. Calhoun as Secretary of War, 1817–1825." Ph.D. dissertation, Louisiana State University, 1977.

**1398.** Stephenson, Nathaniel W. "Calhoun, 1812, and After." *American Historical Review* 31 (July 1926): 701–707.

**1399.** Styron, Arthur. *The Cast-Iron Man: John C. Calhoun and American Democracy.* New York: Longmans, Green, 1935.

**1400.** Thomas, John L., ed. *John Calhoun: A Profile.* New York: Hill and Wang, 1968.

**1401.** Trent, William P. "John Caldwell Calhoun." In his *Southern Statesmen of the Old Regime: Washington, Jefferson, Randolph, Calhoun, Stephens, Toombs, and Jefferson Davis,* 153–196. New York: Crowell, 1897.

**1402.** Von Holst, Hermann E. *John C. Calhoun.* Boston: Houghton Mifflin, 1899.

**1403.** Walker, Mary M. "Problems of Majority Rule in the Political Thought of James Madison and John C. Calhoun." Ph.D. dissertation, Indiana University, 1971.

**1404.** Walmsley, James E. "The Return of John C. Calhoun to the Senate in 1845." *American Historical Association Annual Report* 1 (1913): 159–165.

**1405.** Waring, Alice N., ed. "Letters of John C. Calhoun to Patrick Noble, 1812–1837." *Journal of Southern History* 16 (February 1950): 64–73.

**1406.** White, Henry A. "John Caldwell Calhoun." In *Library of Southern Literature,* vol. 2, edited by Edwin A. Alderman and Joel C. Harris, 673–679. New Orleans, LA: Martin and Hoyt, 1909.

**1407.** ———. "John Caldwell Calhoun's Service to His Country." In his *The Making of South Carolina,* 188–205. New York: Silver, Burdett, 1906.

**1408.** Wiltse, Charles M. "Calhoun and the Modern State." *Virginia Quarterly Review* 13 (Summer 1937): 396–408.

**1409.** ———. "Calhoun's Democracy." *Journal of Politics* 3 (May 1941): 210–223.

**1410.** ———. *John C. Calhoun.* 3 vols. Indianapolis: Bobbs-Merrill, 1944–1951.

**1411.** Woods, John A. "The Political Philosophy of John C. Calhoun." Ph.D. dissertation, University of Rochester, 1953.

**1412.** Young, Donald. "John C. Calhoun—Martin Van Buren." In his *American Roulette: The History and Dilemma of the Vice Presidency,* 24–41. New York: Holt, Rinehart and Winston, 1965.

**CALL, RICHARD KEITH** (1792–1862) FL, House 1823–1825.

**1413.** Doherty, Herbert J., Jr. *Richard Keith Call: Southern Unionist.* Gainesville: University of Florida Press, 1961.

**CAMBRELENG, CHURCHILL CALDOM** (1786–1862) D-NY, House 1821–1839.

**1414.** Carey, Mathew. *Essays On Political Economy: Or, the Most Certain Means of Promoting the Wealth, Power, Resources, and Happiness of States, Applied Particularly to the United States.* New York: A. M. Kelley, 1968.

**CAMDEN, JOHNSON NEWLON** (1828–1908) D-WV, Senate 1881–1887, 1893–1895.

**1415.** Summers, Festus P. *Johnson Newlon Camden: A Study in Individualism.* New York: Putnam's, 1937.

**CAMERON, JAMES DONALD** (1833–1918) R-PA, Senate 1877–1897.

**1416.** Harrison, Robert. "Blaine and the Camerons: A Study in the Limits of Machine Power." *Pennsylvania History* 49 (July 1982): 157–175.

**CAMERON, RALPH HENRY** (1863–1953) R-AZ, House 1909–1912, Senate 1921–1927.

**1417.** Lamb, Blaine P. "A Many Checkered Toga: Arizona Senator Ralph H. Cameron, 1921–1927." *Arizona and the West* 19 (Spring 1977): 47–64.

**1418.** Strong, Douglas H. "Man Who Owned Grand Canyon." *American West* 6 (September 1969): 33–40.

**1419.** ———. "Ralph H. Cameron and the Grand Canyon." *Arizona and the West* 20 (Spring/Summer 1978): 41–64, 155–172.

**CAMERON, SIMON** (1799–1889) R-PA, Senate 1845–1849, 1857–1861, 1867–1877.

**1420.** Bradley, Erwin S. *Simon Cameron, Lincoln's Secretary of War: A Political Biography.* Philadelphia: University of Pennsylvania Press, 1966.

**1421.** Crippen, Lee F. *Simon Cameron, Ante-Bellum Years.* Oxford, OH: Mississippi Valley Press, 1942.

**1422.** Kelly, Brooks M. "Simon Cameron and the Senatorial Nomination of 1867." *Pennsylvania Magazine of History and Biography* 87 (October 1963): 375–392.

**1423.** Libhart, Lemar L. "Simon Cameron's Political Exile as United States Minister to Russia." *Journal of the Lancaster County Historical Society* 72 (1968): 189–228.

**1424.** Macartney, Clarence E. "Simon Cameron: Lincoln and the Pennsylvania Boss." In his *Lincoln and His Cabinet,* 23–46. New York: Scribner's, 1931.

**1425.** McClure, Alexander K. "Lincoln & Cameron." In his *Abraham Lincoln and Men of War-Times,* 147–168. Philadelphia: Times Publishing Company, 1892.

**1426.** McNair, James B. *Simon Cameron's Adventure in Iron,* 1837–1846. Los Angeles: The author, 1949.

**1427.** Page, Elwin L. *Cameron for Lincoln's Cabinet.* Boston: Boston University Press, 1954.

**1428.** Stewart, John D. "The Great Winnebago Chieftan: Simon Cameron's Rise to Power." *Pennsylvania History* 39 (January 1972): 20–39.

**CAMINETTI, ANTHONY (1854–1923)**
**D-CA, House 1891–1895.**

**1429.** Giovinco, Joseph P. "The California Career of Anthony Caminetti, Italian-American Politician." Ph.D. dissertation, University of California, 1973.

**1430.** Young, Miriam E. "Anthony Caminetti and His Role in the Development of a Complete System of Free Public Education in California." Ph.D. dissertation, University of Denver, 1966.

**CAMPBELL, ED HOYT (1882–1969) R-IA, House 1929–1933.**

**1431.** Porter, David L. "Iowa Congressional Delegation and the Great Economic Issues, 1929–1933." *Annals of Iowa* 46 (Summer 1982): 337–354.

**CAMPBELL, GEORGE WASHINGTON (1769–1848) R-TN, House 1803–1809, Senate 1811–1814, 1815–1818.**

**1432.** Jordan, Weymouth T. *George Washington Campbell of Tennessee, Western Statesman.* Tallahassee: Florida State University, 1955.

**1433.** ———. "The Private Interests and Activities of George Washington Campbell." *East Tennessee Historical Society's Publications* 13 (1941): 47–65.

**1434.** ———. "The Public Career of George Washington Campbell." *East Tennessee Historical Society's Publications* 10 (1938): 3–18.

**CAMPBELL, JAMES EDWIN (1843–1924)**
**D-OH, House 1884–1889.**

**1435.** Doyle, James T. "James Edwin Campbell: Conservative Democratic Congressman, Governor and Statesman." Ph.D. dissertation, Ohio State University, 1967.

**1436.** Smith, Ophia D. "James E. Campbell, 1890–1892." In *Governors of Ohio,* 124–127. Columbus: Ohio Historical Society, 1954.

**CAMPBELL, JOHN WILSON (1782–1833) R-OH, House 1817–1827.**

**1437.** "A Sketch of the Life of the Late Judge Campbell." In *Biographical Sketches,* compiled by Eleanor W. Campbell, 1–13, 271–274. Columbus, OH: Scott and Gallagher, 1838.

**CAMPBELL, LEWIS DAVIS (1811–1882)**
**W/D-OH, House 1849–1858, 1871–1873.**

**1438.** Van Horne, William E. "Lewis D. Campbell and the Know Nothing Party in Ohio." *Ohio History* 76 (Autumn 1967): 202–221.

**CAMPBELL, THOMPSON (1811–1868)**
**D-IL, House 1851–1853.**

**1439.** Linder, Usher F. "Thompson Campbell." In his *Reminiscences of the Early Bench and Bar of Illinois,* 319–332. Chicago: Chicago Legal News Company, 1879.

**CANNON, CLARENCE ANDREW (1879–1964) D-MO, House 1923–1964.**

**1440.** Cannon, Clarence. "Congressional Responsibilities." *American Political Science Review* 42 (April 1948): 307–316.

**1441.** Fulkerson, William M. "A Rhetorical Study of the Appropriations Speaking of Clarence Andrew Cannon in the House of Representatives, 1923–1964." Ph.D. dissertation, Michigan State University, 1970.

**1442.** Jarvis, Charles A. "Clarence Cannon, the Corn Cob Pipe, and the Hawley-Smoot Tariff." *Missouri History* 84 (January 1990): 151–166.

**1443.** Lilley, Stephen R. "The Early Career of Clarence Cannon, 1879–1924." Master's thesis, Northeast Missouri State University, 1976.

**1444.** ———. "A Minuteman for Years: Clarence Cannon and the Spirit of Volunteerism." *Missouri Historical Review* 75 (1980): 33–50.

**CANNON, GEORGE QUAYLE**
**(1827–1901) R-UT, House 1873–1881.**

**1445.** Cannon, Mark W. "The Mormon Issue in Congress 1872–1882: Drawing on the Experience of Territorial Delegate George Q. Cannon." Ph.D. dissertation, Harvard University, 1961.

**CANNON, HOWARD WALTER (1912–   )**
**D-NV, Senate 1959–1983.**

**1446.** Fenno, Richard F. "The Changing Senate in the Cannon Years." *Halcyon* 11 (1989): 65–84.

**1447.** Titus, A. Costandina. "Howard Cannon, the Senate and Civil Rights Legislation, 1959–1968." *Nevada Historical Society Quarterly* 33 (Winter 1990): 13–29.

**CANNON, JOSEPH GURNEY**
**(1836–1926) R-IL, House 1873–1891,**
**1893–1913, 1915–1923.**

**1448.** Atkinson, Charles R. "The Committee on Rules and the Overthrow of Speaker Cannon." Ph.D. dissertation, Columbia University, 1911.

**1449.** Barfield, Claude E. "Our Share of the Booty: The Democratic Party, Cannonism, and the Payne-Aldrich Tariff." *Journal of American History* 57 (September 1970): 308–323.

**1450.** Bentley, Judith. "Joe Cannon and Progress." In her *Speakers of the House*, 73–92. New York: Franklin Watts, 1994.

**1451.** Bolles, Blair. *Tyrant from Illinois: Uncle Joe Cannon's Experiment with Personal Power.* New York: Norton, 1951.

**1452.** Braden, Waldo W. "The Cummins-Cannon Controversy of 1909." *Iowa Journal of History* 49 (July 1951): 211–220.

**1453.** Busbey, L. White. *Uncle Joe Cannon: The Story of a Pioneer American.* New York: Holt, 1927.

**1454.** Carmichael, Otto. "Uncle Joe Cannon as Speaker." *World's Work* 7 (December 1903): 4195–4199.

**1455.** Clark, Champ. "The Rules Revolution." In his *My Quarter Century of American Politics*, vol. 2, 271–283, 358–391. New York: Harper and Brothers, 1920.

**1456.** Fitch, George. "A Survey and Diagnosis of Uncle Joe Cannon." *American Magazine* 65 (December 1907): 185–192.

**1457.** Fuller, Hubert B. "Joseph G. Cannon—The Present Speaker." In his *The Speakers of the House*, 250–272. Boston: Little, Brown, 1909.

**1458.** Gwinn, William R. *Uncle Joe Cannon, Arch-Foe of Insurgency: A History of the Rise and Fall of Cannonism.* New York: Bookman Associates, 1957.

**1459.** Hale, William B. "The Speaker of the People?" *World's Work* 19 (April 1910): 12805–12812.

**1460.** Hard, William. "Uncle Joe Cannon: Unmasking the Czar in the House." In *The Muckrakers*, edited by Arthur M. Weinberg and Lila Weinberg, 87–98. New York: Simon and Schuster, 1961.

**1461.** Hatch, Carl E. *Big Stick and the Congressional Gavel: A Study of Theodore Roosevelt's Relations with His Last Congress, 1907–1909.* New York: Pageant Press, 1967.

**1462.** Hechler, Kenneth. *Insurgency.* New York: Columbia University Press, 1941.

**1463.** Jones, Charles O. "Joseph G. Cannon and Howard W. Smith: An Essay on the Limits of Leadership in the House of Representatives." *Journal of Politics* 30 (August 1968): 617–646.

**1464.** Leupp, Francis E. "The New Speaker." *Outlook* 21 (November 1903): 617–646.

**1465.** Lucas, William D. "A Study of the Speaking and Debating of Joseph Gurney Cannon." Ph.D. dissertation, Northwestern University, 1948.

**1466.** Mayhill, George R. "Speaker Cannon under the Roosevelt Administration, 1903–1907." Ph.D. dissertation, University of Illinois, 1942.

**1467.** Messenger, North O. "The Speaker Prospective of the Next House." *Independent* 5 (February 1903): 306–311.

**1468.** Mooney, Booth. "Uncle Joe: Joseph G. Cannon." In his *Mr. Speaker: Four Men Who Shaped the United States House of Representatives,* 89–128. Chicago: Follett, 1964.

**1469.** Moore, Joseph H. *With Speaker Cannon through the Tropics: A Descriptive Story of a Voyage to the West Indies, Venezuela and Panama.* Philadelphia: Book Print, 1907.

**1470.** Osborn, George C. "Joseph G. Cannon and John Sharp Williams." *Indiana Magazine of History* 35 (September 1939): 283–294.

**1471.** Parshall, Gerald. "Czar Cannon." *American History Illustrated* 11 (June 1976): 34–41.

**1472.** Petterchak, Janice A. "Conflict of Ideals: Samuel Gompers vs. Uncle Joe Cannon." *Journal of the Illinois State Historical Society* 74 (Spring 1981): 31–40.

**CANNON, NEWTON** (1781–1841) R-TN, House 1814–1817, 1819–1823.

**1473.** Cassell, Robert B. *Public Career of Newton Cannon.* Nashville, TN: Cassell, 1938.

**1474.** Harkins, John E. "Newton Cannon, Jackson Nemesis." *Tennessee Historical Quarterly* 43 (Winter 1984): 355–375.

**CAPEHART, HOMER EARL** (1897–1979) R-IN, Senate 1945–1963.

**1475.** Pickett, William B. "The Capehart Cornfield Conference and the Election of 1938: Homer E. Capehart's Entry into Politics." *Indiana Magazine of History* 73 (December 1977): 251–275.

**1476.** ———. *Homer E. Capehart, A Senator's Life, 1897–1979.* Indianapolis: Indiana Historical Society, 1990.

**1477.** Taylor, John R. "Homer E. Capehart: United States Senator, 1944–1962." Ph.D. dissertation, Ball State University, 1977.

**CAPPER, ARTHUR** (1865–1951) R-KS, Senate 1919–1949.

**1478.** Capper, Arthur. *The Agriculture Bloc.* New York: Harcourt, Brace, 1922.

**1479.** Clugston, William G. "Capper: The Christ-Like Statesman." In his *Rascals in Democracy,* 221–245. New York: R. R. Smith, 1940.

**1480.** O'Brien, Patrick G. "Validity of Historical Characterizations: Capper and Curtis." *Southwestern Social Science Quarterly* 48 (March 1968): 624–631.

**1481.** Partin, John W. "The Dilemma of a Good Very Good Man: Capper and Non-interventionism, 1936–1941." *Kansas History* 2 (Summer 1979): 86–95.

**1482.** Socolofsky, Homer E. *Arthur Capper, Publisher, Politician, and Philanthropist.* Lawrence: University of Kansas Press, 1962.

**1483.** ———. "Arthur Capper: Votegetter, Par Excellence." *Journal of the West* 13 (October 1974): 26–39.

**1484.** ———. "Capper Farm Press Experience in Western Agricultural Journalism." *Journal of the West* 19 (April 1980): 22–29.

**1485.** ———. "Development of the Capper Farm Press." *Agricultural History* 31 (October 1957): 34–43.

**1486.** ———. "Twenty-One and All Is Well: Arthur Capper in Topeka, 1886." *Kansas History* 6 (Winter 1983/1984): 202–211.

**CARAWAY, HATTIE WYATT** (1878–1950) **D-AR, Senate 1931–1945.**

**1487.** Caraway, Hattie W. *Silent Hattie Speaks: The Personal Journal of Senator Hattie Caraway.* Westport, CT: Greenwood, 1979.

**1488.** Malone, David. *Hattie and Huey: An Arkansas Tour.* Fayetteville: University of Arkansas Press, 1989.

**1489.** Towns, Stuart. "A Louisiana Medicine Show: The King Fish Elects an Arkansas Senator." *Arkansas Historical Quarterly* 25 (Summer 1966): 117–127.

**CARAWAY, THADDEUS HORATIUS** (1871–1931) **D-AR, House 1913–1921, Senate 1921–1931.**

**1490.** Adams, Horace. "Thaddeus H. Caraway in the United States Senate." Ph.D. dissertation, George Peabody College for Teachers, 1936.

**1491.** McNutt, Walter S. "Thomas H. Caraway." In his *Great Statesmen of Arkansas,* 98–106. Jefferson, TX: Four States Publication House, 1954.

**CAREY, JOHN** (1792–1875) **R-OH, House 1859–1861.**

**1492.** Kinney, Muriel. "John Carey, an Ohio Pioneer." *Ohio State Archaeological and Historical Quarterly* 46 (April 1937): 166–198.

**CAREY, JOSEPH MAULL** (1845–1924) **R-WY, House 1885–1890, Senate 1890–1895.**

**1493.** Peters, Betsy R. "Joseph M. Carey and the Progressive Movement in Wyoming." Ph.D. dissertation, University of Wyoming, 1971.

**CARLISLE, JOHN GRIFFIN** (1835–1910) **D-KY, House 1877–1890, Senate 1890–1893.**

**1494.** Barnes, James A. *John G. Carlisle: Financial Statesman.* New York: Dodd, Mead, 1931.

**1495.** Fuller, Hubert B. "Kerr, Randall, Keifer, and Carlisle." In his *The Speakers of the House,* 193–213. Boston: Little, Brown, 1909.

**CARMACK, EDWARD WARD** (1858–1908) **D-TN, House 1897–1901, Senate 1901–1907.**

**1496.** Bass, Frank E. "The Work of Edward Ward Carmack in Congress." Master's thesis, George Peabody College, 1930.

**1497.** Bumpus, Paul F. *Carmack: The Edward Carmack Story.* Franklin, TN: Distributed by Bumpus, 1977.

**1498.** Faries, Clyde J. "Carmack Versus Patterson: The Genesis of a Political Feud." *Tennessee Historical Quarterly* 38 (Fall 1979): 332–347.

**1499.** Lanier, Robert A. "The Carmack Murder Case." *Tennessee Historical Quarterly* 40 (Fall 1981): 272–285.

**1500.** Majors, William R. *Editorial Wild Oats: Edward Ward Carmack and Tennessee Politics.* Macon, GA: Mercer University Press, 1984.

**1501.** Smith, Will D. *The Carmack-Patterson Campaign and Its Aftermath in Tennessee Politics.* Nashville, TN: Smith, 1939.

**CARMICHAEL, WILLIAM** (?–1795) MD, Continental Congress 1778–1780.

**1502.** Coe, Samuel G. *The Mission of William Carmichael to Spain.* Baltimore: Johns Hopkins University Press, 1928.

**CARPENTER, CYRUS CLAY** (1829–1898) R-IA, House 1879–1883.

**1503.** Swisher, Jacob A. "Cyrus C. Carpenter." In his *Governors of Iowa,* 53–54. Mason City, IA: Klipto Loose Leaf Company, 1946.

**1504.** Throne, Mildred. *Cyrus Clay Carpenter and Iowa Politics, 1854–1898.* Iowa City: State Historical Society of Iowa, 1974.

**CARPENTER, MATTHEW HALE** (1824–1881) R-WI, Senate 1869–1875, 1879–1881.

**1505.** Deutsch, Herman J. "Carpenter and the Senatorial Election of 1875 in Wisconsin." *Wisconsin Magazine of History* 16 (September 1932): 26–46.

**1506.** ———. "Matt Carpenter: A Senator of the Seventies." *Proceedings of the Pacific Coast Branch of the American Historical Society* (1929): 187–199.

**1507.** Flower, Frank A. *Life of Matthew Hale Carpenter.* Madison, WI: Atwood, 1883.

**1508.** Thompson, Edwin B. *Matthew Hale Carpenter, Webster of the West.* Madison: State Historical Society of Wisconsin, 1954.

**CARROLL, CHARLES** (1737–1832) MD, Senate 1789–1792, Continental Congress 1776–1778.

**1509.** Brougham, Henry. "Carroll." In his *Historical Sketches of Statesmen Who Flourished in the Time of George III,* vol. 5 of *Works*

of Henry, Lord Brougham, 275–279. London: R. Griffin, 1856.

**1510.** Dulany, Daniel. *Maryland and the Empire, 1773: The Antilon-First Citizen Letters.* Baltimore: Johns Hopkins University Press, 1974.

**1511.** Essary, J. Frederick. "Charles Carroll of Carrollton." In his *Maryland in National Politics,* 18–37. Baltimore: John Murphy, 1915.

**1512.** Gurn, Joseph. *Charles Carroll of Carrollton, 1737–1832.* New York: P. J. Kenedy, 1932.

**1513.** Hanely, Thomas O. *Charles Carroll of Carrollton: The Making of a Revolutionary Gentleman.* Washington, DC: Catholic University of America, 1970.

**1514.** ———. *Revolutionary Statesman: Charles Carroll and the War.* Chicago: Loyola University Press, 1983.

**1515.** Maier, Pauline. "Charles Carroll of Carrollton, Dutiful Son and Revolutionary Politician." In her *The Old Revolutionaries,* 201–268. New York: Knopf, 1980.

**1516.** Rowland, Kate M. *The Life of Charles Carroll of Carrollton, 1737–1832, with His Correspondence and Public Papers.* 2 vols. New York: Putnam's, 1893.

**1517.** Sanderson, John. "Charles Carroll." In *Sanderson's Biography of the Signers of the Declaration of Independence,* edited by Robert T. Conrad, 623–630. Philadelphia: Thomas, Cowperthwait, 1848.

**1518.** Smith, Ellen H. *Charles Carroll of Carrollton.* Cambridge, MA: Harvard University Press, 1945.

**1519.** Van Devanter, Ann C. "Anywhere So Long as There Be Freedom." In *Charles Carroll of Carrollton, His Family and His Maryland: An Exhibition and Catalogue.* Baltimore: Baltimore Museum of Art, 1975.

**CARROLL, DANIEL (1730–1796) MD, House 1789–1791, Continental Congress 1781–1783.**

**1520.** Geiger, Mary V. "Daniel Carroll, a Framer of the Constitution." Ph.D. dissertation, Catholic University of America, 1943.

**1521.** Schauinger, Joseph H. "The Signers of the Constitution." In his *Profiles in Action*, 36–48. Milwaukee, WI: Bruce, 1966.

**CARTER, CHARLES DAVID (1868–1929) D-OK, House 1907–1927.**

**1522.** Grant, Philip A., Jr. "'Save the Farmer': Oklahoma Congressmen Farm Relief Legislation, 1924–1928." *Chronicles of Oklahoma* 64 (Spring 1986): 74–87.

**CARTER, THOMAS HENRY (1854–1911) R-MT, House 1889–1891, Senate 1895–1901, 1905–1911.**

**1523.** Roeder, Richard B. "Thomas H. Carter, Spokesman for Western Development." *Montana* 39 (Spring 1989): 23–29.

**CASE, FRANCIS HIGBEE (1896–1962) R-SD, House 1937–1951, Senate 1951–1962.**

**1524.** Chenoweth, Richard R. "Francis Case: A Political Biography." Ph.D. dissertation, University of Nebraska, 1977.

**CASS, LEWIS (1782–1866) D-MI, Senate 1845–1848, 1849–1857.**

**1525.** Burns, Virginia. *Lewis Cass, Frontier Soldier.* Bath, MI: Enterprise Press, 1980.

**1526.** Carmony, Donald F., and Francis P. Prucha, eds. "A Memorandum of Lewis Cass Concerning a System for the Regulation of Indian Affairs." *Wisconsin Magazine of History* 52 (Autumn 1968): 35–50.

**1527.** Dunbar, Willis F. *Lewis Cass.* Grand Rapids, MI: Eerdmans, 1970.

**1528.** Einstein, Lewis. "Lewis Cass." In *The American Secretaries of State and Their Diplomacy,* edited by Samuel F. Bemis, vol. 6, 295–384. New York: Knopf, 1928.

**1529.** Emery, Benjamin F. "Fort Saginaw." *Michigan History* 30 (July 1946): 476–503.**1530.** Hewlett, Richard G. "Lewis Cass in National Politics, 1842–1861." Ph.D. dissertation, University of Chicago, 1953.

**1531.** Hickman, George H. *The Life of General Lewis Cass.* Baltimore: N. Hickman, 1848.

**1532.** Klunder, Willard C. "Lewis Cass and Slavery Expansion: 'The Father of Popular Sovereignty' and Ideological Infanticide." *Civil War History* 32 (December 1986): 293–317.

**1533.** ———. "Lewis Cass, 1782–1866: A Political Biography." Ph.D. dissertation, University of Illinois, 1981.

**1534.** ———. "The Seeds of Popular Sovereignty: Governor Lewis Cass and Michigan Territory." *Michigan Historical Review* 17 (Spring 1991): 64–81.

**1535.** Magoon, Elias L. "Lewis Cass." In his *Living Orators in America,* 271–301. New York: Baker and Scribner, 1849.

**1536.** McLaughlin, Andrew C. "The Influence of Governor Cass on the Development of the Northwest." *American Historical Association Papers* 3 (1889): 65–83.

**1537.** ———. *Lewis Cass.* Boston Houghton Mifflin, 1891.

**1538.** Miriani, Ronald G. "Lewis Cass and Indiana Administration in the Old Northwest, 1815–1836." Ph.D. dissertation, University of Michigan, 1974.

**1539.** Prucha, Francis P. *Lewis Cass and American Indian Policy.* Detroit, MI: Wayne State University Press, 1967.

**1540.** Seitz, Don C. "Lewis Cass." In his *The "Also Rans": Great Men Who Missed Making the Presidential Goal,* 95–109. NewYork: Crowell, 1928.

**1541.** Shewmaker, Kenneth E. "The War of Words: The Cass-Webster Debate of 1842–43." *Diplomatic History* 5 (Spring 1981): 151–163.

**1542.** Smith, William L. *Fifty Years of Public Life: The Life and Time of Lewis Cass.* New York: Derby & Jackson, 1856.

**1543.** Spencer, Donald S. "Lewis Cass and Symbolic Intervention: 1848–1852." *Michigan History* 53 (Spring 1969): 1–17.

**1544.** Stevens, Walter W. "Lewis Cass and the Presidency." *Michigan History* 49 (June 1965): 123–134.

**1545.** ———. "Michigan's Lewis Cass." *Filson Club Historical Quarterly* 39 (October 1965): 320–325.

**1546.** Unger, Robert W. "Lewis Cass: Indian Superintendent of the Michigan Territory, 1813–1831." Ph.D. dissertation, Ball State University, 1967.

**1547.** Williams, Mentor L. "Shout of Derision: A Sidelight on the Presidential Campaign of 1848." *Michigan History* 32 (March 1948): 66–77.

**1548.** Willson, Beckles. "Cass and King (1836–1846)." In his *America's Ambassadors to France (1777–1927),* 198–207. New York: Frederick A. Stokes, 1928.

**1549.** Woodford, Frank B. *Lewis Cass, the Last Jeffersonian.* New Brunswick, NJ: Rutgers University Press, 1950.

**1550.** Young, William T. *Sketch of the Life and Public Services of General Lewis Cass.* Detroit, MI: Markham and Elwood, 1852.

## CATRON, THOMAS BENTON
**(1840–1921) R-NM, House 1895–1897, Senate 1912–1917.**

**1551.** Duran, Tobias. "Francisco Chaves, Thomas B. Catron and Organized Political Violence in Santa Fe in the 1890's." *New Mexico Historical Review* 59 (July 1984): 291–310.

**1552.** Hefferan, Vioalle C. "Thomas Benton Catron." Master's thesis, University of New Mexico, 1940.

**1553.** Sluga, Mary E. "The Political Life of Thomas Benton Catron, 1896–1921." Master's thesis, University of Mexico, 1941.

**1554.** Westphall, Victor. *Thomas Benton Catron and His Era.* Tucson: University of Arizona Press, 1973.

## CELLER, EMANUEL (1888–1981) D-NY, House 1923–1973.

**1555.** Celler, Emanuel. *You Never Leave Brooklyn: The Autobiography of Emanuel Celler.* New York: John Day, 1953.

## CHAFFEE, JEROME BUNTY (1825–1886) R-CO, House 1871–1875, Senate 1876–1879.

**1556.** West, Elliott. "Jerome B. Chaffee and the McCook-Elbert Fight." *Colorado Magazine* 46 (Spring 1969): 145–165.

## CHALMERS, JAMES RONALD
**(1831–1898) I-MS, House 1877–1882, 1884–1885.**

**1557.** Halsell, Willie D. "James R. Chalmers and Mahoneism in Mississippi." *Journal of Southern History* 10 (February 1944): 37–58.

## CHAMBERLAIN, GEORGE EARLE
**(1854–1928) D-OR, Senate 1909–1921.**

**1558.** Robert, Frank. "The Public Speaking of George Earle Chamberlain, A Study of the Utilization of Speech by a Prominent Politician." Ph.D. dissertation, Stanford University, 1955.

**1559.** Turnbull, George S. "George Earle Chamberlain." In his *Governors of Oregon,* 56–57. Portland, OR: Binfords, 1959.

**CHAMBERS, JOHN** (1780–1852) W-KY, House 1828–1829, 1835–1839.

**1560.** Chambers, John. *Autobiography of John Chambers,* edited by John C. Parish, Iowa City: State Historical Society of Iowa, 1908.

**1561.** Swisher, Jacob A. "John Chambers." In his *Governors of Iowa,* 13–14. Mason City, IA: Klipto Loose Leaf Company, 1946.

**CHANDLER, ALBERT BENJAMIN "HAPPY"** (1898–1991) D-KY, Senate 1939–1945.

**1562.** Boyd, Stephen D. "The Campaign Speaking of A. B. Chandler." *Register of the Kentucky Historical Society* 79 (Summer 1981): 227–239.

**1563.** Chandler, Albert B. *Heroes, Plain Folks, and Skunks: The Life and Times of Happy Chandler: An Autobiography.* Chicago: Bonus Books, 1989.

**1564.** Hixson, Walter L. "The 1938 Kentucky Senate Election: Alben W. Barkley, 'Happy' Chandler, and the New Deal." *Register of the Kentucky Historical Society* 80 (Summer 1982): 309–329.

**1565.** Mann, Arthur W. *Baseball Confidential: Secret History of the War among Chandler, Durochur, MacPhail, and Rickey.* New York: McKay, 1951.

**1566.** Roland, Charles P. "Happy Chandler." *Register of the Kentucky Historical Society* 85 (Spring 1987): 138–161.

**1567.** Shannon, Jasper B. "Happy Chandler: A Kentucky Epic." In *The American Politician,* edited by John T. Salter, 175–191. Chapel Hill: University of North Carolina Press, 1938.

**CHANDLER, JOSEPH RIPLEY** (1792–1880) W-PA, House 1849–1855.

**1568.** Gerrity, Frank. "The Disruption of the Philadelphia Whigocracy: Joseph R. Chandler, Anti-Catholicism, and the Congressional Election of 1854." *Pennsylvania Magazine* 111 (April 1987): 161–194.

**1569.** ———. "Joseph R. Chandler and the Politics of Religion, 1848–1860." *Catholic Historical Review* 74 (April 1988): 226–247.

**1570.** ———. "Joseph Ripley Chandler and the 'Temporal Power of the Pope'" *Pennsylvania History* 49 (April 1982): 106–120.

**CHANDLER, WILLIAM EATON** (1835–1917) R-NH, Senate 1887–1889, 1889–1901.

**1571.** Lacy, Harriet S. "The William E. Chandler Papers, 1829–1917." *Historical New Hampshire* 23 (Autumn 1968): 51–63.

**1572.** Richardson, Leon B. *William E. Chandler, Republican.* New York: Dodd, Mead, 1940.

**1573.** Thompson, Carol L. "William E. Chandler: A Radical Republican." *Current History* 23 (November 1952): 304–311.

**CHANDLER, ZACHARIAH** (1813–1879) R-MI, Senate 1857–1875, 1879.

**1574.** George, Mary K. *Zachariah Chandler: A Political Biography.* East Lansing: Michigan State University Press, 1969.

**1575.** Harbison, Winfred A. "Zachariah Chandler's Part in the Re-election of Abraham Lincoln." *Mississippi Valley Historical Review* 22 (September 1935): 267–276.

**1576.** Harris, Wilmer C. *The Public Life of Zachariah Chandler, 1851–1875.* Lansing: Michigan Historical Commission, 1917.

**CHANLER, WILLIAM ASTOR**
(1867–1934) D-NY, House 1899–1901.

**1577.** Thomas, Lately. *Pride of Lions: The Astor Orphans: The Chanler Chronicle.* New York: Morrow, 1971.

**CHAPIN, CHESTER WILLIAMS**
(1798–1883) D-MA, House 1875–1877.

**1578.** Cochran, Thomas C. "Chester Williams Chapin." In his *Railroad Leaders, 1845–1890,* 288–289. Cambridge, MA: Harvard University Press, 1953.

**CHAPMAN, JOHN GRANT** (1798–1856) W-MD, House 1845–1849.

**1579.** Wheeler, John G. "Chapman, John Grant." In his *History of Congress,* vol. 1, 527–545. New York: Harper, 1848.

**CHAPMAN, WILLIAM WILLIAMS**
(1808–1892) D-IA, House 1838–1840.

**1580.** Colton, Kenneth E. "W. W. Chapman, Delegate to Congress from Iowa Territory." *Annals of Iowa* 21 (April 1938): 283–295.

**CHASE, SALMON PORTLAND**
(1808–1873) R-OH, Senate 1849–1855, 1861.

**1581.** Banker, Charles A. "Salmon P. Chase, Legal Counsel for Fugitive Slaves: Antislavery Ideology as a Lawyer's Creation." Ph.D. dissertation, Rice University, 1986.

**1582.** Bartlett, David V. "Salmon P. Chase." In his *Presidential Candidates Containing Sketches, Biographical, Personal and Political of Prominent Candidates for the Presidency,* 95–117. New York: A. B. Burdick, 1859.

**1583.** Belden, Thomas G. "The Salmon P. Chase Family in the Civil War and Reconstruction: A Study in Ambition and Corruption." Ph.D. dissertation, University of Chicago, 1952.

**1584.** Belden, Thomas G., and Marva R. Belden. *So Fell the Angels.* Boston: Little, Brown, 1956.

**1585.** Benedict, Michael L. "Salmon P. Chase and Mid-nineteenth Century America." *Northwest Ohio Quarterly* 60 (Summer 1988): 119–123.

**1586.** Benson, John S. *The Judicial Record of the Late Chief Justice Chase.* New York: Baker, Voorhis and Company, 1882.

**1587.** Blue, Frederick J. "Kate's Paper Chase: The Race to Publish the First Biography of Salmon P. Chase." *Old Northwest* 8 (Winter 1982–1983): 353–363.

**1588.** ———. *Salmon P. Chase: A Life in Politics.* Kent, OH: Kent State University Press, 1987.

**1589.** Brockett, Linus P. "Salmon Portland Chase." In his *Men of Our Day: Biographical Sketches of Patriots, Orators, Statesmen, Generals, Reformers, Financiers, and Merchants, Now on the State of Action. . . ,* 179–200. Philadelphia: Ziegler and McCurdy, 1872.

**1590.** Brooks, Noah. "Lincoln, Chase, and Grant." *Century Magazine* 49 (February 1845): 607–619.

**1591.** ———. "Salmon P. Chase." In his *Statesman,* 143–174. New York: Scribner's, 1893.

**1592.** Chase, Salmon P. *Inside Lincoln's Cabinet: The Civil War Diaries of Salmon P. Chase.* Edited by David Donald. New York: Longmans, 1954.

**1593.** Chittenden, Lucius E. "Secretary Chase and His Financial Policy." In *Personal Reminiscences, 1840–1890, Including Lincoln,* 99–100. New York: Richmond, Croscup, 1984.

**1594.** Coleman, Charles H. "Chase and the Democratic Nomination." In his *The Election of 1868,* 102–140. New York: Columbia University Press, 1933.

**1595.** ———. "Chief Justice Chase and the Republican Party." In his *The Election of 1868*, 68–83. New York: Columbia University Press, 1933.

**1596.** Coles, Harry L. "Salmon P. Chase, 1856–1860." In *Governors of Ohio*, 72–75. Columbus: Ohio Historical Society, 1954.

**1597.** Cutler, H. M. Tracy. "Salmon Portland Chase." *Chicago Times* 1 (November 1886): 1–10.

**1598.** Dodson, Samuel H., ed. *Diary and Correspondence of Salmon P. Chase*. Washington, DC: Government Printing Office, 1903.

**1599.** Dunne, Gerald T. "President Grant and Chief Justice Chase: A Footnote to the Legal Tender Cases." *St. Louis University Law Journal* 5 (Fall 1959): 539–553.

**1600.** Foraker, Joseph B. "Salmon P. Chase." *Ohio Archaeological and Historical Society Publications* 15 (July 1906): 311–340.

**1601.** Foulke, William D. "Hart: Salmon Portland Chase." *American Historical Review* 5 (April 1900): 583–588.

**1602.** Futch, Ovid L. "Salmon P. Chase and Radical Politics in Florida, 1862–1865." Master's thesis, University of Florida, 1952.

**1603.** Gara, Larry. "Antislavery Congressmen, 1848–1856: Their Contribution to the Debate between the Sections." *Civil War History* 32 (September 1986): 197–207.

**1604.** Gerteis, Louis S. "Salmon P. Chase, Radicalism, and the Politics of Emancipation, 1861–1864." *Journal of American History* 60 (June 1973): 42–62.

**1605.** Gienapp, William E. "Salmon P. Chase, Nativism, and the Formation of the Republican Party in Ohio." *Ohio History* 93 (Winter/Spring 1984): 5–39.

**1606.** Graves, Harmon S. "Chief Justice Chase." *Yale Law Journal* 4 (October 1894): 27–31.

**1607.** Grayson, Theodore J. "Salmon P. Chase and Jay Cooke—Financing the Civil War." In his *Leaders and Periods of American Finance*, 234–265. New York: Wiley, 1932.

**1608.** Gruber, Robert H. "Salmon P. Chase and the Politics of Reform." Ph.D. dissertation, University of Maryland, 1969.

**1609.** Hale, Frank W. "A Rhetorical Exegesis of the Life and Speeches of Salmon Portland Chase." Ph.D. dissertation, Ohio State University, 1955.

**1610.** ———. "Salmon Portland Chase: Rhetorician of Abolition." *Negro History Bulletin* 26 (February 1963): 165–168.

**1611.** Hamlin, Edward S. "Salmon Portland Chase." *International Review* 2 (September 1875): 662–691.

**1612.** Hart, Albert B. *Salmon Portland Chase*. Boston: Houghton Mifflin, 1899.

**1613.** Hoadly, George. "Honorable George Hoadly's Oration of Salmon P. Chase, October 14, 1886." *Weekly Law Bulletin* 16 (November 1, 1886): 321–329.

**1614.** Hollingsworth, Harold M. "The Confirmation of Judicial Review under Taney and Chase." Ph.D. dissertation, University of Tennessee, 1966.

**1615.** Hughes, David F. "Chief Justice Chase at the Impeachment Trial of Andrew Johnson." *New York State Bar Journal* 41 (April 1969): 218–233.

**1616.** ———. "Salmon P. Chase, Chief Justice." Ph.D. dissertation, Princeton University, 1963.

**1617.** ———. "Salmon P. Chase: Chief Justice." *Vanderbilt Law Review* 18 (March 1965): 569–614.

**1618.** Johnson, Bradley T. *Reports on Cases Decided by Chief Justice Chase in the Circuit Court of the United States for the Fourth Circuit*. New York: Da Capo, 1972.

**1619.** Johnson, Dick. "The Role of Salmon P. Chase in the Formation of the

Republican Party." *Old Northwest* 3 (March 1977): 23–38.

**1620.** Jones, Francis R. "Salmon Portland Chase." *Green Bag* 14 (April 1902): 155–165.

**1621.** Lloyd, Henry D. "The Home Life of Salmon Portland Chase." *Atlantic Monthly* 32 (November 1873): 526–538.

**1622.** Luthin, Reinhard H. "Salmon P. Chase's Career before the Civil War." *Mississippi Valley Historical Review* 29 (March 1943): 520–527.

**1623.** Macartney, Clarence E. "Salmon P. Chase: Lincoln and the Man Who Wanted His Place." In his *Lincoln and His Cabinet,* 205–276. New York: Scribner's, 1931.

**1624.** McClure, Alexander K. "Lincoln and Chase." In his *Abraham Lincoln and Men of War-Times,* 132–146. Philadelphia: Times Publishing Company, 1892.

**1625.** McCulloch, Hugh. "Salmon P. Chase." In his *Men and Measures of Half a Century,* 181–188. New York: Scribner's, 1888.

**1626.** Middleton, Stephen. *Ohio and the Antislavery Activities of Attorney Salmon Portland Chase, 1830–1849.* New York: Garland, 1990.

**1627.** Owen, Robert D. "Letter from Honorable S. P. Chase to the Loyal National League." In his *The Conditions of Reconstruction,* 22–24. New York: W. C. Bryant and Company, 1863.

**1628.** Palmer, Beverly W. "From Small Minority to Great Cause: Letters of Charles Sumner to Salmon P. Chase." *Ohio History* 93 (Summer/Autumn 1984): 164–183.

**1629.** Perdue, M. Kathleen. "Salmon P. Chase and the Impeachment Trial of Andrew Johnson." *Historian* 27 (November 1964): 75–92.

**1630.** Perkins, Frederic B. "S. P. Chase." In his *The Picture and the Men,* 137–155. New York: A. J. Johnson, 1867.

**1631.** Phelps, Mary M. *Kate Chase, Dominant Daughter: The Life Story of a Brilliant Woman and Her Famous Father.* New York: Crowell, 1935.

**1632.** Piatt, Donn. "Salmon P. Chase." In his *Memories of the Men Who Saved the Union,* 95–131. New York: Belford, Clarke, 1887.

**1633.** ———. "Salmon P. Chase." *North American Review* 143 (December 1886): 599–614.

**1634.** Pike, James S. *Chief Justice Chase.* New York: Powers, Macgowan and Slipper, 1973.

**1635.** Redfield, Isaac F. "Chief Justice Chase." *North American Review* 122 (April 1876): 337–357.

**1636.** Rice, Clinton. "Salmon Portland Chase, Chief Justice of the United States." In *Sketches of Representative Men, North and South,* edited by Augustus C. Rogers, 129–134. New York: Atlantic Publishing Company, 1872.

**1637.** Savage, John. "Salmon P. Chase, of Ohio." In his *Our Living Representative Men,* 102–173. Philadelphia: Childs and Peterson, 1860.

**1638.** Schlesinger, Arthur M., Sr. *Salmon Portland Chase, Undergraduate and Pedagogue.* Columbus, OH: F. J. Heer Printing Company, 1919.

**1639.** Schuckers, Jacob W. *The Life and Public Services of Salmon Portland Chase.* New York: Appleton, 1874.

**1640.** Scott, Henry W. "Salmon Portland Chase." In his *Distinguished American Lawyers,* 133–142. New York: C. L. Webster, 1891.

**1641.** Sefton, James E., ed. "Chief Justice Chase as an Advisor on Presidential Reconstruction." *Civil War History* 12 (September 1967): 247–264.

**1642.** Smith, Donald V. *Chase and Civil War Politics.* Columbus, OH: F. J. Heer, 1931.

**1643.** ———. "Salmon P. Chase and the Nomination of 1861." In *Essays in Honor of William E. Dodd, by His Former Students at the University of Chicago,* edited by Avery Craven, 291–319. Chicago: University of Chicago, 1935.

**1644.** Stowe, Harriet B. "Salmon P. Chase." In her *Men of Our Times,* 241–266. Hartford, CT: Hartford Publishing Company, 1868.

**1645.** Townshend, Norton S. "Salmon P. Chase." *Ohio Archaeological and Historical Quarterly* 1 (September 1887): 111–126.

**1646.** Umbreit, Kenneth B. "Salmon Portland Chase." In his *Our Eleven Chief Justices,* 247–292. New York: Harper and Brothers, 1938.

**1647.** Viele, Egbert L. "A Trip with Lincoln, Chase and Stanton." *Scribner's Monthly* 16 (October 1878): 813–822.

**1648.** Wambaugh, Eugene. "Salmon Portland Chase." In *Great American Lawyers.* Vol. 5. Edited by William D. Lewis, 327–371. Philadelphia: J. C. Winston, 1908.

**1649.** Warden, Robert B. *An Account of the Private Life and Public Services of Salmon Portland Chase.* Cincinnati, OH: Wilstach, Baldwin, 1874.

**CHASE, SAMUEL** (1741–1811) MD, Continental Congress 1774–1778.

**1650.** Adams, Henry. "Yazoo and Judge Chase." In *John Randolph,* edited by Henry Adams, 122–152. Boston: Houghton Mifflin, 1908.

**1651.** Atwood, Edward W. "Chase's Trial." *Portland University Law Review* 2 (Spring 1951): 11–23.

**1652.** Bair, Robert R., and Robin D. Coblentz. "The Trials of Mr. Justice Samuel Chase." *Maryland Law Review* 27 (Fall 1967): 365–386.

**1653.** Blackmar, Charles B. "On the Removal of Judges: The Impeachment Trial of Samuel Chase." *Judicature* 48 (February 1965): 183–187.

**1654.** Dwight, Nathaniel. "Samuel Chase." In his *The Lives of the Signers of the Declaration of Independence,* 245–252. New York: Barnes, 1876.

**1655.** Elsmere, Jane S. "The Impeachment Trial of Justice Samuel Chase." Ph.D. dissertation, Indiana University, 1962.

**1656.** ———. *Justice Samuel Chase.* Muncie, IN: Janevar Publishing Company, 1980.

**1657.** Essary, J. Frederick. "Samuel Chase." In his *Maryland in National Politics,* 77–95. Baltimore: John Murphy, 1915.

**1658.** Evans, Charles. *Report of the Trial of Samuel Chase before the Senate of the United States for High Crimes and Misdemeanors.* Baltimore: S. Butler and G. Keatince, 1805.

**1659.** Goodrich, Charles A. "Samuel Chase." In his *Lives of the Signers of the Declaration of Independence,* 338–346. New York: W. Reed and Company, 1824.

**1660.** Gould, Ashley M. "Luther Martin and the Trials of Chase and Burr." *Georgetown Law Journal,* 1 (January 1912): 13–19; 1 (November 1912): 17–22.

**1661.** Harris, Charles D. "The Impeachment Trial of Samuel Chase." *American Bar Association Journal* 57 (January 1971): 53–57.

**1662.** Haw, James A. "Samuel Chases's Objections to the Federal Government." *Maryland Historical Magazine* 76 (Fall 1981): 272–285.

**1663.** ———. *Stormy Patriot: The Life of Samuel Chase.* Baltimore: Maryland Historical Society, 1980.

**1664.** Judson, L. Carroll. "Samuel Chase." In his *A Biography of the Signers of the Declaration of Independence and of Washington and Patrick Henry,* 236–248. Philadelphia:

J. Dobson and Thomas, Cowperthwait, 1839.

**1665.** ———. "Samuel Chase." In his *Sages and Heroes of the American Revolution*, 68–77. Philadelphia: Mass and Brother, 1853.

**1666.** Lillich, Richard B. "The Chase Impeachment." *American Journal of Legal History* 4 (January 1960): 49–72.

**1667.** Lossing, Benson J. "Samuel Chase." In his *Lives of the Signers of the Declaration of American Independence*, 146–150. Philadelphia: Evans, Stoddart, and Company, 1870.

**1668.** Presser, Stephen B. "A Tale of Two Judges: Richard Peters, Samuel Chase, and the Broken Promise of Federalist Jurisprudence." *New York University Law Review* 73 (March/April 1978): 26–111.

**1669.** Presser, Stephen B., and Becky B. Hurley. "Saving God's Republic: The Jurisprudence of Samuel Chase." *University of Illinois Law Review* (Summer 1984): 771–882.

**1670.** Rehnquist, William H. *Grand Inquests: The Historic Impeachments of Justice Samuel Chase and President Andrew Johnson.* New York: Morrow, 1992.

**1671.** Sanderson, John. "Samuel Chase." In *Sanderson's Biography of the Signers of the Declaration of Independence*, edited by Robert T. Conrad, 580–601. Philadelphia: Thomas, Cowperthwait, 1848.

## CHATHAM, RICHARD THURMOND (1896–1957) D-NC, House 1949–1957.

**1672.** Christian, Ralph J. "The Folber-Chatham Congressional Primary of 1946." *North Carolina Historical Review* 53 (January 1976): 25–54.

## CHAVES, JOSE FRANCISCO (1833–1904) R-NM, House 1865–1867, 1869–1871.

**1673.** Duran, Tobias. "Francisco Chaves, Thomas B. Catron, and Organized Politi-cal Violence in Sante Fe in the 1890s." *New Mexico Historical Review* 59 (July 1984): 291–310.

## CHAVEZ, DENNIS (1888–1962) D-NM, House 1931–1935, Senate 1935–1962.

**1674.** Crouch, Barry A. "Dennis Chavez and Roosevelt's Court-Packing Plan." *New Mexico Historical Review* 42 (October 1967): 261–280.

**1675.** Fox, Richard L. "New Mexico Senators: A History of Power." *New Mexico Magazine* 63 (November 1985): 82–90.

**1676.** Pickens, William H. "Bronson Cutting vs. Dennis Chavez: Battle of the Patrones in New Mexico, 1934." *New Mexico Historical Review* 46 (January 1971): 5–36.

**1677.** Vigil, Maurilio, and Roy Lujan. "Parallels in the Career of Two Hispanic U.S. Senators." *Journal of Ethnic Studies* 13 (Winter 1986): 1–20.

## CHEATHAM, HENRY PLUMMER (1857–1935) R-NC, House 1889–1893.

**1678.** Christopher, Maurine. "John A. Hyman, James E. O'Hara, and Henry P. Cheatam/North Carolina." In her *Black Americans in Congress*, 149–159. Rev. ed. New York: Thomas Y. Crowell, 1976.

**1679.** Reid, George W. "Four in Black: North Carolina's Black Congressmen, 1874–1901." *Journal of Negro History* 64 (Summer 1979): 229–243.

## CHENOWETH, JOHN EDGAR (1897–1986) R-CO, House 1941–1949, 1951–1965.

**1680.** Mehls, Carol J. "Into the Frying Pan: J. Edgar Chenoweth and the Frying-Pan-Arkansas Reclamation Project." Ph.D. dissertation, University of Colorado at Boulder, 1986.

**CHESNUT, JAMES, JR.** (1815–1885) D-SC, Senate 1858–1860.

**1681.** Chesnut, Mary B. *Mary Chesnut's Civil War.* Edited by C. Vann Woodward. New Haven, CT: Yale University Press, 1981.

**CHEVES, LANGDON** (1776–1857) R-SC, House 1810–1815.

**1682.** Abbot, Abiel. "The Abiel Abbot Journals: A Yankee Preacher in Charleston Society, 1818–1827." *South Carolina Historical Magazine* 68 (April/October 1967): 51–73, 115–139, 232–254.

**1683.** Bennett, Susan S. "The Cheves Family of South Carolina." *South Carolina Historical and Genealogical Magazine* 35 (July 1934): 79–95; 35 (October 1938): 130–152.

**1684.** Diffenderfer, Frank R. "Langdon Cheves." *Historical Papers and Addresses of the Lancaster County Historical Society* 11 (January 1907): 45–58.

**1685.** Haskell, Louisa P. "Langdon Cheves and the United States Bank: A Study from Neglected Sources." In *Annual Report of the American Historical Association, 1896,* 361–371. Washington, DC: Government Printing Office, 1897.

**1686.** Hensel, William U. "A Reminiscence of Langdon Cheves." *Historical Papers and Addresses of the Lancaster County Historical Society* 15 (April 1911): 120–122.

**1687.** Huff, Archie V. "Langdon Cheves and the War of 1812: Another Look at National Honor in South Carolina." In *Proceedings of the South Carolina Historical Association* 17 (1970): 8–20.

**1688.** ———. *Langdon Cheves of South Carolina.* Columbia: University of South Carolina Press, 1977.

**1689.** Wright, David M. "Langdon Cheves and Nicholas Biddle: New Data for a New Interpretation." *Journal of Economic History* 13 (Summer 1953): 305–319.

**CHILTON, HORACE** (1891–1932) D-TX, Senate 1881–1892, 1895–1901.

**1690.** Welch, June R. "Chilton Served in Both Lines." In his *The Texas Senator,* 102–105. Dallas, TX: G. L. A. Press, 1978.

**1691.** ———. "Chilton Was the First Native Texan to Serve in Congress." In his *The Texas Senator,* 40–41. Dallas, TX: G. L. A. Press, 1978.

**CHILTON, THOMAS** (1798–1854) W-KY, House 1827–1831, 1833–1835.

**1692.** Hannum, Sharon E. "Thomas Chilton: Lawyer, Politician, Preacher." *Filson Club Historical Quarterly* 38 (January 1964): 97–114.

**CHIPMAN, NATHANIEL** (1752–1843) F-VT, Senate 1797–1803.

**1693.** Bauer, Elizabeth. "Nathaniel Chipman." In her *Commentaries on the Constitution, 1790–1860,* 114–124. New York: Columbia University Press, 1952.

**1694.** Chipman, Daniel. *The Life of Hon. Nathaniel Chipman.* Boston: Little, Brown, 1846.

**1695.** Hansen, Allen O. "Nathaniel Chipman's Plan for a National System of Education." In his *Liberalism and American Education in the Eighteenth Century,* 89–104. New York: Macmillan, 1926.

**CHISHOLM, SHIRLEY ANITA** (1924– ) D-NY, House 1969–1983.

**1696.** Brownmiller, Susan. *Shirley Chisholm.* Garden City, NY: Doubleday, 1970.

**1697.** Chisholm, Shirley. *The Good Fight.* New York: Harper and Row, 1973.

**1698.** ———. *Unbought and Unbossed.* Boston: Houghton Mifflin, 1970.

**1699.** Christopher, Maurine. "Shirley Chisholm/New York." In her *Black Americans in Congress,* 255–261. Rev. ed. New York: Thomas Y. Crowell, 1976.

**1700.** Drotning, Phillip T., and Wesley W. South. "Shirley Chisholm: Tempest on Capitol Hill." In their *Up from the Ghetto*, 132–142. New York: Cowles, 1970.

**1701.** Flynn, James J. "Shirley Anita Chisholm: Congresswoman." In his *Negroes of Achievement in Modern America*, 200–209. New York: Dodd, Mead, 1970.

**1702.** Hicks, Nancy. *The Honorable Shirley Chisholm: Congresswoman from Brooklyn.* New York: Lion Press, 1971.

**1703.** Kuriansky, Joyce A., and Catherine Smith. *Shirley Chisholm.* Washington, DC: Grossman, 1972.

**1704.** Metcalf, George R. "Shirley Chisholm." In his *Up from Within*, 113–148. New York: McGraw-Hill, 1971.

**1705.** Toppin, Edgar A. "Chisholm, Shirley." In his *Biographical History of Blacks in America Since 1528*, 270–271. New York: McKay, 1971.

**CHOATE, RUFUS (1799–1859) W-MA, House 1831–1834, Senate 1841–1845.**

**1706.** Brown, Samuel G. *The Life of Rufus Choate.* 3d ed. Boston: Little, Brown, 1891.

**1707.** Choate, Rufus. *The Works of Rufus Choate, with a Memoir of His Life.* 2 vols. Edited by Samuel G. Brown. Boston: Little, Brown, 1862.

**1708.** Fuess, Claude M. *Rufus Choate, the Wizard of the Law.* New York: Minton, Balch, 1928.

**1709.** Matthews, Jean V. *Rufus Choate, the Law and Civic Virtue.* Philadelphia: Temple University Press, 1980.

**1710.** Parker, Edward G. *Reminiscences of Rufus Choate, the Great American Advocate.* New York: Mason Brothers, 1860.

**1711.** Parton, James, ed. "College Life of Rufus Choate." In his *Some Noted Princes, Authors, and Statesmen of Our Time*, 277–283. New York: Crowell, 1885.

**1712.** Stubbs, Roy S. "Rufus Choate." *Canadian Bar Review* 17 (December 1939): 716–731.

**1713.** Walker, David B. "Rufus Choate, An American Whig." Ph.D. dissertation, Brown University, 1956.

**1714.** ———. "Rufus Choate: A Case Study in Old Whiggery." *Essex Institute Historical Collections* 94 (October 1958): 334–355.

**1715.** Whipple, Edwin P. "Rufus Choate." In his *Essays and Reviews,* vol. 2, 130–151. Boston: Houghton Mifflin, 1883.

**CHURCH, FRANK FORRESTER (1924–1984) D-ID, Senate 1957–1981.**

**1716.** Ashby, Leroy. *Fighting the Odds: The Life of Senator Frank Church.* Pullman: Washington State University Press, 1994.

**1717.** ———. "Frank Church Goes to the Senate: The Idaho Election of 1956." *Pacific Northwest Quarterly* 78 (January/April 1987): 17–31.

**1718.** Brock, Gustaf J. "'Congress Must Draw the Line': Senator Frank Church and the Cooper-Church Amendment of 1970." *Idaho Yesterdays* 35 (Summer 1991): 27–36.

**1719.** Church, Frank F. *Father and Son: A Personal Biography of Senator Frank Church of Idaho.* New York: Harper and Row, 1985.

**1720.** Hatzenbuehler, Ronald L., and Bert W. Marley. "Why Church Lost: A Preliminary Analysis of the Church-Symms Election of 1980." *Pacific Historical Review* 56 (February 1987): 99–112.

**CHURCHWELL, WILLIAM MONTGOMERY (1826–1862) D-TN, House 1851–1855.**

**1721.** Turner, Ruth O. "The Public Career of William Montgomery Churchwell." Master's thesis, University of Tennessee, 1954.

**CILLEY, JONATHAN (1802–1838) D-ME, House 1837–1838.**

**1722.** Hawthorne, Nathaniel. "Jonathan Cilley." In his *Complete Works,* vol. 12, 264–275. Boston: Houghton Mifflin, 1909.

**CLAIBORNE, JOHN FRANCIS HAMTRAMCK (1807–1884) J-MS, House 1835–1837, 1837–1838.**

**1723.** Williams, Frederich D. "The Career of J. F. H. Claiborne, States' Rights Unionist." Ph.D. dissertation, Indiana University, 1953.

**CLAIBORNE, WILLIAM CHARLES COLE (1775–1817) D-LA, House 1797–1801, Senate 1817.**

**1724.** Bradley, Jared W. "William C. C. Claiborne, The Old Southwest and the Development of the American Indian Policy." *Tennessee Historical Quarterly* 33 (Fall 1974): 265–278.

**1725.** Hatfield, Joseph T. "William C. C. Claiborne: Claiborne, Congress, and Republicanism, 1797–1804." *Tennessee Historical Quarterly* 24 (Summer 1965): 157–181.

**1726.** ———. *William Claiborne: Jeffersonian Centurion in the American Southwest.* LaFayette: University of Southwestern Louisiana, 1976.

**1727.** Holmes, Jack D., ed. "William C. C. Claiborne Predicts the Future of Tennessee." *Tennessee Historical Quarterly* 24 (Summer 1965): 181–184.

**1728.** Reeves, Miriam G. "William Charles Cole Claiborne." In her *Governors of Louisiana,* 40–42. Gretna, LA: Pelican, 1972.

**1729.** Winters, John D. "William C. C. Claiborne: Profile of a Democrat." *Louisiana History* 10 (Summer 1969): 189–210.

**CLARK, ABRAHAM (1726–1794) NJ, House 1791–1794, Continental Congress 1776–1778, 1780–1783, 1786–1788.**

**1730.** Bogin, Ruth. *Abraham Clark and the Quest for Equality in the Revolutionary Era, 1774–1794.* Rutherford, NJ: Fairleigh Dickinson University Press, 1982.

**1731.** ———. "New Jersey's True Policy: The Radical Republican Vision of Abraham Clark." *William and Mary Quarterly* 39 (January 1978): 100–109.

**1732.** Hart, Ann C. *Abraham Clark, Signer of the Declaration of Independence.* San Francisco: Pioneer Press, 1923.

**1733.** Sanderson, John. "Abraham Clark." In *Sanderson's Biography of the Signers of the Declaration of Independence,* edited by Robert T. Conrad, 331–335. Philadelphia: Thomas, Cowperthwait, 1848.

**CLARK, DANIEL (1766–1813) Orleans, House 1806–1809.**

**1734.** Wohl, Michael S. "A Man in the Shadow: The Life of Daniel Clark." Ph.D. dissertation, Tulane University, 1984.

**CLARK, JAMES BEAUCHAMP "CHAMP" (1850–1921) D-MO, House 1893–1895, 1897–1921.**

**1735.** Clark, Champ. *My Quarter Century of American Politics.* 2 vols. New York: Harper, 1920.

**1736.** Hollister, Wilfred R., and Harry Norman. "Champ Clark." In their *Five Famous Missourians.* Kansas City, MO: Hudson-Kimberley Publishing Company, 1900.

**1737.** Lathrop, John E. "The Views of Champ Clark." *Outlook* 11 (May 1912): 65–73.

**1738.** Morrison, Geoffrey. "Champ Clark and the Rules Revolution of 1910." *Capitol Studies* 2 (Winter 1974): 43–56.

**1739.** ———. "A Political Biography of Champ Clark." Ph.D. dissertation, St. Louis University, 1972.

**1740.** Watson, James E. "William Jennings Bryan and Champ Clark." In his *As I Knew Them,* 171–183. Indianapolis: Bobbs-Merrill, 1936.

**1741.** Webb, William L. *Champ Clark.* New York: Neale, 1912.

**1742.** White, Hollis L. "Champ Clark, the Leather-Bound Orator." *Missouri Historical Review* 56 (October 1961): 25–39.

**1743.** ———. "A Rhetorical Criticism of the Speeches of Speaker Champ Clark of Missouri." Ph.D. dissertation, University of Missouri, 1950.

**CLARK, JOSEPH SILL** (1901–1990) D-PA, Senate 1957–1969.

**1744.** Kolodziej, Edward A. "Joe Clark: Profile of a New Senatorial Style." *Antioch Review* 23 (Winter 1963): 463–476.

**CLARK, WILLIAM ANDREWS** (1839–1925) D-MT, Senate 1899–1900, 1901–1907.

**1745.** Farrington, Clayton. "The Political Life of William Andrews Clark." Master's thesis, Montana State University, 1942.

**1746.** Foot, Forrest L. "The Senatorial Aspirations of William A. Clark, 1898–1901: A Study in Montana Politics." Ph.D. dissertation, University of California, 1941.

**1747.** Glasscock, Carl B. *The War of the Copper Kings: Builders of Butte and Wolves of Wall Street.* New York: Blue Ribbon Books, 1935.

**1748.** Malone, Michael P. "Midas of the West: The Incredible Career of William Andrews Clark." *Montana* 33 (Autumn 1983): 2–17.

**1749.** Mangam, William D. *The Clarks, an American Phenomenon.* New York: Silver Bow Press, 1941.

**1750.** Redmond, George F. "William A. Clark." In his *Financial Giants of America,* vol. 2, 181–192. Boston: Stratford Company, 1922.

**CLAY, BRUTUS JUNIUS** (1808–1878) U-KY, House 1863–1865.

**1751.** Hood, James L. "The Union and Slavery: Congressman Brutus J. Clay of the Bluegrass." *Register of the Kentucky Historical Society* 75 (July 1977): 214–221.

**CLAY, CLEMENT CLAIBORNE, JR.** (1816–1882) D-AL, Senate 1853–1861.

**1752.** Bleser, Carol K., and Frederick M. Heath. "The Impact of the Civil War on a Southern Marriage: Clement and Virginia Tunstall Clay of Alabama." *Civil War History* 30 (September 1984): 197–220.

**1753.** Clay-Clopton, Virginia. *A Belle of the Fifties.* New York: Da Capo, 1969.

**1754.** Nuermberger, Ruth A. *The Clays of Alabama: A Plantation-Lawyer-Politician Family.* Lexington: University of Kentucky Press, 1958.

**CLAY, CLEMENT COMER** (1789–1866) D-AL, House 1829–1835, Senate 1837–1841.

**1755.** Nuermberger, Ruth A. *The Clays of Alabama: A Plantation-Lawyer-Politician Family.* Lexington: University of Kentucky Press, 1958.

**CLAY, HENRY** (1777–1852) W-KY, Senate 1806–1807, 1810–1811, 1831–1842, 1849–1852, House 1811–1814, 1815–1821, 1823–1825.

**1756.** Alexander, Holmes M. "Henry Clay." In his *The Famous Five,* 1–43. New York: Bookmailer, 1958.

**1757.** Barton, Tom K. "Henry Clay, Amos Kendall, and Gentlemen's Education: State-Supported Higher Education as a Political Issue in Kentucky, 1815–1825." *Rocky Mountain Social Science Journal* 3 (April 1966): 44–57.

**1758.** Bearss, Sara B. "Henry Clay and the American Claims against Portugal, 1850." *Journal of the Early Republic* 7 (Summer 1987): 167–180.

**1759.** Bentley, Judith. "Henry Clay and Slavery." In his *Speakers of the House,* 73–92. New York: Franklin Watts, 1994.

**1760.** Binkley, Robert W. "The American System: An Example of Nineteenth-Century Economic Thinking—Its Definition by Its Author, Henry Clay." Ph.D. dissertation, Columbia University, 1950.

**1761.** Blakey, George T. "Rendezvous with Republicanism: John Pope vs. Henry Clay in 1816." *Indiana Magazine of History* 62 (September 1966): 233–250.

**1762.** Bolton, Sarah K. "Henry Clay." In her *Famous American Statesmen,* 230–267. New York: Crowell, 1888.

**1763.** Bradford, Gamaliel. "Henry Clay." In his *As God Made Them: Portraits of Some Nineteenth-Century Americans,* 43–86. Boston: Houghton Mifflin, 1929.

**1764.** Breckinridge, Robert J. *Report of the Ceremonies on the Fourth of July, 1857, at the Laying of the Corner Stone of a National Monument, To Be Erected Near Lexington, Kentucky, To the Memory of Henry Clay.* Cincinnati, OH: Cincinnati Gazette, 1857.

**1765.** Brooks, Noah. "Henry Clay." In his *Statesmen,* 9–38. New York: Scribner's, 1893.

**1766.** Brown, James. "Letters of James Brown to Henry Clay, 1804–1835." Edited by James A. Padgett. *Louisiana Historical Quarterly* 24 (October 1941): 921–1177.

**1767.** Burnside, Ronald D. "Henry Clay and the Bank Question, 1804–1832." Master's thesis, Indiana University, 1959.

**1768.** Burton, Theodore E. "Henry Clay." In *The American Secretaries of State and Their Diplomacy,* edited by Samuel F. Bemis, vol. 4, 113–158. New York: Knopf, 1928.

**1769.** Campbell, Randolph B. "Henry Clay and the Emerging Nations of Spanish America, 1815–1829." Ph.D. dissertation, University of Virginia, 1966.

**1770.** ———. "Henry Clay and the Poinsett Pledge Controversy of 1826." *Americas* 28 (April 1972): 429–440.

**1771.** ———. "The Spanish American Aspect of Henry Clay's American System." *Americas* 24 (June 1967): 3–17.

**1772.** Chandler, Charles L. "The Pan-Americanism of Henry Clay." In his *Inter-American Acquaintances.* Sewanee, TN: University Press, 1915.

**1773.** Clay, Henry. *Papers.* Edited by James F. Hopkins and Mary W. M. Hargreaves. 10 vols. Lexington: University of Kentucky Press, 1959–1992.

**1774.** ———. *The Works of Henry Clay, Comprising His Life, Correspondence, and Speeches.* Edited by Calvin Colton. 10 vols. New York: Putnam's, 1904.

**1775.** Clay, Thomas H. *Henry Clay.* Philadelphia: Jacobs, 1910.

**1776.** Coleman, John W. *Henry Clay's Last Criminal Case: An Interesting Episode of Lexington History in 1846.* Lexington, KY: Winburn Press, 1950.

**1777.** ———. *Last Days, Death and Funeral of Henry Clay, with Some Remarks on the Clay Monument in the Lexington Cemetery.* Lexington, KY: Henry Clay Memorial Foundation, 1951.

**1778.** Colton, Calvin. *Life and Times of Henry Clay.* 2 vols. New York: Garland, 1974.

**1779.** Corts, Paul R. "Randolph vs. Clay: A Duel of Words and Bullets." *Filson Club History Quarterly* 43 (April 1969): 151–157.

**1780.** Coulter, E. Merton. "The Genesis of Henry Clay's American System." *South Atlantic Quarterly* 25 (January 1926): 45–54.

**1781.** ———. "Henry Clay." In *American Plutarch,* edited by Edward T. James, 195–208. New York: Scribner's, 1965.

**1782.** Donald, David H. "The Papers of Henry Clay." *Register of the Kentucky Historical Society* 82 (Winter 1984): 72–76.

**1783.** Eaton, Clement. *Henry Clay and the Art of American Politics.* Boston: Little, Brown, 1957.

**1784.** Eichert, Magdalen. "Henry Clay's Policy of Distribution of the Proceeds from Public Land Sales." *Register of the Kentucky Historical Society* 52 (January 1954): 25–32.

**1785.** Estes, J. Worth. "Henry Clay as a Livestock Breeder." *Filson Club History Quarterly* 32 (October 1958): 350–355.

**1786.** Follett, Mary P. "Henry Clay as Speaker of the United States House of Representatives." In *Annual Report of the American Historical Association, 1891,* 257–265. Washington, DC: Government Printing Office, 1892.

**1787.** Franklin, Earl R. "Henry Clay's Visit to Raleigh." *Trinity College Historical Society Papers* 7 (1907): 55–63.

**1788.** Fuller, Hubert B. "Muhlenberg the First and Henry Clay the Greatest of American Speakers." In his *The Speakers of the House,* 22–58. Boston: Little, Brown, 1909.

**1789.** Gantz, Richard A. "Henry Clay and the Harvest of Bitter Fruit: The Struggle with John Tyler, 1841–1842." Ph.D. dissertation, Indiana University, 1986.

**1790.** Grattan, Thomas C. "Henry Clay." In his *Civilized America,* vol. 2, 395–408. London: Bradbury and Evans, 1859.

**1791.** Gunderson, Robert G. "The Magnanimous Mr. Clay." *Southern Speech Journal* 16 (December 1950): 133–140.

**1792.** Hendricks, Rickey L. "Henry Clay and Jacksonian Indian Policy: A Political Anachronism." *Filson Club History Quarterly* 60 (April 1986): 218–238.

**1793.** Hopkins, James F., ed. "Henry Clay, Farmer and Stockman." *Journal of Southern History* 15 (February 1949): 89–96.

**1794.** Hoskins, Halford L. "The Hispanic American Policy of Henry Clay, 1816–1828." *Hispanic American Historical Review* 7 (August 1927): 460–478.

**1795.** Hoyt, Edwin P. "Henry Clay." In his *Lost Statesmen,* 67–88. Chicago: Reilly and Lee, 1961.

**1796.** Hubbard, Elbert. "Henry Clay." In his *Little Journeys to the Homes of the Great,* vol. 3, 207–227. New York: W. H. Wise, 1916.

**1797.** Hulbert, Archer B. "Henry Clay: Promoter of the First American Highway." In his *Pilots of the Republic,* 179–206. Chicago: A. C. McClurg, 1906.

**1798.** Jones, Thomas B. "Henry Clay and Continental Expansion, 1820–1844." *Register of the Kentucky Historical Society* 73 (July 1975): 241–262.

**1799.** Kenworthy, Leonard S. "Henry Clay at Richmond in 1842." *Indiana Magazine of History* 30 (December 1934): 353–359.

**1800.** Kirwan, Albert D. "Congress Elects a President: Henry Clay and the Campaign of 1824." *Kentucky Review* 4 (Winter 1983): 3–26.

**1801.** Klein, Larry D. "Henry Clay: Nationalist." Ph.D. dissertation, University of Kentucky, 1977.

**1802.** Krueger, David W. "The Clay-Tyler Feud, 1841–1842." *Filson Club History Quarterly* 42 (April 1968): 162–175.

**1803.** Lightfoot, Alfred. "Henry Clay and the Missouri Question 1819–1821: American Lobbyist for Unity." *Missouri Historical Review* 61 (January 1967): 143–165.

**1804.** Lindley, Harlow. "The Anti-Slavery Separation in Indiana and the Henry Clay Incident in 1842." *Bulletin of Friends Historical Society* 6 (May 1915): 34–48.

**1805.** Lindsey, David. *Henry Clay, Andrew Jackson: Democracy and Enterprise.* Cleveland, OH: Allen, 1962.

**1806.** Littell, John S. *The Clay Minstrel: Or, National Songster: To Which Is Prefixed a*

*Sketch of the Life, Public Services, and Character of Henry Clay.* 2d ed. Philadelphia: Thomas, Cowperthwait, 1844.

**1807.** Lockey, Joseph B. "Attitude of the United States." In his *Pan-Americanism*, 404–427. New York: Macmillan, 1920.

**1808.** Magoon, Elias L. "Henry Clay." In his *Living Orators in America*, 117–181. New York: Baker and Scribner, 1849.

**1809.** Maness, Lonnie E. "Henry Clay and the Problem of Slavery." Ph.D. dissertation, Memphis State University, 1980.

**1810.** Mathias, Frank F. "Henry Clay and His Kentucky Power Base." *Register of the Kentucky Historical Society* 78 (Spring 1980): 123–139.

**1811.** Mayo, Bernard. *Henry Clay, Spokesman for the New West.* Boston: Houghton Mifflin, 1937.

**1812.** McElroy, Robert M. "Last Days of the 'Great Commoner.'" In *Kentucky in the Nation's History*, 454–482. New York: Moffat, Yard and Company, 1909.

**1813.** Mooney, Booth. "Star of the West: Henry Clay." In his *Mr. Speaker: Four Men Who Shaped the United States House of Representatives*, 21–48. Chicago: Follett, 1964.

**1814.** Moore, John B. "Henry Clay and Pan-Americanism." *Columbia University Quarterly* 17 (September 1915): 346–362.

**1815.** Morgan, William G. "The Corrupt Bargain Charge against Clay and Adams: An Historiographical Analysis." *Filson Club Historical Quarterly* 42 (April 1968): 132–149.

**1816.** ———. "Henry Clay's Biographers and the Corrupt Bargain Charge." *Register of the Kentucky Historical Society* 66 (July 1968): 242–258.

**1817.** Morley, Margaret R. "The Edge of Empire: Henry Clay's American System and the Formulation of American Foreign Policy, 1810–1833." Ph.D. dissertation, University of Wisconsin, 1972.

**1818.** Neely, Mark E., Jr. "American Nationalism in the Image of Henry Clay: Abraham Lincoln's Eulogy on Henry Clay in Context." *Register of the Kentucky Historical Society* 73 (January 1975): 31–60.

**1819.** Orth, Samuel P. "Henry Clay, Master and Victim of Compromise and Coalition." In his *Five American Politicians: A Study in the Evolution of American Politics*, 171–294. Cleveland, OH: Burrows Brothers, 1906.

**1820.** Parker, Edward A. "Henry Clay as an Orator." *Putnam's Monthly* 3 (May 1854): 493–502.

**1821.** Parton, James. "Henry Clay." In his *Famous Americans of Recent Times*, 1–52. Boston: Houghton Mifflin, 1895.

**1822.** Peck, Charles H. "The Speeches of Henry Clay." *Magazine of History* 16 (July 1886): 58–67.

**1823.** Peterson, Merrill D. *The Great Triumvirate: Webster, Clay and Calhoun.* New York: Oxford University Press, 1987.

**1824.** Picklesimer, Dorman. "To Campaign or Not to Campaign: Henry Clay's Speaking Tour through the South." *Filson Club History Quarterly* 42 (July 1968): 235–242.

**1825.** Poage, George R. *Henry Clay and the Whig Party.* Chapel Hill: University of North Carolina Press, 1936.

**1826.** Prentice, George D. *Biography of Henry Clay.* Hartford, CT: Samuel Hammer and John J. Phelps, 1831.

**1827.** Remini, Robert V. *Henry Clay: Statesman for the Union.* New York: W. W. Norton, 1991.

**1828.** Rochester, Sue C. "Henry Clay's Latin American Policy." Master's thesis, Indiana University, 1944.

**1829.** Rogers, Joseph M. *The True Henry Clay.* Philadelphia: Lippincott, 1904.

**1830.** Sargent, Epes. *The Life and Public Services of Henry Clay down to 1848.* Edited by Horace Greeley. Philadelphia: Porter and Coats, 1852.

**1831.** Sargent, Nathan. *Life of Henry Clay.* Philadelphia: R. G. Berford, 1844.

**1832.** Schmucker, Samuel M. *The Life and Times of Henry Clay.* Philadelphia: J. E. Potter, 1860.

**1833.** Schurz, Carl. *Life of Henry Clay.* 2 vols. Boston: Houghton Mifflin, 1887.

**1834.** Schweikart, Larry. "Focus on Power: A Reappraisal of Speaker Henry Clay." *Alabama Historian* 2 (Spring 1981): 18–24.

**1835.** Seager, Robert. "Henry Clay and the Politics of Compromise and Non-compromise." *Register of the Kentucky Historical Society* 85 (Winter 1987): 1–28.

**1836.** Seitz, Don C. "Henry Clay." In his *The "Also Rans": Great Men Who Missed Making the Presidential Goal,* 77–94. New York: Crowell, 1928.

**1837.** Shannon, Jasper B. "Henry Clay as a Political Leader." Ph.D. dissertation, University of Wisconsin, 1934.

**1838.** Smith, Zachariah F. "Henry Clay." In *Library of Southern Literature,* edited by Edwin A. Alderman and Joel C. Harris, vol. 3, 937–946. New Orleans, LA: Martin and Hoyt, 1909.

**1839.** Smith, Zachariah F., and Mary R. Clay. *The Clay Family.* Louisville, KY: John P. Morton, 1899.

**1840.** Sparks, Edwin E. "Henry Clay, The Father of Public Improvements." In his *The Men Who Made the Nation,* 255–281. New York: Macmillan, 1901.

**1841.** Spaulding, Myra L. "Dueling in the District of Columbia." *Columbia Historical Society Records* 29–30 (1928): 117–210.

**1842.** Spaulding, Thomas M. "Clay Versus Randolph." *Michigan Quarterly Review* 1 (Winter 1962): 8–13.

**1843.** Sterling, Carlos M. "Henry Clay: Forerunner of Pan-Americanism." *Americas* 16 (May 1964): 1–6.

**1844.** Stevens, Harry R. "Henry Clay, the Bank, and the West in 1824." *American Historical Review* 60 (July 1955): 843–848.

**1845.** Teague, William J. "An Appeal to Reason: Daniel Webster, Henry Clay, and Whig Presidential Politics, 1836–1848." Ph.D. dissertation, North Texas State University, 1977.

**1846.** Troutman, Richard L. "Emancipation of Slaves by Henry Clay." *Journal of Negro History* 40 (April 1955): 179–181.

**1847.** ———. "Henry Clay and His Ashland Estate." *Filson Club History Quarterly* 30 (April 1956): 159–174.

**1848.** Van Deburg, William L. "Henry Clay: The Right of Petition, and Slavery in the Nation's Capital." *Register of the Kentucky Historical Society* 68 (April 1970): 132–146.

**1849.** Van Deusen, Glyndon G. *Henry Clay.* Morristown, NJ: Silver Burdett, 1967.

**1850.** ———. *The Life of Henry Clay.* Boston: Little, Brown, 1937.

**1851.** Winkler, James R. "Henry Clay: A Current Assessment." *Kentucky Historical Society Register* 70 (July 1972): 179–186.

**CLAY, JOSEPH (1741–1804) GA,**
**Continental Congress 1778–1780.**

**1852.** Clay, Joseph. *Letters of Joseph Clay, Merchant of Savannah, 1776–1793, and a List of Ships and Vessels Entered at the Port of Savannah, for May 1765, 1766 and 1767.* Savannah, GA: Morning News, Printers, 1913.

**CLAY, WILLIAM LACY, SR. (1931– )**
**D-MO, House 1969–**

**1853.** Christopher, Maurine. "William L. Clay/Missouri." In her *Black Americans in Congress,* 249–254. Rev. ed. New York: Thomas Y. Crowell, 1976.

**CLAYTON, HENRY DE LAMAR**
**(1857–1929) D-AL, House 1897–1914.**

**1854.** Alsobrook, David E. "Remember the Maine!: Congressman Henry D. Clayton Comments on the Impending Conflict with Spain, April, 1898." *Alabama Review* 30 (July 1977): 227–231.

**1855.** Rodabaugh, Karl. "Congressman Henry D. Clayton and the Dothan Post Office Fight: Patronage and Politics in the Progressive Era." *Alabama Review* 33 (April 1980): 124–149.

**1856.** ———. "Congressman Henry D. Clayton, Patriarch in Politics: A Southern Congressman During the Progressive Era." *Alabama Review* 31 (April 1978): 110–120.

**CLAYTON, JOHN MIDDLETON**
**(1796–1856) W-DE, Senate 1829–1936, 1845–1849, 1853–1856.**

**1857.** Comegys, Joseph P. *Memoir of John M. Clayton*. Wilmington: Historical Society of Delaware, 1882.

**1858.** Williams, Mary W. "John Middleton Clayton." In *The American Secretaries of State and Their Diplomacy*, edited by Samuel F. Bemis, vol. 6, 1–74. New York: Knopf, 1928.

**1859.** ———. *John Middleton Clayton*. New York: Knopf, 1928.

**1860.** Wire, Richard A. "John M. Clayton and the Search for Order: A Study in Whig Politics and Diplomacy." Ph.D. dissertation, University of Maryland, 1971.

**1861.** Wire, Richard A. "John M. Clayton and Whig Politics During the Second Jackson Administration." *Delaware History* 18 (Spring/Summer 1978): 1–16.

**1862.** Wire, Richard A. "Young Senator Clayton and the Early Jackson Years." *Delaware History* 17 (Fall/Winter 1976): 104–126.

**CLAYTON, POWELL (1833–1914) R-AR,**
**Senate 1871–1877.**

**1863.** Burnside, William H. *The Honorable Powell Clayton*. Conway, AR: UCA Press, 1991.

**1864.** ———. "Powell Clayton: Politician and Diplomat, 1897–1905." Ph.D. dissertation, University of Arkansas, 1978.

**CLEMENS, JEREMIAH (1814–1865) D-AL,**
**Senate 1849–1853.**

**1865.** Martin, John M. "Jeremiah Clemens: Unionist as Southerner." *West Georgia College Review* 13 (1981): 12–21.

**1866.** ———. "The Senatorial Career of Jeremiah Clemens, 1849–1853." *Alabama Historical Quarterly* 43 (Fall 1981): 186–235.

**CLEMENTS, EARLE CHESTER**
**(1896–1985) D-KY, House 1945–1948, Senate 1950–1957.**

**1867.** Syvertsen, Thomas H. "Earle Chester Clements and the Democratic Party, 1920–1950." Ph.D. dissertation, University of Kentucky, 1982.

**CLIFFORD, NATHAN (1803–1881) D-ME,**
**House 1839–1843.**

**1868.** Bradbury, James W. "Memoir of Nathan Clifford." *Maine Historical Society Collections* 9 (1887): 235–257.

**1869.** Chandler, Walter. "Nathan Clifford: A Triumph of Untiring Effort." *American Bar Association Journal* 11 (January 1925): 57–60.

**1870.** Clifford, Philip G. *Nathan Clifford, Democrat, 1803–1881*. New York: Putnam's, 1922.

**1871.** Hunt, William. "Nathan Clifford." In his *American Biographical Sketch Book*, 128–129. New York: Cornish, Lamport and Company, 1848.

## CLINCH, DUNCAN LAMONT
**(1787–1849) W-GA, House 1844–1845.**

**1872.** Patrick, Rembert W. *Aristocrat in Uniform, General Duncan L. Clinch.* Gainesville: University of Florida Press, 1963.

## CLINGMAN, THOMAS LANIER
**(1812–1897) D-NC, House 1843–1845, 1847–1858, Senate 1858–1861.**

**1873.** Bassett, John S. "The Congressional Career of Thomas L. Clingman." *Trinity College Historical Society Papers* 4 (1900): 48–63.

**1874.** Inscoe, John C. "Thomas Clingman, Mountain Whiggery, and the Southern Cause." *Civil War History* 33 (March 1987): 42–62.

**1875.** Jeffrey, Thomas E. "Thunder from the Mountains: Thomas Lanier Clingman and the End of Whig Supremacy in North Carolina." *North Carolina Historical Review* 56 (October 1979): 366–395.

**1876.** Kruman, Marc. "Thomas L. Clingman and the Whig Party: A Reconsideration." *North Carolina Historical Review* 64 (January 1987): 1–18.

## CLINTON, DE WITT
**(1769–1828) R-NY, Senate 1802–1803.**

**1877.** Bobbe, Dorothie. *De Witt Clinton.* New York: Minton, Balch, 1933.

**1878.** Campbell, William W. *The Life and Writings of De Witt Clinton.* New York: Baker and Scribner, 1849.

**1879.** Fitzpatrick, Edward A. *Educational Views and Influence of De Witt Clinton.* New York: Columbia University Teachers College, 1911.

**1880.** Hancock, John. *De Witt Clinton and the Late War.* New York, 1816.

**1881.** Hanyan, Craig R. "De Witt Clinton and Partisanship: The Development of Clintonianism from 1811 to 1820." *New York Historical Society Quarterly* 56 (April 1972): 109–131.

**1882.** ———. "De Witt Clinton, Years of Molding, 1769–1807." Ph.D. dissertation, Harvard University, 1964.

**1883.** Harris, Jonathan. "De Witt Clinton as Naturalist." *New York Historical Society Quarterly* 56 (October 1972): 264–268.

**1884.** Hopkins, Vivian C. "Governor and the Western Recluse: De Witt Clinton and Francis Adrian Van der Kemp." *American Philosophical Society Proceedings* 105 (1961): 315–333.

**1885.** ———. "John Jacob Astor and De Witt Clinton: Correspondence from Jan. 25, 1908, to Dec. 23, 1827." *New York Public Library Bulletin* 68 (December 1964): 654–673.

**1886.** Hulbert, Archer B. "Morris and Clinton: Fathers of the Erie Canal." In his *Pilots of the Republic,* 207–232. Chicago: A. C. McClurg, 1906.

**1887.** Lagana, Michael P. "De Witt Clinton: Politician toward a New Political Order." Ph.D. dissertation, Columbia University, 1972.

**1888.** ———. "The Political Career of De Witt Clinton: A Need for Reinterpretation." *Niagara Frontier* 22 (Winter 1975): 74–77.

**1889.** McBain, Howard L. *De Witt Clinton and the Origin of the Spoils System in New York.* New York: AMS Press, 1967.

**1890.** Mitchill, Samuel L. *A Discourse on the Character and Scientific Attainments of De Witt Clinton, Late Governor of the State of New York.* New York: E. Concord, 1828.

**1891.** Orth, Samuel P. "De Witt Clinton, Father of the Spoils System." In his *Five American Politicians: A Study in the Evolution of American Politics,* 69–119. Cleveland, OH: Burrows Brothers, 1906.

**1892.** Renwick, James. *Life of De Witt Clinton.* New York: Harper and Brothers, 1840.

**1893.** Siry, Steven E. *De Witt Clinton and the American Political Economy: Sectionalism, Politics, and Republican Ideology, 1787–1828.* New York: P. Lang, 1990.

**1894.** ———. "The Sectional Politics of 'Practical Republicanism': De Witt Clinton's Presidential Bid, 1810–1812." *Journal of the Early Republic* 5 (Winter 1985): 441–462.

**1895.** Slosson, Edwin E. "De Witt Clinton and the Free School." In his *The American Spirit in Education,* 141–154. New Haven, CT: Yale University Press, 1921.

**1896.** Spaulding, Ernest W. "Clintonian Democracy and Reconstruction in New York, 1783–88." Ph.D. dissertation, Harvard University, 1930.

**1897.** Yengo, Carmine A. "A Study of the Significance of DeWitt Clinton's Views in the Educational Development of New York State, 1800–1828." Ph.D. dissertation, Cornell University, 1958.

**CLINTON, GEORGE** (1739–1812) DR-NY, Continental Congress 1775–1776.

**1898.** Barzman, Sol. "George Clinton." In his *Madmen and Geniuses: The Vice-Presidents of the United States,* 35–46. Chicago: Follett, 1974.

**1899.** Cragg, Saunders. *George Clinton, Next President, and Our Republican Institutions Rescued from Destruction: Addressed to the Citizens of the United States, or, James Madison Unmasked.* New York: Henry C. Southwick Printer, 1808.

**1900.** Kaminski, John P. *George Clinton: Yeoman Politician of the New Republic.* Madison, WI: Madison House, 1992.

**1901.** Pagano, Frances B. "An Historical Account of the Military and Political Career of George Clinton, 1739–1812." Ph.D. dissertation, St. John's University, 1956.

**1902.** Spaulding, Ernest W. *His Excellency George Clinton, Critic of the Constitution.* New York: Macmillan, 1938.

**1903.** ———. *New York in the Critical Period, 1783–1789.* Port Washington, NY: Empire State Historical Publications, 1963.

**CLYMER, GEORGE** (1739–1813) PA, House 1789–1791, Continental Congress 1776–1777, 1780–1782.

**1904.** Grundfest, Jerry. "George Clymer, Philadelphia Revolutionary, 1739–1813." Ph.D. dissertation, Columbia University, 1973.

**1905.** Mohr, Walter H. "George Clymer." *Pennsylvania History* 5 (October 1935): 282–285.

**1906.** Sanderson, John. "George Clymer." In *Sanderson's Biography of the Signers of the Declaration of Independence,* edited by Robert T. Conrad, 455–474. Philadelphia: Thomas, Cowperthwait, 1848.

**CLYMER, HIESTER** (1827–1884) D-PA, House 1873–1881.

**1907.** Joachim, Walter. "Hiester Clymer and the Belknap Case." *Historical Review of Berks County* 36 (Winter 1970/1971): 24–31.

**COBB, AMASA** (1823–1905) R-WI, House 1863–1871.

**1908.** Nelson, Meredith K. "Amasa Cobb." *Nebraska Law Bulletin* 14 (November 1935): 197–213.

**COBB, HOWELL** (1815–1868) D-GA, House 1843–1851, 1855–1857.

**1909.** Bartlett, David V. "Howell Cobb." In his *Presidential Candidates Containing Sketches, Biographical, Personal and Political of Prominent Candidates for the Presidency,* 333–335. New York: A. B. Burdick, 1859.

**1910.** Boykin, Samuel, ed. *A Memorial Volume of the Hon. Howell Cobb of Georgia.* Philadelphia: Lippincott, 1870.

**1911.** Franklin, John H. "The Southern Expansionists of 1846." *Journal of Southern History* 25 (August 1959): 323–338.

**1912.** Gannon, Nell W. "Howell Cobb Winfield: A Political Biography." Ph.D. dissertation, University of California, 1933.

**1913.** Greene, Helene I. "Politics in Georgia, 1853–54: The Ordeal of Howell Cobb." *Georgia Historical Quarterly* 30 (September 1946): 185–211.

**1914.** Johnson, Zachary T. *Political Policies of Howell Cobb.* Nashville, TN: George Peabody College for Teachers, 1929.

**1915.** Lamar, J. R. "Howell Cobb." In *Men of Mark in Georgia,* edited by William T. Northern, vol. 3, 596–581. Atlanta, GA: A. B. Caldwell, 1910.

**1916.** Montgomery, Horace. "Georgia's Howell Cobb Stumps for James Buchanan in 1856." *Pennsylvania History* 29 (January 1962): 40–52.

**1917.** ———. "Howell Cobb and the Secession Movement in Georgia." *Papers of the Athens Historical Society* 1 (1963): 35–39.

**1918.** ———. *Howell Cobb's Confederate Career.* Tuscaloosa, AL: Confederate Publishing, 1959.

**1919.** ———. "Two Howell Cobbs: A Case of Mistaken Identity." *Journal of Southern History* 28 (August 1962): 348–355.

**1920.** Ramage, C. J. "Howell Cobb." *Virginia Law Register* 8 (November 1922): 486–491.

**1921.** Simpson, John E. "A Biography of Howell Cobb, 1815–1861." Ph.D. dissertation, University of Georgia, 1971.

**1922.** ———. *Howell Cobb: The Politics of Ambition.* Chicago: Adams Press, 1973.

**1923.** ———. "Howell Cobb's Bid for the Presidency in 1860." *Georgia Historical Quarterly* 55 (Spring 1971): 102–113.

**1924.** ———. "Prelude to Compromise: Howell Cobb and the House Speakership Battle of 1849." *Georgia Historical Quarterly* 58 (Winter 1974): 389–399.

**COBB, WILLIAMSON ROBERT WINFIELD** (1807–1864) D-AL, House 1847–1861.

**1925.** Atkins, Leah R. "Williamson R. W. Cobb and the Graduation Act of 1854." *Alabama Review* 28 (January 1975): 16–31.

**COBURN, JOHN** (1825–1908) R-IN, House 1867–1875.

**1926.** Barnes, William H. "John Coburn." In his *Lives of Gen. Ulysses S. Grant and Hon. Henry Wilson, Together with Sketches of Republican Candidates for Congress in Indiana,* 57–60. New York: H. H. Barnes, 1872.

**COCKRAN, WILLIAM BOURKE** (1854–1923) D-NY, House 1887–1889, 1891–1895, 1904–1909, 1921–1923.

**1927.** Bloom, Florence T. "The Political Career of William Bourke Cockran." Ph.D. dissertation, City University of New York, 1970.

**1928.** Dau, William H. *The Logical and Historical Inaccuracies of the Hon. Bourke Cockran in His Review of the Lutheran Letter of Protest to President Roosevelt.* 2d ed. St. Louis, MO: Concordia Publishing House, 1909.

**1929.** Kennedy, Ambrose. *American Orator, Bourke Cockran: His Life and Politics.* Boston: Humphries, 1948.

**1930.** McGurrin, James. *Bourke Cockran, a Free Lance in American Politics.* New York: Scribner's, 1948.

**COCKRELL, FRANCIS MARION** (1834–1915) D-MO, Senate 1875–1905.

**1931.** Clark, Champ. "Lame Ducks." In his *My Quarter Century of American Politics,* 98–106. New York: Harper and Brothers, 1920.

**1932.** Cockrell, Francis M. *The Senator from Missouri: The Life and Times of Francis Marion Cockrell.* New York: Exposition Press, 1962.

**1933.** Cockrell, Monroe F. *Francis Marion Cockrell of Warrensburg, Missouri and Alexander Cockrell I of Dallas, Texas*. Chicago: N.p., 1947.

**1934.** Williamson, Hugh P. "Correspondence of Senator Francis Marion Cockrell: December 23, 1885–March 24, 1888." *Bulletin of the Missouri Historical Society* 28 (July 1969): 296–305.

**COELHO, ANTHONY LEE "TONY"**
(1942–  ) D-CA, House 1979–1989.

**1935.** Hart, Benjamin. "Tip's Iceberg: The Emerging Democratic Leadership in the House." *Policy Review* 35 (Winter 1986): 66–70.

**COFFIN, FRANK MOREY** (1919–  )
D-ME, House 1957–1961.

**1936.** Coffin, Frank. *Witness for AID*. Boston: Houghton Mifflin, 1964.

**1937.** Donovan, John C. *Congressional Campaign: Maine Elects a Democrat*. New York: McGraw-Hill, 1960.

**COHEN, WILLIAM SEBASTIAN**
(1940–  ) R-ME, House 1973–1979,
Senate 1979–  .

**1938.** Cohen, William S. *Roll Call: One Year in the United States Senate*. New York: Simon and Schuster, 1981.

**COIT, JOSHUA** (1758–1798) F-CT, House 1793–1798.

**1939.** Destler, Chester M. *Joshua Coit, American Federalist, 1758–1798*. Middletown, CT: Wesleyan University Press, 1962.

**COKE, RICHARD** (1829–1897) D-TX, Senate 1877–1895.

**1940.** Fett, B. J. "Early Life of Richard Coke." *Texana* 4 (1972): 310–320.

**1941.** Welch, June R. "Coke Restored the People to Their Constitutional Rights." In his *The Texas Senator,* 98–101. Dallas, TX: G. L. A. Press, 1978.

**1942.** ————. "Richard Coke Threw the Rascals Out." In his *The Texas Governor,* 74–79. Irving, TX: G. L. A. Press, 1977.

**COLDEN, CADWALLADER DAVID**
(1769–1834) NY, House 1821–1823.

**1943.** Boyer, Lee R. "Lobster Backs, Liberty Boys, and Laborers in the Streets: New York's Golden Hill and Nassau Street Riots." *New York Historical Society Quarterly* 57 (October 1973): 281–308.

**1944.** Keys, Alice M. "Cadwallader Colden, a Representative Eighteenth-Century Official." Ph.D. dissertation, Columbia University, 1906.

**COLE, CORNELIUS** (1822–1924) R-CA,
House 1863–1865, Senate 1867–1873.

**1945.** Cole, Cornelius. *Memoirs of Cornelius Cole, Ex-Senator of the United States*. New York: McLoughlin, 1908.

**1946.** ————. *Senator Cornelius Cole and the Beginning of Hollywood*. Rev. ed. Los Angeles: Crescent, 1980.

**1947.** Hunt, Rockwell D. "Cornelius Cole, Distinguished Centenarian." In his *California's Stately Hall of Fame*, 261–264. Stockton, CA: College of the Pacific, 1950.

**1948.** Phillips, Catherine. *Cornelius Cole, California Pioneer and United States Senator: A Study in Personality and Achievements Bearing Upon the Growth of a Commonwealth*. San Francisco: J. H. Nash, 1929.

**COLE, CYRENUS** (1863–1939) R-IA,
House 1921–1933.

**1949.** Cole, Cyrenus. *I Remember, I Remember: A Book of Recollections*. Iowa City: State Historical Society of Iowa, 1936.

**1950.** Porter, David L. "Iowa Congressional Delegation and the Great Economic Issues, 1929–1933." *Annals of Iowa* 46 (Summer 1982): 337–354.

**COLFAX, SCHUYLER** (1823–1885) R-IN, House 1855–1869.

**1951.** Barzman, Sol. "Schuyler Colfax." In his *Madmen and Geniuses: The Vice-Presidents of the United States,* 115–122. Chicago: Follett, 1974.

**1952.** Brisbin, James S. *The Campaign Lives of Ulysses S. Grant and Schuyler Colfax.* Cincinnati, OH: C. F. Vent, 1868.

**1953.** Fuller, Hubert B. "Grow and Colfax Dominated by Thaddeus Stevens." In his *The Speakers of the House,* 149–168. Boston: Little, Brown, 1909.

**1954.** Furlong, Patrick J., and Gerald E. Hartdagen. "Schuyler Colfax: A Reputation Tarnished." In *Gentlemen from Indiana: National Party Candidates, 1836–1940,* edited by Ralph D. Gray, 55–82. Indianapolis: Indiana Historical Bureau, 1977.

**1955.** Goldman, Jacob. *Schuyler Colfax, A Short Resume of His Life As an Odd Fellow and Statesman.* South Bend, IN: R. H. Hildebrand, 1923.

**1956.** Hollister, Ovando J. *Life of Schuyler Colfax.* New York: Funk and Wagnalls, 1886.

**1957.** Mansfield, Edward D. *Popular and Authentic Lives of Ulysses S. Grant and Schuyler Colfax.* Cincinnati, OH: R. W. Carroll, 1868.

**1958.** McCabe, James D. *The Life and Public Services of Schuyler Colfax: Together with His Most Important Speeches.* New York: United States Publishing Co., 1868.

**1959.** Moore, Ambrose Y. *The Life of Schuyler Colfax.* Philadelphia: T. B. Peterson and Brothers, 1868.

**1960.** Smith, Willard H. "The Colfax-Turpie Congressional Campaigns, 1862–1866." *Indiana Magazine of History* 38 (June 1942): 123–142.

**1961.** ———. *The Life and Times of Hon. Schuyler Colfax.* Indianapolis: Indiana Historical Bureau, 1952.

**1962.** ———. "The Political Career of Schuyler Colfax to His Election as Vice-President in 1868." Ph.D. dissertation, Indiana University, 1939.

**1963.** ———. *Schuyler Colfax: The Changing Fortunes of a Political Idol.* Indianapolis: Indiana Historical Bureau, 1952.

**1964.** ———. "Schuyler Colfax and the Political Upheaval of 1854–1855." *Mississippi Valley Historical Review* 28 (December 1941): 383–398.

**1965.** ———. "Schuyler Colfax and Reconstruction Policy." *Indiana Magazine of History* 39 (December 1943): 323–344.

**1966.** ———. "Schuyler Colfax: Whig Editor, 1845–1855." *Indiana Magazine of History* 34 (September 1938): 262–282.

**1967.** Stowe, Harriet B. "Schuyler Colfax." In her *Men of Our Times,* 347–362. Hartford, CT: Hartford Publishing Company, 1868.

**COLLAMER, JACOB** (1791–1865) R-VT, House 1843–1849, Senate 1855–1865.

**1968.** Kelly, Mary L. *Jacob Collamer.* Woodstock, VT: Woodstock Historical Society, 1944.

**1969.** Sumner, Charles. "The Late Senator Collamer." In his *Works,* vol. 10, 38–46. Boston: Lee and Shephard, 1880.

**COLLIER, JOHN ALLEN** (1787–1873) AMAS-NY, House 1831–1833.

**1970.** Hecht, Robert A. "Oliver La Farge, John Collier, and the Hopi Constitution of 1936." *Journal of Arizona History* 26 (Summer 1985): 145–162.

**1971.** Kelly, Lawrence C. "John Collier and the Pueblo Lands Board Act." *New Mexico Historical Review* 58 (January 1983): 5–34.

**1972.** Philip, Kenneth R. "John Collier and the Indians of the Americas: The Dream and the Reality." *Prologue* 11 (Spring 1979): 5–21.

**COLLINS, CARDISS** (1931– ) D-IL, House 1973– .

**1973.** Christopher, Maurine. "Cardiss Collins/Illinois." In her *Black Americans in Congress,* 278. Rev. ed. New York: Thomas Y. Crowell, 1976.

**COLLINS, GEORGE WASHINGTON** (1925–1972) D-IL, House 1970–1972.

**1974.** Christopher, Maurine. "George Collins/Illinois." In her *Black Americans in Congress,* 262. Rev. ed. New York: Thomas Y. Crowell, 1976.

**COLLINS, PATRICK ANDREW** (1844–1905) D-MA, House 1883–1889.

**1975.** Curran, Michael P. *Life of Patrick A. Collins.* Norwood, MA: Norwood Press, 1906.

**COLLINS, ROSS ALEXANDER** (1880–1968) D-MS, House 1921–1935, 1937–1943.

**1976.** Grant, Philip A., Jr. "The Mississippi Congressional Delegation and the Formation of the Conservative Coalition." *Journal of Mississippi History* 50 (February 1988): 21–28.

**COLMER, WILLIAM MEYERS** (1890–1980) D-MS, House 1933–1973.

**1977.** Grant, Philip A., Jr. "The Mississippi Congressional Delegation and the Formation of the Conservative Coalition." *Journal of Mississippi History* 50 (February 1988): 21–28.

**1978.** Schlauch, Wolfgang. "Representative William Colmer and Senator James O. Eastland and the Reconstruction of Germany, 1945." *Journal of Mississippi History* 34 (August 1972): 193–214.

**COLQUITT, ALFRED HOLT** (1824–1894) D-GA, House 1853–1855, Senate 1883–1894.

**1979.** Wynne, Lewis. "The Bourbon Triumvirate: A Reconsideration." *Atlanta Historical Journal* 24 (Summer 1980): 39–56.

**COLT, LEBARON BRADFORD** (1846–1924) R-RI, Senate 1913–1924.

**1980.** Schlup, Leonard. "A Senator of Principle: Some Correspondence between Lebaron Bradford Colt and William Howard Taft." *Rhode Island History* 42 (February 1983): 2–16.

**CONGER, OMAR DWIGHT** (1818–1898) R-MI, House 1869–1881, Senate 1881–1887.

**1981.** Rubinstein, Bruce A. "Omar D. Conger: Michigan's Forgotten Favorite Son." *Michigan History* 66 (September/October 1982): 32–39.

**CONKLING, ALFRED** (1789–1874) NY, House 1821–1823.

**1982.** Jonas, Harold J. "Alfred Conkling, Jurist and Gentleman." *New York History* 20 (July 1939): 295–305.

**CONKLING, ROSCOE** (1829–1888) R-NY, House 1859–1863, 1865–1867, Senate 1867–1881.

**1983.** Burlingame, Sara L. "The Making of a Spoilsman: The Life and Career of Roscoe Conkling from 1829 to 1873." Ph.D. dissertation, Johns Hopkins University, 1974.

**1984.** Chidsey, Donald B. *The Gentleman from New York: A Life of Roscoe Conkling.* New Haven, CT: Yale University Press, 1935.

**1985.** Conkling, Alfred R. *The Life and Letters of Roscoe Conkling, Orator, Statesman, Advocate.* New York: C. L. Webster, 1889.

**1986.** Depew, Chauncey M. "Roscoe Conkling." In his *My Memories of Eighty Years,* 75–86. New York: Scribner's, 1922.

**1987.** Jager, Ronald B. "Stanley Matthews for the Supreme Court: 'Lord Roscoe's' Downfall." *Cincinnati Historical Society Bulletin* 38 (Fall 1980): 191–208.

**1988.** Jordan, David M. *Roscoe Conkling of New York: Voice in the Senate.* Ithaca, NY: Cornell University Press, 1971.

**1989.** McClain, Charles J. "From the Huntington Papers: The Huntington-Conkling Connection." *Pacific Historian* 29 (Winter 1985): 30–46.

**1990.** Powers, George C. "The Blaine-Conkling Feud." Master's thesis, Indiana University, 1927.

**1991.** Shores, Venila L. *The Hayes-Conkling Controversy, 1877–1879.* Northampton, MA: Department of History, Smith College, 1919.

**1992.** Swindler, William F. "Roscoe Conkling and the Fourteenth Amendment." *Supreme Court Historical Society Yearbook* (1983): 46–52.

## CONNALLY, THOMAS TERRY "TOM"
**(1877–1963) D-TX, House 1917–1929, Senate 1929–1953.**

**1993.** Connally, Thomas T., and Alfred Steinberg. *My Name Is Tom Connally.* New York: Crowell, 1954.

**1994.** Gulick, Merle L. "Tom Connally as a Founder of the United Nations." Ph.D dissertation, Georgetown University, 1955.

**1995.** Matheny, David L. "A Comparison of Selected Foreign Policy Speeches of Senator Tom Connally." Ph.D. dissertation, University of Oklahoma, 1965.

**1996.** Miller, Otis, and Anita F. Alpern. "Tom Connally." In *Public Men In and Out of Office,* edited by John T. Salter, 311–321. Chapel Hill: University of North Carolina Press, 1946.

**1997.** Smyrl, Frank H. "Tom Connally and the New Deal." Ph.D. dissertation, University of Oklahoma, 1968.

**1998.** Welch, June R. "Tom Connally Signed the United Nations Charter." In his *The Texas Senator,* 56–59. Dallas, TX: G. L. A. Press, 1978.

## CONNOLLY, JAMES AUSTIN
**(1843–1914) R-IL, House 1895–1899.**

**1999.** Connolly, James A. *Three Years in the Army of the Cumberland: The Letters and Diary of Major James A. Connolly.* Edited by Paul M. Angle. Bloomington: Indiana University Press, 1959.

## CONYERS, JOHN JR. (1929– ) D-MI,
**House 1965– .**

**2000.** Christopher, Maurine. "John Conyers, Jr./Michigan." In her *Black Americans in Congress,* 237. Rev. ed. New York: Thomas Y. Crowell, 1976.

**2001.** Metcalf, George R. "John Conyers, Jr." In his *Up from Within,* 1–38. New York: McGraw-Hill, 1971.

**2002.** Wormley, Stanton L., and Lewis H. Fenderson, eds. "John Conyers, Jr." In their *Many Shades of Black,* 3–4. New York: Morrow, 1969.

## COOK, DANIEL POPE (1794–1827) IL,
**House 1819–1827.**

**2003.** De Love, Sidney L. *Cook County and Daniel Pope Cook: Their Story.* Chicago: Independence Hall, 1968.

**2004.** Hubbs, Barbara B. "First Attorney General—Daniel Pope Cook." In *Idols of Egypt,* edited by Will Griffith, 171–180. Carbondale, IL: Egypt Book House, 1947.

## COOPER, JOHN SHERMAN
**(1901–1991) R-KY, Senate 1946–1949, 1952–1955, 1956–1973.**

**2005.** Brock, Gustaf J. "'Congress Must Draw the Line': Senator Frank Church and the Cooper-Church Amendment of 1970." *Idaho Yesterdays* 35 (Summer 1991): 27–36.

**2006.** Cooper, William. "John Sherman Cooper: A Senator and His Constituents." *Register of the Kentucky Historical Society* 84 (Spring 1986): 192–210.

**2007.** Maddox, Robert F. "John Sherman Cooper and the Vietnam War." *Journal of the West Virginia Historical Association* 11, no. 1 (1987): 52–76.

**2008.** Mitchner, Clarice J. *Senator John Sherman Cooper, Consummate Statesman.* New York: Arno Press, 1982.

**2009.** Schulman, Robert. *John Sherman Cooper: The Global Kentuckian.* Lexington: University Press of Kentucky, 1976.

**2010.** Smoot, Richard C. "John Sherman Cooper: The Paradox of a Liberal Republican in Kentucky Politics." Ph.D. dissertation, University of Kentucky, 1988.

**COPELAND, ROYAL SAMUEL** (1868–1938) D-NY, Senate 1923–1938.

**2011.** Potter, Raymond J. "Royal Samuel Copeland, 1868–1928: A Physician in Politics." Ph.D. dissertation, Case Western Reserve University, 1967.

**CORNING, ERASTUS** (1794–1872) D-NY, House 1857–1859, 1861–1863.

**2012.** Cochran, Thomas C. "Erastus Corning." In his *Railroad Leaders, 1845–1890,* 303–304. Cambridge, MA: Harvard University Press, 1953.

**2013.** Neu, Irene D. *Erastus Corning, Merchant and Financier, 1794–1872.* Ithaca, NY: Cornell University Press, 1960.

**CORWIN, THOMAS** (1794–1865) R-OH, House 1831–1840, 1859–1861, Senate 1845–1850.

**2014.** Auer, John J. "Thomas Corwin, 1840–1842." In *Governors of Ohio,* 46–49. Columbus: Ohio Historical Society, 1954.

**2015.** Bochin, Hal W. "Tom Corwin's Speech against the Mexican War: Courageous, But Misunderstood." *Ohio History* 90 (Winter 1981): 33–54.

**2016.** Carroll, Stephen G. "Thomas Corwin and the Agonies of the Whig Party." Ph.D. dissertation, University of Colorado, 1970.

**2017.** Graebner, Norman A. "Thomas Corwin and the Election of 1848: A Study in Conservative Politics." *Journal of Southern History* 17 (May 1951): 162–179.

**2018.** ———. "Thomas Corwin and the Sectional Crisis." *Ohio History* 86 (Autumn 1977): 229–247.

**2019.** Magoon, Elias L. "Thomas Corwin." In his *Living Orators in America,* 408–462. New York: Baker and Scribner, 1849.

**2020.** Morrow, Josiah, ed. *Life and Speeches of T. Corwin, Orator, Lawyer, and Statesman.* Cincinnati, OH: W. H. Anderson, 1896.

**2021.** Pendergraft, Daryl. "The Public Career of Thomas Corwin." Ph.D. dissertation, University of Iowa, 1943.

**2022.** Russell, Addison P. *Thomas Corwin, a Sketch.* Cincinnati, OH: R. Clarke, 1881.

**COSTIGAN, EDWARD PRENTISS** (1874–1939) D-CO, Senate 1931–1937.

**2023.** Brockway, Ronald S. "Edward P. Costigan: A Study of a Progressive and the New Deal." Ph.D. dissertation, University of Colorado, 1974.

**2024.** Costigan, Edward P. *Papers, 1902–1917.* Edited by Colin B. Goodykoontz. Boulder: University of Colorado, 1941.

**2025.** Goodykoontz, Colin B. "Edward P. Costigan and the Tariff Commission, 1917–1928." *Pacific Historical Review* 16 (November 1947): 410–419.

**2026.** Greenbaum, Fred. *Fighting Progressive: A Biography of Edward P. Costigan.* Washington, DC: Public Affairs Press, 1971.

**2027.** Snyder, John R. "Edward P. Costigan and the United States Tariff Commission." Ph.D. dissertation, University of Colorado, 1966.

**COTTON, NORRIS H.** (1900–1989) R-NH, House 1947–1954, Senate 1954–1974, 1975.

**2028.** Bixby, Roland. *Standing Tall: The Life Story of Senator Norris Cotton.* Crawfordsville, IN: Lakeside Press, 1988.

**2029.** Cotton, Norris. *In the Senate: Amidst the Conflict and the Turmoil.* New York: Dodd, Mead, 1978.

**2030.** Morrissey, Charles T. "Memory, Like Congress, Is a Forest Full of Trees: The Recollections of Two New Hampshiremen in Washington, Norris H. Cotton and Chester E. Merrow." *Historical New Hampshire* 33 (Fall 1978): 246–257.

**COUDERT, FREDERICK RENE, JR.** (1898–1972) R-NY, House 1947–1959.

**2031.** Coudert, Paula M. *Frederick R. Coudert, Jr: A Biography.* New York: P. M. Coudert, 1985.

**COUSINS, ROBERT GORDON** (1859–1933) R-IA, House 1893–1909.

**2032.** Swisher, Jacob A. *Robert Gordon Cousins.* Iowa City: State Historical Society of Iowa, 1938.

**COUZENS, JAMES** (1872–1936) R-MI, Senate 1922–1936.

**2033.** Bernard, Harry. *Independent Man: The Life of Senator James Couzens.* New York: Scribner's, 1958.

**2034.** Dickinson, Roy. *Wages and Wealth: This Business Roller-Coaster.* Princeton, NJ: Princeton University Press, 1931.

**2035.** MacManus, Theodore F. *Men, Money, and Motors: The Drama of the Automobile.* New York: Harper and Brothers, 1930.

**2036.** Richards, William C., and William J. Norton. "About the Donor." In their *Biography of a Foundation: The Story of the Children's Fund of Michigan, 1929–1954,* 11–23. Detroit, MI: The Fund, 1957.

**COVODE, JOHN** (1808–1871) R-PA, House 1855–1863, 1867–1869, 1870–1871.

**2037.** Chester, Edward. "The Impact of the Covode Congressional Investigation." *Western Pennsylvania Historical Magazine* 42 (December 1959): 343–350.

**COX, JACOB DOLSON** (1828–1900) R-OH, House 1877–1879.

**2038.** Cox, Jacob D. *Military Reminiscences of the Civil War.* 2 vols. New York: Scribner's, 1900.

**2039.** Rhodes, James F. "Jacob D. Cox." In his *Historical Essays,* 183–188. New York: Macmillan, 1909.

**2040.** Schmiel, Eugene D. "The Career of Jacob Dolson Cox, 1828–1900." Ph.D. dissertation, Ohio State University, 1969.

**COX, JAMES MIDDLETON** (1870–1957) D-OH, House 1909–1913.

**2041.** Cebula, James E. *James M. Cox, Journalist and Politician.* New York: Garland, 1985.

**2042.** Cox, James M. *Journey Through My Years.* New York: Simon and Schuster, 1946.

**2043.** Grant, Philip A. "Congressional Campaigns of James M. Cox, 1908 and 1910." *Ohio History* 81 (Winter 1972): 4–14.

**2044.** Kent, Frank R. "Cox's Nomination and Defeat." In *The Democratic Party, a History,* 449–463. New York: Century, 1928.

**2045.** Morris, Charles E. *The Progressive Democracy of James M. Cox.* Indianapolis: Bobbs-Merrill, 1920.

**COX, SAMUEL SULLIVAN** (1824–1889) D-OH/NY, House (OH) 1857–1865; (NY) 1869–1873, 1873–1885, 1886–1889.

**2046.** Cox, Samuel S. *Eight Years in Congress from 1857 to 1865: Memoir and Speeches.* New York: Appleton, 1865.

**2047.** ———. *Union, Disunion, Reunion: Three Decades of Federal Legislation.* Providence, RI: Reid, 1885.

**2048.** Lindsey, David. *"Sunset" Cox: Irrepressible Democrat.* Detroit, MI: Wayne State University Press, 1959.

**COXE, TENCH** (1755–1824) PA, Continental Congress 1787, 1788.

**2049.** Cooke, Jacob E. *Tench Coxe and the Early Republic.* Chapel Hill: University of North Carolina Press, 1978.

**2050.** Hutcheson, Harold. *Tench Coxe: A Study in American Economic Development.* Baltimore: Johns Hopkins University Press, 1938.

**CRANE, WINTHROP MURRAY** (1853–1920) R-MA, Senate 1904–1913.

**2051.** Griffin, Solomon B. "Mr. Crane's Record as Governor and Senator." In his *People and Politics, Observed by a Massachusetts Editor,* 415–426. Boston: Little, Brown, 1923.

**2052.** ———. *W. Murray Crane, a Man and Brother.* Boston: Little, Brown, 1926.

**2053.** Johnson, Carolyn W. *Winthrop Murray Crane: A Study in Republican Leadership, 1892–1920.* North Hampton, MA: Smith College, 1967.

**CRANSTON, ALAN** (1914– ) D-CA, Senate 1969–1993.

**2054.** Fowle, Eleanor. *Cranston: The Senator from California.* Rev. ed. Los Angeles: J. P. Tarcher, 1984.

**CRAWFORD, COE ISAAC** (1858–1944) R-SD, Senate 1909–1915.

**2055.** Armin, Calvin P. "Coe I. Crawford and the Progressive Movement in South Dakota." Ph.D. dissertation, University of Colorado, 1957.

**2056.** Meyer, Edward L. "Coe I. Crawford and the Persuasion of Progressive Movement in South Dakota." Ph.D. disserta-

tion, University of Minnesota, 1975.

**2057.** Schlup, Leonard. "Coe I. Crawford and the Progressive Campaign of 1912." *South Dakota History* 9 (Spring 1979): 116–130.

**CRAWFORD, GEORGE WASHINGTON** (1798–1872) W-GA, House 1843.

**2058.** Cleveland, Len G. "George W. Crawford of Georgia, 1798–1872." Ph.D. dissertation, University of Georgia, 1974.

**CRAWFORD, WILLIAM HARRIS** (1772–1834) GA, Senate 1807–1813.

**2059.** Campbell, Harold. "William H. Crawford and the Election of 1824." *Southern Historian* 10 (Spring 1989): 43–52.

**2060.** Cutler, Everett W. "William H. Crawford: A Contextual Biography." Ph.D. dissertation, University of Texas, 1971.

**2061.** Green, Philip J. *Life of William Harris Crawford.* Chapel Hill: University of North Carolina, 1965.

**2062.** ———. "Public Career of William Harris Crawford, 1807–1825." Ph.D. dissertation, University of Chicago, 1936.

**2063.** Mooney, Chase C. *William H. Crawford: 1772–1834.* Lexington: University Press of Kentucky, 1974.

**2064.** Seitz, Don C. "William H. Crawford, Last of a Dynasty." In his *The "Also Rans,"* 38–52. New York: Crowell, 1928.

**2065.** Shepard, Helen L. "The National Political Career of William H. Crawford, 1807–1825." Master's thesis, Indiana University, 1940.

**2066.** Shipp, John E. *Giant Days: Or the Life and Times of William H. Crawford.* Americus, GA: Southern Printers, 1909.

**2067.** Williams, William H., ed. "Ten Letters from William Harris Crawford to Martin Van Buren." *Georgia Historical Quarterly* 49 (1965): 65–81.

**2068.** Willson, Beckles. "Crawford (1813–15)." In his *America's Ambassadors to France (1777–1927)*, 118–134. New York: Frederick A. Stokes, 1928.

**CRISP, CHARLES FREDERICK**
**(1845–1896) D-GA, House 1883–1896.**

**2069.** Malone, Preston S. "The Political Career of Charles Frederick Crisp." Ph.D. dissertation, University of Georgia, 1962.

**2070.** Martin, S. Walter. "Charles F. Crisp: Speaker of the House." *Georgia Review* 8 (Summer 1954): 167–177.

**CRITTENDEN, JOHN JORDAN**
**(1786–1863) U-KY, Senate 1817–1819,**
**1835–1841, 1842–1848, 1855–1861,**
**House 1861–1863.**

**2071.** Coleman, Ann M., ed. *The Life of John J. Crittenden, with Selections from His Correspondence and Speeches*. 2 vols. Philadelphia: Lippincott, 1871.

**2072.** Kirwan, Albert D. *John J. Crittenden: The Struggle for the Union*. Lexington: University of Kentucky Press, 1962.

**2073.** Ledbetter, Patsy S. "John J. Crittenden and the Compromise Debacle." *Filson Club History Quarterly* 51 (April 1977): 125–142.

**CRITTENDEN, THOMAS THEODORE**
**(1832–1909) D-MO, House 1873–1875,**
**1877–1879.**

**2074.** Crittenden, Henry H., comp. *The Crittenden Memoirs*. New York: Putnam's, 1936.

**2075.** Powers, Joseph P. "Yours Very Truly, Thos. T. Crittenden: A Missouri Democrats' Observations of the Election of 1896." *Missouri Historical Review* 68 (January 1974): 186–203.

**2076.** Scholes, Walter V. "Mexico in 1896 as Viewed by an American Consul." *Hispanic American Historical Review* 30 (May 1950): 250–257.

**CROCKER, ALVH (1801–1874) R-MA,**
**House 1872–1874.**

**2077.** Wheelwright, William B. *Life and Times of Alvah Crocker.* Boston: Privately printed, 1923.

**CROCKETT, DAVID (1786–1836) AJ-TN,**
**House 1827–1831, 1833–1835.**

**2078.** Abbott, John S. *David Crockett: His Life and Adventures*. New York: Dodd, Mead, 1874.

**2079.** Albanese, Catherine L. *King Crockett: Nature and Civility on the American Frontier.* Charlottesville: University Press of Virginia, 1979.

**2080.** Arpad, Joseph J. "David Crockett, an Original Eccentricity and Early American Character." Ph.D. dissertation, Duke University, 1969.

**2081.** Blair, Walter. *Davy Crockett, Frontier Hero: The Truth as He Told It, the Legend as Friends Built It*. New York: Coward-McCann, 1955.

**2082.** Brady, Cyrus T. "David Crockett and the Most Desperate Defence in American History." In his *Border Fights and Fighters*, 307–326. Garden City, NY: Doubleday, 1913.

**2083.** Burke, James W. *David Crockett, the Man Behind the Myth*. Austin, TX: Eakin Press, 1984.

**2084.** Catron, Anna G. "The Public Career of David Crockett." Master's thesis, University of Tennessee, 1955.

**2085.** Cattermole, E. G. "Davy Crockett." In his *Famous Frontiersmen, Pioneers and Scouts*, 257–304. Tarrytown, NY: W. Abbatt, 1926.

**2086.** Connelly, Thomas L. "Did David Crockett Surrender at the Alamo? A Contemporary Letter." *Journal of Southern History* 26 (August 1960): 368–376.

**2087.** Crockett, Davy. *The Adventures of Davy Crockett, Told Mostly by Himself.* New York: Scribner's, 1934.

**2088.** ———. *Life of David Crockett, the Original Humorist and Irrepressible Backwoodsman.* Philadelphia: Porter and Coates, 1865.

**2089.** ———. *Narrative of the Life of David Crockett of the State of Tennessee.* Knoxville: University of Tennessee Press, 1973.

**2090.** Derr, Mark. *The Frontiersman: The Real Life and Many Legends of Davy Crockett.* New York: Morrow, 1993.

**2091.** Dorson, Richard M., ed. *Davy Crockett, American Comic Legend.* Westport, CT: Greenwood, 1977.

**2092.** Driskill, Frank A. *Davy Crockett: The Untold Story.* Austin, TX: Eakin Press, 1981.

**2093.** Ellis, Edward S. *Life of Colonel David Crockett.* Philadelphia: Parter and Coates, 1884.

**2094.** ———. *Sockdolager! A Tale of Davy Crockett, in Which the Old Tennessee Bear Hunter Meets Up with the Constitution of the United States.* Richmond: Virginia Commission on Constitutional Government, 1961.

**2095.** Folmsbee, Stanley J. "David Crockett and His Autobiography." *East Tennessee Historical Society Publications* 43 (1971): 3–17.

**2096.** ———. "David Crockett and West Tennessee." *West Tennessee Historical Society Papers* 28 (1974): 5–24.

**2097.** ———. "David Crockett in Texas." *East Tennessee Historical Society Publications* 30 (1958): 48–74.

**2098.** ———. "The Early Career of David Crockett." *East Tennessee Historical Society Publications* 28 (1956): 58–85.

**2099.** Folmsbee, Stanley J., and Anna G. Catron. "David Crockett: Congressman." *East Tennessee Historical Society's Publications* 29 (1957): 40–78.

**2100.** Heale, M. J. "The Role of the Frontier in Jacksonian Politics: David Crockett and the Myth of the Self-Made Man." *Western Historical Quarterly* 4 (October 1973): 405–423.

**2101.** Hoffman, Daniel G. "Deaths and Three Resurrections of Davy Crockett." *Antioch Review* 21 (Spring 1961): 5–13.

**2102.** Hough, Emerson. *The Way to the West, and the Lives of Three Early Americans, Boone-Crockett-Carson.* Indianapolis: Bobbs-Merrill, 1903.

**2103.** Hubbell, Jay B. "David Crockett." In his *South in American Literature, 1607–1900,* 662–666. Durham, NC: Duke University, 1954.

**2104.** Kelsey, D. M. "Colonel David Crockett." In his *History of Our Wild West,* 167–194. New York: Wiley, 1928.

**2105.** Kilgore, Dan. *How Did Davy Die?* College Station: Texas A&M University Press, 1978.

**2106.** Loomis, C. Grant. "Davy Crockett Visits Boston." *New England Quarterly* 20 (September 1947): 396–400.

**2107.** Mason, Augustus L. "David Crockett." In his *True Stories of Our Pioneers,* 607–619. Springfield, MA: E. A. Merriam, 1904.

**2108.** Miles, Guy S. "David Crockett Evolves, 1821–1824." *American Quarterly* 8 (Spring 1956): 53–60.

**2109.** Null, Marion M. *The Forgotten Pioneer: The Life of Davy Crockett.* New York: Vantage, 1954.

**2110.** Paine, Gregory L. "David Crockett." In his *Southern Prose Writers,* 135–146. New York: American Book Company, 1947.

**2111.** Parrington, Vernon L. "The Davy Crockett Myth." In his *Main Currents in American Thought,* 172–179. New York: Harcourt, Brace, 1927.

**2112.** Shackford, James A. *David Crockett: The Man and the Legend.* Chapel Hill: University of North Carolina Press, 1986.

**2113.** Watterson, Henry. "Davy Crockett." In his *Oddities in Southern Life and Character,* 245–264. Boston: Houghton Mifflin, 1910.

**2114.** Wecter, Dixon. "Winning of the Frontier: Boone, Crockett and Johnny Appleseed." In his *Hero in America,* 181–198. New York: Scribner's, 1972.

**CROSSER, ROBERT (1874–1957) D-OH, House 1913–1919, 1923–1955.**

**2115.** Tribe, Henry F. "Disciple of 'Progress and Poverty': Robert Crosser and Twentieth Century Reform." Ph.D. dissertation, Bowling Green State University, 1990.

**CROWNINSHIELD, JACOB (1770–1808) R-MA, House 1803–1808.**

**2116.** Reinhoel, John H., ed. "Some Remarks on the American Trade: Jacob Crowninshield to James Madison, 1806." *William and Mary Quarterly* 16 (January 1959): 83–118.

**CRUMP, EDWARD HULL (1874–1954) D-TN, House 1931–1935.**

**2117.** Kitchens, Allen H. "Political Upheaval in Tennessee: Boss Crump and the Senatorial Election of 1948." *West Tennessee Historical Society Papers* 16 (1962): 104–126.

**2118.** Miller, William D. *Mr. Crump of Memphis.* Baton Rouge: Louisiana State University Press, 1964.

**2119.** Steinberg, Alfred. "Ed Crump: Plan Your Work and Work Your Plan." In his *The Bosses,* 72–133. New York: Macmillan, 1972.

**CULBERSON, CHARLES ALLEN (1855–1925) D-TX, Senate 1899–1923.**

**2120.** Hughes, Pollyanna, and Elizabeth Harrison. "Charles Culberson: Not a Shadow of Hogg." *East Texas Historical Journal* 11 (Fall 1973): 41–52.

**2121.** Madden, James W. *Charles Allen Culberson, His Life, Character and Public Service, as County Attorney, Attorney General, Governor of Texas and United States Senator.* Austin, TX: Gammel's Book Store, 1929.

**2122.** Welch, June R. "Culberson Spent 32 Years in Public Life." In his *The Texas Governor,* 104–107. Irving, TX: G. L. A. Press, 1977.

**2123.** ———. "The Culbersons Spent 54 Years in Public Office." In his *The Texas Senator,* 48–51. Dallas, TX: G. L. A. Press, 1978.

**CULLOM, SHELBY MOORE (1829–1914) R-IL, House 1865–1871, Senate 1883–1913.**

**2124.** Converse, Henry A. "The Life and Services of Shelby M. Cullom." *Transactions of the Illinois State Historical Society* 20 (1914): 55–79.

**2125.** Cullom, Shelby M. *Fifty Years of Public Service: Personal Recollections of Shelby M. Cullom.* Chicago: McClurg, 1911.

**2126.** Neilson, James W. *Shelby M. Cullom, Prairie State Republican.* Champaign: University of Illinois Press, 1962.

**2127.** Pitkin, William A. "Shelby M. Cullom: Presidential Prospect." *Journal of the Illinois State Historical Society* 49 (Winter 1956): 375–386.

**CULVER, JOHN CHESTER (1932– ) D-IA, House 1965–1975, Senate 1975–1981.**

**2128.** Drew, Elizabeth B. *Senator.* New York: Simon and Schuster, 1979.

**CUMMINS, ALBERT BAIRD** (1850–1926)
**R-IA, Senate 1908–1926.**

**2129.** Bray, Thomas. "The Cummins Leadership." *Annals of Iowa* 32 (April 1954): 241–296.

**2130.** Harrington, Elbert W. "Albert Baird Cummins: An Analysis of a Logical Speaker." In *American Public Address,* edited by Loren Reid, 99–110. Columbia: University of Missouri Press, 1961.

**2131.** ———. "The Public Speaking Career of Albert W. Cummins." Ph.D. dissertation, University of Iowa, 1987.

**2132.** Margulies, Herbert F. "Senate Moderates in the League of Nations Battle: Case of Albert B. Cummins." *Annals of Iowa* 50 (Spring 1990): 333–358.

**2133.** Sayre, Ralph M. "Albert Baird Cummins and the Progressive Movement in Iowa." Ph.D. dissertation, Columbia University, 1958.

**2134.** Swisher, Jacob A. "Albert B. Cummins." In his *Governors of Iowa,* 87–89. Mason City, IA: Klipto Loose Leaf Company, 1946.

**CURLEY, JAMES MICHAEL** (1874–1958)
**D-MA, House 1911–1914, 1943–1947.**

**2135.** Angoff, Charles. "Curley and the Boston Irish." *American Mercury* 69 (November 1949): 619–627.

**2136.** Beatty, Jack. *The Rascal King: The Life and Times of James Michael Curley, 1874–1958.* Addison-Wesley, 1992.

**2137.** Curley, James M. *I'd Do It Again: A Record of All My Uproarious Years.* Englewood Cliffs, NJ: Prentice-Hall, 1957.

**2138.** Dinneen, Joseph F. *Purple Shamrock: The Honorable James Michael Curley of Boston.* New York: Norton, 1949.

**2139.** Kenneally, James. "Prelude to the Last Hurrah: The Massachusetts Senatorial Election of 1936." *Mid-America* 62 (January 1980): 3–20.

**2140.** Luthin, Reinhard H. "James M. Curley: The Boston Brahmin-Baiter." In his *American Demagogues: Twentieth Century,* 17–43. Boston: Beacon Press, 1954.

**2141.** Steinberg, Alfred. "James Michael Curley: The Joyous Plague of Boston." In his *The Bosses,* 134–197. New York: Macmillan, 1972.

**2142.** Wind, Herbert W. "On the Veranda with James Michael Curley." In his *Gilded Age of Sport,* 467–478. New York: Simon and Schuster, 1961.

**CURRY, GEORGE** (1861–1947) **R-NM,**
**House 1912–1913.**

**2143.** Curry, George. *George Curry, 1861–1947: An Autobiography.* Edited by Horace B. Hening. Albuquerque: University of New Mexico Press, 1958.

**2144.** Larson, Robert W. "Ballinger vs. Rough Rider George Curry: The Other Feud." *New Mexico Historical Review* 43 (October 1968): 271–290.

**CURRY, JABEZ LAMAR MONROE**
(1825–1903) **D-AL, House 1857–1861.**

**2145.** Alderman, Edwin A. *J. L. M. Curry: A Biography.* New York: Macmillan, 1911.

**2146.** ———. "Jabez Lamar Monroe Curry." In *Library of Southern Literature,* edited by Edwin A. Alderman and Joel C. Harris, vol. 3, 1111–1115. New Orleans, LA: Martin and Hoyt, 1909.

**2147.** Rice, Jessie P. *J. L. M. Curry, Southerner, Statesman and Educator.* New York: King's Crown Press, 1949.

**CURTIN, ANDREW GREGG** (1815–1894)
**D-PA, House 1881–1887.**

**2148.** Albright, Rebecca G. "The Civil War Career of Andrew Gregg Curtin, Governor of Pennsylvania." *Western Pennsylvania Historical Magazine* 47 (October 1964): 323–341; 48 (January 1965): 51–73.

**2149.** McClure, Alexander K. "Lincoln and Curtin." In his *Abraham Lincoln and Men of War-Times*, 248–275. Philadelphia: Times Publishing Company, 1892.

**CURTIS, CARL THOMAS** (1905– ) **R-NE, House 1939–1954, Senate 1955–1979.**

**2150.** Curtis, Carl T. *Forty Years against the Tide: Congress and Welfare State.* Chicago: Regnery Gateway, 1986.

**CURTIS, CHARLES** (1860–1936) **R-KS, House 1893–1907, Senate 1907–1913, 1915–1929.**

**2151.** Allen, Robert S., and Andrew R. Pearson. "Egg Charley." In his *Washington Merry-Go-Round*, 78–102. New York: H. Liveright, 1931.

**2152.** Barzman, Sol. "Charles Curtis." In his *Madmen and Geniuses: The Vice-Presidents of the United States*, 213–220. Chicago: Follett, 1974.

**2153.** Ewy, Marvin. *Charles Curtis of Kansas: Vice President of the United States, 1929–1933.* Emporia: Kansas State Teachers College, 1961.

**2154.** Seitz, Don C. *From Kaw Teepee to Capitol: The Life Story of Charles Curtis, Indian, Who Has Risen to High Estate.* New York: Frederick A. Stokes, 1928.

**2155.** Unrau, William E. *Mixed-Bloods and Tribal Dissolution: Charles Curtis and the Quest for Indian Identity.* Lawrence: University of Kansas Press, 1989.

**2156.** Villard, Oswald G. "Charles Curtis." In his *Prophets True and False*, 150–157. New York: Knopf, 1928.

**CURTIS, NEWTON MARTIN** (1835–1910) **R-NY, House 1891–1897.**

**2157.** Curtis, Newton M. *From Bull Run to Chancellorsville.* New York: Putnam's, 1906.

**CUSHING, CALEB** (1800–1879) **W-MA, House 1835–1843.**

**2158.** Baldasty, Gerald J. "Political Stalemate in Essex County: Caleb Cushing's Race for Congress, 1830–1832." *Essex Institute of Historical Collections* 117 (January 1981): 54–70.

**2159.** Fuess, Claude M. *The Life of Caleb Cushing.* New York: Harcourt, Brace, 1923.

**2160.** Hodgson, Michael C. *Caleb Cushing, Attorney General of the United States, 1853–1857.* Washington, DC: Catholic University of America Press, 1955.

**CUTLER, MANASSEH** (1742–1823) **F-MA, House 1801–1805.**

**2161.** Brown, Robert E. *Manasseh Cutler and the Settlement of Ohio, 1788.* Marietta, OH: Marietta College Press, 1938.

**2162.** Cutler, William P. *Life, Journals and Correspondence of Rev. Manasseh Cutler by His Grandchildren W. P. and J. P. Cutler.* Cincinnati, OH: R. Clarke, 1888.

**2163.** Newcomer, Lee N. "Manasseh Cutler's Writings: A Note on Editorial Practice." *Mississippi Valley Historical Review* 47 (June 1960): 88–101.

**2164.** Potts, Louis W. "Manasseh Cutler, Lobbyist." *Ohio History* 96 (Summer/Autumn 1987): 101–123.

**CUTLER, WILLIAM PARKER** (1812–1889) **R-OH, House 1861–1863.**

**2165.** Bogue, Allan G. "William Parker Cutler's Congressional Diary of 1862–63." *Civil War History* 33 (December 1987): 315–330.

**CUTTING, BRONSON MURRAY**
(1888–1935) R-NM, Senate 1927–1928,
1929–1935.

**2166.** Armstrong, Patricia C. *Portrait of Bronson Cutting through His Papers, 1910–1927.* Albuquerque: Division of Research, Department of Government, University of New Mexico, 1959.

**2167.** Dickens, William. "Bronson Cutting vs. Dennis Chavez: Battle of the Patrones in New Mexico, 1934." *New Mexico Historical Journal* 46 (January 1971): 5–36.

**2168.** Fox, Richard L. "New Mexico Senators: A History of Power." *New Mexico Magazine* 63 (November 1985): 82–90.

**2169.** Lowitt, Richard. *Bronson M. Cutting: Progressive Politician.* Albuquerque: University of New Mexico Press, 1992.

**2170.** Seligmann, Gustav L., Jr. "The Political Career of Senator Bronson M. Cutting." Ph.D. dissertation, University of Arizona, 1967.

**DAGGETT, DAVID** (1764–1851) F-CT,
Senate 1813–1819.

**2171.** Hicks, Frederick C. *Yale Law School: The Founders and the Founders' Collection.* New Haven, CT: Yale University Press, 1935.

**DAGGETT, ROLLIN MALLORY**
(1831–1901) R-NV, House 1879–1881.

**2172.** Weisenburger, Francis P. *Idol of the West: The Fabulous Career of Rollin Mallory Daggett.* Syracuse, NY: Syracuse University Press, 1965.

**DALLAS, GEORGE MIFFLIN**
(1792–1864) D-PA, Senate 1831–1833.

**2173.** Ambacher, Bruce I. "George M. Dallas: Leader of the Family Party." Ph.D. dissertation, Temple University, 1971.

**2174.** Barzman, Sol. "George Mifflin Dallas." In his *Madmen and Geniuses: The Vice-Presidents of the United States,* 79–84. Chicago: Follett, 1974.

**2175.** Belohlavek, John M. *George Mifflin Dallas: Jacksonian Patrician.* University Park: Pennsylvania State University Press, 1977.

**2176.** Dallas, George M. *Diary of George Mifflin Dallas, United States Minister to Russia, 1837–1839.* New York: Arno Press, 1970.

**D'AMATO, ALFONSE MARTELLO**
(1937– ) R-NY, Senate 1981– .

**2177.** Lurie, Leonard. *Senator Pothole: The Unauthorized Biography of Al D'Amato.* Secaucus, NJ: Carol, 1994.

**DANA, FRANCIS** (1743–1811) MA,
Continental Congress 1776–1778, 1784.

**2178.** Cresson, William P. *Francis Dana: A Puritan Diplomat at the Court of Catherine the Great.* New York: Dial, 1930.

**DANA, JUDAH** (1772–1845) D-ME, Senate
1836–1837.

**2179.** Spalding, James. "The School and College Life of Judah Dana." *Dartmouth Alumni Magazine* 9 (February 1917): 155–166.

**DANAHER, JOHN ANTHONY**
(1899–1990) R-CT, Senate 1939–1945.

**2180.** Clifford, J. Garry, and Robert Griffiths. "Senator John A. Danaher and the Battle against American Intervention in World War II." *Connecticut History* 25 (1984): 39–63.

**2181.** Kammerman, David. "Reflections upon an Ante-World War II Letter: John A. Danaher and United States Intervention in World War II." *Connecticut History* 23 (1982): 46–55.

**DANE, NATHAN** (1752–1835) MA, Continental Congress 1785–1788.

**2182.** Bauer, Elizabeth. "Nathan Dane." In her *Commentaries on the Constitution, 1790–1860,* 124–132. New York: Columbia University Press, 1952.

**2183.** Johnson, Andrew J. *The Life and Constitutional Thought of Nathan Dane.* New York: Garland, 1987.

**DANIEL, JOHN WARWICK** (1842–1910) D-VA, House 1885–1887, Senate 1887–1910.

**2184.** Doss, Richard. "John Warwick Daniel: A Study in the Virginia Democracy." Ph.D. dissertation, University of Virginia, 1955.

**DANIEL, PRICE MARION** (1910–1988) D-TX, Senate 1953–1957.

**2185.** Banks, Jimmy. "Time and Tides." In his *Money, Marbles and Chalk,* 143–175. Austin: Texas Publishing Company, 1971.

**2186.** Murph, David R. "Price Daniel: The Life of a Public Man, 1910–1956." Ph.D. dissertation, Texas Christian University, 1975.

**2187.** Welch, June R. "Price Daniel Fought for the Tidelands." In his *The Texas Senator,* 60–63. Dallas, TX: G. L. A. Press, 1978.

**2188.** ———. "Price Daniel Ran for a Fourth Term." In his *The Texas Governor,* 176–177. Irving, TX: G. L. A. Press, 1977.

**DARBY, JOHN FLETCHER** (1803–1882) W-MO, House 1851–1853.

**2189.** Darby, John F. *Personal Recollections.* New York: Arno Press, 1975.

**DARLINGTON, WILLIAM** (1782–1863) R-PA, House 1815–1817, 1819–1823.

**2190.** Lansing, Dorothy I. *That Magnificent Cestrian: Dr. William Darlington, 1782–1983.* Paoli, PA: Serpentine Press, 1985.

**DAVENPORT, FREDERICK MORGAN** (1866–1956) R-NY, House 1925–1933.

**2191.** Teti, Frank M. "Profile of a Progressive: The Life of Frederick Morgan Davenport." Ph.D. dissertation, Syracuse University, 1967.

**DAVEY, MARTIN LUTHER** (1884–1946) D-OH, House 1918–1921, 1923–1929.

**2192.** Donaldson, Ralph J. "Martin L. Davey, 1935–1939." In *Governors of Ohio,* 179–183. Columbus: Ohio Historical Society, 1954.

**2193.** Vazzano, Frank P. "Harry Hopkins and Martin Davey: Federal Relief and Ohio Politics during the Great Depression." *Ohio History* 96 (Summer/Autumn 1987): 124–139.

**DAVIS, CUSHMAN KELLOGG** (1838–1900) R-MN, Senate 1887–1900.

**2194.** Baker, James H. "Cushman Kellogg Davis." *Minnesota Historical Society Collections* 13 (1908): 189–223.

**2195.** Coy, Dwight R. "Cushman K. Davis and American Foreign Policy, 1887–1900." Ph.D. dissertation, University of Minnesota, 1965.

**2196.** Kreuter, Kent. "The Presidency or Nothing: Cushman K. Davis and the Campaign of 1896." *Minnesota History* 41 (Fall 1969): 301–316.

**2197.** Stuhler, Barbara. "The March of Empire in Step with Cushman K. Davis." In her *Ten Men of Minnesota and American Foreign Policy, 1898–1968,* 15–31. St. Paul: Minnesota Historical Society, 1973.

**DAVIS, DAVID** (1815–1886) I-IL, Senate 1877–1883.

**2198.** Brockett, Linus P. "David Davis, Associate Justice of the Supreme Court of the U.S." In his *Men of Our Day: Biographical Sketches of Patriots, Orators, Statesmen, Generals, Reformers, Financiers, and*

*Merchants, Now on the Stage of Action. . . . ,* 346–351. Philadelphia: Ziegler and McCurdy, 1872.

**2199.** Dent, Thomas. "David Davis of Illinois: A Sketch." *American Law Review* 53 (July/August 1919): 535–560.

**2200.** King, Willard L. *Lincoln's Manager, David Davis.* Cambridge, MA: Harvard University Press, 1960.

**2201.** Linder, Usher F. "David Davis." In his *Reminiscences of the Early Bench and Bar in Illinois,* 181–188. Chicago: Chicago Legal News, 1879.

**2202.** Pratt, Harry E. "David Davis, 1815–1886." Ph.D. dissertation, University of Illinois, 1930.

**DAVIS, GLENN ROBERT (1914–1988) R-WI, House 1947–1957, 1965–1974.**

**2203.** Smith, Kevin B. *The Iron Man: The Life and Times of Congressman Glenn R. Davis.* Lanham, MD: University Press of America, 1994.

**DAVIS, HENRY GASSAWAY (1823–1916) D-WV, Senate 1871–1883.**

**2204.** Caruso, John A. "Henry Gassaway Davis and the Pan American Railway." Ph.D. dissertation, West Virginia University, 1949.

**2205.** Pepper, Charles M. *The Life and Times of Henry Gassaway Davis, 1823–1916.* New York: Century, 1920.

**2206.** Williams, John A. "Davis and Elkins of West Virginia: Businessmen in Politics." Ph.D. dissertation, Yale University, 1967.

**DAVIS, HENRY WINTER (1817–1865) UU-MD, House 1855–1861, 1863–1865.**

**2207.** Belz, Herman. "Henry Winter Davis and the Origins of Congressional Reconstruction." *Maryland History Magazine* 67 (Summer 1972): 129–143.

**2208.** Essary, J. Frederick. "Henry Winter Davis." In his *Maryland in National Politics.* Baltimore: John Murphy, 1915.

**2209.** Henig, Gerald S. *Henry Winter Davis: Antebellum and Civil War Congressman from Maryland.* Boston: Twayne, 1973.

**2210.** ———. "Henry Winter Davis and the Speakership Contest of 1859–1860." *Maryland History Magazine* 68 (Spring 1973): 1–19.

**2211.** Steiner, Bernard C. *Life of Henry Winter Davis.* Baltimore: John Murphy, 1916.

**2212.** Tyson, Raymond W. "Henry Winter Davis: Orator for the Union." *Maryland Historical Magazine* 58 (March 1963): 1–19.

**2213.** ———. "A Southerner Who Spoke for the Union." *Southern Speech Journal* 30 (Winter 1964): 117–132.

**DAVIS, JAMES JOHN (1873–1947) R-PA, Senate 1930–1945.**

**2214.** Beard, Annie E. "An Iron Puddler Who Became Secretary of Labor." In her *Our Foreign-Born Citizens,* 118–130. New York: Crowell, 1932.

**2215.** Chapple, Joseph M. *'Our Jim': A Biography.* Boston: Chapple, 1928.

**2216.** Davis, James J. *The Iron Puddler: My Life in the Rolling Mills and What Came of It.* Indianapolis: Bobbs-Merrill, 1922.

**2217.** Dennis, Alfred P. "Puddler Jim." In his *Gods and Little Fishes,* 298–323. Indianapolis: Bobbs-Merrill, 1931.

**2218.** Zieger, Robert H. "The Career of James J. Davis." *Pennsylvania Magazine of History and Biography* 98 (January 1974): 67–89.

**DAVIS, JEFF (1862–1913) D-AR, Senate 1907–1913.**

**2219.** Arsenault, Raymond. *The Wild Ass of the Ozarks: Jeff Davis and the Social Bases of Southern Politics.* Philadelphia: Temple University Press, 1984.

**2220.** Jacobson, Charles. *Great Statesmen of Arkansas,* compiled by Walter S. McNutt, 10–45. Jefferson, TX: Four States Publication House, 1954.

**2221.** ———. *The Life Story of Jeff Davis, The Stormy Petrel of Arkansas Politics.* Little Rock, AR: Parke-Harper, 1925.

**2222.** Ledbetter, Cal. "Jeff Davis and the Politics of Combat." *Arkansas Historical Quarterly* 33 (Spring 1974): 16–37.

**2223.** Niswonger, Richard L. "A Study in Southern Demagoguery: Jeff Davis of Arkansas." *Arkansas Historical Quarterly* 39 (Summer 1980): 114–124.

## DAVIS, JEFFERSON FINIS (1808–1889)
**D-MS, House 1845–1846, Senate 1847–1851, 1857–1861.**

**2224.** Anders, Curt. "Jefferson Davis: The Splendid Failure." In his *Fighting Confederates,* 15–66. New York: Dorset Press, 1968.

**2225.** Ballard, Michael B. *A Long Shadow: Jefferson Davis and the Final Days of the Confederacy.* Jackson: University Press of Mississippi, 1986.

**2226.** Bartlett, David V. "Jefferson Davis." In his *Presidential Candidates: Containing Sketches, Biographical, Personal and Political, of Prominent Candidates for the Presidency,* 295–304. New York: A. B. Burdick, 1859.

**2227.** Bradford, Gamaliel. "Lee and Davis." In his *Lee the American,* 48–73. Boston: Houghton Mifflin, 1927.

**2228.** Burger, Nash K. "The Unreconstructible Jefferson Davis." In his *South of Appomattox,* 302–336. New York: Harcourt, Brace, 1959.

**2229.** Canfield, Cass. *The Iron Will of Jefferson Davis.* New York: Harcourt Brace Jovanovich, 1978.

**2230.** Catton, William B. *Two Roads to Sumter.* New York: McGraw-Hill, 1963.

**2231.** Chancellor, William E. "Jefferson Davis." In his *Our Presidents and Their Office,* 473–482. New York: Neale Publishing Company, 1912.

**2232.** Clark, James C. *Last Train South: The Flight of the Confederate Government from Richmond.* Jefferson, NC: McFarland, 1984.

**2233.** Collins, Kathleen, and Ann Wilsher. "Petticoat Politics: The Capture of Jefferson Davis." *History of Photography* 8 (July/September 1984): 237–243.

**2234.** Crist, Lynda L. "A 'Duty Man' Jefferson Davis as Senator." *Journal of Mississippi History* 51 (November 1989): 281–295.

**2235.** Cutting, Elizabeth B. *Jefferson Davis, Political Soldier.* New York: Dodd, Mead, 1930.

**2236.** Davis, Burke. *The Long Surrender.* New York: Random House, 1985.

**2237.** Davis, Jefferson. *Jefferson Davis, Constitutionalist: His Letters, Papers and Speeches.* 10 vols. Jackson: Mississippi Department of Archives and History, 1923.

**2238.** ———. *Messages and Papers, 1861–1865.* 2 vols. Edited by James D. Richardson. New York: Chelsea House, 1966.

**2239.** ———. *Papers.* 2 vols. Edited by Haskell M. Monroe and James T. McIntosh. Baton Rouge: Louisiana State University Press, 1971–1974.

**2240.** ———. *Private Letters, 1823–1889.* Edited by Hudson Strode. New York: Harcourt, Brace and World, 1966.

**2241.** Davis, Varina H. *Jefferson Davis, Expresident of the Confederate States of America: A Memoir by His Wife.* 2 vols. New York: Belford, 1890.

**2242.** Davis, William C. *Jefferson Davis: The Man and His Hour.* New York: HarperCollins, 1991.

**2243.** Dixon, Thomas. *The Victim: A Romance of the Real Jefferson Davis.* New York: Appleton, 1914.

**2244.** Dodd, William E. "Jefferson Davis." In his *Statesmen of the Old South: Or, from Radicalism to Conservative Revolt,* 171–238. New York: Macmillan, 1911.

**2245.** ———. *Jefferson Davis.* Philadelphia: Jacobs, 1907.

**2246.** Eaton, Clement. *Jefferson Davis.* New York: Free Press, 1977.

**2247.** Eckenrode, Hamilton J. *Jefferson Davis, President of the South.* New York: Macmillan, 1923.

**2248.** Escott, Paul D. *After Secession: Jefferson Davis and the Failure of Confederate Nationalism.* Baton Rouge: Louisiana State University Press, 1978.

**2249.** ———. "Jefferson Davis and Slavery in the Territories." *Journal of Mississippi History* 39 (May 1977): 97–116.

**2250.** Gordon, Armistead C. *Jefferson Davis.* New York: Scribner's, 1918.

**2251.** Greeley, Horace. "Jefferson Davis." In his *Recollections of a Busy Life,* 410–416. New York: J. B. Ford, 1869.

**2252.** Hendrick, Burton J. *Statesmen of the Lost Cause: Jefferson Davis and His Cabinet.* Boston: Little, Brown, 1939.

**2253.** Johnson, Byron B. *Abraham Lincoln and Boston Corbett, with Personal Recollections of Each: John Wilkes Booth and Jefferson Davis, a True Story of Their Capture.* Waltham, MA: B. B. Johnson, 1914.

**2254.** Jones, J. William. "Jefferson Davis." In *Library of Southern Literature,* edited by Edwin A. Alderman and Joel C. Harris, vol. 3, 1243–1248. New Orleans, LA: Martin and Hoyt, 1909.

**2255.** Lindsey, David. *Lincoln/Jefferson Davis: The House Divided.* Cleveland, OH: H. Allen, 1960.

**2256.** Maurice, Frederick B. "Jefferson Davis and J. E. Johnston, Jefferson Davis and Lee." In his *Governments and War,* 13–65. London: W. Heinemann, 1926.

**2257.** McElroy, Robert M. *Jefferson Davis: The Unreal and the Real.* 2 vols. New York: Harper and Brothers, 1937.

**2258.** Patrick, Rembert W. *Jefferson Davis and His Cabinet.* Baton Rouge: Louisiana State University Press, 1944.

**2259.** Sanders, Phyllis M. "Jefferson Davis: Reactionary Rebel, 1808–1861." Ph.D. dissertation, University of California, 1976.

**2260.** Sansing, David. "A Happy Interlude: Jefferson Davis and the War Department, 1853–1857." *Mississippi History* 51 (November 1989): 297–312.

**2261.** Seitz, Don C. "Bailing Jefferson Davis." In his *Horace Greeley, Founder of the New York Tribune,* 274–288. Indianapolis: Bobbs-Merrill, 1926.

**2262.** Shelton, William A. "The Young Jefferson Davis, 1808–1846." Ph.D. dissertation, University of Kentucky, 1977.

**2263.** Strode, Hudson. *Jefferson Davis.* 3 vols. New York: Harcourt, Brace, 1955–1964.

**2264.** Tate, Allen. *Jefferson Davis: His Rise and Fall, a Biographical Narrative.* New York: Minton, Balch, 1929.

**2265.** Trent, William P. "Jefferson Davis." In his *Southern Statesmen of the Old Regime: Washington, Jefferson, Randolph, Calhoun, Stephens, Toombs, and Jefferson Davis,* 257–293. New York: Crowell, 1897.

**2266.** Vandiver, Frank E. *Jefferson Davis and the Confederate State.* Oxford: Clarendon Press, 1964.

**2267.** Warren, Robert P. *Jefferson Davis Gets His Citizenship Back.* Lexington: University Press of Kentucky, 1980.

**2268.** Werstein, Irving. *Abraham Lincoln Versus Jefferson Davis.* New York: Crowell, 1959.

**2269.** Wiley, Bell I. *The Road to Appomattox.* Memphis, TN: Memphis State College Press, 1956.

**2270.** Winston, Robert W. *High Stakes and Hair Trigger: The Life of Jefferson Davis.* New York: Holt, 1930.

**DAVIS, JOHN** (1787–1854) W-MA, House 1825–1834, Senate 1835–1841, 1845–1853.

**2271.** Kribbs, Jayne K. "Setting the Record Straight on the Real John Davis." *Bibliographical Society of America Papers* 68 (July 1974): 329–330.

**DAVIS, JOHN WESLEY** (1799–1859) D-IN, House 1835–1837, 1839–1841, 1843–1847.

**2272.** Bedford, Hope. "John Wesley Davis." Master's thesis, Butler University, 1930.

**2273.** Beeler, Dale. "The Election of 1852 in Indiana." *Indiana Magazine of History* 11 (December 1915): 301–323; 12 (March 1916): 34–52.

**2274.** Turnbull, George S. "John Wesley Davis." In his *Governors of Oregon,* 26–27. Portland, OR: Binfords, 1959.

**2275.** Woollen, William W. "John W. Davis." In his *Biographical and Historical Sketches of Early Indiana,* 233–240. Indianapolis: Hammond, 1883.

**DAVIS, JOHN WILLIAM** (1873–1955) D-WV, House 1911–1913.

**2276.** Bullock, Charles S., and Catherine Rudder. "The Case of the Right-Wing Urologist: The Seventh District of Georgia." In *The Making of Congressmen: Seven Campaigns of 1974,* edited by Alan L. Clem, 55–92. North Scituate, MA: Duxbury Press, 1976.

**2277.** Davis, John W. *The Ambassadorial Diary of John W. Davis: The Court of St. James's, 1918–1921,* edited by Julia Davis and Dolores A. Fleming. Morgantown: West Virginia University Press, 1993.

**2278.** Davis, Julia. *The Embassy Girls.* Morgantown: West Virginia University Press, 1992.

**2279.** Harbaugh, William H. *Lawyer's Lawyer: The Life of John W. Davis.* New York: Oxford University Press, 1973.

**DAVIS, REUBEN** (1813–1890) D-MS, House 1857–1861.

**2280.** Davis, Reuben. *Recollections of Mississippi and Mississippians.* Rev. ed. Hattiesburg: University College Press of Mississippi, 1972.

**DAWES, HENRY LAURENS** (1816–1903) R-MA, House 1857–1875, Senate 1875–1893.

**2281.** Arcanti, Steven J. "To Secure the Party: Henry L. Dawes and the Politics of Reconstruction." *Historical Journal of Western Massachusetts* 5 (Spring 1977): 33–45.

**2282.** Nicklason, Fred H. "The Early Career of Henry L. Dawes, 1816–1871." Ph.D. dissertation, Yale University, 1967.

**DAWES, RUFUS** (1838–1899) R-OH, House 1881–1883.

**2283.** Dawes, Rufus R. *A Memoir: Rufus R. Dawes.* New York: DeVinne Press, 1900.

**DAWSON, WILLIAM LEVI** (1886–1970) D-IL, House 1943–1970.

**2284.** Christopher, Maurine. "William L. Dawson/Illinois." In her *Black Americans in Congress,* 185–193. Rev. ed. New York: Thomas Y. Crowell, 1976.

**2285.** Clayton, Edward T. "Dawson: The Master Politician." In his *Negro Politician: His Success and Failure,* 68–91. Lincoln, NE: Johnson, 1964.

**2286.** Stone, Chuck. "Four Black Men in the White Power Structure." In his *Black Political Power in America,* 175–184. Indianapolis: Bobbs-Merrill, 1968.

**2287.** Toppin, Edgar A. "Dawson, William L." In his *Biographical History of Blacks in America since 1528,* 277–278. New York: McKay, 1971.

**2288.** Wilson, James Q. "Two Negro Politicians: An Interpretation." *Midwest Journal of Political Science* 4 (November 1960): 346–369.

**DAYTON, JONATHAN (1760–1824) F-NJ, House 1791–1799, Senate 1799–1805, Continental Congress 1787–1788.**

**2289.** McCormick, Richard P. "New Jersey's First Congressional Election, 1789: A Case Study in Political Skullduggery." *William and Mary Quarterly* 6 (April 1949): 237–250.

**2290.** Nelson, William E. "The Election of Congressmen from New Jersey." *Proceedings of the New Jersey Historical Society* 8 (July 1913): 80–83.

**2291.** Thayer, Theodore. *As We Were: The Story of Elizabethtown.* Elizabeth, NJ: Grassman, 1964.

**DAYTON, WILLIAM LEWIS (1807–1864) W-NJ, Senate 1842–1851.**

**2292.** Elmer, Lucius Q. "Judges I Have Known: William L. Dayton." In his *The Constitution and Government of the Province and State of New Jersey*, 372–396. Newark, NJ: M. R. Dennis, 1872.

**DEANE, SILAS (1737–1789) CT, Continental Congress 1774–1776.**

**2293.** Bloom, Richard. "Silas Deane: Patriot or Renegade?" *American History Illustrated* 13 (November 1978): 32–42.

**2294.** Boyd, Julian P. "Silas Deane: Death by a Kindly Teacher of Treason?" *William and Mary Quarterly* 16 (April 1959): 165–187.

**2295.** Clark, George L. *Silas Deane: A Connecticut Leader in the American Revolution.* New York: Putnam's, 1913.

**2296.** Davidson, Alexander, Jr. "James Rivington and Silas Deane." *Bibliographical Society of America Papers* 52 (July/September 1958): 173–178.

**2297.** Flegal, Fred G. "Silas Deane: Revolutionary or Profiteer?" Master's thesis, Western Michigan University, 1976.

**2298.** James, Coy H. *Silas Deane: Patriot or Traitor?* East Lansing: Michigan State University Press, 1975.

**2299.** Morton, Brian N. "Roderigue Hortalez to the Secret Committee: An Unpublished French Policy Statement of 1777." *French Review* 50 (May 1977): 875–890.

**2300.** Paine, Thomas. "The Affair of Silas Deane." In his *Life and Works*, 281–361. New Rochelle, NY: Thomas Paine National Historical Association, 1925.

**2301.** Stinchcombe, William. "A Note on Silas Deane's Death." *William and Mary Quarterly* 32 (October 1975): 619–624.

**DEARBORN, HENRY (1751–1829) D-MA, House 1793–1797.**

**2302.** Coffin, Charles C., comp. *The Lives and Services of Major General John Thomas, Colonel Thomas Knowlton, Colonel Alexander Scammell, Major General Henry Dearborn.* New York: Egbert, Hovey and King, 1845.

**2303.** Dearborn, Henry A. *Defence of Gen. Henry Dearborn, against the Attack of Gen. William Hull.* Boston: E. W. Davies, 1824.

**2304.** Erney, Richard A. *The Public Life of Henry Dearborn.* New York: Arno Press, 1957.

**DEARBORN, HENRY ALEXANDER SCAMMELL (1783–1851) AJ-MA, House 1831–1833.**

**2305.** Goodwin, Daniel. *The Dearborns: A Discourse Commemorative of the Eightieth Anniversary of the Occupation of Fort Dearborn, and the First Settlement at Chicago.* Chicago: Fergus, 1884.

**DE LA MATYR, GILBERT** (1825–1892)
**G-IN, House 1879–1881.**

**2306.** Doolen, Richard M. "Pastor in Politics: The Congressional Career of Reverend Gilbert De La Matyr." *Indiana Magazine of History* 68 (June 1972): 103–124.

**DE LARGE, ROBERT CARLOS**
(1842–1874) **R-SC, House 1871–1873.**

**2307.** Christopher, Maurine. "Robert C. De Large/South Carolina." In her *Black Americans in Congress,* 97–103. Rev. ed. New York: Thomas Y. Crowell, 1976.

**DELLUMS, RONALD VERNIE** (1935– )
**D-CA, House 1971– .**

**2308.** Christopher, Maurine. "Ronald V. Dellums/California." In her *Black Americans in Congress,* 262–277. Rev. ed. New York: Thomas Y. Crowell, 1976.

**2309.** James, Victor V., Jr. "Cultural Pluralism and the Quest for Black Citizenship: The 1970 Ronald V. Dellums Congressional Primary Campaign." Ph.D. dissertation, University of California, 1975.

**DENHOLM, FRANK EDWARD** (1923– )
**D-SD, House 1971–1975.**

**2310.** Clem, Alan L. "The Case of the Upstart Republican: The First District of South Dakota." In *The Making of Congressmen: Seven Campaigns of 1974,* edited by Alan L. Clem, 127–165. North Scituate, MA: Duxbury Press, 1976.

**DENNY, HARMAR** (1794–1852) **AMAS-PA,**
**House 1829–1837.**

**2311.** Backofen, Catherine. "Congressman Harmar Denny." *Western Pennsylvania Historical Magazine* 23 (June 1940): 65–78.

**DENTON, JEREMIAH ANDREW, JR.**
(1924– ) **R-AL, Senate 1981–1987.**

**2312.** Denton, Jeremiah A. *When Hell Was in Session.* New York: Readers Digest Press, 1976.

**DENVER, JAMES WILLIAM** (1817–1892)
**D-CA, House 1855–1857.**

**2313.** Taylor, Edward T. "General James W. Denver, an Appreciation." *Colorado Magazine* 17 (March 1940): 41–51.

**DEPEW, CHAUNCEY MITCHELL**
(1834–1928) **R-NY, Senate 1899–1911.**

**2314.** Depew, Chauncey M. *My Memories of Eighty Years.* New York: Scribner's, 1922.

**2315.** Murphy, Arthur F. "The Political Personality of Chauncey Mitchell Depew." Ph.D. dissertation, Fordham University, 1959.

**DE PRIEST, OSCAR** (1871–1951) **R-IL,**
**House 1929–1935.**

**2316.** Christopher, Maurine. "Oscar De Priest." In her *Black Americans in Congress,* 168–175. Rev. ed. New York: Thomas Y. Crowell, 1976.

**2317.** Day, David S. "Herbert Hoover and Racial Politics: The De Priest Incident." *Journal of Negro History* 65 (Winter 1980): 6–17.

**2318.** Gosnell, Harold F. *Negro Politicians: The Rise of Negro Politics in Chicago.* Chicago: University of Chicago Press, 1967.

**2319.** Mann, Kenneth E. "Oscar Stanton De Priest: Persuasive Agent for the Black Masses." *Negro History Bulletin* 35 (October 1972): 134–137.

**2320.** Rudwick, Elliott M. "Oscar De Priest and the Jim Crow Restaurant in the U.S. House of Representatives." *Journal of Negro Education* 35 (Winter 1966): 77–82.

**DESHA, JOSEPH** (1768–1842) **D-KY,**
**House 1807–1819.**

**2321.** Doutrich, Paul E. "A Pivotal Decision: The 1824 Gubernatorial Election in Kentucky." *Filson Club Historical Quarterly* 56 (January 1982): 14–29.

**2322.** Padgett, James A., ed. "Joseph Desha, Letters and Papers." *Register of the*

*Kentucky Historical Society* 51 (October 1953): 286–304.

**DEXTER, SAMUEL** (1761–1816) F-MA, House 1793–1795, Senate 1799–1800.

**2323.** Sargent, Lucius. *Reminiscences of Samuel Dexter.* Boston: Dutton, 1857.

**DIAL, NATHANIEL BARKSDALE** (1862–1940) D-SC, Senate 1919–1925.

**2324.** Dial, Rebecca. *True to His Colors: A Story of South Carolina's Senator Nathaniel Barksdale Dial.* New York: Vantage, 1974.

**2325.** Slaunwhite, Jerry L. "The Public Career of Nathaniel Barksdale Dial." Ph.D. dissertation, University of South Carolina, 1979.

**DICKERSON, MAHLON** (1770–1853) R-NJ, Senate 1817–1829.

**2326.** Beckwith, Robert R. "Mahlon Dickerson of New Jersey, 1770–1853." Ph.D. dissertation, Columbia University, 1964.

**DICKINSON, DANIEL STEVENS** (1800–1866) D-NY, Senate 1844–1851.

**2327.** Bartlett, David V. "Daniel S. Dickinson." In his *Presidential Candidates: Containing Sketches, Biographical, Personal and Political, of Prominent Candidates for the Presidency,* 127–149. New York: A. B. Burdick, 1859.

**2328.** Hinman, Marjory B. *Daniel S. Dickinson, Defender of the Constitution.* Windsor, NY: M. B. Hinman, 1987.

**DICKINSON, EDWARD** (1803–1874) W-MA, House 1853–1855.

**2329.** Bingham, Millicent. *Emily Dickinson's Family: Letters of Edward Dickinson and His Family.* New York: Harper and Row, 1955.

**2330.** Thomas, Owen. "Father and Daughter: Edward and Emily Dickinson." *American Literature* 40 (January 1969): 510–523.

**DICKINSON, JOHN** (1732–1808) PA/DE, Continental Congress 1774–1776, 1776, 1777, 1779, 1780.

**2331.** Flower, Milton E. *John Dickinson, Conservative Revolutionary.* Charlottesville: University Press of Virginia, 1983.

**2332.** Hutson, James H. "John Dickinson at the Federal Constitutional Convention." *William and Mary Quarterly* 40 (April 1983): 256–282.

**2333.** Jacobson, David L. *John Dickinson and the Revolution in Pennsylvania, 1764–1776.* Berkeley: University of California Press, 1965.

**2334.** Knollenberg, Bernhard. "John Dickinson v. John Adams, 1774–1776." *Proceeding of the American Philosophical Society* 107 (April 1963): 138–144.

**2335.** Parrington, Vernon L. "John Dickinson: The Mind of the American Whig." In his *Main Currents in American Thought,* vol. 1, 219–232. New York: Harcourt, Brace, 1927.

**2336.** Richards, Robert H. *The Life and Character of John Dickinson.* Wilmington: Historical Society of Delaware, 1901.

**2337.** Slotten, Martha C. "John Dickinson on Independence, July 25, 1776." *Manuscripts* 28 (Summer 1976): 188–194.

**2338.** Stille, Charles J. *The Life and Times of John Dickinson.* Philadelphia: Historical Society of Pennsylvania, 1891.

**DIEKEMA, GERRIT JOHN** (1859–1930) R-MI, House 1908–1911.

**2339.** Schrier, William. *Gerrit J. Diekema, Orator: A Rhetorical Study of the Political and Occasional Addresses of Gerrit J. Diekema.* Grand Rapids, MI: Eerdmans, 1950.

**2340.** Vander Hill, Charles W. *Gerrit J. Diekema.* Grand Rapids, MI: Eerdmans, 1970.

**DIES, MARTIN, JR.** (1900–1972) D-TX, House 1931–1945, 1953–1959.

2341. Alexander, Albert. "The President and the Investigator: Roosevelt and Dies." *Antioch Review* 15 (March 1955): 106–117.

2342. Dies, Martin. *Martin Dies' Story.* New York: Bookmailer, 1963.

2343. Gellermann, William. *Martin Dies.* New York: Da Capo Press, 1972.

2344. McDaniel, Dennis K. "Martin Dies of Un-American Activities: His Life and Times." Ph.D. dissertation, University of Houston, 1988.

2345. Ogden, August R. *The Dies Committee: A Study of the Special House Committee for the Investigation of Un-American Activities, 1938–1944.* Washington, DC: Catholic University of America Press, 1945.

2346. Seldes, George. "The Triumph of Dies." In his *Witch Hunt,* 271–280. New York: Modern Age Books, 1940.

**DIGGS, CHARLES COLES, JR.** (1922– ) D-MI, House 1955–1980.

2347. Christopher, Maurine. "Charles C. Diggs/Michigan." In her *Black Americans in Congress,* 209–214. Rev. ed. New York: Thomas Y. Crowell, 1976.

**DILL, CLARENCE CLEVELAND** (1884–1978) D-WA, House 1915–1919, Senate 1923–1935.

2348. Barkley, Frederick R. "Clarence Dill: The Hometown Boy Who Made Good." In *Sons of the Wild Jackass,* by Ray T. Tucker and Frederick R. Barkley, 245–268. Boston: L. C. Page, 1932.

**DILLINGHAM, WILLIAM PAUL** (1843–1923) R-VT Senate 1900–1923.

2349. Schlup, Leonard. "William Paul Dillingham: A Vermont Republican in National Politics." *Vermont History* 54 (Winter 1986): 20–36.

**DINGELL, JOHN DAVID** (1894–1955) D-MI, House 1933–1955.

2350. Banister, Gerald G. "The Longest-Tenured Polish-American Congressman." *Polish American Studies* 21 (January/June 1964): 38–40.

**DINGLEY, NELSON, JR.** (1832–1899) R-ME, House 1881–1899.

2351. Clark, Champ. "Dingley." In *My Quarter Century of American Politics,* vol. 2, 10–19. New York: Harper and Brothers, 1920.

2352. Dingley, Edward N. *The Life and Times of Nelson Dingley, Jr.* Kalamazoo, MI: Ihling Brothers and Everard, 1902.

**DINSMOOR, SAMUEL** (1766–1835) R-NH, House 1811–1813.

2353. Tilly, Bette B. "The Jackson-Dinsmoor Feud: A Paradox in a Minor Key." *Journal of Mississippi History* 39 (May 1977): 117–131.

**DIOGUARDI, JOSEPH J.** (1940– ) R-NY, House 1985–1989.

2354. DioGuardi, Joseph J. *Unaccountable Congress: It Doesn't Add Up.* Washington, DC: Regnery Gateway, 1992.

**DIRKSEN, EVERETT McKINLEY** (1896–1969) R-IL, House 1933–1949, Senate 1951–1969.

2355. Cronin, Jean T. "Minority Leadership in the United States Senate: The Role and Style of Everett Dirksen." Ph.D. dissertation, Johns Hopkins University, 1973.

2356. Dirksen, Louella. *The Honorable Mr. Marigold: My Life with Everett Dirksen.* Garden City, NY: Doubleday 1972.

2357. Fonsino, Frank J. "Everett McKinley Dirksen: The Roots of an American Statesman." *Journal of the Illinois State Historical Society* 76 (Spring 1983): 17–34.

**2358.** Keynes, Edward. "The Dirksen Amendment: A Study of Legislative Strategy, Tactics and Public Policy." Ph.D. dissertation, University of Wisconsin, 1967.

**2359.** Loomis, Burdett. "The Consummate Minority Leader." In *First Among Equals: Outstanding Senate Leaders of the Twentieth Century,* edited by Richard A. Baker and Roger H. Davidson, 236–263. Washington, DC: Congressional Quarterly, 1991.

**2360.** MacNeil, Neil. *Dirksen: Portrait of a Public Man.* New York: World Publishing Company, 1970.

**2361.** Nixon, Richard M. "Everett Dirksen." In his *Four Great Americans: Tributes Delivered by President Nixon,* 29–40. New York: Doubleday, 1972.

**2362.** Penney, Annette C. *Golden Voice of the Senate.* Washington, DC: Acropolis Books, 1968.

**2363.** Rosenberger, Francis C. "Washington's Jim Berryman, 1902–1971: Cartoons of Senator Dirksen." *Records of the Columbia Historical Society of Washington, DC* 48 (1973): 758–775.

**2364.** Schapsmeier, Edward L., and Frederick H. Schapsmeier. *Dirksen of Illinois: Senatorial Statesman.* Urbana: University of Illinois Press, 1985.

**2365.** ———. "Everett M. Dirksen of Pekin: Politician Par Excellence." *Journal of the Illinois State Historical Society* 76 (Spring 1983): 2–16.

**2366.** ———. "Senator Everett M. Dirksen and American Foreign Policy: From Isolationism to Cold War." *Old Northwest* 7 (Winter 1981/1982): 359–372.

**2367.** Torcom, Jean E. "Leadership: The Role and Style of Senator Everett Dirksen." In *To Be a Congressman: The Promise and the Power,* edited by Sven Groennings, 185–223. Washington, DC: Acropolis Books, 1973.

**2368.** Viorst, Milton. "Everett McKinley Dirksen: Pied Piper of the Hinterland." In his *Hustlers and Heroes: An American Political Panorama,* 38–57. New York: Simon and Schuster, 1971.

**DIX, JOHN ADAMS** (1798–1879) D-NY, Senate 1845–1849.

**2369.** Dix, Morgan, ed. *Memoirs of John Dix.* 2 vols. New York: Harper and Brothers, 1883.

**2370.** Lichterman, Martin. "John Adams Dix: 1798–1897." Ph.D. dissertation, Columbia University, 1952.

**DIXON, JAMES** (1814–1873) R-CT, House 1845–1849, Senate 1857–1869.

**2371.** Albright, Claude. "Dixon, Doolittle, and Norton: The Forgotten Republican Votes on Andrew Johnson's Impeachment." *Wisconsin Magazine of History* 59 (Winter 1975/1976): 91–100.

**2372.** Burr, Nelson R. "United States Senator James Dixon, 1814–1873: Episcopalian Anti-slavery Statesman." *Historical Magazine of the Protestant Episcopal Church* 50 (March 1981): 29–72.

**DIXON, JOSEPH MOORE** (1867–1934) R-MT, House 1903–1907, Senate 1907–1913.

**2373.** Karlin, Jules A. *Joseph M. Dixon of Montana.* 2 vols. Missoula: University of Montana, 1974.

**DODD, THOMAS JOSEPH** (1907–1971) D-CT, House 1953–1957, Senate 1959–1971.

**2374.** Boyd, James. *Above the Law.* New York: New American Library, 1968.

**2375.** Wenger, Paul E. "A Study of Legislative Discourse in the Censure Debate Concerning Senator Thomas J. Dodd." Ph.D. dissertation, University of Iowa, 1972.

**DODDRIDGE, PHILIP** (1773–1832) VA,
House 1829–1832.

**2376.** Willey, Waitman T. *A Sketch of the Life of Philip Doddridge.* Morgantown, WV: Morgan and Hoffman, 1875.

**DODGE, AUGUSTUS CAESAR**
(1812–1883) D-IA, House 1840–1846, Senate 1848–1855.

**2377.** Pelzer, Louis. *Augustus Caesar Dodge.* Iowa City: State Historical Society of Iowa, 1908.

**DODGE, GRENVILLE MELLEN**
(1831–1916) R-IA, House 1867–1869.

**2378.** Ashby, George F. *Major General Grenville M. Dodge (1831–1916): Maker of History in the Great West.* New York: Newcomen Society of England, American Branch, 1947.

**2379.** Farnham, Wallace D. "Grenville Dodge and the Union Pacific: A Study of Historical Legends." *Journal of American History* 51 (March 1965): 632–650.

**2380.** Granger, John T. *A Brief Biographical Sketch of the Life of Major-General Grenville M. Dodge, Compiled from Official Records by J. T. Granger, Private Secretary.* New York: Press of Styles and Cash, 1893.

**2381.** Hirshson, Stanley P. *Grenville M. Dodge, Soldier, Politician, Railroad Pioneer.* Bloomington: Indiana University Press, 1967.

**2382.** Perkins, Jacob R. *Trails, Rails and War: The Life of General G. M. Dodge.* Indianapolis: Bobbs-Merrill, 1929.

**DODGE, HENRY** (1782–1867) D-WI,
House 1841–1845, Senate 1848–1857.

**2383.** Clark, James I. *Henry Dodge, Frontiersman: First Governor of Wisconsin Territory.* Madison: State Historical Society of Wisconsin, 1957.

**2384.** Kingsbury, Gaines P. *Journal of the Expedition of Dragoons under the Command of Col. Henry Dodge to the Rocky Mountains, During the Summer of 1835.* Washington, DC: Gales and Seaton, 1836.

**2385.** Pelzer, Louis. "Henry Dodge." In his *Augustus Caesar Dodge,* 11–37. Iowa City: State Historical Society of Iowa, 1908.

**2386.** ———. *Henry Dodge.* Iowa City: State Historical Society of Iowa, 1911.

**DODGE, WILLIAM EARLE** (1805–1883)
R-NY, House 1866–1867.

**2387.** Dodge, David S., comp. *Memorials of William E. Dodge.* New York: A. D. F. Randolph, 1887.

**2388.** Lowitt, Richard. *A Merchant Prince of the Nineteenth Century: William E. Dodge.* New York: Columbia University Press, 1954.

**DOLE, ROBERT JOSEPH** (1923– ) R-KS,
House 1961–1969, Senate 1969– .

**2389.** Dole, Robert J. *The Doles: Unlimited Partners.* New York: Simon and Schuster, 1988.

**2390.** Hilton, Stanley G. *Bob Dole: American Political Phoenix.* Chicago: Contemporary Books, 1988.

**2391.** Thompson, Jake H. *Bob Dole: The Republican's Man for All Seasons.* New York: Fine, 1994.

**DOLLIVER, JONATHAN PRENTISS**
(1858–1910) R-IA, House 1889–1900, Senate 1900–1910.

**2392.** Ross, Thomas R. *Jonathan Prentiss Dolliver: A Study in Political Integrity and Independence.* Iowa City: State Historical Society of Iowa, 1958.

**DOLPH, JOSEPH NORTON** (1835–1897)
R-OR, Senate 1883–1895.

**2393.** Roth, Frederick M. "A Biographical Sketch of Joseph Norton Dolph." Master's thesis, University of Oregon, 1940.

**DONAHEY, ALVIN VICTOR** (1873–1946) **D-OH, Senate 1935–1941.**

**2394.** Meckstroth, Jacob A. "A. Victor Donahey, 1923–1929." In *Governors of Ohio,* 166–169. Columbus: Ohio Historical Society, 1954.

**2395.** Villard, Oswald G. "A. Victor Donahey: Governor of Ohio." In his *Prophets True and False,* 125–138. New York: Knopf, 1928.

**DONNELLY, IGNATIUS** (1831–1901) **R-MN, House 1863–1869.**

**2396.** Abrahams, Edward H. "Ignatius Donnelly and the Apocalyptic Style." *Minnesota History* 46 (Fall 1978): 102–111.

**2397.** Anderson, David D. *Ignatius Donnelly.* Boston: Twayne, 1980.

**2398.** Beals, Carleton. "The Sage of Nininger." In his *Great Revolt and Its Leaders,* 115–138. New York: Abelard-Schuman, 1968.

**2399.** Hicks, John D. "The Political Career of Ignatius Donnelly." *Mississippi Valley Historical Review* 8 (June 1921): 80–132.

**2400.** Holbrook, Stewart H. "Apostles of Protest." In his *Lost Men of American History,* 267–277. New York: Macmillan, 1946.

**2401.** ———. "The Populist Revolt." In his *Dreamers of the American Dream,* 151–160. Garden City, NY: Doubleday, 1957.

**2402.** Johnson, Gerald W. "Ignatius Donnelly." In his *Lunatic Fringe,* 123–138. New York: Lippincott, 1957.

**2403.** Kennedy, Roger G. "Ignatius Donnelly." In his *Men on the Moving Frontier,* 103–132. Palo Alto, CA: American West, 1969.

**2404.** ———. "Ignatius Donnelly and the Politics of Discontent: An Inquiry into the Career of a Populist." *American West* 6 (March 1969): 10–14+.

**2405.** Moore, Jack B. "Donnelly, Ignatius." In *American Literature to 1900,* 104–106. New York: St. Martin's Press, 1980.

**2406.** Nydahl, Theodore L. "The Diary of Ignatius Donnelly, 1859–1884." Ph.D. dissertation, University of Minnesota, 1942.

**2407.** O'Connor, William D. *Mr. Donnelly's Reviewers.* Chicago: Belford, Clarke, 1889.

**2408.** Parrington, Vernon L. "The Politician Considers Utopia." In his *American Dreams,* 104–110. Providence, RI: Brown University, 1947.

**2409.** Peterson, Larry R. "Ignatius Donnelly: A Psychohistorical Study in Moral Development Psychology." Ph.D. dissertation, University of Minnesota, 1977.

**2410.** Ridge, Martin. "Ignatius Donnelly and the Granger Movement in Minnesota." *Mississippi Valley History Review* 42 (March 1956): 693–709.

**2411.** ———. *Ignatius Donnelly: The Portrait of a Politician.* Chicago: University of Chicago Press, 1962.

**2412.** Warren, Sidney. "Ignatius Donnelly and the Populists." *Current History* 28 (June 1955): 336–342.

**DOOLITTLE, JAMES ROOD** (1815–1897) **R-WI, Senate 1857–1869.**

**2413.** Albright, Claude. "Dixon, Doolittle and Norton: The Forgotten Republican Vote on Johnson Impeachment." *Wisconsin Magazine of History* 59 (Winter 1975–1976): 91–100.

**2414.** Doolittle, James R. "Letter of Senator James Rood Doolittle." *Wisconsin Magazine of History* 6 (September 1922): 95–101.

**2415.** Mowry, Duane. "An Appreciation of James Rood Doolittle." *Wisconsin State Historical Society Proceedings* 57 (1909): 281–296.

**2416.** ———. "Robert T. Lincoln and James R. Doolittle: Interesting Political and Historical Letter from the James R. Doolittle Correspondence." *Illinois Historical Society Journal* 13 (January 1921): 464–475.

**2417.** White, Lonnie J., ed. *Chronicle of a Congressional Journey: The Doolittle Committee in the Southwest, 1865.* Boulder, CO: Pruett, 1975.

**DORN, WILLIAM JENNINGS BRYAN**
**(1916– ) D-SC, House 1947–1949, 1951–1974.**

**2418.** Dorn, William J., and Scott Derks. *Dorn of the People, a Political Way of Life.* Columbia, SC: Sandlapper, 1988.

**DORSEY, STEPHEN WALLACE**
**(1842–1916) R-AR, Senate 1873–1879.**

**2419.** Caperton, Thomas J. *Rogue: Being an Account of Life and High Times of Stephen W. Dorsey, United States Senator and New Mexico Cattle Baron.* Santa Fe: Museum of New Mexico Press, 1978.

**2420.** Lowry, Sharon K. "Mirrors and Blue Smoke: Stephen Dorsey and the Santa Fe Ring in the 1880s." *New Mexico Historical Review* 59 (October 1984): 395–409.

**2421.** ———. "Portrait of an Age: The Political Career of Stephen W. Dorsey, 1868–1889." Ph.D. dissertation, North Texas State University, 1980.

**DOTY, JAMES DUANE (1799–1865)**
**D-WI, House 1839–1841, 1849–1853.**

**2422.** Ellis, Albert G. "Life and Public Services of J. D. Doty." *Wisconsin State Historical Society Collections* 5 (1868): 369–377.

**2423.** Smith, Alice E. *James Duane Doty, Frontier Promoter.* Madison: State Historical Society of Wisconsin, 1954.

**DOUGHTON, ROBERT LEE**
**(1863–1954) D-NC, House 1911–1953.**

**2424.** Rankin, Robert S. "Robert L. Doughton." In *Public Men In and Out of Office,* edited by John T. Salter, 167–180. Chapel Hill: University of North Carolina Press, 1946.

**DOUGLAS, HELEN GAHAGAN**
**(1900–1980) D-CA, House 1945–1951.**

**2425.** Douglas, Helen G. *A Full Life.* Garden City, NY: Doubleday, 1982.

**2426.** O'Connor, Colleen M. "Imagine the Unimaginable: Helen Gahagan Douglas, Women, and the Bomb." *Southern California Quarterly* 67 (Spring 1985): 35–50.

**2427.** ———. "Through the Valley of Darkness: Helen Gahagan Douglas' Congressional Years." Ph.D. dissertation, University of California, San Diego, 1982.

**2428.** Scobie, Ingrid W. *Center Stage: The Life of Helen Gahagan Douglas.* New York: Oxford University Press, 1992.

**2429.** ———. "Helen Gahagan Douglas: Broadway Star as California Politician." *California History* 66 (December 1987): 242–261, 310–413.

**2430.** ———. "Helen Gahagan Douglas and Her 1950 Senate Race with Richard M. Nixon." *Southern California Quarterly* 58 (Spring 1976): 113–126.

**DOUGLAS, LEWIS WILLIAMS**
**(1894–1974) D-AZ, House 1927–1933.**

**2431.** Browder, Robert P. *Independent: A Biography of Lewis W. Douglas.* New York: Knopf, 1986.

**2432.** Smith, Thomas G. "From the Heart of the American Desert to the Court of St. James's: The Public Career of Lewis W. Douglas of Arizona, 1894–1974." Ph.D. dissertation, University of Connecticut, 1977.

**2433.** ———. "Lewis Douglas, Arizona Politics and the Colorado River Controversy." *Arizona and the West* 22 (Summer 1980): 125–162.

## DOUGLAS, PAUL HOWARD (1892–1976)
**D-IL, Senate 1949–1967.**

**2434.** Allen, Devere. "Economist of Tomorrow: Paul Douglas." In his *Adventurous Americans,* 179–191. New York: Farrar and Rinehart, 1932.

**2435.** Anderson, Jerry M. "Paul H. Douglas: Insurgent Senate Spokesman for Humane Causes, 1949–1963." Ph.D. dissertation, Michigan State University, 1964.

**2436.** Douglas, Paul H. *In the Fullness of Time: The Memoirs of Paul H. Douglas.* New York: Harcourt Brace Jovanovich, 1972.

**2437.** Schapsmeier, Frederick H. "Paul H. Douglas: From Pacifist to Soldier-Statesman." *Journal of the Illinois State Historical Society* 67 (June 1974): 307–323.

**2438.** Smith, Mortimer B. "Senator Paul H. Douglas." *American Mercury* 71 (July 1950): 25–32.

**2439.** Tavlas, George S. "Chicago Tradition Revisited: Some Neglected Monetary Contributions: Senator Paul Douglas (1892–1976)." *Journal of Money, Credit and Banking* 9 (November 1977): 529–535.

## DOUGLAS, STEPHEN ARNOLD
**(1813–1861) D-IL, House 1843–1847, Senate 1847–1861.**

**2440.** Bartlett, David V. "Stephen A. Douglas." In his *Presidential Candidates: Containing Sketches, Biographical, Personal and Political, of Prominent Candidates for the Presidency,* 51–94. New York: A. B. Burdick, 1859.

**2441.** Barton, William E. *Lincoln and Douglas in Charleston, an Address.* Charleston, IL: Charleston Daily Courier, 1922.

**2442.** ———. "The Lincoln-Douglas Debates." In his *The Life of Abraham Lincoln,* vol. 1, 364–403, 497–505. Indianapolis: Bobbs-Merrill, 1925.

**2443.** Bell, George W. "The Early Career of Stephen Arnold Douglas." Ph.D. dissertation, Boston University, 1911.

**2444.** Bowers, John H. *Lincoln-Douglas Debate.* Girand, KS: Haldeman-Julius, 1923.

**2445.** Brown, William G. *Stephen Arnold Douglas.* Boston: Houghton Mifflin, 1902.

**2446.** Capers, Gerald M. *Stephen Douglas: Defender of the Union.* Boston: Little, Brown, 1959.

**2447.** Carey, Rita M. *First Campaigner: Stephen A. Douglas.* New York: Vantage, 1964.

**2448.** Carr, Clark E. *Stephen A. Douglas, His Life, Public Services, Speeches and Patriotism.* Chicago: McClurg, 1909.

**2449.** Carter, Orrin N. "Lincoln and Douglas as Lawyers." *Mississippi Valley Historical Association Proceedings* 4 (1910–1911): 213–240.

**2450.** Clinton, Anita. "Stephen Arnold Douglas—His Mississippi Experience." *Journal of Mississippi History* 50 (June 1988): 56–88.

**2451.** Coleman, Charles H. *Lincoln-Douglas Debate at Charleston, Ill., Sept. 18, 1858.* Charleston: Eastern Illinois University, 1957.

**2452.** Davis, Granville D. "Douglas and the Chicago Mob." *American Historical Review* 54 (April 1949): 553–556.

**2453.** Denault, Patricia. "The Little Giant: Stephen Douglas." *American History Illustrated* 5 (October 1970): 22–33.

**2454.** Dennis, Frank L. *Lincoln-Douglas Debates.* New York: Mason and Lipscomb, 1974.

**2455.** Dickerson, Oliver M. "Stephen A. Douglas and the Split in the Democratic Party." *Mississippi Valley Historical Association Proceedings* 7 (1913/1914): 196–211.

**2456.** Douglas, Stephen A. *Letters.* Edited by Robert W. Johannsen. Champaign: University of Illinois Press, 1961.

**2457.** Flint, Henry M. *Life of Stephen A. Douglas, United States Senator from Illinois.* New York: Derby and Jackson, 1860.

**2458.** Greeman, Elizabeth D. "Stephen A. Douglas and Herschel V. Johnson: Examples of National Men in the Section Crisis of 1860." Ph.D. dissertation, Duke University, 1974.

**2459.** Heckman, Richard A. *Lincoln vs. Douglas: The Great Debates Campaign.* Washington, DC: Public Affairs Press, 1967.

**2460.** ———. "Out-of-State Influences and the Lincoln-Douglas Campaign of 1858." *Journal of Illinois State Historical Society* 59 (Spring 1966): 30–47.

**2461.** ———. "Political Fortunes of Lincoln and Douglas in 1858–1859." *Lincoln Herald* 67 (Winter 1965): 161–170.

**2462.** ———. "Some Impressions of Lincoln and Douglas During the Campaign of 1858." *Lincoln Herald* 66 (Fall 1964): 135–139.

**2463.** Herriott, Frank I. "Senator Stephen A. Douglas and the Germans in 1854." *Illinois State Historical Society Transactions* 17 (1912): 142–158.

**2464.** Howland, Louis. *Stephen A. Douglas.* New York: Scribner's, 1920.

**2465.** Hoyt, Edwin P. "Stephen A. Douglas." In his *Lost Statesmen,* 89–108. Chicago: Reilly and Lee, 1961.

**2466.** Jaffa, Harry V. *Crisis of the House Divided: An Interpretation of the Issues in the Lincoln-Douglas Debates.* Garden City, NY: Doubleday, 1959.

**2467.** Johannsen, Robert W. *The Frontier, the Union, and Stephen A. Douglas.* Urbana: University of Illinois Press, 1989.

**2468.** ———. "The Lincoln-Douglas Campaign of 1858: Background and Perspective." *Journal of the Illinois State Historical Society* 73 (Winter 1980): 242–262.

**2469.** ———. *Stephen A. Douglas.* New York: Oxford University Press, 1973.

**2470.** ———. "Stephen A. Douglas and the South." *Journal of Southern History* 33 (February 1967): 26–50.

**2471.** ———. "Stephen A. Douglas, *Harper's Magazine,* and Popular Sovereignty." *Mississippi Valley Historical Review* 45 (March 1959): 606–631.

**2472.** Johnson, Allen. *Stephen A. Douglas: A Study in American Politics.* New York: Macmillan, 1908.

**2473.** Lusk, David W. "Douglas and Lincoln—1858, Stephen A. Douglas." In his *Eighty Years of Illinois Politics and Politicians,* 45–94, 136–142. 3d ed. Springfield, IL: H. W. Bokker, 1889.

**2474.** Lynch, William O. "The Character and Leadership of Stephen A. Douglas." *Mississippi Valley Historical Association Proceedings* 10 (1920/1921): 454–467.

**2475.** Milton, George F. *The Eve of Conflict: Stephen A. Douglas and the Needless War.* Boston: Houghton Mifflin, 1934.

**2476.** Newton, Joseph F. "The Revolt of Douglas: The Great Debates: The Closing Debates." In his *Lincoln and Herndon,* 127–236. Cedar Rapids, IA: Torch Press, 1910.

**2477.** Nolan, Jeannette C. *The Little Giant: The Story of Stephen A. Douglas and Abraham Lincoln.* New York: Messner, 1942.

**2478.** Orth, Samuel P. "Stephen A. Douglas, Defender of State's Rights and of Nationalism." In his *Five American Politicians: A Study in the Evolution of American Politics,* 295–447. Cleveland, OH: Burrows Brothers, 1906.

**2479.** Reilly, Tom. "Lincoln-Douglas Debates of 1858 Forced New Role on the Press." *Journalism Quarterly* 56 (Winter 1979): 734–743.

**2480.** Schapsmeier, Edward L., and Frederick H. Schapsmeier. "Lincoln and Douglas: Their Versions of the West." *Journal of the West* 7 (October 1968): 542–552.

**2481.** Seitz, Don C. "Stephen A. Douglas." In his *The "Also Rans": Great Men Who Missed Making the Presidential Goal,* 167–191. New York: Crowell, 1928.

**2482.** Sigelschiffer, Saul. *American Conscience: The Drama of the Lincoln-Douglas Debates.* New York: Horizon Press, 1973.

**2483.** Smith, Howard W. "The Early Public Career of Stephen A. Douglas." Ph.D. dissertation, Indiana University, 1963.

**2484.** Stevens, Frank E. *Life of Stephen Arnold Douglas.* Springfield: Illinois State Historical Society, 1924.

**2485.** Stevenson, Adlai E. "Stephen A. Douglas." In his *Something of Men I Have Known,* 92–127. Chicago: A. C. McClurg, 1909.

**2486.** Temple, Wayne C. *Stephen A. Douglas, Freemason.* Bloomington: Masonic Book Club, Illinois Lodge of Research, 1982.

**2487.** Weatherman, Donald V. "Partisanship and Principles in the American Party System: A Study of the Pamphlet War between Stephen A. Douglas and Jeremiah S. Black." Ph.D. dissertation, Claremont Graduate School, 1978.

**2488.** Weisbord, Marvin R. "Democratic Demise: Stephen A. Douglas." In his *Campaigning for President: A New Look at the Road to the White House,* 33–40. Washington, DC: Public Affairs Press, 1964.

**2489.** Wells, Damon. *Stephen Douglas: The Last Years, 1857–1861.* Austin: University of Texas Press, 1971.

**2490.** Wheeler, Henry G. "Douglas, Stephen Arnold (Senator)." In his *History of Congress,* vol. 1, 60–172. New York: Harper, 1848.

**2491.** Willis, Henry P. *Stephen A. Douglas.* Philadelphia: G. W. Jacobs, 1910.

### DRAKE, CHARLES DANIEL (1811–1892) R-MO, Senate 1867–1870.

**2492.** Bourke, Paul F. "The London Ballot Society, and the Senate Debate of March 1867." *Perspectives in American History* 1 (1984): 343–357.

**2493.** March, David D. "The Life and Times of Charles Daniel Drake." Ph.D. dissertation, University of Missouri, 1949.

### DRAPER, WILLIAM FRANKLIN (1842–1910) R-MA, House 1893–1897.

**2494.** Draper, William F. *Recollections of a Varied Career.* Boston: Little, Brown, 1908.

### DRAYTON, WILLIAM HENRY (1742–1779) SC, Continental Congress 1778–1779.

**2495.** Dabney, William M. "Drayton and Laurens in the Continental Congress." *South Carolina Historical Magazine* 60 (April 1959): 74–82.

**2496.** ———. *William Henry Drayton and the American Revolution.* Albuquerque: University of New Mexico Press, 1962.

### DRINAN, ROBERT FREDERICK (1920– ) D-MA, House 1971–1981.

**2497.** Fenton, John H., and Donald M. Austern. "The Case of the Priestly Zealot: The Fourth District of Massachusetts." In *The Making of Congressmen: Seven Campaigns of 1974,* edited by Alan L. Clem, 93–106. North Scituate, MA: Duxbury Press, 1976.

**2498.** Grant, Philip A. "The Election of Father Robert F. Drinan to the House of Representatives." *Historical Journal of Massachusetts* 14 (June 1986): 114–121.

**2499.** Lapomarda, Vincent A. "A Jesuit Runs for Congress: The Rev. Robert F. Drinan, S. J. and His 1970 Campaign." *Journal of Church and State* 15 (Spring 1973): 205–222.

**2500.** Leventman, Paula G., and Seymore Leventman. "Congressman Drinan, S. J. and His Jewish Constituents." *American Jewish Historical Quarterly* 66 (December 1976): 215–248.

**2501.** Westin, Alan F. "I Gave Up Beating on the Justice Department for Lent: Conversation with Congressman R. F. Drinan." *Civil Liberties Review* 1 (Fall 1973): 75–95.

## DRYDEN, JOHN FAIRFIELD
(1839–1911) R-NJ, Senate 1902–1907.

**2502.** Reynolds, Robert D. "The 1906 Campaign to Sway Muckraking Periodicals." *Journalism Quarterly* 56 (Autumn 1979): 513–520, 589.

**2503.** Shanks, Carroll M. *Security with Opportunity and Freedom, a Brief History of the Prudential Insurance Company of America, 1875–1950.* New York: Newcomen Society in North America, 1950.

## DUANE, JAMES (1733–1797) NY,
Continental Congress 1774–1784.

**2504.** Alexander, Edward P. *A Revolutionary Conservative, James Duane of New York.* New York: Columbia University Press, 1938.

## DUBOIS, FRED THOMAS (1851–1930)
D-ID, House 1887–1890, Senate 1891–1897, 1901–1907.

**2505.** Clements, Louis J., ed. *Fred T. Dubois's "The Making of a State."* Rexburg, ID: Eastern Idaho Publishing Company, 1971.

**2506.** Cook, Rufus G. "The Political Suicide of Senator Fred T. DuBois of Idaho." *Pacific Northwest Quarterly* 60 (October 1969): 193–198.

**2507.** Graff, Leo W., Jr. "Fred T. DuBois and the Silver Issue, 1896." *Pacific Northwest Quarterly* 53 (October 1962): 138–144.

**2508.** ———. *The Senatorial Career of Fred T. DuBois of Idaho, 1890–1907.* New York: Garland Publications, 1988.

**2509.** Wells, Merle W. "Fred T. DuBois and the Idaho Progressives." *Idaho Yesterday* 4 (Summer 1960): 24–31.

## DUER, WILLIAM (1805–1879) W-NY,
House 1847–1851.

**2510.** Jones, Robert F. "The Public Career of William Duer: Rebel, Federalist Politician, Entrepreneur and Speculator 1775–1792." Ph.D. dissertation, University of Notre Dame, 1967.

## DULLES, JOHN FOSTER (1888–1959)
R-NY, Senate 1949.

**2511.** Beal, John R. *John Foster Dulles: A Biography.* New York: Harper and Row, 1957.

**2512.** ———. *John Foster Dulles: 1888–1959.* Rev. ed. New York: Harper and Row, 1959.

**2513.** Bell, Coral. "The Diplomacy of Mr. Dulles." *International Journal* 20 (Winter 1964–1965): 90–96.

**2514.** Berding, Andrew H. *Dulles on Diplomacy.* Princeton, NJ: Van Nostrand, 1965.

**2515.** Challener, Richard D. "John Foster Dulles: The Moralist Armed." *Proceedings of the Fourth Military History Symposium* (1973): 1431–1461.

**2516.** Cheng, Peter P. "A Study of John Foster Dulles: Diplomatic Strategy in the Far East." Ph.D. dissertation, Southern Illinois University, 1964.

**2517.** Comfort, Mildred H. *John Foster Dulles, Peacemaker: A Biographical Sketch of the Former Secretary of State.* Minneapolis, MN: Denison, 1960.

**2518.** Drummond, Roscoe, and Gaston Coblentz. *Duel at the Brink: John Foster Dulles' Command of American Power.* Garden City, NY: Doubleday, 1960.

**2519.** Dulles, Eleanor L. *American Foreign Policy in the Making.* New York: Harper and Row, 1968.

**2520.** ———. *John Foster Dulles: The Last Year.* New York: Harcourt, 1963.

**2521.** Dulles, John F. *The Spiritual Legacy of John Foster Dulles: Selections from His Articles and Addresses.* Philadelphia: Westminster, 1960.

**2522.** Dulles, Michael G. *John Foster Dulles: A Statesman and His Time.* The Hague: Nijhoff, 1972.

**2523.** Finer, Herman. *Dulles Over Suez: The Theory and Practice of His Diplomacy.* Chicago: Quadrangle Books, 1964.

**2524.** Gerson, Louis L. *John Foster Dulles.* New York: Cooper Square, 1967.

**2525.** Gilbert, Jerry D. "John Foster Dulles' Perceptions of the People's Republic of China: A Study of Belief Systems and Perception in the Analysis of Foreign Policy Decision-Making." Ph.D. dissertation, Texas Tech University, 1973.

**2526.** Goold-Adams, Richard J. *John Foster Dulles: A Reappraisal.* New York: Appleton, 1962.

**2527.** ———. *The Time of Power: A Reappraisal of John Foster Dulles.* London: Weidenfield, 1962.

**2528.** Guhin, Michael A. *John Foster Dulles: A Statesman and His Times.* New York: Columbia University Press, 1972.

**2529.** Harsch, Joseph C. "John Foster Dulles: A Very Complicated Man." *Harper's* 213 (September 1956): 27–34.

**2530.** Heller, Deane F., and David A. Heller. *John Foster Dulles, Soldier for Peace.* New York: Rinehart and Winston, 1960.

**2531.** Holsti, Ole R. "The Belief System and National Images: John Foster Dulles and the Soviet Union." Ph.D. dissertation, Stanford University, 1962.

**2532.** ———. "The Operational Code Approach to the Study of Political Leaders: John Foster Dulles' Philosophical and Instrumental Beliefs." *Canadian Journal of Political Science* 3 (March 1970): 123–137.

**2533.** Hoopes, Townsend. *Devil and John Foster Dulles.* Boston: Little, Brown, 1973.

**2534.** ———. "God and John Foster Dulles." *Foreign Policy* 13 (Winter 1973/1974): 154–177.

**2535.** Hostetter, John H. "John Foster Dulles and the French Defeat in Indochina." Ph.D. dissertation, Rutgers University, 1972.

**2536.** Immerman, Richard H. *John Foster Dulles and the Diplomacy of the Cold War: A Reappraisal.* Princeton, NJ: Princeton University Press, 1990.

**2537.** Jones, Henry P. "John Foster Dulles and United States Involvement in Vietnam." Ph.D. dissertation, University of Oklahoma, 1972.

**2538.** Joynt, Carey B. "John Foster Dulles and the Suez Crisis." In *Statesmen and Statecraft of the Modern West,* edited by Gerald H. Grob, 203–250. Barre, MA: Barre Publishers, 1967.

**2539.** Keim, Albert N. "John Foster Dulles and the Protestant World Order Movement on the Eve of World War II." *Journal of Church and State* 21 (Winter 1979): 73–89.

**2540.** Ladenburger, John F. "The Philosophy of International Politics of John Foster Dulles, 1919–1952." Ph.D. dissertation, University of Connecticut, 1969.

**2541.** Lead, Daniel. "Dulles at the Brink: Some Diverse Reactions from 10 Years Ago." *Journalism Quarterly* 43 (Autumn 1966): 547–550.

**2542.** May, Joseph T. "John Foster Dulles and the European Defense Community." Ph.D. dissertation, Kent State University, 1969.

**2543.** Monroe, Elizabeth. "John Foster Dulles and the Middle East: Appraisal of the Late Secretary of State's Accomplishments." *Western World* 2 (August 1959): 41–44.

**2544.** Morgenthau, Hans J. "John Foster Dulles." In *Uncertain Tradition: American Secretaries of State in the Twentieth Century,* edited by Norman A. Graebner, 289–308. New York: McGraw, 1961.

**2545.** Mosley, Leonard. *Dulles: A Biography of Eleanor, Allen, and John Foster Dulles and Their Family Network.* New York: Dial, 1978.

**2546.** Mulder, John M. "The Moral World of John Foster Dulles: A Presbyterian Layman and International Affairs." *Journal of Presbyterian History* 49 (Summer 1971): 157–182.

**2547.** Newcomer, James R. "Acheson, Dulles, and Rusk: Information, Coherence and Organization in the Department of State." Ph.D. dissertation, Stanford University, 1976.

**2548.** Nimer, Benjamin. "Dulles, Suez, and Democratic Policy." *Western Political Quarterly* 12 (September 1959): 784–798.

**2549.** Nixon, Richard M. "Appreciation of John Foster Dulles." In *Life: Great Reading from Life,* 433–436. New York: Harper and Row, 1960.

**2550.** Parmet, Herbert S. "Power and Reality: John Foster Dulles and Political Diplomacy." In *Makers of American Diplomacy,* edited by Frank J. Merli and Theodore A. Wilson, 589–619. New York: Scribner's, 1974.

**2551.** Peeters, Paul. "John Foster Dulles: The Man and His Work." *Modern Age* 4 (Summer 1960): 235–242.

**2552.** Pruessen, Ronald W. *John Foster Dulles: The Road to Power.* New York: Free Press, 1982.

**2553.** ———. "Woodrow Wilson to John Foster Dulles: A Legacy." *Princeton University Library Chronicle* 34 (Winter 1973): 109–130.

**2554.** Randall, Clarence B. "John Foster Dulles." In his *Adventures in Friendship,* 51–58. Boston: Little, Brown, 1965.

**2555.** Ruskoff, Bennett C. "Eisenhower, Dulles and the Quemoy-Matsu Crisis, 1954–1955." *Political Science Quarterly* 96 (Fall 1981): 465–480.

**2556.** Smith, Gaddis. "The Shadow of John Foster Dulles." *Foreign Affairs* 52 (January 1974): 403–408.

**2557.** Stang, Alan. *Actor: The True Story of John Foster Dulles, Secretary of State, 1953–1959.* Belmont, MA: Western Islands, 1968.

**2558.** Stassen, Glen H. "Individual Preference versus Role-Constraint in Policy-Making: Senatorial Response to Secretaries Acheson and Dulles." *World Politics* 25 (October 1972): 96–119.

**2559.** Thomas, Ivor B. "Unfair to Foster Dulles?" *Twentieth Century* 177 (1969): 39–40.

**2560.** Thompson, Dean K. "World Community Epitomized: Henry Pitney Van Dusen on John Foster Dulles and Dag Hammarskjold." *Journal of Presbyterian History* 48 (Winter 1970): 293–315.

**2561.** Toulouse, Mark G. *The Transformation of John Foster Dulles: From Prophet of Realism to Priest of Nationalism.* Macon, GA: Mercer University Press, 1985.

**2562.** Van Dusen, Henry P., ed. *The Spiritual Legacy of John Foster Dulles.* Philadelphia: Westminster, 1960.

**2563.** Wright, Esmond. "Foreign Policy Since Dulles." *Political Quarterly* 33 (April/June 1962): 114–128.

## DUNN, WILLIAM McKEE (1814–1887)
R-IN, House 1859–1863.

**2564.** Woollen, William W. *William McKee Dunn, Brigadier-General, U.S.A.: A Memoir.* New York: Putnam's, 1892.

**du PONT, HENRY ALGERNON**
(1838–1926) R-DE, Senate 1906–1917.

**2565.** Johnson, William G. "The Senatorial Career of Henry Algernon du Pont." *Delaware History* 13 (April 1969): 234–251.

**du PONT, THOMAS COLEMAN**
(1863–1930) R-DE, Senate 1921–1922, 1925–1928.

**2566.** Rae, John B. "Coleman du Pont and His Road." *Delaware History* 16 (Spring/Summer 1975): 171–183.

**2567.** Redmond, George F. "T. Coleman du Pont." In his *Financial Giants of America,* vol. 2, 25–35. Boston: Stratford Company, 1922.

**DURKIN, JOHN ANTHONY** (1936– ) D-NH, Senate 1975–1980.

**2568.** Kuter, Luis. "Due Process in the Contested New Hampshire Senate Election: Fact, Fiction or Farce." *New England Law Review* 11 (Fall 1975): 25–54.

**2569.** Tibbetts, Donn. *The Closest U.S. Senate Race in History: Durkin v. Wyman.* Manchester, NH: Donn Tibbetts and J. W. Cummings Enterprises, 1976.

**DUVAL, WILLIAM POPE** (1784–1854) R-KY, House 1813–1815.

**2570.** Snyder, Frank L. "William Pope DuVal: An Extraordinary Folklorist." *Florida Historical Quarterly* 69 (October 1990): 195–212.

**DUVALL, GABRIEL** (1752–1844) R-MD, House 1794–1796.

**2571.** Currie, David P. "The Most Insignificant Justice: A Preliminary Inquiry." *University of Chicago Law Review* 50 (Spring 1983): 466–480.

**DYER, ELIPHALET** (1721–1807) CT, Continental Congress 1774–1779, 1780–1783.

**2572.** Miller, Francis T., ed. "The Expenses of a Congressman in 1777." *Connecticut Magazine* 10 (January/March 1906): 28–32.

**2573.** Morris, Richard B., ed. "Eliphalet Dyer: Connecticut Revolutionist." In his *The Era of the American Revolution,* 290–304. New York: Columbia University Press, 1939.

**2574.** Willingham, William F. *Connecticut Revolutionary.* Hartford: American Revolutionary Bicentennial Commission of Connecticut, 1977.

≈⬦

**EAGLETON, THOMAS FRANCIS** (1929– ) D-MO, Senate 1968–1987.

**2575.** Altheide, David L. "Mental Illness and the Law: The Eagleton Story." *Sociology and Social Research* 61 (January 1977): 138–155.

**2576.** Barzman, Sol. "The Eagleton Affair." In his *Madmen and Geniuses: The Vice-Presidents of the United States,* 301–306. Chicago: Follett ,1974.

**2577.** Bormann, Ernest G. "Eagleton Affair: A Fantasy Theme Analysis." *Quarterly Journal of Speech* 59 (April 1973): 143–159.

**2578.** Einsiedel, Edna F. "Television Network News Coverage of the Eagleton Affair: A Case Study." *Journalism Quarterly* 52 (Spring 1975): 56–60.

**2579.** MacDonald, A. P., and Ranjit K. Majumder. "On the Resolution and Tolerance of Cognitive Inconsistency in Another Naturally Occurring Event: Attitudes and Beliefs Following the Senator Eagleton Incident." *Journal of Applied Social Psychology* 3 (April 1973): 132–143.

**EASTLAND, JAMES OLIVER** (1904–1986) D-MS, Senate 1941, 1943–1978.

**2580.** Schlauch, Wolfgang. "Representative William Colmer and Senator James O. Eastland and the Reconstruction of Germany, 1945." *Journal of Mississippi History* 34 (August 1972): 193–213.

**EATON, CHARLES AUBREY**
(1868–1953) R-NJ, House 1925–1953.

**2581.** Kerr, J. Ernest. "Dr. Charles A. Eaton: Congressional Foreign Affairs Committee Chairman." In his *Imprint of the Maritimes*, 85–86. Boston: Christopher Publishing House, 1959.

**EATON, JOHN HENRY (1790–1856)**
R-TN, Senate 1818–1821, 1821–1829.

**2582.** Lowe, Gabriel L. "John H. Eaton, Jackson's Campaign Manager." *Tennessee Historical Quarterly* 11 (June 1952): 99–147.

**EDGE, WALTER EVANS (1873–1956)**
R-NJ, Senate 1919–1929.

**2583.** Edge, Walter E. *A Jersey Man's Journal: Fifty Years of American Business and Politics.* Princeton, NJ: Princeton University Press, 1948.

**EDGERTON, SIDNEY (1818–1900)**
R-OH, House 1859–1863.

**2584.** Plassmann, M. E. "Biographical Sketch of Hon. Sidney Edgerton, First Territorial Governor." *Montana Historical Society Contributions* 3 (1900): 331–340.

**EDMONDSON, JAMES HOWARD**
(1925–1971) D-OK, Senate 1963–1964.

**2585.** Davis, Billy J. "J. Howard Edmondson: A Political Biography." Ph.D. dissertation, Texas Tech University, 1980.

**EDMUNDS, GEORGE FRANKLIN**
(1828–1919) R-VT, Senate 1866–1891.

**2586.** Adler, Selig. "The Senatorial Career of George Franklin Edmunds, 1866–1891." Ph.D. dissertation, University of Illinois, 1934.

**2587.** Kuntz, Norbert. "Edmunds' Contrivance: Senator George Edmunds of Vermont and the Electoral Compromise of 1877." *Vermont History* 38 (Autumn 1970): 305–315.

**2588.** Welch, Richard E. "George Edmunds of Vermont: Republican Half-Breed." *Vermont History* 36 (Spring 1968): 64–73.

**EDWARDS, EDWARD IRVING**
(1863–1931) D-NJ, Senate 1923–1929.

**2589.** Stickle, Warren E. "Edward I. Edwards and the Urban Coalition of 1919." *New Jersey History* 90 (Summer 1972): 83–96.

**EDWARDS, MARVIN HENRY "MICKEY" (1937– ) R-OK, House 1977–1993.**

**2590.** Edwards, Mickey. *Behind Enemy Lines.* Chicago: Regnery Gateway, 1983.

**EDWARDS, NINIAN (1775–1833) R-IL, Senate 1818–1824.**

**2591.** Bakalis, Michael J. "Ninian Edwards and Territorial Politics in Illinois: 1775–1818." Ph.D. dissertation, Northwestern University, 1966.

**2592.** Edwards, Ninian W. *History of Illinois from 1778 to 1833: And Life and Times of Ninian Edwards.* Springfield: Illinois State Journal, 1870.

**2593.** "Ninian Edwards." In *Bench and Bar of Illinois: Historical and Reminiscent*, edited by John M. Palmer, vol. 2, 1139–1156. Chicago: Lewis, 1899.

**2594.** Pease, Theodore C. "The War on Ninian Edwards." In his *The Frontier State, 1818–1848*, 92–113. Springfield: Illinois Centennial Commission, 1918.

**2595.** Wixon, Richard L. "Ninian Edwards: A Founding Father of Illinois." Ph.D. dissertation, Southern Illinois University at Carbondale, 1983.

**ELKINS, STEPHEN BENTON**
(1841–1911) R-NM/WV, House (NM)
1873–1877, Senate (WV) 1895–1911.

**2596.** Lambert, Oscar D. *Stephen Benton Elkins.* Pittsburgh, PA: University of Pittsburgh, 1955.

**2597.** Marquess, Earl L. "The Political Career of Stephen Benton Elkins, Businessman in Politics." Master's thesis, Indiana University, 1951.

**2598.** Williams, John A. "Davis and Elkins of West Virginia: Businessmen in Politics." Ph.D. dissertation, Yale University, 1967.

**2599.** ———. "New York's First Senator from West Virginia: How Stephen B. Elkins Found a New Political Home." *West Virginia History* 31 (January 1970): 73–87.

**ELLENDER, ALLEN JOSEPH**
(1890–1972) D-LA, Senate 1937–1972.

**2600.** Becnel, Thomas A. "Fulbright of Arkansas v. Ellender of Louisiana: The Politics of Sugar and Rice, 1937–1974." *Arkansas Historical Quarterly* 43 (Winter 1984): 289–303.

**2601.** ———. "Louisiana Senator Allen J. Ellender and IWW Leader Covington Hall: An Agrarian Dichotomy." *Louisiana History* 23 (Summer 1982): 259–275.

**ELLERY, WILLIAM** (1727–1820) RI,
Continental Congress 1776–1781, 1783–1785.

**2602.** Sparks, Jared, ed. "William Ellery." In *American Biography,* vol. 9, 131–205. New York: Harper, 1902.

**ELLIOTT, CARL ATWOOD** (1913– )
D-AL, House 1949–1965.

**2603.** Elliott, Carl, and Mike D'Orso. *The Cost of Courage: The Journey of an American Congressman.* New York: Doubleday, 1992.

**2604.** Silveri, Louis. "Pushing the Fence Back Too Far: The Defeat of Congressman Carl Elliott in 1964." *Alabama Review* 45 (January 1992): 3–17.

**ELLIOTT, JAMES** (1775–1839) F-VT House
1803–1809.

**2605.** Huddleston, Eugene L. "Indians and Literature of the Federalist Era: The Case of James Elliott." *New England Quarterly* 44 (June 1971): 221–237.

**ELLIOTT, ROBERT BROWN**
(1842–1884) R-SC, House 1871–1874.

**2606.** Christopher, Maurine. "Robert Brown Elliott/South Carolina." In her *Black Americans in Congress,* 69–76. Rev. ed. New York: Thomas Y. Crowell, 1976.

**2607.** Lamson, Peggy. *The Glorious Failure: Black Congressman Robert Brown Elliott and the Reconstruction of South Carolina.* New York: Norton, 1973.

**2608.** Miller, M. Sammy. "Elliott of South Carolina: Lawyer and Legislator." *Negro History Bulletin* 36 (May 1973): 112–114.

**2609.** Simmons, William J. "Robert B. Elliott." In his *Men of Mark,* 310–314. Cleveland, OH: Rewell, 1887.

**ELLIS, POWHATAN** (1790–1863) MS,
Senate 1825–1826, 1827–1832.

**2610.** Cobb, Edwin L. "Powhatan Ellis of Mississippi: A Reappraisal." *Journal of Mississippi History* 30 (May 1968): 91–110.

**ELLSWORTH, OLIVER** (1745–1807) CT,
Senate 1789–1796, Continental Congress
1778–1783.

**2611.** Brown, William G. "A Continental Congressman: Oliver Ellsworth, 1777–1783." *American Historical Review* 10 (July 1905): 751–781.

**2612.** ———. "The Early Life of Oliver Ellsworth." *American Historical Review* 10 (April 1905): 534–564.

**2613.** ———. *The Life of Oliver Ellsworth.* New York: Macmillan, 1905.

**2614.** Buel, Elizabeth C. "Oliver Ellsworth." *New England Magazine* 30 (July 1904): 611–626.

**2615.** Cook, Frank G. "Oliver Ellsworth and Federation." *Atlantic Monthly* 89 (April 1902): 524–536.

**2616.** ———. "Oliver Ellsworth, 1745–1807." In *Great American Lawyers: The Lives and Influence of Judges and Lawyers Who Have Acquired Permanent National Reputation, and Have Developed the Jurisprudence of the United States,* edited by William D. Lewis, vol. 1, 305–354. Philadelphia: J. C. Winston, 1907.

**2617.** Flanders, Henry. "The Life of Oliver Ellsworth." In his *The Lives and Times of the Chief Justices of the Supreme Court of the United States.* Vol. 2, 53–276. Philadelphia: T. and J. W. Johnson, 1881.

**2618.** Jones, Francis R. "Oliver Ellsworth." *Green Bag* 13 (November 1901): 503–508.

**2619.** Lettieri, Ronald J. *Connecticut's Young Man of the Revolution, Oliver Ellsworth.* Hartford: American Revolution Bicentennial Commission of Connecticut, 1978.

**2620.** Lossing, Benson J. "Oliver Ellsworth." In his *Eminent Americans,* 102–103. New York: Hurst, 1886.

**2621.** McLachlan, James. "Oliver Ellsworth." In his *Princetonians, 1748–1768,* 555–559. Princeton, NJ: Princeton University Press, 1976.

**2622.** Perry, Benjamin F. "Oliver Ellsworth." In his *Biographic Sketches of Eminent American Statesmen,* 403–409. Philadelphia: Ferree Press, 1887.

**2623.** Raymond, Edward A. "Oliver Ellsworth and the Constitution." *Daughters of the American Revolution Magazine* 123 (March 1989): 249, 284–285, 364.

**2624.** Shepard, Henry M. "Oliver Ellsworth." *Chicago Law Times* 2 (April 1888): 109–128.

**2625.** Uhle, John B. "Oliver Ellsworth." *Current Comment* 2 (February 15, 1890): 65–76.

**2626.** Umbreit, Kenneth B. "Oliver Ellsworth." In his *Our Eleven Chief Justices,* 79–110. New York: Harper and Brothers, 1938.

**2627.** Verplanck, Julian C. "Biographical Memoir of Oliver Ellsworth." *Analectic Magazine* 3 (May 1814): 382–403.

**ELMORE, FRANKLIN HARPER (1799–1850) D-SC, House 1836–1839, Senate 1850.**

**2628.** Birney, James. *Correspondence between the Honorable F. H. Elmore and James G. Birney.* New York: Arno Press, 1969.

**ENGLE, CLAIR (1911–1964) D-CA, House 1943–1959, Senate 1959–1964.**

**2629.** Sayles, Stephen. "Clair Engle and His Political Development in Tehama County, 1911–1944." *California Historical Quarterly* 54 (Winter 1975): 293–314.

**2630.** ———. *Clair Engle: The Forging of a Public Servant: A Study of Sacramento Valley Politics, 1933–1943.* Chico: Association for Northern California Records and Research, 1976.

**2631.** ———. "Clair Engle and the Politics of California Reclamation, 1943–1960." Ph.D. dissertation, University of New Mexico, 1978.

**ENGLISH, THOMAS DUNN (1819–1902) D-NJ, House 1891–1895.**

**2632.** Moss, Sidney P. *Poe's Major Crisis: His Libel Suit and New York's Literary World.* Durham, NC: Duke University Press, 1970.

**ENGLISH, WILLIAM HAYDEN (1822–1896) D-IN, House 1853–1861.**

**2633.** Cole, J. R. *The Life and Public Services of Winfield Scott Hancock, Major-General, U.S.A., Also, the Life and Services of Hon. William H. English.* Cincinnati, OH: Douglass Brothers, 1880.

**2634.** Schimmel, Elliot L. "William H. English and the Politics of Self-Deception, 1845–1861." Ph.D. dissertation, Florida State University, 1986.

**ERVIN, SAMUEL JAMES, JR.**
**(1896–1985) D-NC, House 1946–1947,**
**Senate 1954–1974.**

**2635.** Clancy, Paul R. *Just a Country Lawyer: A Biography of Senator Sam Ervin.* Bloomington: Indiana University Press, 1974.

**2636.** Dabney, Dick. *A Good Man: The Life of Sam J. Ervin.* Boston: Houghton Mifflin, 1976.

**2637.** Dash, Samuel. *Chief Counsel: Inside the Ervin Committee: The Untold Story of Watergate.* New York: Random House, 1976.

**2638.** Ervin, Jean C. *The Sam Ervin I Know.* Chapel Hill: North Carolinian Society, 1980.

**2639.** Ervin, Samuel J. *Humor of a Country Lawyer.* Chapel Hill: University of North Carolina Press, 1983.

**2640.** ———. *Preserving the Constitution: The Autobiography of Sam Ervin.* Charlottesville, VA: Michie, 1984.

**2641.** ———. *Quotations from Chairman Sam: The Wit and Wisdom of Senator Sam Ervin.* Edited by Herb Altman. New York: Harper and Row, 1973.

**2642.** ———. *The Whole Truth: The Watergate Conspiracy.* New York: Random House, 1980.

**2643.** Stem, Thad, and Alan Butler. *Senator Sam Ervin's Best Stories.* Durham, NC: Moore, 1973.

**2644.** Van Sickle, Clifford K. "The Oral Communication of Senator Sam J. Ervin, Jr. in the Watergate Hearings: A Study in Consistency." Ph.D. dissertation, Michigan State University, 1976.

**ETHERIDGE, EMERSON (1819–1902)**
**O-TN, House 1853–1857, 1859–1861.**

**2645.** Belz, Herman. "Etheridge Conspiracy of 1863: A Projected Conservative Coup." *Journal of Southern History* 36 (November 1970): 549–567.

**2646.** Maness, Lonnie E. "Emerson Etheridge and the Union." *Tennessee History Quarterly* 48 (Summer 1989): 97–110.

**EUSTIS, GEORGE, JR. (1828–1872)**
**AP-LA, House 1855–1859.**

**2647.** Tregle, Joseph G. "George Eustis, Jr., Non-mythic Southerner." *Louisiana History* 16 (Fall 1975): 383–390.

**EVANS, DANIEL JACKSON (1925– )**
**R-WA, Senate 1983–1989.**

**2648.** Warren, James R. "The Pioneer Roots of Daniel Jackson Evans." *Portage* 10, no. 1 (1989): 9–12, 31.

**EVANS, HENRY CLAY (1843–1921) R-TN,**
**House 1889–1891.**

**2649.** Seehorn, John B. "The Life and Public Career of Henry Clay Evans." Master's thesis, University of Tennessee, 1970.

**EVARTS, WILLIAM MAXWELL**
**(1818–1901) R-NY, Senate 1885–1891.**

**2650.** Barrows, Chester L. *William M. Evarts: Lawyer, Diplomat, Statesman.* Chapel Hill: University of North Carolina Press, 1941.

**2651.** Bowers, Claude G., and Helen D. Reid. "William M. Evarts." In *The American Secretaries of State and Their Diplomacy,* edited by Samuel F. Bemis, vol. 7, 215–259. New York: Knopf, 1928.

**2652.** Dyer, Brainerd. *The Public Career of William M. Evarts.* Berkeley: University of California Press, 1933.

**2653.** Evarts, William M. *Arguments and Speeches.* Edited by Sherman Evarts. 3 vols. New York: Macmillan, 1919.

**2654.** Pennanen, Gary A. "The Foreign Policy of William Maxwell Evarts." Ph.D. dissertation, University of Wisconsin, 1969.

## EVERETT, EDWARD (1794–1865) W-MA, House 1825–1835, Senate 1853–1854.

**2655.** Brooks, Van W. "George Ticknor's Wanderjahre." In his *The Flowering of New England,* 73–88. New York: Dutton, 1936.

**2656.** Brown, Thomas H. "Edward Everett and the Constitution Union Party of 1860." *Historical Journal of Massachusetts* 11 (June 1983): 69–81.

**2657.** Frotingham, Paul R. *Edward Everett: Orator and Statesman.* Boston: Houghton Mifflin, 1925.

**2658.** Geiger, John O. "Scholar Meets John Bull: Edward Everett as United States Minister to England, 1841–1845." *New England Quarterly* 49 (December 1976): 577–595.

**2659.** Grattan, Thomas C. "Edward Everett." In his *Civilized America,* vol. 1, 137–150. London: Bradbury and Evans, 1859.

**2660.** Hale, Edward E. "Edward Everett." In his *Memories of a Hundred Years.* Vol. 2, 9–25. New York: Macmillan, 1902.

**2661.** Horn, Stuart J. "Edward Everett and American Nationalism." Ph.D. dissertation, City University of New York, 1973.

**2662.** Reid, Ronald F. "Edward Everett: Rhetorician of Nationalism, 1824–1855." *Quarterly Journal of Speech* 42 (October 1956): 273–282.

**2663.** ———. *Edward Everett: Unionist Orator.* New York: Greenwood, 1990.

**2664.** Soulis, George C. "Everett-Kapodistrias Correspondence." *Journal of Modern History* 26 (September 1954): 272–273.

**2665.** Sterns, Foster. "Edward Everett." In *The American Secretaries of State and Their Diplomacy,* edited by Samuel F. Bemis, vol. 6, 115–141. New York: Knopf, 1928.

**2666.** Varg, Paul. *Edward Everett: The Intellectual in the Turmoil of Politics.* Selinsgrove, PA: Susquehanna University Press, 1992.

**2667.** Whipple, Edwin P. "Edward Everett." In his *Character and Characteristic Men,* 243–252. Boston: Houghton Mifflin, 1884.

**2668.** Willson, Beckles. "Everett and McLane (1841–1846)." In his *America's Ambassadors to England (1785–1928),* 229–241. New York: Frederick A. Stokes, 1929.

**2669.** Yanikoski, Richard A. "Edward Everett and the Advancement of Higher Education and Adult Learning in Antebellum Massachusetts." Ph.D. dissertation, University of Chicago, 1987.

## EVINS, JOSEPH LANDON (1910–1984) D-TN, House 1947–1977.

**2670.** Graves, Susan B. *Evins of Tennessee: Twenty-Five Years in Congress.* New York: Popular Library, 1971.

## EWING, THOMAS (1789–1871) W-OH, Senate 1831–1837, 1850–1851.

**2671.** Gilbert, Abby L. "Thomas Ewing, Sr.: Ohio's Advocate for a National Bank." *Ohio History* 82 (Winter/Spring 1973): 5–24.

**2672.** Sherman, Ellen B., ed. *Memorial of Thomas Ewing of Ohio.* New York: Catholic Publication Society, 1873.

**2673.** Zsoldos, Sylvia. "Thomas Ewing, Sr., A Political Biography." Ph.D. dissertation, University of Delaware, 1933.

## EWING, THOMAS, Jr. (1829–1896) D-OH, House 1877–1881.

**2674.** Miller, Paul I. "Thomas Ewing, Last of the Whigs." Ph.D. dissertation, Ohio State University, 1934.

**2675.** Taylor, David G. "The Business and Political Career of Thomas Ewing, Jr.: A Study of Frustrated Ambition." Ph.D. dissertation, University of Kansas, 1970.

ح‍

**FAIR, JAMES GRAHAM (1831–1894)**
**D-NE, Senate 1881–1887.**

**2676.** Baur, John E. "Senator's Happy Thought." *American West* 10 (January 1973): 35–39, 62–63.

**2677.** Johnson, Kenneth M. *Fair Will Case.* Los Angeles: Dawsons Book Shop, 1964.

**2678.** Lewis, Oscar. "Fair." In his *Silver Kings: The Lives and Times of Mackay, Fair, Flood, and O'Brien Lords of the Nevada Comstock Lode,* 115–216. New York: Knopf, 1947.

**FAIRBANKS, CHARLES WARREN**
**(1852–1918) R-IN, Senate 1897–1905.**

**2679.** Barzman, Sol. "Charles W. Fairbanks." In his *Madmen and Geniuses: The Vice-Presidents of the United States,* 175–182. Chicago: Follett, 1974.

**2680.** Gould, Lewis L., ed. "Charles Warren Fairbanks and the Republican National Convention of 1900: A Memoir." *Indiana Magazine of History* 77 (December 1981): 358–372.

**2681.** Rissler, Herbert J. "Charles Warren Fairbanks: Conservative Hoosier." Ph.D. dissertation, Indiana University, 1961.

**2682.** Smith, William H. *The Life and Speeches of Hon. Charles Warren Fairbanks, Republican Candidate for Vice-President.* Indianapolis: W. B. Burford, 1904.

**FAIRFIELD, JOHN (1797–1847) D-ME,**
**House 1835–1838, Senate 1843–1847.**

**2683.** Fairfield, John. *The Letters of John Fairfield.* Edited by Arthur G. Staples. Lewiston, ME: Lewiston Journal, 1922.

**FALL, ALBERT BACON (1861–1944)**
**R-NM, Senate 1912–1921.**

**2684.** Busch, Francis X. "Trial of Albert B. Fall and Others." In his *Enemies of State,* 91–170. Indianapolis: Bobbs-Merrill, 1954.

**2685.** Fall, Albert B. *Memoirs of Albert B. Fall.* Edited by David H. Stratton. El Paso, TX: Western College Press, 1966.

**2686.** Gilderhus, Mark T. "Senator Albert B. Fall and the Plot against Mexico." *New Mexico Historical Review* 48 (October 1973): 299–311.

**2687.** Ravage, Marcus E. *The Story of Teapot Dome.* New York: Republic Publishing Company, 1924.

**2688.** Stratton, David H. "Albert B. Fall and the Teapot Dome Affair." Ph.D. dissertation, University of Colorado, 1955.

**2689.** ———. "Two Western Senators and Teapot Dome: Thomas J. Walsh and Albert B. Fall." *Pacific Northwest Quarterly* 65 (April 1974): 57–65.

**2690.** Trow, Clifford W. "Senator Albert B. Fall and Mexican Affairs: 1912–1921." Ph.D. dissertation, University of Colorado, 1966.

**2691.** ———. "'Tired of Waiting': Senator Albert B. Fall's Alternative to Woodrow Wilson's Mexican Policies, 1920–1921." *New Mexico Historical Review* 57 (April 1982): 159–182.

**2692.** Weisner, Herman B. *The Politics of Justice, A. B. Fall and the Teapot Dome Scandal: A New Perspective.* Albuquerque, NM: Creative Designs, 1988.

**2693.** Werner, Morris R., and John Starr. *Teapot Dome.* New York: Viking, 1959.

**FARLEY, JAMES INDUS (1871–1948)**
**D-IN, House 1933–1939.**

**2694.** Syrett, John. "Jim Farley and Carter Glass: Allies against a Third Term." *Prologue* 15 (Summer 1983): 88–102.

## FARWELL, CHARLES BENJAMIN
(1823–1903) R-IL, House 1871–1876,
1881–1883, Senate 1887–1891.

**2695.** Wallis, George A. "The Farwells of XIT." In his *Cattle Kings of the Staked Plains,* 30–41. Dallas, TX: American Guild Press, 1957.

## FAULKNER, CHARLES JAMES
(1847–1929) D-WV, Senate 1887–1899.

**2696.** McVeigh, Donald R. "Charles James Faulkner: Reluctant Rebel." Ph.D. dissertation, West Virginia University, 1955.

## FAUNTROY, WALTER EDWARD
(1933– ) D-DC, 1971–1991.

**2697.** Christopher, Maurine. "Walter E. Fauntroy/District of Columbia." In her *Black Americans in Congress,* 289. Rev. ed. New York: Thomas Y. Crowell, 1976.

## FEINSTEIN, DIANNE (1933– ) D-CA,
Senate 1992– .

**2698.** Roberts, Jerry. *Dianne Feinstein: Never Let Them See You Cry.* New York: HarperCollins, 1994.

## FELL, JOHN (1721–1798) NJ, Continental
Congress 1778–1780.

**2699.** Fell, John. *Delegate from New Jersey: The Journal of John Fell.* Edited by Donald W. Whisenhunt. Port Washington, NY: Kennikat, 1973.

## FELTON, REBECCA LATIMER
(1835–1930) D-GA, Senate 1922.

**2700.** Eaton, Clement. "Breaking a Path for the Liberation of Women in the South." *Georgia Review* 28 (Summer 1974): 190–191.

**2701.** Felton, Rebecca L. *Country Life in Georgia in the Days of My Youth.* Atlanta, GA: Index Printing Company, 1919.

**2702.** Kaufman, Janet E. "Rebecca Latimer Felton." In *American Women Writers,* edited by Lina Mainiero, vol. 2, 21–23. New York: Frederick Ungar, 1980.

**2703.** Talmadge, John E. "Rebecca Latimer Felton." In *Georgians in Profile,* edited by Horace Montgomery, 277–302. Athens: University of Georgia Press, 1958.

**2704.** ———. *Rebecca Latimer Felton: Nine Stormy Decades.* Athens: University of Georgia Press, 1960.

## FELTON, WILLIAM HARRELL
(1823–1909) ID-GA, House 1875–1881.

**2705.** Jones, George L. "William H. Felton and the Independent Democratic Movement in Georgia, 1870–1890." Ph.D. dissertation, University of Georgia, 1971.

**2706.** Roberts, William P. "The Public Career of Dr. William Harrell Felton." Ph.D. dissertation, University of North Carolina, 1953.

## FENTON, REUBEN EATON (1819–1885)
R-NY, House 1853–1855, 1857–1864, Senate 1869–1875.

**2707.** McMahon, Helen. "Reuben Eaton Fenton." Ph.D. dissertation, Cornell University, 1939.

## FENWICK, MILLICENT HAMMOND
(1910–1992) R-NJ, House 1975–1983.

**2708.** Fenwick, Millicent. *Speaking Up.* New York: Harper & Row, 1982.

**2709.** Lamson, Peggy. "Millicent Fenwick: Congresswoman from New Jersey." In her *In the Vanguard,* 1–36. Boston: Houghton Mifflin, 1979.

## FERRARO, GERALDINE ANNE (1935– )
D-NY, House 1979–1985.

**2710.** Breslin, Rosemary, and Joshua Hammer. *Gerry!: A Woman Making History.* New York: Pinnacle Books, 1984.

**2711.** Ferraro, Geraldine. *Ferraro, My Story.* New York: Bantam Books, 1985.

**2712.** Katz, Lee M. *My Name Is Geraldine Ferraro: An Unauthorized Biography.* New York: New American Library, 1984.

**2713.** Lawson, Don. *Geraldine Ferraro.* New York: J.-Messner, 1985.

**FESS, SIMEON DAVISON (1861–1936)**
**R-OH, House 1913–1923, Senate 1923–1935.**

**2714.** Nethers, John L. "Simeon D. Fess: Educator and Politician." Ph.D. dissertation, Ohio State University, 1964.

**FESSENDEN, WILLIAM PITT**
**(1806–1869) R-ME, House 1841–1843,**
**Senate 1854–1864, 1865–1869.**

**2715.** Fessenden, Francis. *Life and Public Services of William Pitt Fessenden.* 2 vols. Boston: Houghton Mifflin, 1907.

**2716.** Jellison, Charles A. *Fessenden of Maine, Civil War Senator.* Syracuse, NY: Syracuse University Press, 1962.

**FIELD, DAVID DUDLEY (1805–1894)**
**D-NY, House 1877.**

**2717.** Field, Henry M. *The Life of David Dudley Field.* New York: Scribner's, 1898.

**2718.** Hicks, Frederick C., ed. "A Great Lawsuit and a Field Fight." In his *High Finance in the Sixties,* 351–386. New Haven, CT: Yale University Press, 1929.

**2719.** ———, ed. "The Lawyer and His Clients: The Truth of a Great Lawsuit." In his *High Finance in the Sixties,* 213–245. New Haven, CT: Yale University Press, 1929.

**FIELD, WALBRIDGE ABNER**
**(1833–1899) R-MA, House 1877–1878,**
**1879–1881.**

**2720.** Noble, John. "Memoir of Walbridge A. Field." *Massachusetts Historical Society Proceedings* 19 (1905): 61–82.

**FILLMORE, MILLARD (1800–1874)**
**W-NY, House 1833–1835, 1837–1843.**

**2721.** Barre, W. L. *The Life and Public Services of Millard Fillmore.* Buffalo, NY: Wanzer, McKim, 1856.

**2722.** Barzman, Sol. "Millard Fillmore." In his *Madmen and Geniuses: The Vice-Presidents of the United States,* 85–90. Chicago: Follett, 1974.

**2723.** Chamberlain, Ivory. *Biography of Millard Fillmore.* Buffalo, NY: Thomas and Lathrops, 1856.

**2724.** Fillmore, Millard. *Millard Fillmore Papers.* Edited by Frank H. Severance. Buffalo, NY: Buffalo Historical Society, 1907.

**2725.** Grayson, Benson L. *The Unknown President: The Administration of President Millard Fillmore.* Washington, DC: University Press of America, 1981.

**2726.** Griffs, William E. *Millard Fillmore, Constructive Statesman, Defender of the Constitution, President of the United States.* Ithaca, NY: Andrus and Church, 1915.

**2727.** Hinton, Wayne K. "Millard Fillmore, Utah's Friend in the White House." *Utah History Quarterly* 48 (Spring 1980): 112–128.

**2728.** Rayback, Robert J. "Biography of Millard Fillmore, 13th President of the United States." Ph.D. dissertation, University of Wisconsin, 1948.

**2729.** ———. *Millard Fillmore: Biography of a President.* Buffalo, NY: H. Stewart, 1959.

**2730.** Schelin, Robert C. "Millard Fillmore, Anti-Mason to Know-Nothing: A Moderate in New York Politics, 1828–1856." Ph.D. dissertation, State University of New York, 1975.

**2731.** ———. "A Whig's Final Quest: Fillmore and the Know-Nothings." *Niagara Frontier* 26 (1979): 1–11.

**2732.** Smith, Elbert B. *The Presidencies of Zachary Taylor and Millard Fillmore.*

Lawrence: University of Kansas Press, 1988.

**FINDLEY, PAUL** (1921– ) R-IL, House 1961–1983.

**2733.** Findley, Paul. *They Dare to Speak Out: People and Institutions Confront Israel's Lobby.* Westport, CT: Lawrence Hill, 1985.

**FINO, PAUL ALBERT** (1913– ) R-NY, House 1953–1968.

**2734.** Fino, Paul A. *My Life in Politics and Public Service.* Great Neck, NY: Todd & Honeywell, 1986.

**FISH, HAMILTON** (1808–1893) W-NY, House 1843–1845, Senate 1851–1857.

**2735.** Chapin, James B. "Hamilton Fish and American Expansion." In *Makers of American Diplomacy,* edited by Frank A. Merli and Theodore A. Wilson, 223–251. New York: Scribner's, 1974.

**2736.** Davis, John C. *Mr. Fish and the Alabama Claims: A Chapter in Diplomatic History.* Freeport, NY: Books for Libraries, 1969.

**2737.** Fuller, Joseph V. "Hamilton Fish." In his *The American Secretaries of State and Their Diplomacy,* edited by Samuel F. Bemis, vol. 7, 123–214. New York: Knopf, 1928.

**2738.** Nevins, Allan. *Hamilton Fish: The Inner History of the Grant Administration.* New York: Dodd, Mead, 1936.

**2739.** Spann, Edward K. "Gotham in Congress: New York's Representatives and the National Government, 1840–1854." *New York History* 67 (July 1986): 304–329.

**2740.** Vail, Robert W. "Ninety More Years of the Society's History." *New York Historical Society Quarterly* 39 (April 1955): 129–131.

**FISH, HAMILTON** (1888–1991) R-NY, House 1920–1945.

**2741.** Current, Richard N. "Hamilton Fish: 'Crusading Isolationist.'" In *Public Men In and Out of Office,* edited by John T. Salter, 210–224. Chapel Hill: University of North Carolina Press, 1946.

**2742.** Fish, Hamilton. *Memoir of an American Patriot.* Washington, DC: Regnery Gateway, 1991.

**2743.** Hanks, Richard K. "Hamilton Fish and the American Isolationism, 1920–1944." Ph.D. dissertation, University of California, Riverside, 1971.

**FISHER, GEORGE PURNELL** (1817–1899) U-DE, House 1861–1863.

**2744.** Lore, Charles B. *The Life and Character of George P. Fisher.* Wilmington: Historical Society of Delaware, 1902.

**FITCH, THOMAS** (1838–1923) R-NV, House 1869–1871.

**2745.** Fitch, Thomas. *Western Carpetbagger: The Extraordinary Memoirs of "Senator" Thomas Fitch.* Edited by Eric N. Moody. Reno: University of Nevada Press, 1978.

**FITZGERALD, JOHN FRANCIS** (1863–1950) D-MA, House 1895–1901, 1919.

**2746.** Cutler, John H. *"Honey Fitz": Three Steps to the White House: The Life and Times of John F. (Honey Fitz) Fitzgerald.* Indianapolis: Bobbs-Merrill, 1962.

**2747.** Fraser, James W. "Mayor John F. Fitzgerald and Boston's Schools, 1905–1913." *Historical Journal of Massachusetts* 12 (June 1984): 117–130.

**2748.** Goodwin, Doris K. *The Fitzgeralds and the Kennedys.* New York: Simon and Schuster, 1987.

**FITZSIMONS, THOMAS** (1741–1811) PA, House 1789–1795, Continental Congress 1782–1783.

**2749.** Schauinger, Joseph H. "The Signers of the Constitution." In his *Profiles in Action*, 36–48. Milwaukee, WI: Bruce, 1966.

**FLANDERS, BENJAMIN FRANKLIN** (1816–1896) U-LA, House 1862–1863.

**2750.** Reeves, Miriam G. "Benjamin Franklin Flanders." In her *Governors of Louisiana*, 73–74. Gretna, LA: Pelican Publishing, 1972.

**FLANDERS, RALPH EDWARD** (1880–1970) R-VT Senate 1946–1959.

**2751.** Flanders, Ralph E. *Senator from Vermont.* Boston: Little, Brown, 1961.

**2752.** Grattan, Clinton H. "Senator Flanders: Intelligent Conservative." *Harper's* 200 (January 1950): 79–86.

**2753.** Griffith, Robert W. "Ralph Flanders and the Censure of Senator Joseph R. McCarthy." *Vermont History* 39 (Winter 1971): 5–20.

**FLETCHER, DUNCAN UPSHAW** (1859–1936) D-FL, Senate 1909–1936.

**2754.** Flynt, Wayne. *Duncan Upshaw Fletcher: Dixie's Reluctant Progressive.* Tallahassee: Florida State University Press, 1971.

**2755.** ———. "Florida's 1926 Senatorial Primary." *Florida Historical Quarterly* 42 (October 1963): 142–153.

**2756.** Stephens, Gertrude H. "Senator Duncan U. Fletcher—Legislator." Master's thesis, University of Florida, 1951.

**2757.** Wells, William J. "Duncan Upshaw Fletcher: Florida's Grand Old Man." Master's thesis, Stetson University, 1942.

**FLOOD, HENRY DE LA WARR** (1865–1921) D-VA, House 1901–1921.

**2758.** Kaufman, Burton I. "Henry De La Warr Flood: A Case Study of Organization Politics in an Era of Reform." Ph.D. dissertation, Rice University, 1966.

**2759.** Treon, John A. "The Political Career of Henry De La Warr Flood: A Biographical Sketch, 1865–1921." *Essays in History* (University of Virginia) 10 (1964–1965): 44–65.

**FLOWER, ROSWELL PETTIBONE** (1835–1899) D-NY, House 1881–1883, 1889–1891.

**2760.** Collin, Charles A. "Administration of Roswell P. Flower." In his *Official New York, from Cleveland to Hughes,* edited by Charles E. Fitch, vol. 1, 103–114. New York: Hurd, 1911.

**FLOYD, JOHN** (1783–1837) R-VA, House 1817–1829.

**2761.** Ambler, Charles H. *The Life and Diary of John Floyd, Governor of Virginia, an Apostle of Secession, and the Father of the Oregon Country.* Richmond, VA: Richmond Press, 1918.

**FLOYD, WILLIAM** (1734–1821) NY, House 1789–1791, Continental Congress 1774–1776, 1779–1783.

**2762.** Sanderson, John. "William Floyd." In *Sanderson's Biography of the Signers of the Declaration of Independence,* edited by Robert T. Conrad, 261–265. Philadelphia: Thomas, Cowperthwait, 1848.

**FLYNN, DENNIS THOMAS** (1861–1939) R-OK, House 1893–1897, 1899–1903.

**2763.** Murdock, Victor. "Dennis T. Flynn." *Chronicles of Oklahoma* 18 (June 1940): 107–113.

**FOCHT, BENJAMIN KURTZ** (1863–1937)
R-PA, House 1907–1913, 1915–1923,
1933–1937.

**2764.** Baumgartner, Donald J. "Benjamin K. Focht: Union County Politician." Ph.D. dissertation, Pennsylvania State University, 1975.

**FOGARTY, JOHN EDWARD** (1913–1967)
D-RI, House 1941–1944, 1945–1967.

**2765.** Bair, Barbara. "The Full Light of This Dawn: Congressman John Fogarty and the Historical Cycle of Community Mental Health Policy in Rhode Island." *Rhode Island History* 41 (November 1982): 126–138.

**2766.** Healey, James S. *John E. Fogarty: Political Leadership for Library Development.* Metuchen, NJ: Scarecrow, 1974.

**FOLEY, THOMAS STEPHEN** (1929–  )
D-WA, House 1965–1995.

**2767.** Bentley, Judith. "Tom Foley and the Deficit." In her *Speakers of the House,* 19–31. New York: Franklin Watts, 1994.

**FONG, HIRAM LEONG** (1907–  ) R-HI,
Senate 1959–1977.

**2768.** Chou, Michaelyn. "The Education of a Senator: Hiram L. Fong from 1906–1954." Ph.D. dissertation, University of Hawaii, 1980.

**FOOT, SOLOMON** (1802–1866) R-VT
House 1843–1847, Senate 1851–1866.

**2769.** Sumner, Charles. "The Late Solomon Foot, Senator from Vermont." In his *Works,* vol. 10, 409–416. Boston: Lee and Shephard, 1880.

**FOOTE, HENRY STUART** (1804–1880)
D-MS, Senate 1847–1852.

**2770.** Borome, Joseph, ed. "Two Letters of Robert Charles Winthrop." *Mississippi Valley Historical Review* 38 (September 1951): 294–296.

**2771.** Coleman, James P. "Two Irascible Antebellum Senators: George Poindexter and Henry S. Foote." *Journal of Mississippi History* 46 (February 1984): 17–27.

**2772.** Foote, Henry S. *Casket of Reminiscences.* Washington, DC: Chronicle Publishing Company, 1874.

**2773.** Gonzales, John E. "Henry Stuart Foote: Confederate Congressman and Exile." *Civil War History* 11 (December 1965): 384–395.

**2774.** ———. "The Public Career of Henry Stuart Foote (1804–1880)." Ph.D. dissertation, University of North Carolina, 1958.

**2775.** Van Der Weele, Wayne J. "Henry Stuart Foote: Stentorian Statesman of the Old South." Master's thesis, Indiana University, 1952.

**FORAKER, JOSEPH BENSON**
(1846–1917) R-OH, Senate 1897–1909.

**2776.** Beck, Earl R. "The Political Career of Joseph Benson Foraker." Ph.D. dissertation, Ohio State University, 1943.

**2777.** Foraker, Joseph B. *Notes on a Busy Life.* 2 vols. Cincinnati, OH: Stewart and Kidd, 1916.

**2778.** Foraker, Julia B. *I Would Live It Again: Memoirs of a Vivid Life.* New York: Harper and Brothers, 1932.

**2779.** Kendrick, Benjamin B. "McKinley and Foraker." *Political Science Quarterly* 31 (December 1916): 590–604.

**2780.** Libby, Justin H. " 'Our Plain Duty': Senator Joseph B. Foraker and the First Civil Government of Puerto Rico." *Mid-America* 69 (January 1987): 39–56.

**2781.** Murray, Percy E. "Harry C. Smith-Joseph B. Foraker Alliance: Coalition Politics in Ohio." *Journal of Negro History* 68 (Spring 1983): 171–184.

**2782.** Tinsley, James A. "Roosevelt, Foraker, and the Brownsville Affray." *Journal of Negro History* 41 (January 1956): 43–65.

**2783.** Walters, Everett. "Joseph B. Foraker, 1886–1890." In *Governors of Ohio,* 120–123. Columbus: Ohio Historical Society, 1954.

**2784.** ———. *Joseph Benson Foraker: An Uncompromising Republican.* Columbus: Ohio History Press, 1948.

## FORD, GERALD RUDOLPH, JR.
**(1913– ) R-MI, House 1949–1973.**

**2785.** Aaron, Jan. *Gerald R. Ford, President of Destiny.* New York: Fleet, 1975.

**2786.** Barzman, Sol. "Gerald R. Ford." In his *Madmen and Geniuses: The Vice-Presidents of the United States,* 1293–1300. Chicago: Follett, 1974.

**2787.** Cannon, James M. *Time and Chance: Gerald Ford's Appointment with History; 1913–1974.* New York: HarperCollins, 1993.

**2788.** Collins, Paul. *Gerald R. Ford: A Man in Perspective: As Portrayed in the Gerald R. Ford Mural by Paul Collins.* Grand Rapids, MI: Eerdmans, 1976.

**2789.** Ford, Gerald R. *A Time to Heal: The Autobiography of Gerald R. Ford.* New York: Harper and Row, 1979.

**2790.** Greene, John R. *The Limits of Power: The Nixon and Ford Administrations.* Bloomington: Indiana University Press, 1992.

**2791.** Hartmann, Robert T. *Palace Politics: An Inside Account of the Ford Years.* New York: McGraw-Hill, 1980.

**2792.** Hersey, John. *The President.* New York: Knopf, 1975.

**2793.** Jones, Charles O. *Minority Party Leadership in Congress.* Boston: Little, Brown, 1970.

**2794.** LeRoy, Dave. *Gerald Ford: Untold Story.* Arlington, VA: R. W. Beatty, 1974.

**2795.** MacDougall, Malcolm D. *We Almost Made It.* New York: Crown, 1977.

**2796.** Mollenhoff, Clark R. *The Man Who Pardoned Nixon.* New York: St. Martin's Press, 1976.

**2797.** Natoli, Marie D. "The Vice Presidency: Gerald Ford as Healer?" *Presidential Studies Quarterly* 10 (Fall 1980): 662–664.

**2798.** Reeves, Richard. *A Ford, Not a Lincoln.* New York: Harcourt Brace Jovanovich, 1975.

**2799.** Rozell, Mark J. *The Press and the Ford Presidency.* Ann Arbor: University of Michigan, 1992.

**2800.** Schapsmeier, Edward L. "President Gerald R. Ford's Roots in Omaha." *Nebraska History* 68 (Summer 1987): 56–62.

**2801.** Syers, William A. "The Political Beginnings of Gerald R. Ford: Anti-Bossism, Internationalism, and the Congressional Campaign of 1948." *Presidential Studies Quarterly* 20 (Winter 1990): 127–142.

**2802.** TerHorst, Jerald F. *Gerald Ford and the Future of the Presidency.* New York: Third Press, 1974.

**2803.** Thompson, Kenneth W., ed. *The Ford Presidency: Twenty-Two Intimate Perspectives of Gerald R. Ford.* Lanham, MD: University Press of America, 1988.

**2804.** Vestal, Bud. *Jerry Ford, Up Close: An Investigative Biography.* New York: Coward, McCann and Geoghegan, 1974.

**2805.** Watson, Christopher, ed. *Gerald R. Ford: Our 38th President.* New York: Mayfair Publications, 1974.

## FORD, HAROLD EUGENE **(1945– )**
**D-TN, House 1975– .**

**2806.** Christopher, Maurine. "Harold E. Ford/Tennessee." In her *Black Americans in Congress,* 289. Rev. ed. New York: Thomas Y. Crowell, 1976.

## FORD, WENDELL HAMPTON **(1924– )**
**D-KY, Senate 1974– .**

**2807.** Ford, Wendell H. *The Public Papers of Governor Wendell H. Ford 1971–1974.* Edited by W. Landis Jones. Lexington: University Press of Kentucky, 1978.

## FORDNEY, JOSEPH WARREN (1853–1932) R-MI, House 1899–1923.

**2808.** Russell, John A. *Joseph Warner Fordney: An American Legislator.* Boston: Stratford, 1928.

## FORSYTH, JOHN (1780–1841) JGA, House 1813–1818, 1823–1827, Senate 1818–1819, 1829–1834.

**2809.** Duckett, Alvin L. *John Forsyth, Political Tactician.* Athens: University of Georgia Press, 1962.

**2810.** McCormac, Eugene I. "John Forsyth." In his *The American Secretaries of State and Their Diplomacy,* edited by Samuel F. Bemis, vol. 4, 299–343. New York: Knopf, 1928.

## FOSTER, ABIEL (1735–1806) F-NH, House 1789–1791, 1795–1803, Continental Congress 1783–1785.

**2811.** Roberts, Daniel A. *Hon. Abiel Foster of Canterbury, New Hampshire.* Chicago: D. A. Roberts, 1957.

## FOSTER, CHARLES (1828–1904) R-OH, House 1871–1879.

**2812.** Downes, Randolph C. "Charles Foster, 1880–1884." In *Governors of Ohio,* 112–114. Columbus: Ohio Historical Society, 1954.

## FOSTER, MURPHY JAMES (1849–1921) D-LA, Senate 1901–1913.

**2813.** Reeves, Miriam G. "Murphy James Foster." In her *Governors of Louisiana,* 85–88. Gretna, LA: Pelican Publishing Company, 1972.

## FOWLER, JOHN (1755–1840) R-KY, House 1797–1807.

**2814.** Fowler, Ila E. *Captain John Fowler of Virginia and Kentucky, Patriot, Soldier, Pioneer, Statesman, Land Baron and Civic Leader.* Cynthiana, KY: Hobson Press, 1942.

## FOWLER, JOSEPH SMITH (1820–1902) U-TN, Senate 1866–1871.

**2815.** Durham, Walter T. "How Say You, Senator Fowler?" *Tennessee Historical Quarterly* 42 (Spring 1983): 39–57.

## FRANKLIN, BENJAMIN (1706–1790) PA, Continental Congress 1775, 1776.

**2816.** Aldridge, Alfred O. *Benjamin Franklin and Nature's God.* Durham, NC: Duke University Press, 1967.

**2817.** ———. *Benjamin Franklin, Philosopher and Man.* Philadelphia: Lippincott, 1965.

**2818.** ———. *Franklin and His French Contemporaries.* New York: New York University Press, 1957.

**2819.** Amacher, Richard E. *Benjamin Franklin.* New York: Twayne, 1962.

**2820.** Becker, Carl L. *Benjamin Franklin, a Biographical Sketch.* Ithaca, NY: Cornell University Press, 1946.

**2821.** Bolton, Sarah K. "Benjamin Franklin." In her *Famous American Statesmen,* 38–66. New York: Thomas Y. Crowell, 1888.

**2822.** Bowen, Catherine D. *The Most Dangerous Man in America: Scenes from the Life of Benjamin Franklin.* Boston: Little, Brown, 1974.

**2823.** Breitwieser, Mitchell R. *Cotton Mather and Benjamin Franklin: The Price of Representative Personality.* New York: Cambridge University Press, 1984.

**2824.** Brougham, Henry. "Franklin." In his *Historical Sketches of Statesmen Who Flourished in the Time of George III,* vol. 5 of *Works of Henry, Lord Brougham,* 291–295. London: R. Griffin, 1856.

**2825.** Bruce, William C. *Benjamin Franklin, Self-Revealed: A Biographical and Critical Study Based Mainly on His Own Writings.* New York: Putnam's, 1923.

**2826.** Burlingame, Roger. *Benjamin Franklin, Envoy Extraordinary.* New York: Coward-McCann, 1967.

**2827.** Buxbaum, Melvin H. *Benjamin Franklin and the Zealous Presbyterians.* University Park: Pennsylvania State University Press, 1975.

**2828.** Carey, Lewis J. *Franklin's Economic Views.* Garden City, NY: Doubleday, Doran, 1928.

**2829.** Carr, William G. *The Oldest Delegate: Franklin in the Constitutional Convention.* Newark: University of Delaware Press, 1990.

**2830.** Clark, Ronald W. *Benjamin Franklin: A Biography.* New York: Random House, 1983.

**2831.** Clark, William B. *Ben Franklin's Privateers: A Naval Epic of the American Revolution.* Baton Rouge: Louisiana State University Press, 1956.

**2832.** Cloyd, David E. *Benjamin Franklin and Education: His Ideal of Life and His System of Education for the Realization of That Ideal.* Boston: D. C. Heath, 1902.

**2833.** Cohen, I. Bernard. *Benjamin Franklin: His Contribution to the American Tradition.* Indianapolis: Bobbs-Merrill, 1953.

**2834.** ———. *Benjamin Franklin, Scientist and Statesman.* New York: Scribner's, 1975.

**2835.** ———. *Franklin and Newton: An Inquiry into Speculative Newtonian Experimental Science and Franklin's Work in Electricity as an Example Thereof.* Philadelphia: American Philosophical Society, 1956.

**2836.** Conner, Paul W. *Poor Richard's Politics: Benjamin Franklin and His New American Order.* New York: Oxford University Press, 1965.

**2837.** Crane, Verner W. *Benjamin Franklin and a Rising People.* Boston: Little, Brown, 1954.

**2838.** Currey, Cecil B. *Code Number 72/Ben Franklin: Patriot or Spy?* Englewood Cliffs, NJ: Prentice-Hall, 1972.

**2839.** ———. *Road to Revolution: Benjamin Franklin in England, 1765–1775.* Garden City, NY: Anchor Books, 1968.

**2840.** Daugherty, James H. *Poor Richard.* New York: Viking, 1941.

**2841.** Dudley, Edward L. *Benjamin Franklin.* New York: Macmillan, 1915.

**2842.** Dull, Jonathan R. *Franklin the Diplomat: The French Mission.* Philadelphia: American Philosophical Society, 1982.

**2843.** Eiselen, Malcolm R. *Franklin's Political Theories.* Garden City, NY: Doubleday, 1928.

**2844.** Eliot, Charles W. "Franklin." In his *Charles W. Eliot, the Man and His Beliefs,* 478–492. New York: Harper and Brothers, 1926.

**2845.** ———. "Franklin." In his *Four American Leaders,* 10–30. Boston: American Unitarian Association, 1906.

**2846.** Farrand, Max. "Benjamin Franklin's Memoirs." *Huntington Library Bulletin* 10 (October 1936): 49–78.

**2847.** Fay, Bernard. *Bernard Fay's Franklin, the Apostle of Modern Times.* Boston: Little, Brown, 1929.

**2848.** ———. *Bernard Fay's The Two Franklins: Fathers of American Democracy.* Boston: Little, Brown, 1933.

**2849.** Fleming, Thomas J. *The Man Who Dared the Lightning: A New Look at Benjamin Franklin.* New York: Morrow, 1971.

**2850.** Flora, Alice E. "Benjamin Franklin as Colonial Agent." Master's thesis, Indiana University, 1934.

**2851.** Forbes, Allen, and Paul F. Cadman. "Memories of Franklin in Passy and Paris." In their *France and New England,* vol. 2, 67–96. Boston: State Street Trust Company, 1927.

**2852.** Ford, Paul L. *The Many-Sided Franklin.* New York: Century, 1899.

**2853.** Franklin, Benjamin. *Autobiography and Other Writings.* Edited by Kenneth Silverman. New York: Penguin, 1986.

**2854.** Fulton, Maurice G. "Franklin, The Citizen." In his *National Ideals and Problems,* 58–67. New York: Macmillan, 1918.

**2855.** Granger, Bruce I. *Benjamin Franklin, an American Man of Letters.* Norman: University of Oklahoma Press, 1976.

**2856.** Guedalla, Philip. "Dr. Franklin." In his *Fathers of the Revolution,* 213–234. New York: Putnam's, 1926.

**2857.** Hall, Max. *Benjamin Franklin and Polly Baker: The History of a Literary Deception.* Chapel Hill: University of North Carolina Press, 1960.

**2858.** Hanna, William S. *Benjamin Franklin and Pennsylvania Politics.* Stanford, CA: Stanford University Press, 1964.

**2859.** Hawke, David F. *Franklin.* New York: Harper and Row, 1976.

**2860.** Hayden, Sidney S. "Benjamin Franklin." In his *Washington and His Masonic Compeers,* 281–299. New York: Masonic Publishing and Manufacturing Company, 1867.

**2861.** Hill, George C. *Benjamin Franklin: A Biography.* Philadelphia: Claxton, Remsen and Haffelfinger, 1869.

**2862.** Hornberger, Theodore. *Benjamin Franklin.* Minneapolis: University of Minnesota Press, 1962.

**2863.** Hubbard, Elbert. "Benjamin Franklin." In his *Little Journeys to the Homes of the Great,* vol. 3, 31–51. New York: W. H. Wise, 1916.

**2864.** Jacobs, Wilbur R. *Benjamin Franklin: Statesman-Philosopher or Materialist?* New York: Holt, Rinehart and Winston, 1972.

**2865.** Johansen, Bruce E. *Forgotten Founders: Benjamin Franklin, the Iroquois, and the Rationale for the American Revolution.* Ipswich, MA: Gambit, 1982.

**2866.** ———. "Franklin, Jefferson and American Indians: A Study in the Cross-Cultural Communication of Ideas." Ph.D. dissertation, University of Washington, 1979.

**2867.** Jusserand, Jean J. "Franklin in France." In *Essays Offered to Herbert Putnam,* edited by William W. Bishop and Andrew Keogh, 226–247. New Haven, CT: Yale University Press, 1929.

**2868.** Ketcham, Ralph L. *Benjamin Franklin.* New York: Washington Square Press, 1965.

**2869.** Keyes, Nelson B. *Ben Franklin, an Affectionate Portrait.* Garden City, NJ: Hanover House, 1956.

**2870.** Korty, Margaret B. *Benjamin Franklin and Eighteenth-Century American Libraries.* Philadelphia: American Philosophical Society, 1965.

**2871.** Lemay, J. A. Leo, ed. *Reappraising Benjamin Franklin: A Bicentennial Perspective.* Newark: University of Delaware Press, 1993.

**2872.** Levin, David, ed. *The Puritan in the Enlightenment: Franklin and Edwards.* Chicago: Rand McNally, 1963.

**2873.** Livingston, Luther S. *Franklin and His Press at Passy.* New York: Grolier Club, 1914.

**2874.** Lodge, Henry C. "Franklin." In his *A Frontier Town,* 249–264. New York: Scribner's, 1906.

**2875.** Lopez, Claude A. *Mon Cher Papa, Franklin and the Ladies of Paris.* New Haven, CT: Yale University Press, 1966.

**2876.** Lopez, Claude A., and Eugenia W. Herbert. *The Private Franklin: The Man and His Family.* New York: Norton, 1975.

**2877.** Lucas, Frank L. "Benjamin Franklin." In his *The Art of Living: Four Eighteenth-Century Minds: Hume, Horace Walpole, Burke, Benjamin Franklin,* 203–260. London: Cassell, 1959.

**2878.** Lynch, Dorothea M. "Benjamin Franklin, Colonial Agent." Master's thesis, Indiana University, 1938.

**2879.** MacKay, Charles. "Franklin." In his *The Founders of the American Republic: A History and Biography, with a Supplementary Chapter on Ultra-Democracy,* 293–322. Edinburgh: W. Blackwood, 1885.

**2880.** MacLaurin, Lois M. *Franklin's Vocabulary.* Garden City, NY: Doubleday, 1928.

**2881.** Maurois, Andre. *Franklin, the Life of an Optimist.* New York: Didier, 1945.

**2882.** McKown, Robin. *Benjamin Franklin.* New York: Putnam's, 1963.

**2883.** McMaster, John B. *Benjamin Franklin as a Man of Letters.* New York: Arno Press, 1970.

**2884.** Meador, Roy. *Franklin, Revolutionary Scientist.* Ann Arbor, MI: Ann Arbor Science Publishers, 1975.

**2885.** Montgomery, Thomas H. "Franklin." In his *History of the University of Pennsylvania,* 11–40, 73–83. Philadelphia: G. W. Jacobs, 1900.

**2886.** More, Paul E. *Benjamin Franklin.* Boston: Houghton Mifflin, 1900.

**2887.** Morse, John T. *Benjamin Franklin.* Boston: Houghton Mifflin, 1894.

**2888.** Myers, J. Jay. "Benjamin Franklin: Mr. America." In his *The Revolutionists,* 84–107. New York: Washington Square Press, 1971.

**2889.** Newcomb, Benjamin H. *Franklin and Galloway: A Political Partnership.* New Haven, CT: Yale University Press, 1972.

**2890.** Nolan, James B. *Benjamin Franklin in Scotland and Ireland, 1759 and 1771.* Philadelphia: University of Pennsylvania Press, 1938.

**2891.** ———. *General Benjamin Franklin: The Military Career of a Philosopher.* Philadelphia: University of Pennsylvania Press, 1956.

**2892.** Ogg, Frederic A. "Benjamin Franklin." In his *Builders of the Republic,* 131–143. New Haven, CT: Yale University Press, 1927.

**2893.** O'Higgins, Harvey J., and Edward H. Reede. "Benjamin Franklin." In their *The American Mind in Action,* 155–179. New York: Harper and Brothers, 1924.

**2894.** Oswald, John C. *Benjamin Franklin, Printer.* Detroit, MI: Gale, 1974.

**2895.** O'Toole, George. *Poor Richard's Game.* New York: Delacorte Press, 1982.

**2896.** Pace, Antonia. *Benjamin Franklin and Italy.* Philadelphia: American Philosophical Society, 1958.

**2897.** Parker, Theodore. "Benjamin Franklin." In his *Works,* vol. 7, 41–96. Boston: American Unitarian Association.

**2898.** ———. " In his *Historic Americans,* 13–72. 2d ed. Boston: H. B. Fuller, 1871.

**2899.** Parrington, Vernon L. "Benjamin Franklin." In his *Main Currents in American Thought,* vol. 1, 164–178. New York: Harcourt, Brace, 1927.

**2900.** Phelps, William L. "The Man of the World and the Man of God." In his *Some Makers of American Literature,* 1–33. Boston: Marshall Jones Company, 1923.

**2901.** Preston, Howard W., ed. "Franklin's Plan of Union, 1754." In his *Documents Illustrative of American History,* 170–187. New York: Putnam's, 1893.

**2902.** Randall, Willard S. *A Little Revenge: Benjamin Franklin and His Son.* Boston: Little, Brown, 1984.

**2903.** Remsburg, John E. "Benjamin Franklin." In his *Six Historic Americans: Paine, Jefferson, Washington, Franklin, Lincoln, Grant, the Fathers and Saviors of Our Republic, Freethinkers,* 158–182. New York: Truth Seeker Company, 1906.

**2904.** Russell, Phillips. *Benjamin Franklin, the First Civilized American.* New York: Brentano's, 1926.

**2905.** Sainte-Beauve, Charles A. "Franklin." In his *Portraits of the Eighteenth Century,* 309–375. New York: Putnam's, 1905.

**2906.** Sanderson, John. "Benjamin Franklin." In *Sanderson's Biography of the Signers of the Declaration of Independence,* edited by Robert T. Conrad, 393–448. Philadelphia: Thomas, Cowperthwait, 1848.

**2907.** Sanford, Charles L., ed. *Benjamin Franklin and the American Character.* Boston: Heath, 1955.

**2908.** Sappenfield, James A. *A Sweet Instruction: Franklin's Journalism as a Literary Apprenticeship.* Carbondale: Southern Illinois University Press, 1973.

**2909.** Schlereth, Thomas J. *The Cosmopolitan Ideal in Enlightenment Thought, Its Form and Function in the Ideas of Franklin, Hume, and Voltaire, 1694–1790.* Notre Dame, IN: University of Notre Dame Press, 1977.

**2910.** Schoenbrun, David. *Triumph in Paris: The Exploits of Benjamin Franklin.* New York: Harper and Row, 1976.

**2911.** Seeger, Raymond J. *Men of Physics: Benjamin Franklin, New World Physicist.* New York: Pergamon, 1973.

**2912.** Sherman, Stuart P. "Franklin and the Age of Enlightenment." In his *Americans,* 28–62. New York: Scribner's, 1923.

**2913.** Skemp, Sheila L. *Benjamin and William Franklin: Father and Son, Patriot and Loyalist.* Boston: St. Martin's Press, 1994.

**2914.** Smyth, John H., ed. *The Amazing Benjamin Franklin.* New York: Frederick A. Stokes, 1929.

**2915.** Sparks, Edwin E. "Benjamin Franklin, the Colonial Agent in England." In his *The Men Who Made the Nation,* 1–46. New York: Macmillan, 1901.

**2916.** Stebbing, William. "An American Revolutionist: Benjamin Franklin." In his *Some Verdicts of History Reviewed,* 255–299. London: J. Murray, 1887.

**2917.** Steell, Willis. *Benjamin Franklin of Paris, 1776–1785.* New York: Minton, Balch, 1928.

**2918.** Stevens, Henry. *Benjamin Franklin's Life and Writings.* London: Davy and Sons, 1881.

**2919.** Stifler, James M. *The Religion of Benjamin Franklin.* New York: Appleton, 1925.

**2920.** Stourzh, Gerald. *Benjamin Franklin and American Foreign Policy.* Chicago: University of Chicago Press, 1954.

**2921.** Thompson, Holland. "Benjamin Franklin and His Times." In his *The Age of Invention,* 1–31, 220–225. New Haven, CT: Yale University Press, 1921.

**2922.** Thorpe, James E. *The Autobiography of B. Franklin.* San Marino, CA: Huntington Library, 1976.

**2923.** Tourtellot, Arthur B. *Benjamin Franklin: The Shaping of Genius: The Boston Years.* Garden City, NY: Doubleday, 1977.

**2924.** Van Doren, Carl C. *Benjamin Franklin.* New York: Viking, 1938.

**2925.** Weems, Mason L. *The Life of Benjamin Franklin: With Many Choice Anecdotes and Admirable Sayings of This Great Man, Never Before Published by Any of His Biographers.* Louisville, KY: Morton, 1829.

**2926.** Wendel, Thomas. *Benjamin Franklin and the Politics of Liberty: A Biography with Readings.* Woodbury, NY: Barron's Educational Series, 1974.

**2927.** Wildman, Edwin. "Benjamin Franklin: Father of the Revolution." In *The Founders of America in the Days of the Revolution,* 3–26. Freeport, NY: Books for Libraries, 1968.

**2928.** Willson, Beckles. "Franklin (1777–85)." In his *America's Ambassadors to France (1777–1927),* 1–16, 20–22. New York: Frederick A. Stokes, 1928.

**2929.** Wilstach, Paul. "Benjamin Franklin." In his *Patriots off Their Pedestals,* 47–77. Indianapolis: Bobbs-Merrill, 1927.

**2930.** Woody, Thomas, ed. *Educational Views of Benjamin Franklin.* New York: McGraw-Hill, 1931.

**2931.** Wright, Esmond. *Benjamin Franklin and American Independence.* London: English Universities Press, 1966.

**2932.** ———. *Benjamin Franklin: His Life as He Wrote It.* Cambridge, MA: Harvard University Press, 1990.

**2933.** ———. *Franklin of Philadelphia.* Cambridge, MA: Harvard University Press, 1986.

**FRAZIER, LYNN JOSEPH (1874–1947) R-ND, Senate 1923–1941.**

**2934.** Briley, Ronald F. "Lynn J. Frazier and Progressive Reform: A Plodder in the Ranks of a Ragged Regiment." *South Dakota History* 7 (Fall 1977): 438–454.

**2935.** Erickson, Nels. *The Gentleman from North Dakota, Lynn J. Frazier.* Bismark: State Historical Society of North Dakota, 1986.

**2936.** Erickson, Nels. "Prairie Pacifist: Senator Lynn J. Frazier and America's Global Mission, 1927–1940." *North Dakota History* 52 (Fall 1985): 26–32.

**FRELINGHUYSEN, THEODORE (1787–1862) NJ, Senate 1829–1835.**

**2937.** Eells, Robert. *Forgotten Saint: The Life of Theodore Frelinghuysen: A Case Study of Christian Leadership.* Lanham, MD: University Press of America: 1987.

**2938.** ———. "Theodore Frelinghuysen, Voluntarism and the Pursuit of the Public Good." *American Presbyterians* 69 (Winter 1991): 257–270.

**2939.** Elmer, Lucius Q. "Lawyers I Have Known: Theodore Frelinghuysen." In his *The Constitution and Government of the Province and State of New Jersey,* 440–456. Newark, NJ: Dennis, 1872.

**FREMONT, JOHN CHARLES (1813–1890) D-CA, Senate 1850–1851.**

**2940.** Bartlett, David V. "John C. Fremont." In his *Presidential Candidates: Containing Sketches, Biographical, Personal and Political, of Prominent Candidates for the Presidency,* 346–360. New York: A. B. Burdick, 1859.

**2941.** Bartlett, Ruhl J. *John C. Fremont and the Republican Party.* Columbus: Ohio State University, 1930.

**2942.** Bashford, Herbert, and Harr Wagner. *A Man Unafraid: The Story of John Charles Fremont.* San Francisco: Harr Wagner, 1927.

**2943.** Bidwell, John. *Fremont in the Conquest of California.* New York: Century, 1891.

**2944.** Bigelow, John. *Memoir on the Life and Public Services of John Charles Fremont.* New York: Derby and Jackson, 1856.

**2945.** Bradley, Glenn D. "John C. Fremont." In his *Winning the Southwest: A Story of Conquest,* 199–225. Chicago: McClurg, 1912.

**2946.** Brandon, William. *Men and the Mountain: Fremont's Fourth Expedition.* New York: Morrow, 1955.

**2947.** Burleigh, George S. *Signal Fires on the Trail of the Pathfinder.* New York: Dayton and Burdick, 1856.

**2948.** Carvalho, Solomon N. *Incidents of Travel and Adventure in the Far West.* New York: Derloy and Jackson, 1859.

**2949.** Cleland, Robert G. "John Charles Fremont." In his *Pathfinders,* 311–343. Los Angeles: Powell, 1929.

**2950.** Creel, George. "A Rocket in the West." In his *Sons of the Eagle,* 187–199. Indianapolis: Bobbs-Merrill, 1927.

**2951.** Dellenbaugh, Frederick S. *Fremont and '49.* New York: Putnam's, 1914.

**2952.** Denslow, Van Buren. *Fremont and McClellan, Their Political and Military*

*Careers Reviewed.* Yonkers, NY: Semiweekly Clarion, 1862.

**2953.** Des Montaignes, François. *The Plains.* Norman: University of Oklahoma Press, 1972.

**2954.** Dillon, Richard. "John C. Fremont." In his *Humbugs and Heroes,* 94–101. Garden City, NY: Doubleday, 1970.

**2955.** Egan, Ferol. *Fremont, Explorer for Restless Nation.* Garden City, NY: Doubleday, 1977.

**2956.** Eldredge, Zoeth S. "John C. Fremont." In his *The Beginnings of San Francisco,* 374–427. San Francisco: Z. S. Eldredge, 1912.

**2957.** Ewan, Joseph A. "John Charles Fremont." In his *Rocky Mountain Naturalists,* 21–33. Denver: University of Denver Press, 1950.

**2958.** Eyre, Alice. *Famous Fremonts and Their America.* Boston: Christopher, 1961.

**2959.** Fremont, Jessie. *Souvenirs of My Time.* Boston: D. Lothrop, 1887.

**2960.** Fremont, John C. *Expeditions of John Charles Fremont: The Bear Flag Revolt and the Court Martial.* Urbana: University of Illinois Press, 1973.

**2961.** ———. *Expeditions of John Charles Fremont: Travels from 1838 to 1844.* Edited by Donald Jackson and Mary L. Spence. Urbana: University of Illinois Press, 1970.

**2962.** ———. *Memoirs of My Life by John Charles Fremont.* Chicago: Belford, Clarke, 1889.

**2963.** Goodwin, Cardinal L. *John Charles Fremont, an Explanation of His Career.* Stanford, CA: Stanford University Press, 1930.

**2964.** Greeley, Horace. *Life of John Charles Fremont.* New York: Greeley and M'Elrath, 1856.

**2965.** Grinnell, George B. "Fremont." In his *Trails of the Pathfinders,* 393–451. New York: Scribner's, 1911.

**2966.** Hagwood, John A. *John C. Fremont and the Bear Flag Revolution.* Birmingham, England: University of Birmingham, 1959.

**2967.** Hall, Benjamin F. "Biographical Sketch of Colonel John C. Fremont." In his *Republican Party,* 473–504. New York: Miller, Orton and Mulligan, 1856.

**2968.** Hawthorne, Hildegarde. *Born to Adventure: The Story of John Charles Fremont.* New York: Appleton-Century, 1947.

**2969.** Hebard, Grace R. "Fremont's Explorations." In his *The Pathbreakers from River to Oceans,* 133–155. Chicago: University Publishing Company, 1917.

**2970.** Herr, Pamela. *Jessie Benton Fremont: A Biography.* New York: Watts, 1987.

**2971.** Horton, Lilburn H. *Fremont's Expeditions through Kansas, 1842–1854.* Hays: Kansas State College, 1962.

**2972.** Hunt, Rockwell D. "John Charles Fremont." In his *California's Stately Hall of Fame,* 175–180. Stockton, CA: College of the Pacific, 1950.

**2973.** Lewis, Ernest A. *The Fremont Cannon—High Up and Far Back.* Glendale, CA: A. H. Clark, 1981.

**2974.** Macartney, Clarence E. "Lincoln and Fremont." In his *Lincoln and His Generals,* 29–45. Philadelphia: Dorrance, 1925.

**2975.** Mack, Effie M. "With Fremont in Nevada." In her *Nevada,* 79–102. Glendale, CA: Arthur H. Clark Company, 1936.

**2976.** Magoon, James. *The Life of Major-Gen. John C. Fremont, the Rocky Mountain Explorer.* New York: Beadle, 1861.

**2977.** McNeil, Everett. *Fighting with Fremont: A Tale of the Conquest of California.* New York: Dutton, 1910.

**2978.** Nevins, Allan. *Fremont, Pathmarker of the West.* New York: Appleton-Century, 1939.

**2979.** ———. *Fremont, the West's Greatest Adventurer.* New York: Harper and Brothers, 1928.

**2980.** Nicholas, Edward. "The Imperialists." and "The Republicans." In his *Hours and the Ages,* 225–292. New York: Sloane Associates, 1949.

**2981.** Pickett, Charles E. *John C. Fremont: His Character, Achievements, and Qualifications for the Presidency; and Other Matters Connected Therewith.* N.p., 1856.

**2982.** Preuss, Charles. *Exploring with Fremont: The Private Diaries of Charles Preuss, Cartographer for John C. Fremont on His First, Second, and Fourth Expeditions to the Far West.* Edited by Erwin G. and Elisabeth K. Gudde. Norman: University of Oklahoma Press, 1972.

**2983.** Richmond, Patricia J. *Trail to Disaster.* Denver: Colorado Historical Society, 1990.

**2984.** Rolle, Andrew F. *John Charles Fremont: Character As Destiny.* Norman: University of Oklahoma Press, 1991.

**2985.** Schmucker, Samuel M. "John Charles Fremont." In his *The Life of Dr. Elisha Kent Kane, and of Distinguished American Explorers,* 151–260. Philadelphia: Evans, 1858.

**2986.** Seitz, Don C. "John Charles Fremont, a Pathfinder Who Lost His Way." In his *The "Also Rans": Great Men Who Missed Making the Presidential Goal,* 144–166. New York: Thomas Y. Crowell, 1928.

**2987.** Talbot, Theodore. *The Journals of Theodore Talbot, 1843 and 1849–52.* Portland, OR: Metropolitan Press, 1931.

**2988.** ———. *Soldier in the West: Letters of Theodore Talbot during His Services in California, Mexico, and Oregon, 1854–53.* Edited by Robert V. Hine and Savoie Lottinville. Norman: University of Oklahoma Press, 1972.

**2989.** Upham, Charles W. *Life, Explorations, and Public Services of John Charles Fremont.* Boston: Ticknor and Fields, 1956.

**2990.** Wilford, John N. "Mapping America: Westward the Topographers." In his *Mapmakers,* 190–215. New York: Knopf, 1981.

**2991.** Willard, Emma C. *Late American History: Containing a Full Account of the Courage, Conduct and Success of John C. Fremont.* New York: Barnes, 1856.

**2992.** Wiltsee, Ernest A. *The Truth about Fremont.* San Francisco: J.H. Nash, 1936.

**2993.** Zabriskie, George A. *The Pathfinder.* Ormond Beach, FL: Privately printed, 1947.

## FULBRIGHT, JAMES WILLIAM
**(1905–1995) D-AR, House 1943–1945, Senate 1945–1974.**

**2994.** Becnel, Thomas A. "Fulbright of Arkansas v. Ellender of Louisiana: The Politics of Sugar and Rice, 1937–1974." *Arkansas Historical Quarterly* 43 (Winter 1984): 289–303.

**2995.** Berman, William C. *William Fulbright and the Vietnam War: The Dissent of a Political Realist.* Kent, OH: Kent State University Press, 1988.

**2996.** Brown, Eugene J. "Fulbright and the Premises of American Foreign Policy." Ph.D. thesis, State University of New York at Binghamton, 1982.

**2997.** ———. *William Fulbright: Advice and Dissent.* Iowa City: University of Iowa Press, 1985.

**2998.** Bullert, Gary B. "Jackson, Fulbright, and the Senatorial Critique of Detente." *Journal of Social, Political and Economic Studies* 13 (Spring 1988): 61–86.

**2999.** Bullert, Gary B., and Francis M. Casey. "The Foreign Policy of Senator William J. Fulbright: From Cold Warrior to Neo-Isolationist." *Journal of Social, Political, and Economic Studies* 8 (Winter 1983): 449–469.

**3000.** Coffin, Tristram. *Senator Fulbright: Portrait of a Public Philosopher.* New York: Dutton, 1966.

**3001.** Downs, Calvin W. "A Thematic Analysis of Speeches on Foreign Policy of Senator J. W. Fulbright." Ph.D. dissertation, Michigan State University, 1963.

**3002.** Fairlie, Henry. "The Senator and World Power." *Encounter* 30 (May 1968): 57–66.

**3003.** Fulbright, James W. *The Arrogance of Power.* New York: Random House, 1966.

**3004.** ———. "The Most Significant and Important Activity I Have Been Privileged to Engage in during My Years in the Senate." *Annals of the American Academy of Political and Social Science* 424 (March 1976): 1–5.

**3005.** Grundy, Kenneth W. "The Apprenticeship of J. William Fulbright." *Virginia Quarterly Review* 43 (Summer 1967): 382–399.

**3006.** Gunn, Herb. "The Continuing Friendship of James William Fulbright and Ronald Buchanan McCallum." *South Atlantic Quarterly* 83 (Autumn 1984): 416–433.

**3007.** Hall, Max. "J. William Fulbright." In *Public Men In and Out of Office,* edited by John T. Salter, 181–295. Chapel Hill: University of North Carolina Press, 1946.

**3008.** Jeffrey, Harry P. "Legislative Origins of the Fulbright Program." *Annals of the American Academy of Political and Social Science* 491 (1987): 36–46.

**3009.** Johnson, Haynes B., and Bernard M. Gwertzman. *Fulbright: The Dissenter.* Garden City, NY: Doubleday, 1968.

**3010.** Johnson, Willie S. "The Bumpers-Fulbright Senate Race: A Rhetorical Analysis." Ph.D. dissertation, University of Illinois, 1981.

**3011.** Lippmann, Walter. "William J. Fulbright." In his *Public Persons,* 173–175. New York: Liveright, 1976.

**3012.** Lynn, Naomi B. "Senator J. William Fulbright's Views on Presidential Power in Foreign Policy." Ph.D. dissertation, University of Kansas, 1970.

**3013.** Lynn, Naomi B., and Arthur F. McClure. *The Fulbright Premise: Senator J. William Fulbright's View on Presidential Power.* Lewisburg, PA: Bucknell University Press, 1973.

**3014.** O'Grady, Joseph P. "J. W. Fulbright and the Fulbright Program in Ireland." *Arkansas Historical Quarterly* 47 (Spring 1988): 47–69.

**3015.** Perry, Bruce. "Senator J. William Fulbright on European and Atlantic Unity." Ph.D. dissertation, University of Pennsylvania, 1968.

**3016.** Powell, Lee R. *J. William Fulbright and America's Lost Crusade: Fulbright's Opposition to the Vietnam War.* Little Rock, AR: Rose, 1984.

**3017.** Ritchie, Donald A. "Making Fulbright Chairman: Or How the 'Johnson Treatment' Nearly Backfired." *Society for Historians of American Foreign Relations Newsletter* 15 (1984): 21–28.

**3018.** Rogers, Jimmie N. "An Investigation of Senator J. William Fulbright's Attitudes towards President Lyndon B. Johnson as Demonstrated in Selected Foreign Policy Addresses: An Evaluative Assertion Analysis." Ph.D. dissertation, Florida State University, 1972.

**3019.** Smith, Harold T. "J. William Fulbright and the Arkansas 1974 Senatorial Election." *Arkansas Historical Quarterly* 44 (Summer 1985): 103–117.

**3020.** Trask, David F. "The Congress as Classroom: J. William Fulbright and the Crises of American Power." In *Makers of American Diplomacy from Benjamin Franklin to Henry Kissinger,* edited by Frank J. Merli and Theodore A. Wilson, 649–675. New York: Scribner's, 1974.

**3021.** Turesky, Stanley F. "A Time to Talk and a Time to Listen: A Study of the Relationship between the Chairman of the Senate Foreign Relations Committee and the President of the United States." Ph.D. dissertation, Brown University, 1973.

**3022.** Tweraser, Kurt K. "The Advice and Dissent of Senator Fulbright: A Longitudinal Analysis of His Images of International Politics and His Political Role Conception." Ph.D. dissertation, American University, 1971.

**3023.** ———. *Changing Patterns of Political Beliefs: The Foreign Policy Operational Codes of J. William Fulbright, 1943–1967.* Beverly Hills, CA: Sage, 1974.

**3024.** Woods, Randall B. "Fulbright Internationalism." *Annals of the American Academy of Political and Social Science* 491 (1987): 22–35.

**FULLER, CLAUDE ALBERT** (1876–1968) D-AR, House 1929–1939.

**3025.** Beals, Frank L. *Backwoods Baron: The Life Story of Claude Albert Fuller.* Denver: Morton, 1951.

৯৶

**GADSDEN, CHRISTOPHER** (1723–1805) SC, Continental Congress 1774–1976.

**3026.** Godbold, E. Stanly. *Christopher Gadsden and the American Revolution.* Knoxville: University of Tennessee Press, 1982.

**GALLATIN, ALBERT** (1761–1849) D-PA, Senate 1793–1794, House 1795–1801.

**3027.** Adams, Henry. *The Life of Albert Gallatin.* Philadelphia: Lippincott, 1879.

**3028.** Andrews, W. "Gallatin Revisited." *New York Historical Society Quarterly* 34 (April 1950): 135–139; 35 (July 1951): 221–226.

**3029.** Badollet, John L. *Correspondence of John Badollet and Albert Gallatin, 1804–1836.* Edited by Gayle Thornbrough. Indianapolis: Indiana Historical Society, 1963.

**3030.** Balinky, Alexander. *Albert Gallatin: Fiscal Theories and Policies.* New Brunswick, NJ: Rutgers University Press, 1958.

**3031.** Boxall, James A. "Albert Gallatin and American Foreign Policy: A Study in Thought and Action." Ph.D. dissertation, Michigan State University, 1967.

**3032.** Burrows, Edwin G. *Albert Gallatin and the Political Economy of Republicanism, 1761–1800.* New York: Garland, 1986.

**3033.** Dater, Henry M. "Albert Gallatin, Land Speculator." *Mississippi Valley Historical Review* 26 (June 1939): 21–38.

**3034.** De Terra, Helmut. "Alexander von Humboldt's Correspondence with Jefferson, Madison, and Gallatin." *American Philosophical Society Proceedings* 103 (December 1959): 783–806.

**3035.** Ewing, Frank E. *America's Forgotten Statesman: Albert Gallatin.* New York: Vantage, 1959.

**3036.** Gallatin, Albert. *The Writings of Albert Gallatin.* 3 vols. Philadelphia: Lippincott, 1879.

**3037.** Gallatin, James. *The Diary of James Gallatin, Secretary to Albert Gallatin, a Great Peace Maker, 1813–1827.* New York: Scribner's, 1916.

**3038.** Grayson, Theodore J. "Albert Gallatin: Republican Finance, Reduction of the National Debt, and Financial Provisions for the War of 1812." In his *Leaders and Periods of American Finance*, 83–114. New York: J. Wiley, 1932.

**3039.** Hay, Robert P. "The Pillorying of Albert Gallatin: The Public Response to His 1824 Vice-Presidential Nomination." *Western Pennsylvania Historical Magazine* 65 (July 1982): 181–202.

**3040.** Kehl, James A. "Albert Gallatin: Man of Moderation." *Western Pennsylvania Historical Magazine* 61 (January 1978): 31–45.

**3041.** Knudson, Jerry W. "The Case of Albert Gallatin and Jeffersonian Patronage." *Western Pennsylvania Historical Magazine* 52 (July 1969): 241–250.

**3042.** Mai, Chien T. *The Fiscal Policies of Albert Gallatin.* New York: N.p., 1930.

**3043.** Mannix, Richard. "Albert Gallatin and the Movement for Peace with Mexico." *Social Studies* 60 (December 1969): 310–318.

**3044.** ———. "Albert Gallatin in Washington, 1801–1813." *Records of the Columbia Historical Society* 48 (1971/1972): 60–80.

**3045.** Merk, Frederick. *Albert Gallatin and the Oregon Problem: A Study.* Cambridge, MA: Harvard University Press, 1950.

**3046.** Neidle, Cecyle S. "Albert Gallatin." In her *Great Immigrants,* 1–22. Boston: Twayne, 1973.

**3047.** Nolan, James B. "The Baiting of Albert Gallatin." In his *Annals of the Penn Square,* 31–42. Philadelphia: University of Pennsylvania Press, 1933.

**3048.** Stevens, John A. *Albert Gallatin, American Statesman.* Boston: Houghton Mifflin, 1884.

**3049.** Vail, Robert W. "Society Grows Up." *New York Historical Society Quarterly* 38 (October 1954): 445–449.

**3050.** Walter, Raymond. *Albert Gallatin: Jeffersonian Financier and Diplomat.* New York: Macmillan, 1957.

**3051.** ———. "Gentleman from Geneva, Albert Gallatin, Jeffersonian Democrat." *New York Historical Society Quarterly* 36 (July 1952): 289–299.

**3052.** Willson, Beckles. "Gallatin (1816–23)." In his *America's Ambassadors to France (1777–1927),* 135–151. New York: Frederick A. Stokes, 1928.

**3053.** ———. "King and Gallatin (1825–1827)." In his *America's Ambassadors to England (1785–1928),* 165–179. London: Murray, 1928.

## GALLEGOS, JOSE MANUEL (1815–1875) D-NM, House 1853–1856, 1871–1873.

**3054.** Chavez, Angelico. *Tres Macho—He Said: Padre Gallegos of Albuquerque, New Mexico's First Congressman.* Santa Fe, NM: William Gannon, 1985.

## GALLOWAY, JOSEPH (1731–1803) PA, Continental Congress 1775.

**3055.** Boyd, Julian P. *Anglo-American Union: Joseph Galloway's Plans to Preserve the British Empire, 1774–1788.* Philadelphia: University of Pennsylvania Press, 1941.

**3056.** Calhoon, Robert M. "I Have Deduced Your Rights: Joseph Galloway's Concept of His Role 1774–1775." *Pennsylvania History* 35 (October 1968): 365–378.

**3057.** Ferling, John E. "Joseph Galloway: A Reassessment of the Motivations of a Pennsylvania Loyalist." *Pennsylvania History* 39 (April 1972): 163–186.

**3058.** ———. *The Loyalist Mind: Joseph Galloway and the American Revolution.* University Park: Pennsylvania State University Press, 1977.

**3059.** Goddard, William. *The Partnership.* Philadelphia, PA: Printed by author, 1770.

**3060.** Kuntzleman, Oliver C. "Joseph Galloway, Loyalist." Ed.D. dissertation, Temple University, 1941.

**3061.** Lively, Bruce R. "The Speaker and His House: Joseph Galloway and the Pennsylvania Assembly, 1755–1776." Ph.D. dissertation, University of Southern California, 1976.

**3062.** Newcomb, Benjamin H. *Franklin and Galloway: A Political Partnership.* New Haven, CT: Yale University Press, 1972.

**GARBER, MILTON CLINE (1867–1948) R-OK, House 1923–1933.**

**3063.** Grant, Philip A., Jr. "'Save the Farmer': Oklahoma Congressmen and Farm Relief Legislation, 1924–1928." *Chronicles of Oklahoma* 64 (Spring 1986): 74–87.

**GARDNER, AUGUSTUS PEABODY (1865–1918) R-MA, House 1902–1917.**

**3064.** Gardner, Augustus P. *Some Letters of Augustus Peabody Gardner.* Edited by Constance Gardner. Boston: Houghton Mifflin, 1920.

**GARFIELD, JAMES ABRAM (1831–1881) R-OH, House 1863–1880.**

**3065.** Bates, Richard O. *The Gentleman from Ohio: An Introduction to Garfield.* Durham, NC: Moore Publishing Company, 1973.

**3066.** Booraem, Hendrik. *The Road to Respectability: James A. Garfield and His World.* Lewisburg, PA: Bucknell University Press, 1988.

**3067.** Brisbin, James S. *The Early Life and Public Career of James A. Garfield, Major General, U.S.A.: The Record of a Wonderful Career.* Philadelphia: J. C. McCurdy, 1880.

**3068.** Brisbin, James S., and William R. Balch. *The Life and Public Career of Gen. James A. Garfield.* Philadelphia: Hubbard, 1880.

**3069.** Brooks, Noah. "James A. Garfield." In his *Statesman,* 313–332. New York: Scribner's, 1893.

**3070.** Brown, Harry J. "Garfield's Congress." *Hayes Historical Journal* 3 (Fall 1981): 57–77.

**3071.** Bundy, Jonas M. *The Life of Gen. James A. Garfield.* New York: Barnes, 1880.

**3072.** Caldwell, Robert G. *James A. Garfield, Party Chieftain.* New York: Dodd, Mead, 1931.

**3073.** Coffin, Charles C. *The Life of James A. Garfield, with a Sketch of the Life of Chester A. Arthur.* Boston: J. H. Earle, 1880.

**3074.** Conwell, Russell H. *The Life, Speeches, and Public Services of James A. Garfield.* Boston: B. B. Russel, 1881.

**3075.** Cottom, Robert I. "To Be Among the First: The Early Career of James A. Garfield, 1831–1868." Ph.D. dissertation, Johns Hopkins University, 1975.

**3076.** Dawes, Henry L. "Garfield and Conkling." *Century* 47 (January 1894): 341–344.

**3077.** Doenecke, Justus D. *The Presidencies of Garfield & Charles A. Arthur.* Lawrence: Regents Press of Kansas, 1981.

**3078.** Doyle, Burton T., and Homer H. Swaney. *Lives of James A. Garfield and Chester A. Arthur, with a Brief Sketch of the Assassin.* Washington, DC: R. H. Darby, 1881.

**3079.** Garfield, James A. *The Diary of James Abram Garfield.* 2 vols. Edited by Harry J. Brown and Frederick D. Williams. East Lansing: Michigan State University Press, 1964.

**3080.** Gilmore, James R. *The Life of James A. Garfield, Republican Candidate for the Presidency.* New York: Harper and Brothers, 1880.

**3081.** Green, Francis M. *A Royal Life, or the Eventful History of James A. Garfield.* Chicago: Central Book Concern, 1882.

**3082.** Harmon, Joseph. *Garfield, the Lawyer.* Yonkers, NY: Riverview Press, 1929.

**3083.** Hawkins, Seth C. "Garfield at the Bar: An Architectonic Rhetorical Criticism of Selected Speeches by James A. Garfield before the U.S. Supreme Court." Ph.D. dissertation, Bowling Green State University, 1975.

**3084.** Hinsdale, Burke A. *President Garfield and Education: Hiram College Memorial.* Boston: J. R. Osgood, 1882.

**3085.** Holm, James N. "A Rhetorical Study of the Public Speaking of James A. Garfield, 1851–1859." Ph.D. dissertation, Western Reserve University, 1958.

**3086.** Hosterman, Arthur D. *Life and Times of James Abram Garfield.* Springfield, OH: Farm and Fireside Publishing, 1882.

**3087.** Ketchen, John C. "Hale and Strong and Utterly Wholesome of Soul: James A. Garfield as Preacher." Master's thesis, Indiana University, 1978.

**3088.** Leech, Margaret, and Harry J. Brown. *The Garfield Orbit: The Life of James A. Garfield.* New York: Harper and Row, 1978.

**3089.** Lossing, Benson J. *A Biography of James A. Garfield.* New York: H. S. Goodspeed, 1882.

**3090.** McCabe, James D. *The Life and Public Service of Gen. James A. Garfield.* Chicago: G. W. Borland, 1881.

**3091.** North, Ira L. "A Rhetorical Criticism of the Speaking of James Abram Garfield, 1876–1880." Ph.D. dissertation, Louisiana State University, 1954.

**3092.** Ogilvie, John S. *The Life and Death of James A. Garfield, from the Tow Path to the White House.* Cincinnati, OH: Cincinnati Publishing Company, 1881.

**3093.** Peskin, Allan. "Blaine, Garfield, and Latin America." *Americas* 36 (July 1979): 79–89.

**3094.** ———. "The Elections of 1880." *Wilson Quarterly* 4 (Spring 1980): 172–181.

**3095.** ———. "From Log Cabin to Oblivion." *American History Illustrated* 11 (May 1976): 25–34.

**3096.** ———. *Garfield.* Kent, OH: Kent State University Press, 1978.

**3097.** ———. "Garfield and Hayes, Political Leaders of the Gilded Age." *Ohio Historical Quarterly* 77 (Winter/Spring/Summer 1968): 111–224.

**3098.** ———. "James A. Garfield: 1831–1863." Ph.D. dissertation, Case Western Reserve University, 1965.

**3099.** ———. "President Garfield and the Southern Question: The Making of the Policy That Never Was." *Southern Quarterly* 16 (July 1978): 375–386.

**3100.** Ridpath, John C. *The Life and Work of James A. Garfield, Twentieth President of the United States.* Cincinnati, OH: Jones Brothers, 1881.

**3101.** Ringenbery, William C. "The Religious Thought and Practice of James A. Garfield." *Old Northwest Genealogical Quarterly* 8 (Winter 1982–1983): 365–382.

**3102.** Rushford, Jerry B. "Political Disciple: The Relationship between James A. Garfield and the Disciples of Christ." Ph.D. dissertation, University of California, Santa Barbara, 1977.

**3103.** Sawyer, Robert W. "James A. Garfield and the Classics." *Hayes Historical Journal* 3 (Fall 1981): 47–56.

**3104.** Shaw, John. "A Shooting Star: The Life and Achievements of James A. Garfield: A Recital Drama for Five Voices." *Hayes Historical Journal* 3 (Spring 1982): 21–46.

**3105.** Short, Howard E. "President Garfield's Religious Heritage and What He Did With It." *Hayes Historical Journal* 4 (Fall 1983): 5–19.

**3106.** Smalley, Eugene V. "Characteristics of President Garfield." *Century Illustrated Monthly Magazine* 23 (November 1881): 168–176.

**3107.** Smith, Theodore C. "General Garfield at Chickamauga." *Massachusetts Historical Society Proceedings* 48 (June 1915): 268–280.

**3108.** ———. *The Life and Letters of James Abram Garfield.* 2 vols. New Haven, CT: Yale University Press, 1925.

**3109.** Smith, Thomas A. "A Pictorial Album: Garfield in Pen and Ink." *Hayes Historical Journal* 3 (Fall 1981): 31–46.

**3110.** Swing, David. "James A. Garfield." In his *The Message of David Swing to His Generation: Addresses and Papers,* 72–87. New York: Revell, 1913.

**3111.** Taylor, John M. *Garfield of Ohio: The Available Man.* New York: Norton, 1970.

**3112.** ———. "With More Sorrow Than I Can Tell: A Future President Turned on His Commander." *Civil War Times Illustrated* 20 (April 1981): 20–29.

**3113.** Thayer, William M. *From Log Cabin to the White House: Life of James A. Garfield.* Rev. ed. Norwich, CT: H. Bill Publishing Company, 1882.

**3114.** Thompson, Jack M. "James R. Garfield: The Making of a Progressive." *Ohio History* 74 (Spring 1965): 79–89.

**3115.** Wasson, Woodrow W. *James A. Garfield: His Religion and Education: A Study in the Religious and Educational Thought and Activity of an American Statesman.* Nashville: Tennessee Book Company, 1952.

**3116.** Wyatt-Brown, Bertram. "Reform and Anti-reform in Garfield's Ohio." *Hayes Historical Journal* 3 (Spring 1982): 63–78.

## GARLAND, AUGUSTUS HILL
### (1832–1899) D-AR, Senate 1877–1885.

**3117.** McNutt, Walter S. "Augustus Hill Garland." In his *Great Statesman of Arkansas,* 7–9. Jefferson, TX: Four States Publishing House, 1954.

**3118.** Newberry, Farrar. *A Life of Mr. Garland of Arkansas.* Arkadelhia, AR: N.p., 1908.

**3119.** Schlup, Leonard. "Augustus Hill Garland: Gilded Age Democrat." *Arkansas Historical Quarterly* 40 (Winter 1981): 338–346.

**3120.** Watkins, Beverly N. "Augustus Hill Garland, 1832–1899: Arkansas Lawyer to United States Attorney-General." Ph.D. dissertation, Auburn University, 1985.

## GARNER, JOHN NANCE (1868–1967)
### D-TX, House 1903–1933.

**3121.** Arnett, Alex M. "Garner versus Kitchin: A Study of Craft and Statecraft." In *The Walter Clinton Jackson Essays in the Social Science,* edited by Vera Largent, 133–145. Chapel Hill: University of North Carolina Press, 1942.

**3122.** Barr, C. Alwyn. "John Nance Garner's First Campaign for Congress." *West Texas Historical Association Year Book* 48 (1972): 105–110.

**3123.** Baulch, Joe R. "Garner Held the Cow While Jim Wells Milked Her." *West Texas Historical Association Year Book* 56 (1980): 91–99.

**3124.** Bell, Ulric. "Little Jack Garner." *American Mercury* 47 (May 1939): 1–8.

**3125.** Brown, George R. *The Speaker of the House: The Romantic Story of John N. Garner.* New York: Putnam's, 1932.

**3126.** Fisher, Ovie C. *Cactus Jack.* Waco, TX: Texian Press, 1982.

**3127.** Gilbert, Clinton W. "John N. Garner." *Forum* 87 (May 1932): 312–317.

**3128.** James, Marquis. *Mr. Garner of Texas.* Indianapolis: Bobbs-Merrill, 1939.

**3129.** Milburn, George. "The Statesmanship of Mr. Garner." *Harper's Magazine* 165 (November 1932): 669–682.

**3130.** Patenaude, Lionel V. "Garner, Sumners, and Connally: The Defeat of the Roosevelt Court Bill in 1937." *Southwestern Historical Quarterly* 74 (July 1970): 36–51.

**3131.** Romano, Michael J. "The Emergence of John Nance Garner as a Figure in American National Politics, 1924–1941." Ph.D. dissertation, St. John's University, 1974.

**3132.** Schwartz, Jordan A. "John Nance Garner and the Sales Tax Rebellion of 1932." *Journal of Southern History* (May 1964): 162–180.

**3133.** Timmons, Bascom N. *Garner of Texas: A Personal History.* New York: Harper, 1948.

**GARNETT, MUSCOE RUSSELL HUNTER (1821–1864) D-VA, House 1856–1861.**

**3134.** Clemons, Harry. *The Home Library of the Garnetts of Elmwood.* Charlottesville: University of Virginia Press, 1957.

**GASTON, WILLIAM (1778–1884) F-NC, House 1813–1817.**

**3135.** Schauinger, Joseph H. "Legislators." In his *Profiles in Action,* 55–71. Milwaukee, WI: Bruce, 1966.

**3136.** ———. *William Gaston, Carolinian.* Milwaukee, WI: Bruce, 1949.

**GEAR, JOHN HENRY (1825–1900) R-IA, House 1887–1891, 1893–1895, Senate 1895–1900.**

**3137.** Swisher, Jacob A. "John H. Gear." In his *Governors of Iowa,* 59–60. Macon City, IA: Klipto Loose Leaf Company, 1946.

**GENTRY, MEREDITH POINDEXTER (1809–1866) W-TN, House 1839–1843, 1845–1853.**

**3138.** Temple, Oliver P. "Meredith Poindexter Gentry." In *Notable Men of Tennessee, from 1833 to 1875,* compiled by Mary B. Temple, 233–245. New York: Cosmopolitan Press, 1912.

**GEORGE, JAMES ZACHARIAH (1826–1897) D-MS, Senate 1881–1897.**

**3139.** Peck, Lucy. "The Life and Times of James Z. George." Ph.D. dissertation, Mississippi State University, 1964.

**GEORGE, WALTER FRANKLIN (1878–1957) D-GA, Senate 1922–1957.**

**3140.** Moore, Glen. "An Analysis of Georgia's 1938 Senate Race." *Proceedings and Papers of the Georgia Association of Historians* 6 (1985): 87–95.

**3141.** Zeigler, Luther H. "Senator Walter George's 1938 Campaign." *Georgia Historical Quarterly* 43 (December 1959): 333–352.

**GERRY, ELBRIDGE (1744–1814) MA, House 1789–1793, Continental Congress 1776–1780, 1783–1785.**

**3142.** Austin, James T. *The Life of Elbridge Gerry, with Contemporary Letters to the Close of the American Revolution.* Boston: Wells and Lilly, 1829.

**3143.** Barzman, Sol. "Elbridge Gerry." In his *Madmen and Geniuses: The Vice-Presidents of the United States,* 41–46. Chicago: Follett, 1974.

**3144.** Billias, George A. *Elbridge Gerry, Founding Father and Republican Statesman.* New York: McGraw-Hill, 1976.

**3145.** Kramer, Eugene. "The Public Career of Elbridge Gerry." Ph.D. dissertation, Ohio State University, 1955.

**3146.** Ringer, James H. "Political Career of Elbridge Gerry." Master's thesis, Indiana University, 1942.

**3147.** Sanderson, John. "Elbridge Gerry." In *Sanderson's Biography of the Signers of the Declaration of Independence,* edited by Robert T. Conrad, 144–167. Philadelphia: Thomas, Cowperthwait, 1848.

**3148.** Warren, James. *A Study in Dissent: The Warren-Gerry Correspondence, 1776–1792.* Edited by C. Harvey Gardiner. Carbondale: Southern Illinois University Press, 1968.

**GIBSON, ERNEST WILLARD (1872–1940) R-VT, House 1923–1933, Senate 1933–1940.**

**3149.** Hand, Ernest. *Friends, Neighbors and Political Allies: Reflections on the Gibson-Aiken Connection.* Burlington: Center for Research on Vermont, University of Vermont, 1986.

**GIBSON, RANDALL LEE** (1832–1892)
D-LA, House 1875–1883, Senate 1883–1892.

**3150.** McBride, Mary M. "Senator Randall Lee Gibson and the Establishment of Tulane University." *Louisiana History* 28 (Summer 1987): 245–262.

**GIDDINGS, JOSHUA REED** (1795–1864)
R-OH, House 1838–1859.

**3151.** Gamble, Douglas A. "Joshua Giddings and the Ohio Abolitionists: A Study in Radical Politics." *Ohio History* 88 (Winter 1979): 37–56.

**3152.** Julian, George W. *The Life of Joshua R. Giddings.* Chicago: McClurg, 1892.

**3153.** Ludlum, Robert P. "Joshua R. Giddings, Antislavery Radical (1795–1844)." Ph.D. dissertation, Cornell University, 1936.

**3154.** Solberg, Richard W. "Joshua Giddings, Politician and Idealist." Ph.D. dissertation, University of Chicago, 1952.

**3155.** Stewart, James B. *Joshua R. Giddings and the Tactics of Radical Politics.* Cleveland, OH: Press of Case Western Reserve University, 1970.

**3156.** Wheeler, Henry G. "Giddings, Joshua Reed." In his *History of Congress,* vol. 1, 268–327. New York: Harper and Brothers, 1848.

**GILES, WILLIAM BRANCH** (1762–1830)
R-VA, House 1790–1798, 1801–1803, Senate 1804–1815.

**3157.** Anderson, Dice R. *William Branch Giles: A Study in the Politics of Virginia and the Nation from 1790 to 1830.* Menasha, WI: George Banta Publishing Company, 1914.

**3158.** Giunta, Mary A. "The Public Life of William Branch Giles, Republican, 1790–1815." Ph.D. dissertation, Catholic University of America, 1980.

**GILLETT, FREDERICK HUNTINGTON** (1851–1935) R-MA, House 1893–1925, Senate 1925–1931.

**3159.** Russell, Henry B. "Frederick H. Gillett: American Statesman." *Amherst Graduates' Quarterly* 21 (November 1931): 3–17.

**GILLETT, JAMES NORRIS** (1860–1937)
R-CA, House 1903–1906.

**3160.** Melendy, Howard B., and Benjamin F. Gilbert. "James N. Gillett." In their *Governors of California: Peter H. Burnett to Edmund G. Brown,* 288–304. Georgetown, CA: Talisman Press, 1965.

**GILLETTE, GUY MARK** (1879–1973)
D-IA, House 1933–1936, Senate 1936–1945, 1949–1955.

**3161.** Harrington, Jerry. "Senator Guy Gillette Foils the Execution Committee." *Palimpsest* 62 (November/December 1981): 170–180.

**GILLIGAN, JOHN JOYCE** (1921– )
D-OH, House 1965–1967.

**3162.** Larson, David R. "Ohio's Fighting Liberal: A Political Biography of John J. Gilligan." Ph.D. dissertation, Ohio State University, 1982.

**GILMER, GEORGE ROCKINGHAM** (1790–1859) J-GA, House 1821–1823, 1827–1829, 1833–1835.

**3163.** Coulter, E. Merton. "Dispute over George R. Gilmer's Election to Congress in 1928." *Georgia Historical Quarterly* 52 (June 1968): 159–186.

**3164.** Gilmer, George R. *Sketches of Some of the First Settlers of Upper Georgia, of the Cherokees, and the Author.* New York: Appleton, 1855.

## GILMER, JOHN ADAMS (1805–1868) O-NC, House 1857–1861.

**3165.** Crofts, Daniel W. "A Reluctant Unionist: John A. Gilmer and Lincoln's Cabinet." *Civil War History* 24 (September 1978): 225–249.

## GILMER, THOMAS WALKER (1802–1844) D-VA, House 1841–1844.

**3166.** Gilmer, Francis W. "Letters of Francis Walker Gilmer to Thomas Walker Gilmer." *Tyler's Quarterly Historical and Genealogical Magazine* 6 (April 1925): 240–249.

## GLASS, CARTER (1858–1946) D-VA, House 1902–1918, Senate 1920–1946.

**3167.** Glass, Carter. *An Adventure in Constructive Finance.* Garden City, NY: Doubleday, 1927.

**3168.** Heinemann, Ronald L. "The Politics of *Status Quo.*" In his *Depression and New Deal in Virginia: The Enduring Dominion,* 129–154. Charlottesville: University Press of Virginia, 1983.

**3169.** Koeniger, A. Cash. "Carter Glass and the National Recovery Administration." *South Atlantic Quarterly* 74 (Summer 1975): 349–364.

**3170.** ———. "The Politics of Independence: Carter Glass and the Elections of 1936." *South Atlantic Quarterly* 80 (Winter 1981): 95–106.

**3171.** ———. "Unreconstructed Rebel: Political Thought and Senate Career of Carter Glass, 1929–1936." Ph.D. dissertation, Vanderbilt University, 1980.

**3172.** Lyle, John D. "The United States Senate Career of Carter Glass of Virginia, 1919–1939." Ph.D. dissertation, University of South Carolina, 1974.

**3173.** Palmer, James A. *Carter Glass: Unreconstructed Rebel.* Roanoke, VA: Institute of American Biography, 1938.

**3174.** Patterson, Michael S. "Fall of a Bishop: James Cannon, Jr., Versus Carter Glass, 1909–1934." *Journal of Southern History* 39 (November 1973): 493–518.

**3175.** Poindexter, Harry E. "From Copy Desk to Congress: The Pre-congressional Career of Carter Glass." Ph.D. dissertation, University of Virginia, 1966.

**3176.** Smith, Rixey, and Norman Beasley. *Carter Glass: A Biography.* New York: Longman's, Green, 1939.

**3177.** Syrett, John. "Jim Farley and Carter Glass: Allies against a Third Team." *Prologue* 15 (Summer 1983): 88–102.

## GLENN, JOHN HERSCHEL, JR. (1921– ) D-OH, Senate 1974– .

**3178.** Fenno, Richard F. *The Presidential Odyssey of John Glenn.* Washington, DC: Congressional Quarterly, 1990.

**3179.** Margolis, Jon. *John Glenn.* Washington, DC: Political Profiles, 1984.

**3180.** Van Riper, Frank. *Glenn: The Astronaut Who Would Be President.* New York: Empire, 1983.

## GOFF, GUY DESPARD (1866–1933) R-WV, Senate 1925–1931.

**3181.** Smith, Gerald W. *Nathan Goff, Jr.: A Biography, with Some Account of Guy Despard Goff and Brazilla Carroll Reece,* 304–340. Charleston, WV: Education Foundation, 1959.

## GOFF, NATHAN (1843–1920) R-WV, House 1883–1889, Senate 1913–1919.

**3182.** Davis, Leonard M. "The Speeches and Speaking of Nathan Goff, Jr." Ph.D. dissertation, Northwestern University, 1958.

**3183.** Davis, Leonard M., and James H. Henning. "Nathan Goff—West Virginia Orator and Statesman." *West Virginia History* 12 (July 1951): 299–337.

**3184.** Smith, Gerald W. *Nathan Goff, Jr.: A Bibliography.* Charleston, WV: Educational Foundation, 1959.

**3185.** ———. *Nathan Goff, Jr.: A Biography, with Some Account of Guy Despard Goff and Brazillla Carroll Reece.* Charleston, WV: Education Foundation, 1959.

**3186.** ———. "Nathan Goff, Jr. and the Solid South." *West Virginia History* 16 (October 1955): 5–21.

## GOLDWATER, BARRY MORRIS
**(1909– ) R-AZ, Senate 1953–1965, 1969–1987.**

**3187.** Annunziata, Frank. "The Revolt against the Welfare State: Goldwater Conservatism and the Election of 1964." *Presidential Studies Quarterly* 10 (Spring 1980): 254–265.

**3188.** Arcese, Anthony E. *Conservatism and Conscience.* Philadelphia: Dorrance, 1968.

**3189.** Bell, Jack. *Mr. Conservative: Barry Goldwater.* Garden City, NY: Doubleday, 1962.

**3190.** Blunt, Barrie E. "The Goldwater Candidacy: Its Effect on Racial Liberalism in the House of Representatives." *Presidential Studies Quarterly* 15 (Winter 1985): 119–127.

**3191.** Castle, David S. "Goldwater's Presidential Candidacy and Political Realignment." *Presidential Studies Quarterly* 20 (Winter 1990): 103–110.

**3192.** Cook, Fred J. *Barry Goldwater: Extremist of the Right.* New York: Grove, 1964.

**3193.** Cosman, Bernard. *Five States for Goldwater: Continuity and Change in Southern Presidential Voting Patterns.* University: University of Alabama Press, 1966.

**3194.** De Toledano, Ralph. *Winning Side: The Case for Goldwater Republicanism.* New York: Putnam's, 1963.

**3195.** Donovan, Frank R. *The Americanism of Barry Goldwater.* New York: MacFadden Books, 1964.

**3196.** Ericson, Jon L. "The Reporting by the Prestige Press of Selected Speeches by Senator Goldwater in the 1964 Presidential Campaign." Ph.D. dissertation, University of Wisconsin, 1966.

**3197.** Goldwater, Barry M. *The Conscience of a Conservative.* Sheperdsville, KY: Victor Publishing Company, 1960.

**3198.** ———. *The Conscience of a Majority.* Englewood Cliffs, NJ: Prentice-Hall, 1970.

**3199.** ———. *Goldwater from A to Z, a Critical Handbook.* Compiled by Arthur Frommer. New York: Frommer/Pasmantier, 1964.

**3200.** ———. *With No Apologies: The Personal and Political Memoirs of United States Senator Barry M. Goldwater.* New York: Morrow, 1979.

**3201.** Goldwater, Barry M., and Jack Casserly. *Goldwater.* New York: Doubleday, 1988.

**3202.** Hammerback, John C. "Barry Goldwater's Rhetoric of Rugged Individualism." *Quarterly Journal of Speech* 58 (April 1972): 175–183.

**3203.** Hess, Karl. *In a Cause That Will Triumph: The Goldwater Campaign and the Future of Conservatism.* Garden City, NY: Doubleday, 1967.

**3204.** Howell, Millard L. *An Answer to Goldwater.* New York: Vantage, 1961.

**3205.** Kessel, John H. *Goldwater Coalition: Republican Strategies in 1964.* Indianapolis: Bobbs-Merrill, 1968.

**3206.** Lokos, Lionel. *Hysteria 1964: The Fear Campaign against Goldwater.* New Rochelle, NY: Arlington House, 1967.

**3207.** Mattar, Edward P. *Barry Goldwater: A Political Indictment.* Riverdale, MD: Century Twenty One Limited, 1964.

**3208.** McDowell, Edwin. *Barry Goldwater: Portrait of an Arizonian.* Chicago: Regnery, 1964.

**3209.** Moore, Mark P. "Individuals Unite: Paradox as a Rhetorical Strategy in the Political Discourse of Barry Goldwater and the Resurgence of Conservatism in American Politics, 1950–1964." Ph.D. dissertation, Indiana University, 1983.

**3210.** Novak, Robert D. *The Agony of the G.O.P. 1964.* New York: Macmillan, 1965.

**3211.** Perry, James M. *Barry Goldwater: A New Look at a Presidential Candidate.* Silver Spring, MD: National Observer, 1964.

**3212.** Porter, Sharon B. "A Rhetorical Analysis of the Speaking of Barry Morris Goldwater, 1969–1974." Ph.D. dissertation, Louisiana State University and Agricultural and Mechanical College, 1980.

**3213.** Rovere, Richard H. *Goldwater Caper: With Cartoons by Bill Mauldin.* New York: Harcourt, 1965.

**3214.** Shadegg, Stephen C. *Barry Goldwater: Freedom Is His Flight Plan.* New York: Fleet Publishing Corporation, 1962.

**3215.** ———. *What Happened to Goldwater? The Inside Story of the 1964 Republican Campaign.* New York: Holt, Rinehart and Winston, 1965.

**3216.** Shirey, Keith F. *Barry Goldwater: His Political Philosophy.* Los Angeles: Brewster, 1963.

**3217.** Smith, James W. *Goldwater and the Republic That Was.* New York: Carlton Press, 1965.

**3218.** Vidal, Gore. "Barry Goldwater: A Chat." In *First Person Singular,* edited by Herbert Gold, 232–250. New York: Dial, 1963.

**3219.** Wagner, Ronnie L. "The Conservative Vision of American Politics in the Campaign of Barry Goldwater." Ph.D. dissertation, University of Arizona, 1976.

**3220.** White, F. Clifton, and William J. Gill. *Suite 3505: The Story of the Draft Goldwater Movement.* New Rochelle, NY: Arlington House, 1967.

**3221.** Wood, Rob, and Dean Smith. *Barry Goldwater: The Biography of a Conservative.* New York: Avon, 1961.

## GONZALEZ, HENRY BARBOSA
(1916– ) D-TX, House 1961– .

**3222.** Rodriguez, Eugene. *Henry B. Gonzalez: A Political Profile.* New York: Arno Press, 1976.

## GOODWIN, JOHN NOBLE (1824–1887)
R-AZ, House 1861–1863, 1865–1867.

**3223.** Poston, Lawrence, ed. "Poston vs. Goodwin: A Document on the Congressional Election of 1865." *Arizona and the West* 3 (Winter 1961): 351–354.

## GORDON, JOHN BROWN (1832–1904)
D-GA, Senate 1873–1880, 1891–1897.

**3224.** Anderson, William. "The Resignation of John B. Gordon from the United States Senate in 1880." *Georgia Historical Quarterly* 52 (December 1968): 438–442.

**3225.** Culpepper, Grady S. "The Political Career of John Brown Gordon, 1868 to 1897." Ph.D. dissertation, Emory University, 1981.

**3226.** Deaderick, John B. "Gordon, John Brown." In his *Strategy in the Civil War,* 164–165. Harrisburg, PA: Military Service, 1946.

**3227.** Dorgan, Howard. "Case Study in Reconciliation: General John B. Gordon and the Last Days of the Confederacy." *Quarterly Journal of Speech* 60 (February 1974): 83–91.

**3228.** Eckert, Ralph L. "The Breath of Scandal: John B. Gordon, Henry W. Grady, and the Resignation-Appointment Controversy of May 1880." *Georgia Historical Quarterly* 69 (Fall 1985): 315–337.

**3229.** ———. *John Brown Gordon: Soldier, Southerner, American.* Baton Rouge: Louisiana State University Press, 1989.

**3230.** Gordon, John B. *Reminiscences of the Civil War.* New York: Scribner's, 1903.

**3231.** Smith, Francis G. "John B. Gordon" In *Library of Southern Literature,* edited by Edwin A. Alderman and Joel C. Harris, vol. 5, 1939–1942. New Orleans: Martin and Hoyt, 1909.

**3232.** Tankersley, Allen P. *John B. Gordon: A Study in Gallantry.* Atlanta, GA: Whitehall Press, 1955.

**GORE, ALBERT ARNOLD** (1907– )
D-TN, House 1939–1944, 1945–1953, Senate 1953–1971.

**3233.** Gardner, James B. "Political Leadership in a Period of Transition: Frank G. Clement, Albert Gore, Estes Kefauver, and Tennessee Politics, 1948–1956." Ph.D. dissertation, Vanderbilt University, 1978.

**3234.** Gore, Albert. *The Eve of the Storm: A People's Politics for the Seventies.* New York: Herder and Herder, 1970.

**3235.** ———. *Let the Glory Out: My South and Its Politics.* New York: Viking, 1972.

**GORE, ALBERT ARNOLD, JR.** (1948– )
D-TN, House 1977–1985, Senate 1985–1993.

**3236.** Hillin, Hank. *Al Gore, Jr.: Born to Lead.* Nashville, TN: Pine Hall Press, 1988.

**3237.** ———. *Al Gore, Jr.: His Life and Career.* Secaucus, NJ: Carol Publishing Group, 1992.

**GORE, CHRISTOPHER** (1758–1827)
F-MA, Senate 1813–1816.

**3238.** Pinkney, Helen. *Christopher Gore, Federalist of Massachusetts, 1758–1827.* Waltham, MA: Gore Place Society, 1969.

**GORE, THOMAS PRYOR** (1870–1949)
D-OK, Senate 1907–1921, 1931–1937.

**3239.** Billington, Monroe L. "Senator Thomas P. Gore." *Chronicles of Oklahoma* 35 (Autumn 1957): 265–287.

**3240.** ———. "Senator Thomas P. Gore: Southern Isolationist." *Southwest Social Science Quarterly* 42 (March 1962): 381–389.

**3241.** ———. "T. P. Gore and Agricultural Legislation." *Agricultural History* 31 (January 1957): 29–39.

**3242.** ———. "Thomas P. Gore and Oklahoma Public Opinion, 1917–1918." *Journal of Southern History* 27 (August 1961): 344–353.

**3243.** ———. *Thomas P. Gore: The Blind Senator from Oklahoma.* Lawrence: University of Kansas Press, 1967.

**GORMAN, ARTHUR PUE** (1839–1906)
D-MD, Senate 1881–1899, 1903–1906.

**3244.** Essary, J. Frederick. "Arthur P. Gorman." In his *Maryland in National Politics,* 243–263. Baltimore: John Murphy, 1915.

**3245.** Lambert, John R. *Arthur Pue Gorman.* Baton Rouge: Louisiana State University, 1953.

**3246.** ———. "Arthur Pue Gorman: Practical Politician." Ph.D. dissertation, Princeton University, 1947.

**3247.** ———. "The Autobiographical Writing of Senator Arthur Pue Gorman." *Maryland Historical Magazine* 58 (June 1963): 93–122; (September 1963): 233–246.

**3248.** Sanderlin, Walter S. "Arthur P. Gorman and the Chesapeake and Ohio Canal: An Episode in the Rise of the Political Boss." *Journal of Southern History* 13 (February 1947): 323–327.

## GORMAN, WILLIS ARNOLD
(1816–1876) D-IN, House 1849–1853.

**3249.** Baker, James H. "Willis Arnold Gorman." *Minnesota Historical Society Collections* 13 (1908): 47–63.

## GRAHAM, FRANK PORTER (1886–1972)
D-NC, Senate 1949–1950.

**3250.** Ashby, Warren. *Frank Porter Graham, a Southern Liberal.* Winston-Salem, NC: J. F. Blair, 1980.

**3251.** Douglas, Paul H. "Three Saints in Politics." *American Scholar* 40 (Spring 1971): 223–232.

**3252.** Pleasants, Julian M. "The Last Hurrah: Bob Reynolds and the U.S. Senate Race in 1950." *North Carolina Historical Review* 65 (January 1988): 52–75.

**3253.** Pleasants, Julian M., and Augustus M. Burns III. *Frank Porter Graham and the 1950 Senate Race in North Carolina.* Chapel Hill: University of North Carolina Press, 1990.

## GRAHAM, WILLIAM ALEXANDER
(1804–1875) W-NC, Senate 1840–1843.

**3254.** Conner, Robert D. "William Alexander Graham." In *Library of Southern Literature,* edited by Edwin A. Alderman and Joel C. Harris, vol. 5, 1987–1991. New Orleans: Martin and Hoyt, 1909.

**3255.** Graham, William A. *The Papers of William Alexander Graham.* Edited by J. G. de Roulhac Hamilton and Max R. Williams. Raleigh, NC: State Department of Archives and History, 1957.

**3256.** Williams, Max R. "The Education of William A. Graham." *North Carolina Historical Review* 40 (Winter 1963): 1–14.

**3257.** ———. "William A. Graham, North Carolina Whig Party Leader, 1804–1849." Ph.D. dissertation, University of North Carolina, 1965.

## GRAMM, WILLIAM PHILIP (1942– )
R-TX, House 1979–1983, 1983–1985, Senate 1985–

**3258.** Baker, Ross K. "Party and Institutional Sanctions in the U.S. House: The Case of Congressman Graham." *Legislative Studies Quarterly* 10 (August 1985): 315–337.

**3259.** Meyerson, Adam. "The Genius of Ordinary People: Senator Phil Gramm on Conservatism; Winning Ideas." *Policy Review* 50 (Fall 1989): 6–12.

**3260.** ———. "Submitting with the Enemy: Senator Phil Gramm Defends the Budget Deal." *Policy Review* 56 (Spring 1991): 44–47.

## GRASSO, ELLA TAMBUSSI (1919–1981)
D-CT, House 1971–1975.

**3261.** Lamson, Peggy. "Two from Connecticut: City Hall and the Capitol Dome, Ann Uccello and Ella T. Grasso." In her *Few Are Chosen: American Women in Political Life,* 215–226. Boston: Houghton Mifflin, 1968.

## GRAVEL, MAURICE ROBERT "MIKE"
(1930– ) D-AK, Senate 1969–1981.

**3262.** Gravel, Mike. *Citizen Power: A People's Platform.* New York: Holt, Rinehart and Winston, 1972.

**3263.** Velvel, Lawrence R. "Supreme Court Tramples Gravel." *Kentucky Law Journal* 61 (Winter 1972): 525–537.

## GRAVES, WILLIAM JORDAN
(1805–1848) W-KY, House 1835–1841.

**3264.** Thayer, Shelly A. "The Delegate and the Duel: The Early Political Career of George Wallace Jones." *Palimpsest* 65 (September/October 1984): 178–188.

**GRAY, GEORGE** (1840–1925) D-DE,
Senate 1885–1899.

**3265.** Crosslin, Michael P. "The Diplomacy of George Gray." Ph.D. dissertation, Oklahoma State University, 1980.

**GRAY, WILLIAM HERBERT III**
(1941–1991) D-PA, House 1979–1991.

**3266.** Hirschoff, Paula. "Congressman William H. Gray, III." *Africa Report* 30 (May/June 1985): 49.

**GRAYSON, WILLIAM** (1740–1790) VA,
Senate 1789–1790, Continental Congress 1785–1787.

**3267.** Bristow, Weston. "William Grayson, a Study in Virginia Biography of the Eighteenth Century." *Richmond College Papers* 2 (June 1917): 74–117.

**3268.** DuPriest, James E. *William Grayson: A Political Biography of Virginia's First United States Senator.* Manassas, VA: Prince William County Historical Commission, 1977.

**3269.** Esposito, Joseph A. "William Grayson of Prince William County." *Northern Virginia Heritage* 10, no. 2 (1988): 15–20.

**3270.** Horrell, Joseph. "New Light on William Grayson." *Magazine of Virginia History and Biography* 92 (October 1984): 423–443.

**3271.** Kukla, Jon. "'Freedom and Good Government': Antifederalist William Grayson's Intended Amendments to the United Sates Constitution." *Virginia Cavalcade* 36 (Spring 1987): 184–191.

**GRAYSON, WILLIAM JOHN** (1788–1863)
N-SC, House 1833–1837.

**3272.** Bass, Robert D. "The Autobiography of William J. Grayson." Ph.D. dissertation, University of South Carolina, 1933.

**3273.** Grayson, William J. *The Hireling and the Slave.* Charleston, VA: Russell, 1854.

**3274.** ———. *Witness to Sorrow: The Antebellum Autobiography of William J. Grayson.* Edited by Richard J. Calhoun. Columbia: University of South Carolina Press, 1990.

**3275.** Hubbell, Jay B. "William J. Grayson." In his *The South in American Literature 1607–1900,* 438–446, 933–934. Durham, NC: Duke University Press, 1954.

**3276.** Jarrett, Thomas D. "The Literary Significance of William J. Grayson's 'The Hireling and the Slave.'" *Georgia Review* 5 (Winter 1951): 487–494.

**3277.** ———. "William Grayson's 'The Hireling and the Slave': A Study of Ideas, Form, Reception, and Editions." Ph.D. dissertation, University of Chicago, 1947.

**3278.** Parks, Edd W. "William J. Grayson, Neo-classicist." In his *Ante-Bellum Southern Literary Critics,* 185–191. Athens: University of Georgia Press, 1962.

**3279.** Parrington, Vernon L. "William J. Grayson." In his *Main Currents of American Thought,* vol. 2, 103–108. New York: Harcourt, Brace, 1927.

**3280.** Taylor, William R. "Southern Mugwumps." In his *Cavalier and Yankee: The Old South and American National Character,* 55–65. New York: Braziller, 1961.

**3281.** Wauchope, George A. "William J. Grayson." In *A Library of Southern Literature,* edited by Edwin A. Alderman and Joel C. Harris, vol. 5, 2011–2013. Atlanta: Martin and Hoyt, 1909–1913.

**3282.** Wilson, Edmund. "Diversity of Opinion in the South: William J. Grayson, George Fitzhugh, and Hilton R. Helper." In his *Patriotic Gore: Studies in the Literature of the American Civil War,* 336–374. New York: Oxford University Press, 1966.

**GREELEY, HORACE** (1811–1872) W-NY,
House 1848–1849.

**3283.** Bradford, Gamaliel. "Horace Greeley." In his *As God Made Them: Portraits of Some Nineteenth-Century Americans,* 129–166. Boston: Houghton Mifflin, 1929.

**3284.** Cary, Samuel F. "Hon. Horace Greeley." In *The National Temperance Offering*, 310–317. New York: R. Vandien, 1850.

**3285.** Commons, John R. *Horace Greeley and the Working Class Origins of the Republican Party*. Boston: Ginn, 1909.

**3286.** Depew, Chauncey M. "Horace Greeley." In his *My Memories of Eighty Years*, 87–98. New York: Scribner's, 1922.

**3287.** Fahrney, Ralph R. *Horace Greeley and the Tribune in the Civil War*. Cedar Rapids, IA: Torch Press, 1936.

**3288.** Godkin, Edwin L. "Horace Greeley." In his *Reflections and Comments, 1865–1895*, 48–55. New York: Scribner's, 1895.

**3289.** Greeley, Horace. *The Autobiography of Horace Greeley*. New York: Treat, 1872.

**3290.** ———. *Greeley on Lincoln, with Mr. Greeley's Letters to Charles A. Dana and a Lady Friend, to Which Are Added Reminiscences of Horace Greeley*. Edited by Joel Benton. New York: Baker and Taylor, 1893.

**3291.** ———. *Recollections of a Busy Life*. New York: J. B. Ford 1868.

**3292.** Hale, William H. *Horace Greeley: Voice of the People*. New York: Collier Books, 1950.

**3293.** Hall, Abraham O. *Horace Greeley Decently Dissected, in a Letter on Horace Greeley*. New York: Ross and Tovsey, 1862.

**3294.** Horner, Harlan H. *Lincoln and Greeley*. Westport, CT: Greenwood, 1971.

**3295.** Ingersoll, Lurton D. *The Life of Horace Greeley: Founder of the New York Tribune, with Extended Notices of Many of His Contemporaries*. Chicago: Union Publishing Company, 1873.

**3296.** Isely, Jeter A. *Horace Greeley and the Republican Party, 1853–1861: A Study of the New York Tribune*. Princeton, NJ: Princeton University Press, 1947.

**3297.** Kirkland, Edward C. "The Peace Missions of Two Northern Journalists." In his *The Peacemakers of 1864*, 51–86. New York: Macmillan, 1864.

**3298.** Kleber, Louis C. "Horace Greeley, 1811–1872." *History Today* 26 (September 1976): 569–575.

**3299.** Lillard, Richard G. *Hank Monk and Horace Greeley, an Enduring Episode in Western History and Detective Work in the Old Files*. Georgetown, CA: Wilmac Press, 1973.

**3300.** Linn, William A. *Horace Greeley, Founder and Editor of the New York Tribune*. New York: Appleton, 1912.

**3301.** Lunde, Erik S. *Horace Greeley*. Boston: Twayne, 1981.

**3302.** Myers, Joseph S. *The Genius of Horace Greeley*. Columbus: Ohio State University Press, 1929.

**3303.** Parrington, Vernon L. "Horace Greeley, Yankee Radical." In his *Main Currents in American Thought*, vol. 2, 247–258. New York: Harcourt, Brace, 1927.

**3304.** Parton, James. *The Life of Horace Greeley*. New York: Mason, 1855.

**3305.** Payne, George H. "Greeley and the Tribune: The Times and Greeley's Triumph." In his *History of Journalism in the United States*, 269–294. New York: Appleton, 1920.

**3306.** Robbins, Roy M. "Horace Greeley and the Quest for Social Justice, 1837–1862." *Indiana History Bulletin* 16 (February 1939): 68–84.

**3307.** Rourke, Constance M. "Horace Greeley." In her *Trumpets of Jubilee*, 239–365. New York: Harcourt, Brace, 1927.

**3308.** Schulze, Suzanne. *Horace Greeley: A Bio-bibliography*. New York: Greenwood, 1992.

**3309.** Seitz, Don C. *Horace Greeley, Founder of the New York Tribune*. Indianapolis: Bobbs-Merrill, 1926.

**3310.** ———. "Horace Greeley, Old White Hat." In his *The "Also Rans,"* 242–254. New York: Thomas Y. Crowell, 1928.

**3311.** Sotheran, Charles. *Horace Greeley and Other Pioneers of American Socialism.* New York: Kennerley, 1915.

**3312.** Spann, Edward K. "Gotham in Congress: New York's Representatives and the National Government, 1840–1854." *New York History* 67 (July 1986): 304–329.

**3313.** Sparks, Edwin E. "Horace Greeley, the Anti-Slavery Editor." In his *The Men Who Made the Nation*, 347–377. New York: Macmillan, 1901.

**3314.** Stockett, Julia C. "Horace Greeley: New York Tribune, 1841–1862." In her *Masters of American Journalism*, 24–33. New York: H. W. Wilson, 1916.

**3315.** Stoddard, Henry L. *Horace Greeley: Printer, Editor, Crusader.* New York: Putnam's, 1946.

**3316.** Stowe, Harriet B. "Horace Greeley." In her *Men of Our Times*, 293–310. Hartford, CT: Hartford Publishing Company, 1868.

**3317.** Strauss, James H. "The Political Economy of Horace Greeley." *Southwestern Social Science Quarterly* 19 (March 1939): 399–408.

**3318.** Sutherland, Daniel E. "Edwin DeLeon and Liberal Republicanism in Georgia: Horace Greeley's Campaign for President in a Southern State." *Historian* 47 (November 1984): 38–57.

**3319.** Van Deusen, Glyndon G. *Horace Greeley, Nineteenth Century Crusader.* Philadelphia: University of Pennsylvania Press, 1953.

**3320.** Zabriskie, Francis N. *Horace Greeley, the Editor.* New York: Geekman Publishers, 1974.

**GREEN, EDITH STARRETT** (1910–1987) **D-OR, House 1955–1975.**

**3321.** Rosenberg, Marie B. "The Campaigns and Elections of Congresswomen Edith Green and Julia Butler Hanson." *Politics* 24 (May 1989): 42–55.

**3322.** ———. "Women in Politics: A Comparative Study of Congresswomen Edith Green and Julia Butler Hansen." Ph.D. dissertation, University of Washington, 1973.

**3323.** Ross, Naomi V. "Congresswoman Edith Green on Federal Aid to Schools and Colleges." Ph.D. dissertation, Pennsylvania State University, 1980.

**GREEN, THEODORE FRANCIS** **(1867–1966) D-RI, Senate 1937–1961.**

**3324.** Levine, Erwin L. *Theodore Francis Green.* 2 vols. Providence, RI: Brown University Press, 1963–1971.

**GREEN, WILLIAM JOSEPH** (1938– ) **D-PA, House 1964–1977.**

**3325.** Green, William J. *Congressman.* New York: McGraw-Hill, 1969.

**GREENWOOD, ARTHUR HERBERT** **(1880–1963) D-IN, House 1923–1939.**

**3326.** Kraus, Rene. "Empire Builder, New Style: Arthur Greenwood." In his *The Men Around Churchill*, 198–207. Philadelphia: Lippincott, 1941.

**GRIFFITHS, MARTHA WRIGHT** **(1912– ) D-MI, House 1955–1974.**

**3327.** George, Emily. *Martha W. Griffiths.* Washington, DC: University Press of America, 1982.

**3328.** Lamson, Peggy. "Three Congresswomen: What Makes Them Run." In her *Few Are Chosen: American Women in Political Life Today*, 87–98. Boston: Houghton Mifflin, 1968.

## GRIMES, JAMES WILSON (1816–1872) R-IA, Senate 1859–1869.

**3329.** Boeck, George A. "Senator Grimes and the Iowa Press, 1867–1868." *Mid-America* 48 (July 1966): 147–161.

**3330.** Christoferson, Eli C. "The Life of James W. Grimes." Ph.D. dissertation, State University of Iowa, 1924.

**3331.** Herriott, Frank I. "James W. Grimes Versus the Southrons." *Annals of Iowa* 15 (July 1926): 323–357; 15 (October 1926): 403–432.

**3332.** Salter, William. *The Life of James W. Grimes.* New York: Appleton, 1876.

## GRINNELL, JOSIAH BUSHNELL (1821–1891) R-IA, House 1863–1867.

**3333.** Grinnell, Josiah B. *Men and Events of Forty Years.* Boston: Lothrop, 1891.

**3334.** Payne, Charles E. *Josiah Bushnell Grinnell.* Iowa City: State Historical Society of Iowa, 1938.

## GRISWOLD, DWIGHT PALMER (1893–1954) R-NE, Senate 1952–1954.

**3335.** Paul, Justus F. "Butler, Griswold, Wherry: The Struggle for Dominance of Nebraska Republicanism, 1941–1946." *North Dakota Quarterly* 43 (Autumn 1975): 51–61.

## GRISWOLD, ROGER (1762–1812) F-CT, House 1795–1805.

**3336.** McBride, Rita M. "Roger Griswold: Connecticut Federalist." Ph.D. dissertation, Yale University, 1948.

## GRONNA, ASLE JORGENSON (1858–1922) R-ND, House 1905–1911, Senate 1911–1921.

**3337.** Phillips, William W. "The Life of Asle J. Gronna: A Self-Made Man of the Prairies." Ph.D. dissertation, University of Missouri, 1958.

## GROVER, LA FAYETTE (1823–1911) D-OR, House 1859, Senate 1877–1883.

**3338.** Turnbull, George S. "La Fayette Grover." In his *Governors of Oregon,* 37–39. Portland, OR: Binfords, 1959.

## GROW, GALUSHA AARON (1823–1907) R-PA, House 1851–1863, 1894–1903.

**3339.** Dubois, James T., and Gertrude S. Mathews. *Galusha A. Grow: Father of the Homestead Law.* Boston: Houghton Mifflin, 1917.

**3340.** Fuller, Hubert B. "Grow and Colfax Dominated by Thaddeus Stevens." In his *The Speakers of the House,* 149–168. Boston: Little, Brown, 1909.

**3341.** Iliserich, Robert D. *Galusha A. Grow: The People's Candidate.* Pittsburgh, PA: University of Pittsburgh Press, 1988.

**3342.** ———. "Galusha Grow: Pennsylvania's Champion of the Homestead Act." *Western Pennsylvania Historical Magazine* 40 (Fall 1957): 205–216.

## GRUENING, ERNEST (1887–1974) D-AK, Senate 1959–1969.

**3343.** Gruening, Ernest. *Many Battles: The Autobiography of Ernest Gruening.* New York: Liveright, 1973.

**3344.** Naske, Claus M. "Governor Ernest Gruening, the Federal Government, and the Economic Development of Territorial Alaska." *Pacific Historian* 28 (Winter 1984): 4–16.

**3345.** Ross, Sherwood. *Gruening of Alaska.* New York: Best Books, 1968.

## GRUNDY, FELIX (1777–1840) D-TN, House 1811–1814, Senate 1829–1838, 1839–1840.

**3346.** Baylor, Orval W. "The Career of Felix Grundy, 1777–1840." *Filson Club History Quarterly* 16 (April 1942): 88–110.

**3347.** Biddle, Charles. *Senator Grundy's Political Conduct Reviewed.* Nashville, TN: Republican and Gazette Office, 1832.

**3348.** Ewing, Frances H. "The Senatorial Career of Felix Grundy, 1829–1840." Master's thesis, Vanderbilt University, 1931.

**3349.** ———. "The Senatorial Career of the Honorable Felix Grundy." *Tennessee Historical Magazine* 2 (October 1931): 3–27; 2 (January 1932): 111–135; 2 (April 1932): 220–224; 2 (July 1932): 270–291.

**3350.** Howell, Robert B. "Felix Grundy." *Tennessee Law Review* 16 (June 1941): 828–842.

**3351.** Parks, Joseph H. *Felix Grundy: Champion of Democracy.* Baton Rouge: Louisiana State University Press, 1940.

**3352.** ———. "Felix Grundy of Tennessee." Ph.D. dissertation, Ohio State University, 1938.

**GRUNDY, JOSEPH RIDGWAY** (1863–1961) R-PA, Senate 1929–1930.

**3353.** Hutton, Ann H. *Pennsylvanian: Joseph R. Grundy.* Ardmore, PA: Dorrance, 1962.

**GUBSER, CHARLES SAMUEL** (1916– ) R-CA, House 1953–1974.

**3354.** Duram, James C. "Ambivalence at the Top: California Congressman Charles Gubser and Federal Aid for Classroom Construction during the Eisenhower Presidency." *California History* 68 (Spring/ Summer 1989): 26–35.

**GUFFEY, JOSEPH F.** (1870–1959) D-PA, Senate 1935–1947.

**3355.** Guffey, Joseph F. *Seventy Years on the Red-Fire Wagon: From Tilden to Truman, through New Freedom and New Deal.* N.p.: 1952.

**3356.** Halt, Charles E. "Joseph F. Guffy, New Deal Politician from Pennsylvania." Ph.D. dissertation, Syracuse University, 1965.

**GUGGENHEIM, SIMON** (1867–1941) R-CO, Senate 1907–1913.

**3357.** Davis, John H. "Senator Simon, or Democracy in America." In his *The*

*Guggenheims: An American Epic,* 243–251. New York: Morrow, 1978.

**3358.** Hoyt, Edwin P. *The Guggenheims and the American Dream.* New York: Funk and Wagnalls, 1967.

**GUTHRIE, JAMES** (1792–1869) D-KY, Senate 1865–1868.

**3359.** Cotterill, Robert S. "James Guthrie: Kentuckian, 1792–1869." *Register of the Kentucky State Historical Society* 20 (September 1922): 290–296.

**GWIN, WILLIAM McKENDREE** (1805–1885) D-CA/MS, House (MS) 1841–1843, Senate (CA) 1850–1855, 1857–1861.

**3360.** Gwin, William M. *The Rivals: William Gwin, David Broderick, and the Birth of California.* New York: Crown, 1994.

**3361.** Hunt, Rockwell D. "William McKendree Gwin." In his *California's Stately Hall of Fame,* 249–253. Stockton, CA: College of the Pacific, 1950.

**3362.** Hynding, Alan A. "William Gwin." In his *California Historymakers,* 33–38. Dubuque, IA: Kendall/Hunt, 1976.

**3363.** McPherson, Hallie M. "William McKendree Gwin, Expansionist." Ph.D. dissertation, University of California, 1931.

**3364.** Stanley, Gerald. "Senator William Gwin: Moderate or Racist?" *California Historical Quarterly* 50 (September 1971): 243–255.

**3365.** Steele, Robert V. *Between Two Empires: The Life Story of California's First Senator.* Boston: Houghton Mifflin, 1969.

**GWINNETT, BUTTON** (1732–1777) GA, Continental Congress 1776–1777.

**3366.** Jenkins, Charles F. *Button Gwinnett.* Garden City, NY: Doubleday, 1926.

**3367.** Sanderson, John. "Button Gwinnett." In *Sanderson's Biography of the Signers of the Declaration of Independence,* edited by Robert T. Conrad, 819–824. Philadelphia: Thomas, Cowperthwait, 1848.

## HAGER, JOHN SHARPENSTEIN
### (1818–1890) D-CA, Senate 1873–1875.

**3368.** Stewart, George R. "John Sharpenstein Hager: Forty-Niner in the Social Register." In *Lives of Eighteen from Princeton,* edited by Willard Thorp, 232–242. Princeton, NJ: Princeton University Press, 1946.

## HAHN, MICHAEL (1830–1886) R-LA,
### House 1862–1863, 1885–1886.

**3369.** Baker, Vaughn. "Michael Hahn: Steady Patriot." *Louisiana History* 13 (Summer 1972): 229–252.

## HALE, JOHN PARKER (1806–1873)
### FS-NH, House 1843–1845, Senate 1847–1853, 1855–1865.

**3370.** Lowden, Lucy. "Black as Ink—Bitter as Hell: John P. Hales's Mutiny in New Hampshire." *Historical New Hampshire* 27 (Spring 1972): 27–50.

**3371.** Sewell, Richard H. "John P. Hale and the Liberty Party, 1847–1848." *New England Quarterly* 37 (June 1964): 200–223.

**3372.** ———. *John P. Hale and the Politics of Abolition.* Cambridge, MA: Harvard University Press, 1965.

**3373.** ———. "Walt Whitman, John P. Hale, and the Free Democracy: An Unpublished Letter." *New England Quarterly* 34 (June 1961): 239–241.

## HALL, KATIE BEATRICE GREEN
### (1938– ) D-IN, House 1982–1985.

**3374.** Catlin, Robert A. "Organizational Effectiveness and Black Political Participation: The Case of Katie Hall." *Phylon* 46 (September 1985): 179–192.

## HALL, LYMAN (1724–1790) GA,
### Continental Congress 1775–1778, 1780.

**3375.** Sanderson, John. "Lyman Hall." In *Sanderson's Biography of the Signers of the Declaration of Independence,* edited by Robert T. Conrad, 825–827. Philadelphia: Thomas, Cowperthwait, 1848.

## HALL, NATHAN KELSEY (1810–1874)
### W-NY, House 1847–1849.

**3376.** Putnam, James O. "Nathan Kelsey Hall." *Buffalo Historical Society Publications* 4 (1896): 285–298.

## HALL, WILLARD (1780–1875) R-DE,
### House 1817–1821.

**3377.** Bates, Daniel M. *Memorial Address on the Life and Character of Willard Hall.* Wilmington: Historical Society of Delaware, 1879.

**3378.** Harris, Charles R. *From Apathy to Awareness: The Contributions of Willard Hall to Delaware Education.* Philadelphia: Dorrance, 1968.

## HALLECK, CHARLES ABRAHAM
### (1900–1986) R-IN, House 1935–1969.

**3379.** Peabody, Robert L. *The Ford-Halleck Minority Leadership Contest, 1965.* New York: McGraw-Hill, 1966.

**3380.** Scheele, Henry Z. *Charlie Halleck: A Political Biography.* Hicksville, NY: Exposition, 1966.

**3381.** Womack, Steven D. "Charles A. Halleck and the New Frontier: Political Opposition through the Madisonian Model." Ph.D. dissertation, Ball State University, 1980.

## HAMILTON, ALEXANDER (1757–1804)
### NY, Continental Congress 1782–1783, 1787–1788.

**3382.** Adams, James T. "The Fight with Hamilton." In his *The Living Jefferson,* 227–253. New York: Scribner's, 1936.

**3383.** ———. "Jefferson and Hamilton Today." In his *Our Business Civilization*, 81–97. New York: Boni, 1929.

**3384.** Aly, Bower. *The Rhetoric of Alexander Hamilton*. New York: Columbia University Press, 1941.

**3385.** Atherton, Gertrude F. *The Conqueror: Being the True and Romantic Story of Alexander Hamilton*. New York: Macmillan, 1902.

**3386.** Bailey, Ralph E. *An American Colossus: The Singular Career of Alexander Hamilton*. Boston: Lothrop, Lee and Shepard, 1933.

**3387.** Bowers, Claude G. *Jefferson and Hamilton: The Struggle for Democracy in America*. Boston: Houghton Mifflin, 1925.

**3388.** Boyd, Julian P. *Number 7, Alexander Hamilton's Secret Attempts to Control American Foreign Policy, with Supporting Documents*. Princeton, NJ: Princeton University Press, 1964.

**3389.** Burr, Samuel E. *The Burr-Hamilton Duel and Related Matters*. San Antonio, TX: Naylor, 1971.

**3390.** Butler, Nicholas M. "Alexander Hamilton, Nation-Builder." In his *Is America Worth Saving?*, 285–313. New York: Scribner's, 1920.

**3391.** Caldwell, Lynton K. *The Administrative Theories of Hamilton and Jefferson: Their Contribution to Thought on Public Administration*. Chicago: University of Chicago Press, 1944.

**3392.** Cantor, Milton, comp. *Hamilton*. Englewood Cliffs, NJ: Prentice-Hall, 1971.

**3393.** Clemens, Jeremiah. *The Rivals: A Tale of the Times of Aaron Burr and Alexander Hamilton*. Philadelphia: Lippincott, 1860.

**3394.** Cooke, Jacob E. *Alexander Hamilton*. New York: Scribner's, 1982.

**3395.** ———, comp. *Alexander Hamilton: A Profile*. New York: Hill and Wang, 1967.

**3396.** Creel, George. "The Brat Who Climbed to the Stars." In his *Sons of the Eagle*, 79–90. Indianapolis: Bobbs-Merrill, 1927.

**3397.** Culbertson, William S. *Alexander Hamilton: An Essay*. New Haven, CT: Yale University Press, 1911.

**3398.** Daniels, Jonathan. *Ordeal of Ambition: Jefferson, Hamilton, Burr.* Garden City, NY: Doubleday, 1970.

**3399.** Elliott, Edward. "Alexander Hamilton: Growth through Administrative Organization." In his *Biographical Story of the Constitution*, 27–51. New York: Putnam's, 1910.

**3400.** Emery, Noemie. *Alexander Hamilton: An Intimate Portrait*. New York: Putnam's, 1982.

**3401.** Fiske, John. "Alexander Hamilton and the Federalist Party." In his *Essays, Historical and Literary*, 99–142. New York: Macmillan, 1902.

**3402.** Flexner, James T. *The Young Hamilton: A Biography*. Boston: Little, Brown, 1978.

**3403.** Ford, Henry J. *Alexander Hamilton*. New York: Scribner's, 1920.

**3404.** Frisch, Morton J. *Alexander Hamilton and the Political Order: An Interpretation of His Political Thought and Practice*. Lanham, MD: University Press of America, 1991.

**3405.** Grayson, Theodore J. "Alexander Hamilton, Reconstruction after Revolution." In his *Leaders and Periods of American Finance*, 46–82. New York: John Wiley and Sons, 1932.

**3406.** Griggs, Edward H. "Hamilton and the Making of Our Government." In his *American Statesmen: An Interpretation of Our History and Heritage*, 175–234. Croton-On-Hudson, NY: Orchard Hill Press, 1927.

**3407.** Guedalla, Philip. "Mr. Alexander Hamilton." In his *Fathers of the Revolution*, 251–262. New York: Putnam's, 1926.

**3408.** Hacker, Louis M. *Alexander Hamilton in the American Tradition.* New York: McGraw-Hill, 1957.

**3409.** Hamilton, Alexander. *Alexander Hamilton: A Biography in His Own Words.* Edited by Mary-Jo Kline. New York: Newsweek, 1973.

**3410.** ———. *Industrial and Commercial Correspondence of Alexander Hamilton, Anticipating His Report on Manufactures.* Edited by Arthur H. Cole. Chicago: A. W. Shaw, 1928.

**3411.** ———. *The Law Practice of Alexander Hamilton: Documents and Commentary.* New York: Columbia University Press, 1964.

**3412.** ———. *The Works of Alexander Hamilton.* Edited by John C. Hamilton. New York: J. F. Trow, 1850.

**3413.** Hamilton, Allan M. *The Intimate Life of Alexander Hamilton, Based Chiefly upon Original Family Letters and Other Documents, Many of Which Have Never Been Published.* New York: Scribner's, 1910.

**3414.** Hecht, Marie B. *Odd Destiny, the Life of Alexander Hamilton.* New York: Macmillan, 1982.

**3415.** Hendrickson, Robert A. *Hamilton.* New York: Mason/Charter, 1976.

**3416.** ———. *The Rise and Fall of Alexander Hamilton.* New York: Van Nostrand Reinhold, 1981.

**3417.** Hirst, Francis W. "The Quarrel with Alexander Hamilton." In his *Life and Letters of Thomas Jefferson,* 264–289. New York: Macmillan, 1926.

**3418.** Kerns, Gerald E. "The Hamiltonian Constitution: An Analysis of the Interpretation Given to Various Provisions of the United States Constitution." Ph.D. dissertation, Indiana University, 1969.

**3419.** Konefsky, Samuel J. *John Marshall and Alexander Hamilton, Architects of the American Constitution.* New York: Macmillan, 1964.

**3420.** Lodge, Henry C. *Alexander Hamilton.* Boston: Houghton Mifflin, 1898.

**3421.** Looze, Helene J. *Alexander Hamilton and the British Orientation of American Foreign Policy, 1783–1803.* The Hague: Mouton, 1969.

**3422.** Loss, Richard. *The Modern Theory of Presidential Power: Alexander Hamilton and the Corwin Thesis.* New York: Greenwood, 1990.

**3423.** Loth, David G. *Alexander Hamilton: Portrait of a Prodigy.* New York: Carrick and Evans, 1939.

**3424.** Lycan, Gilbert L. *Alexander Hamilton and American Foreign Policy: A Design for Greatness.* Norman: University of Oklahoma Press, 1970.

**3425.** Magoon, Elias L. "Alexander Hamilton, the Master of Political Sagacity." In his *Orators of the American Revolution,* 283–310. New York: Scribner's, 1853.

**3426.** McDonald, Forrest. *Alexander Hamilton: A Biography.* New York: Norton, 1979.

**3427.** Miller, John C. *Alexander Hamilton and the Growth of the New Nation.* New York: Harper and Row, 1964.

**3428.** Miroff, Bruce. "Alexander Hamilton: The Aristocratic Statesman and the Constitution of American Capitalism." In his *Icons of Democracy: American Leaders as Heroes, Aristocrats, Dissenters, and Democrats,* 11–49. New York: Basic Books, 1993.

**3429.** Mitchell, Broadus. *Alexander Hamilton: A Concise Biography.* New York: Oxford University Press, 1976.

**3430.** ———. *Alexander Hamilton: The Revolutionary Years.* New York: Crowell, 1970.

**3431.** ———. *Alexander Hamilton: Youth to Maturity, 1755–1788.* New York: Macmillan, 1957.

**3432.** ———. *Heritage from Hamilton.* New York: Columbia University Press, 1957.

**3433.** Morris, Richard B. "Alexander Hamilton and the Quest for Fame." In his *Witnesses at the Creation: Hamilton, Madison, Jay, and the Constitution,* 24–47. New York: Holt, Rinehart and Winston, 1985.

**3434.** Morse, John T. *The Life of Alexander Hamilton.* Boston: Little, Brown, 1882.

**3435.** Munro, William B. "Alexander Hamilton and the Economic Supremacy of the Federal Government." In his *The Makers of the Unwritten Constitution,* 25–50. New York: Macmillan, 1930.

**3436.** Nevins, Allan. "Hamilton and the Founding of the 'Evening Post.'" In his *The Evening Post,* 9–34. New York: Boni and Liveright, 1922.

**3437.** Nott, Eliphalet. *A Discourse, on the Death of Gen. Alexander Hamilton.* Boston: David Carlisle, 1805.

**3438.** Oliver, Frederick S. *Alexander Hamilton: An Essay on American Union.* London: A. Constable, 1906.

**3439.** Pancake, John S. *Thomas Jefferson and Alexander Hamilton.* Woodbury, NY: Barron's Educational Series, 1974.

**3440.** Parks, Robert J. *European Origins of the Economic Ideas of Alexander Hamilton.* New York: Arno Press, 1977.

**3441.** Parrington, Vernon L. "Alexander Hamilton: The Leviathan State." In his *Main Currents in American Thought,* vol. 1, 292–307. New York: Harcourt, Brace, 1927.

**3442.** Peterson, Charles J. "Alexander Hamilton." In his *The Military Heroes of the Revolution,* 469–476. Philadelphia: J. B. Smith, 1856.

**3443.** Ridpath, John C. *Alexander Hamilton: A Study of the Revolution and the Union.* Cincinnati, OH: Jones Brothers, 1883.

**3444.** Risher, James F. *Interview with Honor: The Burr-Hamilton Duel.* Philadelphia: Dorrance, 1975.

**3445.** Rocher, Rosane. *Alexander Hamilton, 1762–1824: A Chapter in the Early History of Sanskrit Philology.* New Haven, CT: American Oriental Society, 1968.

**3446.** Root, Elihu. "Alexander Hamilton." In *Men and Policies,* edited by Robert Bacon and James B. Scott, 76–87. Cambridge, MA: Harvard University Press, 1925.

**3447.** Rossiter, Clinton L. *Alexander Hamilton and the Constitution.* New York: Harcourt, Brace and World, 1964.

**3448.** Schachner, Nathan. *Alexander Hamilton.* New York: Appleton-Century, 1946.

**3449.** Sherlock, Chesla C. "Alexander Hamilton: Comparison of Alexander Hamilton and James Madison." In her *Tall Timbers,* 233–237. Boston: Stratford Company, 1926.

**3450.** Stourzh, Gerald. *Alexander Hamilton and the Idea of Republican Government.* Stanford, CA: Stanford University Press, 1970.

**3451.** Swanson, Donald F. *The Origins of Hamilton's Fiscal Policies.* Gainesville: University of Florida Press, 1963.

**3452.** Syrett, Harold C., and Jean G. Cooke, ed. *Interview in Weehawken: The Burr-Hamilton Duel, as Told in the Original Documents.* Middletown, CT: Wesleyan University Press, 1960.

**3453.** Warshow, Robert I. *Alexander Hamilton, First American Business Man.* New York: Greenberg, 1931.

**3454.** Wharton, Leslie. "Alexander Hamilton and American Nationalism." In her *Polity and the Public Good,* 57–84. Ann Arbor, MI: UMI Research Press, 1980.

**3455.** Wilbur, William A. "Crisis in Leadership: Alexander Hamilton, Timothy Pickering and the Politics of Federalism, 1795–1804." Ph.D. dissertation, Syracuse University, 1969.

**3456.** Wilstach, Paul. "Alexander Hamilton." In his *Patriots off Their Pedestals,* 97–117. Indianapolis: Bobbs-Merrill, 1927.

**3457.** Wise, William. *Alexander Hamilton.* New York: Putnam's, 1963.

**HAMILTON, ANDREW JACKSON** (1815–1875) ID-TX, House 1859–1961.

**3458.** Carter, Katherine D. "Isaac Noris II's Attack on Andrew Hamilton." *Pennsylvania Magazine of History and Biography* 104 (April 1980): 139–161.

**3459.** Kunstler, William M. "Andrew Hamilton." In his *The Case for Courage,* 17–45. New York: William Morrow, 1962.

**3460.** Waller, John L. *Colossal Hamilton of Texas: A Biography of Andrew Jackson Hamilton, Militant Unionist and Reconstruction Governor.* El Paso, TX: Western Press, 1968.

**HAMILTON, JAMES, JR.** (1786–1857) SC, House 1822–1829.

**3461.** Glenn, Virginia L. "James Hamilton, Jr., of South Carolina: A Biography." Ph.D. dissertation, University of North Carolina, 1964.

**3462.** Kell, Carl L. "A Rhetorical History of James Hamilton, Jr.: The Nullification Era in South Carolina." Ph.D. dissertation, University of Kansas, 1971.

**3463.** Sibley, Manly M. "James Hamilton, Jr. vs. Sam Houston: Repercussions of the Nullification Controversy." *Southwestern Historical Quarterly* 89 (October 1985): 165–180.

**HAMLIN, HANNIBAL** (1809–1891) R-ME, House 1843–1847, Senate 1848–1857, 1857–1861, 1869–1881.

**3464.** Bartlett, David V. *Life and Public Services of Hon. Abraham Lincoln, with a Portion on Steel: To Which Is Added a Biographical Sketch of Hon. Hannibal Hamlin.* Philadelphia: Bradley, 1860.

**3465.** Hamlin, Charles E. *The Life and Times of Hannibal Hamlin.* Cambridge, MA: Riverside Press, 1899.

**3466.** Howells, William D. *Lives and Speeches of Abraham Lincoln and Hannibal Hamlin.* Columbus: Follett, Foster, 1860.

**3467.** Hunt, H. Draper. *Hannibal Hamlin: Lincoln's First Vice-President.* Syracuse, NY: Syracuse University Press, 1969.

**3468.** ———. "President Lincoln's First Vice-President: Hannibal Hamlin of Maine." *Lincoln Herald* 88 (Winter 1986): 137–144.

**3469.** Kazarian, Richard, Jr. "Working Radicals: The Early Political Careers of William Seward, Thaddeus Stevens, Henry Wilson, Charles Sumner, Salmon P. Chase and Hannibal Hamlin." Ph.D. dissertation, Brown University, 1981.

**3470.** McClure, Alexander K. "Lincoln and Hamlin." In his *Abraham Lincoln and Men of War-Times,* 115–130. Philadelphia: Times Publishing Company, 1892.

**3471.** Rudolph, Jack. "The Old Carthaginian: Hannibal Hamlin, Possible President." *Civil War Times Illustrated* 20 (February 1982): 22–27.

**3472.** Scroggins, Mark. *Hannibal: The Life of Abraham Lincoln's First Vice President.* Lanham, MD: University Press of America, 1994.

**HAMMOND, JAMES HENRY** (1807–1864) D-SC, House 1835–1836, Senate 1857–1860.

**3473.** Barnwell, John. "'In the Hands of the Compromisers': Letters of Robert W. Barnwell to James H. Hammond." *Civil War History* 29 (June 1983): 154–168.

**3474.** Bartlett, David V. "James H. Hammond." In his *Presidential Candidates,* 322–332. New York: A. B. Burdick, 1859.

**3475.** Bleser, Carol K. "A Legacy Besieged: The Hammond Family in an Era of Crisis and Change, 1865–1916." *Southern Studies* 22 (Spring 1983): 21–31.

**3476.** ———, ed. *The Hammonds of Red-cliffe*. New York: Oxford University Press, 1981.

**3477.** Faust, Drew G. *James Henry Hammond and the Old South: A Design for Mastery*. Baton Rouge: Louisiana State University Press, 1982.

**3478.** Hammond, James H. *Secret and Sacred: The Diaries of James Henry Hammond: A Southern Slaveholder*. Edited by Carol K. Bleser. New York: Oxford University Press, 1988.

**3479.** McDonnell, Lawrence T. "Struggle against Suicide: James Henry Hammond and the Secession of South Carolina." *Southern Studies* 22 (Summer 1983): 109–137.

**3480.** Merritt, Elizabeth. *James Henry Hammond, 1807–1864*. Baltimore: Johns Hopkins University Press, 1923.

**3481.** Stegmaier, Mark J. "Intensifying the Sectional Conflict: William Seward versus James Hammond on the Decompton Debate of 1858." *Civil War History* 31 (September 1985): 197–221.

**3482.** Tucker, Robert C. "James Henry Hammond, South Carolina." Ph.D. dissertation, University of North Carolina, 1958.

**3483.** Wakelyn, John L. "The Changing Loyalties of James Henry Hammond: A Reconsideration." *South Carolina Historical Magazine* 75 (January 1975): 1–13.

**HAMMOND, SAMUEL** (1757–1842) D-GA, House 1803–1805.

**3484.** Morris, Michael P. "Samuel Hammond: Liberator of Spanish Florida." *Richmond County History* 18 (Winter 1986): 8–15.

**HAMPTON, WADE** (1752–1835) R-SC, House 1795–1797, 1803–1805.

**3485.** Bridwell, Ronald E. "The South's Wealthiest Planter: Wade Hampton I of South Carolina, 1752–1835." Ph.D. dissertation, University of South Carolina, 1980.

**3486.** Cauthern, Charles E., ed. *Family Letters of the Three Wade Hamptons, 1782–1901*. Columbia: University of South Carolina Press, 1953.

**HAMPTON, WADE** (1818–1902) D-SC, Senate 1879–1891.

**3487.** Butler, M. C. "Wade Hampton." In *Library of Southern Literature*, edited by Edwin A. Alderman and Joel C. Harris, vol. 5, 2061–2067. New Orleans: Martin and Hoyt, 1909.

**3488.** Cauthern, Charles E., ed. *Family Letters of the Three Wade Hamptons, 1782–1901*. Columbia: University of South Carolina Press, 1953.

**3489.** Jerrell, Hampton M. *Wade Hampton and the Negro: The Road Not Taken*. Columbia: University of South Carolina Press, 1949.

**3490.** Wellman, Manly W. *Giant in Gray: A Biography of Wade Hampton of South Carolina*. New York: Scribner's, 1945.

**3491.** Wells, Edward L. *Hampton and His Cavalry in '64*. Richmond, VA: B. F. Johnson, 1899.

**3492.** White, Henry A. "Wade Hampton and the Carolina Horsemen in the Confederate War." In his *Making of South Carolina*, 263–279. New York: Silver, Burdett, 1906.

**3493.** Williams, Alfred B. *Hampton and His Red Shirts: South Carolina's Deliverance in 1876*. Freeport, NY: Books for Libraries, 1970.

**HANCOCK, JOHN** (1737–1793) MA, Continental Congress 1775–1780, 1785–1786.

**3494.** Allan, Herbert S. *John Hancock: Patriot in Purple*. New York: Macmillan, 1949.

**3495.** Baxter, William T. *The House of Hancock: Business in Boston, 1724–1775*. Cambridge, MA: Harvard University Press, 1945.

**3496.** Fowler, William M. *The Baron of Beacon Hill: A Biography of John Hancock.* Boston: Houghton Mifflin, 1980.

**3497.** Hunt, Freeman, ed. "John Hancock." In his *Lives of American Merchants,* vol. 2, 583–594. New York: Derby and Jackson, 1858.

**3498.** Magoon, Elias L. "John Hancock, Dignified Cavalier of Liberty." In his *Orators of the American Revolution,* 139–154. New York: Scribner's, 1853.

**3499.** Sanderson, John. "John Hancock." In *Sanderson's Biography of the Signers of the Declaration of Independence,* edited by Robert T. Conrad, 53–64. Philadelphia: Thomas, Cowperthwait, 1848.

**3500.** Sears, Lorenzo. *John Hancock, the Picturesque Patriot.* Boston: Little, Brown, 1912.

**3501.** Umbreit, Kenneth B. "John Hancock." In his *Founding Fathers: Men Who Shaped Our Tradition,* 162–174. Port Washington, NY: Kennikat, 1969.

**3502.** Wagner, Frederick. *Patriot's Choice: The Story of John Hancock.* New York: Dodd, Mead, 1964.

## HANNA, MARCUS ALONZO
(1837–1904) R-OH, Senate 1897–1904.

**3503.** Beer, Thomas. *Hanna.* New York: Knopf, 1929.

**3504.** Beveridge, Albert J. "Marcus A. Hanna: The Business Man in Statesmanship." In his *The Meaning of the Times,* 244–247. Indianapolis: Bobbs-Merrill, 1908.

**3505.** Clark, Champ. "The Sherman-McKinley-Hanna Feud." In his *My Quarter Century of American Politics,* 407–422. New York: Harper and Brothers, 1920.

**3506.** Croly, Herbert. *Marcus Alonzo Hanna.* New York: Macmillan, 1919.

**3507.** Dibble, Roy F. "Mark Hanna." In his *Strenuous Americans,* 336–370. London: Routledge, 1925.

**3508.** Felt, Thomas E. "The Rise of Mark Hanna." Ph.D. dissertation, Michigan State University, 1960.

**3509.** Flynn, John T. "Mark Hanna—Big Business in Politics." *Scribner's Magazine* 94 (July 1933): 85–90, 118–128.

**3510.** Hanna, Marcus A. *Mark Hanna: His Book.* Boston: Chapple, 1904.

**3511.** Howe, Frederic C. "Mark Hanna." In his *The Confessions of a Reformer,* 146–156. New York: Scribner's, 1925.

**3512.** O'Higgins, Harvey J., and Edward H. Reede. "Walt Whitman and Mark Hanna." In their *American Mind in Action,* 225–234. New York: Harper and Brothers, 1924.

**3513.** Rhodes, James F. *The McKinley and Roosevelt Administrations, 1897–1909.* New York: Macmillan, 1922.

**3514.** Russell, Francis. "The Red Boss of Cleveland: Marcus Alonzo Hanna." In his *President Makers: From Mark Hanna to Joseph P. Kennedy,* 1–41. Boston: Little, Brown, 1976.

**3515.** Stern, Clarence A. *Resurgent Republicanism: The Handiwork of Hanna.* Arbor, MA: Edwards Brothers, 1963.

**3516.** Thompson, Charles W. "Hanna-McKinley." In his *Presidents I've Known and Two Near Presidents,* 15–40. Indianapolis: Bobbs-Merrill, 1929.

**3517.** White, William A. "Mark Hanna." In his *Masks in a Pageant,* 191–232. New York: Macmillan, 1928.

## HANNEGAN, EDWARD ALLEN
(1807–1859) D-IN, House 1833–1837, Senate 1843–1849.

**3518.** Martin, John B. "Senator Hannegan: Son of the West." In his *Indiana,* 43–52. New York: Knopf, 1947.

**HANSBROUGH, HENRY CLAY**
(1848–1933) R-ND, House 1889–1891, Senate
1891–1909.

**3519.** Schlup, Leonard. "Henry C. Hansbrough and the Fight against the Tariff in 1894." *North Dakota History* 45 (Winter 1978): 4–9.

**3520.** ———. "Political Maverick: Senator Hansbrough and Republican Party Politics, 1907–1912." *North Dakota History* 45 (Fall 1978): 32–39.

**3521.** ———. "Quiet Imperialist: Henry C. Hansbrough and the Question of Expansion." *North Dakota History* 45 (Spring 1978): 26–31.

**HANSEN, GEORGE VERNON** (1930– )
R-ID, House 1965–1969, 1975–1985.

**3522.** Kelly, Colleen E. "The 1984 Campaign Rhetoric of Representative George Hanson: A Pentadic Analysis." *Western Journal of Speech Communication* 51 (Spring 1987): 204–217.

**HANSEN, JULIA BUTLER** (1907–1988)
D-WA, House 1960–1974.

**3523.** Anderson, Lynda R. "Julia Butler Hansen: The Grand Lady of Washington Politics." Ph.D. dissertation, Seattle University, 1992.

**3524.** Hansen, Julia B. *Singing Paddles.* New York: Holt, 1931.

**3525.** Rosenberg, Marie B. "The Campaigns of Congresswomen Edith Green and Julia Butler Hansen." *Politics* 24 (May 1989): 42–55.

**3526.** ———. "Women in Politics: A Comparative Study of Congresswomen Edith Green and Julia Butler Hansen." Ph.D. dissertation, University of Washington, 1973.

**HANSON, JOHN** (1715–1783) MD,
Continental Congress 1780–1783.

**3527.** Levering, Ralph B. "John Hanson, Public Servant." *Maryland Historical Magazine* 71 (Summer 1976): 113–133.

**3528.** Smith, Seymour W. *John Hanson: Our First President.* New York: Brewer, Warren, and Putnam, 1932.

**HARALSON, HUGH ANDERSON**
(1805–1854) D-GA, House 1843–1851.

**3529.** Wheeler, Henry G. "Haralson, Hugh Anderson." In his *History of Congress,* vol. 1, 251–267. New York: Harper, 1848.

**HARALSON, JEREMIAH** (1846–1916)
R-AL, House 1875–1877.

**3530.** Christopher, Maurine. "Benjamin S. Turner, James T. Rapier, and Jeremiah Haralson/Alabama." In her *Black Americans in Congress,* 123–136. Rev. ed. New York: Thomas Y. Crowell, 1976

**HARDING, WARREN GAMALIEL**
(1865–1923) R-OH, Senate 1915–1921.

**3531.** Adams, Samuel H. *Incredible Era: The Life and Times of Warren Gamaliel Harding.* Boston: Houghton Mifflin, 1939.

**3532.** Alderfer, Harold F. "The Personality and Politics of Warren G. Harding." Ph.D. dissertation, Syracuse University, 1929.

**3533.** Asher, Cash, comp. *He Was "Just Folks": The Life and Character of Warren Gamaliel Harding, as Mirrored in the Tributes of the American Press.* Chicago: Laird and Lee, 1923.

**3534.** Bagby, Wesley M. "The Smoke Filled Room and the Nomination of Warren G. Harding." *Mississippi Valley Historical Review* 41 (June 1955): 657–674.

**3535.** Blanchard, Sherman. "President Harding: A Reappraisal." *Current History* 35 (October 1931): 41–47.

**3536.** Boatman, Ellis G. "Evolution of a President: The Political Apprenticeship of Warren G. Harding." Ph.D. dissertation, University of South Carolina, 1966.

**3537.** Brainerd, Lawrence. "President Warren Gamaliel Harding." *New England Historical and Genealogical Register* 77 (October 1923): 243–249.

**3538.** Britton, Nan. *The President's Daughter.* New York: Elizabeth Ann Guild, 1927.

**3539.** Chapple, Joseph M. *Life and Times of Warren G. Harding, Our After-War President.* Boston: Chapple, 1924.

**3540.** Cottrill, Dale E. *The Conciliator.* Philadelphia: Dorrance, 1969.

**3541.** Cuneo, Sherman A. *From Printer to President.* Philadelphia: Dorrance, 1922.

**3542.** Daugherty, Harry M., and Thomas Dixon. *The Inside Story of the Harding Tragedy.* New York: Churchill, 1932.

**3543.** Downes, Randolph C. "The Harding Muckfest: Warren G. Harding—Chief Victim of the Muck-for-Muck's Sake Writers and Readers." *Northwest Ohio Quarterly* 39 (Summer 1967): 5–37.

**3544.** ———. "A Newspaper's Childhood—The *Marion Star* from Hume to Harding." *Northwest Ohio Quarterly* 36 (Summer 1964): 134–145.

**3545.** ———. *The Rise of Warren Gamaliel Harding, 1865–1920.* Columbus: Ohio State University Press, 1970.

**3546.** ———, ed. "President Making: The Influence of Newton H. Fairbanks and Harry M. Daugherty on the Nomination of Warren G. Harding for the Presidency." *Northwest Ohio Quarterly* 31 (Fall 1959): 170–178.

**3547.** ———, ed. "Some Correspondence between Warren G. Harding and William Allen White during the Presidential Campaign of 1920." *Northwest Ohio Quarterly* 37 (Autumn 1965): 121–132.

**3548.** Galbreath, Charles B. *The Story of Warren G. Harding.* Dansville, NY: F. A. Owen, 1922.

**3549.** ———. "Warren Gamaliel Harding." *Ohio Archaeological and Historical Society Publications* 32 (October 1923): 555–570.

**3550.** Gross, Edwin J. *Vindication for Mr. Normalcy: A 100th Birthday Memorial.* Buffalo, NY: American Society for the Faithful Recording of History, 1965.

**3551.** Harris, Ray B. "Background and Youth of the Seventh Ohio President." *Ohio State Archaeological and Historical Quarterly* 52 (July 1943): 260–275.

**3552.** Hartwell, Alena. *Hardings: History of the Harding Family.* Boston: Chapple, 1936.

**3553.** Jennings, David H. "Historiography and Warren G. Harding." *Ohio History* 78 (Winter 1969): 46–49.

**3554.** Johnson, Evans C. "Underwood and Harding: A Bipartisan Friendship." *Alabama Historical Quarterly* 30 (Spring 1968): 65–78.

**3555.** Johnson, Willis F. *The Life of Warren G. Harding from the Simple Life of the Farm to the Glamor and Power of the White House.* Chicago: John C. Winston, 1923.

**3556.** Kurland, Gerald. *Warren Harding: President Betrayed by Friends.* Charlottesville, NY: SamHar Press, 1971.

**3557.** Martin, Dorothy V. "An Impression of Harding in 1916." *Ohio State Archaeological and Historical Quarterly* 62 (September 1953): 179–180.

**3558.** Means, Gaston B. *The Strange Death of President Harding.* New York: Guild, 1930.

**3559.** Mee, Charles L. *The Ohio Gang: The World of Warren G. Harding.* New York: Evans, 1981.

**3560.** Moran, Philip R., ed. *Warren G. Harding, 1865–1923: Chronology, Documents, Biographic Aids.* Dobbs Ferry, NY: Oceana, 1970.

**3561.** Murray, Robert K. *The Harding Era: Warren G. Harding and His Administration.* Minneapolis: University of Minnesota Press, 1969.

**3562.** ———. "Harding on History." *Journal of American History* 53 (March 1967): 781–785.

**3563.** Norris, James D., and Arthur H. Shaffer, eds. *Politics and Patronage in the Gilded Age: The Correspondence of James A. Garfield and Charles H. Henry.* Madison: State Historical Society of Wisconsin, 1970.

**3564.** Potts, Louis W. "Who Was Warren G. Harding?" *Historian* 36 (August 1974): 621–645.

**3565.** Russell, Francis. *The Shadow of Blooming Grove: Warren G. Harding in His Times.* New York: McGraw-Hill, 1968.

**3566.** ———. "The Shadow of Warren Harding." *Antioch Review* 36 (Winter 1978): 57–76.

**3567.** Schruben, Francis W. "An Even Stranger Death of President Harding." *Southern California Quarterly* 48 (Spring 1966): 57–78.

**3568.** Sinclair, Andrew. *The Available Man: The Life behind the Masks of Warren Gamaliel Harding.* New York: Macmillan, 1965.

**3569.** Slosson, Preston W. "Warren G. Harding: A Revised Estimate." *Current History* 33 (November 1930): 174–179.

**3570.** Thacker, May. *The Strange Death of President Harding.* New York: Guild, 1930.

**3571.** Trani, Eugene P., and David L. Wilson. *The Presidency of Warren G. Harding.* Lawrence: Regents Press of Kansas, 1977.

**3572.** Walker, Kenneth R., and Randolph C. Downes. "The Death of Warren G. Harding." *Northwest Ohio Quarterly* 35 (Winter 1962–1963): 7–17.

**3573.** Werner, Morris R., and John Starr. *Teapot Dome.* New York: Viking, 1959.

**3574.** Whitaker, W. Richard. "The Working Press and the Harding Myth." *Journalism History* 2 (Autumn 1975): 90–97.

**3575.** Wood, Clement. *Warren Gamaliel Harding: An American Comedy.* New York: Faro, 1932.

**HARKIN, THOMAS RICHARD** (1939– )
**D-IA, House 1975–1985, Senate 1985– .**

**3576.** Boyte, Harry. "The Making of a Democratic Populist: A Profile of Senator Tom Harkin." *Social Policy* 16 (Fall 1985): 34–37.

**HARLAN, JAMES** (1820–1899) **R-IA, Senate 1855–1857, 1857–1865, 1867–1873.**

**3577.** Brigham, Johnson. *James Harlan.* Iowa City: State Historical Society of Iowa, 1913.

**HARNETT, CORNELIUS** (1723–1781)
**NC, Continental Congress 1777–1780.**

**3578.** Morgan, David T. "Cornelius Harnett: Revolutionary Leader and Delegate to the Continental Congress." *North Carolina Historical Review* 49 (July 1972): 229–241.

**HARPER, ROBERT GOODLOE**
**(1765–1825) MD, House 1795–1801, Senate 1816.**

**3579.** Cox, Joseph W. *Champion of Southern Federalism: Robert Goodloe Harper of South Carolina.* Port Washington: Kennikat, 1972.

**3580.** Harper, Robert G. *Select Works of Robert Goodloe Harper, Consisting of Speeches on Political and Forensic Subjects.* Baltimore: Neilson, 1814.

**3581.** Sommerville, Charles W. *Robert Goodloe Harper.* Washington, DC: Neale, 1899.

**HARRELD, JOHN WILLIAM** (1872–1950) **R-OK, House 1919–1921, Senate 1921–1927.**

**3582.** Grant, Philip A., Jr. "'Save the Farmer': Oklahoma Congressmen and Farm Relief Legislation, 1924–1928." *Chronicles of Oklahoma* 64 (Spring 1986): 74–87.

**3583.** Jones, Stephen. *Once Before: The Political and Senatorial Careers of Oklahoma's First Two Republican Senators, John W. Harreld and W. B. Pine.* Enid, OK: The Dougherty Press, 1986.

**HARRIS, FRED ROY** (1930– ) **D-OK, Senate 1964–1973.**

**3584.** Harris, Fred R. *Alarms and Holes: A Personal Journey, a Personal View.* New York: Harper and Row, 1968.

**3585.** ———. *America's Democracy: The Ideal and the Reality.* Glenview, IL: Scott, Foresman, 1980.

**3586.** ———. *The New Populism.* New York: Saturday Review Press, 1973.

**3587.** ———. *Now Is the Time: A New Populist Call to Action.* New York: McGraw-Hill, 1971.

**3588.** ———. *Potomac Fever.* New York: Norton, 1977.

**HARRIS, ISHAM GREEN** (1818–1897) **D-TN, House 1849–1953, Senate 1877–1897.**

**3589.** Looney, John T. "Isham G. Harris of Tennessee: Bourbon Senator, 1877–1897." Master's thesis, University of Tennessee, 1970.

**3590.** McLeary, Ila. "The Life of Isham G. Harris." Master's thesis, University of Tennessee, 1930.

**3591.** Watters, George W. "Isham Green Harris, Civil War Governor and Senator from Tennessee, 1818–1897." Ph.D. dissertation, Florida State University, 1977.

**HARRIS, SAMPSON WILLIS** (1809–1857) **D-AL, House 1847–1857.**

**3592.** McGregor, Robert C. "Between the Two Wars: Alabama in the House of Representatives 1849–1861." *Alabama Historical Quarterly* 42 (Fall/Winter 1980): 167–200.

**HARRISON, BENJAMIN** (1833–1901) **R-IN, Senate 1881–1887.**

**3593.** Campbell-Copeland, Thomas. *Harrison and Reid: Their Lives and Record, the Republican Campaign Book for 1892.* 3 vols. New York: Charles L. Webster, 1892.

**3594.** Dozer, Donald M. "Benjamin Harrison and the Presidential Campaign of 1892." *American Historical Review* 54 (October 1948): 49–77.

**3595.** Farnum, George R. "Benjamin Harrison: Man of the Law, Soldier of the Republic, and Gentleman in Politics." *American Bar Association Journal* 29 (September 1943): 514–515, 527.

**3596.** Harney, Gilbert L. *The Lives of Benjamin Harrison and Levi P. Morton: With a History of the Republican Party, and a Statement of Its Position on the Great Issues.* Providence, RI: J. A. and R. A. Reid, 1888.

**3597.** Harrison, Benjamin. *The Correspondence between Benjamin Harrison and James G. Blaine, 1882–1893.* Edited by Albert T. Volwiler. Philadelphia: American Philosophical Society, 1940.

**3598.** ———. *Speeches of Benjamin Harrison, Twenty-Third President of the United States.* Compiled by Charles Hedges. New York: United States Book Company, 1892.

**3599.** ———. *This Country of Ours.* New York: Scribner's, 1897.

**3600.** Hirshson, Stanley P. "James S. Clarkson versus Benjamin Harrison, 1891–1893: A Political Saga." *Iowa Journal of History* 58 (July 1960): 219–227.

**3601.** Knox, Thomas W. *The Republican Party and Its Leaders: Lives of Harrison and Reid.* New York: P. F. Collier, 1892.

**3602.** Sievers, Harry J. *Benjamin Harrison.* 3 vols. New York: University Publishers, 1966.

**3603.** ———. *Benjamin Harrison: Hoosier President: The White House and After.* New York: University Publishers, 1968.

**3604.** ———. *Benjamin Harrison: Hoosier Statesman from the Civil War to the White House: 1865–1888.* New York: University Publishers, 1959.

**3605.** ———. *Benjamin Harrison: Hoosier Warrior: 1833–1865, through the Civil War Years.* 2d ed. New York: University Publishers, 1960.

**3606.** ———. "The Early Life and Career of Benjamin Harrison, Twenty-Third President of the United States." Ph.D. dissertation, Georgetown University, 1950.

**3607.** Socolofsky, Homer E., and Allan B. Spetter. *The Presidency of Benjamin Harrison.* Lawrence: University Press of Kansas, 1987.

**3608.** Wallace, Lew. *Life of Gen. Ben Harrison.* Philadelphia: Hubbard, 1888.

## HARRISON, BYRON PATTON
**(1881–1941) D-MS, House 1911–1919, Senate 1919–1941.**

**3609.** Coker, William S. "Pat Harrison: Strategy for Victory." *Journal of Mississippi History* 28 (November 1966): 267–285.

**3610.** ———. "Pat Harrison: The Formative Years, 1911–1919." Master's thesis, University of Southern Mississippi, 1962.

**3611.** Edmonson, Ben G. "Pat Harrison and Mississippi in the Presidential Elections of 1924 and 1928." *Journal of Mississippi History* 33 (November 1971): 333–350.

**3612.** ———. "Pat Harrison: The Gadfly of the Senate, 1918, 1932." Master's thesis, University of Mississippi, 1967.

**3613.** Grant, Philip A., Jr. "The Mississippi Congressional Delegation and the Formation of the Conservative Coalition." *Journal of Mississippi History* 50 (February 1988): 21–28.

**3614.** Gregory, Chellis O. "Pat Harrison and the New Deal." Master's thesis, University of Mississippi, 1960.

**3615.** Porter, David L. "Senator Pat Harrison of Mississippi and the Reciprocal Trade Act of 1940." *Journal of Mississippi History* 36 (November 1974): 363–376.

**3616.** Swain, Martha. "The Harrison Education Bills, 1936–1941." *Mississippi Quarterly* 31 (Winter 1977–1978): 119–131.

**3617.** ———. "The Lion and the Fox: The Relationship of President Franklin D. Roosevelt and Senator Pat Harrison." *Journal of Mississippi History* 38 (November 1976): 333–359.

**3618.** ———. "Pat Harrison and the Social Security Act of 1935." *Southern Quarterly* 15 (October 1976): 1–14.

**3619.** ———. *Pat Harrison: The New Deal Years.* Jackson: University Press of Mississippi, 1978.

## HARRISON, CARTER HENRY
**(1825–1893) D-IL, House 1875–1879.**

**3620.** Harrison, Carter H. *Stormy Years: The Autobiography of Carter H. Harrison, Five Times Mayor of Chicago.* Indianapolis: Bobbs-Merrill, 1935.

**3621.** Johnson, Claudius O. *Carter Henry Harrison I, Political Leader.* Chicago: University of Chicago Press, 1928.

## HARRISON, JOHN SCOTT (1804–1878)
**R-OH, House 1853–1857.**

**3622.** Perling, Joseph J. "Son and Father of Presidents." In his *President's Sons,* 73–85. New York: Odyssey, 1947.

## HARRISON, WILLIAM HENRY
### (1773–1841) OH, House 1799–1800, 1816–1819, Senate 1825–1828.

**3623.** Bond, Beverly W. "William Henry Harrison and the Old Northwest." *Bulletin of the Historical and Philosophical Society of Ohio* 7 (January 1949): 10–17.

**3624.** ———. "William Henry Harrison in the War of 1812." *Mississippi Valley Historical Review* 13 (March 1967): 499–516.

**3625.** Booth, Edward T. "William Henry Harrison: Ohio Alluvial." In his *Country Life in American as Lived by Ten Presidents of the U.S.*, 148–168. New York: Knopf, 1947.

**3626.** Burr, Samuel J. *The Life and Times of William Henry Harrison.* New York: L. W. Ranson, 1840.

**3627.** Carter, Clarence E., ed. "William Henry Harrison and the Mexican Appointment, 1823–1824." *Mississippi Valley Historical Review* 25 (September 1938): 251–262.

**3628.** Cleaves, Freeman. *Old Tippecanoe: William Henry Harrison and His Time.* New York: Scribner's, 1939.

**3629.** Cushing, Caleb. *Outlines of the Life and Public Services, Civil and Military, of William Henry Harrison.* Boston: Weeks, Jordan and Company, 1840.

**3630.** Fabian, Monroe H. "A Portrait of William Henry Harrison." *Prologue* 1 (Winter 1969): 29–32.

**3631.** Gay, James T. "Harrison, Blaine, and Cronyism." *Alaska Journal* 3 (Winter 1973): 12–19.

**3632.** Goebel, Dorothy B. "William Henry Harrison: A Political Biography." Ph.D. dissertation, Columbia University, 1926.

**3633.** Green, James A. *William Henry Harrison: His Life and Times.* Richmond, VA: Garret and Massie, 1941.

**3634.** Hall, James. *A Memoir of the Public Services of William Henry Harrison, of Ohio.* Philadelphia: Edward C. Biddle, 1836.

**3635.** Isely, Bliss. "William Henry Harrison." In her *Presidents, Men of Faith*, 67–73. Boston: Wilde, 1953.

**3636.** Jackson, Isaac R. *General William Henry Harrison.* Philadelphia: Jesper Harding, 1840.

**3637.** ———. *A Sketch of the Life and Public Services of William Henry Harrison.* Columbus, OH: Scott and Wright, 1836.

**3638.** Lewis, Edward S. "The Death and Funeral of President William Henry Harrison." *Ohio Archaeological and Historical Quarterly* 37 (October 1928): 605–612.

**3639.** Montgomery, Henry. *The Life of Major-General William H. Harrison, Ninth President of the United States.* Philadelphia: Porter and Coates, 1852.

**3640.** Peckham, Howard H. "Tears for Old Tippecanoe: Religious Interpretations of President Harrison's Death." *American Antiquarian Society Proceedings* 69 (April 1959): 17–36.

**3641.** ———. *William Henry Harrison: Young Tipppecanoe.* Indianapolis: Bobbs-Merrill, 1951.

**3642.** Peterson, Norma L. *The Presidencies of William Henry Harrison and John Tyler.* Lawrence: University Press of Kansas, 1989.

**3643.** Stoddard, William O. *William Henry Harrison, John Tyler, and James Knox Polk.* New York: Stokes, 1888.

**3644.** Todd, Charles S. *Sketches of the Civil and Military Services of William Henry Harrison.* Cincinnati, OH: U. P. James, 1840.

**3645.** Walker, Kenneth R. "The Death of a President." *Northwestern Ohio Quarterly* 28 (Summer 1956): 157–162.

**3646.** Webster, Homer J. *William Henry Harrison's Administration of Indiana Territory.* Indianapolis: Sentinel Printing Company, 1907.

**HART, GARY WARREN** (1936– ) D-CO, Senate 1975–1987.

**3647.** Blake, R. Roy, and George R. Walters. *The Gary Hart Set-Up.* Aurora, CO: Laramide Productions, 1992.

**3648.** Hart, Gary W. *The Good Fight: The Education of an American Reformer.* New York: Random House, 1993.

**3649.** ———. *The New Democracy.* New York: Morrow, 1983.

**HART, THOMAS CHARLES** (1877–1971) R-CT, Senate 1945–1946.

**3650.** Leutze, James R. *A Different Kind of Victory: A Biography of Admiral Thomas C. Hart.* Annapolis, MD: Naval Institute Press, 1981.

**HARTKE, RUPERT VANCE** (1919– ) D-IN, Senate 1959–1977.

**3651.** Hartke, Vance. *You and Your Senator.* New York: Coward-McCann, 1970.

**3652.** Hartke, Vance, and John M. Redding. *Inside the New Frontier.* New York: MacFadden-Bartell, 1962.

**3653.** Meyer, Nancy J. "Vance Hartke: A Political Biography." Ph.D. dissertation, Ball State University, 1987.

**HARTLEY, FRED ALLAN, JR.** (1902–1969) R-NJ, House 1929–1949.

**3654.** Hartley, Fred A. *Our New National Labor Policy: The Taft-Hartley Act and the Next Steps.* New York: Funk and Wagnalls, 1948.

**HARVEY, RALPH** (1901– ) R-IN, House 1947–1959, 1961–1967.

**3655.** Harvey, Ralph. *Autobiography of a Hoosier Congressman.* Greenfield, IN: Mitchell-Fleming, 1975.

**HASTINGS, WILLIAM WIRT** (1866–1938) D-OK, House 1915–1921, 1923–1935.

**3656.** Grant, Philip A., Jr. "'Save the Farmer': Oklahoma Congressmen and Farm Relief Legislation, 1924–1928." *Chronicles of Oklahoma* 64 (Spring 1986): 74–87.

**HATCH, CARL ATWOOD** (1889–1963) D-NM, Senate 1933–1949.

**3657.** Fox, Richard L. "New Mexico Senators: A History of Power." *New Mexico Magazine* 63 (November 1985): 82–90.

**3658.** Porter, David L. "Senator Carl Hatch and the Hatch Act of 1939." *New Mexico Historical Review* 48 (April 1973): 151–164.

**HATCH, ORRIN GRANT** (1934– ) R-UT, Senate 1977– .

**3659.** Roderick, Lee. *Leading the Charge: Orrin Hatch and 20 Years of America.* Carson City, NV: Gold Leaf Press, 1994.

**3660.** Vetterli, Richard. *Orrin Hatch: Challenging the Washington Establishment.* Chicago: Regnery Gateway, 1982.

**HATFIELD, HENRY DRURY** (1875–1962) R-WV, Senate 1929–1935.

**3661.** Karr, Carolyn. "A Political Biography of Henry Hatfield." *West Virginia History* 28 (October 1966): 35–63, 28 (January 1967): 137–170.

**3662.** Penn, Neil S. "Henry D. Hatfield and Reform Politics: A Study of West Virginia Politics from 1908 to 1917." Ph.D. dissertation, Emory University, 1973.

**HATFIELD, MARK ODOM** (1922– ) R-OR, Senate 1967– .

**3663.** Eells, Robert, and Bartell Nyberg. *Lonely Walk: The Life of Senator Mark Hatfield.* Chappaqua, NY: Christian Herald Books, 1979.

**3664.** Hatfield, Mark O. *Between a Rock and a Hard Place.* Waco, TX: Work Books, 1976.

**3665.** ———. *Not Quite So Simple.* New York: Harper and Row, 1968.

**HATTON, ROBERT HOPKINS**
**(1826–1862) O-TN, House 1859–1861.**

**3666.** Cummings, Charles M. "Robert Hopkins Hatton: Reluctant Rebel." *Tennessee Historical Quarterly* 23 (June 1964): 169–181.

**3667.** Threatte, Bernard B. "The Public Life of Robert Hatton, 1855–1862." Master's thesis, Vanderbilt University, 1931.

**HAUGEN, GILBERT NELSON**
**(1859–1933) R-IA, House 1899–1933.**

**3668.** Harstad, Peter T. *Gilbert N. Haugen: Norwegian-American Farm Politician.* Iowa City: State Historical Society of Iowa, 1992.

**3669.** Michael, Bonnie. "Gilbert N. Haugen: Apprentice Congressman." *Palimpsest* 59 (July/August 1978): 118–129.

**3670.** Porter, David L. "Iowa Congressional Delegation and the Great Economic Issues, 1929–1933." *Annals of Iowa* 46 (Summer 1982): 337–354.

**HAUGEN, NILS PEDERSON**
**(1849–1931) R-WI, House 1887–1895.**

**3671.** Brandes, Stuart D. "Nils P. Haugen and the Wisconsin Progressive Movement." Master's thesis, University of Wisconsin, 1925.

**HAWKINS, AUGUSTUS FREEMAN**
**(1907– ) D-CA, House 1963–1991.**

**3672.** Christopher, Maurine. "Augustus F. Hawkins/California." In her *Black Americans in Congress,* 221–227. Rev. ed. New York: Thomas Y. Crowell, 1976

**HAWKINS, BENJAMIN (1754–1816) NC,**
**Senate 1789-1795, Continental Congress**
**1781–1783, 1787.**

**3673.** Grant, Charles L. "Senator Benjamin Hawkins: Federalist or Republican." *Journal of the Early Republic* 1 (Fall 1981): 233–247.

**3674.** Hawkins, Benjamin. "Introduction, the Author." In his *A Sketch of the Creek Country, in 1798 and 99,* 3–11. Savannah: Georgia Historical Society, 1848.

**3675.** ———. *Letters, Journals, and Writings of Benjamin Hawkins.* Edited by Charles L. Grant. Savannah, GA: Beehive Press, 1980.

**3676.** ———. *Letters of Benjamin Hawkins, 1796–1806.* Savannah, GA: Georgia Historical Society, 1916.

**3677.** Henri, Florette. *The Southern Indians and Benjamin Hawkins, 1796–1816.* Norman: University of Oklahoma Press, 1986.

**3678.** Melton, Mabel. "War Trail of the Red Sticks." *American History Illustrated* 10 (February 1976): 33–42.

**3679.** Pound, Merritt B. "Benjamin Hawkins." In *Georgians in Profile,* edited by Horace Montgomery, 89–113. Athens: University of Georgia Press, 1958.

**3680.** Pound, Merritt B. *Benjamin Hawkins, Indian Agent.* Athens: University of Georgia Press, 1951.

**3681.** Pound, Merritt B. "The Public Career of Benjamin Hawkins." Ph.D. dissertation, University of North Carolina, 1940.

**HAWKINS, ISAAC ROBERTS**
**(1818–1880) R-TN, House 1866–1871.**

**3682.** Lufkin, Charles L. "West Tennessee Unionists in the Civil War: A Hawkins Family Letter." *Tennessee Historical Quarterly* 46 (Spring 1987): 33–42.

**HAY, JAMES** (1856–1931) D-VA, House 1897–1916.

**3683.** Herring, George C. "James Hay and the Preparedness Controversy 1915–1916." *Journal of Southern History* 30 (November 1964): 383–404.

**HAY, JOHN BREESE** (1834–1916) R-IL, House 1869–1873.

**3684.** Dennett, Tyler. *John Hay: From Poetry to Politics.* New York: Dodd, Mead, 1933.

**3685.** Hay, John. *Lincoln and the Civil War in the Diaries and Letters of John Hay.* Edited by Tyler Dennet. New York: Dodd, Mead, 1939.

**HAYAKAWA, SAMUEL ICHIYE** (1906–1992) R-CA, Senate 1977–1983.

**3686.** Diehl, Digby. "S. I. Hayakawa." In his *Supertalk,* 243–255. Garden City, NY: Doubleday, 1974.

**HAYDEN, CARL TRUMBULL** (1877–1972) D-AZ, House 1912–1927, Senate 1927–1969.

**3687.** August, Jack L., Jr. "Carl Hayden, Arizona, and the Politics of Water Development in the Southwest, 1923–1928." *Pacific Historical Review* 58 (May 1989): 195–216.

**3688.** ———. "Carl Hayden: Born a Politician." *Journal of Arizona History* 26 (Summer 1985): 117–144.

**3689.** ———. "'Sterling Young Democrat': Carl Hayden's Road to Congress, 1900–1912." *Journal of Arizona History* 28 (Autumn 1987): 217–242.

**3690.** Colley, Charles C. "Carl Hayden: Phoenician." *Journal of Arizona History* 18 (Autumn 1977): 247–257.

**3691.** ———. "Papers of Carl T. Hayden: Arizona's Silent Senator on Record." *Journal of the West* 14 (December 1975): 5–14.

**3692.** Rice, Ross R. *Carl Hayden: Builder of the American West.* Lanham, MD: University Press of America, 1993.

**HAYES, RUTHERFORD BIRCHARD** (1822–1893) R-OH, House 1865–1867.

**3693.** Barnard, Harry. "Biographical Memories, *in re* RBH." *Hayes Historical Journal* 2 (Fall 1978): 89–96.

**3694.** ———. *Rutherford B. Hayes and His America.* Indianapolis: Bobbs-Merrill, 1954.

**3695.** Conwell, Russell H. *Life and Public Services of Gov. Rutherford B. Hayes.* Boston: B. B. Russell, 1876.

**3696.** Eckenrode, Hamilton J., and Pocahontas W. Wight. *Rutherford B. Hayes, Statesman of Reunion.* New York: Dodd, Mead, 1930.

**3697.** Farnum, George R. "Rutherford B. Hayes in War and in Peace." *American Bar Association Journal* 29 (August 1943): 435–436, 474.

**3698.** Geer, Emily A. "The Rutherford B. Hayes Family." *Hayes Historical Journal* 2 (Spring 1978): 46–51.

**3699.** Hayes, Rutherford B. *Diary and Letters of Rutherford Birchard Hayes.* 5 vols. Edited by Charles R. Williams. Columbus: Ohio State Archeological and Historical Society, 1922–1926.

**3700.** ———. *The Diary of a President, 1875–1881.* Edited by T. Harry Williams. New York: McKay, 1964.

**3701.** Hayes, Walter S., Jr. "Rutherford B. Hayes and the Ohio State University." *Ohio History* 77 (Winter/Spring/Summer 1968): 168–183.

**3702.** Hendricks, Gordon. "Eakins' Portrait of Rutherford B. Hayes." *American Art Journal* 1 (Spring 1969): 104–114.

**3703.** Hickerson, Frank R. "The Educational Contribution of Rutherford B. Hayes." *Northwest Ohio Quarterly* 33 (Winter 1960/1961): 46–53.

**3704.** Hoogenboom, Ari A. *The Presidency of Rutherford B. Hayes.* Lawrence: University Press of Kansas, 1988.

**3705.** ——. "Rutherford B. Hayes: 'Real and Substantial Greatness.'" *Hayes Historical Journal* 7 (Spring 1988): 28–36.

**3706.** Howard, James Q. *The Life, Public Services, and Select Speeches of Rutherford B. Hayes.* Cincinnati, OH: Robert Clarke and Company, 1876.

**3707.** Keeler, Lucy E. "Excursion to Baltimore, Md., and Washington, D.C., January 19–February 15, 1881." Edited by Watt P. Marchman. *Hayes Historical Journal* 1 (Spring 1976): 6–21.

**3708.** Marchman, Watt P. "Collections of the Rutherford B. Hayes State Memorial." *Ohio History* 71 (July 1962): 151–157.

**3709.** ——. *The Hayes Memorial.* Columbus: Ohio State Archaeological and Historical Society, 1950.

**3710.** ——. "Rutherford B. Hayes: Attorney at Law." *Ohio History* 77 (Winter/Spring/Summer 1968): 5–32.

**3711.** ——. "Rutherford B. Hayes in Lower Sandusky, 1845–1859." *Hayes Historical Journal* 1 (Fall 1976): 123–132.

**3712.** ——, comp. "Colleges Costs: What Rutherford B. Hayes Spent as a Student at Kenyon, 1838–1841." *Hayes Historical Journal* 2 (Spring 1978): 14–20.

**3713.** ——, comp. "Rutherford B. Hayes as Painted by William Merritt Chase: The Documentary Story." *Hayes Historical Journal* (Spring 1976): 36–44.

**3714.** ——, ed. "Hayes Album: Fourteen Panels Depicting Scenes from the Life of President Hayes." *Hayes Historical Journal* 1 (Spring 1976): 45–59.

**3715.** Myers, Elisabeth P. *Rutherford B. Hayes.* Chicago: Reilly and Lee, 1969.

**3716.** Pad, Dennis N. "The Educational Contributions and Activities of Rutherford B. Hayes." Ph.D. dissertation, Ohio State University, 1970.

**3717.** Parker, Wyman W. "The College Reading of a President." *Library Quarterly* 21 (April 1951): 107–112.

**3718.** Payne, Alma J. "William Dean Howells and Other Early Biographers of Rutherford B. Hayes." *Hayes Historical Journal* 2 (Fall 1978): 78–88.

**3719.** Peskin, Allan. "Garfield and Hayes, Political Leaders of the Gilded Age." *Ohio Historical Quarterly* 77 (Winter/Spring/Summer 1968): 111–124.

**3720.** Porter, Daniel R. "Governor Rutherford B. Hayes." *Ohio History* 77 (Winter/Spring/Summer 1968): 58–75.

**3721.** Ranson, Frederick D. "The Great Unknown: Governor Rutherford B. Hayes of Ohio." Ph.D. dissertation, West Virginia University, 1978.

**3722.** Smith, Thomas A. "Governor Hayes Visits the Centennial." *Hayes Historical Journal* 1 (Spring 1977): 159–164.

**3723.** Smith, William H. "Conversations with Hayes: A Biographer's Notes." Edited by Curtis W. Carrison. *Mississippi Valley Historical Review* 25 (December 1938): 369–380.

**3724.** Swint, Henry L. "Rutherford B. Hayes, Educator." *Mississippi Valley Historical Review* 39 (June 1952): 45–60.

**3725.** Townsend, Samuel C. *Spiegel Grove: Home of Rutherford Birchard Hayes.* Fremont, OH: Lesher Printers, 1965.

**3726.** Van Sickle, Clinton E., and James T. May. "The Birthplace of President Hayes: A Study in Oral Tradition." *Ohio State Archaeological and Historical Quarterly* 61 (April 1952): 167–172.

**3727.** West, Richard S. "The Kenyon Experience of R. B. Hayes." *Hayes Historical Journal* 2 (Spring 1978): 6–13.

**3728.** Williams, Charles R. *The Life of Rutherford Birchard Hayes, Nineteenth President of the United States.* 2 vols. Boston: Houghton Mifflin, 1914.

**3729.** Williams, T. Harry. *Hayes of the Twenty-Third: The Civil War Volunteer Officer.* New York: Knopf, 1965.

**HAYNE, ROBERT YOUNG (1791–1839) J-SC, Senate 1823–1832.**

**3730.** Bancroft, Frederic. "The Webster-Hayne Debate." In his *Calhoun and the South Carolina Nullification Movement,* 55–74. Baltimore: Johns Hopkins Press, 1928.

**3731.** Devens, Richard M. "The 'Great Debate' between Webster and Hayne, in Congress, 1830." In his *The National Memorial Volume,* 205–213. Chicago: Hugh Heron, 1880.

**3732.** Fields, Wayne. "The Reply to Hayne: Daniel Webster and the Rhetorica of Stewardship." *Political Theory* 11 (February 1983): 5–28.

**3733.** Garnett, James M. "Robert Young Hayne." In *Library of Southern Literature,* edited by Edwin A. Alderman and Joel C. Harris, vol. 5, 2299–2305. New Orleans: Martin and Hoyt, 1909.

**3734.** Jervey, Theodore D. *Robert Y. Hayne and His Times.* New York: Macmillan, 1909.

**3735.** Johnson, Alexander, ed. "In Reply to Hayne. . . ." In his *American Orations,* vol. 1, 248–302. New York: Putnam's, 1896.

**3736.** Langley, Harold D. "Robert Y. Hayne and the Navy." *South Carolina Historical Magazine* 82 (October 1981): 311–330.

**3737.** Ogg, Frederic A. "The Webster-Hayne Debate." In his *The Reign of Andrew Jackson,* 137–157. New Haven, CT: Yale University Press, 1919.

**3738.** Patterson, Lane. "The Battle of the Giants: Webster and Hayne: Orators at Odds." *American History Illustrated* 17 (February 1983): 18–22.

**HAYS, CHARLES (1834–1879) R-AL, House 1869–1877.**

**3739.** Rogers, William W. *Black Belt Scalawag: Charles Hays and the Southern Republicans in the Era of Reconstruction.*

Athens: University of Georgia, 1993.

**3740.** ———. "Politics Is Mighty Uncertain: Charles Hays Goes to Congress." *Alabama Review* 30 (July 1977): 163–190.

**HAYS, LAWRENCE BROOKS (1898–1981) D-AR, House 1943–1959.**

**3741.** Baker, James T. *Brooks Hays.* Macon, GA: Mercer Press, 1989.

**3742.** Barnhill, John H. "Politician, Social Reformer, and Religious Leader: The Public Career of Brooks Hays." Ph.D. dissertation, Oklahoma State University, 1981.

**3743.** Hays, Brooks. *Hotbed of Tranquility: My Life in Five Worlds.* New York: Macmillan, 1968.

**3744.** ———. *Politics Is My Parish: An Autobiography.* Baton Rouge: Louisiana State University Press, 1981.

**3745.** Routh, Porter. "Brooks Hays." In his *Chosen for Leadership,* 76–79. Nashville, TN: Broadman, 1976.

**HEARST, GEORGE (1820–1891) D-CA, Senate 1886–1891.**

**3746.** Older, Fremont, and Cara M. Older. *George Hearst, California Pioneer.* Los Angeles: Westernlore, 1966.

**HEARST, WILLIAM RANDOLPH (1863–1951) D-NY, House 1903–1907.**

**3747.** Bent, Silas. "Hearst and the Mexico Forgeries." In his *Strange Bedfellows,* 218–230. New York: H. Liveright, 1928.

**3748.** Carlisle, Rodney P. *Hearst and the New Deal—the Progressive as Reactionary.* New York: Garland, 1979.

**3749.** ———. "The Political Ideas and Influence of William Randolph Hearst, 1928–1936." Ph.D. dissertation, University of California, 1965.

**3750.** Carlson, Oliver, and Ernest S. Bates. *Hearst, Lord of San Simeon.* New

York: Viking, 1936.

**3751.** Chaney, Linsday, and Michael Cieply. *The Hearsts: Family and Empire: The Later Years.* New York: Simon and Schuster, 1981.

**3752.** Davies, Marion. *The Times We Had: Life with William Randolph Hearst.* Indianapolis: Bobbs-Merrill, 1975.

**3753.** Hearst, William R., Jr., and Jack Casserly. *The Hearsts: Father & Son.* West Cork, Republic of Ireland: Rinehart, Roberts, Publishers, 1991.

**3754.** Hynding, Alan A. "William Randolph Hearst." In his *California History-makers,* 107–114. Dubuque, IA: Kendall/Hunt Publishing Company, 1976.

**3755.** Kelly, Florence F. "Three Journalists of Genius." In her *Flowing Stream: The Story of Fifty-Six Years in American Newspaper Life,* 467–516. New York: Dutton, 1939.

**3756.** Littlefield, Roy E. *William Randolph Hearst, His Role in American Progressivism.* Lanham, MD: University Press of America, 1980.

**3757.** Lundberg, Ferdinand. *Imperial Hearst: A Social Biography.* New York: Avon, 1970.

**3758.** Murray, Ken. *The Golden Days of San Simeon.* Garden City, NY: Doubleday, 1971.

**3759.** Myatt, James A. "William Randolph Hearst and the Progressive Era, 1900–1912." Ph.D. dissertation, University of Florida, 1960.

**3760.** Older, Cara M. *William Randolph Hearst, American.* New York: Appleton-Century, 1936.

**3761.** O'Loughlin, Edward T. *Hearst and His Enemies.* New York: Arno Press, 1970.

**3762.** Robinson, Judith. *The Hearsts: An American Dynasty.* Newark: University of Delaware Press, 1991.

**3763.** Smith, Arthur D. "William Randolph Hearst, the Demagogue of the Printed Word." In his *Men Who Run America,* 201–209. Indianapolis: Bobbs-Merrill, 1936.

**3764.** Swanberg, William A. *Citizen Hearst, a Biography of William Randolph Hearst.* New York: Scribner's, 1961.

**3765.** Tebbel, John W. *The Life and Good Times of William Randolph Hearst.* New York: Dutton, 1952.

**3766.** Villard, Oswald G. "William R. Hearst: Failure." In his *Prophets True and False,* 300–320. New York: Knopf, 1928.

**3767.** ———. "William Randolph Hearst and His Moral Press." In his *Some Newspapers and Newspapermen,* 14–41. New York: Knopf, 1923.

**3768.** Winkler, John K. *W. R. Hearst, an American Phenomenon.* New York: Simon and Schuster, 1928.

**3769.** Winkler, John K. *William Randolph Hearst, a New Appraisal.* New York: Hastings House, 1955.

**HEBERT, FELIX EDWARD (1901–1979) D-LA, House 1941–1977.**

**3770.** Conrad, Glenn R. *Creed of a Congressman: F. Edward Hebert of Louisiana.* Lafayette: The USL History Series, University of Southwestern Louisiana, 1970.

**3771.** Hebert, Felix E. *Last of the Titans: The Life and Times of Congressman F. Edward Hebert of Louisiana.* Edited by Glenn R. Conrad. Lafayette: University of Southwestern Louisiana, 1976.

**HECHLER, KEN (1914– ) D-WV, House 1959–1977.**

**3772.** Hechler, Kenneth. *Working with Truman: A Personal Memoir of the White House Years.* New York: Putnam's, 1982.

**3773.** Moffatt, Charles H. *Ken Hechler: Maverick Public Servant.* Charleston, WV: Mountain State Press, 1987.

**HECKLER, MARGARET MARY O'SHAUGHNESSY** (1931– ) R-MA, House 1967–1983.

**3774.** Lamson, Peggy. "Three Congresswomen: What Makes Them Run." In her *Few Are Chosen: American Women in Political Life Today*, 109–126. Boston: Houghton Mifflin, 1968.

**HEFLIN, JAMES THOMAS** (1869–1951) D-AL, House 1904–1920, Senate 1920–1931.

**3775.** Harper, Glenn T. "Cotton Tom, Heflin and the Election of 1930: The Price of Party Disloyalty." *Historian* 30 (May 1968): 389–411.

**3776.** Tanner, Ralph M. "James Thomas Heflin: United States Senator, 1920–31." Ph.D. dissertation, University of Alabama, 1967.

**3777.** ———. "The Wonderful World of Tom Heflin." *Alabama Review* 36 (July 1983): 163–174.

**3778.** Thornton, J. Mills. "Alabama Politics, J. Thomas Heflin, and the Expulsion Movement in 1929." *Alabama Review* 21 (April 1968): 83–112.

**HEFTEL, CECIL LANDAU** (1924– ) D-HA House 1977–1986.

**3779.** Folen, Robert. "Interview with Representative Cecil Heftel." *American Psychologist* 40 (October 1985): 1131–1136.

**3780.** Rosen, Sidney M. "Cec Heftel: New Politics and the Media Man." Ph.D. dissertation, University of Hawaii, 1985.

**HELMS, JESSE ALEXANDER** (1921– ) R-NC, Senate 1973– .

**3781.** Furguson, Ernest B. *Hard Right: The Rise of Jesse Helms*. New York: Norton, 1986.

**3782.** Gaillard, Frye. "It's Jesse Again." *Southern Changes* 6, no. 6 (1984): 1–3.

**3783.** Garrow, David J. "The Helms Attack on King." *Southern Exposure* 12 (February 1984): 12–15.

**3784.** Hall, Bob. "Jesse Helms: The Meaning of His Money, Campaign Finance Project: Institute for Southern Studies Special Report." *Southern Exposure* 13 (February 1985): 14–23.

**3785.** Helms, Jesse. *When Free Men Shall Stand*. Grand Rapids, MI: Zondervan, 1976.

**3786.** Snider, William D. *Helms and Hunt: The North Carolina's Senate Race, 1984*. Chapel Hill: University of North Carolina Press, 1984.

**HEMPHILL, JOHN** (1803–1862) SRD-TX, Senate 1859–1861.

**3787.** Curtis, Rosalee M. *John Hemphill, First Chief Justice of the State of Texas*. Austin, TX: Jenkins Publishing Company, 1971.

**HENDERSON, ARCHIBALD** (1768–1822) F-NC, House 1799–1803.

**3788.** Murphey, Archibald D. "Sketch of the Character of Archibald Henderson as a Lawyer." In *The Papers of Archibald D. Murphey*, edited by William H. Hoyt, vol. 2, 312–319. Raleigh, NC: E. M. Uzzell, 1914.

**HENDERSON, DAVID BREMNER** (1840–1906) R-IA, House 1883–1903.

**3789.** Chapple, Joseph M. "The Personal Side of Speaker Henderson." *National Magazine* 11 (October 1899): 3–8.

**3790.** Clark, Champ. "Mr. Speaker Henderson." In his *My Quarter Century of American Politics*, 372–381. New York: Harper, 1920.

**3791.** Hoing, Willard L. "David B. Henderson, Speaker of the House." *Iowa Journal of History* 55 (January 1957): 1–34.

**3792.** Richards, Julian W. "Henderson and His Critics." *Independent* 54 (March 20, 1902): 677–679.

**3793.** ———. "The Passing of Speaker Henderson." *Independent* 55 (March 19, 1903): 651–655.

## HENDERSON, JAMES PINCKNEY
(1808–1858) D-TX, Senate 1857–1858.

**3794.** Morris, Elizabeth. "James Pinckney Henderson." Master's thesis, University of Texas, 1931.

**3795.** Welch, June R. "Henderson Led the Texans Off to War." In his *The Texas Governor,* 24–27. Irving, TX: G. L. A. Press, 1977.

**3796.** Winchester, Robert. "James Pinckney Henderson." Master's thesis, Texas College of Arts and Industries, 1952.

**3797.** ———. *James Pinckney Henderson, Texas' First Governor.* San Antonio, TX: Naylor, 1971.

## HENDERSON, JOHN BROOKS
(1826–1913) D-MO, Senate 1862–1869.

**3798.** Mattingly, Arthur H. "Senator John Brooks Henderson, United States Senator from Missouri." Ph.D. dissertation, Kansas State University, 1971.

## HENDRICKS, THOMAS ANDREWS
(1819–1885) D-IN, House 1851–1855, Senate 1863–1869.

**3799.** Barnum, Augustine. *The Lives of Grover Cleveland and Thomas A. Hendricks, Democratic Presidential Candidates of 1884.* Hartford, CT: Hartford Publishing Company, 1884.

**3800.** Evarts, William M. "Thomas A. Hendricks, Vice-President of the United States." In *Arguments and Speeches,* edited by Sherman Evarts, vol. 3, 212–217. New York: Macmillan, 1919.

**3801.** Graham, Hope W. "Thomas A. Hendricks in Reconstruction." Master's thesis, Indiana University, 1912.

**3802.** Holcombe, John W., and Hubert M. Skinner. *Life and Public Services of Thomas A. Hendricks with Selected Speeches and Writings.* Indianapolis: Carlon and Hollenbeck, 1886.

## HENDRICKS, WILLIAM (1782–1850) IN,
House 1816–1822, Senate 1825–1837.

**3803.** Hill, Frederick D. "William Hendricks' Political Circulars to His Constituents: First Senatorial Term, 1826–1831." *Indiana Magazine of History* 71 (June 1975): 124–180.

**3804.** ———. "William Hendricks' Political Circulars to His Constituents: Second Senatorial Term, 1831–1837." *Indiana Magazine of History* 71 (December 1975): 319–374.

## HENNINGS, THOMAS CAREY, JR.
(1903–1960) D-MO, House 1935–1940, Senate 1951–1960.

**3805.** Kemper, Donald J. *Decade of Fear: Senator Hennings and Civil Liberties.* Columbia: University of Missouri Press, 1965.

**3806.** ———. "Senator Hennings and Civil Liberties." Ph.D. dissertation, University of Missouri, 1963.

## HENRY, JOHN (1750–1798) MD, Senate
1789-1797, Continental Congress 1778–1780, 1785–1786.

**3807.** Henry, John. *Letters and Papers of Governor John Henry.* Baltimore: G. W. King, 1904.

## HENRY, PATRICK (1736–1799) VA,
Continental Congress 1774–1776.

**3808.** Axelrad, Jacob. *Patrick Henry, the Voice of Freedom.* New York: Random House, 1947.

**3809.** Beeman, Richard R. *Patrick Henry: A Biography.* New York: McGraw-Hill, 1974.

**3810.** Blunt, Charles P. *Patrick Henry: The Henry County Years, 1779–1784.* Danville, VA: Blunt, 1976.

**3811.** Bordelon, J. Michael. "Visions of Disorder: Patrick Henry and the American Founding." *Occasional Review* 4 (Winter 1976): 99–120.

**3812.** Bruce, Philip A. "Patrick Henry." In his *The Virginia Plutarch,* vol. 1, 173–194. Chapel Hill: University of North Carolina Press, 1929.

**3813.** Campbell, Norine D. *Patrick Henry: Patriot and Statesman.* New York: Devin-Adair, 1969.

**3814.** Creel, George. "His Words Were Flames." In his *Sons of the Eagle,* 50–62. Indianapolis: Bobbs-Merrill, 1927.

**3815.** Erskine, John. *Give Me Liberty: The Story of an Innocent Bystander.* New York: Frederick A. Stokes, 1940.

**3816.** Hart, William S. *A Lighter of Flames.* New York: Crowell, 1923.

**3817.** Henry, William W. *Patrick Henry: Life, Correspondence and Speeches.* New York: Scribner's, 1891.

**3818.** Howe, Henry. "The Two Orators of Our Revolutionary Era: James Otis of Massachusetts and Patrick Henry of Virginia." In his *Adventures and Achievements of Americans,* 200–212. Cincinnati, OH: H. Howe, 1860.

**3819.** Magoon, Elias L. "Patrick Henry, the Incarnation of Revolutionary Zeal." In his *Orators of the American Revolution,* 234–265. New York: Scribner's, 1853.

**3820.** Mayer, Henry. *A Son of Thunder: Patrick Henry and the American Republic.* New York: Watts, 1986.

**3821.** Mayo, Bernard. *Myths and Men: Patrick Henry, George Washington and Thomas Jefferson.* Athens: University of Georgia Press, 1959.

**3822.** Meade, Robert D. *Patrick Henry.* 2 vols. Philadelphia: Lippincott, 1957–1969.

**3823.** Morgan, George. *The True Patrick Henry.* Philadelphia: Lippincott, 1907.

**3824.** Myers, J. Jay. "Patrick Henry: Son of Thunder." In his *The Revolutionists,* 47–64. New York: Pocket Books, 1971.

**3825.** Sparks, Jared, and Alexander H. Everett. *Lives of Robert Cavelier de La Salle and Patrick Henry.* Boston: C. C. Little and J. Brown, 1844.

**3826.** Tyler, Moses C. *Patrick Henry.* Boston: Houghton Mifflin, 1887.

**3827.** Umbreit, Kenneth B. "Patrick Henry." In his *Founding Fathers: Men Who Shaped Our Tradition,* 200–234. Port Washington, NY: Kennikat, 1969.

**3828.** Willison, George F. *Patrick Henry and His World.* Garden City, NY: Doubleday, 1969.

**3829.** Wilstach, Paul. "Patrick Henry." In his *Patriots Off Their Pedestals,* 78–96. Indianapolis: Bobbs-Merrill, 1927.

**3830.** Wirt, William. *Sketches of the Life and Character of Patrick Henry.* New York: Derby and Jackson, 1858.

## HEPBURN, WILLIAM PETERS (1833–1916) R-IA, House 1881–1887, 1893–1909.

**3831.** Briggs, John E. *William Peters Hepburn.* Iowa City: State Historical Society of Iowa, 1919.

## HERBERT, HILARY ABNER (1834–1919) D-AL, House 1877–1893.

**3832.** Davis, Hugh C. "Hilary A. Herbert: Bourbon Apologist." *Alabama Review* 20 (July 1967): 216–225.

**3833.** Fourtin, Maurice S. "Hilary Abner Herbert: Post Reconstruction Southern Politician." Master's thesis, University of Maryland, 1965.

**3834.** Hammett, Hugh B. *Hilary Abner Herbert: A Southerner Returns to the Union.* Philadelphia: American Philosophical Society, 1976.

**3835.** Royall, Dora C. "Sketch of Col. Hilary Abner Herbert." *Researcher: A Magazine of History and Genealogical Exchange* 2 (1927): 45–47.

**3836.** Stabler, Carey V. "The Career of Hilary Abner Herbert." Master's thesis, University of Alabama, 1932.

**HERRICK, MANUEL** (1876–1952) R-OK, House 1921–1923.

**3837.** Aldrich, Gene. *Okie Jesus Congressman: The Life of Manuel Herrick.* Oklahoma City, OK: Times-Journal Publishing Company, 1974.

**HERRING, CLYDE LAVERNE** (1879–1945) D-IA, Senate 1937–1943.

**3838.** Swisher, Jacob A. "Clyde Herring." In his *Governors of Iowa,* 119–120. Mason City, IA: Klipto Loose Leaf Company, 1946.

**HERTER, CHRISTIAN ARCHIBALD** (1895–1966) R-MA, House 1943–1953.

**3839.** Noble, George B. *Christian A. Herter.* New York: Cooper Square, 1970.

**HEWES, JOSEPH** (1730–1779) NC, Continental Congress 1774–1777, 1779.

**3840.** Sanderson, John. "Joseph Hewes." In *Sanderson's Biography of the Signers of the Declaration of Independence,* edited by Robert T. Conrad, 768–775. Philadelphia: Thomas, Cowperthwait, 1848.

**HEWITT, ABRAM STEVENS** (1822–1903) D-NY, House 1875–1879, 1881–1886.

**3841.** Hewitt, Abram S. *Selected Writings of Abram S. Hewitt.* Edited by Allan Nevins. New York: Columbia University Press, 1937.

**3842.** Nevins, Allan. *Abram S. Hewitt: With Some Account of Peter Cooper.* New York: Harper and Brothers, 1935.

**3843.** Post, Louis F., and Fred C. Leubuscher. *Henry George's 1886 Campaign: An Account of the George-Hewitt Campaign in the New York Municipal Election of 1886.* Westport, CT: Hyperion Press, 1976.

**HEYBURN, WELDON BRINTON** (1852–1912) R-ID, Senate 1903–1912.

**3844.** Cook, Rufus G. "Pioneer Portraits: Weldon B. Heyburn." *Idaho Yesterdays* 10 (Spring 1966): 22–26.

**3845.** ———. "Senator Heyburn's War against the Forest Service." *Idaho Yesterdays* 14 (Winter 1970/1971): 12–15.

**3846.** Cox, Thomas R. "Weldon Heyburn, Lake Chatcolet and the Evolving Concept of Public Parks." *Idaho Yesterdays* 24 (Summer 1980): 2–15.

**3847.** Simpson, John A. "Weldon Heyburn and the Image of the Bloody Shirt." *Idaho Yesterdays* 24 (Winter 1981): 20–28.

**HEYWARD, THOMAS JR.** (1746–1809) SC, Continental Congress 1776–1778.

**3848.** Sanderson, John. "Thomas Heyward." In *Sanderson's Biography of the Signers of the Declaration of Independence,* edited by Robert T. Conrad, 793–798. Philadelphia: Thomas, Cowperthwait, 1848.

**HICKENLOOPER, BOURKE BLAKEMORE** (1896–1971) R-IA, Senate 1945–1969.

**3849.** Schapsmeier, Edward L., and Frederick H. Schapsmeier. "A Strong Voice for Keeping America Strong: A Profile of Senator Bourke Hinkenlooper." *Annals of Iowa* 47 (Spring 1984): 362–376.

**3850.** Swisher, Jacob A. "Bourke B. Hickenlooper." In his *Governors of Iowa,* 131–132. Mason City, IA: Klipto Loose Leaf Company, 1946.

**HICKS, THOMAS HOLLIDAY** (1798–1865) U-MD, Senate 1862–1865.

**3851.** Radcliffe, George L. *Governor Thomas H. Hicks of Maryland and the Civil Way.* Baltimore: Johns Hopkins University Press, 1901.

**HIGGINS, ANTHONY** (1840–1912) R-DE, Senate 1889–1895.

**3852.** Higgins, John C. *The Life and Public Services of Hon. Anthony Higgins of Delaware.* Wilmington: Historical Society of Delaware, 1913–1914.

**HIGGINSON, STEPHEN** (1743–1828) MA, Continental Congress 1782–1783.

**3853.** Higginson, Thomas W. *Life and Times of Stephen Higginson, Member of the Continental Congress (1783).* Boston: Houghton Mifflin, 1907.

**HILL, BENJAMIN HARVEY** (1823–1882) D-GA, House 1875–1877, Senate 1877–1882.

**3854.** Hill, Benjamin, Jr. *Senator Benjamin H. Hill of Georgia: His Life, Speeches and Writings.* Atlanta, GA: Hudgins, 1891.

**3855.** Pearce, Haywood J. *Benjamin Hill: Secession and Reconstruction.* Chicago: University of Chicago Press, 1928.

**HILL, DAVID BENNETT** (1843–1910) D-NY, Senate 1892–1897.

**3856.** Bass, Herbert J. "David B. Hill and the Steel of the Senate, 1891." *New York History* 41 (July 1960): 299–311.

**3857.** ———. *"I Am a Democrat": The Political Career of David Bennett Hill.* Syracuse, NY: Syracuse University Press, 1961.

**HILL, ISAAC** (1788–1851) J-NH, Senate 1831–1836.

**3858.** Bradley, Cyrus. *Biography of Isaac Hill.* Concord: J. F. Brown, 1935.

**3859.** Cole, Donald B. *Jacksonian Democracy in New Hampshire, 1800–1851.* Cambridge, MA: Harvard University Press, 1970.

**HILL, JOSEPH LISTER** (1894–1984) D-AL, House 1923–1938, Senate 1938–1969.

**3860.** Hamilton, Virginia V. *Lister Hill: Statesman From the South.* Chapel Hill: University of North Carolina Press, 1987.

**HILL, JOSHUA** (1812–1891) R-GA, House 1857–1861, Senate 1871–1873.

**3861.** Roberts, Lucien E. "The Political Career of Joshua Hill, Georgia Unionist." *Georgia Historical Quarterly* 21 (March 1937): 50–72.

**HILLHOUSE, JAMES** (1754–1832) CT, House 1791–1796, Senate 1796–1810.

**3862.** Bacon, Leonard. *Sketch of the Life and Public Services of Hon. James Hillhouse of New Haven: With a Notice of His Son, Augustus Lucas Hillhouse.* New Haven: N.p., 1860.

**HILLIARD, HENRY WASHINGTON** (1808–1892) W-AL, House 1845–1851.

**3863.** Golden, James L. "Hilliard vs. Yancey: Prelude to the Civil War." *Quarterly Journal of Speech* 42 (February 1956): 35–44.

**3864.** Jackson, Carlton L. "Alabama's Hilliard: A Nationalistic Rebel of the Old South." *Alabama Historical Quarterly* 31 (Fall/Winter 1969): 183–205.

**3865.** McGregor, Robert C. "Between the Two Wars: Alabama in the House of Representatives 1849–1861." *Alabama Historical Quarterly* 42 (Fall/Winter 1980): 167–200.

**3866.** Shields, Johanna N. "An Antebellum Alabama Maverick—Henry Washington Hilliard, 1845–1851." *Alabama Review* 30 (July 1977): 191–212.

**HILLYER, JUNIUS** (1807–1886) D-GA, House 1851–1855.

**3867.** Vinson, Frank B. "Junius Hillyer's 1838 Union Party Letter." *Georgia Historical Quarterly* 64 (Summer 1980): 204–215.

**HINDMAN, THOMAS CARMICHAEL** (1828–1868) D-AR, House 1859–1861.

**3868.** Nash, Charles E. *Biographical Sketches of Gen. Pat Cleburne and Gen. T. C.*

*Hindman, together with Humorous Anecdotes and Reminiscences of the Late Civil War.* Dayton, OH: Press of Morningside Bookshop, 1977.

**HINDMAN, WILLIAM** (1743–1822) F-MD, House 1793–1799, Senate 1800–1801, Continental Congress 1785–1788.

**3869.** Harrison, Samuel A. *A Memoir of the Hon. William Hindman: A Paper Read before the Maryland Historical Society, March 10th, 1879.* Baltimore: J. Murphy, 1880.

**HITCHCOCK, GILBERT MONELL** (1859–1934) D-NE, House 1903–1905, 1907–1911, Senate 1911–1923.

**3870.** Christensen, Walter. "Gilbert M. Hitchcock: The Newspaperman." *Nebraska History* 17 (July/September 1936): 189–191.

**3871.** Coletta, Paolo E. "The Patronage Battle between Bryan and Hitchcock." *Nebraska History* 49 (Summer 1965): 121–137.

**3872.** Johnson, John R. "Gilbert Monell Hitchcock (Publisher) 1859–1934." In his *Representative Nebraskans,* 94–98. Lincoln, NE: Johnsen, 1954.

**3873.** Patterson, Robert F. "Gilbert M. Hitchcock: A Story of Two Careers." Ph.D. dissertation, University of Colorado, 1940.

**3874.** Wimer, Kurt. "Senator Hitchcock and the League of Nations." *Nebraska History* 44 (September 1963): 189–204.

**HOAGLAND, PETER** (1941–  ) D-NE, House 1989–1995.

**3875.** Cwiklik, Robert. *House Rules: A Freshman Congressman's Initiation to the Backslapping, Backpeddling, and Backstrapping Ways of Washington.* New York: Villard Books, 1993.

**HOAR, EBENEZER ROCKWOOD** (1816–1895) R-MA, House 1873–1875.

**3876.** Storey, Moorfield. "Memoir of Ebenezer Rockwood Hoar." *Massachusetts Historical Society Proceedings* 45 (1911): 531–540.

**3877.** Storey, Moorfield, and Edward W. Emerson. *Ebeneezer Rockwood Hoar: A Memoir.* Boston: Houghton Mifflin, 1911.

**HOAR, GEORGE FRISBIE** (1826–1904) R-MA, House 1869–1877, Senate 1877–1904.

**3878.** Beisner, Robert L. "George F. Hoar: The Trials of Dissent." In his *Twelve against Empire: The Anti-imperialists, 1898–1900,* 139–164. New York: McGraw-Hill, 1968.

**3879.** Garraty, John A. "Holmes's Appointment to the US Supreme Court." *New England Quarterly* 22 (September 1949): 291–303.

**3880.** Gillett, Frederick H. *George Frisbie Hoar.* Boston: Houghton Mifflin, 1934.

**3881.** Hess, James W. "George F. Hoar, 1826–1884." Ph.D. dissertation, Harvard University, 1964.

**3882.** Hoar, George F. *Autobiography of Seventy Years.* 2 vols. New York: Scribner's, 1963.

**3883.** Lodge, Henry C. "Senator Hoar." In his *A Frontier Town and Other Essays,* 169–209. New York: Charles Scribner's Sons, 1906.

**3884.** Vandenbusche, Duane L. "Aspects of Domestic Issues in the Senatorial Career of George F. Hoar." Ed.D. dissertation, Oklahoma State University, 1964.

**3885.** Welch, Richard E. *George F. Hoar and the Half-Breed Republicans.* Cambridge, MA: Harvard University Press, 1971.

**3886.** ———. "Opponents and Colleagues: George Frisbie Hoar and Henry Cabot Lodge, 1898–1904." *New England Quarterly* 39 (June 1966): 182–209.

**3887.** ———. "Senator George Frisbie Hoar and the Defeat of Anti-imperialism, 1898–1900." *Historian* 26 (May 1964): 362–380.

**HOAR, SAMUEL (1778–1856) W-MA, House 1835–1837.**

**3888.** Emerson, Ralph W. "Samuel Hoar." In his *Complete Works,* vol. 10, 435–448. Boston: Houghton Mifflin, 1904.

**HOBSON, RICHMOND PEARSON (1870–1937) D-AL, House 1907–1915.**

**3889.** Halliborton, Richard. "Eight Volunteers for Death." In his *Seven League Boots,* 34–46. Indianapolis: Bobbs-Merrill, 1935.

**3890.** Pittman, Walter E. *Navalist and Progressive: The Life of Richmond P. Hobson.* Manhattan: Kansas State University, 1981.

**3891.** ———. "Richmond P. Hobson, Crusader." Ph.D. dissertation, University of Georgia, 1969.

**3892.** Sheldon, Richard N. "Richard Pearson Hobson as a Progressive Reformer." *Alabama Review* 25 (October 1972): 243–261.

**3893.** ———. "Richmond Pearson Hobson: The Military Hero as Reformer During the Progressive Era." Ph.D. dissertation, University of Arizona, 1970.

**HOEY, CLYDE ROARK (1877–1954) D-NC, House 1919–1921, Senate 1945–1954.**

**3894.** Hatcher, Susan A. "The Senatorial Career of Clyde R. Hoey." Ph.D. dissertation, Duke University, 1983.

**HOFFMAN, CLARE EUGENE (1875–1967) R-MI, House 1935–1963.**

**3895.** Walker, Donald E. "The Congressional Career of Clare E. Hoffman, 1935–63." Ph.D. dissertation, Michigan State University, 1982.

**HOFFMAN, HAROLD GILES (1896–1954) R-NJ, House 1927–1931.**

**3896.** Dutch, Andrew K. *Hysteria: Lindbergh Kidnap Case.* Ardmore, PA: Dorrance, 1976.

**HOLIFIELD, CHESTER EARL (1903– ) D-CA, House 1943–1974.**

**3897.** Dyke, Richard W. *Mr. Atomic Energy: Congressman Chet Holifield and Atomic Energy Affairs, 1945–1974.* New York: Greenwood, 1989.

**HOLMAN, WILLIAM STEELE (1822–1897) D-IN, House 1859–1865, 1867–1877, 1881–1895, 1897.**

**3898.** Blake, Israel G. *The Holmans of Veraestau.* Oxford, OH: Mississippi Valley Press, 1943.

**3899.** ———. "The Lives of William Steele Holman and His Father, Jesse Lynch Holman." Ph.D. dissertation, Indiana University, 1940.

**3900.** Clark, Champ. "How Reputations Are Made in Congress." In his *My Quarter Century of American Politics,* vol. 2, 56–62. New York: Harper, 1920.

**HOLMES, DAVID (1770–1832) R-VA/MS, House (VA) 1797–1809, Senate (MS) 1820–1825.**

**3901.** Conrad, David H. "David Holmes: First Governor of Mississippi." In *Publications of the Mississippi Historical Society,* vol. 4. Jackson: Mississippi Historical Society, 1921.

**3902.** Horton, William B. "Life of David Holmes." Ph.D. dissertation, University of Colorado, 1935.

**HOLMES, ISAAC EDWARD (1796–1867) D-SC, House 1839–1851.**

**3903.** Wheeler, Henry G. "Holmes, Isaac Edward." In his *History of Congress,* vol. 1, 9–30. New York: Harper, 1848.

**HOLSEY, HOPKINS** (1779–1859) D-GA, House 1835–1839.

**3904.** Montgomery, Horace. "Hopkins Holsey." In *Georgians in Profile*, edited by Horace Montgomery, 192–219. Athens: University of Georgia Press, 1958.

**HOLT, RUSH DEW** (1905–1955) D-WV, Senate 1935–1941.

**3905.** Coffey, William E. "Rush Dew Holt: The Boy Senator, 1905–1942." Ph.D. dissertation, West Virginia University, 1970.

**HOLTZMAN, ELIZABETH** (1941– ) D-NY, House 1973–1981.

**3906.** Feith, Douglas. "Arms and the Congresswomen." *World Affairs* 143 (Summer 1980): 71–84.

**3907.** Lamson, Peggy. "Elizabeth Holtzman: Congresswoman from New York." In her *In the Vanguard*, 69–108. Boston: Houghton Mifflin, 1979.

**HOOPER, WILLIAM** (1742–1790) NC, Continental Congress 1774–1777.

**3908.** Kneif, Robert C. "William Hooper, 1742–1790, Misunderstood Patriot." Ph.D. dissertation, Tulane University, 1980.

**3909.** Sanderson, John. "William Hooper." In *Sanderson's Biography of the Signers of the Declaration of Independence*, edited by Robert T. Conrad, 758–767. Philadelphia: Thomas, Cowperthwait, 1848.

**HOPE, CLIFFORD RAGSDALE** (1893–1970) R-KS, House 1927–1957.

**3910.** Duram, James C., and Eleanor A. Duram. "Congressman: Clifford Hope's Correspondence with His Constituents: A Conservative View of the Court-Packing of 1937." *Kansas Historical Quarterly* 37 (Spring 1971): 64–80.

**3911.** Forsythe, James L. "Clifford Hope of Kansas: Practical Congressman and Agrarian Idealist." *Agricultural History* 51 (April 1977): 406–420.

**HOPKINS, STEPHEN** (1707–1785) RI, Continental Congress 1774–1780.

**3912.** Foster, William E. *Stephen Hopkins, a Rhode Island Statesman: A Study in the Political History of the Eighteenth Century.* Providence, RI: S. S. Rider, 1884.

**3913.** Sanderson, John. "Stephen Hopkins." In *Sanderson's Biography of the Signers of the Declaration of Independence*, edited by Robert T. Conrad, 195–205. Philadelphia: Thomas, Cowperthwait, 1848.

**HOPKINSON, FRANCIS** (1737–1791) NJ, Continental Congress 1776.

**3914.** Hastings, George E. *The Life and Works of Francis Hopkinson.* Chicago: University of Chicago Press, 1926.

**3915.** Sanderson, John. "Francis Hopkinson." In *Sanderson's Biography of the Signers of the Declaration of Independence*, edited by Robert T. Conrad, 317–322. Philadelphia: Thomas, Cowperthwait, 1848.

**HOPKINSON, JOSEPH** (1770–1842) F-PA, House 1815–1819.

**3916.** Browne, C. A. "Hail, Columbia." In his *The Story of Our National Ballads*, 33–48. Rev. ed. New York: Crowell, 1931.

**3917.** Konkle, Burton A. *Joseph Hopkinson, 1770–1842, Jurist: Scholar: Inspirer of the Arts: Author of "Hail Columbia."* Philadelphia: University of Pennsylvania Press, 1931.

**HOUGHTON, ALANSON BIGELOW** (1863–1941) R-NY, House 1919–1922.

**3918.** Houghton, Adelaide L. *London Years: The Diary of Adelaide Wellington Houghton, 1925–1929.* New York: Privately printed, 1963.

**HOUK, JOHN CHILES** (1860–1923) R-TN, House 1891–1895.

**3919.** Archer, Claude J. "The Life of John Chiles Houk." Master's thesis, University of Tennessee, 1941.

**HOUK, LEONIDAS CAMPBELL**
(1836–1891) R-TN, House 1879–1891.

**3920.** Gentry, Amos L. "The Public Career of Leonidas Campbell Houk." Master's thesis, University of Tennessee, 1939.

**3921.** Temple, Oliver P. "Leonidas C. Houk." In *Notable Men of Tennessee, from 1833 to 1875,* edited by Mary B. Temple, 128–136. New York: Cosmopolitan Press, 1912.

**HOUSTON, ANDREW JACKSON**
(1854–1941) D-TX, Senate 1941.

**3922.** Houston, Andrew J. *Texas Independence.* Houston: Anson Jones Press, 1938.

**3923.** Welch, June R. "Andrew Jackson Houston Succeeded to His Father's Seat." In his *The Texas Senator,* 120–123. Dallas: G. L. A. Press, 1978.

**HOUSTON, GEORGE SMITH**
(1811–1879) D-AL, House 1841–1849, 1851–1861, Senate 1879.

**3924.** Draughon, Ralph B. "George Smith Houston and Southern Unity, 1846–1849." *Alabama Review* 19 (July 1966): 187–207.

**3925.** McGregor, Robert C. "Between the Two Wars: Alabama in the House of Representatives 1849–1861." *Alabama Historical Quarterly* 42 (Fall/Winter 1980): 167–200.

**HOUSTON, SAMUEL** (1793–1863)
TN/D-TX, House (TN) 1823–1827, Senate (TX) 1846–1859.

**3926.** Bradley, Glenn D. "Sam Houston." In his *Winning the Southwest: A Story of Conquest,* 104–144. Chicago: McClurg, 1912.

**3927.** Brady, Cyrus T. "Sam Houston and Freedom." In his *Border Fights and Fighters,* 347–367. Garden City, NY: Doubleday, 1913.

**3928.** Braider, Donald. *Solitary Star: A Biography of Sam Houston.* New York: Putnam's, 1974.

**3929.** Bruce, Henry. *Life of General Houston.* New York: Dodd, Mead, 1891.

**3930.** Bruce, Philip A. "General Samuel Houston." In his *Virginia Plutarch,* vol. 2, 133–150. Chapel Hill: University of North Carolina Press, 1929.

**3931.** Campbell, Randolph B. *Sam Houston and the American Southwest.* New York: HarperCollins, 1993.

**3932.** Cattermole, E. G. "Gen. Samuel Houston." In his *Famous Frontiersmen, Pioneers and Scouts,* 305–345. Tarrytown, NY: W. Abbatt, 1926.

**3933.** Corn, James F. "Sam Houston: The Raven." *Journal of Cherokee Studies* 6 (Spring 1981): 34–39.

**3934.** Crane, William C. *Life and Select Literary Remains of Sam Houston of Texas.* Philadelphia: Lippincott, 1884.

**3935.** Creel, George. "The Playboy of the Plains." In his *Sons of the Eagle,* 150–162. Indianapolis: Bobbs-Merrill, 1927.

**3936.** ———. *Sam Houston: Colossus in Buckskin.* New York: Cosmopolitan, 1928.

**3937.** De Bruhl, Marshall. *Sword of San Jacinto: A Life of Sam Houston.* New York: Random House, 1993.

**3938.** Doegey, Lorayne M. *Sam Houston: Southern Spokesman for the Cause of Union.* Ph.D. dissertation, Southern Illinois University of Carbondale, 1968.

**3939.** Flanagan, Sue. *Sam Houston's Texas.* Austin: University of Texas Press, 1964.

**3940.** Frantz, Joe B. "Texas Giant of Contradictions: Sam Houston." *American West* 27 (July/August 1980): 1, 4–13, 61–65.

**3941.** Friend, Lierena B. *Sam Houston, the Great Designer.* Austin: University of Texas Press, 1954.

**3942.** Gregory, Jack, and Rennard Strickland. *Sam Houston with the Cherokees, 1829–1833.* Austin: University of Texas Press, 1967.

**3943.** Hopewell, Clifford. *Sam Houston Man of Destiny: A Biography.* Austin, TX: Eakin Press, 1986.

**3944.** Houston, Samuel. *The Autobiography of Sam Houston.* Westport: Greenwood, 1980.

**3945.** ———. *Ever Thine Truly: Love Letters from Sam Houston to Anna Raquet.* Austin, TX: Jenkins Garrett Press, 1975.

**3946.** James, Marquis. *The Raven: A Biography of Sam Houston.* Indianapolis: Bobbs-Merrill, 1929.

**3947.** Kennedy, John F. *Sam Houston and the Senate.* Austin, TX: Pemberton Press, 1970.

**3948.** Lester, Charles E. *Sam Houston and His Republic.* New York: Burgess, Stringer, 1846.

**3949.** Oskison, John M. *A Texas Titan: The Story of Sam Houston.* Garden City, NY: Doubleday, 1929.

**3950.** Roberts, Madge T. *Star of Destiny: The Private Life of Sam and Margaret Houston.* Denton: University of North Texas, 1993.

**3951.** Seymour, Flora W. *Sam Houston, Patriot.* New York: Century, 1930.

**3952.** Shearer, Ernest C. "The Mercurial Sam Houston." *East Tennessee Historical Society's Publication* 35 (1963): 3–20.

**3953.** Sibley, Manly M. "James Hamilton, Jr. vs. Sam Houston: Repercussions of the Nullification Controversy." *Southwestern Historical Quarterly* 89 (October 1985): 165–180.

**3954.** Stephenson, Nathaniel W. "Texas Secedes." In his *Texas and the Mexican War,* 65–86. New Haven, CT: Yale University Press, 1921.

**3955.** Waldrop, Charles P. "The Conquest of Sam Houston." *American History Illustrated* 21, no. 9 (1987): 36–43.

**3956.** Welch, June R. "Sam Houston Established His Big Rancho." In his *The Texas Governor,* 10–15, 44–47. Irving, TX: G. L. A. Press, 1977.

**3957.** Westwood, Howard C. "President Lincoln's Overture to Sam Houston." *Southwestern Historical Quarterly* 88 (October 1984): 125–144.

**3958.** Williams, Alfred M. *Sam Houston and the War of Independence in Texas.* Boston: Houghton Mifflin, 1893.

**3959.** Williams, Amelia W., and Eugene C. Barker, eds. *The Writings of Sam Houston, 1813–1863.* Austin, TX: Pemberton Press, 1970.

**3960.** Williams, John H. *Sam Houston: A Biography of the Father of Texas.* New York: Simon and Schuster, 1993.

**3961.** Winkler, Ernest W. "Sam Houston and Williamson Simpson Oldham." *Southwestern Historical Quarterly* 20 (October 1916): 146–150.

**3962.** Wisehart, Marion K. *Sam Houston, American Giant.* Washington, DC: R. B. Luce, 1962.

**3963.** Worrell, John. *A Diamond in the Rough: Embracing Anecdote Biography, Romance and History.* Indianapolis: W. B. Burford, 1906.

**HOWARD, EDGAR (1858–1951) D-NE, House 1923–1935.**

**3964.** Johnson, John R. "Edgar Howard (Country Editor) 1858–1951." In his *Representative Nebraskans,* 99–104. Lincoln, NE: Johnsen, 1954.

**HOWARD, JAMES JOHN (1927–1988) D-NJ, House 1965–1988.**

**3965.** Lyons, Kathleen. *Dear Congressman Howard.* Washington, DC: Acropolis Books, 1971.

## HOWARD, MILFORD WRIARSON
(1862–1937) P-AL, House 1895–1899.

**3966.** Harris, D. Alan. "Campaigning in the Bloody Seventh: The Election of 1894 in the Seventh Congressional District." *Alabama Review* 27 (April 1974): 127–138.

## HOWE, ALLAN TURNER (1927– ) D-UT, House 1975–1977.

**3967.** Hollstein, Milton. "Congressman Howe in the Salt Lake Media: A Case Study of the Press as Pillory." *Journalism Quarterly* 54 (Autumn 1977): 454–458, 465.

## HOWELL, ROBERT BEECHER
(1864–1933) R-NE, Senate 1923–1933.

**3968.** O'Brien, Patrick G. *Senator Robert B. Howell: A Midwestern Progressive and Insurgent During Normalcy.* Emporia: Kansas State Teachers College, 1970.

## HUDDLESTON, GEORGE (1869–1960) D-AL, House 1915–1937.

**3969.** Barnard, William D. "George Huddleston, Sr., and the Political Tradition of Birmingham." *Alabama Review* 36 (October 1983): 243–258.

**3970.** Packer, Nancy H. *In My Father's House: Tales of an Uncomfortable Man.* Santa Barbara, CA: J. Daniel, 1988.

## HUDNUT, WILLIAM HERBERT III
(1932– ) R-IN, House 1973–1975.

**3971.** Hudnut, William H. *Minister/Mayor/William H. Hudnut III.* Philadelphia: Westminster Press, 1987.

## HUGHES, DUDLEY MAYS (1848–1927) D-GA, House 1909–1917.

**3972.** Jones, Billy W. *Vocational Legacy: Biography of Dudley Mays Hughes.* Macon, GA: The author, 1976.

## HUGHES, HAROLD EVERETT (1922– ) D-IA, Senate 1969–1975.

**3973.** Hughes, Harold E. *Man from Ida Grove: A Senator's Personal Story.* Waco, TX: Wood Books, 1979.

**3974.** King, Larry L. "Harold E. Hughes: Evangelist from the Prairies." *Harper's* 238 (March 1969): 50–57.

**3975.** Larew, James C. "A Party Reborn: Harold Hughes and the Iowa Democrats." *Palimpsest* 59 (September/October 1978): 148–161.

## HULL, CORDELL (1871–1955) D-TN, House 1907–1921, 1923–1931, Senate 1931–1933.

**3976.** Akins, Bill. "A Time of Testing: The Tennessee Career of Cordell Hull." *East Tennessee Historical Society's Publications* 54/55 (1982/1983): 26–46.

**3977.** Bowers, Robert E. "Hull, Russian Subversion in Cuba, and Recognition of the U.S.S.R." *Journal of American History* 53 (December 1966): 542–554.

**3978.** Buell, Raymond L. *The Hull Trade Agreement Program and the American Slave System.* New York: Foreign Policy Association, 1938.

**3979.** Burns, Richard D. "Cordell Hull: A Study in Diplomacy, 1933–1941." Ph.D. dissertation, University of Illinois, 1961.

**3980.** Chu, Yung-Chao. "A History of the Hull Trade Program, 1934–1939." Ph.D. dissertation, Columbia University, 1957.

**3981.** Drummond, Donald F. "Cordell Hull." In *Uncertain Tradition: American Secretaries of State in the Twentieth Century,* edited by Norman A. Graebner, 184–209. New York: McGraw-Hill, 1961.

**3982.** Furdell, William J. "Cordell Hull and the London Economic Conference of 1933." Ph.D. dissertation, Kent State University, 1970.

**3983.** Gray, Tony. "Cordell Hull." In his *Champions of Peace,* 198–200. New York: Paddington Press, 1976.

**3984.** Grollman, Catherine A. "Cordell Hull and His Concept of a World Organization." Ph.D. dissertation, University of North Carolina, 1965.

**3985.** Hinton, Harold B. *Cordell Hull: A Biography.* Garden City, NY: Doubleday, 1942.

**3986.** Hull, Cordell. *The Memoirs of Cordell Hull.* 2 vols. New York: Macmillan, 1948.

**3987.** Jablon, Howard. "Cordell Hull, His Associates and Relations with Japan, 1933–1936." *Mid-America* 56 (July 1974): 160–174.

**3988.** ———. "Cordell Hull, the State Department, and the Foreign Policy of the First Roosevelt Administration, 1933–1936." Ph.D. dissertation, Rutgers University, 1967.

**3989.** Johnson, Joseph L. "Congressional Career of Cordell Hull." Master's thesis, University of Tennessee, 1965.

**3990.** Milner, Cooper. "The Public Life of Cordell Hull, 1907–1924." Ph.D. dissertation, Vanderbilt University, 1960.

**3991.** Pratt, Julius W. *Cordell Hull, 1933–44.* 2 vols. New York: Cooper Square, 1964.

**3992.** ———. "The Ordeal of Cordell Hull." *Review of Politics* 28 (January 1966): 76–98.

**3993.** Schatz, Arthur W. "The Anglo-American Trade Agreement and Cordell Hull's Search for Peace, 1936–1938." *Journal of American History* 57 (June 1970): 85–103.

**3994.** ———. "Cordell Hull and the Struggle for the Reciprocal Trade Agreement Program, 1932–1940." Ph.D. dissertation, University of Oregon, 1965.

**3995.** Stanley, Judith M. "Cordell Hull and Democratic Party Unity." *Tennessee Historical Quarterly* 32 (Summer 1973): 169–187.

**3996.** Utley, Jonathan G. *Going to War with Japan, 1937–1941.* Knoxville: University of Tennessee Press, 1985.

**3997.** Wertenbaker, Charles C. "Hull Makes It Personal." In his *A New Doctrine for the Americas,* 97–115. New York: Viking, 1941.

**3998.** Woods, Randall B. "Hull and Argentina: Wilsonian Diplomacy in the Age of Roosevelt." *Journal of Interamerican Studies and World Affairs* 16 (August 1974): 350–371.

## HUMPHREY, HUBERT HORATIO, JR.
**(1911–1978) D-MN, Senate 1949–1964, 1971–1978.**

**3999.** Amrine, Michael. *This Is Humphrey: The Story of the Senator.* Garden City, NY: Doubleday, 1960.

**4000.** Barzman, Sol. "Hubert H. Humphrey." In his *Madmen and Geniuses,* 273–280. Chicago: Follett, 1974.

**4001.** Berman, Edgar. *Hubert: The Triumph and Tragedy of the Humphrey I Knew.* New York: Putnam's, 1979.

**4002.** Cohen, Daniel. *Undefeated: The Life of Hubert H. Humphrey.* Minneapolis, MN: Lerner, 1978.

**4003.** Curtin, Mary T. "Hubert H. Humphrey and the Politics of the Cold War, 1943–1954." Ph.D. dissertation, Columbia University, 1986.

**4004.** Eisele, Albert A. *Almost to the Presidency: A Biography of Two American Politicians.* Blue Earth, MN: Piper, 1972.

**4005.** Engelmayer, Sheldon D., and Robert J. Wagman. *Hubert Humphrey: The Man and His Dream 1911–1978.* New York: Methuen, 1978.

**4006.** Erlanger, Ellen. *Hubert H. Humphrey: The Happy Warrior.* Minneapolis, MN: Lerner Publications Company, 1979.

**4007.** Fleming, Daniel B. *Kennedy vs. Humphrey, West Virginia, 1960: The Pivotal Battle for the Democratic Presidential Nomination*. Jefferson, NC: McFarland, 1992.

**4008.** Garrettson, Charles L. *Hubert H. Humphrey and the Politics of Joy: A Case Study in Religious-Political Ethics*. New Brunswick, NJ: Transaction Books, 1992.

**4009.** Griffith, Winthrop. *Humphrey: A Candid Biography*. New York: William Morrow, 1965.

**4010.** Haynes, John E. "Farm Coops and the Election of Hubert Humphrey to the Senate." *Agricultural History* 57 (April 1983): 201–211.

**4011.** Humphrey, Hubert H. *The Education of a Public Man: My Life and Politics*. New York: Doubleday, 1976.

**4012.** ———. *Hubert Humphrey: The Man and His Dream*. New York: Methuen, 1978.

**4013.** Manfred, Frederick. "Hubert Horatio Humphrey: A Memoir." *Minnesota History* 46 (Fall 1978): 87–101.

**4014.** Martin, Ralph G., and Hubert H. Humphrey. *A Man for All People: Hubert H. Humphrey*. New York: Grosset and Dunlap, 1968.

**4015.** Nordstrom, Marty. *Humphrey*. Washington, DC: Luce, 1964.

**4016.** Polsby, Nelson W. *The Citizen's Choice: Humphrey or Nixon*. Washington, DC: Public Affairs Press, 1968.

**4017.** Pomper, Gerald. "Nomination of Hubert Humphrey for Vice-President." *Journal of Politics* 28 (August 1966): 639–659.

**4018.** Ryskind, Allan H. *Hubert: An Unauthorized Biography of the Vice-President*. New Rochelle, NY: Arlington House, 1968.

**4019.** Sherrill, Robert G., and Harry W. Ernst. *The Drugstore Liberal*. New York: Grossman, 1968.

**4020.** Solberg, Carl. *Hubert Humphrey: A Biography*. New York: Norton, 1984.

**4021.** Stuhler, Barbara. "A Tale of Two Democrats: Hubert H. Humphrey and Eugene J. McCarthy." In her *Ten Men of Minnesota and American Foreign Policy, 1898–1968*, 194–200. St. Paul: Minnesota Historical Society, 1973.

**4022.** Webb, Robert N. "Hubert Horatio Humphrey." In his *Leaders of Our Time*, 23–31. New York: Watts, 1966.

**4023.** Westman, Paul. *Hubert H. Humphrey, the Politics of Joy*. Minneapolis, MN: Dillon Press, 1978.

## HUMPHREYS, BENJAMIN GRUBB
**(1865–1923) D-MS, House 1903–1923.**

**4024.** Rainwater, Percy L., ed. "The Autobiography of Benjamin Grubb Humphreys, August 26, 1808–December 20, 1882." *Mississippi Valley Historical Review* 21 (September 1934): 231–255.

## HUNT, LESTER CALLAWAY (1892–1954)
**D-WY, Senate 1949–1954.**

**4025.** Ewig, Rick. "McCarthy Era Politics: The Ordeal of Senator Lester Hunt." *Annals of Wyoming* 55 (Spring 1983): 9–21.

## HUNT, WASHINGTON (1811–1867)
**W-NY, House 1843–1849.**

**4026.** Wheeler, Henry G. "Hunt, Washington." In his *History of Congress*, vol. 1, 341–365. New York: Harper, 1848.

## HUNTER, MORTON CRAIG
**(1825–1896) R-IN, House 1867–1869, 1873–1879.**

**4027.** Barnes, William H. "Morton C. Hunter." In his *Lives of Gen. Ulysses S. Grant and Hon. Henry Wilson, together with Sketches of Republican Candidates for Congress in Indiana*, 51–53. New York: W. H. Barnes, 1872.

## HUNTER, ROBERT MERCER TALIAFERRO (1809–1887) VA, House 1837–1843, 1845–1847, Senate 1847–1861.

**4028.** Anderson, James L. "Robert Mercer Taliaferro Hunter." *Virginia Cavalcade* 18 (Autumn 1968): 9–13.

**4029.** Anderson, James L., and W. Edwin Hemphill. "1843 Biography of John C. Calhoun: Was R. M. T. Hunter Its Author?" *Journal of Southern History* 38 (August 1972): 469–474.

**4030.** Crow, Jeffrey J. "R. M. T. Hunter and the Secession Crisis, 1860–1861: A Southern Plan for Reconstruction." *West Virginia History* 34 (April 1973): 374–390.

**4031.** Fisher, John E. "The Dilemma of a State's Rights Whig: The Congressional Career of R. M. T. Hunter, 1837–1841." *Virginia Magazine of History and Biography* 81 (October 1973): 387–404.

**4032.** ———. "Statesman of the Lost Cause: R. M. T. Hunter and the Sectional Controversy, 1847–1887." Ph.D. dissertation, University of Virginia, 1968.

**4033.** Garnett, Theodore S. "Address of Hon. T. S. Garnett upon Presenting the Portrait of Hon. R. M. T. Hunter, to the Circuit Court of Essex County, at Tappahanock, Va., June 20, 1898." *Southern Historical Society Papers* 27 (1899): 151–155.

**4034.** Hitchcock, William S. "Southern Moderates and Succession: Senator Robert M. T. Hunter's Call for Union." *Journal of American History* 59 (March 1973): 871–884.

**4035.** Hunter, Martha T. *A Memoir of Robert M. T. Hunter.* Washington, DC: Neale, 1903.

**4036.** Hunter, Robert M. *Correspondence of Robert M. T. Hunter, 1826–1876.* Edited by Charles H. Ambler. New York: Da Capo Press, 1971.

**4037.** Jones, Charles C. *Hon. R. M. T. Hunter.* Augusta, GA: Chronicle Publishing Company, 1887.

**4038.** Moore, R. Randall. "Robert M. T. Hunter and the Crisis of the Union, 1860–1861." *Southern Historian* 13 (1992): 25–35.

**4039.** ———. "In Search of a Safe Government: A Biography of R. M. T. Hunter of Virginia." Ph.D. dissertation, University of South Carolina, 1993.

**4040.** Scanlon, James E. "A Life of Robert Hunter." Ph.D. dissertation, University of Virginia, 1969.

**4041.** Shields, Johanna N. "The Making of American Congressional Mavericks: A Contrasting of the Cultural Attitudes of Mavericks and Conformists in the United States House of Representatives, 1836–1860." Ph.D. dissertation, University of Alabama, 1973.

**4042.** Simms, Henry H. *Life of Robert M. T. Hunter: A Study in Sectionalism and Succession.* Richmond, VA: William Byrd Press, 1935.

**4043.** Washington, L. Quinton. "Hon. R. M. T. Hunter." *Southern Historical Society Papers* 25 (1897): 193–205.

## HUNTINGTON, EBENEZER (1754–1834) F-CT, House 1810–1811, 1817–1819.

**4044.** Huntington, Ebenezer. *Letters Written by Ebenezer Huntington during the American Revolution.* New York: C. F. Heartman, 1915.

## HUNTINGTON, SAMUEL (1731–1796) CT, Continental Congress 1776, 1778–1783.

**4045.** Gerlach, Larry R. *Connecticut Congressman: Samuel Huntington, 1731–1796.* Hartford: American Revolution Bicentennial Commission of Connecticut, 1977.

**4046.** Sanderson, John. "Samuel Huntington." In *Sanderson's Biography of the Signers of the Declaration of Independence,* edited by Robert T. Conrad, 243–248. Philadelphia: Thomas, Cowperthwait, 1848.

**HUNTSMAN, ADAM** (1786–1849) J-TN, House 1835–1837.

**4047.** Monney, Chase C. "The Political Career of Adam Huntsman." *Tennessee Historical Quarterly* 10 (June 1951): 99–126.

**HURD, FRANK HUNT** (1840–1896) D-OH, House 1875–1877, 1879–1881, 1883–1885.

**4048.** Folk, Patrick A. "Our Frank: The Congressional Career of Frank Hurd." *Northwest Ohio Quarterly* 41 (Spring 1969): 45–69.

**4049.** ———. "Our Frank: The Congressional Career of Frank Hurd." *Northwest Ohio Quarterly* 42 (Summer 1970): 47–63.

**4050.** ———. "Our Frank: The Congressional Career of Frank Hurd." *Northwest Ohio Quarterly* 47 (Fall 1975): 151–169.

**4051.** ———. "Our Frank: The Congressional Career of Frank Hurd." *Northwest Ohio Quarterly* 48 (Winter 1975–1976): 24–34.

**4052.** ———. "Our Frank: The Congressional Career of Frank Hurd." *Northwest Ohio Quarterly* 48 (Spring 1976): 55–79.

**4053.** ———. "Our Frank: The Congressional Career of Frank Hurd." *Northwest Ohio Quarterly* 48 (Fall 1976): 143–152.

**HURLBUT, STEPHEN AUGUSTUS** (1815–1882) R-IL, House 1873–1877.

**4054.** Lash, Jeffrey N. "Stephen Augustus Hurlbut: A Military and Diplomatic Politician, 1815–1882." Ph.D. dissertation, Kent State University, 1980.

**HUTCHISON, KATHRYN "KAY" BAILEY** (1943–  ) R-TX, Senate 1993–  .

**4055.** Ide, Arthur F. *From Stardom to Scandal: The Rise and Fall of Kay Bailey Hutchison.* Las Colinas, TX: Monument Press, 1993.

**HYMAN, JOHN ADAMS** (1840–1891) R-NC, House 1875–1877.

**4056.** Christopher, Maurine. "John A. Hyman, James E. O'Hara, and Henry P. Cheatham/North Carolina." In her *Black Americans in Congress,* 149–159. Rev. ed. New York: Thomas Y. Crowell, 1976

**4057.** Reid, George W. "Four in Black: North Carolina's Black Congressmen, 1874–1901." *Journal of Negro History* 64 (Summer 1979): 229–243.

**INGALLS, JOHN JAMES** (1833–1900) R-KS, Senate 1873–1891.

**4058.** Connelley, William E. *Ingalls of Kansas.* Topeka, KS: Privately printed, 1901.

**4059.** Connelley, William E., ed. *A Collection of the Writing of John James Ingalls: Essays, Addresses, and Orations.* Kansas City, MO: Hudson-Kimberly Publishing Company, 1902.

**4060.** Williams, Burton J. "John James Ingalls: Geographic Determinism and Kansas." *Midwest Quarterly* 6 (Spring 1965): 285–291.

**4061.** ———. Williams, Burton J. "Mormons, Mining and the Golden Trumpet of Moroni." *Midwest Quarterly* 8 (October 1966): 67–77.

**4062.** ———. *Senator John James Ingalls: Kansas' Iridescent Republican.* Lawrence: University Press of Kansas, 1972.

**INGERSOLL, CHARLES JARED** (1782–1862) D-PA, House 1813–1815, 1841–1849.

**4063.** Dwight, Timothy. *Remarks on the Review of Inchiquin's Letters.* New York: Garrett Press, 1970.

**4064.** Meigs, William M. *The Life of Charles Jared Ingersoll.* Philadelphia: Lippincott, 1897.

**4065.** Paulding, James K. *The United States and England: Being a Reply to the Criticism on Inchiquin's Letters.* New York: Van Winkle and Wiley, 1815.

**4066.** Stevens, Kenneth R. "The Webster-Ingersoll Feud: Politics and Personality in the New Nation." *Historical New Hampshire* 37 (Summer/Fall 1982): 174–192.

**INGERSOLL, JARED** (1749–1822) PA,
Continental Congress 1780–1781.

**4067.** Gipson, Lawrence H. *American Loyalist: Jared Ingersoll.* New Haven, CT: Yale University Press, 1971.

**INGERSOLL, JOSEPH REED**
(1786–1868) W-PA, House 1835–1837,
1841–1849.

**4068.** Wheeler, Henry G. "Ingersoll, Joseph Reed." In his *History of Congress,* vol. 1, 36–52. New York: Harper, 1848.

**INOUYE, DANIEL KEN** (1924–  ) D-HI,
House 1959–1963, Senate 1963–  .

**4069.** Inouye, Daniel K. *Journey to Washington.* Englewoods Cliffs, NJ: Prentice-Hall, 1967.

**IRVINE, WILLIAM** (1741–1804) PA, House
1793–1795, Continental Congress 1786–1788.

**4070.** Butterfield, Consul W. *An Historical Account of the Expedition against Sandusky under Col. William Crawford in 1782.* Cincinnati, OH: R. Clarke, 1873.

**4071.** Butterfield, Consul W. "Biographical Sketch of William Irvine." In his *Washington-Irvine Correspondence,* 65–70. Madison, WI: D. Atwood, 1882.

**IVES, IRVING MCNEIL** (1896–1962)
R-NY, Senate 1947–1959.

**4072.** Carter, John F. *Republicans on the Potomac,* 263–266. New York: McBride, 1953.

**IZARD, RALPH** (1742–1804) SC, Senate
1789–1795, Continental Congress 1782–1783.

**4073.** Deas, Anne I., ed. *Correspondence of Mr. Ralph Izard of South Carolina, from the Year 1774–1804, with a Short Memoir.* New York: C. S. Francis, 1844.

**4074.** Rumble, Fred. "The Life of Ralph Izard, 1742–1804." Master's thesis, Indiana University, 1935.

❧

**JACKSON, ANDREW** (1767–1845) R-TN,
House 1796–1797, Senate 1797–1798,
1823–1825.

**4075.** Abernethy, Thomas P. "Andrew Jackson and the Rise of Southwestern Democracy." *American Historical Review* 33 (October 1927): 64–77.

**4076.** Bassett, John S. *The Life of Andrew Jackson.* Rev. ed. 2 vols. New York: Macmillan, 1931.

**4077.** ———. "Major Lewis on the Nomination of Andrew Jackson." *American Antiquarian Society Proceedings* 33 (April 1923): 12–33.

**4078.** Bassett, John S., and J. Franklin Jameson, eds. *Correspondence of Andrew Jackson.* 7 vols. Washington, DC: Carnegie Institute of Washington, 1926–1935.

**4079.** Binder, Frederick M. "The Color Problem in Early National America as Viewed by John Adams, Jefferson, and Jackson." Ed.D. dissertation, Columbia University, 1962.

**4080.** Bonner, James C., ed. "Andrew Jackson Comments on Polk's Cabinet." *Tennessee Historical Quarterly* 27 (Fall 1968): 287–288.

**4081.** Bowers, Claude G. *The Party Battles of the Jackson Period.* Boston: Houghton Mifflin, 1922.

**4082.** Brady, Cyrus T. *The True Andrew Jackson.* Philadelphia: Lippincott, 1906.

**4083.** Brasington, George F., Jr. "Representative Government in Jacksonian Political Thought." Ph.D. dissertation, University of Illinois, 1958.

**4084.** Brent, Robert A. "The Triumph of Jacksonian Democracy in the United States." *Southern Quarterly* 7 (October 1968): 43–57.

**4085.** Brown, Richard H. *The Hero and the People: The Meaning of Jacksonian Democracy.* New York: Macmillan, 1964.

**4086.** ———. "The Missouri Crisis, Slavery, and the Politics of Jacksonianism." *South Atlantic Quarterly* 65 (Winter 1966): 55–72.

**4087.** Brown, William G. *Andrew Jackson.* Boston: Houghton Mifflin, 1900.

**4088.** Buell, Augustus C. *History of Andrew Jackson, Pioneer, Patriot, Soldier, Politician, President.* 2 vols. New York: Scribner's, 1904.

**4089.** Bugg, James L., and Peter C. Stewart, eds. *Jacksonian Democracy: Myth or Reality?* 2d ed. New York: Praeger, 1976.

**4090.** Burke, John E. "Andrew Jackson as Seen by Foreigners." *Tennessee Historical Quarterly* 10 (March 1951): 25–45.

**4091.** Cabral, Peter C. "United States vs. Major General Andrew Jackson." *Loyola University of Los Angeles Law Review* 7 (July 1926): 133–144.

**4092.** Cain, Marvin R. "William Wirt against Andrew Jackson: Reflection on an Era." *Mid-America* 47 (April 1965): 113–138.

**4093.** Caldwell, Joshua W. "Last Days of Andrew Jackson." In *Joshua William Caldwell: A Memorial Volume, Containing His Biography, Writings, and Addresses,* 153–162. Nashville, TN: Brandon Printing Company, 1909.

**4094.** Caldwell, Mary F. *Andrew Jackson's Hermitage.* Nashville, TN: Ladies' Hermitage Association, 1933.

**4095.** Canfield, Frederick A. "The Figurehead of Jackson." *Tennessee Historical Magazine* 8 (July 1924): 144–145.

**4096.** Cave, Alfred A. *Jacksonian Democracy and the Historians.* Gainesville: University of Florida Press, 1964.

**4097.** Chase, James S. "Jacksonian Democracy and the Rise of the Nominating Convention." *Mid-America* 45 (October 1963): 229–249.

**4098.** Chidsey, Donald B. *Andrew Jackson: Hero.* Nashville, TN: T. Nelson, 1976.

**4099.** Clark, Thomas D. "The Jackson Purchase: A Dramatic Chapter in Southern Indiana Policy and Relations." *Filson Club Historical Quarterly* 50 (July 1976): 302–320.

**4100.** Cobbett, William. *The Life of Andrew Jackson, President of the USA.* Baltimore: J. Robinson, 1834.

**4101.** Cohalan, Daniel F. "Andrew Jackson." *Journal of the American Irish Historical Society* 28 (1929/1930): 173–187.

**4102.** Coit, Margaret L. *Andrew Jackson.* Boston: Houghton Mifflin, 1965.

**4103.** Cole, Donald B. *The Presidency of Andrew Jackson.* Lawrence: University Press of Kansas, 1993.

**4104.** Colyar, Arthur S. *Life and Times of Andrew Jackson, Soldier, Statesman, President.* Nashville, TN: Marshall and Bruce, 1904.

**4105.** Craven, Avery O., ed. "Letters of Andrew Jackson." *Huntington Library Bulletin* 3 (February 1933): 109–134.

**4106.** Cubberly, Frederick. "Andrew Jackson, Judge." *American Law Review* 56 (September/October 1922): 686–701.

**4107.** Curtis, James C. *Andrew Jackson and the Search for Vindication.* Boston: Little, Brown, 1976.

**4108.** Davis, Andrew M. "A Tempest in a Teapot: Jackson's 'LL.D.'" *Tennessee Historical Magazine* 8 (October 1924): 191–210.

**4109.** Davis, Burke. *Old Hickory: A Life of Andrew Jackson.* New York: Dial, 1977.

**4110.** Deutsch, Eberhard P. "The United States versus Major General Andrew Jackson." *American Bar Association Journal* 46 (September 1960): 966–972.

**4111.** DeWitt, John H., Jr. "Andrew Jackson and His Ward, Andrew Jackson Hutchings: A History Hitherto Unpublished." *Tennessee Historical Magazine* 1 (January 1931): 83–106.

**4112.** Didier, Eugene L. "Andrew Jackson as a Lawyer." *Green Bag* 15 (August 1903): 349–356.

**4113.** Dodd, William E. "Andrew Jackson and His Enemies, and the Great Noise They Made in the World." *Century Magazine* 111 (April 1926): 734–745.

**4114.** ———. "The Making of Andrew Jackson: All Things Worked Together for Good to Old Hickory." *Century Magazine* 111 (March 1926): 531–538.

**4115.** Doherty, Herbert J., Jr. "Andrew Jackson on Manhood Suffrage." *Tennessee Historical Quarterly* 15 (March 1956): 57–60.

**4116.** ———. "The Governorship of Andrew Jackson." *Florida Historical Quarterly* 33 (July 1954): 3–31.

**4117.** Dorris, Mary C. *The Hermitage, Home of General Andrew Jackson.* Nashville, TN: Brandon Printing Company, 1913.

**4118.** Downing, Jack. *The Life of Andrew Jackson.* Philadelphia: T. K. Greenbank, 1834.

**4119.** Dunlap, John R. *Jeffersonian Democracy, Which Means the Democracy of Thomas Jefferson, Andrew Jackson, and Abraham Lincoln.* New York: Jeffersonian Society, 1903.

**4120.** Dyer, Oliver. *General Andrew Jackson.* New York: R. Bonner's Sons, 1891.

**4121.** Eaton, Clement, ed. *The Leaven of Democracy: The Growth of the Democratic Spirit in the Time of Jackson.* New York: Braziller, 1963.

**4122.** Eaton, John H. *The Life of Andrew Jackson, Major General in the Service of the United States.* Philadelphia: Samuel F. Bradford, 1824.

**4123.** ———. *Memoirs of Andrew Jackson, Late Major-General and Commander in Chief of the Southern Division of the Army of the United States.* Boston: Charles Ever, 1828.

**4124.** Elliott, Edward. "Andrew Jackson: Growth through Democratization." In his *Biographical Story of The Constitution: A Study of the Growth of the American Union,* 147–166. New York: G. P. Putnam's, 1910.

**4125.** Ely, James W., Jr. "Andrew Jackson as Tennessee State Court Judge, 1798–1804." *Tennessee Historical Quarterly* 40 (Summer 1981): 144–157.

**4126.** ———. "The Legal Practice of Andrew Jackson." *Tennessee Historical Quarterly* 38 (Winter 1979): 421–435.

**4127.** Farrell, Brian. "Bellona and the General: Andrew Jackson and the Affair of Mrs. Eaton." *History Today* 7 (July 1958): 474–484.

**4128.** Faust, Richard H. "Another Look at General Jackson and the Indians of the Mississippi Territory." *Alabama Review* 28 (July 1975): 202–217.

**4129.** Fellman, Michael. "The Earthbound Eagle: Andrew Jackson and the American Pantheon." *American Studies* 12 (Fall 1971): 67–76.

**4130.** Frost, John. *Old Hickory.* New York: C. T. Dillingham, 1887.

**4131.** Gerry, Margarita S. "The Real Andrew Jackson." *Century Magazine* 115 (November 1927): 54–64, 115 (December 1927): 218–230.

**4132.** Goff, Reda C. "A Physical Profile of Andrew Jackson." *Tennessee Historical Quarterly* 28 (Fall 1969): 297–309.

**4133.** Goodwin, Philo A. *Biography of Andrew Jackson, President of the United States, Formerly Major General in the Army of the*

*United States.* Hartford, CT: Clapp and Benton, 1832.

**4134.** Graf, LeRoy P., and Ralph W. Haskins, eds. *Papers of Andrew Jackson.* 3 vols. Knoxville: University of Tennessee Press, 1967–1972.

**4135.** Grayson, Theodore J. "Andrew Jackson and Nicholas Biddle: The Fight over the Bank." In his *Leaders and Periods of American Finance,* 169–210. New York: John Wiley and Sons, 1932.

**4136.** Green, John W. "Judges Overton, Jackson, and White." *Tennessee Law Review* 18 (December 1944): 413–427.

**4137.** Hay, Robert P. "The Case for Andrew Jackson in 1824: Eaton's 'Wyoming Letters.'" *Tennessee Historical Quarterly* 29 (Summer 1970): 139–157.

**4138.** ———. "John Fitzgerald: Presidential Image-Maker for Andrew Jackson in 1823." *Tennessee Historical Quarterly* 42 (Summer 1983): 138–150.

**4139.** Headley, Joel T. *The Lives of Winfield Scott and Andrew Jackson.* New York: Scribner's, 1852.

**4140.** Heiskell, Samuel G. *Andrew Jackson and Early Tennessee History.* 2d ed. 3 vols. Nashville, TN: Ambrose Printing Company, 1920–1921.

**4141.** Hellegers, John F. "Some Bases of Early Pro-Jackson Sentiment in Western Pennsylvania." *Western Pennsylvania Historical Magazine* 45 (March 1962): 31–46.

**4142.** Herd, Elmer D., Jr. *Andrew Jackson, South Carolinian: A Study of the Enigma of His Birth.* Lancaster, SC: Lancaster County Historical Commission, 1963.

**4143.** Hickey, Donald R. "Andrew Jackson and the Army Haircut: Individual Rights vs. Military Discipline." *Tennessee Historical Quarterly* 35 (Winter 1976): 365–375.

**4144.** Hill, Isaac. *Brief Sketch of the Life, Character, and Services of Major General Andrew Jackson.* Concord, MA: Manahan, Hoag, 1828.

**4145.** Hoffman, William S. *Andrew Jackson and North Carolina Politics.* Chapel Hill: University of North Carolina Press, 1958.

**4146.** Hofstadter, Richard. "Andrew Jackson and the Rise of Liberal Capitalism." In his *The American Political Tradition and the Men Who Made It,* 44–66. New York: Knopf, 1948.

**4147.** Hoogenboom, Ari M., and Olive Hoogenboom. "Francis Preston Blair and the Image of Andrew Jackson." *Reviews in American History* 9 (March 1981): 76–81.

**4148.** Horn, Stanley F., ed. "Some Jackson-Overton Correspondence." *Tennessee Historical Quarterly* 6 (June 1947): 161–175.

**4149.** Jackson, Carlton L. "The Internal Improvement Vetoes of Andrew Jackson." *Tennessee Historical Quarterly* 25 (Fall 1966): 261–280.

**4150.** James, Marquis. *Andrew Jackson: Portrait of a President.* Indianapolis, IN: Bobbs-Merrill, 1937.

**4151.** ———. *Andrew Jackson: The Border Captain.* Indianapolis: Bobbs-Merrill, 1933.

**4152.** ———. *The Life of Andrew Jackson.* Indianapolis, IN: Bobbs-Merrill, 1938.

**4153.** Jenkins, John S. *Jackson and the Generals of the War of 1812.* Philadelphia: J. B. Smith, 1856.

**4154.** ———. *Life and Public Services of Gen. Andrew Jackson.* Buffalo, NY: G. H. Derby, 1852.

**4155.** ———. *The Life of Gen. Andrew Jackson.* Buffalo, NY: Derby and Hewson, 1847.

**4156.** Johnson, Gerald W. *Andrew Jackson: An Epic in Homespun.* New York: Minton, Balch, 1927.

**4157.** Judson, Clara I. *Andrew Jackson, Frontier Statesman.* Chicago: Follett, 1954.

**4158.** Karsner, David. *Andrew Jackson, the Gentle Savage.* New York: Brentano's, 1929.

**4159.** Klingberg, Frank J. "The Americanism of Andrew Jackson." *South Atlantic Quarterly* 21 (April 1922): 127–143.

**4160.** Lebowitz, Michael A. "The Jacksonians: Paradox Lost?" In *Towards a New Past: Dissenting Essays in American History,* edited by Barton J. Bernstein, 565–589. New York: Pantheon Books, 1968.

**4161.** Lewis, Alfred H. *When Men Grew Tall: Or, the Story of Andrew Jackson.* New York: Appleton, 1907.

**4162.** Lindsey, David. *Andrew Jackson and John C. Calhoun.* Woodbury, NY: Barron's Educational Series, 1973.

**4163.** Mayo, Edward L. "Republicanism, Antipartyism, and Jacksonian Party Politics: A View from the Nation's Capital." *American Quarterly* 31 (Spring 1979): 3–20.

**4164.** McFaul, John M. *The Politics of Jacksonian Finance.* Ithaca, NY: Cornell University Press, 1972.

**4165.** McMahon, Edward J. "Was Jackson a Political Opportunist?" *Social Studies* 46 (February 1955): 49–54.

**4166.** Mellen, George F. "Sidelights on Andrew Jackson." *Methodist Quarterly Review* 67 (July 1918): 494–505.

**4167.** Meyers, Marvin. *The Jacksonian Persuasion: Politics and Belief.* Stanford, CA: Stanford University Press, 1957.

**4168.** Miles, Edwin A. "Andrew Jackson and Senator George Poindexter." *Journal of Southern History* 24 (February 1958): 51–66.

**4169.** ———. *Jacksonian Democracy in Mississippi.* New York: Da Capo Press, 1970.

**4170.** Miller, Douglas T. *Jacksonian Aristocracy: Class and Democracy in New York, 1830–1860.* New York: Oxford University Press, 1967.

**4171.** Moody, Robert E. "The Influence of Martin Van Buren on the Career and Acts of Andrew Jackson." *Michigan Academy of Science, Arts and Letters Papers* 7 (1926): 225–240.

**4172.** Morgan, William G. "John Quincy Adams versus Andrew Jackson: Their Biographers and the 'Corrupt Bargain' Charge." *Tennessee Historical Quarterly* 26 (Spring 1967): 43–58.

**4173.** Myers, Elisabeth P. *Andrew Jackson.* Chicago: Reilly and Lee, 1970.

**4174.** Neufeld, Maurice F. "The Size of the Jacksonian Labor Movement: A Cautionary Account." *Labor History* 23 (Fall 1982): 599–607.

**4175.** Nolan, Jeannette C. *Andrew Jackson.* New York: Messner, 1961.

**4176.** Parton, James. *General Jackson.* New York: Appleton, 1893.

**4177.** ———. *Life of Andrew Jackson.* 3 vols. New York: Mason Brothers, 1860.

**4178.** ———. *The Presidency of Andrew Jackson.* Edited by Robert V. Remini. New York: Harper and Row, 1967.

**4179.** Pessen, Edward. "Did Labor Support Jackson? The Boston Story." *Political Science Quarterly* 64 (June 1949): 262–274.

**4180.** ———. *Jacksonian America: Society, Personality, and Politics.* Rev. ed. Homewood, IL: Dorsey Press, 1978.

**4181.** ———. "Should Labor Have Supported Jackson? Or Questions the Quantitative Studies Do Not Answer." *Labor History* 13 (Summer 1972): 427–437.

**4182.** ———. *The Many-Faceted Jacksonian Era: New Interpretations.* Westport, CT: Greenwood, 1977.

**4183.** Phillips, Kim T. "The Pennsylvania Origins of the Jackson Movement." *Political Science Quarterly* 91 (Fall 1976): 489–508.

**4184.** Prucha, Francis P. "Andrew Jackson's Indian Policy: A Reassessment." *Jour-*

*nal of American History* 56 (December 1969): 529–539.

**4185.** ———. "General Jackson, Expansionist." *Reviews in American History* 6 (September 1978): 331–336.

**4186.** Purdy, Virginia C. "Your Zealous Friend, Andrew Jackson." *Prologue* 1 (Winter 1969): 36–37.

**4187.** Quinn, Yancey M., Jr. "Jackson's Military Road." *Journal of Mississippi History* 41 (November 1979): 335–350.

**4188.** Quitt, Martin H. "Jackson, Indians, and Psycho-History: Review Essay." *History of Childhood Quarterly* 3 (Spring 1976): 543–551.

**4189.** Read, Allen W. "Could Andrew Jackson Spell?" *American Speech* 38 (October 1963): 188–195.

**4190.** Reid, John, and John H. Eaton. *The Life of Andrew Jackson*. Edited by Frank L. Owsley. University: University of Alabama Press, 1974.

**4191.** Remini, Robert V. *The Age of Jackson*. Columbia: University of South Carolina Press, 1972.

**4192.** ———. *Andrew Jackson*. New York: Twayne, 1966.

**4193.** ———. *Andrew Jackson and the Course of American Democracy, 1833–1845*. New York: Harper and Row, 1984.

**4194.** ———. *Andrew Jackson and the Course of American Empire, 1767–1821*. New York: Harper and Row, 1977.

**4195.** ———. *Andrew Jackson and the Course of American Freedom: 1822–1832*. New York: Harper and Row, 1981.

**4196 .** ———. "The Final Days and Hours in the Life of General Andrew Jackson." *Tennessee Historical Quarterly* 39 (Summer 1980): 167–177.

**4197.** ———. *The Legacy of Andrew Jackson: Essays on Democracy, Indian Removal, and Slavery*. Baton Rouge: Louisiana State University Press, 1988.

**4198.** Robbins, Peggy. "Andrew and Rachel Jackson." *American History Illustrated* 12 (August 1977): 22–28.

**4199.** Rogin, Michael P. *Fathers and Children: Andrew Jackson and the Subjugation of the American Indian*. New York: Knopf, 1975.

**4200.** Schlesinger, Arthur M., Jr. *The Age of Jackson*. Boston: Little, Brown, 1945.

**4201.** Sellers, Charles G. "Andrew Jackson versus the Historians." *Mississippi Valley Historical Review* 44 (March 1958): 615–634.

**4202.** ———. "Jackson Men with Feet of Clay." *American Historical Review* 62 (April 1957): 537–551.

**4203.** ———. *Jacksonian Democracy*. Washington, DC: American Historical Association, 1958.

**4204.** ———, ed. *Andrew Jackson: A Profile*. New York: Hill and Wang, 1971.

**4205.** Shalhope, Robert E. "Republicanism and Early American Historiography." *William and Mary Quarterly* 39 (April 1982): 334–356.

**4206.** Singletary, Michael W. "The New Editorial Voice for Andrew Jackson: Happenstance or Plan?" *Journalism Quarterly* 53 (Winter 1976): 672–678.

**4207.** Smith, Culver H. "Propaganda Technique in the Jackson Campaign of 1828." *East Tennessee Historical Society's Publications* 6 (1934): 44–66.

**4208.** Smith, Graeme M. "Fearless Fighters and Learning People: Andrew Jackson and Rachel Donelson Jackson as Revealed by Their Ancestors." *National Historical Magazine* 73 (September 1939): 60–61.

**4209.** Smyth, Clifford. *Andrew Jackson, the Man Who Preserved Union and Democracy*. New York: Funk and Wagnalls, 1931.

**4210.** Somit, Albert. "Andrew Jackson: Legend and Reality." *Tennessee Historical Quarterly* 7 (December 1948): 291–313.

**4211.** ———. "Andrew Jackson as Political Theorist." *Tennessee Historical Quarterly* 8 (June 1949): 99–126.

**4212.** ———. "The Political and Administrative Ideas of Andrew Jackson." Ph.D. dissertation, University of Chicago, 1947.

**4213.** Sprague, Lynn T. "'Old Hickory' and His Indian Campaigns." *Outing: An Illustrative Monthly Magazine of Recreations* 49 (November 1906): 223–231.

**4214.** Stark, Bruce P. "The Historical Irrelevance of Heroes: Henry Adams's Andrew Jackson." *American Literature* 46 (May 1974): 170–181.

**4215.** Steiner, Bernard C. "Jackson and the Missionaries." *American Historical Review* 29 (July 1924): 722–723.

**4216.** Stenberg, Richard R. "Jackson, Anthony Butler, and Texas." *Southwestern Social Science Quarterly* 13 (December 1932): 264–287.

**4217.** ———. "Jackson, Buchanan, and the 'Corrupt Bargain' Calumny." *Pennsylvania Magazine of History and Biography* 58 (1934): 61–85.

**4218.** ———. "Jackson's 'Rhea Letter' Hoax." *Journal of Southern History* 2 (November 1936): 480–496.

**4219.** ———. "The Texas Schemes of Jackson and Houston." *Southwestern Social Science Quarterly* 15 (December 1934): 229–250.

**4220.** Sullivan, John L. "Jackson Caricatured: Two Historical Errors." *Tennessee Historical Quarterly* 31 (Spring 1972): 39–44.

**4221.** ———. "Politics and Personality: The Development of the Counter-Image of Andrew Jackson." Ph.D. dissertation, Indiana University, 1970.

**4222.** Sullivan, William A. "Did Labor Support Andrew Jackson?" *Political Science Quarterly* 62 (December 1947): 579–580.

**4223.** Sumner, William G. *Andrew Jackson.* Rev. ed. Boston: Houghton Mifflin, 1900.

**4224.** ———. *Andrew Jackson as a Public Man: What He Was, What Chances He Had, and What He Did with Them.* Boston: Houghton Mifflin, 1882.

**4225.** Syrett, Harold C. *Andrew Jackson: His Contributions to the American Tradition.* Indianapolis: Bobbs-Merrill, 1953.

**4226.** Temin, Peter. *Jacksonian Economy.* New York: Norton, 1969.

**4227.** Thompson, Arthur W. *Jacksonian Democracy on the Florida Frontier.* Gainesville: University Press of Florida, 1961.

**4228.** Tilly, Bette B. "The Jackson-Dinsmoor Feud: A Paradox in a Minor Key." *Journal of Mississippi History* 39 (May 1977): 117–131.

**4229.** Tregle, Joseph G. "Andrew Jackson and the Continuing Battle of New Orleans." *Journal of the Early Republic* 1 (Winter 1981): 373–393.

**4230.** Van Deusen, Glyndon G. *The Rise and Decline of Jacksonian Democracy.* Melbourne, FL: Krieger, 1979.

**4231.** Waldo, Samuel P. *Memoirs of Andrew Jackson.* Hartford, CT: Silas Andrus, 1819.

**4232.** Walker, Arda S. "Andrew Jackson: Frontier Democrat." *East Tennessee Historical Society's Publications* 18 (1946): 59–86.

**4233.** ———. "Andrew Jackson: Planter." *East Tennessee Historical Society's Publications* 15 (1943): 19–34.

**4234.** ———. "The Educational Training and Views of Andrew Jackson." *East Tennessee Historical Society's Publications* 16 (1944): 22–29.

**4235.** ———. "The Religious Views of Andrew Jackson." *East Tennessee Historical Society's Publications* 17 (1945): 61–70.

**4236.** Ward, John W. *Andrew Jackson, Symbol for an Age.* New York: Oxford University Press, 1955.

**4237.** Wason, James R. "Labor and Politics in Washington in the Early Jacksonian Era." Ph.D. dissertation, American University, 1964.

**4238.** Watson, Harry L. *Liberty and Power: The Politics of Jacksonian America.* New York: Hill and Wang, 1990.

**4239.** Watson, Thomas E. *The Life and Times of Andrew Jackson.* Thomson, GA: Press of the Jeffersonian Publishing Company, 1912.

**4240.** Wert, Jeffry D. "Old Hickory and the Seminoles." *American History Illustrated* 15 (October 1980): 28–35.

**4241.** Wilson, Major L. "Andrew Jackson: The Great Compromiser." *Tennessee Historical Quarterly* 26 (Spring 1967): 64–78.

**4242.** Worner, William F. "Andrew Jackson in Lancaster." *Lancaster County Historical Society Papers* 33 (1929): 83–84.

**4243.** Wright, Frances F. *Andrew Jackson Fighting Frontiersman.* New York: Abingdon Press, 1958.

## JACKSON, HENRY MARTIN (1912–1983) D-WA, House 1941–1953, Senate 1953–1983.

**4244.** Bullert, Gary B. "Jackson, Fulbright, and the Senatorial Critique of Detente." *Journal of Social, Political and Economic Studies* 13 (Spring 1988): 61–86.

**4245.** Gelb, Leslie H., and Anthony Lake. "Age of Jackson?" *Foreign Policy* 14 (Spring 1974): 178–188.

**4246.** Lubalin, Eve. "Presidential Ambition and Senatorial Behavior: The Impact of Ambition on the Behavior of Incumbent Politicians." Ph.D. dissertation, Johns Hopkins University, 1981.

**4247.** Ognibene, Peter J. *Scoop: The Life and Politics of Senator Henry M. Jackson.* New York: Stein and Day, 1975.

**4248.** Prochnau, William W., and Richard W. Larsen. *Certain Democrat: Senator Henry M. Jackson: A Political Biography.* Englewood Cliffs, NJ: Prentice-Hall, 1972.

**4249.** Roberts, Brian E. "A Dead Senator Tells No Lies: Seniority and the Distribution of Federal Benefits." *American Journal of Political Science* 34 (February 1990): 31–58.

**4250.** Robson, John S. "Henry Jackson, the Jackson-Vanik Amendment and Detente: Ideology, Ideas, and United States Foreign Policy in the Nixon Era." Ph.D. dissertation, University of Texas, 1989.

**4251.** Stern, Paula. *Water's Edge: Domestic Politics and the Making of American Foreign Policy.* Westport, CT: Greenwood, 1979.

## JACKSON, HOWELL EDMUNDS (1832–1895) D-TN, Senate 1881–1886.

**4252.** Calvani, Terry. "The Early Legal Career of Howell Jackson." *Vanderbilt Law Review* 30 (January 1977): 39–72.

**4253.** Doak, Henry M. "Howell Edmunds Jackson." *Green Bag* 5 (May 1893): 209–215.

**4254.** Green, John W. "Two United States Circuit Judges." *Tennessee Law Review* 18 (June 1944): 311–322.

**4255.** Hardaway, Roger D. "Howell Edmunds Jackson: Tennessee Legislator and Jurist." *West Tennessee Historical Society Papers* 30 (October 1976): 104–119.

## JACKSON, JAMES (1757–1806) R-GA, House 1789–1791, Senate 1793–1795, 1801–1806.

**4256.** Charlton, Thomas. *The Life of Major General James Jackson.* Augusta: G. F. Randolph, 1809.

**4257.** Foster, William O. *James Jackson, Duelist and Militant Statesman, 1757–1806.* Athens: University of Georgia Press, 1960.

**4258.** Lamplugh, George R. "'Oh the Colossus! The Colossus!': James Jackson and the Jeffersonian Republican Party in Georgia." *Journal of the Early Republic* 9 (Fall 1989): 315–334.

**JACKSON, JOHN GEORGE** (1777–1825) D-VA, House 1803–1810, 1813–1817.

**4259.** Brown, Stephen W. "Congressman John George Jackson and Republican Nationalism. 1813–1817." *West Virginia History* 38 (January 1977): 93–125.

**4260.** ———. "Satisfaction at Bladensburg: The Pearson-Jackson Duel of 1809." *North Carolina Historical Review* 58 (Winter 1981): 23–43.

**4261.** ———. *Voice of the New West: John G. Jackson, His Life and Times.* Macon, CA: Mercer, 1985.

**4262.** Davis, Dorothy. *John George Jackson.* Parsons, WV: McClain Printing Company, 1976.

**JACOBSEN, BERNHARD MARTIN** (1862–1936) D-IA, House 1931–1936.

**4263.** Porter, David L. "Iowa Congressional Delegation and the Great Economic Issues, 1929–1933." *Annals of Iowa* 46 (Summer 1982): 337–354.

**JAMES, OLLIE MURRAY** (1871–1918) D-KY, House 1903–1913, Senate 1913–1918.

**4264.** McCalister, Virginia M. "The Political Career of Ollie M. James." Master's thesis, Indiana University, 1933.

**JARMAN, JOHN** (1915–1982) R-OK, House 1951–1977.

**4265.** Grant, Philip A., Jr. "A Tradition of Political Power: Congressional Committee Chairmen from Oklahoma, 1945–1972." *Chronicles of Oklahoma* 60 (Winter 1982/1983): 438–447.

**JAVITS, JACOB KOPPEL** (1904–1986) R-NY, House 1947–1954, Senate 1957–1981.

**4266.** Capell, Frank A. *Strange Case of Jacob Javits.* Zarephath, NJ: Herald of Freedom, 1966.

**4267.** Javits, Jacob K. *Discrimination, USA.* Rev. ed. New York: Washington Square Press, 1962.

**4268.** ———. "How I Used a Poll in Campaigning for Congress." *Public Opinion Quarterly* 11 (Summer 1947): 222–232.

**4269.** Javits, Jacob K., and Rafael Steinberg. *Javits: The Autobiography of a Public Man.* Boston: Houghton Mifflin, 1981.

**4270.** ———. "Scenes from a Political Marriage." *Washington Monthly* 12 (December 1980): 20–29.

**4271.** Viorst, Milton. "Jacob K. Javits: Jewish Republican in a Presidential Fantasy." In his *Hustlers and Heroes: An American Political Panorama,* 13–37. New York: Simon and Schuster, 1971.

**JAY, JOHN** (1745–1829) NY, Continental Congress 1774–1777, 1778–1779.

**4272.** Barre, W. L. "John Jay." In his *Lives of Illustrious Men of America: Distinguished in the Annals of the Republic as Legislators, Warriors, and Philosophers,* 334–348. Cincinnati, OH: W. A. Clarke, 1859.

**4273.** Baxter, Katharine S. "John Jay: Statesman and First Chief Justice of the United States." In her *Godchild of Washington: A Picture of the Past,* 87–94. New York: F. T. Neely, 1897.

**4274.** Becker, Carl L. "John Jay and Peter Van Schaak." *New York State Historical Association Journal* 50 (October 1969): 1–12.

**4275.** Bemis, Samuel F. *Jay's Treaty.* New York: Macmillan, 1924.

**4276.** ———. "John Jay." In his *The American Secretaries of State and Their Diplomacy,* vol. 1, 191–285. New York: Knopf, 1927.

**4277.** Bhagat, G. "The Jay Treaty and Indian Trade." *Essex Institute Historical Collections* 208 (April 1972): 153–172.

**4278.** Clarfield, Gerald H. "Postscript to the Jay Treaty: Timothy Pickering and Anglo-American Relations, 1795–1797." *William and Mary Quarterly* 23 (January 1966): 106–120.

**4279.** Dietze, Gottfried. "Jay's Federalist: Treatise for Free Government." *Maryland Law Review* 17 (Summer 1957): 217–230.

**4280.** Dorfman, Joseph H., and Rexford G. Tugwell. "John Jay: Revolutionary Conservative." In their *Early American Policy: Six Columbia Contributions*, 43–98. New York: Columbia University Press, 1960.

**4281.** Durham, G. Homer. "John Jay and the Judicial Powers." *Brigham Young University Studies* 16 (Spring 1976): 349–361.

**4282.** Farnham, Thomas J. "The Virginia Amendments of 1795: An Episode in the Opposition to Jay's Treaty." *Virginia Magazine of History and Biography* 75 (January 1967): 75–88.

**4283.** Flanders, Henry. "The Life of John Jay." In his *The Lives and Times of the Chief Justices of the Supreme Court of the United States*, 11–429. Philadelphia: T. and J. W. Johnson, 1881.

**4284.** Gruver, Rebecca B. "The Diplomacy of John Jay." Ph.D. dissertation, University of California, Berkeley, 1964.

**4285.** Hackett, William H. "Sketch of the Life and Character of John Jay." *American Review* 2 (July 1845): 59–68.

**4286.** Hammett, Hugh B. "The Jay Treaty: Crisis Diplomacy in the New Nation." *Social Studies* 65 (January 1974): 10–17.

**4287.** Herring, James. "John Jay." In his *The National Portrait Gallery*, vol. 2, 47–62. Philadelphia: Henry Perkins, 1835.

**4288.** Hubbard, Elbert. "John Jay." In his *Little Journeys to the Homes of American Statesmen*, 327–361. New York: Putnam's, 1898.

**4289.** Jay, John. *The Correspondence and Public Papers of John Jay*. Edited by Henry P. Johnston. New York: Putnam's, 1890–1893.

**4290.** ———. *The Diary of John Jay during the Peace Negotiations of 1782*. New Haven, CT: Yale University Library, 1934.

**4291.** ———. *The Life of John Jay, with Selections from His Correspondence and Miscellaneous Papers*. New York: Harper, 1833.

**4292.** Jenkins, John S. "John Jay." In his *Lives of the Governors of the State of New York*, 74–131. Auburn, NY: Derby and Miller, 1851.

**4293.** Johnson, Herbert A. "Civil Procedure in John Jay's New York." *American Journal of Legal History* 11 (January 1967): 69–80.

**4294.** ———. "John Jay: Colonial Lawyer." Ph.D. dissertation, Columbia University, 1965.

**4295.** ———. "John Jay: Lawyer in a Time of Transition 1764–1775." *University of Pennsylvania Law Review* 124 (May 1976): 1260–1292.

**4296.** Lossing, Benson J. "John Jay." In his *Eminent Americans*, 171–172. New York: Hurst, 1886.

**4297.** Monaghan, Frank. "Anti-slavery Papers of John Jay." *Journal of Negro History* 17 (October 1932): 481–497.

**4298.** ———. *The Diary of John Jay during the Peace Negotiations of 1782*. New Haven, CT: Bibliographical Press, Yale University, 1934.

**4299.** ———. *John Jay: Defender of Liberty*. Indianapolis: Bobbs-Merrill, 1935.

**4300.** ———. *Unpublished Correspondence of William Livingston and John Jay*. Newark: New Jersey Historical Society, 1934.

**4301.** Morris, Richard B. "John Jay and the Adoption of the Federal Constitution in New York: A New Reading of Persons and Events." *New York History* 63 (April 1982): 133–164.

**4302.** ———. "John Jay and the New England Connection." *Massachusetts Historical Society Proceedings* 80 (February 1968): 16–37.

**4303.** ———. "John Jay: Aristocrat as Nationalist." In his *Witness at the Creation:*

Hamilton, Madison, Jay, and the Constitution, 48–75. New York: Holt, Rinehart and Winston, 1985.

**4304.** ———. *John Jay, the Nation, and the Court.* Boston: Boston University Press, 1967.

**4305.** ———. *John Jay: The Making of a Revolutionary: Unpublished Papers, 1745–1780.* New York: Harper and Row, 1975.

**4306.** Pellow, George. *John Jay.* Boston: Houghton Mifflin, 1892.

**4307.** Perry, Benjamin F. "John Jay." In his *Biographical Sketches of Eminent American Statesmen*, 393–402. Philadelphia: Ferree Press, 1887.

**4308.** Renwick, Henry B., and James Renwick. *Lives of John Jay and Alexander Hamilton.* New York: Harper and Brothers, 1840.

**4309.** Scott, James B. "John Jay." *Columbia Law Review* 6 (May 1906): 289–325.

**4310.** Smith, Donald L. *John Jay: Founder of a State and Nation.* New York: Teachers College Press, Columbia University, 1968.

**4311.** Tuckerman, Henry T. "Violations of Literary Property: *The Federalist:* Life and Character of John Jay." *Continental Monthly* 6 (September 1864): 336–355.

**4312.** Umbreit, Kenneth B. "John Jay." In his *Our Eleven Chief Justices*, 1–50. New York: Harper and Brothers, 1938.

**4313.** VanBurkleo, Sandra F. "Honour, Justice, and Interest: John Jay's Republican Politics and Statesmanship of the Federal Bench." *Journal of the Early Republic* 4 (Fall 1984): 239–274.

**4314.** Waite, Charles B. "John Jay." *Chicago Law Times* 1 (July 1887): 215–223.

**4315.** Wheeler, Charles B. "John Jay, 1926." *New York Historical Association Proceedings* 7 (July 1926): 180–194.

**4316.** Whitelock, William. *The Life and Times of John Jay, Secretary of Foreign Affairs under the Confederation and First Chief Justice of the United States, with a Sketch of Public* Events from the Opening of the Revolution to the Election of Jefferson. New York: Dodd, Mead, 1887.

**4317.** Wildman, Edwin. "John Jay: The Counsellor of American Liberty." In his *The Founders of America in the Days of the Revolution*, 238–257. Freeport, NY: Books for Libraries, 1968.

**4318.** Willson, Beckles. "Pinckney and Jay (1792–1796)." In his *America's Ambassadors to England (1785–1928)*, 41–54. London: Murray, 1928.

## JEFFERSON, THOMAS (1743–1826) VA, Continental Congress 1775–1776, 1783–1785.

**4319.** Alexander, Edward P. "Jefferson and Kosciuszko: Friends of Liberty and of Man." *Pennsylvania Magazine of History and Biography* 92 (January 1968): 87–103.

**4320.** Allison, John M. *Adams and Jefferson: The Story of a Friendship.* Norman: University of Oklahoma Press, 1966.

**4321.** Andrews, Stuart. "Jefferson and the French Revolution." *History Today* 18 (May 1968): 299–306, 368.

**4322.** Arrowood, Charles F. *Thomas Jefferson and Education in a Republic.* New York: McGraw-Hill, 1930.

**4323.** Banning, Lance. "Jeffersonian Ideology and the French Revolution: A Question of Liberticide at Home." *Studies in Burke and His Time* 17 (Winter 1976): 5–26.

**4324.** Barzman, Sol. "Thomas Jefferson." In his *Madmen and Geniuses: The Vice-Presidents of the United States*, 21–26. Chicago: Follett, 1974.

**4325.** Berkhofer, Robert F. "Jefferson, the Ordinance of 1784, and the Origins of the American Territorial System." *William and Mary Quarterly* 29 (April 1972): 231–262.

**4326.** Boorstin, Daniel J. *The Lost World of Thomas Jefferson.* Boston: Beacon Press, 1960.

**4327.** Bowers, Claude G. *Jefferson and Hamilton: The Struggle for Democracy in America.* Boston: Houghton Mifflin, 1925.

**4328.** Bowling, Kenneth R. "Dinner at Jefferson's: A Note on Jacob E. Cooke's 'The Compromise of 1790'." *William and Mary Quarterly* 28 (October 1971): 629–648.

**4329.** Brodie, Fawn M. "Jefferson Biographers and the Psychology of Canonization." *Journal of Interdisciplinary History* 2 (Summer 1971): 155–172.

**4330.** ———. *Thomas Jefferson: An Intimate History.* New York: Norton, 1974.

**4331.** Burstein, Meyer L. *Understanding Thomas Jefferson: Studies in Economics, Law, and Philosophy.* New York: St. Martin's Press, 1993.

**4332.** Chaudhuri, Joyotpaul. "Jefferson's Unheavenly City: A Bicentennial Look." *American Journal of Economics and Sociology* 34 (October 1975): 397–410.

**4333.** Chiang, C. Y. Jesse. "Understanding Thomas Jefferson." *International Review of History and Political Science* 14 (August 1977): 51–61.

**4334.** Commager, Henry S. *Jefferson, Nationalism and the Enlightenment.* New York: G. Braziller, 1975.

**4335.** Cooke, Jacob E. "The Collaboration of Tench Coxe and Thomas Jefferson." *Pennsylvania Magazine of History and Biography* 100 (October 1976): 468–490.

**4336.** Cunningham, Noble E. *In Pursuit of Reason: The Life of Thomas Jefferson.* Baton Rouge: Louisiana State University Press, 1987.

**4337.** Dearmont, Nelson S. "Federalist Attitudes toward Governmental Secrecy in the Age of Jefferson." *Historian* 37 (February 1975): 222–240.

**4338.** Dewey, Frank L. *Thomas Jefferson, Lawyer.* Charlottesville: University Press of Virginia, 1986.

**4339.** Elliott, Edward. "Thomas Jefferson: Growth through Acquiescence." In his *Biographical Story of The Constitution: A Study of the Growth of the American Union,* 77–100. New York: G. P. Putnam's, 1910.

**4340.** Fishwick, Marshall W. "Thomas Jefferson." In his *Gentlemen of Virginia,* 125–143. New York: Dodd, Mead, 1961.

**4341.** Hay, Robert P. "The Glorious Departure of the American Patriarchs: Contemporary Reactions to the Deaths of Jefferson and Adams." *Journal of Southern History* 35 (November 1969): 543–555.

**4342.** Hellenbrand, Harold. *The Unfinished Revolution: Education and Politics in the Thought of Thomas Jefferson.* Newark: University of Delaware Press, 1990.

**4343.** Honeywell, Roy J. *The Educational Work of Thomas Jefferson.* New York: Russell & Russell, 1964.

**4344.** Hoskins, Jania W. "A Lesson Which All Our Countrymen Should Study: Jefferson Views Poland." *Quarterly Journal of the Library of Congress* 33 (January 1976): 29–46.

**4345.** Jefferson, Thomas. *The Writings of Thomas Jefferson.* Edited by Andrew J. Lipscomb and Albert E. Bergh. Washington, DC: Thomas Jefferson Memorial Association of the United States, 1905.

**4346.** ———. *The Writings of Thomas Jefferson.* Edited by Paul L. Ford. New York: Putnam's, 1892–1900.

**4347.** Johnstone, Robert M. *Jefferson and the Presidency: Leadership in the Young Republic.* Ithaca, NY: Cornell University Press, 1978.

**4348.** Kaplan, Lawrence S. "Consensus of 1789: Jefferson and Hamilton on American Foreign Policy." *South Atlantic Quarterly* 71 (Winter 1972): 91–105.

**4349.** ———. "Jefferson's Foreign Policy and Napoleon's Ideologies." *William and Mary Quarterly* 19 (July 1962): 344–359.

**4350.** Koch, Adrienne. *Jefferson and Madison: The Great Collaboration.* New York: Knopf, 1950.

**4351.** Lehman, Karl. *Thomas Jefferson, American Humanist.* New York: MacMillan, 1947.

**4352.** Luttrell, Clifton B. "Thomas Jefferson on Money and Banking: Disciple of David Hume and Forerunner of Some Modern Monetary Views." *History of Political Economy* 7 (Summer 1975): 156–173.

**4353.** Lynd, Staughton. "Beard, Jefferson and the Tree of Liberty." *American Studies* 9 (Spring 1968): 8–22.

**4354.** Malone, Dumas. *Jefferson and His Time.* 5 vols. Boston: Little, Brown, 1948.

**4355.** ———. *Jefferson the President: Second Term, 1805–1809.* Boston: Little, Brown, 1974.

**4356.** ———. "Mr. Jefferson and the Traditions of Virginia." *Virginia Magazine of History and Biography* 75 (April 1967): 131–142.

**4357.** ———. *The Sage of Monticello.* Boston: Little, Brown, 1981.

**4358.** ———. *Thomas Jefferson as Political Leader.* Berkeley: University of California Press, 1963.

**4359.** Mannix, Richard. "Gallatin, Jefferson, and the Embargo of 1808." *Diplomatic History* 3 (Spring 1979): 151–172.

**4360.** Martin, Edwin T. *Thomas Jefferson: Scientist.* New York: H. Schuman, 1952.

**4361.** Matthew, Richard K. *The Radical Politics of Thomas Jefferson: A Revisionist View.* Lawrence: University Press of Kansas, 1984.

**4362.** Mayer, David N. *The Constitutional Thought of Thomas Jefferson.* Charlottesville: University Press of Virginia, 1994.

**4363.** Mayo, Bernard. *Myths and Men: Patrick Henry, George Washington, Thomas Jefferson.* Athens: University of Georgia Press, 1959.

**4364.** McLaughlin, Jack. *Jefferson and Monticello: The Biography of a Builder.* New York: H. Holt, 1988.

**4365.** McLoughlin, William G. "Thomas Jefferson and the Beginning of Cherokee Nationalism, 1806 to 1809." *William and Mary Quarterly* 32 (October 1975): 547–580.

**4366.** Midgley, Louis. "The Brodie Connection: Thomas Jefferson and Joseph Smith." *Brigham Young University Studies* 19 (Fall 1979): 59–67.

**4367.** Morgan, Edmund S. *The Meaning of Independence: John Adams, George Washington, Thomas Jefferson.* New York: Norton, 1978.

**4368.** Myers, J. Jay. "Thomas Jefferson: Constructive Revolutionist." In his *The Revolutionists,* 65–83. New York: Washington Square Press, 1971.

**4369.** Padover, Saul K. "The American as Democrat: Thomas Jefferson." In his *The Genius of America: Men Whose Ideas Shaped Our Civilization,* 55–68. New York: McGraw-Hill, 1960.

**4370.** Peterson, Merrill D. "Adams and Jefferson: A Revolutionary Dialogue." *Wilson Quarterly* 1 (Autumn 1976): 108–125.

**4371.** ———. "Thomas Jefferson and Commercial Policy, 1783–1793." *William and Mary Quarterly* 22 (October 1965): 584–610.

**4372.** ———. *Thomas Jefferson and the New Nation: A Biography.* New York: Oxford University Press, 1970.

**4373.** ———, ed. *Thomas Jefferson: A Profile.* New York: Hill and Wang, 1967.

**4374.** Prince, Carl E. "The Passing of the Aristocracy: Jefferson's Removal of the Federalists, 1801–1805." *Journal of American History* 57 (December 1970): 563–575.

**4375.** Randall, Willard S. *Thomas Jefferson: A Life.* New York: Holt, 1993.

**4376.** Randolph, Sarah N. *The Domestic Life of Thomas Jefferson.* Charlottesville: University Press of Virginia, 1978.

**4377.** Scanlon, James E. "A Sudden Conceit: Jefferson and the Louisiana Government Bill of 1804." *Louisiana History* 9 (Spring 1968): 139–162.

**4378.** Shalhope, Robert E. "Thomas Jefferson's Republicanism and Antebellum Southern Thought." *Journal of Southern History* 42 (November 1976): 529–556.

**4379.** Sheldon, Garrett W. *The Political Philosophy of Thomas Jefferson.* Baltimore: Johns Hopkins University Press, 1991.

**4380.** Shurr, George H. "Thomas Jefferson and the French Revolution." *American Society Legion of Honor Magazine* 50 (Winter 1979/1980): 161–182.

**4381.** Spivak, Burton. *Jefferson's England Crisis: Commerce, Embargo, and the Republican Revolution.* Charlottesville: University Press of Virginia, 1979.

**4382.** Stuart, Reginald C. "Thomas Jefferson and the Function of War: Policy or Principle?" *Canadian Journal of History* 11 (August 1976): 155–171.

**4383.** Szasz, Paul C. "Thomas Jefferson Conceives an International Organization." *American Journal of International Law* 75 (January 1981): 138–140.

**4384.** Trent, William P. "Thomas Jefferson." In his *Southern Statesmen of the Old Regime,* 49–88. New York: Thomas Y. Crowell, 1897.

**4385.** Tucker, Robert W., and David C. Hendrickson. *Empire of Liberty: The Statecraft of Thomas Jefferson.* New York: Oxford University Press, 1990.

**4386.** Umbreit, Kenneth B. "Thomas Jefferson." In his *Founding Fathers: Men Who Shaped Our Tradition,* 1–103. Port Washington, NY: Kennikat, 1968.

**4387.** Vossler, Otto. *Jefferson and the American Revolutionary Ideal.* Washington, DC: University Press of America, 1980.

**4388.** Weymouth, Lally, ed. *Thomas Jefferson: The Man, His World, His Influence.* London: Weidenfeld and Nicolson, 1973.

**4389.** Wildman, Edwin. "Thomas Jefferson: The Father of Democracy." In his *The Founders of America in the Days of the Revolution,* 258–281. Freeport, NY: Books for Libraries, 1968.

**4390.** Wills, Garry. *Inventing America: Jefferson's Declaration of Independence.* New York: Vintage Books, 1979.

**4391.** Winston, Alexander. "Mr. Jefferson in Paris." *American Society Legion of Honor Magazine* 35 (Winter 1964): 139–150.

**4392.** Wood, Gordon S. "Problem of Jefferson." *Virginia Quarterly Review* 47 (Winter 1971): 137–141.

**4393.** Woolery, William K. *The Relations of Thomas Jefferson to American Foreign Policy, 1783–1793.* Baltimore: Johns Hopkins University Press, 1927.

## JENCKES, THOMAS ALLEN (1818–1875) R-RI, House 1863–1871.

**4394.** Hoogenboom, Ari A. "Thomas A. Jenckes and Civil Service Reform." *Mississippi Valley Historical Review* 47 (March 1961): 636–658.

## JENNER, WILLIAM EZRA (1908–1985) R-IN, Senate 1944–1945, 1947–1959.

**4395.** Poder, Michael P. "The Senatorial Career of William E. Jenner." Ph.D. dissertation, University of Notre Dame, 1976.

**4396.** Ross, Rodney J. "Senator William E. Jenner: A Study in Cold War Isolationism." D.Ed. dissertation, Pennsylvania State University, 1973.

## JENNINGS, JONATHAN (1784–1834) IN, House 1822–1831.

**4397.** Jennings, Jonathan. *Unedited Letters of Jonathan Jennings.* Indianapolis: Indiana Historical Society, 1932.

**4398.** Long, Eleanor R. *Wilderness to Washington: An 1811 Journey on Horseback.* Bloomington: Reflections Press, 1981.

**JOHNSON, ANDREW (1808–1875) R-TN, House 1843–1853, Senate 1857–1862, 1875.**

**4399.** Abernethy, Thomas P. *From Frontier to Plantation in Tennessee.* Chapel Hill: University of North Carolina Press, 1932.

**4400.** Alexander, Thomas B. "Strange Bedfellows: The Interlocking Careers of T. A. R. Nelson, Andrew Johnson and W. G. (Parson) Brownlow." *East Tennessee Historical Society's Publications* 51 (1979): 54–77.

**4401.** Barzman, Sol. "Andrew Johnson." In his *Madmen and Geniuses: The Vice-Presidents of the United States,* 109–114. Chicago: Follett, 1974.

**4402.** Beauregard, Erving E. "The Chief Prosecutor of President Andrew Johnson." *Midwest Quarterly* 31 (Summer 1990): 408–422.

**4403.** Bentley, H. Blair. "Andrew Johnson and the Tennessee State Penitentiary, 1853–1857." *East Tennessee Historical Society's Publications* 47 (1975): 28–45.

**4404.** Berwanger, Eugene R. "Three against Johnson: Colorado Republican Editors React to Reconstruction." *Social Science Journal* 12 (October 1975/January 1976): 149–158.

**4405.** Bowen, David W. "Andrew Johnson and the Negro." Ph.D. dissertation, University of Tennessee, 1977.

**4406.** Bowers, Claude G. *The Tragic Era: Revolution after Lincoln.* Boston: Houghton Mifflin, 1929.

**4407.** Brownlow, Paul C. "The Northern Protestant Pulpit and Andrew Johnson." *Southern Speech Communication Journal* 39 (Spring 1974): 248–259.

**4408.** Caskey, Willie M. "First Administration of Governor Andrew Johnson." *East Tennessee Historical Society's Publications* 1 (1929): 43–59.

**4409.** ———. "The Second Administration of Governor Andrew Johnson." *East Tennessee Historical Society's Publications* 2 (1930): 34–54.

**4410.** Castel, Albert E. "Andrew Johnson: His Historiographical Rise and Fall." *Mid-America* 45 (July 1963): 175–184.

**4411.** ———. "Andrew Johnson—A Profile." *American History Illustrated* 4 (October 1969): 4–11, 47.

**4412.** ———. *The Presidency of Andrew Johnson.* Lawrence: Regents Press of Kansas, 1979.

**4413.** Chadsey, Charles E. "The Struggle between President Johnson and Congress over Reconstruction." Ph.D. dissertation, Columbia University, 1896.

**4414.** Cimprich, John. "Military Governor Johnson and Tennessee Blacks, 1862–1865." *Tennessee Historical Quarterly* 39 (Winter 1980): 459–470.

**4415.** Connally, Ernest A. "The Andrew Johnson Homestead at Greenville, Tennessee." *East Tennessee Historical Society's Publications* 29 (1957): 118–140.

**4416.** Cox, John H., and LaWanda C. Cox. "Andrew Johnson and His Ghost Writers." *Mississippi Valley Historical Review* 48 (December 1961): 460–479.

**4417.** Crane, William D. *Andrew Johnson, Tailor from Tennessee.* New York: Dodd, Mead, 1968.

**4418.** Dewitt, David M. *Impeachment and Trial of Andrew Johnson.* New York: Macmillan, 1903.

**4419.** DeWitt, John H., Jr. "Andrew Johnson and the Hermit." *Tennessee Historical Quarterly* 27 (Spring 1968): 50–61.

**4420.** Dobson, Wayne W. "Some Phases of the Congressional Career of Andrew Johnson." Master's thesis, East Tennessee State University, 1952.

**4421.** Dunning, William A. "A Little More Light on Andrew Johnson." *Massachusetts*

*Historical Society Proceedings* 19 (November 1906): 395–405.

**4422.** ———. "More Light on Andrew Johnson." *American Historical Review* 11 (April 1906): 574–594.

**4423.** Foster, Lillian. *Andrew Johnson, President of the United States: His Life and Speeches.* New York: Richardson, 1866.

**4424.** Freshly, Dwight L. "Vacillation and Venom: Andrew Johnson vs. William L. Yancey." *Southern Speech Communication Journal* 28 (Winter 1962): 98–108.

**4425.** Gloneck, James F. "Lincoln, Johnson, and the Baltimore Ticket." *Lincoln Quarterly* 6 (March 1951): 255–271.

**4426.** Graf, LeRoy P. "Andrew Johnson and the Coming of the War." *Tennessee Historical Quarterly* 19 (September 1960): 208–221.

**4427.** Graf, LeRoy P., and Ralph W. Haskins, eds. *The Papers of Andrew Johnson.* Knoxville: University of Tennessee Press, 1967.

**4428.** Green, Michael S. "Diehard or Swing Man: Senator James W. Nye and Andrew Johnson's Impeachment and Trial." *Nevada Historical Society Quarterly* 29 (Fall 1986): 174–191.

**4429.** Hager, Paul A. "Andrew Johnson of East Tennessee." Ph.D. dissertation, Johns Hopkins University, 1975.

**4430.** Hall, Clifton R. "Andrew Johnson, Military Governor of Tennessee." Ph.D. dissertation, Princeton University, 1914.

**4431.** Hardison, Edwin T. "In the Toils of War: Andrew Johnson and the Federal Occupation of Tennessee, 1862–1865." Ph.D. dissertation, University of Tennessee, 1981.

**4432.** Harris, William C. "Andrew Johnson's First 'Swing around the Circle': His Northern Campaign of 1863." *Civil War History* 35 (June 1989): 153–171.

**4433.** Harrison, James T. "A Mississippian's Appraisal of Andrew Johnson: Letters of James T. Harrison, December 1865." *Journal of Mississippi History* 17 (January 1955): 43–48.

**4434.** Haskins, Ralph W. "Andrew Johnson and the Preservation of the Union." *East Tennessee Historical Society's Publications* 33 (December 1961): 43–60.

**4435.** ———. "Internecine Strife in Tennessee: Andrew Johnson versus Parson Brownlow." *Tennessee Historical Quarterly* 24 (Winter 1965): 321–340.

**4436.** Hays, Willard. "Andrew Johnson's Reputation." *East Tennessee Historical Society's Publications* 31 (1959): 1–21, 32 (1960): 18–50.

**4437.** Jones, James S. *Life of Andrew Johnson, Seventeenth President of the United States.* Greenville, TN: East Tennessee Publishing Company, 1902.

**4438.** Kilar, Jeremy W. "The Blood-Rugged Issue Is Impeachment or Anarchy: Michigan and the Impeachment and Trial of Andrew Johnson." *Old Northwest* 6 (Fall 1980): 245–269.

**4439.** Lawing, Hugh A. "Andrew Johnson National Monument." *Tennessee Historical Quarterly* 20 (June 1961): 103–119.

**4440.** Lomask, Milton. *Andrew Johnson: President on Trial.* New York: Farrar, Straus, 1960.

**4441.** Majeske, Penelope K. "Johnson, Stanton, and Grant: A Reconsideration of the Events Leading to the First Reconstruction Act." *Southern Studies* 22 (Winter 1983): 340–350.

**4442.** Marshall, Lynn L. "The Genesis of Grass-Roots Democracy in Kentucky." *Mid-America* 47 (October 1965): 269–287.

**4443.** McKitrick, Eric L. *Andrew Johnson and Reconstruction.* Chicago: University of Chicago Press, 1960.

**4444.** ———, comp. *Andrew Johnson: A Profile.* New York: Hill and Wang, 1969.

**4445.** Milton, George F. *The Age of Hate: Andrew Johnson and the Radicals.* New York: Coward-McCann, 1930.

**4446.** ———. "Andrew Johnson—Man of Courage." *East Tennessee Historical Society's Publications* 3 (January 1931): 23–34.

**4447.** Miscamble, Wilson D. "Andrew Johnson and the Election of William G. ("Parson") Brownlow as Governor of Tennessee." *Tennessee Historical Quarterly* 37 (Fall 1978): 308–320.

**4448.** Nettels, Curtis P. "Andrew Johnson and the South." *South Atlantic Quarterly* 25 (January 1926): 55–64.

**4449.** Notaro, Carmen A. "History of the Biographic Treatment of Andrew Johnson in the Twentieth Century." *Tennessee Historical Quarterly* 24 (Summer 1965): 143–155.

**4450.** Oder, Brock N. "Andrew Johnson and the 1866 Illinois Election." *Journal of the Illinois State Historical Society* 73 (Autumn 1980): 189–200.

**4451.** Parks, Joseph H. "Memphis under Military Rule." *East Tennessee Historical Society's Publications* 14 (1942): 31–58.

**4452.** Rable, George C. "Anatomy of a Unionist: Andrew Johnson in the Secession Crisis." *Tennessee Historical Quarterly* 32 (Winter 1973): 332–354.

**4453.** ———. "Forces of Darkness, Forces of Light: The Impeachment of Andrew Johnson and the Paranoid Style." *Southern Studies* 17 (Summer 1978): 151–173.

**4454.** Rayner, Kenneth. *Life and Times of Andrew Johnson, Seventeenth President of the United States.* New York: Appleton, 1866.

**4455.** Reece, Brazilla C. *The Courageous Commoner: A Biography of Andrew Johnson.* Charleston, WV: Education Foundation, 1962.

**4456.** Rehnquist, William H. *Grand Inquests: The Historic Impeachments of Justice Samuel Chase and President Andrew Johnson.* New York: Morrow, 1992.

**4457.** Riches, William T. "The Commoners: Andrew Johnson and Abraham Lincoln to 1861." Ph.D. dissertation, University of Tennessee, 1976.

**4458.** Robinson, Daniel M. "Andrew Johnson on the Dignity of Labor." *Tennessee Historical Quarterly* 23 (March 1964): 80–85.

**4459.** Ross, Edmund G. *History of the Impeachment of Andrew Johnson.* Santa Fe, NM: New Mexican Printing Company, 1896.

**4460.** Russell, Robert G. "Andrew Johnson and the Charleston Convention of 1860." *Eastern Tennessee Historical Society Publications* 47 (1975): 46–75.

**4461.** ———. "Prelude to the Presidency: The Election of Andrew Johnson to the Senate." *Tennessee Historical Quarterly* 26 (Summer 1967): 148–176.

**4462.** Sefton, James E. *Andrew Johnson and the Uses of Constitutional Power.* Boston: Little, Brown, 1980.

**4463.** Severn, William. *In Lincoln's Footsteps: The Life of Andrew Johnson.* New York: I. Washburn, 1966.

**4464.** Shofner, Jerrell H. "Andrew Johnson and the Fernandina Unionists." *Prologue* 10 (Winter 1978): 211–223.

**4465.** Smith, Gene. *High Crimes and Misdemeanors: The Impeachment and Trial of Andrew Johnson.* New York: Morrow, 1977.

**4466.** Stampp, Kenneth M. *Andrew Johnson and the Failure of the Agrarian Dream.* Oxford: Clarendon Press, 1962.

**4467.** Steele, Robert V. *The First President Johnson: The Three Lives of the Seventeenth President of the United States of America.* New York: Morrow, 1968.

**4468.** Stryker, Lloyd P. *Andrew Johnson: A Study in Courage.* New York: Macmillan, 1929.

**4469.** Temple, Oliver P. "Andrew Johnson." In *Notable Men of Tennessee from 1833–1875,* 357–467. New York: Cosmopolitan Press, 1912.

**4470.** Trefousse, Hans L. *Andrew Johnson: A Biography.* New York: Norton, 1989.

**4471.** Wagstaff, Thomas. "Andrew Johnson and the National Union Movement, 1865–1866." Ph.D. dissertation, University of Wisconsin, 1967.

**4472.** Wells, Ruth M. "Andrew Johnson: Senator from Tennessee, 1857–1862." Master's thesis, University of Pennsylvania, 1933.

**4473.** Williams, Harry. "Andrew Johnson as a Member of the Committee on the Conduct of the War." *East Tennessee Historical Society's Publications* 2 (1940): 70–83.

**4474.** Winston, Robert W. *Andrew Johnson, Plebeian and Patriot.* New York: Holt, 1928.

**4475.** Young, Donald. "Andrew Johnson." In his *American Roulette: The History and Dilemma of the Vice Presidency,* 66–88. New York: Holt, Rinehart and Winston, 1965.

**JOHNSON, BEN** (1858–1950) D-KY, House 1907–1927.

**4476.** Klotter, James C., and John W. Muir. "Boss Ben Johnson, the Highway Commission, and Kentucky Politics, 1927–1937." *Register of the Kentucky Historical Society* 84 (Winter 1986): 18–50.

**JOHNSON, CAVE** (1793–1866) D-TN, House 1829–1837, 1839–1845.

**4477.** Grant, Clement L. "Congressional Years of Cave Johnson of Tennessee, 1829–1845." Master's thesis, Vanderbilt University, 1948.

**4478.** ———. "The Public Career of Cave Johnson." Ph.D. dissertation, Vanderbilt University, 1951.

**4479.** Sioussat, St. George L., ed. "Letters of James K. Polk to Cave Johnson, 1833–1848." *Tennessee Historical Magazine* 1 (September 1915): 209–256.

**JOHNSON, HENRY** (1783–1864) W-LA, Senate 1818–1824, 1844–1849, House 1834–1839.

**4480.** Reeves, Miriam G. "Henry S. Johnson." In her *Governors of Louisiana,* 46–47. Gretna, LA: Pelican, 1972.

**JOHNSON, HERSCHEL VESPASIAN** (1812–1880) D-GA, Senate 1848–1849.

**4481.** Flippin, Percy S. *Herschel V. Johnson of Georgia, State Rights Unionist.* Richmond, VA: Dietz Printing, 1931.

**4482.** Greeman, Elizabeth D. "Stephen A. Douglas and Herschel V. Johnson: Examples of National Men in the Section Crisis of 1860." Ph.D. dissertation, Duke University, 1974.

**JOHNSON, HIRAM WARREN** (1866–1945) R-CA, Senate 1917–1945.

**4483.** Boyle, Peter G. "The Study of an Isolationist: Hiram Johnson." Ph.D. dissertation, University of California, 1970.

**4484.** Burke, Robert E. "A Friendship in Adversity: Burton K. Wheeler and Hiram W. Johnson." *Montana* 36 (Winter 1986): 12–25.

**4485.** ———. "Hiram Johnson's Impressions of William E. Borah." *Idaho Yesterdays* 17 (Spring 1973): 2–11.

**4486.** ———. "The Political Oratory of Hiram Johnson." *Journal of the West* 27 (April 1988): 20–27.

**4487.** ———, ed. *The Diary Letters of Hiram Johnson, 1917–1945.* New York: Garland, 1983.

**4488.** Davenport, Frederick M. "Did Hughes Snub Johnson?—An Inside Story." *American Political Science Review* 43 (April 1949): 321–332.

**4489.** DeWitt, Howard A. "Hiram Johnson and Early New Deal Diplomacy,

1933–1934." *California Historical Quarterly* 53 (Winter 1974): 377–386.

**4490.** ———. "Hiram Johnson and World War I: A Progressive in Transition." *Southern California Quarterly* 56 (Fall 1974): 295–305.

**4491.** ———. "Hiram W. Johnson and American Foreign Policy, 1917–1941." Ph.D. dissertation, University of Arizona, 1972.

**4492.** Dillon, Richard. "Hiram Johnson." In his *Humbugs and Heroes,* 177–181. Garden City, NY: Doubleday, 1968.

**4493.** Finney, Ruth. "Hiram Johnson of California." *American History Illustrated* 1 (November 1966): 20–28.

**4494.** Fitzpatrick, John J. "Senator Hiram W. Johnson: A Life History, 1866–1945." Ph.D. dissertation, University of California, 1975.

**4495.** Greenbaum, Fred. "Hiram Johnson and the New Deal." *Pacific Historian* 18 (Fall 1974): 20–35.

**4496.** Johnson, Hiram. *The Diary Letters of Hiram Johnson, 1917–1945.* 7 vols. New York: Garland, 1983.

**4497.** Lepore, Herbert P. "Prelude to Prejudice: Hiram Johnson, Woodrow Wilson, and the California Alien Land Law Controversy of 1913." *Southern California Quarterly* 61 (Spring 1979): 99–110.

**4498.** Liljekuist, Clifford B. "Senator Hiram Johnson." Ph.D. dissertation, University of Southern California, 1953.

**4499.** Lincoln, A. "My Dear Senator: Letters between Theodore Roosevelt and Hiram Johnson in 1917." *California Historical Society Quarterly* 42 (September 1963): 221–239.

**4500.** ———. "Theodore Roosevelt, Hiram Johnson, and the Vice-Presidential Nomination of 1912." *Pacific Historical Review* 28 (August 1959): 267–283.

**4501.** Lower, Richard C. *A Bloc of One: The Political Career of Hiram W. Johnson.* Stanford, CA: Stanford University Press, 1993.

**4502.** ———. "Hiram Johnson and the Progressive Denouement, 1910–1920." Ph.D. dissertation, University of California, 1969.

**4503.** ———. "Hiram Johnson: The Making of an Irreconcilable." *Pacific Historical Review* 41 (November 1972): 505–526.

**4504.** McKee, Irving. "Background and Early Career of Hiram Warren Johnson, 1866–1910." *Pacific Historical Review* 19 (February 1950): 17–30.

**4505.** Melendy, Howard B., and Benjamin F. Gilbert. "Hiram W. Johnson." In their *Governors of California: Peter H. Burnett to Edmund G. Brown,* 306–321. Georgetown, CA: Talisman Press, 1965.

**4506.** Olin, Spencer C. *California's Prodigal Sons: Hiram Johnson and Progressivism 1911–1917.* Berkeley: University of California Press, 1968.

**4507.** ———. "Hiram Johnson, the California Progressives and the Hughes Campaign of 1916." *Pacific Historical Review* 31 (November 1962): 403–412.

**4508.** ———. "Hiram Johnson, the Lincoln-Roosevelt League, and the Election of 1910." *California Historical Society Quarterly* 45 (September 1966): 225–240.

**4509.** ———. "Hiram W. Johnson: The California Years, 1911–1917." Ph.D. dissertation, Claremont Graduate School, 1965.

**4510.** Putnam, Jackson K. "Hiram Johnson and His 'Diary Letter': A Review Essay." *Southern California Quarterly* 68 (Winter 1986): 387–394.

**4511.** Weatherson, Michael A. "A Political Revivalist: The Public Speaking of Hiram W. Johnson, 1866–1945." Ph.D. dissertation, Indiana University, 1985.

**4512.** Weatherson, Michael A., and Hal W. Bochin. *Hiram W. Johnson: A Bio-bibliography.* New York: Greenwood, 1988.

## JOHNSON, JED JOSEPH, JR.
(1939–1993) D-OK, House 1965–1967.

**4513.** Grant, Philip A., Jr. "A Tradition of Political Power: Congressional Committee Chairmen from Oklahoma, 1945–1972." *Chronicles of Oklahoma* 60 (1982/1983): 438–447.

## JOHNSON, JOSEPH (1785–1877) D-VA,
House 1823–1827, 1833, 1835–1841, 1845–1847.

**4514.** Squires, William H. "Joseph Johnson, an Executive of High Decision." In his *The Land of Decision,* 271–287. Portsmouth, VA: Printcraft Press, 1931.

## JOHNSON, LYNDON BAINES
(1908–1973) D-TX, House 1937–1949, Senate 1949–1961.

**4515.** Adler, Bill, ed. *The Johnson Humor.* New York: Simon and Schuster, 1965.

**4516.** Altschuler, Bruce E. *LBJ and the Polls.* Gainesville: University of Florida Press, 1990.

**4517.** Amrine, Michael. *This Awesome Challenge: The Hundred Days of Lyndon Johnson.* New York: Putnam's, 1964.

**4518.** Baker, Leonard. *The Johnson Eclipse, a President's Vice Presidency.* New York: Macmillan, 1966.

**4519.** Bannette, Carole. *Partners to the President.* New York: Citadel Press, 1966.

**4520.** Barrett, David M. *Uncertain Warriors: Lyndon Johnson and His Vietnam Advisors.* Lawrence: University Press of Kansas, 1993.

**4521.** Barzman, Sol. "Lyndon Baines Johnson." In his *Madmen and Geniuses: The Vice-Presidents of the United States,* 109–114. Chicago: Follett, 1974.

**4522.** Bearss, Edwin C. *Lyndon B. Johnson National Historic Site.* Washington, DC: U.S. National Park Service, 1971.

**4523.** Bishop, James A. *A Day in the Life of President Johnson.* New York: Random House, 1967.

**4524.** Bornet, Vaughn D. *The Presidency of Lyndon B. Johnson.* Lawrence: University Press of Kansas, 1983.

**4525.** Bourgeois, Christine L. "Lyndon Johnson and Texas Politics, 1937–1945." Ph.D. dissertation, University of Texas at Austin, 1992.

**4526.** Burns, James M. *To Heal and to Build: The Programs of President Lyndon B. Johnson.* New York: McGraw-Hill, 1968.

**4527.** Burns, Mary H. "Theoretical Aspects and Applications of Leadership: The Senate Years of Lyndon B. Johnson." Master's thesis, University of Texas, 1971.

**4528.** Caidin, Martin, and Edward Hymoff. *Mission.* New York: Lippincott, 1964.

**4529.** Califano, Joseph A. *The Triumph and Tragedy of Lyndon Johnson: The White House Years.* New York: Simon and Schuster, 1992.

**4530.** Caro, Robert A. *The Years of Lyndon Johnson: Means of Ascent.* New York: Knopf, 1990.

**4531.** ———. *The Years of Lyndon Johnson: The Path to Power.* New York: Knopf, 1982.

**4532.** Carpenter, Liz. *Ruffles and Flourishes: The Warm and Tender Story of a Simple Girl Who Found Adventure in the White House.* Garden City, NY: Doubleday, 1970.

**4533.** Conklin, Paul K. *Big Daddy from the Pedernales: Lyndon B. Johnson.* Boston: Twayne, 1986.

**4534.** Cooper, Jacqueline. "Lyndon Johnson and Civil Rights: The Senate Years." Master's thesis, University of Texas, 1975.

**4535.** Cormier, Frank. *LBJ: The Way He Was.* Garden City, NY: Doubleday, 1977.

**4536.** Dallek, Robert. *Lone Star Rising: Lyndon Johnson and His Times, 1908–1960.* Oxford: Oxford University Press, 1991.

**4537.** Davie, Michael. *LBJ: A Foreign Observer's Viewpoint.* New York: Duell, Sloan and Pearce, 1966.

**4538.** Dugger, Ronnie. *The Politician: The Life and Times of Lyndon Johnson.* New York: Norton, 1982.

**4539.** Dyer, Stanford P. "Lyndon B. Johnson and the Politics of Civil Rights, 1935–1960: The Art of Moderate Leadership." Ph.D. dissertation, Texas A&M, 1978.

**4540.** Dyer, Stanford P., and Merrell A. Knighten. "Discrimination after Death: Lyndon Johnson and Felix Longoria." *Southern Studies* 17 (Winter 1978): 411–426.

**4541.** Elliott, Bruce. *The Johnson Story.* New York: Macfadden-Bartell, 1964.

**4542.** Evans, Rowland, and Robert D. Novak. *Lyndon B. Johnson: The Exercise of Power: A Political Biography.* New York: New American Library, 1966.

**4543.** Faber, Harold, ed. *The Road to the White House: The Story of the 1964 Election, by the Staff of the New York Times.* New York: McGraw-Hill, 1965.

**4544.** Fite, Gilbert C. "Richard B. Russell and Lyndon B. Johnson: The Story of a Strange Friendship." *Missouri Historical Review* 83 (January 1989): 125–138.

**4545.** Frantz, Joe B. *LBJ: Images of a Vibrant Life.* Austin, TX: Friends of the LBJ Library, 1973.

**4546.** ———. "Opening a Curtain: The Metamorphosis of Lyndon B. Johnson." *Journal of Southern History* 45 (February 1979): 3–26.

**4547.** ———. "Why Lyndon?" *Western Historical Quarterly* 11 (January 1980): 5–15.

**4548.** ———, comp. *37 Years of Public Service: The Honorable Lyndon B. Johnson.* Austin, TX: Shoal Creek Publishers, 1974.

**4549.** Fredericks, Janet P. "The Educational Views of Lyndon Baines Johnson Prior to His Presidency." Ph.D. dissertation, Loyola University, 1982.

**4550.** Gaskin, Thomas M. "Senator Lyndon B. Johnson and United States Foreign Policy." Ph.D. dissertation, University of Washington, 1989.

**4551.** Geyelin, Philip L. *Lyndon B. Johnson and the World.* New York: Praeger, 1966.

**4552.** Goldman, Eric F. *The Tragedy of Lyndon Johnson.* New York: Knopf, 1969.

**4553.** Gomolak, Louis S. "Prologue: LBJ's Foreign Affairs Background, 1908–1948." Ph.D. dissertation, University of Texas, 1989.

**4554.** Gorden, William L., and Robert Bunker. "The Sentimental Side of Mr. Johnson." *Southern Speech Communication Journal* 32 (Autumn 1966): 58–66.

**4555.** Gray, Charles H. "A Scale Analysis of the Voting Records of Senators Kennedy, Johnson, and Goldwater, 1957–1960." *American Political Science Review* 59 (September 1965): 615.

**4556.** Haley, James E. *A Texan Looks at Lyndon: A Study in Illegitimate Power.* Canyon, TX: Palo Duro Press, 1964.

**4557.** Hall, Robert N. "Lyndon B. Johnson's Speaking in the 1941 Senate Campaign." *Southern Speech Journal* 30 (Fall 1964): 15–23.

**4558.** ———. "Lyndon B. Johnson's Speech Preparation." *Quarterly Journal of Speech* 51 (April 1965): 168–176.

**4559.** ———. "A Rhetorical Analysis of Selected Speeches of Senator Lyndon B. Johnson, 1955–1961." Ph.D. dissertation, University of Michigan, 1963.

**4560.** Hammond, Paul Y. *LBJ and the Presidential Management of Foreign Relations.* Austin: University of Texas Press, 1992.

**4561.** Harwood, Richard, and Haynes B. Johnson. *Lyndon.* New York: Praeger, 1973.

**4562.** Heleniak, Roman. "Lyndon Johnson in New Orleans." *Louisiana History* 21 (Summer 1980): 263–275.

**4563.** Hendrix, Jerry A. "A Comparative Analysis of Selected Public Addresses by Allan Shivers and Lyndon B. Johnson in the Texas Pre-Convention Campaign of 1956." Master's thesis, University of Oklahoma, 1957.

**4564.** Herring, George C. *LBJ and Vietnam: A Different Kind of War.* Austin: University of Texas Press, 1994.

**4565.** Huitt, Ralph K. "Democratic Party Leadership in the Senate." *American Political Science Review* 55 (June 1961): 333–344.

**4566.** ———. "Lyndon B. Johnson and Senate Leadership." In *The Presidency and the Congress: A Shifting Balance of Power?*, edited by William S. Livingston, Lawrence C. Dodd, and Richard L. Schott, 253–264. Austin: Lyndon B. Johnson School of Public Affairs, University of Texas, 1979.

**4567.** Humphreys, Milton E. "LBJ—Senate Majority Leader." Master's thesis, East Texas State University, 1969.

**4568.** Janeway, Michael C. "Lyndon Johnson and the Rise of Conservatism in Texas." Honor's thesis, Harvard University, 1962.

**4569.** Janeway, Sharon K. "Making of a Senator from Texas—1948." Master's thesis, Southwest Texas State University, 1970.

**4570.** Johnson, Carolyn M. "A Southern Response to Civil Rights: Lyndon Baines Johnson and Civil Rights Legislation, 1956–1960." Master's thesis, University of Houston, 1975.

**4571.** Johnson, Lyndon B. *This America.* New York: Random House, 1966.

**4572.** ———. *The Vantage Point: Perspectives of the Presidency, 1963–1969.* New York: Holt, Rinehart and Winston, 1971.

**4573.** Johnson, Sam H. *My Brother Lyndon.* New York: Cowles, 1970.

**4574.** Kahl, Mary. *Ballot Box 13: How Lyndon Johnson Won His 1948 Senate Race by 87 Contested Votes.* Jefferson, NC: McFarland, 1983.

**4575.** Kearns, Doris. *Lyndon Johnson and the American Dream.* New York: Harper and Row, 1976.

**4576.** King, Larry L. "Bringing Up Lyndon." *Texas Monthly* 4 (January 1976): 78–85, 107–109.

**4577.** Kluckhohn, Frank L. *The Inside on LBJ.* Derby, CT: Monarch Books, 1964.

**4578.** Knippa, Edwin W. "The Early Political Life of Lyndon B. Johnson, 1931–1937." Master's thesis, Southwest Texas State University, 1967.

**4579.** Kowert, Art. "LBJ's Boyhood among the German-Americans in Texas." *American-German Review* 34 (August/September 1968): 2–6.

**4580.** Leighton, Francis S., ed. *The Johnson Wit.* New York: Citadel Press, 1965.

**4581.** Lucier, Jim. "Johnson and the Dead Men Who Voted." *American Opinion* 7 (April 1964): 1–9.

**4582.** Maguire, Jack R. *A President's Country: A Guide to the LBJ Country of Texas.* Austin, TX: Shoal Creek Publishers, 1973.

**4583.** McKinney, R. Kay. *LBJ: His Home and Heritage.* San Angelo, TX: Anchor, 1964.

**4584.** Miller, Merle. *Lyndon Johnson: An Oral Biography.* New York: Putnam's, 1980.

**4585.** Mooney, Booth. *LBJ: An Irreverent Chronicle.* New York: Crowell, 1976.

**4586.** ———. *The Lyndon Johnson Story.* Rev. ed. New York: Farrar, Straus, and Cudahy, 1964.

**4587.** Muslin, Hyman L., and Thomas H. Jobe. *Lyndon Johnson: The Tragic Self: A Psychohistorical Portrait.* New York: Insight Books, 1991.

**4588.** Newlon, Clarke. *LBJ: The Man from Johnson City.* New York: Dodd, Mead, 1964.

**4589.** Olds, Helen. *Lyndon Baines Johnson.* New York: Putnam's, 1965.

**4590.** Opotowsky, Stan. "The Vice President." In his *Kennedy Government,* 38–48. New York: Dutton, 1961.

**4591.** Partin, James W. "The Texas Senatorial Election of 1941." Master's thesis, Texas Technological College, 1941.

**4592.** Payne, Alvin N. "A Study of the Persuasive Efforts of Lyndon Baines Johnson in the Southern States in the Presidential Campaign of 1960." Master's thesis, Albilene Christian College, 1968.

**4593.** Podell, Jack, ed. *The Johnson Story.* New York: Macfadden-Bartell, 1964.

**4594.** Pool, William E., and David E. Conrad. *Lyndon Baines Johnson: The Formative Years.* San Marcos: Southwest Texas State College Press, 1965.

**4595.** Porterfield, Bill. "Farewell to LBJ: A Hill Country Valediction." *Texas Monthly* 1 (May 1973): 37–43.

**4596.** ———. *LBJ Country.* Garden City, NY: Doubleday, 1965.

**4597.** Provence, Harry. *Lyndon B. Johnson: A Biography.* New York: Fleet, 1964.

**4598.** Reedy, George E. *Lyndon B. Johnson: A Memoir.* Kansas City, MO: Andrews and McMeel, 1982.

**4599.** Riccards, Michael P. "Rare Counsel: Kennedy, Johnson, and the Civil Rights Bill of 1963." *Presidential Studies Quarterly* 11 (Summer 1981): 395–398.

**4600.** Riley, Philip. "Lyndon B. Johnson: The Long, Tall Texan." *Southwestern Journal of Social Education* 12 (Fall/Winter 1981): 9–12.

**4601.** Ritchie, Donald A. "Making Fulbright Chairman: Or How the 'Johnson Treatment' Nearly Backfired." *Society for Historians of American Foreign Relations Newsletter* 15 (September 1984): 21–28.

**4602.** Roberts, Charles W. *LBJ's Inner Circle.* New York: Delacorte, 1965.

**4603.** Roell, Craig H. "Image and Power: Lyndon B. Johnson and the 1957 Civil Rights Act." Master's thesis, University of Texas, 1980.

**4604.** Rulon, Philip R. *The Compassionate Samaritan: The Life of Lyndon Baines Johnson.* Chicago: Nelson-Hall, 1981.

**4605.** ———. "The Education of Lyndon Baines Johnson." *Presidential Studies Quarterly* 12 (Summer 1982): 400–406.

**4606.** Schander, Herbert Y. *The Unmaking of a President: Lyndon Johnson and Vietnam.* Princeton, NJ: Princeton University Press, 1977.

**4607.** Schmertz, Mildred F. "In Praise of a Monument to Lyndon B. Johnson." *Architectural Record* 150 (November 1971): 113–120.

**4608.** Sherrill, Robert G. *The Accidental President.* New York: Grossman, 1967.

**4609.** Shuman, Howard E. "Lyndon B. Johnson: The Senate's Powerful Persuader." In *First Among Equals: Outstanding Senate Leaders of the Twentieth Century,* edited by Richard A. Baker and Roger H. Davidson, 199–235. Washington, DC: Congressional Quarterly, 1991.

**4610.** Sidey, Hugh. *A Very Personal Presidency: Lyndon Johnson in the White House.* New York: Atheneum, 1968.

**4611.** Singer, Kurt D., and Jane Sherrod. *Lyndon Baines Johnson, Man of Reason.* Minneapolis, MN: T. S. Denison, 1964.

**4612.** Soloveytchik, George. "Contemporary Profile Vice-President Lyndon B. Johnson." *Contemporary Review* 203 (May 1963): 223–229.

**4613.** Steinberg, Alfred. *Sam Johnson's Boy: A Close-Up of the President from Texas.* New York: Macmillan, 1968.

**4614.** Stern, Mark. "Lyndon Johnson and Richard Russell: Institutions, Ambitions and Civil Rights." *Presidential Studies Quarterly* 21 (Fall 1991): 687–704.

**4615.** Stewart, John G. "Two Strategies of Leadership: Johnson and Mansfield." In *Congressional Behavior,* edited by Nelson W. Polsby, 61–92. New York: Random House, 1971.

**4616.** Sullivan, Austin P., Jr. "Lyndon Johnson and the Senate Majority Leadership." Honor's thesis, Princeton University, 1964.

**4617.** Thompson, Pat. *Lady Bird's Man.* Los Angeles: Holloway House, 1964.

**4618.** Valenti, Jack. *A Very Human President.* New York: Norton, 1975.

**4619.** Welch, June R. "Lyndon Johnson Became the 36th President." In his *The Texas Senator,* 130–143. Dallas, TX: G. L. A. Press, 1978.

**4620.** White, Theodore H. *The Making of the President.* New York: Atheneum, 1965.

**4621.** White, William S. "Lyndon B. Johnson." In his *The Responsibles,* 215–275. New York: Harper and Row, 1972.

**4622.** ———. *The Professional: Lyndon B. Johnson.* Boston: Houghton, 1964.

**4623.** Whitney, David C. *Let's Find Out about Lyndon Baines Johnson.* New York: Franklin Watts, 1967.

**4624.** Young, Donald. "Lyndon B. Johnson." In his *American Roulette: The History and Dilemma of the Vice Presidency,* 286–311. New York: Holt, Rinehart and Winston, 1965.

**4625.** Zeiger, Henry A. *Lyndon B. Johnson: Man and President.* New York: Popular Library, 1963.

**JOHNSON, REVERDY** (1796–1876)
D-MD, Senate 1845–1849, 1863–1868.

**4626.** Essary, J. Frederick. "Reverdy Johnson." In his *Maryland in National Politics.* Baltimore: John Murphy, 1915.

**4627.** Kunstler, William M. "Reverdy Johnson." In his *Case for Courage,* 120–157. New York: Morrow, 1962.

**4628.** Steiner, Bernard C. *Life of Reverdy Johnson.* Baltimore: Norman, Remington, 1914.

**JOHNSON, RICHARD MENTOR**
(1780–1850) R-KY, House 1807–1819,
1829–1837, Senate 1819–1829.

**4629.** Barzman, Sol. "Richard Mentor Johnson." In his *Madmen and Geniuses: The Vice-Presidents of the United States,* 67–71. Chicago: Follett, 1974.

**4630.** Bolt, Robert. "Vice-President Richard M. Johnson of Kentucky: Hero of the Thames—Or the Great Amalgamator?" *Register of the Kentucky Historical Society* 75 (July 1977): 191–203.

**4631.** Emmons, William. *Authentic Biography of Colonel Richard M. Johnson, of Kentucky.* New York: H. Mason, 1833.

**4632.** Meyer, Leland W. *The Life and Times of Colonel Richard M. Johnson of Kentucky.* New York: Columbia University Press, 1932.

**4633.** Padgett, James A., ed. "The Letters of Colonel Richard M. Johnson of Kentucky." *Register of the Kentucky Historical Society* 38 (July 1940): 186–201, 38 (October 1940): 323–339, 39 (January 1941): 22–46, 39 (April 1941): 172–188, 39 (July 1941): 260–274, 39 (October 1941): 358–367, 40 (January 1942): 69–91.

**4634.** Rouse, Shelly D. "Colonel Dick Johnson's Choctan Academy: A Forgotten Educational Experiment." *Ohio Valley Historical Association Annual Report* 6 (1916): 88–117.

## JOHNSON, THOMAS (1732–1819) MD, Continental Congress 1774–1777.

**4635.** Delaplaine, Edward S. *The Life of Thomas Johnson.* New York: Hitchock, 1927.

**4636.** Offult, T. Scott. "Thomas Johnson and Constitutional Government." *Constitutional Review* 13 (October 1929): 204–211.

## JOHNSON, TOM LOFTIN (1854–1911) D-OH, House 1891–1895.

**4637.** Allen, Philip L. "Cleveland and the Three-Cent Fare." In his *America's Awakening,* 182–198. New York: F. H. Revell Company, 1906.

**4638.** Howe, Frederic C. "I Enter Politics, a Rude Awakening, a Ten Years' War, Tom Johnson." In his *The Confessions of a Reformer,* 85–145. New York: Scribner's, 1925.

**4639.** Johnson, Tom L. *My Story.* Edited by Elizabeth J. Hauser. Seattle: University of Washington Press, 1970.

**4640.** Lorenz, Carl. *Tom L. Johnson, Mayor of Cleveland.* New York: Barnes, 1911.

**4641.** Massouh, Michael. "Innovations in Street Railways before Electric Traction: Tom L. Johnson's Contributions." *Technology and Culture* 18 (April 1977): 202–217.

**4642.** Murdock, Eugene C. "Life of Tom L. Johnson." Ph.D. dissertation, Columbia University, 1951.

## JOHNSON, WILLIAM SAMUEL (1727–1819) CT, Senate 1789–1791, Continental Congress 1785–1787.

**4643.** Beardsley, Eben E. *Life and Times of William Samuel Johnson, LL.D., First Senator in Congress from Connecticut, and President of Columbia College, New York.* New York: Hurd and Houghton, 1876.

**4644.** Groce, George C. *William Samuel Johnson: A Maker of the Constitution.* New York: Columbia University Press, 1937.

**4645.** McCaughey, Elizabeth P. *From Loyalist to Founding Father: The Political Odyssey of William Samuel Johnson.* New York: Columbia University Press, 1980.

## JOHNSTON, JOSEPH EGGLESTON (1807–1891) D-VA, House 1879–1881.

**4646.** Anders, Curt. "Joseph E. Johnston, A Professional President." In his *Fighting Confederates,* 67–109. New York: Putnam's, 1968.

**4647.** Burger, Nash K., and John K. Bettersworth. "Subdued But Unrepentant: 'Old Joe' Johnson." In their *South of Appomattox,* 208–235. New York: Harcourt, 1959.

**4648.** Govan, Gilbert E., and James W. Livingood. *A Different Valor: The Story of General Joseph E. Johnston, C.S.A.* Indianapolis: Bobbs-Merrill, 1956.

**4649.** Hughes, Robert M. *General Johnston.* New York: Appleton, 1897.

**4650.** Maurice, Frederick B. "Jefferson Davis and J. E. Johnston." In his *Statesmen and Soldiers of the Civil War,* 3–30. Boston: Little, Brown, 1926.

**4651.** McMurry, Richard M. "Atlanta Campaign of 1864: A New Look." *Civil War History* 22 (March 1976): 5–15.

**4652.** ———. "Mackall Journal and Its Antecedents." *Civil War History* 20 (December 1974): 311–328.

**4653.** Mitchell, Joseph B. "Joseph E. Johnson." In his *Military Leaders in the Civil War,* 174–192. New York: Putnam's, 1972.

**4654.** Sanger, Donald B. "Some Problems Facing Joseph E. Johnston in the Spring of 1863." In *Essays in Honor of William E. Dodd,* edited by Avery O. Craven, 257–290. Chicago: University of Chicago Press, 1935.

**JOHNSTON, OLIN DEWITT TALMADGE** (1896–1965) D-SC, Senate 1945–1965.

**4655.** Huss, John E. *Senator for the South: A Biography of Olin D. Johnston.* Garden City, NY: Doubleday, 1961.

**4656.** Leemhuis, Roger P. "Olin D. Johnston Runs for the Senate, 1938 to 1962." *Proceedings of the South Carolina Historical Association* 56 (1986): 57–69.

**4657.** Miller, Anthony B. "Palmetto Politician: The Early Political Career of Olin D. Johnston, 1896–1945." Ph.D. dissertation, University of North Carolina, 1976.

**JOHNSTON, RIENZI MELVILLE** (1849–1926) D-TX, Senate 1913.

**4658.** Welch, June R. "Rienzi Johnston Managed the *Houston Post.*" In his *The Texas Senator,* 114–115. Dallas, TX: G. L. A. Press, 1978.

**JOHNSTON, SAMUEL** (1733–1816) NC, Senate 1789–1793, Continental Congress 1780–1781.

**4659.** Allen, T. M. "Samuel Johnston in Revolutionary Times." *Trinity College Historical Society Papers* (1905): 39–49.

**JONES, BURR W.** (1846–1935) D-WI, House 1883–1885.

**4660.** Birge, Edward A. "Burr W. Jones." *Wisconsin Magazine of History* 21 (September 1937): 63–67.

**4661.** Jones, Burr W. "Reminiscences of Nine Decades." *Wisconsin Magazine of History* 20 (September 1936): 10–33, 20 (December 1936): 143–184, 20 (March 1937): 270–290, 20 (June 1937): 404–436, 21 (September 1937): 39–62.

**JONES, CHARLES WILLIAM** (1834–1897) D-FL, Senate 1875–1887.

**4662.** Etemadi, Judy N. "A Love-Maid Man: Senator Charles W. Jones of Flori-da." *Florida Historical Quarterly* 56 (October 1977): 123–137.

**JONES, FRANK** (1832–1902) D-NH, House 1875–1879.

**4663.** Brighton, Ray. *Frank Jones: King of the Alemakers.* Nashville, TN: Randall, 1976.

**JONES, GEORGE WALLACE** (1804–1896) D-MI/WI/IA, House (MI) 1835–1836, (WI)1837–1839, Senate (IA)1848–1859.

**4664.** Parish, John C. *George Wallace Jones.* Iowa City: State Historical Society of Iowa, 1912.

**4665.** Thayer, Shelly A. "The Delegate and the Duel: The Early Political Career of George Wallace Jones." *Palimpsest* 65 (September/October 1984): 178–188.

**JONES, JAMES CHAMBERLAIN** (1809–1859) W-TN, Senate 1851–1857.

**4666.** Crittenden, John R. "The Public Life of James C. Jones." Master's thesis, University of Tennessee, 1927.

**4667.** Osborne, Ray G. "Political Career of James Chamberlain Jones, 1840–1857." *Tennessee Historical Quarterly* 7 (September 1948): 195–228, 7 (December 1948): 322–334.

**4668.** Temple, Oliver P. "The Races of Jones and Polk in 1841 and 1843." In *Notable Men of Tennessee, from 1833 to 1875,* edited by Mary B. Temple, 246–261. New York: Cosmopolitan Press, 1912.

**4669.** Woods, Raymond P. "The Political Life of James Chamberlain Jones." Master's thesis, George Peabody College, 1928.

**JONES, JAMES KIMBROUGH** (1839–1908) D-AR, House 1881–1885, Senate 1885–1903.

**4670.** Newberry, Farrar. *James K. Jones.* Arkadelphia, AK: Siftings-Herald Printing Company, 1913.

**JONES, JOHN MARVIN** (1886–1976)
**D-TX, House 1917–1940.**

**4671.** May, Irvin M. "Marvin Jones: Agrarian and Politician." *Agricultural History* 51 (April 1977): 421–440.

**4672.** ———. "Marvin Jones: Representative of and for the Panhandle." *West Texas Historical Association Year Book* 52 (1976): 91–104.

**4673.** ———. *Marvin Jones: The Public Life of an Agrarian Advocate.* College Station: Texas A & M University Press, 1980.

**JONES, JOHN WINSTON** (1791–1848)
**D-VA, House 1835–1845.**

**4674.** Fothergill, Augusta B. *Peter Jones and Richard Jones Genealogies.* Richmond, VA: Old Dominion Press, 1924.

**4675.** Kennedy, Mary S. *Seldens of Virginia and Allied Families.* 2 vols. New York: Frank Allaben Genealogical, 1911.

**4676.** Lutz, Francis E. *Chesterfield: An Old Virginia County.* Richmond, VA: William Byrd Press, 1954.

**JONES, NOBLE WIMBERLY** (1723–1805)
**GA, Continental Congress 1775, 1781–1782.**

**4677.** Kelso, William M. *Captain Jones's Wormslow: A Historical Archaeological, and Architectural Study of an Eighteenth-Century Plantation Site Near Savannah, Georgia.* Athens: University of Georgia Press, 1979.

**JONES, WALTER** (1745–1815) **R-VA,**
**House 1797–1799, 1803–1811.**

**4678.** Mason, Thomas A. "The Luminary of the Northern Neck: Walter Jones, 1745–1815." *Northern Neck of Virginia Historical Magazine* 35 (1985): 3978–3983.

**JONES, WESLEY LIVSEY** (1863–1932)
**R-WA, House 1899–1909, Senate 1909–1932.**

**4679.** Forth, William S. "Wesley L. Jones: A Political Biography." Ph.D. dissertation, University of Washington, 1962.

**JONES, WILLIAM** (1760–1831) **R-PA,**
**House 1801–1803.**

**4680.** Corrigan, M. Saint Pierre. "William Jones of the Second Bank of the United States: A Reappraisal." Ph.D. dissertation, University of St. Louis, 1966.

**JONES, WILLIAM ATKINSON**
**(1849–1918) D-VA, House 1891–1918.**

**4681.** Shelton, Charlotte J. "William Atkinson Jones, 1849–1918: Independent Democracy in Gilded Age Virginia." Ph.D. dissertation, University of Virginia, 1980.

**JORDAN, BARBARA CHARLINE**
**(1936– ) D-TX, House 1973–1979.**

**4682.** Bryant, Ira B. *Barbara Charline Jordan: From the Ghetto to the Capital.* Houston, TX: Armstrong, 1977.

**4683.** Christopher, Maurine."Barbara Jordan/Texas." In her *Black Americans in Congress,* 289. Rev. ed. New York: Thomas Y. Crowell, 1976.

**4684.** Green, Robert L. *Barbara Jordan: Daring Black Leader.* Milwaukee, WI: Franklin, 1974.

**4685.** Haskins, James S. *Barbara Jordan.* New York: Dial, 1977.

**4686.** Jacobs, Linda. *Barbara Jordan: Keeping Faith.* St. Paul, MN: EMC Corporation, 1978.

**4687.** Jordan, Barbara, and Shelby Hearon. *Barbara Jordan: A Self-Portrait.* Garden City, NY: Doubleday, 1979.

**4688.** Kelin, Norman. *Barbara Jordan.* Los Angeles: Melrose Square Press, 1993.

**4689.** Kirk, Rita G. "Barbara Jordan: The Rise of a Black Woman Politician." Master's thesis, University of Arkansas, 1978.

**4690.** Lashar, Patricia. *Texas Women,* 98–103. Austin, TX: Shoal Creek, 1980.

**4691.** Martin, Donald R. "Barbara Jordan's Symbolic Use of Language in the Keynote Address to the National Women's Conference." *Southern Speech Communication Journal* 49 (Summer 1984): 319–330.

**4692.** Thompson, Wayne N. "Barbara Jordan's Keynote Address: The Juxtaposition of Contradictory Values." *Southern Speech Communication Journal* 44 (Spring 1979): 223–232.

**JORDAN, BENJAMIN EVERETT** (1896–1974) D-NC, Senate 1958–1973.

**4693.** Bulla, Ben F. *Textiles and Politics: The Life of B. Everett Jordan: From Saxapahaw to the United States Senate.* Durham, NC: Carolina Academic Press, 1992.

**JORDAN, LEONARD BECK** (1899–1983) R-ID, Senate 1962–1973.

**4694.** Jordan, Grace. *Unintentional Senator.* Boise, ID: Syms-York Company, 1972.

**JUDD, WALTER HENRY** (1898–1994) R-MN, House 1943–1963.

**4695.** Edwards, Lee. *Missionary for Freedom: The Life and Times of Walter Judd.* New York: Paragon House, 1990.

**4696.** Goodno, Floyd R. "Walter H. Judd: Spokesman for China in the United States House of Representatives." Ed.D. dissertation, Oklahoma State University, 1970.

**4697.** Judd, Walter H. *Walter H. Judd: Chronicles of a Statesman.* Edited by Edward J. Rozek. Denver: Grier, 1980.

**4698.** Stuhler, Barbara. "The Foreign Policy Mission of Walter H. Judd." In her *Ten Men of Minnesota and American Foreign Policy, 1898–1968,* 169–193. St. Paul: Minnesota Historical Society, 1973.

**JULIAN, GEORGE WASHINGTON** (1817–1899) R-IN, House 1849–1851, 1861–1871.

**4699.** Clarke, Grace G. *George W. Julian.* Indianapolis: Indiana Historical Commission, 1923.

**4700.** ———. "George W. Julian: Some Impression." *Indiana Magazine of History* 2 (June 1906): 57–69.

**4701.** Fox, Henry C., ed. "George W. Julian." In his *Memoirs of Wayne County and the City of Richmond, Indiana* vol. 1, 199–213. Madison, WI: Western Historical Association 1912.

**4702.** Julian, George W. *Political Recollections, 1840 to 1872.* Chicago: Jansen, McClurg, 1884.

**4703.** Riddleberger, Patrick W. *George Washington Julian, Radical Republican.* Indianapolis: Indiana Historical Bureau, 1966.

❧

**KAHN, JULIUS** (1861–1924) R-CA, House 1899–1903, 1905–1924.

**4704.** Adams, Willi P. "Ethnic Politicians and American Nationalism during the First World War: Four German-Born Members of the U.S. House of Representatives." *American Studies International* 29 (April 1991): 20–34.

**4705.** Kramer, William M., and Robert J. Hoffman. "Congressman Julius Kahn of California." *Western States Jewish History* 19 (October 1989): 3–22.

**KANE, ELIAS KENT** (1794–1835) IL, Senate 1825–1835.

**4706.** Hubbs, Barbara B. "Father of Illinois Constitution—Elias Kent Kane." In *Idols of Egypt,* edited by Will Griffith, 77–92. Carbondale, IL: Egypt Book House, 1947.

**KASSON, JOHN ADAM** (1822–1910) R-IA, House 1863–1867, 1873–1877, 1881–1884.

**4707.** Schoonover, Thomas. "John A. Kasson's Opposition to the Lincoln Administration's Mexican Policy." *Annals of Iowa* 40 (Spring 1971): 584–593.

**4708.** Younger, Edward. *John A. Kasson: Politics and Diplomacy from Lincoln to McKinley.* Iowa City: State Historical Society of Iowa, 1955.

**KASTENMEIER, ROBERT WILLIAM**
**(1924– ) D-WI, House 1959–1991.**

**4709.** Kidwell, John A. "Congressman Robert Kastenmeier and Professor John Stedman: A Thirty-Five Year Relationship." *Law and Contemporary Problems* 55 (Spring 1992): 129–137.

**KAVANAGH, EDWARD (1795–1844) J-ME,**
**House 1831–1835.**

**4710.** Lucey, William L. *Edward Kavanagh, Catholic, Statesman, Diplomat, from Maine, 1795–1844.* Francestown, NH: Marshall Jones, 1947.

**KAVANAUGH, WILLIAM MARMADUKE**
**(1866–1915) D-AR, Senate 1913.**

**4711.** Jacobson, Charles. "Arkansas Trinity." In *Great Statesmen of Arkansas,* edited by Walter S. McNutt, 41–46. Jefferson, TX: Four States Publication House, 1954.

**KEATING, EDWARD (1875–1965) D-CO,**
**House 1913–1919.**

**4712.** Keating, Edward. *Gentleman from Colorado: A Memoir.* Beverly Hills, CA: Sage, 1964.

**KEATING, KENNETH BARNARD**
**(1900–1975) R-NY, House 1947–1959, Senate 1959–1965.**

**4713.** Paterson, Thomas G. "The Historian as Detective: Senator Kenneth Keating, the Missles in Cuba, and His Mysterious Sources." *Diplomatic History* 11 (Winter 1987): 67–70.

**KEE, JOHN (1874–1951) D-WV, House**
**1933–1951.**

**4714.** Hardin, William H. "John Kee and the Point Four Compromise." *West Virginia History* 41 (Fall 1979): 40–56.

**KEE, MAUDE ELIZABETH (1895–1975)**
**D-WV, House 1951–1965.**

**4715.** Hardin, William H. "Elizabeth Kee: West Virginia's First Woman in Congress." *West Virginia History* 45 (1984): 109–123.

**KEFAUVER, CAREY ESTES (1903–1963)**
**D-TN, House 1939–1949, Senate 1949–1963.**

**4716.** Anderson, Jack, and Frederick G. Blumenthal. *The Kefauver Story.* New York: Dial, 1956.

**4717.** Derr, Jeanine. "'The Biggest Show on Earth': The Kefauver Crime Committee Hearings." *Maryland Historian* 17 (Fall/Winter 1986): 19–37.

**4718.** Dishman, Robert D. "New Hampshire in the Limelight: The 1952 Kefauver-Truman Presidential Primary Campaign." *Historical New Hampshire* 42 (Fall 1987): 214–252.

**4719.** Doig, Ivan. "Kefauver versus Crime: Television Boosts a Senator." *Journalism Quarterly* 39 (Autumn 1962): 483–490.

**4720.** Fontenay, Charles L. *Estes Kefauver: A Biography.* Knoxville: University of Tennessee Press, 1980.

**4721.** Gorman, Joseph B. "The Early Career of Estes Kefauver." *East Tennessee Historical Society's Publications* 42 (1970): 57–84.

**4722.** ———. *Kefauver: A Political Biography.* New York: Oxford University Press, 1971.

**4723.** Graham, Hugh D. "Kefauver: A Political Biography." *Tennessee Historical Quarterly* 30 (Winter 1971): 413–418.

**4724.** Grant, Philip A. "Senator Estes Kefauver and the 1956 Minnesota Presidential Primary." *Tennessee Historical Quarterly* 42 (Winter 1983): 383–392.

**4725.** Harris, Richard. *Real Voice.* New York: Macmillan, 1964.

**4726.** Lisby, Gregory C. "Early Television on Public Watch: Kefauver and His Crime

Investigation." *Journalism Quarterly* 62 (Summer 1985): 236–242.

**4727.** McFadyen, Richard E. "Estes Kefauver and the Drug Industry." Ph.D. dissertation, Emory University, 1973.

**4728.** ———. "Estes Kefauver and the Tradition of Southern Progressivism." *Tennessee Historical Quarterly* 37 (Winter 1978): 430–443.

**4729.** Moore, William H. *The Kefauver Committee and the Politics of Crime, 1950–1952.* Columbia: University of Missouri Press, 1974.

**4730.** ———. "Was Estes Kefauver 'Blackmailed' during the Chicago Crime Hearings? A Historian's Perspective." *Public Historian* 4 (Winter 1982): 5–28.

**4731.** Swados, Harvey. *Standing Up for the People: The Life and Work of Estes Kefauver.* New York: Dutton, 1972.

**KEIFER, JOSEPH WARREN** (1836–1932) R-OH, House 1877–1885, 1905–1911.

**4732.** Fuller, Hubert B. "Kerr, Randall, Keifer, and Carlisle." In his *The Speakers of the House*, 193–213. Boston: Little, Brown, 1909.

**4733.** Galbreath, Charles B. "General Keifer Honored." *Ohio Archaeological and Historical Quarterly* 35 (April 1926): 418–426.

**KEITT, LAURENCE MASSILLON** (1824–1864) D-SC, House 1853–1856, 1856–1860.

**4734.** Merchant, John H., Jr. "Laurence M. Keith: South Carolina Fire Eater." Ph.D. dissertation, University of Virginia, 1976.

**KELLER, KENT ELLSWORTH** (1867–1954) D-IL, House 1931–1941.

**4735.** Weiss, Stuart L. "Kent Keller, the Liberal Bloc, and the New Deal." *Journal of the Illinois State Historical Society* 68 (April 1975): 143–158.

**KELLEY, WILLIAM DARRAH** (1814–1890) R-PA, House 1861–1890.

**4736.** Brown, Ira V. "William D. Kelley and Radical Reconstruction." *Pennsylvania Magazine of History and Biography* 85 (July 1961): 316–329.

**4737.** Nicklas, Floyd W. "William Kelley: The Congressional Years, 1861–1890." Ph.D. dissertation, Northern Illinois University, 1983.

**KELLOGG, FRANK BILLINGS** (1856–1937) R-MN, Senate 1917–1923.

**4738.** Bryn-Jones, David. *Frank B. Kellogg, a Biography.* New York: Putnam's, 1937.

**4739.** Cleaver, Charles G. "Frank B. Kellogg: Attitudes and Assumptions Influencing His Foreign Policy Decisions." Ph.D. dissertation, University of Minnesota, 1956.

**4740.** Debenedetti, Charles. "Borah and the Kellogg-Briand Pact." *Pacific Northwest Quarterly* 63 (January 1972): 22–29.

**4741.** Ellis, Lewis E. "Frank B. Kellogg." In *Uncertain Tradition: American Secretaries of State in the Twentieth Century*, edited by Norman A. Graebner, 149–167. New York: McGraw, 1961.

**4742.** ———. *Frank B. Kellogg and American Foreign Relations, 1925–1929.* New Brunswick, NJ: Rutgers University Press, 1961.

**4743.** Ferrell, Robert H. "Frank B. Kellogg." In his *The American Secretaries of State and Their Diplomacy*, vol. 11, 1–135. New York: Knopf, 1963.

**4744.** ———. *Frank B. Kellogg and Henry L. Stimson.* New York: Cooper Square, 1963.

**4745.** Gray, Tony. "Frank Billings Kellogg." In his *Champions of Peace*, 154–155. New York: Paddington Press, 1976.

**4746.** Kennedy, Roger G. "Frank Billings Kellogg." In his *Men on the Moving Frontier*,

133–151. Palo Alto, CA: American West Publishing Company, 1969.

**4747.** Lippmann, Walter. "The Kellogg Doctrine: Vested Rights and Nationalism in Latin America." In his *Men of Destiny*, 196–224. New York: Macmillan, 1927.

**4748.** Stuhler, Barbara. "The Impassionate Diplomacy of Frank B. Kellogg." In her *Ten Men of Minnesota and American Foreign Policy, 1898–1968*, 99–122. St. Paul: Minnesota Historical Society, 1973.

**4749.** Traphagen, Jeanne C. "The Inter-American Diplomacy of Frank B. Kellogg." Ph.D. dissertation, University of Minnesota, 1956.

**KELLOGG, WILLIAM PITT** (1830–1918) **R-LA, Senate 1868–1872, 1877–1883, House 1883–1885.**

**4750.** Reeves, Miriam G. "William Pitt Kellogg." In her *Governors of Louisiana*, 79–80. Gretna, LA: Pelican, 1972.

**KELLY, JOHN** (1822–1886) **D-NY, House 1855–1858.**

**4751.** Zink, Harold. "'Honest John' Kelley." In his *City Bosses in the United States*, 113–127. Durham, NC: Duke University Press, 1930.

**KELLY, MELVILLE CLYDE** (1883–1935) **R-PA, House 1913–1915, 1917–1935.**

**4752.** Larner, John W., Jr. "Braddock's Congressman M. Clyde Kelly and Indian Policy Reform, 1919–1928." *Western Pennsylvania Historical Magazine* 66 (April 1983): 97–111.

**KEM, JAMES PRESTON** (1890–1965) **R-MO, Senate 1947–1953.**

**4753.** Atwell, Mary W. "A Conservative Response to the Cold War: Senator James P. Kem and Foreign Aid." *Capital Studies* 4 (Fall 1976): 53–65.

**KEMBLE, GOUVERNEUR** (1786–1875) **D-NY, House 1837–1841.**

**4754.** Emerson, Everett H., and Katherine T. Emerson. "Some Letters of Washington Irving, 1833–1843." *American Literature* 35 (May 1963): 156–172.

**KENDRICK, JOHN BENJAMIN** (1857–1933) **D-WY, Senate 1917–1933.**

**4755.** Carroll, Eugene T. "John B. Kendrick, Cowpoke to Senator, 1879–1917." *Annals of Wyoming* 54 (Spring 1982): 51–57.

**4756.** ———. "John B. Kendrick's Fight for Western Water Legislation, 1917–1933." *Annals of Wyoming* 50 (Fall 1978): 319–333.

**4757.** ———. "Wyoming Senator John Benjamin Kendrick: The Politics of Oil, Public Land and National Park Legislation in the 1920's." *Annals of Wyoming* 58 (Fall 1986): 22–29.

**4758.** Fley, Jo Ann. "John B. Kendrick's Career in the United States Senate." Master's thesis, University of Wyoming, 1953.

**KENNEDY, EDWARD MOORE** (1932– ) **D-MA, Senate 1962– .**

**4759.** Aschburner, Steve. *Ted Kennedy, the Politician and the Man*. Milwaukee, WI: Raintree, 1980.

**4760.** Burke, Richard E. *The Senator: My Ten Years with Ted Kennedy*. New York: St. Martin's Press, 1992.

**4761.** Burner, David, and Thomas R. West. *The Torch Is Passed: The Kennedy Brothers and American Liberalism*. New York: Atheneum, 1984.

**4762.** Burns, James M. *Edward Kennedy and the Camelot Legacy*. New York: Norton, 1976.

**4763.** Chellis, Marcia. *Living with the Kennedys: The Joan Kennedy Story*. New York: Simon and Schuster, 1985.

**4764.** David, Lester. *Good Ted, Bad Ted: The Two Faces of Edward M. Kennedy.* Secaucus, NJ: Carol Pub. Group, 1993.

**4765.** ———. *Ted Kennedy: Triumphs and Tragedies.* New York: Grosset, 1972.

**4766.** Galloway, John. "Edward Moore Kennedy." In his *The Kennedys and Vietnam,* 129–140. New York: Facts on File, 1971.

**4767.** Hart, John. "Kennedy, Congress, and Civil Rights." *Journal of American Studies* 13 (August 1979): 165–178.

**4768.** Hersh, Burton. *The Education of Edward Kennedy: A Family Biography.* New York: Morrow, 1972.

**4769.** Honan, William H. *Ted Kennedy: Profile of a Survivor: Edward Kennedy after Bobby, after Chappaquiddick, and after Three Years of Nixon.* New York: Quadrangle Books, 1972.

**4770.** Leamer, Laurence. "The Lion and the Waterhole." In his *Playing for Keeps in Washington,* 75–139. New York: Dial, 1977.

**4771.** Lerner, Max. *Ted and the Kennedy Legend: A Study in Character and Destiny.* New York: St. Martin's Press, 1980.

**4772.** Levin, Murray B. *Kennedy Campaigning: The System and Style as Practiced by Senator Edward Kennedy.* Boston: Beacon Press, 1966.

**4773.** Levin, Murray B., and T. A. Repak. *Edward Kennedy: The Myth of Leadership.* Boston: Houghton Mifflin, 1980.

**4774.** Lippman, Theo. *Senator Ted Kennedy.* New York: Norton, 1976.

**4775.** McGinniss, Joe. *The Last Brother: The Rise and Fall of Teddy Kennedy.* New York: Simon and Schuster, 1993.

**4776.** Mervin, David. "United States Senate Norms and the Majority Whip Election of 1969." *Journal of American Studies* 9 (December 1975): 321–333.

**4777.** Olsen, Jack. *The Bridge at Chappaquiddick.* New York: Ace Books, 1970.

**4778.** Reybold, Malcolm. *The Inspector's Opinion: The Chappaquiddick Incident.* New York: Saturday Review Press, 1975.

**4779.** Rust, Zad. *Teddy Bare: The Last of the Kennedy Clan.* Belmont, MA: Western Islands, 1971.

**4780.** Shaffer, William R. "A Discriminant Function Analysis of Position-Taking: Carter vs. Kennedy." *Presidential Studies Quarterly* 10 (Summer 1980): 451–468.

**4781.** Sherrill, Robert G. *Last Kennedy.* New York: Dial, 1976.

**4782.** Tedrow, Thomas L., and Richard L. Tedrow. *Death at Chappaquiddick.* Ottawa, IL: Green Hill, 1976.

**4783.** Wayne, Stephen J., Cheryl Beil, and Jay Falk. "Public Perceptions about Ted Kennedy and the Presidency." *Presidential Studies Quarterly* 12 (Winter 1982): 84–90.

## KENNEDY, JOHN FITZGERALD
**(1917–1963) D-MA, House 1947–1953, Senate 1953–1960.**

**4784.** Altschuler, Bruce E. "Kennedy Decides to Run: 1968." *Presidential Studies Quarterly* 10 (Summer 1980): 348–352.

**4785.** Berry, Joseph P. *John F. Kennedy and the Media: The First Television President.* Lanham, MD: University Press of America, 1987.

**4786.** Beschloss, Michael R. *The Crisis Years: Kennedy and Khrushchev, 1960–1963.* New York: Edward Burlingame Books, 1991.

**4787.** Bilainkin, George. "Contemporary Profile—President Kennedy—1940 and 1961." *Contemporary Review* 199 (November 1961): 113–119, 141.

**4788.** Blair, Joan, and Clay Blair. *The Search for J.F.K.* New York: Berkley, 1976.

**4789.** Bowles, Chester. "The Foreign Policy of Senator Kennedy." *America* 104 (October 15, 1960): 69–73.

**4790.** Bradford, Richard H. "John F. Kennedy and the 1960 Presidential Primary in West Virginia." *South Atlantic Quarterly* 75 (Spring 1976): 161–172.

**4791.** Bradlee, Benjamin C. *Conversations with Kennedy.* New York: Norton, 1975.

**4792.** ———. *That Special Grace.* New York: Lippincott, 1964.

**4793.** Brauer, Carl M. *John F. Kennedy and the Second Reconstruction.* New York: Columbia University Press, 1977.

**4794.** Brennan, John F. *The Evolution of Everyman: Ancestral Lineage of John F. Kennedy.* Dundalk, Ireland: Dundalgan Press, 1968.

**4795.** Briggs, William D. "John F. Kennedy and the Formation of Limited War Policy, 1952–1961: 'Outsiders' as a Factor in Decisionmaking." Ph.D. dissertation, George Washington University, 1989.

**4796.** Brown, Thomas. *JFK: History of an Image.* Bloomington: Indiana University Press, 1988.

**4797.** Burner, David. *John F. Kennedy and a New Generation.* Boston: Little, Brown, 1988.

**4798.** ———. *The Torch Is Passed: The Kennedy Brothers and American Liberalism.* New York: Atheneum, 1984.

**4799.** Burns, James M. *John Kennedy: A Political Profile.* New York: Harcourt Brace, 1960.

**4800.** Carr, William H. *JFK: A Complete Biography, 1917–1963.* New York: Lancer, 1964.

**4801.** ———. *JFK: An Informal Biography.* New York: Lancer, 1962.

**4802.** Clinch, Nancy G. *The Kennedy Neurosis: A Psychological Portrait of an American Dynasty.* New York: Grossett and Dunlap, 1973.

**4803.** Coffin, Tristram. "John Kennedy: Young Man in a Hurry." *Progressive Magazine* 23 (December 1959): 10–18.

**4804.** Collier, Peter, and David Horowitz. *The Kennedys: An American Drama.* New York: Summit Books, 1984.

**4805.** Dallas, Rita, and Jeanira Ratcliffe. *The Kennedy Case.* New York: Putnam's, 1973.

**4806.** Damore, Leo. *The Cape Cod Years of John Fitzgerald Kennedy.* Englewood Cliff, NJ: Prentice-Hall, 1967.

**4807.** Davis, John H. *The Kennedys: Dynasty and Disaster, 1848–1984.* New York: McGraw-Hill, 1984.

**4808.** Dickerson, Nancy, and Robert Drew. *Being with John F. Kennedy.* Los Angeles: Direct Cinema, 1983.

**4809.** Dinneen, Joseph F. *The Kennedy Family.* Boston: Little, Brown, 1959.

**4810.** Dollen, Charles. *John F. Kennedy, American.* Boston: St. Paul Editions, 1965.

**4811.** Donovan, Robert J. *PT 109: John F. Kennedy in World War II.* New York: McGraw-Hill, 1961.

**4812.** Dunleavy, Stephen, and Peter Brennan. *Those Wild, Wild Kennedy Boys!* New York: Pinnacle Books, 1976.

**4813.** Ekirch, Arthur A., Jr. "Eisenhower and Kennedy: The Rhetoric and the Reality." *Midwest Quarterly* 17 (April 1976): 279–290.

**4814.** Fay, Paul B. *The Pleasure of His Company.* New York: Harper and Row, 1966.

**4815.** Fleming, Daniel B. *Kennedy vs. Humphrey, West Virginia, 1960: The Pivotal Battle for the Democratic Presidential Nomination.* Jefferson, NC: McFarland, 1992.

**4816.** Fox, Douglas M., and Charles H. Clapp. "The House Rules Committee and the Programs of the Kennedy and Johnson Administration." *Midwest Journal of Political Science* 14 (November 1970): 667–672.

**4817.** Gadney, Reg. *Kennedy.* New York: Holt, Rinehart and Winston, 1983.

**4818.** Galloway, John. "John Fitzgerald Kennedy." In his *The Kennedys and Vietnam,* 5–54. New York: Facts on File, 1971.

**4819.** Giglio, James N. *The Presidency of John F. Kennedy.* Lawrence: University Press of Kansas, 1991.

**4820.** Godden, Richard, and Richard A. Maidment. "Anger, Language and Politics: John F. Kennedy and the Steel Crisis." *Presidential Studies Quarterly* 10 (Summer 1980): 317–331.

**4821.** Gray, Charles H. "A Scale Analysis of the Voting Records of Senators Kennedy, Johnson, and Goldwater, 1957–1960." *American Political Science Review* 59 (September 1965): 615.

**4822.** Hamilton, Nigel. *JFK: Reckless Youth.* New York: Random House, 1992.

**4823.** Hanff, Helene. *John F. Kennedy: Young Man of Destiny.* Garden City, NY: Doubleday, 1965.

**4824.** Hirsh, Phil, and Edward Hymoff, eds. *The Kennedy Courage.* New York: Pyramid, 1965.

**4825.** Hoover, Judith. "An Early Use of Television as a Political Tool: The 1961 News Conference of President John F. Kennedy and the Republican Opposition." *Journal of Popular Film and Television* 16 (Spring 1988): 41–48.

**4826.** Ions, Edmund S. *The Politics of John F. Kennedy.* New York: Barnes and Noble, 1967.

**4827.** Kelly, Regina Z. *John F. Kennedy.* Chicago: Follett, 1969.

**4828.** Kennedy, Rose F. *Times to Remember.* Garden City, NY: Doubleday, 1974.

**4829.** Kern, Montague. *The Kennedy Crises: The Press, the Presidency, and Foreign Policy.* Chapel Hill: University of North Carolina, 1983.

**4830.** Lands, Guy. "John F. Kennedy's Southern Strategy, 1956–1960." *North Carolina Historical Review* 56 (January 1979): 41–63.

**4831.** Larrabee, Harold A. "New England Family: The Kennedys." *New England Quarterly* 42 (September 1969): 436–445.

**4832.** Lasky, Victor. *JFK: The Man and the Myth.* New York: Macmillan, 1963.

**4833.** ———. *John F. Kennedy: What's behind the Image?* Washington, DC: Free World Press, 1960.

**4834.** Lemke, William E. "The Political Thought of John F. Kennedy: To the Inaugural Address." Ph.D. dissertation, University of Maine, 1973.

**4835.** Levine, Israel E. *Young Man in the White House: John Fitzgerald Kennedy.* New York: Messner, 1964.

**4836.** Lincoln, Evelyn. *My Twelve Years with John F. Kennedy.* New York: McKay, 1965.

**4837.** Longford, Frank P. *Kennedy.* London: Weidenfeld and Nicholson, 1976.

**4838.** Lowe, Jacques. *Kennedy: A Time Remembered.* Topsfield, MA: Merrimack, 1983.

**4839.** ———. *Portrait: The Emergence of John F. Kennedy.* New York: McGraw-Hill, 1961.

**4840.** Lyons, Louis M. "The Legend of John Kennedy." *Massachusetts Review* 5 (Winter 1964): 209–212.

**4841.** Manchester, William R. *One Brief Shining Moment: Remembering Kennedy.* Boston: Little, Brown, 1983.

**4842.** ———. *Portrait of a President: John F. Kennedy in Profile.* Boston: Little, Brown, 1967.

**4843.** Markmann, Charles L., and Mark Sherwin. *John F. Kennedy: A Sense of Purpose.* New York: St. Martin's Press, 1961.

**4844.** Marvin, Richard. *The Kennedy Curse.* New York: Belmont, 1969.

**4845.** McCarthy, Joseph W. *The Remarkable Kennedys.* New York: Dial, 1960.

**4846.** McEvoy, Kevin, comp. *Two Kennedys.* Glen Rock, NJ: Paulist Press, 1969.

**4847.** Menendez, Albert J. *John F. Kennedy: Catholic and Humanist.* Buffalo, NY: Prometheus Books, 1979.

**4848.** Meyers, Joan S., ed. *John Fitzgerald Kennedy as We Remember Him.* New York: Macmillan, 1965.

**4849.** Miroff, Bruce. "John F. Kennedy: Heroic Leadership for a Television Age." In his *Icons of Democracy: American Leaders as Heroes, Aristocrats, Dissenters, and Democrats,* 273–307. New York: Basic Books, 1993.

**4850.** ———. *Pragmatic Illusions: The Presidential Politics of John F. Kennedy.* New York: McKay, 1976.

**4851.** Muravchik, Joshua. "Kennedy's Foreign Policy: What the Record Shows." *Commentary* 68 (December 1979): 31–43.

**4852.** Nurse, Ronald J. "America Must Not Sleep: The Development of John F. Kennedy's Foreign Policy Attitudes, 1947–1960." Ph.D. dissertation, Michigan State University, 1971.

**4853.** O'Donnell, Kenneth P., and David F. Powers. *Johnny, We Hardly Knew Ye: Memories of John Fitzgerald Kennedy.* Boston: Little, Brown, 1972.

**4854.** Paper, Lewis J. *The Promise and the Performance: The Leadership of John F. Kennedy.* New York: Crown, 1975.

**4855.** Parmet, Herbert S. *Jack: The Struggles of John F. Kennedy.* New York: Dial, 1980.

**4856.** ———. *JFK: The Presidency of John F. Kennedy.* New York: Dial, 1983.

**4857.** Paterson, Thomas G., ed. *Kennedy's Quest for Victory: American Foreign Policy, 1961–1963.* New York: Oxford University Press, 1989.

**4858.** Reeves, Richard. *President Kennedy: Profile of Power.* New York: Simon and Schuster, 1993.

**4859.** Rosenberg, Hyman S. *Short Biography of President John F. Kennedy.* Newark, NJ: Alpco, 1963.

**4860.** Salinger, Pierre. *With Kennedy.* Garden City, NY: Doubleday, 1966.

**4861.** Salisbury, Harrison. *The Kennedys: A New York Times Profile.* New York: Arno Press, 1980.

**4862.** Sanghvi, Ramesh. *John F. Kennedy: A Political Biography.* Bombay: Perennial Press, 1961.

**4863.** Saunders, Frank, and James Southwood. *Torn Lace Curtains.* New York: Holt, Rinehart and Winston, 1982.

**4864.** Schlesinger, Arthur M., Jr. *A Thousand Days: John F. Kennedy in the White House.* Boston: Houghton Mifflin, 1965.

**4865.** Schneidman, J. Lee. *John F. Kennedy.* Boston: G. K. Hall, 1974.

**4866.** Schwab, Peter, and J. Lee Sheidman. *John F. Kennedy.* New York: Twayne, 1974.

**4867.** Shank, Alan. *Presidential Policy Leadership: Kennedy and Social Welfare.* Lanham, MD: University Press of America, 1980.

**4868.** Shaw, Mark. *The John F. Kennedys: A Family Album.* New York: Farrar, 1964.

**4869.** Snyder, J. Richard, ed. *John F. Kennedy: Person, Policy, Presidency.* Wilmington, DE: SR Books, 1988.

**4870.** Sorenson, Theodore C. *Kennedy.* New York: Harper and Row, 1965.

**4871.** Sorenson, Theodore C. *The Kennedy Legacy.* New York: Macmillan, 1969.

**4872.** ———. *175 Little-Known Facts about JFK.* New York: Citadel Press, 1964.

**4873.** Stern, Mark. "John F. Kennedy and Civil Rights: From Congress to the Presidency." *Presidential Studies Quarterly* 19 (Fall 1989): 797–824.

**4874.** Stewart, Charles J., and Bruce Kendall, eds. *A Man Named John F.*

*Kennedy: Sermons on His Assassination.* Glen Rock, NJ: Paulist Press, 1964.

**4875.** Tregaskis, Richard W. *John F. Kennedy and PT–109.* New York: Random House, 1962.

**4876.** ———. *John F. Kennedy: War Hero.* New York: Dell, 1962.

**4877.** Turner, Russell. "Senator Kennedy: The Perfect Politician." *American Mercury* 84 (March 1957): 33–40.

**4878.** Van Gelder, Lawrence. *The Untold Story: Why the Kennedys Lost the Book Battle.* New York: Award Books, 1967.

**4879.** Webb, Robert N. *The Living JFK.* New York: Grossett and Dunlap, 1964.

**4880.** Whalen, Richard J. *The Founding Father: The Story of Joseph P. Kennedy and the Family He Raised to Power.* New York: New American Library, 1964.

**4881.** Whipple, Chandler. *Lt. John F. Kennedy—Expendable!* New York: Universal, 1962.

**4882.** White, Theodore H. *The Making of the President, 1960.* New York: Atheneum, 1988.

**4883.** White, William S. "John F. Kennedy." In his *The Responsibles,* 163–214. New York: Harper and Row, 1972.

**4884.** Wicker, Tom. *JFK and LBJ: The Influence of Personality Upon Politics.* New York: Morrow, 1968.

**4885.** ———. *Kennedy, without Tears: The Man beneath the Myth.* New York: Morrow, 1964.

**4886.** Wofford, Harris. *Of Kennedys and Kings: Making Sense of the Sixties.* New York: Farrar, Straus and Giroux, 1980.

**4887.** Wolin, Howard E. "Grandiosity and Violence in the Kennedy Family." *Psychohistory Review* 8 (Winter 1979): 27–37.

**KENNEDY, JOHN PENDLETON**
**(1795–1870) W-MD, House 1838–1839, 1841–1845.**

**4888.** Bohner, Charles H. *John Pendleton Kennedy, Gentleman from Baltimore.* Baltimore, MD: Johns Hopkins University, 1961.

**4889.** Button, Roland C., ed. "John Pendleton Kennedy and the Civil War: An Uncollected Letter." *Journal of Southern History* 29 (August 1963): 373–376.

**4890.** Gwathmey, Edward M. *John Pendleton Kennedy.* New York: Nelson, 1931.

**4891.** Hubbell, Jay B. "John Pendleton Kennedy." In his *South in American Literature, 1607–1900,* 481–495. Durham, NC: Duke University Press, 1954.

**4892.** Parrington, Vernon L. "John Pendleton Kennedy, a Southern Whig." In his *Main Currents in American Thought,* vol. 2, 46–56. New York: Harcourt, Brace, 1927.

**4893.** Ridgely, Joseph V. *John Pendleton Kennedy.* New York: Twayne, 1966.

**4894.** ———, comp. "John Pendleton Kennedy 1795–1870." In *Bibliographical Guide to the Study of Southern Literature,* edited by Louis D. Rubin, 233–234. Baton Rouge: Louisiana State University Press, 1969.

**4895.** Ringe, Donald A. "Kennedy, John Pendleton." In *American Literature to 1900,* 210–211. New York: St. Martin's Press, 1980.

**4896.** Spelman, Georgia P. "The Whig Rhetoric of John Pendleton Kennedy." Ph.D. dissertation, Indiana University, 1974.

**4897.** Terrell, A. W. "John Pendleton Kennedy." In *Library of Southern Literature,* edited by Edwin A. Alderman and Joel C. Harris, vol. 7, 2987–2991. New Orleans: Martin and Hoyt, 1909.

**4898.** Tuckerman, Henry T. *The Life of John Pendleton Kennedy.* New York: Putnam's, 1871.

**KENNEDY, ROBERT FRANCIS**
**(1925–1968) D-NY, Senate 1965–1968.**

**4899.** Adler, Bill, ed. *Dear Senator Kennedy.* New York: Dodd, Mead, 1966.

**4900.** ———, ed. *New Day: Robert F. Kennedy.* New York: New American Library, 1968.

**4901.** Altschuler, Bruce E. "Kennedy Decides to Run: 1968." *Presidential Studies Quarterly* 10 (Summer 1980): 348–352.

**4902.** Bickers, William P. "Robert Kennedy and the American Press." Ph.D. dissertation, Ball State University, 1984.

**4903.** Brown, Stuart G. *Presidency on Trial: Robert Kennedy's 1968 Campaign and Afterwards.* Honolulu: University Press of Hawaii, 1972.

**4904.** Burner, David, and Thomas R. West. *The Torch Is Passed: The Kennedy Brothers and American Liberalism.* New York: Atheneum, 1984.

**4905.** Cassiday, Bruce, and Bill Adler. *RFK: A Special Kind of Man.* Chicago: Playboy Press, 1977.

**4906.** David, Lester, and Irene David. *Bobby Kennedy: The Making of a Folk Hero.* New York: Dodd, Mead, 1986.

**4907.** De Toledano, Ralph. *RFK: Man Who Would Be President.* New York: Putnam's, 1967.

**4908.** Fairlie, Henry. *Kennedy Promise: The Politics of Expectation.* Garden City, NY: Doubleday, 1973.

**4909.** Galloway, John. "Robert Francis Kennedy." In his *The Kennedys and Vietnam,* 53–127. New York: Facts on File, 1971.

**4910.** Gardner, Gerald C. *Robert Kennedy in New York.* New York: Random House, 1965.

**4911.** Gordon, Gary. *Robert F. Kennedy, Assistant President: The Dramatic Life Story of the Second Most Powerful Man in Washington.* Derby, CT: Monarch Books, 1962.

**4912.** Guthman, Edwin. *We, Band of Brothers.* New York: Harper and Row, 1971.

**4913.** Halberstam, David. *Unfinished Odyssey of Robert Kennedy.* New York: Random House, 1968.

**4914.** Houghton, Robert A. *Special Unit Senator: The Investigation of the Assassination of Senator Robert F. Kennedy.* New York: Random House, 1970.

**4915.** Jansen, Godfrey. *Why Robert Kennedy Was Killed: The Story of Two Victims.* Stamford, CT: Third Press, 1970.

**4916.** Jenkins, Roy. "Robert Kennedy." In his *Nine Men of Power,* 207–223. London: Hamilton, 1974.

**4917.** Kaiser, Robert B. *RFK Must Die! A History of the Robert Kennedy Assassination and Its Aftermath.* New York: Dutton, 1970.

**4918.** Kennedy, Robert F. *Bobby Kennedy Off-Guard.* New York: Grosset, 1968.

**4919.** ———. *The Quotable Robert F. Kennedy.* Anderson, SC: Droke House, 1967.

**4920.** ———. *Robert F. Kennedy Wit.* New York: Berkley, 1968.

**4921.** Kimball, Penn. *Bobby Kennedy and the New Politics.* Englewood Cliffs, NJ: Prentice-Hall, 1968.

**4922.** Kimbrough, Jack, comp. *Killing of Robert Kennedy.* Los Angeles: Privately printed, 1972.

**4923.** Klagsbrun, Francine, and David C. Whitney, eds. *Assassination: Robert F. Kennedy, 1925–1968.* New York: Cowles, 1968.

**4924.** Koch, Thilo. *Fighters for a New World: John F. Kennedy, Martin Luther King, Robert F. Kennedy.* New York: Putnam's, 1969.

**4925.** Laing, Margaret. *The Next Kennedy.* New York: Coward-McCann, 1968.

**4926.** ———. *Robert Kennedy.* London: Macdonald, 1968.

**4927.** Lasky, Victor. *Robert F. Kennedy: The Myth and the Man.* New York: Trident, 1968.

**4928.** Lee, Ronald E. "The Rhetoric of the New Politics: A Case Study of Robert F. Kennedy's 1968 Presidential Primary Campaign." Ph.D. dissertation, University of Iowa, 1981.

**4929.** Marvin, Susan. *Women around RFK.* New York: Lancer Books, 1967.

**4930.** Moldea, Dan E. *The Killing of Robert Kennedy: An Investigation of Motive, Means, and Opportunity.* New York: Norton, 1995.

**4931.** Murphy, John M. "Renewing the National Covenant: The Presidential Campaign Rhetoric of Robert F. Kennedy." Ph.D. dissertation, University of Kansas, 1986.

**4932.** Navasky, Victor S. *Kennedy Justice.* New York: Atheneum, 1971.

**4933.** Newfield, Jack. *Robert Kennedy: A Memoir.* New York: Dutton, 1969.

**4934.** Nicholas, William. *The Bobby Kennedy Nobody Knows.* New York: Fawcett, 1967.

**4935.** Nixon, Diane S. "Providing Access to Controversial Public Records: The Case of Robert Kennedy Assassination Investigation Files." *Public Historian* 11 (Summer 1989): 28–44.

**4936.** Noyes, Peter. *Legacy of Doubt.* Los Angeles: Pinnacle Books, 1973.

**4937.** Quirk, Lawrence J. *Robert Francis Kennedy: The Man and the Politician.* Los Angeles: Holloway House, 1968.

**4938.** Roberts, Allen. *Robert Francis Kennedy: Biography of a Compulsive Politician.* Brookline Village, MA: Branden Press, 1984.

**4939.** Rogers, Warren. *When I Think of Bobby: A Personal Memoir of the Kennedy Years.* New York: HarperCollins, 1993.

**4940.** Ross, Douglas. *Robert F. Kennedy: Apostle of Change: A Review of His Public Record.* New York: Simon and Schuster, 1968.

**4941.** Salinger, Pierre, ed. *Honorable Profession: A Tribute to Robert F. Kennedy.* Garden City, NY: Doubleday, 1968.

**4942.** Schaap, Dick. *RFK.* New York: New American Library, 1967.

**4943.** Schlesinger, Arthur M., Jr. *Robert Kennedy and His Times.* 2 vols. Boston: Houghton Mifflin, 1978.

**4944.** Shannon, William V. *Heir Apparent: Robert Kennedy and the Struggle for Power.* New York: Macmillan, 1967.

**4945.** Sorenson, Theodore C. *Kennedy Legacy.* New York: Macmillan, 1969.

**4946.** Stein, Jean. *American Journey: The Times of Robert Kennedy: Interviews.* New York: Harcourt, 1970.

**4947.** Steinbacher, John A. *Robert Francis Kennedy, the Man, the Mysticism, the Murder.* San Luis Obispo, CA: Impact, 1968.

**4948.** Swinburne, Laurence. *RFK, the Last Knight.* New York: Pyramid Books, 1969.

**4949.** Thimmesch, Nick, and William O. Johnson. *Robert Kennedy at 40.* New York: Norton, 1965.

**4950.** Thompson, Robert E., and Hortense Myers. *Robert F. Kennedy: The Brother Within.* New York: Macmillan, 1962.

**4951.** Turner, William W., and John G. Christian. *Assassination of Robert F. Kennedy: A Searching Look at the Conspiracy and Cover-Up, 1968–1978.* New York: Random House, 1978.

**4952.** Vanden Heuvel, William J. *On His Own: Robert F. Kennedy, 1964–1968.* Garden City, NY: Doubleday, 1970.

**4953.** Viorst, Milton. "Robert F. Kennedy: Good Night, Sweet Prince." In his *Hustlers and Heroes,* 221–239. New York: Simon and Schuster, 1971.

**4954.** Webb, Robert N. "Robert Francis Kennedy." In his *Leaders of Our Time,* 32–41. New York: Watts, 1966.

**4955.** White, Theodore H. "Robert F. Kennedy: Requiescat in Pacem." In his *Making of the President, 1968,* 150–187. New York: Atheneum, 1969.

**4956.** Witcover, Jules. *85 Days: The Last Campaign of Robert Kennedy.* New York: Putnam's, 1969.

**4957.** Wofford, Harris. *Of Kennedys and Kings: Making Sense of the Sixties.* New York: Farrar, Straus, and Giroux, 1980.

**4958.** Zeiger, Henry A. *Robert F. Kennedy: A Biography.* New York: Meredith Press, 1968.

**KENT, WILLIAM (1864–1928) I-CA, House 1911–1917.**

**4959.** Nash, Roderick. "John Muir, William Kent, and the Conservative Schism." *Pacific Historical Review* 36 (November 1967): 423–433.

**4960.** Woodbury, Robert L. "William Kent: Progressive Gadfly, 1864–1928." Ph.D. dissertation, Yale University, 1967.

**KENYON, WILLIAM SQUIRE (1869–1933) R-IA, Senate 1911–1922.**

**4961.** Margulies, Herbert F. "The Moderates in the League of Nations Battle: The Case of William S. Kenyon." *Midwest Review* 12 (1990): 16–33.

**4962.** Potts, E. Daniel. "William Squire Kenyon and the Iowa Senatorial Election of 1911." *Annals of Iowa* 38 (Fall 1966): 206–222.

**KERN, JOHN WORTH (1849–1917) D-IN, Senate 1911–1917.**

**4963.** Bowers, Claude G. *The Life of John Worth Kern.* Indianapolis: Hollenbeck Press, 1918.

**4964.** Haughton, Virginia F. "John W. Kern: Senate Majority Leader and Labor Legislation, 1913–1917." *Mid-America* 57 (July 1975): 184–194.

**4965.** ———. "John Worth Kern and Wilson's New Freedom: A Study of a Senate Majority Leader." Ph.D. dissertation, University of Kentucky, 1973.

**4966.** Oleszek, Walter J. "John Worth Kern: Portrait of a Floor Leader." In *First Among Equals: Outstanding Senate Leaders of the Twentieth Century,* edited by Richard A. Baker and Roger H. Davidson, 7–37. Washington, DC: Congressional Quarterly, 1991.

**4967.** Roberts, George C. "Woodrow Wilson, John W. Kern and the 1916 Indiana Election: Defeat of a Senate Majority Leader." *Presidential Studies Quarterly* 10 (Winter 1980): 63–73.

**KERNAN, FRANCIS (1816–1892) D-NY, House 1863–1865, Senate 1875–1881.**

**4968.** Schauinger, Joseph H. "Francis Kernan." In his *Profiles in Action: American Catholics in Public Life,* 155–164. Milwaukee, WI: Bruce, 1966.

**KERR, ROBERT SAMUEL (1896–1963) D-OK, Senate 1949–1963.**

**4969.** Cox, Joe D. "Senator Robert S. Kerr and the Arkansas River Navigation Project: A Study in Legislative Leadership." Ph.D. dissertation, University of Oklahoma, 1972.

**4970.** English, William B. "Robert S. Kerr: A Study in Ethos." Ph.D. dissertation, University of Oklahoma, 1966.

**4971.** Fuller, Hubert B. "Kerr, Randall, Keifer, and Carlisle." In his *The Speakers of* *the House*, 193–213. Boston: Little, Brown, 1909.

**4972.** Grant, Philip A., Jr. "A Tradition of Political Power: Congressional Committee Chairmen from Oklahoma, 1945–1972." *Chronicles of Oklahoma* 60 (Winter 1982/1983): 438–447.

**4973.** Horn, Gary C. "The Modes of Proof in Selected Speeches of Governor Robert S. Kerr, 1943–1947." Master's thesis, Kansas State College of Pittsburg, 1968.

**4974.** Kerr, Robert S. *Land, Wood, and Water.* Edited by Malvina Stephenson and Tris Coffin. New York: Fleet Publishing, 1960.

**4975.** Morgan, Anne H. *Robert S. Kerr: The Senate Years.* Norman: University of Oklahoma Press, 1977.

**4976.** Nabors, John H. "Robert S. Kerr, Baptist Layman: A Study of the Impact of Religion on the Life of an Oklahoma Leader." Master's thesis, University of Oklahoma, 1964.

**4977.** Reynolds, Thomas L. "Senator Robert S. Kerr and the Arkansas Navigation Project." Master's thesis, Oklahoma State University, 1964.

**4978.** Seligman, Daniel. "Senator Bob Kerr, the Oklahoma Gusher." *Fortune* 59 (March 1959): 136–138, 179–188.

**4979.** Sullivan, Otis. "Robert S. Kerr." In *Public Men In and Out of Office*, edited by John T. Salter, 415–427. Chapel Hill: University of North Carolina Press, 1946.

**4980.** Thorpe, Claude R. "Robert S. Kerr's 1948 Senatorial Campaign." Master's thesis, University of Oklahoma, 1967.

**KERREY, ROBERT** (1943– ) D-NE, Senate 1989– .

**4981.** Harper, Ivy. *Waltzing Matilda: The Life and Times of Nebraska Senator Robert Kerrey.* New York: St. Martin's Press, 1992.

**KERSTEN, CHARLES JOSEPH** (1902–1972) R-WI, House 1947–1949, 1951–1955.

**4982.** Mayer, James A. "Gentleman from Milwaukee." *American Mercury* 77 (November 1953): 93–95.

**KETTNER, WILLIAM** (1864–1930) D-CA, House 1913–1921.

**4983.** Duvall, Lucille C. "William Kettner: San Diego's Dynamic Congressman." *Journal of San Diego History* 25 (Summer 1979): 191–207.

**4984.** Jensen, Joan M. "The Politics and History of William Kettner." *Journal of San Diego History* 11 (June 1965): 26–36.

**KEY, DAVID MCKENDREE** (1824–1900) D-TN, Senate 1875–1877.

**4985.** Abshire, David M. *The South Rejects a Prophet: The Life of Senator D. M. Key, 1824–1900.* New York: Praeger, 1967.

**KEY, PHILIP BARTON** (1757–1815) F-MD, House 1807–1813.

**4986.** Sparrow, Gerald. "Winter in Washington." In his *Great Assassins*, 98–106. New York: Arco, 1969.

**KILBOURNE, JAMES** (1770–1850) R-OH, House 1813–1817.

**4987.** Berquist, Goodwin F. *The New Eden: James Kilbourne and the Development of Ohio.* Lanham, MD: University Press of America, 1983.

**KILGORE, HARLEY MARTIN** (1893–1956) D-WV, Senate 1941–1956.

**4988.** Maddox, Robert F. "The Politics of World War II Science: Senator Harley M. Kilgore and the Legislative Origins of the National Science Foundation." *West Virginia History* 41 (Fall 1979): 20–39.

**4989.** Maddox, Robert F. *The Senatorial Career of Harley Martin Kilgore.* New York: Garland, 1981.

**KING, EDWARD JOHN (1867–1929) R-IL, House 1915–1929.**

**4990.** VanderMeer, Philip R. "Congressional Decision-Making and World War I: A Case Study of Illinois." *Congressional Studies* 8, no. 2 (1981): 59–79.

**KING, JAMES GORE (1791–1853) W-NJ, House 1849–1851.**

**4991.** Hunt, Freeman, ed. "James Gore King." In his *Lives of American Merchants*, vol. 1, 185–214. Cincinnati, OH: H. W. Derby, 1858.

**KING, PRESTON (1806–1865) R-NY, House 1843–1847, 1849–1853, Senate 1857–1863.**

**4992.** Muller, Ernest P. "Preston King: A Political Biography." Ph.D. dissertation, Columbia University, 1957.

**KING, RUFUS (1755–1827) F-NY, Senate 1789–1796, 1813–1825, Continental Congress 1784–1787.**

**4993.** Arbena, Joseph L. "Politics or Principle? Rufus King and the Opposition to Slavery, 1785–1825." *Essex Institute Historical Collections* 101 (January 1965): 56–77.

**4994.** Egerton, Cecil B. "Rufus King and the Missouri Question: A Study in Political Mythology." Ph.D. dissertation, Claremont Graduate School, 1968.

**4995.** Ernst, Robert. *Rufus King: American Federalist.* Chapel Hill: University of North Carolina Press, 1968.

**4996.** King, Charles R., ed. *Life and Correspondence of Rufus King: Comprising His Letters, Private and Official, His Public Documents, and His Speeches.* 6 vols. New York: Putnam's, 1894–1900.

**4997.** Reeser, Robert E. "Rufus King and the Federalist Party." Ph.D. dissertation, University of California, 1948.

**4998.** Willson, Beckles. "Rufus King (1796–1802)." In his *America's Ambassadors to England (1785–1928)*, 58–76. London: Murray, 1928.

**KING, THOMAS BUTLER (1800–1864) W-GA, House 1839–1843, 1845–1850.**

**4999.** Steel, Edward M. *Butler King of Georgia.* Athens: University of Georgia Press, 1964.

**5000.** Wheeler, Henry G. "King, Thomas Butler." In his *History of Congress*, vol. 2, 9–63. New York: Harper, 1848.

**KING, WILLIAM HENRY (1863–1949) D-UT, House 1897–1899, 1900–1901, Senate 1917–1941.**

**5001.** Hauptman, Lawrence M. "Utah Anti-imperialist: Senator William H. King and Haiti, 1921–34." *Utah Historical Quarterly* 41 (Spring 1973): 116–127.

**5002.** Libby, Justin H. "Senators King and Thomas and the Coming War with Japan." *Utah Historical Quarterly* 42 (Fall 1974): 370–380.

**KING, WILLIAM RUFUS deVANE (1786–1853) D-NC/AL, House (NC) 1811–1816, Senate (AL) 1819–1844, 1848–1852.**

**5003.** Barzman, Sol. "William Rufus deVane King." In his *Madmen and Geniuses: The Vice-Presidents of the United States*, 91–95. Chicago: Follett, 1974.

**5004.** Martin, John M. "William R. King: Jacksonian Senator." *Alabama Review* 18 (October 1965): 243–267.

**5005.** ———. "William Rufus King: Southern Moderate." Ph.D. dissertation, University of North Carolina, 1956.

**5006.** Willson, Beckles. "Cass and King (1836–46)." In his *America's Ambassadors to France (1777–1927)*, 207–216. New York: Frederick A. Stokes, 1928.

**KIRBY, WILLIAM FOSGATE** (1867–1934) D-AR, Senate 1916–1921.

**5007.** Niswonger, Richard L. "William F. Kirby, Arkansas's Maverick Senator." *Arkansas Historical Quarterly* 37 (Autumn 1978): 252–263.

**KIRKWOOD, SAMUEL JORDAN** (1813–1894) R-IA, Senate 1866–1867, 1877–1881.

**5008.** Clark, Dan E. *Samuel Jordan Kirkwood*. Iowa City: State Historical Society of Iowa, 1917.

**5009.** Hake, Herbert V. "The Political Firecracker: Samuel J. Kirkwood." *Palimpsest* 56 (January/February 1975): 2–14.

**5010.** Swisher, Jacob A. "Samuel J. Kirkwood." In his *Governors of Iowa*, 39–42. Mason City, IA: Klipto Loose Leaf Company, 1946.

**KITCHIN, CLAUDE** (1869–1923) D-NC, House 1901–1923.

**5011.** Arnett, Alex M. *Claude Kitchin and the Wilson War Policies*. Boston: Little, Brown, 1937.

**5012.** Ingle, Homer L. "Pilgrimage to Reform: A Life of Claude Kitchin." Ph.D. dissertation, University of Wisconsin, 1967.

**KITCHIN, WILLIAM HODGES** (1837–1901) D-NC, House 1879–1881.

**5013.** Ingle, Homer L. "A Southern Democrat at Large: William Hodges Kitchin and the Populist Party." *North Carolina Historical Review* 45 (April 1968): 178–194.

**KITTREDGE, ALFRED BEARD** (1861–1911) R-SD, Senate 1901–1909.

**5014.** Coursey, Oscar W. *Biography of Senator Alfred Beard Kittredge, His Complete Life Work*. Mitchell, SD: Educator Supply Company, 1915.

**5015.** Roberts, Thomas B. "Senator A. B. Kittredge: A Sketch of His Private Life and of His Public Service." *South Dakota Historical Collections* 6 (1912): 49–62.

**KNIGHT, CHARLES LANDON** (1867–1933) R-OH, House 1921–1923.

**5016.** Stewart, Kenneth N., and John W. Tebbel. "Out of Ohio: Knight and Cox." In their *Makers of Modern Journalism*, 295–309. Englewood Cliffs, NJ: Prentice-Hall, 1952.

**KNOTT, JAMES PROCTOR** (1830–1911) D-KY, House 1867–1871, 1875–1883.

**5017.** Crocker, Helen B. "Proctor Knott's Education in Missouri Politics, 1850–1862." *Missouri Historical Society Bulletin* 30 (January 1974): 101–116.

**5018.** Mills, Edwin W. "The Career of James Proctor Knott in Missouri." *Missouri Historical Review* 31 (April 1937): 288–294.

**5019.** Tapp, Hambleton, comp. "James Proctor Knott and the Duluth Speech." *Kentucky Historical Society Register* 70 (April 1972): 177–193.

**KNOWLAND, JOSEPH RUSSELL** (1873–1966) R-CA, House 1904–1915.

**5020.** Gothberg, John A. "The Local Influence of J. R. Knowland's Oakland Tribune." *Journalism Quarterly* 45 (Autumn 1968): 487–495.

**KNOX, PHILANDER CHASE** (1853–1921) R-PA, Senate 1904–1909, 1917–1921.

**5021.** Dodds, Archie J. "The Public Services of Philander Chase Knox." Ph.D. dissertation, University of Pittsburgh, 1950.

**5022.** Mulhollan, Paige E. "Philander C. Knox and Dollar Diplomacy, 1909–1913." Ph.D. dissertation, University of Texas, 1966.

**5023.** Scholes, Walter V. "Philander C. Knox." In *Uncertain Tradition: American Secretaries of State in the Twentieth Century,* edited by Norman A. Graebner, 59–78. New York: McGraw, 1961.

**5024.** Villard, Oswald G. "Philander C. Knox: Dollar Diplomat." In his *Prophets True and False,* 247–257. New York: Knopf, 1928.

**5025.** Wright, Herbert F. "Philander Chase Knox. . . ." In his *The American Secretaries of State and Their Diplomacy,* edited by Samuel F. Bemis, vol. 9, 301–357. New York: Knopf, 1929.

**KNUTSON, COYA GJESDAL** (1912– )
**DFL-MN, House 1955–1959.**

**5026.** Beito, Gretchen U. *Coya Come Home: A Congresswoman's Journey.* Los Angeles: Pomegranate Press, 1990.

**5027.** Fraser, Arvonne S., and Sue E. Holbert. "Women in the Minnesota Legislature." In *Women of Minnesota,* edited by Barbara Stuhler and Gretchen Kreuter, 265–267. St. Paul: Minnesota Historical Society Press, 1977.

**KNUTSON, HAROLD** (1880–1953) R-MN, **House 1917–1949.**

**5028.** Stuhler, Barbara. "Harold Knutson and His Constituents: A Trusted Alliance." In her *Ten Men of Minnesota and American Foreign Policy, 1898–1968,* 54–75. St. Paul: Minnesota Historical Society, 1973.

**KOCH, EDWARD IRVING** (1924– )
**D/L-NY, House 1969–1977.**

**5029.** Browne, Arthur, Dan Collins, and Michael Goodwin. *I, Koch: A Decidedly Unauthorized Biography of the Mayor of New York City, Edward I. Koch.* New York: Dodd, Mead, 1985.

**5030.** Koch, Edward I. *Mayor.* New York: Simon and Schuster, 1984.

**5031.** Koch, Edward I., and Daniel Paisner. *Citizen Koch.* New York: St. Martin's Press, 1992.

**5032.** Mollenkopf, John H. *A Phoenix in the Ashes: The Rise and Fall of the Koch Coalition in New York City Politics.* Princeton, NJ: Princeton University Press, 1992.

**5033.** Newfield, Jack. *City for Sale: Ed Koch and the Betrayal of New York.* New York: Harper and Row, 1988.

**5034.** O'Connor, John J. *His Eminence and Hizzoner: A Candid Exchange.* New York: Morrow, 1989.

**KOPP, WILLIAM FREDERICK**
**(1869–1938) R-IA, House 1921–1933.**

**5035.** Porter, David L. "Iowa Congressional Delegation and the Great Economic Issues, 1929–1933." *Annals of Iowa* 46 (Summer 1982): 337–354.

**KREMER, GEORGE** (1775–1854) PA, **House 1823–1829.**

**5036.** Russ, William A. "The Political Ideas of George Kremer." *Pennsylvania History* 7 (October 1940): 201–212.

**KYLE, JAMES HENDERSON** (1854–1901) **I-SD, Senate 1891–1901.**

**5037.** Quinion, Harold. "James H. Kyle, United States Senator from South Dakota, 1891–1901." *South Dakota Historical Collections* 13 (1926): 311–321.

ॐ

**LACEY, JOHN FLETCHER** (1841–1913) **R-IA, House 1889–1891, 1893–1907.**

**5038.** Gallagher, Mary A. "Citizen of the Nation: John Fletcher Lacey, Conservationist." *Annals of Iowa* 46 (Summer 1981): 9–24.

**5039.** ———. "John F. Lacey: A Study in Organizational Politics." Ph.D. dissertation, University of Arizona, 1970.

**LACOCK, ABNER (1770–1837) R-PA, House 1811–1813, Senate 1813–1819.**

**5040.** Houtz, Harry. "Abner Lacock, Beaver County's Exponent of the American System." *Western Pennsylvania Historical Magazine* 22 (September 1939): 177–187.

**LA FOLLETTE, ROBERT MARION (1855–1925) R-WI, House 1885–1891, Senate 1906–1925.**

**5041.** Alexander, Holmes M. "Robert Marion La Follette." In his *Famous Five,* 122–164. New York: Bookmailer, 1958.

**5042.** Allen, Philip L. "La Follette's Up-Hill Fight." In his *America's Awakening,* 59–89. New York: Revell, 1906.

**5043.** Bliven, Bruce. "Robert M. La Follette's Place in Our History." *Current History* 22 (August 1925): 716–722.

**5044.** Burdick, Walter E., Jr. "Robert M. La Follette: A Political Revolution in Wisconsin." Master's thesis, Southern Illinois University at Carbondale, 1964.

**5045.** Burgchardt, Carl R. *Robert M. La Follette, Sr.: The Voice of Conscience.* Westport, CT: Greenwood, 1992.

**5046.** Chamberlain, John. "The Progressive Mind in Action, La Follette." In his *Farewell to Reform,* 234–262, 272–274. New York: Liveright, 1932.

**5047.** Chandler, Madelynne K. "Robert M. La Follette and American Foreign Affairs." Master's thesis, Butler University, 1966.

**5048.** Clark, James I. *Robert M. La Follette and Wisconsin Progressivism.* Madison: State Historical Society of Wisconsin, 1956.

**5049.** Cooper, John M. "Robert M. La Follette: Political Prophet." *Wisconsin Magazine of History* 69 (Winter 1985/1986): 90–105.

**5050.** Doane, Edward N. *The La Follettes and the Wisconsin Idea.* New York: Rinehart, 1947.

**5051.** Greenbaum, Fred. *Robert Marion La Follette.* Boston: Twayne, 1975.

**5052.** Haynes, Frederick E. "The Pioneer Progressives: Bryan and La Follette." In his *Third Party Movements Since the Civil War,* 390–394. Iowa City: State Historical Society of Iowa, 1916.

**5053.** Hesseltine, William B. "Robert Marion La Follette and the Principles of Americanism." *Wisconsin Magazine of History* 31 (March 1948): 261–267.

**5054.** Hostettler, Gordon F. "Political Speaking of Robert M. La Follette." In *American Public Address,* edited by Loren Reid, 111–131. Columbia: University of Missouri Press, 1961.

**5055.** Kent, Alan E. "Portrait in Isolationism: The La Follettes and Foreign Policy." Ph.D. dissertation, University of Wisconsin, 1956.

**5056.** La Follette, Bella C., and Fola La Follette. *Robert M. La Follette, 1855–1925.* 2 vols. New York: Macmillan, 1953.

**5057.** La Follette, Philip F. *Adventure in Politics: The Memoirs of Philip La Follette.* Edited by Donald Young. New York: Holt, Rinehart and Winston, 1970.

**5058.** La Follette, Robert M. *Autobiography: A Personal Narrative of Political Experiences.* Madison: University of Wisconsin Press, 1960.

**5059.** Lahman, Carrol P. "Robert Marion La Follette as Public Speaker and Political Leader, 1855–1905." Ph.D. dissertation, University of Wisconsin, 1940.

**5060.** Lovejoy, Allen F. *La Follette and the Establishment of the Direct Primary in Wisconsin, 1800–1904.* New Haven, CT: Yale University Press, 1941.

**5061.** Madison, Charles A. "Robert M. La Follette: The Radical in Politics." In *American Radicals,* edited by Harvey Goldberg, 91–110. New York: Monthly Review, 1957.

**5062.** Madison, Charles A. "Robert M. La Follette: Uncompromising Progressive." In his *Leaders and Liberals in 20th Century America,* 135–172. New York: Ungar, 1961.

**5063.** Margulies, Herbert F. "La Follette, Roosevelt and the Republican Presidential Nomination of 1912." *Mid-America* 58 (January 1976): 54–76.

**5064.** ———. "Robert La Follette Goes to the Senate, 1905." *Wisconsin Magazine of History* 59 (Spring 1976): 214–225.

**5065.** Maxwell, Robert S. *La Follette and the Rise of Progressivism in Wisconsin.* Madison: State Historical Society of Wisconsin, 1956.

**5066.** ———, ed. *Great Lives Observed: La Follette.* Englewood Cliffs, NJ: Prentice-Hall, 1969.

**5067.** Rowell, Chester H. "La Follette, Shipstead, and the Embattled Farmers." *World's Work* 46 (August 1923): 408–420.

**5068.** Sanford, Harold E. "The Political Liberalism of Robert Marion La Follette." Ph.D. dissertation, Boston College, 1938.

**5069.** Sutton, Walter A. "Bryan, La Follette, Norris: Three Mid-Western Politicians." *Journal of the West* 8 (October 1969): 613–630.

**5070.** Thelen, David P. *The Early Life of Robert M. La Follette, 1855–1884.* Chicago: Loyola University Press, 1966.

**5071.** ———. *Robert M. La Follette and the Insurgent Spirit.* Boston: Little, Brown, 1976.

**5072.** Torelle, Ellen, comp. *The Political Philosophy of Robert M. La Follette.* Madison, WI: Robert M. La Follette Company, 1920.

**5073.** Twombley, Robert C. "The Reformer as Politician: Robert M. La Follette in the Election of 1900." Master's thesis, University of Wisconsin, 1964.

**5074.** Unger, Nancy C. "The Righteous Reformer: A Life History of Robert M. La Follette, Sr., 1855–1925." Ph.D. disserta-tion, University of Southern California, 1985.

**5075.** Villard, Oswald G. "Robert M. La Follette: A Great American." In his *Prophets True and False,* 187–201. New York: Knopf, 1928.

**5076.** Weisberger, Bernard A. *The La Follettes of Wisconsin: Love and Politics in Progressive America.* Madison: University of Wisconsin Press, 1994.

## LA FOLLETTE, ROBERT MARION, JR.
### (1895–1953) PROG-WI, Senate 1925–1935.

**5077.** Auerbach, Jerold. *Labor and Liberty: The La Follette Committee and the New Deal.* Indianapolis: Bobbs-Merrill, 1960.

**5078.** Doane, Edward N. *The La Follettes and the Wisconsin Idea.* New York: Rinehart, 1947.

**5079.** Johnson, Roger T. *Robert M. La Follette, Jr. and the Decline of the Progressive Party in Wisconsin.* Madison: State Historical Society of Wisconsin, 1964.

**5080.** Kent, Alan E. "Portrait in Isolationism: The La Follettes and Foreign Policy." Ph.D. dissertation, University of Wisconsin, 1956.

**5081.** Madison, Charles A. "Robert M. La Follette: Uncompromising Progressive." In his *Leaders and Liberals in 20th Century America,* 135–172. New York: Frederick Ungar Publishing Co., 1961.

**5082.** Maney, Patrick J. *"Young Bob" La Follette: A Biography of Robert M. La Follette, Jr., 1895–1953.* Columbia: University of Missouri Press, 1978.

**5083.** Rosenof, Theodore. "The Ideology of Senator Robert M. La Follette, Jr." Master's thesis, University of Wisconsin, 1966.

**5084.** ———. "Young Bob La Follette on American Capitalism." *Wisconsin Magazine of History* 55 (Winter 1971/1972): 130–139.

**5085.** Sayre, William S. "Robert M. La Follette, a Study in Political Methods." Ph.D. dissertation, New York University, 1930.

## LA GUARDIA, FIORELLO HENRY
**(1882–1947) R-NY, House 1917–1919, 1923–1933.**

**5086.** Bayor, Ronald H. *Fiorello H. La Guardia: Ethnicity and Reform.* Arlington Heights, IL: Harlan Davidson, 1993.

**5087.** Capeci, Dominic J. "Fiorello H. La Guardia and the American Dream: A Document." *Italian Americana* 4 (Fall/Winter 1978): 1–21.

**5088.** ———. "Fiorello H. La Guardia and the Harlem Crime Wave of 1941." *New York Historical Society Quarterly* 64 (January 1980): 7–29.

**5089.** ———. "From Different Liberal Perspectives: Fiorello H. La Guardia, Adam Clayton Powell, Jr., and Civil Rights in New York City, 1941–1943." *Journal of Negro History* 62 (April 1977): 160–173.

**5090.** ———. *The Harlem Riot of 1943.* Philadelphia: Temple University Press, 1977.

**5091.** Cuneo, Ernest. "I Remember Fiorello." In *Fabulous Yesterday,* edited by Lewis W. Gillenson, 212–214. New York: Harper and Row, 1961.

**5092.** ———. "Life with Fiorello." In *Thirties,* edited by Don Congdon, 179–201. New York: Simon and Schuster, 1962.

**5093.** ———. *Life with Fiorello: A Memoir.* New York: Macmillan, 1955.

**5094.** Cusella, Louis P. "Biography as Rhetorical Artifact: The Affirmation of Fiorello H. La Guardia." *Quarterly Journal of Speech* 69 (August 1983): 302–316.

**5095.** Elliot, Lawrence. *Little Flower: The Life and Times of Fiorello La Guardia.* New York: Morrow, 1983.

**5096.** Esposito, David M., and Jackie R. Esposito. "La Guardia and the Nazis, 1933–1938." *American Jewish History* 78 (September 1988): 38–53.

**5097.** Garrett, Charles. *La Guardia Years: Machine and Reform Politics in New York City.* New Brunswick, NJ: Rutgers University Press, 1961.

**5098.** Hargrove, Edwin C., Jr. "The Tragic Hero in Politics: Theodore Roosevelt, David Lloyd, and Fiorello La Guardia." Ph.D. dissertation, Yale University, 1963.

**5099.** Heckscher, August, and Phyllis Robinson. *When La Guardia Was Mayor: New York's Legendary Years.* New York: Norton, 1978.

**5100.** Kamen, Gloria. *Fiorello: His Honor, the Little Flower.* New York: Atheneum, 1981.

**5101.** Kaufman, Herbert. "Fiorello H. La Guardia, Political Maverick: A Review Essay." *Political Science Quarterly* 105 (Spring 1990): 113–122.

**5102.** Kessner, Thomas. *Fiorello H. La Guardia: And the Making of Modern New York.* New York: McGraw-Hill, 1989.

**5103.** La Guardia, Fiorello H. *The Making of an Insurgent.* Philadelphia: Lippincott, 1948.

**5104.** Limpus, Lowell M., and Burr N. Leyson. *This Man La Guardia.* New York: Dutton, 1938.

**5105.** Mann, Arthur. *La Guardia: A Fighter against His Times, 1882–1933.* Chicago: University of Chicago Press, 1969.

**5106.** ———. *La Guardia Comes to Power, 1933.* Chicago: University of Chicago Press, 1969.

**5107.** Manners, William. *Patience and Fortitude: Fiorello La Guardia: A Biography.* New York: Harcourt Brace Jovanovich, 1976.

**5108.** Moses, Robert. *La Guardia: A Salute and a Memoir.* New York: Simon and Schuster, 1957.

**5109.** Rodman, Bella, and Philip Sterling. *Fiorello La Guardia.* New York: Hill and Wang, 1962.

**5110.** Tugwell, Rexford G. *The Art of Politics as Practiced by Three Great Americans: Franklin Delano Roosevelt, Luis Munoz Marin, and Fiorello La Guardia.* Garden City, NY: Doubleday, 1958.

**5111.** Weston, Paul B. *Hammer in the City.* Port Washington, NY: Regency, 1962.

**5112.** Zinn, Howard. *La Guardia in Congress.* New York: Norton, 1969.

## LAIRD, MELVIN ROBERT (1922– )
R-WI, House 1953–1969.

**5113.** Kinnard, Douglas. "Laird Winds Down the War." In his *Secretary of Defense,* 113–152. Lexington: University of Kentucky Press, 1980.

## LAMAR, LUCIUS QUINTUS CINCINNATUS (1825–1893) D-MS, House 1857–1860, 1873–1877, Senate 1877–1885.

**5114.** Burger, Nash K., and John K. Bettersworth. "Artificer of Reconciliation." In *Mississippi Heroes,* edited by Dean F. Wells and Hunter Cole, 106–142. Jackson: University Press of Mississippi, 1980.

**5115.** ———. "Artificer of Reconciliation: L. Q. C. Lamar." In their *South of Appomattox,* 173–207. New York: Harcourt, 1959.

**5116.** Cate, Wirt A. *Lamar and the Frontier Hypothesis.* Baton Rouge, LA: Franklin Press, 1935.

**5117.** ———. "Lamar and the Frontier Hypothesis." *Journal of Southern History* 1 (November 1935): 497–501.

**5118.** ———. *Lucius Q. C. Lamar: Secession and Reunion, 1825–1893.* Chapel Hill: University of North Carolina, 1935.

**5119.** Galloway, Charles B. "Lucius Q. C. Lamar." In *Library of Southern Literature,* edited by Edwin A. Alderman and Joel C. Harris, vol. 7, 2963–2968. New Orleans, LA: Martin and Hoyt, 1909.

**5120.** Gilbert, S. Price. "The Lamars of Georgia: L. Q. C., Mirabeau B., and Joseph R. Lamar." *American Bar Association Journal* 34 (December 1948): 1100–1102, 1156–1158.

**5121.** Halsell, Willie D. "Appointment of L. Q. C. Lamar to the Supreme Court: A Political Battle of Cleveland's Administration." *Mississippi Valley Historical Review* 28 (December 1941): 399–412.

**5122.** ———. "The Friendship of L. Q. C. Lamar and Jefferson Davis." *Journal of Mississippi History* 6 (July 1944): 131–144.

**5123.** ———. "L. Q. C. Lamar, Associate Justice of the Supreme Court." *Journal of Mississippi History* 5 (April 1943): 59–78.

**5124.** ———. "L. Q. C. Lamar's Taylor Farm: An Experiment in Diversified Farming." *Journal of Mississippi History* 5 (January 1943): 185–196.

**5125.** ———. "A Mississippi 'Habeas Corpus' Case and Justice L. Q. C. Lamar." *Journal of Mississippi History* 4 (January 1942): 31–33.

**5126.** Hamilton, Joseph G. "Lamar of Mississippi." *Virginia Quarterly Review* 8 (January 1932): 77–89.

**5127.** Hill, Walter B. "L. Q. C. Lamar." *Green Bag* 5 (April 1893): 153–165.

**5128.** ———. "Sketch of Mr. Justice L. Q. C. Lamar." *Georgia Bar Association Report* 11 (1894): 149–169.

**5129.** Kennedy, John F. "'Today I Must Be True or False. . . ': Lucius Quintus Cincinnatus Lamar." In his *Profiles in Courage,* 152–177. New York: Harper and Row, 1956.

**5130.** Knight, Lucian L. "L. Q. C. Lamar, of Mississippi." In his *Reminiscences of Famous Georgians,* 176–193. Atlanta: Franklin-Turner, 1907.

**5131.** Mayes, Edward. *Lucius Q. C. Lamar: His Life, Times, and Speeches, 1825–1893.* Nashville, TN: Publishing House of the Methodist Episcopal Church, 1896.

**5132.** Meador, Daniel J. "Lamar and the Law at the University of Mississippi." *Mississippi Law Journal* 34 (May 1963): 227–256.

**5133.** Murphy, James B. *L. Q. C. Lamar: Pragmatic Patriot.* Baton Rouge: Louisiana State University Press, 1973.

**5134.** Reeves, Bennie L. "Lucius Quintus Cincinnatus Lamar: Reluctant Secessionist and Spokesman for the South, 1860–1885." Ph.D. dissertation, University of North Carolina, 1973.

**5135.** Sibley, Samuel H. *Georgia's Contribution to Law, the Lamars.* New York: Newcomen Society of England, 1948.

**5136.** Smith, Frank E., and Audrey Warren. "Lucius Q. C. Lamar." In their *Mississippians All,* 59–74. Gretna, LA: Pelican, 1968.

**5137.** Stone, James H. "L. Q. C. Lamar's Letters to Edward Donaldson Clark, 1868–1885, Part III." *Journal of Mississippi History* 43 (May 1981): 135–164.

**LANE, HARRY** (1855–1917) D-OR, Senate 1913–1917.

**5138.** Holbo, Paul S. "Senator Harry Lane: Independent Democrat in Peace and War." In *Experiences in a Promised Land,* edited by Thomas Edwards and Carlos Schwantes, 242–259. Seattle: University of Washington Press, 1986.

**LANE, HENRY SMITH** (1811–1881) R-IN, House 1840–1843, Senate 1861–1867.

**5139.** Barringer, Graham. "The Life and Letters of Henry S. Lane." Ph.D. dissertation, Indiana University, 1927.

**5140.** Gronert, Theodore G. "Senator Henry S. Lane." *Kentucky Historical Society Register* 35 (July 1937): 260–264.

**5141.** Sharp, Walter R. "Henry S. Lane and the Formation of the Republican Party in Indiana." *Mississippi Valley Historical Review* 7 (September 1920): 93–112.

**LANE, JAMES HENRY** (1814–1866) D-IN/R-KS, House (IN) 1853–1855, Senate (KS) 1861–1866.

**5142.** Bailes, Kendall E. *Rider on the Wind: Jim Lane and Kansas.* Shawnee Mission, KS: Wagon Wheel Press, 1962.

**5143.** Connelley, William E. *James Henry Lane, the "Grim Chieftain" of Kansas.* Topeka, KS: Crane, 1899.

**5144.** ———. "The Lane-Jenkins Claim Contest." *Kansas State Historical Society Collections* 16 (1925): 21–176.

**5145.** Lewis, Lloyd. "The Man Historians Forgot." In his *It Takes All Kinds,* 149–176. New York: Harcourt, 1947.

**5146.** ———. "The Man the Historians Forgot." *Kansas Historical Quarterly* 8 (February 1939): 85–103.

**5147.** Noble, Glenn. *John Brown and the Jim Lane Trail.* Broken Bow, NE: Purcells, 1977.

**5148.** Speer, John. *Life of Gen. James H. Lane, "The Liberator of Kansas," with Corroborative Incidents of Pioneer History.* Cargen City, KS: J. Speer, 1897.

**5149.** Stephenson, Wendell H. "The Political Career of General James H. Lane." Ph.D. dissertation, University of Michigan, 1928.

**LANE, JOSEPH** (1801–1881) D-OR, House 1851–1859, Senate 1859–1861.

**5150.** Brancett, Albert G. *General Lane's Brigade in Central Mexico.* Cincinnati, OH: H. W. Derby, 1854.

**5151.** Fowdy, Stephen B. "The Political Rise and Fall of Joseph Lane." Master's thesis, Indiana University, 1949.

**5152.** Hendrickson, James E. *Joe Lane of Oregon: Machine Politics and the Sectional Crisis of 1849–1861.* New Haven, CT: Yale University Press, 1967.

**5153.** Kelly, Margaret J. *The Career of Joseph Lane, Frontier Politician.* Washington, DC:

Catholic University of America Press, 1942.

**5154.** Rogers, Louisa K. *The Lanes, Cavaliers of the South.* Reno, NV: White, 1910.

**5155.** Turnbull, George S. "Joseph Lane." In his *Governors of Oregon,* 17–19. Portland, OR: Binfords, 1959.

**LANGDON, JOHN** (1741–1819) NH,
**Senate 1789–1801, Continental Congress 1775–1776, 1787.**

**5156.** Camden, Thomas E. "The Langdon-Elwyn Family Papers." *Historical New Hampshire* 36 (Winter 1981): 350–356.

**5157.** Cleary, B. A. "Governor John Langdon Mansion Memorial: New Perspectives in Interpretation." *Old-Time New England* 69 (Summer 1978): 22–36.

**5158.** Mayo, Lawrence S. *John Langdon of New Hampshire.* Concord, NH: Rumford Press, 1937.

**LANGER, WILLIAM** (1886–1959) R-ND,
**Senate 1941–1959.**

**5159.** Geelan, Agnes. *Dakota Maverick: The Political Life of William Langer, Also Known as Wild Bill Langer.* Fargo, ND: Geelan, 1975.

**5160.** Hjalmervik, Gary L. "William Langer's First Administration, 1932–1934." Master's thesis, University of North Dakota, 1966.

**5161.** Horne, Robert M. "The Controversy over the Seating of Senator William Langer: 1940–1942." Master's thesis, University of North Dakota, 1964.

**5162.** Larsen, Lawrence H. "William Langer: A Maverick in the Senate." *Wisconsin Magazine of History* 44 (Spring 1961): 189–198.

**5163.** Smith, Glenn H. *Langer of North Dakota: A Study in Isolationism, 1940–1959.* New York: Garland, 1979.

**5164.** Wilkins, Robert P. "Senator William Langer and National Priorities: An Agrarian Radical's View of American Foreign Policy, 1945–1952." *North Dakota Quarterly* 42 (Autumn 1974): 42–59.

**LANGLEY, KATHERINE GUDGER** (1888–1948) R-KY, House 1927–1931.

**5165.** Gilfond, Duff. "Gentlewomen of the House." *American Mercury* 18 (October 1929): 151–163.

**LANGSTON, JOHN MERCER** (1829–1897) R-VA, House 1890–1891.

**5166.** Blomfield, Maxwell H. "John Mercer Langston and the Training of Black Lawyers." In his *American Lawyers in a Changing Society, 1776–1876,* 302–339. Cambridge, MA: Harvard University Press, 1976.

**5167.** Bromberg, Alan B. "John Mercer Langston: Black Congressman from the Old Dominion." *Virginia Cavalcade* 30 (Autumn 1980): 60–67.

**5168.** Cheek, William F. "Forgotten Prophet: The Life of John Mercer Langston." Ph.D. dissertation, University of Virginia, 1961.

**5169.** ———. "A Negro Runs for Congress: John Mercer Langston and the Virginia Campaign of 1888." *Journal of Negro History* 52 (January 1967): 14–35.

**5170.** Christopher, Maurine. "John Mercer Langston/Virginia." In her *Black Americans in Congress,* 137–146. Rev. ed. New York: Thomas Y. Crowell, 1876.

**5171.** Haynes, Elizabeth. "John Mercer Langston, Scholar and Congressman." In her *Unsung Heroes,* 269–279. New York: Dubois and Dill, 1921.

**5172.** Logan, Rayford W. "Frederic Douglass and John M. Langston." In his *Howard University: The First Hundred Years,* 71–80. New York: New York University Press, 1968.

**5173.** Nelson, Larry E. "Black Leaders and the Presidential Election of 1864." *Journal of Negro History* 63 (January 1978): 42–58.

**5174.** Simmons, William J. "John Mercer Langston." In his *Men of Mark,* 510–523. New York: Arno Press, 1968.

**LARRABEE, CHARLES HATHAWAY**
(1820–1883) D-WI, House 1859–1861.

**5175.** Draper, Lyman C. "Sketch of Hon. Charles H. Larrabee." *Wisconsin State Historical Society Collections* 9 (1882): 366–388.

**LARRAZOLO, OCTAVIANO AMBROSIO** (1859–1930) R-NM, Senate 1928–1929.

**5176.** Cordova, Alfred C., and Charles Judah. *Octavian Larrazolo: A Political Portrait.* Albuquerque: University of New Mexico, 1952.

**LATHAM, MILTON SLOCUM**
(1827–1882) D-CA, House 1853–1855, Senate 1860–1863.

**5177.** Latham, Milton. "The Day Journal of Milton S. Latham, January 1 to May 6, 1860." Edited by Edgar Robinson. *Quarterly of the California Historical Society* 11 (March 1932): 3–28.

**5178.** Melendy, Howard B., and Benjamin F. Gilbert. "Milton S. Latham." In their *Governors of California: Peter H. Burnett to Edmund G. Brown,* 92–99. Georgetown, CA: Talisman Press, 1965.

**LAURENS, HENRY** (1724–1792) SC, Continental Congress 1777–1778.

**5179.** Hunt, Freeman, ed. "Henry Laurens." In his *Lives of American Merchants,* vol. 1, 577–588. New York: Derby and Jackson, 1858.

**5180.** Laurens, Henry. "The Republicanism of Henry Laurens." *South Carolina Historical Magazine* 76 (April 1975): 68–79.

**5181.** Wallace, David D. "Henry Laurens." In *Library of Southern Literature,* edited by Edwin A. Alderman and Joel C. Harris, vol. 7, 3079–3084. New Orleans: Martin and Hoyt, 1909.

**5182.** ———. *The Life of Henry Laurens, with a Sketch of the Life of Lieutenant-Colonel John Laurens.* New York: Putnam's, 1915.

**LAUSCHE, FRANK JOHN** (1895–1990) D-OH, Senate 1957–1969.

**5183.** Bittner, William. *Frank J. Lausche: A Political Biography.* New York: Studia Slovenica, 1975.

**LAWRENCE, ABBOTT** (1792–1855) W-MA, House 1835–1837, 1839–1840.

**5184.** Brauer, Kinley J. "Webster-Lawrence Feud: A Study in Politics and Ambitions." *Historian* 29 (November 1966): 34–59.

**5185.** Everett, Edward. "Abbott Lawrence: Obituary Notice of Abbott Lawrence." In his *Orations,* 365–381. Boston: Little, Brown, 1885.

**5186.** Willson, Beckles. "Bancroft and Lawrence (1846–1852)." In his *America's Ambassadors to England (1785–1928),* 260–270. London: Murray, 1928.

**LEA, LUKE** (1879–1945) D-TN, Senate 1911–1917.

**5187.** Tidwell, Cromwell. "Luke Lea and the American Legion." *Tennessee Historical Quarterly* 28 (Spring/Winter 1968): 70–83.

**LEAKE, WALTER** (1762–1825) R-MS, Senate 1817–1820.

**5188.** Fike, Claude. "The Administration of Walter Leake." *Journal of Mississippi History* 32 (May 1970): 103–115.

**LEE, ARTHUR** (1740–1792) VA,
**Continental Congress 1781–1784.**

**5189.** Potts, Louis W. *Arthur Lee, A Virtuous Revolutionary.* Baton Rouge: Louisiana State University Press, 1981.

**5190.** Riggs, A. R., and Edward M. Riley. *The Nine Lives of Arthur Lee, Virginia Patriot.* Williamsburg: Virginia Independence Bicentennial Commission, 1976.

**LEE, FRANCIS LIGHTFOOT**
(1734–1797) VA, **Continental Congress**
**1775–1780.**

**5191.** Dill, Alonzo T. *Francis Lightfoot Lee, the Improbable Signer.* Williamsburg: Virgina Independence Bicentennial Commission, 1977.

**5192.** Sanderson, John. "Francis Lightfoot Lee." In *Sanderson's Biography of the Signers of the Declaration of Independence,* edited by Robert T. Conrad, 745–747. Philadelphia: Thomas, Cowperthwait, 1848.

**LEE, GIDEON** (1778–1841) J-NY, **House**
**1835–1837.**

**5193.** Hunt, Freeman, ed. "Gideon Lee." In his *Lives of American Merchants,* vol. 1, 401–412. Cincinnati, OH: H. W. Derby, 1858.

**LEE, HENRY** (1756–1818) F-VA, **House**
**1799–1801, Continental Congress 1786–1788.**

**5194.** Boyd, Thomas A. *Light-Horse Harry Lee.* New York: Scribner's, 1931.

**5195.** Crowl, Philip A. "Henry Lee: Light-Horse Harry." In *Lives of Eighteen from Princeton,* edited by Willard Thorp, 111–136. Princeton, NJ: Princeton University Press, 1946.

**5196.** Gerson, Noel B. *Light-Horse Harry: A Biography of Washington's Great Cavalryman, General Henry Lee.* Garden City, NY: Doubleday, 1966.

**5197.** Lee, Henry. *The Campaign of 1781 in the Carolinas.* Chicago: Quadrangle Books, 1962.

**5198.** ———. "Life of General Henry Lee." In his *Memoir of the War in the Southern Department of the United States,* 11–79. New York: University Publishing Company, 1870.

**5199.** ———. *Observations on the Writings of Thomas Jefferson, with Particular Reference to the Attack They Contain on the Memory of the Late Gen. Henry Lee.* 2d ed. Philadelphia: Dobson, 1839.

**5200.** Royster, Charles. "Penniless Leaders." In his *Light-Horse Henry Lee and Legacy of the American Revolution.* New York: Knopf, 1981.

**5201.** Swiggett, Howard G. "Knox, Lee, Duer." In his *Forgotten Leaders of the Revolution,* 155–161. Garden City, NY: Doubleday, 1955.

**LEE, RICHARD HENRY** (1732–1794) VA,
**Senate 1789–1792, Continental Congress,**
**1774–1779, 1784–1785, 1787.**

**5202.** Archer, Jules. "Grand Climax Independence." In his *They Made a Revolution: 1776,* 145–147. New York: St. Martin's Press, 1973.

**5203.** Ballagh, James C., ed. *The Letters of Richard Henry Lee.* 2 vols. New York: Macmillan, 1911.

**5204.** Bowers, Paul C. "Richard Henry Lee and the Continental Congress: 1774–1779." Ph.D. dissertation, Duke University, 1965.

**5205.** Bruce, Philip A. "Richard Henry Lee." In his *The Virginia Plutarch,* vol. 1, 229–250. Chapel Hill: University of North Carolina Press, 1929.

**5206.** Chitwood, Oliver P. *Richard Henry Lee: Statesman of the Revolution.* Morgantown: West Virginia University Library, 1967.

**5207.** Hubbell, Jay B. "Richard Henry Lee." In his *South in American Literature, 1607–1900,* 110–114. Durham, NC: Duke University Press, 1954.

**5208.** Magoon, Elias L. "Richard Henry Lee, the Polished Statesman." In his *Orators of the American Revolution,* 266–282. New York: Scribner's, 1853.

**5209.** Maier, Pauline. "A Virginian as Revolutionary: Richard Henry Lee." In her *The Old Revolutionaries,* 164–200. New York: Knopf, 1980.

**5210.** Sanderson, John. "Richard Henry Lee." In *Sanderson's Biography of the Signers of the Declaration of Independence,* edited by Robert T. Conrad, 642–662. Philadelphia: Thomas, Cowperthwait, 1848.

**LEGARE, HUGH SWINTON** (1797–1843) **D-SC, House 1837–1839.**

**5211.** Bullen, Mary S., ed. *Writings of Hugh Swinton Legare.* 2 vols. Charleston, SC: Burges and James, 1845–1846.

**5212.** Cain, Marvin R. "Return of Republicanism: A Reappraisal of Hugh Swinton Legare and the Tyler Presidency." *South Carolina Historical Magazine* 79 (October 1978): 264–280.

**5213.** Davis, Curtis C. *That Ambitious Mr. Legare.* Columbia: University of South Carolina Press, 1971.

**5214.** O'Brien, Michael. *A Character of Hugh Legare.* Knoxville: University of Tennessee Press, 1985.

**5215.** Parrington, Vernon L. "Hugh Swinton Legare, Charleston Intellectual." In his *Main Currents in American Thought,* vol. 2, 114–124. New York: Harcourt, Brace, 1927.

**5216.** Ramage, B. J. "Hugh Swinton Legare." In *Library of Southern Literature,* edited by Edwin A. Alderman and Joel C. Harris, vol. 7, 3169–3171. New Orleans: Martin and Hoyt, 1909.

**5217.** Rhea, Linda. *Hugh Swinton Legare, a Charleston Intellectual.* Chapel Hill: University of North Carolina, 1934.

**LEHMAN, HERBERT HENRY** (1878–1963) **D-NY, Senate 1949–1957.**

**5218.** Benedict, John. "Reign of the Lehman Brothers." *American Mercury* 89 (November 1959): 97–115.

**5219.** Douglas, Paul H. "Three Saints in Politics." *American Scholar* 40 (Spring 1971): 223–232.

**5220.** Ingalls, Robert P. *Herbert H. Lehman and New York's Little New Deal.* New York: New York University Press, 1975.

**5221.** Levitan, Tina. "Herbert Lehman: Governor, Senator and Philanthropist." In her *Jews in American Life,* 240–243. New York: Hebrew Publishing Company, 1969.

**5222.** Madison, Charles A. "Herbert H. Lehman: Banker, Politician, Humanitarian." In his *Eminent American Jews,* 259–280. New York: Ungar, 1970.

**5223.** Nevins, Allan. *Herbert H. Lehman and His Era.* New York: Scribner's 1963.

**5224.** Vorspan, Albert. "Herbert Lehman: Public Servant." In his *Giants of Justice,* 220–235. Scranton, PA: Crowell, 1960.

**LEIGH, BENJAMIN WATKINS** (1781–1849) **W-VA, Senate 1834–1836.**

**5225.** Dunn, Joseph B. "Benjamin Watkins Leigh." In *Library of Southern Literature,* edited by Edwin A. Alderman and Joel C. Harris, vol. 7, 3205–3208. New Orleans: Martin and Hoyt, 1909.

**LELAND, GEORGE THOMAS** **"MICKEY"** (1944–1989) **D-TX, House 1979–1989.**

**5226.** Kennedy, Edward M. "Humanitarianism and the Legacy of Mickey Leland." *TransAfrica Forum* 7 (Spring 1990): 30–37.

## LEMKE, WILLIAM (1878–1950) R-ND, House 1933–1941.

**5227.** Bennett, David H. "William Lemke and the Nonpartisan League." In his *Demagogues in the Depression: American Radicals and the Union Party, 1932–1936,* 85–109. New Brunswick, NJ: Rutgers University Press, 1969.

**5228.** Blackorby, Edward C. *Prairie Rebel: The Public Life of William Lemke.* Lincoln: University of Nebraska Press, 1963.

**5229.** ———. "William Lemke: Agrarian Radical and Union Party Presidential Candidate." *Mississippi Valley Historical Review* 49 (June 1962): 67–84.

## LENROOT, IRVINE LUTHER (1869–1949) R-WI, House 1909–1918, Senate 1918–1927.

**5230.** Griffith, Robert W. "Prelude to Insurgency: Irvine L. Lenroot and the Republican Primary of 1908." *Wisconsin Magazine of History* 49 (Autumn 1965): 16–28.

**5231.** Margulies, Herbert F. "The Collaboration of Herbert Hoover and Irvine Lenroot, 1921–1928." *North Dakota Quarterly* 45 (Summer 1977): 30–46.

**5232.** ———. "Irvine L. Lenroot and the Republican Vice-Presidential Nomination of 1920." *Wisconsin Magazine of History* 61 (Autumn 1977): 21–31.

**5233.** ———. *Senator Lenroot of Wisconsin: A Political Biography, 1900–1929.* Columbia: University of Missouri Press, 1977.

## LETCHER, JOHN (1813–1884) D-VA, House 1851–1859.

**5234.** Bean, William G. "John Letcher and the Slavery Issue in Virginia's Gubernatorial Contest of 1858–1859." *Journal of Southern History* 20 (February 1954): 22–49.

**5235.** Boney, Francis N. *John Letcher of Virginia: The Story of Virginia's Civil War Governor.* University: University of Alabama Press, 1966.

## LETCHER, ROBERT PERKINS (1788–1861) KY, House 1823–1833, 1834–1835.

**5236.** Gilliam, William D. "The Public Career of Robert Perkins Letcher." Ph.D. dissertation, Indiana University, 1941.

## LETTS, FRED DICKINSON (1875–1965) R-IA, House 1925–1931.

**5237.** Porter, David L. "Iowa Congressional Delegation and the Great Economic Issues, 1929–1933." *Annals of Iowa* 46 (Summer 1982): 337–354.

## LEWIS, DAVID JOHN (1869–1952) D-MD, House 1911–1917, 1931–1939.

**5238.** Masterson, Thomas D. "David J. Lewis of Maryland: Formative and Progressive Years, 1869–1917." Ph.D. dissertation, Georgetown University, 1976.

## LEWIS, FRANCIS (1713–1802) NY, Continental Congress 1774–1779.

**5239.** Sanderson, John. "Francis Lewis." In *Sanderson's Biography of the Signers of the Declaration of Independence,* edited by Robert T. Conrad, 276–281. Philadelphia: Thomas, Cowperthwait, 1848.

## LIEB, CHARLES (1852–1928) D-IN, House 1913–1917.

**5240.** Adams, Willi P. "Ethnic Politicians and American Nationalism during the First World War: Four German-Born Members of the U.S. House of Representatives." *American Studies International* 29 (April 1991): 20–34.

## LIEBERMAN, JOSEPH I. (1942– ) D-CT, Senate 1989– .

**5241.** Meyerson, Adam. "Scoop Jackson Democrat: Senator Joseph Lieberman's Case for Economic and Military Strength." *Policy Review* 53 (Summer 1990): 26–33.

**LINCOLN, ABRAHAM** (1809–1865) R-IL, House 1847–1849.

**5242.** Abbott, John S. *Life of Abraham Lincoln.* Chicago: Illustrated Book Company, 1900.

**5243.** ———. *The Life of Abraham Lincoln.* New York: T. W. Dawley, 1864.

**5244.** Agar, Herbert. *Abraham Lincoln.* New York: Macmillan, 1952.

**5245.** Allen, Eric R. "Abraham Lincoln: An Interpretation." *Hartford Seminary Record* 19 (April 1909): 103–112.

**5246.** Ander, Oscar F. *Lincoln Images: Augustana College Centennial Essays.* Rock Island, IL: Augustana College Library, 1960.

**5247.** Anderson, David D. *Abraham Lincoln.* New York: Twayne, 1970.

**5248.** Anderson, Dwight G. *Abraham Lincoln: The Quest for Immortality.* New York: Knopf, 1982.

**5249.** Anderson, James W. "The Real Issue: An Analysis of the Final Lincoln-Douglas Debate." *Lincoln Herald* 69 (Spring 1967): 27–38.

**5250.** Anderson, Levere. "The Forgotten Lincoln." *Mankind* 1 (February 1969): 84–94.

**5251.** Anderson, Marcus. "Father Abraham, Analysis of a Myth." *Tyler's Quarterly Historical and Genealogical Magazine* 20 (July 1938): 77–98.

**5252.** Angle, Paul M. "The Changing Lincoln." In *The John H. Hauberg Historical Essays,* edited by O. Fritiof Ander, 1–17. Rock Island, IL: Augustana Book Concern, 1954.

**5253.** ———. *Created Equal? The Complete Lincoln-Douglas Debate of 1858.* Chicago: University of Chicago Press, 1958.

**5254.** ———. *Here I Have Lived: A History of Lincoln's Springfield, 1821–1865.* Springfield, IL: Abraham Lincoln Association, 1935.

**5255.** Arnold, Isaac N. *The Life of Abraham Lincoln.* Chicago: Jansen, McClurg, 1885.

**5256.** ———. *Sketch of the Life of Abraham Lincoln.* Chicago: Rand McNally, 1942.

**5257.** Ashe, Samuel A. "Lincoln the Lawyer." *Tyler's Quarterly Historical and Genealogical Magazine* 16 (July 1934): 15–20.

**5258.** Auble, John L. "Abraham Lincoln and the American Liberal Tradition." Ph.D. dissertation, Northwestern University, 1960.

**5259.** Auer, John J. "Cooper Institute: Tom Corwin and Abraham Lincoln." *New York History* 32 (October 1951): 399–413.

**5260.** Bachelder, Louise, ed. *Abraham Lincoln: Wisdom and Wit.* Mount Vernon, NY: Peter Pauper Press, 1965.

**5261.** Bailey, Bernadine F. *The Story of Abraham Lincoln.* Chicago: Rand McNally, 1942.

**5262.** Baldwin, James. *Abraham Lincoln.* New York: American Book Company, 1904.

**5263.** Ballard, Colin R. *The Military Genius of Abraham Lincoln.* London: Oxford University Press, 1926.

**5264.** Barbee, David R. "Lincoln, Chase, and the Rev. Dr. Richard Fuller." *Maryland Historical Magazine* 46 (June 1951): 108–123.

**5265.** Baringer, William E. *A House Dividing: Lincoln as President Elect.* Springfield, IL: Abraham Lincoln Association, 1945.

**5266.** ———. "Lincoln as President Elect: Springfield Phase." Ph.D. dissertation, University of Illinois, 1940.

**5267.** ———. *Lincoln's Rise to Power.* Boston: Little, Brown, 1937.

**5268.** Barker, Harry E. *Abraham Lincoln, His Life in Illinois.* New York: Barrows, 1940.

**5269.** Barnard, George G. *Barnard's Lincoln.* Cincinnati, OH: Stewart and Kidd, 1917.

**5270.** Barnwell, Robert W. *The Lines and Nature of Lincoln's Greatness.* Columbia, SC: State Company, 1931.

**5271.** Bartlett, David V. *Life and Public Services of Hon. Abraham Lincoln.* Boston: Thayer and Eldridge, 1860.

**5272.** ———. *Life of Abraham Lincoln.* Philadelphia: Bradley, 1860.

**5273.** Barton, William E. "Abraham Lincoln and New Salem." *Illinois State Historical Society Journal* 19 (October/January 1926/1927): 74–101.

**5274.** ———. "Abraham Lincoln's Ancestry." *Indiana Historical Bulletin* 2 (January 1925): 55–74.

**5275.** ———. "The Ancestry of Abraham Lincoln." *Illinois State Historical Society Transactions* 31 (1924): 123–138.

**5276.** ———. *A Beautiful Blunder: The True Story of Lincoln's Letter to Mrs. Lydia A. Bixby.* Indianapolis: Bobbs-Merrill, 1926.

**5277.** ———. "The Enduring Lincoln." *Illinois State Historical Society Journal* 20 (July 1927): 243–254.

**5278.** ———. *The Greatness of Abraham Lincoln.* Chicago: Munsell Publishing Company, 1922.

**5279.** ———. "The Influence of Illinois in the Development of Abraham Lincoln." *Illinois State Historical Transactions* 28 (1921): 32–53.

**5280.** ———. "Is Lincoln among the Aristocrats?" *Illinois State Historical Society Journal* 22 (April 1929): 65–78.

**5281.** ———. *The Life of Abraham Lincoln.* 2 vols. Indianapolis, IN: Bobbs-Merrill, 1925.

**5282.** ———. *Lincoln at Gettysburg: What He Intended to Say, What He Said, What He Was Reported to Have Said, What He Wished He Had Said.* Indianapolis: Bobbs-Merrill, 1930.

**5283.** ———. *The Lineage of Lincoln.* Indianapolis: Bobbs-Merrill, 1929.

**5284.** ———. "A Noble Fragment: Beveridge's Life of Lincoln." *Mississippi Valley Historical Review* 15 (March 1929): 497–510.

**5285.** ———. *The Paternity of Abraham Lincoln.* New York: Doran, 1920.

**5286.** ———. *The Soul of Abraham Lincoln.* New York: Doran, 1920.

**5287.** Basler, Roy P. "Abraham Lincoln—Artist." *North American Review* 245 (Spring 1938): 144–153.

**5288.** ———. *Lincoln.* New York: Grove Press, 1962.

**5289.** ———. *The Lincoln Legend: A Study in Changing Conceptions.* Boston: Houghton Mifflin, 1938.

**5290.** ———, ed. *The Collected Works of Abraham Lincoln.* 9 vols. New Brunswick, NJ: Rutgers University Press, 1953–1955.

**5291.** Bassett, Margaret B. *Abraham and Mary Todd Lincoln.* New York: Crowell, 1973.

**5292.** Becker, Lucien. "Abraham Lincoln: Influences That Produced Him." *Filson Club History Quarterly* 33 (April 1955): 125–138.

**5293.** Belz, Herman. "Lincoln and the Constitution: The Dictatorship Question Reconsidered." *Congress and the Presidency* 15 (Autumn 1989): 147–64.

**5294.** Beveridge, Albert J. *Abraham Lincoln, 1809–1858.* 2 vols. Boston: Houghton Mifflin, 1928.

**5295.** Binns, Henry B. *Abraham Lincoln.* New York: Dutton, 1907.

**5296.** ———. *The Life of Abraham Lincoln.* New York: Dutton, 1927.

**5297.** Bishop, James A. *The Day Lincoln Was Shot.* New York: Harper, 1955.

**5298.** Bissett, Clark P. *Abraham Lincoln, a Universal Man.* San Francisco: J. Howell, 1923.

**5299.** Blacknall, Oscar W. *Lincoln as the South Should Know Him.* Raleigh, NC: Edwards and Broughton, 1915.

**5300.** Blegen, Theodore C. "Lincoln's Imagery." In *Abraham Lincoln: A New Portrait,* edited by Henry B. Kranz, 123–128. New York: Putnam's, 1959.

**5301.** Bloom, Robert L. "The Lincoln Image—Then and Now." *Lincoln Herald* 85 (Fall 1983): 175–187.

**5302.** Blue, Merle D. "Sleuthing Lincoln Myths." *Indiana Social Studies Quarterly* 29 (Spring 1976): 43–51.

**5303.** Borit, Gabor S. "Lincoln and Taxation during His Illinois Legislative Years." *Illinois State Historical Society Journal* 61 (Autumn 1968): 365–373.

**5304.** ———. "Lincoln and the Economics of the American Dream: The Whig Years, 1832–1854." Ph.D. dissertation, Boston University, 1968.

**5305.** ———. "Lincoln's Opposition to the Mexican War." *Illinois State Historical Society Journal* 67 (February 1974): 79–100.

**5306.** ———. "The Right to Rise." In *The Public and the Private Lincoln: Contemporary Perspectives,* edited by Cullom Davis, Charles B. Strozier, Rebecca M. Veach, and Geoffrey C. Ward, 57–70. Carbondale: Southern Illinois University Press, 1979.

**5307.** ———. "Was Lincoln a Vulnerable Candidate in 1860?" *Civil War History* 27 (March 1981): 32–48.

**5308.** ———, ed. *Lincoln's Generals.* New York: Oxford University Press, 1994.

**5309.** Borst, William A. "Lincoln's Historical Perspective." *Lincoln Herald* 76 (Winter 1974): 195–203.

**5310.** Bowers, John H. *Life of Abraham Lincoln.* Girard, KS: Haldeman-Julius, 1922.

**5311.** Braden, Waldo W. "Lincoln's Delivery." *Lincoln Herald* 85 (Fall 1983): 167–174.

**5312.** Bradford, M. E. "Lincoln and the Language of Hate and Fear: A View from the South." *Continuity* 9 (1985): 87–108.

**5313.** Bramantip, Bocardo. *The Abraham Lincoln Myth.* New York: Mascot Publishing Company, 1894.

**5314.** Brandt, Keith. *Abe Lincoln: The Young Years.* Mahwah, NJ: Troll Associates, 1982.

**5315.** Breiseth, Christopher N. "Lincoln and Frederick Douglass: Another Debate." *Illinois State Historical Society Journal* 68 (February 1975): 9–26.

**5316.** Brogan, Denis W. *Abraham Lincoln.* New York: Schocken, 1963.

**5317.** Brooks, Noah. "Abraham Lincoln." In his *Statesmen,* 175–222. New York: Scribner's, 1893.

**5318.** ———. *Abraham Lincoln, His Youth and Early Manhood, with a Brief Account of His Later Life.* New York: Putnam's, 1901.

**5319.** Brown, Charles R. *Lincoln, the Greatest Man of the Nineteenth Century.* New York: Macmillan, 1922.

**5320.** Browne, Francis F., comp. *The Every-Day Life of Abraham Lincoln: Abraham Lincoln's Life and Character Portrayed by Those Who Knew Him.* Rev. ed. New York: N. D. Thompson, 1913.

**5321.** Browne, Ray B., ed. *Lincoln-Lore: Lincoln in the Popular Mind.* Bowling Green, OH: Popular Press, 1975.

**5322.** Browne, Robert H. *Abraham Lincoln and the Men of His Time.* New York: Easton and Mains, 1901.

**5323.** Bruce, Robert V. *Lincoln and the Tools of War.* Indianapolis: Bobbs-Merrill, 1956.

**5324.** Bryan, George S. *The Great American Myth.* New York: Carrick and Evans, 1940.

**5325.** Bryner, Byron L. *Abraham Lincoln in Peoria, Ill.* Peoria, IL: Lincoln Historical Publishing Company, 1926.

**5326.** Buck, Solon J. "Lincoln and Minnesota." *Minnesota History* 6 (December 1925): 355–361.

**5327.** Bullard, F. Lauriston. *Abraham Lincoln and the Widow Bixby.* New Brunswick, NJ: Rutgers University Press, 1946.

**5328.** ———. "Lincoln as a Jeffersonian." *More Books* 23 (October 1948): 283–300.

**5329.** ———. "The New England Ancestry of Abraham Lincoln." *New England Magazine* 39 (February 1909): 685–691.

**5330.** Burlingame, Michael A. *The Inner World of Abraham Lincoln.* Urbana: University of Illinois Press, 1994.

**5331.** Burr, Nelson R. "Abraham Lincoln: Western Star over Connecticut." *Lincoln Herald* 85 (Spring 1983): 21–36; 85 (Fall 1983): 133–151; 86 (Spring 1984): 6–18; 86 (Summer 1984): 77–92.

**5332.** Cardiff, Ira D. *The Deification of Lincoln.* Boston: Christopher Publishing House, 1943.

**5333.** Carleton, William G. "Sources of the Lincoln Legend." *Prairie Schooner* 25 (Summer 1951): 184–190.

**5334.** Carman, Harry J., and Reinhard H. Luthin. *Lincoln and the Patronage.* New York: Columbia University Press, 1943.

**5335.** Carnegie, Dale B. *Lincoln, the Unknown.* New York: Century, 1932.

**5336.** Carpenter, Francis B. *Six Months at the White House with Abraham Lincoln: The Story of a Picture.* New York: Hurd and Houghton, 1866.

**5337.** Carruthers, Olive, and R. Gerald McMurtry. *Lincoln's Other Mary.* New York: Ziff-Davis, 1946.

**5338.** Carson, Steven L. "Lincoln and the Mayor of New York." *Lincoln Herald* 67 (Winter 1965): 184–191.

**5339.** Carter, Orrin N. "Lincoln and Douglas as Lawyers." *Mississippi Valley Historical Association Proceedings* 4 (1910/1911): 213–240.

**5340.** Cary, Barbara. *Meet Abraham Lincoln.* New York: Random House, 1965.

**5341.** Cathey, James H. *The Genesis of Lincoln.* Atlanta, GA: Franklin, 1904.

**5342.** Chafin, Eugene W. *Lincoln, the Man of Sorrow.* Chicago: Lincoln Temperance Press, 1908.

**5343.** Chandler, Josephine C. *New Salem: Early Chapters in Lincoln's Life.* Springfield, IL: Journal Print Company, 1930.

**5344.** Chapman, Francis. "Lincoln, the Lawyer." *Temple Law Quarterly* 9 (April 1935): 277–291.

**5345.** Charbonneau, Louis H. "Lincoln the Lawyer." *Detroit Lawyer* 16 (February 1948): 27–32, 36.

**5346.** Charnwood, Godfrey R. *Abraham Lincoln.* London: Constable, 1916.

**5347.** Chipperfield, Burnett M. "Abraham Lincoln." *American Law Review* 57 (March/April 1923): 292–302.

**5348.** Choate, Joseph H. *Abraham Lincoln.* New York: Crowell, 1901.

**5349.** Clark, Leon P. *Lincoln: A Psycho-Biography.* New York: Scribner's, 1933.

**5350.** ———. "Unconscious Motives Underlying the Personalities of Great Statesmen and Their Relating to Epoch-Making Events: A Psychoanalytic Study of Abraham Lincoln." *Psychoanalytic Review* 8 (January 1921): 1–21.

**5351.** Clarke, Philip. *Abraham Lincoln.* Hove, East Sussex, England: Wayland, 1981.

**5352.** Coffin, Charles C. *Abraham Lincoln.* New York: Harper and Brothers, 1893.

**5353.** Coleman, Charles H. "Was Lincoln Eligible for Election to the United States Senate in 1855?" *Lincoln Herald* 60 (Fall 1958): 91–93.

**5354.** Coleman, Christopher B. "The Lincoln Legend." *Indiana Magazine of History* 29 (December 1933): 277–286.

**5355.** Collins, Bruce. "The Lincoln-Douglas Contest of 1858 and Illinois' Electorate." *Journal of American Studies* 20 (December 1986): 391–420.

**5356.** Colver, Anne. *Abraham Lincoln: For the People.* New York: Dell, 1960.

**5357.** Cooper, Homer H. "The Lincoln-Thornton Debate of 1856 at Shelbyville, Illinois." *Illinois State Historical Society Journal* 10 (April 1917): 101–122.

**5358.** Corlett, William S., Jr., and Glen E. Thurow. "The Availability of Lincoln's Political Religion." *Political Theory* 10 (November 1982): 520–546.

**5359.** Corson, Oscar T. "Loyalty as Exemplified in Abraham Lincoln." *Ohio Educational Monthly* 68 (January 1919): 7–15.

**5360.** Cottman, George S. "Lincoln in Indianapolis." *Indiana Magazine of History* 24 (March 1928): 1–14.

**5361.** Courtenay, Calista. *Abraham Lincoln.* New York: M. A. Donohue, 1917.

**5362.** Cravens, Francis. *The Story of Lincoln.* Bloomington, IL: Public School Publishing Company, 1898.

**5363.** Crocker, Lionel. *An Analysis of Lincoln and Douglas as Public Speakers and Debaters.* Springfield, IL: Thomas, 1968.

**5364.** Crosby, Franklin. *Life of Abraham Lincoln.* New York: International Book Company, 1865.

**5365.** Current, Richard N. "Lincoln and Daniel Webster." *Illinois State Historical Society Journal* 48 (Autumn 1955): 307–321.

**5366.** ———. "Lincoln, Husband and Father." In *Abraham Lincoln: A New Portrait,* edited by Henry B. Kranz, 134–139. New York: Putnam's, 1959.

**5367.** ———. *The Lincoln Nobody Knows: A Portrait in Contrast of the Greatest American.* New York: McGraw-Hill, 1958.

**5368.** ———. *The Political Thought of Abraham Lincoln.* Indianapolis: Bobbs-Merrill, 1967.

**5369.** Curtis, William E. *Abraham Lincoln.* Philadelphia: Lippincott, 1902.

**5370.** Daugherty, James H. *Abraham Lincoln.* New York: Viking, 1943.

**5371.** D'Aulaire, Ingri M. *Abraham Lincoln.* Garden City, NY: Doubleday, 1957.

**5372.** David, Michael. *The Image of Lincoln in the South.* Knoxville: University of Tennessee Press, 1971.

**5373.** Davis, Burnett V. "President Abraham Lincoln and the Perpetuation of a Republican Regime." Ph.D. dissertation, University of Chicago, 1973.

**5374.** Davis, Cullom, Charles B. Strozier, Rebecca M. Veach, and Geoffrey C. Ward, eds. *The Public and the Private Lincoln: Contemporary Perspectives.* Carbondale: Southern Illinois University Press, 1979.

**5375.** Davis, Edwin. "Lincoln and Macon Country, Illinois, 1830–1831." *Illinois State Historical Society Journal* 25 (April/July 1932): 63–107.

**5376.** Delahay, Mark W. *Abraham Lincoln.* New York: P. H. Newhadd, 1939.

**5377.** Dennis, Frank L. *The Lincoln-Douglas Debates.* New York: Mason and Lipscomb, 1974.

**5378.** Dewitt, David M. *The Assassination of Abraham Lincoln and Its Expiation.* New York: Macmillan, 1909.

**5379.** Dickson, Edward A. "Lincoln and Baker: The Story of a Great Friendship." *Historical Society of Southern California Quarterly* 34 (September 1952): 229–242.

**5380.** Dodd, William E. "The Rise of Abraham Lincoln." *Century Magazine* 113 (March 1927): 569–584.

**5381.** Dodge, Daniel K. *Abraham Lincoln, Master of Words.* New York: Appleton, 1924.

**5382.** Donald, David H. *Lincoln Reconsidered: Essays on the Civil War Era.* New York: Knopf, 1956.

**5383.** Dondero, George A. "Lincoln the Lawyer." *Michigan State Bar Journal* 38 (February 1959): 22–30.

**5384.** ———. "Why Lincoln Wore a Beard." *Illinois State Historical Society Journal* 24 (July 1931): 321–332.

**5385.** Douglas, Paul H. "Lincoln and Douglas." In *Lincoln for the Ages,* edited by Ralph G. Newman, 124–129. Garden City, NY: Doubleday, 1960.

**5386.** Dowd, Morgan D. "Abraham Lincoln, the Rule of Law and Crisis Government: A Study of His Constitutional Law Theories." *University of Detroit Law Journal* 39 (June 1962): 633–649.

**5387.** Drinkwater, John. *The World's Lincoln.* New York: Bowling Green Press, 1928.

**5388.** Duff, John J. *A. Lincoln: Prairie Lawyer.* New York: Rinehart, 1960.

**5389.** Dunne, Edward F. "Abraham Lincoln." *Illinois State Historical Society Journal* 9 (April 1915): 8–22.

**5390.** Eaton, Vincent L. "Abraham Lincoln: His Hand and Pen." *Manuscripts* 11 (Winter 1955): 5–12.

**5391.** Ehrmann, Bess V. *The Missing Chapter in the Life of Abraham Lincoln.* Chicago: W. M. Hill, 1938.

**5392.** Einhorn, Lois J. *Abraham Lincoln, the Orator: Penetrating the Lincoln Legend.* New York: Greenwood, 1992.

**5393.** Eisenschiml, Otto. *Why Was Lincoln Murdered?* Boston: Little, Brown, 1937.

**5394.** Elazar, Daniel J. "The Constitution, the Union, and the Liberties of the People: Abraham Lincoln's Teaching about the American Political System as Articulated on His Tour from Springfield to Washington in February, 1861." *Publius* 8 (Summer 1978): 141–176.

**5395.** Elias, Edith. *Abraham Lincoln.* New York: Stokes, 1920.

**5396.** Elliott, Edward. "Abraham Lincoln: Growth through Civil War." In his *Biographical Story of the Constitution: A Study of the Growth of the American Union,* 209–228, New York: Putnam's Sons, 1910.

**5397.** Ellsworth, Edward W. "Lincoln and the Education Convention: Education in Illinois—a Jeffersonian Heritage." *Lincoln Herald* 80 (Summer 1978): 69–78.

**5398.** Endy, Melvin B., Jr. "Abraham Lincoln and American Civil Religion: A Reinterpretation." *Church History* 44 (June 1975): 229–241.

**5399.** Ensor, Allison R. "Lincoln, Mark Twain, and Lincoln Memorial University." *Lincoln Herald* 78 (Summer 1976): 43–51.

**5400.** Erikson, Gary L. "Lincoln's Civil Religion and the Lutheran Heritage." *Lincoln Herald* 75 (Winter 1973): 158–171.

**5401.** Evans, Joseph F. "Lincoln at Galesburg—a Sketch Written on the One Hundred and Seventh Anniversary of the Birthday of Abraham Lincoln." *Illinois State Historical Society Journal* 8 (January 1916): 559–568.

**5402.** Fairbanks, Avard T. "The Face of Abraham Lincoln." In *Lincoln for the Ages,* edited by Ralph G. Newman, 160–165. Garden City, NY: Doubleday, 1960.

**5403.** Fehrenbacher, Don E. "The Anti-Lincoln Tradition." *Abraham Lincoln Association Papers* 4 (1982): 7–28.

**5404.** ———. "The Historical Significance of the Lincoln-Douglas Debates." *Wisconsin Magazine of History* 42 (Spring 1959): 193–199.

**5405.** ———. "Lincoln and the Mayor of Chicago." *Wisconsin Magazine of History* 40 (Summer 1961): 237–244.

**5406.** ———. "Lincoln, Douglas, and the 'Freeport Question.'" *American Historical Review* 66 (April 1961): 599–617.

**5407.** ———. "Lincoln's Wartime Leadership: The First Hundred Days." *Journal of Abraham Lincoln Association* 9 (1987): 1–18.

**5408.** ———. "The Origins and Purpose of Lincoln's House-Divided Speech." *Mississippi Valley Historical Review* 46 (March 1960): 615–643.

**5409.** ———. *Prelude to Greatness: Lincoln in the 1850's.* Stanford, CA: Stanford University Press, 1962.

**5410.** Findley, Paul. *Lincoln, the Crucible of Congress.* New York: Crown, 1979.

**5411.** Fiore, Jordan D. *Abraham Lincoln Visits the Old Colony.* Taunton, MA: Old Colony Historical Society, 1978.

**5412.** Fleming, Thomas J. *The Living Land of Lincoln.* New York: Reader's Digest Press, 1980.

**5413.** Forgie, George B. *Patricide in the House Divided: A Psychological Interpretation of Lincoln and His Age.* New York: Norton, 1979.

**5414.** Foster, Genevieve. *Abraham Lincoln.* New York: Scribner's, 1950.

**5415.** Fox, Edward J. "Influence of Law on the Life of Abraham Lincoln." *Case and Comment* 33 (March 1927): 1–6.

**5416.** Frank, John P. *Lincoln as a Lawyer.* Urbana: University of Illinois Press, 1961.

**5417.** Franklin, John H. "Lincoln and Public Morality." *Topic* 9 (Spring 1965): 27–43.

**5418.** Freeman, Andrew A. *Abraham Lincoln Goes to New York.* New York: Coward-McCann, 1960.

**5419.** French, Charles W. *Abraham Lincoln.* New York: Funk and Wagnalls, 1891.

**5420.** Friend, Henry G. *Abraham Lincoln's Commercial Practice: A Series of Articles by Henry C. Friend.* Chicago: Commercial Law Foundation, 1970.

**5421.** Frisch, Morton J. "The Principles of Lincoln's Statecraft." Ph.D. dissertation, Pennsylvania State University, 1953.

**5422.** Gallardo, Florence. "'Til Death Do Us Part': The Marriage of Abraham Lincoln and Mary Todd." *Lincoln Herald* 84 (Spring 1982): 3–10.

**5423.** Garner, Wayne L. "Abraham Lincoln and the Uses of Humor." Ph.D. dissertation, University of Iowa, 1963.

**5424.** Gates, Arnold F. "Abraham Lincoln: Great Image of America." In *Abraham Lincoln: A New Portrait,* edited by Henry B. Branz, 166–174. New York: Putnam's, 1959.

**5425.** ———. *Amberglow of Abraham Lincoln and Ann Rutledge.* West Leisinring, PA: Griglak Printer, 1939.

**5426.** George, Marian M. *Lincoln and Washington.* Chicago: Flanagan, 1899.

**5427.** Gernon, Blaine B. "The Lincolns in Chicago." *Illinois State Historical Society Journal* 27 (October 1934): 243–284.

**5428.** ———. "Lincoln's Visits to Chicago." *Chicago Historical Society Bulletin* 1 (February 1935): 33–41.

**5429.** Goodhart, Arthur L. "Lincoln and the Law." *American Bar Association Journal* 50 (May 1964): 433–441.

**5430.** Goodman, James F. *Lincoln at Heart: Or His Moral and Religious Life.* Albion, MI: Art Craft Press, 1931.

**5431.** Gordy, Wilbur F. *Abraham Lincoln.* New York: Scribner's, 1917.

**5432.** Graebner, Norman A. "The Apostle of Progress." In *The Public and the Private Lincoln: Contemporary Perspectives,* edited by Cullom Davis, Charles B. Strozier, Rebecca M. Veach, and Geoffrey C. Ward, 71–85. Carbondale: Southern Illinois University Press, 1979.

**5433.** ———. "Lincoln's Humility." In *Lincoln for the Ages,* edited by Ralph G. Newman, 384–389. Garden City, NY: Doubleday, 1960.

**5434.** Gray, William C. *Life of Abraham Lincoln.* Cincinnati, OH: Western Tract and Book Society, 1867.

**5435.** Gridley, Eleanor. *The Story of Abraham Lincoln.* New York: M. A. Donohue and Company, 1900.

**5436.** Grierson, Francis. *Abraham Lincoln, the Practical Mystic.* New York: Lane, 1918.

**5437.** ———. *The Valley of Shadows.* New York: History Book Club, 1948.

**5438.** Griffith, Albert H. *The Heart of Abraham Lincoln.* Madison: Lincoln Fellowship of Wisconsin Historical Bulletin, 1950.

**5439.** Gruber, Michael. *Abraham Lincoln.* New York: American R. D. M. Corporation, 1965.

**5440.** Gunderson, Robert G. "Reading Lincoln's Mail." *Indiana Magazine of History* 55 (December 1959): 379–392.

**5441.** ———. "Stoutly Argufy: Lincoln's Legal Speaking." *Wisconsin Magazine of History* 46 (Winter 1962): 109–117.

**5442.** Haerdter, Robert. "Abraham Lincoln." *Mount* 17 (April 1965): 29–36.

**5443.** Hamilton, Holman. "Abraham Lincoln and Zachary Taylor." *Lincoln Herald* 53 (Fall 1951): 14–19.

**5444.** Hamilton, Joseph G. "Lincoln and the South." *Sewanee Review* 17 (April 1909): 129–138.

**5445.** ———. "The Many-Sired Lincoln." *American Mercury* 5 (June 1925): 129–135.

**5446.** Hamilton, Mary A. *The Story of Abraham Lincoln.* New York: Dutton, 1906.

**5447.** Hanaford, Phebe A. *Abraham Lincoln.* New York: Werner, 1895.

**5448.** Hanchett, William. *Out of the Wilderness: The Life of Abraham Lincoln.* Urbana: University of Illinois Press, 1994.

**5449.** Handlin, Oscar, and Lilian Handlin. *Abraham Lincoln and the Union.* Boston: Little, Brown, 1980.

**5450.** Hanna, William F. "This Side of the Mountains: Abraham Lincoln's 1848 Visit to Massachusetts." *Lincoln Herald* 80 (Summer 1978): 56–65.

**5451.** Hapgood, Norman. *Abraham Lincoln, the Man of the People.* New York: Macmillan, 1899.

**5452.** Harper, Ellahue A. "Lincoln, the Lawyer." *Dickinson Law Review* 28 (January 1924): 95–112.

**5453.** Harper, Robert S. *Lincoln and the Press.* New York: McGraw-Hill, 1951.

**5454.** Hart, Hugh. *Lincoln, the Man of the Ages.* Monmouth, IL: F. L. Seybald and Company, 1945.

**5455.** Harwell, Richard B. "Lincoln and the South." In *Lincoln for the Ages,* edited by Ralph G. Newman, 203–207. Garden City, NY: Doubleday, 1960.

**5456.** Havlik, Robert J. "Abraham Lincoln and the Technology of 'Young America.'" *Lincoln Herald* 79 (Spring 1977): 3–11.

**5457.** Hein, David. "The Calvinistic Tenor of Abraham Lincoln's Religious Thought." *Lincoln Herald* 85 (Winter 1983): 212–220.

**5458.** ———. "Lincoln and Political Decision-Making." *Lincoln Herald* 85 (Spring 1983): 3–6.

**5459.** Hendrick, Burton J. *Lincoln's War Cabinet.* Boston: Little, Brown, 1946.

**5460.** Herndon, William H. *The Hidden Lincoln: From the Letters and Papers of William H. Herndon.* Edited by Emanuel Hertz. New York: Viking, 1938.

**5461.** Herndon, William H., and Jesse W. Weik. *Abraham Lincoln: The True Story of a Great Life.* 2 vols. New York: Appleton, 1916.

**5462.** ———. *Herndon's Lincoln: The True Story of a Great Life, the History and Personal Recollections of Abraham Lincoln.* 3 vols. Chicago: Belford, Clarke, 1889.

**5463.** Herrick, Cheesman A. "The Americanism of Lincoln." *North American Review* 215 (February 1922): 179–187.

**5464.** ———. "How Abraham Lincoln Was Educated." *Educational Review* 71 (February 1926): 78–86.

**5465.** Hertz, Emanuel. *Abraham Lincoln: A New Portrait.* 2 vols. New York: Liveright, 1931.

**5466.** ———. *Abraham Lincoln, More Than a Country Lawyer.* New York: Bronx Country Bar Association, 1928.

**5467.** ———. "Lawyer Lincoln, a Review." *St. John's Law Review* 11 (April 1937): 354–359.

**5468.** Hesseltine, William B. *Lincoln and the War Governors.* New York: Knopf, 1948.

**5469.** Hickey, James T. "The Lincoln Account at the Corneau and Diller Drug Store, 1849–1861, a Springfield Tradition." *Illinois State Historical Society Journal* 77 (Spring 1984): 60–66.

**5470.** ———. "Lincolniana: A Small Receipt Reveals a Large Story." *Illinois State Historical Society Journal* 75 (February 1982): 73–80.

**5471.** Hill, Frederick T. "The Lincoln-Douglas Debates, Fifty Years After." *Century Magazine* 77 (November 1908): 3–19.

**5472.** ———. *Lincoln the Lawyer.* New York: Century, 1906.

**5473.** ———. *Lincoln's Legacy of Inspiration.* New York: Stokes, 1909.

**5474.** Hill, John W. *Abraham Lincoln: Man of God.* 2d ed. New York: Putnam's, 1922.

**5475.** ———. *If Lincoln Were Here.* New York: Putnam's, 1925.

**5476.** Hillis, Newell D. "Abraham Lincoln: His Religious Attitude." In his *All the Year Round: An Outlook upon Its Great Days,* 36–55. New York: Revell, 1912.

**5477.** Hobson, Jonathan T. *Footprints of Abraham Lincoln: Presenting Many Interesting Facts, Reminiscences, and Illustrations, Never before Published.* Dayton, OH: Otterbein Press, 1909.

**5478.** Holland, Josiah G. *The Life of Abraham Lincoln.* Springfield, MA: G. Bill, 1866.

**5479.** Holliday, Carl. "Lincoln's First Levee." *Illinois State Historical Society Journal* 11 (October 1918): 386–390.

**5480.** ———. "Lincoln's God." *South Atlantic Quarterly* 18 (January 1919): 15–23.

**5481.** Holmes, Frederick L. *Abraham Lincoln Traveled This Way: The Log Book of a Pilgrim to the Lincoln Country.* Boston: Page, 1930.

**5482.** Holzer, Harold. "The Imagemakers: Portraits of Lincoln in the 1860 Campaign." *Chicago History* 7 (Winter 1978/1979): 198–207.

**5483.** Hope, Eva. *New World Heroes, Lincoln and Garfield: The Life Story of Two Self-Made Men, Whom the People Made Presidents.* London: W. Scott, 1884.

**5484.** Horgan, Paul. *Abraham Lincoln: Citizen of New Salem.* New York: Macmillan, 1961.

**5485.** Horner, Harlan H. *The Growth of Lincoln's Faith.* New York: Abingdon Press, 1939.

**5486.** ———. *Lincoln and Greeley.* Urbana: University of Illinois Press, 1953.

**5487.** ———. "Lincoln Replies to William Henry Seard." *Lincoln Herald* 54 (Spring 1952): 3–11; 54 (Summer 1952): 33–40.

**5488.** Horowitz, Murray M. "That Presidential Grub: Lincoln versus His Generals." *Lincoln Herald* 79 (Winter 1977): 157–168.

**5489.** Houser, Martin L. *The Education of Abraham Lincoln.* Peoria, IL: L. O. Schriver, 1938.

**5490.** ———. *Lincoln's Education and Other Essays.* New York: Bookman Associates, 1957.

**5491.** Howard, James Q. *The Life of Abraham Lincoln: With Extracts from His Speeches.* Columbus, OH: Follett, Foster, 1860.

**5492.** Howe, Beverly W. *Abraham Lincoln in Great Britain.* Chicago: Winslow Publishing Company, 1940.

**5493.** Howells, William D. *Life of Abraham Lincoln.* Bloomington: Indiana University Press, 1960.

**5494.** Howells, William D., and John L. Hayes. *Lives and Speeches of Abraham Lincoln and Hannibal Hamlin.* Columbus, OH: Follett, Foster, 1860.

**5495.** Hubbard, George U. "Abraham Lincoln as Seen by the Mormons." *Utah Historical Quarterly* 31 (Spring 1963): 91–108.

**5496.** Hurt, James. "All the Living and the Dead: Lincoln's Imagery." *American Literature* 52 (November 1980): 351–380.

**5497.** Ingersoll, Robert G. *Abraham Lincoln.* New York: Lane, 1894.

**5498.** Jackson, H. LeRoy. "Concerning the Financial Affairs of Abraham Lincoln, Esquire." *Connecticut Bar Journal* 35 (September 1960): 240–248.

**5499.** Jackson, Samuel T. *Lincoln's Use of the Bible.* New York: Jennings, 1909.

**5500.** Jaffa, Harry V. *Crisis of the House Divided: An Interpretation of the Issues in the Lincoln-Douglas Debates.* Garden City, NY: Doubleday, 1959.

**5501.** ———. "Value Consensus in Democracy: The Issue in the Lincoln-Douglas Debates." *American Political Science Review* 52 (September 1958): 745–753.

**5502.** Jayne, William. *Abraham Lincoln.* Chicago: Grand Army Hall and Memorial Association, 1908.

**5503.** Jennings, Janet. *Abraham Lincoln, the Greatest American.* Madison, WI: Cantwell Print Company, 1909.

**5504.** Jennison, Keith W. *Humorous Mr. Lincoln.* New York: Bonaza, 1965.

**5505.** Johannsen, Robert W. "In Search of the Real Lincoln, or Lincoln at the Crossroads." *Illinois State Historical Society Journal* 61 (Autumn 1968): 229–247.

**5506.** ———. *Lincoln-Douglas Debates of 1858.* New York: Oxford University Press, 1965.

**5507.** Johnson, George B. "The Quakerism of Abraham Lincoln." *Friends Historical Association Bulletin* 38 (Spring 1939): 63–67.

**5508.** Johnson, Ludwell H. "Abraham Lincoln and the Development of Presidential War-Making Powers." *Civil War History* 35 (September 1989): 208–224.

**5509.** Johnson, Ludwell H. "Lincoln and Equal Rights: The Authenticity of the Wadsworth Letter." *Journal of Southern History* 32 (February 1966): 83–87.

**5510.** Jones, Edgar D. *The Influence of Henry Clay upon Abraham Lincoln.* Lexington, KY: Henry Clay Memorial Foundation, 1952.

**5511.** ———. *Lincoln and the Preachers.* New York: Harper and Row, 1948.

**5512.** Jones, Henry C. "Abraham Lincoln's Attitude towards Education." *Iowa Law Review* 12 (June 1927): 336–392.

**5513.** Jones, Jenkin L. "Abraham Lincoln, 1808–1909." *Methodist Quarterly Review* 58 (July 1909): 534–547.

**5514.** Jordan, Harriet P. "The Lincoln-Douglas Debates of 1858: A Presentation of the Rhetorical Scene and Setting with a Plot Film Script of the Ottowa Debate." Ph.D. dissertation, University of Illinois, 1958.

**5515.** Judson, Clara I. *Abraham Lincoln, Friend of the People.* Chicago: Wilcox and Follett, 1950.

**5516.** Jusserand, Jean J. "Abraham Lincoln." In his *With Americans of Past and Present Days,* 277–306. New York: Scribner's, 1916.

**5517.** Kelley, William D. *Lincoln and Stanton.* New York: Putnam's, 1885.

**5518.** Kempf, Edward J. "Abraham Lincoln's Organic and Emotional Neurosis." *Archives of Neurology and Psychiatry* 67 (April 1952): 419–433.

**5519.** ———. *Abraham Lincoln's Philosophy of Common Sense: An Analytical Biography of a Great Mind.* 3 vols. New York: New York Academy of Sciences, 1965.

**5520.** Ketcham, Henry. *The Life of Abraham Lincoln.* New York: A. L. Burt, 1901.

**5521.** Kharas, Theodore. *Lincoln, a Master of Efficiency.* Wilkes-Barre, PA: T. L. Printery, 1921.

**5522.** Kimmel, Stanley O. *Mr. Lincoln's Washington.* New York: Coward-McCann, 1957.

**5523.** Kincaid, Robert L. "The Self-Education of Abraham Lincoln." In *Lincoln for the Ages,* edited by Ralph G. Newman, 150–154. Garden City, NY: Doubleday, 1960.

**5524.** King, Willard L. "Lincoln and the Illinois Copperheads." *Lincoln Herald* 80 (Fall 1978): 132–137.

**5525.** Knowles, Robert E. "The Mystery of Lincoln." *Canadian Magazine* 32 (February 1909): 345–351.

**5526.** Kolpas, Norman. *Abraham Lincoln.* New York: McGraw-Hill, 1981.

**5527.** Komroff, Manuel. *Abraham Lincoln.* New York: Putnam's, 1959.

**5528.** Kooker, Arthur R. "Abraham Lincoln: Spokesman for Democracy." *Journal of the West* 4 (April 1965): 260–271.

**5529.** Kubicek, Earl C. "Abraham Lincoln's Faith." *Lincoln Herald* 85 (Fall 1983): 188–194.

**5530.** ———. "The Case of the Mad Hatter." *Lincoln Herald* 83 (Fall 1981): 708–719.

**5531.** Kunhardt, Dorothy M. *Twenty Days.* New York: Harper and Row, 1965.

**5532.** Kunkel, Mable. *Abraham Lincoln, Unforgettable American.* Charlotte, NC: Delmar, 1976.

**5533.** Lake, Harry F. "The Influence of Douglas on the Life of Lincoln." *Granite Monthly* 60 (March 1928): 149–157.

**5534.** Lamon, Ward H. *The Life of Abraham Lincoln from His Birth to His Inauguration as President.* Boston: J. R. Osgood, 1872.

**5535.** Landis, Frederick. "Lincoln the Lawyer." *Lawyer and Banker* 19 (July 1926): 246–257.

**5536.** Larned, Josephus N. "Abraham Lincoln." *Buffalo Historical Society Publications* 19 (1915): 49–54.

**5537.** ———. "Lincoln: Simplest in Greatness." In his *A Study of Greatness in Men,* 221–303. Boston: Houghton Mifflin, 1911.

**5538.** Lawson, McEwan. *Here Greatness Stands: The Story of Abraham Lincoln.* London: Butterworth, 1948.

**5539.** Learned, Marion D. *Abraham Lincoln: An American Migration.* Philadelphia: W. J. Campbell, 1909.

**5540.** Leibiger, Stuart. "Lincoln's 'White Elephants': The Trent Affair." *Lincoln Herald* 84 (Summer 1982): 84–92.

**5541.** Lemmon, Walter M. "The Bible on the Tongue of Lincoln." *Methodist Review* 89 (January 1907): 93–108.

**5542.** Levy, T. Aaron. *Lincoln, the Politician.* Boston: R. G. Badger, 1918.

**5543.** Lewis, Joseph. *Lincoln the Freethinker.* New York: Lincoln Publishing Company, 1924.

**5544.** Lewis, Lloyd. *Myths after Lincoln.* New York: Blue Ribbon Books, 1929.

**5545.** Lincoln, Robert T. *A Portrait of Abraham Lincoln in Letters by His Oldest Son.*

Edited by Paul M. Angle. Chicago: Chicago Historical Society, 1968.

**5546.** Lincoln, Waldo. *History of the Lincoln Family.* Worchester, MA: Commonwealth Press, 1923.

**5547.** Lindstrom, Ralph G. *Lincoln Finds God.* New York: Longmans, Green, 1958.

**5548.** Locke, Charles E. "Lincoln Not an Unbeliever." *Methodist Review* 89 (September 1907): 737–744.

**5549.** Lockridge, Ross F. *Lincoln.* New York: World Books, 1930.

**5550.** Lodge, Henry C. "The Democracy of Abraham Lincoln." In his *The Democracy of the Constitution, and Other Addresses and Essays,* 122–159. New York: Scribner's, 1915.

**5551.** Lonergan, Thomas S. "Abraham Lincoln: An Example of Patriotism and Self Education." *Americana* 7 (February 1912): 123–129.

**5552.** Long, John D. *The Life Story of Abraham Lincoln.* Chicago: Revell, 1930.

**5553.** Longford, Frank P. *Abraham Lincoln.* New York: Putnam's, 1975.

**5554.** Lorant, Stefan. *The Life of Abraham Lincoln: A Short Illustrated Biography.* New York: McGraw-Hill, 1954.

**5555.** Ludwig, Emil. *Abraham Lincoln: The Full Life Story of Our Martyred President.* New York: Liveright, 1949.

**5556.** ———. *Lincoln.* Boston: Little, Brown, 1930.

**5557.** Luthin, Reinhard H. *The First Lincoln Campaign.* Cambridge, MA: Harvard University Press, 1944.

**5558.** ———. *The Real Abraham Lincoln.* Englewood Cliffs, NJ: Prentice-Hall, 1960.

**5559.** Lynch, William O. "The Convergence of Lincoln and Douglas." *Illinois State Historical Society Transactions* 32 (1925): 155–173.

**5560.** Macartney, Clarence E. *Lincoln and the Bible.* New York: Abingdon Press, 1949.

**5561.** Mace, William H. *Lincoln, the Man of the People.* New York: Rand McNally, 1912.

**5562.** Madison, Lucy F. *Lincoln.* Philadelphia: Penn Publishing Company, 1928.

**5563.** Mallam, William D. "Lincoln and the Conservatives." *Journal of Southern History* 28 (February 1962): 31–45.

**5564.** Malone, Dumas. "Jefferson and Lincoln." *Abraham Lincoln Quarterly* 5 (June 1949): 327–347.

**5565.** Maltby, Charles. *The Life and Public Services of Abraham Lincoln.* Stockton, CA: Daily Independent Steam Power Plant, 1884.

**5566.** Markens, Isaac. "Lincoln and the Jews." *American Jewish Historical Society Publications* 17 (1909): 109–165.

**5567.** Martin, Patricia M. *Abraham Lincoln.* New York: Putnam's, 1964.

**5568.** Masters, Edgar L. *Lincoln the Man.* New York: Dodd, Mead, 1931.

**5569.** McClure, Alexander K. *The Lincoln Ideals, His Personality and Principles as Reflected in His Own Words.* Washington, DC: Lincoln Sesquicentennial Commission, 1959.

**5570.** ———. *Portrait for Posterity: Lincoln and His Biographers.* New Brunswick, NJ: Rutgers University Press, 1947.

**5571.** McGregor, Thomas B. "Some New Facts about Abraham Lincoln's Parents." *Kentucky Historical Society Register* 20 (May 1922): 213–218.

**5572.** McLaughlin, Robert. *Washington and Lincoln.* New York: Putnam's, 1912.

**5573.** McPherson, James M. *Abraham Lincoln and the Second American Revolution.* New York: Oxford University Press, 1991.

**5574.** Meadowcroft, Enid. *Abraham Lincoln.* New York: Crowell, 1942.

**5575.** Meany, Edmond S., ed. *Lincoln Esteemed Washington.* Seattle, WA: F. McCaffrey, 1933.

**5576.** Mearns, David C. *Largely Lincoln.* New York: St. Martin's Press, 1961.

**5577.** ———. "Our Reluctant Contemporary: Abraham Lincoln." *Abraham Lincoln Quarterly* 6 (June 1950): 73–102.

**5578.** ———, ed. *The Lincoln Papers.* 2 vols. Garden City, NY: Doubleday, 1948.

**5579.** Meeklenburg, George. "The Soul of Lincoln's America." *Methodist Review* 44 (July 1928): 561–568.

**5580.** Meese, William A. *Abraham Lincoln: Incidents in His Life Relating to Waterways.* Moline, IL: Desaulniers and Company, 1908.

**5581.** Merriam, Charles E. "Abraham Lincoln." In his *Four American Party Leaders,* 1–21. New York: Macmillan, 1926.

**5582.** Miller, Francis T. *Portrait Life of Lincoln: Life of Abraham Lincoln, the Greatest American.* Springfield, MA: Patriot Publishing Company, 1910.

**5583.** Miller, Marion M., ed. *Life and Works of Abraham Lincoln.* 9 vols. New York: Current Literature Publishing Company, 1907.

**5584.** Miller, William L. "Lincoln's Second Inaugural: The Zenith of Statecraft." *Center Magazine* 13 (July/August 1970): 53–64.

**5585.** Milton, George F. *Abraham Lincoln and the Fifth Column.* New York: Vanguard Press, 1942.

**5586.** Minger, Ralph E. "Abraham Lincoln: His Philosophy of Politics and His Leadership Qualities." *Journal of the West* 4 (April 1965): 272–276.

**5587.** Minor, Charles L. *The Real Lincoln.* Richmond, VA: Everett Waddey, 1901.

**5588.** Minor, Wilma F. "Lincoln, the Lover." *Atlantic Monthly* 142 (December 1928): 838–856; 143 (January 1929): 1–14; 143 (February 1929): 215–225.

**5589.** Miroff, Bruce. "Abraham Lincoln: Democratic Leadership and the Tribe of the Eagle." In his *Icons of Democracy: American Leaders as Heroes, Aristocrats, Dissenters, and Democrats,* 83–124. New York: Basic Books, 1993.

**5590.** Mitchell, Wilmot B. *Abraham Lincoln: The Man and the Crisis.* Portland, ME: Smith and Sale, 1910.

**5591.** Mitgang, Herbert. *The Fiery Trail: A Life of Lincoln.* New York: Viking, 1974.

**5592.** ———, ed. *Lincoln as They Saw Him.* New York: Rinehart, 1956.

**5593.** Mohrmann, Gerald P., and Michael C. Leff. "Lincoln at Cooper Union: A Rationale for Neo-classical Criticism." *Quarterly Journal of Speech* 60 (December 1974): 459–467.

**5594.** Monaghan, Jay. *Diplomat in Carpet Slippers: Abraham Lincoln Deals with Foreign Affairs.* Indianapolis: Bobbs-Merrill, 1945.

**5595.** Moores, Charles W. *Abraham Lincoln.* Greenfield, IN: William Mitchell, 1922.

**5596.** ———. "Abraham Lincoln, Lawyer." *Indiana Historical Society Publications* 7 (1922): 483–535.

**5597.** ———. "The Career of a Country Lawyer—Abraham Lincoln." *American Bar Association Report* 35 (August/September 1910): 440–477.

**5598.** Morgan, James. *Abraham Lincoln, the Boy and the Man.* New York: Macmillan, 1908.

**5599.** Morse, John T. *Abraham Lincoln.* 2 vols. Boston: Houghton Mifflin, 1893.

**5600.** ———. "Lord Charnwood's 'Life of Abraham Lincoln.'" *Massachusetts Historical Society Proceedings* 51 (1918): 90–105.

**5601.** Moses, Elbert R. *Abraham Lincoln: From Cabin to Capitol.* Daytona Beach, FL: College Publishing Company, 1955.

**5602.** Mowry, Duane. "Abraham Lincoln." *Green Bag* 15 (February 1903): 53–61.

**5603.** Mulder, Gerhard E. "Abraham Lincoln and the Doctrine of Necessity." *Lincoln Herald* 66 (Summer 1964): 59–66.

**5604.** Mumford, Mary E. *A Sketch of the Life and Times of Abraham Lincoln.* Philadelphia: Bradley, 1865.

**5605.** Murr, J. Edward. "Lincoln in Indiana." *Indiana Magazine of History* 13 (December 1917): 307–348; 14 (March 1918): 13–75; 14 (June 1918): 148–182.

**5606.** Neely, Mark E., Jr. *The Abraham Lincoln Encyclopedia.* New York: Da Capo Press, 1984.

**5607.** ———. "Abraham Lincoln's Nationalism Reconsidered." *Lincoln Herald* 76 (Spring 1974): 12–28.

**5608.** ———. "American Nationalism in the Image of Henry Clay: Abraham Lincoln's Eulogy on Henry Clay in Context." *Kentucky Historical Society Register* 73 (January 1975): 31–60.

**5609.** ———. *The Fate of Liberty: Abraham Lincoln and Civil Liberties.* New York: Oxford University Press, 1991.

**5610.** ———. *The Last Best Hope of Earth: Abraham Lincoln and the Promise of America.* Cambridge, MA: Harvard University Press, 1993.

**5611.** ———. "Lincoln and the Mexican War: An Argument by Analogy." *Civil War History* 24 (March 1978): 5–24.

**5612.** ———. "The Lincoln Theme since Randall's Call: The Promise and Perils of Professionalism." *Abraham Lincoln Association Papers* 1 (1979): 10–70.

**5613.** ———. "War and Partisanship: What Lincoln Learned from James K. Polk." *Journal of Illinois State Historical Society* 74 (Autumn 1981): 199–216.

**5614.** Nevins, Allan. *The Emergence of Lincoln.* 2 vols. New York: Scribner's, 1950.

**5615.** ———. "Lincoln's Ideals of Democracy." *Topic* (Spring 1965): 11–26.

**5616.** Nevins, Allan, and Irving Stone, eds. *Lincoln: A Contemporary Portrait.* Garden City, NY: Doubleday, 1962.

**5617.** Newton, Joseph F. *Abraham Lincoln: An Essay.* Cedar Rapids, IA: Torch Press, 1910.

**5618.** ———. *Lincoln and Herndon.* Cedar Rapids, IA: Torch Press, 1910.

**5619.** Nichols, Roy F. "Abraham Lincoln: Master Politician." In *Lincoln for the Ages,* edited by Ralph G. Newman, 236–241. Garden City, NY: Doubleday, 1960.

**5620.** Nicolay, Helen. *Personal Traits of Abraham Lincoln.* New York: Century, 1912.

**5621.** Nicolay, John G. *A Short Life of Abraham Lincoln, Condensed from Nicolay and Hay's Abraham Lincoln: A History.* New York: Century, 1902.

**5622.** Nicolay, John G., and John Hay. *Abraham Lincoln: A History.* 10 vols. New York: Century, 1890.

**5623.** Nolan, Jeannette C. *Abraham Lincoln.* New York: Messner, 1965.

**5624.** Norton, Eliot. *Abraham Lincoln: A Lover of Mankind: An Essay.* New York: Moffat, Yard, 1911.

**5625.** Oakleaf, Joseph B. *Abraham Lincoln, His Friendship for Humanity, and Sacrifice for Others.* Moline, IL: Desaulniers, 1910.

**5626.** Oates, Stephen B. *Abraham Lincoln: The Man behind the Myths.* New York: Harper and Row, 1984.

**5627.** ———. "Lincoln: The Man, the Myth." *Civil War Times Illustrated* 22 (February 1984): 10–19.

**5628.** ———. "Toward a New Birth of Freedom: Abraham Lincoln and Reconstruction, 1854–1865." *Lincoln Herald* 82 (Spring 1980): 287–296.

**5629.** ———. "Wilderness Fugue: Lincoln's Journey to Manhood on the Kentucky and Indiana Frontier." *American West* 13 (March/April 1976): 4–13.

**5630.** ———. *With Malice toward None: The Life of Abraham Lincoln.* New York: Harper and Row, 1977.

**5631.** Oberholtzer, Ellis P. *Abraham Lincoln.* Philadelphia: G. W. Jacobs, 1904.

**5632.** O'Connell, Margaret J. *Lincoln Lives.* New York: Vantage, 1957.

**5633.** Ogden, James M. "Lincoln's Early Impressions of the Law in Indiana." *Notre Dame Lawyer* 7 (March 1932): 325–329.

**5634.** Olson, Julius E. "Lincoln in Wisconsin." *Wisconsin Magazine of History* 4 (September 1920): 44–54.

**5635.** Ostendorf, Lloyd. "A Relic from His Last Birthday: The Mills Life-Mask of Lincoln." *Lincoln Herald* 75 (Fall 1973): 79–85.

**5636.** Owen, G. Frederick. *Abraham Lincoln: The Man and His Faith.* Wheaton, IL: Tyndale, 1981.

**5637.** Packard, Roy D. *Lincoln.* Cleveland, OH: Carpenter Print, 1948.

**5638.** ———. *The Lincoln of the Thirtieth Congress.* Boston: Christopher Publishing House, 1950.

**5639.** Padover, Saul K. "The American: Abraham Lincoln." In his *The Genius of America: Men Whose Ideas Shaped Our Civilization,* 156–178. New York: McGraw-Hill, 1960.

**5640.** Paludan, Phillip S. "Lincoln, the Rule of Law, and the American Revolution." *Illinois State Historical Society Journal* 70 (February 1977): 10–17.

**5641.** ———. *The Presidency of Abraham Lincoln.* Lawrence: University Press of Kansas, 1994.

**5642.** Paradise, Frank I. *Abraham Lincoln, Democrat.* London: Mills and Boon, 1921.

**5643.** Pargellis, Stanley M. "Lincoln's Political Philosophy." *Abraham Lincoln Quarterly* 3 (June 1945): 275–290.

**5644.** Paul, Eden, and Cedar Paul. *Abraham Lincoln and the Times That Tried His Soul.* New York: Fawcett, 1956.

**5645.** Paullin, Charles O. "Abraham Lincoln in Congress, 1847–1849." *Illinois State Historical Society Journal* 14 (April/July 1921): 85–89.

**5646.** Pennypacker, Isaac R. "The Lincoln Legend." *American Mercury* 1 (January 1924): 1–7.

**5647.** Peters, Madison C. *Abraham Lincoln's Religion.* Boston: R. G. Badger, 1909.

**5648.** Petersen, William F. *Lincoln-Douglas: The Weather as Destiny.* Springfield, IL: Thomas, 1943.

**5649.** Peterson, Gary L. "A Critical Edition of the Lincoln-Douglas Debates of 1858." Ph.D. dissertation, Ohio University, 1965.

**5650.** Peterson, Gloria. *An Administrative History of Abraham Lincoln Birthplace National Historic Site.* Washington, DC: Division of History, Office of Archaeology and Historic Preservation, 1968.

**5651.** Peterson, Merrill D. *Lincoln in American Memory.* New York: Oxford University Press, 1994.

**5652.** Phillips, Charles. "Abraham Lincoln." *Catholic World* 128 (February 1929): 513–522; 128 (April 1929): 513–522; 129 (April 1930): 48–59.

**5653.** Phillips, Daniel T. *A Prize Treatise on the Character of Abraham Lincoln.* New York: John M. Davis, 1884.

**5654.** Piatt, Donn. "Abraham Lincoln." In his *Memories of the Men Who Saved the Union,* 27–49. New York: Belford, Clarke and Company, 1887.

**5655.** Potter, David M. *The Lincoln Theme and American National Historiography, an Inaugural Lecture Delivered before the University of Oxford on 19 November 1947.* Oxford: Clarendon Press, 1948.

**5656.** Power, John C. *Abraham Lincoln.* Springfield, IL: E. A. Wilson, 1875.

**5657.** Pratt, Harry E. "Abraham Lincoln in Bloomington, Illinois." *Illinois State Historical Society Journal* 29 (April 1936): 42–69.

**5658.** ———. "Abraham Lincoln's First Murder Trial." *Illinois State Historical Society Journal* 37 (September 1944): 242–249.

**5659.** ———. "Judge Abraham Lincoln." *Illinois State Historical Society Journal* 48 (Spring 1955): 28–39.

**5660.** ———. *Lincoln, 1809–1839.* Springfield, IL: Abraham Lincoln Association, 1941.

**5661.** ———. *Lincoln, 1840–1846.* Springfield, IL: Abraham Lincoln Association, 1939.

**5662.** ———. *The Personal Finances of Abraham Lincoln.* Springfield, IL: Abraham Lincoln Association, 1943.

**5663.** ———, ed. *Concerning Mr. Lincoln: In Which Abraham Lincoln Is Pictured as He Appeared to Letter Writers of His Time.* Springfield, IL: Abraham Lincoln Association, 1944.

**5664.** Pratt, Silas G. *Lincoln in Story.* New York: Appleton, 1901.

**5665.** Pressly, Thomas J. "Bullets and Ballots: Lincoln and the Right of Revolution." *American Historical Review* 67 (January 1962): 647–662.

**5666.** Prioli, Carmine A. "'Wonder Girl from the West': Vinnie Ream and the Congressional Statute of Abraham Lincoln." *Journal of American Culture* 12 (Winter 1989): 1–20.

**5667.** Purvis, Thomas L. "The Making of a Myth: Abraham Lincoln's Family Background in the Perspective of Jacksonian Politics." *Illinois State Historical Society Journal* 75 (Summer 1982): 149–160.

**5668.** Putnam, George H. *Abraham Lincoln: The People's Leader in the Struggle for National Existence.* New York: Putnam's, 1909.

**5669.** Quarles, Benjamin. *Lincoln and the Negro.* New York: Oxford University Press, 1962.

**5670.** Randall, James G. *Constitutional Problems under Lincoln.* New York: Appleton, 1926.

**5671.** ———. "Has the Lincoln Theme Been Exhausted?" *American Historical Review* 41 (January 1936): 270–294.

**5672.** ———. "Lincoln and the Governance of Men." *Abraham Lincoln Quarterly* 6 (June 1951): 327–352.

**5673.** ———. *Lincoln and the South.* Baton Rouge: Louisiana State University Press, 1946.

**5674.** ———. *Lincoln, the Liberal Statesman.* New York: Dodd, Mead, 1947.

**5675.** ———. *Lincoln the President: Last Full Measure.* Urbana: University of Illinois Press, 1991.

**5676.** ———. *Mr. Lincoln.* Edited by Richard N. Current. New York: Dodd, Mead, 1957.

**5677.** Randall, James G., and Richard N. Current. *Lincoln the President.* 4 vols. New York: Dodd, Mead, 1945–1955.

**5678.** Rankin, Henry B. "Comments and Corrections on 'The Lincoln Life-Mask and How It Was Made.'" *Illinois State Historical Society Journal* 8 (July 1915): 249–259.

**5679.** ———. "The First American—Abraham Lincoln." *Illinois State Historical Society Journal* 8 (July 1915): 260–267.

**5680.** ———. *Intimate Character Sketches of Abraham Lincoln.* Philadelphia: Lippincott, 1924.

**5681.** Rasmussen, Della M. *The Power of Trying Again: The Story of Abe Lincoln.* Antioch, CA: Power Tales, Eagle Systems International, 1981.

**5682.** Rawley, James A. "Lincoln and Governor Morgan." *Abraham Lincoln Quarterly* 6 (March 1951): 272–300.

**5683.** ———. "The Nationalism of Abraham Lincoln." *Civil War History* 9 (September 1963): 283–298.

**5684.** Raymond, Henry J., and John Savage. *The Life of Abraham Lincoln, and of Andrew Johnson*. New York: National Union Executive Committee, 1864.

**5685.** Reid, Whitelaw. *Abraham Lincoln*. London: Harrison and Sons, 1910.

**5686.** Rennick, Percival G. *Abraham Lincoln and Ann Rutledge: An Old Salem Romance*. Peoria, IL: E. J. Jacob, 1932.

**5687.** Rice, Allen T., ed. *Reminiscences of Abraham Lincoln by Distinguished Men of His Time*. New York: North American Publishing Company, 1885.

**5688.** Richards, John T. *Abraham Lincoln, the Lawyer-Statesman*. Boston: Houghton Mifflin, 1916.

**5689.** Riches, William T. "The Commoners: Andrew Johnson and Abraham Lincoln to 1861." Ph.D. dissertation, University of Tennessee, 1976.

**5690.** Riddle, Donald W. *Congressman Abraham Lincoln*. Urbana: University of Illinois Press, 1957.

**5691.** ———. "Congressman Abraham Lincoln from Illinois, 1846–48." In *Lincoln for the Ages*, edited by Ralph G. Newman, 96–100. Garden City, NY: Doubleday, 1960.

**5692.** ———. *Lincoln Runs for Congress: A Publication of the Abraham Lincoln Association, Springfield, IL*. New Brunswick, NJ: Rutgers University Press, 1948.

**5693.** Ridley, Maurice R. *Abraham Lincoln*. London: Blackie and Son, 1945.

**5694.** Roberts, Octavia. *Lincoln in Illinois*. Boston: Houghton Mifflin, 1918.

**5695.** Rogers, Kate B. "The Name of Lincoln." *Illinois State Historical Society Journal* 7 (July 1914): 60–69.

**5696.** Roske, Ralph J. "Lincoln and Lyman Trumbull." In *Lincoln Images: Augustana College Centennial Essays*, edited by O. Fritiof Ander, 61–81. Rock Island, IL: Augustan College Library, 1960.

**5697.** Ross, Earle D. "Lincoln and Agriculture." *Agricultural History* 3 (April 1929): 51–66.

**5698.** Rothschild, Alonzo. *"Honest Abe": A Study in Integrity Based on the Early Life of Abraham Lincoln*. Boston: Houghton Mifflin, 1917.

**5699.** ———. *Lincoln, Master of Men: A Study in Character*. Boston: Houghton Mifflin, 1906.

**5700.** Rubinger, Naphtali J. *Abraham Lincoln and the Jews*. New York: J. David, 1962.

**5701.** Ruiz, Ramon E. "A Commentary on Morality: Lincoln, Justin Smith, and the Mexican War." *Illinois State Historical Society Journal* 69 (February 1976): 26–34.

**5702.** Ryan, Daniel J. *Lincoln and Ohio*. Columbus: Ohio State Archaeological and Historical Society, 1923.

**5703.** Ryan, Joseph F. "Abraham Lincoln and New York City, 1861–1865: War and Politics." Ph.D. dissertation, St. Johns University, 1969.

**5704.** Samuels, Ernest. "Abraham Lincoln: Strategist of Conciliation." *Lincoln Herald* 64 (Summer 1962): 70–79.

**5705.** Sanchez-Torrento, Eugenio. *A Modern Biography of Abraham Lincoln*. Miami: Impresso Editorial A. I. P., 1970.

**5706.** Sandburg, Carl. *Abe Lincoln Grows Up*. New York: Harcourt, Brace, 1928.

**5707.** ———. *Abraham Lincoln, the Prairie Years*. 2 vols. New York: Harcourt, Brace and World, 1926.

**5708.** ———. *Abraham Lincoln: The War Years*. 4 vols. New York: Harcourt, Brace, 1939.

**5709.** Schapsmeier, Edward L., and Frederick H. Schapsmeier. "Lincoln and Douglas: Their Versions of the West." *Journal of the West* 7 (October 1968): 542–552.

**5710.** Schurz, Carl. *Abraham Lincoln, a Biographical Essay: With an Essay on the Portraits of Lincoln by Truman H. Bartlett.* Boston: Houghton Mifflin, 1907.

**5711.** ———. *Abraham Lincoln, an Essay.* Boston: Houghton Mifflin, 1891.

**5712.** Schwartz, Thomas F. "An Egregious Political Blunder: Justin Butterfield, Lincoln, and Illinois Whiggery." *Papers of the Abraham Lincoln Association* 8 (1986): 9–19.

**5713.** Scovill, Samuel, Jr. *Abraham Lincoln: His Story.* Philadelphia: American Sunday-School Union, 1918.

**5714.** Scripps, John L. *Life of Abraham Lincoln.* New York: Greenwood, 1961.

**5715.** Searcher, Victor. *Lincoln Today: An Introduction to Modern Lincolniana.* New York: T. Yoseloff, 1969.

**5716.** Segal, Charles M., ed. *Conversations with Lincoln.* New York: Putnam's, 1961.

**5717.** Seitz, Don C. *Lincoln the Politician: How the Rail-Splitter and Flatboatman Played the Great American Game.* New York: Coward-McCann, 1931.

**5718.** Sharp, Alfred. *Abraham Lincoln.* London: Epworth Press, 1919.

**5719.** Shaw, Archer H., ed. *The Lincoln Encyclopedia: The Spoken and Written Words of A. Lincoln, Arranged for Ready Reference.* New York: Macmillan, 1950.

**5720.** Sheppard, Robert D. *Abraham Lincoln, Character Sketch.* Milwaukee, WI: H. G. Campbell, 1899.

**5721.** Sherlock, Richard K. "Liberalism, Public Policy, and the Life Not Worth Living: Abraham Lincoln on Beneficent Euthanasia." *American Journal of Jurisprudence* 26 (1981): 47–65.

**5722.** Shirley, Ralph. *A Short Life of Abraham Lincoln.* New York: Funk and Wagnalls, 1919.

**5723.** Short, Isaac M. *Abraham Lincoln: Early Days in Illinois, Reminiscences of Different Persons Who Became Eminent in American History.* Kansas City, MO: Simpson Publishing Company, 1927.

**5724.** Shutes, Milton H. *Abraham Lincoln and the New Almaden Mine.* San Francisco: L. Kennedy, 1936.

**5725.** ———. *Lincoln and the Doctors: A Medical Narrative of the Life of Abraham Lincoln.* New York: Pioneer Press, 1933.

**5726.** Shutes, Milton H. *Lincoln's Emotional Life.* Philadelphia: Dorrance, 1957.

**5727.** Sigelschiffer, Saul. *The American Conscience: The Drama of the Lincoln-Douglas Debate.* New York: Horizon, 1973.

**5728.** Silver, David M. *Lincoln's Supreme Court.* Urbana: University of Illinois Press, 1956.

**5729.** Simon, Paul. *Lincoln's Preparation for Greatness: The Illinois Legislature Years.* Norman: University of Oklahoma Press, 1965.

**5730.** Smiley, David L. "Abraham Lincoln Deals with Cassius M. Clay—Portrait of a Patient Politician." *Lincoln Herald* 55 (Winter 1953): 15–23.

**5731.** Smith, Dwight L., ed. "Robert Livingston Stanton's Lincoln." *Lincoln Herald* 76 (Winter 1974): 172–180.

**5732.** Smith, Harvey G. *Lincoln and the Lincolns.* New York: Pioneer Publications, 1931.

**5733.** Smith, Samuel G. "Abraham Lincoln." *Methodist Review* 41 (January 1925): 81–90.

**5734.** Smith, Thomas V. *Abraham Lincoln and the Spiritual Life.* Boston: Beacon Press, 1951.

**5735.** ———. "Lincoln and Democracy." In *Abraham Lincoln: A New Portrait,* edited by Henry B. Kranz, 69–74. New York: Putnam's, 1959.

**5736.** ———. *Lincoln, Living Legend.* Chicago: University of Chicago Press, 1940.

**5737.** Smyser, George H. "The Lincoln Family in 1861: A History of the Painting and Engraving by Mr. J. C. Buttre." *Illinois State Historical Society Journal* 22 (July 1929): 357–361.

**5738.** Snider, Denton J. *Abraham Lincoln, an Interpretation in Biography.* St. Louis, MO: Sigma Publishing Company, 1908.

**5739.** Sparks, Edwin E. *The Lincoln-Douglas Debates of 1858.* Springfield: Trustees of the Illinois State Historical Library, 1908.

**5740.** Spears, Zarel C., and Robert S. Barton. *Berry and Lincoln, Frontier Merchants: The Store That "Winked Out."* New York: Stratford House, 1947.

**5741.** Spencer, Omar C. "Abraham Lincoln, the Lawyer." *Oregon Law Review* 4 (April 1925): 177–187.

**5742.** Starr, John W. *Lincoln and the Railroads: A Biographical Study.* New York: Dodd, Mead, 1927.

**5743.** ———. *Lincoln's Last Day.* New York: Stokes, 1922.

**5744.** ———. "What Was Abraham Lincoln's Religion?" *Magazine of History* 15 (January 1912): 18–31.

**5745.** Stephenson, Nathaniel W. *Lincoln: An Account of His Personal Life, Especially of Its Springs of Action as Revealed and Deepened by the Ordeals of War.* Indianapolis: Bobbs-Merrill, 1922.

**5746.** Stern, Philip V. "Lincoln's Journey to Greatness." In *Abraham Lincoln: A New Portrait,* edited by Henry B. Kranz, 158–165. New York: Putnam's, 1959.

**5747.** Stewart, Charles J. "The People and the Lincoln-Douglas Campaign of 1858." *Register of the Kentucky Historical Society* 65 (October 1967): 284–293.

**5748.** Stewart, Thomas D. "An Anthropologist Looks at Lincoln." *Smithsonian Institute Annual Report* (1952): 419–437.

**5749.** Stoddard, William O. *Abraham Lincoln.* New York: Fords, Howard, and Hulbert, 1888.

**5750.** ———. *Abraham Lincoln and Andrew Johnson.* New York: Stokes, 1888.

**5751.** ———. "Face to Face with Lincoln, by His Secretary William O. Stoddard." Edited by William O. Stoddard, Jr. *Atlantic Monthly* 135 (March 1925): 332–339.

**5752.** ———. *Lincoln at Work, Sketches from Life.* Boston: United Society of Christian Endeavor, 1900.

**5753.** Strozier, Charles B. *Lincoln's Quest for Union: Public and Private Meanings.* New York: Basic Books, 1982.

**5754.** Strunsky, Rose. *Abraham Lincoln.* London: Methuen, 1914.

**5755.** ———. "Abraham Lincoln's Social Ideals." *Century Magazine* 87 (February 1914): 588–592.

**5756.** Stubbs, Roy St. George. "Lawyer Lincoln—A Canadian Estimate." *Connecticut Bar Journal* 27 (September 1953): 335–358.

**5757.** Stutler, Boyd B. "Abraham Lincoln and John Brown—A Parallel." *Civil War History* 8 (September 1962): 290–299.

**5758.** Sumner, Charles. "Promises of the Declaration of Independence, and Abraham Lincoln." In his *The Works of Charles Sumner,* vol. 9, 367–428. Boston: Lee and Shepard, 1875.

**5759.** Sumner, Guy L. *Meet Abraham Lincoln.* New York: Harper and Row, 1946.

**5760.** Suppiger, Joseph E. *The Intimate Lincoln.* Lanham, MD: University Press of America, 1985.

**5761.** Tarbell, Ida M. *The Early Life of Abraham Lincoln.* New York: McClure, 1896.

**5762.** ———. *In the Footsteps of the Lincolns.* New York: Harper and Row, 1924.

**5763.** ———. *The Life of Abraham Lincoln.* 2 vols. New York: Doubleday, 1900.

**5764.** ———. *The Life of Abraham Lincoln, Drawn from Original Sources and Containing Many Speeches, Letters, and Telegrams Hitherto Unpublished.* 2 vols. Rev. ed. New York: Macmillan, 1917.

**5765.** Taylor, Hannis. "The Lincoln-Douglas Debates and Their Application to Present Problems." *North American Review* 189 (February 1909): 161–173.

**5766.** Temple, Wayne C. *Lincoln and Bennett: The Story of a Store Account.* Harrogate, TN: Lincoln Memorial University, 1967.

**5767.** ———. "Lincoln and W. H. W. Cushman." *Lincoln Herald* 68 (Summer 1966): 81–87.

**5768.** ———. *Lincoln the Railsplitter.* La Cross, WI: Willow Press, 1961.

**5769.** ———. "Lincoln's Fence Rails." *Illinois State Historical Society Journal* 32 (Spring 1954): 20–34.

**5770.** Thayer, William M. *From Pioneer Home to White House: Life of Abraham Lincoln.* Rev. ed. Norwich, CT: Henry Bill Publishing Company, 1882.

**5771.** ———. *Life and Character of Abraham Lincoln.* Boston: Walker, Wise, 1864.

**5772.** Thomas, Benjamin P. *Abraham Lincoln: A Biography.* New York: Knopf, 1952.

**5773.** ———. *Lincoln.* Springfield, IL: Abraham Lincoln Association, 1936.

**5774.** ———. "Lincoln and New Salem, a Study in Environment." *Illinois State Historical Society Transactions* 41 (1934): 61–75.

**5775.** ———. *Portrait for Posterity: Lincoln and His Biographers.* New Brunswick, NJ: Rutgers University Press, 1947.

**5776.** Thompson, David D. *Abraham Lincoln.* New York: Hunt and Eaton, 1894.

**5777.** Thompson, Seymour D. "Lincoln and Douglas: The Great Freeport Debate." *American Law Review* 39 (March/April 1905): 161–177.

**5778.** Thurow, Glen E. *Abraham Lincoln and American Political Religion.* Albany: State University of New York Press, 1976.

**5779.** Tilley, John S. *Lincoln Takes Command.* Chapel Hill: University of North Carolina Press, 1941.

**5780.** Townsend, William H. *Abraham Lincoln, Defendant: Lincoln's Most Interesting Lawsuit.* Boston: Houghton Mifflin, 1924.

**5781.** ———. "Lincoln, the Lawyer." In *Abraham Lincoln: A New Portrait,* edited by Henry B. Kranz, 42–47. New York: Putnam's, 1959.

**5782.** ———. *Lincoln, the Litigant.* Boston: Houghton Mifflin, 1925.

**5783.** ———. "'Old Abe' and the 'Little Giant'?" *American Bar Association Journal* 13 (February 1927): 99–104.

**5784.** Trueblood, David E. *Abraham Lincoln: Theologian of American Anguish.* New York: Harper and Row, 1973.

**5785.** Turner, Justin G. "Lincoln and the Cannibals." *Lincoln Herald* 77 (Winter 1975): 212–218.

**5786.** Tyler, Lyon G. "How Lincoln Got Rich." *Tyler's Quarterly Historical and Genealogical Magazine* 17 (July 1935): 3–9.

**5787.** ———. "Was Lincoln an Ideal?" *Tyler's Quarterly Historical and Genealogical Magazine* 8 (January 1927): 145–155.

**5788.** Van Doren, Mark A. "A Playwright Looks at Lincoln." In *Lincoln for the Ages,* edited by Ralph G. Newman, 395–399. Garden City, NY: Doubleday, 1960.

**5789.** Van Hoesen, Henry B. "Lincoln and John Hay." *Books at Brown* 18 (October 1960): 141–180.

**5790.** Van Natter, Francis M. *Lincoln's Boyhood: A Chronicle of His Indiana Years.* Washington, DC: Public Affairs Press, 1964.

**5791.** Vannest, Charles G. *Lincoln the Hoosier: Abraham Lincoln's Life in Indiana.* St. Louis, MO: Edin Publishing House, 1928.

**5792.** Victor, Orville J. *The Private and Public Life of Abraham Lincoln.* New York: Beadle, 1864.

**5793.** Viele, Egbert L. "A Trip with Lincoln, Chase, and Stanton." *Scribner's Monthly* 16 (October 1878): 813–822.

**5794.** Volk, Leonard W. "The Lincoln Life-Mask and How It Was Made." *Illinois State Historical Society Journal* 8 (July 1915): 238–248.

**5795.** Wade, Mary H. *Abraham Lincoln.* Boston: R. G. Badger, 1914.

**5796.** Walton, Clyde C. "Abraham Lincoln: Illinois Legislator." In *Lincoln for the Ages,* edited by Ralph G. Newman, 74–78. Garden City, NY: Doubleday, 1960.

**5797.** Wanamaker, Reuben M. *The Voice of Lincoln.* New York: Scribner's, 1920.

**5798.** Warde, William F. "Jefferson, Lincoln, and Dewey." In *Marxist Essays in American History,* edited by Robert Himmel, 124–128. New York: Merit Publishers, 1966.

**5799.** Warren, Louis A. *Abraham Lincoln, a Concise Biography.* Fort Wayne, IN: Lincoln National Life Insurance Company, 1934.

**5800.** ———. "Lincoln's Early Political Background." *Illinois State Historical Society Journal* 23 (May 1931): 618–629.

**5801.** ———. "Lincoln's Hoosier Schoolmasters." *Indiana Magazine of History* 27 (June 1931): 104–118.

**5802.** ———. *Lincoln's Parentage and Childhood: A History of the Kentucky Lincolns Supported by Documentary Evidence.* New York: Century, 1926.

**5803.** ———. *Lincoln's Youth: Indiana Years, Seven to Twenty-One, 1816–1830.* New York: Appleton, 1959.

**5804.** ———. "The Religious Background of the Lincoln Family." *Filson Club History Quarterly* 6 (January 1932): 72–88.

**5805.** Warren, Raymond. *Abe Lincoln, Kentucky Boy.* Chicago: Reilly and Lee, 1931.

**5806.** ———. *Abraham Lincoln as a Spiritual Influence.* Chicago: Progressive Century Company, 1933.

**5807.** ———. *The Prairie President.* Chicago: Reilly and Lee, 1930.

**5808.** Weik, Jesse W. *The Real Lincoln: A Portrait.* Boston: Houghton Mifflin, 1922.

**5809.** Weisenburger, Francis P. "Lincoln and His Ohio Friends." *Ohio Historical Quarterly* 68 (July 1955): 223–256.

**5810.** Westwood, Howard C. "Lincoln and the Hampton Roads Peace Conference." *Lincoln Herald* 81 (Winter 1979): 243–256.

**5811.** Wham, George D. "The Education of Abraham Lincoln." *Chicago Schools Journal* 12 (February 1930): 225–231.

**5812.** Wheare, Kenneth C. *Abraham Lincoln and the United States.* New York: Macmillan, 1949.

**5813.** Wheeler, Daniel E. *Abraham Lincoln.* New York: Macmillan, 1916.

**5814.** Whipple, Wayne. *The Story of Young Abraham Lincoln.* Philadelphia: Henry Altemus, 1915.

**5815.** Whitcomb, Paul S. "Lincoln and Democracy." *Tyler's Quarterly Historical and Genealogical Magazine* 9 (July 1927): 5–33.

**5816.** Whitlock, Brand. *Abraham Lincoln.* New York: Appleton, 1930.

**5817.** Whitney, Henry C. *Life of Abraham Lincoln.* 2 vols. New York: Baker and Taylor, 1908.

**5818.** ——. *Life on the Circuit with Lincoln.* Caldwell, ID: Caxton, 1940.

**5819.** Wiest, Walter E. "Lincoln's Political Ethic: An Alternative to American Millennialism." *American Journal of Theology and Philosophy* 4 (September 1983): 116–126.

**5820.** Wiley, Bell I. "Lincoln, Plain Man of the People." *Emory University Quarterly* 14 (December 1958): 195–206.

**5821.** Wiley, Earl W. *Abraham Lincoln: Portrait of a Speaker.* New York: Vantage Press, 1970.

**5822.** ——. "Lincoln in the Campaign of 1856." *Illinois State Historical Society Journal* 22 (January 1930): 582–592.

**5823.** ——. "Lincoln the Speaker." *Quarterly Journal of Speech* 21 (June 1935): 305–322.

**5824.** ——. "Lincoln the Speaker—1816–1830." *Quarterly Journal of Speech* 20 (February 1934): 1–15.

**5825.** ——. "Motivation as a Factor in Lincoln's Rhetoric." *Quarterly Journal of Speech* 24 (December 1938): 615–621.

**5826.** Williams, Francis H. *The Burden Bearer: An Epic of Lincoln.* Philadelphia: Jacobs, 1908.

**5827.** Williams, Gary L. "Lincoln's Neutral Allies: The Case of the Kentucky Unionists." *South Atlantic Quarterly* 73 (Winter 1974): 70–84.

**5828.** Williams, T. Harry. *Lincoln and His Generals.* New York: Grossett and Dunlap, 1952.

**5829.** Williams, T. Harry. *Lincoln and the Radicals.* Madison: University of Wisconsin Press, 1941.

**5830.** ——. *A Rail Splitter for President.* Denver: University of Denver Press, 1951.

**5831.** Wills, Garry. *Lincoln at Gettysburg: The Words That Remade American.* New York: Simon and Schuster, 1992.

**5832.** Woldman, Albert A. "The Centennial of Lincoln's Admission to the Bar—An Historic Event." *American Bar Association Journal* 23 (March 1937): 167–171.

**5833.** ——. *Lawyer Lincoln.* Boston: Houghton Mifflin, 1936.

**5834.** ——. *Lincoln and the Russians.* Cleveland, OH: World Publishing Company, 1952.

**5835.** Wolf, George D. "Lincoln, the Master Politician." *Lincoln Herald* 81 (Fall 1979): 163–168.

**5836.** Wolf, William J. *Lincoln's Religion.* New York: Pilgrim Press, 1970.

**5837.** ——. *The Religion of Abraham Lincoln.* Rev. ed. New York: Seabury Press, 1963.

**5838.** Wood, Harry. "How Both Abraham Lincolns Helped Found Arizona." *Lincoln Herald* 78 (Fall 1976): 109–116.

**5839.** Wood, Leonora W. *Abraham Lincoln.* Piedmont, WV: Herald Printing House, 1942.

**5840.** Woody, Robert H. "Inexhaustible Lincoln." *South Atlantic Quarterly* 52 (October 1953): 587–610.

**5841.** Wright, Allen H., ed. "A New Light on Lincoln as an Advocate." *Green Bag* 20 (February 1908): 78–90.

**5842.** Yarborough, Ralph W. "Lincoln as a Liberal Statesman." In *Lincoln for the Ages,* edited by Ralph G. Newman, 279–283. Garden City, NY: Doubleday, 1960.

**5843.** Zane, John M. *Lincoln, the Constitutional Lawyer.* Chicago: Caxton Club, 1932.

**5844.** Zilversmit, Arthur. *Lincoln on Black and White: A Documentary History.* Melbourne, FL: Krieger, 1983.

**5845.** Zinsmeister, Robert, Jr. "A Lincoln Presidential Library Issue: Colonel Harland Sanders Center for Lincoln Studies." *Lincoln Herald* 75 (Summer 1973): 33–38, 43, 50–67, 75–76.

**5846.** Zornow, William F. *Lincoln and the Party Divided.* Norman: University of Oklahoma Press, 1954.

**5847.** ———. "The Unwanted Mr. Lincoln." *Illinois State Historical Society Journal* 45 (Summer 1952): 146–163.

**LINCOLN, LEVI (1749–1820) R-MA, House 1800–1801.**

**5848.** Petroelje, Marvin J. "Lincoln Levi, Sr.: Jeffersonian Republican of Massachusetts." Ph.D. dissertation, Michigan State University, 1969.

**5849.** Quincy, Josiah. "The Governor at Nantucket." In his *Figures of the Past from the Leaves of Old Journals,* 146–157. Boston: Little, Brown, 1926.

**5850.** Washburn, Emory. *Memoir of Hon. Levi Lincoln Prepared Agreeably to a Resolution of the Massachusetts Historical Society.* Cambridge, MA: J. Wilson, 1869.

**LIND, JOHN (1854–1930) D-MN, House 1887–1893, 1903–1905.**

**5851.** Baker, James H. "John Lind." *Minnesota Historical Society Collections* 13 (1908): 373–394.

**5852.** Stephenson, George M. *John Lind of Minnesota.* Minneapolis: University of Minnesota Press, 1935.

**LINDBERGH, CHARLES AUGUSTUS (1859–1924) R-MN, House 1907–1917.**

**5853.** Haines, Lynn, and Dora B. Haines. *The Lindberghs.* New York: Vanguard, 1931.

**5854.** Larsen, Bruce K. *Lindbergh of Minnesota: A Political Biography.* New York: Harcourt, 1973.

**5855.** Lucas, Richard B. *Charles August Lindbergh, Sr.: A Case Study of Congressional Insurgency, 1906–1912.* Stockholm: Uppsala University, 1974.

**5856.** Stuhler, Barbara. "Charles A. Lindbergh: Radical Isolationist." In her *Ten Men of Minnesota and American Foreign Policy, 1898–1968,* 32–53. St. Paul: Minnesota Historical Society, 1973.

**LINDSAY, JOHN VLIET (1921– ) R-NY, House 1959–1965.**

**5857.** Buckley, William F. *The Unmaking of a Major.* New York: Viking, 1966.

**5858.** Button, Daniel E. *Lindsay: A Man for Tomorrow.* New York: Random House, 1965.

**5859.** Citron, Casper. *John V. Lindsay and the Silk Stocking Story.* New York: Fleet Publishing Corporation, 1955.

**5860.** Davis, Perry. "The New York City Institutionalized Mayoralty: Development in the Lindsay Years." Ph.D. dissertation, Columbia University, 1975.

**5861.** Gottehrer, Barry. *The Mayor's Man.* Garden City, NY: Doubleday, 1975.

**5862.** Hentoff, Nat. *A Political Life: The Education of John V. Lindsay.* New York: Knopf, 1969.

**5863.** Klein, Woody. *Lindsay's Promise: The Dream That Failed: A Personal Account.* New York: Macmillan, 1970.

**5864.** Lindsay, John V. *Journey into Politics.* New York: Dodd, Mead, 1967.

**5865.** Pilat, Oliver R. *Lindsay's Campaign: A Behind-the-Scenes Diary.* Boston: Beacon Press, 1968.

**LINDSAY, WILLIAM (1835–1909) D-KY, Senate 1893–1901.**

**5866.** Schlup, Leonard. "William Lindsay and the 1896 Party Crisis." *Register of the Kentucky Historical Society* 76 (January 1978): 22–33.

**LINN, LEWIS FIELDS (1796–1843) J-MO, Senate 1833–1843.**

**5867.** Husband, Michael B. "Senator Lewis F. Linn and the Oregon Question." *Missouri Historical Review* 66 (October 1971): 1–19.

**5868.** Linn, Elizabeth A., and Nathan Sargent. *The Life and Public Services of L. F. Linn.* New York: Appleton, 1857.

**LITTAUER, LUCIUS NATHAN**
**(1859–1944) R-NY, House 1897–1907.**

**5869.** Boxerman, Burton A. "Lucius Nathan Littauer." *American Jewish Historical Quarterly* 66 (June 1977): 498–512.

**LITTLETON, MARTIN WILEY**
**(1872–1934) D-NY, House 1911–1913.**

**5870.** Levy, Louis S. "Martin Littleton." In his *Yesterdays*, 71–77. New York: Library Publishers, 1954.

**LITTON, JERRY LON (1937–1976)**
**D-MO, House 1973–1976.**

**5871.** Mitchell, Bonnie. *Jerry Litton, 1937–1976: A Biography.* Chillicothe, MO: Jerry Litton Family Memorial Foundation, 1978.

**LIVERMORE, SAMUEL (1732–1803)**
**F-NH, House 1789–1793, Senate 1793–1801, Continental Congress 1780–1782.**

**5872.** McLachlan, James. "Samuel Livermore." In his *Princetonians, 1748–1768*, 56–59. Princeton, NJ: Princeton University Press, 1976.

**LIVINGSTON, EDWARD (1764–1836)**
**NY/LA, House 1795–1801 (NY), 1823–1829 (LA), Senate 1829–1831 (LA).**

**5873.** Carosso, Vincent P., and Lawrence H. Leder. "Edward Livingston and Jacksonian Diplomacy." *Louisiana History* 7 (Summer 1966): 241–248.

**5874.** Hatcher, William B. *Edward Livingston: Jeffersonian Republican and Jacksonian Democrat.* Baton Rouge: Louisiana State University Press, 1940.

**5875.** Hunt, Charles H. *Life of Edward Livingston.* New York: Appleton, 1864.

**5876.** Mackey, Philip E. "Edward Livingston and the Origins of the Movement to Abolish Capital Punishment in America." *Louisiana History* 16 (Spring 1975): 145–166.

**5877.** Pound, Roscoe. *The Formative Era of American Law.* Boston: Little, Brown, 1938.

**5878.** Rawle, Francis. "Edward Livingston." In *The American Secretaries of State and Their Diplomacy*, edited by Samuel F. Bemis, vol. 4, 205–263. New York: Knopf, 1928.

**5879.** Willson, Beckles. "Edward Livingston (1833–35)." In his *America's Ambassadors to France (1777–1927)*, 180–197. New York: Frederick A. Stokes, 1928.

**LIVINGSTON, PHILIP (1716–1778) NY,**
**Continental Congress 1774–1778.**

**5880.** Sanderson, John. "Philip Livingston." In *Sanderson's Biography of the Signers of the Declaration of Independence*, edited by Robert T. Conrad, 266–275. Philadelphia: Thomas, Cowperthwait, 1848.

**LIVINGSTON, ROBERT R. (1746–1813)**
**NY, Continental Congress 1775–1777, 1779–1781.**

**5881.** Alexander, DeAlva S. "Robert R. Livingston: The Author of the Louisiana Purchase." *New York State Historical Association Proceedings* 6 (1906): 100–114.

**5882.** Bonham, Milledge R., Jr. "Robert R. Livingston." In *The American Secretaries of State and Their Diplomacy*, edited by Samuel F. Bemis, vol. 1, 113–189. New York: Knopf, 1927.

**5883.** Dangerfield, George. *Chancellor Robert R. Livingston of New York, 1746–1813.* New York: Harcourt, Brace, 1960.

**5884.** Stecker, H. Dora. "Constructing a Navigation System in the West." *Ohio Valley Historical Association Annual Report* 5 (1912): 18–29.

**LIVINGSTON, WILLIAM (1723–1790) NJ, Continental Congress 1774–1776.**

**5885.** Dillon, Dorothy R. *The New York Triumvirate: A Study of the Legal and Political Careers of William Livingston, John Morin Scott, William Smith, Jr.* New York: Columbia University Press, 1949.

**5886.** Elmer, Lucius Q. "Governors During the War for Independence: William Livingston." In his *The Constitution and Government of the Province and State of New Jersey,* 56–76. Newark, NJ: M. R. Dennis, 1872.

**5887.** Livingston, William. *The Papers of William Livingston.* 5 vols. Trenton: New Jersey Historical Commission, 1979–1988.

**5888.** Sedgwick, Theodore. *A Memoir of the Life of William Livingston.* New York: J. and J. Harper, 1833.

**LODGE, HENRY CABOT (1850–1924) R-MA, House 1887–1893, Senate 1893–1924.**

**5889.** Carrol, John M. "Henry Cabot Lodge's Contributions to the Shaping of Republican European Diplomacy 1920–1924." *Capital Studies* 3 (Fall 1975): 153–165.

**5890.** Crowley, John W. "E. A. Robinson and Henry Cabot Lodge." *New England Quarterly* 43 (March 1970): 115–124.

**5891.** Fischer, Robert J. "Henry Cabot Lodge and the Taft Arbitration Treaties." *South Atlantic Quarterly* 78 (Spring 1979): 244–258.

**5892.** ———. "Henry Cabot Lodge's Concept of Foreign Policy and the League of Nations." Ph.D dissertation, University of Georgia, 1971.

**5893.** Garraty, John A. *Henry Cabot Lodge, a Biography.* New York: Knopf, 1953.

**5894.** ———. "Henry Cabot Lodge and the Alaskan Boundary Tribunal." *New England Quarterly* 24 (December 1951): 469–494.

**5895.** Hewes, James E. "Henry Cabot Lodge and the League of Nations." *American Philosophical Society Proceedings* 114 (August 1970): 245–255.

**5896.** Hill, Thomas M. "The Senate Leadership and International Policy from Lodge to Vandenberg." Ph.D. dissertation, Washington University, 1970.

**5897.** Lodge, Henry C. *Early Memories.* New York: Arno Press, 1975.

**5898.** ———. *The Senate and the League of Nations.* New York: Scribner's, 1925.

**5899.** ———. *The Senate of the United States, and Other Essays and Addresses Historical and Literary.* New York: Scribner's, 1921.

**5900.** Meyerhuber, Carl I., Jr. "Henry Cabot Lodge, Massachusetts and the New Manifest Destiny." Ph.D. dissertation, University of California, 1972.

**5901.** Miller, William J. *Henry Cabot Lodge: A Biography.* New York: Heineman, 1967.

**5902.** Roosevelt, Theodore. *Selections from the Correspondence of Theodore Roosevelt and Henry Cabot Lodge, 1884–1918.* 2 vols. Edited by Henry C. Lodge and Charles F. Redmond. New York: Da Capo Press, 1971.

**5903.** Sachs, Andrew A. "The Imperialist Style of Henry Cabot Lodge." Ph.D. dissertation, University of Wisconsin, 1992.

**5904.** Saveth, Edward N. "Henry Cabot Lodge." In his *American Historians and European Immigrants, 1875–1925,* 51–64. New York: Columbia University Press, 1948.

**5905.** Schorer, Calvin E. "Letter from Henry Cabot Lodge." *New England Quarterly* 25 (September 1952): 391–394.

**5906.** Schriftgiesser, Karl. *The Gentleman from Massachusetts: Henry Cabot Lodge.* Boston: Little, Brown, 1944.

**5907.** Villard, Oswald G. "Henry Cabot Lodge: A Scholar in Politics." In his *Prophets True and False,* 258–266. New York: Knopf, 1928.

**5908.** Welch, Richard E. "Opponents and Colleagues: George Frisbie Hoar and Henry Cabot Lodge, 1898–1904." *New England Quarterly* 39 (June 1966): 182–209.

**5909.** Werking, Richard H. "Senator Henry Cabot Lodge and the Philippines: A Note on American Territorial Expansion." *Pacific Historical Review* 42 (May 1973): 234–240.

**5910.** Widenor, William C. *Henry Cabot Lodge and the Search for an American Foreign Policy.* Berkeley: University of California Press, 1980.

**5911.** ———. "Henry Cabot Lodge: The Astute Parliamentarian." In *First Among Equals: Outstanding Senate Leaders of the Twentieth Century,* edited by Richard A. Baker and Roger H. Davidson, 38–62. Washington, DC: Congressional Quarterly, 1991.

## LODGE, HENRY CABOT, JR.
**(1902–1985) R-MA, Senate 1937–1944, 1947–1953.**

**5912.** Brown, John M. "Lodge of the United Nations." In his *Through These Men,* 141–166. New York: Harper and Row, 1956.

**5913.** Finger, Seymour M. "Henry Cabot Lodge." In his *Your Man at the UN,* 72–108. New York: New York University Press, 1980.

**5914.** Hatch, Alden. *The Lodges of Massachusetts.* New York: Hawthorn Books, 1973.

**5915.** Lodge, Henry C. *As It Was: An Inside View of Politics and Power in the '50s and '60s.* New York: Norton, 1976.

**5916.** ———. *The Storm Has Many Eyes: A Personal Narrative.* New York: Norton, 1973.

**5917.** Vasilew, Eugene. "New Style in Political Campaigns: Lodge in New Hampshire, 1964." *Review of Politics* 30 (April 1968): 131–152.

**5918.** Zeiger, Henry A. *The Remarkable Henry Cabot Lodge.* New York: Popular Library, 1964.

## LOGAN, GEORGE (1753–1821) R-PA,
**Senate 1801–1807.**

**5919.** Logan, Deborah. *Memoir of Dr. George Logan of Stenton, by His Widow Deborah Norris Logan.* Philadelphia: Historical Society of Pennsylvania, 1899.

**5920.** Tolles, Frederick B. "George Logan and the Agricultural Revolution." *American Philosophical Society Proceedings* 95 (1951): 589–596.

**5921.** ———. *George Logan of Philadelphia.* New York: Oxford University Press, 1953.

## LOGAN, JOHN ALEXANDER
**(1826–1886) R-IL, House 1859–1862, 1867–1871, Senate 1871–1877, 1879–1886.**

**5922.** Balestier, Charles W. *James G. Blaine, a Sketch of His Life: With a Brief Record of the Life of John A. Logan.* New York: J. W. Lovell, 1984.

**5923.** Boutwell, George S. "Public Services of John A. Logan." In his *Why I Am a Republican,* 185–195. Hartford, CT: Betts, 1884.

**5924.** Cooke, Vincent S. *The Life and Public Services of Our Greatest Living Statesmen, Hon. James G. Blaine, 'the Plumed Knight':* . . . *To Which Is Added the Life of Gen'l John A. Logan. . . . Also Contains an Account of the Election and Administration of Every President from Washington to Arthur.* Rochester: H. B. Graves, 1884.

**5925.** Cullom, Shelby M. "General John A. Logan." In his *Fifty Years of Public Service,* 180–189. Chicago: A. C. McClurg, 1911.

**5926.** Dawson, George F. *Life and Service of Gen. John A. Logan as Soldier and Statesman.* Washington, DC: National Tribune, 1884.

**5927.** Haughton, Walter R. *Early Life and Public Career of Hon. James G. Blaine, Patriot, Statesman, and Historian: Including a Biography of Gen'l John A. Logan, and Embracing a History of the Principles and Achievements of the Republican Party, with Platforms of Both Parties from 1856, and Other Valuable Political Documents.* Chicago: A. G. Nettleson and Co., 1884.

**5928.** "John A. Logan." In *Bench and Bar of Illinois: Historical and Reminiscent,* edited by John M. Palmer, vol. 2, 1139–1156. Chicago: Lewis, 1899.

**5929.** Jones, James P. *"Black Jack": John A. Logan and Southern Illinois in the Civil War Era.* Tallahassee: Florida State University, 1967.

**5930.** ———. "John A. Logan and the Election of 1864 in Illinois." *Mid-America* 42 (October 1960): 219–230.

**5931.** ———. "John A. Logan, Freshman in Congress, 1859–1861." *Journal of the Illinois State Historical Society* 56 (Spring 1963): 36–60.

**5932.** ———. *John A. Logan: Stalwart Republican from Tennessee.* Tallahassee: University Presses of Florida, 1982.

**5933.** ———. "Radical Reinforcement: John A. Logan Returns to Congress." *Journal of the Illinois State Historical Society* 68 (September 1975): 324–336.

**5934.** Knox, Thomas W. *The Lives of James G. Blaine and John A. Logan, Republican Presidential Candidates of 1884.* Hartford, CT: Hartford Publishing Company, 1884.

**5935.** Logan, John A. *The Volunteer Soldier of America, with Memoir of the Author and Military Reminiscences from General Logan's Private Journal.* Chicago: R. S. Peale, 1877.

**5936.** Logan, Mary S. *Reminiscences of a Soldier's Wife: An Autobiography.* New York: Scribner's, 1916.

**5937.** Messamore, Fred. "John A. Logan: Democrat and Republican." Ph.D. dissertation, University of Kentucky, 1940.

**5938.** Poore, Benjamin P. "Life of John Alexander Logan, Nominee for the Vice-Presidency of the U.S." In *Life and Public Services of Hon. James G. Blaine,* edited by Henry J. Ramsdell, 533–632. Deposit, NY: Phillips and Burrows, 1884.

**LONDON, MEYER** (1871–1926) SOC-NY, House 1915–1919, 1921–1923.

**5939.** Cohen, Julius H. "Meyer London." In his *They Built Better Than They Knew,* 215–222. New York: Messner, 1946.

**5940.** Goldberg, Gordon J. "Meyer London: A Political Biography." Ph.D. dissertation, Lehigh University, 1971.

**5941.** ———. "Meyer London and the National Social Insurance Movement, 1914–1922." *American Jewish Historical Quarterly* 65 (September 1975): 59–73.

**5942.** Rogoff, Harry. *An East Side Epic: The Life and Work of Meyer London.* New York: Vanguard Press, 1930.

**LONG, CHESTER ISAIAH** (1860–1934) R-KS, House 1895–1897, 1899–1903, Senate 1903–1909.

**5943.** Flory, Raymond L. "The Political Career of Chester I. Long." Ph.D. dissertation, University of Kansas, 1955.

**LONG, GEORGE SHANNON** (1883–1958) D-LA, House 1953–1958.

**5944.** Leppert, George M. "Long Live the Kingfishes!" *American Mercury* 83 (October 1956): 93–100.

**LONG, GILLIS WILLIAM** (1923–1985) D-LA, House 1963–1965, 1973–1985.

**5945.** Fullerton, W. H., Jr. "Long Versus Long: The Congressional Race in the Eighth District of Louisiana, 1964." *North Louisiana Historical Association Journal* 16 (1985): 1–13.

## LONG, HUEY PIERCE "the Kingfish" (1893–1935) D-LA, Senate 1932–1935.

**5946.** Beals, Carleton. *The Story of Huey P. Long*. Philadelphia: Lippincott, 1935.

**5947.** Bormann, Ernest G. "A Rhetorical Analysis of the National Radio Broadcasts of Senator Huey P. Long." Ph.D. dissertation, University of Iowa, 1957.

**5948.** Briley, Richard. *Death of the Kingfish*. Dallas, TX: Triangle, 1960.

**5949.** Brinkley, Alan. "Comparative Biography as Political History: Huey Long and Father Coughlin." *History Teacher* (Long Beach) 18 (November 1984): 9–16.

**5950.** ———. "Huey Long, the Share Our Wealth Movement, and the Limits of Depression Dissidence." *Louisiana History* 22 (Spring 1981): 117–134.

**5951.** ———. *Voices of Protest: Huey Long, Father Coughlin and the Great Depression*. New York: Vintage Books, 1983.

**5952.** Carter, Hodding. "Huey Long: American Dictator." In *The Thirties*, edited by Don Congdon, 307–320. New York: Simon and Schuster, 1962.

**5953.** ———. "Portrait of an American Dictator." In *These Were the Years*, edited by Frank Brookhauser, 443–446. Garden City, NY: Doubleday, 1959.

**5954.** Cassity, Michael J. "Huey Long: Barometer of Reform in the New Deal." *South Atlantic Quarterly* 72 (Spring 1973): 255–269.

**5955.** Clay, Floyd M. *Coozan Dudley LeBlanc: From Huey Long to Hadacol*. Gretna, LA: Pelican, 1973.

**5956.** Davenport, Walter. "How Huey Long Gets Away with It." In *Cavalcade of Colliers*, edited by Kenneth McArdle, 314–324. New York: Barnes, 1959.

**5957.** Dethloff, Henry. "Huey Pierce Long: Interpretations." *Louisiana Studies* 3 (Summer 1964): 219–232.

**5958.** ———, comp. *Huey P. Long: Southern Demagogue or American Democrat?* Lexington, MA: Heath, 1967.

**5959.** Deutsch, Hermann B. *Huey Long Murder Case*. Garden City, NY: Doubleday, 1963.

**5960.** Fields, Harvey G. *A True History of the Life, Works, Assassination, and Death of Huey Pierce Long*. Farmerville, LA: Fields Publishing Agency, 1945.

**5961.** Graham, Hugh D. "The Enigma of Huey Long: An Essay Review." *Journal of Southern History* 36 (May 1970): 205–211.

**5962.** ———, comp. *Huey Long*. Englewood Cliffs, NJ: Prentice-Hall, 1970.

**5963.** Hair, William I. *The Kingfish and His Realm: The Life and Times of Huey P. Long*. Baton Rouge: Louisiana State University Press, 1991.

**5964.** Harmlin, Fred. "The Rainbow Boys." In his *Land of Liberty*, 252–272. Scranton, PA: Crowell, 1947.

**5965.** Harris, Thomas O. *The Kingfish, Huey P. Long, Dictator*. New York: Pelican, 1938.

**5966.** Hess, Stephen. "The Long Dynasty." In his *America's Political Dynasties from Adams to Kennedy*. Garden City, NY: Doubleday, 1966.

**5967.** Howell, Roland B. *Louisiana Sugar Plantations, Mardi Gras and Huey P. Long: Reminiscences*. Baton Rouge, LA: Claitor's Publishing Division, 1969.

**5968.** Irey, Elmer L., and William J. Slocum. "End of the Kingfish." In *Fabulous Yesterday*, edited by Lewis W. Gillenson, 214–217. New York: Harper and Row, 1961.

**5969.** Jeansonne, Glen. "Challenge to the New Deal: Huey P. Long and the Redistribution of National Wealth." *Louisiana History* 21 (Fall 1980): 331–339.

**5970.** ———. *Messiah of the Masses: Huey P. Long and the Great Depression*. New York: HarperCollins College Publishers, 1993.

**5971.** Jones, Terry L. "An Administration under Fire: The Long-Farley Affair of 1935." *Louisiana History* 28 (Winter 1987): 5–17.

**5972.** Kane, Harnett T. *Huey Long's Louisiana Hayride: The American Rehearsal for Dictatorship, 1928–1940.* Gretna, LA: Pelican, 1970.

**5973.** King, Peter J. "Huey Long: Louisiana Kingfish." *History Today* 14 (March 1964): 151–160.

**5974.** Leppert, George M. "Long Live the Kingfishes." *American Mercury* 83 (October 1956): 93–100.

**5975.** Long, Huey P. *Everyman a King: The Autobiography of Huey P. Long.* New Orleans: National Book Company, 1933.

**5976.** ———. *My First Days in the White House.* New York: Da Capo Press, 1972.

**5977.** Luthin, Reinhard H. "Huey P. Long: The Louisiana Kingfish." In his *American Demagogues,* 236–271. Boston: Beacon Press, 1954.

**5978.** Malone, David. *Hattie and Huey: An Arkansas Tour.* Fayetteville: University of Arkansas Press, 1989.

**5979.** Moreau, John A. "Huey Long and His Chroniclers." *Louisiana History* 6 (Spring 1965): 121–140.

**5980.** Opotowsky, Stan. *Longs of Louisiana.* New York: Dutton, 1960.

**5981.** Parrington, Vernon L. "The Depression Years." In his *American Dreams,* 197–199. Providence, RI: Brown University, 1947.

**5982.** Reeves, Miriam G. "Huey Pierce Long." In her *Governors of Louisiana,* 100–102. Gretna, LA: Pelican, 1972.

**5983.** Riesmeyer, James F. "The Senate Record of Huey Pierce Long: 1932 to 1935." Master's thesis, Indiana University, 1959.

**5984.** Sindler, Allan P. *Huey Long's Louisiana: State Politics, 1920–1952.* Baltimore: Johns Hopkins Press, 1956.

**5985.** Smith, Webster. *The Kingfish, a Biography of Huey P. Long.* New York: Putnam's, 1933.

**5986.** Snyder, Robert E. "Huey Long and the Cotton-Holiday Plan of 1931." *Louisiana History* 18 (Spring 1977): 133–160.

**5987.** Steinberg, Alfred. "Huey Long: A Storm for My Bride." In his *The Bosses,* 198–259. New York: Macmillan, 1972.

**5988.** Swan, George S. "A Preliminary Comparison of Long's Louisiana and Duplessis's Quebec." *Louisiana History* 25 (Summer 1984): 289–319.

**5989.** Vaughn, Courtney A. "The Legacy of Huey Long." *Louisiana History* 20 (Winter 1979): 93–101.

**5990.** Whisenhunt, Donald W. "Huey Long and the Texas Cotton Acreage Control Law of 1931." *Louisiana Studies* 13 (Summer 1974): 142–153.

**5991.** Williams, Elizabeth E. "A South Dakota Agrarian's Views of Huey Long: A Rhetorical Approach to Emil Loriks." *Midwest Review* 8 (Spring 1986): 40–55.

**5992.** Williams, T. Harry. "Gentleman from Louisiana: Demagogue or Democrat?" *Journal of Southern History* 26 (February 1960): 3–21.

**5993.** ———. *Huey Long.* New York: Knopf, 1969.

**5994.** ———. *Huey P. Long: An Inaugural Lecture Delivered before the University of Oxford on 26 Jan. 1967.* Oxford: Clarendon, 1967.

**5995.** Zinman, David H. *The Day Huey Long Was Shot, September 8, 1935.* New York: I. Obolensky, 1963.

## LONG, JEFFERSON FRANKLIN
**(1836–1901) R-GA, House 1870–1871.**

**5996.** Christopher, Maurine. "Jefferson F. Long/Georgia." In her *Black Americans in Congress,* 25–37. Rev. ed. New York: Thomas Y. Crowell, 1876.

**5997.** Matthews, James M. "Jefferson Franklin Long: The Public Career of Georgia's First Black Congressman." *Phylon* 42 (June 1981): 145–156.

**LONG, JOHN DAVIS** (1838–1915) R-MA, House 1883–1889.

**5998.** Hess, James W. "John D. Long and Reform Issues in Massachusetts Politics, 1870–1889." *New England Quarterly* 33 (March 1960): 57–73.

**5999.** Long, John D. *America of Yesterday, as Reflected in the Journal of John Davis Long.* Edited by Lawrence S. Mayo. Boston: Atlantic Monthly Press, 1923.

**6000.** ———. *Journal.* Edited by Margaret Long. Rindge, NH: R. R. Smith, 1956.

**LONG, RUSSELL BILLIU** (1918– ) D-LA, Senate 1948–1987.

**6001.** Leppert, George M. "Long Live the Kingfishes!" *American Mercury* 83 (October 1956): 93–100.

**6002.** Mann, Robert. *Legacy to Power: Senator Russell Long of Louisiana.* New York: Paragon House, 1992.

**LONG, SPEEDY OTERIA** (1928– ) D-LA, House, 1965–1973.

**6003.** Fullerton, W. H., Jr. "Long Versus Long: The Congressional Race in the Eighth District of Louisiana, 1964." *North Louisiana Historical Association Journal* 16 (1985): 1–13.

**LONGWORTH, NICHOLAS** (1869–1931) R-OH, House 1903–1913, 1915–1931.

**6004.** Chambrun, Clara. *The Making of Nicholas Longworth: Annals of an American Family.* New York: R. Long and R. R. Smith, 1933.

**6005.** Cross, Wilbur, and Ann Novotny. "The Princess." In their *White House Weddings,* 134–161. New York: McKay, 1967.

**6006.** Gilfond, Duff. "Mr. Speaker." *American Mercury* 11 (August 1927): 451–458.

**6007.** Page, William T. "Mr. Speaker Longworth." *Scribner's* 83 (March 1928): 272–280.

**6008.** Shaw, Albert. "The Progress of the World: The Late Nicholas Longworth." *Review of Reviews* 83 (May 1931): 23–24.

**6009.** Stimson, George P. "The Speaker—and the Longworths." In *The Law in Southwestern Ohio,* compiled by Frank G. Davis, 154–164. Cincinnati, OH: Cincinnati Bar Association, 1972.

**LORE, CHARLES BROWN** (1831–1911) D-DE, House 1883–1887.

**6010.** Pennewill, James. *The Life and Public Services of Hon. Charles B. Lore, of Delaware.* Wilmington: Historical Society of Delaware, 1913.

**LORIMER, WILLIAM** (1861–1934) R-IL, House 1895–1901, 1903–1909, Senate 1909–1912.

**6011.** Adams, Frederick U. *The Plot That Failed, Official Records.* Washington, DC: National Publishing Company, 1912.

**6012.** Root, Elihu. "The Case of Senator Lorimer: Address in the Senate of the United States, Feb. 3, 1911." In his *Addresses on Government and Citizenship,* 291–321. Cambridge, MA: Harvard University Press, 1916.

**6013.** Tarr, Joel A. *Study in Boss Politics: William Lorimer of Chicago.* Champaign: University of Illinois Press, 1971.

**LOVEJOY, OWEN** (1811–1864) R-IL, House 1857–1864.

**6014.** Magdol, Edward. *Owen Lovejoy Abolitionist in Congress.* New Brunswick, NJ: Rutgers University Press, 1967.

**LOVELL, JAMES** (1737–1814) MA, Continental Congress 1777–1782.

**6015.** Jones, Helen F. "James Lovell in the Continental Congress 1777–1782." Ph.D. dissertation, Columbia University, 1968.

**LOWDEN, FRANK ORREN** (1861–1943) R-IL, House 1906–1911.

**6016.** Hutchinson, William T. *Lowden of Illinois: The Life of Frank O. Lowden.* 2 vols. Chicago: University of Chicago Press, 1957.

**6017.** Villard, Oswald G. "Frank O. Lowden: Farmer and Candidate." In his *Prophets True and False,* 78–88. New York: Knopf, 1928.

**LOWENSTEIN, ALLARD KENNETH** (1929–1980) D-NY, House 1969–1971.

**6018.** Chafe, William H. *Never Stop Running: Allard Lowenstein and the Struggle to Save American Liberalism.* New York: Basic, 1993.

**6019.** Cummings, Richard. *The Pied Piper: Allard K. Lowenstein and the Liberal Dread.* New York: Grove Press, 1985.

**6020.** Harris, David. *Dreams Die Hard.* New York: St. Martin's Press, 1982.

**6021.** Stone, Gregory, and Douglas Lowenstein. *Lowenstein: Acts of Courage and Belief.* San Diego: Harcourt Brace Jovanovich, 1983.

**LOWNDES, WILLIAM** (1782–1822) R-SC, House 1811–1822.

**6022.** Ravenel, Harriott H. *Life and Times of William Lowndes.* Boston: Houghton Mifflin, 1901.

**6023.** Vipperman, Carl J. *William Lowndes and the Transition of Southern Politics.* Chapel Hill: University of North Carolina Press, 1989.

**LOWRIE, WALTER** (1784–1868) D-PA, Senate 1819–1825.

**6024.** Lowrie, Walter. *Memoirs of the Honorable Walter Lowrie.* New York: Baker and Taylor, 1896.

**LUCAS, SCOTT WIKE** (1892–1968) D-IL, House 1935–1939, Senate 1939–1951.

**6025.** Schapsmeier, Edward L., and Frederick H. Schapsmeier. "Scott W. Lucas of Havana: His Rise and Fall as Majority Leader in the United States Senate." *Journal of the Illinois State Historical Society* 70 (November 1977): 302–320.

**LUCE, CLARE BOOTHE** (1903–1987) R-CT, House 1943–1947.

**6026.** Diehl, Digby. "Clare Booth Luce." In his *Supertalk,* 15–33. Garden City, NY: Doubleday, 1974.

**6027.** Gray, James. "Clare Boothe Luce." In his *On Second Thought,* 191–195. Minneapolis: University of Minnesota Press, 1946.

**6028.** Hatch, Alden. *Ambassador Extraordinary: Clare Boothe Luce.* New York: Holt, 1956.

**6029.** Henle, Faye. *Au Clare de Luce: Portrait of a Luminous Lady.* New York: S. Daye, 1943.

**6030.** Luce, Clare B. *Europe in the Spring.* New York: Knopf, 1941.

**6031.** Martin, Ralph G. *Henry and Clare: An Intimate Portrait of the Luces.* New York: Putnam's, 1991.

**6032.** Roosevelt, Felicia W. "Clare Boothe Luce." In her *Doers and Dowagers,* 157–175. Garden City, NY: Doubleday, 1975.

**6033.** St. Johns, Adela. *Some Are Born Great,* 282–297. Garden City, NY: Doubleday, 1974.

**6034.** Shadegg, Stephen C. *Clare Boothe Luce: A Biography.* New York: Simon and Schuster, 1970.

**6035.** Sheed, Wilfred. *Clare Boothe Luce.* New York: Dutton, 1982.

**6036.** Willis, Ronald G. "The Persuasion of Clare Boothe Luce." Ph.D. dissertation, Indiana University, 1993.

**LUCKEY, HENRY CARL (1868–1956) D-NE, House 1935–1939.**

**6037.** Luckey, Henry C. *85 American Years: Memoirs of a Nebraska Congressman.* Hicksville, NY: Exposition, 1955.

**LUDLOW, LOUIS LEON (1873–1950) D-IN, House 1929–1949.**

**6038.** Ludlow, Louis. *From Cornfield to Press Gallery.* Washington, DC: W. F. Roberts, 1924.

**LUMPKIN, JOHN HENRY (1812–1860) D-GA, House 1843–1849, 1855–1857.**

**6039.** Wheeler, Henry G. "Lumpkin, John Henry." In his *History of Congress,* vol. 1, 328–340. New York: Harper, 1848.

**LUMPKIN, WILSON (1783–1870) GA, House 1815–1817, 1827–1831, Senate 1837–1841.**

**6040.** McPherson, Robert G. "Wilson Lumpkin." In *Georgians in Profile,* edited by Horace Montgomery, 144–167. Athens: University of Georgia Press, 1958.

**6041.** Vipperman, Carl J. "The 'Particular Mission' of Wilson Lumpkin." *Georgia Historical Quarterly* 66 (Fall 1982): 295–316.

**LYMAN, THEODORE (1833–1897) IR-MA, House 1883–1885.**

**6042.** Adams, Charles F. "Memoir of Theodore Lyman." *Massachusetts Historical Society Proceedings* 40 (1907): 147–177.

**6043.** Lyman, Theodore. *Meade's Headquarters, 1863–1865: Letters of Colonel Theodore Lyman from the Wilderness to Appomattox.* Edited by George R. Agassiz. Freeport, NY: Books for Libraries, 1970.

**LYNCH, JOHN ROY (1847–1939) R-MS, House 1873–1877, 1882–1883.**

**6044.** Bell, Frank C. "The Life and Times of John R. Lynch: A Case Study 1847–1939." *Journal of Mississippi. History* 38 (February 1976): 53–67.

**6045.** Christopher, Maurine. "John R. Lynch/Mississippi." In her *Black Americans in Congress,* 55–68. Rev. ed. New York: Thomas Y. Crowell, 1876.

**6046.** Lynch, John R. *Reminiscences of an Active Life.* Edited by John H. Franklin. Chicago: University of Chicago Press, 1970.

**6047.** Mann, Kenneth E. "John Roy Lynch: US Congressman from Mississippi." *Negro History Bulletin* 37 (April 1974): 238–241.

**6048.** McLaughlin, James H. "John R. Lynch, the Reconstruction Politician: A Historical Perspective." Ph.D. dissertation, Ball State University, 1981.

**6049.** Simmons, William J. "John R. Lynch." In his *Men of Mark,* 749–751. Lincoln, NE: Johnson, 1970.

**6050.** Thornbrough, Emma L. "Lynch, John Roy." In her *Black Reconstructionists,* 175–176. Englewood Cliffs, NJ: Prentice-Hall, 1972.

**6051.** Thorpe, Earl E. "John R. Lynch." In his *Black Historians,* 147–148. New York: Morrow, 1971.

**LYNCH, THOMAS JR. (1749–1779) SC, Continental Congress 1776–1777.**

**6052.** Sanderson, John. "Thomas Lynch." In *Sanderson's Biography of the Signers of the Declaration of Independence,* edited by Robert T. Conrad, 801–806. Philadelphia: Thomas, Cowperthwait, 1848.

**LYON, LUCIUS (1800–1851) D-MI, House 1833–1835, 1843–1845, Senate 1837–1839.**

**6053.** Dodge, Elise F. "Lucius Lyon, Pioneers of the Statehood Era." *Michigan History* 71 (November/December 1987): 39–40.

**6054.** Shirigian, John. "Lucius Lyon: His Place in Michigan History." Ph.D. dissertation, University of Michigan, 1960.

**LYON, MATTHEW (1746–1822) R-VT/KY, House 1797–1801 (VT), 1803–1811 (KY).**

**6055.** Austin, Aleine. *Matthew Lyon: New Man of the Democratic Revolution, 1749–1822.* University Park: Pennsylvania State University Press, 1981.

**6056.** Fox, Loyal S. "Colonel Matthew Lyon, Biographical and Genealogical Notes." *Vermont Quarterly* 12 (July 1944): 163–180.

**6057.** Gragg, Larry. "Ragged Mat, the Democrat." *American History Illustrated* 12 (May 1977): 20–25.

**6058.** Herrick, Hudee Z. "Matthew Lyon, the Vermont Years." Master's thesis, University of Vermont, 1952.

**6059.** Mayo, Bernard. "The Lyon of Democracy." *North American Review* 244 (Winter 1937/1938): 251–269.

**6060.** McLaughlin, J. Fairfax. *Matthew Lyon, the Hampden of Congress.* New York: Wynkoop Hallenbeck Crawford Company, 1900.

**6061.** Montagno, George L. "Growing Pains of the New Republic: Congressional Cakewalk." *William and Mary Quarterly* 17 (July 1960): 345–349.

**6062.** ———. "Matthew Lyon, Radical Jeffersonian, 1796–1801: A Case Study in Partisan Politics." Ph.D. dissertation, University of California, 1954.

**6063.** Williams, Robert P. *By the Bulls That Redamed Me: The Odyssey of Matthew Lyon.* Hicksville, NY: Exposition, 1972.

**MACDONALD, WILLIAM JOSIAH (1873–1946) PROG-WI, House 1913–1915.**

**6064.** Boyer, Hugh E. "The Decline of the Progressive Party in Michigan's Upper Peninsula: The Case of Congressman William J. MacDonald in 1914." *Michigan Historical Review* 13 (Fall 1987): 75–94.

**MACLAY, WILLIAM (1737–1804) PA, Senate 1789–1791.**

**6065.** Maclay, William. *The Journal of W. Maclay, United States Senator from Pennsylvania, 1789–1791.* New York: Boni, 1927.

**6066.** Shannon, Gerald L. "William Maclay, Pioneer-Statesman." Master's thesis, Indiana University, 1948.

**MACLAY, WILLIAM BROWN (1812–1882) D-NY, House 1843–1849, 1857–1861.**

**6067.** Spann, Edward K. "Gotham in Congress: New York's Representatives and the National Government, 1840–1854." *New York History* 67 (July 1986): 304–329.

**6068.** Wheeler, Henry G. "Maclay, William Brown." In his *History of Congress,* vol. 1, 187–235. New York: Harper, 1848.

**MACON, NATHANIEL (1757–1837) R-NC, House 1791–1815, Senate 1815–1828.**

**6069.** Bassett, John S., ed. "Some Unpublished Letters of Nathaniel Macon." *Trinity College Historical Papers* 6 (1906): 57–65.

**6070.** Battle, Kemp P., ed. *Letters of Nathaniel Macon, John Steele and William Barry Grove.* Chapel Hill: University of North Carolina Press, 1902.

**6071.** Cotten, Edward R. *Life of Hon. Nathaniel Macon of North Carolina.* Baltimore: Lucas and Deaver, 1840.

**6072.** Cunningham, Noble E. "Nathaniel Macon and the Southern Protest against Consolidation." *North Carolina Historical Review* 32 (July 1955): 376–384.

**6073.** Daniels, Josephus. "Nathaniel Macon." In *Publications of the North Carolina Historical Commission*, 80–93. Raleigh, NC: Edwards and Broughton, 1913.

**6074.** Dodd, William E. *Life of Nathaniel Macon.* Raleigh, NC: Edwards and Broughton, 1903.

**6075.** ———. "Nathaniel Macon Correspondence." *John P. Branch Historical Society Papers* 3 (1909): 27–93.

**6076.** ———. "The Place of Nathaniel Macon in Southern History." *American Historical Review* 7 (April 1902): 663–675.

**6077.** Helms, James M. "The Early Career of Nathaniel Macon: A Study in Pure Republicanism." Ph.D. dissertation, University of Virginia, 1962.

**6078.** McPherson, Elizabeth G., ed. "Letters from Nathaniel Macon to John Randolph of Roanoke." *North Carolina Historical Review* 39 (April 1962): 195–211.

**6079.** Miller, Zane L. "Senator Macon and the Public Domain, 1815–1828." *North Carolina Historical Review* 38 (October 1961): 482–499.

**6080.** Pittman, Thomas M. *Nathaniel Macon.* Greensboro, NC: Guilford Battle Ground, 1902.

**6081.** Poe, Clarence. "Nathaniel Macon, the Cincinnatus of America." *South Atlantic Quarterly* 37 (January 1938): 12–21.

**6082.** Wilson, Edwin M. *The Congressional Career of Nathaniel Macon.* Chapel Hill, NC: University Press, 1900.

## MADDEN, MARTIN BARNABY
(1855–1928) R-IL, House 1905–1928.

**6083.** Bullard, Thomas R. "From Businessman to Congressman: The Careers of Martin B. Madden." Ph.D. dissertation, University of Illinois, 1973.

## MADISON, JAMES (1751–1836) R-VA,
Continental Congress 1780–1783, 1787–1788; House 1789–1797.

**6084.** Adair, Douglass. "That Politics May Be Reduced to a Science: David Hume, James Madison, and the Tenth Federalist." *Huntington Library Quarterly* 20 (August 1957): 343–360.

**6085.** ———, ed. "James Madison's Autobiography." *William and Mary Quarterly* 2 (April 1945): 191–209.

**6086.** Agresto, John. "A System without a President—James Madison and the Revolution in Republican Liberty." *South Atlantic Quarterly* 82 (Spring 1983): 129–144.

**6087.** Alderman, Edwin A. "A Madison Letter and Some Digressions." *North American Review* 217 (June 1923): 785–796.

**6088.** Allen, William B. *Let the Advice Be Good: A Defense of Madison's Nationalism.* Lanham, MD: University Press of America, 1993.

**6089.** Alley, Robert S. *James Madison on Religious Liberty.* Buffalo, NY: Prometheus Books, 1985.

**6090.** Armstrong, Walter P. "James Madison: Virginia Revolutionist and Ardent Nationalist." *American Bar Association Journal* 34 (May 1948): 356–359.

**6091.** Banning, Lance. "The Hamiltonian Madison: A Reconsideration." *Virginia Magazine of History and Biography* 92 (January 1984): 3–28.

**6092.** ———. "James Madison and the Nationalists, 1780–1783." *William and Mary Quarterly* 40 (April 1983): 227–255.

**6093.** ———. "Moderate as Revolutionary: An Introduction to Madison's Life." *Library of Congress Quarterly Journal* 37 (Spring 1980): 162–175.

**6094.** Baskin, Darryl B. "The Pluralist Vision in American Political Thought: Adams, Madison, and Calhoun on Community, Citizenship, and the Public Interest." Ph.D. dissertation, University of California, 1966.

**6095.** Bell, Rudolph M. "Mr. Madison's War and Long-Term Congressional Voting Behavior." *William and Mary Quarterly* 36 (July 1979): 373–395.

**6096.** Beloff, Max. "James Madison." *History Today* 1 (February 1957): 68–73.

**6097.** Bonn, Franklyn G., Jr. "The Ideas of Political Party in the Thought of Thomas Jefferson and James Madison." Ph.D. dissertation, University of Minnesota, 1964.

**6098.** Bourke, Paul F. "The Pluralist Reading of James Madison's Tenth Federalist." *Perspectives in American History* 9 (1975): 271–295.

**6099.** Bradley, Jared W. "W. C. C. Claiborne and Spain: Foreign Affairs under Jefferson and Madison, 1801–1811." *Louisiana History* 12 (Fall 1971): 297–314; 13 (Winter 1972): 5–28.

**6100.** Branson, Roy. "Madison and the Scottish Enlightenment." *Journal of the History of Ideas* 40 (April/June 1979): 235–250.

**6101.** Brant, Irving. *The Fourth President: The Life of James Madison.* Indianapolis: Bobbs-Merrill, 1970.

**6102.** ———. *James Madison and American Nationalism.* Princeton, NJ: Van Nostrand, 1968.

**6103.** ———. "James Madison and His Times." *American Historical Review* 57 (July 1952): 853–870.

**6104.** ———. "James Madison as Founder of the Constitution." *New York University Law Review* 27 (April 1952): 248–264.

**6105.** ———. *James Madison: Commander in Chief, 1812–1836.* Indianapolis: Bobbs-Merrill, 1961.

**6106.** ———. *James Madison: Father of the Constitution, 1787–1800.* Indianapolis: Bobbs-Merrill, 1950.

**6107.** ———. "James Madison: His Greatness Emerges after Two Centuries." *American Bar Association Journal* 37 (August 1951): 563–566.

**6108.** ———. *James Madison: Secretary of State, 1801–1809.* Indianapolis: Bobbs-Merrill, 1953.

**6109.** ———. *James Madison: The Nationalist, 1780–1787.* Indianapolis: Bobbs-Merrill, 1948.

**6110.** ———. *James Madison: The President, 1809–1812.* Indianapolis: Bobbs-Merrill, 1956.

**6111.** ———. *James Madison: The Virginia Revolutionist.* Indianapolis: Bobbs-Merrill, 1941.

**6112.** ———. "Madison and the War of 1812." *Virginia Magazine of History and Biography* 74 (January 1966): 51–67.

**6113.** ———. "The Madison Heritage." *New York University Law Review* 35 (April 1960): 882–902.

**6114.** ———. "Madison on the Separation of Church and State." *William and Mary Quarterly* 8 (January 1951): 3–24.

**6115.** Burns, Edward M. *James Madison, Philosopher of the Constitution.* New Brunswick, NJ: Rutgers University Press, 1938.

**6116.** Cahn, Edmond N. "Madison and the Pursuit of Happiness." *New York University Law Quarterly Review* 27 (April 1952): 265–275.

**6117.** Carey, George W. "Majority Tyranny and the Extended Republic Theory of James Madison." *Modern Age* 20 (Winter 1976): 40–54.

**6118.** Clinton, Robert L. *Marbury v. Madison and Judicial Review.* Lawrence: University Press of Kansas, 1989.

**6119.** Colbourn, H. Trevor. "Madison Eulogized." *William and Mary Quarterly* 8 (January 1951): 108–119.

**6120.** Conniff, James. "The Enlightenment and American Political Thought: A Study of the Origins of Madison's *Federalist Number 10.*" *Political Theory* 8 (August 1980): 381–402.

**6121.** ———. "On the Obsolescence of the General Will: Rousseau, Madison, and the Evolution of Republican Political Thought." *Western Political Quarterly* 28 (March 1975): 32–58.

**6122.** Corwin, Edward S. "James Madison: Layman, Publicist, and Exegete." *New York University Law Review* 27 (April 1952): 277–298.

**6123.** ———. "The Posthumous Career of James Madison (1751–1836) as Lawyer." *American Bar Association Journal* 25 (October 1939): 821–824.

**6124.** Crosskey, William W. "The Ex-post Facto and the Contracts Clauses in the Federal Convention: A Note on the Editorial Ingenuity of James Madison." *University of Chicago Law Review* 35 (1968): 248–254.

**6125.** De Leon, Daniel. *James Madison and Karl Marx, a Contrast and a Similarity.* New York: New York Labor News Company, 1932.

**6126.** De Terra, Helmut. "Alexander von Humboldt's Correspondence with Jefferson, Madison, and Gallatin." *American Philosophical Society Proceedings* 103 (December 1959): 783–806.

**6127.** Dewey, Donald O. "James Madison Helps Clio Interpret the Constitution." *American Journal of Legal History* 15 (January 1971): 38–55.

**6128.** ———. "Madison's Response to Jackson's Foes." *Tennessee Historical Quarterly* 20 (June 1961): 167–176.

**6129.** ———. "Madison's Views on Electoral Reform." *Western Political Quarterly* 15 (March 1962): 140–145.

**6130.** ———. "The Sage of Montpelier: James Madison's Constitutional and Political Thought, 1817–1836." Ph.D. dissertation, University of Chicago, 1961.

**6131.** Dietze, Gottfried. "Madison's Federalist: A Treatise for Free Government." *Georgetown Law Journal* 46 (Fall 1957): 21–51.

**6132.** Donovan, Frank R. *Mr. Madison's Constitution.* New York: Dodd, Mead, 1965.

**6133.** Einhorn, Lois J. "Basic Assumptions in the Virginia Ratification Debates: Patrick Henry vs. James Madison on the Nature of Man and Reason." *Southern Speech Communication Journal* 46 (Summer 1981): 327–340.

**6134.** Elliott, Edward. "James Madison: Growth through Formulation." In his *Biographical Story of the Constitution,* 101–124. New York: Putnam's Sons, 1910.

**6135.** Farnell, Robert S. "Positive Valuations of Politics and Government in the Thought of Five American Founding Fathers: Thomas Jefferson, John Adams, James Madison, Alexander Hamilton, and George Washington." Ph.D. dissertation, Cornell University, 1970.

**6136.** Farrand, Max. "If James Madison Had a Sense of Humor." *Pennsylvania Magazine of History* 62 (April 1938): 130–139.

**6137.** Fornoff, Charles W. "Madison on the Nature of Politics." Ph.D. dissertation, University of Illinois, 1926.

**6138.** Gay, Sydney H. *James Madison.* Boston: Houghton Mifflin, 1899.

**6139.** Hagan, Horace H. "James Madison: Constructive Political Philosopher." *American Bar Association Journal* 16 (January 1930): 51–56.

**6140.** Hobson, Charles F. "The Negative on State Laws: James Madison, the Constitution, and the Crisis of Republican Government." *William and Mary Quarterly* 36 (April 1979): 215–235.

6141. Hughes, Charles E. "James Madison." *American Bar Association Journal* 18 (January 1932): 854–858.

6142. Hunt, Gaillard I. *The Life of James Madison.* Garden City, NY: Doubleday, 1902.

6143. ———. "Madison and Religious Liberty." *American Historical Association Annual Report* 1 (1902): 163–171.

6144. ———, ed. *The Writings of James Madison.* 9 vols. New York: Putnam's, 1900–1910.

6145. Ingersoll, David E. "Machiavelli and Madison: Perspectives on Political Stability." *Political Science Quarterly* 85 (June 1970): 259–280.

6146. Jillson, Calvin C. "The Representation Question in the Federal Convention of 1787: Madison's Virginia Plan and Its Opponents." *Congressional Studies* 8 (1981): 21–41.

6147. Kaplan, Lawrence S. "France and Madison's Decision for War, 1812." *Journal of American History* 50 (March 1964): 652–671.

6148. Kennedy, Patrick J. "The Profound Politician and Scholar: An Examination of the Charges of Inconsistency within the Political Theory of President James Madison." Ph.D. dissertation, Fordham University, 1970.

6149. Ketcham, Ralph L. *James Madison: A Biography.* New York: Macmillan, 1971.

6150. ———. "James Madison and the Nature of Man." *Journal of the History of Ideas* 16 (January 1958): 62–76.

6151. ———. "James Madison: The Unimperial President." *Virginia Quarterly Review* 54 (Winter 1978): 116–136.

6152. ———. "Jefferson and Madison and the Doctrines of Interposition and Nullification: A Letter of John Quincy Adams." *Virginia Magazine of History and Biography* 66 (April 1958): 178–182.

6153. ———. "The Mind of James Madison, D.S.S." Ph.D. dissertation, Syracuse University, 1956.

6154. ———. "Notes on James Madison's Sources for the Tenth Federalist Papers." *Midwest Journal of Political Science* 1 (May 1957): 20–25.

6155. ———, ed. "James Madison and Religion: A New Hypothesis." *Journal of the Presbyterian Historical Society* 38 (June 1960): 65–91.

6156. Koch, Adrienne. "James Madison and the Library of Congress." *Library of Congress Quarterly Journal* 37 (Spring 1980): 158–161.

6157. ———. "James Madison and the Politics of Republicanism." In *The Federalists vs. the Jefferson Republicans,* edited by Paul Goodman, 66–76. New York: Holt, Reinhart and Winston, 1967.

6158. ———. *Jefferson and Madison: The Great Collaboration.* New York: Oxford University Press, 1964.

6159. ———. "Madison and the Workshop of Liberty." In his *Power, Morals, and the Founding Fathers: Essays in the Interpretation of the American Enlightenment,* 103–121. Ithaca, NY: Cornell University Press, 1961.

6160. ———. *Madison's "Advice to My Country."* Princeton, NJ: Princeton University Press, 1966.

6161. ———. "Philosopher-Statesmen of the Republic." *Sewanee Review* 55 (Summer 1947): 384–405.

6162. Koch, Adrienne, and Harry Ammon. "The Virginia and Kentucky Resolutions: An Episode in Jefferson's and Madison's Defense of Civil Liberties." *William and Mary Quarterly* 5 (April 1948): 145–176.

6163. Landi, Alexander R. *The Politics of James Madison.* Dallas, TX: University of Dallas, 1973.

**6164.** Lindsay, Thomas. "James Madison on Religion and Politics: Rhetoric and Reality." *American Political Science Review* 85 (December 1991): 1321–1340.

**6165.** Lodge, Henry C. "James Madison." In his *Historical and Political Essays*, 47–74. Boston: Houghton Mifflin, 1892.

**6166.** Lutz, Donald S. "James Madison as a Conflict Theorist: The Madisonian Model Extended." Ph.D. dissertation, Indiana University, 1969.

**6167.** Madison, James. *The Papers of James Madison.* Edited by William Hutchinson, Robert Rutland, and William M. Rachal. Chicago: University of Chicago Press, 1962–1977.

**6168.** McCoy, Drew R. "Jefferson and Madison on Malthus: Population Growth in Jefferson Political Economy." *Virginia Magazine of History and Biography* 88 (July 1980): 259–275.

**6169.** ———. *The Last of the Fathers: James Madison and the Republican Legacy.* New York: Cambridge University Press, 1989.

**6170.** ———. "Madison's America: Polity, Economy, and Society." *Library of Congress Quarterly Journal* 37 (Spring 1980): 259–264.

**6171.** ———. "Republicanism and American Foreign Policy: James Madison and the Political Economy of Commercial Discrimination, 1789 to 1794." *William and Mary Quarterly* 31 (October 1974): 633–646.

**6172.** McGrath, Dennis R. "James Madison and Social Choice Theory: The Possibility of Republicanism." Ph.D. dissertation, University of Maryland, 1783.

**6173.** Mead, Sidney E. "Neither Church nor State: Reflections on James Madison's Line of Separation." *Journal of Church and State* 10 (Autumn 1968): 349–364.

**6174.** Meyers, Marvin. "Revolution and Founding: On Publius-Madison and the American Genesis." *Library of Congress Quarterly Journal* 37 (Spring 1980): 192–200.

**6175.** ———, ed. *Mind of the Founder: Sources of the Political Thought of James Madison.* Rev. ed. Hanover, NH: University Press of New England, 1981.

**6176.** Miller, William L. *The Business of May Next: James Madison and the Founding.* Charlottesville: University Press of Virginia, 1992.

**6177.** Moore, Virginia. *The Madisons: A Biography.* New York: McGraw-Hill, 1979.

**6178.** Morgan, Robert J. *James Madison on the Constitution and the Bill of Rights.* New York: Greenwood, 1988.

**6179.** ———. "Madison's Analysis of the Sources of Political Authority." *American Political Science Review* 75 (September 1981): 613–625.

**6180.** ———. "Madison's Theory of Representation in the Tenth Federalist." *Journal of Politics* 36 (November 1974): 852–885.

**6181.** Morris, Richard B. "James Madison: Republican Champion of the Rights of Man." In his *Witnesses at the Creation: Hamilton, Madison, Jay, and the Constitution*, 94–118. New York: Holt, Rinehart and Winston, 1985.

**6182.** Myers, J. Jay. "James Madison: The Last Revolutionist." In his *The Revolutionists*, 108–125. New York: Washington Square Press, 1971.

**6183.** Padover, Saul K. "The American as Republican: James Madison." In his *The Genius of America: Men Whose Ideas Shaped Our Civilization*, 118–137. New York: McGraw-Hill, 1960.

**6184.** ———, ed. *The Complete Madison: His Basic Writings.* New York: Harper, 1953.

**6185.** Paulding, James K. "An Unpublished Sketch of James Madison." Edited by Ralph L. Ketcham. *Virginia Magazine of*

*History and Biography* 67 (October 1955): 432–437.

**6186.** Rachal, William M. "James Madison, Father of the Constitution." *Virginia Cavalcade* 1 (Winter 1951): 26–31.

**6187.** Riemer, Neal. *James Madison.* New York: Washington Square Press, 1968.

**6188.** ———. *James Madison: Creating the American Constitution.* Washington, DC: Congressional Quarterly, 1986.

**6189.** ———. "James Madison's Theory of the Self-Destructive Features of Republican Government." *Ethics* 65 (October 1954): 34–43.

**6190.** ———. "The Republicanism of James Madison." *Political Science Quarterly* 69 (March 1954): 45–64.

**6191.** Rives, William C. *History of the Life and Times of James Madison.* 3 vols. Boston: Little, Brown, 1859–1868.

**6192.** Rogow, Arnold A. "The Federal Convention: Madison and Yates." *American Historical Review* 60 (January 1955): 323–335.

**6193.** Ross, Michael. "Homogeneity and Heterogeneity in Jefferson and Madison." *International Review of History and Political Science* 13 (November 1976): 47–50.

**6194.** Rutland, Robert A. *James Madison and the Search for Nationhood.* Washington, DC: Library of Congress, 1981.

**6195.** ———. *James Madison: The Founding Father.* New York: Macmillan, 1987.

**6196.** ———. "Madison's Bookish Habits." *Library of Congress Quarterly Journal* 37 (Spring 1980): 176–191.

**6197.** Schaedler, Louis C. "James Madison, Literary Craftsman." *William and Mary Quarterly* 3 (October 1946): 515–533.

**6198.** Schultz, Harold S. *James Madison.* New York: Twayne, 1970.

**6199.** ———. "James Madison: Father of the Constitution?" *Library of Congress Quarterly Journal* 37 (Spring 1980): 215–222.

**6200.** Scott, James B. *James Madison's Notes of Debates in the Federal Convention of 1787 and Their Relation to a More Perfect Society of Nations.* New York: Oxford University Press, 1918.

**6201.** Singleton, Marvin K. "Colonial Virginia as First Amendment Matrix: Henry, Madison, and the Establishment Clause." *Journal of Church and State* 8 (Autumn 1966): 344–364.

**6202.** Smith, Abbot E. *James Madison: Builder.* New York: Wilson-Erickson, 1937.

**6203.** Smith, Loren E. "The Library List of 1783: Being a Catalogue of Books, Composed and Arranged by James Madison and Others, and Recommended for the Use of Congress on January 24, 1783, with Notes and an Introduction." Ph.D. dissertation, Claremont Graduate School, 1968.

**6204.** Spengler, Joseph J. "The Political Economy of Jefferson, Madison, and Adams." In *American Studies in Honor of William Kenneth Boyd,* edited by David K. Jackson, 3–59. Durham, NC: Duke University Press, 1940.

**6205.** Stagg, John C. *Mr. Madison's War: Politics, Diplomacy, and Warfare in the Early American Republic, 1783–1830.* Princeton, NJ: Princeton University Press, 1983.

**6206.** Stuart, Reginald C. "James Madison and the Militants: Republican Disunity and Replacing the Embargo." *Diplomatic History* 6 (Spring 1982): 145–168.

**6207.** Ulmer, S. Sidney. "James Madison and the Pinckney Plan." *South Carolina Law Quarterly* 9 (Spring 1957): 415–444.

**6208.** Vanderoef, John S. "The Political Thought of James Madison." Ph.D. dissertation, Princeton University, 1968.

**6209.** Walker, Mary M. "Problems of Majority Rule in the Political Thought of

James Madison and John C. Calhoun." Ph.D. dissertation, Indiana University, 1971.

**6210.** Weber, Paul J. "James Madison and Religious Equality: The Perfect Separation." *Review of Politics* 44 (April 1982): 163–186.

**6211.** Woodburn, James A. *The Making of the Constitution, a Syllabus of "Madison's Journal of the Constitutional Convention," Together with a Few Outlines Based on "The Federalist."* Chicago: Scott Foresman, 1908.

**6212.** Wright, Esmond. "The Political Education of James Madison." *History Today* 31 (December 1981): 17–23.

**6213.** Young, John W. "Madison's Answer to Machiavelli: Concerning the Legal Relation of Organized Religion to Government in a Republic." *Freeman* 27 (July 1977): 421–431.

**6214.** Zvesper, John. "The Madisonian Systems." *Western Political Quarterly* 37 (June 1984): 236–256.

## MAGNUSON, WARREN GRANT
**(1905–1989) D-WA, House 1937–1944, Senate 1944–1981.**

**6215.** Hagner, Paul, and William F. Mullen. "Washington: More Republican, Yes; More Conservative, No." *Social Science Journal* 18 (October 1981): 115–129.

## MAGRUDER, PATRICK (1768–1819)
**R-MD, House 1805–1807.**

**6216.** Gordon, Martin K. "Patrick Magruder: Citizen, Congressman, Librarian of Congress." *Quarterly Journal of the Library of Congress* 32 (July 1975): 154–157.

## MAHONE, WILLIAM (1826–1895)
**READ-VA, Senate 1881–1887.**

**6217.** Blake, Nelson M. *William Mahone of Virginia: Soldier and Political Insurgent.* Richmond, VA: Garret and Massie, 1935.

**6218.** Dufour, Charles L. "Every Inch a Soldier: General Billy Mahone." In his *Nine Men in Gray*, 231–266. Garden City, NY: Doubleday, 1963.

**6219.** Smith, Robert H. *General William Mahone, Frederick Kimball and Others: A Short History of the Norfolk and Western Railway.* New York: Newcomen Society in North America, 1949.

**6220.** Squires, William H. "Major General William Mahone." In his *The Land of Decision*, 168–203. Portsmouth, VA: Printcraft Press, 1931.

## MALLARY, ROLLIN CAROLAS
**(1784–1831) VT, House 1820–1831.**

**6221.** Graffagnino, J. Kevin. "I Saw the Ruin All Around and a Comical Spot You May Depend: Orasmus C. Merrill, Rollin C. Mallary, and the Disputed Congressional Election of 1818." *Vermont History* 49 (Summer 1981): 159–168.

## MALLORY, STEPHEN RUSSELL
**(1813–1873) D-FL, Senate 1851–1861.**

**6222.** Durkin, Joseph T. *Stephen R. Mallory: Confederate Navy Chief.* Chapel Hill: University of North Carolina Press, 1954.

## MANGUM, WILLIE PERSON
**(1792–1861) W-NC, House 1823–1826, Senate 1831–1836, 1840–1853.**

**6223.** McDuffie, Penelope. "Chapters in the Life of Willie Person Mangum." *Trinity College Historical Society Historical Papers* 15 (1925): 5–54.

**6224.** Shanks, T. Henry, ed. *Willie P. Mangum Papers.* 5 vols. Raleigh, NC: State Department of Archives and History, 1950–1956.

## MANKIN, HELEN DOUGLAS
**(1896–1956) D-GA, House 1946–1947.**

**6225.** Spritzer, Lorraine N. *The Belle of Ashby Street: Helen Douglas Mankin and Georgia Politics.* Athens: University of Georgia Press, 1982.

## MANN, HORACE (1796–1859) FS-MA, House 1848–1853.

**6226.** Campbell, Macy. "Horace Mann and the Battle for Better Schools." In his *Rural Life at the Crossroads,* 274–293. Boston: Ginn, 1927.

**6227.** Cassara, Ernest. "Reformer as Politician: Horace Mann and the Antislavery Struggle in Congress, 1848–1853." *Journal of American Studies* 5 (December 1971): 247–264.

**6228.** Clifton, John L. "Horace Mann." In his *Ten Famous American Educators,* 2–27. Columbus, OH: R. G. Adams, 1933.

**6229.** Compayre, Gabriel. *Horace Mann and the Public School in the United States.* New York: Crowell, 1907.

**6230.** Culver, Raymond B. *Horace Mann and Religion in the Massachusetts Public Schools.* New Haven, CT: Yale University Press, 1929.

**6231.** Curti, Merle E. "Education and Social Reform: Horace Mann." In his *The Social Ideas of American Educators,* 101–138. New York: Scribner's, 1935.

**6232.** Downs, Robert B. *Horace Mann: Champion of Public Schools.* New York: Twayne, 1974.

**6233.** Edwards, Cecile P. *Horace Mann: Sower of Learning.* Boston: Houghton Mifflin, 1958.

**6234.** Gara, Larry. "Antislavery Congressmen, 1848–1856: Their Contribution to the Debate between the Sections." *Civil War History* 32 (September 1986): 197–207.

**6235.** ———. "Horace Mann: Anti-slavery Congressman." *Historian* 32 (November 1969): 19–33.

**6236.** Hoyt, Charles O. "Horace Mann and School Administration." In his *Studies in the History of Modern Education,* 147–175. New York: Silver Burdett, 1910.

**6237.** Hubbell, George A. *Horace Mann in Ohio: A Study of the Application of His Public School Ideals to College Administration.* New York: Macmillan, 1900.

**6238.** McCluskey, Neil G. *Public Schools and Moral Education: The Influence of Horace Mann, William Torrey Harris, and John Dewey.* New York: Columbia University Press, 1958.

**6239.** Messerli, Jonathan. *Horace Mann: A Biography.* New York: Knopf, 1972.

**6240.** Morgan, Joy E. *Horace Mann, His Ideas and Ideals.* Washington, DC: National Home Library Foundation, 1936.

**6241.** ———. *The School That Built a Nation.* Pittsburgh: University of Pittsburgh Press, 1954.

**6242.** Slosson, Edwin E. "Horace Mann and the American School." In his *The American Spirit in Education,* 124–140. New Haven, CT: Yale University Press, 1921.

**6243.** Tharp, Louise H. *Until Victory: Horace Mann and Mary Peabody.* Boston: Little, Brown, 1953.

**6244.** Williams, Edward I. *Horace Mann, Educational Statesman.* New York: Macmillan, 1937.

## MANNING, JAMES (1738–1791) RI, Continental Congress 1785–1786.

**6245.** Guild, Reuben A. *Early History of Brown University.* Providence, RI: Snow and Farnham, 1897.

## MANSFIELD, MICHAEL JOSEPH (1903– ) D-MT, House 1943–1953, Senate 1953–1977.

**6246.** Baker, Ross K. "Mike Mansfield and the Birth of the Modern Senate." In *First Among Equals: Outstanding Senate Leaders of the Twentieth Century,* edited by Richard A. Baker and Roger H. Davidson, 264–296. Washington, DC: Congressional Quarterly, 1991.

**6247.** Baldwin, Louis. *Hon. Politician: Mike Mansfield of Montana.* Missoula, MT: Mountain Press, 1979.

**6248.** Hood, Charles E. "'China Mike' Mansfield: The Making of a Congressional Authority on the Far East." Ph.D. dissertation, Washington State University, 1980.

**6249.** Schwartz, James E. "Senator Michael J. Mansfield and United States Military Disengagement from Europe: A Case Study in American Foreign Policy: The Majority Leader, His Amendment, and His Influence Upon the Senate." Ph.D. dissertation, University of North Carolina, 1977.

**6250.** Stewart, John G. "Two Strategies of Leadership: Johnson and Mansfield." In *Congressional Behavior,* edited by Nelson W. Polsby, 61–92. New York: Random House, 1971.

**6251.** Stolar, Mark A. "Aiken, Mansfield and the Tonkin Gulf Crisis: Notes from the Congressional Leadership Meeting at the White House, August 4, 1964." *Vermont History* 50 (Spring 1982): 80–94.

**6252.** Williams, Phillip. "Isolationism or Discerning Internationalism: Robert Taft, Mike Mansfield and US Troops in Europe." *Review of International Studies (Great Britain)* 8 (January 1982): 27–38.

**MARCANTONIO, VITO ANTHONY** (1902–1954) AL-NY, House 1935–1937, 1939–1951.

**6253.** Jackson, Peter. "Vito Marcantonio and Ethnic Politics in New York." *Ethnic and Racial Studies* 6 (January 1983): 50–71.

**6254.** LaGumina, Salvatore J. "The New Deal, the Immigrants and Congressman Vito Marcantonio." *International Migration Review* 4 (Spring 1970): 57–73.

**6255.** ———. "Vito Marcantonio: A Study in the Functional and Ideological Dynamics of a Labor Politician." *Labor History* 13 (Summer 1972): 374–399.

**6256.** ———. *Vito Marcantonio: The People's Politician.* Dubuque, IA: Kendall/Hunt, 1969.

**6257.** Luthin, Reinhard H. "Vito Marcantonio: New York's Leftist Laborite." In his *American Demagogues,* 208–235. Boston: Beacon Press, 1954.

**6258.** Meyer, Gerald J. *Vito Marcantonio: Radical Politician, 1902–1954.* Albany: State University of New York Press, 1989.

**6259.** Sasuly, Richard. "Vito Marcantonio: The People's Politician." In *American Radicals,* edited by Harvey Goldberg, 145–159. New York: Monthly Review, 1957.

**6260.** Schaffer, Alan L. *Vito Marcantonio, Radical in Congress.* Syracuse, NY: Syracuse University Press, 1966.

**MARCHANT, HENRY** (1741–1796) RI, Continental Congress 1777–1780, 1783–1784.

**6261.** Lovejoy, David S. "Henry Marchant and the *Mistress of the World.*" *William and Mary Quarterly* 12 (June 1955): 375–398.

**MARCY, WILLIAM LEARNED** (1786–1857) J-NY, Senate 1831–1833.

**6262.** Learned, H. Barrett. "William Learned Marcy." In *The American Secretaries of State and Their Diplomacy,* edited by Samuel F. Bemis, vol. 6, 143–294. New York: Knopf, 1929.

**6263.** Mattina, Benjamin J. "The Early Life of William Learned Marcy, 1789–1832." Ph.D. dissertation, Georgetown University, 1949.

**6264.** Scribner, Robert L. "The Diplomacy of William L. Marcy, Secretary of State, 1853–1857." Ph.D. dissertation, University of Virginia, 1949.

**6265.** Spann, Edward K. "Gotham in Congress: New York's Representatives and the National Government, 1840–1854." *New York History* 67 (July 1986): 304–329.

**6266.** Spencer, Ivor D. *The Victor and the Spoils: A Life of William L. Marcy.* Providence, RI: Brown University Press, 1959.

**MARLAND, ERNEST WHITWORTH**
**(1874–1941) D-OK, House 1933–1935.**

**6267.** Mathews, John J. *Life and Death of an Oilman: The Career of E. W. Marland.* Norman: University of Oklahoma Press, 1951.

**MARSH, GEORGE PERKINS**
**(1801–1882) W-VT, House 1843–1849.**

**6268.** Lowenthal, David. "George Perkins Marsh and the American Geographical Tradition." *Geographical Review* 43 (April 1953): 207–213.

**6269.** Lowenthal, David. *George Perkins Marsh, Versatile Vermonter.* New York: Columbia University Press, 1958.

**6270.** Trauth, Mary P. *Italo-American Diplomatic Relations, 1861–1882: The Mission of George Perkins Marsh, First American Minister to the Kingdom of Italy.* Westport, CT: Greenwood, 1980.

**MARSHALL, HUMPHREY (1760–1841)**
**F-KY, Senate 1795–1801.**

**6271.** Meredith, Howard. "The Historical Thought of Humphrey Marshall: A Note on Frontier Historicism." *Filson Club History Quarterly* 47 (October 1973): 349–354.

**6272.** Quisenberry, Anderson C. *The Life and Times of Honorable Humphrey Marshall.* Winchester, KY: Sun Publishing Company, 1892.

**MARSHALL, HUMPHREY (1812–1872)**
**AP-KY, House 1849–1852, 1855–1859.**

**6273.** Bain, Chester A. "Commodore Matthew Perry, Humphrey Marshall, and the Taiping Rebellion." *Far-East Quarterly* 10 (May 1951): 258–270.

**6274.** Rea, Kenneth W. "Humphrey Marshall's Commissionership to China, 1852–1854." Ph.D. dissertation, University of Colorado, 1970.

**MARSHALL, JOHN (1755–1835) F-VA,**
**House 1799–1800.**

**6275.** Abbott, Lawrence F. "John Marshall, the Democrat." In his *Twelve Great Modernists,* 125–147. New York: Doubleday, Page, 1927.

**6276.** Anderson, Dice R. "The Teacher of Jefferson and Marshall." *South Atlantic Quarterly* 15 (October 1916): 327–342.

**6277.** Baker, Leonard. *John Marshall: A Life in Law.* New York: Macmillan, 1974.

**6278.** Barkley, Alben W. "The Lessons of John Marshall." *Federal Bar Association Journal* 3 (April 1937): 3–11.

**6279.** Bartosic, Florian. "With John Marshall from William and Mary to Dartmouth College." *William and Mary Law Review* 7 (May 1966): 259–266.

**6280.** Beck, James M. "Memory of Marshall." *American Bar Association Journal* 21 (June 1955): 345–351.

**6281.** Belgrad, Eric A. "John Marshall's Contribution to American Neutrality Doctrines." *William and Mary Law Review* 9 (Winter 1967): 430–457.

**6282.** Bell, Landon C. "John Marshall: Albert J. Beveridge as a Biographer." *Virginia Law Register* 12 (February 1927): 640–655.

**6283.** Berger, Raoul. "Jefferson v. Marshall in the Burr Case." *American Business Law Journal* 14 (Winter 1977): 391–404.

**6284.** Beveridge, Albert J. "Commentaries on the Life of John Marshall." *Journal of Missouri Bar* 3 (June 1947): 115–117, 126–127.

**6285.** ———. "Development of the American Constitution under John Marshall." *American Law Review* 56 (November/December 1922): 921–948.

**6286.** ——. "Development of the American Constitution under John Marshall." *American Law Review* 61 (May/June 1927): 449–477.

**6287.** ——. "Development of the American Constitution under John Marshall." In *Proceedings of the Bar Association of the State of New Hampshire 1923,* 7–49. Concord, NH: Rumford Press, 1924.

**6288.** ——. "John Marshall: His Personality and Development." *Ohio Law Report* 14 (February 21, 1916): 24–32.

**6289.** ——. "John Marshall, the Man and the Lawyer." *Case and Comment* 23 (March 1917): 809–812.

**6290.** ——. *The Life of John Marshall.* Boston: Houghton Mifflin, 1916–1919.

**6291.** Black, John C. "John Marshall." *Albany Law Journal* 54 (July 25, 1896): 55–62.

**6292.** ——. "John Marshall." *Illinois State Bar Association Proceedings* 20 (July 1896): 25–45.

**6293.** Bloch, Susan L., and Maeva Marcus. "John Marshall's Selective Use of History in *Marbury v. Madison.*" *Wisconsin Law Review* 1986, no. 2 (1986): 301–337.

**6294.** Bonaparte, Charles J. *John Marshall as Lawyer and Judge.* Baltimore: Williams, 1901.

**6295.** Boudin, Louis B. "John Marshall and Roger B. Taney." *Georgetown Law Journal* 24 (May 1936): 864–909.

**6296.** Boyd, Julian P. "The Chasm That Separated Thomas Jefferson and John Marshall." *Essays on the American Constitution: A Commemorative Volume in Honor of Alpheus T. Mason,* edited by Gottfried Dietze, 3–20. Englewood Cliffs, NJ: Prentice-Hall, 1964.

**6297.** Brant, Irving. "John Marshall and the Lawyers and Politicians." In *Chief Justice John Marshall: A Reappraisal,* edited by William M. Jones, 38–60. Ithaca, NY: Cornell University Press, 1956.

**6298.** Brisbin, Richard A. "John Marshall and the Nature of Law in the Early Republic." *Virginia Magazine History* 98 (January 1990): 57–80.

**6299.** Brown, Neal. *Critical Confessions and John Marshall and His Times.* Wausau, WI: Philosopher Press, 1902.

**6300.** Browne, Irving. "John Marshall." In his *Short Studies of Great Lawyers,* 201–217. Albany, NY: Albany Law Journal, 1878.

**6301.** Brownell, Herbert, Jr. "John Marshall, the Chief Justice." *Cornell Law Quarterly* 41 (Fall 1955): 93–104.

**6302.** Bruce, Philip A. "Chief Justice John Marshall." In his *The Virginia Plutarch,* vol. 2, 76–96. Chapel Hill: University of North Carolina Press, 1929.

**6303.** Burton, Harold H. "John Marshall: The Man." *University of Pennsylvania Law Review* 104 (October 1955): 3–8.

**6304.** ——. "Justice, the Guardian of Liberty: John Marshall at the Trial of Aaron Burr." *American Bar Association Journal* 37 (October 1951): 735–738.

**6305.** Byran, George. *The Imperialism of John Marshall: A Study in Expediency.* Boston: Stratford, 1924.

**6306.** Caldwell, Russell L. "The Influence of the Federal Bar upon the Interpretation of the Constitution by the Supreme Court under John Marshall." Ph.D. dissertation, University of Southern California, 1948.

**6307.** Campbell, Bruce A. "John Marshall, the Virginia Political Economy and the Dartmouth College Decision." *American Journal of Legal History* 19 (January 1975): 40–65.

**6308.** Campbell, Thomas P., Jr. "Chancellor Kent, Chief Justice Marshall and the Steamboat Cases." *Syracuse Law Review* 25 (Spring 1974): 497–534.

**6309.** Carlton, Mabel M. *John Marshall, the Great Chief Justice.* Boston: John Hancock Mutual Life Insurance Company, 1925.

**6310.** Carson, Hampton L. "John Marshall." *Western Reserve Law Journal* 7 (March 1901): 31–47.

**6311.** Cassoday, John B. "John Scott and John Marshall." *American Law Review* 33 (January/February 1899): 1–27.

**6312.** Conant, Harrison J. "John Marshall and the Recall." *Central Law Journal* 81 (August 1927): 147–154.

**6313.** Cook, Fred J. *Fighting for Justice: John Marshall.* Chicago: Kingston House, 1961.

**6314.** Corwin, Edward S. *John Marshall and the Constitution: A Chronicle of the Supreme Court.* New Haven, CT: Yale University Press, 1919.

**6315.** ———. "John Marshall, Revisionist *Malgre Lui.*" *University of Pennsylvania Law Review* 104 (October 1955): 9–22.

**6316.** Coxe, Alfred C. "In Marshall's Day and Ours." *Columbia Law Review* 3 (February 1903): 88–107.

**6317.** Craighill, Robert T. "John Marshall." In his *The Virginia "Peerage": Sketches of Virginians,* 231–284. Richmond, VA: Jones, 1880.

**6318.** Craigmyle, Thomas S. *John Marshall in Diplomacy and in Law.* New York: Scribner's, 1933.

**6319.** Crosskey, William W. "John Marshall and the Constitution." *University of Chicago Law Review* 23 (Spring 1956): 377–397.

**6320.** ———. *Mr. Chief Justice Marshall.* Chicago: University of Chicago Press, 1956.

**6321.** Cullen, Charles T. "New Light on John Marshall's Legal Education and His Admission to the Bar." *American Journal of Legal History* 16 (October 1972): 345–351.

**6322.** ———. "St. George Tucker, John Marshall, and Constitutionalism in the Post-Revolutionary South." *Vanderbilt Law Review* 32 (January 1979): 341–345.

**6323.** Cuneo, John R. *John Marshall, Judicial Statesman.* New York: McGraw-Hill, 1975.

**6324.** Cunningham, Joe. *Remember John Marshall: A Biography of the Great Chief Justice.* Dallas, TX: Biographic Press, 1956.

**6325.** Cushman, Robert E. "Marshall and the Constitution." *Minnesota Law Review* 5 (December 1920): 1–31.

**6326.** Custer, Lawrence B. "Bushrod Washington and John Marshall: A Preliminary Inquiry." *American Journal of Legal History* 4 (January 1960): 34–78.

**6327.** Day, Edward M. "John Marshall." *Connecticut Bar Journal* 9 (April 1935): 95–113.

**6328.** Deniston, Elinore. *John Marshall: Famous Makers of America.* New York: Dodd, Mead, 1963.

**6329.** Dewey, Donald O. *Marshall versus Jefferson: The Political Background of Marbury v. Madison.* New York: Knopf, 1970.

**6330.** Dickinson, Marquis F., ed. *John Marshall.* Boston: Little, Brown, 1901.

**6331.** Dillon, John F. "A Commemorative Address on Chief Justice Marshall." *American Law Review* 35 (March/April 1901): 161–189.

**6332.** ———. *John Marshall: Life, Character, and Judicial Services as Portrayed in the Centenary and Memorial Addresses and Proceedings throughout the United States on Marshall Day, 1901, and the Classic Orations of Binney, Phelps, Waite, and Rawle.* 3 vols. Chicago: Callaghan, 1903.

**6333.** Dixon, Owen. "Marshall and the Australian Connection." *Australian Law Journal* 29 (December 1955): 420–427.

**6334.** Dodd, William E. *Chief Justice Marshall and Virginia, 1813–1821.* New York: Macmillan, 1907.

**6335.** Donnan, Elizabeth, and Leo F. Stock, eds. "Senator Beveridge, J. Franklin Jameson, and John Marshall." *Mississippi*

*Valley Historical Review* 35 (December 1948): 463–492; 36 (March 1949): 639–673.

**6336.** Dorfman, Joseph H. "John Marshall: Political Economist." In *Chief Justice John Marshall: A Reappraisal,* edited by William M. Jones, 124–144. Ithaca, NY: Cornell University Press, 1956.

**6337.** Douglas, William O. "John Marshall, a Life in Law: An Essay Review." *Louisiana History* 16 (Spring 1975): 193–200.

**6338.** Dumbauld, Edward. "John Marshall and the Law of Nations." *University of Pennsylvania Law Review* 104 (October 1955): 38–56.

**6339.** ———. "John Marshall and Treaty Law." *American Journal of International Law* 50 (January 1956): 69–80.

**6340.** Elliott, Edward. "John Marshall: Growth through Legal Interpretation." In his *Biographical Story of the Constitution,* 125–146. New York: Putnam's, 1910.

**6341.** Farr, Chester N., Jr. "John Marshall." *University of Pennsylvania Law Review* 42 (June 1894): 426–434.

**6342.** Faulkner, Robert K. "John Marshall and the Burr Trial." *Journal of American History* 53 (September 1966): 247–258.

**6343.** ———. *The Jurisprudence of John Marshall.* Princeton, NJ: Princeton University Press, 1968.

**6344.** Finch, Francis M. *Chief Justice John Marshall.* Philadelphia: T. and J. W. Johnson, 1905.

**6345.** ———. "John Marshall." *Yale Law Journal* 10 (March 1901): 171–183.

**6346.** Flanders, Henry. "The Life of John Marshall." In his *The Lives and Times of the Chief Justices of the Supreme Court of the United States,* vol. 2, 277–550. Philadelphia: T. and J. W. Johnson, 1881.

**6347.** ———. *The Life of John Marshall.* Philadelphia: T. and J. W. Johnson, 1905.

**6348.** Foran, William A. "John Marshall as a Historian." *American Historical Review* 43 (October 1937): 51–64.

**6349.** Fordham, Jefferson B., and Theodore Husted, Jr. "John Marshall and the Rule of Law." *University of Pennsylvania Law Review* 104 (October 1955): 57–68.

**6350.** Frankfurter, Felix. *The Commerce Clause under Marshall, Taney and Waite.* Chapel Hill: University of North Carolina Press, 1937.

**6351.** ———. "John Marshall and the Judicial Function." *Harvard Law Review* 69 (December 1955): 217–238.

**6352.** Frierson, William L. "Chief Justice John Marshall." *Tennessee Law Review* 12 (April 1934): 167–173.

**6353.** Frisch, Morton J. "John Marshall's Philosophy of Constitutional Republicanism." *Review of Politics* 20 (January 1958): 34–45.

**6354.** Gaines, Clarence H. "John Marshall and the Spirit of America." *North American Review* 205 (February 1917): 287–292.

**6355.** Garvey, Gerald. "The Constitutional Revolution of 1837 and the Myth of Marshall's Monolith." *Western Political Quarterly* 18 (March 1965): 27–34.

**6356.** Gordon, Douglas H. "John Marshall: The Fourth Chief Justice." *American Bar Association Journal* 41 (August 1955): 698–702, 766–771.

**6357.** Griswold, Rufus W. "John Marshall." In his *The Prose Writers of America,* 85–88. Philadelphia: Carey and Hart, 1847.

**6358.** Gunther, Gerald, comp. *John Marshall's Defense of McCulloch v. Maryland.* Stanford, CA: Stanford University Press, 1969.

**6359.** Hardy, Sallie E. "Chief Justice John Marshall." *Magazine of American History* 12 (July 1884): 62–71.

**6360.** ———. "John Marshall, Third Chief Justice of the United States, as Son, Brother, Husband, and Friend." *Green Bag* 8 (December 1896): 479–492.

**6361.** Haskins, George L. *Foundations of Power: John Marshall, 1801–15.* New York: Macmillan, 1981.

**6362.** ———. "John Marshall and the Commerce Clause of the Constitution." *University of Pennsylvania Law Review* 104 (October 1955): 23–68.

**6363.** Hatcher, William H. "John Marshall and States' Rights." *Solicitor Quarterly* 3 (April 1965): 207–216.

**6364.** Haymond, Frank C. "John Marshall: His Influence on the Constitution and the Courts." *West Virginia Law Quarterly* 42 (December 1935): 14–30.

**6365.** Holcombe, Arthur N. "John Marshall as Politician and Political Theorist, 1788–1835." In *Chief Justice John Marshall: A Reappraisal,* edited by William M. Jones, 24–37. Ithaca, NY: Cornell University Press, 1956.

**6366.** Houghton, Walter R. "John Marshall." In his *Kings of Fortune,* 437–456. Chicago: A. E. Davis, 1885.

**6367.** Hughes, Robert M. "Chief Justice John Marshall and His Work." In *Genesis and Birth of the Federal Constitution: Addresses and Papers in the Marshall-Wythe School of Government and Citizenship of the College of William and Mary,* edited by Julian A. Chandler, 351–374. New York: Macmillan, 1924.

**6368.** Isaacs, Nathan. "John Marshall on Contracts: Study in Early Juristic Theory." *Virginia Law Review* 7 (March 1921): 413–428.

**6369.** Jaeger, Walter. "John Marshall: The Man, the Judge and the Law of Nations." *American University Law Review* 8 (January 1959): 28–33.

**6370.** Johnson, Herbert A. "The Tribulations of Conway Robinson, Jr.: John Mar-

shall's 'Washington Lotts'." *Virginia Magazine of History and Biography* 79 (October 1971): 427–435.

**6371.** Jones, Francis R. "John Marshall." *Green Bag* 13 (February 1901): 53–64.

**6372.** Jones, William M., ed. *Chief Justice John Marshall: A Reappraisal.* New York: Da Capo Press, 1971.

**6373.** Karst, Kenneth L. "Justice Marshall and the First Amendment." *Black Law Journal* 6 (Fall 1979): 26–42.

**6374.** Keeble, John B. "Influence of John Marshall on American Jurisprudence." *Tennessee Bar Association Proceedings* 32 (1913): 169–196.

**6375.** Keefe, Arthur J. "John Marshall, Magnificent Mugwump." *Catholic University of America Law Review* 6 (December 1956): 103–115.

**6376.** Klinkhamer, Marie C. "John Marshall's Use of History." *Catholic University of America Law Review* 6 (December 1956): 78–96.

**6377.** Konefsky, Samuel J. *John Marshall and Alexander Hamilton: Architects of the American Constitution.* New York: Macmillan, 1967.

**6378.** Kurland, Philip B., ed. *James Bradley Thayer, Oliver Wendell Holmes, and Felix Frankfurter on John Marshall.* Chicago: University of Chicago Press, 1967.

**6379.** Kutler, Stanley I., comp. *John Marshall.* Englewood Cliffs, NJ: Prentice-Hall, 1972.

**6380.** Lerner, Max. "John Marshall and the Campaign of History." *Columbia Law Review* 39 (March 1939): 396–431.

**6381.** ———. "John Marshall's Long Shadow." In his *Ideas Are Weapons: The History and Uses of Ideas,* 27–37. New York: Viking, 1939.

**6382.** Levy, Martin L. "Supreme Court in Retreat: Wealth Discrimination and Mr. Justice Marshall." *Texas Southern University Law Review* 4 (Spring 1977): 209–242.

**6383.** Lewis, William D. "John Marshall." In his *Great American Lawyers,* vol. 2, 311–408. Philadelphia: John C. Winston Company, 1907–1909.

**6384.** Lossing, Benson J. "John Marshall." In his *Eminent Americans,* 216–218. New York: Hurst, 1886.

**6385.** Loth, David G. *Chief Justice: John Marshall and the Growth of the Republic.* New York: Norton, 1949.

**6386.** MacDonald, William. "The Indebtedness of John Marshall to Alexander Hamilton." *Massachusetts Historical Society Proceedings* 46 (1913): 412–426.

**6387.** Magruder, Allan B. *John Marshall.* Boston: Houghton Mifflin, 1899.

**6388.** Maltbie, William M. "John Marshall: A Tribute." *Connecticut Bar Journal* 29 (December 1955): 335–349.

**6389.** Marshall, John. *The Papers of John Marshall.* Edited by Herbert A. Johnson. 7 vols. Chapel Hill: University of North Carolina Press, 1974– .

**6390.** Martini, Teri. *John Marshall.* Philadelphia: Westminster Press, 1974.

**6391.** Mason, Frances N. *My Dearest Polly: Letters of Chief Justice John Marshall to His Wife, with Their Background, Political and Domestic, 1779–1831.* Richmond, VA: Garrett and Massie, 1961.

**6392.** McCabe, James D. "John Marshall." In his *Great Fortunes,* 417–434. Cincinnati, OH: Hannaford, 1871.

**6393.** McClain, Emlin. "Chief Justice Marshall as a Constructive Statesman." *Iowa Journal of History* 1 (October 1903): 427–466.

**6394.** McGinty, Brian. "The Great Chief Justice." *American History Illustrated* 21 (September 1986): 8–14, 46–47.

**6395.** McLaughlin, Andrew C. "The Life of John Marshall." *American Bar Association Journal* 7 (May 1921): 231–233.

**6396.** Mendelson, Wallace. "Chief Justice John Marshall and the Mercantile Tradition." *Southwestern Social Science Quarterly* 29 (June 1948): 27–37.

**6397.** ———. "John Marshall's Short Way with Statutes: A Study in the Judicial Use of Legislation to Expound the Constitution." *Kentucky Law Journal* 36 (March 1948): 284–289.

**6398.** Montague, Andrew J. "John Marshall." In *The American Secretaries of State and Their Diplomacy,* edited by Samuel F. Bemis, vol. 2, 245–284. New York: Knopf, 1927.

**6399.** ———. "John Marshall." In *Library of Southern Literature,* edited by Edwin A. Alderman and Joel C. Harris, vol. 8, 3369–3373. New Orleans: Martin and Hoyt, 1909.

**6400.** Moore, Frank. "John Marshall." In his *American Eloquence,* vol. 2, 1–32. New York: D. Appleton and Company, 1862.

**6401.** Moore, John B. *John Marshall.* Boston: Ginn, 1901.

**6402.** Morgan, Donald G. "Marshall, the Marshall Court, and the Constitution." In *Chief Justice John Marshall: A Reappraisal,* edited by William M. Jones, 168–185. Ithaca, NY: Cornell University Press, 1956.

**6403.** Moses, Adolf. "The Friendship between Marshall and Story." *American Law Review* 35 (May/June 1901): 321–342.

**6404.** Moses, Belle. *John Marshall, Our Greatest Chief Justice.* New York: Appleton-Century, 1938.

**6405.** Munro, William B. "John Marshall and the Achievement of Nationalism." In his *The Makers of the Unwritten Constitution,* 51–81. New York: Macmillan, 1930.

**6406.** Myers, Gustavus. "The Authentic John Marshall." In his *History of the Supreme Court of the United States,* 228–354. Chicago: C. H. Kerr, 1918.

**6407.** Nelson, William E. "The Eighteenth Century Background of John Marshall's Constitutional Jurisprudence." *Michigan Law Review* 76 (May 1978): 893–960.

**6408.** Newmyer, R. Kent. *The Supreme Court under Marshall and Taney.* New York: Crowell, 1968.

**6409.** Nurick, Gilbert. "Impeach John Marshall." *North Carolina Central Law Journal* 2 (Spring 1970): 100–109.

**6410.** Olney, Warren. "Chief Justice Marshall." *American Law Review* 34 (July/August 1900): 550–561.

**6411.** Oster, John E. *The Political and Economic Doctrines of John Marshall.* New York: Neale Publishing Company, 1914.

**6412.** Padover, Saul K. "The American as Federalist." In his *The Genius of America: Men Whose Ideas Shaped Our Civilization,* 118–137. New York: McGraw-Hill, 1960.

**6413.** ———. "Political Ideas of John Marshall." *Social Research* 26 (Spring 1956): 47–70.

**6414.** Palmer, Benjamin W. *Marshall and Taney: Statesmen of the Law.* Minneapolis: University of Minnesota Press, 1939.

**6415.** Parrington, Vernon L. "John Marshall, Last of the Virginia Federalists." In his *Main Currents in American Thought,* vol. 2, 20–27. New York: Harcourt, Brace, 1927.

**6416.** Perry, Benjamin F. "John Marshall." In his *Biographical Sketches of Eminent American Statesmen,* 467–477. Philadelphia: Ferree Press, 1887.

**6417.** Powell, Thomas R. "The Great Chief Justice: His Leadership in Judicial Review." *William and Mary Law Review* 2 (July 1955): 72–93.

**6418.** Prentice, E. Parmalee. "Chief Justice Marshall on Federal Regulations of Interstate Carriers." *Cleveland Bar Association Journal* 5 (February 1905): 77–106.

**6419.** Richards, Gale L. "Alexander Hamilton's Influence on John Marshall's Judiciary Speech in the 1788 Virginia Federal Ratifying Convention." *Quarterly Journal of Speech* 44 (February 1958): 31–39.

**6420.** ———. "A Criticism of the Public Speaking of John Marshall Prior to 1801." Ph.D. dissertation, State University of Iowa, 1954.

**6421.** ———. "Invention in John Marshall's Legal Speaking." *Southern Speech Journal* 19 (December 1953): 108–115.

**6422.** Roche, John P. *John Marshall: Major Opinions and Other Writings.* Indianapolis: Bobbs-Merrill, 1966.

**6423.** Rudko, Frances H. *John Marshall and International Law: Statesman and Chief Justice.* New York: Greenwood, 1991.

**6424.** Russell, Alfred. "John Marshall." *American Law Review* 35 (January/February 1901): 1–7.

**6425.** Seddig, Robert G. "John Marshall and the Origins of Supreme Court Leadership." *University of Pittsburgh Law Review* 36 (Summer 1975): 785–835.

**6426.** Severn, William. *John Marshall, the Man Who Made the Court Supreme.* New York: D. McKay, 1969.

**6427.** Shevory, Thomas C. *John Marshall's Law: Interpretation, Ideology, and Interest.* Westport, CT: Greenwood, 1994.

**6428.** ———, ed. *John Marshall's Achievement: Law, Politics, and Constitutional Interpretations.* Westport, CT: Greenwood, 1989.

**6429.** Siegel, Adrienne. *The Marshall Court, 1801–1835.* Port Washington, NY: Associated Faculty Press, 1987.

**6430.** Smith, William R. "John Marshall: National Historian." In his *History as Argument: Three Patriot Historians of the American Revolution,* 120–172. The Hague: Mouton, 1966.

**6431.** Smyth, Clifford. *John Marshall, Father of the Supreme Court.* New York: Funk and Wagnalls, 1931.

**6432.** Stanard, Mary N. *John Marshall: An Address.* Richmond, VA: William Ellis Jones's Sons Printers, 1913.

**6433.** Stebbins, Calvin. *John Marshall: A Discourse.* Framingham, MA: Printed by Request, 1901. Np.

**6434.** Steinberg, Alfred. *John Marshall.* New York: Putnam's, 1962.

**6435.** Stinson, Joseph W. "Marshall and the Supremacy of the Unwritten Law." *American Law Review* 58 (November/December 1942): 856–871.

**6436.** ———. "Marshall on the Jurisdiction of the Littoral Sovereign over Territorial Waters." *American Law Review* 57 (July/August 1923): 567–578.

**6437.** Stites, Francis N. *John Marshall, Defender of the Constitution.* Boston: Little, Brown, 1981.

**6438.** Story, Joseph. *Discourse upon the Life, Character and Services of the Honorable John Marshall.* Boston: J. Munro, 1835.

**6439.** Strong, Frank R. "John Marshall: Hero or Villain?" *Ohio State Law Journal* 6 (December 1939): 42–62; 7 (March 1940): 158–189.

**6440.** Surrency, Erwin C., ed. *The Marshall Reader: The Life and Contributions of Chief Justice John Marshall.* New York: Oceana Publications, 1955.

**6441.** Swindler, William F. *The Constitution and Chief Justice Marshall.* New York: Dodd, Mead, 1978.

**6442.** ———. "John Marshall's Preparation for the Bar: Some Observations on His Law Notes." *American Law Journal of Legal History* 11 (April 1967): 207–273.

**6443.** Swisher, Carl B. "The Achievement of John Marshall." *Thought* 31 (Spring 1956): 5–26.

**6444.** Thayer, James B. *John Marshall.* Boston: Houghton Mifflin, 1901.

**6445.** Thompson, William D. "John Marshall: His Constitutional Decisions." *Marquette Law Review* 7 (April 1923): 111–130.

**6446.** Thorpe, Francis N. "Hamilton's Ideas in Marshall's Decisions." *Boston University Law Review* 1 (April 1921): 60–98.

**6447.** Tillet, Paul. "Mr. Justice Black, Chief Justice Marshall and the Commerce Clause." *Nebraska Law Review* 43 (December 1963): 1–26.

**6448.** Tucker, Caroline. *John Marshall, the Chief Justice.* New York: Ariel Books, 1962.

**6449.** Tunstall, Robert B. "John Marshall: One Hundred Years After." *American Bar Association Journal* 21 (September 1935): 561–567.

**6450.** Turner, Kathryn. "The Appointment of Chief Justice Marshall." *William and Mary Quarterly* 17 (April 1960): 143–163.

**6451.** Umbanhowar, Charles W. "Marshall on Judging." *American Journal of Legal History* 7 (July 1963): 210–227.

**6452.** Umbreit, Kenneth B. "John Marshall." In his *Our Eleven Chief Justices,* 111–196. New York: Harper, 1938.

**6453.** Waite, Catherine V. "John Marshall." *Chicago Law Times* 1 (April 1887): 109–121.

**6454.** Warren, Aldice G. "A Comparison of the Tendencies in Constitutional Construction Shown by the Supreme Court under Chief Justices Marshall and Taney Respectively." Ph.D. dissertation, New York University, 1913.

**6455.** Warren, Charles. *The Story-Marshall Correspondence.* New York: New York University, 1942.

**6456.** White, Edward J. "The Life of John Marshall." *American Law Review* 55 (July 1921): 503–511.

**6457.** White, G. Edward. *The Marshall Court and Cultural Change: 1815–35.* Vol. 3 of *The History of the Supreme Court of the United States,* edited by Paul A. Freund and Stanley N. Katz. New York: Macmillan, 1988.

**6458.** Wildman, Edwin. "John Marshall: The Interpreter of the Constitution." In his *The Founders of America in the Days of the Revolution,* 282–299. Freeport, NY: Books for Libraries, 1968.

**6459.** Wilson, Andrew. "The Influence of John Marshall on the Political History of the U.S." Ph.D. dissertation, George Washington University, 1904.

**6460.** Wilson, Henry H. "The Influence of Chief Justice Marshall on American Institutions." *Nebraska Law Bulletin* 6 (February 1928): 327–354.

**6461.** Wilson, John R. "John Marshall." *American Law Review* 22 (September/October 1988): 706–730.

**6462.** Wilstach, Paul. "John Marshall." In his *Patriots Off Their Pedestals,* 182–210. Indianapolis: Bobbs-Merrill, 1927.

**6463.** Wolfe, Christopher. "John Marshall and Constitutional Law." *Polity* 15 (Spring 1982): 5–25.

**6464.** Woodbridge, Dudley W. "John Marshall in Perspective." *Pennsylvania Bar Association Quarterly* 27 (January 1956): 192–204.

**6465.** Ziegle, Benjamin M. *The International Law of John Marshall: A Study in First Principles.* Chapel Hill: University of North Carolina Press, 1939.

## MARSHALL, THOMAS FRANCIS
### (1801–1864) W-KY, House 1841–1843.

**6466.** Duke, Basil W. "Thomas Francis Marshall." In *Library of Southern Literature,* edited by Edwin A. Alderman and Joel C. Harris, vol. 8, 3395–3399. New Orleans: Martin and Hoyt, 1909.

## MARTIN, ALEXANDER (1740–1807) NC, Senate 1793–1799.

**6467.** McLachlan, James. "Alexander Martin." In his *Princetonians, 1748–1768,* 157–160. Princeton, NJ: Princeton University Press, 1976.

## MARTIN, CHARLES HENRY
### (1863–1946) D-OR, House 1931–1935.

**6468.** Turnbull, George S. "Charles Henry Martin." In his *Governors of Oregon,* 82–84. Portland, OR: Binfords, 1959.

## MARTIN, EDWARD (1879–1967) R-PA, Senate 1947–1959.

**6469.** Early, Elizabeth A. "In the Public's Best Interest." *Pennsylvania Heritage* 15, no. 3 (1989): 12–19.

**6470.** Martin, Edward W. *Always Be on Time: An Autobiography.* Harrisburg, PA: Telegraph Press, 1959.

## MARTIN, JOSEPH WILLIAM JR.
### (1884–1968) R-MA, House 1925–1967.

**6471.** Hasenfus, William A. "Managing Partner: Joseph W. Martin, Jr., Republican Leader of the United States House of Representatives, 1939–1959." Ph.D. dissertation, Boston College, 1986.

**6472.** Martin, Joseph W. *My First Fifty Years in Politics as told to Robert J. Donovan.* New York: McGraw-Hill, 1960.

## MARTIN, LUTHER (1744–1826) MD,
### Continental Congress 1784–1785.

**6473.** Clarkson, Paul S. *Luther Martin of Maryland.* Baltimore: Johns Hopkins University Press, 1970.

**6474.** Essary, J. Frederick. "Luther Martin." In his *Maryland in National Politics.* Baltimore: John Murphy, 1915.

**6475.** Goddard, Henry P. *Luther Martin: The "Federal Bulldog."* Baltimore: John Murphy, 1887.

## MARTIN, THOMAS STAPLES
(1847–1919) D-VA, Senate 1895–1919.

**6476.** Cox, Harold E. "The Jones-Martin Senatorial Campaign of 1911." In *Essays in History*, 38–56. Charlottesville: University of Virginia, 1954.

**6477.** Fishwick, Marshall W. "Thomas Martin." In his *Gentlemen of Virginia*, 194–209. New York: Dodd, Mead, 1961.

**6478.** Holt, Wyeth W. "The Senator from Virginia and the Democratic Floor Leadership: Thomas S. Martin and Conservatism in the Progressive Era." *Virginia Magazine of History and Biography* 83 (January 1975): 3–21.

**6479.** Reeves, Pascal. "Thomas S. Martin: Committee Statesman." *Virginia Magazine of History and Biography* 68 (July 1960): 344–364.

## MASON, JAMES MURRAY (1798–1871)
D-VA, House 1837–1839, Senate 1847–1861.

**6480.** Bugg, James L. "The Political Career of James Murray Mason." Ph.D. dissertation, University of Virginia, 1950.

**6481.** Mason, Virginia. *The Public Life and Diplomatic Correspondence of James M. Mason.* Roanoke, VA: Stone Printing, 1903.

## MASON, JEREMIAH (1768–1848) F-NH,
Senate 1813–1817.

**6482.** Hillard, George S., ed. *Memoir and Correspondence of Jeremiah Mason.* Cambridge, MA: Riverside, 1973.

**6483.** Stubbs, Roy St. George. "Jeremiah Mason." *Canadian Bar Review* 24 (October 1946): 678–692.

## MASON, JOHN YOUNG (1799–1859)
J-VA, House 1831–1837.

**6484.** Williams, Frances L. "The Heritage and Preparation of a Statesman, John Young Mason, 1799–1859." *Virginia Magazine of History and Biography* 75 (July 1967): 305–330.

## MASON, NOAH MORGAN (1882–1965)
R-IL, House 1937–1963.

**6485.** Samosky, Jack A. "Congressman Noah Morgan Mason: From Wales to Washington." *Journal of the Illinois State Historical Society* 71 (November 1978): 252–263.

**6486.** Samosky, Jack A. "Congressman Noah Morgan Mason: Illinois' Conservative Spokesman." *Journal of the Illinois State Historical Society* 76 (Spring 1983): 35–48.

## MASON, STEVENS THOMSON
(1760–1803) R-VA, Senate 1794–1803.

**6487.** Grigsby, Hugh B. "Stevens Thomson Mason." In his *History of the Virginia Federal Convention*, vol. 2, 225–264. Richmond: Virginia Historical Society, 1891.

## MASON, WILLIAM ERNEST (1850–1921)
R-IL, House 1887–1891, 1917–1921, Senate 1897–1903.

**6488.** Mason, William E. *John, the Unafraid.* Chicago: A. C. McClurg, 1913.

**6489.** VanderMeer, Philip R. "Congressional Decision-Making and World War I: A Case Study of Illinois." *Congressional Studies* 8, no. 2 (1981): 59–79.

## MATHEWS, GEORGE (1739–1812) GA,
House 1789–1791.

**6490.** Kruse, Paul. "Secret Agent in East Florida: General George Mathews and the Patriot War." *Journal of Southern History* 18 (May 1952): 193–217.

## MATHIAS, ROBERT BRUCE (1930– )
R-CA, House 1967–1975.

**6491.** Bortstein, Larry. "Bob Mathias." In his *After Olympic Glory*, 50–67. New York: Warne, 1978.

**MATTHEWS, STANLEY** (1824–1889)
R-OH, Senate 1877–1879.

**6492.** Helfman, Harold M. "The Contested Confirmation of Stanley Matthews to the United States Supreme Court." *Historical and Philosophical Society of Ohio* 8 (July 1958): 154–170.

**6493.** Jager, Ronald B. "Stanley Matthews for the Supreme Court: Lord Roscoe's Downfall." *Cincinnati Historical Society Bulletin* 38 (Fall 1980): 191–208.

**MAVERICK, FONTAINE MAURY**
(1895–1954) D-TX, House 1935–1939.

**6494.** Doyle, Judith K. "Maury Maverick and Racial Politics in San Antonio, Texas, 1938–1941." *Journal of Southern History* 53 (May 1987): 194–224.

**6495.** Henderson, Richard B. *Maury Maverick: A Political Biography.* Austin: University of Texas Press, 1970.

**6496.** Weiss, Stuart L. "Maury Maverick and the Liberal Bloc." *Journal of American History* 57 (March 1971): 880–895.

**MAXEY, SAMUEL BELL** (1825–1895)
D-TX, Senate 1875–1887.

**6497.** Horton, Louise. *Samuel Bell Maxey: A Biography.* Austin: University of Texas Press, 1974.

**6498.** Maxey, Samuel B. *Maxey's Texas.* Austin, TX: Pemberton Press, 1965.

**6499.** Welch, June R. "Maxey Was a Confederate General." In his *The Texas Senator,* 26–29. Dallas, TX: G. L. A. Press, 1978.

**MAY, CATHERINE DEAN BARNES**
(1914–  ) R-WA, House 1959–1971.

**6500.** Parshalle, Eve. "Catherine May." In her *Kashmir Bridge-Women,* 213–217. New York: Oxford University Press, 1965.

**MAYBANK, BURNET RHETT**
(1899–1954) D-SC, Senate 1941–1954.

**6501.** Cann, Marvin L. "Burnett Rhett Maybank and the New Deal in South Carolina, 1931–1941." Ph.D. dissertation, University of North Carolina, 1967.

**MAYFIELD, EARLE BRADFORD**
(1881–1964) D-TX, Senate 1923–1929.

**6502.** O'Neill, Eugene G. *Eugene O'Neill and the Senator from Texas.* New Haven, CT: Yale University Library Gazette, 1961.

**6503.** Welch, June R. "Earle Mayfield Was the Klan Candidate." In his *The Texas Senator,* 52–55. Dallas, TX: G. L. A. Press, 1978.

**MAYNARD, HORACE** (1814–1882) R-TN,
House 1857–1863.

**6504.** Marshall, Kendrick. "Horace Maynard: A Tennessee Statesman." Master's thesis, Tennessee State A & I University, 1960.

**6505.** Temple, Oliver P. "Horace Maynard." In *Notable Men of Tennessee, From 1833 to 1875,* edited by Mary B. Temple, 137–149. New York: Cosmopolitan Press, 1912.

**6506.** Williams, Gladys I. "The Life of Horace Maynard." Master's thesis, University of Tennessee, 1931.

**McADOO, WILLIAM GIBBS** (1863–1941)
D-CA, Senate 1933–1938.

**6507.** Allen, Lee N. "The McAdoo Campaign for the Presidential Nomination in 1924." *Journal of Southern History* 29 (May 1963): 211–228.

**6508.** Bagby, Wesley M. "William Gibbs McAdoo and the 1920 Democratic Presidential Nominations." *East Tennessee Historical Society Publications* 31 (1959): 43–58.

**6509.** Broesamle, John J. *William Gibbs McAdoo: A Passion for Change, 1863–1917.* Port Washington, NY: Kennikat, 1973.

**6510.** Cross, Wilbur, and Ann Novotny. "A Simple Event." In their *White House Weddings,* 190–202. New York: McKay, 1967.

**6511.** Gelbert, Herbert A. "The Anti-McAdoo Movement of 1924." Ph.D. dissertation, New York University, 1978.

**6512.** Kent, Frank R. "McAdoo's 1924 Campaign." In his *The Democratic Party, a History,* 464–475. New York: Century Company, 1928.

**6513.** Kerr, K. Austin. "Decision for Federal Control: Wilson, McAdoo, and the Railroads, 1917." *Journal of American History* 54 (December 1967): 550–560.

**6514.** Lippmann, Walter. "An Early Estimate of Mr. McAdoo." In his *Men of Destiny,* 112–119. New York: Macmillan, 1927.

**6515.** McAdoo, William G. *Crowded Years: The Reminiscences of William G. McAdoo.* Boston: Houghton Mifflin, 1931.

**6516.** McKinney, Gordon B. "East Tennessee Politics: An Incident in the Life of William Gibbs McAdoo, Jr." *East Tennessee Historical Society Publications* 48 (1976): 34–39.

**6517.** Prude, James C. "William Gibbs McAdoo and the Democratic National Convention of 1924." *Journal of Southern History* 38 (November 1972): 621–628.

**6518.** Shook, Dale N. *William G. McAdoo and the Development of National Economic Policy, 1913–1918.* New York: Garland, 1987.

**6519.** Synon, Mary. *McAdoo: The Man and His Times.* Indianapolis: Bobbs-Merrill, 1924.

## McARTHUR, DUNCAN (1772–1839) OH, House 1813, 1823–1825.

**6520.** Cramer, Clarence H. "Duncan McArthur: First Phase, 1772–1812." *Ohio State Archaeological and Historical Quarterly* 45 (January 1936): 27–33.

**6521.** Smith, S. Winifred. "Duncan McArthur, 1830–1832." In *Governors of Ohio,* 31–34. Columbus: Ohio Historical Society, 1954.

## McCARRAN, PATRICK ANTHONY (1876–1954) D-NV, Senate 1933–1954.

**6522.** Cole, David. "McCarran-Walter." *Constitution* 2 (Winter 1990): 51–52, 54–59.

**6523.** Edwards, Jerome E. "Nevada Power Broker: Pat McCarran and His Political Machine." *Nevada Historical Society Quarterly* 27 (Fall 1984): 182–198.

**6524.** ———. *Pat McCarran, Political Boss of Nevada.* Reno: University of Nevada Press, 1982.

**6525.** ———. "The Sun and the Senator." *Nevada Historical Society Quarterly* 24 (Spring 1981): 3–16.

**6526.** Green, Michael S. "Senator McCarran and the Roosevelt Court-Packing Plan." *Nevada Historical Society Quarterly* 33 (Winter 1990): 30–48.

**6527.** McCarran, Margaret P. "Patrick Anthony McCarran." *Nevada Historical Society Quarterly* 11 (Winter 1968): 3–66; 12 (Spring 1969): 5–75.

**6528.** Pittman, Von V. "Senator Patrick A. McCarran and the Politics of Containment." Ph.D. dissertation, University of Georgia, 1979.

**6529.** ———. "Three Crises: Senator Patrick McCarran in Mid-Career." *Nevada Historical Society Quarterly* 24 (Fall 1981): 221–234.

**6530.** Steinberg, Alfred. "McCarran, Lone Wolf of the Senate." *Harper's* 201 (November 1950): 89–95.

**6531.** Whited, Fred E. "Senator Patrick A. McCarran: Orator from Nevada." *Nevada Historical Society Quarterly* 17 (Winter 1974): 181–202.

## McCARTHY, EUGENE JOSEPH (1916– )
D-MN, House 1949–1959, Senate 1959–1971.

**6532.** Eisele, Albert A. *Almost to the Presidency: A Biography of Two American Politicians.* Blue Earth, NM: Piper, 1972.

**6533.** Herzog, Arthur. *McCarthy for President.* New York: Viking, 1969.

**6534.** Hoeh, David C. "The Biography of a Campaign Strategy, Management, Result: McCarthy in New Hampshire 1968." Ph.D. dissertation, University of Massachusetts, 1978.

**6535.** Larner, Jeremy. *Nobody Knows: Reflections on the McCarthy Campaign of 1968.* New York: Macmillan, 1969.

**6536.** McCarthy, Abigail. *Private Faces/Public Places.* Garden City, NY: Doubleday, 1972.

**6537.** McCarthy, Eugene J. *Up 'Til Now: A Memoir of the Decline of the Democratic Party.* San Diego, CA: Harcourt Brace Jovanovich, 1987.

**6538.** McDonald, William P., and Jerry G. Smoke. *Peasants' Revolt: McCarthy 1968.* Mt. Vernon, OH: Noe-Bixby, 1969.

**6539.** Richards, Carmen. "Eugene J. McCarthy." In her *Minnesota Writers,* 219–220. Minneapolis, MN: Denison, 1961.

**6540.** Stavis, Ben. *We Were the Campaign: New Hampshire to Chicago for McCarthy.* Boston: Beacon Press, 1969.

**6541.** Stout, Richard T. *People.* New York: Harper and Row, 1970.

**6542.** Stuhler, Barbara. "A Tale of Two Democrats: Hubert H. Humphrey and Eugene J. McCarthy." In her *Ten Men of Minnesota and American Foreign Policy, 1898–1968,* 194–220. St. Paul: Minnesota Historical Society, 1973.

**6543.** White, Theodore H. "The Democrats: The Struggle for Inheritance." In his *Making of the President, 1968,* 62–90. New York: Atheneum, 1969.

## McCARTHY, JOSEPH RAYMOND
(1908–1957) R-WI, Senate 1947–1957.

**6544.** Adams, John G. *Without Precedent: The Story of the Death of McCarthyism.* New York: Norton, 1983.

**6545.** Anderson, Jack, and Ronald W. May. *McCarthy: The Man, the Senator, the "Ism."* Boston: Beacon Press, 1952.

**6546.** Bayley, Edwin R. *Joe McCarthy and the Press.* Madison: University of Wisconsin Press, 1981.

**6547.** Belfrage, Cedric. *The American Inquisition, 1945–1960.* Indianapolis: Bobbs-Merrill, 1973.

**6548.** Bornet, Vaughn D. "An Eyewitness Account of Senator Joseph R. McCarthy on the Hustings, San Mateo County, February 10, 1954." *Pacific Historian* 29 (Spring 1985): 68–74.

**6549.** Buckley, William F., and L. Brent Bozell. *McCarthy and His Enemies: The Record and Its Meaning.* Chicago: Regnery, 1954.

**6550.** Cohn, Roy. *McCarthy.* New York: New American Library, 1968.

**6551.** Cook, Fred J. *Nightmare Decade: The Life and Times of Joe McCarthy.* New York: Random House, 1971.

**6552.** Crandell, William F. "Eisenhower the Strategist: The Battle of the Bulge and the Censure of Joe McCarthy." *Presidential Studies Quarterly* 17 (Summer 1987): 487–501.

**6553.** Crosby, Donald F. "The Catholic Bishops and Senator Joseph McCarthy." *Records of the American Catholic Historical Society of Philadelphia* 86 (March/December 1975): 132–148.

**6554.** Crosby, Donald F. *God, Church, and Flag: Senator Joseph R. McCarthy and the Catholic Church, 1950–1957.* Chapel Hill: University of North Carolina Press, 1978.

**6555.** Deaver, Jean F. "A Study of Senator Joseph R. McCarthy and 'McCarthyism' as Influences upon the News Media and the Evolution of Reportorial Method." Ph.D. dissertation, University of Texas, 1969.

**6556.** DeFuria, Guy G. "McCarthy Censure Case: Some Legal Aspects." *American Bar Association Journal* 42 (April 1956): 329–332, 395–397.

**6557.** Dembitz, Nanette. "Was Senator McCarthy's Good Name Damaged?" *South Atlantic Quarterly* 52 (April 1953): 228–237.

**6558.** Dulles, Eleanor L. "Footnote to History: A Day in the Life of Senator Joe McCarthy." *World Affairs* 143 (Fall 1980): 156–162.

**6559.** Evans, Medford. *Assassination of Joe McCarthy.* Belmont, MA: Western Islands, 1970.

**6560.** Ewald, William B. *McCarthyism and Consensus?* Lanham, MD: University Press of America, 1986.

**6561.** ———. *Who Killed Joe McCarthy?* New York: Simon and Schuster, 1984.

**6562.** Ezell, Macel D. *McCarthyism: Twentieth Century Witch-hunt.* Austin, TX: Steck-Vaughn, 1970.

**6563.** Feuerlicht, Roberta S. *Joe McCarthy and McCarthyism: The Hate That Haunts America.* New York: McGraw-Hill, 1972.

**6564.** Ford, Sherman. *McCarthy Menace: An Evaluation of the Facts and an Interpretation of the Evidence.* New York: William-Frederick Press, 1954.

**6565.** Fried, Richard M. "McCarthyism without Tears: A Review Essay." *Wisconsin Magazine of History* 66 (Winter 1982–1983): 143–146.

**6566.** ———. *Men Against McCarthy.* New York: Columbia University Press, 1976.

**6567.** ———. *Nightmare in Red: The McCarthy Era in Perspective.* New York: Oxford University Press, 1990.

**6568.** Goldston, Robert. *American Nightmare: Senator Joseph R. McCarthy and the Politics of Hate.* Indianapolis: Bobbs-Merrill, 1973.

**6569.** Gore, Leroy. *Joe Must Go.* New York: Messner, 1954.

**6570.** Grant, Philip A. "Bishop Bernard J. Sheil's Condemnation of Senator Joseph R. McCarthy." *Records of the American Catholic Historical Society of Philadelphia* 97 (March/December 1986): 43–50.

**6571.** Griffith, Robert W. *Politics of Fear, Joseph R. McCarthy and the Senate.* Lexington: University Press of Kentucky, 1970.

**6572.** Griffith, Robert W., and Athan G. Theoharis, eds. *The Specter: Original Essays on the Cold War and the Origins of McCarthyism.* New York: New Viewpoints, 1974.

**6573.** Halliday, Terence C. "The Idiom of Legalism in Bar Politics: Lawyers, McCarthyism, and the Civil Rights Era." *American Bar Foundation Research Journal* (Fall 1982): 911–988.

**6574.** Haynes, John E. "The 'Spy' on Joe McCarthy's Staff: The Forgotten Case of Paul H. Hughes." *Continuity* 14 (Spring/Fall 1990): 21–61.

**6575.** Ingalls, Robert P. *Point of Order: A Profile of Senator Joe McCarthy.* New York: Putnam's, 1981.

**6576.** Jenkins, Roy. "Joseph R. McCarthy." In his *Nine Men of Power,* 109–131. London: Hamilton, 1974.

**6577.** Kendrick, Frank J. "McCarthy and the Senate." Ph.D. dissertation, University of Chicago, 1962.

**6578.** Kew, D. A. "The Decline and Fall of Senator McCarthy." *Political Quarterly* 37 (October/December 1966): 394–415.

**6579.** Knecht, Richard J. "The Ethos of Senator Joseph McCarthy." *Michigan Academician* 20 (Fall 1988): 429–438.

**6580.** Landis, Mark. *Joseph McCarthy: The Politics of Chaos.* Cranbury, NJ: Associated University Presses, 1987.

**6581.** Latham, Carl, ed. *The Meaning of McCarthyism.* Lexington, MA: D. C. Heath, 1973.

**6582.** Lattimore, Owen. *Ordeal by Slander.* Boston: Little, Brown, 1950.

**6583.** Leslie, Larry Z. "Newspaper and Photo Coverage of Censure of McCarthy." *Journalism Quarterly* 63 (Winter 1986): 850–853.

**6584.** Luthin, Reinhard H. "Joseph R. McCarthy: Wisconsin's Briefcase Demagogue." In his *American Demagogues,* 272–301. Boston: Beacon Press, 1954.

**6585.** Mandelbaum, Seymour J. *The Social Setting of Intolerance: The Know-Nothings, the Red Scare, and McCarthyism.* Chicago: Scott Foresman, 1964.

**6586.** Marlow, Lon D. "The Roots of McCarthyism: The House of Representatives and Internal Security Legislation, 1945–1950." Ph.D. dissertation, University of Georgia, 1981.

**6587.** Matusow, Allen J., ed. *Joseph R. McCarthy.* Englewood Cliffs, NJ: Prentice-Hall, 1970.

**6588.** Mooney, Booth. "Everything Coming Loose." In his *Politicians: 1945–1960,* 101–111. New York: Lippincott, 1970.

**6589.** Morton, Joseph. *McCarthy, the Man and the Ism.* San Francisco: Pacific Publishing Foundation, 1953.

**6590.** Nodine, Thad R. "Detecting Community: Joseph McCarthy, the Detective Form, and Recent American Fiction." Ph.D. dissertation, University of California, Santa Cruz, 1990.

**6591.** O'Brien, Michael J. *McCarthy and McCarthyism in Wisconsin.* Columbia: University of Missouri Press, 1980.

**6592.** O'Connor, John E. "Edward R. Murrow's Report on Senator McCarthy: Image as Artifact." *Film and History* 16 (September 1986): 55–72.

**6593.** O'Reilly, Kenneth. "Adlai E. Stevenson, McCarthyism, and the FBI." *Illinois Historical Journal* 81 (Spring 1988): 45–60.

**6594.** Oshinsky, David M. *A Conspiracy So Immense: The World of Joe McCarthy.* New York: Free Press, 1983.

**6595.** ———. *Senator Joe McCarthy and the American Labor Movement.* Columbia: University of Missouri Press, 1976.

**6596.** Peterson, Arthur L. "McCarthyism: Its Ideology and Foundations." Ph.D. dissertation, University of Minnesota, 1962.

**6597.** Potter, Charles E. *Days of Shame.* New York: Coward-McCann, 1965.

**6598.** Reeves, Thomas C. *The Life and Times of Joe McCarthy: A Biography.* New York: Stein and Day, 1982.

**6599.** ———. *McCarthyism.* Hinsdale, IL: Dryden Press, 1973.

**6600.** ———. "The Search for Joe McCarthy." *Wisconsin Magazine of History* 60 (Spring 1977): 185–196.

**6601.** ———. "Tail Gunner Joe: Joseph R. McCarthy and the Marine Corps." *Wisconsin Magazine of History* 62 (Summer 1979): 300–313.

**6602.** Ricks, John A. "Mr. Integrity and McCarthyism: Senator Robert A. Taft and Senator Joseph R. McCarthy." Ph.D. dissertation, University of North Carolina, 1974.

**6603.** Rogin, Michael P. *The Intellectuals and McCarthy: The Radical Specter.* Cambridge, MA: MIT Press, 1967.

**6604.** ———. "McCarthyism and Agrarian Radicalism." Ph.D. dissertation, University of Chicago, 1963.

**6605.** Rorty, James, and Moshe Decter. *McCarthy and the Communists.* Boston: Beacon Press, 1954.

**6606.** Rosteck, Thomas. "Irony, Argument, and Reportage in Television Documentary: *See It Now* versus Senator McCarthy." *Quarterly Journal of Speech* 75 (August 1989): 277–298.

**6607.** ———. *See It Now Confronts Mc-Carthyism: Television Documentary and the Politics of Representation.* Tucaloosa: University of Alabama Press, 1994.

**6608.** Rovere, Richard H. *Senator Joe McCarthy.* New York: Harcourt, 1959.

**6609.** Schmidt, Godfrey P., and Herbert A. Kenny. "Senator McCarthy: A Summing Up." *Catholic World* 185 (September 1957): 440–451.

**6610.** Schrecker, Ellen. *The Age of McCarthyism: A Brief History with Documents.* Boston: St. Martin's Press, 1994.

**6611.** Sniegoski, Stephen J. "Joseph R. McCarthy and the Historians." *Modern Age* 29 (Spring 1985): 132–142.

**6612.** Steinke, John. "The Rise of McCarthyism." Master's thesis, University of Wisconsin, 1960.

**6613.** Strada, Michael J. "McCarthy's Wheeling Speech: Catalyst to Mayhem." *Upper Ohio Valley Historical Review* 15, no. 2 (1986): 33–41.

**6614.** Straight, Michael W. "Fanaticism of Joseph McCarthy." In *Faces of Five Decades,* edited by Robert B. Luce, 342–346. New York: Simon and Schuster, 1964.

**6615.** Theoharis, Athan G. *Seeds of Repression: Harry S. Truman and the Origins of McCarthyism.* New York: Quadrangle Books, 1971.

**6616.** Thelen, David P., and Esther S. Thelen. "Joe Must Go: The Movement to Recall Senator Joseph R. McCarthy." *Wisconsin Magazine of History* 49 (Spring 1966): 185–209.

**6617.** Thomas, Lately. *When Even Angels Wept; The Senator Joseph McCarthy Affair: A Story without a Hero.* New York: Morrow, 1973.

**6618.** Trow, Martin A. *Right-Wing Radicalism and Political Intolerance: A Study of Support for McCarthy in a New England Town.* New York: Arno Press, 1980.

**6619.** Varney, Harold L. "Truth about Joe McCarthy." *American Mercury* 77 (September 1953): 3–11.

**6620.** Watkins, Arthur V. *Enough Rope: The Inside Story of the Censure of Senator Joe McCarthy by His Colleagues, the Controversial Hearings That Signaled the End of a Turbulent Career and a Fearsome Era in American Public Life.* Englewood Cliffs, NJ: Prentice-Hall, 1969.

**6621.** Weintraub, Rebecca. "Joseph McCarthy as Leader: An Image Analysis." Ph.D. dissertation, University of Southern California, 1983.

**6622.** Yarnell, Allen. "Eisenhower and McCarthy: An Appraisal of Presidential Strategy." *Presidential Studies Quarterly* 10 (Winter 1980): 90–98.

## McCLELLAN, GEORGE BRINTON
(1865–1940) D-NY, House 1895–1903.

**6623.** McClellan, George B. *Gentleman and the Tiger: Autobiography.* Edited by Harold C. Syrett. New York: Lippincott, 1956.

## McCLELLAN, JOHN LITTLE
(1896–1977) D-AR, House 1935–1939, Senate 1943–1977.

**6624.** Dos Passos, John. "Backcountry Lawyer." In his *Midcentury,* 271–277. Boston: Houghton Mifflin, 1961.

## McCLERNAND, JOHN ALEXANDER
(1812–1900) D-IL, House 1843–1851, 1859–1861.

**6625.** Hicken, Victor. "John A. McClernand and the House Speakership Struggle of 1859." *Journal of the Illinois State Historical Society* 53 (Summer 1960): 163–178.

**6626.** Longacre, Edward G. "The Rise of John A. McClernand: Congressman Becomes General." *Civil War Times Illustrated* 21 (November 1982): 30–39.

**6627.** Macartney, Clarence E. "Grant and McClernand." In his *Grant and His Generals,* 223–244. New York: McBride, 1953.

**6628.** Wheeler, Henry G. "M'Clernand, John Alexander." In his *History of Congress,* vol. 1, 510–526. New York: Harper and Brothers, 1848.

**McCLOSKEY, FRANCIS XAVIER**
**(1939– ) D-IN, House 1983–1995.**

**6629.** Herzberg, Roberta. "McCloskey Versus McIntyre: Implications of Contested Elections in a Federal Democracy." *Publius* 16 (Summer 1986): 93–109.

**McCLOSKEY, PAUL NORTON "PETE,"**
**JR. (1927– ) R-CA, House 1967–1983.**

**6630.** Cannon, Lou. *McCloskey Challenge.* New York: Dutton, 1972.

**6631.** Minott, Rodney G. *Sinking of the Lollipop: Shirley Temple vs. Pete McCloskey.* Berkeley, CA: Diablo Press, 1968.

**McCLURG, JOSEPH WASHINGTON**
**(1818–1900) R-MO, House 1863–1868.**

**6632.** Morrow, Lynn. "Joseph Washington McClurg: Entrepreneur, Politician, Citizen." *Missouri Historical Review* 78 (January 1984): 168–201.

**McCONNELL, FELIX GRUNDY**
**(1809–1846) D-AL, House 1843–1846.**

**6633.** Atkins, Leah R. "Felix Grundy McConnell: Old South Demagogue." *Alabama Review* 30 (April 1977):83–100.

**McCORMACK, JOHN WILLIAM**
**(1891–1980) D-MA, House 1928–1971.**

**6634.** Gordon, Lester I. "John McCormack and the Roosevelt Era." Ph.D. dissertation, Boston University, 1976.

**McCORMICK, RICHARD**
**CUNNINGHAM (1832–1901) AZ/NY,**
**House 1869–1875 (AZ), 1895–1897 (NY).**

**6635.** Goff, John S. *Richard C. McCormick.* Cave Creek, AZ: Black Mountain Press, 1983.

**McCORMICK, RUTH HANNA**
**(1880–1944) R-IL, House 1929–1931.**

**6636.** Gilfond, Duff. "Gentlewomen of the House." *American Mercury* 18 (October 1929): 151–163.

**6637.** Miller, Kristie. *Ruth Hanna McCormick: A Life in Politics, 1880–1944.* Albuquerque: University of New Mexico Press, 1992.

**6638.** ———. "Ruth Hanna McCormick and the Senatorial Election of 1930." *Illinois Historical Journal* 81 (Autumn 1988): 191–210.

**McCUMBER, PORTER JAMES**
**(1858–1933) R-ND, Senate 1899–1923.**

**6639.** Schlup, Leonard. "Philosophical Conservative: Porter James McCumber and Political Reform." *North Dakota History* 45 (Summer 1978): 16–21.

**6640.** Wilkins, Robert P. "Tory Isolationist: Porter J. McCumber and World War I, 1914–1917." *North Dakota History* 34 (Summer 1967): 192–207.

**McDONALD, LAWRENCE PATTON**
**(1935–1983) D-GA, House 1975–1983.**

**6641.** Bullock, Charles S., and Catherine Rudder. "The Case of the Right-Wing Urologist: The Seventh District of Georgia." In *The Making of Congressmen: Seven Campaigns of 1974,* edited by Alan L. Clem, 55–92. North Scituate, MA: Duxbury Press, 1976.

**6642.** McDonald, Lawrence P. *We Hold These Truths.* Seal Beach, CA: '76 Press, 1976.

## McDONOUGH, GORDON LEO (1895–1968) R-CA, House 1945–1963.

**6643.** Mitchell, Franklin D. "An Act of Presidential Indiscretion: Harry S. Truman, Congressman McDonough, and the Marine Corps Incident of 1950." *Presidential Studies Quarterly* 11 (Fall 1981): 565–575.

## McDOUGALL, ALEXANDER (1731–1786) NY, Continental Congress 1781–1782, 1784–1785.

**6644.** Champagne, Roger J. *Alexander McDougall and the American Revolution in New York.* Schenectady, NY: Union College Press, 1975.

**6645.** MacDougall, William L. *American Revolutionary: A Biography of General Alexander McDougall.* Westport, CT: Greenwood, 1977.

**6646.** Shannon, Anna M. "General Alexander McDougall: Citizen and Soldier, 1732–1786." Ph.D. dissertation, Fordham University, 1957.

## McDOUGALL, JAMES ALEXANDER (1817–1867) D-CA, House 1853–1855, Senate 1861–1867.

**6647.** Buchanan, Russell. "James A. McDougall, a Forgotten Senator." *California Historical Society Quarterly* 15 (September 1936): 199–212.

**6648.** Farr, James. "Not Exactly a Hero: James Alexander McDougall in the United States Senate." *California History* 65 (June 1986): 104–113, 132–133.

**6649.** Shaw, William L. "United States Senator James A. McDougall." *Pacific Historian* 6 (November 1962): 181–187.

## McDOWELL, JAMES (1795–1851) D-VA, House 1846–1851.

**6650.** Collier, James G. "The Political Career of James McDowell, 1830–1851." Ph.D. dissertation, University of North Carolina, 1963.

## McDUFFIE, GEORGE (1790–1851) D-SC, House 1821–1834, Senate 1842–1846.

**6651.** Burlin, Ann E. "The Rhetoric of George McDuffie, 'One of the People' and Nullifer." Master's thesis, Indiana University, 1977.

**6652.** Green, Edwin L. *George McDuffie.* Columbia, SC: State Company, 1936.

**6653.** Green, Edwin L. "George McDuffie." In *Library of Southern Literature,* edited by Edwin A. Alderman and Joel C. Harris, vol. 8, 3547–3549. New Orleans: Martin and Hoyt, 1909.

**6654.** Magoon, Elias L. "George McDuffie." In his *Living Orators in America,* 246–270. New York: Baker and Scribner, 1849.

## McDUFFIE, JOHN (1883–1950) D-AL, House 1919–1935.

**6655.** Brannen, Ralph N. "John McDuffie: State Legislator, Congressman, Federal Judge, 1883–1950." Ph.D. dissertation, Auburn University, 1975.

## McENERY, SAMUEL DOUGLAS (1837–1910) D-LA, Senate 1897–1910.

**6656.** Reeves, Miriam G. "Samuel Douglas McEnery." In his *Governors of Louisiana,* 83–85. Gretna, LA: Pelican, 1972.

## McFARLAND, ERNEST WILLIAM (1894–1984) D-AZ, Senate 1941–1953.

**6657.** McFarland, Ernest W. *Mac: The Autobiography of Ernest W. McFarland.* McFarland, 1979.

**6658.** McMillan, James E. "Ernest W. McFarland: Southwestern Progressive, the United States Senate Years, 1940–1952." Ph.D. dissertation, Arizona State University, 1990.

**6659.** ———. "McFarland and the Movies." *Journal of Arizona History* 29 (Autumn 1988): 277–302.

**McGEE, GALE WILLIAM** (1915–1992)
D-WY, Senate 1959–1977.

**6660.** McGee, Gale. *The Responsibilities of World Power.* Washington, DC: National Press, 1968.

**McGEHEE, DANIEL RAYFORD** (1883–1962) D-MS, House 1935–1947.

**6661.** Grant, Philip A., Jr. "The Mississippi Congressional Delegation and the Formation of the Conservative Coalition." *Journal of Mississippi History* 50 (February 1988): 21–28.

**McGILL, GEORGE** (1879–1963) D-KS, Senate 1930–1939.

**6662.** McCoy, Donald R. "George S. McGill of Kansas and the Agricultural Adjustment Act of 1938." *Historian* 45 (February 1983): 186–205.

**6663.** ———. "Senator George S. McGill and the Election of 1938." *Kansas History* 4 (Spring 1981): 2–19.

**6664.** Shockley, Dennis M. "George McGill of Kansas: Depression Senator." Ph.D. dissertation, Kansas State University, 1986.

**McGOVERN, GEORGE STANLEY** (1922– ) D-SD, House 1957–1961, Senate 1963–1981.

**6665.** Anson, Robert S. *McGovern: A Biography.* New York: Holt, Rinehart and Winston, 1972.

**6666.** Clem, Alan L. *The Nomination of Joe Bottom: Analysis of a Committee Decision to Nominate a United States Senator.* Vermillion, SD: Governmental Research Bureau, University of South Dakota, 1963.

**6667.** Courtney, Phoebe. *How Dangerous Is McGovern?* Littleton, CO: Independent American Newspaper, 1972.

**6668.** Dougherty, Richard. *Goodbye, Mr. Christian: A Personal Account of McGovern's Rise and Fall.* Garden City, NY: Doubleday, 1973.

**6669.** Hart, Gary W. *Right from the Start: A Chronicle of the McGovern Campaign.* New York: Quadrangle, 1973.

**6670.** Mailer, Norman. *St. George and the Godfather.* New York: Arbor House, 1983.

**6671.** Max, Nicholas. *President McGovern's First Term.* Garden City, NY: Doubleday, 1973.

**6672.** McGovern, Eleanor S., and Mary Finch. *Uphill: A Personal Story.* Boston: Houghton Mifflin, 1974.

**6673.** McGovern, George S. *An American Journey: The Presidential Campaign Speeches of George McGovern.* New York: Random House, 1974.

**6674.** ———. *Grassroots: The Autobiography of George McGovern.* New York: Random House, 1977.

**6675.** ———. *McGovern: The Man and His Beliefs.* Edited by Shirley MacLaine. New York: Norton, 1972.

**6676.** ———. *A Time of War, a Time of Peace.* New York: Random House, 1968.

**6677.** Tobier, Arthur. *How McGovern Won the Presidency, and Why the Polls Were Wrong.* New York: Ballantine, 1972.

**6678.** Weil, Gordon L. *Long Shot: George McGovern Runs for President.* New York: Norton, 1973.

**6679.** Witker, Kristi. *How to Lose Everything in Politics Except Massachusetts.* New York: Mason, 1974.

**McHENRY, JAMES** (1753–1816) MD, Continental Congress 1783–1786.

**6680.** Brown, Frederick J. *A Sketch of the Life of Dr. James McHenry, a Paper Read before the Maryland Historical Society, November 13th, 1876.* Baltimore: John Murphy, 1877.

**6681.** Essary, J. Frederick. "James McHenry." In his *Maryland in National Politics,* 38–57. Baltimore: John Murphy, 1915.

**6682.** Steiner, Bernard C. *The Life and Correspondence of James McHenry, Secretary of War under Washington and Adams.* Cleveland, OH: Burrows Brothers Company, 1907.

## McILVAINE, ABRAHAM ROBINSON
(1804–1863) W-PA, House 1843–1849.

**6683.** Wheeler, Henry G. "M'Ilvaine, Abraham Robinson." In his *History of Congress,* vol. 1, 236–250. New York: Harper, 1848.

## McINTOSH, LACHLAN (1725–1806) GA, Continental Congress 1784.

**6684.** Jackson, Harvey H. *Lachlan McIntosh and the Politics of Revolutionary Georgia.* Athens: University of Georgia Press, 1979.

**6685.** Lawrence, Alexander A. "General Lachlan McIntosh and His Suspension from the Continental Command during the Revolution." *Georgia Historical Quarterly* 38 (June 1954): 101–141.

**6686.** McIntosh, Lachlan. *Lachlan McIntosh Papers in the University of Georgia Libraries.* Edited by Lilla M. Hawes. Athens: University of Georgia Press, 1968.

## McINTYRE, THOMAS JAMES
(1915–1992) D-NH, Senate 1962–1979.

**6687.** McIntyre, Thomas J. *The Fear Brokers.* New York: Pilgrim Press, 1979.

## McKEAN, THOMAS (1734–1817) DE, Continental Congress 1774–1776, 1778–1783.

**6688.** Cobbett, William. *The Democratic Judge: Or, the Equal Liberty of the Press.* New York: Arno Press, 1970.

**6689.** Coleman, John M. *Thomas McKean: Forgotten Leader of the Revolution.* Rockaway, NJ: American Faculty Press, 1975.

**6690.** Rowe, Gail S. *Thomas McKean: The Shaping of an American Republicanism.* Boulder: Colorado Associated University Press, 1978.

**6691.** ———. "A Valuable Acquisition in Congress: Thomas McKean, Delegate from Delaware to the Continental Congress, 1774–1783." *Pennsylvania History* 38 (July 1971): 225–264.

**6692.** Sanderson, John. "Thomas M'Kean." In *Sanderson's Biography of the Signers of the Declaration of Independence,* edited by Robert T. Conrad, 561–579. Philadelphia: Thomas, Cowperthwait, 1848.

## McKELLAR, KENNETH DOUGLAS
(1869–1957) D-TN, House 1911–1917, Senate 1917–1953.

**6693.** Bridges, Lamar W. "Tennessee Representative Kenneth McKellar and the Sixty-Second Congress (1911–1913)." *West Tennessee Historical Society Papers* 27 (1973): 63–80.

**6694.** Graham, Jeanne. "Kenneth D. McKellar's 1934 Campaign: Issues and Events." *West Tennessee Historical Society Papers* 18 (1964): 107–129.

**6695.** McKellar, Kenneth D. *Tennessee Senators as Seen by One of Their Successors.* Kingsport, TN: Southern, 1942.

**6696.** Pope, Dean. "The Senator from Tennessee." *West Tennessee Historical Society Papers* 22 (1968): 102–122.

**6697.** Pope, Robert D. "Senatorial Baron: The Long Political Career of Kenneth D. McKellar." Ph.D. dissertation, Yale University, 1976.

**6698.** Riggs, Joseph H. *Calendar of Political and Occasional Speeches by Senator Kenneth D. McKellar, 1928–1940.* Memphis, TN: Memphis Public Library, 1962.

## McKENNA, JOSEPH (1843–1926) R-CA, House 1885–1892.

**6699.** Danelski, David J. "Supreme Court Justice Steps Down." *Yale Review* 54 (Spring 1965): 411–425.

**6700.** McDevitt, Matthew. *Joseph McKenna, Associate Justice of the United States.* Washington, DC: Catholic University of America Press, 1946.

**6701.** Schauinger, Joseph H. "The Supreme Court." In his *Profiles in Action,* 179–184. Milwaukee, WI: Bruce, 1966.

**McKEOWN, THOMAS DEITZ**
**(1878–1951) D-OK, House 1917–1921,**
**1923–1925.**

**6702.** Grant, Philip A., Jr. "'Save the Farmer': Oklahoma Congressmen and Farm Relief Legislation, 1924–1928." *Chronicles of Oklahoma* 64 (Summer 1986): 74–87.

**McKINLEY, JOHN (1780–1852) J-AL,**
**Senate 1826–1831, 1837, House 1833–1835.**

**6703.** Hicks, Jimmie. "Associate Justice John McKinley: A Sketch." *Alabama Review* 18 (1965): 227–233.

**6704.** Martin, John M. "John McKinley: Jacksonian Phase." *Alabama Historical Quarterly* 28 (Spring/Summer 1966): 7–31.

**McKINLEY, WILLIAM, JR. (1843–1901)**
**R-OH, House 1877–1884, 1885–1891.**

**6705.** Brush, Edward H. "In Remembrance of William McKinley: The Birthplace Memorial at Niles, Ohio, and Other Tributes." *National Magazine* 46 (June 1917): 386–390.

**6706.** Chapple, Joseph M. "The Real McKinley." *National Magazine* 44 (July 1916): 569–584.

**6707.** Corning, A. Elwood. *William McKinley, a Biographical Study, with Introductory Address by President Roosevelt.* New York: Broadway Publishing Company, 1907.

**6708.** Damiani, Brian P. *Advocates of Empire: William McKinley, the Senate, and American Expansion, 1898–1899.* New York: Garland Publishers, 1987.

**6709.** Dobson, John. *Reticent Expansionism: The Foreign Policy of William McKinley.* Pittsburgh: Duquesne University Press, 1988.

**6710.** Ellis, Edward S. *From Tent to White House, or How a Poor Boy Became President.* New York: Street and Smith, 1899.

**6711.** ———. *The Life of William McKinley, the Twenty-Fifth President of the United States.* New York: Street and Smith, 1901.

**6712.** Glad, Paul W. *McKinley, Bryan, and the People.* Philadelphia: Lippincott, 1964.

**6713.** Gordon, Charles U. *William McKinley, Commemorative Tributes.* Waterloo, WI: Courier Printing Company, 1942.

**6714.** Gould, Lewis L. *The Presidency of William McKinley.* Lawrence: University Press of Kansas, 1980.

**6715.** ———. *The Spanish-American War and President McKinley.* Lawrence: University Press of Kansas, 1982.

**6716.** ———. "William McKinley and the Expansion of Presidential Power." *Ohio History* 87 (Winter 1978): 5–20.

**6717.** Grosvenor, Charles H. *William McKinley, His Life and Work.* Washington, DC: Continental Assembly, 1901.

**6718.** Halstead, Murat. *The Illustrious Life of William McKinley.* Chicago: Donohue, 1901.

**6719.** Heald, Edward T. *The William McKinley Story.* Canton, OH: Stark County Historical Society, 1964.

**6720.** Hoyt, Edwin P. *William McKinley.* Chicago: Reilly and Lee, 1967.

**6721.** Latchman, John S. "President McKinley's Active Positive Character: A Comparative Revision with Barber's Typology." *Presidential Studies Quarterly* 12 (Fall 1982): 491–521.

**6722.** Leech, Margaret. *In the Days of McKinley.* New York: Harper, 1959.

**6723.** Miller, Charles R. "William McKinley, the Lawyer." *Ohio Law Reporter* 14 (May 1916): 195–202.

**6724.** Morgan, H. Wayne. "The Congressional Career of William McKinley." Ph.D. dissertation, University of California at Los Angeles, 1960.

**6725.** Morgan, H. Wayne. *From Hayes to McKinley: National Party Politics, 1877–1896.* Syracuse, NY: Syracuse University Press, 1969.

**6726.** Morgan, H. Wayne. "Governor McKinley's Misfortune: The Walker-McKinley Fund of 1893." *Ohio Historical Quarterly* 69 (April 1960): 103–120.

**6727.** ———. *William McKinley and His America.* Syracuse, NY: Syracuse University Press, 1963.

**6728.** ———. "William McKinley as a Political Leader." *Review of Politics* 28 (October 1966): 417–432.

**6729.** Neil, Henry. *Complete Life of William McKinley and Story of His Assassination.* Chicago: Historical Press, 1908.

**6730.** Olcott, Charles S. *The Life of William McKinley.* 2 vols. Boston: Houghton Mifflin, 1916.

**6731.** Porter, Robert P. *Life of William McKinley: Soldier, Lawyer, Statesman.* Cleveland, OH: N. G. Hamilton Publishing Company, 1896.

**6732.** Roe, Edward T. *The Life of William McKinley, Twenty-Fifth President of the United States, 1897–1901: With a Complete Chronology of His Life and Public Services.* Chicago: Laird and Lee, 1913.

**6733.** Snow, Jane E. *The Life of William McKinley, Twenty-Fifth President of the United States.* Cleveland, OH: Gardner Printing Company, 1908.

**6734.** Spielman, William C. *William McKinley, Stalwart Republican: A Biographical Study.* New York: Exposition Press, 1954.

**6735.** Townsend, George W. *Our Martyred President, Memorial Life of William McKinley.* Philadelphia: National Publishing Company, 1901.

**6736.** Tyler, John. *The Life of William McKinley, Soldier, Statesman, and President.* Philadelphia: P. W. Ziegler and Company, 1901.

**6737.** Waksmudski, John. "Governor McKinley and the Workingman." *Historian* 38 (August 1976): 629–647.

**6738.** Weisbord, Marvin R. "Republican Revolutionary: William McKinley." In his *Campaigning for President: A New Look at the Road to the White House,* 71–80. Washington, DC: Public Affairs Press, 1964.

**6739.** Weisenburger, Francis P. "The Time of Mark Hann's First Acquaintance with McKinley." *Mississippi Valley Historical Review* 21 (June 1934): 78–80.

**6740.** West, Henry L. "William McKinley." *Forum* 32 (October 1901): 131–137.

**6741.** White, William A. "McKinley." In his *Masks in a Pageant,* 152–190. New York: Macmillan, 1928.

**McLANE, LOUIS (1786–1857) DE, House 1817–1827, Senate 1827–1829.**

**6742.** Blackburn, George M. "The Public Career of Louis McLane." Master's thesis, Indiana University, 1950.

**6743.** McCormac, Eugene I. "Louis McLane." In *The American Secretaries of State and Their Diplomacy,* edited by Samuel F. Bemis, vol. 4, 265–298. New York: Knopf, 1928.

**6744.** Munroe, John A. *Louis McLane: Federalist and Jacksonian.* New Brunswick, NJ: Rutgers University Press, 1973.

**McLANE, ROBERT MILLIGAN (1815–1898) D-MD, House 1847–1851, 1879–1883.**

**6745.** McLane, Robert M. *Reminiscences, 1827–1897, Governor Robert M. McLane.*

Wilmington, DE: Scholarly Resources, 1972.

## McLAURIN, ANSELM JOSEPH
(1848–1909) D-MS, Senate 1894–1895, 1901–1909.

**6746.** Faries, Clyde J. "Redneck Rhetoric and the Last of the Redeemers: The 1899 McLaurin-Allen Campaign." *Journal of Missouri History* 33 (November 1971): 283–298.

## McLAURIN, JOHN LOWNDES
(1860–1934) D-SC, House 1892–1897, Senate 1897–1903.

**6747.** Stroup, Rodger E. "John L. McLaurin: A Political Biography." Ph.D. dissertation, University of South Carolina, 1980.

## McLEAN, JOHN (1785–1861) R-OH,
House 1813–1816.

**6748.** Bartlett, David V. "John McLean." In his *Presidential Candidates,* 218–232. New York: A. B. Burdick, 1859.

**6749.** Livingstone, John A. "Honorable John McLean." In his *Portraits of Eminent Americans Now Living,* vol. 2, 789–796. New York: Cornish, Lamport, 1853.

**6750.** Longacre, James B., and James Herring. "John McLean." In their *The National Portrait Gallery,* vol. 4, 257–262. Philadelphia: Robert E. Peterson and Company, 1839.

**6751.** Maury, Sarah M. "The Honorable John McLean, Associate-Justice in the Supreme Court of the United States." In her *The Statesmen of America in 1847,* 164–182. London: Brown, Green, and Longmans, 1847.

**6752.** Savage, John. "John McLean of Ohio." In his *Our Living Representative Men,* 373–381. Philadelphia: Childs and Peterson, 1860.

**6753.** Weisenburger, Francis P. "John McLean, Postmaster-General." *Mississippi Valley Historical Review* 18 (June 1931): 23–33.

**6754.** ———. *The Life of John McLean.* Columbus: Ohio State University Press, 1937.

## McMILLAN, JAMES (1838–1902) R-MI,
Senate 1889–1902.

**6755.** Heyda, Marie. "Senator James McMillan and the Flowering of the Spoils System." *Michigan History* 54 (Fall 1970): 183–200.

**6756.** Moore, Charles. "James McMillan, United States Senator from Michigan." *Michigan Historical Collections* 39 (1915): 173–187.

**6757.** Peterson, John A. "The Nation's First Comprehensive City Plan: A Political Analysis of the McMillan Plan for Washington, D.C., 1900–1902." *Journal of the American Planning Association* 51 (Spring 1985): 134–150.

## McMILLIN, BENTON (1845–1933) D-TN,
House 1879–1899.

**6758.** Braden, Kenneth S. "Ambition or Service: Benton McMillin's Political Races in Tennessee." *Tennessee Historical Quarterly* 49 (Spring 1990): 53–63.

## McNARY, CHARLES LINZA (1874–1944)
R-OR, Senate 1917–1918, 1918–1944.

**6759.** DeWitt, Howard A. "Charles L. McNary and the 1918 Congressional Election." *Oregon Historical Quarterly* 68 (June 1967): 125–140.

**6760.** Hoffman, George C., Jr. "The Early Political Career of Charles McNary, 1917–1924." Ph.D. dissertation, University of Southern California, 1952.

**6761.** ———. "Political Arithmetic: Charles L. McNary and the 1914 Election." *Oregon Historical Quarterly* 66 (December 1965): 363–378.

**6762.** Johnson, Roger T. "Charles L. Mc-Nary and the Republican Party during Prosperity and Depression." Ph.D. dissertation, University of Wisconsin, 1967.

**6763.** ———. "Part-Time Leader: Senator Charles L. McNary and the McNary-Haugen Bill." *Agricultural History* 54 (October 1980): 527–541.

**6764.** Neal, Steve. "Charles L. McNary: The Quiet Man." In *First Among Equals: Outstanding Senate Leaders of the Twentieth Century,* edited by Richard A. Baker and Roger H. Davidson, 98–126. Washington, DC: Congressional Quarterly, 1991.

**6765.** ———. *McNary of Oregon: A Political Biography.* Portland, OR: Western Imprints, 1985.

**6766.** Roberts, Walter K. "The Political Career of Charles L. McNary, 1924–1944." Ph.D. dissertation, University of North Carolina, 1954.

**MEAD, JAMES MICHAEL** (1885–1964) **D-NY, House 1919–1938, Senate 1938–1947.**

**6767.** Mead, James M. *Tell the Folks Back Home.* New York: Appleton-Century, 1944.

**MEDILL, WILLIAM** (1802–1865) **R-OH, House 1839–1843.**

**6768.** Smith, Dwight L. "William Medill, 1853–1856." In *Governors of Ohio,* 68–71. Columbus: Ohio Historical Society, 1954.

**MEIGS, RETURN JONATHAN, JR.** (1764–1825) **R-OH, Senate 1808–1810.**

**6769.** Campbell, John W. "Return J. Meigs." In *Biographical Sketches,* compiled by Eleanor Campbell, 65–91. Columbus, OH: Scott and Gallagher, 1838.

**6770.** McKeown, James S. "Return J. Meigs: United States Agent in the Cherokee Nation, 1801–1823." Ph.D. dissertation, Pennsylvania State University, 1984.

**6771.** Smith, S. Winifred. "Return J. Meigs, Jr., 1810–1814." In *Governors of Ohio,* 11–13. Columbus: Ohio Historical Society, 1954.

**MELLEN, PRENTISS** (1764–1840) **MA, Senate 1818–1820.**

**6772.** Greenleaf, Simon. "Memoir of the Life and Character of the Late Chief Justice Mellen." *Maine Reports* 17 (1841): 467–476.

**MENEFEE, RICHARD HICKMAN** (1809–1841) **W-KY, House 1837–1839.**

**6773.** Marshall, Thomas F. "Life and Character of Richard H. Menefee." In *Library of Southern Literature,* edited by Edwin A. Alderman and Joel C. Harris, vol. 8, 3400–3407. New Orleans: Martin and Hoyt, 1909.

**6774.** Townsend, John W. *Richard Hickman Menefee.* New York: Neale Publishing Company, 1907.

**MERCER, CHARLES FENTON** (1778–1858) **W-VA, House 1817–1839.**

**6775.** Carter, Robert A. "Virginia Federalist in Dissent: A Life of Charles Fenton Mercer." Ph.D. dissertation, University of Virginia, 1988.

**6776.** Dunaway, Wayland F. "Charles Fenton Mercer." Master's thesis, University of Chicago, 1917.

**6777.** Egerton, Douglas R. "Charles Fenton Mercer and the Foundations of Modern American Conservatism." Ph.D. dissertation, Georgetown University, 1985.

**6778.** ———. *Charles Fenton Mercer and the Trial of National Conservatism.* Jackson: University Press of Mississippi, 1989.

**6779.** ———. "To the Tombs of the Capulets: Charles Fenton Mercer and Public Education in Virginia." *Virginia Magazine of History and Biography* 93 (April 1985): 155–174.

**6780.** Hulbert, Archer B. "Thomas and Mercer: Rival Promoters of Canal and Railway." In his *Pilots of the Republic,* 233–255. Chicago: A. C. McClurg, 1906.

**MERCER, JOHN FRANCIS** (1759–1821)
MD, House 1792–1794, Continental Congress
1783–1784.

**6781.** Brown, Dorothy M. "John Francis
Mercer: Two Election Broadsides, 1792."
*Maryland Historical Magazine* 62 (June
1967): 193–196.

**MERIWETHER, DAVID** (1800–1893)
D-KY, Senate 1852.

**6782.** Meriwether, David. *My Life on the
Mountains and on the Plains: The Newly Dis-
covered Autobiography.* Edited by Robert A.
Griffen. Norman: University of Oklahoma
Press, 1965.

**MERRILL, ORSAMUS COOK**
(1775–1865) R-VT, House 1817–1820.

**6783.** Graffagnino, J. Kevin. "I Saw Ruin
All Around and a Comical Spot You May
Depend: Orsamus C. Merrill, Rollin C.
Mallary, and the Disputed Congressional
Election of 1818." *Vermont History* 49
(Summer 1981): 159–168.

**MERRIMON, AUGUSTUS
SUMMERFIELD** (1830–1892) D-NC, Senate
1873–1879.

**6784.** Merrimon, Maud. *A Memoir of Augustus Summerfield Merrimon.* Raleigh, NC:
E. M. Uzzell, 1894.

**MERROW, CHESTER EARL** (1906–1974)
R-NH, House 1943–1963.

**6785.** Merrow, Chester E. *My Twenty Years
in Congress.* N.p.: 1968.

**METCALF, LEE WARREN** (1911–1978)
D-MT, House 1953–1961, Senate 1961–1978.

**6786.** Metcalf, Lee, and Vic Reinemer.
*Overcharge.* New York: McKay, 1967.

**6787.** Warden, Richard D. *How a Senator
Makes Government Work: Metcalf of Montana.* Washington, DC: Acropolis Books,
1965.

**METCALFE, RALPH HAROLD**
(1910–1978) D-IL, House 1971–1978.

**6788.** Chalk, Ocania. "Black Olympians."
In his *Black College Sport,* 352–356. New
York: Dodd, Mead, 1976.

**6789.** Christopher, Maurine. "Ralph H.
Metcalfe/Illinois." In her *Black Americans
in Congress,* 262. Rev. ed. New York:
Thomas Y. Crowell Company, 1976.

**MEZVINSKY, EDWARD MAURICE**
(1937– ) D-IA, House 1973–1977.

**6790.** Mezvinsky, Edward M. *Term to Remember.* New York: Coward-McCann, 1977.

**MIDDLETON, ARTHUR** (1742–1787) SC,
Continental Congress 1776–1778, 1781–1783.

**6791.** Sanderson, John. "Arthur Middleton." In *Sanderson's Biography of the Signers
of the Declaration of Independence,* edited by
Robert T. Conrad, 809–818. Philadelphia:
Thomas, Cowperthwait, 1848.

**MIDDLETON, HENRY** (1770–1846) R-SC,
House 1815–1819.

**6792.** Bergquist, Harold E., Jr. "Russo-
American Economic Relations in the
1820's: Henry Middleton as a Protector of
American Economic Interests in Russia
and Turkey." *East European Quarterly* 11
(Spring 1977): 27–41.

**MIFFLIN, THOMAS** (1744–1800) PA,
Continental Congress 1774–1776, 1782–1784.

**6793.** Rossman, Kenneth R. *Thomas Mifflin and the Politics of the American Revolution.* Chapel Hill: University of North Carolina Press, 1952.

**MILLER, DANIEL FRY** (1814–1895) W-IA,
House 1850–1851.

**6794.** Schmidt, Louis B. "The Miller-
Thompson Election Contest." *Iowa Journal
of History* 12 (January 1914): 34–127.

## MILLER, SAMUEL FRANKLIN
(1827–1892) R-NY, House 1863–1865, 1875–1877.

**6795.** Fairman, Charles. *Mr. Justice Miller and the Supreme Court, 1862–1890.* Cambridge, MA: Harvard University Press, 1939.

## MILLER, THOMAS EZEKIEL
(1849–1938) R-SC, HOUSE 1890–1891.

**6796.** Christopher, Maurine. "Thomas E. Miller/South Carolina." In her *Black Americans in Congress,* 113–122. Rev. ed. New York: Thomas Y. Crowell Company, 1976.

## MILLS, OGDEN LIVINGSTON
(1884–1937) R-NY, House 1921–1927.

**6797.** McKnight, Gerald D. "The Perils of Reform Politics: The Abortive New York State Constitutional Reform Movement of 1915." *New York Historical Society Quarterly* 63 (July 1979): 203–227.

## MILLS, ROGER QUARLES (1832–1911)
D-TX, House 1873–1892, Senate 1892–1899.

**6798.** Barr, C. Alwyn. "The Making of a Secessionist: The Antebellum Career of Roger Q. Mills." *Southwestern Historical Quarterly* 79 (October 1975): 129–144.

**6799.** Roberts, Myrtle. "Roger Quarles Mills." Master's thesis, University of Texas, 1929.

**6800.** Welch, June R. "An Oklahoma County Was Named for Mills." In his *The Texas Senator,* 42–47. Dallas, TX: G. L. A. Press, 1978.

## MILLS, WILBUR DAIGH (1909–1992)
D-AR, House 1939–1977.

**6801.** Manley, John F. *The Politics of Finance: The House Committee on Ways and Means.* Boston: Little, Brown, 1970.

**6802.** ———. "Wilbur D. Mills: A Study in Congressional Influence." *American Political Science Review* 63 (June 1969): 442–464.

## MINK, PATSY TAKEMOTO (1927–  )
D-HI, House 1965–1977, 1990–  .

**6803.** Lamson, Peggy. "Three Congresswomen: What Makes Them Run—Martha W. Griffiths, Patsy T. Mink, Margaret M. Heckler." In her *Few Are Chosen: American Women in Political Life Today,* 99–107. Boston: Houghton Mifflin, 1968.

## MINTON, SHERMAN (1890–1965) D-IN,
Senate 1935–1941.

**6804.** Atkinson, David N. "From New Deal Liberal to Supreme Court Conservative: The Metamorphosis of Justice Sherman Minton." *Washington University Law Quarterly* 1975 (Spring 1975): 361–394.

**6805.** ———. "Justice Sherman Minton and Behavior Patterns Inside the Supreme Court." *Northwestern University Law Review* 69 (November/December 1975): 716–739.

**6806.** ———. "Justice Sherman Minton and the Balance of Liberty." *Indiana Law Journal* 50 (Fall 1974): 34–59.

**6807.** ———. "Justice Sherman Minton and the Protection of Minority Rights." *Washington and Lee Law Review* 34 (Winter 1977): 97–117.

**6808.** ———. "Mr. Justice Minton and the Supreme Court, 1949–1956." Ph.D. dissertation, University of Iowa, 1969.

**6809.** ———. "Opinion Writing on the Supreme Court, 1949–1956: The Views of Justice Sherman Minton." *Temple Law Quarterly* 49 (Fall 1975): 105–118.

**6810.** Braden, George D. "Mr. Justice Minton and the Truman Bloc." *Indiana Law Journal* 26 (Winter 1951): 153–168.

**6811.** Corcoran, David H. "Sherman Minton: New Deal Senator." Ph.D. dissertation, University of Kentucky, 1977.

**6812.** Hull, Elizabeth A. "Sherman Minton and the Cold War Court." Ph.D. dissertation, New School for Social Research, 1977.

**6813.** Wallace, Henry L. "Mr. Justice Minton: Hoosier Justice on the Supreme Court." *Indiana Law Journal* 54 (Winter 1959): 145–205; 54 (Spring 1959): 377–424.

**MITCHELL, ALEXANDER (1817–1887) D-WI, House 1871–1875.**

**6814.** Butler, James D. "Alexander Mitchell, the Financier." *Wisconsin State Historical Society Collections* 11 (1888): 435–450.

**MITCHELL, ARTHUR WERGS (1883–1968) D-IL, House 1935–1943.**

**6815.** Christopher, Maurine. "Arthur W. Mitchell/Illinois." In her *Black Americans in Congress,* 176–184. Rev. ed. New York: Thomas Y. Crowell Company, 1976.

**MITCHELL, JOHN HIPPLE (1835–1905) R-OR, Senate 1873–1879, 1885–1897, 1901–1905.**

**6816.** O'Callaghan, Jerry A. "Senator John H. Mitchell and the Oregon Land Frauds, 1905." *Pacific Historical Review* 21 (August 1952): 255–261.

**MITCHELL, PARREN JAMES (1922– ) D-MD, House 1971–1987.**

**6817.** Christopher, Maurine. "Parren J. Mitchell/Maryland." In her *Black Americans in Congress,* 289. Rev. ed. New York: Thomas Y. Crowell Company, 1976.

**MITCHILL, SAMUEL LATHAM (1764–1831) R-NY, House 1801–1804, 1810–1813, Senate 1804–1809.**

**6818.** Aberbach, Alan D. *In Search of an American Identity: Samuel Latham Mitchill, Jeffersonian Nationalist.* New York: P. Lang, 1988.

**6819.** Hall, Courtney R. "A Scientist in the Early Republic: Samuel Latham Mitchill, 1764–1831." Ph.D. dissertation, Columbia University, 1938.

**6820.** Kastner, Joseph. "A Chaos of Knowledge." In his *Species of Eternity,* 194–206. New York: Knopf, 1977.

**MONDALE, WALTER FREDERICK "FRITZ" (1928– ) D-MN, Senate 1964–1976.**

**6821.** Gillon, Steven M. *The Democrats' Dilemma: Walter F. Mondale and the Liberal Legacy.* New York: Columbia University Press, 1992.

**6822.** Lewis, Finlay. *Mondale: Portrait of an American Politician.* New York: Harper and Row, 1980.

**6823.** Marmor, Theodore R. "The Lessons of Mondale's Defeat." *Political Quarterly* 56 (April/June 1985): 153–166.

**6824.** Schneider, Tom. *Walter Mondale: Serving All the People.* Minneapolis, MN: Dillon Press, 1984.

**MONROE, JAMES (1758–1831) VA, Senate 1790–1794, Continental Congress 1783–1786.**

**6825.** Alderman, Edwin A. "James Monroe." *University of Virginia Alumni Bulletin* 17 (July 1924): 323–325.

**6826.** Ammon, Harry. "James Monroe and the Election of 1808 in Virginia." *William and Mary Quarterly* 20 (January 1963): 33–56.

**6827.** ———. "James Monroe and the Era of Good Feelings." *Virginia Magazine of History and Biography* 66 (October 1958): 387–398.

**6828.** ———. *James Monroe: The Quest for National Identity.* New York: McGraw-Hill, 1971.

**6829.** ———. "The Monroe Doctrine: Domestic Politics or National Decision?" *Diplomatic History* 5 (Winter 1981): 53–73.

**6830.** Angel, Edward. "James Monroe's Mission to Paris, 1794–1796." Ph.D. dissertation, George Washington University, 1979.

**6831.** Berkeley, Dorothy S., and Edmund Berkeley. "The Piece Left Behind: Monroe's Authorship of a Political Pamphlet Revealed." *Virginia Magazine of History and Biography* 75 (April 1967): 174–180.

**6832.** Bond, Beverly W. *The Monroe Missions to France 1794–1796.* Baltimore: Johns Hopkins University Press, 1907.

**6833.** Cox, Isaac J. "Monroe and the Early Mexican Revolutionary Agents." *American Historical Association Annual Report* 1 (1911): 199–215.

**6834.** Cresson, William P. *James Monroe.* Chapel Hill: University of North Carolina Press, 1946.

**6835.** Dickson, Charles E. "James Monroe's Defense of Kentucky's Interests in the Confederation Congress: An Example of Early North/South Party Alignment." *Kentucky Historical Society Register* 74 (October 1976): 261–280.

**6836.** ———. "Politics in a New Nation: The Early Career of James Monroe." Ph.D. dissertation, Ohio State University, 1971.

**6837.** Gilman, Daniel C. *James Monroe.* Boston: Houghton Mifflin, 1909.

**6838.** ———. *James Monroe in His Relations to the Public Service during Half a Century, 1776 to 1826.* Boston: Houghton Mifflin, 1883.

**6839.** Hay, Robert P. "The Meaning of Monroe's Death: The Contemporary Response." *West Virginia History* 30 (January 1969): 427–435.

**6840.** Hoes, Ingrid W. "James Monroe—Neglected Son of Virginia." *Virginia and the Virginia Record* 76 (December 1954): 18–19.

**6841.** Hooes, Rose G. "James Monroe—Soldier: His Part in the War of the American Revolution." *Daughters of the American Revolution Magazine* 57 (December 1923): 721–727.

**6842.** Johnson, Monroe. "James Monroe, Soldier." *William and Mary Quarterly* 9 (April 1928): 110–117.

**6843.** ———. "The Maryland Ancestry of James Monroe." *Maryland Historical Magazine* 23 (June 1928): 193–195.

**6844.** Manning, Clarence A. "The Meaning of the Monroe Doctrine." *Ukrainian Quarterly* 18 (Autumn 1962): 246–254.

**6845.** May, Ernest R. *The Making of the Monroe Doctrine.* Cambridge, MA: Harvard University Press, 1979.

**6846.** Mitchell, Mary H. "'With Appropriate Honors': The Reburial of James Monroe." *Virginia Cavalcade* 35 (Autumn 1985): 52–63.

**6847.** Monroe, James. *The Autobiography of James Monroe.* Edited by Stuart B. Brown. Syracuse, NY: Syracuse University Press, 1959.

**6848.** ———. *The Memoirs of James Monroe, Esq. Relating to His Unsettled Claims upon the People and Government of the United States.* Charlottesville, VA: Gilmer, Davis, 1828.

**6849.** ———. *The Writings of James Monroe.* Edited by Stanislaus M. Hamilton. New York: Putnam's, 1898–1903.

**6850.** Morgan, George. *The Life of James Monroe.* Boston: Small, Maynard, 1921.

**6851.** Nadler, Solomon. "The Green Bag: James Monroe and the Fall of DeWitt Clinton." *New York Historical Society Quarterly* 59 (July 1975): 202–225.

**6852.** Pratt, Julius W. "James Monroe, Secretary of State, November 25, 1811, to March 3, 1817 (ad interim, April 3 to November 25, 1811)." In *The American Secretaries of State and Their Diplomacy,* edited by Samuel F. Bemis, vol. 3, 201–277. New York: Knopf, 1927.

**6853.** Rachal, William M. "President Monroe's Return to Virginia." *Virginia Cavalcade* 3 (Summer 1953): 43–57.

**6854.** Skeen, C. Edward. "Monroe and Armstrong: A Study in Political Rivalry." *New York Historical Society Quarterly* 57 (April 1973): 121–147.

**6855.** Steel, Anthony. "Impressment in the Monroe-Pinckney Negotiation, 1806–1807." *American Historical Review* 57 (January 1952): 352–369.

**6856.** Styron, Arthur. *The Last of the Cocked Hats: James Monroe and the Virginia Dynasty.* Norman: University of Oklahoma Press, 1945.

**6857.** Waldo, Samuel P. *The Tour of James Monroe.* 2d ed. Hartford, CT: Silas Andrus, 1820.

**6858.** Wilmerding, Lucius, Jr. "James Monroe and the Furniture Fund." *New York Historical Society Quarterly* 44 (April 1960): 132–149.

**6859.** ———. *James Monroe: Public Claimant.* New Brunswick, NJ: Rutgers University Press, 1960.

**6860.** Wolfe, Maxine G. "Where Monroe Practiced Law." *American Bar Association Journal* 59 (November 1973): 1282–1284.

**MONRONEY, ALMER STILLWELL MIKE (1902–1980) D-OK, House 1939–1951, Senate 1951–1969.**

**6861.** Grant, Philip A., Jr. "A Tradition of Political Power: Congressional Committee Chairmen from Oklahoma, 1945–1972." *Chronicles of Oklahoma* 60 (Winter 1982/1983): 348–447.

**MONTAGUE, ANDREW JACKSON (1862–1937) D-VA, House 1913–1937.**

**6862.** Larsen, William E. *Montague of Virginia: The Making of a Southern Progressive.* Baton Rouge: Louisiana State University Press, 1965.

**MONTGOMERY, SAMUEL JAMES (1896–1957) R-OK, House 1925–1927.**

**6863.** Grant, Philip A., Jr. "'Save the Farmer': Oklahoma Congressmen and Farm Relief Legislation, 1924–1928." *Chronicles of Oklahoma* 64 (Spring 1986): 74–87.

**MONTOYA, JOSEPH MANUEL (1915–1978) D-NM, House 1957–1964, Senate 1964–1977.**

**6864.** Vigil, Maurilio, and Roy Lujan. "Parallels in the Careers of Two Hispanic U.S. Senators." *Journal of Ethics Studies* 13 (Winter 1964): 1–20.

**MOODY, WILLIAM HENRY (1853–1917) R-MA, House 1895–1902.**

**6865.** Heffron, Paul T. "Profile of a Public Man." *Supreme Court Historical Society Yearbook* 1980 (1980): 30–31, 48.

**6866.** ———. "Theodore Roosevelt and the Appointment of Mr. Justice Moody." *Vanderbilt Law Review* 18 (March 1965): 545–568.

**6867.** McDonough, Judith R. "William Henry Moody (Massachusetts)." Ph.D. dissertation, Auburn University, 1983.

**6868.** Morrow, James B. "The Honorable William H. Moody the New Justice of the United States Supreme Court." *Law Students Helper* 15 (February 1907): 42–46.

**6869.** Paradise, Scott H. "William Henry Moody." In his *Men of the Old School,* 111–130. Andover, MA: Phillips Academy, 1956.

**6870.** Whitelock, George. "Mr. Justice Moody, Lately Attorney General." *Green Bag* 21 (June 1909): 263–266.

**6871.** Wiener, Frederick B. "The Life and Judicial Career of William Henry Moody." Master's thesis, Harvard University Law School, 1937.

**MOORE, ARTHUR HARRY (1879–1952) D-NJ, Senate 1935–1938.**

**6872.** Bloodgood, Fred L. *The Quiet Hour.* Trenton, NJ: MacCrellish and Quigley, 1940.

**MOORE, ELY (1798–1860) D-NY, House 1835–1839.**

**6873.** Hugins, Walter E. "Ely Moore: The Case History of a Jacksonian Labor Leader." *Political Science Quarterly* 65 (March 1950): 105–125.

**MOORE, GABRIEL (1785–1845) AL, House 1821–1829, Senate 1831–1837.**

**6874.** Martin, John M. "The Early Career of Gabriel Moore." *Alabama Historical Quarterly* 29 (Fall/Winter 1967): 89–105.

**6875.** ———. "The Senatorial Career of Gabriel Moore." *Alabama Historical Quarterly* 26 (Summer 1964): 249–281.

**MOORE, JOSEPH HAMPTON (1864–1950) R-PA, House 1906–1920.**

**6876.** Drayer, Robert E. "J. Hampton Moore: An Old Fashioned Republican." Ph.D. dissertation, University of Pennsylvania, 1961.

**MOREHEAD, JAMES TURNER (1797–1854) W-KY, Senate 1841–1847.**

**6877.** Jillson, Willard R., ed. "Early Political Papers of Governor James T. Morehead." *Register of the Kentucky State Historical Society* 22 (September 1924): 272–300; 23 (January 1925): 36–61.

**MOREHEAD, JOHN MOTLEY (1866–1923) R-NC, House 1909–1911.**

**6878.** Steelman, Joseph F. "Republicanism in North Carolina: John Motley Morehead's Campaign to Revive a Moribund Party, 1908–1910." *North Carolina Historical Review* 62 (April 1965): 153–168.

**MORGAN, DANIEL (1736–1802) F-VA, House 1797–1799.**

**6879.** Brandon, John H. "General Daniel Morgan's Part in the Burgoyne Campaign." *New York State Historical Association Proceedings* 12 (1913): 119–138.

**6880.** Bruce, Philip A. "General Daniel Morgan." In his *The Virginia Plutarch,* 287–305. Chapel Hill: University of North Carolina Press, 1929.

**6881.** Callahan, North. *Daniel Morgan, Ranger of the Revolution.* New York: Holt, Rinehart and Winston, 1961.

**6882.** Graham, James. *The Life of General Daniel Morgan.* New York: Derby and Jackson, 1856.

**6883.** Griswold, Rufus W. "Brigadier-General Daniel Morgan." In his *Washington and the Generals of the American Revolution,* vol. 2, 84–104. Philadelphia: Cary and Hart, 1848.

**6884.** Higginbotham, Don. *Daniel Morgan: Revolutionary Rifleman.* Chapel Hill: University of North Carolina Press, 1961.

**6885.** McConkey, Rebecca. *The Hero of Cowpens: A Centennial Sketch.* New York: Barnes, 1881.

**MORGAN, EDWIN DENNISON (1811–1883) R-NY, Senate 1863–1869.**

**6886.** Rawley, James A. *Edwin D. Morgan, 1811–1883: Merchant in Politics.* New York: Columbia University Press, 1955.

**MORGAN, JOHN TYLER (1824–1907) D-AL, Senate 1877–1907.**

**6887.** Anders, James M. "The Senatorial Career of John Tyler Morgan." Ph.D. dissertation, George Peabody College for Teachers, 1956.

**6888.** Baylen, Joseph O. "Senator John Tyler Morgan, E. D. Morel, and the Congo Reform Association." *Alabama Review* 15 (April 1962): 117–132.

**6889.** Baylen, Joseph O., and John H. Moore. "Senator John Tyler Morgan and Negro Colonization in the Philippines, 1901–1902." *Phylon* 29 (Spring 1968): 65–75.

**6890.** Burnette, O. Lawrence. "John Tyler Morgan and Expansionist Settlement in the New South." *Alabama Review* 18 (July 1965): 163–182.

**6891.** Clayton, Lawrence A. "John Tyler Morgan and the Nicaraguan Canal, 1897–1900." *Anuario Estudios Centroamericanos (Costa Rica)* 9 (1983): 37–53.

**6892.** Fry, Joseph A. "Governor Johnston's Attempt to Unseat Senator Morgan, 1899–1900." *Alabama Review* 38 (October 1985): 243–279.

**6893.** ———. *John Tyler Morgan and the Search for Southern Autonomy.* Knoxville: University of Tennessee Press, 1992.

**6894.** ———. "John Tyler Morgan's Southern Expansionism." *Diplomatic History* 9 (Fall 1985): 329–346.

**6895.** ———. "Strange Expansionist Bedfellows: Newlands, Morgan, and Hawaii." *Halcyon* 11 (1989): 105–124.

**6896.** Radke, August C. "John Tyler Morgan, an Expansionist Senator, 1877–1907." Ph.D. dissertation, University of Washington, 1953.

**MORRIL, DAVID LAWRENCE**
**(1772–1849) R-NH, Senate 1817–1823.**

**6897.** Brown, William H. "David Lawrence Morril." *Historical New Hampshire* 19 (Summer 1964): 3–26.

**MORRILL, JUSTIN SMITH (1810–1898)**
**R-VT, House 1855–1867, Senate 1867–1898.**

**6898.** Brown, Rita. "Justin Smith Morrill." *Vermont History* 31 (January 1963): 65–71.

**6899.** Dies, Edward J. *Titans of the Soil,* 85–93. Chapel Hill: University of North Carolina Press, 1949.

**6900.** Fisher, Dorothy C. "Justin Morrill." In her *Vermont Tradition,* 346–357. Boston: Little, Brown, 1953.

**6901.** Hoyer, Randal L. "The Gentleman from Vermont: The Career of Justin S. Morrill in the United States House of Representatives." Ph.D. dissertation, Michigan State University, 1974.

**6902.** Parker, William B. *The Life and Public Service of Justin Smith Morrill.* Boston: Houghton Mifflin, 1924.

**MORRILL, LOT MYRICK (1813–1883)**
**R-ME, Senate 1861–1869, 1869–1876.**

**6903.** Talbot, George F. "Lot M. Morrill." *Collections and Proceedings of the Maine Historical Society* 5 (1894): 225–275.

**MORRIS, GOUVERNEUR (1752–1816)**
**F-NY, Senate 1800–1803, Continental Congress 1778–1779.**

**6904.** Best, Mary A. "A Yankee Tory in Paris." In her *Thomas Paine: Prophet and Martyr of Democracy,* 287–297. New York: Harcourt Brace, 1927.

**6905.** Hulbert, Archer B. "Morris and Clinton: Fathers of the Erie Canal." In his *Pilots of the Republic,* 207–232. Chicago: A. C. McClurg, 1906.

**6906.** Kline, Mary J. "Gouverneur Morris and the New Nation, 1775–1788." Ph.D. dissertation, Columbia University, 1970.

**6907.** Lodge, Henry C. "Gouverneur Morris." In his *Historical and Political Essays,* 75–113. Boston: Houghton Mifflin, 1892.

**6908.** Massaro, Dominic R. "Gouverneur Morris: The Constitutional Penman Revisited." *Bronx County Historical Society Journal* 24, no. 2 (1987): 67–83.

**6909.** Mintz, Max M. *Gouverneur Morris and the American Revolution.* Norman: University of Oklahoma Press, 1970.

**6910.** Morris, Anne C., ed. *The Diary and Letters of Gouverneur Morris.* 2 vols. New York: Scribner's, 1888.

**6911.** Roosevelt, Theodore. *Gouverneur Morris.* Boston: Houghton Mifflin, 1893.

**6912.** Sparks, Jared. *The Life of G. Morris, with Selections from His Correspondence.* Boston: Gray and Bowen, 1832.

**6913.** Swiggett, Howard G. *The Extraordinary Mr. Morris.* Garden City, NY: Doubleday, 1952.

**6914.** Walther, Daniel. *Gouverneur Morris: Witness of Two Revolutions.* New York: Funk and Wagnalls, 1934.

**6915.** Willson, Beckles. "Morris (1790–1792)." In his *America's Ambassadors to England (1785–1928)*, 20–35. London: Murray, 1928.

**6916.** ———. "Morris (1792–94)." In his *America's Ambassadors to France (1777–1927)*, 40–62. New York: Frederick A. Stokes, 1928.

**MORRIS, LEWIS** (1726–1798) NY, **Continental Congress 1775–1777.**

**6917.** Sanderson, John. "Lewis Morris." In *Sanderson's Biography of the Signers of the Declaration of Independence,* edited by Robert T. Conrad, 159–180. Philadelphia: Thomas, Cowperthwait, 1848.

**MORRIS, ROBERT** (1734–1806) PA, **Senate 1789–1795, Continental Congress 1775–1778.**

**6918.** Chernon, Barbara A. *Robert Morris, Land Speculator, 1790–1801.* New York: Arno Press, 1978.

**6919.** Grayson, Theodore J. "Robert Morris, the Financier of the Revolution." In his *Leaders and Periods of American Finance,* 21–45. New York: J. Wiley, 1932.

**6920.** Hunt, Freeman, ed. "Robert Morris." In his *Lives of American Merchants,* 595–605. New York: Derby and Jackson, 1858.

**6921.** Morris, Robert. *Papers of Robert Morris, 1781–1784.* Edited by E. James Ferguson. Pittsburgh: University of Pittsburgh Press, 1978.

**6922.** Oberholtzer, Ellis P. *Robert Morris, Patriot and Financier.* New York: Macmillan, 1903.

**6923.** Sanderson, John. "Robert Morris." In *Sanderson's Biography of the Signers of the Declaration of Independence,* edited by Robert T. Conrad, 336–377. Philadelphia: Thomas, Cowperthwait, 1848.

**6924.** Schappes, Morris U. "Excerpts from Robert Morris Diaries in the Office of Finance, 1781–1784, Referring to Haym Solomon and Other Jews." *American Jewish Historical Quarterly* 67 (September 1977): 9–49; 67 (December 1977): 140–161.

**6925.** Sparks, Edwin E. "Robert Morris, the Financier of the Revolution." In his *The Men Who Made the Nation,* 119–150. New York: Macmillan, 1901.

**6926.** Sumner, William G. *Financier and the Finances of the American Revolution.* 2 vols. New York: Dodd, Mead, 1891.

**6927.** Swiggett, Howard G. "The Patriot Financier: Robert Morris." In his *The Forgotten Leaders of the Revolution,* 105–118, 145–154. Garden City, NY: Doubleday, 1955.

**6928.** Ver Steeg, Clarence L. *Robert Morris: Revolutionary Financier, with an Analysis of His Early Career.* Philadelphia: University of Pennsylvania Press, 1954.

**6929.** Wagner, Frederick. *Robert Morris: Audacious Patriot.* New York: Dodd, Mead, 1976.

**6930.** Westcott, Thompson. "Robert Morris's Folly: The Hills." In his *The Historic Mansions and Buildings of Philadelphia,* 351–380. Philadelphia: Porter and Coates, 1877.

**6931.** Wildman, Edwin. "Robert Morris: The Patriotic Financier of the Revolution." In his *The Founders of America in the Days of the Revolution,* 300–318. Freeport, NY: Books for Libraries, 1968.

**6932.** Young, Eleanor M. *Forgotten Patriot: Robert Morris.* New York: Macmillan, 1950.

**MORRIS, THOMAS** (1776–1844) J-OH,
**Senate 1833–1839.**

**6933.** Morris, Benjamin F. *The Life of Thomas Morris, Pioneer and Long a Legislator of Ohio and U.S. Senator from 1833 to 1839.* Cincinnati, OH: Moore, Wilstach, Keys and Overend, 1856.

**6934.** Nevenschwander, John A. "Senator Thomas Morris: Antagonist of the South, 1836–39." *Cincinnati Historical Society Bulletin* 32 (Fall 1974): 123–139.

**MORRISON, WILLIAM RALLS**
(1824–1909) D-IL, House 1863–1865,
**1873–1887.**

**6935.** Robbins, David E. "The Congressional Career of William Ralls Morrison." Ph.D. dissertation, University of Illinois, 1963.

**MORRISSEY, JOHN** (1831–1878) D-NY,
**House 1867–1871.**

**6936.** Asbury, Herbert. "John Morrissey and His Times." In his *Sucker's Progress,* 358–418. New York: Dodd, Mead, 1938.

**6937.** Fleischer, Nathaniel S. "The Second Trojan War." In his *Heavyweight Championship,* 55–68. New York: Putnam's, 1949.

**6938.** Kofoed, John C. *Brandy for Heroes: A Biography of the Honorable John Morrissey, Champion Heavyweight of America and State Senator.* New York: Dutton, 1938.

**MORROW, DWIGHT WHITNEY**
(1873–1931) R-NJ, Senate 1930–1931.

**6939.** Allen, Robert S., and Andrew R. Pearson. "Little Nemo, the Wonder-Worker." In their *Washington Merry-Go-Round,* 268–292. New York: H. Liveright, 1931.

**6940.** Howland, Hewitt H. *Dwight Whitney Morrow, a Sketch in Admiration.* New York: Century, 1930.

**6941.** McBride, Mary M. *The Story of Dwight W. Morrow.* New York: Farrar and Rinehart, 1930.

**6942.** Melzer, Richard A. "Dwight Morrow's Role in the Mexican Revolution: Good Neighbor or Meddling Yankee?" Ph.D. dissertation, University of New Mexico, 1979.

**6943.** Nicolson, Harold G. *Dwight Morrow.* New York: Harcourt, Brace, 1935.

**MORROW, JEREMIAH** (1771–1852)
W-OH, House 1803–1813, 1840–1843, Senate
**1813–1819.**

**6944.** Smith, S. Winifred. "Jeremiah Morrow." In *Governors of Ohio,* 27–30. Columbus: Ohio Historical Society, 1954.

**MORSE, WAYNE LYMAN** (1900–1974)
D-OR, Senate 1945–1969.

**6945.** Davis, James R. "An Examination of the Views of Senator Wayne Morse on Federal Aid to Higher Education." Ph.D. dissertation, Michigan State University, 1969.

**6946.** Morse, Harold. "An Analysis of the Published Statements of Senator Wayne Morse on Education, 1947–1965." Ph.D. dissertation, University of Washington, 1969.

**6947.** Neuberger, Richard L. "Wayne Morse: Republican Gadfly." *American Mercury* 65 (July 1947): 16–24.

**6948.** Smith, Arthur R. *Tiger in the Senate: The Biography of Wayne Morse.* Garden City, NY: Doubleday, 1962.

**6949.** Swiggett, Howard G. *Extraordinary Mr. Morse.* Garden City, NY: Doubleday, 1952.

**6950.** Unrah, Gail Q. "Eternal Liberal: Wayne L. Morse and the Politics of Liberalism." Ph.D. dissertation, University of Oregon, 1987.

**6951.** ———. "Republican Apostate: Senator Wayne L. Morse and His Quest for Independent Liberalism." *Pacific Northwest Quarterly* 82 (July 1991): 82–91.

**6952.** Wilkins, Lee. "Wayne Morse: The Childhood of an American Adam." *Journal of Psychohistory* 10 (Fall 1982): 189–211.

**6953.** Wilkins, Lee, and Lee R. Alton. *Wayne Morse: A Bibliography.* Westport, CT: Greenwood, 1985.

**6954.** Wilkins, Lillian C. "Wayne Morse: An Exploratory Biography." Ph.D. dissertation, University of Oregon, 1982.

**MORTON, JACKSON** (1794–1874) W-FL, Senate 1849–1855.

**6955.** Rucker, Brian R. *Jackson Morton: West Florida's Soldier, Senator, and Secessionist.* Milton, FL: Patagonia Press, 1990.

**MORTON, JOHN** (1724–1777) PA, Continental Congress 1774–1777.

**6956.** Sanderson, John. "John Morton." In *Sanderson's Biography of the Signers of the Declaration of Independence,* edited by Robert T. Conrad, 449–452. Philadelphia: Thomas, Cowperthwait, 1848.

**6957.** Springer, Ruth L. *John Morton in Contemporary Records.* Harrisburg, PA: Pennsylvania History and Museum Commission, 1967.

**MORTON, LEVI PARSONS** (1824–1920) R-NY, House 1879–1881.

**6958.** Barzman, Sol. "Levi Parsons Morton." In his *Madmen and Geniuses: The Vice-Presidents of the United States,* 147–152. Chicago: Follett Publishing Company, 1974.

**6959.** Harney, Gilbert L. *The Lives of Benjamin Harrison and Levi P. Morton.* Providence, RI: J. A. and R. A. Reid, 1888.

**6960.** Lincoln, Charles Z. "Administration of Levi P. Morton." In *Official New York, from Cleveland to Hughes,* vol. 1, edited by Charles E. Fitch. New York: Hurd, 1911.

**6961.** McElroy, Robert M. *Levi Parsons Morton: Banker, Diplomat and Statesman.* New York: Putnam's, 1930.

**6962.** Wallace, Lew. "Levi P. Morton, a Biography." In his *Life of Gen. Ben Harrison,* 349–438. Philadelphia: Hubbard Brothers, 1888.

**6963.** Willson, Beckles. "Noyes, Morton and McLane (1877–1889)." In his *America's Ambassadors to France (1777–1927),* 317–327. New York: Frederick A. Stokes, 1928.

**MORTON, OLIVER HAZARD PERRY THROCK** (1823–1877) R-IN, Senate 1867–1877.

**6964.** Beveridge, Albert J. "Morton, the Nationalist." In his *The Meaning of the Times,* 89–100. Indianapolis: Bobbs-Merrill, 1908.

**6965.** Dye, Charity. "Oliver Perry Morton: Who Bore the Torch of Patriotism for Indiana in '61." In her *Some Torch Bearers in Indiana,* 84–91. Indianapolis: Hollenbeck Press, 1917.

**6966.** Foulke, William D. *Life of Oliver P. Morton, Including His Important Speeches.* 2 vols. Indianapolis: Bowen-Merrill, 1898.

**6967.** Fox, Henry C., ed. "Oliver P. Morton." In his *Memoirs of Wayne County and the City of Richmond, Indiana,* 183–198. Madison, WI: Western Historical Association, 1912.

**6968.** French, William M., ed. *Life, Speeches, State Papers and Public Services of Gov. Oliver P. Morton.* Cincinnati, OH: Moore, Wilstach, and Baldwin, 1866.

**6969.** Morrison, Olin D. "The Administration of Oliver Perry Morton, Governor of Indiana, 1860–1865." Master's thesis, Indiana University, 1917.

**6970.** Morton, Oliver P. *Oliver P. Morton, of Indiana: A Sketch of His Life and Public Services.* Indianapolis: Journal Company, 1876.

**6971.** Sylvester, Lorna L. "Oliver P. Morton and Hoosier Politics during the Civil War." Ph.D. dissertation, Indiana University, 1968.

**6972.** Walker, Charles M. *Sketch of the Life, Character and Public Services of O. P. Morton, Prepared for the Indianapolis Journal.* Indianapolis: Indianapolis Journal, 1878.

**MORTON, THRUSTON BALLARD**
**(1907–1982) R-KY, House 1947–1953,**
**Senate 1957–1969.**

**6973.** Smiley, Sara J. "The Political Career of Thruston B. Morton: The Senate Years, 1956–1968." Ph.D. dissertation, University of Kentucky, 1975.

**MOSES, GEORGE HIGGINS**
**(1869–1944) R-NH, Senate 1918–1933.**

**6974.** Gallagher, Edward J. *George H. Moses: A Profile.* Laconia, NH: Citizen Publishing House, 1975.

**6975.** Symonds, Merrill A. "George Higgins Moses of New Hampshire: The Man and the Era." Ph.D. dissertation, Clark University, 1955.

**MOSHER, CHARLES ADAMS**
**(1906–1984) R-OH, House 1961–1977.**

**6976.** Flinn, Thomas A. "The Case of the Quiescent Campaign: The Thirteenth District of Ohio." In *The Making of Congressmen: Seven Campaigns of 1974*, edited by Alan L. Clem, 107–125. North Scituate, MA: Duxbury Press, 1976.

**MOSS, JOHN EMERSON** (1915–  ) D-CA, **House 1953–1978.**

**6977.** Moss, John E. "Future Problems and Prospects." In *The Voice of Government*, edited by Ray E. Hiebert and Carloon E. Spitzer, 25–36. New York: Wiley, 1968.

**MOUTON, ALEXANDER** (1804–1885) **D-LA, Senate 1837–1842.**

**6978.** Reeves, Miriam G. "Alexander Mouton." In her *Governors of Louisiana*, 55–57. Gretna, LA: Pelican, 1972.

**MOYNIHAN, DANIEL PATRICK**
**(1927–  ) D-NY, Senate 1977–  .**

**6979.** Finger, Seymour M. "Daniel Patrick Moynihan." In his *Your Man at the UN*, 235–248. New York: New York University Press, 1980.

**6980.** Gerson, Allan. "Senator Moynihan and Allan Gerson's Correspondence on the World Court." *World Affairs* 148 (Summer 1985): 31–33.

**6981.** Loury, Glenn C. "The Family, the Nation, and Senator Moynihan." *Commentary* 81 (June 1986): 21–26.

**6982.** Moynihan, Daniel P. *A Dangerous Place.* Boston: Little, Brown, 1978.

**6983.** Schoen, Douglas. *Pat: A Biography of Daniel Patrick Moynihan.* New York: Harper and Row, 1979.

**6984.** Williams, C. Dickerman. "Senator Moynihan and the World Court." *World Affairs* 148 (Summer 1985): 27–30.

**6985.** Winston, Henry. *The Moynihan-Kissinger Doctrine and the "Third World."* New York: New Outlook Publishers, 1975.

**MUHLENBERG, FREDERICK**
**AUGUSTUS CONRAD (1750–1801) PA,**
**House 1789–1797, Continental Congress**
**1779–1780.**

**6986.** Fuller, Hubert B. "Muhlenberg the First and Henry Clay the Greatest of American Speakers." In his *The Speakers of the House*, 22–58. Boston: Little, Brown, 1909.

**6987.** Muhlenberg, Henry A. *The Life of Major-General Peter Muhlenberg of the Revolutionary War.* Philadelphia: Carey and Hart, 1849.

**6988.** Richards, Henry M. "Famous Pennsylvania-Germans: Frederick Augustus Conrad Muhlenberg." *Pennsylvania-German* 3 (April 1902): 51–60.

**6989.** Seidensticker, Oswald. "Frederick Augustus Conrad Muhlenberg: Speaker of the House of Representatives, in the First Congress, 1789." *Pennsylvania Magazine of History and Biography* 13 (July 1889): 184–206.

**6990.** Wallace, Paul A. *The Muhlenbergs of Pennsylvania.* Philadelphia: University of Pennsylvania Press, 1950.

**MUNDT, KARL EARL** (1900–1974) R-SD, House 1939–1948, Senate 1948–1973.

**6991.** Heidepriem, Scott. *A Fair Chance for Free People: Biography of Karl E. Mundt, United States Senator.* Madison, SD: Leader Printing, 1988.

**6992.** Lange, Gerald. "Mundt vs. McGovern: The 1960 Senate Election." *Heritage of the Great Plains* 15 (Fall 1982): 33–41.

**6993.** Lee, R. Alton. "New Dealers, Fair Dealers, Misdealers and Hiss Dealers: Karl Mundt and the Internal Security Act of 1950." *South Dakota History* 10 (Fall 1980): 277–290.

**MURPHY, GEORGE LLOYD** (1902–1992) R-CA, Senate 1965–1971.

**6994.** Murphy, George. *"Say . . . Didn't You Used to Be George Murphy?"* New York: Bartholomew House, 1970.

**MURPHY, JOHN MICHAEL** (1926– ) D-NY, House 1963–1981.

**6995.** Reeder, Russell P. "John Murphy and Warren Hearnes: Two Uncommon Statesmen." In his *Heroes and Leaders of West Point,* 132–140. New York: Nelson, 1970.

**MURRAY, GEORGE WASHINGTON** (1853–1926) R-SC, House 1893–1895, 1896–1897.

**6996.** Christopher, Maurine. "George W. Murray/South Carolina." In her *Black Americans in Congress,* 113–122. Rev. ed. New York: Thomas Y. Crowell Company, 1976.

**6997.** Gaboury, William J. "George Washington Murray and the Fight for Political Democracy in South Carolina." *Journal of Negro History* 62 (July 1977): 258–269.

**MURRAY, JAMES EDWARD** (1876–1961) D-MT, Senate 1934–1961.

**6998.** Evans, William B. "Senator James E. Murray: A Voice of the People in Foreign Affairs." *Montana* 32 (Winter 1982): 25–35.

**6999.** Spritzer, Donald E. "New Dealer from Montana: The Senate Career of James E. Murray." Ph.D. dissertation, University of Montana, 1980.

**7000.** ———. *Senator James E. Murray and the Limits of Post-War Liberalism.* New York: Garland, 1985.

**MURRAY, WILLIAM HENRY DAVID** (1869–1956) D-OK, House 1913–1917.

**7001.** Bryant, Keith L. *Alfalfa Bill Murray.* Norman: University of Oklahoma Press, 1968.

**7002.** ———. "Alfalfa Bill Murray: Apostle of Agrarianism." Ph.D. dissertation, University of Missouri, 1965.

**7003.** Hines, Gordon. *Alfalfa Bill, an Intimate Biography.* Oklahoma City: Oklahoma Press, 1932.

**7004.** Luthin, Reinhard H. "William H. Murray: 'Alfalfa Bill' of Oklahoma." In his *American Demagogues,* 102–126. Boston: Beacon Press, 1954.

**7005.** Schruben, Francis W. "The Return of Alfalfa Bill Murray." *Chronicles of Oklahoma* 4 (Spring 1963): 38–65.

**7006.** Vaughn, Courtney A. "By Hook or By Crook: Alfalfa Bill Murray, Colonizer in Bolivia." *Journal of the West* 18 (January 1979): 67–73.

**MURRAY, WILLIAM VANS (1760–1803)**
**F-MD, House 1791–1797.**

**7007.** DeConde, Alexander. "William Vans Murray and Diplomacy of Peace, 1797–1800." *Maryland Historical Magazine* 48 (March 1953): 1–26.

**7008.** Hill, Peter P. *William Vans Murray, Federalist Diplomat: The Shaping of Peace with France 1797–1801.* Syracuse, NY: Syracuse University Press, 1971.

**MUSKIE, EDMUND SIXTUS (1914– )**
**D-ME, Senate 1959–1980.**

**7009.** Lippman, Theo, and Donald C. Hansen. *Muskie.* New York: Norton, 1971.

**7010.** Muskie, Edmund S. *Journeys.* Garden City, NY: Doubleday, 1972.

**7011.** Nevin, David R. *Muskie of Maine.* New York: Random House, 1972.

**7012.** Pilarski, Laura. "Edmond S. Muskie and John A. Gronouski: They Rank High in Politics." In her *They Came from Poland,* 131–146. New York: Dodd, Mead, 1969.

**MYERS, HENRY LEE (1862–1943) D-MT,**
**Senate 1911–1923.**

**7013.** Myers, Henry L. *The United States Senate: What Kind of a Body?* Philadelphia: Dorrance, 1939.

❧

**NASH, CHARLES EDMUND (1844–1913)**
**R-LA, House 1875–1877.**

**7014.** Christopher, Maurine. "Charles E. Nash and P. B. S. Pinchback/Louisiana." In her *Black Americans in Congress,* 104–112. Rev. ed. New York: Thomas Y. Crowell Company, 1976.

**NEAL, JOHN RANDOLPH (1836–1889)**
**D-TN, House 1885–1889.**

**7015.** Fisher, Gilbert M. "John Randolph Neal, Esq., the Great Objector." Master's thesis, Tennessee State A & I University, 1960.

**7016.** Hicks, Bobby E. "The Great Objector: The Life and Public Career of Dr. John R. Neal." *East Tennessee Historical Society's Publications* 41 (1969): 33–66.

**7017.** ———. "The Great Objector: The Public Career of Dr. John R. Neal." Master's thesis, University of Tennessee, 1968.

**NELSON, GAYLORD ANTON (1916– )**
**D-WI, Senate 1963–1981.**

**7018.** Shapiro, Walter. "Gaylord Nelson and the Myth of the White Knight." *Washington Monthly* 7 (July 1975): 23–34.

**NELSON, KNUTE (1843–1923) R-MN,**
**House 1883–1889, Senate 1895–1923.**

**7019.** Baker, James H. "Knute Nelson." *Minnesota Historical Society Collections* 13 (1908): 327–355.

**7020.** Gieske, Millard L. "The Politics of Knute Nelson, 1912–1920." Ph.D. dissertation, University of Minnesota, 1965.

**7021.** Odland, Martin. *The Life of Knute Nelson.* Minneapolis: Lund Press, 1926.

**7022.** Preus, Jacob. "Knute Nelson." *Minnesota History Bulletin* 5 (February 1924): 329–347.

**NELSON, THOMAS, JR. (1738–1789) VA,**
**Continental Congress 1775–1777, 1779–80.**

**7023.** Evans, Emery G. *Thomas Nelson of Yorktown: Revolutionary Virginian.* Charlottesville: University Press of Virginia, 1975.

**7024.** Sanderson, John. "Thomas Nelson." In *Sanderson's Biography of the Signers of the Declaration of Independence,* edited by Robert T. Conrad, 730–744. Philadelphia: Thomas, Cowperthwait, 1848.

**NELSON, THOMAS AMOS ROGERS**
**(1812–1873) O-TN, House 1859–1861.**

**7025.** Alexander, Thomas B. "Strange Bedfellows: The Interlocking Careers of T. A. R. Nelson, Andrew Johnson and W. G. (Parson) Brownlow." *East Tennessee Historical Society's Publications* 51 (1979): 54–77.

**7026.** ———. *Thomas A. R. Nelson of East Tennessee.* Nashville: Tennessee Historical Commission, 1956.

**7027.** Temple, Oliver P. "Thomas A. R. Nelson." In *Notable Men of Tennessee, from 1833 to 1875,* compiled by Mary B. Temple, 166–181. New York: Cosmopolitan Press, 1912.

**NEUBERGER, MAURINE BROWN**
**(1907–  ) D-OR, Senate 1960–1967.**

**7028.** Parshalle, Eve. "U.S. Senator Maurine Neuberger." In her *Kashmir Bridge-Women,* 159–160. New York: Oxford University Press, 1965.

**NEUBERGER, RICHARD LEWIS**
**(1912–1960) D-OR, Senate 1955–1960.**

**7029.** Neuberger, Richard L. *Adventures in Politics: We Go to the Legislature.* New York: Oxford University Press, 1954.

**7030.** Wagner, J. Richard. "Congress and United States-Canada Water Problems: Senator Neuberger and the Columbia River Treaty." *Rocky Mountain Social Science Journal* 11 (October 1974): 51–60.

**NEW, HARRY STEWART (1858–1937)**
**R-IN, Senate 1917–1923.**

**7031.** McMains, Howard F., ed. "Booth Tarkington and the League of Nations: Advice for Senator Harry S. New." *Indiana Magazine of History* 84 (December 1988): 343–352.

**NEWBERRY, TRUMAN HANDY**
**(1864–1945) R-MI, Senate 1919–1922.**

**7032.** Ervin, Spencer. *Henry Ford vs. Truman H. Newberry: The Famous Senate Election Contest: A Study in American Politics, Legislation and Justice.* New York: Smith, 1935.

**NEWELL, WILLIAM AUGUSTUS**
**(1817–1901) R-NJ, House 1847–1851, 1865–1867.**

**7033.** Rogers, Fred B. "William Augustus Newell (1817–1901): Physician, Governor, Congressman." In his *Help-Bringers: Versatile Physicians of New Jersey,* 81–86. New York: Vantage, 1960.

**NEWLANDS, FRANCIS GRIFFITH**
**(1848–1917) D-NV, House 1893–1903, Senate 1903–1917.**

**7034.** Atwood, Albert W. *Francis G. Newlands, a Builder of the Nation.* Washington, DC: The author, 1969.

**7035.** Carrnell, Richard S. "Francis G. Newlands and the National Incorporation of the Railroads." *Nevada Historical Society Quarterly* 19 (Spring 1976): 3–25.

**7036.** Darling, Arthur B., ed. *The Public Papers of Francis G. Newlands.* 2 vols. Boston: Houghton Mifflin, 1932.

**7037.** Hudson, Millard, ed. *Senator Francis G. Newlands, His Work.* Washington, DC: Carnahon Press, 1914.

**7038.** Lilley, William. "The Early Years of Francis G. Newlands, 1848–1897." Ph.D. dissertation, Yale University, 1965.

**7039.** Rowley, William D. "Francis G. Newlands: A Westerner's Search for a Progressive and White America." *Nevada Historical Society Quarterly* 17 (Summer 1974): 69–79.

**7040.** ———. "Francis G. Newlands and the Promises of American Life." *Nevada History Society Quarterly* 32 (Fall 1989): 169–180

**7041.** ———. "Sen. Newlands and the Modernization of the Democratic Party." *Nevada Historical Society Quarterly* 15 (Summer 1972): 25–36.

**NICHOLSON, ALFRED OSBORN POPE** (1808–1876) D-TN, Senate 1840–1842, 1859–1861.

**7042.** Clark, Patricia P. "A. O. P. Nicholson of Tennessee: Editor, Statesman, and Jurist." Master's thesis, University of Tennessee, 1965.

**NILES, NATHANIEL** (1741–1828) VT, House 1791–1795.

**7043.** McLachlan, James. "Nathaniel Niles." In his *Princetonians, 1748–1768,* 585–587. Princeton, NJ: Princeton University Press, 1976.

**NIX, ROBERT NELSON CORNELIUS, SR.** (1905–1987) D-PA, House 1958–1979.

**7044.** Christopher, Maurine. "Robert N. C. Nix/Pennsylvania." In her *Black Americans in Congress,* 215–220. Rev. ed. New York: Thomas Y. Crowell Company, 1976.

**NIXON, RICHARD MILHOUS** (1913–1994) R-CA, House 1947–1950, Senate 1950–1953.

**7045.** Abrahamsen, David. *Nixon vs. Nixon: An Emotional Tragedy.* New York: Farrar, Straus and Giroux, 1977.

**7046.** Aitken, Jonathan. *Nixon: A Life.* Washington, DC: Regnery, 1994.

**7047.** Allen, Gary. *Richard Nixon: The Man behind the Mask.* Belmont, MA: Western Islands, 1971.

**7048.** Alsop, Stewart. *Nixon and Rockefeller: A Double Portrait.* Garden City, NY: Doubleday, 1960.

**7049.** Ambrose, Stephen E. *Nixon: The Education of a Politician 1913–1962.* New York: Simon and Schuster, 1987.

**7050.** ———. *Nixon: The Triumph of a Politician 1962–1972.* New York: Simon and Schuster, 1989.

**7051.** Anderson, Walt. "Self-Actualization of Richard N. Nixon." *Journal of Humanistic Psychology* 15 (Winter 1975): 27–35.

**7052.** Andrews, Phillip. *This Man Nixon: The Life Story of California Senator Richard M. Nixon, Republican Candidate for Vice President of the U.S., His Rise to Fame, His Prosecution of the Hiss Case, His Nomination, Including the Text of the Famous Radio and TV Vindication Speech.* Philadelphia: Winston, 1952.

**7053.** Anson, Robert S. *Exile: The Unquiet Oblivion of Richard M. Nixon.* New York: Simon and Schuster, 1984.

**7054.** Arnold, William A. *Back When It All Began: The Early Nixon Years: Being Some Reminiscences of President Nixon's Early Political Career by His First Administrative Assistant and His Press Secretary.* New York: Vantage, 1975.

**7055.** Barzman, Sol. "Richard M. Nixon." In his *Madmen and Geniuses: The Vice-Presidents of the United States,* 253–262. Chicago: Follett, 1974.

**7056.** Benoit, William L. "Richard M. Nixon's Rhetorical Strategies in His Public Statements on Watergate." *Southern Speech Communication Journal* 47 (Winter 1982): 192–211.

**7057.** Brodie, Fawn M. *Richard Nixon: The Shaping of His Character.* Cambridge, MA: Harvard University Press, 1983.

**7058.** Brown, Steven R. "Richard Nixon and the Public Conscience: The Struggle for Authenticity." *Journal of Psychohistory* 6 (Summer 1978): 93–111.

**7059.** Bullock, Paul. "Rabbits and Radicals: Richard Nixon's 1946 Campaign against Jerry Voorhis." *Southern California Quarterly* 55 (Fall 1973): 319–359.

**7060.** Cavan, Sherri. *20th Century Gothic: America's Nixon.* San Francisco: Wigan Pier Press, 1979.

**7061.** Chesen, Eli S. *President Nixon's Psychiatric Profile: A Psychodynamic-Genetic Interpretation.* New York: P. H. Wyden, 1973.

**7062.** Colodny, Len, and Robert Gettlin. *Silent Coup: The Removal of a President.* New York: St. Martin's Press, 1991.

**7063.** Costello, William A. *The Facts about Nixon: An Unauthorized Biography.* New York: Viking, 1960.

**7064.** Dailey, Joseph M. "The Eisenhower-Nixon Campaign Organization of 1952." Ph.D. dissertation, University of Illinois, 1975.

**7065.** De Toledano, Ralph. *Nixon.* Rev. ed. New York: Duell, Sloan and Pearce, 1960.

**7066.** ———. *One Man Alone: Richard Nixon.* New York: Funk and Wagnalls, 1969.

**7067.** Diamond, Edwin. "Psychojournalism: Nixon on the Couch." *Columbia Journal Review* 12 (March/April 1974): 7–11.

**7068.** Ehrlichman, John. *Witness to Power: The Nixon Years.* New York: Simon and Schuster, 1982.

**7069.** Eisenhower, Julie N., comp. *Eye on Nixon: A Photographic Study of the President and the Man.* New York: Hawthorn, 1972.

**7070.** Evans, Rowland. *Nixon in the White House: The Frustration of Power.* New York: Random House, 1971.

**7071.** Flaningam, Carl D. "Complementary Images: The Off-Year Election Campaigns of Richard Nixon in 1954 and Spiro Agnew in 1970." Ph.D. dissertation, Purdue University, 1973.

**7072.** Friedman, Leon, and William F. Levantrosser. *Cold War Patriot and Statesman, Richard M. Nixon.* Westport, CT: Greenwood, 1993.

**7073.** ———, eds. *Watergate and Afterward: The Legacy of Richard M. Nixon.* Westport, CT: Greenwood, 1992.

**7074.** Frost, David. *"I Gave Them a Sword:" Behind the Scenes of the Nixon Interviews.* New York: Morrow, 1978.

**7075.** Greene, John R. *The Limits of Power: The Nixon and Ford Administrations.* Bloomington: Indiana University Press, 1992.

**7076.** Grofman, Bernard. "Richard Nixon as Pinocchio, Richard II, and Santa Claus: The Use of Allusion in Political Satire." *Journal of Politics* 51 (February 1989): 167–173.

**7077.** Hart, Roderick P. "Absolutism and Situation: Prolegomena to a Rhetorical Biography of Richard M. Nixon." *Communication Monographs* 43 (August 1976): 204–228.

**7078.** Herr, Donald F. "Presidential Influence and Bureaucratic Politics: Nixon's Policy toward Cuba." Ph.D. dissertation, Yale University, 1978.

**7079.** Hess, Stephen, and Earl Mazo. *Nixon: A Political Portrait.* New York: Harper and Row, 1968.

**7080.** Higgins, George. *The Friends of Richard Nixon.* Boston: Little, Brown, 1975.

**7081.** Hoff, Joan. *Nixon Reconsidered.* New York: Basic Books, 1994.

**7082.** Hofstetter, C. Richard, and Cliff Zukin. "TV Network News and Advertising in the Nixon and McGovern Campaigns." *Journalism Quarterly* 56 (Spring 1979): 106–115, 152.

**7083.** Hoyt, Edwin P. *The Nixons: An American Family.* New York: Random House, 1972.

**7084.** Hughes, Arthur J. *Richard M. Nixon.* New York: Dodd, Mead, 1972.

**7085.** Johnson, George. *Richard Nixon: An Intimate and Revealing Portrait of One of America's Key Political Figures.* Derby, CT: Monarch Press, 1961.

**7086.** Johnson, James P. "Nixon and the Psychohistorians: A Review Essay." *Psychohistory Review* 7 (Summer/Fall 1979): 38–42.

**7087.** Keogh, James. *This Is Nixon.* New York: Putnam's 1956.

**7088.** Kissel, Bernard C. "Richard M. Nixon: Definition of an Image." *Quarterly Journal of Speech* 46 (December 1960): 353–361.

**7089.** Klein, Herbert G. *Making It Perfectly Clear.* Garden City, NY: Doubleday, 1980.

**7090.** Kleinau, Marvin D. "The Role of Rhetoric in the Political Resurrection of Richard M. Nixon: 1963–1968." Ph.D. dissertation, Southern Illinois University, 1978.

**7091.** Kornitzer, Bela. *The Real Nixon: An Intimate Biography.* New York: Rand McNally, 1960.

**7092.** Kutler, Stanley I. *The Wars of Watergate: The Last Crisis of Richard Nixon.* New York: Knopf, 1990.

**7093.** Lasky, Victor. *Richard Nixon.* New York: Putnam's, 1984.

**7094.** Lee, Ronald E. *The Featuring of Will in History: A Rhetorical Exploration of Richard Nixon's Post Presidential Writings.* Quarterly Journal of Speech 75 (November 1989): 453–66.

**7095.** Longford, Frank P. *Nixon, a Study in Extremes of Fortune.* London: Weidenfeld and Nicolson, 1980.

**7096.** Mankiewicz, Frank. *Perfectly Clear: Nixon from Whittier to Watergate.* New York: Praeger, 1975.

**7097.** Mazlish, Bruce. *In Search of Nixon: A Psychological Inquiry.* Baltimore: Penguin, 1972.

**7098.** ———. "Toward a Psychohistorical Inquiry: The Real Richard Nixon." *Journal of Interdisciplinary History* 1 (Autumn 1970): 49–105.

**7099.** Mazo, Earl. *Richard Nixon: A Political and Personal Portrait.* New York: Harper, 1959.

**7100.** Mazon, Mauricio. "Young Richard Nixon: A Study in Political Precocity." *His-*

*torian* 41 (November 1978): 21–40.

**7101.** Morris, Roger. *Richard Milhous Nixon: The Rise of an American Politician.* New York: Holt, 1990.

**7102.** Nixon, Richard M. *Beyond Peace.* New York: Random House, 1994.

**7103.** ———. *In the Arena: A Memoir of Victory, Defeat and Renewal.* New York: Simon and Schuster, 1990.

**7104.** ———. *RN: The Memoirs of Richard Nixon.* New York: Grosset and Dunlap, 1978.

**7105.** ———. *Six Crises.* Garden City, NY: Doubleday, 1962.

**7106.** Nuechterlein, James A. "Richard Nixon's Character and Fate." *Queen's Quarterly* 86 (Spring 1979): 16–25.

**7107.** Parmet, Herbert S. *Richard Nixon and His America.* Boston: Little, Brown, 1990.

**7108.** Reichley, James. *Conservatives in an Age of Change: The Nixon and Ford Administrations.* Washington, DC: Brookings Institution, 1981.

**7109.** Renshon, Stanley A. "Psychological Analysis and Presidential Personality: The Case of Richard Nixon." *History of Childhood Quarterly* 2 (Winter 1975): 415–450.

**7110.** Reuben, William A. *The Honorable Mr. Nixon.* 2d ed. New York: Action Books, 1958.

**7111.** Rogin, Michael P., and John Lottier. "The Inner History of Richard Milhous Nixon." *Trans-Action* 9 (November/December 1971): 19–28.

**7112.** Rowse, Arthur E. *Slanted News: A Case Study of the Nixon and Stevenson Fund Stories.* Boston: Beacon Press, 1957.

**7113.** Schulte, Renee K., ed. *The Young Nixon: An Oral Inquiry.* Fullerton: Oral History Program, California State University, 1978.

**7114.** Schurmann, Franz. *The Foreign Politics of Richard Nixon: The Grand Design.* Berkeley: Institute of International Studies, University of California, 1987.

**7115.** Scobie, Ingrid W. "Helen Gahagan Douglas and Her 1950 Senate Race with Richard M. Nixon." *Southern California Quarterly* 58 (Spring 176): 113–126.

**7116.** Seelye, John. "The Measure of His Company: Richard M. Nixon in Amber." *Virginia Quarterly Review* 53 (Autumn 1977): 585–606.

**7117.** Szulc, Tad. *The Illusion of Peace: Foreign Policy in the Nixon Years.* New York: Viking, 1978.

**7118.** Thompson, Kenneth W., ed. *The Nixon Presidency: Twenty-Two Intimate Perspectives of Richard Nixon.* Lanham, MD: University Press of America, 1987.

**7119.** Thornton, Richard C. *The Nixon-Kissinger Years: Reshaping America's Foreign Policy.* New York: Paragon House,1989.

**7120.** Voorhis, Horace J. *The Strange Case of Richard Milhous Nixon.* New York: Popular Library, 1972.

**7121.** White, Theodore H. *Breach of Faith: The Fall of Richard Nixon.* New York: Atheneum Publishers, 1975.

**7122.** ———. *The Making of the President, 1972.* New York: Bantam Books, 1973.

**7123.** Wicker, Tom. *One of Us: Richard Nixon and the American Dream.* New York: Random House, 1991.

**7124.** Wills, Garry. *Nixon Agonistes: The Crisis of the Self-Made Man.* Boston: Houghton Mifflin, 1970.

**7125.** Witcover, Jules. *The Resurrection of Richard Nixon.* New York: Putnam's, 1970.

**7126.** Woodstone, Arthur. *Nixon's Head.* New York: St. Martin's Press, 1972.

**7127.** Woodward, Bob, and Carl Bernstein. *The Final Days.* New York: Simon and Schuster, 1976.

**7128.** Young, Donald. "Richard M. Nixon." In his *American Roulette: The History and Dilemma of the Vice Presidency,* 252–285. New York: Holt, Rinehart and Winston, 1965.

## NORBECK, PETER (1870–1936) R-SD, Senate 1921–1936.

**7129.** Fite, Gilbert C. "Peter Norbeck and the Defeat of the Nonpartisan League in South Dakota." *Mississippi Valley History Review* 33 (September 1946): 217–236.

**7130.** ———. *Peter Norbeck: Prairie Statesman.* Columbia: University of Missouri, 1948.

## NORRIS, GEORGE WILLIAM (1861–1944) IR-NE, House 1903–1913, Senate 1913–1943.

**7131.** Budig, Eugene A., and Donald B. Walton. "The Day Senator Norris Died." *Nebraska History* 50 (Spring 1969): 55–64.

**7132.** Clancy, Manus J. "Senator George W. Norris: An Analysis and Evaluation of His Role of Insurgency during the Hoover Years." Ph.D. dissertation, St. John's University, 1965.

**7133.** Clark, Jerome L. "The Contributions of George W. Norris during His Service on the United States Senate Judiciary Committee." Ph.D. dissertation, University of Southern California, 1959.

**7134.** Dahlstrom, Karl A. "The Defeat of George W. Norris in 1942." *Nebraska History* 59 (Summer 1978): 231–258.

**7135.** Fellman, David. "Liberalism of Senator Norris." *American Political Science Review* 40 (February 1946): 27–51.

**7136.** Grant, Philip A., Jr. "Editorial Reaction to the Defeat of Senator George W. Norris of Nebraska." *Midwest Review* 11 (Spring 1989): 37–43.

**7137.** Guinsburg, Thomas N. "The George W. Norris Conversion to Internationalism, 1939–1941." *Nebraska History* 53 (Winter 1972): 477–490.

**7138.** Johnson, John R. "George William Norris (Insurgent Republican) 1861–1944." In his *Representative Nebraskans*, 136–141. Lincoln, NE: Johnsen, 1954.

**7139.** Kennedy, John F. "'I Have Come Home to Tell You the Truth:' George Norris." In his *Profiles in Courage*, 186–210. New York: Harper and Row, 1956.

**7140.** Leuchtenburg, William E. "Roosevelt, Norris and the Seven Little TVAs." *Journal of Politics* 14 (August 1952): 418–441.

**7141.** Lief, Alfred. *Democracy's Norris: The Biography of a Lonely Crusade.* New York: Stackpole Sons Publishers, 1939.

**7142.** Lindeen, Shirley A., and James W. Lindeen. "Bryan, Norris and the Doctrine of Party Responsibility." *American Studies* 11 (Spring 1970): 45–53.

**7143.** Lowitt, Richard. "A Case Study in Biographical Research: George W. Norris." *Journal of Library History, Philosophy and Comparative Librarianship* 4 (April 1969): 123–132.

**7144.** ———. "George Norris, James J. Hill, and the Railroad Rate Bill." *Nebraska History* 40 (June 1959): 137–146.

**7145.** ———. "George W. Norris: A Country Boy in an Urbanizing Nation." *Nebraska History* 52 (Fall 1971): 233–237.

**7146.** ———. "George W. Norris: A Reflective View." *Nebraska History* 70 (Winter 1990): 297–302.

**7147.** ———. "George W. Norris and the Kinkaid Act of 1904: A Footnote." *Nebraska History* 57 (Fall 1976): 399–404.

**7148.** ———. "George W. Norris and the New Deal in Nebraska, 1933–1936." *Agricultural History* 51 (April 1977): 396–405.

**7149.** ———. *George W. Norris: The Making of a Progressive, 1861–1912.* Syracuse, NY: Syracuse University Press, 1963.

**7150.** ———. *George W. Norris: The Persistence of a Progressive, 1913–1933.* Champaign: University of Illinois Press, 1971.

**7151.** ———. *George W. Norris: The Triumph of a Progressive, 1933–1944.* Urbana: University of Illinois Press, 1978.

**7152.** ———. "The Making of an Insurgent." *Mid-America* 42 (April 1960): 105–115.

**7153.** ———. "Nebraska: A Reflective View by George W. Norris." *Nebraska History* 49 (Summer 1968): 139–148.

**7154.** ———. "A Neglected Aspect of the Progressive Movement: George W. Norris and Public Control of Hydroelectric Power, 1913–1919." *Historian* 27 (May 1965): 350–365.

**7155.** ———. "Present at the Creation: George W. Norris, Franklin D. Roosevelt and the TVA Enabling Act." *East Tennessee Historical Society Publications* 48 (1976): 116–126.

**7156.** ———. "Senator Norris and His 1918 Campaign." *Pacific Northwest Quarterly* 57 (July 1966): 113–119.

**7157.** Madison, Charles A. "George W. Norris: Eminent Progressive." In his *Leaders and Liberals in 20th Century America*, 315–362. New York: Ungar, 1961.

**7158.** Madison, Charles A. "George W. Norris: 'The Fighting Liberal'." In his *Critics and Crusaders*, 567–580. New York: Ungar, 1959.

**7159.** Neuberger, Richard L., and Stephen Kahn. *Integrity: The Life of George W. Norris.* New York: Vanguard, 1937.

**7160.** Norris, George W. *Fighting Liberal.* New York: Macmillan, 1945.

**7161.** Owens, John W. "Norris, the Discouraged." In *Faces of Five Decades*, edited by Robert B. Luce, 105–107. New York: Simon and Schuster, 1964.

**7162.** Smallwood, Johnny B. "George W. Norris and the Concept of a Planned Region." Ph.D. dissertation, University of North Carolina, 1963.

**7163.** Sutton, Walter A. "Bryan, La Follette, Norris: Three Mid-Western Politicians." *Journal of the West* 8 (October 1969): 613–630.

**7164.** Villard, Oswald G. "George W. Norris: Noblest of the Romans." In his *Prophets True and False*, 100–111. New York: Knopf, 1928.

**7165.** Zucker, Norman L. *George W. Norris: Gentle Knight of American Democracy.* Urbana: University of Illinois Press, 1966.

**7166.** ———. "George W. Norris: Nebraska Moralist." *Nebraska History* 42 (June 1961): 95–124.

**7167.** ———. "George W. Norris: Progressive from the Plains." *Nebraska History* 45 (June 1964): 147–166.

**7168.** ———. "Political Philosophy of George W. Norris." Ph.D. dissertation, Rutgers University, 1961.

**NORTON, MARY TERESA (1875–1959) D-NJ, House 1925–1951.**

**7169.** Gilfond, Duff. "Gentlewomen in the House." *American Mercury* 18 (October 1929): 151–163.

**7170.** Mitchell, Gary. "Women Standing for Women: The Early Political Career of Mary T. Norton." *New Jersey History* 96 (Spring/Summer 1978): 27–42.

**NUNN, SAMUEL AUGUSTUS (1938– ) D-GA, Senate 1972– .**

**7171.** Roberts, Brian E. "A Dead Senator Tells No Lies: Seniority and the Distribution of Federal Benefits." *American Journal of Political Science* 34 (Summer 1990): 31–58.

**7172.** Williams, Phillip. "The Nunn Amendment, Burden-Sharing and U.S. Troops in Europe." *Survival* 1 (January/February 1985): 2–10.

**NYE, GERALD PRENTICE (1892–1971) R-ND, Senate 1925–1945.**

**7173.** Clifford, J. Garry. "A Note on the Break between Senator Nye and President Roosevelt in 1939." *North Dakota History* 49 (Summer 1982): 14–17.

**7174.** Cole, Wayne S. *Senator Gerald P. Nye and American Foreign Relations.* Minneapolis: University of Minnesota Press, 1962.

**7175.** Horowitz, David. "The Perils of Western Farm Politics: Herbert Hoover, Gerald P. Nye, and Agricultural Reform, 1926–1932." *North Dakota Quarterly* 53 (Fall 1985): 92–110.

**7176.** Larsen, Lawrence H. "Gerald Nye and the Isolationist Argument." *North Dakota History* 47 (Winter 1980): 25–28.

**7177.** Leonard, Robert J. "From County Politics to the Senate: The Learning Years for Senator Nye." *North Dakota History* 39 (Summer 1972): 15–23.

**7178.** Rylance, Daniel. "A Controversial Career: Gerald P. Nye, 1925–1946." *North Dakota Quarterly* 36 (Winter 1968): 5–19.

**7179.** Sayre, J. L. "Gerald P. Nye." In *Public Men In and Out of Office*, edited by John T. Salter, 127–146. Chapel Hill: University of North Carolina Press, 1946.

**NYE, JAMES WARREN (1815–1876) R-NV, Senate 1864–1873.**

**7180.** Green, Michael S. "Diehard or Swing Man: Senator James W. Nye and Andrew Johnson's Impeachment and Trial." *Nevada Historical Society Quarterly* 29 (Fall 1986): 174–191.

**7181.** Higgins, L. James. "A Mystery Cleared: The Diary of James W. Nye." *Nevada Historical Society Quarterly* 26 (Summer 1983): 127–132.

**7182.** Samon, Jud B. "Sagebrush Falstaff: A Biographical Sketch of James Warren Nye." Ph.D. dissertation, University of Maryland, 1979.

❧

## O'CONNOR, JOHN JOSEPH
(1885–1960) D-NY, House 1923–1939.

**7183.** Polenberg, Richard. "Franklin Roosevelt and the Purge of John O'Connor: The Impact of Urban Change on Political Parties." *New York History* 49 (July 1968): 306–326.

## O'CONOR, HERBERT ROMULUS
(1896–1960) D-MD, Senate 1947–1953.

**7184.** Kirwin, Harry W. *Inevitable Success: Herbert R. O'Conor.* Westminster, MD: Newman Press, 1962.

## O'DANIEL, WILBERT LEE "PAPPY"
(1890–1969) D-TX, Senate 1941–1949.

**7185.** Douglas, Claude. *The Life Story of W. Lee O'Daniel.* Dallas: Regional Press, 1938.

**7186.** Welch, June R. "W. Lee O'Daniel Changed Texas Politics." In his *The Texas Governor,* 158–165. Irving, TX: G. L. A. Press, 1977.

**7187.** Welch, June R. "W. Lee O'Daniel Was a Radio Personality." In his *The Texas Senator,* 124–129. Dallas, TX: G.L.A. Press, 1978.

## ODDIE, TASKER LOWNDES
(1870–1950) R-NV, Senate 1921–1933.

**7188.** Chan, Loren B. *Sagebrush Statesman: Tasker L. Oddie of Nevada.* Reno: University of Nevada Press, 1973.

**7189.** Wash-Pickett, Evelyne. "Tasker Oddie in Belmont." *Nevada Historical Society Quarterly* 29 (Summer 1986): 89–108.

## O'DONNELL, JAMES (1840–1915) R-MI,
House 1885–1893.

**7190.** Horan, Kenneth. *Papa Went to Congress.* Garden City, NY: Doubleday, 1946.

## OGDEN, AARON (1756–1839) F-NJ,
Senate 1801–1803.

**7191.** Baxter, Maurice G. *The Steamboat Monopoly: Gibbons v. Ogden, 1824.* New York: Knopf, 1972.

**7192.** Elmer, Lucius Q. "Governors I Have Known: Aaron Ogden." In his *The Constitution and Government of the Province and State of New Jersey,* 136–151. Newark, NJ: M. R. Dennis and Company, 1872.

## OGLESBY, RICHARD JAMES
(1824–1899) R-IL, Senate 1873–1879.

**7193.** Plummer, Mark A. "Richard J. Oglesby, Lincoln's Rail-Splitter." *Illinois Historical Journal* 80 (Spring 1987): 2–12.

**7194.** "Richard Oglesby." In *Bench and Bar of Illinois: Historical and Reminiscent,* edited by John M. Palmer, vol. 2, 1139–1156. Chicago: Lewis, 1899.

**7195.** Wilkie, Frank B. *A Sketch of Richard Oglesby.* Chicago: Shanholtzer, 1884.

## O'HARA, JAMES EDWARD (1844–1905)
R-NC, House 1883–1887.

**7196.** Christopher, Maurine. "John A. Hyman, James E. O'Hara, and Henry P. Cheatham/North Carolina." In her *Black Americans in Congress,* 149–159. Rev. ed. New York: Thomas Y. Crowell Company, 1976.

**7197.** Reid, George W. "Four in Black: North Carolina's Black Congressmen, 1874–1901." *Journal of Negro History* 64 (Summer 1979): 229–243.

## OLNEY, RICHARD (1871–1939) D-MA,
House 1915–1921.

**7198.** Eggert, Gerald G. "Richard Olney and the Income Tax Cases." *Mississippi Valley Historical Review* 48 (June 1961): 24–41.

**7199.** James, Henry. *Richard Olney and His Public Service.* Boston: Houghton Mifflin, 1923.

## O'MAHONEY, JOSEPH CHRISTOPHER (1884–1962) D-WY, Senate 1934–1953, 1954–1961.

**7200.** Coombs, Frank A. "Joseph Christopher O'Mahoney: The New Deal Years." Ph.D. dissertation, University of Illinois, 1969.

**7201.** Gressley, Gene M. "Joseph C. O'Mahoney, FDR, and the Supreme Court." *Pacific Historical Review* 40 (May 1971): 183–202.

**7202.** Moore, Carl. "Joseph Christopher O'Mahoney: A Brief Biography." *Annals of Wyoming* 41 (October 1969): 159–186.

**7203.** Ninneman, Thomas R. "Joseph C. O'Mahoney: The New Deal and the Court Fight." Ph.D. dissertation, University of Wyoming, 1972.

**7204.**———. "Wyoming's Senator Jo-seph C. O'Mahoney." *Annals of Wyoming* 49 (Fall 1977): 193–222.

**7205.** Snow, Julian. "Joseph C. O'Mahoney." In *Public Men In and Out of Office*, edited by John T. Salter, 109–126. Chapel Hill: University of North Carolina Press, 1946.

**7206.** Voight, Barton R. "Joseph C. O'Mahoney and the 1952 Senate Election in Wyoming." *Annals of Wyoming* 45 (Fall 1973): 177–224.

## O'NEILL, THOMAS PHILLIP "TIP," JR. (1912–1994) D-MA, House 1953–1987.

**7207.** Bentley, Judith. "Tip O'Neill and the Contras." In her *Speakers of the House*, 119–136. New York: Franklin Watts, 1994.

**7208.** Clancy, Paul R., and Shirley Elder. *Tip: A Biography of Thomas P. O'Neill, Speaker of the House.* New York: Macmillan, 1980.

**7209.** O'Neill, Thomas P. *Man of the House: The Life and Political Memoirs of Speaker Tip O'Neill.* New York: Random, 1987.

**7210.** Smith, Steven S. "O'Neill's Legacy for the House." *Brookings Review* 9 (Winter 1987): 28–36.

## ORR, JAMES LAWRENCE (1822–1873) D-SC, House 1849–1859.

**7211.** Bartlett, David V. "James L. Orr." In his *Presidential Candidates: Containing Sketches, Biographical, Personal and Political, of Prominent Candidates for the Presidency*, 305–315. New York: A. B. Burdick, 1859.

**7212.** Leemhuis, Roger P. *James L. Orr and the Sectional Conflict.* Washington, DC: University Press of America, 1979.

**7213.** Topping, W. H. "Hon. James L. Orr, of South Carolina." *National Democratic Quarterly Review* 1 (April 1856): 328–342.

## OTIS, HARRISON GRAY (1765–1848) F-MA, House 1797–1801, Senate 1817–1822.

**7214.** Morison, Samuel E. *Harrison Gray Otis, 1765–1848: The Urbane Federalist.* Boston: Houghton Mifflin, 1969.

**7215.** ———. *The Life and Letters of Harrison Gray Otis, Federalist, 1765–1848.* 2 vols. Boston: Houghton Mifflin, 1913.

## OWEN, ROBERT DALE (1801–1877) D-IN, House 1843–1847.

**7216.** Leopold, Richard W. *Robert Dale Owen: A Biography.* Cambridge, MA: Harvard University Press, 1940.

**7217.** Lockwood, George B. "Robert Dale Owen." In his *The New Harmony Movement*, 336–377. New York: D. Appleton and Company, 1905.

**7218.** Pancoast, Elinor, and Anne E. Lincoln. *The Incorrigible Idealist: Robert Dale Owen in America.* Bloomington, IN: Principia Press, 1940.

**7219.** Waterman, William R. "Nashoba Begun: Nashoba Concluded." In his *Frances Wright*, 92–133. New York: Columbia University, 1924.

**OWEN, ROBERT LATHAM** (1856–1947)
**D-OK, Senate 1907–1925.**

**7220.** Brown, Kenny L. "A Progressive from Oklahoma: Senator Robert Latham Owen, Jr." *Chronicles of Oklahoma* 62 (Fall 1984): 232–265.

**7221.** ———. "Robert Latham Owen, Jr.: His Careers as Indian Attorney and Progressive Senator." Ph.D. dissertation, Oklahoma State University, 1985.

**7222.** Keso, Edward E. "The Senatorial Career of Robert Latham Owen." Ph.D. dissertation, George Peabody College for Teachers, 1937.

**7223.** Shaffer, Janet. "Narcissa and Robert Owen: The Point of Honor Years." *Virginia Magazine of History and Biography* 89 (April 1981): 153–169.

**OWEN, RUTH BRYAN** (1885–1954) **D-FL, House 1929–1933.**

**7224.** Gilfond, Duff. "Gentlewoman of the House." *American Mercury* 18 (October 1929): 151–163.

**PACA, WILLIAM** (1740–1799) **MD, Continental Congress 1774–1779.**

**7225.** Sanderson, John. "William Paca." In *Sanderson's Biography of the Signers of the Declaration of Independence,* edited by Robert T. Conrad, 602–611. Philadelphia: Thomas, Cowperthwait, 1848.

**7226.** Stiverson, Gregory A., and Phoebe R. Jacobsen. *William Paca, a Biography.* Baltimore: Maryland Historical Society, 1976.

**PACHECO, ROMUALDO** (1831–1899) **R-CA, House 1877–1878, 1879–1883.**

**7227.** Conmy, Peter T. *Romualdo Pacheco, Distinguished Californian of the Mexican and American Periods.* San Francisco: Grand Parlor, Native Sons of the Golden West, 1957.

**7228.** Genini, Ronald, and Richard Hitchman. *Romualdo Pacheco: A Californio in Two Eras.* San Francisco: Book Club of California, 1985.

**7229.** Melendy, Howard B., and Benjamin F. Gilbert. "Romualdo Pacheco." In their *Governors of California: Peter H. Burnett to Edmund G. Brown,* 166–173. Georgetown, CA: Talisman Press, 1965.

**7230.** Nicholson, Loren. *Romualdo Pacheco's California!: The Mexican-American Who Won.* San Luis Obispo: California Heritage Publishing Associates, 1990.

**7231.** Ramirez, Anthony. *Romualdo Pacheco, Governor of California.* San Francisco: San Francisco Press, 1974.

**PACKARD, JASPER** (1832–1899) **R-IN, House 1869–1875.**

**7232.** Barnes, William H. "Jasper Packard." In his *Lives of Gen. Ulysses S. Grant and Hon. Henry Wilson,* 54–57. New York: W. H. Barnes, 1872.

**PACKER, ASA** (1805–1879) **D-PA, House 1853–1857.**

**7233.** Stuart, Milton C. *Asa Packer, 1805–1879, Captain of Industry, Educator, Citizen.* Princeton, NJ: Princeton University Press, 1938.

**PACKWOOD, ROBERT WILLIAM** (1932– ) **R-OR, Senate 1969–1995.**

**7234.** Kirchmeier, Mark. *Packwood: The Public and Private Life of Acclaim to Outrage.* New York: HarperCollins, 1994.

**PAGE, CARROLL SMALLEY** (1843–1925) **R-VT, Senate 1908–1923.**

**7235.** Barlow, Melvin L. *The Unconquerable Senator Page: The Struggle to Establish Federal Legislation for Vocational Education.* Washington, DC: American Vocational Association, 1976.

## PAINE, ROBERT TREAT (1731–1814)
MA, Continental Congress 1774–1778.

**7236.** Paine, Robert T. *The Papers of Robert Treat Paine.* Edited by Stephen T. Riley and Edward W. Hanson. 2 vols. Boston: Massachusetts Historical Society, 1992.

**7237.** Sanderson, John. "Robert Treat Paine." In *Sanderson's Biography of the Signers of the Declaration of Independence*, edited by Robert T. Conrad, 132–143. Philadelphia: Thomas, Cowperthwait, 1848.

## PALFREY, JOHN GORHAM (1796–1881)
W-MA, House 1847–1849.

**7238.** Gatell, Frank O. "Doctor Palfrey Frees His Slaves." *New England Quarterly* 34 (March 1961): 74–86.

**7239.**———. Gatell, Frank O. *John Gorham Palfrey and the New England Conscience.* Cambridge, MA: Harvard University Press, 1963.

**7240.** ———. "Palfrey's Vote, the Conscience Whigs, and the Election of Speaker Winthrop." *New England Quarterly* 31 (June 1958): 218–231.

## PALMER, ALEXANDER MITCHELL (1872–1936) D-PA, House 1909–1915.

**7241.** Coben, Stanley. *A. Mitchell Palmer: Politician.* New York: Columbia University Press, 1963.

**7242.** ———. "A. Mitchell Palmer and the Reorganization of the Democratic Party in Pennsylvania, 1910–1912." *Pennsylvania Magazine of History and Biography* 84 (April 1960): 175–193.

**7243.** Dunn, Robert W., ed. *Palmer Raids.* New York: International Publishers, 1948.

**7244.** Warth, Robert D. "Palmer Raids." *South Atlantic Quarterly* 48 (January 1949): 1–23.

## PALMER, JOHN McAULEY (1817–1900)
D-IL, Senate 1891–1897.

**7245.** Cullom, Shelby M. "General John M. Palmer." In his *Fifty Years of Public Service*, 190–197. Chicago: A. C. McClurg and Company, 1911.

**7246.** Palmer, George T. *A Conscientious Turncoat: The Story of John M. Palmer, 1817–1900.* New Haven, CT: Yale University Press, 1941.

**7247.** Palmer, John M. *Personal Recollections: The Story of an Earnest Life.* Cincinnati, OH: Clarke, 1901.

## PALMER, THOMAS WITHERELL (1830–1913) R-MI, Senate 1883–1889.

**7248.** Bodman, Henry E. "Thomas Witherell Palmer." In *Michigan and the Cleveland Era*, edited by Earl D. Babst and Lewis G. Vanderveld, 194–206. Ann Arbor: University of Michigan Press, 1948.

**7249.** Burton, M. Agnes. "Thomas W. Palmer." *Michigan Pioneer and Historical Society Collections* 39 (1915): 207–217.

## PARKER, ISAAC (1768–1830) F-MA, House 1797–1799.

**7250.** Drago, Harry S. "Judge Parker Takes Over." In his *Outlaws on Horseback*, 114–143. New York: Dodd, Mead, 1964.

**7251.** Sutherland, Arthur E. "Parker and Sterns: 1817–1829." In his *Law at Harvard*, 43–91. Cambridge, MA: Belknap Press, 1967.

## PARKER, ISAAC CHARLES (1838–1896) R-MO, House 1871–1875.

**7252.** Croy, Homer. *He Hanged Them High: An Authentic Account of the Fanatic Judge Who Hanged Eighty-Eight Men.* New York: Duell, Sloan and Pearce, 1952.

**7253.** Emery, J. Gladston. *Court of the Damned: Being a Factual Story of the Court of Judge Isaac C. Parker and Life and Times of the Indian Territory and Old Fort Smith.* New York: Comet Press Books, 1959.

**7254.** Harman, Samuel W. *Hell on the Border, He Hanged Eighty-Eight Men.* Muskogee, OK: Indian Heritage Publications, 1971.

**7255.** Harrington, Fred H. *Hanging Judge.* Caldwell, ID: Caxton Printers, 1951.

**7256.** Shirley, Glenn. *Law West of Fort Smith: A History of Frontier Justice in the Indian Territory, 1834–1896.* New York: Holt, 1957.

**PARKER, JOHN MASON** (1805–1873) R-NY, House 1855–1859.

**7257.** Schott, Matthew J. "John M. Parker and the Bull Moose Progressive Party in State and Nation." Master's thesis, Tulane University, 1960.

**PASCO, SAMUEL** (1834–1917) D-FL, Senate 1887–1899.

**7258.** Pasco, Samuel. "Jefferson County, Florida." *Florida Historical Society Quarterly* 7 (October 1928): 139–154; 7 (January 1929): 234–257.

**7259.** ———. "Samuel Pasco." *Florida Historical Society Quarterly* 7 (October 1928): 135–138.

**PASSMAN, OTTO ERNEST** (1900–1988) D-LA, House 1947–1977.

**7260.** Jones, Randolph. "Otto Passman and Foreign Aid: The Early Years." *Louisiana History* 26 (Winter 1985): 53–62.

**PASTORE, JOHN ORLANDO** (1907– ) D-RI, Senate 1950–1976.

**7261.** Morgenthau, Ruth S. *Pride without Prejudice: The Life of John O. Pastore.* Providence: Rhode Island Historical Society, 1989.

**PATERSON, WILLIAM** (1745–1806) NJ, Senate 1789–1790.

**7262.** Boyd, Julian P. "William Paterson, Forerunner of John Marshall." In *Lives of Eighteen from Princeton,* edited by Williard

Thorp, 194–196. Princeton, NJ: Princeton University Press, 1946.

**7263.** Degnan, Daniel A. "Justice William Paterson: Founder." *Seton Hall Law Review* 16 (1986): 313–342.

**7264.** Elmer, Lucius Q. "Governors after the War for Independence: William Paterson." In his *The Constitution and Government of the Province and State of New Jersey,* 77–102. Newark, NJ: M. R. Dennis and Company, 1872.

**7265.** Haskett, Richard. "Prosecuting the Revolution." *American Historical Review* 59 (April 1954): 578–587.

**7266.** ———. "Village Clerk and County Lawyer: William Paterson's Legal Experience, 1763–1772." *Proceedings of the New Jersey Historical Society* 66 (October 1948): 155–171.

**7267.** ———. "William Paterson, Attorney General of New Jersey: Public Office and Private Profit in the American Revolution." *William and Mary Quarterly* 7 (January 1950): 26–38.

**7268.** ———. "William Paterson, Counsellor at Law." Ph.D. dissertation, Princeton University, 1952.

**7269.** Honeyman, A. Van Doren. "Early Career of Governor William Paterson, 1745–1806." *Somerset County Historical Quarterly* 1 (July/October 1912): 161–179, 241–256.

**7270.** O'Connor, John E. "William Paterson and the American Revolution, 1763–1787." Ph.D. dissertation, City University of New York, 1974.

**7271.** ———. *William Paterson, Lawyer and Statesman, 1745–1806.* New Brunswick, NJ: Rutgers University Press, 1979.

**7272.** Parker, Cortlandt. "Address on Governor William Paterson." *New Jersey Historical Society Proceedings* 5 (October 1920): 230–236.

**7273.** ———. "Alexander Hamilton and William Paterson." *American Bar Association Reports* 3 (August 1880): 149–166.

**7274.** ———. "William Paterson." In *Great American Lawyers,* edited by William D. Lewis, vol. 1, 223–245. Philadelphia: J. C. Winston, 1907.

**7275.** Rosenberg, Leonard B. "The Political Thought of William Paterson." Ph.D. dissertation, New School for Social Research, 1967.

**7276.** ———. "William Paterson: New Jersey's Nation-Maker." *New Jersey History* 85 (Spring 1967): 7–40.

**7277.** Shriner, Charles A. *William Paterson.* Paterson, NJ: Paterson Industrial Commission, 1940.

**7278.** Wood, Gertrude S. "William Paterson of New Jersey, 1745–1806." Ph.D. dissertation, Columbia University, 1933.

**PATMAN, JOHN WILLIAM WRIGHT (1893–1976) D-TX, House 1929–1976.**

**7279.** Andrews, Frank E. *Patman and Foundations: Review and Assessment.* New York: Foundation Center, 1968.

**7280.** Harrison, William B. "Annals of a Crusade: Wright Patman and the Federal Reserve System." *American Journal of Economics and Sociology* 40 (July 1981): 317–320.

**7281.** Owens, John E. "Extreme Advocacy Leadership in the Pre-reform House: Wright Patman and the House Banking and Currency Committee." *British Journal of Political Science* 15 (April 1985): 187–206.

**7282.** Schmelzer, Janet L. "The Early Life and Early Congressional Career of Wright Patman: 1893–1941." Ph.D. dissertation, Texas Christian University, 1978.

**7283.** Sherwood, Edwin D. "Wright Patman and the Bonus Episode." Master's thesis, Lamar University, 1988.

**7284.** Weintraub, Robert E. "Some Neglected Monetary Contributions: Congressman Wright Patman (1893–1976)." *Journal of Money, Credit and Banking* 9 (November 1977): 517–528.

**PATTERSON, JOSIAH (1837–1904) D-TN, House 1891–1897.**

**7285.** Faries, Clyde J. "Carmack Versus Patterson: The Genesis of a Political Feud." *Tennessee Historical Quarterly* 38 (Fall 1979): 332–347.

**PATTERSON, THOMAS MacDONALD (1839–1916) D-CO, House 1875–1876, 1877–1879, Senate 1901–1907.**

**7286.** Smith, Robert E. "Thomas M. Patterson: Colorado Crusader." Ph.D. dissertation, University of Missouri, 1973.

**PATTISON, JOHN M. (1847–1906) D-OH, House 1891–1893.**

**7287.** Smith, Ophia D. "John M. Pattison, 1906." In *Governors of Ohio,* 144–147. Columbus: Ohio Historical Society, 1954.

**PEARCE, JAMES ALFRED (1805–1862) D-MD, House 1835–1839, 1841–1843, Senate 1843–1862.**

**7288.** Steiner, Bernard C. "James Alfred Pearce." *Maryland Historical Magazine* 16 (December 1921): 319–339; 17 (March 1922): 33–47; 17 (June 1922): 177–190; 17 (September 1922): 269–283; 17 (December 1922): 348–363; 18 (December 1923): 341–357; 19 (March 1924): 13–29; 19 (June 1924): 162–178.

**PEARSON, JOSEPH (1776–1834) F-NC, House 1809–1815.**

**7289.** Brown, Stephen W. "Satisfaction at Bladenburg: The Pearson-Jackson Duel of 1809." *North Carolina Historical Review* 58 (Winter 1981): 23–43.

**PEARSON, RICHMOND** (1852–1923) R-NC, House 1895–1899, 1900–1901.

**7290.** Steelman, Joseph F. "Richmond Pearson, Roosevelt Republicans, and the Campaign of 1912 in North Carolina." *North Carolina Historical Review* 43 (Spring 1966): 122–139.

**PEERY, GEORGE CAMPBELL** (1873–1952) D-VA, House 1923–1929.

**7291.** Fry, Joseph A., and Brent Tarter. "The Redemption of the Ninth: The 1922 Congressional Election in the Ninth District of Virginia and the Origins of the Byrd Organization." *South Atlantic Quarterly* 77 (Summer 1978): 352–370.

**PEFFER, WILLIAM ALFRED** (1831–1912) P-KS, Senate 1891–1897.

**7292.** Argersinger, Peter H. "The Most Picturesque Drama: The Kansas Senatorial Election of 1891." *Kansas Historical Quarterly* 38 (Spring 1972): 43–64.

**7293.** ———. *Populism and Politics: William Alfred Peffer and the People's Party.* Lexington: University Press of Kentucky, 1974.

**7294.** Fischer, Roger A. "Rustic Rasputin: William A. Peffer in Color Cartoon Art, 1891–1899." *Kansas History* 11 (Winter 1988/1989): 222–239.

**PELL, HERBERT CLAIBORNE, JR.** (1884–1961) D-NY, House 1919–1921.

**7295.** Baker, Leonard. *Brahmin in Revolt: A Biography of Herbert C. Pell.* Garden City, NY: Doubleday, 1971.

**7296.** Blayney, Michael S. *Democracy's Aristocrat: The Life of Herbert C. Pell.* Lanham, MD: University Press of America, 1986.

**7297.** ———. "Herbert Pell, War Crimes, and the Jews." *American Jewish Historical Quarterly* 65 (June 1976): 335–352.

**7298.** ———. "Honor Among Gentlmen: Herbert Pell, Franklin Roosevelt, and the

Campaign of 1936." *Rhode Island History* 39 (August 1980): 94–102.

**PELLY, THOMAS MINOR** (1902–1973) R-WA, House 1953–1973.

**7299.** Gore, William, and Robert L. Peabody. "The Functions of the Political Campaign: A Case Study." *Western Political Quarterly* 11 (March 1958): 55–70.

**PENDLETON, EDMUND** (1721–1803) VA, Continental Congress 1774–1775.

**7300.** Hilldrup, Robert L. *The Life and Times of Edmund Pendleton.* Chapel Hill: University of North Carolina Press, 1939.

**7301.** Mays, David J. *Edmund Pendleton, 1721–1803: A Biography.* Cambridge, MA: Harvard University Press, 1952.

**PENDLETON, GEORGE HUNT** (1825–1889) D-OH, House 1857–1865, Senate 1879–1885.

**7302.** Bloss, George. *Life and Speeches of George H. Pendleton.* Cincinnati, OH: Miami Printing and Publishing, 1868.

**7303.** Sageser, Adelbert B. "The First Two Decades of the Pendleton Act: A Study of Civil Service Reform." Ph.D. dissertation, University of Nebraska, 1935.

**PENN, JOHN** (1741–1788) NC, Continental Congress 1775–1776, 1777–1780.

**7304.** Sanderson, John. "John Penn." In *Sanderson's Biography of the Signers of the Declaration of Independence,* edited by Robert T. Conrad, 776–778. Philadelphia: Thomas, Cowperthwait, 1848.

**PENNINGTON, WILLIAM** (1796–1862) R-NJ, House 1859–1861.

**7305.** Elmer, Lucius Q. "Governors I Have Known: William Pennington." In his *The Constitution and Government of the Province and State of New Jersey,* 237–258. Newark, NJ: M. R. Dennis and Company, 1872.

**7306.** Nixon, John T. "Election of William Pennington of New Jersey, as Speaker of the Thirty-Sixth Congress." *Proceedings of the New Jersey Historical Society* 2 (1872): 205–220.

**PENROSE, BOIES** (1860–1921) R-PA, Senate 1897–1921.

**7307.** Bowden, Robert D. *Boies Penrose: Symbol of an Era.* New York: Greenberg, 1937.

**7308.** Davenport, Walter. *Power and Glory: The Life of Boies Penrose.* New York: Putnam's, 1931.

**7309.** Stackpole, Edward J. "The Remarkable Career of Boies Penrose." In his *Behind the Scenes with a Newspaper Man: Fifty Years in the Life of an Editor,* 110–123. Philadelphia: Lippincott, 1927.

**PEPPER, CLAUDE DENSON** (1900–1989) D-FL, Senate 1936–1951, House 1963–1989.

**7310.** Clark, James C. "The 1944 Florida Democratic Senate Primary." *Florida Historical Quarterly* 66 (April 1988): 365–384.

**7311.** Hager, M. "Claude Pepper: An Octogenarian for All Seasons." *Perspectives: The Civil Rights Quarterly* 14 (Fall 1982): 12–15.

**7312.** Locke, Francis P. "Claude D. Pepper." In *Public Men In and Out of Office,* edited by John T. Salter, 257–276. Chapel Hill: University of North Carolina, 1946.

**7313.** Pepper, Claude D. *Pepper: Eyewitness to a Century.* New York: Harcourt Brace Jovanovich, 1987.

**7314.** Stoesen, Alexander R. "The Senatorial Career of Claude D. Pepper." Ph.D. dissertation, University of North Carolina, 1965.

**PEPPER, GEORGE WHARTON** (1867–1961) R-PA, Senate 1922–1927.

**7315.** Jones, Edgar D. "George Wharton Pepper." In his *Royalty of the Pulpit,* 355–359. New York: Harper and Row, 1951.

**7316.** Pepper, George W. *Family Quarrels: The President, the Senate, the House.* New York: Baker, Voorhis, 1931.

**7317.** ———. *In the Senate.* Philadelphia: University of Pennsylvania Press, 1930.

**7318.** ———. *Men and Issues: A Selection of Speeches and Articles.* New York: Duffield, 1924.

**7319.** ———. *Philadelphia Lawyer: An Autobiography.* Philadelphia: Lippincott, 1944.

**7320.** Zieger, Robert H. "Senator George Wharton Pepper and Labor Issues in the 1920's." *Labor History* 9 (Spring 1968): 163–183.

**PERCY, CHARLES HARTING** (1919– ) R-IL, Senate 1967–1985.

**7321.** Cleveland, Martha. *Charles Percy: Strong New Voice from Illinois: A Biography.* Jacksonville, IL: Harris Wolfe, 1968.

**7322.** Hartley, Robert E. *Charles H. Percy: A Political Perspective.* Chicago: Rand-McNally, 1975.

**7323.** Murray, David. *Charles Percy of Illinois.* New York: Harper and Row, 1968.

**PERCY, LE ROY** (1860–1929) D-MS, Senate 1910–1913.

**7324.** Baker, Lewis. *The Percys of Mississippi: Politics and Literature in the New South.* Baton Rouge: Louisiana State University Press, 1983.

**PERKINS, GEORGE CLEMENT** (1839–1923) R-CA, Senate 1893–1915.

**7325.** Melendy, Howard B., and Benjamin F. Gilbert. "George C. Perkins." In their *Governors of California: Peter H. Burnett to Edmund G. Brown*, 188–202. Georgetown, CA: Talisman Press, 1965.

**7326.** Reeves, Andree E. "The Committee during the Perkins Years." In his *Congressional Committee Chairman*, 141–178. Lexington: University Press of Kentucky, 1993.

**PETTENGILL, SAMUEL BARRETT**
(1886–1974) D-IN, House 1931–1939.

**7327.** Pettengill, Samuel B. *My Story.* Edited by Helen M. Pettengill. Grafton, VT: H. M. Pettengill, 1979.

**7328.** ———. *Smoke-screen.* New York: Southern, 1940.

**PETTIGREW, EBENEZER** (1783–1848)
W-NC, House 1835–1837.

**7329.** Wall, Bennett H. "Ebenezer Pettigrew's Efforts to Control the Marketing of His Crops." *Agricultural History* 27 (October 1953): 123–132.

**7330.** ———. "Medical Care of Ebenezer Pettigrew's Slaves." *Mississippi Valley Historical Review* 37 (December 1950): 451–470.

**PETTIGREW, RICHARD FRANKLIN**
(1848–1926) R-SD, House 1881–1883, Senate 1889–1901.

**7331.** Hendrickson, Kenneth E. "The Public Career of Richard F. Pettigrew of South Dakota, 1848–1926." Ph.D. dissertation, University of Oklahoma, 1962.

**7332.** McMahon, Dalton E. "Richard Pettigrew's Opposition to Imperialism." *Midwest Review* 8 (1986): 26–39.

**7333.** Olson, Gary D. "Dakota Resources: The Richard F. Pettigrew Papers." *South Dakota History* 12 (Summer/Fall 1982): 182–187.

**7334.** Pettigrew, Richard F. *Imperial Washington: The Story of American Public Life from 1870 to 1920.* New York: Arno Press, 1970.

**PETTIS, JERRY LYLE** (1916–1975) R-CA,
House 1967–1975.

**7335.** Wood, Miriam. *Congressman Jerry L. Pettis.* Mountain View, CA: Pacific Press Publishing Association, 1977.

**PHELAN, JAMES DUVAL** (1861–1930)
D-CA, Senate 1915–1921.

**7336.** Hennings, Robert E. *James D. Phelan and the Wilson Progressives of California.* New York: Garland, 1985.

**7337.** Hunt, Rockwell D. "James Dural Phelan." In his *California's Stately Hall of Fame*, 477–482. Stockton, CA: College of the Pacific, 1950.

**7338.** Kaucher, Dorothy J. *James Duval Phelan: A Portrait, 1861–1930.* Saratoga, CA: Gallery Committee of the Montalvo Association, 1965.

**7339.** Riley, Martha W. "A Rhetorical Biography of Senator James D. Phelan of California Concentrating on the Ways in Which His Rhetoric Constructed Images and Ideas about Asian Immigrants to the United States." Ph.D. dissertation, University of Pittsburgh, 1992.

**7340.** Walsh, James P. *Legacy of a Native Son: James Duval Phelan and Villa Montalvo.* California: Forbes Mill Press, 1993.

**PHELPS, WILLIAM WALTER**
(1839–1894) R-NJ, House 1873–1875,
1883–1889.

**7341.** Herrick, Hugh M., comp. *William Walter Phelps, His Life and Public Services.* New York: Knickerbacker Press, 1904.

**PHILLIPS, PHILIP** (1807–1884) D-AL,
House 1853–1855.

**7342.** Phillips, Philip. "Philip Phillips: Southern Unionist." In *Memoirs of American Jews, 1775–1865*, edited by Jacob R. Marcus, vol. 3, 133–196. Philadelphia: Jewish Publishing Society of America, 1955.

**7343.** Morgan, David T. "Philip Phillips and Internal Improvements in Mid-Nineteenth-Century Alabama." *Alabama Review* 34 (April 1981): 83–93.

**7344.** Simonhoff, Harry. "Philip and Eugenia Phillips, Southern Loyalists." In his *Saga of American Jewry, 1865–1914*, 14–20. New York: Arco, 1959.

### PHILLIPS, WILLIAM ADDISON
**(1824–1893) R-KA House 1873–1879.**

**7345.** Reuter, Paul. "William Phillips and the Development of Foreign Policy, 1933–1947." Ph.D. dissertation, University of Southern Mississippi, 1979.

### PICKENS, ANDREW (1739–1817) SC,
**House 1793–1795.**

**7346.** Waring, Alice N. *Fighting Elder: Andrew Pickens, 1739–1817*. Columbia: University of South Carolina Press, 1962.

### PICKENS, FRANCIS WILKINSON
**(1805–1869) D-SC, House 1834–1843.**

**7347.** Edmunds, John B. *Francis W. Pickens and the Politics of Destruction*. Chapel Hill: University of North Carolina Press, 1986.

### PICKENS, ISRAEL (1780–1827) R-NC/AL,
**House 1811–1817 (NC), Senate 1826 (AL).**

**7348.** Bailey, Hugh C. "Israel Pickens, People's Politician." *Alabama Review* 17 (April 1964): 83–101.

### PICKERING, TIMOTHY (1745–1829)
**F-MA, Senate 1803–1811, House 1813–1817.**

**7349.** Brown, Jeffrey P. "Timothy Pickering and the Northwest Territory." *Northwest Ohio Quarterly* 12 (Summer 1982): 302–316.

**7350.** Clarfield, Gerald H. "Postscript to the Jay Treaty: Timothy Pickering and Anglo-American Relations, 1795–1797." *William and Mary Quarterly* 23 (January 1966): 106–120.

**7351.** Clarfield, Gerald H. *Timothy Pickering and American Diplomacy, 1795–1800*. Columbia: University of Missouri Press, 1969.

**7352.** ———. *Timothy Pickering and the American Republic*. Pittsburgh: University of Pittsburgh Press, 1980.

**7353.** ———. "Timothy Pickering and French Diplomacy, 1795–1796." *Essex Institute Historical Collections* 104 (January 1968): 58–74.

**7354.** ———. "Victory in the West: A Study of the Role of Timothy Pickering in the Successful Consummation of Pickney's Treaty." *Essex Institute Historical Collections* 101 (October 1965): 333–353.

**7355.** Ford, Henry J. "Timothy Pickering." In *The American Secretaries of State and Their Diplomacy*, edited by Samuel F. Bemis, vol. 2, 161–244. New York: Knopf, 1927.

**7356.** Ingersoll, Lurton D. "Hon. Timothy Pickering, Second Secretary of War." In his *A History of the War Department of the United States*, 409–421. Washington, DC: F. B. Mohun, 1879.

**7357.** McLean, David. "Salem, Timothy Pickering, and the American Revolution." *Essex Institute Historical Collections* 111 (January 1975): 65–78.

**7358.** ———. *Timothy Pickering and the Age of the American Revolution*. New York: Arno Press, 1982.

**7359.** Phillips, Edward H. "Timothy Pickering at His Best: Indian Commissioner, 1790–1794." *Essex Institute Historical Collections* 102 (July 1966): 163–202.

**7360.** Pickering, Octavius, and Charles W. Upham. *The Life of Timothy Pickering*. 4 vols. Boston: Little, Brown, 1867–1873.

**7361.** Prentiss, Harvey P. *Timothy Pickering as the Leader of New England Federalism, 1800–1815*. Evanston: Northwestern University, 1934.

**7362.** Swiggett, Howard G. "The First Civil Servants: Oliver Walcott and Timothy Pickering." In his *Forgotten Leaders of the Revolution*, 197–214. Garden City, NY: Doubleday, 1955.

**7363.** Wayne, Anthony. *Anthony Wayne, a Name in Arms: Soldier, Diplomat, Defender of Expansion Westward of a Nation: The Wayne-Knox-Pickering-McHenry Correspondence.* Edited by Richard C. Knopf. Pittsburgh, PA: University of Pittsburgh Press, 1960.

**7364.** Wilbur, William A. "Crisis in Leadership: Alexander Hamilton, Timothy Pickering and the Politics of Federalism 1795–1804." Ph.D. dissertation, Syracuse University, 1969.

**7365.** ———. "Timothy Pickering, Federalist Politician: An Historiographical Perspective." *Historian* 34 (February 1972): 278–292.

**PIERCE, FRANKLIN** (1804–1869) D-NH, House 1833–1837, Senate 1837–1842.

**7366.** Bartlett, David V. *The Life of General Franklin Pierce, of New Hampshire, the Democratic Candidate for President of the United States.* Buffalo, NY: G. H. Derby, 1852.

**7367.** Bell, Carl I. *They Knew Franklin Pierce.* Springfield, VT: April Hill, 1980.

**7368.** Gara, Larry. *The Presidency of Franklin Pierce.* Lawrence: University Press of Kansas, 1991.

**7369.** Hawthorne, Nathaniel. *Life of Franklin Pierce.* Boston: Ticknor, Reed and Fields, 1852.

**7370.** Hoyt, Edwin P. *Franklin Pierce: The Fourteenth President of the United States.* New York: Harper and Row, 1972.

**7371.** Klement, Frank L. "Franklin Pierce and the Treason Charges of 1861–1862." *Historian* 23 (August 1961): 436–448.

**7372.** Nichols, Roy F. *Franklin Pierce, Young Hickory of the Granite Hills.* 2d ed. Philadelphia: University of Pennsylvania Press, 1958.

**7373.** Page, Elwin L. "Franklin Pierce and Abraham Lincoln: Parallels and Contrasts." *Abraham Lincoln Quarterly* 5 (December 1949): 455–472.

**7374.** Taylor, Lloyd C. "A Wife for Mr. Pierce." *New England Quarterly* 28 (September 1955): 339–348.

**PIERCE, WALTER MARCUS** (1861–1954) D-OR, House 1933–1943.

**7375.** Pierce, Walter M. *Oregon Cattleman/Governor/Congressman: Memoirs and Times of Walter M. Pierce.* Edited by Arthur H. Bone. Portland: Oregon Historical Society, 1981.

**7376.** Schwartz, Gerald. "Walter M. Pierce and the Birth Control Movement." *Oregon Historical Quarterly* 88 (Winter 1987): 370–383.

**7377.** ———. "Walter M. Pierce and the Tradition of Progressive Reform: A Study of Eastern Oregon's Great Democrat." Ph.D. dissertation, Washington State University, 1969.

**7378.** Turnbull, George S. "Walter Marcus Pierce." In his *Governors of Oregon*, 72–74. Portland, OR: Binfords, 1959.

**PINCKNEY, CHARLES** (1757–1824) R-SC, Senate, 1798–1801, House, 1819–1821, Continental Congress 1785–1787.

**7379.** Bethea, Andrew. *Contributions of Charles Pinckney to the Formation of the American Union.* Richmond, VA: Garrett and Massis, 1937.

**7380.** Nott, Charles. *The Mystery of the Pinckney Draught.* New York: Century, 1908.

**7381.** Zahniser, Marvin R. *Charles Cotesworth Pinckney: Founding Father.* Chapel Hill: University of North Carolina Press, 1967.

**PINCKNEY, THOMAS** (1750–1828) F-SC, House 1797–1801.

**7382.** Cross, Jack L. *London Mission: The First Critical Years.* East Lansing: Michigan State University Press, 1968.

**7383.** Pinckney, Charles C. *Life of General Thomas Pinckney.* Boston: Houghton Mifflin, 1895.

**7384.** Williams, Frances L. *A Founding Family: The Pinckneys of South Carolina.* New York: Harcourt Brace Jovanovich, 1978.

**PINE, WILLIAM BLISS** (1877–1942) R-OK, Senate 1925–1931.

**7385.** Grant, Philip A., Jr. "'Save the Farmer': Oklahoma Congressmen and Farm Relief Legislation, 1924–1928." *Chronicles of Oklahoma* 64 (Spring 1986): 74–87.

**7386.** Hanson, Maynard J. "Senator William B. Pine and His Times." Ph.D. dissertation, Oklahoma State University, 1983.

**7387.** Jones, Stephen. *Once Before: The Political and Senatorial Careers of Oklahoma's First Two Republican United States Senators, John W. Harreld and W. B. Pine.* Enid, OK: The Dougherty Press, 1986.

**PINKNEY, WILLIAM** (1764–1822) R-MD, House 1791, 1815–1816, Senate 1819–1822.

**7388.** Allen, Max P. "The Early Career of William Pinkney, Diplomat and Constitutional Lawyer." Ph.D. dissertation, Indiana University, 1944.

**7389.** Essary, J. Frederick. "William Pinkney." In his *Maryland in National Politics,* 112–133. Baltimore: John Murphy, 1915.

**7390.** Ireland, Robert M. "The Legal Career of William Pinkney, 1764–1822." New York: Garland, 1986.

**7391.** ———. "William Pinkney: A Revision and Re-emphasis." *American Journal of Legal History* 14 (1970): 235–246.

**7392.** Magoon, Elias L. "William Pinkney, the Accomplished Counsellor." In his *Orators of the American Revolution,* 343–367. New York: Scribner's, 1853.

**7393.** Pinkney, William. *Life of William Pinkney.* New York: Da Capo Press, 1969.

**7394.** Sparks, Jared. "William Pinkney." In his *American Biography,* vol. 5, 117–200. New York: Harper and Brothers, 1902.

**7395.** Wheaton, Henry. *Some Account of the Life, Writings, and Speeches of William Pinkney.* Philadelphia: Small, 1826.

**7396.** Willson, Beckles. "William Pinkney." In his *America's Ambassadors to England (1785–1928),* 94–110. London: Murray, 1928.

**7397.** Wolfgang, Esther M. "The Monroe-Pinkney Treaty." Master's thesis, Indiana University, 1934.

**PITTMAN, KEY** (1872–1940) D-NV, Senate 1913–1940.

**7398.** Cole, Wayne S. "Senator Key Pittman and American Neutrality Policies, 1933–1940." *Mississippi Valley Historical Review* 46 (March 1960): 644–662.

**7399.** Glad, Betty. *Key Pittman: The Tragedy of a Senate Insider.* New York: Columbia University Press, 1986.

**7400.** Israel, Fred L. "The Fulfillment of Bryan's Dream: Key Pittman and Silver Politics." *Pacific Historical Review* 30 (November 1961): 359–380.

**7401.** ———. "Key Pittman and New Deal Politics." *Nevada Historical Society Quarterly* 14 (Fall 1971): 19–26.

**7402.** ———. *Nevada's Key Pittman.* Lincoln: University of Nebraska Press, 1963.

**7403.** Libby, Justin H. "The Irreconcilable Conflict: Key Pittman and Japan during the Interwar Years." *Nevada Historical Society Quarterly* 18 (Fall 1975): 128–139.

**7404.** Porter, David L. "Key Pittman and the Monetary Act of 1939." *Nevada Historical Society Quarterly* 21 (Fall 1978): 205–213.

**7405.** Sewall, Arthur F. "Key Pittman and the Quest for the China Market, 1933–1940." *Pacific Historical Review* 44 (August 1975): 351–371.

**7406.** ———. "Key Pittman, the Senate Foreign Relations Committee, and American Foreign Policy, 1933–1940." Ph.D. dissertation, University of Delaware, 1974.

**7407.** Smith, Harold T. "Pittman, Creel, and New Deal Politics." *Nevada Historical Society Quarterly* 22 (Winter 1979): 254–270.

**PLATT, ORVILLE HITCHCOCK (1827–1905) R-CT, Senate 1879–1905.**

**7408.** Coolidge, Louis A. *Orville H. Platt of Connecticut: An Old Fashioned Senator.* New York: Putnam's, 1910.

**7409.** Smith, Edwina C. "Conservatism in the Gilded Age: The Senatorial Career of Orville H. Platt." Ph.D. dissertation, University of North Carolina, 1976.

**PLATT, THOMAS COLLIER (1833–1910) R-NY, House 1873–1877, Senate 1881, 1897–1909.**

**7410.** Gosnell, Harold F. *Boss Platt and His New York Machine: A Study of the Political Leadership of Thomas C. Platt, Theodore Roosevelt, and Others.* Chicago: University of Chicago Press, 1924.

**7411.** Gosnell, Harold F. "Thomas C. Platt—Political Manager." *Political Science Quarterly* 38 (September 1923): 443–469.

**7412.** McCormick, Richard L. "The Thomas Collier Platt Papers." *Yale University Library Gazette* 50 (July 1975): 46–58.

**7413.** Platt, Thomas C. *The Autobiography of Thomas Collier Platt.* Edited by Louis J. Lang. New York: Dodge, 1910.

**7414.** Russell, Francis. "The Easy Boss: Thomas Collier Platt." In his *President Makers: From Mark Hanna to Joseph P. Kennedy,* 43–85. Boston: Little, Brown, 1976.

**7415.** White, William A. "Platt." In his *Masks in a Pageant,* 30–60. New York: Macmillan, 1928.

**PLUMB, PRESTON B. (1837–1891) R-KS, Senate 1877–1891.**

**7416.** Connelley, William E. *The Life of Preston B. Plumb, 1837–1891.* Chicago: Browne and Howell, 1913.

**PLUMER, WILLIAM (1759–1850) F-NH, Senate 1802–1807.**

**7417.** Plumer, William, Jr. *Life of William Plumer.* Edited by Andrew P. Peabody. New York: Da Capo Press, 1969.

**7418.** Turner, Lynn W. "Electoral Vote against Monroe in 1820—An American Legend." *Mississippi Valley Historical Review* 42 (September 1955): 250–273.

**7419.** ———. *William Plumer of New Hampshire, 1759–1850.* Chapel Hill: University of North Carolina Press, 1962.

**PLUMER, WILLIAM, JR. (1789–1854) NH, House 1819–1825.**

**7420.** Brown, Everett S. *The Missouri Compromise and Presidential Politics, 1820–1825, from the Letters of William Plumer, Jr.* St. Louis: Missouri Historical Society, 1926.

**PLUMMER, FRANKLIN E. (?–1847) J-MS, House 1831–1835.**

**7421.** Cockrell, Thomas D. "United States Senators and Representatives from Mississippi." *Journal of Mississippi History* 49 (February 1987): 35–48.

**7422.** Miles, Edwin A. "Franklin E. Plummer: Piney Woods Spokesman of the Jackson Era." *Journal of Mississippi History* 14 (January 1952): 2–34.

**POAGE, WILLIAM ROBERT (1899–1987) D-TX, House 1937–1978.**

**7423.** Poage, William R. *My First 85 Years.* Waco, TX: Baylor University, 1985.

**POINDEXTER, GEORGE** (1779–1853)
**MS, House 1807–1813, 1817–1819, Senate
1830–1835.**

**7424.** Cockrell, Thomas D. "The Politics
of Land in Jacksonian Mississippi." *Journal
of Mississippi History* 47 (February 1985):
1–14.

**7425.** ———. "United States Senators
and Representatives from Mississippi."
*Journal of Mississippi History* 49 (February
1987): 35–48.

**7426.** Coleman, James P. "Two Irascible
Antebellum Senators: George Poindexter
and Henry S. Foote." *Journal of Mississippi
History* 46 (February 1984): 17–27.

**7427.** Miles, Edwin A. "Andrew Jackson
and Senator George Poindexter." *Journal
of Southern History* 24 (February 1958):
51–66.

**7428.** Smith, Suanna. "George Poindexter: A Political Biography." Ph.D. dissertation, University of Southern Mississippi,
1980.

**7429.** Swearingen, Mack B. *The Early Life
of George Poindexter.* New Orleans: Tulane
University Press, 1934.

**POINDEXTER, MILES** (1868–1946) R-WA,
**House 1909–1911, Senate 1911–1923.**

**7430.** Allen, Howard W. "Miles Poindexter and the Progressive Movement." *Pacific Northwest Quarterly* 53 (July 1962):
114–122.

**7431.** Allen, Howard W. *Poindexter of
Washington: A Study in Progressive Politics.*
Carbondale: Southern Illinois University
Press, 1981.

**POINSETT, JOEL ROBERTS**
(1779–1851) D-SC, House 1821–1825.

**7432.** Cox, Henry B. "Reasons for Joel R.
Poinsett's Refusal of a Second Mission to
South America." *Hispanic American Histori-
cal Review* 43 (August 1963): 405–408.

**7433.** Hruneni, George A. "Palmetto Yankee: The Public Life and Times of Joel
Roberts Poinsett, 1824–1851." Ph.D. dissertation, University of California, 1972.

**7434.** Parton, Dorothy M. "The Diplomatic Career of Joel Roberts Poinsett
(1779–1851)." Ph.D. dissertation,
Catholic University of America, 1934.

**7435.** Putnam, Herbert E. "Joel R. Poinsett: A Biography." Ph.D. dissertation,
Cornell University, 1930.

**7436.** Rippy, James F. *Joel R. Poinsett, Versatile American.* Durham, NC: Duke University Press, 1935.

**7437.** Stoney, Samuel G., ed. "The Poin-
sett-Campbell Correspondence." *South
Carolina Historical and Genealogical Magazine* 42 (April 1941): 31–52; 42 (July 1941):
122–136; 42 (October 1941): 149–168; 43
(January 1942): 27–34.

**7438.** Weber, Ralph E. "Joel R. Poinsett's
Secret Mexican Dispatch Twenty." *South
Carolina Historical Magazine* 75 (April
1974): 67–76.

**POLK, JAMES KNOX** (1795–1849) D-TN,
**House 1825–1839.**

**7439.** Abernethy, Thomas P. "The Origin
of the Whig Party in Tennessee." *Mississippi Valley Historical Review* 12 (March 1926):
504–522.

**7440.** Bassett, John S., ed. "James K. Polk
and His Constituents, 1831–1832." *American Historical Review* 28 (October 1922):
69–77.

**7441.** ———, ed. *The Southern Plantation
Overseer as Revealed in His Letters.* Northampton, MA: Smith College, 1925.

**7442.** Bergeron, Paul H. "James K. Polk
and the Jacksonian Press in Tennessee."
*Tennessee Historical Quarterly* 41 (Fall
1982): 257–277.

**7443.** ———. *The Presidency of James K.
Polk.* Lawrence: University Press of Kansas,
1987.

7444. Burt, Jesse. "Editor Eastman Writes James K. Polk." *East Tennessee Historical Society's Publications* 39 (1967): 103–117.

7445. Chandler, Walter. "Centenary of James K. Polk and His Administration." *West Tennessee Historical Society Papers* 3 (1949): 27–38.

7446. Everett, Robert B. "James K. Polk and the Election of 1844 in Tennessee." *West Tennessee Historical Society Papers* 16 (1962): 5–28.

7447. Goodpasture, Albert V. "The Boyhood of President Polk." *Tennessee Historical Magazine* 7 (April 1921): 36–50.

7448. Hickman, George H. *The Life and Public Services of the Hon. James Knox Polk, with a Compendium of His Speeches on Various Public Measures.* Baltimore: N. Hickman, 1844.

7449. Jenkins, John S. *James Knox Polk.* Auburn, NY: J. M. Alden, 1851.

7450. McCormac, Eugene I. *James K. Polk: A Political Biography.* Berkeley: University of California Press, 1922.

7451. McCoy, Charles A. *Polk and the Presidency.* Austin: University of Texas Press, 1960.

7452. Moore, Powell. "James K. Polk and Tennessee Politics, 1839–1841." *East Tennessee Historical Society's Publications* 9 (1937): 31–52.

7453. ———. "James K. Polk and the 'Immortal Thirteen.'" *East Tennessee Historical Society Publications* 11 (1939): 20–33.

7454. ———. "James K. Polk: Tennessee Politician." *Journal of Southern History* 17 (November 1951): 493–516.

7455. Morell, Martha M. *"Young Hickory," the Life and Times of President James K. Polk.* New York: Dutton, 1949.

7456. Neely, Mark E., Jr. "War and Partisanship: What Lincoln Learned from James K. Polk." *Journal of the Illinois State Historical Society* 74 (Autumn 1981): 199–216.

7457. Polk, Sarah C. "Letters of Mrs. James K. Polk to Her Husband, 1839–1843." *Tennessee Historical Quarterly* 11 (June 1952): 180–191; 11 (September 1952): 282–288.

7458. Pukl, Joseph M. "James K. Polk's Congressional Campaigns, 1829–1833." *Tennessee Historical Quarterly* 40 (Winter 1981): 348–365.

7459. ———. "James K. Polk's Congressional Campaigns of 1835 and 1837." *Tennessee Historical Quarterly* 41 (Summer 1982): 105–123.

7460. ———. "James K. Polk's Early Congressional Campaigns of 1825 and 1827." *Tennessee Historical Quarterly* 39 (Winter 1980): 440–458.

7461. Sellers, Charles G. "The Early Career of James K. Polk, 1795–1839." Ph.D. dissertation, University of North Carolina, 1950.

7462. ———. *James K. Polk.* Princeton, NJ: Princeton University Press, 1957.

7463. ———. *James K. Polk, Continentalist: 1843–1846.* Princeton, NJ: Princeton University Press, 1966.

7464. ———. *James K. Polk, Jacksonian, 1795–1843.* Princeton, NJ: Princeton University Press, 1957.

7465. ———. "James K. Polk's Political Apprenticeship." *East Tennessee Historical Society's Publications* 25 (1953): 37–53.

7466. Severn, William. *Frontier President: James K. Polk.* New York: I. Washburn, 1965.

7467. Stoddard, William O. *William Henry Harrison, John Tyler, and James Knox Polk.* New York: Stokes, 1888.

7468. Trickey, Katharine S. "Young Hickory and Sarah." *Tennessee Valley Historical Review* 1 (Spring 1972): 49–54.

7469. Weaver, Herbert, ed. *Correspondence of James K. Polk.* Nashville, TN: Vanderbilt University Press, 1969.

**7470.** West, Earl I. "Religion in the Life of James K. Polk." *Tennessee Historical Quarterly* 26 (Winter 1967): 357–371.

**7471.** Williams, Frank B. *Tennessee's Presidents.* Knoxville: University of Tennessee Press, 1981.

**POLK, WILLIAM HAWKINS (1815–1862) D-TN, House 1851–1853.**

**7472.** Bergeron, Paul H. "My Brother's Keeper: William H. Polk Goes to School." *North Carolina Historical Review* 44 (Spring 1967): 188–204.

**POMERENE, ATLEE (1863–1937) D-OH, Senate 1911–1923.**

**7473.** Shriver, Phillip R. "The Making of a Moderate Progressive: Atlee Pomerene." Ph.D. dissertation, Columbia University, 1954.

**7474.** Smith, Thomas H. "The Senatorial Career of Atlee Pomerene of Ohio." Ph.D. dissertation, Kent State University, 1966.

**POMEROY, SAMUEL CLARKE (1816–1891) R-KS, Senate 1861–1873.**

**7475.** Gambone, Joseph. "Samuel C. Pomeroy and the Senatorial Election of 1861, Reconsidered." *Kansas Historical Quarterly* 37 (Spring 1971): 15–32.

**7476.** Kitzhaber, Albert. "Gotterdammerung in Topeka: The Downfall of Senator Pomeroy." *Kansas Historical Quarterly* 18 (August 1950): 243–278.

**7477.** Malin, James C. "Some Reconsiderations of the Defeat of Senator Pomeroy of Kansas, 1873." *Mid-America* 48 (January 1966): 47–57.

**POPE, JAMES PINCKNEY (1884–1966) D-ID, Senate 1933–1939.**

**7478.** Sims, Robert C. "James P. Pope, Senator from Idaho." *Idaho Yesterdays* 15 (Fall 1971): 9–15.

**POPE, JOHN (1770–1845) W-KY, Senate 1807–1813, House 1837–1843.**

**7479.** Baylor, Orval W. *John Pope: Kentuckian, His Life and Times, 1770–1845: A Saga of Kentucky Politics from 1792 to 1850.* Cynthiana, KY: Hobson Press, 1943.

**7480.** Blakey, George T. "Rendezvous with Republicanism: John Pope vs. Henry Clay in 1816." *Indiana Magazine of History* 62 (September 1966): 233–250.

**POPE, NATHANIEL (1784–1850) IL, House 1816–1818.**

**7481.** Bloom, Jo T. "Peaceful Politics: The Delegates from Illinois Territory, 1809–1818." *Old Northwest* 6 (Fall 1980): 203–215.

**PORTER, ALEXANDER (1786–1844) W-LA, Senate 1833–1837.**

**7482.** Stephenson, Wendell H. *Alexander Porter: Whig Planter of Old Louisiana.* Baton Rouge: Louisiana State University Press, 1934.

**PORTER, PETER BUELL (1773–1844) R-NY, House 1809–1813, 1815–1816.**

**7483.** Grande, Joseph A. "The Political Career of Peter Buell Porter, 1797–1829." Ph.D. dissertation, University of Notre Dame, 1971.

**7484.** Roland, Daniel D. "Peter Buell Porter and Self-Interest in American Politics." Ph.D. dissertation, Claremont Graduate School, 1990.

**POSEY, THOMAS (1750–1818) LA, Senate 1812–1813.**

**7485.** Sparks, Jared. "Memoir of Thomas Posey, Major General and Governor of Indiana." In his *Library of American Biography,* vol. 9, 359–403. Boston: Little Brown, 1852.

## POSTON, CHARLES DEBRILLE
(1825–1902) R-AZ, House 1864–1865.

**7486.** Gressinger, Alfred W. *Charles D. Poston, Sunland Seer.* Globe, AZ: D. S. King, 1961.

**7487.** Poston, Lawrence, ed. "Poston vs. Goodwin: A Document on the Congressional Election of 1865." *Arizona and the West* 3 (Winter 1961): 351–354.

## POTTER, ALLEN (1818–1885) D-MI,
House 1875–1877.

**7488.** McCarthy, Joseph P. *A Tribute to Mr. and Mrs. Allen Potter.* Kalamazoo, MI: Inling Bros. Everard Co., 1910.

## POTTER, CHARLES EDWARD
(1916–1979) R-MI, House 1947–1952, Senate 1952–1959.

**7489.** Potter, Charles E. *Days of Shame.* New York: Coward-McCann, 1965.

## POTTER, CLARKSON NOTT
(1825–1882) D-NY, House 1869–1875, 1877–1879.

**7490.** Guenther, Karen. "Potter Committee Investigation of the Disputed Election of 1876." *Florida Historical Quarterly* 16 (January 1983): 281–295.

**7491.** Vazzano, Frank P. "The Louisiana Question Resurrected: The Potter Commission and the Election of 1876." *Louisiana History* 61 (Winter 1975): 39–57.

## POTTER, JOHN FOX (1817–1899) R-WI,
House 1857–1863.

**7492.** Riley, Ben A. "The Pryor-Potter Affair: Nineteenth Century Civilian Conflict as Precursor to Civil War." *Journal of the West Virginia Historical Association* 8 (Spring 1984): 29–40.

## POTTER, ROBERT (1800–1842) JNC,
House 1829–1831.

**7493.** Fisher, Ernest G. *Robert Potter: Founder of the Texas Navy.* Gretna, LA: Pelican, 1976.

**7494.** Shearer, Ernest C. *Robert Potter, Remarkable North Carolinian and Texan.* Houston: University of Houston Press, 1951.

## POTTS, RICHARD (1753–1808) MD,
Senate 1793–1796, Continental Congress 1781.

**7495.** Steiner, Lewis H. "A Memoir of Hon. Richard Potts." *Maryland Historical Magazine* 5 (March 1910): 63–68.

## POWELL, ADAM CLAYTON, JR.
(1908–1972) D-NY, House 1945–1967, 1969–1971.

**7496.** Alexander, E. Curtin. *Adam Clayton Powell, Jr.: A Black Power Political Educator.* New York: ECA Associates, 1983.

**7497.** Capeci, Dominic J. "From Different Liberal Perspectives: Fiorello La Guardia, Adam Clayton Powell, Jr., and Civil Rights in New York City 1941–1943." *Journal of Negro History* 62 (April 1977): 160–173.

**7498.** ———. "From Harlem to Montgomery: The Bus Boycotts and Leadership of Adam Clayton Powell, Jr. and Martin Luther King, Jr." *Historian* 41 (August 1979): 721–737.

**7499.** ———. *Harlem Riot of 1943.* Philadelphia: Temple University Press, 1977.

**7500.** Chapman, Gil. *Adam Clayton Powell, Saint or Sinner?* San Diego: Publishers Export Company, 1967.

**7501.** Christopher, Maurine. "Adam Clayton Powell, Jr./New York." In her *Black Americans in Congress,* 194–208. Rev. ed. New York: Thomas Y. Crowell Company, 1976.

**7502.** Coleman, Emmett. *Rise, Fall, and . . .? of Adam Clayton Powell.* New York: Bee-line Books, 1967.

**7503.** Dionisopoulos, P. Allan. *Rebellion, Racism, and Representation: The Adam Clayton Powell Case and Its Antecedents.* Dekalb: Northern Illinois University Press, 1970.

**7504.** Hamilton, Charles V. *Adam Clayton Powell, Jr., the Political Biography of an American Dilemma.* New York: Macmillan, 1991.

**7505.** Haskins, James S. "Adam Clayton Powell, Jr." In his *Profiles in Black Power,* 31–59. Garden City, NY: Doubleday, 1972.

**7506.** ———. *Adam Clayton Powell: Portrait of a Marching Black.* Trenton, NJ: Africa World Press, 1993.

**7507.** Haygood, Wil. *King of the Cats: The Life and Times of Adam Clayton Powell, Jr.* Boston: Houghton Mifflin, 1993.

**7508.** Hickey, Neil, and Ed Edwin. *Adam Clayton Powell and the Politics of Race.* New York: Fleet Publishing Corporation, 1965.

**7509.** Jacobs, Andy. *The Powell Affair: Freedom Minus One.* Indianapolis: Bobbs-Merrill, 1973.

**7510.** Kindregan, Charles P. "The Cases of Adam Clayton Powell, Jr., and Julian Bond: The Right of Legislative Bodies to Exclude Members-Elect." *Suffolk University Law Review* 2 (Winter 1968): 58–80.

**7511.** Kinney, John W. "Adam Clayton Powell, Sr. and Adam Clayton Powell, Jr.: A Historical Exposition and Theological Analysis." Ph.D. dissertation, Columbia University, 1979.

**7512.** Lewis, Claude. *Adam Clayton Powell.* New York: Fawcett, 1963.

**7513.** Paris, Peter J. *Black Leaders in Conflict: Joseph H. Jackson, Martin Luther King, Jr., Malcolm X, Adam Clayton Powell, Jr.* Princeton, NJ: Pilgrim Press, 1978.

**7514.** Powell, Adam C. *Adam by Adam.* New York: Dial Press, 1971.

**7515.** ———. *Keep the Faith Baby!* New York: Trident Press, 1967.

**7516.** ———. *Marching Blacks.* New York: Dial Press, 1945.

**7517.** Reeves, Andree E. "The Chairmanship of Adam Clayton Powell, Jr." In his *Congressional Committee Chairman.* Lexington: The University Press of Kentucky, 1993.

**7518.** Toppin, Edgar A. "Powell, Adam Clayton, Jr." In his *Biographical History of Blacks in America since 1528,* 388–391. New York: McKay, 1971.

**7519.** Weeks, Kent M. *Adam Clayton Powell and the Supreme Court.* Port Washington, NY: Dunellen, 1971.

**7520.** Wilson, James Q. "Two Negro Politicians: An Interpretation." *Midwest Journal of Political Science* 4 (November 1960): 346–369.

**POWELL, LEVEN** (1737–1810) F-VA, **House 1799–1801.**

**7521.** Powell, Leven. "Correspondence of Col. Leven Powell, M. C., Relating to the Election of 1800." *John P. Branch Historical Papers of Randolph-Macon College* 1 (1901): 54–63.

**7522.** ———. "The Leven Powell Correspondence." *John P. Branch Historical Papers of Randolph-Macon College* 2 (1902): 111–138.

**7523.** ———. "The Leven Powell Correspondence." *John P. Branch Historical Papers of Randolph-Macon College* 3 (1903): 217–253.

**7524.** Powell, Robert C., ed. *A Biographical Sketch of Col. Leven Powell.* Alexandria, VA: G. H. Ramey, 1877.

**PRATT, DANIEL DARWIN** (1813–1877) **R-IN, Senate 1869–1875.**

**7525.** Holliday, Joseph E. "Daniel D. Pratt: Lawyer and Legislator." *Indiana Magazine of History* 57 (June 1961): 99–126.

**7526.** ———. "Daniel D. Pratt: Senator and Commissioner." *Indiana Magazine of History* 58 (March 1962): 17–50.

**PRATT, RUTH SEARS BAKER**
**(1877–1965) R-NY, House 1929–1933.**

**7527.** Gilfond, Duff. "Gentlewomen of the House." *American Mercury* 18 (October 1929): 151–163.

**PRENTISS, SAMUEL (1782–1857) W-VT,**
**Senate 1831–1842.**

**7528.** Binney, Charles J. *Memoirs of Judge Samuel Prentiss of Montpelier, Vermont, and His Wife.* Boston: N.p., 1883.

**PRENTISS, SEARGEANT SMITH**
**(1808–1850) MS, House 1838–1839.**

**7529.** Dickey, Dallas C. *Seargeant S. Prentiss, Whig Orator of the Old South.* Baton Rouge: Louisiana State University Press, 1945.

**7530.** Prentiss, George L. *A Memoir of S. S. Prentiss.* 2 vols. New York: Scribner's, 1855.

**7531.** Rowland, Dunbar. "Seargeant Smith Prentiss." In *Library of Southern Literature,* edited by Edwin A. Alderman and Joel C. Harris, vol. 10, 4209–4214. New Orleans: Martin and Hoyt, 1909.

**7532.** Shields, Joseph D. *Life and Times of Seargeant Smith Prentiss.* Freeport, NY: Books for Libraries, 1971.

**PRESSLER, LARRY LEE (1942– ) R-SD,**
**House 1975–1979, Senate 1979– .**

**7533.** Clem, Alan L. "The Case of the Upstart Republican: The First District of South Dakota." In *The Making of Congressmen: Seven Campaigns of 1974,* edited by Alan L. Clem, 127–165. North Scituate, MA: Duxbury Press, 1976.

**PRESTON, WILLIAM CAMPBELL**
**(1794–1860) W-SC, Senate 1833–1842.**

**7534.** Magoon, Elias L. "William C. Preston: The Inspired Declaimer." In his *Living Orators in America,* 347–407. Dublin: J. M'Glashan, 1849.

**7535.** Preston, William C. *The Reminiscences of William C. Preston.* Edited by Minnie C. Yarborough. Chapel Hill: University of North Carolina Press, 1933.

**7536.** Venable, Francis P. "William Campbell Preston." In *Library of Southern Literature,* edited by Edwin A. Alderman and Joel C. Harris, vol. 10, 4255–4259. New Orleans: Martin and Hoyt, 1909.

**PRICE, DAVID EUGENE (1940– ) D-NC,**
**House 1987–1995.**

**7537.** Price, David E. *The Congressional Experience: A View from the Hill.* Boulder, CO: Westview, 1992.

**PRICE, STERLING (1809–1867) D-MO,**
**House 1845–1846.**

**7538.** Castel, Albert E. *General Sterling Price and the Civil War in the West.* Baton Rouge: Louisiana State University Press, 1968.

**7539.** Rea, Ralph R. *Sterling Price: The Lee of the West.* Little Rock, AK: Pioneer Press, 1959.

**7540.** Shalhope, Robert E. *Sterling Price, Portrait of a Southerner.* Columbia: University of Missouri Press, 1971.

**PRINCE, OLIVER HILLHOUSE**
**(1787–1837) GA, Senate 1828–1829.**

**7541.** Nirenstein, Virginia. *With Kindly Voices: A Nineteenth Century Georgia Family.* Macon, GA: Tullous Books, 1984.

**PROCTOR, REDFIELD (1831–1908)**
**R-VT, Senate 1891–1908.**

**7542.** Bowie, Chester W. "Redfield Proctor: A Biography." Ph.D. dissertation, University of Wisconsin, 1980.

**7543.** Cooley, Roger G. "Redfield Proctor: A Study in Leadership: The Vermont Period." Ph.D. dissertation, University of Rochester, 1955.

**7544.** Partridge, Frank C. "Redfield Proctor, His Public Life and Services." *Vermont Historical Society* (1913–1914): 59–104.

**7545.** Quimby, Rollin W., and Michelle B. Davis. "Senator Proctor's Cuban Speech: Speculations on a Cause of the Spanish-American War." *Quarterly Journal of Speech* 55 (April 1969): 131–141.

**PROXMIRE, WILLIAM (1915–  ) D-WI, Senate 1957–1989.**

**7546.** Proxmire, Ellen. *One Foot in Washington, the Perilous Life of a Senator's Wife.* Washington, DC: Luce, 1963.

**7547.** Sykes, Jay G. *Proxmire.* Washington, DC: Luce, 1972.

**PRYOR, ROGER ATKINSON (1828–1919) D-VA, House 1859–1861.**

**7548.** Holzman, Robert S. *Adapt or Perish: The Life of General Roger A. Pryor, C.S.A.* Hamden, CT: Archon Books, 1976.

**7549.** Pryor, Sara A. *Reminiscences of Peace and War.* Freeport, NY: Books for Libraries, 1970.

**7550.** Riley, Ben A. "The Pryor-Potter Affair: Nineteenth Century Civilian Conflict as Precursor to Civil War." *Journal of The West Virginia Historical Association* 8 (Spring 1984): 29–40.

**PULITZER, JOSEPH (1847–1911) D-NY, House 1885–1886.**

**7551.** Barrett, James W. *Joseph Pulitzer and His World.* New York: Vanguard Press, 1941.

**7552.** ———. *The World, the Flesh and Messrs. Pulitzer.* New York: Vanguard Press, 1931.

**7553.** Beard, Annie E. "A Great Journalist and Philanthropist: Joseph Pulitzer." In her *Our Foreign-Born Citizens,* 194–201. New York: Crowell, 1922.

**7554.** Heaton, John L. *The Story of a Page.* New York: Arno Press, 1913.

**7555.** Ireland, Alleyne. *An Adventure with a Genius: Recollections of Joseph Pulitzer.* New York: Dutton, 1920.

**7556.** ———. *Joseph Pulitzer: Reminiscences of a Secretary.* New York: M. Kennerley, 1914.

**7557.** Juergens, George. *Joseph Pulitzer and the New York World.* Princeton, NJ: Princeton University Press, 1966.

**7558.** Noble, Iris. *Joseph Pulitzer: Front Page Pioneer.* New York: J. Messner, 1957.

**7559.** Payne, George H. "The Melodrama in the News." In his *History of Journalism in the United States,* 360–369. New York: D. Appleton, 1920.

**7560.** Pfaff, Daniel W. *Joseph Pulitzer II and the Post-Dispatch: A Newspaperman's Life.* University Park: Pennsylvania State University Park, 1991.

**7561.** Rammelkamp, Julian S. *Pulitzer's Post-Dispatch, 1878–1883.* Princeton, NJ: Princeton University Press, 1967.

**7562.** Seitz, Don C. *Joseph Pulitzer: His Life and Letters.* Garden City, NJ: Garden City Publishing Company, 1927.

**7563.** Swanberg, William A. *Pulitzer.* New York: Scribner's, 1967.

**QUAY, MATTHEW STANLEY (1833–1904) R-PA, Senate 1887–1899, 1901–1904.**

**7564.** Blair, William A. "A Practical Politician: The Boss Tactics of Matthew Stanley Quay." *Pennsylvania History* 56 (April 1989): 77–92.

**7565.** Kehl, James A. *Boss Rule in the Gilded Age: Matt Quay of Pennsylvania.* Pittsburgh: University of Pittsburgh Press, 1981.

**7566.** Oliver, John W. "Matthew Stanley Quay." *Western Pennsylvania Historical Magazine* 17 (March 1934): 1–12.

**QUAYLE, JAMES DANFORTH "DAN"**
(1947– ) R-IN, House 1977–1981, Senate
1981–1989.

**7567.** Bonafede, Dom. "The Last American Viceroyalty: Dan Quayle and Vice Presidency." *Congress and Presidency* 16 (Spring 1989): 57–66.

**7568.** Broder, David S., and Bob Woodward. *The Man Who Would Be President.* New York: Simon and Schuster, 1992.

**7569.** Fenno, Richard F. *The Making of a Senator: Dan Quayle.* Washington, DC: CQ Press, 1989.

**QUEZON, MANUEL LUIS** (1878–1944)
**NAT-PI House 1909–1916.**

**7570.** Goettel, Elinor. *Eagle of the Philippines: President Manuel Quezon.* New York: J. Messner, 1970.

**7571.** Gopinath, Aruna. *Manuel L. Quezon: The Tutelary Democrat.* Detroit, MI: New Day Publishers, 1987.

**7572.** Gwekoh, Sol H. *Manuel L. Quezon, His Life and Career: A Philippine President Biography.* Manila: University Publishing Company, 1948.

**QUINCY, JOSIAH** (1772–1864) F-MA,
**House 1805–1813.**

**7573.** Chamberlain, Mellen. *Josiah Quincy, the Great Mayor.* Boston: The Society, 1889.

**7574.** Everett, Edward. "Josiah Quincy: The Administration of President Quincy." In his *Orations,* vol. 4, 684–697. Boston: Little, Brown, 1879.

**7575.** Lowell, James R. "A Great Public Character." In his *Complete Writings,* vol. 2, 1–49, 272–312. Boston: Houghton Mifflin, 1904.

**7576.** McCaughey, Robert A. *Josiah Quincy, 1772–1864, the Last Federalist.* Cambridge, MA: Harvard University Press, 1974.

**7577.** Muzzey, Artemas B. "Quincy Family." In his *Reminiscences and Memorials of Men of the Revolution and Their Families,* 81–100. Boston: Estes and Lauriat, 1883.

**7578.** Nash, George H. "From Radicalism to Revolution: The Political Career of Josiah Quincy, Jr." *Proceedings of the American Antiquarian Society* 79 (October 15, 1969): 253–290.

**7579.** Quincy, Edmund. *Life of Josiah Quincy of Massachusetts.* Boston: Ticknor and Fields, 1867.

**7580.** Quincy, Josiah. *Memoir of the Life of Josiah Quincy.* New York: Da Capo Press, 1971.

**QUITMAN, JOHN ANTHONY**
(1799–1858) D-MS, House 1855–1858.

**7581.** Claiborne, John F. *Life and Correspondence of John A. Quitman.* 2 vols. New York: Harper, 1860.

**7582.** May, Robert E. *John A. Quitman: Old South Crusader.* Baton Rouge: Louisiana State University Press, 1985.

**7583.** ———. "Squatter Sovereignty as the Freeport Doctrine: A Note on the Territorial Controversy in the U.S. House of Representatives in the Winter of 1855–1856." *Journal of Southern History* 53 (May 1987): 304–306.

**7584.** McLendon, James H. "John A. Quitman." Ph.D. dissertation, University of Texas, 1949.

෴

**RAILSBACK, THOMAS FISHER**
(1932– ) R-IL, House 1967–1983.

**7585.** Nollen, Shelia H. "Thomas F. Railsback and His Congressional Papers." *Western Illinois Regional Studies* 9 (1986): 59–74.

## RAINEY, HENRY THOMAS (1860–1934)
D-IL, House 1903–1921, 1923–1934.

**7586.** Baker, William E. "The Political Career of Henry T. Rainey, 1903–1934." Master's thesis, University of Maryland, 1953.

**7587.** Block, Marvin W. "Henry T. Rainey of Illinois." *Journal of the Illinois State Historical Society* 65 (Summer 1972): 142–157.

**7588.** ———. "Henry Thomas Rainey: Some Major Aspects of His Legislative Career." Master's thesis, Illinois State Normal University, 1960.

**7589.** Graff, Helen E. "Henry T. Rainey: An American Statesman." Master's thesis, State University of Iowa, 1933.

**7590.** Treadway, Allen T. "The Amherst Illustrious: The Congressional Leaders— Rainey, '83, and Snell, '94." *Amherst Graduates' Quarterly* 22 (May 1933): 209–218.

**7591.** Uhle, Lee. "Gadfly Rainey." *Illinois History* 22 (May 1969): 186–187.

**7592.** Waller, Robert A. *Rainey of Illinois: A Political Biography, 1903–34.* Urbana: University of Illinois Press, 1977.

**7593.** ———. "The Selection of Henry T. Rainey as Speaker of the House." *Capital Studies* 2 (Spring 1973): 37–47.

## RAINEY, JOSEPH HAYNE (1832–1887)
R-SC, House 1870–1879.

**7594.** Christopher, Maurine. "Joseph H. Rainey/South Carolina and Jefferson F. Long/Georgia." In her *Black Americans in Congress,* 25–37. Rev. ed. New York: Thomas Y. Crowell Company, 1976.

**7595.** Packwood, Cyril O. *Detour—Bermuda, Destination—U.S. House of Representatives: The Life of Joseph Hayne Rainey.* Hamilton, Bermuda: Baxter's, 1977.

## RAMSAY, DAVID (1749–1815) SC,
Continental Congress 1782–1783, 1785–1786.

**7596.** Hensel, William U. "Dr. David Ramsay." *Lancaster County Historical Society Papers* 10 (1906): 357–367.

**7597.** Kent, Charles W. "David Ramsay." In *Library of Southern Literature,* edited by Edwin A. Alderman and Joel C. Harriss, vol. 10, 4295–4297. New Orleans: Martin and Hoyt, 1909.

**7598.** Shaffer, Arthur H. *To Be an American: David Ramsay and the Making of the American Consciousness.* Columbia: University of South Carolina Press, 1991.

**7599.** Smith, William R. "David Ramsay: Moral Historian." In his *History as Argument: Three Patriot Historians of the American Revolution,* 42–72. The Hague: Mouton, 1966.

## RAMSEY, ALEXANDER (1815–1903)
R-MN, House 1843–1847, Senate 1863–1875.

**7600.** Baker, James H. "Alexander Ramsey." *Minnesota Historical Society Collections* 13 (1908): 1–46.

**7601.** Guentzel, Richard D. "Alexander Ramsey: First Territorial and Second State Governor of Minnesota." Ph.D. dissertation, University of Nebraska, 1976.

**7602.** Hayland, John C. "Alexander Ramsey and the Republican Party, 1855–1875: A Study in Personal Politics." Ph.D. dissertation, University of Minnesota, 1961.

**7603.** Kennedy, Roger G. "Alexander Ramsey." In his *Men on the Moving Frontier,* 39–73. Palo Alto, CA: American West, 1969.

**7604.** Ryland, William J. "Alexander Ramsey: Frontier Politician." Ph.D. dissertation, Yale University, 1930.

**7605.** Swanholm, Marx. *Alexander Ramsey and the Politics of Survival.* St. Paul: Minnesota Historical Society, 1977.

**RAMSEY, NATHANIEL (1741–1817) MD, Continental Congress 1785–1787.**

**7606.** Brand, William F. *A Sketch of the Life and Character of Nathaniel Ramsey.* Baltimore: J. Murphy, 1887.

**RAMSEYER, CHRISTIAN WILLIAM (1875–1943) R-IA, House 1915–1933.**

**7607.** Porter, David L. "Iowa Congressional Delegation and the Great Economic Issues, 1929–1933." *Annals of Iowa* 46 (Summer 1982): 337–354.

**RANDALL, SAMUEL JACKSON (1828–1890) D-PA, House 1863–1890.**

**7608.** Adams, Thomas R. "The Samuel J. Randall Papers." *Pennsylvania History* 21 (January 1954): 45–54.

**7609.** House, Albert V., Jr. "Contributions of Samuel J. Randall to the Rules of the National House of Representatives." *American Political Science Review* 29 (October 1935): 837–841.

**7610.** ———. "The Political Career of Samuel Jackson Randall." Ph.D. dissertation, University of Wisconsin, 1934.

**RANDALL, WILLIAM HARRISON (1812–1881) UU-KY, House 1863–1867.**

**7611.** Hood, James L. "For the Union: Kentucky's Unconditional Unionist Congressmen and the Development of the Republican Party in Kentucky, 1863–1865." *Register of the Kentucky Historical Society* 76 (July 1978): 197–215.

**RANDOLPH, EDMUND JENNINGS (1753–1813) VA, Continental Congress 1779–1782.**

**7612.** Reardon, John J. *Edmund Randolph.* New York: Macmillan, 1975.

**RANDOLPH, JOHN (1773–1833) VA, House 1799–1813, 1815–1817, 1819–1825, 1827–1829, 1833, Senate, 1825–1827.**

**7613.** Adams, Henry. *John Randolph.* 10th ed. Boston: Houghton Mifflin, 1882.

**7614.** Baldwin, Joseph G. "John Randolph of Roanoke." In his *Party Leaders,* 135–276. New York: D. Appleton and Company, 1855.

**7615.** Bowers, Claude G. "The Leaders, Portrait of Randolph." In his *Jefferson in Power,* 96–113. Boston: Houghton Mifflin, 1936.

**7616.** Bradford, Gamaliel. "John Randolph of Roanoke." In his *Damaged Souls,* 121–156. Boston: Houghton Mifflin, 1923.

**7617.** Bruce, Philip A. "John Randolph." In *Library of Southern Literature,* edited by Edwin A. Alderman and Joel C. Harris, vol. 10, 4329–4334. New Orleans: Martin and Hoyt, 1909.

**7618.** ———. "John Randolph of Roanoke." In his *The Virginia Plutarch,* vol. 2, 115–132. Chapel Hill: University of North Carolina Press, 1929.

**7619.** Bruce, William C. *John Randolph of Roanoke, 1773–1833.* 2 vols. New York: Putnam's, 1922.

**7620.** Carson, David A. "That Ground Called Quiddism: John Randolph's War with the Jefferson Administration." *Journal of American Studies* 20 (April 1986): 71–92.

**7621.** Dawidoff, Robert. *Education of John Randolph.* New York: Norton, 1979.

**7622.** Fishwick, Marshall W. "Randolph of Roanoke." In his *Gentlemen of Virginia,* 160–176. New York: Dodd, Mead, 1961.

**7623.** Garland, Hugh A. *The Life of John Randolph of Roanoke.* 2 vols. New York: Appleton, 1850.

**7624.** Hines, Jack W. "John Randolph and the Growth of Federal Power: The

Opinions of a States Righter on the Political Issues of His Time." Ph.D. dissertation, University of Kansas, 1957.

**7625.** Hubbell, Jay B. "John Randolph of Roanoke." In his *South in American Literature, 1607–1900,* 223–229. Durham, NC: Duke University Press, 1954.

**7626.** Johnson, Gerald W. *Randolph of Roanoke: A Political Fantastic.* New York: Minton, Balch, 1929.

**7627.** Jordan, Daniel P. "John Randolph of Roanoke and the Art of Winning Elections in Jeffersonian Virginia." *Virginia Magazine of History and Biography* 86 (October 1978): 389–407.

**7628.** Kirk, Russell. *John Randolph of Roanoke: A Study in American Politics.* Chicago: Regnery, 1964.

**7629.** ———. *Randolph of Roanoke: A Study in Conservative Thought.* Chicago: University of Chicago Press, 1951.

**7630.** Magoon, Elias L. "John Randolph, the Impersonation of Sarcasm." In his *Orators of the American Revolution,* 421–456. New York: Scribner's, 1853.

**7631.** Parton, James. "John Randolph." In his *Famous Americans of Recent Times,* 773–819. Boston: Houghton Mifflin, 1895.

**7632.** Quincy, Josiah. "Visits to John Randolph: Randolph in the Senate." In his *Figures of the Past from the Leaves of Old Journals,* 175–191. Boston: Little, Brown, 1926.

**7633.** Randolph, John. *Letters of John Randolph, to a Young Relative.* Philadelphia: Carey, Lea and Blanchard, 1834.

**7634.** Sherwood, Henry N. "The Settlement of the John Randolph Slaves in Ohio." *Mississippi Valley Historical Association Proceedings* 5 (1911–1912): 39–59.

**7635.** Spaulding, Myra L. "Dueling in the District of Columbia." *Columbia Historical Society Records* 29/30 (1928): 117–210.

**7636.** Spaulding, Thomas M. "Clay versus Randolph." *Michigan Quarterly Review* 1 (Winter 1962): 8–13.

**7637.** Thomas, Frederick W. *John Randolph, of Roanoke, and Other Sketches of Character, Including William Wirt.* Philadelphia: Carey and Hart, 1853.

**7638.** Trent, William P. "John Randolph of Roanoke." In his *Southern Statesmen of the Old Regime,* 89–152. New York: Crowell, 1897.

## RANDOLPH, PEYTON (1721–1775) VA, Continental Congress 1774–1775.

**7639.** Delaplaine, Joseph. "Life of Peyton Randolph." In his *Delaplaine's Repository of the Lives and Portraits of Distinguished American Characters,* vol. 1, pt. 2, 107–123. Philadelphia: W. Brown, 1817.

**7640.** Hayden, Sidney S. "Peyton Randolph." In his *Washington and His Masonic Compeers,* 260–274. New York: Masonic Publishing and Manufacturing Company, 1867.

**7641.** Reardon, John J. *Peyton Randolph, 1721–1775, One Who Presided.* Durham, NC: Carolina Academic Press, 1982.

## RANDOLPH, THOMAS MANN (1768–1828) R-VA, House 1803–1807.

**7642.** Gaines, William H. *Thomas Mann Randolph: Jefferson's Son-in-Law.* Baton Rouge: Louisiana State University Press, 1966.

## RANGEL, CHARLES BERNARD (1930– ) D-NY, HOUSE 1971– .

**7643.** Christopher, Maurine. "Charles B. Rangel/New York." In her *Black Americans in Congress,* 262. Rev. ed. New York: Thomas Y. Crowell, 1976.

**RANKIN, JEANNETTE** (1880–1973)
**R-MT, House 1917–1919, 1941–1943.**

**7644.** Block, Judy R. *The First Woman in Congress: Jeannette Rankin.* New York: C.P.I., 1978.

**7645.** Board, John C. "Jeannette Rankin: The Lady from Montana." *Montana* 17 (July 1967): 2–17.

**7646.** ———. "The Lady from Montana: Jeannette Rankin." Master's thesis, University of Wyoming, 1964.

**7647.** Giles, Kevin S. *Flight of the Dove: The Story of Jeannette Rankin.* Beaverton, OR: Touchstone Press, 1980.

**7648.** Hardaway, Roger D. "Jeannette Rankin: The Early Years." *North Dakota Quarterly* 48 (Winter 1980): 62–68.

**7649.** Harris, Ted C. "Jeannette Rankin: Suffragist, First Woman Elected to Congress, and a Pacifist." Ph.D. dissertation, University of Georgia, 1972.

**7650.** ———. "Jeannette Rankin, Warring Pacifist." Master's thesis, University of Georgia, 1969.

**7651.** Hinckle, Warren, and Marianne Hinckle. "History of the Rise of the Unusual Movement for Power in the United States, 1961–1968." *Ramparts Magazine* 6 (February 1968): 22–26.

**7652.** Josephson, Hannah. *Jeannette Rankin, First Lady in Congress: A Biography.* Indianapolis: Bobbs-Merrill, 1974.

**7653.** Richey, Elinor. "Jeannette Rankin: Woman of Commitment." In her *Eminent Women of the West*, 181–207. Berkeley, CA: Howell-North Books, 1975.

**7654.** Schaffer, Ronald. "Jeannette Rankin, Progressive Isolationist." Ph.D. dissertation, Princeton University, 1959.

**7655.** White, Florence M. *First Woman in Congress, Jeannette Rankin.* New York: J. Messner, 1980.

**7656.** Wilson, Joan H. "Peace Is a Woman's Job: Jeannette Rankin and American Foreign Policy: The Origins of her Pacifism." *Montana: Magazine of Western History* 30 (January 1980) 28–41.

**RANKIN, JOHN ELLIOTT** (1882–1960)
**D-MS, House 1921–1953.**

**7657.** Grant, Philip A., Jr. "The Mississippi Congressional Delegation and the Formation of the Conservative Coalition." *Journal of Mississippi History* 50 (February 1988): 21–28.

**RANSDELL, JOSEPH EUGENE** (1858–1954) **D-LA, House 1899–1913, Senate 1913–1931.**

**7658.** Flynn, George Q. "A Louisiana Senator and the Underwood Tariff." *Louisiana History* 10 (Winter 1969): 5–39.

**7659.** LaBorde, Adras P. *National Southerner: Ransdell of Louisiana.* New York: Benziger, 1951.

**RANSIER, ALONZO JACOB** (1834–1882)
**R-SC, HOUSE 1873–1875.**

**7660.** Christopher, Maurine. "Robert C. DeLarge and Alonzo J. Ransier/South Carolina." In her *Black Americans in Congress*, 97–103. Rev. ed. New York: Thomas Y. Crowell Company, 1976.

**RANSOM, MATT WHITAKER** (1826–1904) **D-NC, Senate 1872–1895.**

**7661.** Edmunds, Pocahontas W. "Matt Whitaker Ranson: Courtly General and Senator." In her *Tar Heels Track the Century*, 71–93. Raleigh, NC: Edwards and Broughton, 1966.

**RANTOUL, ROBERT, JR.** (1805–1852)
**D-MA, Senate 1851, House 1851–1852.**

**7662.** Buckley, Robert D. "A Democrat and Slavery: Robert Rantoul, Jr." *Essex Institute Historical Collections* 110 (July 1974): 216–238.

**7663.** ———. "Robert Rantoul, Jr., 1805–1852: Politics and Reform in Antebellum

Massachusetts." Ph.D. dissertation, Princeton University, 1971.

**7664.** Hamilton, Luther, ed. *Memoirs, Speeches, and Writings of Robert Rantoul, Jr.* Boston: John P. Jewett, 1854.

## RAPIER, JAMES THOMAS (1837–1883) R-AL, House 1873–1875.

**7665.** Christopher, Maurine. "Benjamin S. Turner, James T. Rapier, and Jeremiah Haralson/Alabama." In her *Black Americans in Congress*, 97–103. Rev. ed. New York: Thomas Y. Crowell Company, 1976.

**7666.** Feldman, Eugene. *Black Power in Old Alabama: The Life and Stirring Times of James Rapier, Black Congressman from Alabama.* Chicago: Museum of African-American History, 1968.

**7667.** ———. "James T. Rapier, Negro Congressman from Alabama." *Phylon Quarterly* 19 (Winter 1958): 417–423.

**7668.** Freeman, Thomas J. "The Life of James T. Rapier." Master's thesis, Auburn University, 1959.

**7669.** Schweninger, Loren. "James Rapier and the Negro Labor Movement, 1869–1872." *Alabama Review* 28 (July 1975): 185–201.

**7670.** ———. *James T. Rapier and Reconstruction.* Chicago: University of Chicago Press, 1978.

**7671.** Walton, Norman W. "James T. Rapier: Congressman from Alabama." *Negro History Bulletin* 30 (November 1967): 6–10.

## RAUM, GREEN BERRY (1829–1909) R-IL, House 1867–1869.

**7672.** Thompson, Josephine, and Scerial Thompson. "Fighter: Military, Political Green Berry Raum." In *Idols of Egypt*, edited by Will Griffith, 181–201. Carbondale, IL: Egypt Book House, 1947.

## RAWLINS, JOSEPH LAFAYETTE (1850–1926) D-UT, House 1893–1895, Senate 1897–1903.

**7673.** Harrow, Joan R. "Joseph L. Rawlins, Father of Utah Statehood." *Utah Historical Quarterly* 44 (Winter 1976): 59–75.

## RAYBURN, SAMUEL TALIAFERRO (1882–1961) D-TX, House 1913–1961.

**7674.** Allen, Edward. *Sam Rayburn: Leading the Lawmakers.* Chicago: Encyclopedia Britannica Press, 1963.

**7675.** Bentley, Judith. "Sam Rayburn and Civil Rights." In her *Speakers of the House*, 93–118. New York: Franklin Watts, 1994.

**7676.** Brown, D. Clayton. "Sam Rayburn and the Development of Public Power in the Southwest." *Southwestern Historical Quarterly* 78 (October 1974): 140–154.

**7677.** Champagne, Anthony. *Congressman Sam Rayburn.* New Brunswick, NJ: Rutgers University Press, 1984.

**7678.** ———. *Sam Rayburn: A Biobibliography.* New York: Greenwood Press, 1988.

**7679.** ———. "Sam Rayburn: Achieving Party Leadership." *Southwestern Historical Quarterly* 90 (April 1987): 373–392.

**7680.** Daniel, Edward O. "Sam Rayburn: Trials of a Party Man." Ph.D. dissertation, North Texas State University, 1979.

**7681.** Dorough, C. Dwight. *Mr. Sam.* New York: Random House, 1962.

**7682.** Dulaney, H. G., and Edward H. Phillips, eds. *Speak, Mr. Speaker.* Bonham, TX: Sam Rayburn Foundation, 1978.

**7683.** Emswiler, Marilyn. "Mr. Speaker: Sam Rayburn." *Texas Historian* 33 (March 1973): 20–25.

**7684.** Hairgrove, Kenneth D. "Sam Rayburn: Congressional Leader, 1940–1952." Ph.D. dissertation, Texas Tech University, 1974.

**7685.** Hardeman, Dorsey B. "Sam Rayburn and the House of Representatives."

In *The Presidency and the Congress: A Shifting Balance of Power?*, edited by William S. Livingston, Lawrence C. Dodd, and Richard L. Schott, 226–252. Austin: Lyndon B. Johnson School of Public Affairs, University of Texas, 1979.

**7686.** Hardeman, Dorsey B., and Donald C. Baum. *Rayburn: A Biography.* Austin: Texas Monthly Press, 1987.

**7687.** Hinga, Don. "Sam Rayburn: Texas Squire." *Southwest Review* 24 (Summer 1944): 471–480.

**7688.** Kornitzer, Bela. "The 'Untalkative Speaker' Talks: About His Father." In his *American Fathers and Sons*, 209–221. Lawrence, MA: Hermitage, 1952.

**7689.** Little, Dwayne L. "The Political Leadership of Speaker Sam Rayburn, 1940–1961." Ph.D. dissertation, University of Cincinnati, 1970.

**7690.** Mooney, Booth. "Man of the House: Sam Rayburn." In his *Mr. Speaker: Four Men Who Shaped the United States House of Representatives*, 129–184. Chicago, Follett, 1964.

**7691.** ———. *Roosevelt and Rayburn: A Political Partnership.* Philadelphia: J. B. Lippincott, 1971.

**7692.** Nash, Walter C. "Sam Rayburn: The Congressman of the Fourth District." Master's thesis, East Texas State Teachers College, 1950.

**7693.** Porter, David L. "The Battle of the Texas Giants: Hatton Sumners, Sam Rayburn, and the Logan-Walter Bill of 1939." *Texana* 12 (1973): 349–361.

**7694.** Riddick, Floyd M. "Sam Rayburn." In *Public Men In and Out of Office*, edited by John T. Salter, 147–166. Chapel Hill: University of North Carolina Press, 1946.

**7695.** Shanks, Alexander G. "Sam Rayburn and the Democratic Convention of 1932." *Texana* 3 (Winter 1965): 321–332.

**7696.** ———. "Sam Rayburn and the New Deal, 1933–1936." Ph.D. dissertation, University of North Carolina, 1965.

**7697.** ———. "Sam Rayburn in the Wilson Administration, 1913–1921." *East Texas Historical Journal* 6 (March 1968): 63–76.

**7698.** ———. "Sam Rayburn: The Texas Politician as New Dealer." *East Texas Historical Journal* 5 (March 1967): 51–59.

**7699.** Smallwood, James. "Sam Rayburn and the Rules Committee Change of 1961." *East Texas Historical Journal* 11 (1973): 51–54.

**7700.** Splawn, Walter. "Rayburn of Texas." *Banker's Monthly* 2 (October 1928): 523–526.

**7701.** Steinberg, Alfred. *Sam Rayburn: A Biography.* New York: Hawthorn Books, 1975.

**7702.** Welch, June R. "Sam Rayburn Served with Eight Presidents." In his *The Texas Senator*, 152–159. Dallas, TX: G.L.A. Press, 1978.

**7703.** Young, Valton J. *Speaker's Agent.* New York: Vantage, 1956.

## RAYMOND, HENRY JARVIS (1820–1869)
**R-NY, House 1865–1867.**

**7704.** Brown, Ernest F. *Raymond of the Times.* New York: Norton, 1951.

**7705.** Dodd, Dorothy. "Henry J. Raymond and the *New York Times* during Reconstruction." Ph.D. dissertation, University of Chicago, 1933.

**7706.** Krout, John A. "Henry J. Raymond on the Republican Caucuses." *American Historical Review* 33 (July 1928): 835–842.

**7707.** Maverick, August. *Henry J. Raymond and the New York Press.* New York: Arno Press, 1970.

**7708.** Stewart, Kenneth N., and John W. Tebbel. "Raymond, Ochs, and the *New York Times.* In their *Makers of Modern Jour-*

*nalism,* 121–137. Englewood Cliffs, NJ: Prentice-Hall, 1952.

## RAYNER, ISIDOR (1850–1912) D-MD, House 1887–1889, 1891–1895, Senate 1905–1912.

**7709.** Essary, J. Frederick. "Isidor Rayner." In his *Maryland in National Politics,* 264–286. Baltimore: John Murphy, 1915.

**7710.** Simonhoff, Harry. "Senator Isidor Rayner." In his *Saga of American Jewry, 1865–1914,* 255–262. New York: Arco, 1959.

## RAYNER, KENNETH (1808–1884) W-NC, House 1839–1845.

**7711.** Cantrell, Gregg. *Kenneth and John B. Rayner and the Limits of Southern Dissent.* Urbana: University of Illinois Press, 1993.

## READ, GEORGE (1733–1798) DE, Senate 1789–1793, Continental Congress 1774–1777.

**7712.** Boughner, D. Terry. "George Read and the Founding of Delaware State, 1781–1798." Ph.D. dissertation, Catholic University, 1970.

**7713.** Read, William T. *Life and Correspondence of George Read.* Philadelphia: Lippincott, 1870.

**7714.** Sanderson, John. "George Read." In *Sanderson's Biography of the Signers of the Declaration of Independence,* edited by Robert T. Conrad, 547–558. Philadelphia: Thomas, Cowperthwait, 1848.

## REAGAN, JOHN HENNINGER (1818–1905) D-TX, House 1857–1861, 1875–1887, Senate 1887–1891.

**7715.** Good, Benjamin H. "John Henninger Reagan." Ph.D. dissertation, University of Texas, 1932.

**7716.** Proctor, Ben H. *Not without Honor: The Life of John H. Reagan.* Austin: University of Texas Press, 1962.

**7717.** Reagan, John H. *Memoirs with Special Reference to Secession and the Civil War.* New York: Neale, 1906.

**7718.** Schuster, Stephen W. "John H. Reagan." In *Ten Texans in Grey,* edited by William C. Nunn, 157–174. Hillsboro, TX: Hill Junior College Press, 1968.

**7719.** Wilson, Georgia P. "John Henninger Reagan and the Texas Constitution of 1876." Master's thesis, Texas Tech University, 1937.

## REDFIELD, WILLIAM COX (1858–1932) D-NY, House 1911–1913.

**7720.** Redfield, William C. *With Congress and Cabinet.* New York: Doubleday, 1924.

## REECE, BRAZILLA CARROLL (1889–1961) R-TN, House 1921–1931, 1933–1947, 1951–1961.

**7721.** Hicks, John H. "Congressional Career of B. Carroll Reece, 1920–1948." Master's thesis, East Tennessee State University, 1968.

**7722.** Smith, Gerald W. "Brazilla Carroll Reece." In his *Nathan Goff, Jr.: A Biography with Some Account of Guy Despard Goff and Brazilla Carroll Reece,* 341–347. Charleston, WV: Education Foundation, 1959.

## REED, DANIEL ALDEN (1875–1959) R-NY, House 1919–1959.

**7723.** Bulkey, Peter B. "Daniel A. Reed: A Study in Conservatism." Ph.D. dissertation, Clark University, 1972.

## REED, JAMES ALEXANDER (1861–1944) D-MO, Senate 1911–1929.

**7724.** Hults, Jan E. "The Senatorial Career of James Alexander Reed (Missouri)." Ph.D. dissertation, University of Kansas, 1987.

**7725.** Meriwether, Lee. *Jim Reed, Senatorial Immortal: A Biography.* Webster Groves, MO: International Mark Twain Society, 1948.

**7726.** Midgley, Wilson. "Senator Reed." In his *Possible Presidents*, 151–162. London: E. Benn Limited, 1928.

**7727.** Mitchell, Franklin D. "The Re-election of Irreconcilable James A. Reed." *Missouri Historical Review* 60 (July 1966): 416–435.

**7728.** Villard, Oswald G. "James A. Reed: A Modern Andrew Jackson." In his *Prophets True and False*, 89–99. New York: Knopf, 1928.

**REED, JOSEPH** (1741–1785) PA,
**Continental Congress 1777–1778.**

**7729.** Bancroft, George. *Joseph Reed: A Historical Essay*. New York: W. J. Middleton, 1867.

**7730.** Griswold, Rufus W. "Brigadier-General Joseph Reed." In his *Washington and the Generals of the American Revolution*, vol. 2, 58–83. Philadelphia: Carey and Hart, 1848.

**7731.** Reed, William B. *President Reed of Pennsylvania: A Reply to Mr. George Bancroft and Others, February 1867*. Philadelphia: H. Challen, 1867.

**7732.** Roche, John F. *Joseph Reed, a Moderate in the American Revolution*. New York: Columbia University Press, 1957.

**7733.** Smith, Horace W., comp. *Nuts for Future Historians to Crack*. Philadelphia: H. W. Smith, 1856.

**7734.** Sparks, Jared. "Life of Joseph Reed." In his *Library of American Biography*, vol. 8, 209–439. Boston: Little, Brown, 1852.

**7735.** Stryker, William S. *The Reed Controversy, Further Facts with Reference to the Character of Joseph Reed*. Trenton, NJ: Naar, Day and Naar, 1885.

**REED, THOMAS BRACKETT**
(1839–1902) R-ME, House 1877–1899.

**7736.** Beisner, Robert L. "Old Chiefs and Stalwarts: The Impotent Protest." In his *Twelve against Empire*, 186–214. New York: McGraw-Hill, 1968.

**7737.** Bentley, Judith. "Thomas Brackett Reed and the Rules." In her *Speakers of the House*, 57–72. New York: Franklin Watts, 1994.

**7738.** Butler, Nicholas M. "Things Seen and Heard in Politics—Speaker Reed on the American Idea of War." *Scribner's* 100 (September 1936): 154–161.

**7739.** Chamberlain, Daniel H. "Counting a Quorum: Or Speaker Reed's Change of Rules." *New Englander and Yale Review* 53 (December 1890): 510–525.

**7740.** De Casseres, Benjamin. "Tom Reed." *American Mercury* 19 (February 1930): 221–228.

**7741.** Fuller, Hubert B. "Czar Reed—The Revolution." In his *The Speakers of the House*, 214–249. Boston: Little, Brown, 1909.

**7742.** Hazeltine, Mayo W. "Speaker Reed and the House of Representatives." *North American Review* 165 (August 1897): 232–239.

**7743.** Knight, Enoch. "Thomas B. Reed: An Appreciation." *New England Magazine* 30 (April 1904): 215–224.

**7744.** Lodge, Henry C. "Thomas Brackett Reed: The Statesman, the Wit, and the Man." *Century Magazine* 81 (February 1911): 613–621.

**7745.** McCall, Samuel W. *The Life of Thomas Brackett Reed*. Boston: Houghton Mifflin, 1914.

**7746.** Montgomery, Kirt E. "Thomas B. Reed's Theory and Practice of Congressional Debating." *Speech Monographs* 17 (March 1950): 65–74.

**7747.** Mooney, Booth. "The Czar: Thomas B. Reed." In his *Mr. Speaker: Four Men Who Shaped the United States House of Representatives*, 49–88. Chicago: Follett, 1964.

**7748.** Munsey, Frank A. "Thomas Brackett Reed." *Munsey's Magazine* 9 (April 1893): 85–88.

**7749.** Offenberg, Richard S. "The Political Career of Thomas Brackett Reed." Ph.D. dissertation, New York University, 1963.

**7750.** Porter, Robert P. "Thomas B. Reed of Maine: The Man and His Home." *McClure's* 1 (October 1893): 374–389.

**7751.** Robinson, William A. *Thomas Brackett Reed: Parliamentarian.* New York: Dodd, Mead, 1930.

**7752.** Roosevelt, Theodore. "Thomas Brackett Reed and the Fifty-First Congress." *Forum* 20 (December 1895): 410–418.

**7753.** ———. "The Vindication of Speaker Reed." In *The Works,* edited by Herman Hagedorn, vol. 14, 169–180. New York: Scribner's, 1926.

**7754.** Strunsky, Simeon. "Czar Reed: Speaker of the House." *Current History* 34 (April 1931): 58–62.

**7755.** Webb, Richard. "Public Career of Thomas B. Reed." *Collections of the Maine Historical Society* 1 (1904): 369–389.

## REEVES, HENRY AUGUSTUS
### (1832–1916) D-NY, House 1869–1871.

**7756.** Bethauser, Margaret O. "Henry A. Reeves: The Career of a Conservative Democratic Editor, 1858–1916." *Journal of Long Island History* 9 (Spring 1973): 34–43.

## REUSS, HENRY SCHOELLKOPF
### (1912– ) D-WI, House 1955–1983.

**7757.** Reuss, Henry S. "Reflections of a Wisconsin Congressman of German Descent." *Yearbook of German-American Studies* 19 (1984): 17–22.

## REVELS, HIRAM RHODES (1827–1901)
### R-MS, Senate 1870–1871.

**7758.** Christopher, Maurine. "Hiram R. Revels/Mississippi." In her *Black Americans in Congress,* 1–14. Rev. ed. New York: Thomas Y. Crowell Company, 1976.

**7759.** Gibbs, Warmoth. "Hiram R. Revels and His Times." *Quarterly Review of Higher Education Among Negroes* 8 (January 1940): 25–37, 8 (April 1940): 64–91.

**7760.** Lawson, Elizabeth. *The Gentleman from Mississippi: Our First Negro Senator, Hiram R. Revels.* New York: The author, 1960.

**7761.** Libby, Billy W. "Senator Hiram Revels of Mississippi Takes His Seat, January-February, 1870." *Journal of Mississippi History* 37 (November 1975): 381–394.

**7762.** Revels, Hiram R. "Hiram R. Revels." In *Black Reconstructionists,* edited by Emma L. Thornbrough, 47–48. Englewood Cliffs, NJ: Prentice-Hall, 1972.

**7763.** Sewell, George A. "Hiram Rhodes Revels: Another Evaluation." *Negro History Bulletin* 38 (December/January 1974/1975): 336–339.

**7764.** Simmons, William J. "Hiram R. Revels." In his *Men of Mark,* 672–673. Lincoln, NE: Johnson, 1970.

**7765.** Singer, Donald L. "For Whites Only: The Seating of Hiram Revels in the United States Senate." *Negro History Bulletin* 35 (March 1972): 60–63.

**7766.** Thompson, Julius E. *Hiram R. Revels, 1827–1901: A Biography.* New York: Arno Press, 1982.

**7767.** Wheeler, Gerald E. "Hiram Rhodes Revels: Negro Educator and Statesman." Master's thesis, University of California, 1949.

**REYNOLDS, JOHN** (1789–1865) D-IL, House 1834–1837, 1839–1843.

**7768.** Harper, Josephine L. "John Reynolds, the Old Ranger of Illinois, 1788–1865." Ph.D. dissertation, University of Illinois, 1949.

**7769.** Stevenson, Adlai E. "The Old Ranger." In his *Something of Men I Have Known*, 182–196. Chicago: A. C. McClurg, 1909.

**REYNOLDS, ROBERT RICE** (1884–1963) D-NC, Senate 1932–1945.

**7770.** Pleasants, Julian M. "The Last Hurrah: Bob Reynolds and the U.S. Senate Race in 1950." *North Carolina Historical Review* 65 (January 1988): 52–75.

**7771.** ———. "The Senatorial Career of Robert Rice Reynolds." Ph.D. dissertation, University of North Carolina, 1971.

**RHEA, JOHN** (1753–1832) D-TN, House 1803–1815, 1817–1823.

**7772.** Bolden, John. "John Rhea, His Views and Voting Record in Congress, 1803–1815 and 1817–1823." Master's thesis, Tennessee State A & I University, 1958.

**7773.** Hamer, Marguerite B. "John Rhea of Tennessee." *East Tennessee Historical Society's Publications* 4 (January 1932): 35–44.

**7774.** Jordan, Robert D. "Some Phases of the Private Life and Public Career of John Rhea." Master's thesis, East Tennessee State University, 1952.

**RHETT, ROBERT BARNWELL** (1800–1876) D-SC, House 1837–1849, Senate 1850–1852.

**7775.** Barnwell, John. "Hamlet to Hotspur: Letters of Robert Woodward Barnwell to Robert Barnwell Rhett." *South Carolina Historical Magazine* 77 (October 1976): 236–256.

**7776.** Niles, Walter B. "Robert Barnwell Rhett, Sr.: His Political Career." Master's thesis, Indiana University, 1922.

**7777.** White, Laura A. "The Life of Barnwell Rhett." Ph.D. dissertation, University of Chicago, 1917.

**7778.** ———. *Robert Barnwell Rhett: Father of Secession.* New York: Century, 1931.

**RIBICOFF, ABRAHAM ALEXANDER** (1910– ) D-CT, House 1949–1953, Senate 1963–1981.

**7779.** Bagdikian, Ben H. "Honest Abe—The Vote Getter." In *Kennedy Circle,* edited by Lester Tanzer, 213–236. Washington, DC: Luce, 1961.

**7780.** Ribicoff, Abraham A. *America Can Make It!* New York: Atheneum, 1972.

**7781.** Ribicoff, Abraham A., and Jon O. Newman. *Politics: The American Way.* Boston: Allyn and Bacon, 1969.

**RICE, HENRY MOWER** (1817–1894) D-MN, House 1853–1857, Senate 1858–1863.

**7782.** Marshall, William. "Henry Mower Rice." *Minnesota Historical Society Collections* 9 (1901): 654–658.

**RICHARD, GABRIEL** (1767–1832) MI, House 1823–1825.

**7783.** Pargellis, Stanley M. *Father Gabriel Richard.* Detroit, MI: Wayne University Press, 1950.

**RICHARDS, JAMES PRIOLEAU** (1894–1979) D-SC, House 1933–1957.

**7784.** Lee, Joseph E. "America Comes First with Me: The Early Political Career of Congressman James P. Richards." *Proceedings of the South Carolina Historical Association* (1986): 48–56.

**7785.** ———. "America Comes First with Me: The Political Career of Congressman James P. Richards, 1932–1957." Ph.D. dissertation, University of South Carolina, 1987.

**7786.** ———. "On the Stump: The Congressional Campaigns of James P.

Richards, 1932–1954." *Proceedings of the South Carolina Historical Association* 1991 (1991): 54–60.

**7787.** ———. "A South Carolinian in the Middle East: Ambassador James P. Richards' 1957 Mission." *Proceedings of the South Carolina Historical Association* 1988 (1988): 103–111.

## RICHARDSON, JOHN PETER
(1801–1864) J-SC, HOUSE 1836–1839.

**7788.** Begley, Paul R. "Governor Richardson Faces the Tillman Challenge." *South Carolina Historical Magazine* 89 (April 1988): 119–126.

## RICHARDSON, WILLIAM ALEXANDER
(1811–1875) D-IL, House 1847–1856, 1861–1863, Senate 1863–1865.

**7789.** Howard, Robert P. "'Old Dick' Richardson, the Other Senator from Quincy." *Western Illinois Regional Studies* 7, no. 1 (1984): 16–27.

**7790.** Tharenet, Denis. "William Alexander Richardson, 1811–1875." Ph.D. dissertation, University of Nebraska, 1967.

## RIDDLE, ALBERT GALLATIN
(1816–1902) R-OH, House 1861–1863.

**7791.** Riddle, Albert G. *Recollections of War Times: Reminiscences of Men and Events in Washington, 1860–1865.* New York: Putnam's, 1895.

## RIDDLEBERGER, HARRISON HOLT
(1844–1890) READ-VA, Senate 1883–1889.

**7792.** Cole, Howson W. "Harrison Holt Riddleberger, Readjuster." Master's thesis, University of Virginia, 1952.

## RIEGLE, DONALD WAYNE, JR. (1938– )
D-MI, House 1967–1976, Senate 1976–1995.

**7793.** Riegle, Donald. *O Congress.* Garden City, NY: Doubleday, 1972.

## RIPLEY, ELEAZAR WHEELOCK
(1782–1839) D-LA, House 1835–1839.

**7794.** Baylies, Nicholas. *Eleazer Wheelock Ripley, of the War of 1812.* Des Moines, IA: Brewster and Company, 1890.

**7795.** Wyatt, Thomas. "Major-General Ripley." In his *Memoirs of the Generals,* 135–146. Philadelphia: Carey and Hart, 1848.

## RIVERS, LUCIUS MENDEL (1905–1970)
D-SC, House 1941–1970.

**7796.** Huntley, Will. "The Controversy Surrounding Mendel Rivers and His Battle with the Bottle." *Proceedings of the South Carolina Historical Association* (1992): 87–94.

## RIVES, WILLIAM CABELL (1793–1868)
W-VA, House 1823–1829, Senate 1832–1834, 1836–1839, 1841–1845.

**7797.** Everett, Joseph W. "William Cabell Rives." In *Library of Southern Literature,* edited by Edwin A. Alderman and Joel C. Harris, vol. 10, 4477–4480. New Orleans: Martin and Hoyt, 1909.

**7798.** Dingledine, Raymond C. "The Political Career of William Cabell Rives." Ph.D. dissertation, University of Virginia, 1947.

**7799.** Gunderson, Robert G. "William C. Rives and the Old Gentlemen's Convention." *Journal of Southern History* 22 (November 1956): 459–476.

**7800.** Liston, Ann E. "W. C. Rives: Diplomat and Politician." Ph.D. dissertation, Ohio State University, 1972.

**7801.** Rives, William C. "Letters of William Rives, 1823–1829." *Tyler's Historical and Genealogical Register* 5 (April 1923): 223–237, 6 (July 1924): 6–15, 6 (October 1924): 97–106, 8 (January 1926): 203–207.

**7802.** Willson, Beckles. "Brown and Rives (1824–32), Rives and Mason (1849–59)." In his *America's Ambassadors to France*

(*1777–1927*), 166–179, 234–244. New York: Frederick A. Stokes, 1928.

**7803.** Wingfield, Russell S. "William Cabell Rives." *Richmond College Historical Papers* 1 (June 1915): 57–72.

## ROACH, WILLIAM NATHANIEL
(1840–1902) D-ND, Senate 1893–1899.

**7804.** Schlup, Leonard. "William N. Roach: North Dakota Isolationist and Gilded Age Senator." *North Dakota History* 57 (Fall 1990): 2–11.

## ROBERTS, BRIGHAM HENRY
(1857–1933) D-UT, House 1899–1900.

**7805.** Bitton, R. Davis. "The B. H. Roberts Case of 1898–1900." *Utah Historical Quarterly* 25 (January 1957): 27–46.

**7806.** White, William G. "The Feminist Campaign for the Exclusion of Brigham Henry Roberts from the Fifty-Sixth Congress." *Journal of the West* 17 (January 1978): 45–52.

## ROBERTS, JONATHAN (1771–1854)
R-PA, House 1811–1814, Senate 1814–1821.

**7807.** Champagne, Raymond W., and Thomas J. Rueter. "Jonathan Roberts and the War Hawk Congress of 1811–1812." *Pennsylvania Magazine of History and Biography* 104 (October 1980): 434–449.

**7808.** Shriver, Philip R., ed. "Memoirs of a Senator from Pennsylvania: Jonathan Roberts, 1771–1854." *Pennsylvania Magazine of History and Biography* 61 (October 1937): 446–474, 62 (January 1938): 64–97, 62 (April 1938): 213–248, 62 (July 1938): 361–409, 62 (October 1938): 502–551.

## ROBERTSON, ALICE MARY (1854–1931)
R-OK, House 1921–1923.

**7809.** James, Louise B. "Alice Mary Robertson—Anti-Feminist Congresswoman." *Chronicles of Oklahoma* 55 (Winter 1977/1978): 454–462.

**7810.** Morris, Cheryl. "Alice M. Robertson: Friend or Foe of the American Soldier?" *Journal of the West* 12 (April 1973): 307–316.

**7811.** Stanley, Ruth M. "Alice M. Robertson, Oklahoma's First Congresswoman." *Chronicles of Oklahoma* 45 (Autumn 1967): 259–289.

## ROBERTSON, THOMAS BOLLING
(1779–1828) R-LA, House 1812–1818.

**7812.** Reeves, Miriam G. "Thomas Bolling Robertson." In her *Governors of Louisiana*, 43–45. Gretna, LA: Pelican, 1972.

## ROBERTSON, WILLIAM HENRY
(1823–1898) R-NY, House 1867–1869.

**7813.** Nevins, Allan. "A Forgotten Hero of Westchester." *Westchester County Historical Society Bulletin* 16 (1940): 1–14.

## ROBINSON, JOSEPH TAYLOR
(1872–1937) D-AR, House 1903–1913, Senate 1913–1937.

**7814.** Bacon, Donald C. "Joseph Taylor Robinson: The Good Soldier." In *First Among Equals: Outstanding Senate Leaders of the Twentieth Century,* edited by Richard A. Baker and Roger H. Davidson, 63–97. Washington, DC: Congressional Quarterly, 1991.

**7815.** Grant, Gilbert R. "Joseph Robinson in Foreign Affairs." *Arkansas Historical Quarterly* 9 (Autumn 1950): 133–171.

**7816.** Ledbetter, Cal. "Joe T. Robinson and the Presidential Campaign of 1928." *Arkansas Historical Quarterly* 45 (Summer 1986): 95–125.

**7817.** McNutt, Walter S. "Joseph Taylor Robinson." In his *Great Statesmen of Arkansas,* 107–133. Jefferson, TX: Four States Publishing House, 1954.

**7818.** Neal, Kevin E. "A Biography of Joseph T. Robinson." Ph.D. dissertation, University of Oklahoma, 1958.

**7819.** Rhodes, Dennis H. "The Political Speaking of Joseph Taylor Robinson." Ph.D. dissertation, Southern Illinois University, 1966.

**7820.** Towns, Stuart. "Joseph T. Robinson and Arkansas Politics: 1912–1913." *Arkansas Historical Quarterly* 24 (Winter 1965): 291–307.

**7821.** Vervack, Jerry J. "The Making of a Politician: Joe T. Robinson, 1872–1921." Ph.D. dissertation, University of Arkansas, 1990.

**7822.** Weller, Cecil E., Jr. "Joseph Taylor Robinson and the Robinson-Patman Act." *Arkansas Historical Quarterly* 72 (Spring 1988): 28–36.

**7823.** ———. "Joseph Taylor Robinson: Keystone of Franklin D. Roosevelt's Supreme Court 'Packing' Plan." *Southern Historian* 7 (Spring 1986): 23–30.

**ROBINSON, MOSES (1741–1813) VT, Senate 1791–1796.**

**7824.** Wood, Richard G. "Moses Robinson: Town Clerk." *American Archivist* 25 (April 1962): 189–191.

**ROBINSON, THOMAS JOHN BRIGHT (1868–1958) R-IA, House 1923–1933.**

**7825.** Porter, David L. "Iowa Congressional Delegation and the Great Economic Issues, 1929–1933." *Annals of Iowa* 46 (Summer 1982): 337–354.

**RODENBERG, WILLIAM AUGUST (1865–1937) R-IL, House 1899–1901, 1903–1913, 1915–1923.**

**7826.** VanderMeer, Philip R. "Congressional Decision-Making and World War I: A Case Study of Illinois." *Congressional Studies* 8, no. 2 (1981): 59–79.

**RODINO, PETER WALLACE, JR. (1909– ) D-NJ, House 1949–1989.**

**7827.** Rapoport, Daniel. *Inside the House: An Irreverent Guided Tour through the House of Representatives, from the Days of Adam Clayton Powell to Those of Peter Rodino.* Chicago: Follett, 1975.

**RODNEY, CAESAR (1728–1784) DE, Continental Congress 1774–1776, 1777–1778, 1782–1784.**

**7828.** Frank, William, and Harold B. Hancock. "Caesar Rodney's Two Hundred and Fiftieth Anniversary: An Evaluation." *Delaware History* 18 (Fall/Winter 1976): 63–76.

**7829.** Sanderson, John. "Caesar Rodney." In *Sanderson's Biography of the Signers of the Declaration of Independence,* edited by Robert T. Conrad, 529–544. Philadelphia: Thomas, Cowperthwait, 1848.

**RODNEY, DANIEL (1764–1846) DE, House 1822–1823, Senate 1826–1827.**

**7830.** Turner, Charles H., ed. *Rodney's Diary and Other Delaware Records.* Philadelphia: Allen, Lane and Scott, 1911.

**RODNEY, THOMAS (1744–1811) DE, Continental Congress 1781–1783, 1785–1787.**

**7831.** Rodney, Thomas. *Anglo-American Law on the Frontier: Thomas Rodney and His Territorial Cases.* Durham, NC: Duke University Press, 1953.

**ROLLINS, EDWARD HENRY (1824–1889) R-NH, House 1861–1867, Senate 1877–1883.**

**7832.** Lyford, James. *Life of Edward H. Rollins.* Boston: D. Estes, 1906.

**ROLLINS, JAMES SIDNEY (1812–1888) U-MO, House 1861–1865.**

**7833.** Wood, James M., Jr. "James Sidney Rollins of Missouri: A Political Biography." Ph.D. dissertation, Stanford University, 1952.

**ROMULO, CARLOS PENA** (1899– ) **PI**
**House 1944–1946.**

**7834.** Romulo, Carlos P. *Forty Years: A Third World Soldier at the UN.* New York: Greenwood, 1986.

**7835.** Yaukey, Grace S. *Romulo: Voice of Freedom.* New York: J. Day Company, 1953.

**ROOSEVELT, FRANKLIN DELANO, JR.**
**(1914–1988) D-NY, House 1949–1955.**

**7836.** Kornitzer, Bela. "As His Sons Saw FDR." In his *American Fathers and Sons,* 257–294. Lawrence, MA: Hermitage, 1952.

**7837.** Perling, Joseph J. "Sons of Franklin D. Roosevelt." In his *Presidents' Sons,* 310–346. New York: Odyssey, 1947.

**ROOSEVELT, JAMES** (1907–1991) **D-CA,**
**House 1955–1965.**

**7838.** Roosevelt, James. *My Parents: A Differing View.* Chicago: Playboy Press, 1976.

**ROOT, ELIHU** (1845–1937) **R-NY, Senate**
**1909–1915.**

**7839.** Brown, James B. "Elihu Root." In his *The American Secretaries of State and Their Diplomacy,* edited by Samuel F. Bemis, vol. 9, 191–282. New York: Knopf, 1929.

**7840.** Cantor, Louis. "Elihu Root and the National Guard: Friend or Foe?" *Military Affairs* 33 (December 1969): 361–373.

**7841.** Cummins, Lejeune. "The Origin and Development of Elihu Root's Latin American Diplomacy." Ph.D. dissertation, University of California, 1964.

**7842.** Curtis, George H. "The Wilson Administration, Elihu Root, and the Founding of the World Court, 1918–1921." Ph.D. dissertation, Georgetown University, 1972.

**7843.** Davis, Jack. "The Latin American Policy of Elihu Root." Ph.D. dissertation, University of Illinois, 1956.

**7844.** DeFroscia, Patrick D. "The Diplomacy of Elihu Root, 1905–1909." Ph.D. dissertation, Temple University, 1976.

**7845.** Dubin, Martin D. "Elihu Root and the Advocacy of a League of Nations, 1914–1917." *Western Political Quarterly* 19 (September 1966): 439–455.

**7846.** Gray, Tony. "Elihu Root." In his *Champions of Peace,* 112–114. New York: Paddington Press, 1976.

**7847.** Hendrickson, Embert J. "Root's Watchful Waiting and the Venezuelan Controversy." *Americas* 23 (October 1966): 115–129.

**7848.** Hewes, James E. *From Root to McNamara: Army Organization and Administration, 1900–1963.* Washington, DC: U.S. Army Center of Military History, 1975.

**7849.** Hopkins, C. Howard, and John W. Long. "American Jews and the Root Mission to Russia in 1917: Some New Evidence." *American Jewish History* 69 (March 1980): 342–354.

**7850.** Ingram, Alton E. "The Root Mission to Russia, 1917." Ph.D. dissertation, Louisiana State University, 1970.

**7851.** Jessup, Philip C. *Elihu Root.* 2 vols. New York: Dodd, Mead, 1938.

**7852.** Law, Frederick H. "Elihu Root, Winner of the Nobel Peace Prize." In his *Modern Great Americans,* 220–233. New York: Century, 1926.

**7853.** Leopold, Richard W. *Elihu Root and the Conservative Tradition.* Boston: Little, Brown, 1954.

**7854.** Lindgren, Homer D. "Speeches Celebrating the Eightieth Birthday of the Honorable Elihu Root: Speech of Introduction." In his *Modern Speeches,* 245–251. New York: F. S. Crofts, 1926.

**7855.** Lockridge, Crystal G. "Elihu Root's Work in Colonial Administration." Master's thesis, Indiana University, 1943.

**7856.** Muth, Edwin A. "Elihu Root: His Role and Concepts Pertaining to United States Policies of Intervention." Ph.D. dissertation, Georgetown University, 1966.

**7857.** Palmer, John M. "Elihu Root." In his *Washington, Lincoln, Wilson: Three War Statesmen,* 282–299. Garden City, NY: Doubleday, Doran, 1930.

**7858.** Schambra, William A. "Elihu Root, the Constitution, and the Election of 1912." Ph.D. dissertation, Northern Illinois University, 1983.

**7859.** Scott, James B. *Elihu Root's Services to International Law.* New York: Carnegie Endowment for International Peace, 1925.

**7860.** Semsch, Philip L. "Elihu Root and the General Staff." *Military Affairs* 27 (Spring 1963): 16–27.

**7861.** Storey, Moorfield, and Julian Codman. *Secretary Root's Record, "Marked Severities" in Philippine Warfare: An Analysis.* Boston: G. H. Ellis, 1902.

**7862.** Toth, Charles W. "Elihu Root." In *Uncertain Tradition: American Secretaries of State in the Twentieth Century,* edited by Norman A. Graebner, 40–58. New York: McGraw-Hill, 1961.

**ROSECRANS, WILLIAM STARKE**
**(1819–1898) D-CA, House 1881–1885.**

**7863.** Lamers, William M. *Edge of Glory: A Biography of General William S. Rosecrans, U.S.A.* New York: Harcourt, 1961.

**7864.** Pletcher, David M. "General William S. Rosecrans and the Mexican Transcontinental Railroad Project." *Mississippi Valley Historical Review* 38 (March 1952): 657–678.

**7865.** Schauinger, Joseph H. "The Civil War: Generals and Statesmen." In his *Profiles in Action,* 118–144. Milwaukee, WI: Bruce, 1966.

**7866.** Smith, Theodore C. "General Garfield at Chickamauga" *Massachusetts Historical Society Proceedings* 48 (1914/1915): 268–280.

**ROSIER, JOSEPH** (1870–1951) D-WV, **Senate 1941–1942.**

**7867.** Maddox, Robert F. "The Martin-Rosier Affair." *Capitol Studies* 5 (Spring 1977): 57–69.

**ROSS, EDMUND GIBSON** (1826–1907) **R-KS, Senate 1866–1871.**

**7868.** Berwanger, Eugene R. "Ross and the Impeachment: A New Look at a Critical Vote." *Kansas History* 1 (Winter 1978): 235–242.

**7869.** Bumgardner, Edward. *The Life of Edmund G. Ross: The Man Whose Vote Saved a President.* Kansas City, MO: Fielding-Turner Press, 1949.

**7870.** Kennedy, John F. "Edmund G. Ross." In his *Profiles in Courage,* 126–151. New York: Harper and Row, 1956.

**7871.** Kubicek, Earl C. "Pioneer, Soldier and Statesman: The Story of Edmund Gibson Ross." *Lincoln Herald* 84 (Fall 1982): 147–154.

**7872.** Plummer, Mark A. "Governor Crawford's Appointment of Edmund G. Ross to the United States Senate." *Kansas Historical Quarterly* 28 (Summer 1962): 145–153.

**7873.** Plummer, Mark A. "Profile in Courage? Edmund G. Ross and the Impeachment Trial." *Midwest Quarterly* 27 (Autumn 1985): 30–48.

**ROSS, GEORGE** (1730–1779) PA, **Continental Congress 1774–1777.**

**7874.** Sanderson, John. "George Ross." In *Sanderson's Biography of the Signers of the Declaration of Independence,* edited by Robert T. Conrad, 523–528. Philadelphia: Thomas, Cowperthwait, 1848.

**ROSS, JAMES** (1762–1847) F-PA, Senate **1794–1803.**

**7875.** Brownson, James I. *The Life and Times of Senator James Ross.* Washington, PA: Historical Society of Washington, 1910.

## ROSTENKOWSKI, DANIEL DAVID "DAN" (1928– ) D-IL, House 1959–1995.

**7876.** Hart, Benjamin. "Tip's Iceberg: The Emerging Democratic Leadership in the House." *Policy Review* 35 (Winter 1986): 66–70.

## ROUSSEAU, LOVELL HARRISON (1818–1869) UU-KY, House 1865–1866, 1866–1867.

**7877.** Dawson, Joseph G. "General Lovell H. Rousseau and Louisiana Reconstruction." *Louisiana History* 20 (Fall 1979): 373–391.

## ROWAN, JOHN (1773–1843) R-KY, House 1807–1809, Senate 1825–1831.

**7878.** Fackler, Stephen W. "John Rowan and the Demise of Jeffersonian Republicanism in Kentucky, 1819–1831." *Register of the Kentucky Historical Society* 78 (Winter 1980): 1–26.

**7879.** Jillson, Willard R. "Autobiography of John Rowan, 1782–1785: The Old Kentucky Home, 1795–1853." In his *Tales of the Dark and Bloody Ground*, 139–144. Louisville, KY: C. T. Dearing Printing Company, 1930.

**7880.** Richards, Frances. "John Rowan." Master's thesis, Indiana University, 1930.

## RUGGLES, BENJAMIN (1783–1857) R-OH, Senate 1815–1833.

**7881.** Stanford, Donald E. "Edward Taylor versus the Young Cockerill Benjamin Ruggles: A Hitherto Unpublished Episode from the Annals of Early New England Church History." *New England Quarterly* 44 (September 1971): 459–468.

## RUMSFELD, DONALD HENRY (1932– ) R-IL, House 1963–1969.

**7882.** Leamer, Laurence. "The Little Engine That Could." In his *Playing for Keeps in Washington*, 139–187. New York: Dial, 1977.

## RUSH, BENJAMIN (1745–1813) PA, Continental Congress 1776–1777.

**7883.** Binger, Carl A. *Revolutionary Doctor: Benjamin Rush, 1746–1813*. New York: Norton, 1966.

**7884.** Butterfield, Lyman H. "Benjamin Rush, the American Revolution and the American Millennium." In *Physician Signers of the Declaration of Independence*, edited by George E. Gifford, 18–42. New York: Science History Publications, 1976.

**7885.** D'Elia, Donald J. *Benjamin Rush, Philosopher of the American Revolution*. Philadelphia: American Philosophical Society, 1974.

**7886.** Deutsch, Albert. "Benjamin Rush: The Father of American Psychiatry." In his *The Mentally Ill in America*, 72–87. Garden City, NY: Doubleday, Dorran, 1937.

**7887.** Flexner, James T. "Saint or Scourge: Benjamin Rush." In his *Doctors on Horseback*, 55–117. New York: Viking, 1937.

**7888.** Goodman, Nathan G. *Benjamin Rush, Physician and Citizen, 1746–1813*. Philadelphia: University of Pennsylvania Press, 1934.

**7889.** Hansen, Allen O. "Benjamin Rush's Plan for a National System of Education." In his *Liberalism and American Education in the Eighteenth Century*, 48–63. New York: Macmillan, 1926.

**7890.** Hawke, David F. *Benjamin Rush: Revolutionary Gadfly*. Indianapolis: Bobbs-Merrill, 1971.

**7891.** King, Lester S. *Transformations in American Medicine: From Benjamin Rush to William Osler*. Baltimore: Johns Hopkins University Press, 1991.

**7892.** Kloos, John M., Jr. *A Sense of Deity: The Republican Spirituality of Dr. Benjamin Rush*. Brooklyn, NY: Carlson Publishers, 1991.

**7893.** Riley, Isaac W. "Benjamin Rush, and Mental Healing." In his *American Thought from Puritanism to Pragmatism,* 104–117. New York: Holt, 1915.

**7894.** Rush, Benjamin. *My Dearest Julia: The Loveletters of Dr. Benjamin Rush to Julia Stockton.* New York: N. Watson Academic Publications, 1979.

**7895.** Sanderson, John. "Benjamin Rush." In *Sanderson's Biography of the Signers of the Declaration of Independence,* edited by Robert T. Conrad, 378–390. Philadelphia: Thomas, Cowperthwait, 1848.

**RUSK, JEREMIAH McLAIN** (1830–1893)
**R-WI, House 1871–1877.**

**7896.** Casson, Henry. *Uncle Jerry, Life of General Jeremiah M. Rusk: Stage Driver, Farmer, Soldier, Legislator, Governor, Cabinet Officer.* Madison, WI: J. W. Hill, 1895.

**RUSK, THOMAS JEFFERSON**
(1803–1857) **D-TX, Senate 1846–1857.**

**7897.** Blount, Lois F. "A Brief Study of Thomas J. Rusk, Based on His Letters to His Brother, David, 1835–1856." *Southwestern Historical Quarterly* 34 (January 1931): 181–202.

**7898.** Clarke, Mary W. *Thomas J. Rusk, Soldier, Statesman, Jurist.* Austin, TX: Pemberton Press, 1971.

**7899.** Huston, Cleburne. *Towering Texan, a Biography of Thomas Jefferson Rusk.* Waco, TX: Texian Press, 1971.

**7900.** Sterrett, Carrie B. "The Life of Thomas Jefferson Rusk." Master's thesis, University of Texas, 1922.

**7901.** Welch, June R. "T. J. Rusk Lived for Texas." In his *The Texas Senator,* 2–7. Dallas, TX: G. L. A. Press, 1978.

**RUSSELL, DANIEL LINDSAY**
(1845–1908) **G-NC, House 1879–1881.**

**7902.** Crow, Jeffrey J., and Robert F. Durden. *Maverick Republican in the Old North State: A Political Biography of Daniel L. Russell.* Baton Rouge: Louisiana State University Press, 1977.

**7903.** Durden, Robert F. *Reconstruction Bonds and Twentieth-Century Politics: South Dakota v. North Carolina, 1904.* Durham, NC: Duke University Press, 1962.

**RUSSELL, RICHARD BREVARD, JR.**
(1897–1971) **D-GA, Senate 1933–1971.**

**7904.** Boney, Francis N. "The Senator's Senator: Richard Brevard Russell, Jr. of Georgia." *Georgia Historical Quarterly* 71 (Fall 1987): 477–490.

**7905.** Fite, Gilbert C. "The Education of a Senator: Richard B. Russell, Jr., in School." *Atlanta Historical Journal* 30 (Summer 1986): 19–31.

**7906.** ———. "Richard B. Russell and Lyndon B. Johnson: The Story of a Strange Friendship." *Missouri Historical Review* 83 (January 1989): 125–138.

**7907.** ———. *Richard B. Russell, Jr., Senator from Georgia.* Chapel Hill: University of North Carolina Press, 1991.

**7908.** Hale, F. Sheffield. "Richard B. Russell's Election to the Senate: The Watershed of Two Political Careers." *Atlanta Historical Journal* 28 (Spring 1984): 5–21.

**7909.** Kelly, Karen K. "Richard B. Russell: Democrat from Georgia." Ph.D. dissertation, University of North Carolina, 1979.

**7910.** Mead, Howard N. "Russell vs. Talmadge: Southern Politics and the New Deal." *Georgia Historical Quarterly* 65 (Spring 1981): 28–45.

**7911.** Potenziani, David D. "Looking to the Past: Richard B. Russell and the Defense of Southern White Supremacy." Ph.D. dissertation, University of Georgia, 1981.

**7912.** ———. "Striking Back: Richard B. Russell and Racial Relocation." *Georgia Historical Quarterly* 65 (Fall 1981): 263–277.

**7913.** Stern, Mark. "Lyndon Johnson and Richard Russell: Institutions, Ambitions, and Civil Rights." *Presidential Studies Quarterly* 21 (Fall 1991): 687–704.

**7914.** Ziemke, Caroline F. "Senator Richard B. Russell and the 'Lost Cause' in Vietnam, 1954–1968." *Georgia Historical Quarterly* 72 (Spring 1988): 30–71.

**RUTLEDGE, EDWARD (1749–1800) SC, Continental Congress 1774–1776.**

**7915.** Sanderson, John. "Edward Rutledge." In *Sanderson's Biography of the Signers of the Declaration of Independence,* edited by Robert T. Conrad, 781–790. Philadelphia: Thomas, Cowperthwait, 1848.

**RUTLEDGE, JOHN (1739–1800) SC, Continental Congress 1774–1775, 1782–1783.**

**7916.** Barnwell, Robert W. "Rutledge, 'the Dictator.'" *Journal of Southern History* 7 (May 1941): 215–224.

**7917.** Barry, Richard H. *Mr. Rutledge of South Carolina.* New York: Duel, Sloan and Pearce, 1942.

**7918.** Flanders, Henry. "Chief Justice Rutledge." *University of Pennsylvania Law Review* 54 (April 1906): 203–213.

**7919.** Lossing, Benson J. "John Rutledge." In his *Eminent Americans,* 153–154. New York: Hurst, 1886.

**7920.** Mendelson, Wallace. "Mr. Justice Rutledge's Mark upon the Bill of Rights." *Columbia Law Review* 50 (January 1950): 48–51.

**7921.** O'Neall, John B. "John Rutledge." In his *Biographical Sketches of the Bench and Bar of South Carolina,* vol. 1, 17–27. Charleston, SC: S. G. Courtnay, 1859.

**7922.** Perry, Benjamin F. "John Rutledge." In his *Biographical Sketches of Eminent American Statesmen,* 254–258. Philadelphia: Ferree Press, 1887.

**7923.** Umbreit, Kenneth B. "John Rutledge." In his *Our Eleven Chief Justices: A History of the Supreme Court in Terms of Their Personalities,* 51–78. New York: Harper and Brothers, 1938.

**7924.** Waite, Charles B. "John Rutledge." *Chicago Law Times* 1 (October 1887): 305–311.

**7925.** Webber, Mabel L. "Dr. John Rutledge and His Descendants." *South Carolina Historical and Genealogical Magazine* 31 (January 1930): 7–25.

**RUTLEDGE, JOHN, JR. (1766–1819) F-SC, House 1797–1803.**

**7926.** Cometti, Elizabeth. "John Rutledge, Jr., Federalist." *Journal of Southern History* 13 (May 1947): 186–219.

**7927.** Furlong, Patrick J. "John Rutledge, Jr., and the Election of a Speaker of the House in 1799." *William and Mary Quarterly* 24 (July 1967): 432–436.

**7928.** Ratzlaff, Robert K. "The Evolution of a Gentleman-Politician: John Rutledge, Jr., of South Carolina." *Midwest Quarterly* 27 (Autumn 1985): 77–95.

**7929.** Ratzlaff, Robert K. "John Rutledge, Jr., South Carolina Federalist." Ph.D. dissertation, University of Kansas, 1975.

❧

**SABATH, ADOLPH JOACHIM (1866–1952) D-IL, House 1907–1952.**

**7930.** Beal, John R. "Adolph J. Sabath." In *Public Men In and Out of Office,* edited by John T. Salter, 196–209. Chapel Hill: University of North Carolina Press, 1946.

**7931.** Boxerman, Burton A. "Adolph Joachim Sabath in Congress: The Early Years, 1907–1932." *Journal of the Illinois State Historical Society* 66 (Autumn 1973): 327–340.

**7932.** ———. "Adolph Joachim Sabath in Congress: The Roosevelt and Truman Years." *Journal of the Illinois State Historical Society* 66 (Winter 1973): 428–443.

**SACKETT, FREDERICK MOSLEY** (1868–1941) R-KY, Senate 1925–1930.

**7933.** Burke, Bernard V. "Senator and Diplomat: The Public Career of Frederick M. Sackett." *Filson Club Historical Quarterly* 61 (April 1987): 185–216.

**SAGE, EBENEZER** (1755–1834) R-NY, House 1809–1815.

**7934.** Harmond, Richard J. "Ebenezer Sage of Sag Harbor: An Old Republican in Young America, 1812–1834." *New York Historical Society Quarterly* 57 (October 1973): 309–325.

**7935.** ———. "A Reluctant War Hawk: Ebenezer Sage of Sag Harbor, Long Island, and the Coming of the War of 1812." *Journal of Long Island History* 14 (Fall 1977): 48–53.

**SAGE, RUSSELL** (1816–1906) W-NY, House 1853–1857.

**7936.** Eddy, Arthur J. "The Russell Sage Fortune." In his *Property*, 83–117. Chicago: A. C. McClurg, 1921.

**7937.** Remsen, Jane. "Russell Sage: Yankee." *New England Quarterly* 11 (March 1938): 4–28.

**7938.** Sarnoff, Paul. *Russell Sage: The Money King*. New York: Obolensky, 1965.

**ST. CLAIR, ARTHUR** (1734–1818) PA, Continental Congress 1785–1787.

**7939.** Bunn, Matthew. "The Life and Adventures of Matthew Bunn." *Buffalo Historical Society Publications* 7 (1904): 377–436.

**7940.** Headley, Joel T. "Major General St. Clair." In his *Washington and His Generals*, vol. 2, 201–224. New York: Baker and Scribner's, 1847.

**7941.** Peterson, Charles J. "Arthur St. Clair." In *The Military Heroes of the Revolution*, 277–284. Philadelphia: J. B. Smith, 1856.

**7942.** Smith, William H. *St. Clair Papers: The Life and Public Services of Arthur St. Clair, Soldier of the Revolutionary War, President of the Continental Congress*. 2 vols. New York: Da Capo Press, 1971.

**7943.** Wilson, Frazer E. *Arthur St. Clair, Rugged Ruler of the Old Northwest: An Epic of the American Frontier*. Richmond, VA: Garrett and Massie, 1944.

**SALINGER, PIERRE EMIL GEORGE** (1925– ) D-CA, Senate 1964.

**7944.** Anderson, Patrick. "Falstaff and the Iceman: Salinger and O'Donnell." In his *The Presidents' Men: White House Assistants of Franklin D. Roosevelt, Harry S. Truman, Dwight D. Eisenhower, John F. Kennedy and Lyndon B. Johnson*, 230–244. Garden City, NY: Doubleday, 1868.

**7945.** Salinger, Pierre. *With Kennedy*. Garden City, NY: Doubleday, 1966.

**SALTONSTALL, LEVERETT** (1783–1845) W-MA, House 1838–1843.

**7946.** Saltonstall, Leverett. *The Papers of Leverett Saltonstall, 1816–1845*. Boston: Massachusetts Historical Society, 1978.

**SALTONSTALL, LEVERETT** (1892–1979) R-MA, Senate 1945–1967.

**7947.** Saltonstall, Leverett. *Salty: Recollections of a Yankee in Politics*. Boston: Boston Globe, 1976.

**SANDERS, BERNARD** (1941– ) I-VT, House 1991– .

**7948.** Conroy, W. J. *Challenging the Boundaries of Reform: Socialism in Burlington*. Philadelphia: Temple University Press, 1990.

**7949.** Rosenfeld, Steven. *Making History in Vermont: The Election of a Socialist to Congress*. Wakefield, NH: Hollowbrook, 1992.

**7950.** Soifer, Steven. *The Socialist Mayor: Bernard Sanders in Burlington, Vermont*. New York: Bergin and Garvey, 1991.

**SANDERS, JARED YOUNG** (1867–1944)
**D-LA, House 1917–1921.**

**7951.** Reeves, Miriam G. "Jared Young Sanders." In her *Governors of Louisiana*, 91–93. Gretna, LA: Pelican, 1972.

**SANDERS, NEWELL** (1850–1939) **R-TN,**
**Senate 1912–1913.**

**7952.** Terral, Rufus. *Newell Sanders: A Biography.* Kingsport, TN: Kingsport Press, 1935.

**SAUND, DALIPH SINGH** (1899–1973)
**D-CA, House 1957–1963.**

**7953.** Glasgow, R. W. "From Chhajalwadi to the United States Congress." In *Nine Who Chose America,* edited by Life International, 77–89. New York: Dutton, 1959.

**7954.** Saund, Dalip S. *Congressman from India.* New York: Dutton, 1960.

**SAWYER, FREDERICK ADOLPHUS**
**(1822–1891) R-SC, Senate 1868–1873.**

**7955.** Rietveld, Ronald D., ed. "Eyewitness Account of Abraham Lincoln's Assassination." *Civil War History* 22 (March 1976): 60–69.

**SAWYER, PHILETUS** (1816–1900) **R-WI,**
**House 1865–1875, Senate 1881–1893.**

**7956.** Current, Richard N. *Pine Logs and Politics: A Life of Philetus Sawyer, 1816–1900.* Madison: State Historical Society of Wisconsin, 1950.

**SAXBE, WILLIAM BART** (1916– ) **R-OH,**
**Senate 1969–1974.**

**7957.** Pollitt, Daniel H. "Senator/Attorney-General Saxbe and the Ineligibility Clause of the Constitution: An Encroachment upon Separation of Powers." *North Carolina Law Review* 53 (November 1974): 111–133.

**SAYERS, JOSEPH DRAPER** (1841–1929)
**D-TX, House 1885–1899.**

**7958.** Welch, June R. "Sayers Was Governor of Catastrophes." In his *The Texas Governor,* 108–111. Irving, TX: G. L. A. Press, 1977.

**SCHENCK, ROBERT CUMMING**
**(1809–1890) R-OH, House 1843–1851,**
**1863–1871.**

**7959.** Havighurst, Walter. "Robert Cumming Schenck: Son of Miami." In his *Men of Old Miami, 1809–1873,* 25–48. New York: Putnam's, 1974.

**7960.** Joyner, Fred B. "Robert Cumming Schenck, First Citizen and Statesman of the Ohio Valley." *Ohio State Archaeological and Historical Quarterly* 58 (July 1949): 286–297.

**7961.** Willson, Beckles. "Schenck, Pierrepont and Welsh (1871–1879)." In his *America's Ambassadors to England (1785–1928),* 358–367. London: Murray, 1928.

**SCHMIDHAUSER, JOHN RICHARD**
**(1922– ) D-IA, House 1965–1967.**

**7962.** Schmidhauser, John R., and Larry L. Berg. *The Supreme Court and Congress: Conflict and Interaction, 1945–1968.* New York: Free Press, 1972.

**SCHMITZ, JOHN GEORGE** (1930– )
**R-CA, House 1970–1973.**

**7963.** Schmitz, John G. *Stranger in the Arena.* Santa Ana, CA: Rayline Printing Company, 1974.

**SCHOEPPEL, ANDREW FRANK**
**(1894–1962) R-KS, Senate 1949–1962.**

**7964.** Koppes, Clayton. "Oscar L. Chapman and McCarthyism." *Colorado Magazine* 56 (Winter/Spring 1979): 35–44.

## SCHURZ, CARL (1829–1906) R-MO, Senate 1869–1875.

**7965.** Adams, Charles F. "Tributes to Hon. Carl Schurz." *Massachusetts Historical Society Proceedings* 40 (January 1906): 395–409.

**7966.** Bancroft, Frederic, ed. *Speeches, Correspondence and Political Papers of Carl Schurz.* 6 vols. New York: Putnam's, 1913.

**7967.** Beard, Annie E. "A True Patriot: Carl Schurz." In her *Our Foreign-Born Citizens,* 235–240. New York: Crowell, 1922.

**7968.** Beisner, Robert L. "Carl Schurz: The Law and the Prophet." In his *Twelve against Empire: The Anti-imperialists, 1898–1900,* 18–34. New York: McGraw-Hill, 1968.

**7969.** Brauer, Kinley J. "Appointment of Carl Schurz as Minister to Spain." *Mid-America* 56 (April 1974): 75–84.

**7970.** Burlingame, Michael A. "The Early Life of Carl Schurz, 1829–1865." Ph.D. dissertation, Johns Hopkins University, 1971.

**7971.** Easum, Chester V. "The Americanization of Carl Schurz." Ph.D. dissertation, University of Wisconsin, 1928.

**7972.** Ely, Margaret. "Carl Schurz: New York Evening Post, 1881–1884." In her *Some Great American Newspaper Editors,* 22–30. White Plains, NY: H. W. Wilson, 1916.

**7973.** Fuess, Claude M. *Carl Schurz, Reformer, 1829–1906.* New York: Dodd, Mead, 1932.

**7974.** ———. "Schurz, Lodge and the Campaign of 1884." *New England Quarterly* 5 (July 1932): 453–482.

**7975.** Husband, Joseph. "Carl Schurz." In his *Americans by Adoption: Brief Biographies of Great Citizens Born in Foreign Lands,* 56–73. Boston: Atlantic Monthly Press, 1920.

**7976.** Lovett, Clara M. *Carl Schurz, 1829–1906: A Biographical Essay and a Selective List of Reading Materials in English.* Washington, DC: Library of Congress, 1983.

**7977.** Morgan, Bayard Q. "Carl Schurz." In *Forty-Eighters,* edited by Adolf E. Zucker, 221–250. New York: Columbia University Press, 1950.

**7978.** Nevins, Allan. "The Villard Purchase: Carl Schurz Editor-in-Chief." In his *The Evening Post,* 438–457. New York: Boni and Liveright, 1922.

**7979.** Peattie, Donald C. "Carl Schurz: German American." In his *Lives of Destiny,* 74–79. Boston: Houghton Mifflin, 1954.

**7980.** Rader, Benjamin G., and Barbara K. Rader. "Carl Schurz: Patriarch of the Anti-imperialism Movement." *Missouri Historical Society Bulletin* 20 (July 1964): 296–306.

**7981.** Schafer, Joseph, ed. *Carl Schurz, Militant Liberal.* Evansville, WI: Antes Press, 1930.

**7982.** Schurz, Carl. *Autobiography.* New York: Scribner's, 1961.

**7983.** ———. *The Intimate Letters of Carl Schurz, 1841–1869.* Edited by Joseph Schafer. Madison: State Historical Society of Wisconsin, 1928.

**7984.** ———. *The Reminiscences of Carl Schurz.* 3 vols. New York: McClure, 1907–1908.

**7985.** ———. *Speeches, Correspondence, and Political Papers of Carl Schurz.* Edited by Frederick Bancroft. New York: Putnam's, 1913.

**7986.** Terzian, James P. *Defender of Human Rights: Carl Schurz.* New York: Messner, 1965.

**7987.** Trefousse, Hans L. *Carl Schurz: A Biography.* Knoxville: University of Tennessee Press, 1982.

**7988.** ———. "Carl Schurz and the Indians." *Great Plains Quarterly* 4 (Spring 1984): 109–120.

**7989.** ———. "Carl Schurz: Myth and Reality." *Yearbook of German-American Studies* 19 (1984): 1–16.

**7990.** Wersich, Rudiger, ed. *Carl Schurz: Revolutionary Statesman, His Life in Personal and Official Documents with Illustrations.* Munchen, Germany: Moos, 1979.

**SCHUYLER, PHILIP JOHN** (1733–1804)
**NY, Senate 1789–1791, 1797–1798,**
**Continental Congress 1775, 1777, 1779–1780.**

**7991.** Bush, Martin H. *Revolutionary Enigma: A Reappraisal of General Philip Schuyler of New York.* Port Washington, NY: Friedman, 1969.

**7992.** Gerlach, Don R. *Philip Schuyler and the American Revolution in New York, 1733–1777.* Lincoln: University of Nebraska Press, 1964.

**7993.** ———. *Philip Schuyler and the Growth of New York, 1733–1804.* Albany, NY: Office of State History, 1968.

**7994.** ———. *Proud Patriot: Philip Schuyler and the War of Independence, 1775–1783.* Syracuse, NY: Syracuse University Press, 1987.

**7995.** Griswold, Rufus W. "Major-General Philip Schuyler." In his *Washington and the Generals of the American Revolution,* vol. 1, 183–193. Philadelphia: Cary and Hart, 1848.

**7996.** Halsey, Francis W. "General Schuyler's Part in the Burgoyne Campaign." *New York State Historical Association Proceedings* 12 (1913): 109–118.

**7997.** Headley, Joel T. "Major General Schuyler." In his *Washington and His Generals,* vol. 1, 229–259. New York: Baker and Scribner's, 1847.

**7998.** Lossing, Benson J. *Life and Times of Philip Schuyler.* 2 vols. New York: Da Capo Press, 1973.

**7999.** Pell, John H. "Philip Schuyler: The General as Aristocrat." In *Washington's Generals,* edited by George A. Billias, 54–78. New York: Morrow, 1964.

**8000.** Peterson, Charles J. "Philip Schuyler." In his *The Military Heroes of the Revolution,* 285–294. Philadelphia: J. B. Smith, 1856.

**8001.** Schuyler, George L. *Correspondence and Remarks upon Bancroft's History of the Northern Campaign of 1779 and the Character of Major Gen. Philip Schuyler.* New York: D. G. Francis, 1867.

**8002.** Tuckerman, Bayard. *Life of General Philip Schuyler, 1733–1804.* Freeport, NY: Books for Libraries, 1969.

**8003.** Wildman, Edwin. "Philip Schuyler: Who Held New York in the Constitutional Course." In his *The Founders of America in the Days of the Revolution,* 175–193. Freeport, NY: Books for Libraries, 1968.

**SCHWEIKER, RICHARD SCHULTZ**
**(1926–  ) R-PA, House 1961–1969, Senate**
**1969–1981.**

**8004.** Landes, Burton R. *Making of a Senator, 1974: A Biography of Richard S. Schweiker.* Trappes, PA: Landes, 1976.

**SCHWELLENBACH, LEWIS BAXTER**
**(1894–1948) D-WA, Senate 1935–1940.**

**8005.** Libby, Justin H. "Anti-Japanese Sentiment in the Pacific Northwest: Senator Schwellenbach and Congressman Coffee Attempt to Embargo Japan, 1937–1941." *Mid-America* 58 (October 1976): 167–174.

**SCOTT, HUGH DOGGETT, JR.**
**(1900–1994) R-PA, House 1941–1945,**
**1947–1959, Senate 1959–1977.**

**8006.** Scott, Hugh D. *Come to the Party.* Englewood Cliffs, NJ: Prentice-Hall, 1968.

**8007.** ———. *How to Go into Politics.* New York: Day, 1949.

**8008.** ———. *How to Run for Public Office and Win!* Washington, DC: National Press, 1968.

**8009.** ———. "The Relationship of a Senator to His Constituency." In *The Senate Institution,* edited by Nathaniel S. Preston, 50–56. New York: Van Nostrand Reinhold, 1969.

**SCOTT, JOHN** (1785–1861) R-MO, House 1816–1817, 1817–1821, 1821–1827.

**8010.** Weiner, Alan S. "John Scott, Thomas Hart Benton, David Barton and the Presidential Election of 1824: A Case Study in Pressure Politics." *Missouri Historical Review* 60 (July 1966): 460–494.

**SCOTT, JOHN MORIN** (1730–1784) NY, Continental Congress 1780–1783.

**8011.** Dillon, Dorothy R. *The New York Triumvirate: A Study of the Legal and Political Careers of William Livingston, John Morin Scott, William Smith, Jr.* New York: Columbia University Press, 1949.

**SCRANTON, WILLIAM WARREN** (1917– ) R-PA, House 1961–1963.

**8012.** Finger, Seymour M. "William W. Scranton." In his *Your Man at the UN,* 249–260. New York: New York University Press, 1980.

**8013.** Wolf, George D. *William Warren Scranton: Pennsylvania Statesman.* University Park: Pennsylvania State University Press, 1981.

**SEDDON, JAMES ALEXANDER** (1815–1880) D-VA, House 1845–1847, 1849–1851.

**8014.** Curry, Roy W. "James A. Seddon, a Southern Prototype." *Virginia Magazine of History and Biography* 63 (April 1955): 123–150.

**8015.** O'Brien, Gerald F. "James A. Seddon, Statesman of the Old South." Ph.D. dissertation, University of Maryland, 1963.

**SEDGWICK, CHARLES BALDWIN** (1815–1883) R-NY, House 1859–1863.

**8016.** Field, Earle. "Charles B. Sedgwick's Letters from Washington, 1859–1861." *Mid-America* 49 (April 1967): 129–139.

**SEDGWICK, THEODORE** (1746–1813) F-MA, House 1789–1796, 1799–1801, Senate 1796–1799, Continental Congress 1785–1786, 1788.

**8017.** Birdsall, Richard D. "Country Gentlemen of the Berkshires." *New-England Galaxy* 3 (Summer 1961): 16–25.

**8018.** Davis, Thomas L. "Aristocrats and Jacobins in Country Towns: Party Formation in Berkshire County, Massachusetts, 1775–1816." Ph.D. dissertation, Boston University, 1975.

**8019.** Dewey, Mary E. *Life and Letters of Catharine M. Sedgwick.* New York: Harper and Brothers, 1871.

**8020.** Field, David A. *A History of the County of Berkshire, Massachusetts.* Pittsfield, MA: Samuel W. Bush, 1829.

**8021.** Furlong, Patrick J. "John Rutledge, Jr., and the Election of a Speaker of the House in 1799." *William and Mary Quarterly* 24 (July 1967): 432–436.

**8022.** Goodwin, Nathaniel. *Genealogical Notes: Or, Contributions to the Family History of Some of the First Settlers of Connecticut and Massachusetts.* Hartford, CT: F. A. Brown, 1856.

**8023.** Jones, Electra F. *Stockbridge, Past and Present: Or, Records of an Old Mission Station.* Springfield, MA: Samuel Bowles, 1854.

**8024.** Sedgwick, Henry D. "The Sedgwicks of Berkshire." *Collections of the Berkshire Historical and Scientific Society* 3 (1900): 91–106.

**8025.** Welch, Richard E. "Mumbet and Judge Sedgwick: A Footnote to the Early History of Massachusetts Justice." *Boston Bar Journal* 8 (January 1964): 12–19.

**8026.** Welch, Richard E. *Theodore Sedgwick, Federalist: A Political Portrait*. Middleton, CT: Wesleyan University Press, 1965.

**SEELYE, JULIUS HAWLEY (1824–1895)**
**I-MA, House 1875–1877.**

**8027.** Patton, Cornelius H., and Walter T. Field. "President Julius H. Seelye." In their *Eight O'Clock Chapel*, 154–160. Boston: Houghton Mifflin, 1927.

**SELVIG, CONRAD GEORGE**
**(1877–1953) R-MN, House 1927–1933.**

**8028.** Selvig, Conrad G. *Tale of Two Valleys: An Autobiography*. Los Angeles: Jones Press, 1951.

**SERGEANT, JONATHAN (1776–1793) NJ,**
**Continental Congress 1776, 1776–1777.**

**8029.** McLachlan, James. "Jonathan Sergeant." In his *Princetonians, 1748–1768*, 407–411. Princeton, NJ: Princeton University Press, 1976.

**SEVIER, AMBROSE HUNDLEY**
**(1801–1848) D-AR, House 1828–1836,**
**Senate 1836–1848.**

**8030.** Walton, Brian G. "Ambrose Hundley Sevier in the United States Senate, 1836–1846." *Arkansas Historical Quarterly* 32 (Spring 1973): 25–60.

**SEVIER, JOHN (1745–1815) R-NC/TN,**
**House 1790–1791 (NC), 1811–1815 (TN).**

**8031.** Bond, Octavia Z. "The Hornet's Nest: On to King's Mountain: A Famous Rescue." In her *Old Tales Retold*, 93–122. Nashville, TN: Smith and Lamar, 1906.

**8032.** Bruce, Philip A. "John Sevier." In his *The Virginia Plutarch*, vol. 1, 306–328. Chapel Hill: University of North Carolina Press, 1929.

**8033.** Driver, Carl S. "John Sevier, a Pioneer of the Old Southwest." Ph.D. dissertation, Vanderbilt University, 1929.

**8034.** Gilmore, James R. *John Sevier as a Commonwealth Builder: A Sequel to the Rear Guard of the Revolution*. New York: Appleton, 1887.

**8035.** Heiskell, Samuel G. "John Sevier." In his *Andrew Jackson and Early Tennessee History*, 311–367. Nashville, TN: Ambrose Printing Company, 1920.

**8036.** Skinner, Constance L. "Sevier, the Statemaker." In her *Pioneers of the Old Southwest*, 226–271. New Haven, CT: Yale University Press, 1919.

**SEWARD, WILLIAM HENRY (1801–1872)**
**R-NY, Senate 1849–1861.**

**8037.** Baker, George E., ed. *The Life of William H. Seward with Selections from His Works*. New York: Houghton Mifflin, 1855.

**8038.** ———, ed. *The Works of William H. Seward*. 5 vols. Boston: Houghton Mifflin, 1853–1884.

**8039.** Bancroft, Frederic. *The Life of William H. Seward*. 2 vols. New York: Harper, 1900.

**8040.** Bartlett, David V. "William H. Seward." In his *Presidential Candidates: Containing Sketches, Biographical, Personal and Political, of Prominent Candidates for the Presidency*, 7–50. New York: A. B. Burdick, 1859.

**8041.** Bradford, Gamaliel. "William Henry Seward." In his *Union Portraits*, 197–230. Boston: Houghton Mifflin, 1916.

**8042.** Brauer, Kinley J. "Seward's Foreign War Panacea: An Interpretation." *New York History* 55 (April 1974): 133–157.

**8043.** Brooks, Noah. "William H. Seward." In his *Statesmen*, 119–142. New York: Scribner's, 1893.

**8044.** Conrad, Earl. *Governor and His Lady: The Story of William Henry Seward and His Wife Frances*. New York: Putnam's, 1960.

**8045.** Coulter, E. Merton. "Seward and the South: His Career as a Georgia Schoolmaster." *Georgia Historical Quarterly* 53 (June 1969): 147–164.

**8046.** Crofts, Daniel W. "Secession Winter: William Henry Seward and the Decision for War." *New York History* 65 (July 1984): 229–256.

**8047.** Curran, Thomas J. "Seward and the Know-Nothings." *New York Historical Society Quarterly* 51 (April 1967): 141–159.

**8048.** Dibble, Ernest F. "War Averters: Seward, Mallory, and Fort Pickens." *Florida Historical Quarterly* 49 (January 1971): 232–244.

**8049.** Estrem, Andrew. "The Statesmanship of William Henry Seward as Seen in His Public Career Prior to 1861." Ph.D. dissertation, Cornell University, 1892.

**8050.** Ferris, Norman B. *Desperate Diplomacy: William H. Seward's Foreign Policy, 1861.* Knoxville: University of Tennessee Press, 1976.

**8051.** Gerdts, William H. "Heads or Tails: The Seward Portrait in City Hall." *Art Quarterly* 21 (Spring 1958): 68–80.

**8052.** Goldwert, Marvin. "Matias Romero and Congressional Opposition to Seward's Policy toward the French Intervention in Mexico." *Americas* 22 (July 1965): 22–40.

**8053.** Hale, Edward E. *William H. Seward.* Philadelphia: G. W. Jacobs, 1910.

**8054.** Hinckley, Ted C. "William H. Seward Visits His Purchase." *Oregon Historical Quarterly* 72 (June 1971): 127–147.

**8055.** Hubbard, Elbert. "William H. Seward." In his *Little Journeys to the Homes of the Great*, vol. 3, 253–276. New York: William H. Wise, 1916.

**8056.** Kunstler, William M. "William Henry Seward." In his *The Case for Courage*, 82–119. New York: Morrow, 1962.

**8057.** Kushner, Howard I. "'Seward's Folly'?: American Commerce in Russian America and the Alaska Purchase." *California Historical Quarterly* 54 (Spring 1975): 4–26.

**8058.** Lannie, Vincent P. *Public Money and Parochial Education: Bishop Hughes, Governor Seward, and the New York School Controversy.* Cleveland, OH: Press of Case Western Reserve University, 1968.

**8059.** ———. "William Seward and Common School Education." *History of Education Quarterly* 4 (September 1964): 181–192.

**8060.** Lodge, Henry C. "William H. Seward." In his *Historical and Political Essays*, 1–46. Boston: Houghton Mifflin, 1892.

**8061.** Lothrop, Thornton K. *William Henry Seward.* Boston: Houghton Mifflin, 1896.

**8062.** Macartney, Clarence E. "William Henry Seward: Lincoln and His Prime Minister." In his *Lincoln and His Cabinet.* 83–179. New York: Scribner's, 1931.

**8063.** Miller, Wayne V. "The Emergence of William Henry Seward as a National Political Leader, 1847–1859." Ph.D. dissertation, University of Southern California, 1957.

**8064.** Nalty, Bernard C., and Truman R. Strobridge. "Mission to Peking, 1870: Captain McLane Tilton's Letter Describing His Trip with the Seward Party to Peking." *American Neptune* 25 (April 1965): 116–127.

**8065.** O'Rourke, Mary M. "The Diplomacy of William H. Seward during the Civil War: His Policies as Related to International Law." Ph.D. dissertation, University of California, Berkeley, 1963.

**8066.** Paolino, Ernest N. *The Foundations of the American Empire: William Henry Seward and U.S. Foreign Policy.* Ithaca, NY: Cornell University Press, 1973.

**8067.** Patterson, Richard S. "William H. Seward as Secretary of State." *U.S. Department of State Bulletin* 44 (May 15, 1961): 728–730.

**8068.** Perkins, Frederic B. "William Henry Seward." In his *The Picture and the Men,* 114–136. New York: A. J. Johnson, 1867.

**8069.** Piatt, Donn. "William H. Seward." In his *Memories of the Men Who Saved the Union,* 132–171. New York: Belford, Clarke, 1887.

**8070.** Scheidenhelm, Richard J. "The Legal and Political Rhetoric of William Henry Seward." Ph.D. dissertation, University of Wisconsin, 1970.

**8071.** Seitz, Don C. "William H. Seward." In his *The "Also Rans": Great Men Who Missed Making the Presidential Goal,* 192–207. New York: Thomas Y. Crowell Company, 1928.

**8072.** Seward, Frederick W., ed. *William H. Seward: An Autobiography from 1801 to 1834, with a Memoir of His Life, and Selections from His Letters.* 3 vols. New York: Derby and Miller, 1890.

**8073.** Sharrow, Walter G. "William Henry Seward: A Study in Nineteenth Century Politics and Nationalism, 1855–1861." Ph.D. dissertation, University of Rochester, 1965.

**8074.** ———. "William Henry Seward and the Basis for American Empire, 1850–1860." *Pacific Historical Review* 36 (August 1967): 325–342.

**8075.** Stegmaier, Mark J. "Intensifying the Sectional Conflict: William Seward versus James Hammond on the Lecompton Debate of 1858." *Civil War History* 31 (September 1985): 197–221.

**8076.** Taylor, John M. *William Henry Seward: The Definitive Biography of Abraham Lincoln's Controversial Secretary of State.* New York: HarperCollins, 1991.

**8077.** Temple, Henry W. "William H. Seward." In *The American Secretaries of State and Their Diplomacy,* edited by Samuel F. Bemis, vol. 7, 1–115. New York: Knopf, 1928.

**8078.** Van Deusen, Glyndon G. *William Henry Seward.* New York: Oxford University Press, 1967.

**8079.** Warren, Gordon H. "Imperial Dreamer: William Henry Seward and American Destiny." In *Makers of American Diplomacy,* edited by Frank J. Merli and Theodore A. Wilson, 195–221. New York: Scribner's, 1974.

**8080.** Welles, Gideon. *Lincoln and Seward.* New York: Sheldon, 1874.

**8081.** Whelan, Joseph G. "William Henry Seward, Expansionist." Ph.D. dissertation, University of Rochester, 1959.

**8082.** Wilson, Major L. "Repressible Conflict: Seward's Concept of Progress and the Free-Soil Movement." *Journal of Southern History* 37 (November 1971): 533–556.

**8083.** Woodward, Isaiah A. "Life of William H. Seward and His Role in the Crisis of 1850 and 1860." *Negro History Bulletin* 25 (November 1961): 27–31.

**SEYMOUR, HORATIO** (1778–1857) VT, Senate 1821–1833.

**8084.** Carroll, Howard. "Horatio Seymour." In his *Twelve Americans: Their Lives and Times,* 1–48. Freeport: Books for Libraries, 1971.

**8085.** Mitchell, Stewart. *Horatio Seymour of New York.* Cambridge, MA: Harvard University Press, 1938.

**SHANKS, JOHN PETER CLEAVER** (1826–1901) R-IN, House 1861–1863, 1867–1875.

**8086.** Barnes, William H. "John P. C. Shanks." In his *Lives of Gen. Ulysses S. Grant and Hon. Henry Wilson, Together with Sketches of Republican Candidates for Congress in Indiana,* 45–50. New York: W. H. Barnes, 1872.

**SHANNON, JOSEPH BERNARD**
**(1867–1943) D-MO, House 1931–1943.**

**8087.** Blackmore, Charles P. "Joseph B. Shannon, Political Boss and Twentieth Century Jeffersonian." Ph.D. dissertation, Columbia University, 1953.

**SHANNON, WILSON (1802–1877) D-OH, House 1853–1855.**

**8088.** Day, Donald E. "A Life of Wilson Shannon, Governor of Ohio, Diplomat, Territorial Governor of Kansas." Ph.D. dissertation, Ohio State University, 1978.

**8089.** Smith, S. Winifred. "Wilson Shannon, 1838–1840, 1842–1844." In *Governors of Ohio*, 42–45. Columbus: Ohio Historical Society, 1954.

**SHARON, WILLIAM (1821–1885) R-NV, Senate 1875–1881.**

**8090.** Eliot, Elizabeth. "The Golden West." In her *Heiresses and Coronets*, 210–253. New York: McDowell, Obolensky, 1959.

**8091.** Kroninger, Robert H. *Sarah and the Senator.* Berkeley, CA: Howell-North, 1964.

**8092.** Roberts, Gary L. "In Pursuit of Duty." *American West* 7 (September 1970): 27–33.

**SHARP, SOLOMON P. (1780–1825) R-KY, House 1813–1817.**

**8093.** Beauchamp, Jereboam O. *The Confession of Jereboam O. Beauchamp.* Philadelphia: University of Pennsylvania Press, 1966.

**8094.** Coleman, John W. *The Beauchamp-Sharp Tragedy: An Episode of Kentucky History during the Middle 1820's.* Frankfort, KY: Roberts Printing Company, 1950.

**8095.** Kallsen, Loren J., ed. *The Kentucky Tragedy: A Problem in Romantic Attitudes.* Indianapolis: Bobbs-Merrill, 1963.

**SHARP, WILLIAM GRAVES (1859–1922) D-OH, House 1909–1914.**

**8096.** Sharp, William G. *The War Memoirs of William Graves Sharp, American Ambassador to France, 1914–1919.* London: Constable and Company, 1931.

**8097.** Willson, Beckles. "Herrick and Sharp (1912–19)." In his *America's Ambassadors to France (1777–1927)*, 397–410. London: Murray, 1928.

**SHELBY, RICHARD CRAIG (1934– ) D-AL, House 1979–1987, Senate 1987– .**

**8098.** Powell, Larry, and Annette Shelby. "A Strategy of Assumed Incumbency: A Case Study." *Southern Speech Communication Journal* 46 (Winter 1981): 105–123.

**SHEPPARD, MORRIS (1875–1941) D-TX, House 1902–1913, Senate 1913–1941.**

**8099.** Bailey, Richard. "Morris Sheppard of Texas: Southern Progressive and Prohibitionist." Ph.D. dissertation, Texas Christian University, 1980.

**8100.** ———. "Troubles in Texas: Senator Morris Sheppard of Texas, 1913–1919." *Red River Valley Historical Review* 7, no. 3 (1982): 30–36.

**8101.** Dude, Escal F. "The Political Career of Morris Sheppard, 1875–1941." Ph.D. dissertation, University of Texas, 1958.

**8102.** Welch, June R. "Sheppard Was the Father of National Prohibition." In his *The Texas Senator,* 116. Dallas, TX: G. L. A. Press, 1978.

**SHERMAN, JAMES SCHOOLCRAFT (1855–1912) R-NY, House 1887–1891, 1893–1909.**

**8103.** Barzman, Sol. "James Schoolcraft Sherman." In his *Madmen and Geniuses: The Vice-Presidents of the United States,* 183–188. Chicago: Follett, 1974.

**SHERMAN, JOHN** (1823–1900) R-OH, House 1855–1861, Senate 1861–1877, 1881–1897.

**8104.** Bridges, Roger D. "The Constitutional World of Senator John Sherman, 1861–1869." Ph.D. dissertation, University of Illinois, 1970.

**8105.** Bronson, Sherlock A. *John Sherman*. Columbus, OH: H. W. Derby, 1880.

**8106.** Burton, Theodore E. *John Sherman*. Boston: Houghton Mifflin, 1906.

**8107.** Crenshaw, Ollinger. "The Speakership Contest of 1859–1860: John Sherman's Election a Cause of Disruption." *Mississippi Valley Historical Review* 29 (December 1942): 323–338.

**8108.** Grayson, Theodore J. "John Sherman: The Resumption of Species Payments." In his *Leaders and Periods of American Finance*, 266–286. New York: J. Wiley, 1932.

**8109.** Kerr, Winfield S. *John Sherman: His Life and Public Service*. 2 vols. Boston: Sherman, French, 1908.

**8110.** Matthews, John H. "John Sherman and American Foreign Relations, 1883–1898." Ph.D. dissertation, Emory University, 1976.

**8111.** Nichols, Jeanette D. "John Sherman: A Study in Inflation." *Mississippi Valley Historical Review* 21 (September 1934): 181–194.

**8112.** ———. "Rutherford B. Hayes and John Sherman." *Ohio Historical Quarterly* 77 (Winter/Spring/Summer 1968): 125–138.

**8113.** ———. "Sherman and the Silver Drive of 1877–78." *Ohio State Archaeological and Historical Quarterly* 46 (April 1937): 148–165.

**8114.** Randall, James G. "John Sherman and Reconstruction." *Mississippi Valley Historical Review* 19 (December 1932): 382–383.

**8115.** Sears, Louis M. "John Sherman." In *The American Secretaries of State and Their Diplomacy*, edited by Samuel F. Bemis, vol. 9, 1–23. New York: Knopf, 1929.

**8116.** Sherman, John. *John Sherman's Recollections of Forty Years in the House, Senate and Cabinet: An Autobiography*. 2 vols. Chicago: Werner, 1895.

**8117.** Thorndike, Rachel S., ed. *The Sherman Letters: Correspondence between General Sherman and Senator Sherman, from 1837 to 1891*. London: Sampson Low, Marston, 1894.

**8118.** Weaver, John B. "John Sherman and the Politics of Economic Change." *Hayes Historical Journal* 6 (Spring 1987): 6–19.

**SHERMAN, LAWRENCE YATES** (1858–1939) R-IL, Senate 1913–1921.

**8119.** Stone, Ralph A. "Two Illinois Senators Among the Irreconcilables." *Mississippi Valley Historical Review* 50 (December 1963): 443–465.

**SHERMAN, ROGER** (1721–1793) CT, House 1789–1791, Senate 1791–1793, Continental Congress 1774–1781, 1784.

**8120.** Beals, Carleton. "Shoemaker Statesman." In his *Our Yankee Heritage*, 150–168. New York: McKay, 1955.

**8121.** Beisner, Robert L. "Pathetic End." In his *Twelve against Empire*, 197–203. New York: McGraw-Hill, 1968.

**8122.** Boardman, Roger S. *Roger Sherman, Signer and Statesman*. Philadelphia: University of Pennsylvania Press, 1938.

**8123.** Boutell, Lewis H. *The Life of Roger Sherman*. Chicago: A. C. McClurg, 1896.

**8124.** Collier, Christopher. *Roger Sherman's Connecticut: Yankee Politics and the American Revolution*. Middletown, CT: Wesleyan University Press, 1971.

**8125.** Rommel, John G. *Connecticut's Yankee Patriot, Roger Sherman*. Hartford, CT: American Revolution Bicentennial Commission of Connecticut, 1979.

**8126.** Sanderson, John. "Roger Sherman." In *Sanderson's Biography of the Signers of the Declaration of Independence,* edited by Robert T. Conrad, 222–240. Philadelphia: Thomas, Cowperthwait, 1848.

**SHIELDS, JAMES** (1810–1879)
**D-IL/MN/MO, Senate 1849 (IL), 1849–1855 (IL), 1858–1859 (MN), 1879 (MO).**

**8127.** Condon, William H. *Life of Major-General James Shields.* Chicago: Blakely Printing Company, 1900.

**8128.** Curran, Judith M. "The Career of James Shields, an Immigrant Irishman in Nineteenth Century America." Ph.D. dissertation, Columbia University Teachers College, 1980.

**8129.** Myers, James E. *The Astonishing Saber Duel of Abraham Lincoln.* Springfield, IL: Lincoln-Herndon Building Publishers, 1968.

**8130.** Schauinger, Joseph H. "James Shields." In his *Profiles in Action: American Catholics in Public Life,* 146–155. Milwaukee, WI: Bruce, 1966.

**SHIELDS, JOHN KNIGHT** (1858–1934)
**D-TN, Senate 1913–1925.**

**8131.** Foster, James P. "The Public Career of John K. Shields." Master's thesis, University of Tennessee, 1965.

**SHIPSTEAD, HENRIK** (1881–1960) **R-MN, Senate 1923–1947.**

**8132.** Lorentz, Mary R. "Henrik Shipstead: Minnesota Independent, 1923–1946." Ph.D. dissertation, Catholic University of America, 1963.

**8133.** Matsen, William E. "William A. Schaper, War Hysteria, and the Price of Academic Freedom." *Minnesota History* 51 (Winter 1988): 130–137.

**8134.** Moose, Malcolm C., and Edwin W. Kenworthy. "Dr. Shipstead Come to Judgement." *Harper's Magazine* 193 (July 1946): 21–27.

**8135.** Ross, Martin. *Shipstead of Minnesota.* Chicago: Packard and Company, 1940.

**8136.** Stuhler, Barbara. "The Political Enigma of Henrik Shipstead." In her *Ten Men of Minnesota and American Foreign Policy, 1898–1968,* 76–98. St. Paul: Minnesota Historical Society, 1973.

**SHOEMAKER, FRANCIS HENRY** (1889–1958) **FL-MN, House 1933–1935.**

**8137.** Johnson, Frederick L. "From Leavenworth to Congress: The Improbable Journey of Francis H. Shoemaker." *Minnesota History* 51 (Spring 1989): 166–177.

**SHORT, DEWEY JACKSON** (1898–1979) **R-MO, House 1929–1931, 1935–1957.**

**8138.** Wiley, Robert S. *Dewey Short, Orator of the Ozarks.* Crane, MO: R. S. Wiley, 1985.

**SHOUP, GEORGE LAIRD** (1836–1904) **R-ID, Senate 1890–1901.**

**8139.** Crowder, David L. "George Laird Shoup." *Idaho Yesterdays* 33 (Winter 1990): 18–23.

**SIBLEY, HENRY HASTINGS** (1811–1891) **WI/MN, House 1848–1849 (WI), 1849–1853 (MN).**

**8140.** Jorstad, Erling T. "The Life of Henry Hastings Sibley." Ph.D. dissertation, University of Wisconsin, 1957.

**8141.** Shortridge, Wilson P. "The Transition of a Typical Frontier, with Illustration from the Life of Henry Hastings Sibley, Fur Trader, First Delegate in Congress from Minnesota Territory, and First Governor of the State of Minnesota." Ph.D. dissertation, University of Minnesota, 1919.

**8142.** West, Nathaniel. *The Ancestry, Life and Times of Hon. Henry Hastings Sibley, LL.D.* St Paul, MN: Pioneer Press Publishing Company, 1889.

**SICKLES, DANIEL EDGAR (1819–1914) D-NY, House 1857–1861, 1893–1895.**

**8143.** Brandt, Nat. *The Congressman Who Got Away with Murder.* Syracuse, NY: Syracuse University Press, 1991.

**8144.** Clark, Champ. "Sixteen Generals-Wheeler and Sickles: The Sickles Trial." In his *My Quarter Century of American Politics,* vol. 2, 37–51. New York: Harper and Brothers, 1920.

**8145.** Morris, Richard B. "The Fate of the Flagrant Adulterer." In his *Fair Trial,* 225–258. New York: Knopf, 1952.

**8146.** Sparrow, Gerald. "Winter in Washington." In his *Great Assassins,* 98–106. New York: Arco, 1969.

**8147.** Swanberg, William A. *Sickles the Incredible.* New York: Scribner's, 1956.

**SIKES, ROBERT LEE FULTON (1906– ) D-FL, House 1941–1944, 1945–1979.**

**8148.** Sikes, Robert. *He-Coon, the Bob Sikes Story: An Autobiography.* Pensacola, FL: Perdido Bay Press, 1984.

**SIMMONS, FURNIFOLD McLENDEL (1854–1940) D-NC, House 1887–1889, Senate 1901–1931.**

**8149.** Edmunds, Pocahontas W. "Furnifold McLendel Simmons." In her *Tar Heels Track the Century,* 203–219. Raleigh, NC: Edwards and Broughton, 1966.

**8150.** Rippy, James F., ed. *F. M. Simmons, Statesman of the New South: Memoirs and Addresses.* Durham, NC: Duke University Press, 1936.

**SIMON, PAUL MARTIN (1928– ) D-IL, House 1975–1985, Senate 1985– .**

**8151.** Gove, Samuel K., and Michael B. Preston. "State-Local (Chicago) Relations in Illinois: The Harold Washington Era, 1984." *Publius* 15 (Summer 1985): 143–154.

**8152.** Simon, Jeanne. *Codename Scarlett: Life on the Campaign Trail.* New York: Continuum, 1989.

**8153.** Simon, Paul. *Winners and Losers: The 1988 Race for the Presidency—One Candidate's Perspective.* New York: Continuum, 1989.

**SIMPSON, JEREMIAH "JERRY" (1842–1905) P-KS, House 1891–1895, 1897–1899.**

**8154.** Beals, Carleton. "Sockless Socrates." In his *Great Revolt and Its Leaders,* 159–182. New York: Abelard-Schuman, 1968.

**8155.** Bicha, Karel D. "Jerry Simpson: Populist without Principle." *Journal of American History* 54 (September 1967): 291–306.

**8156.** Diggs, Annie L. *The Story of Jerry Simpson.* Wichita, KS: Jane Simpson, 1908.

**8157.** Johnson, Gerald W. "Sockless Jerry Simpson." In his *Lunatic Fringe,* 139–151. New York: Lippincott, 1957.

**SIMS, ALEXANDER DROMGOOLE (1803–1848) D-SC, House 1845–1848.**

**8158.** Wheeler, Henry G. "Sims, Alexander Dromgoole." In his *History of Congress,* vol. 1, 366–375. New York: Harper, 1848.

**SISK, BERNICE FREDERIC (1910– ) D-CA, House 1955–1979.**

**8159.** Sisk, Bernice F. *A Congressional Record: The Memoir of Bernie Sisk.* Fresno, CA: Panorama West, 1980.

**SKEEN, JOSEPH RICHARD (1927– ) R-NM, House 1981– .**

**8160.** Vigil, Maurilio E. "Anatomy of a Successful Congressional Write-In Campaign: New Mexico, 1980." *Social Science* 56 (Summer 1981): 146–157.

**SKINNER, CHARLES RUFUS**
**(1844–1928) R-NY, House 1881–1885.**

**8161.** Skinner, Charles R. "How Congress Acted Forty Years Ago: Reminiscences of a Member from New York State." *State Service* 8 (December 1924): 104–110.

**SLAYDEN, JAMES LUTHER (1853–1924)**
**D-TX, House 1897–1919.**

**8162.** Pohl, James W. "Slayden's Defeat: A Texas Congressman Loses Bid as Wilson's Secretary of War." *Military History of Texas and the Southwest* 10 (1972): 43–56.

**SLEMP, CAMPBELL BASCOM**
**(1870–1943) R-VA, House 1907–1923.**

**8163.** Hathorn, Guy B. "C. Bascom Slemp—Virginia Republican Boss, 1907–1932." *Journal of Politics* 17 (May 1955): 248–264.

**8164.** ———. "Congressional Campaign in the Fighting Ninth: The Contest between C. Bascom Slemp and Henry C. Stuart." *Virginia Magazine of History and Biography* 66 (July 1958): 337–344.

**8165.** ———. "The Political Career of C. Bascom Slemp." Ph.D. dissertation, Duke University, 1950.

**SLIDELL, JOHN (1793–1871) D-LA,**
**House 1843–1845, Senate 1853–1861.**

**8166.** Diket, Albert L. *Senator John Slidell and the Community He Represented in Washington, 1853–1861*. Washington, DC: University Press of America, 1982.

**8167.** Sears, Louis M. *John Slidell*. Durham, NC: Duke University Press, 1925.

**8168.** Tregle, Joseph G. "Political Apprenticeship of John Slidell." *Journal of Southern History* 26 (February 1960): 57–70.

**8169.** Willson, Beckles. *John Slidell and the Confederates in Paris, 1862–65*. New York: Minton, Balch, 1932.

**SLOCUM, HENRY WARNER (1827–1894)**
**D-NY, House 1869–1873, 1883–1885.**

**8170.** Deaderick, John B. "Slocum, Henry Warner." In his *Strategy in the Civil War*, 188–189. Harrisburg, PA: Military Service, 1946.

**SMALLS, ROBERT (1839–1915) R-SC,**
**House 1875–1879, 1882–1883, 1884–1887.**

**8171.** Christopher, Maurine. "Robert Smalls/South Carolina." In her *Black Americans in Congress*, 38–54. Rev. ed. New York: Thomas Y. Crowell, 1976.

**8172.** Miller, Edward A. *Gullah Statesman: Robert Smalls from Slavery to Congress*. Columbia: University of South Carolina Press, 1994.

**8173.** Simmons, William J. "Robert Smalls." In his *Men of Mark*, 165–179. New York: Arno Press, 1968.

**SMATHERS, GEORGE ARMISTEAD**
**(1913–  ) D-FL, House 1947–1951,**
**Senate 1951–1969.**

**8174.** Sherrill, Robert G. "Power Game: George Smathers, the Golden Senator from Florida." *Nation* 199 (December 7, 1964): 426–437.

**SMITH, CALEB BLOOD (1808–1864)**
**W-IN, House 1843–1849.**

**8175.** Bochin, Hal W. "Caleb B. Smith's Opposition to the Mexican War." *Indiana Magazine of History* 69 (June 1973): 75–114.

**8176.** Macartney, Clarence E. "Caleb Blood Smith." In his *Lincoln and His Cabinet*, 47–58. New York: Scribner's, 1931.

**8177.** Thomas, Richard J. "Caleb Blood Smith, Whig Orator and Politician Lincoln's Secretary of Interior." Ph.D. dissertation, Indiana University, 1969.

**SMITH, DANIEL** (1748–1818) R-TN, Senate 1798–1799, 1805–1809.

**8178.** Durham, Walter T. *Daniel Smith: Frontier Statesman.* Gallatin, TN: Sumner County Library Board, 1976.

**8179.** Sioussat, St. George L., ed. "The Journal of Daniel Smith." *Tennessee Historical Magazine* 1 (March 1915): 40–65.

**SMITH, ELLISON DURANT** (1866–1944) D-SC, Senate 1909–1944.

**8180.** Plummer, Leonard N. "Ellison Durant Smith." In *Public Men In and Out of Office,* edited by John T. Salter, 344–354. Chapel Hill: University of North Carolina Press, 1946.

**8181.** Smith, Selden K. "Ellison Durant Smith: A Southern Progressive, 1909–1929." Ph.D. dissertation, University of South Carolina, 1970.

**SMITH, FRANCIS ORMAND JONATHAN** (1806–1876) D-ME, House 1833–1839.

**8182.** Gaffney, Thomas L. "Maine's Mr. Smith: A Study of the Career of Francis O. J. Smith, Politician and Entrepreneur." Ph.D. dissertation, University of Maine, 1979.

**SMITH, FRANK ELLIS** (1918– ) D-MS, House 1951–1962.

**8183.** Mitchell, Dennis J. "Frank E. Smith: Mississippi Liberal." *Journal of Mississippi History* 48 (May 1986): 85–104.

**8184.** Smith, Frank E. *Congressman from Mississippi.* New York: Pantheon, 1964.

**8185.** ———. "The Democratic Idea and Southern Congressional Politics." *Mississippi Quarterly* 18 (Fall 1965): 223–230.

**SMITH, FRANK LESLIE** (1867–1950) R-IL, House 1919–1921.

**8186.** Wooddy, Carroll H. *The Case of Frank L. Smith: A Study in Representative Government.* Chicago: University of Chicago Press, 1931.

**SMITH, GERRIT** (1797–1874) FS-NY, House 1853–1854.

**8187.** Harlow, Ralph V. *Gerrit Smith, Philanthropist and Reformer.* New York: Holt, 1939.

**8188.** O'Callaghan, Edmund B. *Controversy between New York Tribune and Gerrit Smith.* New York: John A. Gray, 1855.

**SMITH, GREEN CLAY** (1826–1895) UU-KY, House 1863–1866.

**8189.** Hood, James L. "For the Union: Kentucky's Unconditional Unionist Congressmen and the Development of the Republican Party in Kentucky, 1863–1865." *Register of the Kentucky Historical Society* 76 (July 1978): 197–215.

**SMITH, HOKE** (1855–1931) D-GA, Senate 1911–1921.

**8190.** Bawden, William T. "Leaders in Industrial Education." *Industrial Arts and Vocational Education* 40 (April 1951): 147–148.

**8191.** Carageorge, Ted. "An Evaluation of Hoke Smith and Thomas E. Watson as Georgia Reformers." Ph.D. dissertation, University of Georgia, 1963.

**8192.** Grant, Philip A. "Senator Hoke Smith, Southern Congressmen, and Agricultural Education, 1914–1917." *Agricultural History* 60 (Spring 1986): 111–122.

**8193.** Grantham, Dewey W. "Hoke Smith and the New Freedom, 1913–1917." In *Studies in Southern History,* edited by Joseph C. Sitterson, 139–151. Chapel Hill: University of North Carolina Press, 1957.

**8194.** ———. *Hoke Smith and the Politics of the New South.* Baton Rouge: Louisiana State University Press, 1958.

**8195.** ———. "Hoke Smith: Progressive Governor of Georgia, 1907–1909." *Journal of Southern History* 15 (November 1949): 423–440.

## SMITH, HOWARD ALEXANDER
(1880–1966) R-NJ, Senate 1944–1959.

**8196.** Leary, William M., Jr. "Smith of New Jersey: A Biography of Alexander Smith, United States Senator from New Jersey, 1944–1959." Ph.D. dissertation, Princeton University, 1966.

## SMITH, HOWARD WORTH (1883–1976) D-VA, House 1931–1967.

**8197.** Brauer, Carl M. "Women Activists, Southern Conservatives, and Prohibition of Sex Discrimination in Title VII of the 1964 Civil Rights Act." *Journal of Southern History* 49 (January 1983): 37–57.

**8198.** Dierenfield, Bruce J. *Keeper of the Rules: Congressman Howard W. Smith of Virginia.* Charlottesville: University Press of Virginia, 1986.

## SMITH, ISAAC (1740–1807) F-NJ, House 1795–1797.

**8199.** McLachlan, James. "Isaac Smith." In his *Princetonians, 1748–1768*, 147–150. Princeton, NJ: Princeton University Press, 1976.

## SMITH, JOHN (1735–1824) R-OH, Senate 1803–1808.

**8200.** Wilhelmy, Robert W. "Senator John Smith and the Aaron Burr Conspiracy." *Cincinnati Historical Society Bulletin* 28 (Spring 1970): 39–60.

## SMITH, MARCUS AURELIUS
(1851–1924) D-AZ, House 1887–1895, 1897–1899, 1901–1903, 1905–1909, Senate 1912–1921.

**8201.** Fazio, Steven A. "Marcus Aurelius Smith: Arizona Delegate and Senator." *Arizona and the West* 12 (Spring 1970): 23–62.

## SMITH, MARGARET CHASE
(1897–1995) R-ME, House 1940–1949, Senate 1949–1973.

**8202.** Burton-Norris, Judith. "The Personhood of Margaret Chase Smith: Methodology of a Video Tape Series Inspired by Abraham Maslow's Research on Self-Actualization." Ph.D. dissertation, Union for Experimenting Colleges and Universities, 1986.

**8203.** Fleming, Alice M. *The Senator from Maine: Margaret Chase Smith.* New York: Crowell, 1969.

**8204.** Gallant, Gregory P. "Margaret Chase Smith, McCarthyism and the Drive for Political Purification." Ph.D. dissertation, University of Maine, 1992.

**8205.** Gould, Alberta. *First Lady of the Senate: A Life of Margaret Chase Smith.* Mt. Desert, ME: Windswept House Publishers, 1990.

**8206.** Graham, Frank. *Margaret Chase Smith: Woman of Courage.* New York: Day, 1964.

**8207.** Graham, Mary W. "Margaret Chase Smith." *Quarterly Journal of Speech* 50 (December 1964): 390–394.

**8208.** Lamson, Peggy. "One in a Hundred: Margaret Chase Smith." In her *Few Are Chosen: American Women in Political Life Today*, 3–29. Boston: Houghton Mifflin, 1968.

**8209.** Parshalle, Eve. "Margaret Chase Smith." In her *Kashmir Bridge-Women*, 61–65. New York: Oxford University Press, 1965.

**8210.** Sherman, Janann. "They Either Need Women or They Do Not: Margaret Chase Smith and the Fight for Regular Status in the Military." *Journal of Military History* 54 (January 1990): 47–78.

**8211.** Smith, Margaret C. *Declaration of Conscience.* Edited by William C. Lewis, Jr. Garden City, NJ: Doubleday, 1972.

**8212.** Smith, Margaret C., and H. Paul Jeffers. *Gallant Women.* New York: McGraw-Hill, 1968.

**8213.** Truman, Margaret. "I Speak as a Woman." In her *Women of Courage,* 201–218. New York: Morrow, 1976.

**SMITH, NATHAN** (1770–1835) W-CT, Senate 1833–1835.

**8214.** Smith, Emily, ed. *Life and Letters of Nathan Smith.* New Haven, CT: Yale University Press, 1914.

**SMITH, ROBERT** (1802–1867) D-IL, House 1843–1849, 1857–1859.

**8215.** Wheeler, Henry G. "Smith, Robert." In his *History of Congress,* vol. 1, 464–477. New York: Harper, 1848.

**SMITH, SAMUEL** (1752–1839) R-MD, House 1793–1803, 1816–1822, Senate 1803–1815, 1822–1823.

**8216.** Cassell, Frank A. *Merchant Congressman in the Young Republic: Samuel Smith of Maryland, 1752–1839.* Madison: University of Wisconsin Press, 1971.

**8217.** Essary, J. Frederick. "General Samuel Smith." In his *Maryland in National Politics,* 96–111. Baltimore: John Murphy, 1915.

**8218.** Pancake, John S. *Samuel Smith and the Politics of Business, 1752–1839.* University: University of Alabama Press, 1972.

**SMITH, THOMAS VERNOR** (1890–1964) D-IL, House 1939–1941.

**8219.** Smith, Thomas V. *The Legislative Way of Life.* Chicago: University of Chicago Press, 1940.

**SMITH, WILLIAM** (1762–1840) R-SC, Senate 1816–1823, 1826–1831.

**8220.** Davis, Richard W. "William Smith: A Study in the Politics of Dissent." Ph.D. dissertation, Columbia University, 1964.

**8221.** Smith, Caroline P. "Jacksonian Conservative: The Later Years of William Smith, 1826–1840." Ph.D. dissertation, Auburn University, 1977.

**SMITH, WILLIAM** (1797–1887) D-VA, House 1841–1843, 1853–1861.

**8222.** Fahrner, Alvin A. "The Public Career of William 'Extra Billy' Smith." Ph.D. dissertation, University of North Carolina, 1953.

**SMITH, WILLIAM ALDEN** (1859–1932) R-MI, House 1895–1907, Senate 1907–1919.

**8223.** Goss, Dwight. "William Alden Smith." In his *A History of Grand Rapids and Its Industries,* 801–802. Chicago: C. F. Cooper, 1906.

**8224.** Moore, Charles. "William Alden Smith." In his *A History of Michigan,* vol. 4, 1978–1980. Chicago: Lewis Publishing Co., 1915.

**8225.** Reed, George I., ed. "William Alden Smith." In his *Bench and Bar of Michigan,* 171–173. Chicago: Century, 1897.

**8226.** Sparks, Frank M. "William Alden Smith." In *Men Who Have Made Michigan,* edited by Edwin G. Pipp, 8–9. Detroit, MI: Pipps Magazine, 1928.

**8227.** Thompson, Charles W. "The Stampedes of William Alden Smith." In his *Party Leaders of the Time,* 205–213. New York: Dillingham, 1906.

**8228.** Wade, Wyn C. "The Senator and the Shipwreck." *Michigan History* 63 (November/December 1979): 10–19.

**SMITH, WILLIAM LOUGHTON** (1758–1812) F-SC, House 1789–1797.

**8229.** Rogers, George C. *Evolution of a Federalist: William Loughton Smith of Charleston.* Columbia: University of South Carolina Press, 1962.

**SMITH, WILLIAM RUSSELL** (1815–1896)
AP-AL, House 1851–1857.

**8230.** Fry, Joseph A. "Profit, Reputation and Clio: A Note on William Russell Smith's Debates." *Alabama Review* 37 (October 1984): 271–276.

**8231.** Owen, Thomas M. "William Russell Smith." In *Library of Southern Literature,* edited by Edwin A. Alderman and Joel C. Harris, vol. 11, 4985–4991. New Orleans: Martin and Hoyt, 1909.

**SMITH, WILLIAM STEPHENS**
(1755–1816) F-NY, House 1813–1815.

**8232.** Launitz-Schurer, Leopold S. "Feudal Revival or Republican Government: An Interpretation of the Loyalist Ideology of William Smith of New York." *Australian Journal of Politics and History* 30 (1984): 236–247.

**8233.** Pickering, Timothy. "Lieut. Col. William Stephens Smith." In his *A Review of the Correspondence between John Adams and Wm. Cunningham,* 143–155. Salem: Cushing and Appleton, 1824.

**8234.** Roof, Katharine M. *Colonel William Smith and Lady.* Boston: Houghton Mifflin, 1928.

**SMOOT, REED** (1862–1941) R-UT, Senate 1903–1933.

**8235.** Alexander, Thomas G. "Senator Reed Smoot and Western Land Policy, 1905–1920." *Arizona and the West* 13 (Autumn 1971): 245–264.

**8236.** ———. "Teapot Dome Revisited: Reed Smoot and Conservation in the 1920s." *Utah Historical Quarterly* 45 (Fall 1977): 352–368.

**8237.** Allen, James B. "The Great Protectionist, Senator Reed Smoot of Utah." *Utah Historical Quarterly* 45 (Fall 1977): 325–345.

**8238.** Cardon, A. F. "Senator Reed Smoot and the Mexican Revolutions." *Utah Historical Quarterly* 31 (Spring 1963): 151–163.

**8239.** Dennis, Alfred P. "Senator Smoot—Diligent in Business." In his *Gods and Little Fishes,* 207–227. Indianapolis: Bobbs-Merrill, 1931.

**8240.** Heath, Harvard S. "Reed Smoot: The First Modern Mormon." Ph.D. dissertation, Brigham Young University, 1990.

**8241.** Heinerman, Joseph. "Reed Smoot's Secret Code." *Utah Historical Quarterly* 57 (Summer 1989): 254–263.

**8242.** Hinckley, Bryant S. "Reed Smoot, a Church and Civic Leader." In his *Faith of Our Pioneer Fathers,* 195–208. Salt Lake City, UT: Deseret, 1956.

**8243.** Holsinger, M. Paul. "For God and the American Home: The Attempt to Unseat Senator Reed Smoot, 1903–1907." *Pacific Northwest Quarterly* 60 (July 1969): 154–160.

**8244.** Merrill, Milton R. *Reed Smoot: Apostle in Politics.* Logan: Utah State University Press, 1990.

**8245.** ———. *Reed Smoot, Utah Politician.* Logan: Utah State Agricultural College, 1953.

**SMYTH, ALEXANDER** (1765–1830) R-VA, House 1817–1825, 1827–1830.

**8246.** Severance, Frank H. "The Case of Alexander Smyth." *Buffalo Historical Society Publications* 18 (1914): 213–255.

**SNELL, BERTRAND HOLLIS**
(1870–1958) R-NY, House 1915–1939.

**8247.** Barone, Louis A. "Republican House Minority Leader Bertrand H. Snell and the Coming of the New Deal, 1931–1939." Ph.D. dissertation, State University of New York at Buffalo, 1969.

**SOULE, PIERRE** (1801–1870) D-LA, Senate 1847, 1849–1853.

**8248.** Ettinger, Amos A. *The Mission to Spain of Pierre Soule, 1853–1855: A Study in the Cuban Diplomacy of the United States.* New Haven, CT: Yale University Press, 1932.

**8249.** Moore, John P. "Correspondence of Pierre Soule: The Louisiana Tehuantepec Company." *Hispanic American Historical Review* 32 (February 1952): 59–72.

**8250.** ———. "Pierre Soule: Southern Expansionist and Promoter." *Journal of Southern History* 21 (May 1955): 203–223.

## SOUTHARD, SAMUEL LEWIS
(1787–1842) W-NJ, Senate 1821–1823, 1833–1842.

**8251.** Birkner, Michael J. *Samuel L. Southard: Jeffersonian Whig.* Rutherford, NJ: Fairleigh Dickinson University Press, 1984.

**8252.** Elmer, Lucius Q. "Governors I Have Known: Samuel L. Southard." In his *The Constitution and Government of the Province and State of New Jersey,* 201–234. Newark, NJ: Martin, 1872.

**8253.** Ershkowitz, Herbert. "Samuel L. Southard: A Case Study of Whig Leadership in the Age of Jackson." *New Jersey History* 88 (Spring 1970): 5–24.

## SPALDING, THOMAS (1774–1851) R-GA, House 1805–1806.

**8254.** Coulter, E. Merton. *Thomas Spalding of Sapelo.* Baton Rouge: Louisiana State University Press, 1940.

## SPARKMAN, JOHN JACKSON
(1899–1985) D-AL, House 1937–1946, Senate 1946–1979.

**8255.** Sparkman, Ivo H. *Journeys with the Senator.* Huntsville, AL: Strode, 1977.

**8256.** Walker, Henry, Jr. "Beyond the Call of Duty: Representative John Sparkman of Alabama and World War II, 1939–1945." *Southern Historian* 11 (1990): 24–42.

## SPECTER, ARLEN (1930– ) R-PA, Senate 1981– .

**8257.** Fenno, Richard F. *Learning to Legislate: The Senate Education of Arlen Specter.* Washington, DC: CQ Press, 1991.

## SPENCE, BRENT (1874–1967) D-KY, House 1931–1963.

**8258.** Hedlund, Richard. "Brent Spence and the Bretton Woods Legislation." *Register of the Kentucky Historical Society* 79 (Winter 1981): 40–56.

## SPENCER, GEORGE ELIPHAZ
(1836–1893) R-AL, Senate 1868–1879.

**8259.** Woolfolk, Sarah V. "George E. Spencer: A Carpetbagger in Alabama." *Alabama Review* 19 (January 1966): 41–52.

## SPENCER, SELDEN PALMER
(1862–1925) R-MO, Senate 1918–1925.

**8260.** Margulies, Herbert F. "Selden P. Spencer, Senate Moderates and the League of Nations." *Missouri Historical Review* 83 (July 1989): 373–394.

**8261.** Schlup, Leonard. "The Unknown Senator: Selden Palmer Spencer of Missouri and the League of Nations." *International Review of History and Political Science* 26 (November 1989): 1–9.

## SPOONER, JOHN COIT (1843–1919)
R-WI, Senate 1885–1891, 1897–1907.

**8262.** Fowler, Dorothy G. *John Coit Spooner, Defender of Presidents.* New York: University Publishers, 1961.

**8263.** Parker, James R. "The Business of Politics, the Politics of Business: The Career of John C. Spooner, 1868–1907." *Maryland Historian* 17 (Fall/Winter 1986): 39–53.

**8264.** ———. "Paternalism and Racism: Senator John C. Spooner and American Minorities, 1897–1907." *Wisconsin Magazine of History* 57 (Spring 1974): 195–200.

**8265.** ———. "Senator John C. Spooner: Advocate of the American Empire, 1899–1906." *Maryland Historian* 5 (Fall 1974): 113–129.

**8266.** ———. "Senator John C. Spooner, 1887–1907." Ph.D. dissertation, University of Maryland, 1972.

**SPRAGUE, WILLIAM** (1830–1915) R-RI, Senate 1863–1875.

**8267.** Belden, Marva R., and Thomas G. Belden. *So Fell the Angels.* Boston: Little, Brown, 1956.

**8268.** Sokoloff, Alice H. *Kate Chase for the Defense.* New York: Dodd, Mead, 1971.

**STAEBLER, NEIL OLIVER** (1905– ) D-MI, House 1963–1965.

**8269.** Weideman, Christine. *Neil Staebler: His Career and Legacy.* Ann Arbor, MI: University of Michigan, 1987.

**STANFORD, LELAND** (1824–1893) R-CA, Senate 1885–1893.

**8270.** Bancroft, Hubert H. *History of the Life of Leland Stanford: A Character Study.* Oakland, CA: Biobooks, 1952.

**8271.** Clark, George T. *Leland Stanford, War Governor of California.* Stanford, CA: Stanford University Press, 1931.

**8272.** Dillon, Richard. "Leland Stanford." In his *Humbugs and Heroes,* 294–299. Garden City, NY: Doubleday, 1970.

**8273.** Hoyt, Edwin P. *Leland Stanford.* New York: Abelard-Schuman, 1967.

**8274.** Jordan, David S. *The Days of a Man,* vol. 1, 478–493. Yonkers-on-Hudson, NY: World Book Company, 1922.

**8275.** Lewis, Oscar. *The Big Four: The Story of Huntington, Stanford, Hopkins, and Crocker, and of the Building of the Central Pacific.* New York: Knopf, 1938.

**8276.** Melendy, Howard B., and Benjamin F. Gilbert. "Leland Stanford." In their *Governors of California: Peter H. Burnett to Edmund G. Brown,* 114–127. Georgetown, CA: Talisman Press, 1965.

**8277.** Nagel, Gunther W. "Monument to Elegance: Leland Stanford's Nob Hill Mansion." *American West* 12 (September 1975): 18–25.

**8278.** Schuck, Oscar T., ed. "Leland Stanford." In his *Representative and Leading Men of the Pacific,* 35–46. San Francisco: Bacon and Company, 1870.

**8279.** Tutorow, Norman E. *Leland Stanford: Man of Many Careers.* Menlo Park, CA: Pacific Coast Publishers, 1971.

**STANLEY, AUGUSTUS OWSLEY** (1867–1958) D-KY, House 1903–1915, Senate 1919–1925.

**8280.** Burckel, Nicholas C. "A. O. Stanley and Progressive Reform, 1902–1919." *Register of the Kentucky Historical Society* 79 (Spring 1981): 136–161.

**8281.** Ramage, Thomas. "Augustus Owsley Stanley: Early Twentieth-Century Kentucky Democrat." Ph.D. dissertation, University of Kentucky, 1968.

**STANLY, EDWARD** (1810–1872) W-NC, House 1837–1843, 1849–1853.

**8282.** Brown, Norman D. "Edward Stanly: Federal Whig." Ph.D. dissertation, University of North Carolina, 1963.

**8283.** ———. "Edward Stanly: First Republican Candidate for Governor of California." *California Historical Society Quarterly* 47 (September 1968): 251–272.

**8284.** ———. *Edward Stanly: Whiggery's Tarheel "Conqueror."* University: University of Alabama Press, 1974.

**STEAGALL, HENRY BASCOM** (1873–1943) D-AL, House 1915–1943.

**8285.** Key, Jack B. "Henry B. Steagall: The Conservative as a Reformer." *Alabama Review* 17 (July 1964): 198–209.

**STEARNS, ASAHEL** (1774–1839) F-MA, House 1815–1817.

**8286.** Sutherland, Arthur E. "Parker and Stearns: 1817–1829." In his *Law at Harvard,* 43–91. Cambridge, MA: Belknap Press, 1967.

**STEELE, JOHN** (1764–1815) NC, House 1790–1793.

**8287.** Steele, John. *The Papers of John Steele.* Raleigh, NC: Edwards and Broughton, 1924.

**8288.** West, William S. "John Steele: Portrait of a Moderate Southern Federalist." Ph.D. dissertation, University of North Carolina, 1972.

**STEFAN, KARL** (1884–1951) R-NE, House 1935–1951.

**8289.** Johnson, John R. "Karl Stefan (My Congressman) 1884–1951." In his *Representative Nebraskans,* 171–176. Lincoln, NE: Johnsen, 1954.

**STEIGER, WILLIAM ALBERT** (1938–1978) R-WI, House 1967–1978.

**8290.** Bibby, John F. "The Case of the Young Old Pro: The Sixth District of Wisconsin." In *The Making of Congressmen: Seven Campaigns of 1974,* edited by Alan L. Clem, 209–234. North Scituate, MA: Duxbury Press, 1976.

**STENNIS, JOHN CORNELIUS** (1901– ) D-MS, Senate 1947–1989.

**8291.** Dazey, Mary A. "A Stylistic Study of the Public Addresses of Senator John C. Stennis of Mississippi." Ph.D. dissertation, University of Southern Mississippi, 1981.

**8292.** Downs, Michael S. "A Matter of Conscience: John C. Stennis and the Vietnam War." Ph.D. dissertation, Mississippi State University, 1989.

**STEPHENS, ALEXANDER HAMILTON** (1812–1883) D-GA, House 1843–1859, 1873–1882.

**8293.** Bartlett, David V. "Alexander H. Stephens." In his *Presidential Candidates: Containing Sketches, Biographical, Personal and Political, of Prominent Candidates for the Presidency,* 179–197. New York: A. B. Burdick, 1859.

**8294.** Bolton, Sarah K. "Alexander H. Stephens." In her *How Success Is Won,* 152–173. Boston: D. Lathrop and Company, 1885.

**8295.** Burger, Nash K., and John K. Bettersworth. "The South's Conscience: Alexander H. Stephens." In their *South of Appomattox,* 144–172. New York: Harcourt, 1959.

**8296.** Cleveland, Henry. *Alexander H. Stephens in Public and Private.* Philadelphia: National Publishing Company, 1866.

**8297.** Golden, James L. "Alexander H. Stephens Speaks for the Union." *Quarterly Journal of Speech* 47 (December 1961): 355–362.

**8298.** Johnston, Richard M., and William H. Browne. *Life of Alexander H. Stephens.* Philadelphia: Lippincott, 1878.

**8299.** Parrington, Vernon L. "Alexander H. Stephens, Constitutionalist." In his *Main Currents in American Thought,* vol. 2, 82–93. New York: Harcourt, Brace, 1927.

**8300.** Pendleton, Louis B. "Alexander H. Stephens." In *Library of Southern Literature,* edited by Edwin A. Alderman and Joel C. Harris, vol. 11, 5097–5102. New Orleans: Martin and Hoyt, 1909.

**8301.** ———. *Alexander H. Stephens.* Philadelphia: G. H. Jacobs, 1908.

**8302.** Rabun, James Z. "Alexander H. Stephens: A Biography." Ph.D. dissertation, University of Chicago, 1949.

**8303.** ———. "Alexander H. Stephens and Jefferson Davis." *American Historical Review* 58 (January 1953): 290–321.

**8304.** Richardson, Eudora R. *Little Aleck: A Life of Alexander H. Stephens, the Fighting Vice-President of the Confederacy.* Indianapolis: Bobbs-Merrill, 1932.

**8305.** Schott, Thomas E. *Alexander H. Stephens of Georgia: A Biography.* Baton Rouge: Louisiana State University Press, 1988.

**8306.** Stephens, Alexander H. *A Constitutional View of the Late War between the States.* 2 vols. Philadelphia: National Publishing Company, 1868–1870.

**8307.** ———. *Letter for Posterity: Alex Stephens to His Brother Linton, June 3, 1864.* Edited by James Z. Rabun. Atlanta, GA: Emory University Library, 1954.

**8308.** ———. *Recollections: His Diary Kept When Prisoner at Fort Warren, Boston Harbour, 1865.* Edited by Myrta L. Avary. New York: Da Capo Press, 1971.

**8309.** Trent, William P. "Alexander H. Stephens and Robert Toombs." In his *Southern Statesmen of the Old Regime: Washington, Jefferson, Randolph, Calhoun, Stephens, Toombs, and Jefferson Davis,* 197–256. New York: Crowell, 1897.

**8310.** Von Abele, Rudolph R. *Alexander H. Stephens: A Biography.* New York: Knopf, 1946.

**STEPHENSON, ISAAC** (1829–1918) **R-WI, House 1883–1889, Senate 1907–1915.**

**8311.** Stephenson, Isaac. *Recollections of a Long Life, 1829–1915.* Chicago: Donnelley, 1915.

**STEVENS, ISAAC INGALLS** (1818–1862) **D-WA, House 1857–1861.**

**8312.** Hazard, Joseph T. *Companion of Adventure: A Biography of Isaac Ingalls Stevens, First Governor of Washington Territory.* Portland, OR: Binfords, 1952.

**8313.** Meinig, Donald W. "Isaac Stevens: Practical Geographer of the Early Northwest." *Geographical Review* 45 (October 1955): 542–558.

**8314.** Nicandri, David. *Northwest Chiefs: Gustave Sohon's Views of the 1855 Stevens Treaty Councils.* Tacoma: Washington State Historical Society, 1986.

**8315.** Paradise, Scott H. "Isaac Ingalls Stevens." In his *Men of the Old School,* 163–192. Andover, MA: Phillips Academy, 1956.

**8316.** Richards, Kent D. *Isaac I. Stevens: Young Man in a Hurry.* Salt Lake City, UT: Brigham Young University Press, 1979.

**8317.** Stevens, Hazard. *The Life of Isaac Ingalls Stevens.* Boston: Houghton Mifflin, 1900.

**8318.** Todd, William. *The Seventy-Ninth Highlanders, New York Volunteers in the War of Rebellion, 1861–1865.* Albany, NY: Press of Brandow, Barton, 1886.

**8319.** Trafzer, Clifford E., ed. *Indians, Superintendents, and Councils: Northwestern Indian Policy, 1850–1855.* Lanham, MD: University Press of America, 1986.

**STEVENS, THADDEUS** (1792–1868) **R-PA, House 1849–1853, 1859–1868.**

**8320.** Bennett, Lerone, Jr. "White Architects of Black Liberation: Charles Sumner and Thaddeus Stevens." In his *Pioneers in Protest,* 181–194. Chicago: Johnson, 1968.

**8321.** Boyd, Charles W. *Your Legacy from Thaddeus Stevens: Republican of the First Kind.* Chicago: Bomax Publishers, 1987.

**8322.** Brodie, Fawn M. *Thaddeus Stevens, Scourge of the South.* New York: Norton, 1959.

**8323.** ———. "Tyrant Father." In *Psychological Studies of Famous Americans,* edited by Norman Kiell, 180–189. Boston: Twayne, 1964.

**8324.** Bryand-Jones, Mildred. "The Relation of Thaddeus Stevens to National Developments." Ph.D. dissertation, Loyola University of Chicago, 1940.

**8325.** Callender, Edward B. *Thaddeus Stevens: Commoner.* Boston: Williams, 1882.

**8326.** Crofts, Daniel W. "Reconstruction in Tennessee: An Assessment for Thaddeus Stevens." *West Tennessee Historical Society Papers* 43 (1989): 13–27.

**8327.** Current, Richard N. *Old Thad Stevens: A Story of Ambition.* Madison: University of Wisconsin Press, 1942.

**8328.** Elliott, Edward. "Thaddeus Stevens: Growth through Reconstruction." In his *Biographical Story of the Constitution*, 229–250. New York: Putnam's, 1910.

**8329.** Fuller, Hubert B. "Grow and Colfax Dominated by Thaddeus Stevens." In his *The Speakers of the House*, 149–168. Boston: Little, Brown, 1909.

**8330.** Hensel, William U. "An Early Letter by Thaddeus Stevens." *Lancaster Historical Society Papers* 10 (November 1906): 396–401.

**8331.** Korngold, Ralph. *Thaddeus Stevens: A Being Darkly Wise and Rudely Great*. New York: Harcourt, 1955.

**8332.** Landis, Charles I. *Thaddeus Stevens, a Letter Written to the Daily New Era, Lancaster, PA*. Lancaster, PA: Press of the New Era Printing Company, 1916.

**8333.** Lawson, Elizabeth. *Thaddeus Stevens*. New York: International Publishers, 1942.

**8334.** McCall, Samuel W. *Thaddeus Stevens*. Boston: Houghton Mifflin, 1899.

**8335.** McClure, Alexander K. "Lincoln and Stevens." In his *Abraham Lincoln and Men of War-Times*, 277–295. Philadelphia: Times Publishing Company, 1892.

**8336.** Miller, Alphonse B. *Thaddeus Stevens*. New York: Harper, 1939.

**8337.** Pickens, Donald K. "The Republican Synthesis and Thaddeus Stevens." *Civil War History* 31 (March 1985): 57–73.

**8338.** Robertson, Andrew. "The Idealist as Opportunist: An Analysis of Thaddeus Stevens' Support in Lancaster County, 1843–1866." *Journal of the Lancaster County Historical Society* 84 (Spring 1980): 49–107.

**8339.** Singmaster, Elsie. *I Speak for Thaddeus Stevens*. Boston: Houghton Mifflin, 1947.

**8340.** Thompson, Carol L. "Thaddeus Stevens: Radical Republican." *Current History* 14 (May 1948): 277–282.

**8341.** Trefousse, Hans L. "Old Thad Stevens: 'One of the Strangest Men of the Nation.'" *American History Illustrated* 16, no. 8 (1981): 18–23.

**8342.** Woodburn, James A. "The Attitude of Thaddeus Stevens Towards the Conduct of the Civil War." *American Historical Association Annual Report* (1906): 211–237.

**8343.** ———. *The Life of Thaddeus Stevens: A Study in American Political History*. Indianapolis: Bobbs-Merrill, 1913.

**8344.** Woodley, Thomas F. *Great Leveler: The Life of Thaddeus Stevens*. Freeport, NY: Books for Libraries, 1969.

## STEVENSON, ADLAI EWING
(1835–1914) D-IL, House 1875–1877, 1879–1881.

**8345.** Barzman, Sol. "Adlai Ewing Stevenson." In his *Madmen and Geniuses: The Vice-Presidents of the United States*, 153–157. Chicago: Follett, 1974.

**8346.** Cook, John W. "The Life and Labors of Hon. Adlai Ewing Stevenson." *Journal of the Illinois State Historical Society* 8 (July 1915): 209–231.

**8347.** Schlup, Leonard. "Adlai E. Stevenson and the Bimetalic Monetary Commission of 1897." *International Review of History and Political Science* 14 (August 1977): 41–55.

**8348.** ———. "Adlai E. Stevenson and the 1892 Campaign in Virginia." *Virginia Magazine of History and Biography* 86 (July 1978): 344–354.

**8349.** ———. "Adlai E. Stevenson and the 1900 Campaign in Delaware." *Delaware History* 17 (Spring/Summer 1977): 191–198.

**8350.** ———. "Adlai E. Stevenson and the Presidential Campaign of 1900." *Filson Club Historical Quarterly* 53 (April 1979): 196–208.

**8351.** ———. "Adlai E. Stevenson and the Presidential Election of 1896." *Social Science Journal* 14 (April 1977): 117–128.

**8352.** ———. "Adlai E. Stevenson's Campaign Visits to West Virginia." *West Virginia History* 38 (January 1977): 126–135.

**8353.** Schulp, Leonard. "Democratic Talleyrand: Adlai E. Stevenson and Politics in the Gilded Age and Progressive Era." *South Atlantic Quarterly* 78 (Spring 1979): 182–194.

**8354.** ———. "The Political Career of the First Adlai E. Stevenson." Ph.D. dissertation, University of Illinois, 1973.

**8355.** Stevenson, Adlai E. *Something of Men I Have Known.* Chicago: McClurg, 1909.

## STEVENSON, ADLAI EWING III
(1930– ) D-IL, Senate 1970–1981.

**8356.** Gruenberg, Mark. *Adlai Stevenson, 3d: Democratic Senator from Illinois.* Washington, DC: Grossman, 1972.

## STEVENSON, ANDREW (1784–1857)
J-VA, House 1821–1834.

**8357.** Adams, Charles F. "John Quincy Adams and Speaker Andrew Stevenson of Virginia: An Episode of the Twenty-Second Congress, (1832)." *Proceedings of the Massachusetts Historical Society* 19 (December 1905): 504–553.

**8358.** Chalkley, Lyman. *Chronicles of the Scotch-Irish Settlement in Virginia.* 3 vols. Rosslyn, VA: Commonwealth Printing Company, 1912.

**8359.** Gardner, Eugene N. "Andrew Stevenson." *Richmond College Historical Papers* 1 (June 1915): 259–308.

**8360.** Jordan, Daniel P. "Virginia Congressmen, 1801–1825." Ph.D. dissertation, University of Virginia, 1970.

**8361.** Stevenson, Sarah C. "Mrs. Andrew Stevenson to Dr. Thomas Sewall, 1837, 1840." Edited by Grenville H. Norcross. *Proceedings of the Massachusetts Historical Society* 44 (November 1910): 213–216.

**8362.** Temperley, Howard. "The O'Connell-Stevenson Contretemps: A Reflection of the Anglo-American Slavery Issue." *Journal of Negro History* 47 (October 1962): 217–233.

**8363.** Wayland, Francis F. *Andrew Stevenson, Democrat and Diplomat, 1785–1857.* Philadelphia: University of Pennsylvania Press, 1949.

**8364.** Wayland, Francis F. "Slavebreeding in America: The Stevenson-O'Connell Imbroglio of 1838." *Virginia Magazine of History and Biography* 50 (January 1942): 47–54.

**8365.** Willson, Beckles. "Stevenson (1836–1841)." In his *America's Ambassadors to England (1785–1928),* 212–228. London: Murray, 1928.

## STEWART, WILLIAM MORRIS
(1827–1909) SIL.R-NV, Senate 1864–1875, 1887–1905.

**8366.** Brown, George R. *Reminiscences of William M. Stewart of Nevada.* New York: Neale Publishing Company, 1908.

**8367.** Elliot, Russell R. *Servant of Power: A Political Biography of Senator William M. Stewart.* Reno: University of Nevada Press, 1983.

**8368.** Hermann, Ruth. *Gold and Silver Colossus: William Morris Stewart and His Southern Bride.* Sparks, NV: Dave's Print and Publishing, 1975.

**8369.** Hulse, James W. "Idaho versus Nevada: The 1887 Struggle between Nevada's Senator and Idaho's Governor." *Idaho Yesterdays* 29 (Fall 1985): 26–31.

**8370.** Johnson, David A. "A Case of Mistaken Identity: William M. Stewart and the Rejection of Nevada's First Constitution." *Nevada Historical Society Quarterly* 22 (Fall 1979): 186–198.

**8371.** Mack, Effie M. "William Morris Stewart, 1827–1909." *Nevada Historical Society Quarterly* 7, nos. 1, 2 (1964): 3–121.

**8372.** Stewart, William M. *The Reminiscences of Senator William M. Stewart of Nevada.* New York: Neale, 1908.

**8373.** "William Morris Stewart." In *Representative and Leading Men of the Pacific,* edited by Oscar T. Shuck, 635–644. San Francisco: Bacon and Company, 1870.

**STILES, WILLIAM HENRY (1808–1865)**
**D-GA, House 1843–1845.**

**8374.** Harwell, Christopher L. "William Stiles: Georgia Gentleman-Politician." Ph.D. dissertation, Emory University, 1959.

**STOCKMAN, DAVID ALAN (1946– )**
**R-MI, House 1977–1981.**

**8375.** Greenya, John, and Anne Urban. *The Real David Stockman.* New York: St. Martin's Press, 1986.

**8376.** Greider, William. *The Education of David Stockman and Other Americans.* New York: Dutton, 1982.

**8377.** Ullmann, Owen. *Stockman: The Man, the Myth, the Future.* New York: Kensington, 1986.

**8378.** Urban, Anne. *Inside the Trojan Horse: The Odyssey of David Stockman.* Washington, DC: Presidential Accountability Group, 1983.

**STOCKTON, JOHN POTTER**
**(1826–1900) D-NJ, Senate 1865–1866, 1869–1875.**

**8379.** Stockton, Thomas C. *The Stockton Family of New Jersey.* Washington, DC: Carnahan Press, 1911.

**STOCKTON, RICHARD (1730–1781) NJ,**
**Continental Congress 1776.**

**8380.** Field, Richard S. "Richard Stockton." In his *The Provincial Courts of New Jersey, with Sketches of the Bench and Bar,* 189–202. New York: Bartlett and Welford, 1849.

**8381.** Stockton, Thomas C. *The Stockton Family of New Jersey.* Washington, DC: Carnahan Press, 1911.

**STOCKTON, RICHARD (1764–1828)**
**F-NJ, Senate 1796–1799, House 1813–1815.**

**8382.** Stockton, Thomas C. *The Stockton Family of New Jersey.* Washington, DC: Carnahan Press, 1911.

**STOCKTON, ROBERT FIELD**
**(1795–1866) D-NJ, Senate 1851–1853.**

**8383.** Bayard, Samuel J. *A Sketch of the Life of Com. Robert F. Stockton.* New York: Derby and Jackson, 1856.

**8384.** Bradley, Glenn D. *Winning the Southwest: A Story of Conquest.* Chicago: A. C. McClurg, 1912.

**8385.** Hunt, Rockwell D. "Robert F. Stockton." In his *California's Stately Hall of Fame,* 187–192. Stockton, CA: College of the Pacific, 1950.

**8386.** Quincy, Josiah. "Commodore Stockton: The Supreme Court and the Marianna Flora." In his *Figures of the Past from the Leaves of Old Journals,* 192–211. Boston: Little, Brown, 1926.

**8387.** Stockton, Thomas C. *The Stockton Family of New Jersey.* Washington, DC: Carnahan Press, 1911.

**8388.** Sutherland, Robert T. "Ericsson, Stockton, and the USS Princeton." *U.S. Naval Institute Proceedings* 83 (January 1957): 92–94.

**8389.** Watts, Harry C. "Ericsson, Stockton, and the USS Princeton." *U.S. Naval Institute Proceedings* 82 (September 1956): 961–967.

**STOKES, LOUIS (1925– ) D-OH,**
**House 1969– .**

**8390.** Christopher, Maurine. "Louis Stokes/Ohio." In her *Black Americans in Congress,* 243–248. Rev. ed. New York: Thomas Y. Crowell, 1976.

**STOKES, MONTFORT** (1762–1842) NC, Senate 1816–1823.

**8391.** Foster, William O. "The Career of Montfort Stokes in North Carolina." *North Carolina Historical Review* 16 (July 1939): 237–272.

**STONE, THOMAS** (1743–1787) MD, Continental Congress 1775–1779, 1784–1785.

**8392.** Sanderson, John. "Thomas Stone." In *Sanderson's Biography of the Signers to the Declaration of Independence,* edited by Robert T. Conrad, 612–620. Philadelphia: Thomas, Cowperthwait, 1848.

**STONE, WILLIAM JOEL** (1848–1918) D-MO, House 1885–1891, Senate 1903–1918.

**8393.** Hamilton, Beryl A. "Early Political Career of William Joel Stone." Master's thesis, University of Missouri, 1950.

**8394.** Towne, Ruth W. *Senator William J. Stone and the Politics of Compromise.* Port Washington, NY: Kennikat, 1979.

**STORKE, THOMAS MORE** (1876–1971) D-CA, Senate 1938–1939.

**8395.** Storke, Thomas. *California Editor.* Los Angeles: Western Lore Press, 1958.

**STORY, JOSEPH** (1779–1845) R-MA, House 1808–1809.

**8396.** Bishirjian, Richard. "Justice Story's Influence on American Law." *Intercollegiate Review* 8 (Winter 1972/1973): 127–130.

**8397.** Brown, George S. "A Dissenting Opinion of Mr. Justice Story Enacted as Law within Thirty-Six Days." *Virginia Law Review* 26 (April 1940): 759–767.

**8398.** Buchanan, James M. "A Note on 'Joe Cotton Story.'" *Supreme Court Historical Society Yearbook* 1981 (1981): 92–93.

**8399.** Cassoday, John B. "James Kent and Joseph Story." *Yale Law Journal* 12 (January 1903): 146–153.

**8400.** Commager, Henry S. "Joseph Story." In *Gaspar G. Bacon Lectures on the Constitution of the United States,* edited by Arthur N. Holcombe, 31–94. Boston: Boston University Press, 1953.

**8401.** Dowd, Morgan D. "Justice Joseph Story: A Study of the Contributions of a Jeffersonian Judge to the Development of American Constitutional Law." Ph.D. dissertation, University of Massachusetts, 1964.

**8402.** ———. "Justice Joseph Story: A Study of the Legal Philosophy of a Jeffersonian Judge." *Vanderbilt Law Review* 18 (March 1965): 643–662.

**8403.** ———. "Justice Joseph Story and the Politics of Appointment." *American Journal of Legal History* 9 (October 1965): 265–285.

**8404.** ———. "Justice Story and the Slavery Conflict." *Massachusetts Law Quarterly* 52 (September 1967): 239–253.

**8405.** ———. "Justice Story, the Supreme Court, and the Obligation of Contract." *Case Western Reserve Law Review* 19 (April 1968): 493–527.

**8406.** Dunne, Gerald T. "American Blackstone." *Washington University Law Quarterly* 1963 (June 1963): 321–337.

**8407.** ———. "Joseph Story, 1812 Overture." *Harvard Law Review* 77 (December 1963): 240–278.

**8408.** ———. "Joseph Story: The Age of Jackson." *Missouri Law Review* 34 (Summer 1969): 307–355.

**8409.** ———. "Joseph Story: The Germinal Years." *Harvard Law Review* 75 (February 1962): 707–754.

**8410.** ———. "Joseph Story: The Great Term, 1837." *Harvard Law Review* 79 (March 1966): 877–913.

**8411.** ———. "Joseph Story: The Lowering Storm." *American Journal of Legal History* 13 (January 1969): 1–41.

**8412.** ———. "Joseph Story: The Middle Years." *Harvard Law Review* 80 (June 1967): 1679–1709.

**8413.** ———. "Joseph Story: The Salem Years." *Essex Institute Historical Collection* 101 (October 1965): 307–332.

**8414.** ———. *Justice Joseph Story and the Rise of the Supreme Court.* New York: Simon and Schuster, 1970.

**8415.** ———. "Justice Story and the Modern Corporation: A Closing Circle?" *American Journal of Legal History* 17 (July 1973): 262–270.

**8416.** ———. "Mr. Joseph Story and the American Law of Banking." *American Journal of Legal History* 5 (July 1961): 205–229.

**8417.** ———, ed. "The Story—Livingston Correspondence, 1812–1822." *American Journal of Legal History* 10 (July 1966): 224–236.

**8418.** Eddy, Ruth S. "The Ancestry of Judge Joseph Story: Justice of the Supreme Court of the United States." *Essex Institute of Historical Collections* 83 (January 1947): 59–66.

**8419.** Gould, Elizabeth P. "Joseph Story: An Additional Word." *Chicago Law Times* 3 (July 1889): 231–236.

**8420.** Greenleaf, Simon. "Biographical Sketch of Joseph Story, LL.D." *American Law Magazine* 6 (January 1846): 241–268.

**8421.** ———. *A Discourse Commemorative of the Life and Character of the Honorable Joseph Story.* Boston: Little, Brown, 1845.

**8422.** Griswold, Rufus W. "Joseph Story." In his *The Prose Writers of America,* 138–139. Philadelphia: Carey and Hart, 1847.

**8423.** Guernsey, Rocellus S. *A Key to Story's Equity Jurisprudence.* New York: Diossy, 1876.

**8424.** Heaney, Howell J. "The Letters of Joseph Story, 1779–1845, in the Hampton L. Carson Collection of the Free Library of Philadelphia." *American Journal of Legal History* 2 (April 1958): 75–85.

**8425.** Hillard, George S. "Memoir of Joseph Story, LL.D." *Massachusetts Historical Society Proceedings* 10 (April 1868): 176–205.

**8426.** Hogan, John C. "Blackstone and Joseph Story: Their Influence on the Development of Criminal Law in America." *Minnesota Law Review* 40 (January 1956): 107–124.

**8427.** ———. "Joseph Story on Juries." *Oregon Law Review* 37 (April 1958): 234–255.

**8428.** ———. "Joseph Story's Anonymous Law Articles." *Michigan Law Review* 52 (April 1954): 869–884.

**8429.** ———. "Joseph Story's Essay on 'Domicile.'" *Buffalo Law Review* 35 (April 1955): 215–224.

**8430.** ———. "Joseph Story's Essay on 'Natural Law.'" *Oregon Law Review* 34 (February 1955): 88–105.

**8431.** ———. "Joseph Story's Unsigned Article on Common Law Lines." *Case and Comment* 62 (November/December 1957): 24–26.

**8432.** ———. "Justice Story on Capital Punishment." *California Law Review* 43 (March 1955): 76–84.

**8433.** ———. "Justice Story on the Common Law of Evidence." *Vanderbilt Law Review* 9 (December 1955): 51–67.

**8434.** ———, ed. "Three Essays on the Law by Joseph Story." *Southern California Law Review* 28 (December 1954): 19–32.

**8435.** Howland, Francis. "Story." In *Homes of American Statesmen: With Anecdotal, Personal, and Descriptive Sketches by Various Authors,* 427–445. New York: A. W. Upham, 1858.

**8436.** Joyce, Craig. "Supreme Court Justice Joseph Story: Statesman of the Old Republic." *Michigan Law Review* 84 (February/April 1986): 846–860.

**8437.** Leslie, William R. "The Influence of Joseph Story's Theory of the Conflict of Laws on Constitutional Nationalism." *Mississippi Valley Historical Review* 35 (September 1948): 203–220.

**8438.** Leslie, William R. "Similarities in Lord Mansfield's and Joseph Story's View of Fundamental Law." *American Journal of Legal History* 1 (October 1957): 278–307.

**8439.** Loerenzen, Ernest G. "Story's Commentaries on the Conflict of Laws: One Hundred Years After." *Harvard Law Review* 48 (November 1934): 15–38.

**8440.** Marshall, John. *An Autobiographical Sketch.* Ann Arbor: University of Michigan Press, 1937.

**8441.** ———. *Letters of Joseph Story.* New York: Macmillan, 1958.

**8442.** ———. "Marshall-Story Correspondence." *Massachusetts Historical Society Proceedings* 14 (1901): 324–360.

**8443.** Mathews, William. "Recollections of Judge Story." In his *Hours with Men and Books,* 97–116. Chicago: Scott, Foresman, 1879.

**8444.** McClellan, James. "Comments on Kent Newmyer's Paper, 'Justice Joseph Story, the Charles River Bridge Case, and the Crisis of Republicanism.'" *American Journal of Legal History* 17 (July 1973): 271–273.

**8445.** ———. *Joseph Story and the American Constitution: A Study in Political and Legal Thought.* Norman: University of Oklahoma Press, 1971.

**8446.** McDowell, Gary L. "Joseph Story's 'Science' of Equity." *Supreme Court Review* 1979 (1979): 153–172.

**8447.** Moore, Frank. "Joseph Story." In his *American Eloquence,* vol. 2, 422–437. New York: D. Appleton and Company, 1862.

**8448.** Moses, Adolf. "The Friendship between Marshall and Story." *American Law Review* 35 (May/June 1901): 321–342.

**8449.** Myers, Gustavus. "Marshall and His Chief Coadjutor, Story." In his *History of the Supreme Court of the United States,* 258–282. Chicago: C. H. Kerr and Company, 1918.

**8450.** Nadelmann, Kurt H. "Joseph Story's Sketch of American Law." *American Journal of Comparative Law* 3 (Winter 1954): 3–8.

**8451.** Newell, William. *A Discourse Occasioned by the Death of the Honorable Joseph Story, LL.D.* Cambridge, MA: Metcalf, 1845.

**8452.** Newmyer, R. Kent. "Joseph Story and the War of 1812: A Judicial Nationalist." *Historian* 26 (August 1964): 486–501.

**8453.** ———. "Justice Joseph Story, the Charles River Bridge Case and the Crisis of Republicanism." *American Journal of Legal History* 17 (July 1973): 232–245.

**8454.** ———. "A Note on the Whig Politics of Justice Joseph Story." *Mississippi Valley Historical Review* 48 (December 1961): 480–491.

**8455.** ———. *Supreme Court Justice Joseph Story: Statesman of the Old Republic.* Chapel Hill: University of North Carolina Press, 1985.

**8456.** Peabody, Andrew P. "Joseph Story." In his *Harvard Reminiscences,* 56–60. Boston: Ticknor and Company, 1888.

**8457.** Prager, Frank D. "The Changing Views of Justice Story on the Constitution of Patents." *American Journal of Legal History* 4 (January 1960): 1–21.

**8458.** ———. "The Influence of Mr. Justice Story on American Patent Law." *American Journal of Legal History* 5 (July 1961): 254–264.

**8459.** Quincy, Josiah. "A Journey with Judge Story." In his *Figures of the Past from the Leaves of Old Journals,* 158–166. Boston: Little, Brown, 1926.

**8460.** Robbins, Donald C. "Joseph Story: The Early Years, 1779–1811." Ph.D. dissertation, University of Kentucky, 1965.

**8461.** Schofield, William. "Joseph Story." In *Great American Lawyers*, edited by William D. Lewis. vol. 3, 121–186. Philadelphia: J. C. Winston Company, 1907–1909.

**8462.** Schotten, Peter M. "A Government of Laws: The Constitutional Understanding of Mr. Justice Story." Ph.D. dissertation, Claremont Graduate School, 1974.

**8463.** Schwartz, Mortimer D., and John C. Hogan. "A National Library: Mr. Justice Story Speaks." *Journal of Legal Education* 8 (1955): 328–330.

**8464.** Scott, Henry W. "Joseph Story." In his *Distinguished American Lawyers*, 627–636. New York: C. L. Webster, 1891.

**8465.** Story, Joseph. *Joseph Story: A Collection of Writings by and about an Eminent American Jurist*. Edited by Mortimer D. Schwartz and John C. Hogan. New York: Oceana Publications, 1959.

**8466.** Story, William W. *Life and Letters of Joseph Story*. 2 vols. Boston: Little, Brown, 1851.

**8467.** Sumner, Charles. *The Scholar, the Jurist, the Artist, the Philanthropist: An Address before the Phi Beta Kappa Society of Harvard University, at Their Anniversary, August 27, 1846*. Boston: W. D. Ticknor, 1846.

**8468.** ———. "Some Account of Judge Story of the United States." *Bentleys Miscellany* 29 (1851): 376–384.

**8469.** ———. "Tribute of Friendship: The Scholar, the Jurist, the Artist, the Philanthropist." In his *Works,* vol. 1, 133–148, 241–302. Boston: Lee and Shepard, 1875.

**8470.** Sutherland, Arthur E. "Joseph Story: 1829–1845." In his *Law at Harvard*, 92–139. Cambridge, MA: Belknap Press, 1967.

**8471.** Tucker, Henry S. "Judge Story's Position on the So-Called General Welfare Clause." *Constitutional Review* 13 (January 1929): 13–35.

**8472.** Valladao, Haroldo. "The Influence of Joseph Story on Latin-American Rules of Conflict of Law." *American Journal of Comparative Law* 3 (Winter 1954): 27–41.

**8473.** Waite, Charles B. "Joseph Story." *Chicago Law Times* 3 (January 1889): 1–13.

**8474.** Ware, William. "Joseph Story." In his *American Unitarian Biography*, vol. 2, 175–186. Boston: J. Munroe, 1851.

**8475.** Warren, Charles. *The Story-Marshall Correspondence*. New York: New York University, 1942.

**8476.** ———, ed. "The Story-Marshall Correspondence." *William and Mary Quarterly* 21 (January 1941): 1–25.

**8477.** Waterson, Robert C. "The Character of Joseph Story LL.D.: A Discourse." *Monthly Religious Magazine* 2 (November 1845): 361–370.

**8478.** ———. *A Discourse on the Life and Character of Hon. Joseph Story*. Boston: W. Crosby and H. P. Nichols, 1845.

**8479.** Watson, Alan. *Joseph Story and the Comity of Errors: A Case of Study in Conflict of Laws*. Athens: University of Georgia Press, 1992.

**8480.** Webster, Daniel. "Mr. Justice Story." In his *Writings and Speeches*, vol. 3, 295–302. Boston: Little, Brown, 1903.

## STRATTON, SAMUEL STUDDIFORD (1916–1990) D-NY, House 1959–1989.

**8481.** Cross, Wilbur. *Samuel S. Stratton: A Story of Political Gumption*. New York: James H. Heineman, 1964.

## STRATTON, WILLIAM GRANT (1914– ) R-IL, House 1941–1943, 1947–1949.

**8482.** Kenney, David. *A Political Passage: The Career of Stratton of Illinois*. Carbondale: University of Southern Illinois, 1990.

**STRINGER, LAWRENCE BEAUMONT**
(1866–1942) D-IL, House 1913–1915.

**8483.** Lindstrom, Andrew F. "Lawrence Stringer: A Wilson Democrat." *Journal of the Illinois State Historical Society* 66 (Spring 1973): 20–40.

**STRINGFELLOW, DOUGLAS R.**
(1922–1966) R-UT, House 1953–1955.

**8484.** Jonas, Frank H. *Story of a Political Hoax.* Salt Lake City: University of Utah, 1966.

**STRONG, CALEB** (1745–1819) MA,
Senate 1789–1796.

**8485.** Bradford, Alden. *Biography of the Hon. Caleb Strong, Several Years Governor of the State of Massachusetts.* Boston: West, Richardson and Lord, 1820.

**8486.** Lodge, Henry C. *A Memoir of Caleb Strong.* Cambridge, MA: J. Wilson and Son, 1879.

**STRONG, WILLIAM** (1808–1895) D-PA,
House 1847–1851.

**8487.** Dwight, Benjamin W. *The History of the Descendants of Older John Strong.* Albany, NY: J. Munsell, 1871.

**8488.** Teaford, Jon C. "Toward a Christian Nation: Religion, Law and Justice Strong." *Journal of Presbyterian History* 54 (Winter 1976): 422–437.

**8489.** Teiser, Sidney. "William Strong, Associate Justice of the Territorial Courts." *Oregon Historical Quarterly* 64 (December 1963): 293–308.

**STUART, JOHN TODD** (1807–1885) D-IL,
House 1839–1843, 1863–1865.

**8490.** Angle, Paul M. *One Hundred Years of Law: An Account of the Law Office with John T. Stuart Founded in Springfield, Illinois, a Century Ago.* Springfield, IL: Brown, Hay and Stephens, 1928.

**SULLIVAN, JAMES** (1744–1808) MA,
Continental Congress 1782.

**8491.** Amory, Thomas C. *Life of James Sullivan: With Selections from His Writings.* Boston: Phillips, Sampson and Company, 1859.

**8492.** Hansen, Allen O. "James Sullivan's Plan for a National System of Education." In his *Liberalism and American Education in the Eighteenth Century,* 79–89. New York: Macmillan, 1926.

**8493.** Knapp, Samuel L. "Sullivan." In his *Biographical Sketches of Eminent Lawyers, Statesmen and Men of Letters,* 291–313. Boston: Richardson and Lord, 1821.

**SULLIVAN, JOHN** (1740–1795) NH,
Continental Congress 1774–1775, 1780–1781.

**8494.** Amory, Thomas C. *Daniel Sullivan's Visits, 1781, to Gen. John Sullivan in Phila., to Explain Declarations in Sir Henry Clinton's Secret Journal.* Cambridge, MA: J. Wilson, 1884.

**8495.** ———. *General Sullivan Not a Pensioner of Luzerne (Minister of France at Philadelphia, 1778–1783).* Boston: A. Williams, 1875.

**8496.** ———. *The Military Services and Public Life of Major-General John Sullivan, of the American Revolutionary Army.* Boston: Wiggin and Lunt, 1868.

**8497.** Griswold, Rufus W. "Major-General John Sullivan." In his *Washington and the Generals of the American Revolution,* vol. 1, 194–214. Philadelphia: Carey and Hart, 1848.

**8498.** Hayden, Sidney S. "John Sullivan." In his *Washington and His Masonic Compeers,* 329–339. New York: Masonic Publishing and Manufacturing Company, 1867.

**8499.** Headley, Joel T. "Major General Sullivan." In his *Washington and His Generals,* vol. 2, 180–200. New York: Baker and Scribner, 1847.

**8500.** Norris, Major J. "Major Norris' Journal of Sullivan's Expedition, June to October, 1779." *Buffalo Historical Society Publications* 1 (1879): 217–252.

**8501.** Peabody, Oliver N. "Life of John Sullivan." In *The Library of American Biography*, edited by Jared Sparks, vol. 3, 1–177. Boston: Little, Brown, 1852.

**8502.** Peterson, Charles J. "John Sullivan." In his *The Military Heroes of the Revolution*, 347–354. Philadelphia: J. B. Smith, 1856.

**8503.** Sullivan, John. *Letters and Papers of Major-General John Sullivan: Continental Army.* Concord: New Hampshire Historical Society, 1930–1931.

**SULLIVAN, TIMOTHY DANIEL** (1862–1913) D-NY, House 1903–1906, 1913.

**8504.** Zink, Harold. "Big Tim Sullivan." In his *City Bosses in the United States*, 85–95. Durham, NC: Duke University Press, 1930.

**SULZER, WILLIAM** (1863–1941) D-NY, House 1895–1912.

**8505.** Wesser, Robert F. "Impeachment of a Governor: William Sulzer and the Politics of Excess." *New York History* 60 (October 1979): 407–438.

**SUMNER, CHARLES** (1811–1874) R-MA, Senate 1851–1874.

**8506.** Baylen, Joseph O. "Sumner and Lord Wharncliffe: Some Unpublished Letters." *New England Quarterly* 35 (September 1962): 390–395.

**8507.** Beecher, Henry W. "Charles Sumner." In his *Lectures and Orations*, 183–207. New York: Revell, 1913.

**8508.** ———. "Charles Sumner." In his *Plymouth Pulpit*, vol. 2, 7–20. Boston: Pilgrim Press, 1875.

**8509.** Bennett, Lerone, Jr. "White Architects of Black Liberation: Charles Sumner and Thaddeus Stevens." In his *Pioneers in Protest*, 181–194. Lincoln, NE: Johnsen, 1968.

**8510.** Blue, Frederick J. *Charles Sumner and the Conscience of the North.* Arlington Heights, IL: Harlan Davidson, 1994.

**8511.** Bolton, Sarah K. "Charles Sumner." In her *Famous American Statesmen*, 268–306. New York: Crowell, 1888.

**8512.** Bourke, Paul F., and Donald A. De Bats. "Charles Sumner, the London Ballot Society, and the Senate Debate of March 1867." *Perspectives in American History* 1 (1984): 343–357.

**8513.** Bradford, Gamaliel. "Charles Sumner." In his *Union Portraits*, 231–262. Boston: Houghton Mifflin, 1916.

**8514.** Brooks, Noah. "Charles Sumner." In his *Statesmen*, 223–244. New York: Scribner's, 1893.

**8515.** Chaplin, Jeremiah. *Life of Charles Sumner.* Boston: D. Lothrop Company, 1874.

**8516.** Craven, Avery O. "Charles Sumner and the Crisis of 1860–61." In his *Essays in Honor of William E. Dodd*, 131–193. Chicago: University of Chicago Press, 1935.

**8517.** Curtis, George W. "Charles Sumner." In his *Orations and Addresses of George William Curtis*, vol. 3, 199–250. New York: Harper, 1894.

**8518.** Davis, J. Bancroft. *Mr. Sumner, the Alabama Claims, and Their Settlement.* New York: Taylor, 1878.

**8519.** Donald, David H. *Charles Sumner and the Coming of the Civil War.* New York: Knopf, 1960.

**8520.** ———. *Charles Sumner and the Rights of Man.* New York: Knopf, 1970.

**8521.** ———. "Vacant Chair." In *Psychological Studies of Famous Americans*, edited by Norman Kiell, 160–176. Boston: Twayne, 1964.

**8522.** Emerson, Ralph W. "The Assault Upon Mr. Sumner." In his *Complete Works*, vol. 11, 231–237, 245–252. Boston: Houghton Mifflin, 1884.

**8523.** Gienapp, William E. "The Crime against Sumner: The Caning of Charles Sumner and the Rise of the Republican Party." *Civil War History* 25 (September 1979): 218–245.

**8524.** Gradin, Harlan J. "Losing Control: The Caning of Charles Sumner and the Breakdown of Antebellum Political Culture." Ph.D. dissertation, University of North Carolina at Chapel Hill, 1991.

**8525.** Grimke, Archibald H. *Charles Sumner Centenary, Historical Address.* Washington, DC: The Academy, 1911.

**8526.** ———. *The Life of Charles Sumner, the Scholar in Politics.* New York: Funk and Wagnalls, 1892.

**8527.** Harsha, David A. *The Life of Charles Sumner: With Choice Specimens of His Eloquence, a Delineation of His Oratorical Character, and His Great Speech on Kansas.* New York: Dayton, 1858.

**8528.** Haynes, George H. *Charles Sumner.* Philadelphia: G. W. Jacobs, 1909.

**8529.** Higginson, Thomas W. "Charles Sumner." In his *Contemporaries,* vol. 2, 280–293. Boston: Houghton Mifflin, 1900.

**8530.** Holmes, J. Welford. "Whittier and Sumner: A Political Friendship." *New England Quarterly* 30 (March 1957): 58–72.

**8531.** Jager, Ronald B. "Charles Sumner: The Constitution, and the Civil Rights Act of 1875." *New England Quarterly* 42 (September 1969): 350–372.

**8532.** Palmer, Beverly W. "From Small Minority to Great Cause: Letters of Charles Sumner to Salmon P. Chase." *Ohio History* 93 (Summer/Autumn 1984): 164–183.

**8533.** Pierce, Edward L. *Memoir and Letters of Charles Sumner.* 4 vols. Boston: Roberts Brothers, 1877–1893.

**8534.** Rolle, Andrew F. "Friendship Across the Atlantic: Charles Sumner and William Story." *American Quarterly* 11 (Spring 1959): 40–57.

**8535.** Schurz, Carl. *Charles Sumner: An Essay.* Edited by Arthur R. Hogue. Champaign: University of Illinois Press, 1951.

**8536.** Shotwell, Walter G. *Life of Charles Sumner.* New York: Crowell, 1910.

**8537.** Stearns, Frank P. "Sumner." In his *Cambridge Sketches,* 180–217. Philadelphia: Lippincott, 1905.

**8538.** Storey, Moorfield. *Charles Sumner.* Boston: Houghton Mifflin, 1900.

**8539.** ———. "Memoir of Charles Sumner." *Massachusetts Historical Society Proceedings* 40 (January 1907): 538–549.

**8540.** Stowe, Harriet B. "Charles Sumner." In her *Men of Our Times,* 214–238. Hartford, CT: Hartford Publishing Company, 1868.

**8541.** Sumner, Charles. *Charles Sumner: His Complete Works.* 20 vols. Boston: Lee and Shepard, 1900.

**8542.** White, Laura A. "Was Charles Sumner Shamming, 1856–1859?" *New England Quarterly* 33 (September 1960): 291–324.

## SUMNERS, HATTON WILLIAM
### (1875–1962) D-TX, House 1913–1947.

**8543.** Champagne, Anthony. "Hatton Sumners and the 1937 Court-Packing Plan." *East Texas Historical Journal* 26, no. 1 (1988): 46–49.

**8544.** Law, Ron C. "Congressman Hatton W. Sumners of Dallas, Texas: His Life and Congressional Career, 1875–1937." Ph.D. dissertation, Texas Christian University, 1990.

**8545.** Porter, David L. "The Battle of the Texas Giants: Hatton Sumners, Sam Rayburn, and the Logan-Walter Bill of 1939." *Texana* 12 (1973): 349–361.

**SUMTER, THOMAS** (1734–1832) R-SC, House 1789–1793, 1797–1801, Senate 1801–1810.

**8546.** Bass, Robert D. *Gamecock: The Life and Campaigns of General Thomas Sumter.* New York: Holt, Rinehart and Winston, 1961.

**8547.** Gregorie, Anne. *Thomas Sumter.* Columbia, SC: R. L. Byron Company, 1931.

**8548.** Griswold, Rufus W. "Major-General Thomas Sumter." In his *Washington and the Generals of the American Revolution,* vol. 2, 295–312. Philadelphia: Carey and Hart, 1848.

**SUTHERLAND, GEORGE** (1862–1942) R-UT, House 1901–1903, Senate 1905–1917.

**8549.** Arkes, Hadley. *The Return of George Sutherland: Restoring a Jurisprudence of Natural Rights.* Princeton, NJ: Princeton University Press, 1994.

**8550.** Banner, James. "Mr. Justice Sutherland and the Social Welfare." Master's thesis, Columbia University, 1961.

**8551.** Howell, Ronald F. "Conservative Influence on Constitutional Development, 1923–1937: The Judicial Theory of Justices Van Devanter, McReynolds, Sutherland, and Butler." Ph.D. dissertation, Johns Hopkins University, 1952.

**8552.** Knox, John. "Justice George Sutherland." *Chicago Bar Review* 24 (October 1942): 16–18.

**8553.** Levitan, David M. "The Foreign Relations Power: An Analysis of Mr. Justice Sutherland's Theory." *Yale Law Journal* 55 (April 1946): 467–497.

**8554.** Maidment, Richard A. "A Study in Judicial Motivation: Mr. Justice Sutherland and Economic Regulation." *Utah Law Review* 1973 (Summer 1973): 156–163.

**8555.** Mason, Alpheus T. "Conservative World of Mr. Justice Sutherland, 1883–1910." *American Political Science Review* 32 (June 1938): 445–477.

**8556.** ———. "The Dilemma of Liberalism." *Journal of Social Philosophy* 3 (April 1938): 223–234.

**8557.** Paschal, Joel F. *Mr. Justice Sutherland.* Chicago: University of Chicago Press, 1956.

**8558.** ———. "Mr. Justice Sutherland." In *Mr. Justice,* edited by Allison Dunham and Philip B. Kurland, 123–146. Chicago: University of Chicago Press, 1956.

**8559.** ———. *Mr. Justice Sutherland, a Man against the State.* Princeton, NJ: Princeton University Press, 1951.

**8560.** Saks, Jay B. "Mr. Justice Sutherland." Ph.D. dissertation, Johns Hopkins University, 1940.

**8561.** Sentell, R. Perry, Jr. "The Opinions of Hughes and Sutherland and the Rights of the Individual." *Vanderbilt Law Review* 15 (March 1962): 559–615.

**8562.** Stephens, Harold M. "Mr. Justice Sutherland." *American Bar Association Journal* 31 (September 1945): 446–453.

**8563.** White, G. Edward. "The Four Horsemen: The Sources of Judicial Notoriety." In his *American Judicial Tradition,* 178–199. New York: Oxford University Press, 1978.

**SUTHERLAND, HOWARD** (1865–1950) R-WV, House 1913–1917, Senate 1917–1923.

**8564.** Casdorph, Paul D. "Howard Sutherland's 1920 Bid for the Presidency." *West Virginia History* 35 (October 1973): 1–25.

**SWANK, FLETCHER B.** (1875–1950) D-OK, House 1921–1929, 1931–1935.

**8565.** Grant, Philip A., Jr. "'Save the Farmer': Oklahoma Congressmen and Farm Relief Legislation, 1924–1928." *Chronicles of Oklahoma* 64 (Spring 1986): 74–87.

## SWANSON, CLAUDE AUGUSTUS
(1862–1939) D-VA, House 1893–1906, Senate 1910–1933.

**8566.** Ferrell, Henry C. *Claude A. Swanson of Virginia: A Political Biography.* Lexington: University of Kentucky Press, 1985.

## SWANWICK, JOHN (1740–1798) R-PA, House 1795–1798.

**8567.** Baumann, Ronald M. "John Swanwick: Spokesman for Merchant-Republicanism in Philadelphia, 1790–1798." *Pennsylvania Magazine of History and Biography* 97 (April 1973): 131–182.

## SWING, PHILIP DAVID (1884–1963) R-CA, House 1921–1933.

**8568.** Moeller, Beverley B. *Phil Swing and Boulder Dam.* Berkeley: University of California Press, 1971.

## SYMINGTON, WILLIAM STUART
(1901–1988) D-MO, Senate 1953–1976.

**8569.** Green, Murray. "Stuart Symington and the B–36." Ph.D. dissertation, American University, 1960.

**8570.** Martin, Ralph G., and Ed Plaut. *Front Runner, Dark Horse.* Garden City, NY: Doubleday, 1960.

**8571.** Wellman, Paul I. *Stuart Symington: Portrait of a Man with a Mission.* Garden City, NY: Doubleday, 1960.

## TABER, JOHN (1880–1965) R-NY, House 1923–1963.

**8572.** Henderson, Cary S. "Congressman John Taber of Auburn: Politics and Federal Appropriations, 1923–1962." Ph.D. dissertation, Duke University, 1964.

## TABOR, HORACE AUSTIN WARNER
(1830–1899) R-CO, Senate 1883.

**8573.** Gandy, Lewis C. *The Tabors: A Footnote of Western History.* New York: Press of the Pioneers, 1934.

**8574.** Karsner, David. *Silver Dollar: The Story of the Tabors.* New York: Bonanza Books, 1932.

**8575.** Parkhill, Forbes. "Barren Gain and Bitter Loss." In his *Wildest of the West,* 151–174. Beverly Hills, CA: Sage, 1957.

**8576.** Smith, Duane A. "A Fifty-Niner Miner: The Career of Horace A. W. Tabor." *Colorado Heritage* 1 and 2 (1983): 24–33.

**8577.** ———. Smith, Duane A. *Horace Tabor: His Life and the Legend.* Boulder: Colorado Associated University Press, 1973.

**8578.** ———. "The Kansas Days of Horace Tabor." *Kansas Historical Quarterly* 39 (Autumn 1973): 367–378.

**8579.** Willison, George F. *Here They Dig the Gold.* New York: Reynal and Hitchcock, 1946.

## TAFT, ROBERT ALPHONSO
(1889–1953) R-OH, Senate 1939–1953.

**8580.** Alexander, Holmes M. "Robert Alphonso Taft." In his *Famous Five,* 165–204. New York: Bookmailer, 1958.

**8581.** Ambrose, Stephen E. "The Senator and the General." *Timeline* 4 (February/March 1987): 2–15.

**8582.** Armstrong, John P. "The Enigma of Senator Taft and Foreign Policy." *Review of Politics* 17 (April 1955): 206–231.

**8583.** ———. "Senator Taft and American Foreign Policy." *Review of Politics* 17 (April 1955): 206–231.

**8584.** ———. "Senator Taft and American Foreign Policy: The Period of Opposition." Ph.D. dissertation, University of Chicago, 1953.

**8585.** Berger, Henry W. "Bipartisanship, Senator Taft, and the Truman Administration." *Political Science Quarterly* 90 (Summer 1975): 221–237.

**8586.** Berger, Henry W. "Senator Robert A. Taft Dissents from Military Escalation." In *Cold War Critics: Alternatives to American Foreign Policy in the Truman Years*, edited by Thomas G. Paterson, 167–204. Chicago: University of Chicago Press, 1971.

**8587.** Brown, Charles C. "Robert A. Taft: Champion of Public Housing and National Aid to Schools." *Cincinnati Historical Society Bulletin* 26 (July 1968): 225–253.

**8588.** Burd, Frank A. "Robert A. Taft and the American Understanding of Politics." Ph.D. dissertation, University of Chicago, 1969.

**8589.** Crocker, Lionel. "1948 Presidential Campaign Speakers." *Quarterly Journal of Speech* 34 (October 1948): 1311–1313.

**8590.** Davis, Richard O. "Mr. Republican Turns Socialist: Robert A. Taft and Public Housing." *Ohio History* 73 (Summer 1964): 135–143.

**8591.** De John, Samuel, Jr. "Robert A. Taft, Economic Conservatism, and Opposition to United States Foreign Policy, 1944–1951." Ph.D. dissertation, University of Southern California, 1976.

**8592.** Harnsberger, Caroline T. *A Man of Courage: Robert A. Taft*. Chicago: Wilcox and Follett, 1952.

**8593.** Hoyt, Edwin P. "Robert Alphonso Taft." In his *Lost Statesmen*, 189–208. Chicago: Reilly, 1961.

**8594.** Isaacson, Pauline H. "Robert Alphonso Taft: An Assessment of a Persuader." Ph.D. dissertation, University of Minnesota, 1956.

**8595.** Kennedy, John F. "Robert Taft." In his *Profiles in Courage*, 211–224. New York: Harper and Row, 1956.

**8596.** Kirk, Russell, and James McClellan. *The Political Principles of Robert A. Taft*. New York: Fleet Press, 1967.

**8597.** Kornitzer, Bela. "Son of a President: William Howard Taft—Robert A. Taft." In his *American Fathers and Sons*, 29–40. Lawrence, MA: Hermitage, 1952.

**8598.** Matthews, Geoffrey. "Robert A. Taft, the Constitution and American Foreign Policy, 1939–53." *Journal of Contemporary History* 17 (July 1982): 507–522.

**8599.** Merry, Robert W. "A Study in the Accumulation of Legislative Power." In *First Among Equals: Outstanding Senate Leaders of the Twentieth Century*, edited by Richard A. Baker and Roger H. Davidson, 163–198. Washington, DC: Congressional Quarterly, 1991.

**8600.** Patterson, James T. "Alternatives to Globalism: Robert A. Taft and American Foreign Policy, 1939–1945." *Historian* 36 (August 1974): 670–688.

**8601.** ———. *Mr. Republican: A Biography of Robert A. Taft*. Boston: Houghton Mifflin, 1972.

**8602.** ———. "Robert A. Taft and American Foreign Policy, 1939–1945." In *Watershed of Empire: Essays on New Deal Foreign Policy*, edited by Leonard P. Liggio and James J. Martin, 183–207. Colorado Springs, CO: Ralph Myles, 1976.

**8603.** Perling, Joseph J. "Sons of William Howard Taft." In his *President's Sons: The Prestige of Name in a Democracy*, 274–291. New York: Odyssey Press, 1947.

**8604.** Radosh, Ronald. "Robert A. Taft: A Noninterventionist Faces War." In his *Prophets on the Right: Profiles of Conservative Critics of American Globalism*, 119–146. New York: Simon and Schuster, 1975.

**8605.** ———. "Robert A. Taft and the Emergence of the Cold War." In his *Prophets on the Right: Profiles of Conservative Critics of American Globalism*, 147–196. New York: Simon and Schuster, 1975.

**8606.** Rapp, Noel G. "The Political Speaking of Robert A. Taft, 1939–1953." Ph.D. dissertation, Purdue University, 1955.

**8607.** Ricks, John A. "Mr. Integrity and McCarthyism: Robert A. Taft, Sr. and Joseph R. McCarthy." *Cincinnati Historical Society Bulletin* 37 (Fall 1979): 175–190.

**8608.** ———. "Mr. Integrity and McCarthyism: Senator Robert A. Taft and Senator Joseph R. McCarthy." Ph.D. dissertation, University of North Carolina, 1974.

**8609.** Robbins, Jhan, and June Robbins. *Eight Weeks to Live: The Last Chapter in the Life of Robert A. Taft.* Garden City, NY: Doubleday, 1954.

**8610.** Roper, Elmo B. "Robert A. Taft." In his *You and Your Leaders,* 188–206. New York: Morrow, 1957.

**8611.** Ross, Ishbel. *An American Family: The Tafts, 1678–1964.* Cleveland, OH: World Publishing Company, 1964.

**8612.** Sadler, Christine. "Taft's Two Sons and Daughter." In her *Children in the White House,* 230–236. New York: Putnam's, 1967.

**8613.** Smith, Thomas V., and Robert A. Taft. *Foundations of Democracy: A Series of Debates.* New York: Knopf, 1939.

**8614.** Stolberg, Benjamin. "Robert A. Taft: American Liberal." *American Mercury* 71 (October 1950): 387–399.

**8615.** Van Dyke, Vernon, and Edward L. Davis. "Senator Taft and American Security." *Journal of Politics* 14 (May 1952): 177–202.

**8616.** White, William S. "Robert A. Taft." In his *The Responsibles,* 73–108. New York: Harper and Row, 1971.

**8617.** ———. *The Taft Story.* New York: Harper, 1954.

**8618.** Williams, Phillip. "Isolationism of Discerning Internationalism: Robert Taft, Mike Mansfield and US Troops in Eu-

rope." *Review of International Studies* 8 (January 1982): 27–38.

**TAGGART, SAMUEL** (1754–1825) F-MA, House 1803–1817.

**8619.** Haynes, George H., ed. "Letters of Samuel Taggart: Representative in Congress, 1803–1814." *Proceedings of the American Antiquarian Society* 33 (April 1923): 113–226, 33 (October 1923): 297–438.

**TAGGART, THOMAS** (1856–1929) D-IN, Senate 1916.

**8620.** Ludlow, Louis. "Anecdotes." In his *From Cornfield to Press Gallery: Adventures and Reminiscences of a Veteran Washington Reporter,* 125–132, 138–147. Washington, DC: W. F. Roberts, 1924.

**TAIT, CHARLES** (1768–1835) R-GA, Senate 1809–1819.

**8621.** Moffatt, Charles H. "Charles Tait, Planter, Politician, and Scientist of the Old South." *Journal of Southern History* 14 (May 1948): 206–233.

**8622.** ———. "The Life of Charles Tait." Ph.D. dissertation, Vanderbilt University, 1946.

**TALCOTT, BURT LACKLEN** (1920– ) R-CA, House 1963–1977.

**8623.** Cavala, William. "The Case of the Chicano Challenger: The Sixteenth District of California." In *The Making of Congressmen: Seven Campaigns of 1974,* edited by Alan L. Clem, 25–54. North Scituate, MA: Duxbury Press, 1976.

**TALIAFERRO, BENJAMIN** (1750–1821) F-GA, House 1799–1802.

**8624.** Wallace, Lee A., Jr., ed. *Virginia Infantry. 2nd Regt., 1776–1783: The Orderly Book of Captain Benjamin Taliaferro, 2nd Virginia Detachment, Charleston, South Carolina, 1780.* Richmond: Virginia State Library, 1980.

**TALLMADGE, BENJAMIN** (1754–1835)
**F-CT, House 1801–1817.**

**8625.** Tallmadge, Benjamin. *Memoir of Colonel Benjamin Tallmadge.* New York: New York Times, 1968.

**TALMADGE, HERMAN EUGENE**
(1913– ) **D-GA, Senate 1957–1981.**

**8626.** Anderson, William. *The Wild Man from Sugar Creek: The Political Career of Eugene Talmadge.* Baton Rouge: Louisiana State University Press, 1975.

**8627.** Mead, Howard N. "Russell vs. Talmadge: Southern Politics and the New Deal." *Georgia Historical Quarterly* 65 (Spring 1981): 28–45.

**8628.** Talmadge, Herman E. *Talmadge: A Political Legacy, a Politician's Life: A Memoir.* Atlanta, GA: Peachtree Publishers, 1987.

**TAPPAN, BENJAMIN** (1773–1857) **D-OH, Senate 1839–1845.**

**8629.** Ratcliffe, Donald J., ed. "The Autobiography of Benjamin Tappan." *Ohio History* 85 (Spring 1976): 109–157.

**TAULBEE, WILLIAM PRESTON**
(1851–1890) **D-KY, House 1885–1889.**

**8630.** Klotter, James C. "Sex, Scandal and Suffrage in the Gilded Age." *Historian* 42 (February 1980): 225–243.

**TAYLOR, ALFRED ALEXANDER**
(1848–1931) **R-TN, House 1889–1895.**

**8631.** Fain, Sara P. *Fiddle and the Bow.* Boston: Christopher Publishing House, 1952.

**8632.** Taylor, Robert L., Jr. "Apprenticeship in the First District: Bob and AIF Taylor's Early Congressional Races." *Tennessee Historical Quarterly* 28 (Spring 1969): 24–41.

**TAYLOR, GEORGE** (1716–1781) **PA, Continental Congress 1776–1777.**

**8633.** Sanderson, John. "George Taylor." In *Sanderson's Biography of the Signers of the Declaration of Independence,* edited by Robert T. Conrad, 491–496. Philadelphia: Thomas, Cowperthwait, 1848.

**TAYLOR, GLEN HEARST** (1904–1984)
**D-ID, Senate 1945–1951.**

**8634.** Neuberger, Richard L. "Glen Taylor: Crooner on the Left." *American Mercury* 67 (September 1948): 263–272.

**8635.** Peterson, Frank R. "Glen H. Taylor and the Bilbo Case." *Phylon* 31 (Winter 1970): 344–350.

**8636.** ———. "Liberal from Idaho: The Public Career of Senator Glen H. Taylor." Ph.D. dissertation, Washington State University, 1968.

**8637.** ———. *Prophet without Honor: Glen H. Taylor and the Fight for American Liberalism.* Lexington: University Press of Kentucky, 1974.

**8638.** Pratt, William C. "Glen H. Taylor: Public Image and Reality." *Pacific Northwest Quarterly* 60 (January 1969): 10–16.

**8639.** Taylor, Glen H. *Way It Was with Me.* Secaucus, NJ: Stuart, 1979.

**TAYLOR, JOHN** (1754–1824) **R-VA, Senate 1792–1794, 1803, 1822–1824.**

**8640.** Bailor, Keith M. "John Taylor of Caroline: Continuity, Change, and Discontinuity in Virginia's Sentiments Toward Slavery, 1790–1820." *Virginia Magazine of History and Biography* 75 (July 1967): 290–304.

**8641.** Bauer, Elizabeth. "Southern Ideas of Sovereignty." In her *Commentaries on the Constitution, 1790–1860,* 219–223. New York: Columbia University Press, 1952.

**8642.** Destler, Chester M. "Forward Wheat for New England: The Correspondence of John Taylor of Caroline and Jeremiah Wadsworth, in 1795." *Agricultural History* 42 (July 1961): 201–210.

**8643.** Hill, Charles W. *The Political Theory of John Taylor of Caroline.* Rutherford, NJ: Fairleigh Dickinson University Press, 1976.

**8644.** Hubbell, Jay B. "John Taylor of Caroline." In his *South in American Literature, 1607–1900,* 219–223. Durham, NC: Duke University Press, 1954.

**8645.** Mudge, Eugene T. *The Social Philosophy of John Taylor of Caroline: A Study in Jeffersonian Democracy.* New York: Columbia University Press, 1939.

**8646.** Padover, Saul K. "The American as Agrarian: John Taylor." In his *The Genius of America: Men Whose Ideas Shaped Our Civilization,* 109–117. New York: McGraw-Hill, 1960.

**8647.** Paine, Gregory L. "John Taylor." In his *Southern Prose Writers,* 43–45. New York: American Book Company, 1947.

**8648.** Shalhope, Robert E. *John Taylor of Caroline: Pastoral Republican.* Columbia: University of South Carolina Press, 1980.

**8649.** Simms, Henry H. *Life of John Taylor: The Story of a Brilliant Leader in the Early Virginia State Rights School.* Richmond, VA: William Byrd Press, 1932.

**8650.** Thompson, Carol L. "John Taylor of Caroline: Forgotten Prophet." *Current History* 13 (November 1947): 264–269.

**8651.** Wharton, Leslie. "John Taylor and Southern Agrarianism." In his *Polity and the Public Good: Conflicting Theories of Republican Government in the New Nation.* Ann Arbor, MI: UMI Research Press, 1980.

**8652.** Wright, Benjamin F. "The Philosopher of Jeffersonian Democracy." *American Political Science Review* 22 (November 1928): 870–892.

**TAYLOR, JOHN W.** (1784–1854) D-NY, House 1813–1833.

**8653.** Alexander, DeAlva S. "John W. Taylor." *Quarterly Journal of the New York Historical Association* 1 (January 1920): 14–37.

**8654.** ———. "Only One Speaker from Empire." *State Service* 6 (September/October 1922): 336–342.

**8655.** Grose, Edward F. *Centennial History of the Village of Ballston Spa.* Ballston Spa, NY: Ballston Journal Office, 1907.

**8656.** Spann, Edward K. "John W. Taylor, the Reluctant Partisan, 1784–1854." Ph.D. dissertation, New York University, 1957.

**8657.** ———. "The Souring of Good Feelings: John W. Taylor and the Speakership Election of 1821." *New York History* 41 (October 1960): 379–399.

**8658.** Taylor, Elisha. *Genealogy of Judge John Taylor and His Descendants.* Detroit, MI: Richmond and Backus, 1886.

**TAYLOR, ROBERT LOVE** (1850–1912) D-TN, House 1879–1881, Senate 1907–1912.

**8659.** Fain, Sara P. *Fiddle and the Bow.* Boston: Christopher Publishing House, 1952.

**8660.** Gillespie, Eleanor M. "Robert Love Taylor, 1850–1912, Governor, Senator, Lecturer, Gentleman." *Southern Magazine* 3 (1936): 12–14, 44.

**8661.** Robison, Daniel M. *Bob Taylor and the Agrarian Revolt in Tennessee.* Chapel Hill: University of North Carolina Press, 1935.

**8662.** Taylor, James. *The Life and Career of Senator Robert Love Taylor (Our Bob).* Nashville, TN: Bob Taylor Publishing Company, 1913.

**8663.** Taylor, Robert L., Jr. "Apprenticeship in the First District: Bob and Alf Taylor's Early Congressional Races." *Tennessee Historical Quarterly* 28 (Spring 1969): 24–41.

## TAZEWELL, LITTLETON WALLER
(1774–1860) VA, House 1800–1801, Senate 1824–1832.

**8664.** Grigsby, Hugh B. *Discourse on the Life and Character of Honorable Littleton Waller Tazewell.* Norfolk: J. D. Ghiselin, 1860.

**8665.** Peterson, Norma L. *Littleton Waller Tazewell.* Charlottesville: University Press of Virginia, 1983.

**8666.** Sawers, Timothy R. "The Public Career of Littleton Waller Tazewell, 1824–1836." Ph.D. dissertation, Miami University, 1972.

## TELFAIR, EDWARD (1735–1807) GA,
Continental Congress 1778–1782, 1784–1785, 1788–1789.

**8667.** Coulter, E. Merton. "Edward Telfair." *Georgia Historical Quarterly* 20 (June 1936): 99–124.

## TELLER, HENRY MOORE (1830–1914)
D-CO, Senate 1876–1882, 1885–1909.

**8668.** Ellis, Elmer. *Henry Moore Teller: Defender of the West.* Caldwell, ID: Caxton, 1941.

**8669.** Holsinger, M. Paul. "Henry M. Teller and the Edmunds-Tucker Act." *Colorado Magazine* 48 (Winter 1971): 1–14.

## THAYER, ELI (1819–1899) R-MA, House
1857–1861.

**8670.** Andrews, Horace. "Kansas Crusade: Eli Thayer and the New England Emigrant Aid Company." *New England Quarterly* 35 (December 1962): 497–514.

**8671.** Thayer, Eli. *Six Speeches with a Sketch of the Life of Hon. Eli Thayer.* Boston: Brown and Taggard, 1860.

## THAYER, JOHN MILTON (1820–1906)
R-NE, Senate 1867–1871.

**8672.** Curtis, Earl G. "John Milton Thayer." *Nebraska History* 29 (March/June 1948): 55–68, 134–150.

## THOMAS, CHARLES SPALDING
(1849–1934) D-CO, Senate 1913–1921.

**8673.** Thomas, Sewell. *Silhouettes of Charles S. Thomas, Colorado Governor and United States Senator.* Caldwell, ID: Caxton, 1959.

## THOMAS, ELBERT DUNCAN
(1883–1953) D-UT, Senate 1933–1951.

**8674.** Goldberg, Joyce S. "FDR, Elbert D. Thomas, and American Neutrality." *Mid-America* 68 (January 1986): 35–50.

**8675.** Libby, Justin H. "Senators King and Thomas and the Coming War with Japan." *Utah Historical Quarterly* 42 (Fall 1974): 370–380.

## THOMAS, JESSE BURGESS (1777–1853)
W-IN/IL, House 1808–1809 (IN), Senate 1818–1829 (IL).

**8676.** Suppiger, Joseph E. "Jesse Burgess Thomas: Illinois' Pro-slavery Advocate." Ph.D. dissertation, University of Tennessee, 1970.

## THOMAS, JOHN PARNELL (1895–1970)
R-NJ, House 1937–1950.

**8677.** Carlson, Lewis H. "J. Parnell Thomas and the House Committee on Un-American Activities, 1938–1948." Ph.D. dissertation, Michigan State University, 1967.

## THOMAS, JOHN WILLIAM ELMER
(1876–1965) D-OK, House 1923–1927, Senate 1927–1951.

**8678.** Manheimer, Eric. "The Public Career of Elmer Thomas." Ph.D. dissertation, University of Oklahoma, 1953.

**8679.** Thomas, J. Elmer. *Autobiography of an Enigma.* New York: Pagent Press, 1965.

## THOMPSON, FRANK, JR. (1918–1980)
D-NJ, House 1955–1980.

**8680.** Burns, Joan S. "Superstructures." In her *Awkward Embrace,* 330–350. New York: Knopf, 1975.

**8681.** Wilson, Augusta E. *Liberal Leader in the House: Frank Thompson, Jr.* Washington, DC: Acropolis Books, 1968.

**THOMPSON, RICHARD WIGGINTON** (1809–1900) W-IN, House 1841–1843, 1847–1849.

**8682.** Neely, Mark E., Jr. "Richard W. Thompson: The Persistent Know Nothing." *Indiana Magazine of History* 72 (June 1976): 95–122.

**8683.** Roll, Charles. *Colonel Dick Thompson: The Persistent Whig.* Indianapolis: Indiana Historical Bureau, 1948.

**THOMPSON, WADDY, JR.** (1798–1868) W-SC, House 1835–1841.

**8684.** Pickett, James C. "Hon. Waddy Thompson, Pocahontas, Cortez and Santa Anna." In his *Letters and Dissertations upon Sundry Subjects,* 41–51. Washington, DC: William Greer, 1848.

**THOMPSON, WILLIAM** (1813–1897) D-IA, House 1847–1850.

**8685.** Schmidt, Louis B. "The Miller-Thompson Election Contest." *Iowa Journal of History* 12 (January 1914): 34–127.

**THOMSON, CHARLES MARSH** (1877–1943) PROG-IL, House 1913–1915.

**8686.** Hendricks, J. Edwin. *Charles Thomson and the Making of a New Nation.* Rutherford, NJ: Fairleigh Dickinson University Press, 1979.

**THORNBURGH, JACOB MONTGOMERY** (1837–1890) R-TN, House 1873–1879.

**8687.** McCammon, Charles S. "The Other Thornburgh." *Annals of Wyoming* 56 (Fall 1984): 2–11.

**THORNTON, MATTHEW** (1714–1803) NH, Continental Congress 1776–1777.

**8688.** Estes, J. Worth. "Honest Dr. Thornton: The Path to Rebellion." In *Physician Signers of the Declaration of Independence,* edited by George E. Gifford, 70–98. New York: Science History Publications, 1976.

**8689.** Sanderson, John. "Matthew Thornton." In *Sanderson's Biography of the Signers of the Declaration of Independence,* edited by Robert T. Conrad, 187–194. Philadelphia: Thomas, Cowperthwait, 1848.

**THROCKMORTON, JAMES WEBB** (1825–1894) D-TX, House 1875–1879, 1883–1887.

**8690.** Elliott, Claude. *Leathercoat, the Life History of a Texas Patriot.* San Antonio, TX: Standard Printing Company, 1938.

**8691.** Marten, James. "The Lamentations of a Whig: James Throckmorton Writes a Letter." *Civil War History* 31 (June 1985): 163–170.

**8692.** Welch, June R. "James Throckmorton Voted against Secession." In his *The Texas Governor,* 62–65. Irving, TX: G. L. A. Press, 1977.

**THURMAN, ALLEN GRANBERRY** (1813–1895) D-OH, House 1845–1847, Senate 1869–1881.

**8693.** Carroll, Howard. "Allen Thurman." In *Twelve Americans: Their Lives and Times,* 331–354. Freeport, NY: Books for Libraries, 1971.

**8694.** Goodrich, Frederick E. "Biography of Allen G. Thurman of Ohio, and His Services to the People of His State and His Country." In his *The Life and Public Services of Grover Cleveland,* 515–549. Augusta, ME: E. C. Allen, 1888.

**8695.** Hare, John S. "Allen G. Thurman: A Political Study." Ph.D. dissertation, Ohio State University, 1933.

**THURMOND, JAMES STROM** (1902– )
**R-SC, Senate 1954–1956, 1956– .**

**8696.** Boggs, Doyle W. "A Different Brand of Education: Strom Thurmond Goes to the Senate, 1954." *Proceedings of the South Carolina Historical Association* (1984): 77–85.

**8697.** Cohodas, Nadine. *Strom Thurmond and Politics of Southern Change.* New York: Simon and Schuster, 1993.

**8698.** Ellers, Joseph C. *Strom Thurmond: The Public Man.* Orangeburg, SC: Sandlapper Pub., 1993.

**8699.** Lachicotte, Albert M. *Rebel Senator: Strom Thurmond of South Carolina.* Old Greenwich, CT: Devin-Adair, 1966.

**TIFFIN, EDWARD** (1766–1829) **R-OH, Senate 1807–1809.**

**8700.** Comegys, Cornelius G. *Reminiscences of the Life and Public Services of Edward Tiffin, Ohio's First Governor.* Chillicothe, OH: J. R. S. Bond and Sons Printers, 1869.

**8701.** Gilmore, William E. *Life of Edward Tiffin, First Governor of Ohio.* Chillicothe, OH: Horney and Son, 1897.

**8702.** Lang, William. "Governor Edward Tiffin: A Biography." In *History of Seneca County, From the Close of the Revolutionary War to July 1880,* 196–207. Springfield, OH: Transcript Printing Company, 1880.

**8703.** Smith, S. Winifred. "Edward Tiffin." In *Governors of Ohio,* 1–3. Columbus: Ohio Historical Society, 1954.

**TILLMAN, BENJAMIN RYAN** (1847–1918) **D-SC, Senate 1895–1918.**

**8704.** Begley, Paul R. "Governor Richardson Faces the Tillman Challenge." *South Carolina Historical Magazine* 89 (April 1988): 119–126.

**8705.** Eubanks, John E. *Ben Tillman's Baby: The Dispensary System of South Carolina, 1892–1915.* Augusta, GA: The author, 1950.

**8706.** Neal, Diane. "Benjamin Ryan Tillman: The South Carolina Years, 1847–1894." Ph.D. dissertation, Kent State University, 1976.

**8707.** Simkins, Francis B. "Ben Tillman's View of the Negro." *Journal of Southern History* 3 (May 1937): 161–174.

**8708.** ———. *Pitchfork Ben Tillman.* Baton Rouge: Louisiana State University Press, 1944.

**8709.** ———. *The Tillman Movement in South Carolina.* Durham, NC: Duke University Press, 1926.

**TILSON, JOHN QUILLIN** (1866–1958) **R-CT, House 1909–1913, 1915–1932.**

**8710.** Sweeting, Orville J. "John Q. Tilson and the Reapportionment Act of 1929." *Western Political Quarterly* 9 (June 1956): 434–453.

**TINKHAM, GEORGE HOLDEN** (1870–1956) **R-MA, House 1915–1943.**

**8711.** Burns, Philip J. "'Dear Uncle George': Ezra Pound's Letters to Congressman Tinkham of Massachusetts." Ph.D. dissertation, University of Rhode Island, 1988.

**TIPTON, JOHN** (1786–1839) **D-IN, Senate 1832–1839.**

**8712.** Blackburn, Glen A. "The Papers of John Tipton." Ph.D. dissertation, Indiana University, 1928.

**8713.** Robertson, Nellie A., and Dorothy Riker, eds. *The John Tipton Papers.* 3 vols. Indianapolis: Indiana Historical Bureau, 1942.

**TIPTON, THOMAS WESTON** (1817–1899) **R-NE, Senate 1867–1875.**

**8714.** Tipton, Thomas W. *Forty Years of Nebraska at Home and in Congress.* Lincoln, NE: State Journal, 1902.

## TODD, JOHN BLAIR SMITH
(1814–1872) D-ND, House 1861–1863, 1864–1865.

**8715.** Wilson, Wesley C. "General John B. S. Todd, First Delegate, Dakota Territory." *North Dakota History* 31 (July 1964): 189–194.

## TOMPKINS, CHRISTOPHER
(1780–1858) AJ-KY, House 1831–1835.

**8716.** Doutrich, Paul E. "A Pivotal Decision: The 1824 Gubernatorial Election in Kentucky." *Filson Club Historical Quarterly* 56 (January 1982): 14–29.

## TOMPKINS, DANIEL D. (1774–1825) NY, House 1805.

**8717.** Barzman, Sol. "Daniel D. Tompkins." In his *Madmen and Geniuses: The Vice-Presidents of the United States*, 47–52. Chicago: Follett, 1974.

## TOOMBS, ROBERT (1810–1885) D-GA, House 1845–1853, Senate 1853–1861.

**8718.** Cole, Fred C., and W. Darden Colgate. *Robert Augustus Toombs*. Syracuse, NY: Union College, 1961.

**8719.** Phillips, Ulrich B. *The Life of Robert Toombs*. New York: Macmillan, 1913.

**8720.** ———, ed. *The Correspondence of Robert Toombs, Alexander H. Stephens and Howell Cobb*. Washington, DC: American Historical Association, 1913.

**8721.** Roberts, Derrell C. "Robert Toombs: An Unreconstructed Rebel on Freedmen." *Negro History Bulletin* 28 (Summer 1965): 191–192.

**8722.** Stovall, Pleasant A. "Robert Toombs." In *Library of Southern Literature*, edited by Edwin A. Alderman and Joel C. Harris, vol. 12, 5417–5423. New Orleans: Martin and Hoyt, 1910.

**8723.** ———. *Robert Toombs, Statesman, Speaker, Soldier, Sage: His Career in Congress and on the Hustings—His Work in the Courts—His Record with the Army—His Life at Home*. New York: Cassell, 1892.

**8724.** Thompson, William Y. *Robert Toombs of Georgia*. Baton Rouge: Louisiana State University Press, 1966.

**8725.** Trent, William P. "Alexander H. Stephens and Robert Toombs." In his *Southern Statesmen of the Old Regime: Washington, Jefferson, Randolph, Calhoun, Stephens, Toombs, and Jefferson Davis*, 197–256. New York: Crowell, 1897.

## TOWER, JOHN GOODWIN (1925–1991) R-TX, Senate 1961–1985.

**8726.** Banks, Jimmy. "Double Play." In his *Money, Marbles and Chalk: The Wondrous World of Texas Politics*, 176–186. Austin: Texas Publishing Company, 1971.

**8727.** Tower, John G. *Consequences: A Personal and Political Memoir*. Boston: Little Brown, 1991.

**8728.** ———. *A Program for Conservatives*. New York: MacFadden-Bartell Corporation, 1962.

**8729.** Welch, June R. "Tower Was the First Republican Senator since Reconstruction." In his *The Texas Senator*, 148–151. Dallas, TX: G. L. A. Press, 1978.

## TOWNE, CHARLES ARNETTE
(1858–1928) D-MN/NY, House 1895–1897 (MN), 1905–1907 (NY), Senate 1900–1901 (MN).

**8730.** Schlup, Leonard. "Charles A. Towne and the Vice-Presidential Question of 1900." *North Dakota History* 44 (Winter 1977): 14–20.

## TRAMMELL, PARK (1876–1936) D-FL, Senate 1917–1936.

**8731.** Kerber, Stephen. "Park Trammell and the Florida Democratic Senatorial Primary of 1916." *Florida Historical Quarterly* 58 (January 1980): 255–272.

**8732.** ———. "Park Trammell of Florida: A Political Biography." Ph.D. dissertation, University of Florida, 1979.

**TRIMBLE, JAMES WILLIAM** (1894–1972) **D-AR, House 1945–1967.**

**8733.** Rothrock, Thomas. "Congressman James Trimble." *Arkansas Historical Quarterly* 28 (Spring 1969): 76–85.

**TRIMBLE, WILLIAM ALLEN** (1786–1821) **OH, Senate 1819–1821.**

**8734.** Campbell, John W. "William A. Trimble." In his *Biographical Sketches,* 34–53. Columbus, OH: Scott and Gallagher, 1838.

**TROUP, GEORGE MICHAEL** (1780–1856) **R-GA, House 1807–1815, Senate 1816–1818, 1829–1833.**

**8735.** Fortune, Porter L. "George M. Troup: Leading State Rights Advocate." Ph.D. dissertation, University of North Carolina, 1950.

**8736.** Harden, Edward J. *The Life of George M. Troup.* Savannah, GA: E. J. Purse, 1859.

**TRUMAN, HARRY S.** (1884–1972) **D-MO, Senate 1935–1945.**

**8737.** Barzman, Sol. "Harry S. Truman." In his *Madmen and Geniuses: The Vice-Presidents of the United States,* 237–244. Chicago: Follett, 1974.

**8738.** Blanton, Willard B. "Harry S. Truman and Pendergast Politics." *Gateway Heritage* 11 (Winter 1990/1991): 60–69.

**8739.** Clemens, Cyril. *The Man from Missouri: A Biography of Harry S. Truman.* Webster Groves, MO: International Mark Twain Society, 1945.

**8740.** Cochrane, Bert. *Harry Truman and the Crisis Presidency.* New York: Funk & Wagnalls, 1973.

**8741.** Coffin, Tristram. *Missouri Compromise.* Boston: Little, Brown, 1947.

**8742.** Collins, David R. *Harry S. Truman: People's President.* Easton, MD: Garrard, 1975.

**8743.** Crane, John M. *The Pictorial Biography of Harry S. Truman, Thirty-Second President of the United States.* Philadelphia: Curtis, 1948.

**8744.** Crenshaw, James T. "Harry S. Truman: A Study of the Missouri Democratic Senatorial Primary Races of 1934 and 1940." Ph.D. dissertation, Vanderbilt University, 1976.

**8745.** Daniels, Jonathan. *Man of Independence.* Philadelphia: Lippincott, 1950.

**8746.** Dayton, Eldorous. *Give 'Em Hell Harry: An Informal Biography of the Terrible-Tempered Mr. T.* New York: Devin-Adair, 1956.

**8747.** Dishman, Robert D. "New Hampshire in the Limelight: The 1952 Kefauver-Truman Presidential Primary Campaign." *Historical New Hampshire* 42 (Fall 1987): 214–252.

**8748.** Donovan, Robert J. *Tumultuous Years: The Presidency of Harry S. Truman, 1949–1953.* New York: Norton, 1982.

**8749.** Eaton, Richard O., and LaValle Hart. *Meet Harry S. Truman.* Washington, DC: Dumbarton House, 1945.

**8750.** Faber, Doris. *Harry Truman.* New York: Abelard-Schuman, 1973.

**8751.** Ferrell, Robert H. *Harry S. Truman.* Columbia: University of Missouri Press, 1994.

**8752.** ———. *Truman, a Centenary Remembrance.* New York: Viking, 1984.

**8753.** Fink, Gary M., and James W. Hilty. "Prologue: The Senate Voting Record of Harry S. Truman." *Journal of Interdisciplinary History* 4 (Autumn 1973): 207–235.

**8754.** Gallu, Samuel. *"Give 'Em Hell Harry": Reminiscences.* New York: Viking, 1975.

**8755.** Gardner, Lloyd C. "Harry S. Truman: From San Francisco to Potsdam." In his *Architects of Illusion,* 55–83. Chicago: Quadrangle Books, 1970.

**8756.** Gies, Joseph. *Harry S. Truman, a Pictorial Biography.* Garden City, NY: Doubleday, 1968.

**8757.** Giglio, James N., and Greg G. Thielen. *Truman in Cartoon and Caricature.* Ames: Iowa State University Press, 1984.

**8758.** Goodman, Mark, ed. *Give 'Em Hell, Harry!* New York: Award Books, 1974.

**8759.** Gosnell, Harold F. *Truman's Crises: A Political Biography of Harry S. Truman.* Westport, CT: Greenwood, 1980.

**8760.** Grant, Philip A. "The Election of Harry S. Truman to the United States Senate." *Bulletin of the Missouri Historical Society* 36 (January 1980): 103–109.

**8761.** Hamby, Alonzo L. *Beyond the New Deal: Harry S. Truman and American Liberalism.* New York: Columbia University Press, 1973.

**8762.** ———. "Harry Truman, Small-Town American." *History Today* 39 (December 1989).

**8763.** ———. "'The Modest and Capable Western Statesman': Harry S. Truman in the United States Senate, 1935–1940." *Congress and the Presidency* 17 (Autumn 1990): 109–130.

**8764.** Harris, Edward A. "Harry S. Truman." In *Public Men In and Out of Office,* edited by John T. Salter, 322–343. Chapel Hill: University of North Carolina Press, 1946.

**8765.** Hayman, LeRoy. *Harry S. Truman: A Biography.* New York: Crowell, 1969.

**8766.** Heaster, Brenda L. "Who's on Second: The 1944 Democratic Vice Presidential Nomination." *Missouri Historical Review* 80 (January 1986): 156–175.

**8767.** Hedley, John H. *Harry S. Truman: The "Little" Man from Missouri.* Woodbury, NY: Barron's, 1979.

**8768.** Helicher, Karl. "The Education of Harry S. Truman." *Presidential Studies Quarterly* 14 (Fall 1984): 581–582.

**8769.** Helm, William P. *Harry Truman: A Political Biography.* New York: Duell, Sloan and Pearce, 1947.

**8770.** Jenkins, Roy. *Truman.* New York: Harper and Row, 1986.

**8771.** Kelton, Nancy. *Harry Four Eyes.* Thousand Oaks, CA: Raintree Publishers, 1977.

**8772.** Kempton, Greta. "Painting the Truman Family." *Missouri Historical Review* 67 (April 1973): 335–349.

**8773.** Kirkendall, Richard S. "Harry S. Truman: A Missouri Farmer in the Golden Age." *Agricultural History* 48 (October 1974): 467–483.

**8774.** ———. "Truman and Missouri." *Missouri Historical Review* 81 (January 1987): 127–140.

**8775.** ———. "Truman and the Pendergast Machine: A Comment." *American Studies* 7 (Fall 1966): 36–39.

**8776.** Kish, Francis B. "Citizen-Soldier: Harry S. Truman, 1884–1972." *Military Review* 53 (February 1973): 30–44.

**8777.** Kornitzer, Bela. "The President's Father." In his *American Fathers and Sons,* 11–28. New York: Hermitage House, 1952.

**8778.** Madison, Charles A. "Harry S. Truman: The New Deal in Eclipse." In his *Leaders and Liberals in 20th Century America,* 412–462. New York: Frederick Unger, 1961.

**8779.** Maher, M. Patrick. "The Role of the Chairman of a Congressional Investigating Committee: A Case Study of the Special Committee of the Senate to Investigate the National Defense Program, 1941–1948." Ph.D. dissertation, St. Louis University, 1962.

**8780.** Martin, Ralph G. *President from Missouri: Harry S. Truman.* New York: Messner, 1964.

**8781.** Mason, Frank. *Truman and the Pendergasts.* Evanston, IL: Regency, 1964.

**8782.** McClure, Arthur F., and Donna Costigan. "The Truman Vice Presidency: Constructive Apprenticeship or Brief Interlude?" *Missouri Historical Review* 65 (April 1971): 318–341.

**8783.** McCullough, David G. Truman. New York: Simon & Schuster, 1992.

**8784.** McNaughton, Frank, and Walter Hehmeyer. *Harry Truman, President.* New York: McGraw-Hill, 1948.

**8785.** McNaughton, Frank, and Walter Hehmeyer. *This Man Truman.* New York: Whittlesey House, 1945.

**8786.** Medhurst, Martin J. "Truman's Rhetorical Reticence, 1945–1947: An Interpretive Essay." *Speech* 74 (February 1988): 52–70.

**8787.** Melton, David. *Harry S. Truman: The Man Who Walked with Giants.* Independence, MO: Independence Press, 1980.

**8788.** Miller, Merle. *Plain Speaking: An Oral Biography of Harry S. Truman.* New York: Berkley Publishing Company, 1974.

**8789.** Milligan, Maurice. *The Inside Story of the Pendergast Machine by the Man Who Smashed It.* New York: Scribner's, 1948.

**8790.** Miscamble, Wilson D. "Harry S. Truman, the Berlin Blockade and the 1948 Election." *Presidential Studies Quarterly* 10 (Summer 1980): 306–316.

**8791.** Mitchell, Franklin D. "An Act of Presidential Indiscretion: Harry S. Truman, Congressman McDonough, and the Marine Corps Incident of 1950." *Presidential Studies Quarterly* 11 (Fall 1981): 565–575.

**8792.** ———. "Who Is Judge Truman? The Truman-for-Governor Movement of 1931." *American Studies* 7 (Fall 1966): 3–15.

**8793.** Mitchell, Franklin D., Lyle W. Dorsett, Eugene F. Schmidtlein, and Richard S. Kirkendall. "Truman and the Pendergast Machine." *Midcontinent American Studies Journal* 7 (Fall 1966): 3–39.

**8794.** Mollman, John P. *Harry S. Truman: A Biography.* New York: Monarch Press, 1966.

**8795.** Natoli, Marie D. "Harry S. Truman and the Contemporary Vice Presidency." *Presidential Studies Quarterly* 18 (Winter 1988): 81–84.

**8796.** Pemberton, William E. "Struggle for the New Deal: Truman and the Hoover Commission." *Presidential Studies Quarterly* 26 (Summer 1986): 511–527.

**8797.** Powell, Eugene J. *Tom's Boy Harry: The First Complete, Authentic Story of Harry Truman's Connection with the Pendergast Machine.* Jefferson City, MO: Hawthorn Publishing, 1948.

**8798.** Reddig, William M. *Tom's Town: Kansas City and the Pendergast Legend.* Philadelphia: Lippincott, 1947.

**8799.** Riley, Glenda. "'Dear Mamma': The Family Letters of Harry S. Truman." *Missouri Historical Review* 83 (April 1989): 249–270.

**8800.** Robbins, Charles. *Last of His Kind: An Informal Portrait of Harry S. Truman.* New York: Morrow, 1979.

**8801.** Robbins, Jhan. *Bess and Harry: An American Love Story.* New York: Putnam's, 1980.

**8802.** Rogers, Benjamin F. "Dear Mr. President: The Hoover-Truman Correspondence." *Presidential Studies Quarterly* 26 (Summer 1986): 503–510.

**8803.** Sand, Gregory W. *Truman in Retirement: A Former President Views the Nation & the World.* South Bend, IN: Justice Books, 1993.

**8804.** Schauffler, Edward R. *Harry Truman, Son of the Soil.* Kansas City, KS: Schauffler Publishing Company, 1947.

**8805.** Schmidtlein, Eugene F. "Harry S. Truman and the Pendergast Machine." *American Studies* 7 (Fall 1966): 28–35.

**8806.** ———. "Truman the Senator." Ph.D. dissertation, University of Missouri, 1962.

**8807.** ———. "Truman's First Senatorial Election." *Missouri Historical Review* 57 (January 1962/1963): 128–155.

**8808.** Sheldon, Ted., ed. *Harry S. Truman: The Man from Missouri.* Kansas City, MO: Hallmark, 1970.

**8809.** Steinberg, Alfred. *The Man from Missouri: The Life and Times of Harry S. Truman.* New York: Putnam's, 1962.

**8810.** Street, Kenneth W. "Harry S. Truman: His Role As Legislative Leader, 1945–1948." Ph.D. dissertation, University of Texas, 1963.

**8811.** Tammens, William D. "Harry S. Truman's Courthouse Years: The Missouri Proving Ground for a Future U.S. President." *Gateway Heritage* 4 (Spring 1984): 22–29.

**8812.** Truman, Harry S. *Memoirs, Years of Decision.* Garden City, NY: Doubleday, 1955.

**8813.** Truman, Margaret. *Harry S. Truman.* New York: Morrow, 1973.

**8814.** Van Patten, James J. "Harry S. Truman—Educator." *Educational Forum* 34 (March 1970): 379–381.

**8815.** Weisbord, Marvin R. "'Give 'Em Hell, Harry!': Harry S. Truman." In his *Campaigning for President: A New Look at the Road to the White House,* 133–146. Rev. ed. New York: Washington Square Press, 1966.

**8816.** White, William S. "Harry S. Truman." In his *The Responsibles,* 25–70. New York: Harper and Row, 1971.

**8817.** Wilburn, Mark S. "Keeping the Powder Dry: Senator Harry S. Truman and Democratic Interventions, 1935–1941." *Missouri Historical Review* 84 (April 1990): 311–337.

**8818.** Williams, Robert J. "Harry S. Truman and the American Presidency." *Journal of American Studies* 13 (December 1979): 393–408.

**8819.** Wilson, Donald E. "The History of President Truman's Air Policy Commission and Its Influence on Air Policy, 1947–1949." Ph.D. dissertation, University of Denver, 1978.

**8820.** Wolfson, Victor. *The Man Who Cared: A Life of Harry S. Truman.* New York: Farrar, Straus, 1966.

**8821.** Young, Donald. "Harry S. Truman." In his *American Roulette: The History and Dilemma of the Vice Presidency,* 196–251. New York: Holt, Rinehart and Winston, 1965.

## TRUMBULL, JONATHAN, JR.
### (1740–1809) CT, House 1789–1795, Senate 1795–1796.

**8822.** Dwight, Timothy. *A Discourse Occasioned by the Death of His Excellency Jonathan Trumbull, Esq., Governor.* New Haven, CT: Oliver Steele, 1809.

**8823.** Ely, Zebulon. *The Peaceful End to the Perfect Man: A Discourse Delivered in Lebanon at the Funeral of His Excellency Jonathan Trumbull.* Hartford, CT: Hudson and Goodwin, 1809.

**8824.** Ifkovic, John W. "Jonathan Trumbull, Jr., 1740–1809: A Biography." Ph.D. dissertation, University of Virginia, 1974.

**8825.** Trumbull, Jonathan. *Jonathan Trumbull: Governor of Connecticut, 1769–1784.* Boston: Little, Brown, 1919.

**8826.** Weaver, Glen. *Jonathan Trumbull: Connecticut's Merchant Magistrate, 1710–1785.* Hartford: Connecticut Historical Society, 1956.

**8827.** Wildman, Edwin. "Jonathan Trumbull: The Rebel Governor of Connecticut." In his *The Founders of America in the Days of the Revolution,* 110–130. Freeport, NY: Books for Libraries, 1968.

**TRUMBULL, LYMAN** (1813–1896) IL,
Senate 1855–1873.

**8828.** Dinunzio, Mario R. "Ideology and Party Loyalty: The Political Conversion of Lyman Trumbull." *Lincoln Herald* 79 (Fall 1977): 95–103.

**8829.** ———. "Lyman Trumbull and the Crisis in Congress." *Capitol Studies* 1 (Fall 1972): 29–40.

**8830.** ———. "Lyman Trumbull, the States' Rights Issue and the Liberal Republican Revolt." *Journal of the Illinois State Historical Society* 66 (Winter 1973): 364–375.

**8831.** ———. "Lyman Trumbull, United States Senator." Ph.D. dissertation, Clark University, 1964.

**8832.** Krug, Mark M. "Lyman Trumbull and the Real Issues in the Lincoln-Douglas Debates." *Illinois State Historical Society Journal* 57 (Winter 1964): 380–396.

**8833.** ———. *Lyman Trumbull, Conservative Radical.* New York: Barnes, 1965.

**8834.** Les Callette, Millard G. "Lyman Trumbull and the Democratic Tradition." Ph.D. dissertation, University of Maryland, 1962.

**8835.** Roske, Ralph J. *His Own Counsel: The Life and Times of Lyman Trumbull.* Reno: University of Nevada Press, 1979.

**8836.** ———. "The Post Civil War Career of Lyman Trumbull." Ph.D. dissertation, University of Illinois, 1949.

**8837.** White, Horace. *The Life of Lyman Trumbull.* Boston: Houghton Mifflin, 1913.

**TSONGAS, PAUL EFTHEMIOS** (1941– )
D-MA, House 1975–1979, Senate 1979–1985.

**8838.** Tsongas, Paul. *Heading Home.* New York: Knopf, 1984.

**TUCK, WILLIAM MUNFORD**
(1896–1983) D-VA, House 1953–1969.

**8839.** Crawley, William B. *Bill Tuck: A Political Life in Harry Byrd's Virginia.* Charlottesville: University Press of Virginia, 1978.

**TUCKER, GEORGE** (1775–1861) VA,
House 1819–1825.

**8840.** Harrison, Robert L. "George Tucker." In *Library of Southern Literature,* edited by Edwin A. Alderman and Joel C. Harris, vol. 12, 5515–5519. New Orleans: Martin and Hoyt, 1910.

**8841.** McLean, Robert C. *George Tucker: Moral Philosopher and Man of Letters.* Chapel Hill: University of North Carolina Press, 1961.

**8842.** Snavely, Tipton R. *George Tucker as Political Economist.* Charlottesville: University Press of Virginia, 1964.

**8843.** Turner, John R. "George Tucker." In his *The Ricardian Rent Theory in Early American Economics,* 83–109. New York: New York University Press, 1921.

**TUCKER, HENRY ST. GEORGE**
(1780–1848) R-VA, House 1815–1819.

**8844.** Bauer, Elizabeth. "Henry St. George Tucker." In her *Commentaries on the Constitution, 1790–1860,* 197–207. New York: Columbia University Press, 1952.

**TUCKER, JOHN RANDOLPH**
(1823–1897) D-VA, House 1875–1887.

**8845.** Davis, John W. "John Randolph Tucker: The Man and His Work." In *John Randolph Tucker Lectures,* 11–36. Lexington, VA: Washington and Lee University, 1952.

**TURNER, BENJAMIN STERLING**
(1825–1894) R-AL, House 1871–1873.

**8846.** Christopher, Maurine. "Benjamin S. Turner, James T. Rapier, and Jeremiah

Haralson/Alabama." In her *Black Americans in Congress,* 123–136. Rev. ed. New York: Thomas Y. Crowell, 1976.

## TURNER, GEORGE (1850–1932) FUS/SIL.R-WA, Senate 1897–1903.

**8847.** Johnson, Claudius O. *George Turner, Attorney-at-Law.* Pullman: State College of Washington, 1943.

## TWEED WILLIAM MARCY (1823–1878) D-NY, House 1853–1855.

**8848.** Bales, William A. *Tiger in the Streets.* New York: Dodd, Mead, 1962.

**8849.** Callow, Alexander B. *The Tweed Ring.* New York: Oxford University Press, 1966.

**8850.** Hershkowitz, Leo. *Tweed's New York: Another Look.* Garden City, NY: Anchor Press, 1977.

**8851.** Lynch, Denis T. *"Boss" Tweed: The Story of a Grim Generation.* New York: Boni and Liveright, 1927.

**8852.** Mandelbaum, Seymour J. *Boss Tweed's New York.* New York: J. Wiley, 1965.

**8853.** Zink, Harold. "Honorable William M. Tweed." In his *City Bosses in the United States,* 96–112. Durham, NC: Duke University Press, 1930.

## TYDINGS, MILLARD EVELYN (1890–1961) D-MD, House 1923–1927, Senate 1927–1951.

**8854.** Alexander, Holmes M. "Millard E. Tydings: The Man from Maryland." In *The American Politician,* edited by John Salter, 124–137. Chapel Hill: University of North Carolina Press, 1938.

**8855.** Grant, Philip, A. "Maryland Press Reaction to the Roosevelt-Tyding Confrontation." *Maryland Historical Magazine* 68 (Winter 1973): 422–437.

**8856.** Keith, Caroline H. *For Hell and a Brown Mule: The Biography of Senator Millard E. Tydings.* Lanham, MD: Madison Books, 1991.

**8857.** Miller, Nancy V. "A Political Fraud: The Maryland Senatorial Election, 1950." Master's thesis, Indiana University, 1960.

## TYLER, JOHN (1790–1862) R-VA, House 1817–1821, Senate 1827–1836.

**8858.** Barbee, David R., ed. "Tyler's Intentions Become Achievements." *Tyler's Quarterly Historical and Genealogical Magazine* 31 (April 1950): 219–221.

**8859.** Barzman, Sol. "John Tyler." In his *Madmen and Geniuses: The Vice-Presidents of the United States,* 73–78. Chicago: Follett, 1974.

**8860.** Bradshaw, Herbert C. "A President's Bride at Sherwood Forest." *Virginia Cavalcade* 7 (Spring 1958): 30–39.

**8861.** Chidsey, Donald B. *And Tyler Too.* Nashville, TN: T. Nelson, 1978.

**8862.** Chitwood, Oliver P. *John Tyler: Champion of the Old South.* New York: Appleton, 1939.

**8863.** Coleman, Elizabeth T. *Priscilla Cooper Tyler and the American Scene, 1816–1889.* University: University of Alabama Press, 1955.

**8864.** Ellett, Katherine T. *Young John Tyler.* Richmond, VA: Diety Printing Company, 1957.

**8865.** Gordon, Armistead C. "John Tyler." In his *Virginian Portraits: Essays in Biography,* 1–40. Staunton, VA: McClure, 1924.

**8866.** Hoyt, Edwin P. *John Tyler.* London: Abelard-Schuman, 1969.

**8867.** Morgan, Robert J. *A Whig Embattled: The Presidency under John Tyler.* Lincoln: University of Nebraska Press, 1954.

**8868.** Perling, Joseph J. *A President Takes a Wife.* Middleburg, VA: Denlinger's, 1959.

**8869.** Seager, Robert. *And Tyler Too: A Biography of John Tyler and Julia Gardiner Tyler.* New York: McGraw-Hill, 1963.

**8870.** Tyler, Lyon G. "John Tyler and the Vice-Presidency." *Tyler's Quarterly Historical and Genealogical Magazine* 9 (October 1927): 89–95.

**8871.** ———. *The Letters and Times of the Tylers.* 3 vols. Richmond, VA: Whittel and Shepperson, 1884–1896.

**8872.** Wallace, Sarah A. "Letters of the Presidentess, Julia Gardiner Tyler, 1844–1845." *Daughters of the American Revolution Magazine* 87 (April 1953): 641–646.

**8873.** Wise, Henry A. *Seven Decades of the Union: The Humanities and Materialism, Illustrated by a Memoire of John Tyler, with Reminiscences of Some of His Great Contemporaries.* Philadelphia: Lippincott, 1872.

**8874.** Young, Donald. "John Tyler." In his *American Roulette: The History and Dilemma of the Vice Presidency,* 42–54. New York: Holt, Rinehart and Winston, 1965.

**8875.** Young, Stanley P. *Tippecanoe and Tyler, Too!* New York: Random House, 1957.

**TYNER, JAMES NOBLE (1826–1904) R-IN, House 1869–1875.**

**8876.** Barner, William H. "James N. Tyner." In his *Lives of Gen. Ulysses S. Grant and Hon. Henry Wilson, Together with Sketches of Republican Candidates for Congress in Indiana,* 61–69. New York: W. H. Barnes, 1872.

۶&

**UDALL, MORRIS KING (1922– ) D-AZ, House 1961–1991.**

**8877.** Peabody, Robert L., ed. *Education of a Congressman: The Newsletters of Morris K. Udall.* Indianapolis: Bobbs-Merrill, 1972.

**UDALL, STEWART LEE (1920– ) D-AZ, House 1955–1961.**

**8878.** Leunes, Barbara L. "The Conservative Philosophy of Stewart L. Udall, 1961–1968." Ph.D. dissertation, Texas A&M University, 1977.

**UNDERWOOD, JOSEPH ROGERS (1791–1876) W-KY, House 1835–1843, Senate 1847–1853.**

**8879.** Priest, Nancy L. "Joseph Rogers Underwood: Nineteenth Century Kentucky Orator." *Register of the Kentucky Historical Society* 75 (October 1977): 386–403.

**8880.** Stickles, Arndt M., ed. "Joseph R. Underwood's Fragmentary Journal of the New and Old Court Contest in Kentucky." *Filson Club History Quarterly* 13 (October 1939): 202–210.

**UNDERWOOD, OSCAR WILDER (1862–1929) D-AL, House 1895–1896, 1897–1915, Senate 1915–1927.**

**8881.** Allen, Lee N. "The Underwood Presidential Movement of 1924." *Alabama Review* 15 (April 1962): 83–99.

**8882.** Doyle, Elizabeth J. "The Congressional Career of Oscar W. Underwood of Alabama." Master's thesis, Indiana University, 1948.

**8883.** Fleming, James S. "Re-establishing Leadership in the House of Representatives: The Case of Oscar W. Underwood." *Mid-America* 54 (October 1972): 234–250.

**8884.** Johnson, Evans C. "Oscar Underwood and the Hobson Campaign." *Alabama Review* 16 (April 1963): 125–140.

**8885.** ———. "Oscar Underwood and the Senatorial Campaign of 1920." *Alabama Review* 21 (January 1968): 3–20.

**8886.** ———. *Oscar W. Underwood: A Political Biography.* Baton Rouge: Louisiana State University Press, 1980.

**8887.** ———. "Oscar W. Underwood: The Development of a National Statesman, 1894–1915." Ph.D. dissertation, University of North Carolina, 1953.

**8888.** ———. "Underwood Forces and the Democratic Nomination of 1912." *Historian* 31 (February 1969): 173–193.

**8889.** Link, Arthur S. "The Underwood Presidential Movement of 1912." *Journal of Southern History* 11 (May 1945): 230–245.

**8890.** Torodash, Martin. "Underwood and the Tariff." *Alabama Review* 20 (April 1967): 115–130.

**8891.** Underwood, Oscar W. *Drifting Sands of Party Politics.* New York: Century, 1931.

৵৯

## VALLANDIGHAM, CLEMENT LAIRD (1820–1871) D-OH, House 1858–1863.

**8892.** Benedict, Michael L. "Vallandigham: Constitutionalist and Copperhead." *Timeline* 3 (February/March 1986): 16–25.

**8893.** Klement, Frank L. "Clement L. Vallandigham's Exile in the Confederacy, May 25–June 17, 1863." *Journal of Southern History* 31 (May 1965): 149–163.

**8894.** ———. *Limits of Dissent: Clement L. Vallandigham and the Civil War.* Lexington: University Press of Kentucky, 1970.

**8895.** Nye, Russel B. "Clemet L. Vallandigham." In his *Baker's Dozen,* 185–208. East Lansing: Michigan State University Press, 1956.

**8896.** Vallandigham, James L. *A Life of Clement Vallandigham.* Baltimore: Turnbull Brothers, 1872.

## VAN BUREN, JOHN (1799–1855) D-NY, House 1841–1843.

**8897.** Sadler, Christine. "Van Buren and Sons: All of Them Ladies Men." In her *Children in the White House,* 98–105. New York: Putnam's, 1967.

## VAN BUREN, MARTIN (1782–1862) NY, Senate 1821–1828.

**8898.** Alexander, Holmes M. *The American Talleyrand: The Career and Contemporaries of Martin Van Buren, Eighth President.* New York: Russell and Russell, 1968.

**8899.** Ashby, John H. "The Political Ideas of Martin Van Buren." Master's thesis, American University, 1966.

**8900.** Barzman, Sol. "Martin Van Buren." In his *Madmen and Geniuses: The Vice-Presidents of the United States,* 53–60. Chicago: Follett, 1874.

**8901.** Bassett, John S. "Martin Van Buren." In *American Secretaries of State,* edited by Samuel F. Bemis, vol. 4, 161–204. New York: Knopf, 1928.

**8902.** Brown, Richard H. "Southern Planters and Plain Republicans of the North: Martin Van Buren's Formula for National Politics." Ph.D. dissertation, Yale University, 1955.

**8903.** Butler, William A. *Martin Van Buren: Lawyer, Statesman and Man.* New York: Appleton, 1862.

**8904.** Carleton, William G. "Political Aspects of the Van Buren Era." *South Atlantic Quarterly* 50 (April 1951): 167–185.

**8905.** Cole, Donald B. *Martin Van Buren and the American Political System.* Princeton, NJ: Princeton University Press, 1984.

**8906.** Cone, Leo W. "Martin Van Buren: The Architect of the Democratic Party, 1837–1840." Ph.D. dissertation, University of Chicago, 1951.

**8907.** Crockett, Davy. *The Life of Martin Van Buren: Heir-Apparent to the "Government" and the Appointed Successor of General Andrew Jackson.* Philadelphia: Wright, 1835.

**8908.** Curtis, James C. *The Fox at Bay: Martin Van Buren and the Presidency, 1837–1841.* Lexington: University of Kentucky Press, 1970.

**8909.** Dawson, Moses. *Sketches of the Life of Martin Van Buren, President of the United States.* Cincinnati, OH: J. W. Ely, 1840.

**8910.** Donovan, Herbert D. "The Campaign of 1844." In his *The Barnburners: A Study of the Internal Movements in the Political History of New York State, 1830–1852,* 52–59. New York: Porcupine Press, 1952.

**8911.** Emmons, William. *Biography of Martin Van Buren, President of the United States.* Washington, DC: Jacob Gideon, 1835.

**8912.** Fitzpatrick, John C., ed. *Autobiography of Martin Van Buren.* Washington, DC: American Historical Association, 1920.

**8913.** Gatell, Frank O. "Sober Second Thoughts on Van Buren, the Albany Regency, and the Wall Street Conspiracy." *Journal of American History* 53 (June 1966): 19–40.

**8914.** Grayson, Theodore J. "Martin Van Buren and the Panic of 1837." In his *Leaders and Periods of American Finance,* 211–233. New York: John Wiley and Sons, 1932.

**8915.** Hamilton, James A. *Martin Van Buren's Calumnies Repudiated.* New York: Scribner's, 1870.

**8916.** Harrison, Joseph H., Jr. "Martin Van Buren and His Southern Supporters." *Journal of Southern History* 22 (November 1956): 438–458.

**8917.** Holland, William M. *The Life and Political Opinions of Martin Van Buren, Vice President of the United States.* 2d ed. Hartford, CT: Belknap and Hamersley, 1835.

**8918.** Irelan, John R. *History of the Life, Administration, and Times of Martin Van Buren.* Chicago: Fairbanks and Palmer, 1887.

**8919.** Jacobs, David H. "Martin Van Buren: Political Genius or Failure?" *Concord* 1 (Spring 1989): 63–75.

**8920.** Joline, Adrian H. "Martin Van Buren, The Lawyer." *Law Student's Helper* 18 (November 1910): 328–335.

**8921.** Lynch, Denis T. *An Epoch and a Man: Martin Van Buren and His Times.* 2 vols. New York: Liveright, 1929.

**8922.** Mackenzie, William L. *Life and Times of Martin Van Buren.* Boston: Cooke, 1846.

**8923.** McElhiney, Thomas. *Life of Martin Van Buren.* Pittsburgh: J. T. Shryock, 1853.

**8924.** McPherson, Elizabeth G., ed. "Unpublished Letters from North Carolinians to Van Buren." *North Carolina Historical Review* 15 (January 1938): 53–81.

**8925.** Mintz, Max M. "The Political Ideas of Martin Van Buren." *New York History* 30 (October 1949): 422–428.

**8926.** Moody, Robert E. "The Influence of Martin Van Buren on the Career and Acts of Andrew Jackson." *Michigan Academy of Science, Arts and Letters Papers* 7 (1927): 225–240.

**8927.** Nigro, Felix A. "Van Buren Confirmation before the Senate." *Western Political Quarterly* 14 (March 1961): 148–159.

**8928.** Niven, John. *Martin Van Buren: The Romantic Age of American Politics.* New York: Oxford University Press, 1983.

**8929.** Orth, Samuel P. "Martin Van Buren, Nationalizer of the Machine." In his *Five American Politicians: A Study in the Evolution of American Politics,* 120–170. Cleveland, OH: Burrows Brothers Company, 1906.

**8930.** Parks, Gordon E. "Martin Van Buren and the Re-organization of the Democratic Party, 1841–1844." Ph.D. dissertation, University of Wisconsin, 1965.

**8931.** Rank, Vernon E. "Martin Van Buren's Political Speaking in His Rise to Political Power." Ph.D. dissertation, Pennsylvania State University, 1961.

**8932.** Rayback, Joseph G. *Martin Van Buren.* New York: Eastern Acorn Press, 1982.

**8933.** ———. "Martin Van Buren: His Place in the History of New York and the United States." *New York History* 64 (April 1983): 120–135.

**8934.** ———. "Martin Van Buren's Break with James K. Polk: The Record." *New York History* 36 (January 1955): 51–62.

**8935.** ———. "A Myth Re-examined: Martin Van Buren's Role in the Presidential Election of 1816." *American Philosophical Society Proceedings* 124 (April 29, 1980): 106–118.

**8936.** ———, ed. "Martin Van Buren's Desire for Revenge in the Campaign of 1848." *Mississippi Valley Historical Review* 40 (March 1954): 707–716.

**8937.** Remini, Robert V. "The Albany Regency." *New York History* 39 (October 1958): 341–355.

**8938.** ———. "The Early Political Career of Martin Van Buren, 1782–1828." Ph.D. dissertation, Columbia University, 1951.

**8939.** ———. *Martin Van Buren and the Making of the Democratic Party.* New York: Columbia University Press, 1959.

**8940.** Roper, Donald M. "Martin Van Buren as Tocqueville's Lawyer: The Jurisprudence of Politics." *Journal of the Early Republic* 2 (Summer 1982): 169–189.

**8941.** Shepard, Edward M. *Martin Van Buren.* Rev. ed. Boston: Houghton Mifflin, 1899.

**8942.** Smith, Richard W. "The Career of Martin Van Buren in Connection with the Slavery Controversy through the Election of 1840." Ph.D. dissertation, Ohio State University, 1959.

**8943.** Sullivan, Wilson. "Martin Van Buren: Old Kinderhood the Politician." *Mankind* 3 (June 1972): 34–40.

**8944.** Wilson, Major L. *The Presidency of Martin Van Buren.* Lawrence: University Press of Kansas, 1984.

**VANCE, JOSEPH** (1786–1852) W-OH, House 1821–1835, 1843–1847.

**8945.** Smith, S. Winifred. "Joseph Vance, 1836–1838." In *Governors of Ohio,* 39–41. Columbus: Ohio Historical Society, 1954.

**VANCE, ZEBULON BAIRD** (1830–1894) D-NC, House 1858–1861, Senate 1879–1894.

**8946.** Bromberg, Alan B. "The Worst Muddle Ever Seen in N.C. Politics: The Farmers' Alliance, The Subtreasury, and Zeb Vance." *North Carolina Historical Review* 56 (January 1979): 19–40.

**8947.** Burgwyn, William H. "Zebulon Baird Vance." In *Library of Southern Literature,* edited by Edwin A. Alderman and Joel C. Harris, vol. 12, 5555–5559. New Orleans: Martin and Hoyt, 1910.

**8948.** Camp, Cordelia. *Governor Vance: A Life for Young People.* Raleigh: Division of Archives and History, North Carolina Department of Cultural Resources, 1980.

**8949.** Cannon, Elizabeth R., ed. *My Beloved Zebulon: The Correspondence of Zebulon Baird Vance and Harriet Newell Espy.* Chapel Hill: University of North Carolina Press, 1971.

**8950.** Dowd, Clement. *Life of Zebulon B. Vance.* Charlotte, NC: Observer Printing and Publishing House, 1897.

**8951.** Edmunds, Pocahontas W. "Zebulon Baird Vance: State's Man and Statesman." In her *Tar Heels Track the Century,* 41–69. Raleigh, NC: Edwards and Broughton, 1966.

**8952.** Shirley, Franklin R. *Zebulon Vance: Tarheel Spokesman.* Charlotte, NC: McNally and Loftin, 1963.

**8953.** Tucker, Glenn. *Zeb Vance: Champion of Personal Freedom.* Indianapolis: Bobbs-Merrill, 1966.

**8954.** Vance, Zebulon B. *The Papers of Zebulon Baird Vance.* Edited by Frontis W. Johnston. Raleigh, NC: State Department of Archives and History, 1963.

**8955.** Yates, Richard E. *Confederacy and Zeb Vance.* Tuscaloosa, AL: Confederate Publishing Company, 1958.

**VAN CORTLANDT, PHILIP (1749–1831) R-NY, House 1793–1809.**

**8956.** Van Cortlandt, Pierre. *Correspondence of the Van Cortlandt Family of Cortlandt Manor, 1748–1800.* Edited by Jacob Judd. Tarrytown, NY: Sleepy Hollow Restorations, 1977.

**8957.** ———. *Correspondence of the Van Cortlandt Family of Cortlandt Manor, 1800–1814.* Edited by Jacob Judd. Tarrytown, NY: Sleepy Hollow Restorations, 1978.

**8958.** ———. *Correspondence of the Van Cortlandt Family of Cortlandt Manor, 1815–1848.* Edited by Jacob Judd. Tarrytown, NY: Sleepy Hollow Restorations, 1981.

**VAN CORTLANDT, PIERRE, JR. (1762–1848) R-NY, House 1811–1813.**

**8959.** Van Cortlandt, Pierre. *Correspondence of the Van Cortlandt Family of Cortlandt Manor, 1815–1848.* Edited by Jacob Judd. Tarrytown, NY: Sleepy Hollow Restoration, 1981.

**VANDENBERG, ARTHUR HENDRICK (1884–1951) R-MI, Senate 1928–1951.**

**8960.** Acheson, Dean. "Arthur Vandenberg and the Senate." In *Congressional Behavior,* edited by Nelson W. Polsby, 93–104. New York: Random House, 1971.

**8961.** ———. "Arthur Vandenberg and the Senate." In his *Sketches from Life of Men I Have Known,* 123–146. New York: Harper and Row, 1961.

**8962.** Boulard, Garry. "Arthur H. Vandenberg and the Formation of the United Nations." *Michigan History* 71 (July/August 1987): 38–45.

**8963.** Bradshaw, James S. "Senator Arthur H. Vandenberg and Article 51 of the United Nations Charter." *Mid-America* 57 (July 1975): 145–156.

**8964.** ———. "Three from the *Grand Rapids Herald:* Cobb, Knox, and Vandenberg." *Michigan History* 74 (March/April 1990): 18–24

**8965.** Briggs, Philip J. "Senator Vandenberg, Bipartisanship and the Origin of United Nations Article 51." *Mid-America* 60 (October 1978): 163–169.

**8966.** Caspar, Luzian R. *Senator Vandenberg, 1884–1951.* Zurich: ADAG Administration and Druch, 1979.

**8967.** Dunlap, Aurie N. "The Political Career of Arthur H. Vandenberg." Ph.D. dissertation, Columbia University, 1955.

**8968.** Eldersveld, A. Martin. "A Review and Thematic Analysis of Arthur H. Vandenberg's Senate Addresses on Foreign Policy." Ph.D. dissertation, University of Michigan, 1960.

**8969.** Fetzer, James. "Senator Vandenberg and the American Commitment to China, 1945–50." *Historian* 36 (February 1974): 283–303.

**8970.** Gazell, James A. "Arthur H. Vandenberg, Internationalism, and the United Nations." *Political Science Quarterly* 88 (September 1973): 375–394.

**8971.** Harris, Edward A. "Senator Arthur H. Vandenberg, the Politics of Bipartisanship, and the Origins of Anti-Soviet Consensus, 1941–1946." *World Affairs* 138 (Winter 1975–1976): 219–241.

**8972.** Hill, Thomas M. "The Senate Leadership and International Policy from Lodge to Vandenberg." Ph.D. dissertation, Washington University, 1970.

**8973.** Hudson, Daryl J. "Vandenberg Reconsidered: Senate Resolution 239 and American Foreign Policy." *Diplomatic History* 1 (Winter 1977): 46–63.

**8974.** Meijer, Hank. "Arthur Vandenberg and the Fight for Neutrality, 1939." *Michigan Historical Review* 16 (Fall 1990): 1–21.

**8975.** Moore, Newell S. "The Role of Senator Arthur H. Vandenberg in American Foreign Affairs." Ph.D. dissertation, George Peabody College for Teachers, 1954.

**8976.** Oliver, Robert T. "1948 Presidential Campaign Speakers." *Quarterly Journal of Speech* 34 (October 1948): 317–321.

**8977.** Patterson, J. W. "Arthur Vandenberg's Rhetorical Strategy in Advancing Bipartisan Foreign Policy." *Quarterly Journal of Speech* 56 (October 1970): 284–295.

**8978.** ———. "A Study of the Changing Views in Selected Foreign Policy Speeches of Senator Arthur H. Vandenberg, 1937–1949." Ph.D. dissertation, University of Oklahoma, 1961.

**8979.** Reston, James. "Arthur Vandenberg." *Michigan Quarterly Review* 8 (Spring 1969): 73–81.

**8980.** Shimmel, Lee A. "The Evolution of an Interventionist Senator Arthur H. Vandenberg, 1945–1949." Master's thesis, Eastern Michigan University, 1991.

**8981.** Silverman, Sheldon A. "At the Water's Edge: Arthur Vandenberg and the Foundation of American Bipartisan Foreign Policy." Ph.D. dissertation, University of California, 1967.

**8982.** Tompkins, Clinton D. "Arthur Vandenberg Goes to the Senate." *Michigan History* 51 (Spring 1967): 19–36.

**8983.** ———. *Senator Arthur H. Vandenberg: The Evolution of a Modern Republican, 1884–1945.* East Lansing: Michigan State University Press, 1970.

**8984.** ———. "Senator Arthur Hendrick Vandenberg: Middle Western Isolationist." *Michigan History* 44 (March 1960): 39–58.

**8985.** Vandenberg, Arthur H., and Joe A. Morris, eds. *The Private Papers of Senator Vandenberg.* Boston: Houghton Mifflin, 1952.

**8986.** Wilcox, Francis O. *Arthur H. Vandenberg, His Career and Legacy.* Ann Arbor: University of Michigan, 1975.

**VANDER JAGT, GUY ADRIAN** (1931– ) R-MI, House 1966–1993.

**8987.** Ried, Paul E. *The Orator: Guy Vander Jagt on the Hustings.* Ottawa, IL: Green Hill Publishers, 1984.

**VAN WINKLE, PETER GODWIN** (1808–1872) U-WV, Senate 1863–1869.

**8988.** Bayless, R. W. "Peter G. Van Winkle and Waitman Willey in the Impeachment Trial of Andrew Johnson." *West Virginia History* 13 (January 1952): 75–89.

**8989.** Howard, Thomas W. "Peter G. Van Winkle's Vote in the Impeachment of President Johnson: A West Virginian as a Profile in Courage." *West Virginia History* 35 (July 1974): 290–295.

**VAN WYCK, CHARLES HENRY** (1824–1895) R-NY/NE, House 1859–1863, 1867–1869, 1870–1871 (NY), Senate 1881–1887 (NE).

**8990.** Harmar, Marie U., and James L. Sellers. "Charles Henry Van Wyck." *Nebraska Historical Magazine* 12 (April/June 1929): 80–129, 12 (July/September 1929): 190–246, 12 (October/December 1929): 322–373.

**VARDAMAN, JAMES KIMBLE** (1861–1930) D-MS, Senate 1913–1919.

**8991.** Fortenberry, Joseph E. "James Kimble Vardaman and American Foreign Policy 1913–1919." *Journal of Mississippi History* 35 (May 1973): 127–140.

**8992.** Holmes, William F. *The White Chief: James Kimble Vardaman.* Baton Rouge: Louisiana State University Press, 1970.

**8993.** McLemore, Nannie P. "James K. Vardaman, A Mississippi Progressive." *Journal of Mississippi History* 29 (February 1967): 1–11.

**8994.** Prince, Vinton M., Jr. "Will Women Turn the Tide? Mississippi Women and the 1922 United States Race." *Journal of Mississippi History* 42 (August 1980): 212–220.

**VARE, WILLIAM SCOTT** (1867–1934) R-PA, House 1912–1923, 1923–1927.

**8995.** Salter, John T. *The People's Choice: Philadelphia's William S. Vare.* New York: Exposition Press, 1971.

**8996.** Vare, William S. *My Forty Years in Politics.* Philadelphia: Roland Swain, 1933.

**VARNUM, JAMES MITCHELL** (1748–1789) RI, Continental Congress 1780–1782, 1786–1787.

**8997.** Hildreth, Samuel P. *Memoirs of the Early Pioneer Settlers of Ohio*, 165–183. Cincinnati, OH: H. W. Derby, 1854.

**VARNUM, JOSEPH BRADLEY** (1750–1821) R-MA, House 1795–1811, Senate 1811–1817.

**8998.** Coburn, Frederick W. *General Joseph Bradley Varnum: His Life and Times.* Lowell, MA: Press of the Courier-Citizen, 1933.

**8999.** Coburn, George B. "A Sketch of the Life of General James M. Varnum." *Contributions of the Lowell Historical Society* 1 (November 1907): 69–78.

**9000.** Kaplan, Lawrence S. "Document: A New Englander Defends the War of 1812: Senator Varnum to Judge Thacher." *Mid-America* 46 (October 1964): 269–280.

**9001.** Varnum, John M. *The Varnums of Dracut.* Boston: David Clapp and Son, 1907.

**9002.** Varnum, Joseph. "Autobiography of General Joseph B. Varnum." *Magazine of American History* 20 (November 1888): 405–414.

**9003.** Wood, Frederick A. "A New England Democrat of the Old School." *New England Magazine* 24 (July 1901): 474–486.

**VERPLANCK, GULIAN CROMMELIN** (1786–1870) J-NY, House 1825–1833.

**9004.** Bryant, William C. "Gulian Crommelin Verplanck." In his *Prose Writings William Cullen Bryant,* vol. 1, 394–431. New York: Appleton, 1884.

**9005.** July, Robert W. *Essential New Yorker, Gulian Crommelin Verplanck.* Durham, NC: Duke University Press, 1951.

**9006.** Taft, Kendall B. "Gulian Crommelin Verplanck." In his *Minor Knickerbockers,* 68–69. New York: American Book Company, 1947.

**VEST, GEORGE GRAHAM** (1830–1904) D-MO, Senate 1879–1903.

**9007.** Dawes, Marian E. "The Senatorial Career of George Graham Vest." Master's thesis, University of Missouri, 1932.

**9008.** French, Edwin M. *Senator Vest: Champion the Dog.* Boston: Meador, 1930.

**9009.** Holsinger, M. Paul. "Senator George Graham Vest and the Menace of Mormonism, 1882–1887." *Missouri Historical Review* 65 (October 1970): 23–36.

**9010.** Johnson, Icie F. *The Old Drum Story.* Warrensburg, MO: Chamber of Commerce, 1957.

**9011.** Kramer, Daisy. *Old Drum, Being an Account of George Graham Vest and His Now Famous Eulogy to the Dog.* Kirkwood, MO: Printery, 1970.

**9012.** Philips, John F. "George Graham Vest." In *Library of Southern Literature,* edited by Edwin A. Alderman and Joel C. Harris, vol. 12, 5575–5580. New Orleans: Martin and Hoyt, 1910.

**VILAS, WILLIAM FREEMAN** (1840–1908) D-WI, Senate 1891–1897.

**9013.** Merrill, Horace S. *William Freeman Vilas: Doctrinaire Democrat.* Madison: State Historical Society of Wisconsin, 1954.

**VINSON, CARL** (1883–1981) D-GA, House 1914–1965.

**9014.** Enders, Calvin W. "The Vinson Navy." Ph.D. dissertation, Michigan State University, 1970.

**9015.** Reed, Ralph. "Fighting the Devil with Fire: Carl Vinson's Victory over Tom Watson in the 1918 Tenth District Democratic Primary." *Georgia Historical Quarterly* 67 (Winter 1983): 451–479.

**9016.** Walter, John C. "Congressman Carl Vinson and Franklin D. Roosevelt: Naval Preparedness and the Coming of World War II, 1932–40." *Georgia Historical Quarterly* 64 (Fall 1980): 294–305.

**VINSON, FREDERICK MOORE** (1890–1953) D-KY, House 1924–1929, 1931–1938.

**9017.** Allen, Francis A. "Chief Justice Vinson and the Theory of Constitutional Government: A Tentative Appraisal." *Northwestern University Law Review* 49 (March/April 1954): 3–25.

**9018.** Bolner, James. "Fred M. Vinson: 1890–1938, The Years of Relative Obscurity." *Register of the Kentucky Historical Society* 63 (January 1965): 3–16.

**9019.** ———. "Mr. Chief Justice Fred M. Vinson and Racial Discrimination." *Kentucky Historical Society Register* 64 (January 1966): 29–43.

**9020.** ———. "Mr. Chief Justice Vinson and the Communist Controversy: A Reassessment." *Kentucky Historical Society Register* 66 (October 1968): 378–391.

**9021.** ———. "Mr. Chief Justice Vinson: His Politics and His Constitutional Law." Ph.D. dissertation, University of Virginia, 1963.

**9022.** Frank, John P. "Fred Vinson and the Chief Justiceship." *University of Chicago Law Review* 21 (Winter 1954): 212–246.

**9023.** Grant, Philip A. "Press Reaction to the Appointment of Fred M. Vinson as Chief Justice of the United States." *Kentucky Historical Society Register* 75 (October 1977): 304–313.

**9024.** Hatcher, John H. "The Education of the Thirteenth United States Chief Justice: Frederick Moore Vinson, Part I." *West Virginia History* 39 (July 1978): 285–323.

**9025.** ———. "Fred Vinson: Boyhood and Education in the Big Sandy Valley." *Kentucky Historical Society Register* 72 (July 1974): 243–261.

**9026.** ———. "Fred Vinson, Congressman from Kentucky: A Political Biography, 1890–1938." Ph.D. dissertation, University of Cincinnati, 1967.

**9027.** Kornitzer, Bela. "Chief Justice Vinson's Kentucky Boyhood: James Vinson—Fred M. Vinson." In his *American Fathers and Sons,* 171–190. New York: Hermitage House, 1952.

**9028.** Law Clerks of Justice Vinson. "Chief Justice Vinson and His Law Clerks." *Northwestern University Law Review* 49 (March/April 1954): 26–35.

**9029.** Laws, Bolitha J. "Chief Justice Fred M. Vinson." *American Bar Association Journal* 39 (October 1953): 901–921.

**9030.** Lefberg, Irving F. "Chief Justice Vinson and the Politics of Desegregation." *Emory Law Journal* 24 (Spring 1975): 243–312.

**9031.** Lester, Wilbur R. "Fred M. Vinson in the Executive Branch." *Northwestern University Law Review* 49 (March/April 1954): 36–53.

**9032.** Oliver, William W. "Vinson in Congress." *Northwestern Law Review* 49 (March/April 1954): 62–75.

**9033.** Parker, John J. "Chief Justice Fred M. Vinson: Meeting the Challenge to Law and Order: Evaluates the Work of the Late Chief Justice." *American Bar Association Journal* 41 (April 1955): 324–326, 363.

**9034.** Ries, John C. "Congressman Vinson and the Deputy to JCS Chairman." *Military Affairs* 30 (Spring 1966): 16–24.

**9035.** Schwartz, Marvin, and Edwin M. Zimmerman. "Place of Chief Justice Vinson in the History of the Supreme Court." *Oklahoma Bar Association Journal* 24 (November 28, 1953): 1925–1930.

**9036.** Stephens, Harold M. "The Chief Justice." *American Bar Association Journal* 32 (July 1946): 387–389.

**9037.** ———. "The Chief Justice." *Case and Comment* 51 (November/December 1946): 3–7.

**9038.** ———. "The Chief Justice." *Kentucky State Bar Journal* 10 (September 1946): 212–214.

**VOIGT, EDWARD** (1873–1934) R-WI, House 1917–1927.

**9039.** Adams, Willi P. "Ethnic Politicians and American Nationalism during the First World War: Four German-Born Members of the U.S. House of Representatives." *American Studies International* 29 (April 1991): 20–34.

**VOORHEES, DANIEL WOLSEY** (1827–1897) D-IN, House 1861–1866, 1869–1873, Senate 1877–1897.

**9040.** Jordan, Henry D. "Daniel Wesley Voorhees." *Mississippi Valley Historical Review* 6 (March 1920): 532–555.

**9041.** Kenworthy, Leonard S. *The Tall Sycamore of the Wabash: Daniel Wolsey Voorhees.* Boston: Humphries, 1936.

**VOORHIS, HORACE JERRY "JERRY"** (1901–1984) D-CA, House 1937–1947.

**9042.** Bullock, Paul. *Jerry Voorhis, The Idealist as Politician.* New York: Vantage, 1978.

**9043.** ———. "Rabbits and Radicals: Richard Nixon's 1946 Campaign Against Jerry Voorhis." *Southern California Quarterly* 55 (Fall 1973): 319–359.

**9044.** Douglas, Paul H. "Three Saints in Politics." *American Scholar* 40 (Spring 1971): 223–232.

**9045.** Johnson, Claudius O. "Jerry Voorhis." In *Public Men In and Out of Office,* edited by John T. Salter, 322–343. Chapel Hill: University of North Carolina Press, 1946.

**9046.** Voorhis, Jerry. *Confessions of a Congressman.* Garden City, NY: Doubleday, 1947.

**VORYS, JOHN MARTIN** (1896–1968) R-OH, House 1939–1959.

**9047.** Porter, David L. "Ohio Representative John M. Vorys and the Arms Embargo in 1939." *Ohio History* 83 (Spring 1974): 103–113.

**9048.** Livingston, Jeffrey C. "Ohio Congressman John M. Vorys: A Republican, Conservative Nationalist and Twentieth Century American Foreign Policy." Ph.D. dissertation, University of Toledo, 1989.

**VROOM, PETER DUMONT** (1791–1873) D-NJ, House 1839–1841.

**9049.** Elmer, Lucius Q. "Governors I Have Known: Peter D. Vroom." In his *The Constitution and Government of the Province and State of New Jersey,* 184–200. Newark, NJ: Dennis, 1872.

&

## WADE, BENJAMIN FRANKLIN
(1800–1878) R-OH, Senate 1851–1869.

9050. Brown, Daniel S., Jr. "A Radical Republican in the United States Senate: The Antislavery Speaking of Benjamin Franklin Wade." Ph.D. dissertation, Louisiana State University and Agricultural and Mechanical College, 1987.

9051. Land, Mary. "Bluff Ben Wade's New England Background." *New England Quarterly* 27 (December 1954): 484–509.

9052. Lewis, Lloyd. "He Hated Southern Gentlemen." In his *It Takes All Kinds*, 13–30. New York: Harcourt, 1947.

9053. Riddle, Albert G. *The Life of Benjamin Wade*. Cleveland, CH: Williams, 1886.

9054. Shover, Kenneth B. "The Life of Benjamin F. Wade." Ph.D. dissertation, University of California, Berkeley, 1962.

9055. ———. "Maverick at Bay: Ben Wade's Senate Reelection Campaign, 1862–1863." *Civil War History* 12 (March 1966): 23–42.

9056. Trefousse, Hans L. *Benjamin Franklin Wade, Radical Republican from Ohio*. Boston: Twayne, 1963.

9057. ———. "The Motivation of a Radical Republican: Benjamin F. Wade." *Ohio History* 73 (Spring 1964): 63–74.

9058. Vollweiler, Albert T. "Life in Congress 1850–1861." *Quarterly Journal of North Dakota* 6 (January 1916): 145–158.

9059. Volpe, Vernon L. "Benjamin Wade's Strange Defeat." *Ohio History* 97 (Summer/Autumn 1988): 122–132.

## WADSWORTH, JAMES WOLCOTT, JR.
(1877–1952) R-NY, Senate 1915–1927, House 1933–1951.

9060. Fausold, Martin L. *James W. Wadsworth, Jr.: The Gentleman from New York*. Syracuse, NY: Syracuse University Press, 1975.

9061. Hatch, Alden. *The Wadsworths of the Genesee*. New York: Coward-McCann, 1959.

9062. Holthusen, Henry F. *James W. Wadsworth, Jr., A Biographical Sketch*. New York: Putnam's, 1926.

9063. Porter, David L. "The Man Who Made the Draft—Representative James Wadsworth." *Aerospace Historian* 22 (Spring 1975): 29–32.

## WADSWORTH, JEREMIAH (1743–1804)
CT, Continental Congress 1788, House 1789–1795.

9064. Destler, Chester M. "Forward Wheat for the New England: The Correspondence of John Taylor of Carolina with Jeremiah Wadsworth, in 1795." *Agricultural History* 42 (July 1968): 201–210.

9065. ———. "Gentleman Farmer and the New Agriculture: Jeremiah Wadsworth." *Agricultural History* 46 (January 1972): 135–153.

9066. Platt, John D. "Jeremiah Wadsworth, Federalist Entrepreneur." Ph.D. dissertation, Columbia University, 1955.

9067. Swiggett, Howard G. "A Solid Man of Connecticut: Jeremiah Wadsworth." In his *Forgotten Leaders of the Revolution*, 35–61. Garden City, NY: Doubleday, 1955.

## WADSWORTH, PELEG (1748–1829)
F-MA, House 1793–1807.

9068. Wadsworth, Peleg. *Letters of General Peleg Wadsworth to His Son John, Student at Harvard College, 1796–1798: Biographical Chapter and Notes by George and Margaret Rose*. Portland: Maine Historical Society, 1961.

## WAGGONNER, JOSEPH DAVID, JR.
(1918– ) D-LA, House 1961–1979.

9069. Childs, David W. "Congressman Joe D. Waggonner: A Study in Political Influence." *North Louisiana Historical Association Journal* 13, no. 4 (1982): 118–130.

## WAGNER, ROBERT FERDINAND
(1877–1953) D-NY, Senate 1927–1949.

**9070.** Byrne, Thomas R. "The Social Thought of Senator Robert F. Wagner." Ph.D. dissertation, Georgetown University, 1951.

**9071.** Huthmacher, J. Joseph. *Senator Robert F. Wagner and the Rise of Urban Liberalism.* New York: Atheneum, 1968.

## WALKER, AMASA (1799–1875) R-MA,
House 1862–1863.

**9072.** Mick, Laura A. "The Life of Amasa Walker." Ph.D. dissertation, Ohio State University, 1940.

**9073.** Turner, John R. "Amasa Walker." In his *The Ricardian Rent Theory in Early American Economics,* 165–178. New York: New York University Press, 1921.

## WALKER, JAMES ALEXANDER
(1832–1901) R-VA, House 1895–1899.

**9074.** Campbell, Edward C. "James Alexander Walker: A Biography." Master's thesis, Virginia Polytechnical Institute and State University, 1972.

## WALKER, JOHN WILLIAMS (1783–1823)
D-AL, Senate 1819–1822.

**9075.** Bailey, Hugh C. "John W. Walker and the Land Laws of the 1820's." *Agricultural History* 32 (April 1958): 120–126.

**9076.** ———. *John William Walker: A Study in the Political, Social and Cultural Life of the Old Southwest.* University: University of Alabama Press, 1964.

**9077.** Owsley, Frank L. "John Williams Walker." *Alabama Review* 9 (April 1956): 100–119.

## WALKER, ROBERT JOHN (1801–1869)
D-MS, Senate 1835–1845.

**9078.** Brown, George W. *Reminiscences of Gov. R. J. Walker: With the True Story of the Rescue of Kansas from Slavery.* Westport, CT: Negro Universities Press, 1970.

**9079.** Dodd, William E. *Robert J. Walker, Imperialist.* Chicago: Chicago Literary Club, 1914.

**9080.** Harmon, George D. "Aspects of Slavery and Expansion, 1848–60." *Lehigh University Publication* 3 (July 1929): 3–43.

**9081.** McHenry, George. "Slavery and Abolition in America." In his *The Cotton Trade,* 281–283. London: Saunders, Otley and Company, 1863.

**9082.** Shenton, James P. *Robert John Walker: A Politician from Jackson to Lincoln.* New York: Columbia University Press, 1961.

**9083.** Tick, Frank H. "The Political and Economic Policies of Robert J. Walker." Ph.D. dissertation, University of California, 1947.

**9084.** Wolpow, Meyer S. "For the Greater Glory of the Union: The Last Years of Robert J. Walker." Ph.D. dissertation, New York University, 1960.

## WALKER, WILLIAM ADAMS (1805–1861)
D-NY, House 1853–1855.

**9085.** Greene, Laurence. *The Filibuster: The Career of William Walker.* Indianapolis: Bobbs-Merrill, 1937.

**9086.** Scroggs, William O. *Filibusters and Financiers: The Story of William Walker and His Associates.* New York: Macmillan, 1916.

## WALL, GARRET DORSET (1783–1850)
J-NJ, Senate 1835–1841.

**9087.** Elmer, Lucius Q. "Lawyers I Have Known: Garrett D. Wall." In his *The Constitution and Government of the Province and State of New Jersey,* 419–431. Newark, NJ: Dennis, 1872.

## WALLS, JOSIAH THOMAS (1842–1905)
R-FL, House 1871–1873, 1873–1876.

**9088.** Christopher, Maurine. "Josiah T. Walls/Florida." In her *Black Americans in Congress,* 78–86. Rev. ed. New York: Thomas Y. Crowell, 1976.

**9089.** Klingman, Peter D. "Josiah T. Walls and the Black Tactics of Race in Post Civil War Florida." *Negro History Bulletin* 37 (April 1974): 242–247.

**9090.** Klingman, Peter D. *Josiah Walls, Florida's Black Congressman of Reconstruction.* Gainesville: University of Florida Press, 1976.

**WALSH, DAVID IGNATIUS** (1872–1947)
**D-MA, Senate 1919–1925, 1926–1947.**

**9091.** Byrne, Michael W. "The Walsh Amendment: A Legal Barrier to the Destroyer-Base Deal." *Valley Forge Journal* 3, no. 4 (1987): 320–333.

**9092.** Flannagan, John H. "The Disillusionment of a Progressive: US Senator David I. Walsh and the League of Nations Issue, 1918–1920." *New England Quarterly* 41 (December 1968): 483–504.

**9093.** Grattan, William J. "David I. Walsh and Post War America." Ph.D. dissertation, Harvard University, 1958.

**9094.** Wayman, Dorothy G. *David I. Walsh: Citizen-Patriot.* Milwaukee, WI: Bruce Publishing Company, 1952.

**WALSH, MICHAEL** (1810–1859) D-NY,
**House 1853–1855.**

**9095.** Ernst, R. "One and Only Mike Walsh." *New York Historical Society Quarterly* 36 (January 1952): 43–65.

**WALSH, THOMAS JAMES** (1859–1933)
**D-MT, Senate 1913–1933.**

**9096.** Bates, James L. "Politics and Ideology: Thomas J. Walsh and the Rise of Populism." *Pacific Northwest Quarterly* 65 (April 1974): 49–56.

**9097.** ———. Bates, James L. "Senator Walsh of Montana, 1918–1924: A Liberal under Pressure." Ph.D. dissertation, University of North Carolina, 1952.

**9098.** ———. "T. J. Walsh: His Genius for Controversy." *Montana* 19 (October 1969): 3–15.

**9099.** ———, ed. *Tom Walsh in Dakota Territory: Personal Correspondence of Senator Thomas J. Walsh and Elinor C. McClements.* Champaign: University of Illinois, 1966.

**9100.** Brammer, Clarence L. "Thomas J. Walsh, Spokesman for Montana." Ph.D. dissertation, University of Missouri, 1972.

**9101.** Carter, Paul A. "The Other Catholic Candidate: The 1928 Presidential Bid of Thomas J. Walsh." *Pacific Northwest Quarterly* 55 (January 1964): 1–8.

**9102.** Dunnington, Miles W. "Senator Thomas J. Walsh, Independent Democrat in the Wilson Years." Ph.D. dissertation, University of Chicago, 1941.

**9103.** O'Grady, M. Denis. "The Role of Thomas J. Walsh in the Senatorial Contest, 1913–1926." Ph.D. dissertation, University of Notre Dame, 1951.

**9104.** O'Keane, Josephine. *Thomas J. Walsh: A Senator from Montana.* Francestown, NH: Jones, 1955.

**9105.** Schafer, Joseph. "Thomas James Walsh, A Wisconsin Gift to Montana." *Wisconsin Magazine of History* 23 (June 1940): 448–473.

**9106.** Schauinger, Joseph H. "Senators." In his *Profiles in Action,* 164–171. Milwaukee, WI: Bruce, 1966.

**9107.** Stratton, David H. "Two Western Senators and Teapot Dome: Thomas J. Walsh and Albert B. Fall." *Pacific Northwest Quarterly* 65 (April 1974): 57–65.

**9108.** Villard, Oswald G. "Thomas J. Walsh: A Great Prosecutor." In *Prophets True and False,* 139–149. New York: Knopf, 1928.

**WALTER, FRANCIS EUGENE**
**(1894–1963) D-PA, House 1933–1963.**

**9109.** Cole, David. "McCarran-Walter." *Constitution* 2 (Winter 1990): 51–52, 54–59.

**9110.** Dimmitt, Marius A. "The Enactment of the McCarran-Walter Act of 1952." Ph.D. dissertation, University of Kansas, 1970.

**9111.** Sherman, Richard. "Representative Walter Outsmarts the Reds." *American Mercury* 83 (November 1956): 37–43.

**WALTHALL, EDWARD CARY**
**(1831–1898) D-MS, Senate 1885–1894, 1895–1898.**

**9112.** Helmes, James. "Edward Carey Walthall: Soldier and Statesman." Ph.D. dissertation, Peabody College, 1928.

**WALTON, GEORGE (1749–1804) GA, Senate 1795–1796, Continental Congress 1776–1777, 1780–1781.**

**9113.** Bridges, Edwin. "George Walton: A Political Biography." Ph.D. dissertation, University of Chicago, 1981.

**9114.** Cashin, Edward J. "George Walton and the Forged Letter." *Georgia Historical Quarterly* 62 (Summer 1978): 133–145.

**WARD, ARTEMAS (1727–1800) MA, House 1791–1795, Continental Congress 1780–1781.**

**9115.** Martyn, Charles. *Life of Artemas Ward, The First Commander-In-Chief of the American Revolution.* Port Washington, NY: Kennikat, 1970.

**WARD, MATTHIAS (1805–1861) D-TX, Senate 1858–1859.**

**9116.** Welch, June R. "Matthias Ward." In his *The Texas Senator,* 14–15. Dallas, TX: G. L. A. Press, 1978.

**WARD, SAMUEL (1725–1776) RI, Continental Congress 1774–1776.**

**9117.** Sparks, Jared. "The Life of Samuel Ward." In his *The Library of American Biography,* vol. 9, 231–358. New York: Harper, 1855.

**WARNER, WILLIAM (1840–1916) R-MO, House 1885–1889, Senate 1905–1911.**

**9118.** Ryan, John B., Jr. "William Warner in the California Gold Rush." *Journal of the West* 10 (October 1971): 713–725.

**WARREN, FRANCIS EMROY (1844–1929) R-WY, Senate 1890–1893, 1895–1929.**

**9119.** Gould, Lewis L. "Frances E. Warren and the Johnson County War." *Arizona and the West* 9 (Summer 1967): 131–142.

**9120.** Hansen, Anne C. "The Congressional Career of Senator Francis Warren from 1890–1902." *Annals of Wyoming* 20 (January/July 1948): 3–49, 131–158.

**9121.** Schlup, Leonard. "A Taft Republican: Sen. Francis E. Warren and National Politics." *Annals of Wyoming* 54 (Fall 1982): 62–66.

**WARREN, JOSEPH MABBETT (1813–1896) D-NY, House 1871–1873.**

**9122.** Cary, John. *Joseph Warren: Physician, Politician, Patriot.* Urbana: University of Illinois Press, 1961.

**WARREN, LINDSAY CARTER (1889–1976) D-NC, House 1925–1940.**

**9123.** Porter, David L. "Representative Lindsay Warren, the Water Bloc, and the Transportation Act of 1940." *North Carolina Historical Review* 50 (Summer 1973): 273–288.

**WASHBURN, CADWALLADER COLDEN (1818–1882) R-WI, House 1855–1861, 1867–1871.**

**9124.** Hunt, Gaillard I. *Israel, Elihu, and Cadwallader Washburn: A Chapter in American Biography.* New York: Macmillan, 1925.

**9125.** Marquette, Clare L. "The Business Activities of C. C. Washburn." Ph.D. dissertation, University of Wisconsin, 1940.

## WASHBURN, ISRAEL, JR. (1813–1883)
R-MA, House 1851–1861.

**9126.** Hunt, Gaillard I., comp. *Israel, Elihu and Cadwallader Washburn: A Chapter in American Biography.* New York: Macmillan, 1925.

## WASHBURNE, ELIHU BENJAMIN
(1816–1887) R-IL, House 1853–1869.

**9127.** Hunt, Gaillard I., comp. *Israel, Elihu and Cadwallader Washburn: A Chapter in American Biography.* New York: Macmillan, 1925.

**9128.** Nelson, Russell K. "The Early Life and Congressional Career of Elihu B. Washburne." Ph.D. dissertation, University of North Dakota, 1954.

**9129.** Willson, Beckles. "Washburne (1869–77)." In his *America's Ambassadors to France (1777–1927),* 296–312. New York: Frederick A. Stokes, 1928.

## WASHINGTON, GEORGE (1732–1799)
VA, Continental Congress 1774–1775.

**9130.** Adams, Randolph. *The Dignity of George Washington.* Ann Arbor: G. Wahr, 1932.

**9131.** Alden, John R. *George Washington: A Biography.* Baton Rouge: Louisiana State University Press, 1984.

**9132.** Anderson, Ray M. "George Washington and the Whiskey Insurrection." Master's thesis, American University, 1970.

**9133.** Andrews, William L. *New York as Washington Knew It after the Revolution.* New York: Scribner's 1905.

**9134.** Aulaire, Ingri M. *George Washington.* Garden City, NY: Doubleday, 1957.

**9135.** Bacheller, Irving A., and Herbert Kates. *Great Moments in the Life of Washington.* New York: Grossett and Dunlap, 1932.

**9136.** Baldridge, H. A. "Washington's Visits to Colonial Annapolis." *U.S. Naval Institute Proceedings* 54 (February 18, 1928): 90–104.

**9137.** Beck, James M. "The Political Philosophy of George Washington." *Constitutional Review* 13 (April 1929): 61–74.

**9138.** ———. "Washington's Supreme Achievement." *Constitutional Review* 3 (July 1919): 131–145.

**9139.** Bemis, Samuel F. "John Quincy Adams and George Washington." *Massachusetts Historical Society Proceedings* 67 (1941/1944): 365–384.

**9140.** ———. "Washington's Farewell Address: A Foreign Policy of Independence." *American Historical Review* 39 (January 1934): 250–268.

**9141.** Binney, Horace. *An Enquiry into the Formation of Washington's Farewell Address.* New York: Da Capo, 1969.

**9142.** Boller, Paul F. "Washington and Civilian Supremacy." *Southwestern Review* 39 (Winter 1954): 9–22.

**9143.** Borden, Morton, comp. *George Washington.* Englewood, NJ: Prentice-Hall, 1969.

**9144.** Bowen, Clarence W. "The Inauguration of Washington." *Century Magazine* 37 (April 1889): 803–833.

**9145.** Bowling, Kenneth R. "The Bank Bill, the Capitol City, and President Washington." *Capitol Studies* 1 (Spring 1972): 59–72.

**9146.** Brown, Everett S. "The Inauguration of George Washington." *Michigan Alumnus Quarterly Review* 45 (Spring 1939): 213–221.

**9147.** Callahan, North. *George Washington, Soldier and Man.* New York: Morrow, 1972.

**9148.** Cammerer, H. Paul. "The Sesquicentennial of the Laying of the Cornerstone of the United States Capitol by George Washington." *Columbia Historical Society Records* 44/45 (1944): 161–189.

**9149.** Campbell, Janet. "The First Americans' Tribute to the First President." *Chronicles of Oklahoma* 57 (Summer 1979): 190–195.

**9150.** Carroll, John A. "President Washington and the Challenge of Neutrality, 1793–1794." Ph.D. dissertation, Georgetown University, 1956.

**9151.** Carroll, John A., and Mary W. Ashworth. *George Washington: First in Peace, 1793–1799.* New York: Scribner's, 1957.

**9152.** Carson, Hampton L. "Washington in His Relation to the National Idea." *Magazine of History* 11 (May 1910): 261–272.

**9153.** Cavanagh, John W. *Our First Two Presidents, John Janson-George Washington.* New York: John W. Cavanagh, 1932.

**9154.** Chesterton, Gilbert K. "George Washington." *Fortnightly Review* 131 (March 1932): 303–310.

**9155.** Christensen, Lois E. "Washington's Experience and the Creation of the Presidency." Ph.D. dissertation, University of Nebraska, 1957.

**9156.** Clark, Philip. *Washington.* Hove, East Sussex, England: Wayland, 1981.

**9157.** Clarfield, Gerald H. "Protecting the Frontiers: Defense Policy and the Tariff Question in the First Washington Administration." *William and Mary Quarterly* 32 (July 1975): 443–464.

**9158.** Coe, Edward B. "Washington—The Man." *Magazine of History* 9 (February 1909): 92–103.

**9159.** Corbin, John. *The Unknown Washington: Biographic Origins of the Republic.* New York: Scribner's 1930.

**9160.** ———. "Washington and the American Union." *Scribner's Magazine* 86 (November 1929): 487–497.

**9161.** Coulcomb, Charles A. "George Washington in Recent Biographies." *Historical Outlook* 23 (February 1932): 70–80.

**9162.** Davis, Burke. *George Washington and the American Revolution.* New York: Random House, 1975.

**9163.** DeConde, Alexander. *Entangling Alliance: Politics and Diplomacy under George Washington.* Durham, NC: Duke University Press, 1958.

**9164.** ———. "Washington's Farewell, the French Alliance, and the Election of 1796." *Mississippi Valley Historical Review* 43 (March 1957): 641–658.

**9165.** Dutcher, George M. *George Washington and Connecticut in War and Peace.* New Haven, CT: Yale University Press, 1933.

**9166.** Edwards, George C. "George Washington's Leadership of Congress: Director or Facilitator." *Congress and the Presidency* 18 (Autumn 1991): 163–180.

**9167.** Ellis, Ivan C. "A Study of the Influence of Alexander Hamilton on George Washington." Ph.D. dissertation, University of Southern California, 1957.

**9168.** Emery, Noemie. *Washington: A Biography.* New York: Putnam's, 1976.

**9169.** Engelman, Rose C. "Washington and Hamilton: A Study in the Development of Washington's Political Ideas." Ph.D. dissertation, Cornell University, 1947.

**9170.** Farnell, Robert S. "Positive Valuations of Politics and Government in the Thought of Five American Founding Fathers: Thomas Jefferson, John Adams, James Madison, Alexander Hamilton, and George Washington." Ph.D. dissertation, Cornell University, 1970.

**9171.** Farrand, Max. "George Washington in the Federal Convention." *Yale Review* 16 (November 1907): 280–287.

**9172.** Farrell, Nancy. "George Washington: The Administrator." *Historical and Philosophical Society of Ohio Bulletin* 14 (January 1956): 21–36.

**9173.** Fay, Bernard. *George Washington, Republican Aristocrat.* Boston: Houghton Mifflin, 1931.

**9174.** Ferling, John E. *The First of Men: A Life of George Washington.* Knoxville: University of Tennessee Press, 1988.

**9175.** Fish, Carl R. "George Washington: The Man." *Illinois State Historical Society Transactions* 39 (1932): 21–40.

**9176.** Fishwick, Marshall W. "George Washington." In his *Gentlemen of Virginia,* 85–105. New York: Dodd, Mead, 1961.

**9177.** Fitzpatrick, John C. "Washington's Election as First President of the United States." *Daughters of the American Revolution Magazine* 58 (February 1924): 69–81.

**9178.** Flanagan, Vincent. *George Washington, First President of the United States.* Charlottesville, NY: SamHar Press, 1973.

**9179.** Fleming, Thomas J. *First in Their Hearts: A Biography of George Washington.* New York: Norton, 1968.

**9180.** Flexner, James T. *George Washington and the New Nation.* Boston: Little, Brown, 1970.

**9181.** ———. *George Washington: Anguish and Farewell.* Boston: Little, Brown, 1969.

**9182.** ———. *George Washington in the American Revolution.* Boston: Little, Brown, 1968.

**9183.** ———. *Washington.* New York: New American Library, 1974.

**9184.** ———. *Washington, the Indispensable Man.* Boston: Little, Brown, 1974.

**9185.** Flick, Alexander C. "Washington's Relations to New York State." *New York History* 13 (April 1932): 115–128.

**9186.** Ford, Henry J. *Washington and His Colleagues.* New Haven, CT: Yale University Press, 1921.

**9187.** Foster, Genevieve. *George Washington's World.* New York: Scribner's 1977.

**9188.** Freeman, Douglas S. *George Washington: A Biography.* 7 vols. New York: Scribner's, 1848–1857.

**9189.** ———. *Washington.* Edited by Richard Harwell. New York: Scribner's 1968.

**9190.** Fry, Joseph A. "Washington's Farewell Address and American Commerce." *West Virginia History* 37 (July 1976): 281–290.

**9191.** Grey, Zane. *George Washington, Frontiersman.* Lexington: University Press of Kentucky, 1994.

**9192.** Guedalla, Philip. "General Washington." In his *Fathers of the Revolution,* 189–212. New York: Putnam's Sons, 1926.

**9193.** Hancock, Harold B. "Loaves and Fishes: Applications for Office from Delawareans to George Washington." *Delaware History* 14 (October 1970): 135–158.

**9194.** Hart, Albert B. *Washington as President.* Washington, DC: George Washington Bicentennial Commission, 1931.

**9195.** ———. "Washington or Order." *Massachusetts Historical Society Proceedings* 60 (December 1926): 66–81.

**9196.** ———. *Washington, the Man of Mind.* Washington, DC: George Washington Bicentennial Commission, 1931.

**9197.** Hemphill, W. Edwin. "Virginia to George Washington, Debtor: His Income as a Delegate to the Federal Convention." *Virginia Cavalcade* 1 (Winter 1951): 42–43.

**9198.** Higginbotham, Don. *George Washington and the American Military Tradition.* Athens: University of Georgia Press, 1985.

**9199.** Holcombe, Arthur N. "The Role of Washington in the Framing of the Constitution." *Huntington Library Quarterly* 19 (August 1956): 317–334.

**9200.** Hubbard, Elbert. *George Washington.* New York: Putnam's, 1968.

**9201.** Hughes, Rupert. *George Washington.* 3 vols. New York: Morrow, 1926–1930.

**9202.** Hutchins, Frank, and Cortelle Hutchins. *Washington and the Lafayettes.* New York: Longmans, Green, 1939.

**9203.** Hutchinson, Paul. "Washington." *Tennessee Historical Magazine* 2 (January 1932): 147–152.

**9204.** Irving, Washington. *George Washington: A Biography.* Edited by Charles Neider. Garden City, NY: Doubleday, 1976.

**9205.** Jackson, Joseph. "Washington in Philadelphia." *Pennsylvania Magazine of History* 56 (1932): 110–155.

**9206.** Johnson, Albert W. "George Washington." *Western Pennsylvania Historical Magazine* 11 (October 1928): 203–216.

**9207.** Jones, Robert F. *George Washington.* Boston: Twayne, 1979.

**9208.** ———. "George Washington and the Politics of the Presidency." *Presidential Studies Quarterly* 10 (Winter 1980): 28–34.

**9209.** Kaufman, Burton I., ed. *Washington's Farewell Address: The View from the 20th Century.* Chicago: Quadrangle Books, 1969.

**9210.** Ketchum, Richard M. *The World of George Washington.* New York: American Heritage, 1974.

**9211.** Klein, Rose S. "Washington's Thanksgiving Proclamation." *American Jewish Archives* 20 (November 1968): 156–162.

**9212.** Knollenberg, Bernhard. *George Washington: The Virginia Period, 1732–1775.* Durham, NC: Duke University Press, 1964.

**9213.** Kohn, Richard H. "The Washington Administration's Decision to Crush the Whiskey Rebellion." *Journal of American History* 59 (December 1972): 567–584.

**9214.** Lamb, Martha J. "The Inauguration of Washington, 1789." *Magazine of American History* 20 (December 1888): 433–460.

**9215.** Lawrence, Henry W. "Washington, Capitalism, and Nationalism." *American Scholar* 1 (May 1932): 352–359.

**9216.** Lear, Tobias. "President Washington in New York, 1789." *Pennsylvania Magazine of History and Biography* 32 (October 1908): 498–500.

**9217.** Lewis, Thomas A. *For King and Country: The Maturing of George Washington, 1748–1760.* New York: HarperCollins, 1993.

**9218.** Libby, Orin G. "Political Factions in Washington's Administration." *Quarterly Journal of the University of North Dakota* 3 (July 1913): 293–318.

**9219.** Lieberman, Carl. "George Washington and the Development of American Federalism." *Social Science* 51 (Winter 1976): 3–10.

**9220.** Little, Shelby M. *George Washington.* New York: Minton, Balch, 1929.

**9221.** Lodge, Henry C. *The Life of George Washington.* 2 vols. Boston: Houghton Mifflin, 1920.

**9222.** Lombard, M. E. "The Inauguration of George Washington." *Legion D'Honneur Magazine* 9 (April 1939): 293–300.

**9223.** Longmore, Paul K. *The Invention of George Washington.* Berkeley: University of California Press, 1988.

**9224.** Markowitz, Arthur A. "Washington's Farewell and the Historians: A Critical Review." *Pennsylvania Magazine of History and Biography* 94 (April 1970): 173–191.

**9225.** Marling, Karal A. *George Washington Slept Here: Colonial Revivals and American Culture, 1876–1986.* Cambridge, MA: Harvard University Press, 1988.

**9226.** Matteson, David M. *Washington and the Constitution.* Washington, DC: George Washington Bicentennial Commission, 1931.

**9227.** Matthewson, Timothy M. "George Washington's Policy toward the Haitian Revolution." *Diplomatic History* 3 (Summer 1979): 321–336.

**9228.** Mayo, Bernard. *Myths and Men: Patrick Henry, George Washington, Thomas Jefferson.* Athens: University of Georgia Press, 1959.

**9229.** McCamant, Wallace S. "Washington as a Man." *Oregon Law Review* 12 (December 1932): 22–36.

**9230.** McClure, William E. "Washington and His Relation to the Constitution." *Sons of American Revolution Magazine* 27 (January 1933): 224–227.

**9231.** McDonald, Forrest. *President of George Washington.* Lawrence: University Press of Kansas, 1974.

**9232.** McMaster, John B. "Washington's Inauguration." *Harper's Monthly Magazine* 78 (April 1889): 671–686.

**9233.** Meadowcroft, Enid. *The Story of George Washington.* New York: Grossett and Dunlap, 1952.

**9234.** Morgan, Edmund S. *The Genius of George Washington.* New York: Norton, 1981.

**9235.** ———. "George Washington: The Aloof American." *Virginia Quarterly Review* 52 (Summer 1976): 410–436.

**9236.** ———. *The Meaning of Independence: John Adams, George Washington, Thomas Jefferson.* Charlottesville: University Press of Virginia, 1976.

**9237.** Morris, Richard B. "Washington and Hamilton: A Great Collaboration." *American Philosophical Society Proceedings* 102 (April 1958): 107–116.

**9238.** Myers, J. Jay. "George Washington: The Soul and the Sword." In his *The Revolutionists,* 159–175. New York: Washington Square Books, 1971.

**9239.** Nettels, Curtis P. *George Washington and American Independence.* Boston: Little, Brown, 1951.

**9240.** Nordham, George W. *The Age of Washington: George Washington's Presidency, 1789–1797.* Chicago: Adams Press, 1989.

**9241.** ———. *George Washington and Money.* Washington, DC: University Press of America, 1982.

**9242.** ———. *George Washington and the Law.* Chicago: Adams Press, 1982.

**9243.** Padover, Saul K. "The American as Archetype: George Washington." In his *The Genius of America: Men Whose Ideas Shaped Our Civilization,* 1–22. New York: McGraw-Hill, 1960.

**9244.** Page, Elwin L. *George Washington in New Hampshire.* Boston: Houghton Mifflin, 1932.

**9245.** Palmer, John M. *Washington, Lincoln, Wilson: Three War Statesmen.* Garden City, NY: Doubleday, 1930.

**9246.** Paltsits, Victor H., ed. *Washington's Farewell Address.* New York: New York Public Library, 1935.

**9247.** Partin, Robert. "The Changing Images of George Washington from Weems to Freeman." *Social Studies* 56 (February 1965): 52–59.

**9248.** Pennypacker, Isaac R. "Washington and Lincoln, the Father and the Saviour of the Country." *Pennsylvania Magazine of History* 56 (1932): 97–109.

**9249.** Pew, William A. "Washington—A Great Commander." *Essex Institute of Historical Collections* 68 (April 1932): 225–239.

**9250.** Phelps, Glenn A. "George Washington and the Building of the Constitution: Presidential Interpretation and Constitutional Development." *Congress and the Presidency* 12 (Autumn 1985): 95–110.

**9251.** Phillips, Charles. "The Naked Washington." *Catholic World* 124 (February 1927): 577–586.

**9252.** Randall, James G. "George Washington and Entangling Alliances." *South Atlantic Quarterly* 30 (July 1931): 221–229.

**9253.** Reuter, Frank T. *Trials and Triumphs: George Washington's Foreign Policy.* Forth Worth: Texas Christian University, 1983.

**9254.** Rivoire, Mario. *The Life and Times of Washington.* Philadelphia: Curtis, 1968.

**9255.** Sawyer, Joseph D. *Washington.* 2 vols. New York: Macmillan, 1927.

**9256.** Schafer, Joseph. "Washington and His Biographers." *Wisconsin Magazine of History* 11 (December 1927): 218–228.

**9257.** Schwartz, Barry. "George Washington and the Whip Conception of Heroic Leadership." *American Sociological Review* 48 (February 1983): 18–33.

**9258.** Scott, W. "George Washington: Some Great Public Services Commonly Overlooked." *Magazine of History* 20 (February 1915): 51–56.

**9259.** Scudder, Horace E. *George Washington, an Historical Biography.* Boston: Houghton Mifflin, 1924.

**9260.** Sears, Louis M. *George Washington and the French Revolution.* Detroit, MI: Wayne State University Press, 1960.

**9261.** Seasongood, Murray. "George Washington and Political Parties." *American Scholar* 1 (May 1932): 265–271.

**9262.** Smelser, Marshall. "George Washington and the Alien and Sedition Acts." *American Historical Review* 59 (January 1954): 322–334.

**9263.** ———. "George Washington Declines the Part of El Libertador." *William and Mary Quarterly* 11 (January 1954): 42–51.

**9264.** Smith, F. DuMont. *Washington and the Constitution.* Chicago: American Bar Association, 1931.

**9265.** Smith, James M., ed. *George Washington: A Profile.* New York: Hill and Wang, 1969.

**9266.** Smith, Richard N. *Patriarch: George Washington and the New American Nation.* Boston: Houghton Mifflin, 1993.

**9267.** Smucker, Isaac. "A Great Event of a Century Ago: Washington's Inauguration and Inaugural." *Magazine of Western History* 9 (March 1889): 522–526.

**9268.** Smylie, James H. "The President as Republican Prophet and King: Clerical Reflections on the Death of Washington." *Journal of Church and State* 18 (Spring 1976): 233–252.

**9269.** Smyth, Clifford. *George Washington, the Story of the First American.* New York: Funk and Wagnalls, 1931.

**9270.** Stearns, Clifford B. "National Defense Embodying Patriotic Education: George Washington and the Constitution." *Daughters of the American Revolution Magazine* 66 (September 1932): 577–581.

**9271.** Stephenson, Nathaniel W. "The Romantics and George Washington." *American Historical Review* 39 (January 1934): 274–283.

**9272.** Stephenson, Nathaniel W., and Waldo H. Dunn. *George Washington.* 2 vols. New York: Oxford University Press, 1940.

**9273.** Swiggett, Howard G. *The Great Man: George Washington as a Human Being.* Garden City, NY: Doubleday, 1953.

**9274.** Taylor, Edward M. *George Washington, the Ideal Patriot.* New York: Eaton, 1897.

**9275.** Thayer, William R. *George Washington.* Boston: Houghton Mifflin, 1922.

**9276.** Thorsmar, Thora. *George Washington.* Chicago: Scott, Foresman, 1931.

**9277.** Trent, William P. "George Washington." In his *Southern Statesmen of the Old Regime,* 3–48. New York: Thomas Y. Crowell, 1897.

**9278.** Trotter, Reginald G. "George Washington and the English-Speaking Heritage." *Queen's Quarterly* 29 (Autumn 1932): 297–306.

**9279.** Umbreit, Kenneth B. "George Washington." In his *Founding Fathers: Men*

*Who Shaped Our Tradition,* 235–332. Port Washington, NY: Kennikat, 1969.

**9280.** Van Dyke, Paul. *George Washington, the Son of His Country, 1732–1775.* New York: Scribner's, 1931.

**9281.** ———. "Washington." *American Philosophical Society Proceedings* 71 (1932): 191–205.

**9282.** Vaught, Edgar S. "The Father of His Country." *Oklahoma State Bar Journal* 3 (1933): 276–281.

**9283.** Wall, Charles C. *George Washington, Citizen-Soldier.* Charlottesville: University of Virginia Press, 1980.

**9284.** Washington, W. Lanier. "George Washington and a League of Nations." *Landmark* 2 (February 1920): 89–93.

**9285.** ———. "George Washington's Ideals: Revealed in an Unpublished Letter." *Forum* 61 (February 1919): 129–141.

**9286.** Weems, Mason L. *A History of the Life and Death, Virtues and Exploits of General George Washington.* Cleveland, OH: World Publishing, 1965.

**9287.** ———. *The Life of George Washington.* Cambridge: Belknap Press, 1962.

**9288.** ———. *The Life of Washington the Great.* New York: Garland, 1977.

**9289.** Wildman, Edwin. "George Washington: Father of His Country." In his *The Founders of America in the Days of the Revolution,* 67–91. Freeport, NY: Books for Libraries, 1968.

**9290.** Williamson, Mary L. *George Washington, Soldier and Statesman.* Chicago: Beckley-Cardy, 1951.

**9291.** Wills, Garry. *Cincinnatus: George Washington and the Enlightenment.* Garden City, NY: Doubleday, 1984.

**9292.** ———. "Washington's Citizen Virtue: Greenough and Houdon." *Critical Inquiry* 10 (March 1984): 420–441.

**9293.** ———. "Washington's Farewell Address: An Eighteenth-Century 'Fireside Chat.'" *Chicago History* 10 (Fall 1981): 176–179.

**9294.** Woodward, William E. *George Washington, the Image and the Man.* New York: Boni and Liveright, 1926.

**9295.** Wriston, Henry M. "Washington and the Foundations of American Foreign Policy." *Minnesota History* 8 (March 1927): 3–26.

## WASHINGTON, HAROLD (1922–1987)
**D-IL, House 1981–1983.**

**9296.** Clarel, Pierre, and Wim Wiewel, eds. *Harold Washington and the Neighborhoods: Progressive City Government in Chicago, 1983–1987.* New Brunswick, NJ: Rutgers University Press, 1991.

**9297.** Gove, Samuel K., and Michael B. Preston. "State and Local (Chicago) Relations in Illinois: The Harold Washington Era, 1984." *Publius* 15 (*Summer 1985*): *143–154.*

**9298.** Holli, Melvin G., and Paul M. Green, eds. *The Making of the Mayor, Chicago, 1983.* Grand Rapids, MI: Eerdmans Publishing, 1984.

**9299.** Kleppner, Paul. *Chicago Divided: The Making of a Black Mayor.* DeKalb: Northern Illinois University Press, 1984.

**9300.** Levinsohn, Florence H. *Harold Washington: A Political Biography.* Chicago: Chicago Review Press, 1983.

**9301.** Rivlin, Gary. *Five on the Prairie: Chicago's Harold Washington and the Politics of Race.* New York: Holt, 1992.

## WATKINS, ARTHUR VIVIAN
**(1886–1973) R-UT, Senate 1947–1959.**

**9302.** Watkins, Arthur V. *Enough Rope: The Inside Story of the Censure of Senator Joe McCarthy.* Englewood Cliffs, NJ: Prentice-Hall, 1969.

**WATSON, ALBERT WILLIAM (1922– )**
**R-SC, House 1963–1965, 1965–1971.**

**9303.** Hathorn, Billy B. "The Changing Politics of Race: Congressman Albert William Watson and the S.C. Republican Party, 1965–1970." *South Carolina Historical Magazine* 89 (October 1988): 227–241.

**WATSON, JAMES ELI (1864–1948) R-IN,**
**House 1895–1897, 1899–1909, Senate**
**1916–1933.**

**9304.** Kent, Frank R. "Senator James E. Watson: The Professional Public Servant." *Atlantic Monthly* 149 (February 1932): 183–190.

**9305.** Watson, James E. *As I Knew Them.* Indianapolis: Bobbs-Merrill, 1936.

**WATSON, THOMAS EDWARD**
**(1856–1922) D-GA, House 1891–1893,**
**Senate 1921–1922.**

**9306.** Carageorge, Ted. "An Evaluation of Hoke Smith and Thomas E. Watson as Georgia Reformers." Ph.D. dissertation, University of Georgia, 1963.

**9307.** Cashin, Edward J. "Thomas E. Watson and the Catholic Laymen's Association of Georgia." Ph.D. dissertation, Fordham University, 1962.

**9308.** Crowe, Charles. "Tom Watson, Populists and Blacks Reconsidered." *Journal of Negro History* 55 (April 1970): 99–116.

**9309.** Fingerhut, Eugene R. "Tom Watson, Blacks and Southern Reform." *Georgia Historical Quarterly* 60 (Winter 1976): 324–343.

**9310.** Franzoni, Janet B. "Troubled Tirader: A Psychobiographical Study of Tom Watson." *Georgia Historical Quarterly* 57 (Winter 1973): 493–510.

**9311.** Johnson, Gerald W. "Tom Watson: Who Could Dish It Out, but Couldn't Take It." In his *Lunatic Fringe,* 222–237. New York: Lippincott, 1957.

**9312.** Knight, Lucian L. "Thomas E. Watson." In *Library of Southern Literature,* edited by Edwin A. Alderman and Joel C. Harris, vol. 13, 5681–5687. New Orleans: Martin and Hoyt, 1910.

**9313.** Nelson, Richard. "The Cultural Contradictions of Populism: Tom Watson's Tragic Vision of Power, Politics, and History." *Georgia Historical Quarterly* 72 (Spring 1988): 1–29.

**9314.** Reed, Ralph. "Fighting the Devil with Fire: Carl Vinson's Victory over Tom Watson in the 1918 Tenth District Democratic Primary." *Georgia Historical Quarterly* 67 (Winter 1983): 451–479.

**9315.** Saunders, Robert M. "The Transformation of Tom Watson, 1894–1895." *Georgia Historical Quarterly* 54 (Fall 1970): 339–356.

**9316.** Woodward, Comer V. "The Political and Literary Career of Thomas E. Watson." Ph.D. dissertation, University of North Carolina, 1937.

**9317.** ———. *Tom Watson, Agrarian Rebel.* 2d ed. Savannah, GA: Beehive Press, 1973.

**9318.** ———. "Tom Watson and the Negro." *Journal of Southern History* 4 (February 1938): 14–33.

**WATTERSON, HENRY (1840–1921) D-KY,**
**House 1876–1877.**

**9319.** Bingham, Robert W. "Henry Watterson." In *Library of Southern Literature,* edited by Edwin A. Alderman and Joel C. Harris, vol. 13, 5707–5708. New Orleans: Martin and Hoyt, 1910.

**9320.** Logan, Lena C. "Henry Watterson, Border Nationalist, 1840–1877." Ph.D. dissertation, Indiana University, 1942.

**9321.** Marcosson, Isaac F. *Marse Henry, a Biography of Henry Watterson.* New York: Dodd, Mead, 1951.

**9322.** ———. "Watterson and the Early Days." In *Adventures in Interviewing,* 28–35. New York: John Lane Company, 1920.

**9323.** Pringle, Henry F. "Kentucky Bourbon: Marse Henry Watterson." In *Highlights in the History of the American Press.* Edited by Edwin H. Ford, 211–228. Minneapolis: University of Minnesota Press, 1954.

**9324.** Stewart, Kenneth N., and John W. Tebbel. "Two Southern Gentlemen." In their *Makers of Modern Journalism,* 159–167. Englewood Cliffs, NJ: Prentice-Hall, 1952.

**9325.** Villard, Oswald G. "Henry Watterson and His Courier-Journal." In his *Some Newspapers and Newspaper-Men,* 258–272. New York: Knopf, 1923.

**9326.** Wall, Joseph F. *Henry Watterson, Reconstructed Rebel.* New York: Oxford University Press, 1956.

**9327.** Watterson, Henry. *Marse Henry: An Autobiography.* 2 vols. New York: Doran, 1919.

## WAYNE, ANTHONY (1745–1796) GA, House 1791–1792.

**9328.** Bald, Frederick C. *A Portrait of Anthony Wayne Painted from Life by Jean Pierre Henri Elouis in 1796 and Now Reproduced from a Unique Print for the Schoolchildren of Detroit.* Ann Arbor: Clements Library, University of Michigan, 1948.

**9329.** Boyd, Thomas A. *Mad Anthony Wayne.* New York: Scribner's, 1929.

**9330.** Bradley, Daniel. *Journal of Capt. Daniel Bradley: An Epic of the Ohio Frontier, With Copious Comments by Frazer E. Wilson.* Greenville, OH: F. H. Jobes, 1935.

**9331.** Griswold, Bert J. "Mad Anthony Wayne, Savior of the West-Fallen Timber: The Building and Dedication of Fort Wayne." In his *The Pictorial History of Fort Wayne, Indiana,* 121–149. Chicago: Robert W. Law Company, 1917.

**9332.** Griswold, Rufus W. "Anthony Wayne." In his *Washington and the Generals of the American Revolution,* vol. 1, 105–132. Philadelphia: Carey and Hart, 1848.

**9333.** Headley, Joel T. "Major General Wayne." In his *Washington and His Generals,* vol. 1, 314–340. New York: Scribner's, 1847.

**9334.** McGrane, Reginald C. "Anthony Wayne and James Wilkinson: A Study in Frontier Characters." *Ohio Valley Historical Association Annual Report* 7 (1913): 30–39.

**9335.** Moore, Horatio N. *Life and Services of Gen. Anthony Wayne.* Philadelphia: J. B. Perry, 1845.

**9336.** Nelson, Paul D. *Anthony Wayne, Soldier of the Early Republic.* Bloomington: Indiana University Press, 1985.

**9337.** Pennypacker, Samuel W. *Anthony Wayne.* Philadelphia: Lippincott, 1908.

**9338.** Peterson, Charles J. "Anthony Wayne." In his *The Military Heroes of the Revolution,* 391–402. Philadelphia: J. B. Smith, 1856.

**9339.** Preston, John H. *A Gentleman Rebel: The Exploits of Anthony Wayne.* New York: Farrar and Rinehart, 1930.

**9340.** Sklarsky, I. W. *The Revolution's Boldest Venture: The Story of General "Mad Anthony" Wayne's Assault on Stony Point.* Port Washington, NJ: Kennikat, 1965.

**9341.** Spears, John R. *Anthony Wayne, Sometimes Called Mad Anthony.* New York: Appleton, 1903.

**9342.** Stille, Charles J. *Major-General Anthony Wayne and the Pennsylvania Line in the Continental Army.* Philadelphia: Lippincott, 1893.

**9343.** Victor, Orville J. *The Life, Times and Services of Anthony Wayne.* New York: Beadle and Company, 1861.

**9344.** Wildes, Harry E. *Anthony Wayne, Trouble Shooter of the American Revolution.* New York: Harcourt Brace, 1941.

**9345.** Wood, Charles S. *The Sword of Wayne: A Story of the Way He Smote the Indians and Brought Them to Sue for Peace.* Boston: W. H. Wilde Company, 1903.

**9346.** Wyatt, Thomas. "General Anthony Wayne." In his *Memoirs of the Generals,* 17–39. Philadelphia: Carey and Hart, 1848.

**WAYNE, JAMES MOORE** (1790–1867)
**J-GA, House 1829–1835.**

**9347.** Alexander, Lawrence A. *James Moore Wayne, Southern Unionist.* Chapel Hill: University of North Carolina Press, 1943.

**9348.** Battle, George G. "James Moore Wayne: Southern Unionist." *Fordham Urban Law Journal* 14 (March 1964): 42–59.

**9349.** Candler, Allen D., and Clement A. Evans. "James Moore Wayne." In his *Georgia: Comprising Sketches of Counties, Towns, Events, Institutions, and Persons Arranged in Cyclopedic Form,* vol. 3, 536–537. Atlanta, GA: Atlanta State Historical Association, 1906.

**9350.** Grice, Warren. "James M. Wayne." *Georgia Bar Association Proceedings* (1938): 179–200.

**9351.** Lawrence, Alexander A. *James Moore Wayne, Southern Unionist.* Chapel Hill: University of North Carolina Press, 1943.

**9352.** ———. "Justice Wayne and the *Dred Scott* Case." In *Report of Proceedings of the Fifty-Seventh Annual Session of the Georgia Bar Association,* edited by John B. Harris, 196–218. Macon, GA: W. Burke Company, 1940.

**WEAVER, ARCHIBALD JERARD**
(1843–1887) **R-NE, House 1883–1887.**

**9353.** Snoddy, Donald D. "The Congressional Career of Archibald Jerard Weaver, 1882–1887." *Nebraska History* 57 (Spring 1976): 83–98.

**WEAVER, JAMES BAIRD** (1833–1912)
**G-IA, House 1879–1881, 1885–1889.**

**9354.** Beals, Carleton. "Greenback Moses." In his *Great Revolt and Its Leaders,* 183–212. New York: Abelard-Schuman, 1968.

**9355.** Colbert, Thomas B. "Disgruntled Chronic Office Seeker or Man of Political Integrity: James Baird Weaver and the Republican Party in Iowa, 1857–1877." *Annals of Iowa* 49 (Winter/Spring 1988): 187–207.

**9356.** ———. "Political Fusion in Iowa: The Election of James B. Weaver to Congress in 1878." *Arizona and the West* 20 (Spring 1978): 25–40.

**9357.** Haynes, Frederick E. *James Baird Weaver.* Iowa City: State Historical Society of Iowa, 1916.

**WEBB, WILLIAM ROBERT** (1842–1926)
**D-TN, Senate 1913.**

**9358.** McMillin, Laurence. *The Schoolmaker: Sawney Webb and the Bell Buckle Story.* Chapel Hill: University of North Carolina Press, 1971.

**9359.** Parks, Edd W. "Sawney Webb: Tennessee's Schoolmaster." *North Carolina Historical Review* 12 (July 1935): 233–251.

**WEBSTER, DANIEL** (1782–1852)
**W-NH/MA, House 1813–1817 (NH), 1823–1827 (MA), Senate 1827–1841, 1845–1850 (MA).**

**9360.** Adams, Samuel H. *The Godlike Daniel.* New York: Sears Publishing Company, 1930.

**9361.** Alexander, Holmes M. "Daniel Webster." In his *The Famous Five,* 44–86. New York: Bookmailer, 1958.

**9362.** Bancroft, Frederic. "The Webster-Hayne Debate." In his *Calhoun and the South Carolina Nullification Movement,* 55–74. Baltimore: Johns Hopkins Press, 1928.

**9363.** Barber, James. *The Godlike Black Dan.* Washington, DC: Smithsonian Institution Press, 1982.

**9364.** Bartlett, Irving H. *Daniel Webster.* New York: Norton, 1978.

**9365.** ———. "Daniel Webster as a Symbolic Hero." *New England Quarterly* 45 (December 1972): 484–507.

**9366.** Baxter, Maurice G. *Daniel Webster and the Supreme Court.* Amherst: University of Massachusetts Press, 1966.

**9367.** ———. *One and Inseparable: Daniel Webster and the Union.* Cambridge, MA: Harvard University Press, 1984.

**9368.** Benson, Allan L. *Daniel Webster.* New York: Cosmopolitan Book Corporation, 1929.

**9369.** Birkner, Michael J. "Daniel Webster and the Crisis of Union, 1850." *Historical New Hampshire* 37 (Summer/Fall 1982): 150–173.

**9370.** Bolton, Sarah K. "Daniel Webster." In her *Famous American Statesmen,* 177–229. New York: Crowell, 1888.

**9371.** Bradford, Gamaliel. "Daniel Webster." In his *As God Made Them: Portraits of Some Nineteenth-Century Americans,* 1–42. Boston: Houghton Mifflin, 1929.

**9372.** Bradley, Howard A., and James A. Winans. *Daniel Webster and the Salem Murder.* Columbia, MO: Arteraft Press, 1956.

**9373.** Brauer, Kinley J. "The Webster-Lawrence Feud: A Study in Politics and Ambitions." *Historian* 29 (November 1966): 34–59.

**9374.** Brooks, Noah. "Daniel Webster." In his *Statesmen,* 39–68. New York: Scribner's, 1893.

**9375.** Brown, Norman D. *Daniel Webster and the Politics of Availability.* Athens: University of Georgia Press, 1969.

**9376.** ———. "Webster-Jackson Movement for Constitution and Union Party in 1833." *Mid-America* 46 (July 1964): 147–171.

**9377.** Carey, Robert L. *Daniel Webster as an Economist.* New York: Columbia University Press, 1929.

**9378.** Choate, Rufus. "Remarks before the Circuit Court on the Death of Mr. Webster." In his *Addresses and Orations,* 222–240. Boston: Little, Brown, 1879.

**9379.** Current, Richard N. *Daniel Webster and the Rise of National Conservatism.* Boston: Little, Brown, 1955.

**9380.** Curtis, George T. *The Last Years of Daniel Webster.* New York: Appleton, 1878.

**9381.** ———. *The Life of Daniel Webster.* 2 vols. New York: Appleton, 1870.

**9382.** Dalzell, Robert F. *Daniel Webster and the Trial of American Nationalism, 1843–1852.* Boston: Houghton Mifflin, 1973.

**9383.** ———. "The Rhetoric and Politics of Nationalism: Daniel Webster, 1843–1852." Ph.D. dissertation, Yale University, 1966.

**9384.** Devens, Richard M. "The Great Debate between Webster and Hayne, in Congress, 1830." In his *The National Memorial Volume,* 205–213. Chicago: Hugh Heron, 1880.

**9385.** Dubofsky, Melvyn. "Daniel Webster and the Whig Theory of Economic Growth: 1828–1848." *New England Quarterly* 42 (December 1969): 551–572.

**9386.** Duniway, Clyde A. "Daniel Webster." In *The American Secretaries of State and Their Diplomacy,* edited by Samuel F. Bemis, 1–64. New York: Knopf, 1928.

**9387.** Eichert, Magdalen. "Daniel Webster's Western Land Investments." *Historical New Hampshire* 26 (Fall 1971): 29–39.

**9388.** Elitzer, Michael R. "A Study of Greatness: Daniel Webster and the African Slave Cases." *Journal of Historical Studies* 4 (1980): 43–63.

**9389.** Elliott, Edward. "Daniel Webster: Growth through Rising National Sentiment." In *Biographical Story of the Constitution,* 167–187. New York: Putnam's, 1910.

**9390.** Erickson, Paul D. "Daniel Webster's Myth of the Pilgrims." *New England Quarterly* 57 (March 1984): 44–64.

**9391.** ———. "A Note on Daniel Webster's 'The Character of Washington: The Messiah of Federalism.'" *Historical New Hampshire* 37 (Summer/Fall 1982): 193–198.

**9392.** ———. *The Poetry of Events: Daniel Webster's Rhetoric of the Constitution and the Union.* New York: New York University Press, 1986.

**9393.** Esenwein, Joseph B., and Dale B. Carnegie. "Eulogy of Webster." In their *The Art of Public Speaking,* 464–469. Springfield, MA: Home Correspondence School, 1915.

**9394.** Etulain, Richard W. "Peter Harvey: Confidant and Interpreter of Daniel Webster." *Vermont History* 39 (Winter 1971): 21–30.

**9395.** Evarts, William M. "Mr. Webster's Position." In *Arguments and Speeches,* vol. 2, 401–410, 435–441, vol. 3, 275–283. New York: Macmillan, 1919.

**9396.** Fields, Wayne. "The Reply to Hayne: Daniel Webster and the Rhetoric of Stewardship." *Political Theory* 11 (February 1983): 5–28.

**9397.** Fisher, Sydney G. *The True Daniel Webster.* Philadelphia: Lippincott, 1911.

**9398.** Fiske, John. "Daniel Webster and the Sentiment of Union." In his *Essays, Historical and Literary,* vol. 1, 363–409. New York: Macmillan, 1902.

**9399.** Fuess, Claude M. *Daniel Webster.* 2 vols. Boston: Little, Brown, 1930.

**9400.** Grattan, Thomas C. "Daniel Webster." In his *Civilized America,* vol. 1, 229–255. London: Bradbury and Evans, 1859.

**9401.** Hale, Edward E. "Daniel Webster." In his *Memories of a Hundred Years,* vol. 2, 26–42. New York: Macmillan, 1902.

**9402.** Hubbard, Elbert. "Daniel Webster." In his *Little Journeys to the Homes of the Great,* vol. 3, 183–206. New York: W. H. Wise and Company, 1916.

**9403.** Jones, Howard. "The Attempt to Impeach Daniel Webster." *Capitol Studies* 3 (Fall 1975): 31–44.

**9404.** Kennedy, John F. "'Not as a Massachusetts Man but as an American. . .': Daniel Webster." In his *Profiles in Courage,* 55–80. New York: Harper and Row, 1955.

**9405.** King, James C. "Daniel Webster and Westward Expansion." Ph.D. dissertation, University of Utah, 1952.

**9406.** Kneeland, John, and Henry N. Wheeler, eds. "Daniel Webster." In their *Masterpieces of American Literature,* 313–316. Boston: Houghton Mifflin, 1891.

**9407.** Lanman, Charles. *The Private Life of Daniel Webster.* New York: Harper, 1852.

**9408.** Leduc, Thomas. "The Webster-Ashburton Treaty and the Minnesota Iron Ranges." *Journal of American History* 51 (December 1964): 476–481.

**9409.** Lewis, Walker, ed. *Speak for Yourself, Daniel: A Life of Webster in His Own Words.* Boston: Houghton Mifflin, 1969.

**9410.** Lodge, Henry C. *Daniel Webster.* Boston: Houghton Mifflin, 1899.

**9411.** ———. "Webster." In *The Cambridge History of American Literature,* edited by William P. Trent, John Erskine, Stuart P. Sherman and Carl C. Van Doren, vol. 2, 92–103. New York: Putnam's, 1918.

**9412.** Lyman, Samuel P. *The Public and Private Life of Daniel Webster, Including Most of His Great Speeches, Letters from Marshfield.* Philadelphia: Keystone, 1890.

**9413.** Magoon, Elias L. "Daniel Webster." In his *Living Orators in American,* 1–116. New York: Baker and Scribner, 1849.

**9414.** March, Charles W. *Daniel Webster and His Contemporaries.* New York: Mason, Baker and Pratt, 1873.

**9415.** McClure, Alexander K., and Byron Andrews. "Oration on Daniel Webster, Delivered at the Unveiling of His Statue in Washington, January 18, 1900." In their *Famous American Statesmen and Orators,* vol. 5, 356–380. New York: F. F. Lovell Publishing Company, 1902.

**9416.** McMaster, John B. *Daniel Webster.* New York: Century, 1902.

**9417.** Mondale, Clarence. "Daniel Webster and Technology." *American Quarterly* 14 (Spring 1962): 37–47.

**9418.** Morrow, Honore W. *Black Daniel, The Love Story of a Great Man.* New York: Morrow, 1931.

**9419.** Nathans, Sydney. *Daniel Webster and Jacksonian Democracy.* Baltimore: Johns Hopkins University Press, 1973.

**9420.** ———. "Daniel Webster, Massachusetts Man." *New England Quarterly* 39 (June 1966): 161–181.

**9421.** Ogg, Frederic A. *Daniel Webster.* Philadelphia: Jacobs, 1914.

**9422.** ———. "The Webster-Hayne Debate." In his *The Reign of Andrew Jackson,* 137–157. New Haven, CT: Yale University Press, 1919.

**9423.** Parish, Peter J. "Daniel Webster, New England, and the West." *Journal of American History* 54 (December 1967): 524–549.

**9424.** Parker, Theodore. "Daniel Webster." In his *Works of Theodore Parker,* vol. 7, 266–383. Boston: American Unitarian Association, 1908.

**9425.** Parrington, Vernon L. "Daniel Webster, Realist and Constitutionalist." In his *Main Currents in American Thought,* vol. 2, 304–316. New York: Harcourt, Brace, 1927.

**9426.** Parton, James. "Daniel Webster." In his *Famous Americans of Recent Times,* 53–112. Boston: Houghton Mifflin, 1895.

**9427.** Patterson, Lane. "The Battle of the Giants: Webster and Hayne: Orators at Odds." *American History Illustrated* 17 (February 1983): 18–22.

**9428.** Peterson, Merrill D. *The Great Triumvirate: Webster, Clay and Calhoun.* New York: Oxford University Press, 1987.

**9429.** Phelps, William L. "Political Ideals: Daniel Webster and Abraham Lincoln." In his *Some Makers of American Literature,* 65–84. Boston: Marshal Jones Company, 1923.

**9430.** Prince, Carl E., and Seth Taylor. "Daniel Webster, the Boston Associates, and the U.S. Government's Role in the Industrializing Process, 1815–1830." *Journal of the Early Republic* 2 (Fall 1982): 283–299.

**9431.** Quincy, Josiah. "Daniel Webster at Home." In his *Figures of the Past from the Leaves of Old Journals,* 117–124. Boston: Little, Brown, 1926.

**9432.** Scherer, James A. "Daniel Webster on the Power of Cotton (Extension Quotations)." In his *Cotton as a World Power,* 217–222, 408–413. New York: Frederick A. Stokes Company, 1916.

**9433.** Seitz, Don C. "Daniel Webster." In *The "Also Rans": Great Men Who Missed Making the Presidential Goal,* 110–124. New York: Thomas Y. Crowell, 1928.

**9434.** Shewmaker, Kenneth E. "Daniel Webster and the Politics of Foreign Policy, 1850–1852." *Journal of American History* 63 (September 1976): 303–315.

**9435.** ———. "Untaught Diplomacy: Daniel Webster and the Lobos Islands Controversy." *Diplomatic History* 1 (Fall 1977): 321–340.

**9436.** ———. "The War of Words: The Cass-Webster Debate of 1842–43." *Diplomatic History* 5 (Spring 1981): 151–163.

**9437.** Smith, Craig R. "Daniel Webster's July 17th Address: A Mediating Influence in the 1850 Compromise." *Quarterly Journal of Speech* 71 (August 1985): 349–361.

**9438.** Smith, Craig R. *Defender of the Union: The Oratory of Daniel Webster.* New York: Greenwood, 1989.

**9439.** Smith, Thomas J. "Daniel Webster, A Study in Nationalism." Ph.D. dissertation, Fordham University, 1933.

**9440.** Smyth, Clifford. *Daniel Webster: Spokesman for the Union.* New York: Funk and Wagnalls, 1931.

**9441.** Sparks, Edwin E. "Daniel Webster, The Defender of the Constitution." In his *The Men Who Made the Nation,* 318–346. New York: Macmillan, 1901.

**9442.** Steinberg, Alfred. *Daniel Webster.* New York: Putnam's, 1959.

**9443.** Teague, William J. "An Appeal to Reason: Daniel Webster, Henry Clay, and Whig Presidential Politics, 1836–1848." Ph.D. dissertation, North Texas State University, 1977.

**9444.** Tefft, Benjamin F. *Life of Daniel Webster.* Philadelphia: Porter and Coates, 1854.

**9445.** Van Tyne, Claude H., ed. *The Letters of Daniel Webster.* New York: McClure, Phillips, 1902.

**9446.** Webster, Daniel. *The Great Speeches and Orations of Daniel Webster.* Boston: Little, Brown, 1897.

**9447.** ———. *The Works of Daniel Webster.* 6 vols. Boston: Little, Brown, 1851.

**9448.** Wheeler, Everett P. *Daniel Webster, The Expounder of the Constitution.* New York: Putnam's, 1905.

**9449.** Whipple, Edwin P. "Daniel Webster." In his *Essays and Reviews,* vol. 1, 172–207. Boston: Houghton Mifflin, 1883.

**9450.** ———. "Daniel Webster as a Master of English Style." In his *American Literature and Other Papers,* 139–233. Boston: Ticknor and Company, 1887.

**9451.** Wilkinson, William C. *Daniel Webster: A Vindication, with Other Historical Essays.* New York: Funk and Wagnalls, 1911.

**9452.** Wilson, Major L. "Of Time and the Union: Webster and His Critics in the Crisis of 1850." *Civil War History* 14 (December 1968): 293–306.

**9453.** Wiltse, Charles M. "Daniel Webster and the British Experience." *Massachusetts Historical Society Proceedings* 85 (1973): 58–77.

**9454.** ———. *The Papers of Daniel Webster.* Hanover, NH: University Press of New England, 1974.

## WEEKS, JOHN WINGATE (1860–1926) R-MA, House 1905–1913, Senate 1913–1919.

**9455.** Spence, Benjamin A. "The National Career of John Wingate Weeks (1904–1925)." Ph.D. dissertation, University of Wisconsin, 1971.

**9456.** Washburn, Charles G. *The Life of John W. Weeks.* New York: Houghton Mifflin, 1928.

## WEFALD, KNUD (1869–1936) FL-MN, House 1923–1927.

**9457.** Wefald, Jon M. "Congressman Knud Wefald: A Minnesota Voice for Farm Parity." *Minnesota History* 38 (December 1962): 177–185.

## WELLER, JOHN B. (1812–1875) D-OH/CA, House 1839–1845 (CA), Senate 1852–1857 (OH).

**9458.** Melendy, Howard B., and Benjamin F. Gilbert. "John B. Weller." In their *Governors of California: Peter H. Burnett to Edmund G. Brown,* 80–90. Georgetown, CA: Talisman Press, 1965.

## WELTNER, CHARLES LONGSTREET (1927–1992) D-GA, House 1963–1967.

**9459.** Dimon, Joseph H. "Charles L. Weltner and Civil Rights." *Atlanta History* 24 (Fall 1980): 7–20.

**9460.** Weltner, Charles L. *Southerner.* New York: Lippincott, 1966.

**WENTWORTH, JOHN (1815–1888) R-IL, House 1843–1851, 1853–1855, 1865–1867.**

**9461.** Fehrenbacher, Don E. *Chicago Giant: A Biography of Long John Wentworth.* Madison, WI: American History Research Center, 1957.

**9462.** Wentworth, John. *Congressional Reminiscences.* Chicago: Fergus Printing Company, 1882.

**WHALEN, CHARLES WILLIAM, JR. (1920– ) R-OH, House 1967–1979.**

**9463.** Lynch, Patricia L. "An Analysis of the Rhetorical Dialogue of Charles W. Whalen, Jr., in Ohio's Third Congressional District." Ph.D. dissertation, Ohio State University, 1976.

**WHEELER, BURTON KENDALL (1882–1975) D-MT, Senate 1923–1947.**

**9464.** Anderson, John T. "Senator Burton K. Wheeler and United States Foreign Relations." Ph.D. dissertation, University of Virginia, 1982.

**9465.** Burke, Robert E. "A Friendship in Adversity: Burton K. Wheeler and Hiram W. Johnson." *Montana* 36 (Winter 1986): 12–25.

**9466.** Coleman, Elizabeth W. *Mrs. Wheeler Goes to Washington: Mrs. Burton Kendall Wheeler, Wife of the Senator from Montana.* Helena, MT: Falcon Press Publishers, 1989.

**9467.** Plotkin, David G. *The Plot Against America: Senator Wheeler and the Forces Behind Him.* Missoula, MT: Kennedy, 1946.

**9468.** Ruetten, Richard T. "Burton K. Wheeler and the Montana Connection." *Montana Magazine of Western History* 27 (Summer 1977): 3–19.

**9469.** ———. "Burton K. Wheeler of Montana: A Progressive between the Wars." Ph.D. dissertation, University of Oregon, 1961.

**9470.** ———. "Senator Burton K. Wheeler and the Insurgency in the 1920's." *University of Wyoming Publications* 32 (1966): 111–131, 164–172.

**9471.** Spritzer, Donald E. "B. K. Wheeler and Jim Murray: Senators in Conflict." *Montana Magazine of Western History* 23 (April 1973): 16–33.

**9472.** Wheeler, Burton K., and Paul F. Healy. *Yankee from the West: The Candid, Turbulent Life Story of the Yankee-Born U.S. Senator from Montana.* Garden City, NY: Doubleday, 1962.

**WHEELER, JOSEPH (1836–1906) D-AL, House 1881–1882, 1883, 1885–1900.**

**9473.** Dyer, John P. *From Shiloh to San Juan: The Life of Fightin' Joe Wheeler.* Rev. ed. Baton Rouge: Louisiana State University Press, 1961.

**WHEELER, WILLIAM ALMON (1819–1887) R-NY, House 1861–1863, 1869–1877.**

**9474.** Barzman, Sol. "William Almon Wheeler." In his *Madmen and Geniuses: The Vice-Presidents of the United States,* 129–134. Chicago: Follett, 1974.

**9475.** Otten, James T. "Grand Old Partyman: William A. Wheeler and the Republican Party, 1850–1880." Ph.D. dissertation, University of South Carolina, 1976.

**WHERRY, KENNETH SPICER (1892–1951) R-NE, Senate 1943–1951.**

**9476.** Dahlstrom, Karl A. "Kenneth S. Wherry." Ph.D. dissertation, University of Nebraska, 1965.

**9477.** Paul, Justis F. "Butler, Griswold, Wherry: The Struggle for Dominance of Nebraska Rebublicanism, 1941–1946." *North Dakota Quarterly* 43 (Autumn 1975): 51–61.

**9478.** Stromer, Marvin E. *The Making of a Political Leader: Kenneth S. Wherry and the United States Senate.* Lincoln: University of Nebraska Press, 1969.

**WHIPPLE, WILLIAM (1730–1785) NH, Continental Congress 1775, 1776, 1778.**

**9479.** Sanderson, John. "William Whipple." In *Sanderson's Biography of the Signers of the Declaration of Independence,* edited by Robert T. Conrad, 178–186. Philadelphia: Thomas, Cowperthwait, 1848.

**WHITE, EDWARD DOUGLASS (1845–1921) D-LA, Senate 1891–1894.**

**9480.** Carolyn, Marie. "The Legal Philosophy of Edward Douglass White." *University of Detroit Law Journal* 35 (December 1957): 174–199.

**9481.** Carter, Newman. "Edward D. White in Personal Retrospect." *Supreme Court Historical Society Yearbook* 1979 (1979): 5–7.

**9482.** Cassidy, Lewis C. *The Catholic Ancestry of Chief Justice White.* Philadelphia: Patterson and White, 1927.

**9483.** ———. "An Evaluation of Chief Justice White." *Mississippi Law Journal* 10 (February 1958): 136–153.

**9484.** ———. "The Life of Edward Douglass White: Soldier, Statesmen, Jurist, 1845–1921." Ph.D. dissertation, Georgetown University, 1923.

**9485.** Dart, Henry P. "Chief Justice White." *Louisiana Historical Quarterly* 5 (April 1922): 141–151.

**9486.** ———. "Edward Douglass White." *Loyola Law Journal* 3 (November 1921): 1–13.

**9487.** Davis, John W. "Edward Douglass White." *American Bar Association Journal* 7 (August 1921): 377–382.

**9488.** Dishman, Robert B. "Mr. Justice White and the Rule of Reason." *Review of Politics* 13 (April 1951): 229–243.

**9489.** Fegan, Hugh E. "Edward Douglass White, Jurist and Statesman." *Georgetown Law Journal* 14 (November 1925): 1–21, 15 (January 1926): 148–168.

**9490.** Forman, William H. "Chief Justice Edward Douglass White." *American Bar Association Journal* 56 (May 1970): 260–262.

**9491.** Frankfurter, Felix. *The Commerce Clause under Marshall, Taney and White.* Chapel Hill: University of North Carolina Press, 1937.

**9492.** Gannon, Frank S. "Edward D. White, Chief Justice, 1845–1921." *American Irish Historical Society Journal* 20 (June 1921): 235–257.

**9493.** Hagemann, Gerard. *The Man on the Bench: A Story of Chief Justice Edward Douglass White.* Notre Dame, IN: Dujarie Press, 1962.

**9494.** Hartman, Harold F. "Constitutional Doctrines of Edward D. White." Ph.D. dissertation, Cornell University, 1936.

**9495.** Highsaw, Robert B. *Edward Douglass White: Defender of the Conservative Faith.* Baton Rouge: Louisiana State University Press, 1981.

**9496.** Jesse, Richard H. "Chief Justice White." *American Law Review* 45 (May/June 1911): 321–326.

**9497.** Joyce, Walter E. "Edward Douglass White: The Louisiana Years, Early Life and on the Bench." *Tulane Law Review* 41 (June 1967): 752–768.

**9498.** Klinkhamer, Marie C. "Chief Justice White and Administrative Law." *Fordham Law Review* 14 (November 1944): 194–231.

**9499.** ———. *Edward Douglass White, Chief Justice of the United States.* Washington, DC: Catholic University of America Press, 1943.

**9500.** ———. "Legal Philosophy of Edward Douglass White." *University of Detroit Law Journal* 35 (December 1957): 174–199.

**9501.** Mann, S. H. "Chief Justice White." *American Law Review* 60 (July/August 1926): 620–637.

**9502.** Morris, Jeffrey B. "Chief Justice Edward Douglass White and President Taft's Court." *Supreme Court Historical Society Yearbook* 1982 (1982): 27–45.

**9503.** Myers, Gustavus. "The Supreme Court Under Chief Justice White." In his *History of the Supreme Court of the United States, 695–786.* Chicago: C. H. Kerr and Company, 1918.

**9504.** Ramke, Diedrich. "Edward Douglass White, Statesman and Jurist." Ph.D. dissertation, Louisiana State University, 1940.

**9505.** Ransdell, Joseph E. "Reminiscences of Edward Douglass White." *Loyola Law Journal* 7 (April 1926): 69–73.

**9506.** Spring, Samuel. "Two Chief Justices: Edward Douglass White and William Howard Taft." *Review of Reviews* 64 (August 1921): 161–170.

**9507.** Umbreit, Kenneth B. "Edward Douglass White." In his *Our Eleven Chief Justices*, 359–392. New York: Harper and Brothers, 1938.

**9508.** Williams, Samuel C. "A Remarkable Bench: Campbell, Jackson and White." *Tennessee Law Review* 16 (June 1941): 907–914.

**WHITE, GEORGE** (1872–1953) D-OH, House 1911–1915, 1917–1919.

**9509.** Jones, Robert L. "George White, 1931–1935." In *Governors of Ohio*, 174–178. Columbus: Ohio Historical Society, 1954.

**9510.** Queenan, Thomas J. "The Public Career of George White, 1905–1941." Ph.D. dissertation, Kent State University, 1976.

**WHITE, GEORGE HENRY** (1852–1918) R-NC, House 1897–1901.

**9511.** Christopher, Maurine. "George H. White/North Carolina." In her *Black*

*Americans in Congress,* 160–167. Rev. ed. New York: Thomas Y. Crowell, 1976.

**9512.** Katz, William. "George H. White: A Militant Negro Congressman in the Age of Booker T. Washington." *Negro History Bulletin* 29 (March 1966): 125–126.

**9513.** Reid, George W. "A Biography of George H. White, 1852–1918." Ph.D. dissertation, Johns Hopkins University, 1974.

**9514.** ———. "Congressman George Henry White, His Major Power Base." *Negro History Bulletin* 39 (March 1976): 554–555.

**9515.** ———. "Four in Black: North Carolina's Black Congressmen, 1874–1901." *Journal of Negro History* 64 (Summer 1979): 229–243.

**9516.** ———. "The Post-Congressional Career of George H. White, 1901–1918." *Journal of Negro History* 61 (October 1976): 362–373.

**9517.** Simmons, William J. "George H. White." In his *Men of Mark*, 362–363. Chicago: Johnson, 1970.

**WHITE, HARRY** (1834–1920) R-PA, House 1877–1881.

**9518.** Shankman, Arnold. "John P. Penny, Harry White and the 1864 Pennsylvania Senate Deadlock." *Western Pennsylvania Historical Magazine* 55 (January 1972): 77–86.

**WHITE, HUGH LAWSON** (1773–1840) J-TN, Senate 1825–1840.

**9519.** Atkins, Jonathan M. "The Presidential Candidacy of Hugh Lawson White in Tennessee, 1832–1836." *Journal of Southern History* 58 (February 1992): 27–56.

**9520.** Gresham, L. Paul. "Hugh Lawson White as a Tennessee Politician and Banker, 1807–1827." *East Tennessee Historical Society's Publications* 18 (1946): 25–46.

**9521.** ———. "The Public Career of Hugh Lawson White." Ph.D. dissertation, Vanderbilt University, 1945.

**9522.** ———. "The Public Career of Hugh Lawson White." *Tennessee Historical Quarterly* 3 (December 1944): 291–318.

**9523.** Heiskell, Samuel G. "Hugh Lawson White." In his *Andrew Jackson and Early Tennessee History*, vol. 1, 641–664, vol. 2, 1–63. Nashville, TN: Ambrose Printing Company, 1920.

**9524.** Maybrey, Aileen S. "Hugh Lawson White: A Tennessean in State and National Politics from 1817–1840." Master's thesis, Tennessee A & I University, 1955.

**9525.** McCormac, Eugene I. "Judge White and the Presidency." In his *James K. Polk, A Political Biography*, 62–91. Berkeley: University of California Press, 1922.

**9526.** Rogers, Daniel T. "Biography of Hugh Lawson White." Master's thesis, George Peabody College, 1924.

**9527.** Scott, Nancy N., ed. *A Memoir of Hugh Lawson White*. Philadelphia: Lippincott, 1856.

**WHITE, JOHN** (1802–1845) W-KY, House 1835–1845.

**9528.** Levin, H., ed. *The Lawyers and Lawmakers of Kentucky*. Chicago: Lewis Publishing, 1897.

**WHITE, SAMUEL** (1770–1809) F-DE, Senate 1801–1809.

**9529.** Conrad, Henry C. *Samuel White and His Father Judge Thomas White*. Wilmington: Historical Society of Delaware, 1903.

**WHITE, STEPHEN MALLORY** (1853–1901) D-CA, Senate 1893–1899.

**9530.** Dillon, Richard. "Stephen M. White." In his *Humbugs and Heroes*, 346–351. Garden City, NY: Doubleday, 1970.

**9531.** Dobie, Edith. *The Political Career of Stephen Mallory White: A Study of Party Politics under the Convention System*. Stanford, CA: Stanford University Press, 1927.

**9532.** Grassman, Curtis E. "Prologue to Progressivism: Senator Stephen M. White and the California Reform Impulse, 1875–1905." Ph.D. dissertation, University of California, 1970.

**9533.** Hunt, Rockwell D. "Stephen Mallory White: Father of Los Angeles Harbor." In his *California's Stately Hall of Fame*, 345–350. Stockton, CA: College of the Pacific, 1950.

**WHITEAKER, JOHN** (1820–1902) D-OR, House 1879–1881.

**9534.** Turnbull, George S. "John Whiteaker. In his *Governors of Oregon*, 28–30. Portland, OR: Binfords, 1959.

**WHITEHILL, ROBERT** (1738–1813) R-PA, House 1805–1813.

**9535.** Crist, Robert G. *Robert Whitehill and the Struggle for Civil Rights: A Paper Presented before the Hamilton Library and Historical Association of Cumberland County, Carlisle, Pa., on March 20, 1958*. Lemoyne, PA: Lemoyne Trust Company, 1958.

**WHITEHURST, GEORGE WILLIAM** (1925– ) R-VA, House 1969–1987.

**9536.** Whitehurst, George W. *Diary of a Congressman*. Norfolk, VA: Donning Company, 1983.

**WHITTLESEY, ELISHA** (1783–1863) W-OH, House 1823–1838.

**9537.** Davison, Kenneth E. "Forgotten Ohioan: Elisha Whittlesey." Ph.D. dissertation, Western Reserve University, 1953.

**WICKERSHAM, JAMES** (1857–1939) R-AK, House 1909–1917, 1919, 1921, 1931–1933.

**9538.** Atwood, Evangeline. *Frontier Politics: Alaska's James Wickersham*. Portland, OR: Binford and Mort, 1979.

**WIGFALL, LOUIS TRESVANT**
**(1816–1874) D-TX, Senate 1859–1861.**

**9539.** Hassler, William. "Wildman Wigfall: 'From Whom We Hoped So Much. . . .'" *Civil War Times Illustrated* 23 (April 1984): 24–26, 35–37.

**9540.** King, Alvy L. *Louis T. Wigfall, Southern Fire-Eater.* Baton Rouge: Louisiana State University Press, 1970.

**9541.** Ledbetter, Billy D. "The Election of Louis T. Wigfall to the United States Senate, 1859: A Reevaluation." *Southwestern Historical Quarterly* 77 (October 1973): 241–254.

**9542.** Lord, Clyde. "The Ante Bellum Career of Louis Tresvant Wigfall." Master's thesis, University of Texas, 1925.

**9543.** Seehorn, Beverly J. "Louis Tresvant Wigfall: A Confederate Senator." Master's thesis, Southern Methodist University, 1930.

**9544.** Wirsdorfer, George C. "Louis Wigfall." In *Ten Texans in Gray.* Edited by William C. Nunn, 175–194. Hillsboro, TX: Hill Junior College Press, 1968.

**WIGGLESWORTH, RICHARD**
**BOWDITCH (1891–1960) R-MA, House**
**1928–1958.**

**9545.** Weeks, Sinclair. *Richard Bowditch Wigglesworth: Way-Stations of a Fruitful Life.* N.p.: The author, 1964.

**WILDE, RICHARD HENRY (1789–1847)**
**R-GA, House 1815–1817, 1825, 1827–1835.**

**9546.** Chamberlayne, Lewis P. "Richard Henry Wilde." In *Library of Southern Literature,* edited by Edwin A. Alderman and Joel C. Harris, vol. 13, 5789–5794. New Orleans: Martin and Hoyt, 1910.

**9547.** Hubbell, Jay B. "Richard Henry Wilde." In his *South in American Literature, 1607–1900,* 304–313. Durham, NC: Duke University Press, 1954.

**9548.** Tucker, Edward L. *Richard Henry Wilde: His Life and Selected Poems.* Athens: University of Georgia Press, 1966.

**9549.** ———, comp. "Richard Henry Wilde (1789–1847)." In *Bibliographical Guide to the Study of Southern Literature.* Edited by Louis D. Rubin, Jr., 322–324. Baton Rouge: Louisiana State University Press, 1969.

**WILEY, ALEXANDER (1884–1967) R-WI,**
**Senate 1939–1963.**

**9550.** Wiley, Alexander. *Laughing with Congress.* New York: Crown, 1947.

**WILKINS, WILLIAM (1779–1865) D-PA,**
**Senate 1831–1834, House 1843–1844.**

**9551.** Slick, Sewell E. "The Life of William Wilkins." Ph.D. dissertation, University of Pittsburgh, 1931.

**9552.** Slick, Sewell E. "William Wilkins, Pittsburgher Extraordinary." *Western Pennsylvania Historical Magazine* 22 (December 1939): 217–236.

**WILLEY, WAITMAN THOMAS**
**(1811–1900) R-VA/WV Senate 1861–1863,**
**1863–1871.**

**9553.** Ambler, Charles H. *Waitman Thomas Willey: Orator, Churchman, Humanitarian.* Huntington, WV: Standard Print and Publishing Company, 1954.

**9554.** Bayless, R. W. "Peter Van Winkle and Waitman T. Willey in the Impeachment Trial of Andrew Johnson." *West Virginia History* 13 (January 1952): 75–89.

**WILLIAMS, ALPHEUS STARKEY**
**(1810–1878) D-MI, House 1875–1878.**

**9555.** Charnley, Jeffrey G. "Neglected Honor: The Life of General A. S. Williams of Michigan, 1810–1878." Ph.D. dissertation, Michigan State University, 1983.

**9556.** Williams, Alpheus S. *From the Cannon's Mouth: The Civil War Letters of General*

*Alpheus S. Williams.* Edited by Milo M. Quaife. Detroit, MI: Wayne State University Press, 1959.

**WILLIAMS, DAVID ROGERSON** (1776–1830) R-SC, House 1805–1809, 1811–1813.

**9557.** Cook, Harvey T. *The Life and Legacy of David Rogerson Williams.* New York: N.p., 1916.

**WILLIAMS, GEORGE HENRY** (1823–1910) R-OR, Senate 1865–1871.

**9558.** Teiser, Sidney. "Life of George H. Williams: Almost Chief-Justice." *Oregon Historical Quarterly* 47 (September 1946): 255–280, 47 (December 1946): 417–420.

**WILLIAMS, JOHN BELL** (1918–1983) D-MS, House 1947–1968.

**9559.** Vance, Sandra S. "The Congressional Career of John Bell Williams, 1947–1967." Ph.D. dissertation, Mississippi State University, 1976.

**WILLIAMS, JOHN JAMES** (1904–1988) R-DE, Senate 1947–1970.

**9560.** Heller, Deane F., and David A. Heller. "Senator Williams: Lone Wolf Investigator." *American Mercury* 85 (November 1957): 97–105.

**WILLIAMS, JOHN SHARP** (1854–1932) D-MS, House 1893–1909, Senate 1911–1923.

**9561.** Dickson, Harris. *An Old-Fashioned Senator: A Story-Biography of John Sharp Williams.* New York: Stokes, 1925.

**9562.** Osborn, George C. "Career of John Sharp Williams in the House of Representatives, 1893–1909." Master's thesis, Indiana University, 1932.

**9563.** ———. "John Sharp Williams Becomes a United States Senator." *Journal of Southern History* 6 (May 1940): 222–236.

**9564.** ———. *John Sharp Williams, Planter Statesman of the Deep South.* Atlanta, GA: Smith, 1964.

**WILLIAMS, JONATHAN** (1750–1815) PA, House 1815.

**9565.** Cullum, George W. "Military Education and Causes of the War, with a Biographical Sketch of Brig. General Jonathan Williams." In his *Campaigns of the War of 1812–15,* 9–62. New York: J. Miller, 1879.

**WILLIAMS, WILLIAM** (1731–1811) CT, Continental Congress 1776–1778, 1783–1784.

**9566.** Barnes, William H. "William Williams." In his *Lives of Gen. Ulysses S. Grant and Hon. Henry Wilson, Together with Sketches of Republican Candidates for Congress in Indiana,* 42–44. New York: W. H. Barnes, 1872.

**9567.** Stark, Bruce P. *Connecticut Signer, William Williams.* Chester, CT: Pequot Press, 1975.

**WILLIAMSON, HUGH** (1735–1819) F-NC, Continental Congress 1782–1785, 1788, House 1790–1793.

**9568.** Gilpatrick, Delbert H. "Contemporary Opinion of Hugh Williamson." *North Carolina Historical Review* 17 (January 1940): 26–36.

**9569.** Hosack, David. "A Biographical Memoir of Hugh Williamson." In *New York Historical Society Collections,* vol. 3, 125–179. New York: E. Bliss and E. White, 1821.

**9570.** Neal, John W. "Life and Public Services of Hugh Williamson." In *Trinity College Historical Society Historical Papers,* 62–115. Durham, NC: Trinity College Historical Society, 1919.

**9571.** Potts, Louis W. "Hugh Williamson: The Poor Man's Franklin and the National Domain." *North Carolina Historical Review* 64 (October 1987): 371–393.

**WILLIAMSON, WILLIAM** (1875–1972) R-SD, House 1921–1933.

**9572.** Williamson, William. *William Williamson: Student, Homesteader, Teacher, Lawyer, Judge, Congressman, and Trusted Friend: An Autobiography.* Rapid City, SD: The author, 1964.

**WILLING, THOMAS** (1731–1821) PA, Continental Congress 1775–1776.

**9573.** Konkle, Burton A. *Thomas Willing and the First American Financial System.* Philadelphia: University of Pennsylvania Press, 1937.

**9574.** Slaski, Eugene R. "Thomas Willing: Moderation during the American Revolution." Ph.D. dissertation, Florida State University, 1971.

**9575.** Willing, Thomas. *Willing Letters and Papers, Edited with a Biographical Essay of Thomas Willing of Philadelphia (1731–1821) by Thomas Willing Balch.* Philadelphia: Allen, Lane and Scott, 1922.

**WILLIS, FRANK BARTLETT** (1871–1928) R-OH, House 1911–1915, Senate 1921–1928.

**9576.** Ridinger, Gerald E. "The Political Career of Frank B. Willis." Ph.D. dissertation, Ohio State University, 1957.

**9577.** Smith, S. Winifred. "Frank B. Willis, 1915–1917." In *Governors of Ohio,* 159–162. Columbus: Ohio Historical Society, 1954.

**WILLITS, EDWIN** (1830–1896) R-MI, House 1877–1883.

**9578.** Bald, Frederick C. "Edwin Willits." In *Michigan and the Cleveland Era.* Edited by Earl D. Babst and Lewis G. Vander Velde, 288–304. Ann Arbor: University of Michigan Press, 1948.

**WILMOT, DAVID** (1814–1868) R-PA, House 1845–1851, Senate 1861–1863.

**9579.** Going, Charles B. *David Wilmot, Free-soiler: A Biography of the Great Advocate of the Wilmot Proviso.* N.p.: Smith, 1924.

**WILSON, GEORGE ALLISON** (1884–1953) R-IA, Senate 1943–1949.

**9580.** Swisher, Jacob A. "George A. Wilson." In his *Governors of Iowa,* 127–128. Mason City, IA: Klipto Loose Leaf Company, 1946.

**WILSON, HENRY** (1812–1875) R-MA, Senate 1855–1873.

**9581.** Abbott, Richard H. *Cobbler in Congress: The Life of Henry Wilson, 1812–1875.* Lexington: University of Kentucky Press, 1972.

**9582.** Barzman, Sol. "Henry Wilson." In his *Madmen and Geniuses: The Vice-Presidents of the United States,* 123–127. Chicago: Follett, 1974.

**9583.** Loubert, J. Daniel. "The Orientation of Henry Wilson, 1812–1856." Ph.D. dissertation, Boston University, 1952.

**9584.** McKay, Ernest. *Henry Wilson: Practical Radical: A Portrait of a Politician.* Port Washington, NY: Kennikat, 1971.

**9585.** ———. "Henry Wilson: Unprincipled Know Nothing." *Mid-America* 46 (January 1964): 29–37.

**9586.** Nason, Elias, and Thomas Russell. *Life and Public Services of Henry Wilson, Late Vice-President of the United States.* Westport, CT: Negro Universities Press, 1969.

**WILSON, JAMES** (1742–1798) PA, Continental Congress 1775–1776, 1782–1783, 1785–1787.

**9587.** Adams, Randolph. "The Legal Theories of James Wilson." *University of Pennsylvania Law Review* 68 (June 1920): 337–355.

**9588.** ———, ed. *Selected Political Essays of James Wilson.* New York: Knopf, 1930.

**9589.** Andrews, James D. "James Wilson and His Relation to Jurisprudence and Constitutional Law." *University of Pennsylvania Law Review* 49 (December 1901): 708–728.

**9590.** Carson, Hampton L. "James Wilson and James Iredell: A Parallel and a Contrast." *American Bar Association Journal* 7 (March 1921): 123–136.

**9591.** Cook, Frank G. "James Wilson." *Atlantic Monthly* 64 (September 1889): 316–330.

**9592.** Delahanty, Mary T. *The Integralist Philosophy of James Wilson.* New York: Pageant Press, 1969.

**9593.** Denniston, George M. "Revolutionary Principle: Ideology and the Constitution in the Thought of James Wilson." *Review of Politics* 39 (April 1977): 157–191.

**9594.** Dwight, Nathaniel. "James Wilson." In his *The Lives of the Signers to the Declaration of Independence,* 214–218. New York: Barnes, 1876.

**9595.** Elliott, Edward. "James Wilson: Growth through Speculative Forecast." In his *Biographical Story of the Constitution,* 53–75. New York: Putnam's, 1910.

**9596.** Gallagher, Eugene R. "Two Interpretations of the State and Government: The Pragmatic Skepticism of Mr. Justice Oliver Wendell Holmes Contrasted with the Natural Law Philosophy of Mr. Justice James Wilson." Ph.D. dissertation, Fordham University, 1940.

**9597.** Goodrich, Charles A. "James Wilson." In his *Lives of the Signers of the Declaration of Independence,* 300–309. New York: W. Reed and Company, 1829.

**9598.** Hunt, William. "James Wilson." In his *American Biographical Panorama,* 160. Albany, NY: J. Munsell, 1849.

**9599.** Jezierski, John V. "Parliament or People: James Wilson and Blackstone on the Nature and Location of Sovereignty." *Journal of the History of Ideas* 32 (January/March 1971): 95–106.

**9600.** Judson, L. Carroll. "James Wilson." In his *A Biography of the Signers of the Declaration of Independence,* 394–399. Philadelphia: Cowperthwait and Company, 1839.

**9601.** Kelland, Clarence B. "James Wilson, Expounder and Defender of the Constitution." *Law Student's Helper* 17 (July 1909): 209–213.

**9602.** Klingelsmith, Margaret C. "James Wilson." In *Great American Lawyers,* edited by William D. Lewis, vol. 1, 149–222. Philadelphia: J. C. Winston Company, 1907–1909.

**9603.** ———. "James Wilson and the So-Called Yazoo Frauds." *University of Pennsylvania Law Review* 56 (January 1908): 1–27.

**9604.** Konkle, Burton A. *James Wilson and the Constitution: The Opening Address in the Official Series of Events Known as the James Wilson Memorial: Delivered before the Law Academy of Philadelphia on November 14, 1906.* Philadelphia: Law Academy of Philadelphia, 1907.

**9605.** Leavelle, Arnaud B. "James Wilson and the Relation of Scottish Metaphysics to American Political Thought." *Political Science Quarterly* 57 (September 1942): 394–410.

**9606.** Lossing, Benson J. "James Wilson." In his *Lives of the Signers of the Declaration of American Independence,* 126–129. Philadelphia: Evans, Stoddart, and Company, 1870.

**9607.** McLaughlin, Andrew C. "James Wilson in the Philadelphia Convention." *Political Science Quarterly* 12 (March 1897): 1–20.

**9608.** Mell, Wayne A. "James Wilson, Alexander Hamilton, William Blackstone: Organic Principles of Constitutional Liberty." Ph.D. dissertation, University of Oregon, 1976.

**9609.** Nevin, David R. "James Wilson, of Pennsylvania." In his *Continental Sketches of Distinguished Pennsylvanians,* 76–84. Philadelphia: Porter and Coates, 1875.

**9610.** Obering, William F. *The Philosophy of Law of James Wilson, Associate Justice of the United States Supreme Court, 1789–1798: A Study in Comparative Jurisprudence.* Washington, DC: American Catholic Philosophical Association, Catholic University of America, 1938.

**9611.** O'Donnell, May G. *James Wilson and the Natural Law Basis of Positive Law.* New York: Fordham University Press, 1937.

**9612.** Pierce, James O. "James Wilson as a Jurist." *American Law Review* 38 (January/February 1904): 44–60.

**9613.** Quattrocchi, Anna M. "James Wilson and the Establishment of Federal Government." *Historian* 2 (Spring 1940): 105–117.

**9614.** Rosenberger, Homer T. "James Wilson's Theories of Punishment." *Pennsylvania Magazine of History and Biography* 73 (January 1949): 45–63.

**9615.** Sanderson, John. "James Wilson." In *Sanderson's Biography of the Signers of the Declaration of Independence,* edited by Robert T. Conrad, 499–520. Philadelphia: Thomas, Cowperthwait, 1848.

**9616.** Seed, Geoffrey. *James Wilson.* Millwood, NY: KTO Press, 1978.

**9617.** Smith, Charles P. *James Wilson, Founding Father, 1742–1798.* Chapel Hill: University of North Carolina Press, 1956.

**9618.** Smith, William C. "James Wilson and the Philosophy of Freedom in the American Revolution." *American Catholic Historical Society Records* 51 (September 1939): 65–71.

**9619.** Young, George L. "The Services of James Wilson in the Continental Congress." Ph.D. dissertation, Lehigh University, 1954.

**WILSON, JAMES** (1835–1920) R-IA, House 1873–1877, 1883–1885.

**9620.** Wilcox, Earley V. *Tama Jim.* Boston: Stratford Company, 1930.

**WILSON, WILLIAM BAUCHOP** (1862–1934) D-PA, House 1907–1913.

**9621.** Gengarelly, W. Anthony. "Secretary of Labor William B. Wilson and the Red Scare, 1919–1920." *Pennsylvania History* 47 (October 1980): 311–330.

**9622.** Wilhelm, Clarke L. "William B. Wilson: The First Secretary of Labor." Ph.D. dissertation, Johns Hopkins University, 1967.

**WILSON, WILLIAM LYNE** (1843–1900) D-WV, House 1883–1895.

**9623.** Summers, Festus P. *William L. Wilson and Tariff Reform.* New Brunswick, NJ: Rutgers University Press, 1953.

**9624.** Wilson, William L. *Borderland Confederate.* Edited by Festus P. Summers. Westport, CT: Greenwood, 1973.

**WINDOM, WILLIAM** (1827–1891) R-MN, House 1859–1869, Senate 1870–1871, 1871–1881, 1881–1883.

**9625.** Salisbury, Robert S. "Presidential Politics, 1880: William Windom and the GOP." *Minnesota History* 49 (Fall 1985): 292–302.

**9626.** ———. "William Windom and the Exodus Movement of 1879–1880." *Southern Studies* 26 (Summer 1987): 101–114.

**9627.** ———. "William Windom: The Formative Years." *Old Northwest* 12 (Winter 1986): 439–456.

**9628.** ———. "William Windom, the Republican Party and the Gilded Age." Ph.D. dissertation, University of Minnesota, 1982.

**9629.** ———. "William Windom, the Sioux, and Indian Affairs." *South Dakota History* 17 (Fall/Winter 1987): 202–222.

**WINGATE, PAINE (1739–1838) NH, Senate 1789–1793, House 1793–1795, Continental Congress 1788.**

**9630.** Wingate, Charles E. *Life and Letters of Paine Wingate, One of the Fathers of the Nation.* Medford, MA: Mercury Printing Company, 1930.

**WINTHROP, ROBERT CHARLES (1809–1894) W-MA, House 1840–1842, 1842–1850, Senate 1850–1851.**

**9631.** Bolton, Ethel S. "Two Notable Wax Portraits." *Old Time New England* 13 (July 1922): 3–13.

**9632.** Borome, Joseph, ed. "Two Letters of Robert Charles Winthrop." *Mississippi Valley Historical Review* 38 (September 1951): 289–296.

**9633.** Crawford, Mary C. "Winthrop." In her *Famous Families of Massachusetts,* vol. 1, 52–68. Boston: Little, Brown, 1930.

**9634.** Everett, William. "Robert Charles Winthrop." *Harvard Graduates' Magazine* 3 (March 1895): 294–301.

**9635.** Forbes, Abner, and J. W. Greene. *The Rich Men of Massachusetts.* Boston: Fetridge, 1851.

**9636.** Fowler, William M. "Sloop of War/Sloop of Peace: Robert Bennet Forbes and the USS Jamestown." *Proceedings of the Massachusetts Historical Society* 98 (1986): 49–59.

**9637.** Freiberg, Malcolm. "The Winthrops and Their Papers." *Proceedings of the Massachusetts Historical Society* 80 (1968): 55–70.

**9638.** Goodwin, Daniel. *In Memory of Robert C. Winthrop.* Chicago: R. R. Donnelley and Sons, 1894.

**9639.** Smalley, George W. "Mr. Winthrop." In his *Studies of Men,* 307–314. New York: Harper, 1895.

**9640.** Wheeler, Henry G. "Winthrop, Robert Charles (Speaker)." In his *History of Congress,* vol. 1, 376–424. New York: Harper and Brothers, 1848.

**9641.** Winthrop, Robert C. *A Memoir of Robert C. Winthrop.* Boston: Little, Brown, 1897.

**WISE, HENRY ALEXANDER (1806–1876) D-VA, House 1833–1844.**

**9642.** Adkins, Edwin P. "Henry A. Wise in Sectional Politics, 1833–1860." Ph.D. dissertation, Ohio State University, 1949.

**9643.** Bartlett, David V. "Henry A. Wise." In his *Presidential Candidates: Containing Sketches, Biographical, Personal and Political, of Prominent Candidates for the Presidency in 1860,* 233–243. New York: A. B. Burdick Publishers, 1859.

**9644.** Goldfield, David R. "Marketing a Candidate: Henry A. Wise and the Art of Mass Politics." *Virginia Cavalcade* 26 (Summer 1976): 30–37.

**9645.** Simpson, Craig M. *A Good Southerner: The Life of Henry A. Wise of Virginia.* Chapel Hill: University of North Carolina Press, 1985.

**9646.** Wise, Barton H. *The Life of Henry A. Wise of Virginia, 1806–1876.* New York: Macmillan, 1899.

**9647.** Wise, Henry A. *Seven Decades of the Union.* Philadelphia: Lippincott, 1872.

**WISE, JOHN SERGEANT (1846–1913) READ-VA, House 1883–1885.**

**9648.** Campbell, Otho C. "John Sergeant Wise: A Case Study in Conservative-Readjuster Politics in Virginia, 1869–1889." Ph.D. dissertation, University of Virginia, 1979.

**9649.** Davis, Curtis C. "Very Well-Rounded Republican: The Several Lives of John S. Wise." *Virginia Magazine of History and Biography* 71 (October 1963): 461–487.

**9650.** Lindsay, J. H. "John Sergeant Wise." In *Library of Southern Literature,* edited by Edwin A. Alderman and Joel C. Harris, vol. 13, 5937–5940. New Orleans: Martin and Hoyt, 1910.

462 Withers, Robert Enoch

**9651.** Wise, Barton H. *The Life of Henry A. Wise of Virginia, 1806–1876.* New York: Macmillan, 1899.

**WITHERS, ROBERT ENOCH**
(1821–1907) D-VA, Senate 1875–1881.

**9652.** Withers, Robert E. *Autobiography of an Octogenarian.* Roanoke, VA: Stone Printing Company, 1907.

**WITHERSPOON, JOHN** (1723–1794) NJ, Continental Congress 1776–1779, 1780–1781, 1782.

**9653.** Collins, Varnum L. *President Witherspoon: A Biography.* Princeton, NJ: Princeton University Press, 1925.

**9654.** Sanderson, John. "John Witherspoon." In *Sanderson's Biography of the Signers of the Declaration of Independence,* edited by Robert T. Conrad, 296–314. Philadelphia: Thomas, Cowperthwait, 1848.

**9655.** Woods, David W., Jr. *John Witherspoon.* New York: F. H. Revell, 1906.

**WOLCOTT, EDWARD OLIVER**
(1848–1905) R-CO, Senate 1889–1901.

**9656.** Dawson, Thomas F. *Life and Character of Edward Oliver Wolcott: Late Senator of the United States from the State of Colorado.* 2 vols. New York: Knickerbocker Press, 1911.

**9657.** Horner, John W. *Silver Town.* Caldwell, ID: Caxton Printers, 1950.

**WOLCOTT, OLIVER** (1726–1797) CT, Continental Congress 1775–1778, 1780–1784.

**9658.** Bland, James E. "The Oliver Wolcotts of Connecticut: The National Experience, 1775–1800." Ph.D. dissertation, Harvard University, 1970.

**9659.** Cash, Philip. "Oliver Wolcott of Litchfield: A Temperate Revolutionary." In *Physician Signers of the Declaration of Independence,* edited by George E. Gifford, 43–69. New York: Science History Publications, 1976.

**9660.** Sanderson, John. "Oliver Wolcott." In *Sanderson's Biography of the Signers of the Declaration of Independence,* edited by Robert T. Conrad, 254–258. Philadelphia: Thomas, Cowperthwait, 1848.

**9661.** Swiggett, Howard G. "The First Civil Servants: Oliver Wolcott and Timothy Pickering." In his *Forgotten Leaders of the Revolution,* 197–214. Garden City, NY: Doubleday, 1955.

**WOLF, GEORGE** (1777–1840) PA, House 1824–1829.

**9662.** Steele, Henry J. *The Life and Public Services of Governor George Wolf, Read before the Pennsylvania German Society at Easton, Oct. 12, 1928.* Norristown: Pennsylvania German Society, 1930.

**WOOD, BENJAMIN** (1820–1900) D-NY, House 1861–1865, 1881–1883.

**9663.** Mushkat, Jerome. "Ben Wood's Fort Lafayette: A Source for Studying the Peace Democrats." *Civil War History* 21 (June 1975): 160–171.

**WOOD, FERNANDO** (1812–1881) D-NY, House 1841–1843, 1863–1865, 1867–1881.

**9664.** Anbinder, Tyler G. "Fernando Wood and New York City's Secession from the Union: A Political Reappraisal." *New York History* 68 (January 1987): 67–92.

**9665.** Connable, Alfred, and Edward Silberfarb. "Fernando Wood, the Model Mayor." In their *Tigers of Tammany,* 104–137. New York: Holt, 1967.

**9666.** Lynch, Denis T. "How Wood Was Named Fernando, Local Autonomy: The Amphibious Wood." In his *"Boss" Tweed: The Story of a Grim Generation,* 110–137. New York: Boni and Liveright, 1931.

**9667.** Mushkat, Jerome. *Fernando Wood: A Political Biography.* Kent, OH: Kent State University Press, 1990.

**9668.** Pleasants, Samuel A. *Fernando Wood of New York*. New York: Columbia University Press, 1948.

**9669.** Spann, Edward K. "Gotham in Congress: New York's Representatives and the National Government, 1840–1854." *New York History* 67 (July 1986): 304–329.

**WOODBURY, LEVI (1789–1851) D-NH, Senate 1825–1831, 1841–1845.**

**9670.** Capowski, Vincent J. "The Era of Good Feelings in New Hampshire: The Gubernatorial Campaigns of Levi Woodbury, 1823–1824." *Historical New Hampshire* 21 (Winter 1966): 3–30.

**9671.** Capowski, Vincent J. "The Making of a Jacksonian Democrat: Levi Woodbury 1789–1831." Ph.D. dissertation, Fordham University, 1966.

**9672.** Cole, Donald B. *Jacksonian Democracy in New Hampshire, 1800–1851*. Cambridge, MA: Harvard University Press, 1970.

**9673.** Rantoul, Robert. "Mr. Justice Woodbury." *Law Reporter* 14 (November 1851): 349–361.

**9674.** Watterston, George. "Levi Woodbury." In his *Gallery of American Portraits*, 149–153. 3d ed. Washington, DC: F. Taylor, 1836.

**9675.** Wheaton, Philip D. "Levi Woodbury—Jacksonian Financier." Ph.D. dissertation, University of Maryland, 1955.

**9676.** Woodbury, Charles L. *Memoir of Hon. Levi Woodbury, LL.D*. Boston: David Clapp and Son, 1894.

**9677.** ———. "Memoir of Honorable Levi Woodbury, LL.D." *New England Historical and Genealogical Register* 48 (January 1894): 9–17.

**9678.** Woodbury, Levi. *Writings of Levi Woodbury*. 3 vols. Edited by Naham Capen. Boston: Little, Brown, 1852.

**WOODRUM, CLIFTON ALEXANDER (1887–1950) D-VA, House 1923–1945.**

**9679.** Sargent, James E. "Clifton A. Woodrum of Virginia: A Southern Progressive in Congress, 1923–1945." *Virginia Magazine of History and Biography* 89 (July 1981): 341–364.

**9680.** ———. "Woodrum's Economy Bloc: The Attack on Roosevelt's WPA." *Virginia Magazine of History and Biography* 93 (April 1985): 175–207.

**WORTHINGTON, THOMAS (1773–1827) R-OH, Senate 1803–1807, 1810–1814.**

**9681.** Sears, Alfred B. *Thomas Worthington: Father of Ohio Statehood*. Columbus: Ohio State University Press, 1958.

**9682.** Smith, S. Winifred. "Thomas Worthington, 1814–1818." In *Governors of Ohio*, 17–19. Columbus: Ohio Historical Society, 1954.

**WRIGHT, HENDRICK BRADLEY (1808–1881) G-PA, House 1853–1855, 1861–1863, 1877–1881.**

**9683.** Curran, Daniel J. "Hendrick B. Wright: A Study in Leadership." Ph.D. dissertation, Fordham University, 1962.

**WRIGHT, JAMES CLAUDE, JR. (1922–  ) D-TX, House 1955–1989.**

**9684.** Barry, John M. *The Ambition and the Power*. New York: Viking, 1989.

**9685.** Wright, James C. *Reflections of a Public Man*. Fort Worth, TX: Madison Publishing Company, 1984.

**9686.** ———. *You and Your Congressman*. New York: Coward-McCann, 1965.

**WRIGHT, JOSEPH ALBERT (1810–1867) U-IN, House 1843–1845, Senate 1862–1863.**

**9687.** Crane, Philip M. "Governor Jo Wright: Hoosier Conservative." Ph.D. dissertation, Indiana University, 1963.

**9688.** ———. "Onus with Honor: A Political History of Joseph A. Wright, 1809–1857." Master's thesis, Indiana University, 1961.

**WRIGHT, SILAS, JR.** (1795–1847) J-NY, House 1827–1829, Senate 1833–1844.

**9689.** Bacheller, Irving A. *The Light in the Clearing: A Tale of the North Country in the Time of Silas Wright.* Indianapolis: Bobbs-Merrill, 1917.

**9690.** Chancellor, William E. *A Life of Silas Wright, 1795–1847.* New York: W. C. O'Donnell, Jr., 1913.

**9691.** Garraty, John A. *Silas Wright.* New York: Columbia University Press, 1949.

**9692.** Hammond, Jabez D. *The History of Political Parties in the State of New York, from the Ratification of the Federal Constitution to December, 1840.* Syracuse, NY: Hall, Mills, 1852.

**9693.** ———. *Life and Times of Silas Wright.* Syracuse, NY: Hall and Dickson, 1848.

**9694.** Jenkins, John S. *The Life of Silas Wright, with an Appendix.* 5th ed. Auburn, NY: Alden and Parsons, 1849.

**9695.** Kennedy, Mary C. "Silas Wright and New York Politics, 1795–1847." Ph.D. dissertation, University of Chicago, 1950.

**WYMAN, LOUIS CROSBY** (1917– ) R-NH, House 1963–1965, 1967–1974, Senate 1974–1975.

**9696.** Kuter, Luis. "Due Process in the Contested New Hampshire Senate Election: Fact, Fiction or Farce." *New England Law Review* 11 (Fall 1975): 25–54.

**9697.** Tibbetts, Donn. *Closest U.S. Senate Race in History: Durkin v. Wyman.* Manchester, NH: Cummings Enterprises, 1976.

**WYNKOOP, HENRY** (1737–1816) PA, Continental Congress 1779–1782, House 1789–1791.

**9698.** Beaty, Joseph M., Jr. "The Letters of Judge Henry Wynkoop, Representative from Pennsylvania to the First Congress of the United States." *Pennsylvania Magazine of History and Biography* 38 (January 1914): 39–64, 183–205.

**9699.** McLachlan, James. "Henry Wynkoop." In his *Princetonians, 1748–1768,* 334–338. Princeton, NJ: Princeton University Press, 1976.

**WYTHE, GEORGE** (1726–1806) VA, Continental Congress 1775–1777.

**9700.** Blackburn, Joyce. *George Wythe of Williamsburg.* New York: Harper and Row, 1975.

**9701.** Sanderson, John. "George Wythe." In *Sanderson's Biography of the Signers of the Declaration of Independence,* edited by Robert T. Conrad, 633–641. Philadelphia: Thomas, Cowperthwait, 1848.

🕊

**YANCEY, WILLIAM LOWNDES** (1814–1846) D-AL, House 1844–1846.

**9702.** Draughon, Ralph B. "William Lowndes Yancey: From Unionist to Secessionist 1814–1852." Ph.D. dissertation, University of North Carolina, 1968.

**9703.** Dubose, John W. *The Life and Times of William Lowndes Yancey.* 2 vols. Birmingham, AL: Roberts and Son, 1892.

**9704.** Golden, James L. "Hilliard vs. Yancey: Prelude to the Civil War." *Quarterly Journal of Speech* 42 (February 1956): 35–44.

**9705.** Hergesheimer, Joseph. "The Pillar of Words." In his *Swords and Roses,* 33–64. New York: Knopf, 1929.

**9706.** Mitchell, Rexford S. "William Lowndes Yancey: Orator of Southern Constitutional Rights." Ph.D. dissertation, University of Wisconsin, 1937.

**9707.** Petrie, George. "William Lowndes Yancey." In *Library of Southern Literature*, edited by Edwin A. Alderman and Joel C. Harris, vol. 13, 6021–6028. New Orleans: Martin and Hoyt, 1910.

**9708.** Venable, Austin L. "The Public Career of William Lowndes Yancey." *Alabama Review* 16 (July 1963): 200–212.

**YARBOROUGH, RALPH WEBSTER**
**(1903– ) D-TX, Senate 1957–1971.**

**9709.** Adams, Mark. *Yarborough: Portrait of a People's Senator.* Austin, TX: Chaparral Press, 1957.

**9710.** Banks, Jimmy. "Marathon Runner." In his *Money, Marbles and Chalk,* 54–81. Austin: Texas Publishing Company, 1971.

**9711.** Phillips, William G. *Yarborough of Texas.* Washington, DC: Acropolis Books, 1969.

**9712.** Welch, June R. "Ralph Yarborough Persevered." In his *The Texas Senator,* 66–71. Dallas: G. L. A. Press, 1978.

**YATES, JOHN BARENTSE (1784–1836)**
**R-NY, House 1815–1817.**

**9713.** Aitken, Hugh G. "J. Yates and McIntyre's Lottery Managers." *Journal of Economic History* 13 (Winter 1953): 36–57.

**YATES, RICHARD (1818–1873) R-IL,**
**House 1851–1855, Senate 1865–1871.**

**9714.** Northrup, Jack. "Governor Richard Yates and President Lincoln." *Lincoln Herald* 70 (Winter 1968): 193–205.

**9715.** Northrup, Jack. "Lincoln and Yates: The Climb to Power." *Lincoln Herald* 73 (Winter 1971): 242–253.

**9716.** Reavis, Logan. *The Life and Public Services of Richard Yates.* St. Louis: J. A. Chambers, 1881.

**9717.** Yates, Richard E., and Catherine Y. Pickering. *Richard Yates, Civil War Governor.* Edited by John H. Krenkel. Danville, IL: Interstate, 1966.

**YATES, RICHARD (1860–1936) R-IL,**
**House 1919–1933.**

**9718.** Yates, Richard E. *Serving the Republic: An Autobiography.* Edited by John H. Krenkel. Danville, IL: Interstate, 1968.

**YORTY, SAMUEL WILLIAM (1909– )**
**D-CA, House 1951–1955.**

**9719.** Ainsworth, Edward M. *Maverick Major: A Biography of Sam Yorty of Los Angeles.* Garden City, NY: Doubleday, 1966.

**9720.** Bollens, John C., and Grant B. Geyer. *Yorty: Politics of a Constant Candidate.* Pacific Palisades, CA: Palisades, 1973.

**YOUNG, ANDREW JACKSON, JR.**
**(1932– ) D-GA, House 1973–1977.**

**9721.** Bryant, Ira B. *Andrew Jackson Young, Mr. Ambassador: United States Ambassador to the United Nations.* Houston, TX: Armstrong, 1979.

**9722.** Christopher, Maurine. "Andrew Young/Georgia." In her *Black Americans in Congress,* 289. Rev. ed. New York: Thomas Y. Crowell, 1976.

**9723.** Finger, Seymour M. "Andrew Young." In his *Your Man at the UN,* 260–288. New York: New York University Press, 1980.

**9724.** Gardner, Carl. *Andrew Young: A Biography.* New York: Drake Publishers, 1978.

**9725.** Haskins, James S. *Andrew Young, Man with a Mission.* New York: Lothrop, Lee and Shepard, 1979.

**9726.** Simpson, Janice C. *Andrew Young: A Matter of Choice.* St. Paul, MN: EMC Corporation, 1978.

**9727.** Stone, Eddie. *Andrew Young, Biography of a Realist.* Los Angeles: Holloway House, 1980.

**9728.** Westman, Paul. *Andrew Young, Champion of the Poor.* Minneapolis, MN: Dillon Press, 1983.

**9729.** Young, Andrew J. *Andrew Young at the United Nations.* Edited by Lee Clement. Salisbury, NC: Documentary Publications, 1978.

**9730.** ———. *A Way Out of No Way.* Nashville, TN: Thomas Nelson, 1994.

## YOUNG, MILTON RUBEN (1897–1983) R-ND, Senate 1945–1981.

**9731.** Sylvester, Stephen G. "Water on Both Shoulders: The Political Ascendancy of Milton R. Young." *North Dakota Quarterly* 56 (Fall 1988): 222–244.

## YOUNG, PIERCE MANNING BUTLER (1836–1896) D-GA, House 1868–1869, 1870–1875.

**9732.** Holland, Lynwood M. *Pierce M. B. Young: The Warwick of the South.* Athens: University of Georgia Press, 1964.

## YOUNG, STEPHEN MARVIN (1889–1984) D-OH, House 1933–1937, 1941–1943, 1949–1951, Senate 1959–1971.

**9733.** Young, Stephen M. *Tales Out of Congress.* Philadelphia: Lippincott, 1964.

## YOUNG, THOMAS LOWRY (1832–1888) R-OH, House 1879–1883.

**9734.** Marchman, Watt P. "Thomas L. Young, 1877–1878." In *Governors of Ohio,* 105–107. Columbus: Ohio Historical Society, 1954.

## YULEE, DAVID LEVY (1810–1886) D-FL, House 1841–1845, Senate 1845–1851, 1855–1861.

**9735.** Adler, Joseph G. "The Public Career of Senator David Levy Yulee." Ph.D. dissertation, Case Western Reserve, 1973.

**9736.** Simonhoff, Harry. "David Levy Yulee: Florida's First Senator." In his *Jewish Notables in America, 1776–1865,* 362–365. Sykesville, MD: Greenberg, 1956.

**9737.** Thompson, Arthur W. "David Yulee: A Study of Nineteenth Century American Thought and Enterprise." Ph.D. dissertation, Columbia University, 1954.

**9738.** Whitfield, James B. "Senatorial Contest between David L. Yulee and Stephen R. Mallory, Sr., in 1851." *Florida Law Journal* 19 (October 1945): 251–255.

## ZOLLICOFFER, FELIX KIRK (1812–1862) AP-TN, House 1853–1859.

**9739.** Parks, Edd W. "Zollicoffer: Southern Whig." *Tennessee Historical Quarterly* 11 (December 1952): 346–355.

**9740.** Stamper, James C. "Felix K. Zollicoffer." *Tennessee Historical Quarterly* 28 (Winter 1969): 356–376.

## ZUBLY, JOHN JOACHIM (1724–1781) GA, Continental Congress 1775.

**9741.** Martin, Roger A. "John Joachim Zubly: Preacher, Planter, Politician." Ph.D. dissertation, University of Georgia, 1975.

**9742.** Zubly, John J. *"A Warm and Zealous Spirit": John J. Zubly and the American Revolution: A Selection of His Writings.* Edited by Randall M. Miller. Macon, GA: Mercer University Press, 1982.

# Author Index